W9-AVW-020

THE SEARCH FOR IDENTITY

Modern American History

Consulting Editors   **BENJAMIN QUARLES**

Professor of History
Morgan State University
Baltimore, Maryland

Dr. Quarles is the author of many books and articles, including
The Negro in the Making of America, Black Abolitionists,
and *Allies for Freedom: Blacks and John Brown.* He has been
a consultant in American history to the Library of Congress
and he serves on the editorial board of the *Journal of Negro
History* and many other historical journals. He also is a
member of the American Antiquarian Society and other
professional societies.

RICHARD E. MARSHALL

Chairman, Department of History
   and Political Science
Montgomery County Community College
Blue Bell, Pennsylvania

Dr. Marshall has taught and has been a department chairman
in social studies at the secondary level. He earned an M.S.
degree in the teaching of social studies in secondary
education, and an M.A. and Ph.D. in international relations.
He is co-editor of *The Search for Meaning: Viewpoints in
American History.*

About the Author   Dr. Wiltz is Professor of History at Indiana University. He
has been a visiting lecturer at the University of the East Indies
in Jamaica and a guest professor of history at Hamburg
University in Germany. He is the author of *In Search of
Peace: The Senate Munitions Inquiry, 1934-35; From Isolation
to War: 1931-1941;* and *Books in American History: A Basic
List for High Schools.* Dr. Wiltz also is co-editor of *The Search
for Meaning: Viewpoints in American History.* For five years
Dr. Wiltz was associate director of the Lilly Program in
American History, a project dedicated to improving the
teaching of American history in the secondary schools of
Indiana.

THE SEARCH FOR IDENTITY

MODERN AMERICAN HISTORY

John Edward Wiltz

8109

J. B. LIPPINCOTT COMPANY

Philadelphia · New York · San Jose

Maps, charts, and graphs within the text: Allyn-Mason, Incorporated

Maps within the *Historical Atlas:* Hammond Incorporated

About the Cover

For more than two hundred years the people of the United States
have been searching for a new way of life — a new identity
for themselves and their nation. In their search they have followed
many different dreams: for some it was a better crop or a taller
building; for others it was a new poem, a new road, or a new law.
Together, all the dreams and all the searching have made us
a people unlike any other. What is your dream?

Printed in the United States of America

ISBN-0-397-40253-8

15 . 807 . 2

CONTENTS

SPECIAL LEARNING AIDS

Historical Atlas

SOME THOUGHTS ABOUT HISTORY

THE TWENTIETH-CENTURY INDUSTRIALIST Henry Ford once said that "history is bunk." At another time he remarked, "I don't read history. That's in the past. I'm thinking of the future." The English poet Matthew Arnold wrote in the nineteenth century that history is a "vast Mississippi of falsehood," and Ambrose Bierce in his irreverent *Devil's Dictionary* described it as "an account, mostly false, of events, unimportant, brought about by rulers, mostly knaves, and soldiers, mostly fools." The Iron Chancellor of Germany, Otto von Bismarck, thundered that "the thing is not to write history, but to make it."

Many Americans have felt the same way about history. In an age of moon voyagers and computers, jet airplanes and Salk vaccine, mankind's past seems almost irrelevant to some people.

WHAT HISTORY IS

What is history? The student often thinks of history as a written account of the past. History is more than that. It *is* the past. The *Louisville Courier-Journal* expressed this idea in an editorial on July 20, 1966:

> Whatever it is, history is no dull and dusty thing in a book. It is John Kennedy in Dallas, General Westmoreland in Viet Nam, Einstein in his laboratory. It is a killer loose in Chicago, Liz and Dick in Rome, Lyndon Johnson in Omaha. What happens today is history tomorrow. History is wars and floods and famines and fires, the rise and fall of civilizations. It is also the loves and hopes and tears and sweat and laughs of the men and women who made those civilizations.

Everything that has taken place is history, every step that mankind has taken, every word that has been uttered. The classic definition is that history is the sum of human experience. That is a sobering thought. Even the most erudite scholar, despite academic degrees and titles, can hope to master only the tiniest particle of history.

The enormous expanse of history makes it an exciting enterprise. Other so-called disciplines of knowledge emphasize one part of the universe or human activity. The zoologist concentrates on animals, the political scientist on government, the theologian on religion. But the field of the historian is limitless. History embraces everything that has influenced human activity. The historian examines the effect of science and technology on human society, explores philosophy and economics, literature and architecture, diplomacy and war. The historian is both scientist and artist. The job of the historian is to conduct a scientific search for information, and, from this material, to fashion an account which ideally is a work of art as well as a source of knowledge.

The Value and Use of History

What is the value of history? In ancient times, probably nobody would have thought to ask such a question. Aristotle caught the mood of antiquity when he insisted that the pursuit of knowledge is good in itself and requires no practical justification. Only in the modern era have people demanded that the search for knowledge meet a test of "practicality."

Since modern society wishes a practical justification, what, then, is the use of history? For an answer to this question, each person need only look within. Each of us is a historian. Locked up in the memory of each of us is a fairly detailed account of his or her past, complete with places, names, and dates. Hardly a waking hour passes that we do not flip the pages of our personal histories for guidelines on how to meet problems of the moment. When writing a theme for an English class, the student recalls the mistakes made in a previous theme and tries to avoid them. The football quarterback thinks of the plays that were successful in last week's game.

All of us place great value on our personal histories or experiences, and few of us would elect to wipe the slate clean and face life without benefit of the knowledge of past successes and failures. So it is with human society. History is the sum of human experience, and the works of the historian are the memory of society. Without historical accounts, society would be like a person with amnesia.

The individual, of course, does not confine the use of history to personal affairs. History also is useful in virtually every occupation or profession. Psychiatrists search the pasts of their patients to find the sources of mental illness. Before beginning the construction of a dam or bridge, an engineer examines similar structures designed by other engineers. The carpenter uses methods and materials that have proved successful on previous jobs. The renowned newspaper publisher Joseph Pulitzer understood the importance of the past when he listed knowledge of history as the first requirement of a good editorial writer. Without the "total picture" of events that history provides, Pulitzer knew, no writer can present enlightened opinion in editorial columns.

One of the best statements on the value of history appeared in a report by a committee of the American Historical Association (AHA) in 1964.[1] According to this report, history demonstrates that nothing in human society stands still: "To those caught up in the moment, swept along by mass passions, or blinded by the sudden glare of new dangers, it offers the sovereign antidote of perspective. Men have survived troubles before."

The AHA report noted that history also reveals the complexity of human affairs: "However uncomfortable it may make us, we discover that issues were not all black and white, or one-sided. From history we learn that things are rarely if ever as simple as they seem."

Recalling the words of the modern philosopher George Santayana that "he who does not know history is fated to repeat it," the AHA emphasized that history can provide warnings, indicate circumstances that mankind should take into account, and suggest possible actions: "In an international crisis history will not tell us precisely what to do but rather some things we surely ought not to do."

As for the importance of history to the individual, the same report quoted a great name in the historical literature of the United States, Carl L. Becker. Becker wrote that "the value of history is, indeed, not scientific but moral: by liberalizing the mind, by deepening the sympa-

thies, by fortifying the will, it enables us to control, not society, but ourselves—a much more important thing; it prepares us to live more humanely in the present and to meet rather than to foretell the future."

The AHA committee saw history as a means of civilizing decision-makers in the modern world: "How more effectively than through history can we bring to our citizens and their chosen leaders that experience of other rulers and crises, and that humility in prediction without which the highest statesmanship becomes impossible?"

The report concluded that history also is a reservoir of wisdom for ordinary persons, the nonscholars, helping to guard them against fanatics and demagogues, the latest discovery or novelty: "When a man can know about and think about the past, and becomes aware of alternatives, of the fallibility of human planning, of the danger of oversimplification, of the limitation of dogmas or monistic solutions, then he is a freer man, by so much emancipated from the pressures of fashionable opinion, the tyranny of circumstance, or the false premises of some party line."

Much of the above is summarized in an inscription at the base of a statue on the Pennsylvania Avenue side of the National Archives building in Washington: "What is past is prologue." Put another way, history is the preface to the present. The origins of the present generation are in the past, and to understand the present, one must know its origins.

History enables people to understand their national character and institutions. In the history of ancient Greece and Rome, we find the birth of Western civilization, of which our American heritage is a part. Examining our own country, we see how many of our ideas about liberty and equality derive from Thomas Jefferson. We see the influence of the frontier, the growth of industry and urbanization.

Most important perhaps, when we study history, we explore not only movements, conflicts, or ideas. We study people. The lives of Clara Barton and George Washington Carver might not tell us much about current problems of nuclear weapons or pollution. Still, Barton and Carver were people. When we examine their ambitions and fears and hopes, we learn something about human nature—about ourselves.

The importance of history received an eloquent expression more than two thousand years ago when Cicero wrote that "to be ignorant of what happened before you were born is to be ever a child."

[1] AHA Newsletter. Vol. 11. No. 4, April 1964, pp. 5-7.

PHILOSOPHIES OF HISTORY

Sooner or later every serious student of history encounters the question: "What is your philosophy of history?" Put another way, the question is: "What forces do you think have determined the course of human events?" Or, more simply, "Why do things happen as they do?"

Today, most historians have despaired of identifying the hand of a Supreme Being or fate in human events. They leave that task to the theologian and the philosopher. Even Christian historians who believe in a providential God normally confine themselves to the natural order and seek natural causes for earthly events.

Natural Forces that Affect History

What are some of the natural forces that historians think have had a great bearing on history?

Some thinkers in the nineteenth century concluded that economics was the main influence in history. According to this view, people usually act in accord with their own economic interests — their pocketbooks and their stomachs.

The best-known prophet of economic determinism was Karl Marx, father of modern communism. Not all economic determinists, however, have been Communists. In the United States, particularly from 1900 to 1920, many scholars, including the renowned historian Charles A. Beard, believed economics to be at the base of most human conduct. Most scholars today believe that Marx and Beard went too far — that geography, climate, tradition, religion, and nationalism have greater influence on human affairs than economic determinists have been willing to admit.

There are other philosophies of history, including the hero theory — the idea that a few powerful individuals determine the outline of events. Such scholars as J. G. Fichte, G. W. F. Hegel, and Thomas Carlyle proposed such an interpretation of history. Other historians have gone to the opposite extreme. Events, they think, shape the individual. Both of these theories probably are wrong.

It is true that the person with the ability to mold history must appear at the right moment. One historian has noted that if Alexander the Great had "been born in Macedon three centuries earlier or three centuries later than he was, he could never have embarked on his career of conquest." Still, it would seem that "the times" do not make inevitable the success of the great leader. Napoleon appeared at an opportune time to influence the history of Europe. On the other hand, it is hard to imagine that a person of less daring and talent could have accomplished so much.

One may conclude that there can be no philosophy of history that will satisfy everybody. Your own view of the forces determining events will depend on your religious convictions, your idea of the universe, your conception of human nature. So long as people differ on such matters, there will be different philosophies of history.

THE WRITING OF HISTORY

The student of history ought to have some knowledge of the way in which the historian recreates the past. How do history books come into being? Where do the authors of biographies and other historical works find information?

First, the author of a history book reads books on the topics he or she intends to cover. For example, the author of a book of United States history reads biographies of Christopher Columbus and George Washington, Carry Nation and Theodore Roosevelt, Susan B. Anthony and Martin Luther King, Jr. Other sources which will be used are books on exploration, the American Revolution, the westward movement, the Great Depression, and the cold war. From these studies the historian gathers information and ideas. Such works are the bricks and mortar with which the general author builds a new book.

Finding Specialized Material

Where do the specialized works come from? Perhaps the best way to approach this question is to consider a specific case. Suppose a historian sets out to write a biography of Abraham Lincoln. Where does she or he find the material for a new biography?

The first job would be to examine what other people have written about Lincoln. This would be a heavy task. Since Lincoln's death, thousands of books, pamphlets, and articles on his life and career have appeared. After absorbing the ideas and information in these works, the author would move into what historians call source materials — materials which date from the time when Lincoln lived.

What are some of these source materials? One source would be old newspapers and periodicals. Some libraries have files of out-of-print newspapers such as the *New York Sun* and *Philadelphia Public Ledger* and such periodicals as *Niles' Weekly Register*. The biographer would explore these materials for the years of Lincoln's life. The newspapers and periodicals would have information on what Lincoln did and said, and what other people thought about him. The historian probably would be particularly interested in editorial comment on Lincoln.

Biographers often consult legal records. The Lincoln biographer might examine records in Sangamon County, Illinois, for information such as how much property Lincoln owned. This information might offer insight into Lincoln's political views.

The Lincoln biographer would consult public documents. Many of the documents pertaining to the Lincoln period are in printed form. There is the *Congressional Globe* (the predecessor of today's *Congressional Record*), which set out day-to-day discussion on the floor of Congress. Lincoln was a member of Congress in 1847-49, and statements he made in the House of Representatives (such as those concerning the war with Mexico) would indicate his view on issues, and perhaps indicate his debating skill at that point in his career. During the presidential years the *Globe* would be a treasure house of information on the views of members of Congress toward Lincoln and his program. Printed hearings and reports of congressional committees would supplement the *Globe*. Even more important would be official records that remain unprinted, especially presidential records. These records have been stored in the National Archives in Washington.

The biographer of Lincoln would have special interest in personal letters and diaries. After Lincoln's death, some of his associates wrote memoirs in which they recalled dealings with the Civil War president. Such recollections are useful, although the historian must be cautious. Memoirists who have a habit of casting themselves and their heroes in the best possible light may often depart from fact. Associates, often writing many years after the important events of their lives, may sometimes be the victims of faulty memory.

Interviews with persons who took part in events are another source of historical information. The Lincoln biographer would not be able to use interviews, since there is no one alive today who knew Lincoln. But a historian working on the life of Calvin Coolidge or Franklin D. Roosevelt might talk with many people who had

some part in the subject's career. Again, the historian must be cautious in using the material; interviews may suffer from many of the same shortcomings as memoirs.

Using the Information

After making this survey of source materials — probably stretching over several years — the historian, his or her files bulging with notes, would be ready to write a biography of Lincoln. For long hours, day after day, the writer must work alone in a study, concentrating on the task at hand. Millions of words of notes must be condensed to perhaps one hundred and fifty thousand. At the same time, the writer must give careful thought to organization, arrive at defensible conclusions, and strive for literary excellence.

By the time the historian feels reasonably satisfied with the manuscript, she or he probably will have written four or five drafts. Then other scholars will be asked to scrutinize the work for errors in fact or interpretation and flaws in style. With these comments and criticism, the historian will give the manuscript another revision or two. Like a sculptor, the writer repeatedly turns over each part of the work, striking a sentence here, changing a word there.

At last, perhaps many years after the first thought of writing a Lincoln biography, the author sees the final product — several hundred printed pages neatly bound between two hard covers. The sight, feel, and smell of the new book bring immense satisfaction. The author knows that he or she has made a contribution to knowledge that will add to the enlightenment of mankind for years to come. And the historian who succeeds in capturing Abraham Lincoln with crisp, sparkling prose also has the satisfaction of having produced a work of art.

HISTORY IS NOT A SCIENCE

History is not a science, and the appearance of an idea or conclusion in a book on history does not necessarily make it true. No two historians will consider identical aspects of history and see them in exactly the same light. Compounding the problem is the fact that historians cannot possibly have a total picture of their subject, and indeed their picture is usually much more fragmentary than they would care to admit. Moreover, historians cannot set forth all the information at their disposal. They must select the information and ideas that they intend to record.

Despite historians' determination to be "objective," their origins, education, and prejudices will influence their selection and hence their conclusions.

The student should be cautious. Historians or teachers of history who have spent years, perhaps decades, in careful, systematic study of the past are entitled to respect. But no historian is infallible, and the student should not hesitate to dispute the historian's ideas and conclusions if evidence can be found to support another viewpoint.

Every experienced teacher of history can recall occasions when bright students, bringing their intellects to bear on historical problems, have raised interesting questions and advanced new ideas. Thus in studying the history of your country, you should not be afraid to express and defend your own ideas.

Further Readings

The reference materials listed here are broad in scope and will be helpful throughout the entire course on American history.

General Reference Works

Concise Dictionary of American History by Thomas C. Cochran and Wayne Andrews.
Encyclopedia of American History by Dushkin Publishing Group, Inc.
Encyclopedia Americana (30 vols.) by Grolier, Inc.
Webster's American Biographies by G. & C. Merriam Co.
The Woman in American History by Gerda Lerner.
World Book Encyclopedia (22 vols.) by World Book Encyclopedia Editors.

Atlases and Almanacs

Atlas of American History by Edward W. Fox.

Historical Atlas of the United States by Clifford E. Lord and Elizabeth S. Lord.
Information Please Almanac ed. by Dan Golenpaul. Published annually.
Statistical Abstract of the United States by U. S. Department of Commerce, Bureau of the Census. Published annually.
World Almanac and Book of Facts ed. by George Dulury, Newspaper Enterprise Association. Published annually.

Documents and Source Materials

The Black American: A Brief Documentary History by Leslie H. Fishel, Jr., and Benjamin Quarles.
Documents of American History ed. by Henry Steele Commager.
Great Presidential Decisions: State Papers that Changed the Course of History by Richard B. Morris.

Pictorial History

America's Historylands ed. by National Geographic Society.
American Heritage Guide to Great Historic Places by M. Davidson.
The American Past, 1775-1945 by Roger Butterfield.

The Arts

American Houses: Colonial, Classic, Contemporary by Edwin Hoag.
American Songbag by Carl Sandburg.
Art and Life in America by Oliver Larkin.
Literary History of the United States by Robert E. Spiller and others.
New Complete Book of the American Musical Theater by David A. Ewen.
This Land is Mine: An Anthology of American Verse ed. by Al Hine.

The most important document in the history of the United States, the *Declaration of Independence,* signaled the beginning of a new nation. It states the colonies' reasons for separating from Great Britain, and expresses the basic rights of every citizen—"life, liberty, and the pursuit of happiness." The complete text is reproduced at the end of this book.

A NATION IS ESTABLISHED

IN CONGRESS, JULY 4, 1776.

The unanimous Declaration of the thirteen united States of America.

When in the Course of human events, it becomes necessary for one people to dissolve the political bands which have connected them with another, and to assume among the powers of the earth, the separate and equal station to which the Laws of Nature and of Nature's God entitle them, a decent respect to the opinions of mankind requires that they should declare the causes which impel them to the separation. _____ We hold these truths to be self-evident, that all men are created equal, that they are endowed by their Creator with certain unalienable Rights, that among these are Life, Liberty and the pursuit of Happiness — That to secure these rights, Governments are instituted among Men, deriving their just powers from the consent of the governed, — That whenever any Form of Government becomes destructive of these ends, it is the Right of the People to alter or to abolish it, and to institute new Government, laying its foundation on such principles and organizing its powers in such form, as to them shall seem most likely to effect their Safety and Happiness. Prudence, indeed, will dictate that Governments long established should not be changed for light and transient causes; and accordingly all experience hath shewn, that mankind are more disposed to suffer, while evils are sufferable, than to right themselves by abolishing the forms to which they are accustomed. But when a long train of abuses and usurpations, pursuing invariably the same Object evinces a design to reduce them under absolute Despotism, it is their right, it is their duty, to throw off such Government, and to provide new Guards for their future security. — Such has been the patient sufferance of these Colonies; and such is now the necessity which constrains them to alter their former Systems of Government. The history of the present King of Great Britain is a history of repeated injuries and usurpations, all having in direct object the establishment of an absolute Tyranny over these States. To prove this, let Facts be submitted to a candid world. _____ He has refused his Assent to Laws, the most wholesome and necessary for the public good. _____ He has forbidden his Governors to pass Laws of immediate and pressing importance, unless suspended in their operation till his Assent should be obtained; and when so suspended, he has utterly neglected to attend to them. _____ He has refused to pass other Laws for the accommodation of large districts of people, unless those people would relinquish the right of Representation in the Legislature, a right inestimable to them and formidable to tyrants only. _____ He has called together legislative bodies at places unusual, uncomfortable, and distant from the depository of their public Records, for the sole purpose of fatiguing them into compliance with his measures. _____ He has dissolved Representative Houses repeatedly, for opposing with manly firmness his invasions on the rights of the people. _____ He has refused for a long time, after such dissolutions, to cause others to be elected; whereby the Legislative powers, incapable of Annihilation, have returned to the People at large for their exercise; the State remaining in the mean time exposed to all the dangers of invasion from without, and convulsions within. _____ He has endeavoured to prevent the population of these States; for that purpose obstructing the Laws for Naturalization of Foreigners; refusing to pass others to encourage their migrations hither, and raising the conditions of new Appropriations of Lands. _____ He has obstructed the Administration of Justice, by refusing his Assent to Laws for establishing Judiciary powers. _____ He has made Judges dependent on his Will alone, for the tenure of their offices, and the amount and payment of their salaries. _____ He has erected a multitude of New Offices, and sent hither swarms of Officers to harrass our people, and eat out their substance. _____ He has kept among us, in times of peace, Standing Armies without the Consent of our legislatures. _____ He has affected to render the Military independent of and superior to the Civil power. _____ He has combined with others to subject us to a jurisdiction foreign to our constitution, and unacknowledged by our laws; giving his Assent to their Acts of pretended Legislation: — For Quartering large bodies of armed troops among us: — For protecting them, by a mock Trial, from punishment for any Murders which they should commit on the Inhabitants of these States: — For cutting off our Trade with all parts of the world: — For imposing Taxes on us without our Consent: — For depriving us in many cases, of the benefits of Trial by jury: — For transporting us beyond Seas to be tried for pretended offences — For abolishing the free System of English Laws in a neighbouring Province, establishing therein an Arbitrary government, and enlarging its Boundaries so as to render it at once an example and fit instrument for introducing the same absolute rule into these Colonies: — For taking away our Charters, abolishing our most valuable Laws, and altering fundamentally the Forms of our Governments: — For suspending our own Legislatures, and declaring themselves invested with power to legislate for us in all cases whatsoever. _____ He has abdicated Government here, by declaring us out of his Protection and waging War against us. _____ He has plundered our seas, ravaged our Coasts, burnt our towns, and destroyed the lives of our people. _____ He is at this time transporting large Armies of foreign Mercenaries to compleat the works of death, desolation and tyranny, already begun with circumstances of Cruelty & perfidy scarcely paralleled in the most barbarous ages, and totally unworthy the Head of a civilized nation. _____ He has constrained our fellow Citizens taken Captive on the high Seas to bear Arms against their Country, to become the executioners of their friends and Brethren, or to fall themselves by their Hands. _____ He has excited domestic insurrections amongst us, and has endeavoured to bring on the inhabitants of our frontiers, the merciless Indian Savages, whose known rule of warfare, is an undistinguished destruction of all ages, sexes and conditions. In every stage of these Oppressions We have Petitioned for Redress in the most humble terms: Our repeated Petitions have been answered only by repeated injury. A Prince, whose character is thus marked by every act which may define a Tyrant, is unfit to be the ruler of a free people. _____ Nor have We been wanting in attentions to our British brethren. We have warned them from time to time of attempts by their legislature to extend an unwarrantable jurisdiction over us. We have reminded them of the circumstances of our emigration and settlement here. We have appealed to their native justice and magnanimity, and we have conjured them by the ties of our common kindred to disavow these usurpations, which, would inevitably interrupt our connections and correspondence. They too have been deaf to the voice of justice and of consanguinity. We must, therefore, acquiesce in the necessity, which denounces our Separation, and hold them, as we hold the rest of mankind, Enemies in War, in Peace Friends. _____

We, therefore, the Representatives of the united States of America, in General Congress, Assembled, appealing to the Supreme Judge of the world for the rectitude of our intentions, do, in the Name, and by Authority of the good People of these Colonies, solemnly publish and declare, That these United Colonies are, and of Right ought to be Free and Independent States; that they are Absolved from all Allegiance to the British Crown, and that all political connection between them and the State of Great Britain, is and ought to be totally dissolved; and that as Free and Independent States, they have full Power to levy War, conclude Peace, contract Alliances, establish Commerce, and to do all other Acts and Things which Independent States may of right do. _____ And for the support of this Declaration, with a firm reliance on the protection of divine Providence, we mutually pledge to each other our Lives, our Fortunes and our sacred Honor.

John Hancock   Robt Morris   Geo Read   Josiah Bartlett

CHAPTER 1

DISCOVERY AND SETTLEMENT

IT WAS LATE EVENING, Thursday, October 11, 1492. Three Spanish caravels, their masts and sails straining before a raging easterly wind, rolled and pitched through heavy seas at an almost incredible speed of nine knots. Despite the wind, the sky was clear, stars sparkled, and a brilliant moon enveloped the little fleet in a silvery glow. Charts revealed that the ships, just beginning the sixth week of their voyage, had reached a point in the Atlantic 4,000 miles west and slightly south of the Canary Islands.

From the quarterdeck of the largest vessel, the *Santa Maria,* a ruddy-complexioned navigator with aquiline nose and white hair peered intently into the darkness. An Italian sailing for the sovereigns of Spain, he was scanning the horizon for sight of land. Surely land could not be far away; in recent days he and his crew had observed flocks of birds, leaves and branches bobbing in the water, even a stick with carving that must have been work of human hands. The crew chanted the *Salve Regina.* Midnight. Still no land. One o'clock. Then at two o'clock on the morning of October 12, a lookout on the vessel *Pinta* saw something rising from the sea. It looked like a cliff. "*¡Tierra! ¡Tierra!*" — "Land! Land!" Above the howl of the wind and the snapping of rigging, these magical words, shouted by one seaman after another, reverberated through the decks of the little ship.

Next the boom of a cannon echoed across the water, the *Pinta's* signal that one of its crew had sighted land. Aboard the *Santa Maria* the navigator, Christopher Columbus ordered crews to shorten sail. The little ships proceeded slowly in the choppy sea for the next few hours until dawn, then drifted around the southern tip of an island. The men could hardly attend to duties; as though drawn by a mysterious magnet, their eyes turned to the island, a solid mass of green trees ringed by the white sand of coral beaches. Soon, groups of men, women, and children from the island began to gather along the shore, their attention fixed on the strange objects in the water which they thought to be some kind of sea animals. Along the west coast of the island

Columbus and his men searched for an opening in the barrier reef and shortly before noon found one. After dropping anchor, the admiral and the captains of the *Pinta* and the third vessel, the *Niña,* cast off in small boats and moved through the shallow water toward a beach. The admiral displayed the royal standard of Castile, the two captains carried the flag of the expedition.

Ashore, the men offered a prayer of thanksgiving and knelt down and kissed the sand, shedding tears of joy. While the islanders gathered around, Columbus rose, claimed the island in the name of the Catholic sovereigns, and named it San Salvador — Holy Savior.

EUROPEAN SETTLEMENT AND EXPLORATION

Columbus had arrived in the New World. He was the first European to discover it, but in fact the first migrants from the Old World had arrived there perhaps as long as thirty thousand years earlier.

The First Americans

From where had the original Americans come? It was a long, long story. From man's birthplace in the Near East or Africa, countless generations of tribesmen had slowly made their way eastward across mountain ranges and deserts to present-day Siberia. Often they were retreating in the face of human enemies, famine, or wild beasts. Sometimes they were following the hunt. Shifting patterns of glaciation in Europe and Asia in prehistoric centuries caused migrations of animals, and at one time there was probably an abundance of game in what today are the barren lands of Siberia. In any event, when the tribesmen reached the blue waters of the Pacific they had no place else to go. Or so it seemed. Then — and no anthropologist knows for sure when — some of them discovered present-day Alaska. The new land was not far away. In our own time, Alaska on a clear day is visible across the sixty miles of water that separate it from the Siberian

HEADLINE EVENTS

800s Norsemen occupy Iceland

900s Eric the Red sails to Greenland

986 Eric the Red establishes first European settlement in Western Hemisphere

c. 1003 Lief Ericson reaches Vinland

c. 1013 Thorfinn Karlsefni attempts colony at Vinland

1096-1270 The Crusades

1295 Marco Polo returns from Far East

1453 Constantinople falls to the Ottoman Turks

1394-1460 Prince Henry the Navigator

1488 Dias rounds the African cape

1492 Columbus sails to America

1493 Columbus establishes trading post at Hispaniola on second voyage

1497 John Cabot reaches North America

1498 Vasco da Gama sails to India
Columbus reaches Trinidad and northern coast of South America on third voyage

1502 Columbus explores coast of Central America on fourth voyage

1513 Ponce de Leon reaches Florida

1519-1522 One of Magellan's ships circumnavigates the globe

1524 Verrazano explores North America

1534 Cartier discovers Saint Lawrence River

1539-1543 De Soto explores southeastern United States

1540-1542 Coronado explores southwestern United States

1577-1580 Drake sails around the world

1578 Gilbert unsuccessful in seeking northwest passage

1583 Gilbert claims Newfoundland for England

1584 Raleigh sends expedition to America

1588 Spanish Armada is defeated

1606 Charters given to London and Plymouth companies

1607 Jamestown founded

1609 Henry Hudson explores Hudson River

1612 Tobacco culture begins in Virginia

1614 John Rolfe exports first tobacco crop

1618 Common law is introduced to Jamestown colony

1619 House of Burgesses meets at Jamestown

1620 Pilgrims arrive near Cape Cod; write Mayflower Compact

1620s Swedish begin settlements along Delaware River

1621 Dutch West India Company chartered

1624 Dutch settlers in New Netherland
Virginia becomes royal colony

1629 Massachusetts Bay Colony chartered

1632 Calvert given charter for Maryland

1636 Harvard College founded
Roger Williams establishes Providence

1638 New Haven founded

1639 Fundamental Orders of Connecticut

1643 New England Confederation formed

1649 Act of Toleration passed in Maryland

1655 Dutch annex New Sweden

1662 Connecticut colony formed

1663 Charter given for Carolina

1664 Duke of York receives charter; English take over New York
East and West Jersey formed

1670 Charleston, South Carolina, founded

1682 Penn takes possession of Pennsylvania; selects site for Philadelphia

1691 Plymouth absorbed by Massachusetts Bay Colony

1701 Delaware given separate government
Penn issues Charter of Privileges

1702 New Jersey becomes royal colony

1729 North and South Carolina become royal colonies

1730s-1740s Era of the Great Awakening

1732 George II grants charter for Georgia

1750 Parliament passes Iron Act

1752 Georgia becomes royal colony

1767 Mason and Dixon establish boundary between Maryland and Pennsylvania mainland; thirty thousand years ago the distance may have been less.

How did these first discoverers of the New World travel? Again there is no certainty. Possibly they moved across the water in crude dugouts, proceeding gradually from one island to the next. Perhaps they left Asia when freezing ice caps lowered the shallow northern sea and formed a land bridge across the Bering Strait. Maybe they simply trudged across the ice during the few months of the year when the Arctic cold froze the waters of the strait. Whatever the mode of movement, it was a story that had much repetition. Evidence is clear that many separate groups of Asiatics (or Indians, as Columbus would call them), having different origins and varying racial characteristics, with little or no knowledge that others had gone before, made their way from old homelands in Siberia to North America.

In North America these first colonists continued their primitive existence. In the rushing waters and gentle inlets of Alaska they fished for salmon; in the forests they found herbs and hunted wild game. With crude spears they even challenged such prehistoric beasts as the mammoth and mastodon. They lived in tribal camps, usually finding shelter in caves, and, like their forebears, moved as necessity demanded. Gradually small bands of Indians inched down the Alaska panhandle, fanned through North America, moving along rivers, through tangled forests, and across burning desert. Others migrated along the spine of the Rocky Mountains into Central and South America, and some found their way across miles of ocean to the tropical islands of the Caribbean and western Atlantic.

When Columbus crossed the Atlantic in 1492, several major Indian cultures were flourishing in what has become the present-day United States and Canada. Therefore, one is mistaken if he holds a single image or stereotype of the North American Indian. About all the Indians had in common were straight hair, high cheekbones, brown eyes, and some shade of copper-colored skin. Otherwise some were tall, some squat. They spoke hundreds of different languages and dialects. Some were nomads, moving about the country in an endless search for better hunting grounds. Others, like the Pueblos of the Southwest, lived generation after generation in the same locales, taking food from carefully cultivated fields. Still other Indians subsisted on roots, acorns, and wild berries. Some Indians were warlike, others not. In some tribes women

had great authority. Other tribes had a caste system as rigid as that of recent India. Some worshiped a supreme deity; others saw divine spirits in a myriad of plants and animals.

Despite an absence of evidence, it is possible that communication between inhabitants of Siberia and Alaska continued up to the time of Columbus. But if information about the vast territory to the east and south trickled across the Bering Strait, it failed to get beyond the plains of Siberia. For all practical purposes, the Western Hemisphere remained secluded from the Old World.

The Norsemen

Columbus, it turned out, was not even the first European to behold the New World. That honor belonged to brave seamen from Scandinavia, the Norsemen.

The Norsemen took their first stride toward America in the ninth century, when they occupied Iceland in the North Atlantic. In the next century a fearless seaman-farmer, Eric the Red, migrated from Norway to Iceland, ran into difficulty with the authorities, and received a three-year banishment from the island. With his wife, one or two small children, and a handful of men he boarded his tiny single-masted vessel and without a compass sailed westward into the Atlantic. His purpose was to explore islands far to the west of Iceland that a kinsman had discovered many years before when blown from his course by a storm. Eric found the islands—and also the vast territory of Greenland. He explored along the east coast of the territory and eventually found a suitable place for a settlement, a spot where green grass carpeted the landscape (hence the name Greenland). When the period of his banishment ended, Eric returned to Iceland, recruited colonists, and in 986 established the first European settlement in the Western Hemisphere. The colony soon had three thousand people and survived for more than four hundred years.

Later in 986, the same year that Eric led colonists to Greenland, a young Norseman named Bjarne and a few companions sailed from Iceland, destination Greenland. Bjarne's purpose was to spend the winter with his parents who recently had sailed in Eric's expedition. But his tiny vessel became lost in a storm. Eventually Bjarne sighted land. Noting that it had no mountains and much timber, he decided that it was not Greenland and declined to go ashore. It is possible that he and his men had reached Cape Cod. Hoisting sail, they caught southwesterly winds, moved northward, saw more land (possibly Newfoundland), and eventually reached Greenland.

Mittet Foto, Oslo

Longships similar to this one were used by the Vikings (Norsemen) almost a thousand years ago. Why did their attempts to colonize in North America fail?

Their energies taken up by the Greenland colony, the Norsemen seemed in no hurry to follow up Bjarne's voyage. Then around the year 1003, Leif, the son of Eric the Red (hence, Leif Ericson), determined to explore the territory sighted by Bjarne. A young man, Leif had established a reputation as a fearless and skillful navigator a few years before, in 999, when he became the first seaman to bypass Iceland and sail directly from Greenland to Norway.

In sailing toward North America, Leif retraced the route of Bjarne's return voyage and, when he made his first landing, had probably reached the upper part of Labrador. After a brief stop, he and his men again hoisted sail, caught northeasterly winds, and a few days later found a territory more to their liking, but decided to sail on and soon made a third landing. Where were they? Scholars are not sure. Some have guessed the southern shores of Labrador, others Newfoundland, and a few Cape Cod or Nantucket Island. Wherever they were, the Norsemen took a liking to the area's pleasing climate and long hours of daylight, also to its large trees and long grass. They built houses and spent the winter in this land which Leif named Vinland or Wineland (apparently because of the presence of wild grapes). After returning to Greenland, Leif dreamed of planting a colony in Vinland. His brother Thorwald sailed to North America the following year, only to fall victim to an Indian's arrow. At this point disease swept the Greenland colony, and Leif became so occupied with problems there that he never returned to North America.

A few years later a Norseman named Thorfinn Karlsefni migrated from Iceland to Greenland, met Leif, and became tantalized by the prospect of establishing a colony in Vinland. He had Leif's support, made careful preparations, and probably around 1013 set out with 160 colonists and an assortment of livestock. No one knows for sure where Karlsefni attempted his first colony. Probably it was somewhere in Labrador. The colonists built stout log houses but found life difficult. After passing a hard winter in which they lived on the edge of starvation, they boarded their ships, migrated southward, and established a second colony, possibly in Newfoundland. Here the land was more hospitable, and fish and wild grain provided an adequate supply of food. The Norsemen even struck up a small trade with Indians, but then, inevitably perhaps, they clashed with the natives. Since their weapons were no better than those of the Indians, the Norsemen may have found it difficult to defend themselves. They shortly abandoned the colony and returned to Greenland.

Evidence discovered and evaluated in recent years indicates that the Norsemen returned to North America and attempted other colonies. But communication between Norsemen in the area of Greenland and North America and their kinsmen in Norway was slight and eventually ceased entirely. There was, moreover, virtually no contact between Norway and the rest of Europe. Hence, information about Vinland, such as it may have been, had failed to filter into central and southern Europe. In the time of Columbus, in the second half of the fifteenth century, some European maps showed Greenland, usually as an extension of the Asian mainland. But neither maps nor chronicles disclosed anything about Leif Ericson's Vinland or Norse colonies on a strange continent to the west and south of Greenland.

EXPLORING THE NEW WORLD

1

The Vikings may have been the first Europeans to sail to America. Archeologists are excavating Viking ruins in Newfoundland. Their finds show that the Vikings made a settlement in America about five centuries before Columbus.

2

This page from an Aztec manuscript made in 1576 shows a Spanish warrior facing an Aztec warrior. Behind them, an Aztec beats a ceremonial drum. In the background is the great temple at Tenochtitlán.

3

Indians of the New World developed a variety of languages and cultures. This pipe was carved from soapstone by a Cherokee Indian.

4

The Indians of Middle America based their way of life on agriculture. This "Feathered Serpent" bowl is from Casa Grandes, Mexico.

1

Photo by Emory Kristof © National Geographic Society

2

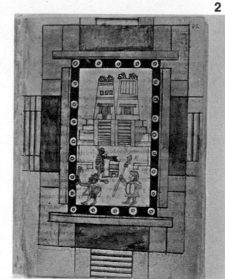

Courtesy of the Trustees of the British Museum

3

Courtesy Museum of the American Indian
Heye Foundation

4

Courtesy Museum of the American Indian
Heye Foundation

5

This map by Nicholas Visscher shows New Belgium, New England, and Virginia. It was drawn before the founding of Philadelphia in 1682. Notice that Visscher has shown New World animals as well as the town of New Amsterdam.

6

John White was one of the colonists who sailed to Roanoke, Virginia, in 1585. He had been commissioned by Raleigh to paint the flora and fauna of the New World. *Harvest Feasts*, a watercolor by John White, is shown here.

6

5

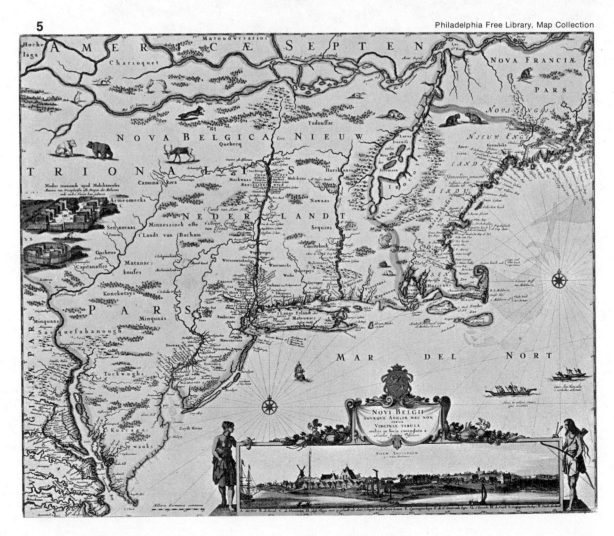

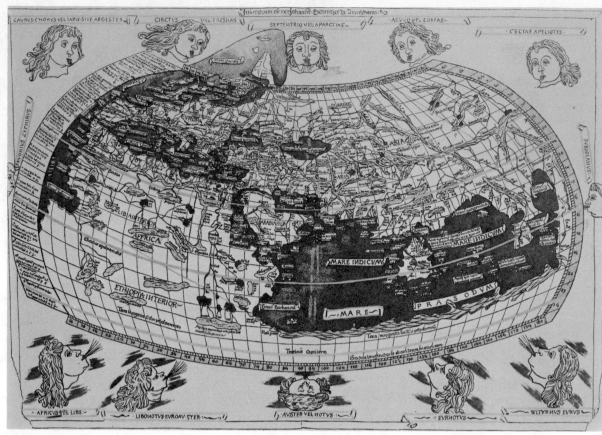

Europe Looks Outward

When the Norsemen ventured onto the shores of North America at the beginning of the eleventh century, Europe was a remote corner of the world. Europeans had few contacts with other peoples or indeed with each other. Population was sparse. For the most part, Europe was a vast forest ruled by feudal barons or lords whose preoccupations were jousting, hunting, and war. Peasants toiled in the fields and after payment of feudal dues had barely enough to live on. There was little industry. Towns were clusters of a few shops and dwellings.

Only one institution brought any measure of unity and intellectual activity: the Roman Catholic church. Most Europeans felt allegiance to Christianity, and many peasants saw the church as a beacon of hope, the only escape from earthly trials. Almost by default the church had become the guardian of European culture.

But the church was weakened by schism, demoralized by Moslem occupation of the holy places of Palestine, and corrupted by a clergy often fascinated by earthly comforts and riches.

As far back as the second century A.D., the famed geographer Claudius Ptolemy drew maps showing that the earth was round. Copies of Ptolemy's maps were printed in Europe during the late 1400s and influenced European mapmakers and explorers.

Then, in the eleventh century, Europe began to change. Agriculture and manufacturing expanded, isolation weakened as Europeans increased trade, and a new commercial class in cities along the northern Mediterranean expanded Europe's dealings in North Africa and the Near East. Next came the Crusades, beginning in the eleventh century and continuing over the next three hundred years. The Crusades failed to wrest the Holy Land from the Moslems, but they helped break down Europe's isolation. Europeans became acquainted with each other while campaigning in the distant East, for under the Christian banner marched men of many nations. Soldiers of the Cross, of course, came in contact with Eastern civilization. They saw the great Moslem centers where scholars studied astronomy, mathematics, philosophy, chemistry, and medicine. They savored Eastern art, tapestries, silk, tea, pepper, cinnamon, precious stones, perfumes, gums, dyes, fragrant woods, ornamental glass, and fine porcelain. They carried their new tastes back home to Europe and inspired more trade with the East.

Almost as important as the Crusades in opening the European mind were journeys by missionaries and travelers in the thirteenth and fourteenth centuries. Where crusaders confined their movements to the Near East, missionaries and travelers ranged thousands of miles to the very interior of Asia and beyond. Inspiring the missionaries was a blend of religion and politics. By the thirteenth century it was clear that Christian arms lacked power to expel the Moslems from the Holy Land. Therefore, Crusade leaders elaborated the idea of converting the Mongols to Christianity and bringing the Mongol Empire into alliance against the Moslems.

European travelers to the Far East recorded what they saw and a great deal of what they did not see. They told of exotic cities with streets of gold, walls of silver, rivers and lakes heaped with pearls and rubies. Easily the most influential of these accounts was that by Marco Polo. In the thirteenth century Polo with his father and uncle, both Venetian merchants, wandered all over Asia, visiting Persia, India, and China, savoring the wonders of the East. Copies of Polo's journals, at once astonishingly accurate and hopelessly exaggerated, circulated through Europe and fired European readers. One can easily envision jeweled European princes poring over Polo's prose, counting the Eastern lands open to conquest, Italian merchants pondering a trade with the Great Khan, and friars in monastery libraries contemplating the souls of Asia's infidels.

About this time Europe began to experience an intellectual awakening known to history as the Renaissance. The Crusades and writings of Polo contributed to this ferment, which started in Italy and spread to other parts of Europe. The Renaissance grew out of increasing interest in man and his surroundings. Hitherto Europeans had focused on God and Heaven. Now they began to search for the origins of European civilization, took up the study of Greek and Latin, and investigated ancient literature, philosophy, science, painting, sculpture, and architecture. There was new interest in geography. The Renaissance gave Europe a new spirit, a new interest in adventure, distant places, and strange people.

During this same period a social and political revolution was taking place. The old feudal system began to deteriorate (although vestiges would linger into the twentieth century). Impoverished by war, feudal lords were losing their controls, while trade and industry increased the power of towns. Townsmen owed nominal allegiance to feudal lords, but lords, often on the verge of bankruptcy, exchanged charters of independence to towns for a monetary settlement. As towns became independent, urban dwellers became more influential.

Europe's kings likewise gathered strength, producing nation states. In the Middle Ages the kings of Europe were nominal rulers, power resting with feudal lords. But lords were perpetually at odds. Petty quarrels and war seemed never-ending. Each principality had its own laws, currency, and trade rules. No one had responsibility for uniform communications. There was little security against a strong enemy, for there was no central military organization. To the middle-class tradesman and merchant of the city, the chaotic conditions were intolerable. As townsmen pondered the problem, there seemed one solution: unify the nation by supporting the king. With middle-class support, several European sovereigns asserted authority, subjugated the lords, and brought national unity. The new nation states had the leadership, organization, and financial resources necessary for sponsoring profitable adventures in distant and exotic parts of the world.

Still, the age of discovery had to await technical developments. Lacking the stout ships and navigational guides to sail uncharted waters, seamen of the Middle Ages dared not venture far from shore. Then, during the Renaissance Europeans invented a compass which enabled mariners to navigate when clouds obscured the stars. From the Moslems they acquired the astrolabe for measuring the altitude of stars and determining latitude. Mathematicians devised longitude tables, and European cartographers, borrowing techniques from the Arabs, prepared new maps and charts. Shipbuilders developed larger, stronger, and faster vessels. At the same time gunpowder appeared, and with it weapons that gave Europeans superiority.

Technical developments may have made it possible, but economic problems produced Europe's discovery of the New World. In the wake of the Crusades, an important trade grew up with the East. Merchants in the Mediterranean, especially Venice, purchased silks, spices, drugs, pearls, and rugs from the East and sold such items at a profit to wealthy Europeans. Goods reached Europe via several trade routes stretching from China and India to the eastern Mediterranean, but movement of cargoes over these routes was expensive and dangerous. It was necessary to transfer cargo from one type of carrier to another several times; cargo had to pass through regions of excessive heat and cold, cross dangerous mountain passes, run the gauntlet of robber bands and pirates. The merchants of western Europe were especially interested in new routes, for they were disturbed that the existing trade routes, ending in the eastern Mediterranean, gave the Italian merchants great advantage.

In the year 1453, Europe's last important outpost in Asia Minor, the great city of Constantinople, fell to the Ottoman Turks, who over the previous 150 years had been extending their empire. The main arteries of Europe's eastern trade now passed through Turkish territory, and the outcome was heavy taxes on cargoes moving between the Far East and Europe. With this development, even the Italian merchants became anxious to discover new routes to travel to the East.

Pondering the problem, Europeans concluded that the best solution would be a water passage, around Africa or due west. The first man to launch a serious search for a sea route to the East was Prince Henry of Portugal. The son of King John I, Henry built a great laboratory in the south of Portugal and surrounded himself with astronomers, cartographers, navigators, and geographers. From this base he encouraged exploration in southern seas. As a result, Portuguese seamen inched down the west coast of Africa. Then, in 1488, twenty-eight years after Henry's death, a violent storm drove Bartholomew Dias around the African cape. Understandably, Dias christened the tip of Africa the Cape of Storms, but King John II renamed it the Cape of Good Hope, for it gave hope of a sea passage to the Far East.

The king's hope achieved fulfillment ten years later, in 1498, when Vasco da Gama sailed around the Cape and across the Indian Ocean to Calicut (Calcutta) in India. Old trade routes to the East quickly fell into disuse; profit and prestige came to Portugal. Still, from the perspective of history, da Gama at best receives only a consolation prize, for six years before, in 1492, sailing for Spain, an Italian navigator had made a far greater discovery.

Columbus

Christopher Columbus was a strongly built, rather tall man with blue eyes and a reddish complexion. He ate and drank moderately, and he did not dress ostentatiously. His son Ferdinand wrote of the admiral that "he was affable in conversation with strangers and very pleasant to the members of his household, though with a certain gravity." Perhaps this gravity derived from the religious convictions which dominated his life. He carefully observed rules of fasting, prayed incessantly, and, according to Ferdinand, "was so great an enemy of swearing and blasphemy that I give my word I never heard him utter any other oath than 'by St. Ferdinand!'"

Whatever his convictions about a world beyond the perception of mortal men, Columbus, who was born at Genoa in Italy in 1451 at the height of the Renaissance, caught the enthusiasms of the age. He took an interest in navigation and geography and went to sea. A turning point in his life came at the age of twenty-five when he sailed in a Genoese merchant convoy, came under attack by French warships off the south coast of Portugal, and had his ship shot from under him. Wounded, he nonetheless made it to the Portuguese shore six miles away. In Portugal the young seaman became a prosperous chartmaker, went to sea again, and made voyages ranging from Iceland and the British Isles to the Equator. He became a master mariner in the Portuguese merchant service. He also established excellent business connections and married into one of the leading families of the realm. By the age of thirty-two a life of wealth and comfort lay before him.

Columbus, however, burned with greater ambition. Over the years he had listened to navigators and geographers discuss the possibility of reaching the fabled East by sailing west, for by the fifteenth century every informed European believed the earth to be spherical in shape.

Such a venture required money and in 1484 Columbus placed his plan before King John II of Portugal. Discussion soon centered on the size of the earth. Columbus calculated the distance from the Canary Islands, in the mid-Atlantic off the west coast of Africa, to Japan as 2,400 miles (it is 10,600). He argued that a voyage of such distance would not be difficult. The king's advisers disagreed. They reckoned that the earth was much larger and persuaded the king that a voyage across such an expanse of sea was impossible.

If the royal rebuff injured Columbus's pride, it did not weaken his determination. Then, in the year 1485, his wife died. With her passing, he no longer felt a strong link with Portugal and turned to Spain to seek support for his great adventure. Securing an audience with the queen, Isabella, he journeyed to the Spanish court at Barcelona and in 1486 explained his idea. The fervor and intelligence of the Genoese navigator captivated the queen, who submitted the matter to a royal commission. Unable to make up its mind, the commission procrastinated—for one year, then two, then three. In his frustration Columbus again communicated with the Portuguese king while his brother Bartholomew sought support in England and France. At length, in 1490, the Spanish commission issued a report. It had reached the same conclusion as had the advisers to the king of Portugal: the earth was much larger than Columbus thought, and no vessel could make the kind of voyage he proposed. Fortunately Isabella continued to have a spark of understanding of the navigator. The queen left the door ajar for possible reconsideration and late in 1491 agreed to entertain a new proposal. Another rejection. With that, Columbus dejectedly packed up maps, charts, and exhibits and set out across the Spanish countryside for Seville.

Then suddenly and dramatically Ferdinand and Isabella, who were known as the Catholic Sovereigns, had a change of heart. The royal treasury could easily bear the expense of the voyage Columbus proposed. And what if by chance he turned out to be right? What if he discovered a new route to the East? What if he found new lands? The reward for Spain might be incalculable. In retrospect, one wonders why it took so long to reach such conclusions. At any rate, Isabella dispatched a messenger to bring Columbus back to the royal court. In April 1492 the crown authorized him "to discover and acquire certain islands and mainlands in the Ocean Sea." If successful, he would become viceroy of lands discovered, receive the title Admiral of the Ocean Sea, share any profit, and pass on his office and rewards to his heirs.

By evening, August 2, 1492, Columbus had completed preparations for his voyage into the Sea of Darkness. The caravels *Santa Maria, Pinta,* and *Niña,* each probably seventy to eighty feet long, were provisioned and riding at anchor at the port of Palos on the Rio Tinto in southwestern Spain, a few miles from the Atlantic. Then, in the early hours of August 3, Columbus boarded the *Santa Maria* and at 8:00 A.M. gave the order to weigh anchor. Chains rattled, and a few minutes later the three vessels were drifting down the Rio Tinto to the sea. Taking advantage of northerly winds, Columbus piloted the little fleet southward along the African coast to the Canary Islands. He tarried a few weeks in the Canaries, taking on water, meat, and other provisions, and also repairing the *Pinta*'s troublesome rudder and replacing the *Niña*'s triangular sails with square ones. On September 6 the ships again weighed anchor, but the epochal voyage did not have an auspicious beginning. The vessels were becalmed and for three days bobbed rather aimlessly in the water a few miles from shore. Then the easterly trade winds began to stir, sails billowed, and in a few hours the Canaries faded from view.

The mid-Atlantic in September-October 1492 was as calm as a millpond, the easterly trade winds blew steadily, and the trio of small ships made excellent speed, averaging 142 miles a day during a five-day stretch. As for life aboard ship, there were few comforts. Rations consisted of salt meat, hardtack, and dried peas washed down with wine or stale water. Only Columbus and the other ship captains had cabins with bunks. The men, when off duty, sprawled about the decks, finding resting places wherever they could. Several times each day all hands assembled for prayers, as was the custom among seamen in those days. Otherwise there were few diversions except storytelling, trolling for fish, and admiring nature's splendor—the deep blue ocean, brilliant sunrise and sunset, stars shimmering in the black sky.

Every man, of course, squinted his eyes several times each day and slowly scanned the horizon in hope of sighting land. Nothing. Then as days turned into weeks and weeks into a month the crew became restive and began to mutter among themselves. They calculated that if they did not make a landfall soon, they would not have enough provisions to return to Spain. Mutiny flared, and on October 9 Columbus promised to turn back if they did not sight land in three days. On that same day, however, the men saw clear evidence that land was not far away—leaves and sticks floating in the water—and thoughts of mutiny evaporated. On October 12 Columbus walked onto the beach of San Salvador.

Although San Salvador yielded no riches and indeed bore no resemblance whatever to the fabled land described in the journals of Marco Polo, Columbus had no doubt that he had reached the Orient. Natives told of other islands to the south, and after a short rest the admiral, in high spirits, steered his little fleet in that direction. He observed luxuriant vegetation and breathtaking tropical landscapes, but no cities with streets of gold. When he came upon Cuba he was sure he had found the Asian mainland and sent members of the crew as emissaries to bear greetings to the Great Khan. But there was no Khan. Still Columbus was not discouraged. He visited other islands and admired the gold ornaments worn by Indians (which they happily traded for beads and hawk's bells). Then, in January 1493, he loaded his exhibits, including several Indians, on the *Niña* and *Pinta*—the *Santa Maria* had fallen victim to a coral reef—and set out for Spain. The return voyage proved one of the most difficult the admiral ever made, and one can speculate on the course of history if the *Niña* and *Pinta* had perished in one of the several storms encountered.

Because of ill wind, Columbus landed first in Portugal and was detained for a short time, but the Portuguese soon permitted him to leave. In March 1493, the *Niña* and *Pinta* made their way into Palos. The Catholic Sovereigns immediately summoned the admiral to Barcelona and, as he trudged across the countryside, crowds gathered to stare at him and his exhibits, particularly the Indians. His son Ferdinand related that when he approached Barcelona in mid-April "all the Court and the city came out to meet him; and the Catholic Sovereigns received him in public, seated with all majesty and grandeur on rich thrones under a canopy of cloth of gold. When he came forward to kiss their hands, they rose from their thrones as if he were a great lord and would not let him kiss their hands, but made him sit down beside them."

Excitement had barely subsided at Barcelona before Columbus was preparing a second voyage, and in September 1493 he sailed with a fleet of seventeen ships. The vessels carried soldiers, colonists, plants, animals, seeds, tools, wine, and trinkets. The object was a trading-post colony on the island of Hispaniola—now the countries of Haiti and the Dominican Republic.

After establishing the colony, Columbus's fortunes began to decline, for the admiral did not prove to be an efficient governor. There was trouble with natives, profits were sparse, and many Spaniards resented Columbus as a Genoese interloper. Columbus made a third voyage to the New World in 1498 and discovered Trinidad and the northern coast of South America. Searching for a strait to the Far East, which he still

thought not far away, he began a fourth voyage in 1502. He explored the coast of Central America on this voyage, moving from present-day Honduras along Nicaragua, Costa Rica, and Panama.

In 1504 the aging and arthritis-ridden admiral returned to Spain. By this time Isabella had died; disgruntled colonists from Hispaniola had undermined his reputation at court; other adventurers had encroached upon his claims. Columbus died a disheartened man in 1506.

In the Wake of Columbus

The mystery of the Sea of Darkness resolved, other seamen ventured along the route of Columbus. In subsequent decades Spanish explorers fanned through the Caribbean and Central and South America. Discovery of North America by Spaniards came in 1513 when Juan Ponce de León, the conqueror of Puerto Rico, set out to explore territory north of Cuba where he thought there was gold and a spring whose waters brought perpetual youth. Touching the east coast of Florida near the St. John's River, Ponce de León sailed around the tip of Florida, discovering the Florida Keys. But he found no gold or fountain of youth.

Other Spanish explorers moved into the southeastern part of the present-day United States. Most important was Hernando de Soto who from 1539 to 1543 wandered about Florida, Georgia, Alabama, Mississippi, and Tennessee, and a few miles south of what is now Memphis discovered the Mississippi River. He crossed into Arkansas, looked for gold in the Ozarks, and discovered the Arkansas River, which much to his disappointment led back to the Mississippi. De Soto died, but what remained of the expedition made its way down the Mississippi to the Gulf of Mexico and thence to Florida. Meanwhile, in 1540-42 de Soto's countryman, Francisco Vásquez de Coronado, led an expedition from Mexico to the present-day southwestern United States in search of the Seven Cities of Cibola, which, according to a Spanish legend, abounded in gold and silver. Ranging as far north as central Kansas, Coronado found nothing more exciting than roving herds of buffalo.

Apart from founding a few scattered missions Spaniards did not follow up North American explorations with colonies. Failure to take interest in the territory that would become the United States is one of the ironies of history. Many a Spaniard has doubtless pondered what course history would have taken if his forebears had made a great effort to occupy the country north of the Rio Grande.

The English—Spain's competitors in the New World—made their first exploration at the end of the fifteenth century. In 1497 King Henry VII dispatched the Venetian navigator John Cabot across the North Atlantic to search out the route to the East that Columbus had failed to find. Cabot struck the North American continent somewhere above present-day New England, probably Labrador. He made a second voyage, sailing as far south as the Carolinas, but apparently foundered in the Atlantic on the return trip.

The English did not follow up Cabot's discovery. Instead, they confined their efforts over the next three-quarters of a century to raiding Spanish treasure ships and searching for the elusive northwest passage through North America to the Pacific. It was after a combined exploratory-pirating venture that Sir Francis Drake in 1577–80 sailed along the California coast to present-day San Francisco. Continuing his voyage, he became the second sea captain to circumnavigate the globe (the Portuguese mariner Fernando Magellan in 1519-22 had been the first).

French activity in North America began in 1524 when an Italian seaman, Giovanni da Verrazano, sailed for King Francis I to find a northwest passage. He moved along the North American coast from the Carolinas to Nova Scotia, but nothing came of his efforts. More important was the voyage of Jacques Cartier ten years later. Also looking for a northwest passage, Cartier discovered the St. Lawrence River and on later voyages explored to the site of Montreal. Cartier thus laid the foundation for the colony of New France, which appeared in the St. Lawrence Valley early in the seventeenth century.

trade grew with the East. Goods reached Europe over land routes. But moving cargoes by land was expensive and dangerous. A water route was needed. Prince Henry of Portugal sent men to find a sea route by sailing along the coast of Africa.

In August 1492, Christopher Columbus, an Italian navigator, undertook a voyage for the king and queen of Spain. He believed he would reach the East by sailing West. His three ships reached San Salvador in the West Indies in October. On later voyages he established a colony on Hispaniola and discovered Trinidad and the northern coast of South America. The Spaniards arrived on the mainland of North America in 1513 when Juan Ponce de León touched the east coast of Florida. Later Hernando de Soto and Francisco Vásquez de Coronado explored southern and southwestern parts of the United States.

In 1497 the English sent John Cabot across the North Atlantic to seek the route to the East that Columbus had failed to find. He landed around Labrador. In 1577, Sir Francis Drake began a voyage that took him to California.

The French government sent Giovanni da Verrazano to look for a northwest passage through North America in 1524. Ten years later Jacques Cartier discovered the Saint Lawrence River.

BEGINNINGS OF ENGLISH SETTLEMENT

The English, as mentioned, were slow to exploit the claim John Cabot had given them in North America. The reasons are not hard to discern. At the turn of the sixteenth century, England was a poor country of some five million people. In preceding decades the country had endured incessant turmoil as rival branches of the royal family sought control of the throne. In the first years of the new century the scars of the recent struggle remained. Next, in the 1530s, came Henry VIII's separation from the Roman Catholic church, which brought to England a long period of religious strife.

Still, England gathered strength through the decades of the sixteenth century. Part of the treasure which Spain took from its growing empire in the New World, particularly from Mexico and Peru, found its way northward to buy the output of English woolen mills. At the

STUDY GUIDE: First migrants to the New World were the Indians, who started coming more than thirty thousand years ago. They traveled either by water or over a land bridge across the Bering Strait. The first known Europeans in the New World were Norsemen. In the tenth century, Eric the Red colonized Greenland. Later his son, Leif Ericson, explored an area he called Vinland.

By the thirteenth century, European travelers were going far into Asia. After the Crusades,

1

2

1. The Winnebago Indians were an eastern woodland tribe who suffered the fate of many American Indians. The advance of the white man forced them to move from the Missouri River area. They were moved many times and finally settled in Nebraska. This catlinite, or red clay, pipe with carved stem was made by a Winnebago Indian. Do you know where the Winnebagos live today?

2. The Chilkat Tlingit Indians were a Northwest Coast tribe living in Alaska. They made ornamental masks and costumes for their religious ceremonies. This dance apron with puffin-beak fringe is typical of the attire created for these ceremonies.

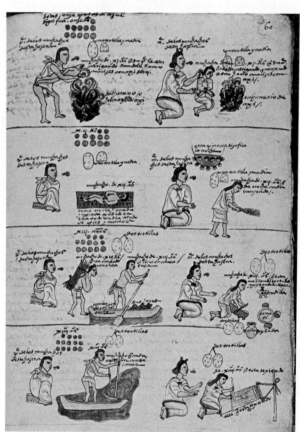

These drawings by an Aztec artist show a father, top center, explaining the vocations open to his son. Among the desirable occupations are those of messenger and musician, top row. At bottom left, the hangman's noose warns the young man that death is the reward of the drunkard or thief.

John White, the leader of a group of settlers sent to Virginia in 1587, was an accomplished artist. His many fine watercolors, such as this scene of Indians fishing, showed Englishmen what life was like in the New World.

same time, English buccaneers, raiding along the Spanish Main, brought in more gold, while the crown's take-over of Catholic monasteries and estates after England's break with Rome provided a financial stimulant.

Until England settled accounts with Spain, however, it could not safely build an empire, at least in the New World. Spain claimed all of North America and was prepared to defend its claim. Spain also was England's rival in Europe, and when in 1588 tension between the two countries led to war, King Philip II decided to dispatch his Armada—a vast fleet of warships which he considered invincible—to English waters. When the clash came, in the Straits of Dover, the Spanish men-of-war, designed for close combat in the calm Mediterranean, were no match for the smaller English ships, which were easier to maneuver in the rough seas off the English coast. Breaking off the one-sided battle, the Armada sailed in disarray northward around the tip of Scotland, only to encounter severe storms. Lashed by wind and waves, nearly half the Armada's ships perished on the rocks off the Scottish coast.

England was now mistress of the seas, meaning that the path was open for establishment of an English empire in the New World.

Even before defeat of the Armada, an aristocrat named Sir Humphrey Gilbert had taken England on its pioneer step toward colonization in the New World. Hoping to find a northwest passage through North America to the Pacific, and also to recoup his sagging fortunes, Gilbert persuaded the crown to authorize him to explore and plant colonies. His first venture, launched in 1578, came to grief at the hands of Spanish cruisers near the Cape Verde Islands. A few years later, in 1583, he tried again, leading three vessels to the shores of Newfoundland (already occupied by Spanish, Portuguese, and English fishermen). Gilbert claimed the territory for England by virtue of John Cabot's voyage. But Gilbert and his men found the climate (and also the fishermen) inhospitable and sailed southward to find a more congenial place for a settlement. After touching Cape Breton Island and Nova Scotia, Gilbert's supplies began to run low, and he set out for England. In the eastern Atlantic the vessels encountered violent storms and Sir Humphrey's ship was lost.

Gilbert's heir was a half-brother, Walter Raleigh, considered by many historians as the outstanding Englishman of his time. Raleigh was a soldier and seaman, also a poet and patron of scholars. He was intelligent, ambitious, and enterprising. He was witty, and his tall, muscular physique, his face that was "long and bold," and beard that turned up, naturally made him a favorite of the ladies, including Queen Elizabeth I.

Raleigh had started for America with Gilbert in 1583 but, much to Sir Humphrey's disgust, had turned his ship around and returned to England. In 1584, after Gilbert's death, Raleigh sent a small expedition to scout the North American coast for a suitable site for a colony. Following Columbus's route from the Canaries to the West Indies, the expedition sailed up the Florida coast to present-day North Carolina. There Raleigh's men explored Pamlico Sound and discovered several islands. The largest island, called Roanoke by the Indians, was sixteen miles long. The men described the soil of the area as "the most plentiful, sweet, fruitful, and wholesome of all the world." So enthusiastic was Elizabeth that she knighted Raleigh and permitted him to name the new land Virginia (for she was known as "the Virgin Queen") in her honor.

Digging into his own pockets and securing support of some other English gentlemen, in 1585 Raleigh recruited 108 men, put them on seven ships, and sent them to Roanoke. The settlers were discouraged by the hardships they encountered in the New World. The following spring when Sir Francis Drake stopped at Roanoke, he offered the settlers transportation to England and they sailed away with him. A few days later supply ships arrived at the island. To retain possession of the area, the captains of the relief expedition left behind fifteen seamen, then sailed off to England.

Undaunted, in 1587 Raleigh sent more than one hundred new settlers to Roanoke. When the new settlers arrived, the fifteen seamen had vanished. The colonists of this third attempt at settlement expected to live on English supplies, and their leader, John White, returned to England for provisions. Unfortunately, the English war with Spain delayed White's return to Roanoke until 1591. When the relief expedition finally arrived it found no trace of the colonists and thus ended Raleigh's attempt to establish a settlement in Virginia.

Raleigh's contribution to eventual settlement of America was larger than it may seem. He made Englishmen aware of the possibilities of establishing an English empire in the North American wilderness. More important, perhaps, he proved that colonial ventures required more than the pooling of meager resources by a few rich men, outfitting some ships, and sending colonists on their way. Colonies needed careful organization, solid financial backing, and regular communication with the mother country.

Virginia

With Elizabeth's death, the new king, James I, divided Raleigh's domain between two joint-stock companies, the London Company and the Plymouth Company. Perhaps the territory allotted to one of the companies would yield a northwest passage to the Pacific, giving that company a tremendous advantage in the Far East trade. Perhaps the company's settlers would find gold. Even if quick riches were not forthcoming, the colonies planted by the companies ought to bring some return from export of food, fiber, and timber to England and the countries of the continent. Recruiting colonists was no problem. There was wide unemployment in England, and many healthy males would jump at the opportunity of a job that also carried the promise of adventure.

First to swing into action was the Plymouth Company, but the first settlers, sent out in summer 1606, returned to England before reaching America. A second expedition established a settlement at the mouth of the Kennebec River in present-day Maine. Then came cold and discouragement, and after a year the colonists boarded their ships and sailed for home.

The London Company launched its venture in December 1606, a few days before Christmas, when three ships drifted down the Thames with 120 men, destination Chesapeake Bay. After a long voyage, with a short rest in the West Indies, the expedition steered northward, picked up the North American coast, and at daybreak, May 6, 1607, sighted the capes of Chesapeake Bay. One of the men wrote that he "was almost ravished at the first sight" of Virginia's meadows and trees. But it was not all peace and quiet. A band of Indians had been watching the English colonists explore the area, and later that day the Indians attacked, wounding two men with arrows.

That evening leaders of the expedition broke open the sealed box containing the company's instructions. These directed the expedition to find a navigable river. The colonists were to proceed inland along the river perhaps a hundred miles and select a site for a colony. The site was to have as few trees as possible so that land would not have to be cleared and so that there

would be no forest to provide cover for enemy attacks. The colony was not to be located in a low or swampy area.

Despite these instructions, the settlers moved only thirty miles up the James River to a low, densely wooded, malarial area and built a fort mounting several cannon. Then they began staking out a village which they called Jamestown in honor of the king.

A week after arrival the captain of the expedition took a group of men to look for gold at the falls of the James River (at present-day Richmond). There was no gold, but the Englishmen did make friendly contact with Powhatan, a powerful leader who exacted tribute from the Algonquin Indian tribes of the region.

Then came disaster. Supplies ran low and settlers failed to meet the problem of providing their own food. There was little fresh water and Indians became increasingly hostile. Within three months Jamestown was a nightmare. By September 1607 only forty-six of the hundred and twenty men who began the expedition the previous December were alive. Over the next year and a half the colony survived only because of supplies delivered by two relief ships from England and the leadership of Captain John Smith. Smith imposed discipline, traded with Indians for food, and ordered the men to raise corn and take fish and oysters from nearby waters.

Directors of the London Company remained optimistic. Securing a new charter, they reorganized the company, and using propaganda full of glowing untruths, recruited more colonists. In the summer of 1609 they dispatched to Jamestown a fleet of nine ships crowded with nearly five hundred colonists, including women and children. Enduring plague and a West Indian hurricane (one ship had gone down and another had been wrecked at Bermuda), seven of the vessels straggled into Jamestown—at the height of the malaria season. Sickness was soon taking a heavy toll of the new arrivals. Then, to make matters worse, an explosion of gunpowder seriously injured Smith, compelling him to return to England.

Now there was nobody to keep discipline, and within weeks famine and death began to overtake the colony. While palisades fell down and buildings lapsed into disrepair, the Jamestown colonists, over the winter of 1609-10 (known to history as the colony's "starving time"), tried to feed themselves on horses, dogs, mice, snakes, and roots. Some hunger-crazed colonists turned to cannibalism, stalking dying comrades, even digging up corpses.

The company soon landed more settlers, and the dreary story of disease, hunger, and death was repeated. In all, more than nine hundred settlers disembarked at Jamestown between 1607 and 1611. About one hundred and fifty survived.

A turn in Virginia's history came with the introduction of tobacco culture. It seems that Sir Walter Raleigh, if he did not introduce smoking in England, at least made the habit popular, despite protests of some individuals who saw tobacco as a hazard to health. (King James I described smoking as "a custome lothsome to the eye, hatefull to the Nose, harmefull to the braine, dangerous to the Lungs, and in the blacke stinking fume thereof, neerest resembling the horrible Stigian smoke of the pit that is bottomelesse.") But the tobacco of North America was harsh and Englishmen preferred the mellower leaf of the West Indies. Then John Rolfe, a youthful aristocrat, acquired seeds from the West Indies, experimented until he cured tobacco he was sure would please the English taste, and in 1614 exported the first consignment of tobacco from Virginia. Englishmen took to the Virginia leaf, and within a decade tobacco had become Virginia's staple crop, the foundation of its economy.

Rolfe performed a second important service for Jamestown when in 1614 he married Pocahontas, the beautiful and intelligent daughter of Powhatan. Powhatan was flattered, and the union brought the colony a respite from Indian attack. At the same time the London Company liquidated the unhappy experiment in communal agriculture which had demoralized early settlers and produced little food. The company now sold or granted land to settlers. In 1618 the company ordered the introduction of common law and a representative assembly with power to enact legislation — subject to company consent.

Still, problems remained. The high death rate continued, and between 1619 and 1622 nearly 3,000 of the colony's 4,200 people died, mostly from malnutrition and disease. Despite efforts by the company to diversify the Virginia economy, the settlers determined to concentrate on the cash crop, tobacco. Thus they remained dependent on trade with the Indians and imports from abroad for much of their food. At the same time the colony tended to spread out, making effective defense impossible, a serious danger when the passing of Powhatan and Pocahontas weakened the truce with the Indians. Then in 1622 a conflict between Indians and colonists resulted in the destruction of the ironworks on the James River, eliminated nearly every settlement outside Jamestown, and resulted in the death of nearly 350 colonists and many Indians. Enemies of the London Company now saw their opportunity. They charged mismanagement and persuaded the king to begin proceedings against the company. Virginia became a royal colony in 1624.

Fluctuating tobacco prices brought ups and downs, but from this point on, Virginia enjoyed increasing prosperity. Settlements moved inland along the James, York, Rappahannock, and Potomac rivers. The population increased, and the colony met its most pressing need, labor, by importing white indentured servants — young

Good tobacco and cheap labor made Virginia a prosperous colony in the 1600s. To plant and harvest the tobacco, colonists began to import growing numbers of African slaves. This diagram of a slave ship shows how closely men and women were crowded together during the long voyage across the Atlantic. Many died during the trip.

Bettmann Archive

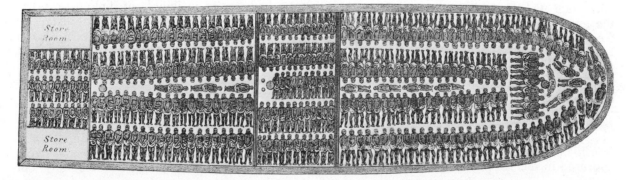

Englishmen who bonded themselves to a master for four to seven years to pay for passage to America—and by importing Negro slaves. Colonial attacks against the Indians subdued them and kept the colony free from conflict for more than twenty years.

What of life in colonial Virginia? The typical Virginia farmer of the seventeenth century owned two hundred to four hundred acres of land which invariably bordered a river or creek, enabling him to move crops and supplies by flatboat. If he concentrated on tobacco, he also raised a few cows and hogs and cultivated a little patch of corn. He lived simply (only a handful of Virginia planters, most of whom had arrived from England with capital, had large plantations and pursued the lives of "gentlemen"). He and his family lived in a story-and-a-half house of brick or wood with a small front porch and a stone chimney at each end, subsisted on a diet of cornbread, hominy, and salt pork, and wore coarse and drab clothing (indeed colonial regulations prohibited him from wearing fancy garments, the "badges" of the aristocracy). He toiled long hours in the fields, working alongside indentured servants and slaves. He was very devout and found comfort and fellowship in attending services of the colony's legal or established church, the Church of England. Apart from religious observances, he found diversion in house-raisings, dancing (Virginians were the most enthusiastic dancers in early America), cock-fighting, and horse racing.

By the eighteenth century the plantation gentry of Virginia had grown and become more influential. And the planter aristocrats, owning large tracts of land, battalions of slaves, and porticoed mansions, gave Virginia the appearance of a colony in which men, emancipated from the desire to accumulate worldly goods, could cultivate learning, the arts, and gracious living. Even for planters, such a picture was distorted; most were occupied with economic problems and few had much time for philosophy and leisure. For the great majority of white Virginians—not to mention Negroes—life was difficult. Most whites were small farmers who owned no slaves and labored in their tobacco fields and corn patches much as had their fathers and grandfathers in the previous century.

Maryland

North of Virginia, across the Potomac, there appeared in the 1630s a new colony, Maryland.

In 1632 Cecilius Calvert, the second Lord Baltimore, inherited the land given to his father in Maryland by King Charles I. Why did religious tensions develop in the Maryland colony?

The men behind the Maryland venture were Sir George Calvert, the first Lord Baltimore, and his son Cecilius, the second lord. The Calverts had two objectives in America: a great feudal estate for the Calvert family and an asylum for English Roman Catholics.

The first Lord Baltimore was a wealthy man who had served in important diplomatic posts under James I. Perhaps because of extended contact with Spaniards, he became a Roman Catholic in the 1620s. Although English law at that time prescribed severe penalties for Roman Catholics, Calvert did not forfeit his influence at the royal court. Thus he secured a grant of lands—a patent—for a colony in Newfoundland. After one winter there he concluded that the climate was too cold. He then sailed down to Virginia. Virginians made it clear that his religion made him unacceptable in the colony, but

Virginia by this time was a royal colony and King Charles I in 1632 granted Calvert some Virginia territory north of the Potomac. The king called the territory "Terra Maria" — or Maryland — in honor of his wife Henrietta Maria. That same year George Calvert died, and the land passed to his son Cecilius, the second Lord Baltimore.

Maryland was to be a proprietary colony, the proprietor Lord Baltimore having about the same authority as the company in a corporate colony or the king in a royal colony. Calvert's only obligation to the crown was the delivery of two Indian arrows at Windsor Castle each year and a promise of a fifth of all gold and silver mined in the colony. Calvert recruited about twenty gentlemen, mostly Roman Catholics, and some two hundred laborers, mostly Protestant. Cecilius Calvert, who never made a voyage to America, directed the Roman Catholics to avoid offending the Protestants and to be silent on matters of religion. With these instructions, emigrants sailed from England in autumn 1633 in two ships, the *Ark* and the *Dove*. The following February their ships entered the Potomac, "in comparison with which" — so one enthusiastic colonist wrote — "the Thames seemed a rivulet." Going ashore, the settlers erected a cross, made friends with the Indians, and staked out the town of St. Mary's.

Thanks to a more healthful climate, nearness of an established colony (Virginia), and good relations with Indians, Maryland had no time of starvation. The first year the colony sent a cargo of corn to New England in exchange for fish and provisions. Still, Maryland had difficulties. Lord Baltimore intended that Maryland should be a Roman Catholic sanctuary but, strangely, few Roman Catholics settled in the colony. Protestants, especially Puritans, migrated in large numbers, and, as time passed, friction developed between the Protestant majority and the Roman Catholic minority. Much of it resulted from Protestant resentment over the privileged position of Roman Catholic aristocrats in the colony's administration. In 1649 the colony passed its famous Act of Toleration guaranteeing religious liberty to all Christians who recognized the Holy Trinity. But Protestant-Catholic discord remained and civil war flared in 1654. Protestant yeomen carried the day, and one of their first acts on taking over the colony was repeal of the Act of Toleration, accompanied by legislation forbidding Roman Catholics free exercise of their religion.

Later the crown restored Calvert's rights in Maryland, but he and his heirs faced unending trouble. There were religious quarrels and disputes with Virginia and Pennsylvania over Maryland's boundaries. At length, in the 1690s, Maryland became a royal colony, the Church of England was established and the capital moved from the Roman Catholic center, St. Mary's, to the Protestant center, Annapolis.

Life in colonial Maryland was generally the same as in Virginia. The colony quickly adopted the tobacco culture of its southern neighbor. It became a settlement of small farms and plantations, concentrated along streams and rivers, supported in part by indentured servants and Negro slaves.

Plymouth

While colonists in Virginia were braving starvation, disease, and Indian arrows, a religious controversy was stirring in England that would have great consequences for America. The controversy was not complicated: a sizable and vocal element of the English population had become disenchanted with the Church of England. In part this dissatisfaction derived from failure of the English church to purge itself of the vestiges of "popery" — hierarchy, ritual, "set" prayers. Critics argued that church organization should be less centralized and religious observance should be simple and more spontaneous. Dissatisfaction also resulted from the corrupt and worldy excesses which critics felt had overtaken the church during the reigns of the first two Stuart kings, James I and Charles I. Among Englishmen who took a critical view of the existing state of the church, there were two positions. One group wanted to reform or purify the Church of England. History knows these people as Puritans. The other group believed reform impossible; the only recourse was separation from the church. These people became Separatists.

In the third and fourth decades of the seventeenth century, Englishmen of both these persuasions settled in North America. First came a band of Separatists — the Pilgrims, as they are better known — who had left England for the Netherlands around 1608. Seeking toleration in the Netherlands, the Pilgrim Separatists encountered barriers because of their lack of skill for Dutch occupations. Furthermore, not being Dutch citizens made them ineligible for membership in craft guilds. Pilgrims, moreover, felt strong attachment to their English heritage and feared that their children, intermarrying with the Dutch, were drifting away from English traditions.

Weighing these problems, Pilgrim leaders eventually looked to the New World. Fortunately the head of the London Company, Sir Edwin Sandys, felt kindly toward Separatists—and also saw that these strong-minded people might prove excellent developers of the company's domain in America. The outcome was an agreement for a Pilgrim settlement in Virginia, confirmed by King James. Supported by London investors, Pilgrims in the Netherlands joined another group of Separatists from England—about one hundred in all—and in mid-September 1620 set sail for America aboard the *Mayflower*.

The Atlantic crossing was stormy. When the Pilgrims arrived near Cape Cod in early November, they were much farther north than intended; indeed, they were outside the limits of Virginia. They turned south but, upon encountering "dangerous shoals and roaring breakers," returned to Cape Cod. Since the group's leaders had no legal authority outside Virginia, some members now threatened defiance, whereupon the leaders and forty-one adults gathered in the ship's cabin, where they signed the Mayflower Compact. This compact pledged just and equal laws for the settlement. An exploring party led by Miles Standish, a hired military leader, investigated the area and decided that a site they named Plymouth would be a proper location for the colony.

The Pilgrims had come upon a barren country at the start of winter and in the initial months the little colony was close to disaster. Cold and disease brought on by exposure eliminated half the settlers that first winter. Sometimes there were only a few individuals able to care for the sick and bury the dead. Fortunately the Indians were friendly. One Indian in particular, called Squanto, acted as a guide and teacher for the colony, showing the white men how to raise corn and catch fish. Another stroke of fortune was the election of William Bradford as governor in spring 1621. A religious zealot, Bradford also was a man of common sense and courage. He remained governor of Plymouth for thirty years.

Plymouth was poorly located for agriculture, fishing, and the fur trade. It failed to prosper, and it made no important contributions to art, literature, or scholarship. Gradually it fell under the shadow of later New England settlements, and in 1691 was absorbed by its illustrious neighbor, the Massachusetts Bay Colony. Still, the Pilgrims proved that simple, intelligent people, girded with ideals and courage, could survive fearsome odds.

Massachusetts Bay Company

In the year 1629 King Charles I confirmed a charter to the Massachusetts Bay Company. Within a decade this company's colony in North America became a citadel of Puritanism. Although a majority of the new company's stockholders were Puritans, they saw their enterprise as a commercial venture patterned after that of the defunct London Company. They hoped for profit from fishing, the fur trade, and farming. A religious refuge was not the original purpose of the colony.

In England, while the king signed the charter, events were stirring which would change the object of the Massachusetts Bay Company. Determined to exercise absolute authority, Charles dissolved Parliment in 1629 and began ten years of arbitrary rule. At the same time, the Archbishop of Canterbury, William Laud, with Charles's support, set out to assert the authority of the Church of England and restore some practices of Roman Catholicism. Adding to the unrest was an economic depression that had lingered from the first years of Charles's reign. Moved mainly by the religious situation, Puritan leaders of the Massachusetts Bay Company changed their minds about profits and resolved to make the projected colony in America a sanctuary for Puritans.

Before the Puritans left England, a new question arose. How could the colony avoid royal interference, especially if officers of the company remained in England, where they would be easy targets for pressure by the crown? Puritans answered with the Cambridge Agreement. The charter and all company officers—that is, the colony's government—would go to America. This agreement concluded, a grand fleet of eleven ships departed for America in the spring of 1630. The fleet anchored at Salem harbor in mid-June. Other ships followed, and, before the end of the year, more than a thousand Puritans had scattered through the region, clearing land and putting up buildings at Boston, Charlestown, Lynn, Medford, Dorchester, Watertown, and Roxbury.

Despite better preparation, Massachusetts Bay, like Virginia and Plymouth, found the going difficult in the New World wilderness. In the first year some two hundred colonists died.

One cannot discuss the early history of Massachusetts Bay without mention of its distinguished leader, John Winthrop, called more than two centuries later by the historian John Fiske "the Moses of the great Puritan exodus." A man of wealth and learning, Winthrop dreamed of a Puritan commonwealth in the American wilderness. Like most great leaders, Winthrop had confidence in his capacity to govern and quite enjoyed the exercise of power. He served as governor of Massachusetts Bay for most of its first twenty years and his intelligence and courage were a source of strength for the colony.

The chief characteristic of daily life in early Massachusetts Bay was a bustling town activity, quite unlike that of such rural colonies as Virginia and Maryland. Many colonists earned their livelihood from the sea; others depended on trade with other colonies and Europe or with African chiefs having slaves for sale. Even farmers lived in towns and villages, walking to and from fields and pastures. A prominent feature of Massachusetts life was the town meeting, chief organ of local government in the colony. The meeting, which was a gathering of all citizens of the town, took up such local problems as roads and schools. Intellectually and culturally, Massachusetts Bay became the leader in English America. In 1636, when the colony was only six years old its government founded Harvard College. For many years Massachusetts Bay had the only printing press in English America. New Englanders also had an appreciation for fine arts, and artisans of the region fashioned beautiful articles for home and church.

The focal point of life in Massachusetts Bay was religion. While some less-devout Puritans had come to America in search of economic opportunity, the colony's leaders determined that Massachusetts Bay should become a city of God on earth. Initially this intent did not imply separation from the Church of England, only a purification. However, after arrival in New England, the Puritans, smarting from persecution under Archbishop Laud, severed ties with the Church of England. In doctrine they borrowed heavily from John Calvin, an early leader of the Protestant Reformation, giving particular emphasis to Calvin's doctrine of predestination — the idea that God from eternity had determined all events in the universe. They acknowledged no church hierarchy; each congregation was independent. Ritual was simple; there were no trappings of "popery."

Church and state from the outset were closely intertwined in Massachusetts Bay. Leaders of the colony, as leaders of the church, saw that every facet of life was subordinated to religion. Such leaders as Cotton Mather spoke out against idleness, which Puritans thought a serious sin, and urged their followers to be thrifty, industrious, and honest. They arranged legislation requiring attendance at Sunday meeting, observance of the Sabbath and measures prohibiting such worldly amusements as mixed dancing, card-playing, and shuffleboard. Non-Puritans were not welcome in the colony.

Still, one should not overemphasize Puritan intolerance in Massachusetts Bay and subsequent Puritan colonies. Intolerance, especially in matters of religion, was the rule among seventeenth-century Europeans. As for their "killjoy" attitude toward worldly pleasures, most Puritans were not "bluenoses." Whatever Cotton Mather and the statute books might prescribe, beer and rum flowed freely, men rolled dice, and families broke the Sabbath. Life in a Puritan colony was a good deal less austere than the pronouncements of Puritan pastors would lead us to believe.

Elsewhere in New England

The religious base of the Massachusetts Bay Colony did not insure harmony, and indeed dissension marked the colony's early history. Debate initially centered on the colony's govern-

The Salem witchcraft trials held in Massachusetts in the 1690s resulted in death to nineteen innocent people. Shown here is one of the original Salem documents accusing two women of practicing witchcraft. Why were more women than men tried for witchcraft?

ment. Puritan clergymen wanted to keep control of civil affairs. They feared that dreams of a Bible commonwealth might go unfulfilled if the colony's ordinary citizens had much say. Farmers, fishermen, and artisans saw matters differently and insisted on a stronger voice in the colony's government. Winthrop and his followers gave ground, but in spite of some concessions to representative government, they managed to direct affairs of the colony as they wished.

More serious were religious differences. In England Puritans had seemed the champions of nonconformity; in Massachusetts Bay they demanded a rigid orthodoxy. Since Protestantism by definition implied protest and the right of each individual to reach his own theological conclusions, conflict in New England was inevitable. The first major clash came when a pious and eloquent young man, Roger Williams, spoke out for religious liberty and separation of church and state. Williams believed, moreover, that Indians were brothers of white men and deserved compensation for land occupied by colonists. Looking on him as a troublemaker as well as a heretic, Puritan authorities planned to expel Williams to England. But, after taking refuge with Indians, Williams and a handful of friends made their way southward in 1636 to present-day Rhode Island. There they established a settlement at Providence.

Williams never had much of a following. Hence he did not give the tree of orthodoxy in Massachusetts a violent shake. The activities of Anne Hutchinson were a different story. An intelligent and kindly woman, Mrs. Hutchinson said that the Holy Spirit illumined every true believer, enabling him to find truth. Such teaching seemed to deny the Puritan view that the Bible was the only source of inspiration. Mrs. Hutchinson's position also questioned the authority of Puritan clergymen to interpret the Bible and impose conclusions on followers.

Leaders of Massachusetts Bay could not tolerate such heresy, especially when Mrs. Hutchinson began to attract support. They brought her to trial and, after proceedings that would do violence to modern principles of jurisprudence, banished her and several followers from the colony. The new heretics followed Williams's path southward and in the year 1639 founded a settlement at Newport. The next year Newport and Williams's colony, Providence, joined. From this union, inspired by fear of Massachusetts Bay, the colony of Rhode Island evolved. It endured dissensions of its own, but for a time

Rhode Island offered more freedom than did its neighbors to the north.

During this time other settlements appeared in New England. Soon after arriving at Massachusetts Bay, Puritans heard alluring stories of fertile land in the valley of the Connecticut River. Ignoring a Dutch claim to the region, several groups of Puritans — about eight hundred in all — migrated to Connecticut between 1635 and 1639. In 1639 the assorted settlements drafted a plan of union. A promoter of the Connecticut migration was a clergyman named Thomas Hooker. In these same years a band of Puritans from England established a small settlement at New Haven. New Haven lost its separate existence in 1662 when King Charles II united the Connecticut River towns and New Haven to form one colony, Connecticut. In manners and customs, Connecticut was a copy of Massachusetts Bay, with only a few minor variations.

To the north of Massachusetts Bay in 1632 a pair of English gentlemen received a grant of land which they divided and called New Hampshire and Maine. Attempts of the promoters to establish settlements in the territories, however, met slight success. Puritans from Massachusetts Bay then moved into the area, and eventually the Bay Colony took control. In 1679 King Charles II detached New Hampshire, making it a royal colony, but Maine continued under authority of Massachusetts until 1820.

New York

The history of the so-called Middle Colonies — New York, New Jersey, Pennsylvania, and Delaware — began in 1609. In that year the English navigator Henry Hudson, sailing for the Dutch East India Company, piloted the *Half Moon* into New York harbor. During that era the Netherlands was one of the world's leading maritime countries. In southeast Asia (present-day Indonesia) the Dutch were busy putting together an empire that was to endure until World War II. The object of Hudson's voyage was to open a westerly route to the new Dutch empire by finding a northwest passage to the Pacific. Sailing up the river that now bears his name, Hudson reached a point beyond present-day Albany. He did not find a northwest passage, and the East India Company took scant interest in his discoveries. Other Dutchmen, however, noted that Hudson had found an area rich in fur-bearing animals, and from 1610 Dutch fur traders exploited the region.

t' Fort nieuw Amsterdam op de Manhatans

The history of the Hudson Valley took an important turn in 1621 when the Dutch government chartered the Dutch West India Company. The new company had two purposes: trade and plundering. After recruiting a few hundred Protestants from the southern Netherlands (a part of present-day Belgium), the company landed its first colonists in America in 1624. The settlers scattered up the valley, but the area around Manhattan Island soon became the focus of New Netherland. To reinforce their position on Manhattan, the Dutch "bought" the island from Indians for merchandise and trinkets worth about twenty-four dollars. The Dutch settlement on the island took the name New Amsterdam.

Affairs did not proceed smoothly in New Netherland. Claiming that John Cabot's discovery had given them all of North America north of New Spain, the British took a dark view of the Dutch presence. Puritan settlers from England and Massachusetts Bay forced the Dutch out of the Connecticut Valley. As Dutch agriculture cut into their hunting ground, the Indians became restive, and the outcome was a series of murderous conflicts with Dutch colonists. Although the Dutch survived, the struggles with the Indians gravely weakened the colony.

While the Dutch labored in New Netherland, a dozen Swedish villages appeared along the

This engraving shows the Dutch settlement of New Amsterdam as it looked about 1626. Forty years later the English took possession and renamed the settlement New York. Did the English have a legitimate claim to this area?

Delaware River, in present-day Delaware. This was the period when Sweden achieved a position of eminence under one of its greatest kings, Gustavus Adolphus. To extend Swedish influence to the New World, the king granted to a trading company a patent to establish a colony on Delaware Bay. The main interest of the four hundred or so settlers in New Sweden was the fur trade. The Swedes lived quietly and in their early years in America had no difficulty with Dutch neighbors at New Amsterdam. But in time the Dutch came to resent the Swedish presence and in 1655 annexed New Sweden. Swedish colonists had the choice of retaining their land under Dutch rule or returning to the homeland. Most stayed in America.

To meet the myriad problems in New Netherland, meanwhile, the Dutch West India Company sent a new governor, Peter Stuyvesant. He took office in 1647. Stuyvesant announced that government should be "as a father over his children," then issued a series of stern decrees, restricting, among other things, the sale and consumption of liquor. Since New Amsterdam was a town of taverns and gin shops, where drunken sailors and Indians were a public nuisance, there was something to be said for Stuyvesant's decrees. Still, the governor was a narrow despot at a time when tact and judgment were essential.

By the middle of the seventeenth century, relations between England and the Netherlands, one-time allies, had become strained. The two countries came to blows early in the 1650s, the war ending just in time to prevent an English expeditionary force from attacking New Netherland. The truce gave Stuyvesant a ten-year respite, but he failed to use the opportunity. Instead he ended the liberal trade policy that had made New Amsterdam a thriving port, alienated the people with arbitrary policies, and failed to resolve the colony's pressing fiscal problems.

Another war broke out between England and the Netherlands and in 1664 King Charles II of England confirmed a grant to his brother, the Duke of York, of all lands between the Connecticut and Delaware rivers. That summer four English vessels carried several companies of soldiers, mostly recruits from New England, into New Amsterdam harbor. The English colonel demanded that the Dutch surrender. Stuyvesant considered making a stand, then thought better of it when he noted that the colony's defenses had lapsed into disrepair and that the settlers were in no mood to fight. Without firing a shot, therefore, the English took over the colony, which they promptly renamed New York.

As proprietor of the colony, the Duke of York, via his appointed governor, ruled with a light hand. His main interest being profit, he sought a harmonious climate in which business could flourish. To maintain the goodwill of Dutch citizens, he promised freedom of worship, non-interference with use of the Dutch language, and protection of Dutch property rights. Still, there was trouble—mainly from Englishmen in the colony who resented the duke's system of rents and taxes and his refusal to grant the people a voice in the colony's government.

Matters did not improve when the Duke of York ascended the English throne as King James II. Then, in 1688, he lost his throne to William and Mary. At the same time a rebellion led by Jacob Leisler, a popular leader in the colony, overthrew King James's regime in New York. The new king, William III, made New York a royal colony, with a representative assembly. Until the end of the colonial period, New York's government was similar to the governments of other royal colonies.

New Jersey, Pennsylvania, and Delaware

The Duke of York's vast domain provided territory for other colonies. When the duke received his grant in 1664 he gave two friends the tract between the Hudson and Delaware rivers. These proprietors divided the land into East Jersey and West Jersey. Then the ownership of the land changed several times. Eventually the King took over and in 1702 New Jersey became a royal colony.

Across the Delaware from New Jersey and north of Maryland lay another great tract of land, part of the Duke of York's grant of 1664. It became the colony of Pennsylvania.

Pennsylvania was created out of the religious turmoil of the mid-seventeenth century. An English mystic, George Fox, denying the need of a trained clergy, believed that Christ taught men through an "inner light." No religious ceremony was necessary, he thought, only "a good conscience toward God." Out of such ideas evolved the Society of Friends, or (derisively) Quakers. The sect thrived in spite of persecution, and soon Fox had thousands of followers, including a young aristocrat named William Penn.

Penn was the son of Sir William Penn, a British admiral. Perhaps it was while in jail for his Quaker beliefs, that the young Penn became interested in establishing in America a proprietary colony where he could try a "holy experiment" in government and society. The colony would rest on religious liberty and political liberalism.

Fortunately Penn had inherited from his father a claim of £16,000 against the royal treasury, and in 1680—in consideration of "debts due to him and his father from the Crown"—Penn petitioned the king for land in America west of the Delaware and north of Maryland. The request was granted.

After announcing his venture Penn's next step was to write a pamphlet which in typical Quaker fashion understated Pennsylvania's advantages. Translated into Dutch, German, and French, and circulated throughout the British Isles and the continent, the pamphlet sought to recruit farmers, carpenters, masons, weavers, shoemakers, and mechanics; Penn wanted no adventurers or speculators. As a lure he promised liberal government, religious freedom, and, most important perhaps, generous terms for acquiring land. Within a short time thousands of English, Welsh, Irish, German, Dutch, and French settlers (mostly non-Quakers) were pouring into Pennsylvania.

Penn sailed to America in 1682 and, after a feudal ceremony in which he took possession of the land, began to explore the Delaware River for a site for his capital city. He decided on a location at a spot near where the Schuylkill and Delaware rivers joined. The town received the name Philadelphia, after a Greek word meaning "brotherly love."

There was no "starving time" in Pennsylvania, and from the outset the colony prospered. The countryside yielded rich harvests, and within a decade the colony was exporting food to Europe and the West Indies. Pennsylvanians enjoyed excellent relations with the Indians, who brought corn to exchange for shoes, guns, blankets, and mirrors. Contributing to the colony's prosperity was high morale stemming from religious liberty and the most liberal legal code in the world. The colony also developed a system of elementary and secondary schools and the best hospitals and charitable institutions in English America.

Still there were problems. For all his liberalism, Penn was no democrat in the present-day sense. He had limited faith in the ability of the people to govern themselves. Hence, he believed in government *by* enlightened gentlemen. His only concession to democracy in the colony's infancy was a small advisory council elected by taxpayers. Colonists chafed under this system, and under heavy pressure Penn in 1701 issued a Charter of Privileges permitting a popular assembly.

To assist Quakers in the homeland, and also to press his case in a dispute with Lord Baltimore over the boundary between Pennsylvania and Maryland (a dispute not settled, incidentally, until 1767 when the surveyors Mason and Dixon established their famous line), after two years in the colony Penn returned to England. And from this point his fortunes began to decline. He lived beyond his means and fell deeply into debt. Then he became a target of widespread criticism in the 1680s because of his close friendship with England's unpopular king, James II. Penn traveled to his colony again in 1699, but after two years sailed back to England, never to return.

Despite Penn's personal problems, quarrels over the colony's government, and occasional failure of the colony to honor its high standards (Roman Catholics, for example, suffered considerable abuse in Pennsylvania), Penn's "holy experiment" foretold the America of the future. It was a colony in which people of diverse ethnic origins, languages, and religions generally lived peaceably and, except for the black man, on equal terms. Pennsylvania's ideas of civil equality, political liberalism, and religious freedom were to become essential principles of American democracy.

Delaware developed along similar lines and was united with Pennsylvania until 1701 when Penn gave it a separate government. Through the end of the colonial period, however, Delaware was a mere appendage of Pennsylvania.

The Carolinas

Walter Raleigh's venture at Roanoke marked the beginning of white settlement in the present-day Carolinas. However, for two generations after failure of Raleigh's colony, white men showed little interest in the region. Then in 1629 Charles I granted Sir Robert Heath title to the land between Virginia and Spanish Florida. The territory was named Carolina in honor of the king, but only a few settlers came. Citing inactivity, Charles II revoked Sir Robert's grant and in 1663 parceled out much of the territory to a group of eight royal favorites who became the "Carolina proprietors." Charles's purpose was to reward his friends and at the same time erect a bulwark between Virginia and the Spaniards in Florida. The proprietors hoped to make money, mainly from rent of land.

The proprietors in the beginning concentrated on the northern part of Carolina. Existing settlements could serve as a foundation for new colonization; there was plenty of level and fertile land; and navigable rivers penetrated the interior. Moreover, the prosperous Virginia colony was nearby. To make settlement more attractive, the Carolina proprietors adopted a liberal policy, including a representative assembly, religious liberty, and generous terms of land distribution. Still, settlement of North Carolina (as people came to call it) lagged, and by 1677 the population was only 3,000. Isolation was the reason for slow growth. Swamps separated North Carolina from Virginia; the wide rivers flowing inland from the sea impeded north-south communication; and the harbors of North Carolina were not deep enough for ocean-going vessels.

Settlement of the southern part of Carolina—or South Carolina—began in 1670 when three vessels of colonists, dispatched by the proprietors, sailed into Charleston harbor. The climate was warm and humid, but the South Carolina colony took root. Charleston was the best port between Virginia and Florida and within a few years it became a center of commerce. The colony had the good fortune to attract several groups of hardy Scotch settlers, as well as a band of French Protestants, Huguenots, whose thrift and industry made them especially desirable. In its pioneer period the colony found markets for its furs and naval stores: pitch, tar, resin, and turpentine. Then, around the turn of the eighteenth century, South Carolinians learned that their climate and soil were ideal for cultivation of indigo and rice. These staples gave South Carolina a firm economic base and assured prosperity.

Until 1712, North and South Carolina were parts of the same colony. Separating them was an expanse of forest and, more important, social and economic differences. North Carolina's economy rested on tobacco and naval stores. Rice and indigo, as mentioned, became the staples of South Carolina. Most North Carolina farmers were small operators, working a few acres, usually without Negro slaves. South Carolina became a colony of sprawling plantations where battalions of slaves toiled in the broiling sun and high humidity of lowland fields. Most of North Carolina's trade was with other colonies, notably Virginia. South Carolina carried on an extensive overseas commerce, especially with the West Indies. Class divisions were not sharp in North Carolina, and it became the most democratic of the southern colonies. The opposite was true in South Carolina, where wealthy planters constituted a social and economic elite. There were few towns in North Carolina and little intellectual or cultural activity. South Carolina had Charleston, one of the most cultured cities in America, and from Charleston radiated considerable interest in learning and art.

The Carolina proprietors never exercised much control over their colony, and, as time passed, their authority became increasingly unpopular. Since their main concern was dividends from renting or (after the 1690s) selling land, they took little interest in the colony's development. Resentment grew in North Carolina when, in 1711-12, the area was attacked by Tuscarora Indians whose lands were being settled by colonists. Colonists blamed the proprietors for the colony's poor defenses. At length, in 1729, the proprietors, concluding that there were more problems than profits, relinquished their charter. The two parts of the colony became the royal provinces of North Carolina and South Carolina.

Georgia

Making North and South Carolina royal colonies did not make their presence any more agreeable to the Spaniards in Florida, so the English crown decided to establish a buffer colony between the Carolinas and the Spanish settlements. To carry out the design, King George II granted a charter in 1732 to a group of proprietors headed by a young aristocrat, James Oglethorpe. The charter gave the proprietors authority over the territory between the Altamaha and Savannah rivers. But Oglethorpe and his associates were to own no land, take no profits from administration of the colony, and were to return control of the province to the crown after twenty-one years. Oglethorpe named the territory Georgia in honor of the king.

Why would the Georgia proprietors accept such an unprofitable arrangement? The explanation is not complicated. Oglethorpe and his associates were patriotic Englishmen who took pride in upholding England's claims in America against the Spaniards. They were also humanitarians who saw America as a sanctuary for persecuted Protestants in Europe and a refuge for outcasts of English society, especially those in debtors' prison. The Georgia proprietors had studied England's penal system, noted injustices in English law, and found that jails were incubators of disease and crime. Destruction of health and spirit was often the fate of prisoners. Worst of all was imprisonment for debt. While in jail, the honest debtor could not pay his obligations and, meanwhile, his family suffered. Oglethorpe and the others believed that with a fresh start in America many of these people could find happiness and at the same time contribute to the well-being of the British empire.

The proprietors set out to recruit colonists and to that end put out publicity grossly exaggerating the advantages of Georgia's climate and soil. There was a modest response and in 1733 – 126 years after Jamestown, only forty-two before the American Revolution – Oglethorpe and some 130 colonists landed at the mouth of the Savannah River and laid out the town of Savannah.

Prosperity came slowly to Georgia. The colony lacked a firm economic base, and from the outset settlers chafed under restrictions imposed by Oglethorpe and the proprietors. Enlightened though they were, the proprietors determined to hold a tight rein on the colony. They set up a land policy that made it impossible for colonists to get clear title to large tracts, granted settlers no voice in government, and forbade the importation of liquor. They also forbade slavery, a restriction which annoyed colonists, who felt that an abundant supply of cheap labor was essential if they were to clear land and cultivate cash crops. Then there was the proximity of South Carolina, a bustling colony whose slave-supported economy was yielding steady returns. For Georgians the comparison between South Carolina and their own struggling enterprise was odious. Many of them packed their belongings, abandoned land and houses, and migrated to the neighboring colony.

Eventually the proprietors relaxed the conditions of land ownership, granted a popular assembly, and lifted prohibitions on liquor. They also permitted the introduction of slavery. Soon Georgians, like South Carolinians, were concentrating on rice and indigo. Still the colony lagged behind other colonies in population growth and economic development. In 1752 the proprietors passed their burden to the crown, and Georgia became a royal colony.

STUDY GUIDE: After destroying the Spanish Armada in 1588, England ruled the seas and began to establish an English empire in the New World. Sir Walter Raleigh tried but failed to colonize Virginia. King James I then divided Raleigh's lands between two joint-stock companies: the London Company and the Plymouth Company. The London Company founded a colony at Jamestown in 1607. After many hardships, the colony learned to farm the land and developed a profitable tobacco trade with England. In 1624 Virginia became a royal colony. The Plymouth Company was unsuccessful in attempts to colonize in present-day Maine.

Colonization of Maryland began in the 1630s when Sir George Calvert, first Lord Baltimore, sought to establish a colony as an asylum for English Roman Catholics. Most of the settlers were Protestant, so friction developed. In 1649 the colony passed the Act of Toleration granting religious liberty, but it was later repealed. In the 1690s Maryland became a royal colony.

Separatists from England and Pilgrims from the Netherlands reached America aboard the *Mayflower* in 1620. Some of them wrote the Mayflower Compact, which set up a civil government for the new Plymouth colony. Gradually the colony was overshadowed by other New England settlements. In 1691 it was absorbed by the Massachusetts Bay Colony.

The Massachusetts Bay Colony was chartered in 1629. Religion played a central role in life there. But dissension marked the colony's early history. When Roger Williams sought religious liberty, he was forced to flee the colony. In 1636 he went southward and established Providence. Mrs. Anne Hutchinson was also sent away because she questioned the authority of the Puritan leaders. She and her followers settled at Newport. In 1640 Newport and Providence joined to become the colony of Rhode Island. In the 1630s a number of Puritans migrated to Connecticut and formed the Connecticut Colony. North of Massachusetts Bay, the land was divided and called New Hampshire and Maine. New Hampshire was made a royal colony in 1679. Maine remained under authority of Massachusetts until 1820.

The Middle Colonies began when Henry Hudson's *Half Moon* sailed into New York harbor in 1609. Hudson was seeking a westerly route to Asia. Later, Dutch colonists settled in the Hudson Valley and called the colony New Netherland. Meanwhile a group of Swedish villages appeared on the Delaware River. The Dutch resented the Swedish intrusion and annexed this land in 1655. In 1664 the Duke of York was granted all lands between the Connecticut and Delaware rivers by his brother, King Charles II. The English took New Netherland from the Dutch and renamed it New York. The duke gave to friends the land between the Hudson and Delaware rivers. The land changed hands many times, but in 1702 the king took over and made New Jersey a royal colony. Pennsylvania was also part of the duke's grant. William Penn, a Quaker, wanted to establish a colony based on religious freedom and political liberalism. Penn was given a tract of land west of the Delaware and north of Maryland. Delaware was part of Pennsylvania until Penn gave it a separate government in 1701.

Charles II granted the Carolinas to a group of proprietors in 1663. Settlement of northern Carolina lagged because of swamps, wide rivers, and shallow harbors. Southern Carolina settlement was more successful. In 1729 the proprietors gave up their charter and the colony became the royal provinces of North Carolina and South Carolina.

Georgia was established as a buffer colony between the Carolinas and the Spanish settlements. King George II granted a charter to James Oglethorpe and a group of proprietors in 1732. They hoped to provide a place where honest debtors could work off their debts. Prosperity came slowly. In 1752 Georgia became a royal colony.

LIFE IN THE EARLY ENGLISH COLONIES

The United States started out as a rural nation. The first settlers were farmers, and during the entire colonial period, the great majority of Americans earned their living from the land.

Agriculture and Industry

The great overriding problem of farmers was clearing the land to plant and harvest crops. Clearing fields from a tangled wilderness was no easy task. The farmer had to fell each tree with an ax, dig out around giant stumps, and, with teams of oxen or horses, extract them from the earth. Little wonder that pioneer farmers seldom cleared enough land to permit the system of crop rotation. Planting and cultivating crops was only slightly less arduous. Such plows as farmers had were wooden implements not much better than those used in Biblical times. To break and level upturned clods of earth the farmer used a crude harrow with wooden teeth. He planted or sowed seed by hand. If he raised wheat or rye, he reaped the grain with a sickle and threshed it with a flail.

Another problem was transportation. To buy salt and gunpowder, pay taxes, and meet mortgage payments the farmer had to get at least part of his crop to markets in towns and villages. Some farms were connected with market centers by rivers and streams, but a great many farmers in colonial days had to move their crops—sometimes for scores of miles—over roads that were nothing more than enlarged paths.

In every colony farmers raised corn, beans, and potatoes; also cattle, hogs, sheep, and horses. Market conditions and variations in climate and soil, of course, created differences from colony to colony, particularly as population increased and the area under cultivation enlarged. In New England agriculture never advanced much beyond the subsistence level,

and farmers through the entire colonial period concentrated on corn and livestock. (The rocky soil of New England discouraged many farmers, who turned to fishing and commerce.)

Farmers in Pennsylvania raised much of their own food, but turned out surpluses of wheat and rye for sale in the markets at Philadelphia. In the southern colonies farmers were the least self-sufficient. While they raised a little corn and a few hogs for their own consumption, most farmers in the South had their eyes on the cash which they could earn from tobacco, rice, or indigo. Hence they depended on other colonies and the mother country for much of their food.

Alongside agriculture, a primitive kind of industry developed in the thirteen colonies, much of it centering in the home. The conditions of life in America, especially in rural or frontier areas, made household industry imperative. To survive, the colonial family had to have food to carry it through the long winter months. Thus it was necessary for most families to smoke and salt meat, dry and preserve fruits and vegetables. Another requirement was clothing. Manufactured garments were not available, and factory-made cloth was difficult to purchase. Hence, most families had spinning wheels for turning flax, hemp, wool, or cotton into thread and small hand looms for turning thread into cloth. From the cloth the housewife fashioned clothing for the entire family. The family also needed furniture and utensils for the kitchen and table. Artisans in some areas turned out such articles— often for the well-to-do—but many farmers could not afford the luxury of ready-made chairs and beds, spoons and bowls. Therefore, they gathered timber from the forest and produced their own household furnishings with crude tools. The family tanned leather and often made their own shoes, gloves, and harnesses for their horses or oxen. Families also made candles and soap, brewed beer, and distilled whiskey.

Some commercial industry existed in households. To raise extra cash, especially in the winter, the farmer and his family often produced such articles as shingles, nails, and barrels for sale to nearby merchants. Other men, perhaps wearied by the labors of farming, decided to earn their bread entirely by industry. Eventually every settlement of consequence had a sawmill, gristmill for grinding grain and sometimes a tannery or brewery. Several commercial industries used the abundance of timber in the colonies. One industry of the forest was production of potash—a form of lye obtained by processing ashes. Potash was used for bleach and fertilizer as well as in the manufacture of soap and glass.

More important were shipbuilding and production of naval stores. Through most of the American colonial period, England sought to reinforce her position as mistress of the seas, and the thirteen colonies contributed to that effort. From American forests came planking, masts, and spars for English cruisers and merchantmen. Much of this material was turned into ships in colonial shipyards, especially in New England. By 1760 the colonies were building up to four hundred vessels annually, and at that time about a third of the tonnage sailing under the Union Jack was American-built. The forest also yielded tar which on distillation produced turpentine and left a residue, pitch. Both of these commodities were important in ship construction and maintenance.

Fishing was another major industry in colonial America. Long before the appearance of English settlements, fishermen from Spain, Portugal, and the British Isles had discovered that the waters from Newfoundland to Long Island were ideal in depth and temperature for such fish as cod, halibut, and mackerel. When the Pilgrims and Puritans arrived in the 1620s and 1630s, they soon decided that the nearby waters of the Atlantic were at least as valuable as the rocky soil of Massachusetts. Before long, fishing villages dotted the New England coast. The most prized fish was the cod, whose head provided feed for hogs and whose liver oil softened leather. The dried body of the cod provided food for tables in New England and other colonies, but codfish of the highest quality often went to southern Europe and the Canary Islands. Fish of lesser quality found its way to the West Indies as food for slaves, in return for which the New Englanders received molasses, used for making rum.

New Englanders found another source of profit in the sea, the whale, and the story of brave men in tiny boats challenging the great mammals of the deep is an American epic. The whale's blubber furnished oil for lubrication and illumination and the waxy sperm oil taken from the head was an ingredient for fine candles, ointments, and cosmetics. The bone of the whale provided stays for corsets. At first colonists took whales that had become stranded on beaches or were swimming in shallow waters near the shore. Eventually, however, New England seamen pursued the whale all around the globe. The most capable and fearless whalers

Courtesy The Corning Museum of Glass, Corning, N. Y.

The colonial period saw the rise of many small industries. Craftsmen produced numerous objects which today are highly prized, such as this blue sugar bowl attributed to the glassworks of William Stiegel of Manheim, Pennsylvania, about 1770.

anywhere, these men made New England the whaling center of the world.

To meet the need for articles of metal—rims for wagon wheels, anvils, kettles, weights, bells, chains, anchors, guns—a few colonial entrepreneurs developed a primitive iron industry. The first iron smeltery appeared in the early years of Jamestown, but was destroyed in the Indian uprising of 1622 and never rebuilt.

Shortly after their arrival in the 1630s, the Puritans of Massachusetts Bay discovered iron at the bottom of marshes of the region, whereupon John Winthrop recruited craftsmen from England who in the 1640s set up a smeltery at Lynn. Other iron works appeared in the hinterland of New England where colonists found rock ore, and by the eighteenth century the iron industry had taken root in New York, New Jersey, Pennsylvania, and Maryland.

With the output of the smelteries, Americans came to meet many of their needs for hardware fashioned from iron. What did authorities in England think of these developments? The mother country had no objection to the production of raw iron in the colonies, but did not like the idea of the Americans converting iron to finished products; the latter process was the job of the mother country. Hence, Parliament in 1750 passed the Iron Act forbidding the colonies to enlarge or build new mills or forges for manufacturing articles from iron.

Labor

The colonists readily saw that the American wilderness offered unmatched opportunity for prosperity, especially if they could exploit its rich soil. But to take advantage of opportunity — to clear fields, build roads and bridges, erect barns and houses — enterprising colonists needed the toil and sweat of many men. And that was the problem; manpower was always in short supply in colonial America. Colonists often sought to meet the problem by pooling local manpower to perform such tasks as raising barns and launching ships. They also put women and children to work in unskilled trades and household crafts, encouraged immigration from Europe, and favored early marriages and many children.

Because of the scarcity of labor, men who would work for pay commanded premium wages. Some skilled workers forced such hard bargains with employers that most colonial legislatures in the seventeenth century fixed ceilings on wages. In their thirst for manpower, however, employers often paid wages above the legal limit and eventually wage codes fell into disuse. The labor shortage also produced good labor-management relations; since the colonial entrepreneur depended on a steady labor supply, he sought to keep hired hands happy.

Still, good wages and favorable working conditions seldom could keep a man in the wage-labor market for a long period. Hired men usually found the lure of cheap, fertile land irresistible, ultimately abandoning the shops or land of employers and staking out farms on the frontier. As Benjamin Franklin expressed it, "No Man continues long a labourer for others, but gets a Plantation of his own, no Man continues long a Journeyman to a Trade, but goes among those new Settlers and sets up for himself."

In the face of the endless labor shortage, colonists in English America turned increasingly to bonded labor. There were two kinds of bonded workers, slaves and indentured servants, and two categories of indentured servants, voluntary and involuntary.

Voluntary indentured servants were usually poor young men and women from England who, dreaming of a life of prosperity in America but lacking money for passage to the colonies, had bound themselves to shipmasters (although they sometimes signed with recruiting agents), usually for a period of four to seven years. The shipmasters thus bore the expense of transporting them to America and on arrival sold their bonds to the highest bidders. Because of the chronic manpower shortage in the colonies, there was never a lack of bidders. The servant worked for his master without pay for the duration of his bond and was a virtual slave, receiving only food, clothing, and shelter.

Involuntary servants were usually debtors, paupers, or criminals sentenced to service in America as a substitute for imprisonment or some other punishment in England. However, importation of convicts aroused much opposition in the thirteen colonies. Benjamin Franklin suggested with tongue in cheek that in return for convicts the colonies might send their poisonous snakes to England. As a result, British officials sent few convicts to North America.

White servitude had its bad side. Considered private property, the servant was subject to lease or sale without restriction, and if his master died, the servant passed to the heirs. To maintain discipline, masters were free to administer corporal punishment, usually by whipping or branding. The largest evil, however, was overwork. Since the servant's bond extended only a few years, masters often broke the health and spirit of servants by trying to extract maximum benefit from their services. Still the system had advantages. It helped meet the need for labor in the colonies and thus hastened development of the country. It also helped many people to get a new start in life in the New World. (One historian estimates that perhaps fifty percent of the migrants from Europe to the colonies arrived as indentured servants).

As for slavery, there were two categories of slaves in colonial America: Indians and Negroes. Indian slavery never became widespread, however, partly because the Indian population, scattered across a vast continent, could not provide a steady supply of workers. Negro slavery was a different proposition. The west coast of

Africa seemed to offer an endless supply of slave workers. Beginning in 1619, when the first shipload of slaves arrived in Virginia, the southern colonies bought slaves regularly.

Every one of the thirteen colonies tolerated slavery, but in the northern provinces, particularly New England, where farms were small and the farmer raised a variety of crops, the slave population was tiny. It was in the South that slavery took root. In the tobacco colonies of Maryland, Virginia, and North Carolina, and the rice and indigo colonies of South Carolina and Georgia, where farms were large and planters concentrated on a few staple crops for export, slavery seemed economically desirable. The planter, particularly if he was a large operator, could utilize large numbers of slaves.

The Middle Passage

Doubtless the most horrifying aspect of the slave system during the colonial period of American history was the transport of slaves from Africa to the New World. The melancholy drama, repeated scores of thousands of times, would begin in West Africa. White slave traders, or blacks tempted by what seemed to be handsome rewards for delivering fellow blacks to the white men, hounded and captured natives. Traders then loaded the terrified captives on ships for the passage to the Western Hemisphere, sometimes packing 350 blacks and more into tiny vessels barely a hundred feet long. Chained hand and foot, the blacks could scarcely move, and their condition was unsanitary in the extreme. In these surroundings, disease was a constant threat and, whenever a slave showed symptoms of a serious disease, especially smallpox, he was thrown overboard for fear that he might contaminate the rest of the cargo. Such drastic action usually came too late, and disease took a fearsome toll. Accurate statistics are impossible to acquire, but it seems likely that of the tens of thousands of black slaves who started on their way to the New World, perhaps one quarter failed to survive the voyage.

Who were the slave traders? Most were Englishmen, operating out of Liverpool, and Americans, sailing from ports in New England. The New England slavers usually engaged in what became known as "the triangular trade." From Boston or Salem they set a course for the west coast of Africa. There they exchanged rum and other goods for slaves. With their human cargoes they sailed along the "middle passage" to a port in the West Indies or North America—perhaps Charleston or Savannah. There they exchanged slaves for sugar, molasses, and tobacco, which they carried home to New England.

Cities

The first villages or towns in English America were little clusters of dwellings intended to provide protection and companionship for the settlers. As trade enlarged—with other colonies, with the mother country, with the West Indies—some towns became important commercial centers. Still, at no time in the colonial period did more than one American in ten live in an urban area.

For many years the most prosperous and bustling city in America was Boston. Like other leading cities in the thirteen colonies, Boston had a good natural harbor. As its importance as a trading center increased, excellent wharves and warehouses appeared. Otherwise, there was little that was impressive about colonial Boston. Streets were narrow and winding, and most were unpaved. Houses were drafty and generally uncomfortable. The architecture of public buildings, churches, and dwellings was plain, even ugly. Still, Boston was an interesting city. At its wharves one could see sailing vessels that had called at ports all across the world: ships bringing luxury goods from England, others engaged in the "triangular trade" between New England, West Africa, and the West Indies, smaller vessels that ran up and down the Atlantic seaboard to New York, Philadelphia, and Charleston. One could also hear the raucous laughter of sailors on shore leave and observe the bargaining between merchants and sea captains.

Similar to Boston, if somewhat smaller, was the port of New York. Originally New Amsterdam, New York had its spacious Broadway, lined with splendid trees, but otherwise it was a drab city of narrow, meandering streets and (except where Dutch influence lingered) uninteresting buildings and houses.

A more attractive city in the view of many visitors to America was Charleston, located along the best harbor in the South, the nerve center of South Carolina's rice-indigo economy. Fortunately Charleston stood in the path of ocean breezes, which kept it relatively free of malaria, the scourge of life on South Carolina's plantations. When the malaria season arrived, wealthy planters gathered their families and

The Pennsylvania Hospital, organized by Benjamin Franklin in Philadelphia and chartered in 1751, was the first city hospital in the English colonies. Philadelphia's medical facilities made it a leading health center in the New World.

Library of Congress

moved to Charleston. The presence of the planter gentry gave the city a social life unmatched by any other colonial city: elegant balls, concerts, and cockfights. Like other port cities, Charleston bustled with ships, sailors, and finely dressed businessmen. The endless coming and going of men and vessels gave the city an aura of excitement that contrasted sharply with the slow pace of life in the countryside.

By the middle of the eighteenth century the largest and most important city in the thirteen colonies was William Penn's City of Brotherly Love, Philadelphia. A hundred miles from the open sea, Philadelphia had access to the Atlantic via the Delaware River and Delaware Bay. It became a leading center for the export of fur, lumber, and grain. Apart from the hubbub of commercial activity, what first caught the eye of any visitor to Philadelphia was the city's handsome streets, many of them paved, shaded by rows of tall trees. At night the best street-lighting system in the colonies illuminated the main thoroughfares. Visitors also admired the many fine brick houses. In medicine and public health, Philadelphia, with its hospitals and medical college, became the most advanced city in the New World. It was the premier American city in music, thanks in part to the many German musicians who had settled in Pennsylvania. And the city's volunteer fire-fighting organization, which was equipped with the best engines, ladders, and hooks of the time, was the finest in the colonies.

As for life in colonial cities, there was much

about the urban environment that sensitive people found repugnant. Despite construction of sewers in such cities as Boston and Philadelphia, urban America was hopelessly unsanitary. Pigs roamed the streets, living on garbage tossed out by housewives. When animals died, their carcasses often lay in the streets for days before being removed. And of course the transient character of much of the urban population— soldiers, seamen, businessmen, adventurers— opened the way in cities for a certain amount of drunkeness, brawling, prostitution, thievery, and vandalism.

Still, there was a brighter side to urban life in the colonies. The city dweller had intellectual and cultural opportunities that were missing in the country. There were discussion clubs—such as Benjamin Franklin's "Junto" of Philadelphia —concerts and the theater, coffeehouses and lodges where merchants and tradesmen exchanged ideas and transacted business. There were dancing schools in most towns, and in every city the well-to-do colonists attended a round of balls where guests danced the minuet, the gavotte, or English square dances. Horse races, fortune-tellers, and magicians offered other diversions. A favorite amusement was group singing, and the increasing preference of Bostonians for lusty English ballads caused the Puritan divine Cotton Mather to lament the demise of the good old religious tunes. At public observances such as Guy Fawkes Day or Pope's Day, Bostonians paraded effigies of the pope and the devil.

Religion

Religion had had much to do with establishment of such colonies as Maryland, Plymouth, Massachusetts Bay, Rhode Island, and Pennsylvania. But religion also had great influence in other colonies. Throughout English America, religious feeling was intense during much of the colonial period. Colonists accepted the Bible as the literal word of God, and most made religious observance a daily part of their lives.

The great majority of inhabitants of the thirteen colonies — more than ninety-five per cent — considered themselves Protestants. There were of course several Protestant groups, and sometimes the hostility of Protestants toward other Protestants was exceeded only by the hostility of Protestants toward Roman Catholics. To an outside observer it may have seemed that about all colonial Protestants had in common was their origin in the Reformation of the sixteenth century and a burning hatred, mingled with fear, of Roman Catholicism.

The first Protestant denomination to appear in English America was the Anglican, at Jamestown in 1607. Anglicanism became the "established" faith (supported by the provincial government) in Virginia and South Carolina and, after the end of Roman Catholic influence, in Maryland. But the Anglican church, despite considerable support from the royal government in London, never became strong in the colonies. The opposition of Puritans kept it from taking root in New England and New York. Even in Virginia and South Carolina the lower economic classes came to scorn it as a handmaiden of royal authority and a friend of the planter gentry.

In Massachusetts, Connecticut, and New Hampshire most colonists belonged to Congregational (Puritan) churches in which each congregation presided over its own affairs. The Congregationalists had little influence beyond the borders of New England. However, Presbyterianism, similar to Congregationalism in doctrine (both were essentially Calvinist) though different in church government, spread throughout English America. After 1700 large numbers of Scotch-Irish Presbyterians began to arrive in the colonies. The Baptists, organized first in Rhode Island, also spread throughout the thirteen colonies. Belief in religious liberty and separation of church and state were the marks of the Baptists' faith. Among the smaller Protestant denominations were the Quaker, Dutch Reformed, German Reformed, Lutheran, and Moravian.

Despite Lord Baltimore's attempt to establish a refuge for Roman Catholics in Maryland, only a few thousand Catholics — about two per cent of the total population — lived in the colonies by the middle of the eighteenth century. Most of these made their homes in Maryland and Pennsylvania. Roman Catholics usually were held in low esteem by their Protestant neighbors. Several colonies had laws excluding them from residence, and in others statutes restricted them in the exercise of their religion. Much of this hostility was a natural, if unfortunate, carry-over from the Protestant Reformation. In part it also derived from fear that in the event of a showdown with the French in Canada — who were militantly Roman Catholic — the Roman Catholics in Maryland and Pennsylvania might side with the French.

As for Judaism, an occasional Jew arrived in the colonies in the first half of the seventeenth century. The first group of Jewish settlers arrived in the Dutch colony of New Netherland in 1654, soon to become the English colony of New York. They had fled persecution in Portugal and made their way to Brazil. Still they did not find peace and freedom, whereupon they migrated to North America. A few years later another Jewish community appeared at Newport, Rhode Island, and over the next century groups of Jews settled in Philadelphia, Richmond, Charleston, and Savannah. Most Jews lived in cities and became merchants. At that, they comprised only a fraction of one per cent of the population of English America. While non-Jewish neighbors tended to view them with suspicion, and even dislike, Jews nonetheless enjoyed a larger measure of liberty in colonial America than anywhere else in the world.

As one would expect, most migrants to America became members of the same religious organizations to which they had been attached in the Old World. Reestablishing the old ties, however, was impossible for one segment of the population in the thirteen colonies: the slaves.

Whether or not to convert slaves to Christianity was a question that weighed on the minds of many colonists, particularly in the South where slavery was a pillar of the economy. Slave owners seemed to fear that admission of slaves to the Christian brotherhood would compel their emancipation. After all, it did not seem Christian to hold one's brother in bondage. To resolve the dilemma of devout slave owners, some colonial legislatures determined that a black could become a Christian and remain a slave. This raised the question of whether black Christians and white Christians would worship together in the same churches, or whether slaves would have their own churches. Most whites did not want to share their churches with blacks. But many white people were afraid that all-black churches might become centers of rebellion by slaves against their white owners. Whites could not agree on what to do, so in some communities slaves joined white congregations, and in other places the churches were segregated.

Because of this issue, few white colonists made any real efforts to convert slaves to Christianity, even though the issue was discussed widely. By the time of the Revolution, in the 1770s, only a small percentage of the black population had formally embraced Christianity.

Certainly the greatest religious happening of the colonial era was the Great Awakening, a religious revival that swept English America in the 1730s and 1740s. The revival followed a period in which colonists had exhibited little interest in affairs of the spirit. Some individuals became alarmed over this religious decline, among them Jonathan Edwards, a pious and brilliant Congregationalist minister in Massachusetts. Edwards was one of a handful of bona fide intellectuals to appear in colonial America. It was he who provided the spark for the Great Awakening.

Despite his intelligence and interest in logical exposition, Edwards aimed his gospel message straight at the emotions, warning listeners of the grim consequences of sin, and conjuring up visions of the torments of hell. The power of his oratory, his piety, and also the mystical quality that seemed to envolop him, gave Edwards great appeal. When a gallery of his old meetinghouse at Northampton collapsed during a sermon without injuring the people below, colonists were sure that he had the approval of God. Another leading spokesman of the Great Awakening was a velvet-tongued Englishman, George Whitefield, who traveled about the colonies, exhorting congregations to put away their sins and walk in the path of the Lord. (When an Anglican cleric, disapproving of Whitefields's simple, emotional appeal, said, "Mr. Whitefield, I am sorry you are here," Whitefield replied: "Yes, and so is the devil.")

By the 1750s the Great Awakening had begun to burn itself out, and once again religion seemed in decline in the colonies.

STUDY GUIDE: The United States began as a rural nation. Clearing land, planting, and cultivating were hard. Farming equipment was primitive. Transportation was also a problem. New England soil was so rocky that farmers turned to fishing and commerce for a livelihood. Middle Colony farmers were able to produce a surplus, but southern colonies had to depend on other colonies and England for much of their food. Shipbuilding and fishing became major industries.

Manpower was always scarce in the colonies. Men who could work demanded high wages. To solve the labor shortage, colonists turned to bonded labor. There were two kinds of bonded workers: indentured servants and slaves. Most slave traders were Englishmen or New Englanders. Some slavers engaged in "triangular trade." Triangular trade was between New England, the West Indies, and the west coast of Africa.

Boston, New York, Charleston, and Philadelphia were the major colonial cities. Religious feeling was strong during much of the colonial period. Most of the colonists were Protestants. Only a small percentage of the population was Catholic or Jewish.

THE EXPANDING BRITISH EMPIRE

The establishment of Georgia rounded out the English colonies that would proclaim independence in 1776 and become the United States. One should note, however, that these thirteen colonies were only part of an expanding British Empire. By the time of the Revolution, they did not necessarily seem to be the most valuable part.

At Calcutta, Madras, and Bombay the English East India Company was finding profits for the mother country and preparing the foundation that would make India a jewel in the British imperial crown. Using the Levant Company and bases at Gibraltar and Minorca, the British were extending influence into the Mediterranean and Middle East. They had a colony at Senegambia (present-day Senegal) on the west coast of Africa and trading posts at Cape Coast (present-day Ghana) and on the island of Saint Helena in the South Atlantic. By 1776 the Em-

COLONIES IN 1750

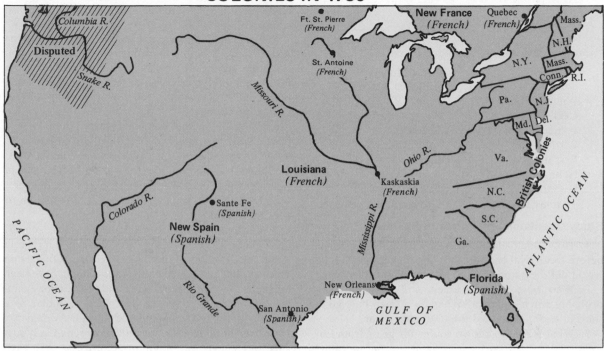

pire in the Western Hemisphere reached from the Arctic Circle to the Falkland Islands off the coast of Argentina. Far to the north the Hudson's Bay Company, chartered in 1670, had founded fur-trading settlements. Following wars with France, the English had gained Nova Scotia, Newfoundland, and, in 1763, Canada—rich in furs, timber, and fish. The English in 1688 had established a colony in Honduras in Central America, noted for dyewood. There was a settlement in Guiana along the north coast of South America (present-day Guyana). Most profitable of all were British holdings in the islands of the western Atlantic and Caribbean.

Settlement of England's island empire in the Western Hemisphere had begun in 1609 when a supply ship bound for Virginia was wrecked at Bermuda. Survivors founded a colony which became an important producer of tobacco. From Bermuda, Puritan malcontents moved on and in 1656 established a settlement in the Bahamas. The English colonized the West Indian islands of Saint Christopher and Barbados, and by 1639 —when Virginia's population was 7,000—Barbados had 20,000 people. Jamaica was captured by William Penn's father in 1655. These tropical islands in the seventeenth and eighteenth centuries contributed more to the mother country's

prosperity than did the thirteen mainland colonies that became the United States. They produced tobacco and later sugar and molasses, which they exchanged for food and manufactured articles. And they had an insatiable appetite for Negro slaves, a source of profit for the mother country.

Thus when English statesmen turned to colonial affairs in the seventeenth and eighteenth centuries, their thoughts did not necessarily center on Massachusetts Bay, Virginia, or South Carolina. Their minds ranged over an empire that girdled more than half the globe, an empire with a wide diversity of people and economic interests.

STUDY GUIDE: The thirteen colonies were only a part of an expanding British Empire. There were colonies also in India, Gibraltar, Minorca, and Africa. In the North, the Hudson's Bay Company founded fur-trading settlements. Most profitable holdings were those in the western Atlantic and Caribbean. Settlement began there in 1609 when a ship was wrecked at Bermuda. An important tobacco-producing colony was founded. In 1656 settlement was started in the Bahamas.

SUMMING UP THE CHAPTER

Names and Terms to Identify

astrolabe	Anne Hutchinson
Bahamas	Thorfinn Karlsefni
William Bradford	*Pinta*
Cecilius Calvert	Savannah River
Jacques Cartier	Roanoke
Bartholomew Dias	John Rolfe
Eric the Red	royal colony
Henry the Navigator	San Salvador
Hispaniola	Peter Stuyvesant
Thomas Hooker	Giovanni da Verrazano

Study Questions and Points to Review

1. How long had the Indians been in the Americas before the arrival of Columbus? From what part of the world did they come? What was their probable route?

2. Who were the Norsemen, and when did they probably reach America? When did Marco Polo go to the Far East? When did the Crusades occur?

3. What were the known routes for going from Europe to the Far East by water and by land in 1400?

4. Briefly explain the differences between English corporate, proprietary, and royal colonies.

5. Name the thirteen original English colonies. When was the first founded?

6. In what ways was the Plymouth colony different from the first colony at Jamestown?

7. What religious and social conditions in Europe encouraged many colonists to come to America?

8. List some products or raw materials that colonies sent back to England. List some products that they had to import from England.

9. What were the major religious groups represented in the colonies?

Topics for Discussion

1. Discuss the justifications Europeans might have given for settling in lands already inhabited by Indians. Consider in your discussion what the Indian viewpoint might have been toward the new settlers.

2. Conduct a panel discussion on economic reasons for the European settlement of the New World. Consider the English, Spanish, French, and Dutch nations in the 1500s and 1600s. Why did each want colonies?

3. What kinds of people do you think might have been attracted to the colonies? (Consider age, sex, occupations, personal qualities in your discussion.) Can you make a case for the idea that the early colonial population did *not* represent a true cross section of European culture? (For example, what skilled workers would not have wanted to go to the colonies?)

4. Compare the settlement of Negroes in Spanish colonies with their settlement in French and English colonies.

5. Exchange opinions (backed by references to the text and reference books) concerning motives for colonization: desire for wealth; religious freedom; desire for adventure. Make a list of reasons suggested and take a poll of the class to see which motive is considered to be strongest.

6. Throughout the colonial period there was a frontier and new lands to which settlers could move. What do you believe our frontiers are today? What are the most important ones: new lands or the realm of new ideas and solutions to social problems? Could new uses for land not presently settled aid in solution of social problems?

7. Our accounts of the Indians are based chiefly upon those given by European explorers who wrote and made drawings of the Indians as they found them. Discuss why and how these accounts might have been influenced by European values and ideas. (For example, Europeans might have described an Indian as a "king"—but the Indian idea of a leader would not have been at all like that of the Europeans.) Is it possible to compare two different cultures, or must each be described and evaluated within the framework of its own values and customs?

Subjects for Reports or Essays

1. Assume that you are a young Englishman in 1740 preparing to come to the American colonies. Write a letter to a friend explaining which colony you have chosen to settle in and why you chose it.

2. Pretend that you are a slave in one of the large colonial cities in 1700. Write a poem or essay expressing your attitude and feelings about your life.

3. Imagine that you are an English visitor to an American colony in 1635. Write a letter home describing differences between life in the colonies and life at home.

4. In your library find references describing the lives of any two people mentioned in this chapter. Try to choose two people whose attitudes and backgrounds were very different. Write an essay or report comparing and contrasting the two.

Projects, Activities, and Skills

1. Make a list of encyclopedias and general reference books in your school library that will be useful in studying United States history. Be sure to include atlases that your library has.

2. Study Map 5 in the Atlas. List the explorers, and their nationalities, who explored present-day United States before settlements were made at Jamestown and Plymouth.

3. Use reference books (encyclopedias or *Webster's New Geographical Dictionary*) to write a short description of one Spanish mission and one French fort shown on Atlas Map 4. Use Map 1 in the Atlas to find a modern city near the mission and fort about which you write your report.

4. Use Table 5 in the Appendix to compare the growth of population in each colony between 1610 and 1700. Which colony had the greatest increase in population? List in order the three colonies that had the largest black populations. Prepare a poster with charts or graphs illustrating the growth of population in the colonies in the period 1610-1700.

5. Refer to Table 6 in the Appendix. In which years between 1697 and 1735 did the colonies import more goods than they exported? Prepare a graph showing colonial imports and exports for the years shown from 1697 through 1735.

6. Prepare a program of music or dances popular in the 1600s.

7. Make a time line indicating major events in America and major events in Europe, Africa, and Asia between 1600 and 1700. (Refer to world history books for information.)

8. Make a book report on a book written in England between 1600 and 1700 and point out references to America or the colonies.

Further Readings

General

The Atlantic Frontier: Colonial American Civilization, 1607-1763 by Louis B. Wright. Social and cultural history.

The Colonial Period of American History: The Settlements (3 vols.) by Charles M. Andrews.

The Devil in Massachusetts: A Modern Inquiry into the Salem Witch Trials by Marion L. Starkey. Interesting study of the Puritan witch hunts.

The European Discovery of America: The Northern Voyages by Samuel Eliot Morison.

Pioneers of France in the New World by Francis Parkman. First published in 1865 and since brought out in many editions. Excellent book on early French activity in America.

They Saw America First by Katherine Bakeless and John Bakeless. The adventures and discoveries of America's explorers, from Columbus to Lewis and Clark.

Biography

Admiral of the Ocean Sea by Samuel Eliot Morison. Massive two-volume work, also published in one volume without maps and charts.

Christopher Columbus, Mariner by Samuel Eliot Morison. To write this story, Morison went to sea in ships similar to those of Columbus and retraced the voyages.

James Edward Oglethorpe by Joyce Blackburn.

Jonathan Edwards and *Master Roger Williams* by Ola E. Winslow.

Puritan Dilemma: The Story of John Winthrop by Edmund S. Morgan.

William Penn: A Biography by Catherine O. Peare. One of the more recent biographies.

Fiction, Drama, and Poetry

The Crucible by Arthur Miller. A modern play about the Salem witch trials.

Evangeline, Hiawatha, and *The Courtship of Miles Standish* by Henry Wadsworth Longfellow. Narrative poetry.

The Fair God by Lew Wallace. Mexico during the conquest of Cortez.

The House of the Seven Gables by Nathaniel Hawthorne. The story of a Salem family curse.

Shadows on the Rock by Willa Cather. Seventeenth-century Quebec.

To Have and To Hold by Mary Johnston. Romance in early Virginia.

Westward Ho! by Charles Kingsley. Adventure on the Spanish main.

The Yemassee by William Gilmore Simms. Written in 1835; describes the conflict between the Yemassee Indians and the British in 1715.

Pictorial History

Age of Exploration by John R. Hale and the editors of Time-Life Books.

Ancient America by Jonathan N. Leonard and the editors of Time-Life Books.

Ebony Pictorial History of Black America, Vol. 1, by the editors of *Ebony.*

CHAPTER 2

THE NEW NATION

IT WAS INEVITABLE that one day Americans would be independent of Great Britain. Over the decades the thirteen colonies slowly achieved a condition which students of colonialism describe as nationhood. On their side of the Atlantic, Americans established a unique society. Their economy gradually matured to the point where it could no longer live satisfactorily within the limits of Britain's imperial policy. Americans had matured politically, understood politics, and were determined to chart their own political destiny.

Americans had come of age. The child had grown to manhood; the time had come to cut the strings binding colonies to mother country. Still one should not judge harshly England's failure to comprehend this fact. No previous imperial power had experienced the growth of colonies into nations. No one indeed had considered such a possibility.

To England's credit, it did not miss the lesson of the American experience. Following loss of the thirteen colonies, the British Empire continued to expand until it became the greatest empire in the world's history, stretching from the British Isles to Canada and the West Indies, to Central and South America, the South Sea Islands, Australia, New Zealand, Hong Kong, Malaya, Burma, India, Ceylon, Africa, the Middle East, and the Mediterranean. Still, the British did not forget that colonies become nations. Instead of thwarting the growth of colonies, in most instances Great Britain nurtured it. And when England concluded that the colony had reached maturity it cut the colonial cord— Canada, Australia, New Zealand, South Africa, India, Pakistan, Ceylon, Burma, Malaya, Ghana, Kenya, Nigeria, Jamaica, Trinidad, Guyana. The fruits of such policy? In most instances the British retained the goodwill—in some cases the fierce loyalty—of the new nations.

THE OLD COLONIAL SYSTEM

More than a century and a half elapsed between establishment of the first permanent English settlement at Jamestown in 1607 and the close of the French and Indian War in 1763. Historians generally mark 1763 as the beginning of the "age of the American Revolution." Up until that time there was little friction between colonies and mother country. The cumbersome system through which the imperial government in London sought to administer the colonies was not oppressive, the powers of colonial assemblies increased steadily, and assemblies became adept at getting around the authority of royal officials. The imperial government did not place many restrictions on the colonies and usually declined to enforce those it did impose.

Mercantilism

English imperial policy—such as it was before 1763—rested on a philosophy called mercantilism. Mercantilism looked to the creation of a self-sufficient empire—an empire that would meet its own needs in food and raw materials, produce its own manufactured goods, provide markets for its industrial output, handle its own shipping. To achieve mercantilist ends, the British government over the years enacted a number of laws. Navigation acts sought to build British sea power by prohibiting non-English ships from carrying cargo in or out of English or colonial ports. Naval stores acts provided bounties for colonial producers of hemp, pitch, tar, and turpentine and restricted the cutting of white pine trees. Another measure sought to assure the mother country profit in trade between colonies and other countries by compelling ships to stop in England to pay tariffs.

To promote self-sufficiency the imperial government decreed that certain "enumerated" articles produced in colonies had to go only to England. Such articles included sugar, tobacco, indigo, rice, molasses, naval stores, beaver skins, and copper. To make certain that the mother country would remain the manufacturing center of the empire, the government passed laws restricting colonial manufacture of wool, hats, and iron goods. To encourage planters in the British West Indies, a molasses act imposed prohibitive duties on rum, molasses, and sugar imported by mainland colonies from the non-English West Indies. To encourage production of dye for the English woolen industry, there were bounties to American indigo planters.

HEADLINE
EVENTS

1689 King William's War begins
1701 Queen Anne's War begins
1713 Treaty of Utrecht
1740s King George's War begins
1748 Treaty of Aix-la-Chapelle
1754 French and Indian War begins
Albany Congress
1755 Braddock defeated
1759 British seize Quebec
1763 Treaty of Paris
Proclamation of 1763
1764 Sugar Act
Currency Act
1765 Quartering Act
Stamp Act
Stamp Act Congress is called
1766 Stamp Act repealed
Declaratory Act
1767 Townshend Acts
1770 Boston Massacre
Townshend Acts repealed except on tea
1773 Parliament passes Tea Act
Boston Tea Party
1774 Parliament passes Intolerable Acts
First Continental Congress meets
1775 Battles of Lexington and Concord
Second Continental Congress meets
Battle of Bunker Hill
Washington takes command of Continental army
1776 Thomas Paine's *Common Sense*
General Howe's troops evacuate Boston
Declaration of Independence
Battle of Long Island
Washington attacks at Trenton
1777 Battle of Princeton
General Howe captures Philadelphia
Burgoyne takes Fort Ticonderoga
St. Leger retreats to Canada
Burgoyne loses Battle of Bennington
Battle of Germantown
Battle of Saratoga
Congress approves Articles of Confederation

1778 Treaty of Alliance with France
Savannah falls to British
1780 British capture Charleston
Americans win at King's Mountain
1781 Nathanael Greene wins at Cowpens
Cornwallis surrenders at Yorktown
Articles of Confederation ratified by all thirteen states
1781-1789 Confederation period
1783 Treaty of Paris
1785 Land Ordinance
1786 Annapolis Convention
1787 Shays's Rebellion
Northwest Ordinance
Constitutional Convention
1788 Constitution ratified by eleven states
1789 Washington unanimously elected as first president
Congress proposes Bill of Rights
Congress creates Departments of State, War, and Treasury
1791 Bank of the United States created
Congress votes whiskey tax
Vermont enters the Union
Bill of Rights ratified
1792 Kentucky enters the Union
War breaks out in Europe
1793 Washington proclaims neutrality
Genêt affair
1794 Whiskey Rebellion
Battle of Fallen Timbers
1795 Jay's Treaty
Pinckney's Treaty
Treaty of Greenville
1796 Tennessee enters the Union
Washington delivers Farewell Address
1797 John Adams inaugurated president
XYZ Affair
1798 Eleventh Amendment ratified
Naturalization, Alien, and Sedition Acts
Department of the Navy is created
Virginia and Kentucky resolutions
1800 National capital moves to Washington
Jefferson wins presidency

The grand objective of this "old colonial system" was to increase the power and wealth of Great Britain and its colonies — in that order. The imperial government considered the colonies part of the English nation, but a subordinate part. The ideal, of course, was that colonies would never compete with the mother country; America and England, for example, should complement one another. Still, the mother country would receive first consideration.

Such a relation between mother country and colonies seems unfair, and one may wonder why the American Revolution was so long in coming. There are several explanations for American patience. Colonists thought of themselves as loyal Englishmen and generally accepted the idea that profits of empire should center in the mother country. Second, the imperial government down to 1763 seldom tried vigorously to enforce mercantilist laws. Third, colonists derived benefit from imperial policy. As mentioned, there were bounties for producing particular commodities. There was also the monopoly of the English market by American tobacco growers and protection of the colonies by the imperial army and navy — supported by taxes paid by Britons, not colonials.

STUDY GUIDE: There was little friction between the colonies and England in the early colonial period. But over the years the British tried to control trade with the colonies under a policy called mercantilism. Mercantilism was based on the idea that colonies should provide wealth for the mother country. Various laws were passed to increase Britain's power. Among these were navigation acts, which prohibited non-British ships from carrying cargo to or from colonial ports. Americans were patient with British laws for a long time because the colonies did benefit from imperial rule. Moreover, until 1763 Britain seldom tried to enforce these mercantilist laws.

THE COLONIAL WARS

Another reason for American patience with English imperial policy down to 1763 was the presence of the French in North America. French settlement of the Saint Lawrence Valley had begun two years after establishment of the colony at Jamestown. While for many years there was no serious conflict, France was the tradi-tional rival of England, and English colonies lived under a threat of attack.

War finally came in 1689 following an outbreak of hostilities in Europe between England and France. Known as King William's War, the conflict was essentially a guerrilla action centered in New England. A second war erupted between England and France in 1701, and again the war in Europe had its American counterpart — Queen Anne's War. This time the English colonists showed more initiative. They attacked Montreal and Quebec, and captured Acadia (present-day Nova Scotia) and the strategic harbor of Port Royal. The war in Europe also went well for the English. By the Treaty of Utrecht (1713) the French gave up Acadia, Newfoundland, and the region around Hudson's Bay.

Peace held for the next quarter-century, during which time the English in America expanded west and south while the French penetrated the Ohio and Mississippi valleys. A war in Europe about 1740 ended the calm, and once more the European conflict had a counterpart in America, King George's War. Guerrilla fighting was again the rule and the war ended in 1748 with no fundamental changes.

The treaty of 1748 proved only a truce, and six years later another conflict broke out. This time it originated in America and spread to Europe. The quarrel that caused the fourth and final "colonial war," known as the French and Indian War (in Europe the Seven Years' War), was ownership of the Ohio Valley. Both France and England claimed the area, although only the French had supported their claim by settlements.

To protest the French activity in the Ohio Valley, the governor of Virginia in 1753 sent twenty-one-year-old George Washington to a French garrison along the shores of Lake Erie. Politely but firmly the French rejected the protest. The next year, 1754, Washington again moved westward, this time as a commander of militia. In western Pennsylvania he clashed with French skirmishers (the first fighting of the war) and retreated to Fort Necessity, which he had prepared against such an emergency. After a one-day battle in a driving rainstorm, he surrendered.

A year later, in 1755, Washington was again on his way to the West, this time as an aide to General Edward Braddock. On orders from London, Braddock was leading British regulars against Fort Duquesne, the French garrison at

FRENCH AND INDIAN WAR

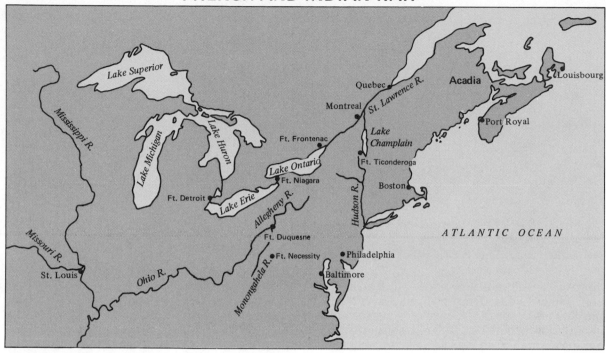

the headwaters of the Ohio (at present-day Pitts-burgh). Eight miles from Duquesne, Braddock's redcoated regiments met French and Indian skirmishers. Scores of redcoats, including Braddock, fell before the murderous fire of the French and Indians. After reading the burial service over Braddock's body, Washington led the rest of the force back to Virginia.

The French retained the initiative in America after Braddock's defeat. Then William Pitt moved to the leadership of the British govern-ment and removed much "dead wood" from the military establishment, whereupon the fortunes of war abruptly turned. Over the next four years British captured Louisbourg and took Fort Frontenac on the northeastern shore of Lake Ontario.

But the great objective was Quebec, keystone of New France. In charge of the Quebec opera-

Use this map to trace the campaigns of the French and Indian War. What routes did the British use to attack Quebec?

Clashes with the Indians continued even after the French and Indian War. In 1763 the Ottawa chieftain Pontiac was defeated by Colonel Henry Bouquet and a force of 1500 men. In this 1766 engraving Colonel Bouquet and his men talk with the Indians at a council fire by the Muskingum River in Ohio. What led to clashes between Indians and colonists?

Library of Congress

The British victory at Quebec in 1759 marked the end of French control in eastern North America. This engraving, published in *London Magazine* in 1760, shows the taking of Quebec by British forces under the command of General James Wolfe.

tion was a frail, thirty-two-year-old British general, James Wolfe. On a high bluff overlooking the Saint Lawrence, Quebec's fortress seemed impregnable and withstood Wolfe's siege throughout the autumn of 1759. Then, as Wolfe was preparing to withdraw to winter quarters, the British discovered a poorly guarded ravine leading up to the Plains of Abraham, just west of the fortress. Under cover of darkness, Wolfe's troops quietly made their way up the ravine. The French awakened to the sight of British troops deployed on the weak side of the fortress. They could see no alternative to a pitched battle in the open. The fight lasted only fifteen minutes, and both Wolfe and the French commander, the Marquis de Montclam, fell mortally wounded, but the result was a total British victory.

The British captured Montreal the following year, and with the fall of Quebec and Montreal the war in America ended. Fighting dragged on in Europe for two more years, but at length came the Treaty of Paris of 1763. France handed over to England all but two of its colonies in India, some West Indian islands, Canada, and all French holdings east of the Mississippi River except the isle of Orléans. To compensate its ally in the war, France in a separate agreement ceded Louisiana and the isle of Orléans to Spain. The Spaniards in turn ceded Florida to England.

STUDY GUIDE: Beginning in 1689, a series of wars broke out in Europe between England and France. At the same time, French and English colonies in America fought. The last of the colonial wars—the French and Indian War—determined ownership of the Ohio Valley. After the British captured Quebec and Montreal, the war in America ended. By a treaty signed in Paris in 1763, France gave up most of its holdings in North America.

A DECADE OF CONTROVERSY

While the Union Jack now waved over an empire stretching from the Ganges to the Mississippi, Britain's victory also brought problems. A larger empire meant enlarged expenses, raising the question: who was to pay? Under existing law, taxpayers in England would bear the burden. But colonists in America and elsewhere had benefited from the recent war. They enjoyed the protection of redcoats and royal cruisers. Why should they be exempt from imperial taxation? The war had stimulated English industry. Textile mills and iron finishing works were humming. Needing markets and raw materials, industrialists naturally looked to the colonies. The result was increasing demand in England for a rigid application—and extension—of mercantilist laws, long dormant.

Sensitive to the plight of English taxpayers and the wishes of industrialists, the government in London began to fashion a new policy of imperial administration. The parts of the British Empire would function as a unit. Royal officials would enforce commercial and industrial regulations, and colonies would share imperial taxation. Such a policy, of course, meant abandonment of the practice of declining to enforce restrictions which had been the salvation of the old colonial system.

For Americans the new imperial policy came at the wrong psychological moment. Colonists were shedding the old idea that the government in London had absolute authority over the empire and were reaching the astounding conclusion that they were under no legal or moral obligation to obey imperial statutes that conflicted with their interests.

The American colonists no longer lived in fear of a French-Indian sweep from the north and west. The victories of Wolfe and others had eliminated the French threat and reduced Indian capacity for attack. With this new feeling of security Americans began to believe they could shift for themselves.

King George III, well-intentioned but shortsighted, and his first minister, a narrow politican named George Grenville (illness having pushed Pitt to the background), forged ahead. In 1764 Parliament passed the Revenue Act, commonly called the Sugar Act. Intended in part to offset expenses of British troops stationed in America, this measure provided for duties on molasses, refined sugar, and other imports from the non-English West Indies, and on luxuries from Europe. If there was logic in expecting the colonies to pay for their own protection, Americans saw the Sugar Act as a dangerous precedent which, unchallenged, might open the way for endless taxation by the imperial government. Hence they attacked the revenue articles, claiming that taxation by a legislature (the Parliament in London) in which they had no representation violated their constitutional rights as Englishmen.

Next came the Currency Act forbidding colonists to issue paper money not supported by precious metal. Since little metallic money circulated in America, the prohibition against paper money was certain to complicate the transaction of ordinary business.

At the same time, Americans began to feel the effect of the Proclamation of 1763 forbidding settlement beyond the crest of the Appalachian Mountains. The intent of the Proclamation Line was to calm the Indians by delaying the inevitable white invasion of their hunting grounds. Whatever the argument for delaying the westward movement, Americans resented the Proclamation Line. In their view the main purpose of the French and Indian War had been to open the territory west of the Appalachians to settlement and speculation. In the late 1760s and early 1770s, several little bands of pioneers, ignoring the edict, trudged over the Proclamation Line and established frontier communities, the best-known of which were the Watauga settlements in the northeastern corner of present-day Tennessee, Fort Harrod in central Kentucky, and Daniel Boone's settlement, Boonesborough, on the banks of the Kentucky River.

The Stamp Act Congress

American protests had no effect on George III and Grenville. In 1765 the imperial government passed the Stamp Act. This act sought to meet expenses of 10,000 British troops in the colonies by requiring colonists to purchase stamps for newspapers, almanacs, pamphlets, legal documents, and broadsides, even for playing cards and dice. Aroused by such orators as Patrick Henry, Americans were soon denouncing the Stamp Act in town meetings, pamphlets, and newspapers as taxation without representation. Responding to a call by the Massachusetts legislature, a Stamp Act Congress met in New York to protest the obnoxious legislation, while secret organizations, known as Sons of Liberty, harassed stamp agents. Merchants in New York, Boston, and Philadelphia pledged to import no goods from England until Parliament repealed the Stamp Act, and there was talk that Americans might repudiate debts to English creditors.

This economic pressure was successful. Anguished appeals came from English bankers and merchants for appeasement of the colonists. Parliament listened, and in March 1766 repealed the Stamp Act, but at the same time passed the Declaratory Act asserting its right to tax colonies. Despite the Declaratory Act, colonists rejoiced in repeal of the Stamp Act and curtailed assaults on the mother country. Trade between England and America revived.

The Townshend Acts

The Stamp Act affair taught authorities in London nothing. On the recommendation of Chancellor of the Exchequer Charles Townshend, Parliament passed the so-called Townshend Acts in 1767. One of these measures suspended the assembly of New York because of the colony's refusal to respect the Quartering Act, a bill passed in 1765 requiring civil authorities to provide barracks and supplies for British troops. More important was the act imposing a duty on glass, lead, paper, and tea imported by the colonies. Townshend knew American feelings about "internal" taxes such as the stamp tax, but he thought the colonists might accept an "external" tax collected at ports of entry. Revenue from the measure would pay salaries of royal governors and judges. Hitherto these officials had been dependent on colonial assemblies for income and hence subject to colonial pressure.

Townshend had miscalculated. Samuel Adams of Massachusetts and other spokesmen raised the old cry of taxation without representation. Merchants of the North and planters of the South pledged to import no British goods until repeal of the Townshend duties. There were fistfights and riots, climaxing in Boston on March 5, 1770 when a British sentry, frightened by jeering Americans, called for reinforcements. A detachment of redcoats appeared, the crowd swelled, and soldiers became targets of snowballs. Then someone gave a command to fire into the crowd. Five Americans, including an Afro-American named Crispus Attucks, died in what has become known as the Boston Massacre.

Again there was pressure in England that Parliament accede to American demands. The imperial government, now headed by Frederick, Lord North, repealed all Townshend duties except the one on tea. Despite appeals by Boston merchants that the colonies stand firm until repeal of the tea tax, importation soon began again, and relations between England and America improved.

Some Americans were determined to keep up the agitation against the mother country. Foremost was Sam Adams, of whom one royal official wrote: "I doubt whether there is a greater incendiary in the King's dominion." Adams organized a "committee of correspondence" in Massachusetts and persuaded other colonies to do likewise. His purpose was to keep the flames of revolt burning.

The Tea Act

A new crisis arose in 1773 when Parliament passed the Tea Act, which was designed to solve the financial difficulties of the English East India Company and eliminate smuggling of tea from Holland to the colonies. The key provision removed the tax the company paid on tea when it entered England prior to shipment to America. Thus the company would be able to undersell Dutch smugglers in the American market. The imperial government also hoped that Americans, lured by cheaper tea, would willingly pay the Townshend tea tax, still in effect. If they did, what would remain of the argument about taxation without representation?

The response in the colonies brought no comfort to leaders in London. Enjoying profits from smuggling, merchants denounced the Tea Act. So did Sam Adams and his followers. Popular assemblies attacked the act, and angry citizens in New York and Philadelphia forced tea ships to return to England. Then came the climax, at Boston, in December 1773. Following a mass meeting, some fifty Bostonians disguised themselves as Mohawk Indians, boarded ships in the harbor, and with approval from a crowd of spectators tossed the cargoes of tea overboard.

Now it was England's turn to erupt. In retaliation for the Boston Tea Party, Parliament in 1774 passed four coercive laws, called Intolerable Acts in the colonies. These measures closed the port of Boston, reformed the government of Massachusetts to increase the power of the royal governor, and permitted trial in England or other colonies of royal officials in Massachusetts accused of certain crimes. They also authorized quartering of royal troops among the people and in barracks.

The Intolerable Acts fell most heavily on Massachusetts, but other colonies rallied in protest. Conferring at the Raleigh Tavern in Williamsburg, members of the Virginia assembly urged a meeting of all continental colonies. In response, delegates of twelve colonies (Georgia sent no representative) gathered at Carpenter's Hall in Philadelphia in September 1774 "to consult upon the present unhappy State of the Colonies." The First Continental Congress had begun its work.

STUDY GUIDE: The expanding British Empire and the wars with France brought more expenses. In England there was an increasing demand to enforce and extend the mercantilists laws. Colonists protested the Sugar Act as a law which might lead to endless taxation without representation. When Parliament passed the Stamp Act in 1765, Americans assembled at a Stamp Act Congress to protest. Later, the Townshend Acts led to rioting in Boston. In 1770 a skirmish between British soldiers and angry Bostonians led to the

Boston Massacre. All the Townshend duties were repealed except the tax on tea. In 1773 colonists disguised as Indians boarded ships in Boston harbor and dumped tea overboard. The Boston Tea Party led the king to pass the Intolerable Acts. These acts sharply limited the freedom of Massachusetts colonists. The acts united the colonies in opposing British rule. The First Continental Congress met in September 1774 with all colonies represented except Georgia.

INDEPENDENCE PROCLAIMED

Representing all shades of colonial opinion, the First Continental Congress declined to move toward independence. Instead it affirmed loyalty to the king and adopted a Declaration of Rights and Grievances claiming that colonies were subject to taxation only by their representative assemblies. The declaration conceded that Parliament could regulate external commerce of colonies—provided such regulation implied no taxation. Congress also prepared a nonintercourse agreement, called the Continental Association, pledging that the colonies would import nothing from England after December 1, 1774. The First Continental Congress adjourned in October 1774, but agreed to meet the following May if necessary.

The focus of events in subsequent months was Massachusetts, where relations with England went from bad to worse. Citizens publicly defied royal officials, Sam Adams stepped up his propaganda, "minutemen" drilled on village commons and patriots gathered munitions.

Finally in April 1775 came the inevitable clash of arms. It was an attempt to seize ammunition and supplies at Concord that provoked the first shots of the American Revolution. There was no hint of high drama on the night of April 18, 1775, when a column of light infantry set out from Boston. The British hoped for surprise, but patriots had anticipated their maneuver, and Paul Revere, Will Dawes, and Samuel Prescott roused the countryside. When the British column marched into Lexington, early the next day, it saw through the morning mist a company of armed militia formed on the village green. The British commander ordered the Americans to disperse. Outnumbered, the militiamen began to withdraw. Then somebody—Briton or American, nobody knows—fired a shot that touched off a skirmish. The British had the better of the exchange, broke off the engagement, and continued the march to Concord where they destroyed the ammunition supplies. But news of the clash at Lexington had spread, and when the redcoats returned to Boston, Americans were lying in wait for them—behind trees, rocks and fences. Sharpshooting Americans turned the march into a rout, and 247 English soldiers lay dead along the road from Concord when the last stragglers trailed into Boston.

The news swept across the colonies. In New England farmers abandoned plows to take up muskets. They hurried to Boston where they joined other militiamen and put the city under siege.

A few weeks later, in May 1775, the Second Continental Congress assembled in Philadelphia. Its mood still cautious, the group issued another appeal to the king to redress grievances. Events, however, were pushing the country away from moderation. Ethan Allen and his Green Mountain Boys had captured Fort Ticonderoga on the same day that Congress convened; revolutionary fervor was increasing in Massachusetts. Unless Congress could get in step with what was becoming a majority sentiment, it would lose what influence it had. Reluctantly Congress assumed authority over the militiamen around Boston and in mid-June 1775 named George Washington commander of the Continental army.

Bunker Hill

Before Washington could take command, a major battle took place near Boston when the British sought to expel American militiamen from several hills. One of these was known as Bunker Hill although much of the fighting was on Breed's Hill. After three assaults the British carried the hill, but not before patriot militia had shot down more than a thousand redcoats. In the face of such losses, the British gave up the attempt to break the American encirclement.

Spurred on by Bunker Hill, Congress authorized an ill-advised overland expedition to capture Quebec, then organized a navy and authorized raids on British islands. Washington's forces around Boston had meanwhile improved fortifications and, with cannon dragged from Ticonderoga, threatened the British position; whereupon the British commander, Sir William Howe, evacuated his army to Nova Scotia in March 1776.

Still hoping the crown might meet American demands, Congress declined to make a final break with the mother country, but over the winter of 1775-76 the flame of independence burned ever brighter. Fanning the flame was a pamphlet entitled *Common Sense,* by a recent immigrant from England, Thomas Paine. Calling George III "the Royal Brute of Great Britain," Paine compared England and America and saw "something absurd in supposing a continent to be perpetually governed by an island." He also saw advantages in separation—freedom from England's European quarrels and freedom from restrictive trade policies. Reinforcing Paine's argument was the news in spring 1776 that the king was dispatching twelve thousand German mercenaries—Hessian hired soldiers—to bring the colonies under control.

The Declaration of Independence

By late spring 1776, when George III gave no hint of compromise, the Second Continental Congress prepared to separate from the mother country. On June 7, 1776, Richard Henry Lee of Virginia moved that "these United Colonies are and of right ought to be, free and independent states." Sharp debate followed and delegates agreed to delay a vote for three weeks. Debate

The Declaration of Independence was largely written by Thomas Jefferson. It was adopted by the Second Continental Congress on July 4, 1776. On what grounds did Jefferson justify the American position to seek independence from Britain? What was Jefferson's attitude toward slavery?

was resumed, and on July 2 Lee's motion carried. Congress, meanwhile, had appointed a committee headed by Thomas Jefferson to draft a proclamation. Jefferson's handiwork, the Declaration of Independence, was adopted on July 4, 1776.

The philosophy of the declaration had received expression in John Locke's *Second Treatise on Government.* Locke and Jefferson believed the only legitimate government was that created by "social compact." They argued that in primitive societies men lived on terms of equality in "a state of nature." As population increased and society became more complex, however, it was necessary to establish instruments of control. At that point, men came together and by popular consent set up a government. The function of government? To protect life, liberty, and property. So long as the government, resting on a compact between rulers and ruled, observed its responsibility, there was no reason for civil disobedience or revolt. But if it failed to do its duty

A NEW NATION FIGHTS FOR RECOGNITION

1

The Tory's Day of Judgement shows New England colonists preparing to tar and feather two Englishmen. This was a common punishment for men who acted as tax collectors for the British government.

2

This mural shows the men who signed the Constitution of the United States of America. The Constitution was written after four months of hard work and compromise.

3

This house served as General Washington's headquarters at Valley Forge during the winter of 1777–78.

4

Exselenc Georg General Waschingdon and Ledy Waschingdon. The name of the artist who made this watercolor is unknown, but the style of the painting and spelling suggest it was done about 1780 by a Pennsylvania German.

1   Library of Congress

2   The National Archives Washington, D.C.

Abby Aldrich Rockefeller
Folk Art Collection

4

3   Montgomery County Tourist Bureau, Pennsylvania

British redcoats won the Battle of Bunker Hill in 1775, using only their bayonets. This engraving was made in 1798 after a painting by John Trumbull.

Library of Congress

—failed to protect life, liberty, and property— the people had a right to alter or abolish it. In Jefferson's view, then, the American colonies and the English crown had made a compact. The crown had violated the compact by infringing upon American liberty. Hence Americans were justified in removing themselves from authority of the crown.

The Declaration of Independence marked the end of the policy of drift and turned the colonies squarely toward independence.

STUDY GUIDE: The First Continental Congress adopted a Declaration of Rights and Grievances claiming that the colonies were subject to taxation only by their representative assemblies. In May 1775, the Second Continental Congress met in Philadelphia and again appealed to the king. The Continental Army was formed with George Washington as commander. To protect Boston from attack, the British tried to expel militiamen from several nearby hills. This fighting became known as the Battle of Bunker Hill. The Americans then tried unsuccessfully to capture Quebec. The pamphlet *Common Sense* urged independence from Britain. In 1776 the Second Continental Congress approved the Declaration of Independence, which stated reasons why the colonists were planning to seek independence from Britain.

THE OPPOSING SIDES

The outlook for the thirteen rebellious colonies did not appear bright when they committed themselves to war against the mother country. England had a large and experienced army, and a hundred ships for every one owned by Americans. It was the richest country in the world, had good credit, and a tax mechanism capable of raising money. The colonies had little capital, poor credit, and no national tax system. As a foundation for an army, there were 13,000 poorly trained militiamen scattered through the colonies. Weapons were scarce, and British control of the sea complicated the task of securing munitions from abroad. There was the added problem of disunity and apathy. Perhaps a fourth to a third of the population sided with the mother country. These people became Loyalists, contributing men and money to the British. Many colonists who favored independence were unwilling to make sacrifices. In the autumn of 1775 Washington wrote that he had never seen and, pray God, never hoped to see again such a dearth of public spirit.

American Advantages

Still, Americans had some advantages. Some Englishmen believed in the justice of the colonial cause. Others saw Americans as their brothers and had no interest in the war. The distance between England and America—it took five weeks to cross the North Atlantic in the 1770s—caused problems of communication between London and America. To subdue the Americans the British would have to gain control of an expanse of territory stretching from New England to Georgia. Finally, to weaken the British Empire, France and Spain might help the Americans.

George Washington

Another advantage for the Americans was George Washington.

Washington was forty-three years old. Born in 1732 in Westmoreland County, Virginia, he was the eldest son of his father's second wife. Contrary to myth, Washington was not born to great wealth and luxury. Like many Virginia planters, his father, a former ship captain, was "land poor." When he died in 1743, he left the family about five thousand acres, twenty-two Negro slaves, and little cash.

Washington's childhood was not particularly happy. Relations with his mother apparently were not marked by great affection. His schooling was irregular (possibly seven or eight years altogether). After his father's death, when he was eleven, he moved about, living with one half-brother and then another. Surveying became a major interest, and at sixteen he journeyed to the Shenandoah Valley to survey lands of his neighbor. He remained in the wilderness of western Virginia three years and wrote in his diary that he had slept under "one thread Bear Blanket with double its Weight in Vermin." Still, the pay was good, and during this time Washington acquired a liking for western lands (eventually he purchased great tracts and became one of the largest landowners in America).

Young Washington's hero at this time was his older half-brother, Lawrence, who had served in the British navy. In the 1740s Lawrence built a mansion beside the Potomac, which he named Mount Vernon in honor of Admiral Edward Vernon, his former commander. After his return from the West, George accompanied his brother on a trip to the island of Barbados in the eastern Caribbean, the only time he ever ventured from the shores of North America. In Barbados he came down with smallpox, which left pock marks on his face but made him immune to the dreaded disease when it ravaged his troops in the War of Independence.

Returning from Barbados, Washington decided to pursue a military career and received an appointment as adjutant in the Virginia militia.

In 1753 he volunteered to carry the governor's protest to the French (see page 46). On the return trip to Virginia, Washington nearly lost his life. While crossing the icy waters of the Allegheny on a raft, he was jolted overboard but managed to swim to a small island in midstream where he and his guide spent a frigid night. Next day the river was solid ice and the two men walked to the opposite shore.

Back in Virginia, Washington was commissioned a lieutenant colonel, led skirmishers to western Pennsylvania, and in 1754, as mentioned, engaged the French in the first fighting of the French and Indian War. The following year, 1755, he marched with General Edward Braddock to expel the French from Fort Duquesne. Violently ill, Washington had fallen behind the march and missed the first hours of the famous battle near present-day Pittsburgh in which the French and their Indian allies defeated Braddock. But he arrived in time to have four musket balls rip through his coat and two horses shot from under him. Braddock died of wounds, whereupon Washington led the remnants of the redcoated force back to Virginia.

For the rest of the French and Indian War, Washington commanded a small band of Virginia militiamen who tried to defend a 350-mile frontier against Indian attack.

By the end of the fighting, around 1760, Washington had reached maturity. For his time he was a giant of a man, standing six feet, two inches, weighing about two hundred pounds. Fair in complexion, with brown hair and blue eyes, he had broad shoulders, large hands, and wore a size thirteen shoe. Although reserved and rather serious, he nonetheless liked to dance, hunt foxes, and bet on horse races. In 1759 he had married Martha Dandridge Custis, a widow with two children. A woman of means, the new Mrs. Washington gave her husband a measure of financial security he had not previously enjoyed.

With the passing of the war with France, Washington settled down to a quiet life at Mount Vernon (which he had inherited from his brother Lawrence). Managing the estate, he enjoyed romping with his stepchildren (he never had any children of his own), fox hunting, and a steady round of social affairs. Like other planters, he became concerned over British imperial policies in the 1760s and 1770s. He thought the government in London was hamstringing the colonies with regulations and exploiting Americans to the advantage of British merchants. As relations between mother country and colonies worsened,

In George Washington the American people found almost exactly the type of military leader that their war for independence required. What qualities combined to make Washington a fine general and president?

he warned that "more blood will be spilt . . . if the ministry are determined to push matters to extremity, than history has ever yet furnished instances of in the annals of North America." He secured election as a delegate to the Second Continental Congress and took command of the Continental army in May 1775.

Despite experience in the French and Indian War, Washington did not have great military talent. He knew little military history or theory and, if he shared dangers and discomforts, did not inspire strong affection from his troops. He kept his distance, accepting the common idea of the time that only "gentlemen" were fit to be officers. He was not a dynamic personality.

Fortunately Washington had other qualities. He was a man of reputation and dignity who demonstrated to the outer world, and also to American aristocrats, that the revolution was not a movement of the rabble of colonial society. He had persistence and never wavered in his determination to win the war. He was a fighter, not excessively cautious, with no qualms about engaging the enemy. He nonetheless understood the essential strategic requirements of the war:

that he must keep his army together, even at the expense of evacuating key positions and avoiding pitched battles. He became skilled in guerrilla tactics, learning the art of strike and run. He appreciated problems of finance and supply. He recognized his limits and never questioned the idea of civil control of the war. Washington, indeed, was almost exactly the type of military leader that America's war of independence required.

Black Soldiers

When he took command of the Continental army, Washington faced many serious problems, one of which was whether to recruit Negro soldiers. This was not a new problem for the colonists. Whites had always been reluctant to put guns in the hands of black men, free or slave, for fear that the guns would become tools of slave insurrections. But under pressure of French and Indian attack, Negroes had usually been given arms. When the quarrel with the mother country reached a crisis in spring 1775, American colonists in Massachusetts had again provided Negroes with weapons. A few New England slave owners liberated their slaves to enable them to serve in the ranks against the British. One former slave, Peter Salem, saw action at Lexington and Concord and later at the Battle of Bunker Hill.

Whatever the heroics of Peter Salem and other Negroes at Bunker Hill, the idea of black soldiers in the patriot army annoyed some whites, particularly in the South, for it was clearly contradictory to use some Negroes to fight for national independence while keeping other Negroes in bondage. Such whites had an ally in George Washington. An owner of many slaves, he shared the views of Virginia planters about the rightness of slavery and the inferiority of Negroes. (One may note that he dealt generously with his slaves when they gave obedient service but directed overseers to be firm with those who gave trouble. On one occasion, he ordered the sale of a particularly strong-willed slave to an owner in the West Indies.) Thus in July 1775 he issued a directive to recruiting officers to enlist no new black soldiers.

Then the royal governor of Virginia, in November 1775, published a proclamation inviting slaves and white indentured servants to join the British army, promising emancipation as a reward. Patriots, including Washington, were aghast when large numbers of slaves left plantations and farms and joined the royal troops. At the same time, a few free Negroes in New England, denied the privilege of joining the Continental army, began to enlist in British regiments. Yielding a bit, Washington directed that free blacks who had been dismissed from the service be permitted to re-enlist.

Despite its limitations, the new order, issued at the end of the year 1776, foreshadowed things to come. Some New England slave owners, as others had done the previous spring, liberated slaves to enable them to enter the patriot service. By 1777–78, white colonists in New England had gone beyond Washington's order. They not only allowed their slaves to join the Continental army, but they also made efforts to recruit slaves for the army. The colonists promised that any slave who joined the army would receive freedom as a reward.

Congress soon became convinced of the need to bring slaves into the Continental army. To encourage southern slaveowners to release their slaves for army duty, it was proposed in 1779 that owners of slaves in South Carolina and Georgia be paid as much as a thousand dollars for each slave enlisted. But to Washington's disgust, South Carolina and Georgia rejected the plan.

Despite these controversies, about five thousand blacks, most of them from the Northeast, served in the Continental army and navy. These black soldiers fought in nearly every important battle of the War for Independence.

STUDY GUIDE: Britain had a large and experienced army and navy. It was the richest nation in the world and had good credit. The colonies had a poorly trained group of militiamen, little money, poor credit, and no tax system. Weapons were scarce. But the colonies had the advantage of Washington's leadership. Washington commanded the Continental army. The army included about five thousand black soldiers.

NEW YORK TO SARATOGA

When General Howe evacuated his army from Boston to Nova Scotia in March 1776, Washington anticipated that the British would next try to divide the middle and southern colonies from New England by attacking New York. He therefore moved his men to Long Island. His guess was correct, for on July 2 Howe led the redcoats ashore at Staten Island. Ferrying his army to Long Island, Howe handed the Americans a stinging defeat in late August. Over the next three months the superior British force compelled Washington to abandon one position after another. The Americans then retreated to New Jersey, the British at their heels, and from there across the Delaware River to Pennsylvania. The British pursuit ended at the water's edge, for Washington cleverly seized all boats for some distance up and down the river.

While gloom spread across the colonies, Washington fashioned a plan for attacking a British garrison—mostly Hessians—at Trenton. Late in December 1776 a ragged force of Americans, braving floating ice, recrossed the Delaware. After a diversionary movement by New Jersey militiamen had drawn away a British force stationed nearby, two columns of Washington's troops marched on the surprised garrison at Trenton in the frigid dawn of December 26. After a brief fight, nearly a thousand Hessians surrendered. But when on January 2, 1777, Lord Cornwallis moved on Trenton with 6,000 British regulars, it seemed that Washington's army, unable to retreat across the Delaware, was finished. Then, as darkness fell, Cornwallis, preferring daylight combat, relaxed pressure. Washington's men left their campfires burning and silently withdrew, filing around the British camp by a side road. They arrived at Princeton the next morning. After a clash with a separate British column (interpreted in the colonies as a victory), Washington evacuated his army to the hills of Morristown and established winter quarters.

Americans had meanwhile scored two successes in the South, where the British hoped to capitalize on widespread Loyalist sentiment. The first blow to British plans came at Moore's Creek Bridge near Wilmington, North Carolina, where a small army of patriots armed with rifles and cannon annihilated a band of Loyalist militia in February 1776. A few months later, in June 1776, a British force attacked Charleston. Colonists had worked tirelessly to strengthen the port's defenses, and they repulsed the assault. The British southern strategy had failed.

British Strategy

Back in the north the British planned the final defeat of the colonies early in 1777. Their strategy was curious. General John Burgoyne, would advance from Canada along Lake Champlain and the Hudson to Albany. Colonel Barry St. Leger would move in a southwesterly direction from Montreal, along the Saint Lawrence to Lake Ontario, then eastward along the Mohawk to Albany where he would join Burgoyne. The purpose of this elaborate maneuver was to isolate New England from the middle colonies.

Logic, it seemed, required General Howe to move northward from New York to join Burgoyne and St. Leger. Instead Howe elected to move on Philadelphia. Capture of the American capital, he fondly thought, would be a staggering blow to the rebels.

Boarding 15,000 soldiers on 260 ships, Howe moved on Philadelphia via Chesapeake Bay in July 1777. Unable to believe that Howe did not intend to join Burgoyne, Washington hesitated before marching his army to defend Philadelphia, but by the time Howe's force landed, Washington's troops had taken positions on the bank of Brandywine Creek. However a series of flanking movements by the British compelled him to withdraw. In late September, the British marched into Philadelphia. In October, Washington launched an assault on British positions at Germantown, just north of Philadelphia, but a British counterattack sent the Americans reeling. When Howe failed to follow up this victory, the Americans went into winter quarters at Valley Forge, twenty miles northwest of Philadelphia.

Burgoyne's Campaign

During these months the campaign to capture Albany had been underway. Burgoyne's army had marched from Canada in summer 1777. A week later St. Leger moved westward from Montreal with 900 men. Burgoyne's first objective was Fort Ticonderoga, near the southern end of Lake Champlain. He took it without a fight. The easy triumph made Burgoyne a hero in England. There was a report that King George burst into Queen Charlotte's dressing room—to the shock of the ladies-in-waiting—and shouted: "I have beat them! I have beat the Americans." Burgoyne was only seventy miles from Albany.

When Burgoyne moved out from Ticonderoga, in late July 1777, his difficulties began to increase. Patriots harassed his supply line and obstructed his advance by rolling huge stones and felling trees across wagon paths. Many Indian and Loyalist troops deserted Burgoyne. Reaching Fort Edward, halfway between Ticonderoga and Albany, the British halted. The Americans meanwhile were regrouping and in August 1777 Congress made General Horatio Gates commander of forces facing Burgoyne. Regulars and militiamen from New York and New England swelled patriot regiments, and Washington dispatched good officers from units around Philadelphia, including Benedict Arnold, one of the most resourceful and daring American leaders.

St. Leger, meanwhile, had entered Lake Ontario and was making his way eastward toward Albany. He was delayed when defenders at Fort Stanwix refused to surrender. Next came disaster. Using a half-witted prisoner named Hon Yost, Benedict Arnold persuaded St. Leger's Indian troops that large numbers of Americans were at hand. The Indians began to desert, and, without his Indians, St. Leger had no choice but to retreat to Montreal. The British attempt to reach Albany from the west had collapsed.

At the same time, in August 1777, the British suffered another shock. It came when Burgoyne sent a raiding party of several hundred men into Vermont to capture horses, cattle, oxen, and flour. By sheer accident the raiders at Bennington, Vermont, collided with an American force of 1,500. Commanded by Brigadier General John Stark, the Americans overwhelmed the British on August 16. The Battle of Bennington was a stinging defeat for Burgoyne.

With misgivings Burgoyne decided to press on toward Albany and in mid-September ferried his force to the west bank of the Hudson. He was opposed by a slightly larger army under the command of General Gates. In a series of battles during September, Burgoyne's army lost more and more men.

Burgoyne's time was running out. He withdrew to Saratoga, taking positions on high ground bounded by open country. But Gates kept his distance and surrounded the British. Supplies running still lower and with no hope of relief, Burgoyne surrendered on October 17, 1777. Thus ended one of the decisive campaigns of military history.

In this American victory two great officers from Poland played an important part: Count Casimir Pulaski and Thaddeus Kosciusko. In building an army and planning fortifications they were invaluable to the American cause.

STUDY GUIDE: Washington tried to prevent the British from taking New York. His army was forced to retreat to New Jersey. The British pursuit ended when Washington crossed into Pennsylvania. In December 1776, Washington successfully attacked the British garrison at Trenton. This was followed by a clash at Princeton. British General Howe captured Philadelphia in July 1777. But in October, General Burgoyne was forced to surrender his entire British army at the Battle of Saratoga.

SOCIETY, POLITICS, DIPLOMACY

The term "revolution" brings visions of social as well as political upheaval, as in France (1789), Russia (1917), and China (1949). This was not entirely true in America. The original purpose of the American Revolution had been to accomplish political reform. However, social changes followed inevitably.

The Revolution brought about several immediate social changes. Perhaps one of the most important was a weakening of aristocracy, resulting in part from popular opposition to upperclass Loyalists. During the Revolution state legislatures changed the laws on land ownership and inheritances and did away with titles of nobility. The Revolution brought a decline in religious fervor (but an increase in religious toleration), and the movement for separation of church and state gathered momentum. There was also a new humanitarian impulse, which produced reform in penal codes and prison conditions.

Revolutionary humanitarianism generally opposed slavery and the slave trade. Many patriots lamented the inconsistency between human bondage and the ringing phrases of the Declaration of Independence. Commenting on slavery, Thomas Jefferson wrote: "I tremble for my country when I reflect that God is just; that his justice cannot sleep forever." The African slave trade was recognized as a prime illustration of man's inhumanity to man, and over the next few decades slavery virtually disappeared in every state north of the Mason-Dixon Line (where slavery was not profitable anyhow). It also seemed that the institution was no longer profitable in the South. The slave trade was an easy target, and eventually every state except Georgia and South Carolina had laws against importation of slaves from foreign shores.

Turning to politics, one of the first tasks facing the colonies on declaring independence was to fashion new state governments. Americans had placed great importance on colonial charters, so the new states determined to have written constitutions. (In Rhode Island and Connecticut the old colonial charters became the state constitutions.) The state constitutions bore marked similarities. Each contained a "bill of rights" guaranteeing moderate bail, humane punishment, trial by jury, and freedom of conscience. All provided for a governor elected by voters or the legislature. The right to vote was given to property owners and taxpayers. Most called for separation of executive, legislative, and judicial powers, but nearly every one gave major authority to the legislature and limited the powers of the executive and judicial branches.

As for national politics, the Second Continental Congress functioned as the general government from 1775 to 1781. It was not strong. A revolutionary creation, it lacked power to enforce decisions or raise revenue and had little more authority than the states cared to delegate. Some historians have likened it to a federal debating society. Still, Congress declared independence, took control over the army, established the navy and marine corps, organized a postal service, and issued currency.

The Articles of Confederation

Congress also drafted the Articles of Confederation. In the same month that it adopted the Declaration of Independence, July 1776, Congress appointed a committee to draft a constitution for a national confederation or union. A month later the committee reported the Articles of Confederation, primarily the handiwork of the Pennsylvanian John Dickinson. Congress approved the document—the first written constitution for a general government in America—in November 1777, but ratification by states came slowly. The last holdout was Maryland, which feared the power of states, especially Virginia, claiming land beyond the Appalachians. When Virginia surrendered its claim, Maryland ratified the Articles on March 1, 1781. Congress declared them in effect the same day.

Benjamin Franklin

In the course of the war the Congress became involved in diplomacy. When friction between colonies and mother country reached the point of crisis in the early 1770s, France encouraged the Americans with vague pledges of support. After Lexington and Concord, the French, aided by the Spaniards, began smuggling muskets and powder to the rebels. The Americans had misgivings about an alliance with France and Spain, hereditary enemies of the colonies and also Roman Catholic, or "papist" countries. Still, they needed foreign support and in autumn 1776 Congress dispatched to Paris a three-man commission to seek French recognition of American independence and a military alliance. Heading the commission was seventy-year-old Benjamin Franklin.

Franklin was one of the most versatile men in American history. He was doubtless the outstanding American down to the time of the Revolution, a man who took an important part in the contest for independence and in launching the new nation.

Franklin was born at Boston in 1706. After only two years of schooling, he became an apprentice printer to his brother, left Boston after a quarrel with his brother, and in 1723 arrived in Philadelphia where he again worked as a printer. Within seven years he was publisher of the *Pennsylvania Gazette,* his deft editorial touch making the newspaper his most profitable venture. In 1732 he published the first number of *Poor Richard's Almanac,* which for more than twenty years was—next to the Bible—the most widely read book in America. The *Almanac,* was, like all almanacs, a book of facts such as astronomical data and weather predictions. But sandwiched between such information were the proverbial sayings of "Poor Richard": "God helps those that help themselves" and "Experience keeps a dear school, yet fools will learn in no other." It was these words of wisdom, usually emphasizing thrift and hard work, written in Franklin's crisp, lucid style, that accounted for the *Almanac*'s popularity and caused people to preface remarks with the words: "As Poor Richard says. . . ."

Franklin was a many-sided individual. He had a strong civic spirit and continually sought to improve the quality of life in Philadelphia. He helped establish a police force for the city, campaigned for better streets, started the Philadelphia Free Library, the American Philosophical Society, and an academy which became the University of Pennsylvania. He was also an inventor and scientist. He invented the Franklin stove, which provided more effective and less expensive household heating. He took special interest

Few American patriots served their country in so many different ways as did Benjamin Franklin. A self-educated man, he won distinction as a statesman, scientist, publisher, and diplomat.

in electricity, performed many experiments, and was the first man to suggest an identity between electricity and lightning, a theory he proved in the summer of 1752 when he flew a kite with a metal point into a storm cloud and drew sparks. Always anxious to apply scientific discovery to everyday problems, Franklin then invented a lightning rod to protect buildings against electrical storms.

Writing, philosophy, science, and civic interests were not enough to consume Franklin's great energies; he also took part in political affairs. In 1754, during the French and Indian War, he was Pennsylvania's delegate to the Albany Congress in New York. He won acclaim when he proposed a plan for uniting the English colonies to meet the French threat, but the colonial legislatures were reluctant to offer support. Three years later he sailed to London to present grievances which the Pennsylvania assembly had against the descendants of William Penn, the proprietors of the colony. His charm and wit made for him a host of friends in England, and it was with reluctance that he returned to America in 1762. Two years later, however, he was again on his way to London to press Pennsylvania's grievances against the proprietors and was there in 1765 when Parliament passed the Stamp Act. The following year he won applause throughout America when his eloquent testimony before the House of Commons helped win repeal of the obnoxious measure.

By that time Franklin was acting as the agent of several colonies and had become something of an ambassador extraordinary for the thirteen colonies in the mother country. He did his best to avert a split between England and the colonies, continually urging compromise and forbearance on Americans and Britons alike. But when the crisis deepened, following passage of the "Intolerable Acts," Franklin sailed for home. He arrived in Philadelphia in the spring of 1775, just in time to win election to the Second Continental Congress. By 1776 he favored separation from England, and in summer of that year served with Thomas Jefferson on the committee to draft the Declaration of Independence. A few months later he was on his way to Paris to court the help of the French government.

Franklin took the French by storm. His likeness appeared on snuffbox lids and medallions. Pictures and busts of Franklin were to be seen in shopwindows and parlors. Scholars and scientists hailed his intellectual and scientific achievements. Others exalted him as a simple Quaker from Pennsylvania (although he actually was a sophisticated deist and freethinker who hoped for a life beyond the grave but rather doubted that it would come to pass). For his part, Franklin was witty and charming. He dressed simply and spoke modestly. He permitted people to think what they wished, all the while using to his country's advantage the fund of goodwill he accumulated.

The French government was cautious, however. American defeats around New York in 1777, Burgoyne's easy conquest of Ticonderoga the following summer, and Howe's capture of Philadelphia in September dampened official enthusiasm for the rebels. Then came Burgoyne's surrender at Saratoga. While Parisians rejoiced, French leaders shuddered lest the British, their ancient enemies, now offer a generous peace to the Americans. After serious negotiations a treaty of alliance was signed in February 1778 between the governments in Paris and Philadelphia.

Britain and France drifted into war in the summer of 1778. Never becoming a formal ally of the United States, Spain declared war the next year. The Netherlands and England came to blows in 1780. Several Baltic states threatened British operations in the Baltic Sea. Thus, the British faced not merely thirteen rebellious colonies, but a coalition of powerful enemies. Without this external assistance, especially that of France, the Americans could not have won the War of Independence.

STUDY GUIDE: One of the social changes brought about by the Revolution was the weakening of aristocracy. New state governments were chartered. States wrote their own constitutions. Each contained a bill of rights and provided for an elected governor. From 1775 to 1781, the Second Continental Congress acted as the general government. In 1781 the Articles of Confederation were ratified. Meanwhile, Benjamin Franklin headed a commission that went to Paris to seek a military alliance with France. England and France went to war in 1778. This external assistance helped America to secure its independence.

TO YORKTOWN AND PEACE

Washington's tattered army, meanwhile, was enduring Valley Forge. Devastated by fighting the previous autumn, Valley Forge was barren of cattle and grain. Worse, the supply system established by Congress had broken down. The result was a severe shortage of food, clothing, blankets, and tenting. Disease and death stalked the army; many troops deserted.

Spring and news of the French alliance revived sagging spirits. Then came word that the British, to concentrate forces at New York against a possible French attack, were evacuating Philadelphia. The new British commander, Sir Henry Clinton, dispatched part of his army from Philadelphia by sea, but a shortage of ships compelled him to send 10,000 of his best troops overland. When the redcoats crossed the Delaware into New Jersey, Washington broke camp at Valley Forge, and set out in pursuit. At Monmouth, in a confusing battle, the Americans narrowly missed disaster, and that night when Clinton resumed his march they did not follow.

The war in the North was now a stalemate. Clinton had a large force at New York but feared to strike into the interior lest he repeat Burgoyne's experience of encountering a countryside in arms. Washington encamped at White Plains, New York. There his troops spent an agonizing winter that was worse than the winter at Valley Forge.

While the war stood on dead center in the North, there was a successful American move in the West. George Rogers Clark, in spring 1778, loaded a small force on rafts at Fort Pitt (Pittsburgh) and floated down the Ohio to the mouth of the Cumberland. There he disembarked and marched his men through a tangled wilderness to the British fort at Kaskaskia in Illinois. After taking Kaskaskia, he wheeled his little army around. In the dead of winter he hacked and splashed his way through forest and flood for 150 miles to another post, Vincennes, held by British Colonel Henry Hamilton. Clark took Vincennes in February 1779. Clark's victories helped relieve new settlements in western Virginia and Kentucky from British-supported Indian attacks.

Meanwhile the British had taken the offensive in the South, sending the forces of Colonel Archibald Campbell from New York to Savannah in autumn 1778. After overrunning the settled area of Georgia and restoring the royal governor, the British turned toward Charleston, burning plantations and kidnapping slaves as they went. At Charleston, patriot defenses held, but a combined American and French force failed to dislodge the British from Savannah.

At this point Clinton's second-in-command, Lord Cornwallis, fashioned a bold strategy which he hoped might end the war. He would send a larger force to capture Charleston, enlist the support of Carolina Loyalists, establish royal governors in the Carolinas, and then strike northward to Virginia. Capture of Virginia and the Chesapeake Bay region, he calculated, would end the rebellion. Thus a great armada of warships and transports ferried 8,500 redcoats from New York to Charleston in January 1780. After overwhelming a tiny American fleet, in May 1780 the British captured the South Carolina capital. A short time later Cornwallis routed a large American army at Camden, South Carolina.

Then American fortunes began to change. At King's Mountain in northwestern South Carolina, a band of sharpshooting frontiersmen overwhelmed a force of Loyalist militia in October 1780. Washington then put General Nathanael Greene, a Rhode Islander, in command of American forces in the South. At Cowpens, not far from King's Mountain, part of Greene's army displayed skill and courage in routing the British in January 1781. Two months later at Guilford Court House in North Carolina the British took such losses that Cornwallis had to withdraw from the interior of the Carolinas and return to the coast.

Reinforced via his ocean supply line, Cornwallis marched northward to Virginia in spring 1781. There he joined Benedict Arnold who, the previous autumn, had gone over to the British and now was a general in their army. The British force raided deep into Virginia and at Charlottesville nearly captured Governor Thomas Jefferson. But an American army under General Anthony Wayne, the Prussian Baron von Steuben, and France's Marquis de Lafayette had moved into position. Cornwallis therefore decided to base his army at Yorktown, on the Chesapeake Bay at the mouth of the York River, where he could maintain sea communication with Clinton at New York. He reached Yorktown on August 1.

Cornwallis Surrenders

By now a French army had joined the Americans under Washington opposite Clinton's fortifications at New York. A French fleet under the Comte de Grasse was in the Caribbean preparing to move northward. Washington wanted to attack Clinton, but the French preferred an assault on Cornwallis at Yorktown. Washington agreed. His army and the French under the Comte de Rochambeau moved to Baltimore and Annapolis, boarded French transports, and sailed down the Chesapeake, cutting off the British from an escape by sea. Cornwallis and his 7,000 redcoats were surrounded. Accepting unconditional surrender, on October 19, 1781, Cornwallis and his men marched through Franco-American lines and put down their arms.

It seemed that the war had ended and Lafayette wrote: "The play is over; the fifth act has just come to an end." The Frenchman was overly optimistic in seeing an end to the war, for some fighting continued.

Most Englishmen, however, had tired of the fight, the war had drained the royal treasury, and the alliance between France and America was increasingly disconcerting. Thus a British agent went to Paris and opened negotiations with Benjamin Franklin.

The Treaty of Paris

After several months of diplomatic fencing, the negotiators reached a preliminary agreement in autumn 1782 — without consent of France as required by the spirit if not the letter of the Franco-American alliance. But Franklin deftly soothed the French and even secured from them a handsome loan to replenish the American treasury! France and Spain came to terms with England in 1783, and in September of that year representatives of the interested nations — Franklin, John Jay, and John Adams for the United States — signed the Treaty of Paris.

The British recognized American independence and a boundary running along the Saint Croix and Saint Lawrence to the Great Lakes and from there to the Mississippi. The boundary extended southward down the middle of the Mississippi to the thirty-first parallel, then roughly along that parallel eastward to the Atlantic. Americans retained fishing privileges in waters around Nova Scotia and Newfoundland.

The treaty made legal all debts due creditors of both countries, an important point for English merchants who held several million pounds of unpaid American bills. The Americans pledged that Congress would "earnestly recommend" to the states a full restoration of the rights and property of Loyalists, an empty promise required by current English politics. Spain received all of Florida, taken by the British in 1763 after the Seven Years' War, but boundaries for the whole unexplored territory beyond the Mississippi were not defined. France got little from the war except revenge. The French gained some fishing privileges around Newfoundland, recovered two islands in the West Indies and several trading posts in India and Africa. But the war had exhausted the French treasury, and the hope soon died of markets in America and a firm alliance with the United States.

STUDY GUIDE: The French alliance brought new hope to the Americans. The British evacuated Philadelphia. Hoping to win the southern states, they concentrated on taking Charleston. British Lord Cornwallis then moved his army to Yorktown, but a combined army of French and American troops forced him to surrender in 1781. In 1783 the war was ended by the Treaty of Paris.

THE CONFEDERATION

The Treaty of Paris had given the United States an expanse of territory stretching from the Atlantic to the Mississippi, from Florida to the Great Lakes. Few independent states in the world were so large. And few countries had such potential for prosperity and power, for in that vast land was fertile soil, seemingly inexhaustible supplies of timber, navigable streams, and unknown other mineral riches.

Still, the new nation faced problems. Since the first loyalty of most Americans was to their states, there was no strong national consciousness. This lack of national purpose was illustrated by the Articles of Confederation. The general government was weak, had no executive branch, could not enforce decisions or raise revenue, and indeed had no more authority than the states granted. As implied in the words "Articles of Confederation," the new nation was a confederacy, a loose partnership of sovereign states.

The Confederation period began two years before the British recognized American independence, in 1781, the year the Articles went into effect, and ended in 1789 with adoption of the federal Constitution. Although the Confederation lasted only eight years, it had some achievements. In 1785 Congress passed the Land Ordinance providing for a systematic, rectangular survey of land in the Northwest Territory (present-day Ohio, Indiana, Michigan, Illinois, and Wisconsin). This ended the haphazard method of marking off boundaries that had prevailed in colonial times (when a pioneer might run his line from a tree to a rock to a stream). The Land Ordinance also provided for sale of public land in the Northwest. The Northwest Ordinance of 1787 set out a formula for dividing the Northwest Territory into smaller territories and, with a minimum of difficulty, bringing the territories to statehood — on equal footing with the original thirteen states.

Achievements in meeting problems in the Northwest unfortunately did not offset the Confederation's failures in other areas. The Confederation Congress was unable to persuade the states to honor the provisions of the Treaty of Paris for restoring rights and property of Loyalists and opening American courts to British subjects seeking to recover debts. It could not compel the British to abandon garrisons in the wilderness of the Northwest. It was not equal to the task of meeting difficulties with Spain:

THE NEW NATION

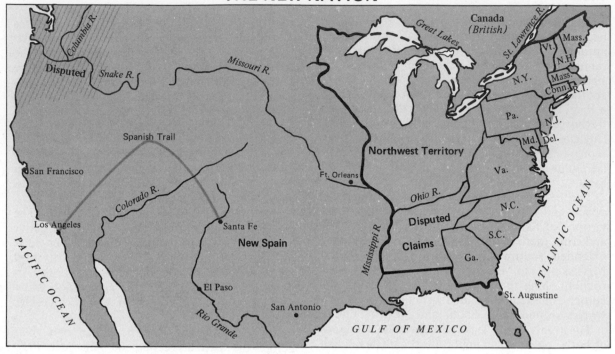

the precise location of the boundary separating the American South from Spanish Florida, harassment of American settlements by Indians based in Florida, and the rights to navigation of the Lower Mississippi. (The Mississippi River was the lifeline of American settlers beyond the Appalachians who produced bulky farm products which they could not easily move eastward over the mountains).

Problems with the Economy

The domestic economy also faced problems, for depression followed independence. Money became "dear," meaning that compared to times of prosperity the value of money increased, a disadvantage to individuals who had contracted debts in more prosperous years. Low prices meant that the debtor, if he was a farmer, had to raise more corn and hogs to secure money for repayment than he had bargained for when contracting the loan. For the creditor the situation was reversed. Deflation worked to his advantage, for the money he now received in repayment would purchase more than that which he had lent. In such circumstances, debtors sent up appeals for relief. Most important were demands for large issues of paper money not supported by

precious metal. Expansion of the money supply with paper currency would bring inflation, reduce the value of money, and hence scale down debts.

Shays's Rebellion

The debtor-creditor problem reached a climax in 1786-87. The focal point was Massachusetts, where the legislature refused appeals for paper currency and creditors began to take over debt-ridden farms. In desperation farmers in the western part of the state began to organize. Led by a former captain in the Continental army, Daniel Shays, they went about in armed bands, breaking up court trials and sheriff's sales. Needing more guns, they advanced on the arsenal at Springfield in January 1787. The state militia stopped Shays's men, killed several, captured many, and sent the rest flying to the hills.

Shays's Rebellion and similar disturbances elsewhere in the country filled some Americans with a dread of radicalism. What would happen if a larger and better equipped rebel force should appear? The states did not have great military power and the Articles of Confederation gave the general government no authority to help states put down disorder. There seemed only one solution: a strong national government.

[64]

STUDY GUIDE: The Articles of Confederation showed that the central government was weak. There was no executive branch. Shays's Rebellion pointed up the need for a strong central government. During the Confederation period the Northwest Ordinance of 1787 was passed. It established a formula for territories to enter the Union as states.

THE FEDERAL CONSTITUTION

Other factors required a stronger national government. The Confederation was unable to resolve differences with England and Spain, and a national economic policy was needed to eliminate such absurdities as tariff barriers between states. A meeting at Annapolis in September 1786, called to study the problems of interstate commerce, issued an invitation to the states to send delegates to a convention at Philadelphia the following spring. The purpose was to "render the constitution of the federal government adequate to the exigencies of the union." The invitation created hardly a ripple until January-February 1787 when word spread across the country of Daniel Shays's attack on the Springfield arsenal.

The Constitutional Convention

In May 1787 fifty-five delegates to the Federal Convention gathered in the Philadelphia State House (now Independence Hall). This modest red brick building had witnessed the signing of the Declaration of Independence and had been the meeting place of the Second Continental Congress.

As weeks passed, the weather became warmer —and so did discussions. The first question was whether to revise the Articles of Confederation in accordance with the convention's mandate or to proceed with a new constitution. The issue came to a head when Edmund Randolph offered the Virginia Plan. Without reference to the Articles, the plan called for a two-house legislature. Representation in the lower house would depend on population. The lower house would elect the upper house and the two chambers would join to elect the executive and judicial branches. Small states recoiled at the Virginia Plan, weighted as it was in favor of large states. They favored the New Jersey Plan, in which Congress would remain the nucleus of the national government and, as under the Articles, each state would have one vote in a one-house legislature. Delegates from large states rejected New Jersey's proposal.

Large and Small States Compromise

Tempers flared and the convention deadlocked. Without the urgings of Washington, the presiding officer, and Benjamin Franklin, the meeting might have dissolved. Then the Connecticut Compromise was introduced. Offered by Oliver Ellsworth of Connecticut, it proposed a "middle way" between the Virginia and New Jersey formulas. In deference to large states, representation in the lower chamber of the national legislature would depend on population. In the upper chamber each state, regardless of population, would have two votes and passage of legislation would require approval of both houses. As for the thorny question of whether to count Negro slaves in determining a state's representation in the House of Representatives and its share of federal taxes to be levied in proportion to a state's population, Ellsworth's plan proposed the "three-fifths compromise": three-fifths of the slave population of each state would count both for representation in the House and national tax levies.

Another point of friction was regulation of foreign trade. Fearing export duties on cotton and tobacco, and also commercial treaties working to the South's disadvantage, southern delegates opposed federal authority over foreign commerce. Again there was compromise. Congress could regulate foreign trade but could impose no export duties, and all treaties, including commercial treaties, would require a two-thirds vote in the Senate, assuring the South of a veto of any treaty not to its liking.

Otherwise the framing of the federal Constitution went smoothly. With little debate delegates agreed that the national government should have authority to regulate commerce between the states, raise and maintain an army and navy, and call out the militia to enforce national laws and put down insurrection. There was no great objection to the idea that states should not have the right to issue money, make treaties, or impose duties on imports or exports.

Remembering the alleged tyranny of George III, Americans feared an executive who had absolute power. Therefore they devised a system of checks on the presidential power. Should the president act outside the law, Congress could check him by its power of impeachment. To reduce the risk of arbitrary use, however, the impeachment power was cleverly divided between the Senate and the House. With this safeguard the convention gave the president power as commander-in-chief over the armed forces and authority to supervise the country's foreign affairs, appoint federal judges, and veto legislation of Congress (although a two-thirds vote of Congress could override). The president was also to recommend to Congress "measures as he shall judge necessary and expedient."

As a safeguard against the choice of a chief executive by uninformed citizens, who might be swayed by the appeal of a demagogue, the electoral college was established. Under this system the people would not vote directly for presidential candidates but for "electors," presumably men who were politically aware. These electors would then cast ballots for presidential candidates. Each state would have the same number of "electoral votes" as it had representatives in Congress. If a candidate received a majority of the electoral votes, he would become president. If nobody won a majority, the House of Representatives, voting by states, would choose the president from the three candidates receiving the most electoral votes.

Ratification of the Constitution

To assure the broadest possible base of support, the federal convention, winding up its work in September 1787, submitted the Constitution for ratification to popularly elected state conventions rather than to state legislatures. When nine states approved, the new government would start to function.

Many Americans continued to fear a strong central government and ratification of the Constitution required a herculean effort. The most persuasive arguments for the new government appeared in a battery of essays, *The Federalist Papers,* written by Alexander Hamilton, James Madison, and John Jay. The views of Madison, Jay, and Hamilton were circulated to the people via pamphlets, handbills, and editorials. Some struck a responsive chord, especially the one which said the Constitution would make possible a vigorous foreign policy. Skillful politicking also helped. Before Anti-Federalists (opponents of the Constitution) could organize, Federalists rushed election of a ratifying convention in Pennsylvania. In December 1798 Pennsylvania approved the Constitution. When Anti-Federalists in Massachusetts complained

that the Constitution contained no "bill of rights," Federalists drafted ten amendments which they recommended to the states. Early in 1788 Massachusetts approved the Constitution by a narrow margin.

In June 1788 New Hampshire became the ninth state to ratify, but Virginia and New York had not acted. Without them the new government stood scant chance of success. In Virginia such spokesmen as Patrick Henry and James Monroe carried the Anti-Federalist argument, conjuring up visions of a federal tyranny akin to that of George III. Rebutting each Anti-Federalist thrust was a brilliant group of Federalists led by James Madison and John Marshall. In the last days of June 1788 Virginia narrowly approved the new government. New York fell into line a month later, thanks largely to Hamilton who argued persuasively before the state convention, "wined and dined" hesitant delegates, and terrified upstate New Yorkers by threatening to detach New York City from the rest of the state and take it into the federal Union.

Only Rhode Island and North Carolina remained outside the Union when the Confederation Congress made ready to transfer authority to the new federal government in September 1788. North Carolina finally ratified the Constitution in November 1789. Rhode Island held out until May 1790 when a resolution for ratification carried by two votes.

STUDY GUIDE: In 1787 delegates to the Federal Convention wrote a new constitution creating a federal Union. A president, a congress, and a judicial system were created. Each branch was to be separate, with the power to check the other branches. Delegates disagreed on state representation in Congress, but a compromise was worked out. Several states opposed the Constitution, fearing a strong central government. The addition of the Bill of Rights and the appeal made by *The Federalist Papers* won its approval.

LAUNCHING THE NEW GOVERNMENT

On April 14, 1789, George Washington learned that the electoral college had unanimously elected him president of the United States. Two days later the president-elect left for New York, the first capital of the new republic. Requiring eight days, the journey to New York immediately took on the appearance of a triumphal procession. At each town and coach stop enthusiastic crowds pressed about the carriage, bells pealed, and guns roared in salute.

For his inauguration on April 30, 1789, Washington wore a brown suit with metal buttons and white stockings. A sword hung at his side. At the appointed time he stepped onto a balcony of Federal Hall, at the corner of Broad and Wall streets, and took the oath. In the street below, several thousand people cheered. The president did not address the crowd outside Federal Hall. Instead he moved inside the building and read his inaugural speech only to the members of Congress.

Washington, the President

Great problems faced the new president. The federal government had no administrative machinery, an empty treasury, and a substantial public debt. Foreign powers, Britain and Spain, maintained spheres of influence on American soil. Beyond the Appalachians, people talked of secession from the federal Union.

The situation had some saving elements. The economic depression was passing and Anti-Federalist hostility to the new government was in decline. (Quick ratification of the first ten amendments to the Constitution—the "bill of rights" guaranteeing "civil liberties"—further soothed Anti-Federalists.)

Most important, the new government had George Washington.

Perhaps the best analysis of the first president came years later, in 1814, from the pen of Thomas Jefferson, secretary of state in Washington's Cabinet: "His mind was great and powerful, without being of the very first order; his penetration was strong, though not so acute as that of a Newton, Bacon, or Locke; and as far as he saw, no judgment was ever sounder. It was slow in operation, being little aided by invention or imagination, but sure in conclusion. . . . Perhaps the strongest feature in his character was prudence, never acting until every circumstance, every consideration, was maturely weighed; refraining if he saw a doubt, but, when once decided, going through with his purpose, whatever obstacles opposed. His integrity was most pure, his justice the most inflexible I have ever known, no motives of interest or consanguinity, of friendship or hatred, being able to bias his decision."

Alexander Hamilton

If Washington brought integrity and judgment to the new government, Alexander Hamilton, only thirty-four, brought genius. Born in the British West Indies, Hamilton had migrated to New York in 1773, fought in the War of Independence, married the daughter of a wealthy businessman, and become active in politics. Recognizing his ability, Washington appointed him secretary of the treasury. Hamilton was an aristocrat who had little faith in common people. He saw the federal government as the only alternative to democracy-run-wild. To succeed, he believed the new government needed continuing support of the most influential and powerful groups in the country—the merchant, shipowning, and financial classes.

To bind financiers to the national interest—and to establish the credit of the new government—Hamilton announced that the government should make good the debts inherited from the Confederation and assume debts incurred by the states during the War of Independence. Such proposals triggered angry debate. Much of the Confederation debt consisted of "certificates of indebtedness" issued by the Continental and Confederation Congresses. Many of the certificates had gone to shopkeepers during the war to pay for supplies, others to soldiers of the Continental army in lieu of pay. During the depression of the 1780s, however, these common people had often sold their certificates at ruinous discount to speculators and bankers. To redeem them at par seemed unfair, even unpatriotic. But Congress agreed with Hamilton that the new government was honor bound to pay its debts. For that reason, Congress approved the secretary's plan for funding the Confederation debt at par with payment of past interest.

As for state debts, Virginians noted that their state had managed to retire most of its wartime obligations. Why should they now pay federal taxes to service the debt of Massachusetts? To end Virginia's opposition to his plan, Hamilton agreed to support a bill to locate the federal capital in the South. Thus in separate acts in 1790 Congress approved Hamilton's bill to assume the debt of states and voted to move the federal capital from New York to Philadelphia for a ten-year period. After this time, in 1800 the government would move to a new capital city along the Potomac, the site to be selected by President Washington.

Hamilton next urged a national bank—"national" in that it would have a federal charter, be the sole depository of federal funds, and be one-fifth government-owned. Such a bank would have the capital and security necessary for an expanding economy. It would also cement the alliance between "influential classes" and the government. Manufacturers and other business-men would benefit from improved credit facilities and wealthy investors would control eighty percent of the bank's stock. Thus they would receive dividends from government balances which actually belonged to all the people. In 1791 Congress voted a twenty-year charter for the Bank of the United States.

Hamilton, meanwhile, wrestled with the problem of raising revenue. Sale of public land was one source of federal income, but could not meet all the government's monetary requirements. The secretary thus settled on increased tariff duties on imports and an excise tax on alcoholic liquors. Characteristically, Hamilton combined economics with politics. A higher tariff would protect domestic manufacturers from foreign competition and tighten their bond with the federal government. A whiskey tax would fall mainly on distillers in the back country of Pennsylvania, Virginia, and North Carolina, where people had scant respect for the national government. If frontiersmen ignored or rebelled against the tax, the new government would have an opportunity to assert authority and demonstrate that it would not tolerate outbreaks like Shays's Rebellion. In 1791 Congress voted Hamilton's whiskey tax and the next year approved his tariff recommendations.

Although Hamilton's policies permitted an orderly and sustained growth of the national economy, they generated opposition, especially in the rural South, where Thomas Jefferson became the champion. The upshot was a running quarrel over the nature of the American republic. While Hamilton argued for a strong central government, Jefferson wanted the principal authority to rest with the states. Hamilton emphasized order and stability, Jefferson liberty and democracy. Hamilton favored government by a wealthy elite; Jefferson believed the people, properly educated, could manage their political affairs. Hamilton wished to encourage manufacturing and shipping and dreamed of making the United States a throbbing industrial nation. Despising cities, the handmaidens of industry, Jefferson wanted the United States to remain a nation of farmers.

As the Hamilton-Jefferson debate sharpened,

two distinct political parties began to take form. People who rallied around Hamilton became Federalists, Jefferson's followers, Republicans. Both groups, however, favored Washington's reelection in 1792. Hamilton was confident that Washington would continue the fiscal and trade policies of the first administration; Jefferson did not think his Republican party sufficiently strong to bid for power and preferred Washington to a Federalist president. Despite a longing to return to the quiet of Mount Vernon, Washington yielded to the appeals of his brilliant subordinates and won unanimous reelection.

STUDY GUIDE: In 1789 George Washington was unanimously elected president by the electoral college. Alexander Hamilton was appointed secretary of the treasury. He proposed ways of establishing credit and raising revenue. One of these was a whiskey tax. He also proposed that a national bank be established. But Thomas Jefferson opposed some of Hamilton's ideas. Serious differences between Hamilton and Jefferson led to the formation of the nation's first political parties, the Federalist and the Republican.

WASHINGTON'S SECOND ADMINISTRATION

In his first term (1789–93) Washington had concentrated on establishing the federal mechanism and securing the finances of the new government. Problems of the western frontier which had plagued the Confederation received only left-over attention. Hence, British garrisons remained in the Northwest Territory, and there was no agreement with Spain on the Florida boundary or passage of American goods down the Lower Mississippi. As he started his second administration, Washington could no longer ignore western problems. Settlers were passing over the mountains and taking up land in the West. The fifteenth state, Kentucky, had entered the federal Union in 1792 (the fourteenth, Vermont, having come in the preceding year). Before long Tennessee would be ready for statehood (achieved in 1796). As population increased, western problems became more pressing.

Before resolving the difficulties with Britain and Spain, the president needed to assure western respect for the federal government. If the link between the West and the rest of the nation should snap, other problems would become academic. Washington saw his opportunity in the so-called Whiskey Rebellion of 1794. Spurred by anger over Hamilton's whiskey tax, farmers in western Pennsylvania began to organize and gather arms. Before they could do much violence, Washington summoned 12,000 state militiamen and personally led them as far as Bedford, Pennsylvania. The would-be rebels dispersed. Other frontier areas "got the message," and the authority of the federal government was secure.

At the same time a military expedition under General Anthony Wayne—sometimes called "Mad Anthony"—was methodically advancing against an army of Indians at the mouth of the Maumee in present-day Ohio. The climax came in mid-August 1794 when the Indians deployed in an area where a tornado had felled many trees. Wayne kept them waiting three days, and with each hour the Indians became a little hungrier, a bit more nervous. Then, as the sun rose on August 20, Wayne signaled the attack. With muskets and bayonets, the federal troops flushed the Indians from the tangled under- growth. In forty minutes the Battle of Fallen Timbers was over. The following summer the Indians signed the Treaty of Greenville and once more were forced to move westward. A few years later, in 1803, Ohio became a state.

Other western problems—those involving Britain and Spain—required a diplomatic solu- tion. However, diplomacy was handicapped in the mid-1790s because a general war had broken out in Europe.

The French Revolution

The war was a consequence of the French Revolution, which had begun in 1789 shortly after Washington became president. Seeking a society resting on "liberty, equality, and fraternity," the French Revolution filled the royal courts of Britain, Russia, Austria, and Prussia with loathing and terror. The inevitable collision between revolution and counterrevolu- tion came in spring 1792 when France went to war with Austria and Prussia. Britain, Spain, and Holland became belligerents the following January (1793).

Americans took keen interest in the goings-on in Europe. Wealthy classes, businessmen, and the clergy—people who mirrored the ideas of Hamilton and the emerging Federalist party— despised the French Revolution as an attack on property and religion. They sided with France's enemies. Workers and farmers—fol- lowers of Jefferson—saw the revolution as a sacred cause, an extension to the Old World of the democratic ideas of the New. They wanted America to help France.

Britain's entry made the war a matter of grave concern to President Washington, who a month later took the oath of office the second time. The Treaty of Alliance of 1778 between the United States and France was still in force and bound the United States to assist in defense of the French West Indies. But the United States was an infant republic and Washington decided that joining in Europe's war might be disastrous. Thus he proclaimed in April 1793 that the United States would be "friendly and impartial toward the belligerent powers."

The neutrality policy met its first test when the new French minister, Edmond Genêt (known to history as Citizen Genêt), who had landed at Charleston a few weeks before, outfitted several privateers and urged such western leaders as George Rogers Clark to attack Spanish outposts in Florida and Louisiana. Determined to keep the country out of war and his patience ex- hausted, Washington ignored protests of Francophiles in the country and demanded re- call of the minister. (Fearing the guillotine, Genêt did not return to France but retired to Long Island, where he married the daughter of Governor George Clinton.)

Now it was Great Britain's turn to try Wash- ington's patience. First, the British informed the United States that they had no intention of evacuating posts in the Northwest. Then in November 1793 came an announcement that the Royal Navy would detain ships carrying produce or supplies to or from French colonies. The purpose of the order was to end trade be- tween the United States and the French West Indies. Before long, British cruisers were chasing down American merchantmen suspected of doing business with French colonies.

Jay's Treaty

Still the British did not seek war with America, and Washington kept his temper. The outcome was a mission to London in spring 1794 by Chief Justice John Jay, which after several months of negotiations led to Jay's Treaty. The treaty was no diplomatic triumph for the United States, the only British concession being a pledge to evacuate the Northwest posts. There was no promise by Britain to stop meddling in Indian affairs south of the Canadian border. Worse, there was no end to the British interference with American shipping. News of Jay's Treaty brought a storm across the United States, one citizen chalking sentiments on a fence: "Damn John Jay! damn every one that won't damn John Jay!!" Although disappointed in Jay's handiwork, Washington concluded that the only alternative was a disastrous war and, because of his urging, the Senate consented to the treaty.

Next came agreement with Spain, via Pinckney's Treaty (1795), named for Thomas Pinckney, the envoy who signed for the United States. The treaty guaranteed Americans freedom to navigate the Mississippi and the privilege for a three-year period of depositing goods at New Orleans for transfer to ocean-going vessels, the privilege to be renewed there or at some equivalent place. It also fixed the Florida boundary at the thirty-first parallel and pledged the Spaniards to curb Indian raids from Spanish territory on American settlements.

By now nearing the end of his second administration and anxious to return to Mount Vernon, Washington determined not to accept a third term. The mechanism of government was humming, the fiscal base of the nation seemed secure, and there was general acceptance of the authority of the federal government. The nation was at peace, and diplomacy had resolved annoying problems of the West. All that remained was the Farewell Address, which Washington published in newspapers in September 1796. The document explained that the interests of Europe and America were different and urged Americans to avoid the "ordinary vicissitudes" of Europe's politics, "the ordinary combinations and collisions of her friendships or enmities."

STUDY GUIDE: By the end of Washington's second term, many problems had been solved. Washington had established the authority of the federal government by stopping the Whiskey Rebellion. The Battle of Fallen Timbers had ended Indian resistance to new white settlements in Ohio. In Jay's Treaty, England had promised to leave the Northwest Territory. In Pinckney's Treaty, Spain had agreed that the Americans could use the lower Mississippi to ship goods to Spanish New Orleans without paying a tax. The treaty also had fixed the boundary between Spanish Florida and the United States.

JOHN ADAMS

By 1796 the Republican and Federalist parties were prepared to contest the presidential election. Among Republicans there was no debate over a presidential candidate. Jefferson, the idol of all Republicans, was the obvious choice. Matters were not so simple for the Federalists. The logical candidate was Hamilton, but his fiscal policies of the preceding eight years had made too many enemies.

Almost by default, then, the Federalist nomination fell to John Adams, vice-president under Washington. Capitalizing on Washington's reputation, Adams managed a majority in the electoral college, but because of sectional rivalry many Federalist electors scratched the party's vice-presidential candidate, Thomas Pinckney of South Carolina. Since at that time each elector simply voted for two individuals (the Constitution failing to distinguish between presidential and vice-presidential candidates), Jefferson received more electoral votes than did Pinckney. This meant that the Republican leader became vice-president in the new Federalist administration of which Adams became the chief.

Early Career

Born in Braintree (later Quincy), Massachusetts in 1735, John Adams was a descendant of early settlers in the Massachusetts Bay Colony. He attended Harvard College, graduated near the head of his class, and, after teaching school for a year, decided to become a lawyer. Soon he was the most prosperous legal practitioner in Massachusetts. In 1764, at age twenty-nine, he married the daughter of a parson, Abigail Smith, an unusually intelligent and witty young woman.

A short time later, in 1765, Parliament passed the Stamp Act. Adams employed his pen against the obnoxious measure, preparing resolutions which won the approval of several Massachusetts towns. In 1770 he attracted considerable attention—and much criticism—when he defended nine British soldiers charged with murder in the so-called Boston Massacre.

Adams might provide legal defense for English soldiers, but in the continuing quarrel with the mother country he upheld the colonial view. When Boston patriots had their famous "tea party" in 1773, he called it "the grandest event which has ever yet happened since the controversy with Britain opened." Several months

Library of Congress

John Adams brought to the presidency a keen mind and wide experience in affairs of state. However, his lack of tact soon lost him popular support. Adams was the first president to live in the White House.

later he went off to Philadelphia as a delegate to the First Continental Congress and, the following year, to the Second. Perhaps his outstanding service in Congress was to urge George Washington's appointment as commander-in-chief of American military forces. By placing a southerner in charge of the army, he hoped to rally the South behind the conflict, which up to this point had centered in New England.

After Congress proclaimed independence, Adams went on diplomatic missions to Europe and in 1782–83 helped negotiate the Treaty of Paris ending the war with Britain. A tireless worker, he proved a capable diplomat. After the war, Adams served as minister to Great Britain, returning home in 1788 in time to be elected vice-president under Washington. Considering himself the intellectual superior of Washington, Adams was unhappy in his role. He found the vice-presidency an inadequate outlet for his energy and talent.

Adams was in some ways admirably equipped for the presidency. He had a brilliant mind, surpassed in his day perhaps only by that of Jef-

ferson, and, like Washington, he was a man of prudence and courage. He understood the mechanism of politics better than most men of the time and could claim wide experience in affairs of state. Particularly important was his experience in diplomacy, for foreign affairs were the central problem of the country when he took the presidential oath in 1797.

Still, Adams had shortcomings. In dealing with other political leaders, he was often tactless and soon lost the support of many influential Federalists. He also lost the support of a high percentage of the national population. To most Americans he seemed cold and distant, a conservative New Englander who felt little commitment to the principles of popular democracy; he simply was unable to communicate his burning patriotism to the country at large.

Trouble with France

When Adams became president in March 1797, relations with the British had become cordial, thanks to Jay's Treaty. The problem now was France.

War with a coalition of enemies had not ended revolutionary turmoil inside the French nation. Leaders had come and gone—their exit often accompanied by the crash of the guillotine—and by 1797 a group called the Directory held the power. Although not apparent to Americans, the Directory had abandoned the idealism of the Revolution and was concentrating on French mastery in Europe. Hence, Jay's Treaty, removing the threat of war between England and the United States, was a setback to France. In retaliation, the Directory ordered French privateers to attack American ships bound for the British Isles.

The United States and France seemed to be edging toward hostilities. Adams, like Washington, believed that war was a catastrophe the young republic must avoid, so he dispatched a three-man peace commission to Paris. When the French foreign minister declined to receive them, three mysterious French officials—identified by Adams by the initials X, Y, and Z—advised the Americans that the Directory would open negotiations if they would apologize for recent anti-French remarks by President Adams, pay a substantial bribe, and arrange a loan to the French government. The American commission refused these insulting terms, and word of the

"X Y Z affair" outraged America. With the co-operation of Congress, the president cut off trade with France, ended the alliance of 1778, and authorized capture of French armed vessels. An undeclared naval war with France followed.

Limited hostilities did not satisfy the "war Federalists" led by Alexander Hamilton. Hamilton and his followers wanted to ally with the British, help beat down what remained of the ideas of the French Revolution, and in the process discredit the pro-French Republican party of Thomas Jefferson. Knowing it would ruin his political career, President Adams rejected appeals of fellow Federalists and instead sent a new peace mission to Paris. The result in 1800 was a settlement with the French government, now headed by Napoleon Bonaparte, who had overthrown the Directory.

The Naturalization, Alien, and Sedition Acts

Federalists, meanwhile, had not ignored their political rivals, the Republicans, and arranged passage in 1798 of the Naturalization, Alien and Sedition Acts. Since most immigrants on becoming citizens joined the Republican party, the Naturalization Act extended the waiting period for citizenship from five to fourteen years. The several Alien Acts gave the president power to expel "undesirable" foreigners, and the Sedition Act prohibited "any false, scandalous and malicious writings" against the government, Congress, or the president. Adams never exercised his authority under the Alien Acts, but about two dozen Republicans, mainly newspaper editors, were tried, and ten were convicted for violating the Sedition Act.

Republican disapproval of the acts led to the Kentucky and Virginia Resolutions of 1798. Drafted by Jefferson and Madison, the resolutions announced that whenever the national government exceeded the authority specifically granted by the Constitution, its acts were "unauthoritative, void, and of no force." Who would decide if the federal government had gone beyond its constitutional limits? The states. Jefferson and Madison, it seems, did not see the consequences of this nullification idea, which, carried to its conclusion, would justify a state in disobeying any federal act not to its liking. Their main purpose was construction of a platform around which the party faithful would rally for the election of 1800. The resolutions, however, were not forgotten after the election, and over the next sixty years advocates of "state rights" would capitalize on their arguments. It would take a great civil war in 1861–65 to end the idea of nullification.

Jefferson's strategy worked, and in 1800 the Republican ticket of Jefferson and Aaron Burr—helped by disenchantment of "war Federalists" with the president—won a narrow victory in the electoral college over Adams and Charles C. Pinckney.

The election was not over, however, because no Republican elector scratched the name of Burr. So the two Republican candidates, Jefferson and Burr, had the same number of electoral votes. The issue went to the House of Representatives, where after many ballots and some last-minute bargaining to swing Delaware, Jefferson secured the presidency.

The Adams presidency was not quite finished, and a recent judiciary act allowed an increase in the number of federal judges. Since the new judges presumably would hold positions for life, Adams determined that they must be Federalists. Most important of these "midnight appointments" (so-called because the president allegedly sat up until midnight on his last day in office signing commissions) was that of John Marshall as chief justice of the Supreme Court. Over the next third of a century Marshall exerted a powerful influence on the American political system.

Embittered by his electoral defeat, Adams got up early on the morning of March 4, 1801, and departed from the capital city. He did not wish to be present when Jefferson took the oath of office. Several days later he settled into the large house on his farm near Quincy, Massachusetts. While he entertained no thoughts of a political comeback, he took continuing interest in the affairs of the country and watched with satisfaction the rising career of his son, John Quincy Adams. This culminated in 1824 in the election of the younger Adams as sixth president of the republic. As time passed, moreover, old political wounds healed and, encouraged by his wife, Abigail, he struck up a correspondence with his old adversary, Jefferson. On the afternoon of his death, Adams, now ninety years old, muttered: "Thomas Jefferson still survives." He was wrong. Jefferson had died a few hours before at Monticello. It was July 4, 1826, the fiftieth anniversary of the signing of the Declaration of Independence.

MAJOR LAND FORMATIONS OF THE UNITED STATES

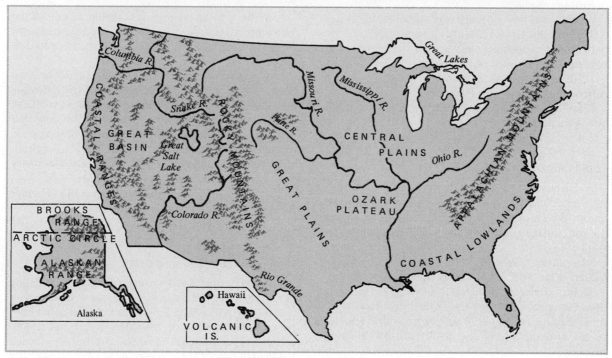

STUDY GUIDE: In 1796 John Adams was elected president. In the XYZ affair, Americans refused to meet the demands of French officials that the United States pay a bribe, lend money, and apologize for anti-French remarks. Relations with France then weakened. Meanwhile, Federalists forced passage of the Naturalization, Alien, and Sedition Acts, designed to keep out aliens and discourage criticism of the government. Republicans disapproved of the acts. Jefferson and Madison drafted the Kentucky and Virginia Resolutions of 1798 declaring that when the federal government exceeded the authority granted by the Constitution, such acts were null and void. The Resolutions insisted that states would decide if the federal government had gone beyond its constitutional limits.

SUMMING UP THE CHAPTER

Names and Terms to Identify

James Wolfe	*Poor Richard's Almanac*
Crispus Attucks	Nathanael Greene
Sons of Liberty	Land Ordinance of 1785

The map above shows major land formations of the United States. As you read the text, find ways in which the geography of regions is reflected in their historical development.

Boston Tea Party	Shays's Rebellion
Ethan Allen	Connecticut Compromise
Common Sense	certificates of indebtedness
Edward Braddock	Battle of Fallen Timbers
Peter Salem	Edmond Genêt
John Burgoyne	Pinckney's Treaty
Barry St. Leger	"midnight appointments"

Study Questions and Points to Review

1. What were the immediate social changes brought about by the American Revolution?

2. List the terms of the treaty signed at Paris in 1783.

3. Why was the electoral college established?

4. When was the Confederation period? What problems faced the domestic economy during the Confederation period?

5. How did the Virginia Plan and the New Jersey Plan differ?

6. What was Ellsworth's "three-fifths compromise"?

7. Who were the Anti-Federalists?

8. How did Alexander Hamilton solve the problem of raising revenue?

9. Why was Jay's Treaty met with a storm of protest across the United States?

10. What important guarantees were given to Americans as a result of Pinckney's Treaty?

11. Explain the XYZ affair. How did it influence American relations with France?

12. Why were the Naturalization, Alien, and Sedition Acts passed?

Topics for Discussion

1. Discuss the advantages and disadvantages of the thirteen colonies at the outset of the American Revolution. Which of those advantages and disadvantages do you consider most critical to the outcome of the war?

2. Analyze George Washington as a military leader. What were his strengths and weaknesses?

3. Both Jefferson and Hamilton sought to safeguard democracy: one through the federal government, the other through the states. Which do you think was right in his attitude toward the nature of the American republic?

4. What was Washington's position toward France during the French Revolution? Do you agree with him? Give reasons for your answer.

5. What was mercantilism? What legislation did the British government enact to achieve mercantilist ends? Imagine that you were a British subject during the Revolutionary period. Justify this legislation.

6. How did the Constitution make the central government stronger than it had been under the Articles of Confederation? Why did many Americans fear a strong central government?

Subjects for Reports or Essays

1. Using Atlas Map 6 and reference material from your school or local library, prepare a descriptive report of one of the major military engagements of the American Revolution between 1775 and 1783.

2. Read the Declaration of Independence. Outline the three main sections. What part discusses rights? What part discusses grievances? Make a list of the reasons given within the Declaration for declaring independence.

3. Imagine you are a soldier in Washington's army. Write an account of your living conditions, weapons you have used, food, clothing available to you, and places you have seen.

4. Read the Preamble to the Constitution of the United States. Make a list of the reasons given for the creation of the federal Constitution. Reword the Preamble in today's language.

5. Write a brief biographical sketch of one of the following: Alexander Hamilton, John Jay, Benjamin Franklin, Aaron Burr, Thomas Paine, Thomas Jefferson.

6. Using reference material in your school or local library, write a short report on one of the following topics: (a) The Negro in the American Revolution; (b) Weapons and military strategy used by opposing sides in the American Revolution; (c) Foreign aid given to Americans during their struggle for independence; (d) Literature written during the Revolutionary period (1765-1800) by American authors.

7. Read one of the selections listed in the "Further Readings" section and report on it to the class.

Projects, Activities, and Skills

1. Make a time line showing a chronological listing of all the major events covered in this chapter.

2. Using Atlas Map 7, trace the campaign in upper New York that led to Burgoyne's surrender. Describe British strategy. How had the British planned the final defeat of the colonies in 1777?

3. On Atlas Map 8, study the major military engagements of the American Revolution between 1779 and 1781. Evaluate the French contribution to the British defeat at Yorktown.

4. Using Atlas Map 9a, trace the rides of Revere, Dawes, and Prescott. How far did each man travel? Prepare a report on their rides. What do you think the three men accomplished by their rides?

5. Study Atlas Map 9b. Trace George Rogers Clark's route from Fort Pitt to Vincennes. Prepare a report on what you consider to be the significance of this western campaign.

6. Make a collection of pictures of architecture and furniture of the Revolutionary period (1765-1800). You may want to show how this style differs from the earlier Colonial period (1700-1765).

7. Prepare a report on the history and architecture of Independence Hall in Philadelphia.

8. Listen to some music that was written during the Revolutionary period (1765-1800). Report on American ballads and folk songs of that era. Are many of these songs sung today?

9. Draw an outline map and show on it the states ultimately carved out of the Northwest Territory.

10. Prepare a report on the meaning of the term *revolution*. Consider the word in the context of the American, French and Russian revolutions, and as used in industrial revolution, cultural revolution, and green revolution.

Further Readings

General

America at 1750: A Social History by Richard Hofstadter.

The American Revolution, 1775-1783 by John R. Alden. Perhaps the best general treatment of the War for Independence.

The Birth of the Republic, 1763-89 by Edmund S. Morgan. Defends the American position in setting out the immediate origins of the Revolution.

The Coming of the Revolution, 1763-1775 by Lawrence H. Gipson. Best one-volume treatment by an author who feels sympathy for the British.

Crisis in Freedom by John C. Miller. Readable study of the Alien and Sedition Acts.

The Declaration of Independence: A Study in the History of Political Ideas by Carl L. Becker. Most important among special studies.

An Economic Interpretation of the Constitution of the United States by Charles A. Beard. Students should be familiar with the argument set forth in this work.

The Federalist Era, 1789-1801 by John C. Miller. Best book on the period.

The Federalist Papers by Alexander Hamilton and others. Available in many editions.

The Framing of the Constitution of the United States by Max Farrand. This little masterpiece has been the standard work on the subject since 1913.

The Great Rehearsal: The Making and Ratifying of the Constitution of the U. S. by Carl Van Doren.

Miracle at Philadelphia: The Story of the Constitutional Convention, May-September 1787 by Catherine Drinker Bowen.

The Negro in the American Revolution by Benjamin Quarles.

Spies of the Revolution by Katherine Bakeless and John Bakeless. True stories of secret agents on both sides of the American Revolution.

Through These Arches by Katherine Milhous. The story of Independence Hall and of the people whose lives were spent in its presence.

Biography

Alexander Hamilton by Nathan Schachner.
Autobiography by Benjamin Franklin.
Benjamin Franklin by Carl Van Doren.

George Washington: Man and Monument by Marcus Cunliffe. A brilliant account.

Honest John Adams by Gilbert Chinard.

John Adams and the American Revolution by Catherine Drinker Bowen.

John Paul Jones: A Sailor's Biography by Samuel Eliot Morison. Prize-winning account of this naval hero.

Patrick Henry: Patriot in the Making and *Patrick Henry: Practical Revolutionary* by Robert Douthat Meade.

Thomas Jefferson by Gilbert Chinard.

Fiction, Drama, and Poetry

Arundel, Northwest Passage, Oliver Wiswell, and *Rabble in Arms* by Kenneth Roberts. Four excellent books by a noted historical novelist; each is set in the period covered in this chapter.

The Conqueror by Gertrude Atherton. The central figure is Alexander Hamilton.

The Devil's Disciple by George Bernard Shaw. A drama set during the American Revolution that pokes fun at the military.

Drums by James Boyd. An adventure set during the Revolution.

Drums Along the Mohawk by Walter D. Edmonds. A story about Mohawk Indians and European settlers.

Hear a Different Drummer by Theodora Koob. The story of a boy on his own in colonial America.

Johnny Tremain by Esther Forbes. The plot revolves around revolutionaries in Boston.

Never No More by Shirley Seifert. A biographical novel about Rebecca Boone.

Poems of Phillis Wheatley by Julian D. Mason. The work of America's first major black woman writer.

The Spy by James Fenimore Cooper. A Yankee peddler is a double agent.

Those Who Love by Irving Stone. A fictional biography of Abigail Adams.

Pictorial History

American Heritage Book of the Revolution ed. by Bruce Catton.

The American Heritage History of the American People by Bernard A. Weisberger and the editors of *American Heritage.*

CHAPTER 3

AGE OF JEFFERSON AND JACKSON

AT THE WHITE HOUSE in the spring of 1962 President John F. Kennedy paid tribute to a group of forty-nine Nobel Prize winners that included physicists, poets, dramatists, mathematicians, and peacemakers. After dinner the president rose, looked out over the distinguished gathering, and announced: "I think this is the most extraordinary collection of human talent, or human knowledge, that has ever been gathered at the White House—with the possible exception of when Thomas Jefferson dined alone." If Kennedy exaggerated the third president's talent and knowledge, he reminded his audience that the Virginian was one of the most brilliant and versatile individuals that America has produced. Jefferson was a philosopher, scientist, inventor, writer, planter, architect, lawyer, musician, politician, and diplomatist. Only one other president has rivaled him in range of ability and achievement: Theodore Roosevelt, who entered the White House exactly a hundred years after Jefferson took the presidential oath.

PRESIDENT JEFFERSON

Jefferson was born on the edge of the Virginia frontier in 1743. His father was a moderately wealthy planter and surveyor, his mother a member of one of Virginia's most prominent families. Although he was the third child in a family of ten, he was the eldest son. Thus, when his father died in 1757, he inherited the entire family estate, which included more than two thousand acres of land and about thirty slaves.

Early Career

A sensitive and intelligent youth (he had mastered Latin and Greek and was an accomplished violinist), Jefferson did not permit management of the estate to interfere with his plans for education. In 1760 he matriculated at the College of William and Mary. After graduation he decided to become a lawyer and over the next few years went to extraordinary lengths to prepare himself for a legal career. The careful training yielded dividends. Within a few years Jefferson was one of the most prosperous attorneys in

Virginia, had enlarged his estate, and begun construction of a mansion, Monticello, atop a little mountain near his birthplace. Tall, sandyhaired, and freckled, he also found time to enjoy the pleasures of a wealthy bachelor and at one point wrote: "Many and great are the comforts of a single state."

Then into his life came a charming and beautiful widow, five years his junior, and in 1772 the couple was married. Tragedy unfortunately marked the union, death claiming three of the six Jefferson children and, in 1782, Mrs. Jefferson. As she lay dying, Mrs. Jefferson extracted a promise from her husband that he would not take a second wife. He kept his word.

Meanwhile, Jefferson, like most successful lawyers of the time, had entered politics. In 1769 he won election to a seat in the Virginia House of Burgesses. By this time, relations between England and the thirteen colonies were strained and, as the controversy with the mother country deepened, he never wavered in his support of the colonial position. Then in 1775 he became a member of the Second Continental Congress. He was not much of an orator, but other delegates soon recognized that he was a master of the written language. The committee assigned to draft the Declaration of Independence gave to him the task of composition. He was only thirty-three years old.

A short time later he left the Congress to return to the Virginia legislature, which in 1779 elected him to succeed his friend Patrick Henry as governor. As chief executive Jefferson persuaded the legislature to revise the state's judicial system, change the inheritance laws, and disestablish the Anglican church. He also sought a system of free public schools for all individuals of talent and ambition and spoke out against Negro slavery. On these matters he was not in tune with most Virginians. In the latter part of his administration he sought to organize Virginia's defenses against Lord Cornwallis and the redcoats. His efforts were ineffectual, and he himself barely avoided capture.

He entered the Confederation Congress in 1783 and drew up proposals that were later incorporated in the famous Northwest Ordinances.

HEADLINE
EVENTS

1789 Judiciary Act of 1789

1801 Adams appoints John Marshall Chief Justice of Supreme Court

Thomas Jefferson inaugurated president

1803 Ohio enters the Union

Marbury v. *Madison* decision

Louisiana Territory purchased

1804 Twelfth Amendment ratified

1804-1806 Lewis and Clark explore far northwest

1805 Jefferson inaugurated for second term

Treaty with Tripoli

1805-1807 Zebulon Pike's explorations

1807 H.M.S. *Leopard* fires on U.S.S. *Chesapeake*

Fulton's *Clermont* sails up the Hudson

Embargo Act

1809 Embargo Act repealed

Non-Intercourse Act

James Madison inaugurated president

United States v. *Judge Peters* decision

1810 Macon's Bill No. 2

1811 Battle of Tippecanoe

1812 Louisiana enters the Union

Congress declares war on Britain

1813 Madison inaugurated for second term

Perry wins Battle of Lake Erie

Harrison wins Battle of Thames

1814 Battle of Horseshoe Bend

Francis Scott Key writes "Star-Spangled Banner"

Macdonough forces British to retreat to Canada

Treaty of Ghent signed

1815 Battle of New Orleans

Era of Good Feeling begins

1816 *Martin* v. *Hunter's Lesee* decision

Indiana enters the Union

Tariff Act of 1816

Second Bank of the United States is chartered

1817 James Monroe inaugurated president

Mississippi enters the Union

Rush-Bagot Agreement

1818 Illinois enters the Union

Treaty with Britain allows ten-year joint occupation of Oregon

1819 Alabama enters the Union

Financial panic

McCulloch v. *Maryland* decision

Treaty with Spain transfers Florida to United States

Tallmadge Amendment

1820 Missouri Compromise

Maine enters the Union

1820s Railroad track laid near Baltimore

1821 Missouri enters the Union

Russia claims jurisdiction of part of Oregon country

1823 Monroe Doctrine proclaimed

1824 John Quincy Adams elected president by House of Representatives

1825 John Quincy Adams inaugurated

Erie Canal completed

Era of Good Feeling ends

1828 Tariff of Abominations

1829 Andrew Jackson inaugurated president

1830 Webster-Hayne debate

1831 Mechanical reaper (McCormick)

1832 Jackson vetoes bill to recharter Bank of the United States

Worcester v. *Georgia*

Black Hawk's War

South Carolina convention nullifies tariff laws

1833 Congress passes Force Bill

Jackson inaugurated for second term

Jackson withdraws funds from Bank; withholds further deposits; Biddle's panic

1835 Repeating revolver (Colt)

Osceola leads Seminole Indian uprising in Florida

1836 Specie Circular

Arkansas enters the Union

1837 Michigan enters the Union

Martin Van Buren inaugurated president

Financial panic

1839 Vulcanized rubber (Goodyear)

1841 William Henry Harrison inaugurated president

John Tyler succeeds to presidency upon death of Harrison

Few presidents can compare with Thomas Jefferson in range of ability and achievement. All areas of human endeavor interested Jefferson, but politics beckoned him most as a means to promote the improvement of society.

He was responsible, for example, for the provision in the Ordinance of 1787 that prohibited slavery in the Northwest Territory. (One may add that he proposed a measure abolishing slavery in all future territories, only to see it fail by one vote. Lamented Jefferson: "The voice of a single individual . . . would have prevented this abominable crime from spreading itself over the new country.") Going to Paris in 1784 to help negotiate a trade treaty with France, Jefferson became American minister in Paris the following year. He had a low opinion of the French monarchy and felt a warm glow when he observed the start of the French Revolution. He returned to America in 1789 and served as secretary of state under Washington and vice-president under Adams.

Although he was a talented political manipulator, Jefferson in some ways seemed ill-suited for the role of politician. He was not dramatic, felt uncomfortable in crowds, and was a poor public speaker. He was modest in dress and manner. He had little taste for the "good living" often associated with politicians, did not smoke, ate and drank sparingly, and did not gamble. He did not enjoy the in-fighting of politics and saw political combat as a necessary evil. In fact, Jefferson even saw government itself as a necessary evil.

Why, then, did he take up politics? Doubtless he found satisfaction in the exercise of power. But, in Jefferson's case, sheer will to power does not provide an adequate answer to the question of why he chose a political career. Equally important was his philosophy. As a young man he had caught the spirit of the eighteenth-century intellectual ferment known as the Enlightenment. He believed in a rational universe—one that intelligent and educated men could understand. The Enlightenment, moreover, led him to the conclusion that men did not have to submit to the blind forces of nature, that by skillful use of intellect and will men could improve the human environment. Who had the wit and wisdom to take the lead in any movement for social regeneration? Obviously not the men down on the farm or in the counting-houses. Only men of intellect and learning—men like Thomas Jefferson—could provide the necessary leadership. Such men indeed had a moral responsibility to apply their superior talents to the task of social betterment. And what was the best medium for promoting the improvement of society? For Jefferson the answer was clear: government. Hence he became and remained a politician.

His Goals as President

Jefferson was fifty-seven years old on March 4, 1801, when he took the oath of office as president. The national government had only recently moved to Washington from Philadelphia, and the new federal city was little more than a village. Streets were unpaved, and the President's House, later renamed the White House, was only partially completed.

The third president sought repeal of the whiskey tax, reduction in appropriations for the army and navy, and repeal of the Alien and Sedition Acts. Contrary to Federalist fears, however, he inaugurated nothing akin to a revolutionary upheaval. He pledged honest payment of the public debt and made clear that he would deviate only slightly from the fiscal programs of his predecessors. He did not even purge the administration of Federalist officeholders (although, of course, as vacancies occurred he filled them with Republicans). The principal changes were in leadership and style. Leadership of the government passed from the businessmen of the Northwest to agrarians of the South. As for style, Jefferson brought "democratic simplicity" to the new federal city of Washington, a contrast with the splendor the Federalists had displayed in the old capital, Philadelphia. The new president set the tone of his administration when he walked to the Capitol for his inauguration, instead of being whisked up Pennsylvania Avenue (a muddy road cut through a swamp) in an ornate coach.

One dark spot marred Jefferson's record in his first years in the presidency: relations with the federal judiciary. Jefferson sought to get rid of the "midnight appointments" of Adams to the judiciary. One tactic was to hold up commissions to Adams appointees which, in the confusion of changing administrations, had remained undelivered. Another was impeachment of judges hostile to the ideas of Jefferson.

Marbury v. Madison

One appointee, William Marbury, petitioned the Supreme Court for a judicial order directing Secretary of State James Madison to deliver his commission. In the case *Marbury* v. *Madison* (1803), Chief Justice John Marshall, in part to avoid a clash with Jefferson that he was sure to lose, held that the Supreme Court was not responsible for delivering Marbury's commission by declaring unconstitutional the part of the Judiciary Act of 1789 which had granted the Court such power. The result was establishment of the principle—not spelled out before this time—that if the Supreme Court found acts of Congress in conflict with the Constitution, it could declare them unconstitutional.

What about the impeachment trials? Of two federal judges, the Senate found only one guilty and acquitted the other. Acquittal of one judge probably increased the independence of federal judges and dissuaded Jefferson from trying to remove Marshall, one of the greatest jurists the United States has produced.

More commendable was Jefferson's firmness toward Tripoli. For many years the so-called Barbary states of North Africa had harassed commerce in the Mediterranean. In the 1780s and 1790s the United States had joined European countries in buying "protection" from the pirates. Then, in the last months of the Adams presidency, the ruler of Tripoli raised the price for protection. When the United States rejected his demands, the ruler in spring 1801 declared war on the United States by chopping down the flagpole of the American consulate. Naval squadrons were sent to attack the pirates and a force of American marines marched across the desert. These actions of Jefferson helped bring

Jefferson took a firm stand toward the Barbary pirates who had been harassing American shipping in the Mediterranean. During the Tripolitan War, Stephen Decatur led a daring attack to set fire to the United States frigate *Philadelphia*, which the pirates had captured.

a new treaty with Tripoli in 1805. The document ended payment of tribute, but exacted $60,000 for release of Americans still in the prisons of Tripoli. Barbary pirates continued to operate in the Mediterranean for another decade —until 1816, when a combined British-Dutch naval force defeated the Algerians.

The Louisiana Purchase

While the Tripolitan War was not a complete triumph for the United States, the purchase of Louisiana in 1803 was that and more.

Originally a part of New France, the Louisiana Territory—stretching 1,800 miles from the Mississippi Delta to the northwestern part of present-day Montana—had passed to Spain in 1762. Then, at the end of the eighteenth century, leaders in Paris began to dream of reviving the French empire in the Western Hemisphere. In autumn 1801 France signed a secret treaty with Spain for the return of Louisiana (although for a time Spain would continue to administer the territory). Hearing rumors of the transaction, Jefferson was disturbed lest the French restrict American use of the lower Mississippi. Hence, he directed the American minister in Paris, Robert Livingston, to negotiate the purchase of a tract of land on the Lower Mississippi where the United States could build a port. A short time later he sent James Monroe to Paris with authorization to pay France $10 million for New Orleans and West Florida (although, unknown to Jefferson, the latter had not been part of the recent transaction).

The French, meanwhile, had been unable to crush an uprising of Negro slaves led by Toussaint L'Ouverture on Santo Domingo, which dampened French enthusiasm for the New World venture and seriously threatened their hold on Louisiana. During a talk with Livingston in spring 1803 the French foreign minister, on instructions from the First Consul, Napoleon Bonaparte, asked what the United States would pay for all the Louisiana Territory. Neither Livingston nor Monroe had authority to make such a purchase, but they knew a bargain when they saw one and signed a treaty buying the territory for $15 million. Since there was nothing in the Constitution about increasing the national domain by treaty, Jefferson felt uneasy. Then word came from Livingston and Monroe that Bonaparte might change his mind, whereupon Jefferson sent the treaty to the Senate. The vote for ratification was overwhelming.

Almost as large as the original United States, the Louisiana Territory passed to the United States in December 1803. The first state carved from the territory, appropriately named Louisiana, entered the Union in 1812.

Lewis and Clark Explore the Far West

Even before the purchase of Louisiana Jefferson had planned an expedition up the Missouri and across Spanish territory to the Pacific. To lead the expedition the president chose his young private secretary, Meriwether Lewis, and, for a colleague, Lewis selected William Clark, the brother of George Rogers Clark.

Starting out from Saint Louis in May 1804, a few months after Louisiana became an American territory, Lewis and Clark pushed up the Missouri to present-day Bismarck, North Dakota, where they spent the winter of 1804-5. From there they crossed the Rockies and went down to the Pacific via the Clearwater, Snake, and Columbia rivers. They arrived back in Saint Louis in September 1806. The expedition brought back scientific data and many specimens of the geology and wildlife of the Far West, including a pair of grizzly cubs for Jefferson. Knowledge about the geography of the western half of the continent was obtained which paved the way for eventual settlement by white men.

Jefferson also sponsored expeditions by Lieutenant Zebulon M. Pike. Pike's first venture (1805-6) was an unsuccessful search for the source of the Mississippi. Next (1806) he set out across the plains of Kansas, sighted what was later to be called Pike's Peak, pushed up the Arkansas River into the Rockies, and after enduring cold and hunger, veered southward toward the upper Rio Grande. Detained by the Spaniards at Santa Fe, he returned to the United States in 1807 and wrote an account of his observations of the Far West.

STUDY GUIDE: When Jefferson became president in 1801, he tried to get rid of Adams's "midnight appointments." The *Marbury* v. *Madison* case established that the Supreme Court had authority to review acts of Congress and declare them unconstitutional if they were in conflict with the Constitution. Jefferson took a firm stand on Tripoli but his major triumph was purchase of the Louisiana Territory. He also sponsored expeditions by Lewis and Clark and Zebulon Pike to explore the West.

THE NATION COMES OF AGE

1

President Jefferson retired from politics in 1809. He insisted that the best foundation for a democratic government was an educated electorate. So Jefferson worked to improve the schools in Virginia. He was responsible for the creation of the University of Virginia. He planned the architecture of the buildings, supervised their construction, hired the faculty, arranged the courses of study, and chose the books for the library. Shown here is the Rotunda at the University of Virginia, which Jefferson designed after the Pantheon in Rome.

2

In 1812 the United States went to war with England for a second time. This painting shows the brig *Armstrong* engaging the British fleet in 1814. The painting was made by an American painter, Edward Moran, who lived from 1829 to 1901.

3

General Andrew Jackson won fame at the Battle of New Orleans during the War of 1812. He was elected to the presidency in 1828. He was the first westerner elected to the office. This portrait of Jackson was painted by the American artist Thomas Sully.

4

During its early years the United States continually expanded westward. Texas became a state after winning independence from Mexico. This painting shows the Texans taking Fort San Antonio de Bexar during their war for independence in 1835.

Courtesy Virginia State Travel Service **1**

Courtesy, U. S. Naval Academy Museum **2**

Texas State Archives **4**

3 National Gallery of Art, Washington, D.C.

WAR OF 1812

Jefferson easily won reelection in 1804, trouncing the Federalist candidate Charles C. Pinckney. Unfortunately his second administration was not fated to be as tranquil or fruitful as the first. The difficulty was Europe. The long European war had died out about the time Jefferson took office in 1801, giving him breathing space and a chance to concentrate on affairs at home. By the time he took the presidential oath a second time, in March 1805, war had again broken out in Europe.

As before, the principal combatants were Britain and France. Also as before, neither took a tolerant view of trade between neutral countries and the enemy. In 1806-7 the French emperor, Napoleon I (formerly Napoleon Bonaparte), announced the "Continental system," closing the European Continent to Britain and ruling that any neutral ships calling at British ports could not land cargoes at any continental ports controlled by France or its allies. American ship captains who defied Napoleon's decrees saw their ships confiscated and their crews thrown into prison.

The British, to destroy trade with France issued a series of orders-in-council announcing that neutral vessels bound for the Continent would have to stop in Britain and buy a license — or be subject to capture by British cruisers. A ship calling in England for a license would, of course, be in violation of Napoleon's decrees and hence liable to seizure if it went on to a continental port.

Impressment

There was also the problem of impressment. Britain's survival depended on its navy. Unable to recruit full crews, ship captains often steered their vessels into British ports and dispatched gangs to scour docks and taverns for able-bodied men who, bound and gagged, were forced into the royal naval service. This kidnapping was called impressment. At sea there was no escape from the "floating hells," but in American ports these British seamen often deserted, sometimes signing on vessels flying the Stars and Stripes. The British found this manpower drain intolerable and stepped up the practice of stopping neutral ships, lining up the crew, and impressing into the British navy any man with a trace of an English accent.

The impressment problem reached a crisis on June 22, 1807. On that date the British warship H.M.S. *Leopard* overhauled the American frigate *Chesapeake* just off the coast of Virginia. The British demanded to search the American frigate for deserters. When the Americans refused, the *Leopard* fired three broadsides, killing three Americans. The American ship, unable to defend herself, struck her colors and was boarded by a British search party. Four men were seized by the British. One was a British deserter. The other three men were Americans who had previously been impressed by the British and had escaped.

Outraged, many Americans urged war, but Jefferson remained calm, confident that he could compel the British and French to respect American rights. He would cut off all American trade with the rest of the world, a punishment Britain and France, needing American materials, could not bear. The result was the Embargo Act of December 1807 prohibiting ships from leaving the United States for any foreign port. But Jefferson miscalculated. The chief victims of the embargo were Americans — merchants, planters, and farmers who needed foreign markets. As ships remained tied to wharves, economic depression swept the country and unemployment increased. Desperate for work, many seamen drifted to the British navy and merchant marine, relieving Britain's manpower problem and, ironically, bringing impressment to a virtual end.

James Madison

Still wallowing in depression, the country faced a presidential election in 1808. Honoring the precedent set by Washington, Jefferson did not seek a third term. Instead he promoted the candidacy of his secretary of state, James Madison. Despite wide displeasure over the embargo, especially in the Northeast, Madison defeated the Federalist candidate, Charles C. Pinckney.

James Madison was born in 1751 at Port Conway in King George County, Virginia, of moderately well-to-do parents. He attended the College of New Jersey (now Princeton), taking a course oriented toward theology, but upon graduation decided to be a lawyer.

Too frail for military service during the War of Independence, Madison soon became active in politics. He took part in the convention to draft a constitution for Virginia, attracting attention with his arguments for religious toleration. He also served in the first state legislature under the new constitution. In 1779 the legislature elected him as a delegate to the Second Continental Congress (after 1781, the Confederation Congress).

Madison left Congress in 1783, returning to Virginia to pursue his law studies. In 1786 he reentered politics as a member of the Virginia legislature where he rendered distinguished service. At this time he began to take a deep interest in problems of commerce, which made him painfully aware of the chaotic state of domestic and foreign trade in this period under the Articles of Confederation.

He was one of the organizers of the Annapolis convention and a delegate to the Constitutional Convention in Philadelphia. During the convention he took such an important part in deliberations that some historians have referred to him as "the father of the Constitution." He also played an outstanding part in securing the document's ratification, being one of the authors of *The Federalist Papers*. Quietly but effectively Madison led pro-Constitution delegates when his own state, Virginia, debated the question of ratification.

When the new federal government began operation in spring 1789, Madison was on hand as a representative from Virginia. He quickly established himself as an influential member of the House and took special pride in his part in the drafting of the first ten amendments to the Constitution, the Bill of Rights. In the struggle between Hamilton and Jefferson over federal policy, Madison fell in easily with his fellow Virginian and became the number two man in Jefferson's emerging Republican party. He headed the State Department when Jefferson assumed the presidency in 1801 and over the next eight years worked closely with the president in shaping foreign policy.

Madison was a quiet and introspective individual, rather shy, who spoke softly, his voice often trailing off to a whisper at the end of a sentence. Still, he was pleasant and a good conversationalist. His strength, of course, was his intellect. At forty-four, he married a charming and attractive widow, Dolley Payne Todd, seventeen years his junior. Dolley Madison was a devoted wife and, when her husband became chief executive, she made the presidential residence the focal point of Washington society.

Madison as President

When Madison took the presidential oath in 1809, he was approaching sixty. Some historians have seen him as a tired old man, long past his physical and intellectual peak. Irving Brant, a historian who devoted many years to study of the fourth president, has different ideas. He thinks Madison was sufficiently alert and energetic in his eight years as president, did not sit by and permit events to determine policies of his administration, and maneuvered as well as anybody might have in situations, particularly diplomatic ones, that were hopelessly tangled.

AMERICAN BUSINESS ACTIVITY: 1790 – 1819

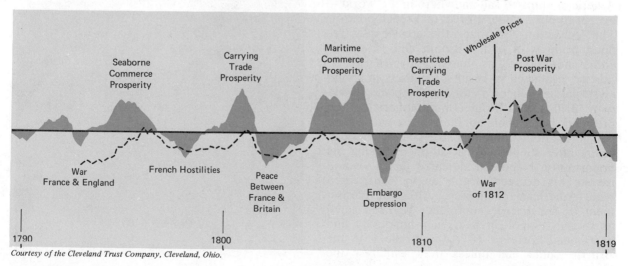

Courtesy of the Cleveland Trust Company, Cleveland, Ohio.

Courtesy Colonial Williamsburg, Williamsburg, Virginia

James Madison became president as the United States was edging toward war with Britain. Madison fell in with the "warhawks" and asked Congress to declare war on Britain. Did he have the support of the majority of Americans during the War of 1812? What evidence of popular reaction is given in the text?

orders-in-council. When he received no encouragement from London, the president executed his threat.

The United States was edging toward war with Britain, but interference with American shipping and impressment were only partly responsible. Some Americans were furious because the British, from forts in Canada, were encouraging Indians to ravage frontier settlements in the Northwest. Others saw rich rewards from war against the British. Should American arms succeed (and with Napoleon also fighting Britain, the chances seemed good), the United States might acquire the great domain of Canada—and perhaps Florida, for Spain was an ally of Britain.

When Congress assembled in autumn 1811, there was considerable sentiment for war. Mar-

As the wife of President James Madison, Dolley Madison won fame as a charming and gracious hostess. The Madisons were forced to flee the White House during the British invasion of Washington in 1814. Mrs. Madison saved the Gilbert Stuart portrait of Washington and some of the White House silverware from destruction by the invaders.

The New-York Historical Society

A few days before Madison's inauguration, Jefferson approved repeal of the embargo. Still, neither he nor Madison had lost faith in peaceful coercion, and the two men persuaded Congress to pass the Non-Intercourse Act, allowing American ships to sail anywhere in the world—except to ports under British or French control. The legislation authorized the president to reopen trade with either Britain and France if either should repeal its obnoxious decrees. When this act produced no results, Congress in spring 1810 passed Macon's Bill No 2, opening trade with Britain and France but authorizing the president to proclaim nonintercourse with either belligerent if it continued to violate American rights after the other had stopped. Seeing his opportunity, Napoleon indicated that he would revoke his decrees insofar as they interfered with American commerce. Although harassment by the French continued, Madison acted as though Napoleon had dealt honorably and announced early in 1811 that trade with the British would end unless they withdrew the

tial enthusiasm was increased by word from the West a few days later proclaiming the victory of Governor William Henry Harrison over Tecumseh's warriors at Tippecanoe Creek in Indiana Territory. Henry Clay, a freshman congressman, boasted that the Kentucky militia alone could conquer Canada. Tired of haggling with the British, Madison fell in with the "warhawks" and on June 1, 1812, asked Congress to declare war. In the House of Representatives a majority (79-49) were for the war. Debate in the Senate was sharper and the vote closer, 19-13 for war.

Clearly a large minority of the population opposed hostilities. Although Madison was elected to another term in the White House, it was by a smaller margin than in 1808. Federalist strength in Congress doubled. Opposition continued through the end of the war, particularly in New England, where people engaged in treasonable trade with the enemy while leaders talked of seceding from the Union and of forming a northeastern confederacy.

Perhaps reflecting the popular mood, United States forces made a poor start in the war.

Instead of concentrating on Montreal, Britain's strategic center in North America, the United States launched a three-pronged invasion of Canada in August–November 1812. One attack started from Detroit under Governor William Hull of the Michigan Territory. After barely penetrating Canada, the governor retreated to Detroit and then surrendered without firing a shot. A second attack aimed across the Niagara River in western New York. It quickly evaporated, in part because the New York militiamen refused to cross the Canadian border. A third invading force moved northward along Lake Champlain, destination Montreal, but turned back when New York militiamen again refused to cross the border. The only consolation for Americans in those dreary months were two spectacular victories at sea by the frigates *Constitution* and *United States*. But the British navy soon drove American warships to cover and clamped a blockade around American ports. A short time later word began to filter across the Atlantic that Napoleon's Grand Army was retreating in disarray through the snows of Russia, raising the fear that soon Britain might be able to turn full attention to the war in America.

This engraving shows a view of the British bombardment of Fort McHenry, near Baltimore, in September 1814. What musical composition was inspired by the battle?

Victories on the Great Lakes

Then, in spring 1813, things took a turn for the better. American ships won control of Lake Ontario, and ships under Oliver Hazard Perry defeated a British fleet on Lake Erie. (Flapping from the mast of Perry's flagship was a banner: "Don't Give Up the Ship.") American victories on the Great Lakes compelled the British to evacuate Detroit. An American army under William Henry Harrison, now a general, set out in pursuit and defeated the retreating British along the Thames River in southwestern Ontario.

Spring 1814 brought another turn—for the worse. His armies broken, Napoleon agreed to retire to the island of Elba in the Mediterranean, and soon British veterans of the European war were on the way to America. The first blow fell when a 4,000-man expeditionary force entered Chesapeake Bay in August 1814. Scattering American militiamen, the British soldiers marched into Washington while President Madison and his aides scurried to surrounding hills. Most public buildings, including the Capitol and the White House, were set on fire. Returning to their ships, the British next moved on Baltimore. But a heavy bombardment failed to subdue Fort McHenry, strongpoint of Baltimore's defenses, whereupon the British withdrew to Jamaica in the Caribbean. Watching through the night of September 13-14, 1814, as bombs fell on Fort McHenry was Francis Scott Key. At "dawn's early light" the Stars and Stripes still flew over the fort, inspiring Key to jot down some verses and set them to a popular drinking song. Thus was born "The Star-Spangled Banner."

The British, meanwhile, had moved 11,000 troops along Lake Champlain from Canada. Supported by four ships and a dozen gunboats, they seemed invincible. But at Plattsburg they met an American naval force commanded by thirty-year-old Thomas Macdonough. With clever tactics Macdonough nullified the enemy's advantage in firepower. After a furious battle on September 11, 1814, the British retreated to Canada.

Jackson at New Orleans

Three months later, in December 1814, 7,500 British regulars landed below New Orleans. Their object was to gain control of the Mississippi Valley, lifeline of the American West.

Awaiting the battle was an irregular force of militiamen from Kentucky and Tennessee, Creoles, free Negroes, and pirates—under command of General Andrew Jackson. The first action came on New Year's Day 1815, an artillery duel in which the Americans outgunned the British. A week later the redcoats attacked, moving in even ranks across an open field. Jackson's men discharged a murderous fire. The battle lasted a half-hour and, when they retreated to their ships, the British left many dead and wounded.

A short time later word traveled across the country that the war was over, and many Americans concluded that Jackson's victory at New Orleans had forced the British to terms. This was not true. Had they wished, the British probably could have defeated the United States. But the long war with Napoleon had drained the British, and they felt no enthusiasm for an exhaustive campaign in North America. Accordingly, representatives of Britain and the United States met at Ghent, Belgium, in December 1814—two weeks before the Battle of New Orleans—and agreed to peace. Except for some articles providing for arbitration of disputed boundaries between the United States and Canada, the peace settlement was a truce. Both sides simply agreed to stop fighting and restore the conditions existing prior to the war. There was no mention of impressment or of neutral rights.

STUDY GUIDE: During Jefferson's second term, there was trouble between England and France. British impressment of American seamen forced Congress to pass the Embargo Act of 1807. Americans suffered from this act. It was repealed a few days before James Madison's inauguration. Madison and Jefferson urged Congress to pass the Non-Intercourse Act allowing U.S. ships to sail anywhere in the world except to ports under British or French control. In 1810 Congress passed Macon's Bill No. 2, opening trade with Britain and France. The Bill stated that the United States would stop trade with either of those nations that continued to violate American rights after the other had stopped. From Canada, the British continued to encourage Indians to attack northwestern frontier settlements.

In 1812, Madison asked Congress to declare war. United States forces made a three-pronged attack on Canada. American victories on the Great Lakes compelled the British to evacuate Detroit. After Napoleon retired to Elba, the British sent an expeditionary force to America. In 1814 the British burned Washington. During the bombing of Fort McHenry, Francis Scott Key composed "The Star-Spangled Banner." In December the British landed near New Orleans, hoping to gain control of the Mississippi Valley. Andrew Jackson led American forces defending New Orleans and forced the British to retreat.

THE ERA OF GOOD FEELING

The year 1815 marked the beginning of a new day for Americans. Seeking to obliterate lingering ideas of the French Revolution, Europe turned away from the New World. Americans returned the favor, settling down to exploiting opportunities inside their own borders. An entire continent was awaiting ax and plow, and even as the country celebrated the feats of General Jackson, cornfields were pressing back the forest. Within a few years after the Treaty of Ghent four new states entered the federal Union: Indiana (1816), Mississippi (1817), Illinois (1818), and Alabama (1819). The nation had achieved political unity. New England's dissenters of 1812-14 became silent, and the Federalist party came to an end. The country was at peace—with itself and the outer world. The Era of Good Feeling had followed a long season of discord and war.

A prevailing theme in the new era was nationalism—concentration on the national interest rather than the sectional. To reinforce national unity, severely strained in the recent war, Henry Clay and John C. Calhoun sponsored the "American system." The idea was to bind people to the nation by appealing to local interests. For businessmen of the Northeast, a higher tariff would encourage manufacturing, and a new Bank of the United States (Hamilton's bank having expired in 1811) would assure fiscal stability. For the West and South the national government would finance "internal improvements," mainly roads and bridges. Better transportation facilities would help farmers take their goods to market quickly and cheaply. Congress responded in 1816 by raising the tariff and voting a twenty-year charter for the Second Bank of the United States. The internal improvements did not fare so well, in part because Presidents Madison and Monroe could find nothing in the Constitution authorizing such an expenditure of federal funds.

John Marshall

Another source of the nationalist impulse during the postwar years was Chief Justice John Marshall.

Born on the Virginia frontier in 1755, Marshall grew up in a crude frontier environment and in his first twenty years hardly got out of the backwoods. Still, he did not live in poverty. His father was a reasonably prosperous planter, held assorted public offices, and provided his family (which eventually included fifteen children, the oldest of whom was John) with a large and comfortable house. As a boy, Marshall, who was strong and rawboned, loved the outdoors and in particular enjoyed exploring the extensive forest. But he also liked to read and was particularly taken with Alexander Pope's *Essay on Man,* many passages of which he memorized.

A few months after the battles at Lexington and Concord, in 1775, twenty-year-old John Marshall joined the Culpeper Minutemen. The following year he entered the Continental army and saw combat at Brandywine, Germantown, Monmouth, and Stony Point. He also endured the agonies of Valley Forge in the winter of 1777-78.

The experience of war had great influence on Marshall. For one thing, he became an admirer of the commander-in-chief, and to the time of Washington's death in 1799 his loyalty never weakened. More important, during the War of Independence he acquired ideas about nationalism.

As he explained many years later, while fighting the mother country Marshall became imbued with the maxim "united we stand, divided we fall." In the army, moreover, he lived intimately with men of different states and regions who were risking everything in the common cause. In such circumstances, he recalled, state boundaries ceased to have much meaning and he fell in with the habit of thinking in national terms: America became his country, and Congress his government. After the war this national spirit became even stronger, and in the 1780s and 1790s when Jefferson and others raised the idea of state rights, Marshall feared disintegration of the infant nation. As he viewed the problem, the only guarantor of national unity was a strong general government. Throughout his entire career, until his death in 1835, Marshall used his extraordinary talent toward strengthening the general government—the government of the nation, of all the people.

Except for a few weeks at the College of William and Mary near the end of the war, Marshall had no formal instruction in law. He gained admission to the bar in 1780; his license was signed by his distant relative, Governor Thomas Jefferson. Two years later Marshall became a member of the Virginia legislature and soon felt disgust for the way Virginia, as well as the rest of the states, was doing as it pleased, without regard for the national interest or the treaty obligations incurred by the Confederation government.

Hence, Marshall favored the new federal Constitution, which looked to a stronger national government, and his eloquence helped carry the Virginia ratifying convention in 1788. When the new general government began to function, he supported the policies of Washington and Hamilton and, of course, gravitated to the Federalist party. In 1797 he was one of the three American commissioners involved in the notorious XYZ affair in France. The following year, on Washington's urging, he ran for Congress, won a close election, and served a distinguished term in the House of Representatives. Then, in 1800, President Adams appointed him secretary of state.

Marshall—New Chief Justice

Near the end of his term, early in 1801, Adams asked Marshall's help in designating a new chief justice of the Supreme Court, and the president and the secretary of state considered one name after another. Finally Adams turned to Marshall and said: "I believe I must nominate you." Many years later in an autobiographical sketch Marshall described his response: "I had never before heard myself named for the office and had not even thought of it. I was pleased as well as surprised, and bowed in silence."

John Marshall was a conservative who placed great stress on the rights of private property. He was mild, gentle, and warmhearted, not a cynic or an angry man. Some historians have compared him with Abraham Lincoln. Like Lincoln, he was tall, loose-jointed, and swarthy in complexion. Like Lincoln also, he was negligent in dress, was good humored, and had simple tastes. Despite his position, he remained unpretentious, as illustrated by the story of the young man who was grumbling because there was no one to carry the turkey he had just purchased. Marshall offered his services (the youth did not recognize him), and down the street walked the young man, rather haughtily, the distinguished chief justice trailing meekly, the turkey under his arm.

Marshall was devoted to his invalid wife and also to their ten children. He had great power of argument and expressed himself in language that, unlike the flowery rhetoric so fashionable at the time, was clear, crisp, and unembellished. Marshall had such talent for persuasion that associate justices of the Court usually accepted his conclusions, to the exasperation of such Republican presidents as Jefferson, Madison, and Monroe, who appointed Republican justices in the hope of diluting the Federalist influence of Marshall. Jefferson confessed that he never admitted anything when conversing with Marshall; as soon as one conceded a point, however remote it seemed from the conclusion the chief justice was trying to establish, the argument was lost. Jefferson said that if Marshall asked him if it were daylight he would reply, "Sir, I don't know, I can't tell."

The Marshall Court

In supporting nationalism, four decisions of the Marshall court stand out. First was the case of *United States* v. *Judge Peters* (1809), which emerged from an attempt by the Pennsylvania legislature to obstruct an action by a federal district judge. The Supreme Court ruled that in case of conflict the power of a federal court was above that of a state legislature, a blow to the idea of state sovereignty. In *Martin* v. *Hunter's Lessee* (1816) and *Cohens* v. *Virginia* (1821), the Marshall court established that the power of the Supreme Court was greater than that of the state courts when federal rights were involved. The outcome was an increase in the power and prestige of the federal judiciary.

McCulloch v. *Maryland* (1819) resulted from Maryland's attempt to tax out of existence the Baltimore branch of the Bank of the United States. Seeing that through taxation a state could undo any federal law it disliked, the Court ruled that the power to tax involved the power to destroy; hence, no state might tax an institution of the federal government. In the McCulloch decision Marshall also spoke out against the theory that the Constitution came from the states; that the government established by it was therefore a creature of the states. He wrote that the federal government was a government of all the people of the nation. Its form and substance came from them, not the states. Since federal power derived from the people, he concluded, the government of the federal Union, if limited in power, was supreme in its sphere of action.

Throughout his entire legal career John Marshall strongly believed in nationalism. How did his major decisions as chief justice of the United States increase the power of the Supreme Court and the federal government?

The chief justice established these principles on the nature of the American Union over a period of thirty-four years. Appointed by the second president, he presided over the Supreme Court during the terms of five other presidents. His ideas on nationalism were in tune with the Era of Good Feeling which began with the election of James Monroe in 1816. Monroe, a Republican, overwhelmed Rufus King, a Federalist. The electoral vote was 183-24. The Federalist party was finished.

James Monroe

Born in Westmoreland County, Virginia in 1758, James Monroe was the son of a planter. At six-teen he entered the College of William and Mary but left the school two years later to join the Continental army. By 1778 he was a lieutenant colonel. On conclusion of the war Monroe studied law, entered politics, and after a year in the Virginia legislature, became a member of the Confederation Congress, where he helped to fashion the famous Northwest Ordinance of 1787. He took a dim view of the Constitution, and with Patrick Henry was a leading opponent of the document when it came before the Virginia ratifying convention.

Upon approval of the Constitution, Monroe ran for a seat in the new Congress, only to lose the election to James Madison. In 1790 the Virginia governor appointed him to the Senate to fill the vacancy created when one of Virginia's senators died. In the Senate he became a vehement critic of the policies of Alexander Hamilton and thus joined Thomas Jefferson's Republican party.

The French Revolution had meanwhile captured Monroe's enthusiasm, and in 1794 President Washington, hoping somehow to improve relations with the government in Paris, appointed Monroe as ambassador to France. Monroe proved to be too friendly toward the French government and Washington ordered him to return home.

Back in Virginia, Monroe composed a long book attacking Washington's policy toward France. In 1799 he won election as governor of Virginia. Four years later, in 1803, he was again on his way to Paris, this time sent by President Jefferson to help Robert Livingston in negotiations with the government of Napoleon. The outcome was the Louisiana Purchase. Monroe remained in Europe for the next four years, trying on the one hand to reach an agreement with Britain to end British violation of American rights on the seas and on the other to arrange the purchase of Florida from Spain. Neither negotiation was successful.

When he returned to the United States in 1807, Monroe fixed his eye on the election of 1808 and hoped that he might succeed Jefferson as president. Instead the election went to James Madison, and Monroe had to settle for the governorship of Virginia.

Then Madison asked him to be secretary of state, whereupon he resigned the governor's office. During the War of 1812, the president asked him to take on the additional responsibilities of secretary of war. As head of the War Department Monroe was energetic and resourceful.

James Monroe was the last of the "Virginia dynasty" of presidents. One of his most notable achievements was the Monroe Doctrine, in which European nations were warned not to intervene in the affairs of the New World. How can you relate the Monroe Doctrine to the Cuban missile crisis in 1962?

After Andrew Jackson's spectacular victory at New Orleans early in 1815, Monroe basked in the warm glow of popular approval, for it was he who had ordered Jackson to New Orleans and helped assemble the forces which "Old Hickory" used to humiliate the British. This new popularity contributed to his election to the presidency in 1816.

Of the men who had taken part in the struggle for independence, Monroe was the last to occupy the presidency. He was also the last of "the Virginia dynasty" of chief executives (Washington, Jefferson, Madison, and Monroe). Unlike the two Republicans who preceded him in office, Jefferson and Madison, Monroe had modest intellectual talent. What, then, accounted for his rise to the top in politics? One can point to several factors. He had good luck, particularly in his first

years as a lawyer-politician when he gained the friendship of Jefferson. He had ambition, determination, and energy, prerequisites for political success in Monroe's time as well as in our own. He was also loyal to political allies, and had integrity. Jefferson said, "Monroe was so honest that if you turned his soul inside out there would not be a spot on it."

The Panic of 1819

Two years after Monroe took office, in 1819, the country fell victim to a severe economic depression. The crisis originated in the speculation that swept the country after the peace of Ghent. Men in those years had wild dreams of agricultural and industrial empires and, to make dreams come true borrowed heavily. No group was more dazzled by such visions than pioneer farmers who since the war had flocked to the West. Prices of cattle, grain, and cotton were climbing and, to take advantage of new opportunities, farmers determined to put more acreage to the plow. To finance expansion they borrowed from small state banks—often "wildcat" banks lacking in both a sense of fiscal responsibility and reserves of gold coin. The small wildcat banks in turn were usually in debt to the large Bank of the United States.

Directors of the Bank of the United States, knowing that runaway speculation could not go on forever, became uneasy. Since it was impossible to deflate the speculative bubble gradually, they popped it by directing all Bank branches late in 1818 to accept no more bills of state banks, to present state bank notes for immediate repayment in coin, and to renew no personal notes or mortgages. Soon the wildcat empire was tumbling like a house of cards, and with it the dreams of western farmers. Westerners saw much of their land pass to the Bank of the United States, and the result was anger—much of it unreasoning—against the "monster bank." Bitterness deepened when in *McCulloch* v. *Maryland* the Supreme Court led by John Marshall headed off any attempt to regain losses by state taxation of the Bank.

The Panic of 1819 seemed to signal a sectional cleavage in the country along vertical lines, East against West. But, even as the dreary economic depression was settling over the country, a new crisis appeared which divided the country horizontally, North against South—the "Missouri controversy" of 1819-20.

Tallmadge Offers an Amendment

Since the birth of the republic in 1789, Congress had taken care to admit free states and slave states alternately. With the entry of Alabama, there was a balance of eleven each. This meant that slave and free states had equal representation in the United States Senate, a guarantee against legislation that was opposed by the South such as bills restricting slavery. Then came an explosion. When Missouri applied for admission as a slave state, Representative James Tallmadge of New York in February 1819 offered an amendment to the statehood bill that would prohibit further entry of slaves into Missouri. His proposed amendment also required that all children henceforth born to slave parents in the new state be given their freedom at the age of twenty-five.

Tallmadge was not thinking of Missouri. It was the rest of the territory purchased from France in 1803 that concerned him. There was no prohibition against slavery in the Louisiana Territory. What if—as in the case of Missouri—southerners took along slaves when they migrated westward and drafted state constitutions protecting slavery? The entire territory would be carved into slave states. The balance between free and slave states would tilt so radically in favor of the latter that the special interests of those opposed to slavery would stand no chance in the high councils of Washington.

When Congress adjourned in March 1819, the Missouri question went to the people, and at mass meetings orators shouted arguments to angry audiences. Newspapers and state legislatures took up the debate. Seldom did the morality of slavery enter discussions; most Americans in 1819 were reconciled to the South's "peculiar institution." The issue was one of sectional politics and power. An occasional "fire-eater" on either side talked wildly of secession, but few people wanted to fracture the federal Union.

The Missouri Compromise

Accordingly, in 1820 Congress approved the Missouri Compromise. Missouri would enter the Union as a slave state without the restric-

Count the number of states where slavery was permitted and also the states where slavery was prohibited. How did the Missouri Compromise affect the balance of power between the states?

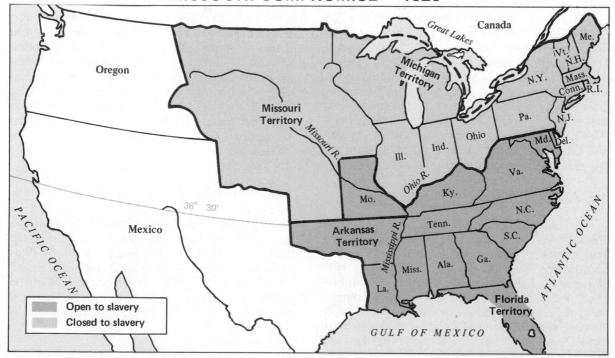

MISSOURI COMPROMISE — 1820

tions of the Tallmadge amendment and, to maintain the balance of free and slave states, Maine, recently detached from Massachusetts, would enter the Union as a free state. Finally, slavery would be prohibited in the remainder of the Louisiana Territory north of the line 36° 30′ (the southern border of present-day Kansas). The South thus gained its immediate objective, admission of Missouri as a slave state. But eighty percent of the Louisiana Territory was closed to slavery.

Across the country the compromise brought applause and a sigh of relief. Still, the Missouri controversy had revealed how fragile was a nation that was half slave and half free. From Monticello, the aging Thomas Jefferson wrote that the angry debate, like a firebell in the night, had awakened him and filled him with terror. John Quincy Adams of Massachusetts confided to his diary that the controversy was the title page of a tragic volume. Forty years later, in 1861-65, Adams's prophecy would come true.

Foreign Affairs

If Americans in the Era of Good Feeling gave first attention to problems at home, they also found time for foreign affairs. The most notable achievements of President Monroe were in the field of diplomacy.

First came two important understandings with the British. The Rush-Bagot agreement (1817) ended the expensive naval rivalry between the United States and Britain on the Great Lakes. The following year, 1818, the two countries signed a treaty opening the waters around Newfoundland to American fishermen and establishing the forty-ninth parallel as the border between the United States and Canada from Lake of the Woods to the crest of the Rockies. The agreement temporarily ended friction over the Oregon country, claimed by both countries, by providing for a ten-year joint occupation.

Trouble in Florida

Americans had been nibbling at Florida for some time. Uninvited migrants from the United States had overthrown Spanish authority in Florida's western regions as early as 1810, and in 1813 Americans had seized the area around Mobile, then in Spanish West Florida. Spain's colonies in Latin America had meanwhile begun a revolt, forcing the withdrawal of most Spanish garrisons from Florida. Bands of outcast Indians and runaway Negro slaves subsequently stormed across the United States border, looting and killing, then returning to their sanctuary in Florida. To end these raids, President Monroe ordered Andrew Jackson to the southeastern frontier. Ignoring Monroe's instructions to respect Spanish sovereignty, "Old Hickory" seized posts at Saint Mark's and Pensacola in 1818 and deposed the Spanish governor.

Monroe prepared to censure Jackson and apologize to Spain, but Secretary of State John Quincy Adams persuaded him to accuse Spain of violating Pinckney's Treaty (1795) by failing to keep order in Florida. Then Adams went another step, advising the Spaniards that they had two choices in Florida: control the troublemakers (which Adams and the government in Madrid knew was impossible) or cede Florida to the United States. Spanish leaders could see the handwriting on the wall, knowing that if they did not hand over Florida the Americans simply would take it. The outcome was a treaty by which Spain in 1819 transferred Florida to the United States, and the United States assumed $5 million of claims held by American citizens against the Spanish government.

Pressure in the West

The United States was at this time feeling the pressure of European autocracy on the western coast of North America, where Russian influence was expanding. Here was an area where Americans hoped one day to plant the Stars and Stripes. The Russians had been in America since the 1720s, when they established themselves in Alaska. But over the decades they had shown no inclination to move southward. Then, in 1812, they set up a trading post at Fort Ross near San Francisco Bay. Next, in 1821, Tsar Alexander I claimed Russian jurisdiction in the Pacific Northwest from Alaska down to the fifty-first parallel, well into the Oregon country.

Meanwhile, Americans feared that the Holy Alliance[1] was planning to move against the newly independent nations of Latin America. Britain, which was profiting from trade with Latin America, seemed to share American fears: in 1823 the British proposed that they and the United States warn the autocrats to keep hands off Latin America. Former-Presidents Jefferson and Madison agreed. But Secretary Adams wondered why Britain, with its powerful navy, wanted the aid of

---

[1] Austria, Russia, Prussia.

the United States. He concluded that what the British really wanted was a pledge that the United States would take no new territory in the Western Hemisphere. Given American ambitions in Oregon and Texas, that would never do. Adams also decided that the Holy Alliance had no serious plans for attacking Latin America, and, if it tried, the British navy would handle the problem.

The Monroe Doctrine

Adams's fertile mind did not stop there. He saw an opportunity to assert American nationalism—to blow a defiant blast at the Old World. The result was the Monroe Doctrine, buried in the president's annual message to Congress in December 1823. The doctrine proclaimed, first, that the era of European colonization in the Western Hemisphere was over. Europeans might keep what territory they already occupied, but must acquire no more. Adams aimed this part of the doctrine at Russian activity along the Pacific coast. The doctrine, second, announced that the nations of the Old World must not interfere in the affairs of the New. This principle of nonintervention was aimed at any plans the Holy Alliance might have for overturning Latin American republics. In return, the United States would keep out of the Old World.

What were the immediate effects of the Monroe Doctrine? The doctrine was not needed to prevent Europe's autocrats from attacking Latin America, for they had never given serious thought to such an operation. The Russians had decided before Monroe's message to withdraw up the Pacific coast. Americans applauded Monroe for twisting Europe's tail, then turned to more pressing matters at home. The doctrine, of course, had no legal standing, and was the subject of no federal statute or treaty. It was simply a statement of policy by one president, James Monroe. But the long-run effects were important as the United States grew stronger and based foreign policy on this doctrine.

In subsequent months the president probably gave scant thought to diplomacy, for 1824 was an election year. In contrast to 1820 when Monroe had run unopposed, the contest for the White House was sharp. There was only one political party. Hence, four Republicans sought the presidency: John Quincy Adams, Henry Clay, William H. Crawford of Georgia, and Andrew Jackson. When returns were in, Jackson had most of the popular vote, but he did not

have a majority in the electoral college, so the election went to the House of Representatives. After much maneuvering, Clay threw support to Adams and, as a result, the son of the second president of the republic gained the victory. The president-elect thereupon named Clay secretary of state in the new administration. Infuriated, Jacksonians accused Adams and Clay of a "corrupt bargain," and, when Adams went to the Capitol in March 1825 to take the oath, the charge of "corrupt bargain" still echoed through the country.

The Era of Good Feeling had ended.

STUDY GUIDE: To strengthen national unity, Henry Clay and John C. Calhoun sponsored the "American system." Chief Justice John Marshall also encouraged nationalistic feelings. He wrote that the federal government was of all the people and that federal power came from the people. As chief justice Marshall established principles that helped determine the nature of the American Union.

In 1817 James Monroe became president. Two years later the nation was hit by the Panic of 1819. This economic crisis showed that there was a conflict between the interests of eastern and western sections of the nation.

The Missouri Compromise of 1819–20 attempted to settle differences between the northern and southern sections of the nation. It provided that Missouri would enter the Union as a slave state without the restrictions of the Tallmadge Amendment. Maine would enter as a free state. Slavery would be prohibited in the remainder of the Louisiana Territory north of the line 36° 30'.

In 1819 Florida was acquired from Spain. In 1821 Russia, a member of the Holy Alliance, claimed land in the Pacific Northwest from Alaska down to Oregon Territory. Fearing overthrow of Latin American nations by the Holy Alliance, the Monroe Doctrine stated that Old World nations must not interfere in the affairs of the New World. In return, the United States would keep out of the Old World.

THE SECOND PRESIDENT ADAMS

The United States was a young and vigorous country in March 1825, and it must have seemed that the man entering the White House was unusally well-equipped to provide national leadership.

Born in Braintree, Massachusetts, in 1767, John Quincy Adams, as a young boy, had watched the smoke of the Battle of Bunker Hill. Later he went off to Paris with his father, who was on a diplomatic mission for the Second Continental Congress. In Europe he mastered several languages and at the age of fourteen became the private secretary and interpreter for the American minister to Russia. Three years later he returned to America, enrolled at Harvard, and at nineteen graduated with honors. As a young lawyer he took a deep interest in politics. He supported Federalist ideas and so impressed President Washington with essays defending the administration's neutrality policies of the 1790s that he received, at twenty-six, appointment as American minister to the Netherlands. During his father's presidency he was moved to the foreign office in Berlin.

Adams won election to the Massachusetts senate in 1802, and the following year the Federalist-controlled legislature elected him to the Senate in Washington. Then Adams ran into trouble with fellow Federalists. He showed no disposition to accept party discipline, separated himself entirely from the party in 1807 when he voted for Jefferson's embargo bill, and in 1808 resigned his seat in the Senate. By then he was moving toward the Republican party, and in 1809 President Madison appointed the ex-Federalist as minister to Russia. He remained at his post in Saint Petersburg during the War of 1812. In 1814, when the governments in Washington and London decided to seek peace, Adams was sent to Ghent in Belgium as chief negotiator for the United States. The outcome of the conversations was the Treaty of Ghent, signed in December 1814. The following year Madison made Adams minister to Great Britain, a post he held until he returned home to become secretary of state in the cabinet of President Monroe. He established a splendid record as head of the State Department from 1817 to 1825.

Unfortunately Adams's personality and political skills did not match his intelligence and experience. He did not enjoy the combat of politics, and had no objection to keeping enemies in his administration if he thought them capable. He was also stubborn. Determined to gear his administration to the nationalism of 1815, he refused to acknowledge that the popular tide by the mid-1820s was running toward state rights and sectionalism.

Despite his intelligence and experience, John Quincy Adams was an unpopular president whose programs failed to win widespread support. What new currents in American thinking led to the rejection of his programs?

The outcome for Adams was four miserable years in the White House. His plans for a national system of roads and canals got nowhere; those for a national university and astronomical observatory provoked laughter and derision. The president alienated the West when he rejected western proposals for a more liberal federal land policy (he thought they would play into the hands of speculators). Frontiersmen denounced him for being "soft on Indians" when he refused to enforce a treaty to remove the Creeks and Cherokees from Georgia. In foreign affairs, where his experience promised the most success, his idea of closer relations with Latin America produced nothing, and his efforts to improve conditions of trade with the British West Indies backfired.

The Tariff Problem

Perhaps the most vexing problem of the Adams presidency was the tariff. To protect infant textile industries from foreign competition, northeasterners wanted to increase duties on imported woolens. But southerners, their prosperity resting on overseas sales of cotton and tobacco, recoiled at any proposal that might jar the delicate mechanism of foreign commerce. The problem reached a climax when supporters of Andrew Jackson, looking to the election of 1828, saw a chance to score a political triumph. They would draft a clever tariff bill to protect domestic woolen manufacturers, but one with other features that Adams would find unacceptable. When the president opposed the bill, he would bring down the wrath of the Northeast. In the South, meanwhile, Jacksonians would pass the word that by a slick maneuver they had prevented new tariff legislation.

Things did not work out as Jacksonians had planned. Despite dissatisfaction with some provisions, Adams grudgingly approved the tariff of 1828. The South was furious and labeled the new measure the "tariff of abominations." Still, the affair did not work out badly for the Jacksonians. While southerners did not feel especially grateful to followers of Jackson, they were incensed at Adams. And in the Northeast people were displeased that the president had failed to get a more satisfactory tariff law.

The Presidential Election of 1828

Still simmering from the tariff debate, the country prepared for a presidential election in 1828. By now the Republicans had divided into two parties, the National Republican led by President Adams and the Democratic Republican headed by Andrew Jackson. Both parties included men of all classes and sections, but National Republican strength centered in the Northeast and among upper economic classes. National Republicans were the heirs of the old Federalist party, forebears of the present-day Republican party. Democratic Republicans carried the traditions of Thomas Jefferson and were ancestors of the present-day Democratic party. Their base was in the South and West and among farmers, wage laborers, and small businessmen.

The presidential campaign hinged on personalities rather than on issues and was the dirtiest up to that time. The most saddening episode was the charge of adultery leveled against Jackson and his shy, sensitive wife, Rachel. It was true that Jackson and Rachel had unwittingly married before Rachel's divorce from her first husband was complete. However, supporters of Adams in 1828 ignored the complexities of the situation and charged that the hero of New Orleans had lived with another man's wife. For their part, Jacksonians accused Adams of similar immoral behavior.

Whatever the evils of the campaign, Jackson won a sweeping victory, carrying the electoral college 178-83. A short time later, Rachel Jackson died, allegedly brokenhearted by the slurs on her honor during the campaign.

STUDY GUIDE: John Quincy Adams's administration was troubled by tariff problems. Easterners wanted increased duties on imported woolens. Southerners feared anything that might affect their overseas sale of cotton and tobacco. The outcome was the Tariff of 1828. Southerners called it the "tariff of abominations."

Republicans divided into two parties in the election of 1828: National Republicans (led by Adams) and Democratic Republicans (led by Andrew Jackson).

ANDREW JACKSON

Andrew Jackson was born the same year as John Quincy Adams, 1767; otherwise, these men who were, respectively, the seventh and sixth presidents, had little in common. Jackson's parents were poor immigrants from Northern Ireland (and their son would be the only first-generation American to achieve the presidency). They settled at the village of Waxhaw along the South Carolina frontier, and it was there, in a log cabin, that Andrew Jackson was born. His father died shortly before his birth, and during Jackson's infancy and early boyhood his family was nearly destitute. Still, he was a precocious youth. Many years later he recalled that at the age of nine he had read a copy of the recently proclaimed Declaration of Independence to a group of illiterate but enthusiastic frontiersmen.

During the war against the mother country, South Carolina became a center of hostilities between British and Loyalists on the one hand and patriots on the other. At thirteen Jackson became a messenger for an American unit, was captured, and on refusing to clean the boots of a British officer received a crashing saber blow on the head, which left a permanent scar. The British released him and his brother, also a captive, when they contracted smallpox. The brother died, and a short time later Jackson lost his mother, a victim of an illness contracted while nursing war prisoners in Charleston. Blaming his misfortunes on the mother country, Jackson hated the British from that time to his death.

As the war drew to a close, Jackson's prospects seemed to take a turn for the better. He inherited more than a thousand dollars from an uncle in Northern Ireland. However, the boy soon squandered the money on fancy clothes, gambling, and revelry. Next he found his way to Salisbury, North Carolina, where he studied law and in 1787 gained admission to the bar. Study did not tame his wild spirit. He delighted in brawling and other amusements of the Carolina frontier. An early biographer described him as "the most roaring, rollicking, game-cocking, horse-racing, card-playing, mischievous fellow, that ever lived in Salisbury . . . the head of the rowdies hereabouts."

Like many other Carolinians, Jackson looked westward and in 1788 joined a wagon train for Nashville, a small village on the Cumberland River in the western district of North Carolina, later the state of Tennessee. At Nashville he opened a law office which soon was yielding a handsome income. He also became acquainted with Rachel Donelson Robards, an attractive, young woman who was estranged from her husband, a Kentuckian named Lewis Robards. Believing that Robards had divorced his wife, Jackson and Rachel were married in 1791, only to learn in 1794 that Robards had not obtained the divorce until 1793. Jackson and Rachel then went through a second ceremony, but the couple never overcame the stigma of having lived together while Rachel was the legal wife of Robards. The union produced no children, although the Jacksons adopted Rachel's nephew and raised the children of several other relatives.

In 1796 Jackson served in the convention that drafted a state constitution for Tennessee, and on the state's admission to the Union he went to Washington as Tennessee's first member of the House of Representatives. A few months later the legislature at Nashville elected him to the Senate, but he resigned in 1797 to become a judge of the Tennesse supreme court. The dignity of the court, one should note, did not restrict Jackson's style; he continued his freewheeling ways and was involved in several duels.

"Old Hickory"

By the turn of the century Jackson was one of the wealthiest men in the West. In 1804 he and Rachel moved into a splendid mansion in Tennessee, the Hermitage near Nashville. His career then went into decline, in part because of his friendship with the former vice-president, Aaron Burr, an implacable enemy of President Jefferson. This association brought him into conflict with the administration in Washington.

But Jackson's fortunes turned in 1813–14 when he pulled himself out of bed (in a recent gunfight he had taken several bullets) and with his left arm in a sling, led Tennessee militiamen against the Creek Indians (allies of the British in the War of 1812). The Battle of Horseshoe Bend in Alabama shattered Creek power. It was in this campaign that Jackson, a tough disciplinarian who shared the privations of his men, earned the nickname "Old Hickory."

The victory over the Creeks brought Jackson a commission as major general in the United States Army. Less than a year later he became the hero of the generation when he directed the defeat of the British invading force at New Orleans. He next won acclaim in 1817–18 when he led a successful campaign against the Seminole Indians in Florida and also created an international incident by hanging two British subjects on Spanish territory.

While the British and Spaniards fumed over Jackson's methods, the people of the United States loved them. Many Americans began to think that General Jackson might make an excellent president. Meanwhile, he served as military governor of Florida, after its acquisition by the United States, and in 1823 returned to Washington as senator from Tennessee. While he lost his bid for the presidency in 1824, he won easily in 1828.

A contemporary writer described Jackson as being "tall, slim and straight. . . . His head was long, but narrow, and covered with thick grey hair that stood erect, as though impregnated with his defiant spirit; his brow was deeply furrowed. . . . His mouth displayed firmness. His whole being conveyed an impression of energy and daring." Still, by the time he entered the White House in 1829, Jackson had mellowed. Some historians have seen him as a man not much more radical in political outlook than John Quincy Adams. No longer a young man (he was past sixty), he was not the roughhewn brawler that the so-called common people of the country thought him to be. The death of his wife, moreover, had drained much of his zest for life. He continued to chew tobacco and sometimes lost his temper (usually to intimidate political opponents or to get his way), but he was a frontier man who had taken on the manners and attitudes of the aristocrats of the South.

Jacksonian Democracy

Although Jackson had lost some of his "commonness," he continued to be the idol of farmers and laborers across the country, particularly in the South and West. He became the symbol of a loose body of ideas known to history as "Jacksonian Democracy."

Jacksonian Democrats wanted, first, to alter the existing political balance, then slanted they thought, in favor of a wealthy elite. To that end they set out to make government more responsive to the "people." They determined to eliminate property qualifications that most states required for voters. They sought to enlarge the number of elective offices, making appointive positions as few as practicable. Officials were to be responsible to the electorate rather than to the executive or agency that appointed them.

Jacksonians were determined to deprive state legislatures of the power, exercised in several states, of choosing presidential electors. To the extent permitted by the Constitution, the president should be responsible to the people. Jacksonians objected to the way of nominating candidates for president and vice-president. Up until this time, caucuses of party representatives in Congress had chosen presidential tickets, but Jacksonians suspected that members of Congress allowed congressional politics to influence choices. It would be better, they thought, to put the nomination of candidates in the hands of a national convention composed of delegates drawn from the "people."

Jacksonians also set about to strengthen the executive branch of government at both state and national levels. Unlike Americans of the Revolutionary generation who had seen a strong executive as a threat to liberty, Jacksonians considered the executive as the representative of all the people; state legislators and congressmen were responsible to their districts.

The "Spoils System"

Finally, there was the "spoils system." Jacksonians thought the professional civil servant was likely to fall into the institutional trap of putting the welfare of his bureau ahead of that of the people. Hence, a frequent turnover of public servants was good for the country. A new ad-ministration, moreover, should not be weighed down by bureaucrats appointed by previous regimes whose programs may have been rejected by the people. It ought to have the privilege of starting afresh with officials of its own choosing—officials loyal to the administration, which in turn was responsible to the people. Jacksonians were, of course, clever politicians who recognized that political parties, particularly now that the electorate was growing, required effective organization. The only way to maintain an organization or "machine" was to provide jobs for the organization faithful.

What faction would hold the power when government became responsive to the people? The Jacksonians—naturally.

On gaining power, Jacksonian Democrats wanted to scale down the strength of what they thought was a selfish business elite. They wanted abolition of imprisonment for debt, a clever device of big capital, they believed, for keeping farmers and laborers in line. They wanted a national bankruptcy law that would make it easier for financially distressed persons to emancipate themselves from difficulties and start anew. They sought downward revision of the tariff, for they saw the protective tariff—which enabled domestic producers to impose higher prices—as a tax, ultimately paid by consumers, for the benefit of manufacturers. They determined to revise public land policies to enable a farmer to buy smaller lots and take longer for payment. In the Jacksonian view, the federal government's conservative land policy was a device of eastern industrialists to hold on to a cheap labor supply by discouraging workers from migrating westward.

The Bank of the United States

Most of all, Jacksonians wanted to destroy the Bank of the United States, a citadel of conservatism which exercised wide control over fiscal affairs.

In those years small banks operating on state charters—often nothing more than wildcat (financially irresponsible) enterprises—issued their own bank notes to circulate as currency. By enlarging the money supply, these notes increased economic activity, particularly in the West where metallic currency was scarce. By adding to the circulating currency, the notes also depressed the value of the dollar, an advantage to debtors—and it seemed that most Jacksonians were debtors. The Bank of the United States was able to keep the wildcatters in check, however, by threatening to collect quantities of their notes and to present them for redemption in specie. If the Bank carried out its threat the wildcatter would go bankrupt. This would eliminate another source of currency and credit and hence would be a blow to farmers and other small capitalists.

The Bank of the United States also had much to say about the issuance of credit by small banks, for most of the latter depended on loans from the Bank. If the small banks overextended credit or granted it recklessly, the Bank would cut them off. Small capitalists, particularly farmers, needed easy credit to expand and felt hemmed in by the tight credit policies of the Bank. Tight money policies of the Bank likewise found opposition among the working classes, who also needed easier credit.

Throughout the 1820s the ideas of Jacksonian Democrats won support, and in some states, particularly in the West, Jacksonians won control of government. Then came the great moment, in March 1829, when Andrew Jackson entered the White House. Jacksonian Democrats now would bring their ideas to fulfillment and terminate the hold of the business elite on the country.

STUDY GUIDE: Andrew Jackson was elected senator from Tennessee in 1823, and won the presidency in 1828. He symbolized Jacksonian Democracy which aimed to make the government more responsive to the people. Believing that a frequent turnover of public servants was good for the country, Jacksonians advocated the "spoils system." This system gave a new administration the chance to start out with officials of its own choosing. Jacksonians also wanted to destroy the powerful Bank of the United States. The tight money policies of the large Bank made it difficult for Jacksonians—most of whom were debtors—to get easy credit.

PRESIDENT JACKSON

Still mourning the death of his wife, Jackson wore a black suit when, on March 4, 1829, he left Gadsby's Hotel and walked to the Capitol for the swearing-in ceremony. On the portico he acknowledged the cheers of enthusiastic followers who had descended on Washington to see their hero installed in the presidency. After the oath and an uninspiring inaugural address, he mounted a horse and splashed through the mud of Pennsylvania Avenue to the White House.

In the East Room the White House staff had prepared a reception for the political and social elite of the capital. Attendants had unfortunately failed to take into account the exuberance of the new president's partisans. Instead of dispersing after the inauguration the Jacksonians swept down Pennsylvania Avenue, pushed past the White House guards, and invaded the mansion. Frontiersmen with muddy boots clambered up on satin-covered chairs to catch a glimpse of the president. Others shoved into the East Room, tearing clothing and shattering china. Jackson slipped out a back door and trudged back to his quarters at Gadsby's Hotel. Attendants meanwhile placed tubs of punch on the White House lawn to lure the throng outside. The spectacle left Washington society aghast, and Justice Joseph Story of the Supreme Court observed that "the reign of 'King Mob' seemed triumphant."

John C. Calhoun

It appeared that a key individual in the Jackson administration would be forty-seven-year-old John C. Calhoun. An aristocrat from South Carolina, Calhoun was handsome, refined, and intelligent. He had been vice-president in 1825–29, but, finding no rapport with President Adams, cast his lot with the Democratic Republicans and won reelection in 1828 as Jackson's running mate. He expected to become president when Jackson's term expired. Then a rival appeared, Secretary of State Martin Van Buren. Of Dutch origin, from a village in New York, Van Buren was not an impressive figure. He was small and quiet, with reddish sideburns. But he was ambitious and clever, as suggested by his nicknames, "the Little Magician" and "the Red Fox." He had served in the Senate and, in 1828, campaigned for Jackson and won election as governor of New York. He resigned the governorship when Jackson asked him to take over the State Department. Before long—to Calhoun's dismay—Van Buren's star began to rise.

Compounding Calhoun's problem was the affair of Peggy O'Neale Eaton. Bright and pretty, Peggy at a young age had married a naval officer and, during her husband's absences, often moved about the capital in the company of Senator John H. Eaton of Tennessee. On the death of her husband, she and Eaton married, which gave rise to considerable gossip. When Jackson appointed Eaton as secretary of war, wives of cabinet members—and Mrs. Calhoun—refused to receive Mrs. Eaton. Remembering the slanders on his beloved Rachel, Jackson was incensed. It made no difference. The cabinet wives held their ground. Since Mrs. Calhoun seemed to be the leader of the boycott of Peggy Eaton, a rift appeared between the president and vice-president. One cabinet member, Secretary Van Buren, however, had no wife. He was a widower. "Little Van" cultivated the Eatons, extending numerous courtesies. Pleased, the president in 1831 appointed Van Buren minister to Britain. The appointment was not popular, and the vote for confirmation in the Senate was a tie, giving the vice-president the privilege of casting a vote. His break with Jackson nearly complete, Calhoun voted against Van Buren's appointment.

Differences between Jackson and Calhoun, however, were not entirely personal; they also disagreed over the nature of the federal Union.

Before his elevation to the presidency, Jackson had given scant thought to the problem that had nagged the republic since its birth: state rights versus federal authority. This was not true of the vice-president. Calhoun had wrestled with the question and, as his chances of succeeding Jackson in the White House dimmed, he brought his views into the open, forcing the president to take a stand. In essence, Calhoun had taken over the theme of the Kentucky and Virginia Resolutions of 1798—that each state could decide for itself whether an act of Congress was constitutional. If it found an act unconstitutional, a state might proclaim the legislation null and void within its borders. But Calhoun went a critical step further: a dissatisfied state also might secede from the federal Union.

Calhoun's ideas reached the stage of public discussion in January 1830 after Senator Samuel A. Foot of Connecticut proposed a suspension of federal land sales. Considering Foot's resolution a crude attempt by New England to prevent factory workers from migrating, westerners were furious. At that point, southern senators saw a chance to win western support against tariff protection and jumped into the debate on the side of the West. A West-South alliance against the Northeast appeared in the making. Thereupon Daniel Webster of Massachusetts cleverly turned the discussion to Calhoun's secessionist ideas.

The Webster-Hayne Debate

Webster then challenged Senator Robert Y. Hayne of South Carolina, a follower of Calhoun, to debate the question of state rights versus federal authority. Webster knew of course that westerners had a strong sense of nationalism and hoped to forestall a West-South alliance by showing that southerners were entertaining ideas about fracturing the Union.

Hayne accepted the challenge and skillfully set forth the argument for nullification and secession. But it was "godlike Dan'l" Webster who prevailed. Tall and muscular, with a rugged face and heavy brows, the Massachusetts senator had an awesome appearance. He also had a deep and melodious voice, an unmatched command of language, and a mastery of imagery. His final response to Hayne took two afternoons. For hour after hour he unleashed his oratorical talents, held his audience spellbound, made them laugh, provoked them to anger, roused their patriotism. He concluded: "Liberty *and* Union, now and forever, one and inseparable!"

Still, the important question was the view of the president. Given his popularity, it seemed that Jackson could carry the country either way —for the ideas of Calhoun or for those of Webster. He gave his answer at a Jefferson Day dinner in April 1830. Offering an after-dinner toast, the president raised his glass, looked squarely at Calhoun, and said: "Our Federal Union; it must be preserved." Calhoun seemed to tremble, then responded: "The Union—next to our liberty, most dear."

Jackson nonetheless had not become an advocate of increased federal power. Proof came a few weeks later when he vetoed a bill that would have provided a federal subsidy for construction of a road in Kentucky from Maysville to Lexington. He also revealed state rights sentiments when Georgia defied rulings of the Supreme Court in controversies with the Cherokee Indians. Following a decision in *Worcester* v. *Georgia* (1832), the president allegedly said: "John Marshall has made his decision; now let him enforce it." He gave the Cherokees no support, and a few years later the Indians felt compelled to sign a treaty exchanging land in Georgia for a section of prairie in the present-day state of Oklahoma.

Treaties with the Indians

Jackson's stance on the Cherokee question, one should add, went beyond state rights. No friend of the Indian, Jackson determined to remove Indians to the Great Plains, thought by whites to be a wasteland. To that end he negotiated about a hundred treaties with assorted tribes. The outcome was an exodus of Indians, sometimes at bayonet point, from ancestral lands in the eastern part of the country to territory beyond the Mississippi. The policy provoked scattered violence, as in western Illinois in 1832 when hungry followers of Chief Black Hawk recrossed the Mississippi to grow corn. The Illinois militia went after the Indians (Black Hawk's War), chased them into Wisconsin, and killed many as they tried to escape down the Wisconsin River. In Florida, beginning in 1835, Chief Osceola led an uprising of Seminole tribesmen and runaway Negro slaves who refused to move west in accordance with a treaty.

While Jackson supported state rights on most questions (and in the Cherokee affair permitted Georgia to nullify an edict of the Supreme Court), he was unwilling to concede anything to the nullification-secessionist theories of John C. Calhoun.

Calhoun's ideas were put to a test in 1832 when Congress passed new tariff legislation which brought little reduction in rates from the "tariff of abominations" of 1828. Prodded by the vice-president, the South Carolina legislature called a state convention in autumn 1832 to consider nullification. The convention voted overwhelmingly to nullify the tariff laws of 1828 and 1832 and forbade the collection of duties in the state. A short time later Calhoun resigned the vice-presidency, and the legislature elected him to the Senate, where hopefully he would present a persuasive case for nullification.

Still, success of nullification depended on the support of other states and a weak response by the president. Neither was forthcoming. Partly out of respect for Jackson and appreciation of his Indian policy, other southern states refused to join South Carolina. As for President Jackson, he announced that nullification was treason. To show he was not bluffing, he then strengthened federal forts in South Carolina and ordered several armed vessels to sail to Charleston. When Congress convened in Washington, Jackson's followers introduced a "force bill" authorizing use of the army and navy to enforce acts of Congress.

Sequoya was a Cherokee Indian who invented an alphabet for his people. After its completion in 1821, Sequoya turned to projects for the advancement of Indians. In 1828 he went to Washington as the representative of western tribes. What did he accomplish in Washington?

South Carolina had lost, but Jackson had no wish to humiliate the nullifiers. When Henry Clay proposed new tariff legislation designed to pacify the South, he made no objection. Clay's measure provided for an annual reduction of tariff duties until 1842, when they would reach the level of 1816. In February 1833 Congress passed the Clay bill but, as a gesture of toughness toward South Carolina, also passed the Force Bill. Satisfied with the tariff compromise, the South Carolina convention repealed the nullification ordinances applying to the tariff. Then, in an act of defiance—and to retain the principle of nullification—the convention also nullified the Force Act. Repeal of the original nullification ordinances made the Force Act meaningless, so Jackson ignored the new act of nullification.

STUDY GUIDE: There was disagreement between Jackson and his vice-president, John C. Calhoun. Calhoun believed that each state should decide whether an act of Congress was constitutional. He insisted that a dissatisfied state had the right to secede from the Union. Daniel Webster challenged Robert Hayne, a Calhoun supporter, to debate state rights versus federal authority.

Jackson was determined to remove Indians west of the Mississippi. Black Hawk's War in 1832 was caused by Indian resistance to Illinois militia.

Congress passed new tariff legislation in 1832, but there was little reduction in rates from the 1828 tariff. South Carolina called a state convention to consider nullification. The vote was overwhelmingly in favor of nullifying the tariff laws of 1828 and 1832. Calhoun resigned his vice-presidency. Other southern states refused to join South Carolina. Henry Clay introduced new legislation providing for an annual reduction of tariff duties until 1842. Satisfied with the compromise, South Carolina repealed the nullification ordinances applying to the tariff.

JACKSON'S SECOND TERM

Nullification was the central issue of Jackson's first term in the White House; the Bank of the United States held the spotlight during the second.

Jacksonian Democrats despised the hard-currency—tight-credit policies of the Bank, the "monster bank" which had triggered the Panic of 1819. They were dedicated to its destruction. Andrew Jackson was no wildcatter and did not share the soft-money—easy-credit ideas of his followers. However, he disliked all banks (the result apparently of a speculating venture in the 1790s that went sour because of a bank panic) and hence looked coldly on the Bank of the United States.

The Bank War

Still, it was not Jackson who fired the first salvo in the "bank war" of the 1830s. It was Henry Clay. Expecting to be the presidential candidate of the National Republican party in 1832, Clay needed an issue. He saw one in the Bank of the United States. Thinking most people of the country favored the Bank, he determined to push through Congress a bill to grant the Bank a new charter (the existing charter would expire in 1836). If Jackson vetoed the bill—and Clay was sure he would—the voters would reject him,

Library of Congress

Jackson's critics agreed with this cartoon portraying the president as a tyrannical king. What policies of the Jackson administration formed the basis of this criticism?

and the National Republican ticket would sweep the election.

Falling in with Clay's tactics, the president of the Bank of the United States, Nicholas Biddle, applied for a new charter. In summer 1832 Congress passed a recharter bill, and, as expected, Jackson used the veto. Clay's plan was functioning smoothly, and at the National Republican convention in Baltimore, the Kentuckian received the party's nomination for president. The Democrats renominated Jackson and for vice-president selected Martin Van Buren. Then Clay learned that he had miscalculated. The Bank was not generally popular and, when returns were in, Jackson had piled up an overwhelming victory.

Now it was Jackson's turn to take the initiative. While he could not destroy the Bank before expiration of its charter in 1836, he had power to weaken it. His main tactic was to reduce federal deposits in the Bank. He put no new federal funds in the Bank and paid all federal bills with money still on deposit there. At the same time he directed the secretary of the treasury to open accounts in state banks across the country. By 1836, federal money was distributed in eighty-nine such banks, labeled "pet banks" by Jackson's critics. In retaliation, Biddle called in loans and made credit scarce. The result was an economic recession in 1833-34, "Biddle's panic." Biddle's scheme achieved nothing; Jackson refused to budge from his opposition to a new charter for the Bank of the United States.

Jackson Right or Wrong?

How does one judge Jackson's determination to rid the country of the Bank?

Jackson surely was correct in his view that the Bank had become too powerful and that it gave a handful of private individuals control over the economic well-being of millions of people. The Biddle panic proved the point. On the other hand, as the early history of the Bank had demonstrated, a strong central bank could perform an important function, compelling fiscal responsibility and thus serving as a stabilizing influence in the national economy. This leads to the obvious conclusion that Jackson should have agreed to rechartering the bank while insisting upon effective public regulation of its affairs.

Subsequent events proved the desirability of the middle way, for, following Jackson's "war" on the Bank, the country experienced a rampaging prosperity resting on easy credit and speculation. Within less than two years, in 1835-36, state banks, no longer restrained by the Bank of the United States, increased bank notes in circulation from $82 million to $120 million. With borrowed money, canals were dug and flimsy railroad tracks were put down hither and yon, with little thought about whether there would be sufficient traffic to make the lines profitable. Large sums were also going into land. Western farmers mortgaged their land to borrow money to buy more land, then used the newly acquired land as collateral for new loans. Sale of public land in 1836 was nine times greater than in 1832, and it was at this time that the phrase "doing a land-office business" came into vogue.

Even the federal government prospered. Revenue from the tariff and land sales was so large that the government paid all its debts and began to accumulate a surplus. Henry Clay thereupon proposed distribution to the states of the proceeds from land sales. Clay's idea was generally welcomed. Then somebody asked, "Why not give away the entire federal surplus?" President Jackson liked this proposal and signed a bill in 1836 to distribute to the states in quarterly installments the surplus accumulated by the end of the year (an estimated $40 million). When distribution began, most states promptly accelerated the economic boom by investing their money in canals, highways, and railroads.

Meanwhile, the president, a "hard money" man since his youth, became concerned about the state bank notes that were flooding into federal accounts as payment for public land. He suspected that many of these were not worth their face value, and thus the government was not receiving fair return for its land. As a result, in summer 1836 he issued a circular announcing that in future land transactions the government would accept only metallic money (specie). The Specie Circular was of course an expression of no confidence in the notes of wildcat banks.

The booming country meanwhile prepared for the election of 1836. By now a tired old man, Jackson did not seek a third term but prevailed on the Democratic convention to nominate his friend and loyal subordinate, Martin Van Buren. The Whig party (successor to the National Republican) was united only in opposition to Jackson and could not agree on a presidential candidate. Whigs finally settled on the curious strategy of nominating three candidates, one from each section: Daniel Webster from the Northeast, Hugh Lawson White from the South, and William Henry Harrison from the West. These men hoped to win enough votes between them to deprive Van Buren of a majority in the electoral college, thus throwing the election into the House of Representatives. In the House perhaps Whig congressmen would be able to muster a majority for a member of the party. The strategy failed; Van Buren won a majority of electoral votes.

STUDY GUIDE: Jacksonian Democrats were dedicated to the destruction of the Bank of the United States. Henry Clay needed an issue for the presidential campaign of 1832. Thinking that most people favored the Bank, he sought to push through Congress a bill granting the Bank a new charter. If Jackson vetoed the bill, Clay would sweep the election. Clay miscalculated. The Bank was not popular with the people, and Jackson piled up an overwhelming victory. To weaken the Bank before its charter expired in 1836, Jackson reduced federal deposits and put no new federal funds into the Bank. He directed the secretary of the treasury to open accounts in state banks across the nation. In retaliation, the Bank called in loans and made credit scarce. The result was an economic depression.

THE VAN BUREN PRESIDENCY

On March 3, 1837, Andrew Jackson recognized the independence of Texas and the following day turned over the government to Van Buren.

Born at Kinderhook, New York, in 1782, "Little Van" was the first president born after the Revolutionary War. Of Dutch ancestry, he was also the first president who did not trace his origins to the British Isles. (As a youth he spoke the Dutch language better than he did English.) Van Buren left school at fourteen to enter a law office. By the time he reached forty his fortune was such that he did not have to worry about finances for the rest of his life.

Like many successful lawyers, Van Buren became a politician. In 1812 he entered the New York state senate as a member of the Democratic-Republican party (Jackson's party). Soon he was party leader. His success resulted from his

Courtesy Chicago Historical Society

Martin Van Buren entered the White House in 1837 just in time to witness the economic collapse of the country. What policies did he propose to overcome the depression?

Use the graph below to follow American business activity during Van Buren's presidency.

AMERICAN BUSINESS ACTIVITY: 1820 — 1849

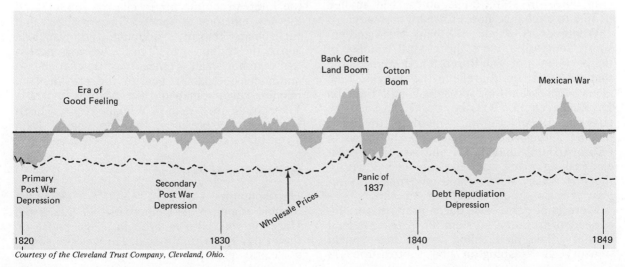

Courtesy of the Cleveland Trust Company, Cleveland, Ohio.

[103]

skillful application of the spoils system. By the 1820s he had set his sights on Washington, and in 1821 he manipulated the New York legislature to secure his election to the United States Senate.

In 1828, while campaigning for governor of New York, he supported the presidential candidacy of Andrew Jackson and helped "Old Hickory" win a majority of New York's large block of electoral votes. Van Buren won the governor's race, but after two months in the governor's mansion in Albany he resigned to accept appointment as secretary of state in the new Jackson administration. He became a favorite of the president and in 1832 was Jackson's choice for the vice-presidency.

The Panic of 1837

When Van Buren entered the White House, the economic system was humming along. Three months later it was a wreck. Reaching the end of their reserves in specie, banks closed their doors, and in the next few years virtually every bank in the country failed. Most canal and railroad companies went into bankruptcy, land sales dwindled, and state governments repudiated bonds. Whigs, of course, blamed the Democratic hero, Andrew Jackson, for the disaster—the Panic of 1837. By destroying the Bank of the United States, Jackson had deprived the country of its best check on the wildcatters. Distribution of the treasury surplus (a Whig idea, although Jackson signed the bill) had accelerated inflation and—by withdrawing funds—weakened the "pet banks." The Specie Circular, a public declaration of no confidence in state bank notes, had invited people to exchange notes for hard currency.

Whatever its origins, the bank panic and ensuing depression were the central features of the presidency of Van Buren. There seemed little that he could do to relieve the distress. Like every depression-time president until Franklin D. Roosevelt in 1933, he worked to keep the government solvent and waited for the crisis to pass. Otherwise he tried without success to reform federal land policy and issued an order establishing a ten-hour day on federal works, the first act by the national government to improve the condition of labor in America.

More important, Van Buren proposed an "independent treasury" system for handling federal finances. The plan called for an independent treasury in Washington and subtreasuries in several cities across the country. All federal funds would be on deposit in these treasuries and could not therefore become instruments of profit and power for private individuals (as in the heyday of the Bank of the United States) or a device for spurring inflation (as in the time of the "pet banks"). Proposed in Van Buren's inaugural address in 1837, an independent treasury bill did not pass Congress until 1840. When the Whigs took over the government the following year, they abolished the independent treasury, but the Democrats reestablished it in 1846. It survived until the Civil War.

STUDY GUIDE: Three months after Martin Van Buren took office in 1837, the nation's economy was a wreck. By destroying the Bank of the United States, Jackson had deprived the nation of a check on wildcatters. Inflation increased. The Specie Circular was a public declaration of no confidence in state bank notes. Van Buren could do little to relieve the distress. But he did propose an independent treasury system for handling federal finances.

THE ELECTION OF 1840

The country was still mired in depression as the election of 1840 approached. All the Democrats could do in such circumstances was renominate Van Buren, praise the independent treasury, and remind voters of the Whigs' past affinity for the dreadful Bank of the United States. The Whigs, however—even though they often supported the interests of the upper classes—understood the new electoral arithmetic. They realized that Jacksonian reforms widening the franchise across the country made it necessary to appeal to the common man. Hence they determined to nominate a "glamor figure" for president—a popular hero, somebody like Andrew Jackson. They found their man in William Henry Harrison. For vice-president they nominated John Tyler of Virginia.

William Henry Harrison

Harrison, the Whig hero, could not claim the humble origins of the Democratic hero, Jackson. Harrison was born in 1773 in a fine house on the James River in Virginia. He was the son of a wealthy planter who three years later would sign the Declaration of Independence. As a youth, Harrison studied classics and history; then he decided to take up medicine and went to Philadelphia to study. But, like many other young Americans of the time, he caught the spirit of adventure, put aside his medical books, and in 1791 received a commission in the army. Soon he was on his way to the Ohio country where he became an aide to General Anthony Wayne and was on hand when "Mad Anthony" defeated the Indians at Fallen Timbers in 1794. Harrison left the army in 1798 and settled on a farm at North Bend, Ohio, a few miles downstream from Cincinnati. In 1800, upon the organization of the Indiana Territory, President Adams appointed him territorial governor.

Before long, the Shawnee Indians in the Indiana Territory became restive. Inspired by a zealot called the Prophet and led by his talented warrior-brother, Tecumseh, the Shawnees argued that past treaties ceding land to white men were invalid and talked of a great confederacy of all Indian tribes. At length, in 1811, the Shawnees heard rumors that the United States would soon be at war with Britain. They decided that the time had come to reclaim their land.

To get the jump on the Indians, Harrison assembled a small force of militiamen at the territorial capital, Vincennes, and marched northward to the Shawnee encampment, Prophet's Town, on Tippecanoe Creek near present-day Lafayette, Indiana. The Indians learned of the impending attack and surprised the militiamen. Harrison rallied his dazed men and, despite 190 casualties, defeated the Indians after three hours of fierce combat. From then on, Harrison was known as "Old Tippecanoe," or just plain "Tip." Two years later Harrison, now a major general in the regular army, led American soldiers against a combined British-Indian force in the Battle of the Thames, north of Lake Erie in Canada. In this latter action the chieftain Tecumseh, who had eluded Harrison at Tippecanoe, was killed.

Harrison resigned his commission in 1814, returning to the Ohio farm. In 1816 he won election to Congress. After one undistinguished term he lost his bid for reelection, then served six years in the Ohio state senate. The Ohio legislature sent him to the United States Senate in 1825, and three years later the second President Adams named him minister to Colombia.

In 1840 settlement of the frontier was a major concern of many Americans.

THE UNITED STATES — 1840

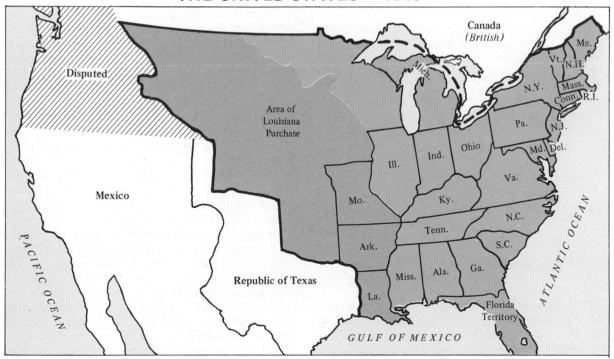

Fearing that the great South American liberator, Simón Bolívar, at that time head of the Colombian government, had imperial ambitions, Harrison sent a friendly but clumsy message to Bolívar urging him to heed the example of George Washington rather than Alexander the Great. Shortly after, because Harrison had been appointed by Adams, President Jackson replaced him. Harrison returned once again to Ohio, for a time served as clerk of Hamilton County, Ohio, and, as mentioned, ran for president in 1836 and in 1840.

Tippecanoe and Tyler Too

The campaign of 1840 turned into the gaudiest political jamboree Americans had ever experienced. To the present day, the Whig slogan "Tippecanoe and Tyler too" connotes political bosses, candidates, and voters, all marching in splendid disarray behind tubas and banners, illumined by hundreds of flickering torches. Nobody tried to appeal to the intellect of voters. Whig orators attacked Van Buren as an aristocrat who used cologne, drank champagne, and ate with gold spoons, whereupon a Democratic reporter wrote of Harrison: "Give him a barrel of hard cider and settle a pension of two thousand a year on him, and my word for it, he will sit the remainder of his days in his log cabin by the side of a 'sea coal' fire, and study moral philosophy."

Whigs gleefully agreed that Harrison—who actually lived in a fine house—was a man of simple tastes who liked log cabins and hard cider. Thenceforth the log cabin became the Whig symbol and at party rallies hard cider was the standard refreshment. Whig tactics worked. When the shouting and hoopla ended, the returns showed 60 electoral votes for Van Buren, 234 for Tippecanoe—and Tyler, too.

STUDY GUIDE: In the political campaign of 1840, William Henry Harrison, Whig candidate, was elected president.

EARLY NINETEENTH-CENTURY AMERICA

The American scene in the first four decades of the nineteenth century—the age of Jefferson and Jackson—was notable for its frenzy of activity. In addition to the flash of gunfire in the War of 1812 and the campaign shenanigans of 1840, an endless stream of people—some walking, others bouncing along in covered wagons or drifting downstream on flatboats—were moving westward across the Appalachians, through the Ohio Valley, beyond the Mississippi, to the rim of the Great Plains.

Forests were steadily disappearing under the frontiersman's ax, to be replaced by brown patches which would soon turn to yellow or white with wheat and cotton. In the country's western regions people celebrated the admission of new states to the federal Union: Arkansas in 1836 and Michigan in 1837.

Industrialization and Immigration

Each year more and more people dotted the American landscape. Ships steering into seaports along the Atlantic seaboard were emptying their holds of thousands of men, women, and children, particularly from Ireland and Germany.

In the eastern half of the Republic, the haze rising from urban-industrial areas continued to increase. From smokestacks piercing skyward, more and more factories were belching forth greater volumes of noxious gases. Protruding from the haze of cities along the ocean were increasing numbers of wharves, and tied to them were scores of wooden sailing ships.

There was also a quickening of activity on rivers and streams in the American hinterland, as boats and barges moved up and down and across the waterways. In 1807, a little steamboat pushed up the Hudson from New York to Albany in thirty-two hours. The name of the vessel was the *Clermont,* the name of its inventor, Robert Fulton. By 1820, an American ship had used steam part of the way in crossing the Atlantic, and steamboats were common in river traffic.

In the upper part of New York, a great engineering project was linking the Hudson River and Lake Erie. In 1825, the great ditch completed, a huge celebration took place as Americans marked the completion of the Erie Canal. In subsequent years, similar ditches scarred the landscape in many parts of the country.

Toward the close of the 1820s some important construction took place just west of the city of Baltimore: two bands of iron, a little more than four feet apart, fastened to evenly spaced cross-members of wood. At first, carriages drawn by horses moved up and down the rails. Then one day there appeared at the head of the carriage a fearsome four-wheeled machine pouring forth black smoke and hissing steam. In the years that followed, similar roads of rail inched out from other towns and cities. By 1840, the future of transportation in the United States had passed from the canal boat to the steam train.

The westward movement, expansion of industry and transportation, and growth of population were destined to have political repercussions. Especially after 1815, the West began to achieve a place alongside the Northeast and the South in the councils of the nation. The appearance of this third factor in the sectional equation opened new opportunities for political maneuver. There was increased rivalry among spokesmen for industry and those who advocated the interests of the farmer. The expanding population of farmers and industrial workers—the "common people"—were insisting that they should have a greater voice in charting the course of the national destiny.

Achievements in Science and the Arts

It is not easy to grasp the full picture of life in America in the age of Jefferson and Jackson. Scientific and technological inquiry claimed the attention of a growing number of people. Americans did important work in botany, zoology, chemistry, paleontology, and geology. Perhaps the outstanding American scientist of the era was Benjamin Silliman, the first professor of chemistry and natural history at Yale who pushed back frontiers in both chemistry and geology. Of inventions in America, several stand out: Robert Fulton's steamboat (1807); the mechanical reaper by Cyrus Hall McCormick (1831); the repeating revolver by Samuel Colt (1835); the steel plow by John Deere

The success of steamboats during the first half of the 1800s led to a great transportation system on the rivers of America. The print below shows a race between two steamboats on the Mississippi. The print was published in 1859.

(1837); and vulcanization of rubber by Charles Goodyear (1839).

In the field of the arts, American painters were usually doing portraits, landscapes, or pictures having historical or religious themes. Architects were designing buildings inspired by the classical models of ancient Greece or Rome. The most prolific writers were Washington Irving and James Fenimore Cooper, but the outstanding literary figure of the first half of the nineteenth century was Ralph Waldo Emerson. At this time Emerson conceived his philosophy of "transcendentalism," an optimistic view of the universe holding that the self-reliant individual, using spiritual resources, could achieve perfection.

Religious Activity and Social Reform

The early nineteenth century was a period of great religious activity. Despite the skepticism of a few national leaders, including Thomas

One of the most important social reformers of the 1800s was Dorothea Dix. In 1841 she visited a jail in Cambridge, Massachusetts, and found that it contained not only criminals, but also those who were insane. Soon she began a crusade for special treatment of the mentally ill. Because of her work, many state hospitals for the insane were founded.

Jefferson, most Americans in 1801-40 maintained some connection with organized religion. Among Protestants, this was a time of "fire-and-brimstone" preaching and revivalism, particularly in the West and South where itinerant preachers moved from one camp meeting to another, assailing the devil and urging sinners to repent. It was also a period marked by the appearance of many new sects and branches of established churches.

Among the new religious groups was the Unitarian Church (1819), stressing the unity of God, and the Church of Jesus Christ of Latter-Day Saints, or Mormon Church (1830). Meeting opposition, the Mormons migrated from New York to Ohio to Missouri, under the leadership of their founder, Joseph Smith. By 1840 they were settled at Nauvoo, Illinois. There, more violence awaited them, and they migrated to Utah a few years later under the leadership of Brigham Young. The influx of immigrants from Ireland and Germany brought growth to the Roman Catholic church in America. This also produced a long period of anti-Catholic agitation, beginning in the late 1820s and produced such acts of violence as the burning of an Ursuline convent in Massachusetts in 1834.

Perhaps the most admirable phenomenon of the Jefferson-Jackson period—and it would continue through the next twenty years, until the Civil War—was the movement for social reform. Abuses and shortcomings in American society gradually aroused the consciences of many Americans. Beginning about the late 1820s, a few determined to do something. Taking note of the widespread illiteracy and ignorance, educational reformers were dismayed to learn that no state in the Union in 1830 had a system of free public education. Tackling the problem with characteristic energy, they made considerable headway in education. Much of it derived from the work of Horace Mann in Massachusetts. As the first secretary of the Massachusetts Board of Education (1837-1848), Mann reorganized that state's school system, lengthened the school year, and improved teachers' salaries. He also upgraded teacher training. Still other reformers cencentrated on penal codes and prison conditions. The outcome was an assault on such evils as imprisonment for debt and public hangings. A particularly nettlesome problem in semifrontier America was drunkenness. In an effort to wipe out the evils of alcohol, a temperance movement gathered momentum in the decades before 1861. Attempts were also made to remedy the terrible mistreatment of the insane, a movement that shifted into high gear in 1841 under the leadership of Dorothea L. Dix. Abolition of Negro slavery claimed the attention of many other humanitarians, a subject which will be discussed more extensively in the following chapter.

Thus, while the age of Jefferson and Jackson closed on a note of economic despair and—for the party of Jefferson and Jackson—political defeat, it was nonetheless a time of growth and achievement matched by only a few eras in American history.

STUDY GUIDE: During the first forty years of the nineteenth century, an endless stream of people headed westward. Thousands of immigrants from Europe arrived in the East. Industrial areas continued to develop. Canals cut into the landscape. The steamship was introduced, and the railroad appeared. Along with scientific and technological advances, there were major contributions in literature and the arts. This was also a period of great religious activity and social reform.

SUMMING UP THE CHAPTER

Names and Terms to Identify

Zebulon M. Pike	"tariff of abominations"
Continental system	Battle of Horseshoe
impressment	Bend
Chesapeake	John C. Calhoun
Tecumseh	Osceola
Oliver Hazard Perry	nullification
Fort McHenry	Force Act
McCulloch v. *Maryland*	"pet banks"
Tallmadge Amendment	Specie Circular
Rush-Bagot Agreement	transcendentalism

Study Questions and Points to Review

1. Why did Jefferson seem to be ill-suited for the role of politician?

2. What was the Enlightenment?

3. What were Jefferson's relations with the federal judiciary during his first years in the presidency?

4. What was Jefferson's position toward Tripoli?

5. Why was Jefferson concerned over the cession of Louisiana to France by Spain? What actions did he take which finally led to the Louisiana Purchase?

6. What was the purpose of the Embargo Act of 1807? How did it affect American commerce?

7. What legislation led to the enactment of Macon's Bill No. 2 in 1810?

8. What effect did the long war with Napoleon have on the British attitude toward war with the United States?

9. Why was the tariff problem the most vexing of the Adams presidency?

10. What is Jacksonian democracy?

11. Explain the Eaton affair.

12. What was Clay's reason for pushing through Congress a bill to grant the Bank of the United States a new charter? How did Jackson react?

13. Why did the South Carolina legislature call a state convention in 1832? What action did Jackson take as a result of this convention?

Topics for Discussion

1. What was the spoils system? Do you think such a system is desirable? Or can you see shortcomings in such an arrangement? Give reasons for your answer.

2. Using Atlas Map 12, trace Jackson's movements during the last stages of the War of 1812. Evaluate the significance of his victory. What was the objective of the British in trying to capture New Orleans?

3. The Monroe Doctrine was an expression of American nationalism. Discuss the provisions of this doctrine.

4. How did the federal government accumulate a surplus during the Jackson administration? What did Clay propose to do with the money? What was the result of his proposal?

5. Why did the Whig party nominate three candidates during the campaign of 1836? Did their strategy work? Evaluate the wisdom of such strategy.

Subjects for Reports or Essays

1. On Atlas Map 11a locate the site of the Battle of Tippecanoe. Using reference material from the library, prepare a report on the results of the battle.

2. Using Atlas Map 11b, locate the Battle of Lake Erie. What was the significance of Perry's victory? Report on this battle.

3. Using Atlas Map 13, prepare a report on the operations against the Barbary states.

4. Using reference materials in your library, prepare a newspaper account of the burning of Washington.

5. Research the origin of the term "Era of Good Feeling." Why was this period in American history called an era of good feeling? What were some of the important events of this period?

6. Prepare a report on one of the following people: John Marshall, Tecumseh, Dorothea L. Dix, Washington Irving, Martin Van Buren.

7. Prepare a book report for class presentation on one of the selections listed under "Further Readings."

Projects, Activities, and Skills

1. Draw an outline map showing the present-day states which comprise the Louisiana Purchase. Indicate the year when each of these states entered the Union.

2. Using reference material from your school library, prepare a map showing the route of Lewis and Clark's expedition. Describe some of their experiences. Who was Sacajewea? How did the expedition cross the Rocky Mountains? What advantage was this expedition to the people of the United States?

3. Imagine you are living during Jackson's administration. How would you have reacted to Jackson's treatment of the American Indians? Write a letter stating your feelings on his action.

4. One of the greatest engineering projects of the early nineteenth century was the Erie Canal. Prepare an illustrated report on the canal considering some of the problems that were encountered during its construction. On a map trace the route of the canal. Explain the economic consequences of the canal. Try to locate the words to a folk song about the Erie Canal.

5. Prepare an illustrated report on one of the following buildings: the Hermitage, Monticello, the White House, the Capitol Building (Washington, D.C.), the Capitol Building (Richmond, Virginia). Or, if you live in an area where there is an outstanding example of American architecture for the period from 1800 to 1840, report on it.

Further Readings

General

The Age of Jackson by Arthur M. Schlesinger, Jr. Interesting interpretation of Jacksonian democracy.
The Awakening of American Nationalism: 1815-1828 by George Dangerfield.
Democracy in America by Alexis de Tocqueville. A classic commentary on American society.

The Era of Good Feelings by George Dangerfield.
Freedom's Ferment: Phases of American Social History from the Revolution to the Outbreak of the Civil War by Alice F. Tyler. Best study of the reform movement.
A History of the Monroe Doctrine by Dexter Perkins.
The Jacksonian Era, 1828-1848 by Glydon Van Deusen.
The Journals of Lewis and Clark ed. by Bernard De Voto. Interesting original account of the Lewis and Clark expedition.
The Nation Takes Shape: 1789-1837 by Marcus Cunliffe. Excellent treatment of the period.
Prologue to War: England and the United States, 1805-1812 by Bradford Perkins.
The United States in 1800 by Henry Adams. The opening chapters contain a splendid picture of the United States at the beginning of the 1800s.
The War of 1812 by Harry L. Coles. The best account of the fighting war.

Biography

Daniel Webster and the Rise of National Conservatism by Richard N. Current.
James Monroe by W. P. Cresson.
John C. Calhoun, Opportunist by Gerald M. Capers.
Martin Van Buren: The Careers and Contemporaries of an American Talleyrand by Holmes Alexander.

Fiction

Captain Caution, The Lively Lady, and *Lydia Bailey* by Kenneth Roberts. All take place in the early 1800s.
Captain from Connecticut and *Lord Hornblower* by Cecil S. Forester. Adventure in the War of 1812.
Immortal Wife by Irving Stone. Historical novel about John Frémont's wife, Jesse.
Lighthouse by Eugenia Price. A young man seeks to fulfill an impossible dream in the early 1800s.
The Man Without a Country by Edward Everett Hale.
The Medicine Man by Shirley Seifert. French doctor joins early settlers around the time of the Louisiana Purchase.
The Prairie by James Fenimore Cooper. The last of the "Leatherstocking Tales."
The President's Lady by Irving Stone. Historical novel about Andrew Jackson's wife, Rachel.

More than six hundred thousand American soldiers died during the Civil War. Cities were burned and families were divided or destroyed. When the war ended in 1865, the job of rebuilding—and reuniting—began. ▶

2
CIVIL WAR AND RECONSTRUCTION

CIVIL WAR

1

In the Battle of Gettysburg Union soldiers forced the Confederate army to retreat. A painting of the battle was made by a French artist, Paul Philippoteaux, in 1881. Part of the painting is shown here.

2

General Ulysses S. Grant was the outstanding leader of the Union army. President Lincoln gave him command of all Northern armies in 1864. This portrait of Grant was painted in 1865.

3

Before he became president of the Confederate States of America, Jefferson Davis had a distinguished military career in the United States Army and as secretary of war. As a senator he spoke out for the southern cause. This photograph of Davis was made in 1861.

4

The watercolor at the right shows the interior of a tent used by Union soldiers. The painting was made at Camp John A. Andrew, near Annapolis, Maryland, in December 1861 by Herbert E. Valentine. Valentine was a private in Company F of the 23rd Massachusetts Volunteers.

5

In 1865 A. A. Lamb made a painting to glorify the Emancipation Proclamation. The painting was not made to record the event but rather to symbolize the effect of Lincoln's action. Compare the style of this painting with the one by Valentine.

Chicago Historical Society **2**

1   Courtesy Gettysburg National Military Park

3

4

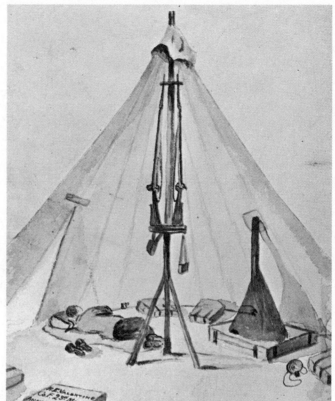

5

CHAPTER 4

THE ROAD TO FORT SUMTER

A COLD, BITING WIND swirled about Washington on March 4, 1841, when William Henry Harrison took office as the ninth president. As a rugged frontiersman, the new chief executive declined to wear an overcoat or hat. He gave one of the longest inaugural addresses on record, then mounted a horse and led the inaugural parade down Pennsylvania Avenue to the White House. A few weeks later the sixty-eight-year-old president, tired by the inauguration festivities and endless interviews with Whig office-seekers, came down with a cold, which developed into pneumonia. On April 4, one month after entering the White House, he died.

Unaware that Harrison was ill, Vice-President Tyler was on his knees shooting marbles with his children when a messenger galloped into his yard at Williamsburg with news that the president was dead. "Honest John" Tyler thus became the first man to take the presidency on the death of a president.

JOHN TYLER, PRESIDENT

Tyler was born in tidewater Virginia in 1790. Like Harrison, he was a member of Virginia's aristocracy and grew up in comfortable circumstances.

The Tyler household was a citadel of Jeffersonian Republicanism. Throughout his life, John Tyler believed in state rights and a rigid interpretation of the Constitution. After graduating from the College of William and Mary, he became a lawyer, served in the House of Representatives (1816-21), was governor of Virginia (1825-27), then a member of the Senate. A Democrat, he supported Andrew Jackson in the presidential elections of 1828 and 1832, then broke with Jackson on the issues of nullification and the Bank of the United States. In 1836 he refused to carry out instructions by the Virginia legislature to vote for a Senate resolution removing a censure of Jackson. Resigning from the Senate, he drifted into the new Whig party, although all he had in common with most Whigs was a dislike of the president. Hoping to attract anti-

Jackson Democrats, the Whigs nominated him for vice-president in 1836 and again in 1840.

Calling him "His Accidency," some people, including the Whig leader Henry Clay, thought the new president should run a "caretaker" administration. Tyler insisted, however, that on Harrison's death he had inherited the full power of the presidential office, setting an important precedent for the future.

The Tyler presidency (1841-45) was not successful. The president was an impatient man of limited ability who soon found himself at odds with Whig leaders, particularly Henry Clay. As the most distinguished Whig, Clay wanted the power of the leader and thought Tyler should serve as a puppet. Most Whigs favored Clay's American system and wanted a strong national government, internal improvements at public expense, and a high tariff. Standing for state rights and agrarianism and opposed to internal improvements and tariff protection, Tyler used his veto freely to thwart the will of the Whig-controlled Congress. After he had vetoed a banking bill sponsored by Clay, a crowd of angry Whigs gathered outside the White House. They booed and hissed, threw stones at the mansion, and burned an effigy of the president. Among Whigs the name Tyler became a swear word and Whig women called their rheumatic pains "Tyler's grip." At length the Whigs put the president out of the party. Before his term ended in 1845 he was, for all practical purposes, back in the Democratic party.

A Thin Record of Achievements

The record of achievements of the Tyler administration is thin. There was the "Log Cabin Bill" (1841) which liberalized federal land policy (making it easier for settlers to acquire land) and a treaty with China (1844) opening China to American traders. Most important, Tyler's first secretary of state, Daniel Webster, negotiated an important treaty with a special British envoy, Lord Ashburton. The Webster-Ashburton agreement ended a dispute over the boundary between Maine and New Brunswick,

HEADLINE EVENTS

1787 Slavery prohibited in Northwest Territory by Confederation Congress

1793 Whitney invents cotton gin

1808 Further importation of slaves from overseas prohibited by Congress

1817 American Colonization Society founded

1821 Austin given charter to establish colony in Texas

1831 William Lloyd Garrison publishes first issue of *The Liberator*

Nat Turner leads slave revolt in Virginia

1834 Slavery abolished in British Empire

1836 Texas declares its independence from Mexico

Fall of the Alamo

Battle of San Jacinto

1837 Jackson recognizes independence of Republic of Texas

1841 William Henry Harrison inaugurated

John Tyler succeeds to the presidency on death of Harrison

Log Cabin Bill

1842 Webster-Ashburton Treaty ends boundary dispute with Canada

1844 Telegraph line between Washington and Baltimore

"Fifty-four—forty-or-fight," Oregon boundary a campaign issue

1845 Texas is annexed

Florida enters the Union

James K. Polk inaugurated president

Slidell Mission

Texas enters the Union

1846 Congress declares war on Mexico

Northwest boundary dispute settled by treaty with Britain

Wilmot Proviso introduced

Bear Flag revolt in California

Frémont and Stockton claim California for United States

Iowa enters the Union

1847 Battle of Buena Vista

Vera Cruz falls to Scott

Scott claims Mexico City

1848 Gold discovered in California

Treaty of Guadalupe Hidalgo

Wisconsin enters the Union

1849 Zachary Taylor inaugurated president

California gold rush

1850 Millard Fillmore succeeds to presidency upon death of Taylor

Compromise of 1850

California enters the Union

1852 *Uncle Tom's Cabin* published

1853 Franklin Pierce inaugurated president

Gadsden Purchase

1854 Kansas-Nebraska Act

Republican party organized

Ostend Manifesto

1855 Civil strife in Kansas, "Bleeding Kansas"

1856 Sumner attacked in Senate

Know-Nothing party appears

1857 James Buchanan inaugurated president

Dred Scott decision

Financial panic

1858 Minnesota enters the Union

Lincoln-Douglas debates; Freeport Doctrine

1859 Oregon enters the Union

John Brown raids Harpers Ferry

1860 Abraham Lincoln is elected president

Crittenden Compromise proposed

South Carolina secedes from Union (December 20)

1861 Mississippi (January 9), Florida (January 10), Alabama (January 11), Georgia (January 19), Louisiana (January 26) Texas (February 1) secede from the Union

Kansas enters the Union

Confederate States of America established; Jefferson Davis chosen as president

Lincoln is inaugurated president

Fort Sumter fired on

Lincoln orders troops to put down the rebellion

Virginia (April 17), Arkansas (May 6), North Carolina (May 21), and Tennessee (June 8) secede from the Union

1886 Presidential Succession Act

settled boundary questions between Canada and New York and Vermont, and established a line between Canada and the United States in the region of Lake Superior that gave the great Mesabi iron range (then unknown) to the United States.

Although John Tyler's Whig party had a majority in Congress, he achieved very little success with his legislative program. What basic differences did he have with his party?

Tyler hoped for the Democratic nomination for president in 1844. When he failed to secure it, he set about organizing a third party, only to drop the idea at the urging of Andrew Jackson, with whom he had become reconciled. On leaving the White House in March 1845, he retired to Virginia. Over the next decade and a half he devoted himself to defending state rights and the interests of southern planters. During the secession crisis of 1860-61 he sought a compromise solution, but when his efforts failed he joined the secessionists. Tyler helped organize the Confederacy, and shortly before his death

IN MEMORY

OF

PRESIDENT

WM. H. HARRISON,

WHO DEPARTED
THIS LIFE,
APRIL 4, 1841,
AGED 68,

Deeply lamented
by 16 Millions of
people.

After a brief illness, William Henry Harrison died only one month after entering the White House. He had caught a cold on inauguration day and the stress of the first few weeks in office brought on pneumonia. He was the first president to die in office and was deeply mourned by his country. In his memory, many Americans wore ribbons like the one above.

in 1862 won election to the Confederate House of Representatives.

STUDY GUIDE: William Henry Harrison died in 1841, a month after he became president. He was succeeded by John Tyler. Tyler insisted that he inherited all the powers of the president and refused to act as a caretaker. The Whigs wanted a strong national government, high tariff and Clay's "American system." Tyler wanted state rights and an agricultural society. He opposed internal improvements at public expense and tariff protection.

SLAVERY

While quarrels with Whig leaders brought bitterness to President Tyler, the two questions that came to occupy national attention during his presidency were slavery and Texas.

Negro slavery had made its appearance in America at Jamestown shortly after 1619, expanded slowly, and by the time of the War of Independence seemed in decline. Without opposition of a single southern member, the Confederation Congress in the Northwest Ordinance of 1787 prohibited slavery in the Northwest Territory. In the next few years, meanwhile, human bondage disappeared in one northeastern state after another. Thomas Jefferson said "nothing is more certainly written in the book of fate than that these people [the slaves] are to be free," and with approval of southern members Congress prohibited further importation of slaves from overseas after January 1, 1808.

Then "King Cotton" arrived.

When Washington took the oath as president, cotton culture was almost unknown in the United States. Four years later in 1793 Eli Whitney invented a gin for separating cotton seed from fiber. Two decades later southern planters were producing nearly two hundred thousand bales of cotton a year, by 1840 more than a million. The opening of new cotton lands created an increased demand for labor. Since cultivation of cotton required battalions of unskilled workers who could toil from sunup to sundown in broiling heat, the planters turned to slave labor. Hence slavery—apparently a declining institution at the close of the eighteenth century—became, in the view of the South, an economic necessity.

The Greatest Era

Meanwhile, an elaborate domestic slave trade sprang up in this country. Over the next half-century thousands of slaves were marched down dusty roads or trundled along in wagons to such trading centers as Washington, Memphis, and New Orleans. At the slave market finely dressed planters in beaver hats would gather about the auction platform while a smooth-tongued auctioneer pointed out the features of the man up for sale—broad shoulders, bulging biceps, straight legs. He might emphasize that the slave was docile, easily controlled. To establish the point, he would note the absence of lash marks on the back. To demonstrate endurance he might order the slave to sprint several hundred yards down the street and back, the planters gathering round on the slave's return to see how hard he was panting. The greatest evil of the trade was separation of families. Someone once asked John Randolph of Virginia to name the greatest orator he had ever heard. He replied: "A slave, sir. She was a mother, and her rostrum was the auction block."

Slave families often were separated by their owners. For example, a slaveowner who needed money might choose one of his women slaves and put her up for sale at an auction, even if the slave had a husband and children.

Slaves had no legal rights to protect them. Once a slave had been sold, she or he was at the mercy of the buyer. Some slaveowners tried to treat their slaves kindly, but a slave could be beaten or lashed at the whim of an owner. Slaves always were treated as servants. They had no hope of gaining their freedom, or of ever owning the land they worked, or of ever being able to sell the crops they harvested.

Everyday life was hard for slaves. It was especially hard for those who were field workers. The slave toiled from sunup to sundown on a monotonous diet of meal, pork, and molasses. He usually lived in a ramshackle hut, often shared by several families. Slave quarters were naturally incubators of disease, and each year malaria, dysentery, and tuberculosis took a fearsome toll. The slave's clothing was of the coarsest quality. Adults usually received one new dress or set of work garments a year; children often wore long-tailed shirts that reached to the knees and went barefooted and bareheaded the year around. Since masters were determined to keep slaves illiterate (on the theory that an educated slave might become rebellious), the slave could not attempt intellectual pursuits.

Slaves often pretended to their owners to be content. But, of course, slaves knew that their position was the lowest in society and longed for something better. The slave often found satisfaction — poignant in its futility — in a subtle competition with the master, the game the present generation calls "one-upmanship." This competition carried over to Negro folklore, as shown in the tales of "Br'er Rabbit." Br'er Rabbit represented the slave, defenseless except for his wits, but always winning out against the schemes of Br'er Fox and Br'er B'ar (the slave masters). Some slaves, it seems, accepted their fate because they could see no alternative. It was hard to run away and, when caught, the fugitive slave received punishment that was severe and swift. Insurrection was next to impossible; restricted movement and communication prevented effective organization and planning and, besides, the whites had all the guns. Other slaves took the advice of the apostle Saint Paul that slaves should obey masters, finding some comfort in the promise of eternal reward in a world beyond for bearing patiently the tribulations of earthly life.

The Abolition Movement

Then came the movement for abolition. From the time of the War of Independence, many thoughtful Americans had observed the conflict between the ringing phrases of the Declaration of Independence and the existence of Negro slavery. In the second decade of the nineteenth century, a few of them, including Henry Clay, became attracted to the idea of abolishing slavery by purchasing the freedom of Negroes and shipping them back to Africa. The outcome was appearance of the American Colonization Society which, over the next two decades, settled several thousand Negroes in a new country, Liberia, on the west coast of Africa. It was clear by 1830, however, that the problems and expense of colonization, coupled with the view of most southerners that slavery was an economic necessity, made resettlement in Africa an inadequate means of eliminating Negro slavery in America.

As the deficiencies of colonization became apparent, other developments were transpiring which would influence the attitudes of many Americans. First, in the mid-1820s, was the beginning of the humanitarian impulse that inspired people to look about at the evils of American society — drunkenness, poverty, inhuman prison conditions. Reformers searched for ways to eliminate these conditions. Inevitably this new humanitarianism produced an attack on the country's worst evil, human bondage. Then, in 1830, the British Parliament began to debate the question of immediate abolition of slavery in the British Empire. Abolitionists in Britain gave little attention to proposals to colonize slaves in Africa or gradually emancipate Negroes (a solution to the slave problem urged by some Americans). The British reformers demanded total abolition at once. Britain abolished slavery in its empire in 1834.

Garrison's Crusade

Among the many Americans, white and black, who caught the new humanitarian spirit and also followed the debates in England was an obscure journalist in Boston, William Lloyd Garrison. In June 1831 he published the first issue of *The Liberator,* a paper dedicated to the immediate abolition of slavery in the United States. In opening his campaign, Garrison gave up his past support of "the popular but pernicious doctrine of *gradual* abolition" and asked "pardon of my God, of my country, and of my brethren the poor slaves, for having uttered a sentiment so full of timidity, injustice, and absurdity." He proclaimed that, on the subject of abolition, "I do not wish to think, or speak, or write, with moderation. No! no! Tell a man whose house is on fire to give a moderate alarm; tell him to moderately rescue his wife from the hands of the ravisher; tell the mother to gradually extricate her babe from the fire into which it has fallen; — but urge me not to use moderation in a cause like the present. I am in earnest — I will not equivocate — I will not excuse — I will not retreat a single inch — AND I WILL BE HEARD."

Garrison's crusade attracted a corps of zealous followers who carried the abolitionist message to every corner of the North. In sermons and pamphlets abolitionists focused on the most terrible aspects of slavery and if the raw truth did not seem sufficiently horrible they were not above inventing a few details. Abolitionists refused to admit that slavemasters were capable of a human impulse. In Garrison's words, "the life of a slaveowner is but one of unbridled lust, of filthy amalgamation, of swaggering braggadocio, of haughty domination, of cowardly ruffianism, of boundless dissipation, of matchless insolence, of infinite self-conceit, of unequalled oppression, of more than savage cruelty."

The Underground Railroad

Impatient with merely arguing against slavery, some abolitionists became "engineers" and "conductors" on the "Underground Railroad" to help runaway slaves ("passengers") make their way to freedom in the North or in Canada. Operating the Underground Railroad was a thrilling and risky enterprise, and abolitionists

Henry "Box" Brown used an ingenious method to escape slavery. He had himself nailed in a wooden crate and shipped from Richmond to Philadelphia. What does this incident tell about the black man's feelings toward slavery?

Harriet Tubman, an escaped slave, helped over 300 slaves gain freedom through the Underground Railroad. She also served as a spy for the Union and as a scout on raids. Were there any "stations" of the Underground Railroad in your area?

often found ingenious ways to manage the escape of Negroes. Sometimes they put slaves in boxes, carried them to the nearest railroad station or wharf, and shipped them northward as freight. Another device was for the abolitionist to pose as master of the Negroes in his company. On one occasion an abolitionist delivered twenty-eight slaves to freedom by organizing them into a funeral procession. Still, most slave passengers traveled on foot or in hidden compartments in wagons, moving under cover of darkness, hiding by day.

Not all operators of the Underground Railroad were white. One of the most famous conductors was a little Negro woman, Harriet Ross Tubman, who, despite her frailty, used her wits and iron nerve to deliver more than three hundred slaves over the Pennsylvania border. Extreme caution was necessary, for "trains" of the Railroad often had to elude bloodhounds, professional slave catchers, and local authorities. And the danger did not end entirely at the Ohio River or the Mason-Dixon line. Some northern whites had no sympathy for Negroes or abolitionists, and slave chasers had a legal right to pursue fugitives all the way to the Canadian border.

The Underground Railroad produced more sound and fury than results. Only a fraction of the South's slave population—fewer than 100,000 altogether, over a period of several decades—ever got aboard. But the psychological consequences were great, for the Railroad roused southern champions of slavery and their northern sympathizers to heights of passion, and fired the spirit of abolitionists.

Nat Turner Leads an Insurrection

Southerners meanwhile rallied to the defense of slavery and over the next three decades fashioned an elaborate proslavery argument. Urging them on (particularly in the 1830s), was the natural tendency to defend one's institutions against alien critics and a fear that if the abolitionist logic were not disproved it might give rise to slave rebellions all over the South. This fear rested in large part on an insurrection in 1831 in Southampton County, Virginia—led by a black man named Nat Turner which resulted in the death of perhaps sixty whites. The first issue of Garrison's *Liberator* had appeared earlier that year, but there is no evidence of any connection between publication of the paper and the slave uprising which Turner, an intelligent and restless Negro, had planned many months before.

Defenders of Slavery

Two of the most brilliant spokesmen for slavery were John C. Calhoun of South Carolina and George Fitzhugh of Virginia. Calhoun announced that slavery was "a good—a positive good." His main argument paralleled that of the ancient Greek philosopher Aristotle who had declared that no advanced community ever existed in which one part of the community did not live off the labor of the other. Calhoun also compared what he thought was the stability and tranquillity of the South with the continuing conflict between capital and labor in the North. Fitzhugh took a similar theme, asserting that "domestic slavery in the Southern States has produced the same results in elevating the character of the master that it did in Greece and Rome." According to Fitzhugh, "we provide for each slave, in old age and infancy, in sickness and health, not according to his labor, but according to his wants." Fitzhugh, of course, did not think the slave's wants were great.

Other defenders of slavery invoked religion and science. The Reverend Thornton Stringfellow of Virginia noted that the patriarchs of the Old Testament had owned slaves, that Jesus of Nazareth apparently had not spoken out against slavery, and that apostles of the New Testament had urged obedience to civil ordinances governing relations of masters and servants. There is sufficient evidence to prove that during this period of history white Christianity forgot about its doctrines of charity and justice where the black man was involved.

STUDY GUIDE: Negro slavery came to America shortly after 1619. It declined during the War of Independence. And Congress banned further importation of slaves as of 1808. But when the cotton industry began to expand in the South, there was an increased demand for slave labor. The abolition movement began during the 1820s as many Americans began to feel a conflict between the Declaration of Independence and slavery. Abolitionist William Lloyd Garrison published *The Liberator,* a paper dedicated to the immediate abolition of slavery. Some abolitionists organized the Underground Railroad to help runaway slaves reach freedom. Some slaves sought their freedom by rebellions.

TEXAS

In the years that slavery was coming under abolitionist attack, events were taking place in the Mexican territory of Texas that reached a point of controversy during the presidency of John Tyler.

American involvement in Texas began in 1821 when authorities in Mexico City granted a charter to Moses Austin permitting him to establish a colony in that part of Mexico which is now east Texas. An enterprising Yankee down on his luck, Austin dreamed of becoming a latter-day Lord Baltimore or William Penn. Austin died in 1822, but the following year the new emperor of Mexico continued the grant to Stephen F. Austin, son of Moses. Over the next decade Austin and a few other Americans lured several thousand settlers from the United States to Texas. Cotton and sugar became the foundation of the Texas economy, and to cultivate these staples the Americans, in violation of Mexican law, introduced slavery—while Mexican authorities obligingly looked the other way.

Although Stephen Austin tried to be a good Mexican, most Americans in Texas felt no attachment to the regime in Mexico City. There was of course the emotional pull of the United

States. Then who could tell when a Mexican leader might try to enforce the laws against slavery? Hence, Texas was ripe for revolt. In 1835 the Mexican dictator, Antonio López de Santa Anna, eliminated local privileges, such as those enjoyed by Americans in Texas. The Americans countered by setting up their own government and expelling the Mexican garrison from San Antonio. On March 2, 1836, they declared the independence of Texas.

Santa Anna meanwhile had swept northward with 5,000 men and on March 6, 1836, hurled his army against a band of 187 Americans who had taken refuge behind the ancient adobe walls of the Alamo Mission in San Antonio. The Mexicans won at a cost of 1,500 casualties, but the Americans never surrendered and apparently every man was killed. (Some scholars think that the Mexicans took some prisoners at the Alamo.) The Texans were not finished. Sam Houston, a former governor of Tennessee who had taken command of Texas forces, lured Santa Anna eastward. The climax came on April 21, 1836, near present-day Houston. Hiding in a grove of trees, Houston's men caught Santa Anna unawares and in twenty minutes routed the Mexican's army.

The Battle of San Jacinto was a conclusive defeat for Mexico. The Texans quickly approved a new constitution legalizing slavery. They also elected Houston their first president and sent an envoy to Washington to gain annexation of Texas to the United States—or, failing that, recognition of Texas as an independent republic. Annexation was not approved, but early the next year, in 1837, Congress recognized Texas as independent.

Texas was an independent republic between 1837 and 1845, and Austin was its capital. This drawing of Austin was made around 1840.

Annexation or Independence

Before long abolitionists began to argue that the Texas revolution had been a clever southern conspiracy to gain new territory for the "peculiar institution." The annexation question thus became tangled in agitation over slavery. There had been no conspiracy, but both the North and South understood sectional arithmetic and knew that if Texas was carved into several slave states, Southern influence would increase substantially. Then, in 1841, John Tyler entered the White House. A Virginian, the president was proslavery and his administration signed a treaty of annexation in 1843. Because of hostility in the North, however, the treaty was rejected by the Senate.

With the impending election of 1844, advocates of annexation hit on a new strategy. Since the country was talking of "manifest destiny," the idea that providence had marked out the entire North American continent for control by the United States, why not remove the Texas question from its slavery setting and make it one of national expansion and prestige? Such an approach, moreover, would make it possible to link Texas with Oregon.

"Fifty-four Forty or Fight!"

As noted in the preceding chapter, Britain and the United States had long maintained conflicting claims to the Oregon country. For more than two decades they had managed to gloss over the difficulty, but movement of settlers into Oregon was about to force the issue. Americans, particularly in the North, were demanding a solution. A few had already shouted, "Fifty-four forty or fight!"—meaning that they wanted all the Oregon country right up to the line 54° 40'. Here, then, was the chance: southerners would

support a strong stand on Oregon if northerners would not oppose annexation of Texas.

The Texas-Oregon strategy was adopted by the Democratic national convention in May 1844. Then (after several ballots) the Democrats nominated for president a firm supporter of expansion, James Knox Polk of Tennessee. The Whigs had met a few weeks before and nominated Henry Clay, then in his sixty-seventh year. The Whigs took no stand on Texas and in the campaign Clay sought to straddle the question. The strategy misfired. Polk was elected by a narrow margin.

Interpreting the election as a mandate to annex Texas, President Tyler determined to act before Polk took office. Congress went along and in February 1845 adopted an annexation resolution permitting Texas to become a state at once without the usual preliminary of territorial status. A convention met at Austin the following July 4. It accepted terms set down in Washington (that Texas would be responsible for debts incurred in the republican period and not more than four new states could emerge from its territory). The voters of Texas a few months later ratified the convention's action and in December 1845 the new state entered the Union.

STUDY GUIDE: In 1821 Mexico granted Moses Austin a permit to establish a colony in Texas. Over the next decade several thousand American settlers went there. They introduced slavery in violation of Mexican laws. Americans in Texas set up their own government and expelled Mexicans from San Antonio. In 1836 they declared the independence of Texas. The Battle of San Jacinto caused Mexico to lose authority in Texas. Annexation of Texas became tangled in the dispute over slavery. In the campaign of 1844, the idea of manifest destiny was introduced—that destiny had marked out the entire American continent for control by the United States. Advocates of manifest destiny insisted that the Texas question was one of national expansion and prestige, not slavery. Texas was annexed by the United States in 1845.

JAMES K. POLK

The day Tyler signed the resolution to annex Texas was the day that Florida became the twenty-seventh state. The next day James K. Polk took the presidential oath. The air was cold, and the driving rain turned Washington's unpaved streets into a sea of mud. John Quincy Adams recorded in his diary that Polk delivered his inaugural address "to a large assemblage of umbrellas."

Of Scotch-Irish descent, James K. Polk was born in 1795 in Mecklenburg County, North Carolina, the son of a prosperous farmer. When he was ten, the family migrated to Tennessee where the elder Polk continued to prosper and became one of the largest landowners in the state. At nineteen the future president, a frail and serious-minded youth, went back over the mountains to his native state to attend the University of North Carolina. He graduated at the head of his class, returned to Tennessee, and became a successful lawyer.

From the legal profession to politics was a short step, and after a brief tenure in the Tennessee legislature Polk won election to the House of Representatives. He served seven terms (1825-39) and established a remarkable record of attendance in the House, missing only one sitting in fourteen years. In Washington he easily slipped into alliance with his fellow Tennesseean, Andrew Jackson. Helping to guide Jacksonian measures through the House, Polk won the special gratitude of "Old Hickory" when he assisted in the fight against the Bank of the United States. He became chairman of the powerful House Ways and Means Committee, chairman of the Democratic majority in the House, and from 1835 to 1839 was speaker of the House, earning the nickname "Young Hickory."

Urged on by Jackson, Polk reluctantly ran for governor of Tennessee in 1839. He won that campaign but lost bids for reelection in 1841 and 1843. His political career seemed in total eclipse when in 1844 the Democratic party convened at Baltimore to nominate a presidential ticket. When the convention deadlocked, word went through the delegations that the party's elder statesman, Andrew Jackson, favored the nomination of Polk for president. On the ninth ballot Polk became the first "dark horse" to carry a national political convention. Samuel F. B. Morse, who had recently invented the telegraph and strung a wire from Baltimore to Washington, immediately tapped out the news. Down in the capital observers hooted and announced that Morse's newfangled instrument now stood exposed as a fake. James K. Polk for president? Impossible, they said.

This presidential campaign poster of 1844 by Currier proclaims James Polk "The Peoples Choice." What actions during his four years in office made this statement truer at the end of his presidency than at the beginning?

Secretive and suspicious, Polk did not get along well with other politicians and, lacking elegance and oratorical skill, failed to establish himself with the country at large. Still, he was a strong president. On taking office he told the historian George Bancroft that he had four goals: reduction of the tariff, restoration of the independent treasury, settlement of the Oregon question, and acquisition of California. He achieved his goals in a single term. But he paid a price. Exhausted and in declining health, he could not campaign for reelection in 1848. Three months after leaving the presidency, in June 1849, he fell victim to a cholera epidemic and died.

Polk and California

Of Polk's achievements, the most important was acquisition of Mexico's province of California. For all its natural riches, California in the mid-1840s was a sparsely settled and undeveloped land. By the time Polk became president, its population was only 18,000—7,000 Mexicans, 4,000 Indians, and 7,000 Americans who had drifted in without invitation. Relations between the Mexican and American communities were

chilly. The Americans thought the Mexicans lazy; the Mexicans thought the Americans uncivilized. California actually was like Texas a decade before, and Polk was quick to see the similarity. The president's first impulse was to buy the territory but if Mexico would not sell perhaps a revolt, like that the Texans had staged, would open the way for bringing California into the United States. Accordingly his secretary of war advised the American consul at Monterey that "if the people [of California] should desire to unite their destiny with ours, they would be received as brethren."

Polk's aims in California, meanwhile, had merged with other issues between the United States and Mexico. One was the matter of $3 million in claims that Americans held against the Mexican government for property that had been damaged or destroyed. Another issue was the boundary between Texas and Mexico. The southern boundary of Texas for a hundred years had been the Nueces River. However, Texans, upheld by Polk, insisted that their territory extended to the Rio Grande.

The Slidell Mission

To strike a deal with Mexico, in autumn 1845 the president commissioned John Slidell as minister to Mexico, instructing him to assume unpaid claims of American citizens against Mexico if the Mexicans would recognize the Rio Grande boundary. He also was to offer $5 million for Mexico's vast territory between Texas and California (present-day Arizona, Nevada, and Utah and parts of New Mexico, Colorado, and Wyoming), and, if the Mexicans would sell California, "money would be no object." Responding to their country's deep hostility toward the United States, the result of the recent annexation of Texas, authorities in Mexico City would not even talk with Slidell.

Learning of the rebuff to Slidell, President Polk in mid-January 1846 ordered General Zachary Taylor to move American troops across the Nueces and establish positions along the left bank of the Rio Grande. He claimed, of course, that the territory between the two rivers, a veritable wasteland, was part of Texas. The president was goading the Mexicans—either to negotiate with Slidell or fight. Several weeks later he learned that leaders in Mexico City had again refused to receive Slidell. Polk then began to draft a message to Congress advocating war with Mexico on the basis of Slidell's rejection and the unpaid claims. Before sending the message, he received word from Taylor that a Mexican force had crossed the Rio Grande and skirmished with American troops. The president rewrote the message and on May 11, 1846, sent it to Capitol Hill. "After reiterated menaces," Polk declared, "Mexico has passed the boundary of the United States, has invaded our territory and shed American blood upon American soil." Congress promptly voted for war.

STUDY GUIDE: James K. Polk was elected president in 1844. He achieved all four of his goals in one term: he reduced the tariff, restored the independent treasury, settled Oregon's border dispute, and acquired California.

In 1845 Polk sent John Slidell to Mexico to try to buy land which Mexico owned but which Texas was claiming. Mexican officials refused to talk with Slidell. Polk then sent troops into the disputed area. Mexican troops soon arrived, and there was a skirmish. At Polk's request, Congress declared war on Mexico.

WAR WITH MEXICO

To defeat the Mexicans the president and his advisers settled on a two-pronged offensive. One force would strike across the Rio Grande and drive southward to Mexico City. The other would move westward to Santa Fe and from there to California. The latter thrust began in June 1846 when Colonel Stephen W. Kearny led an army of volunteers from Fort Leavenworth. They trudged across more than six hundred miles of plains and desert to Santa Fe. Warning the Mexicans (who outnumbered the Americans) that they faced annihilation, Kearny took Santa Fe in mid-August without a fight. He then prepared to push westward, but, he learned shortly, California was already under the Stars and Stripes.

The pot had begun to boil in California the previous spring when Americans in the northern part of the province—mostly ranchers, trappers, and traders—rose up against Mexican authority. Taking part in the affair was Captain John C. Frémont of the United States Army, whose "exploring" expedition had arrived in California early in 1846. Whether Frémont started the revolt is not clear, but the American settlers doubtless took courage from his presence and, when the uprising began, he encouraged it. The climax came at Sonoma on June 14, 1846, when the Americans ran up a white flag emblazoned with the crude likeness of a grizzly bear (hence, the insurrection became the Bear Flag Revolt) and declared the independence of the Republic of California.

A few weeks later Commodore John D. Sloat of the American Pacific Squadron captured Monterey and San Francisco, then made contact with the Bear Flaggers. After completing the conquest of northern California, the Americans turned southward. Moving by sea, forces under Frémont and Commodore Robert F. Stockton proceeded down the coast, one group landing near Los Angeles, the other near San Diego. When the two groups began to converge, the Mexican commander elected to make a stand just below Los Angeles. Sight of the approaching Americans, however, caused his army to break and flee to the south. Frémont and Stockton then marched into Los Angeles and Stockton, in August 1846, proclaimed California a part of the United States.

The Campaign in Northern Mexico

Success was also crowning American efforts in the Texas–northern Mexico theater. Thanks to superior artillery, General Taylor's men in May 1846 beat back a much larger Mexican army that had flung itself against the Americans several miles north of the Rio Grande. A few days later Taylor defeated the Mexicans in a wild hand-to-hand encounter in a ravine called Resaca de la Palma. Gathering reinforcements, Taylor moved across the Rio Grande and took the town of Matamoros, abandoned by the Mexican army. Now Taylor looked 175 miles to the west, to Monterrey, the strategic center of northern Mexico. Advancing deliberately, his 6,000-man army reached Monterrey in mid-September 1846. By skillful feinting, Taylor kept the main Mexican army occupied on the northeast side of the city while a force under General William Jenkins Worth slipped around to the west side to cut the Mexican supply road and infiltrate Monterrey from the rear. In two days, Worth's men had control of all strategic points on the west side of the city. Taylor meanwhile had pressed in from the east and north and after four days of sharp fighting—much of it house-to-house—the Mexicans capitulated.

Taylor's victories brought satisfaction to President Polk, but they also brought concern. For "Old Rough and Ready"—as the troops called Taylor—had become a national hero. And Taylor was a Whig, the kind of Whig, Polk feared, who might rally the forces of Whiggery for victory in the election of 1848, as "Old Tippecanoe" Harrison had done in 1840.

At the same time Polk faced a military problem. The road from Monterrey to Mexico City, across desert and mountains, would be long and difficult. Given his ability and determination, Taylor eventually could make it, but because many Americans opposed the war, the president wanted a quick conclusion to the conflict. So he fell in with the plan of General Winfield Scott who wanted to lead an amphibious movement on the Mexican capital via the port of Vera Cruz. Such an operation had an extra attraction: it would solve Polk's domestic political problem by drawing the spotlight away from Taylor. True, Scott was also a Whig, but he was a vain "spit-and-polish" soldier (called "Old Fuss and Feathers") and was not apt to attract a popular following.

"Old Rough and Ready," it turned out, was not finished. In February 1847 the Mexican leader Santa Anna, recently returned from exile in Cuba, rode northward with a large army in the hope of smashing Taylor. When scouts reported that Santa Anna was advancing with 15,000 men, Taylor ordered his 4,000-man army to take up positions at Buena Vista, a few miles below Monterrey, where a mountain range and a set of gullies provided natural defenses. Santa Anna's first assault at Buena Vista was inconclusive. The following morning (February 23) the Mexicans attacked again. The Americans fell back in confusion and for a time seemed to face annihilation. But reinforcements, mainly volunteers from Mississippi, broke the Mexican charge. Later in the day, in a blinding rainstorm that turned the battlefield to mud, the Mexicans charged again. Beaten back, they rallied for one last attack. By sheer weight of numbers they forced the Americans to give ground, only to be stalled when American artillery began to tear holes in their columns. That night Santa Anna and his men withdrew southward. Fighting in the north of Mexico was over.

Two weeks later a force under General Scott sailed down the Gulf of Mexico and splashed ashore a few miles below Vera Cruz. After heavy fighting and a long siege, Vera Cruz fell. Then with clever maneuvers, Scott fought his way to Mexico City—some three hundred miles through the mountains. On September 14, 1847, General Scott's troops claimed the victory of Mexico City.

The soldiers had achieved the tasks assigned them. The rest was up to the diplomats.

To have somebody available to negotiate whenever the Mexicans might feel an urge to end the war, Polk had assigned Nicholas Trist, a clerk in the State Department, to accompany Scott's army. But after the capture of Mexico City, the president decided that the Mexicans must sue for peace in the American capital, so he sent a dispatch recalling Trist. The Mexicans, meanwhile, had named a peace commission. On receiving his dismissal, Trist faced the question: should he obey Polk's order and return home or take advantage of the new opportunity for a settlement? Fearing the Mexicans might change their minds about making peace, he opened negotiations.

Capture of Veracruz was vital if the Americans were to complete their venture into Mexico. After a long siege by gunboats, the city fell to General Winfield Scott.

The Treaty of Guadalupe Hidalgo

On receipt of a sixty-page explanation from his envoy, Polk flew into a rage, denounced Trist as a scoundrel, and drafted a new dismissal order. But while the message was slowly making its way to Mexico, negotiations continued and on February 2, 1848, Trist and the Mexicans signed the Treaty of Guadalupe Hidalgo. The treaty ceded California and the territory between California and Texas to the United States, confirmed the Rio Grande as the southern boundary of Texas, and provided that the United States would pay Mexico $15 million and assume more than $3 million of claims by American citizens against the Mexican government. Regarding the payment of $15 million and assumption of the claims, some historians, finding no historical parallel for such generosity by a victor toward the vanquished, have concluded that this part of the treaty was intended to ease the consciences of those Americans who thought the United States had been the aggressor in the war. A copy of the treaty went off to Washington and Polk. Despite his rage at Trist, Polk wisely put it before the Senate where it quickly received ratification.

The Mexican Congress consented to the treaty a few months later. The American army in June 1848 marched out of Mexico City, and traveled over the mountains to Vera Cruz. There the troops boarded transports and sailed for home.

STUDY GUIDE: Just as the war against Mexico was beginning, American settlers in the Mexican province of California revolted. In the Bear Flag revolt of 1846, the Americans declared California independent. Then in 1847, United States forces took Mexico City and won the war. The Treaty of Guadalupe Hidalgo extended the Texas boundary south to the Rio Grande and gave California and the land between Texas and California to the United States. The United States paid Mexico $15 million.

THE COMPROMISE OF 1850

Polk and the Democrats had engineered a successful war and added a vast territory to the national domain. Two new states, Iowa (1846) and Wisconsin (1848), had entered the Union. The long dispute over Oregon had been the object of a sensible compromise, a treaty with Great Britain in summer 1846 extending the boundary between the United States and Canada along the forty-ninth parallel from the Rockies to the Pacific. It would seem, therefore, that as the election of 1848 approached, the Democrats should have radiated confidence. They did not. A few Americans had uneasy consciences about the recent war with Mexico. In the North, where "fifty-four forty or fight" had captured an audience, people were angry over the Oregon compromise. Then, addition of California and the adjacent area to the east had reopened the question of slavery in federal territories, dormant since the Missouri controversy of 1819-20.

Scenting victory, the Whigs convened at Philadelphia in summer 1848 and nominated Zachary Taylor for president. Taylor was a southerner who owned slaves and hence had appeal in the South. His military reputation was certain to attract voters in the North. For vice-president the Whigs balanced their ticket geographically by naming a northerner, a lawyer from Buffalo, New York, Millard Fillmore. Taking no stand on the issues of the day, the Whig platform was little more than a recital of the military accomplishments of the party's presidential candidate.

Less than a month before, at Baltimore, the Democrats had faced the task of replacing Polk. Worn out by his duties as president, Polk refused to run. The convention chose Lewis Cass of Michigan. An expansionist who always sought to appease the South, Cass wanted to leave the question of slavery in federal territories with residents of the territories.

While Whigs and Democrats tried to hedge the question of slavery in territories, the Free-Soil party determined to make it a central issue. Organized in summer 1848, the party nominated former President Van Buren on a platform of unyielding opposition to opening California and the New Mexico area to slavery. The Free-Soilers, it turned out, played a decisive part in the election, for in New York "Little Van" won votes of enough antislavery Democrats to enable Taylor to carry the state. As a result, in March 1849, "Old Rough and Ready" became the twelfth president of the Republic.

Zachary Taylor

Born in Orange County, Virginia, in 1784, Zachary Taylor was the son of a Revolutionary War officer and a relative of such famous Virginians as James Madison and Robert E. Lee. When he was nine months old, his father received an appointment as collector of the port of Louisville, and the family migrated across the mountains and down the Ohio to Kentucky. On a plantation near Louisville the younger Taylor grew to manhood, and he always considered himself a Kentuckian.

Thanks to James Madison's influence, Taylor received from President Jefferson a commission in the regular army. During the War of 1812 a force of fifty men under his command repulsed an attack led by the Indian chieftain Tecumseh in Indiana. Nearly two decades later he commanded regulars and militiamen (including Captain Abraham Lincoln) against Sauk and Fox Indians in the Black Hawk War and personally accepted the surrender of Chief Black Hawk. A few years later he led victorious troops against the Seminole Indians in Florida and in 1837 defeated the Seminoles in the Battle of Okeechobee. After their defeat, he was assigned to remove the Seminoles from Florida to territory in the West. In the year 1841 he went to Louisiana as commander of the army's Southwest Department, bought a large house at Baton Rouge, and a plantation with 300 slaves in Mississippi. Then came the climax of his forty-year military career, the victories in 1846-47 during the Mexican War.

"Old Rough and Ready" did not possess an outstanding intellect. As a youth on the Kentucky frontier, he had received only a smattering of formal instruction from private tutors. Over the decades, as he and his family moved from one army post to another, he read few if any books and developed little interest in intellectual pursuits. He had scant knowledge of government, paid little attention to politics, and before 1848 never bothered to vote.

Still, Taylor had qualities that compensated for his intellectual limits. He was a man of prudence or "common sense" — seeming to know instinctively in difficult situations what he could do and also what he must do. He was a man of rare courage who never became rattled when under attack, either on the battlefield or in the political arena, and he had the gift of transferring his "cool" to subordinates. He was a humble man. Finally, he was an uncompromising patriot who without hesitation placed the national interest above that which was purely regional or sectional.

By the time Taylor took the presidential oath, one issue had obscured all others: was the terri-

Zachary Taylor served as a soldier for forty years and never lost a battle. He became a national hero for his outstanding performance in the Mexican War. After the war Taylor won the election for president of the United States.

tory recently acquired from Mexico to be open to slavery? The issue had come to the surface a few months after the first shots of the Mexican War, in summer 1846, when Polk, as part of a design for ending the war and purchasing California, asked Congress for a secret appropriation. Without warning, a little-known congressman from Pennsylvania, David Wilmot, offered an amendment to the appropriation bill — the Wilmot Proviso — that "neither slavery nor involuntary servitude shall ever exist" in any territory purchased from Mexico. Passions exploded. Southerners assailed Wilmot and his proviso. In the North the idea of keeping slavery out of federal territories suddenly became a sacred principle. The Wilmot Proviso did not pass Congress. Neither did any of the other measures proposed after the war to bring political organization to the new territory.

Gold in California

Then came another development, the Gold Rush to California. Word had filtered back East that in January 1848 a workman had discovered gold in the millrace of Sutter's Mill in the Sacramento Valley. Before long hundreds of fortune-seekers were on their way to California—by the Isthmus of Panama, around the tip of South America, overland across plains, mountains, and desert. By the time Taylor took the presidency in March 1849, several thousand miners, equipped with washbowls and other crude implements, were stirring about the streams of California, and more miners were on the way. The need for a government in this territory of expanding population and turbulent mining camps was clear, but Congress, hopelessly deadlocked on the issue of slavery, could agree on no framework for political organization. Urged on by President Taylor, Californians themselves took matters in hand, elected an assembly, and in autumn 1849 accepted a constitution that prohibited slavery. Before Congress could consider an application for statehood, a governor and legislature were elected and a state government began to function.

Southerners erupted. The South had long argued for state rights. Now California, the choicest part of the recent conquest, would be closed to slavery. In their anger and frustration, leaders of the South began to talk of breaking up the Union and putting together a slave-holding confederacy that would extend from the Potomac to the Rio Grande and beyond. They received no encouragement from the president. Taylor warned that secession was treason and that, if necessary, he personally would lead the army to enforce federal authority in the southern states.

Clay Fashions a Compromise

When the Thirty-first Congress convened in December 1849, the atmosphere in Washington was heavy with tension. It appeared that despite the president's brave words against secession, the nation was on the verge of breaking apart. Then early in the year 1850 came a formula for compromise fashioned by a veteran of the political wars, Henry Clay of Kentucky. The central

provision would permit California to enter the Union as a free state. However, to compensate the South, Congress would pass a stronger law for helping slaveowners capture fugitive Negroes. As for the rest of the territory acquired from Mexico, Clay proposed political organization without reference to slavery. Clay's proposal left it to residents of the territories to decide the slavery issue.

But Clay, the master compromiser, did not stop with the issue of slavery in the territory acquired from Mexico. He determined with one great stroke to resolve all disputes that were poisoning relations between North and South. Hence, he proposed to compromise differences over the western boundary of Texas. If Texans would permit the disputed area (which included about half of present-day New Mexico and extended across Colorado into southern Wyoming) to become part of the New Mexico Territory, Congress in return would take over the debt Texas had accumulated during its period of independence.

There was also the matter of slavery and the slave trade in the District of Columbia. Northerners for many years had cringed over the presence of slaves in the federal capital. They had sought abolition of slavery and the slave trade in the District of Columbia. Southerners fought such proposals. Clay proposed a compromise. The slave trade would be ended in the federal capital, but in other respects, the "peculiar institution" would continue unchecked in the capital and would enjoy the protection of the law.

Clay's compromise resolutions triggered one of the most memorable debates in congressional history. The Kentuckian himself, now a frail old man, opened the debate in early February 1850 when he labored up the long stairs leading to the Capitol and delivered an eloquent defense of his measures. When he finished, his admirers swarmed about him to offer congratulations.

Clay's appeal for moderation and compromise failed to move the champion of the South, John C. Calhoun, also old and haggard. Ravaged by tuberculosis (he would be dead within a month), Calhoun on March 4 began his retort to Clay. Then his voice failed, and he had to sit by, his eyes burning with anger, while a fellow southerner read the speech for him. The South Carolinian would accept no compromise. The South must have "equal rights in the acquired territory," and the North must "cease agitation of the slave question." Otherwise the spirit of

COMPROMISE OF 1850

Oregon Territory

Minnesota Territory

Great Lakes

Mich.

Wis.

Me.

Vt.

N.H.

N.Y.

Mass.

Conn. R.I.

Unorganized

Pa.

N.J.

Utah Territory

Iowa

Ind.

Ohio

Md. Del.

Calif.

Ill.

Va.

PACIFIC OCEAN

Mo.

Ky.

N.C.

New Mexico Territory

Indian Territory

Tenn.

S.C.

Ark.

Texas

Miss.

Ala.

Ga.

La.

ATLANTIC OCEAN

Fla.

GULF OF MEXICO

Territories and States Closed to Slavery

Territories and States Open to Slavery

disunion would gather strength and the South would proclaim independence.

Three days later, March 7, Daniel Webster, like Clay and Calhoun a relic of a bygone era, rose in the Senate chamber, paused for a moment, and, after brushing a hand across his forehead, announced in low tones: "I speak today for the preservation of the Union. Hear me for my cause." Although age and illness had muffled the magnificent resonance of Webster's voice, the veteran senator from Massachusetts was still a master speaker. When he finished his long address, which put him on the side of Clay's resolutions, the galleries cheered and clapped and stamped their feet. But spectators had no votes in Congress. When the cheering faded, the gulf between leaders of the North and South remained.

Through the spring of 1850 sentiment for compromise increased across the country, but one obstacle remained. President Taylor did not see why it was necessary to make concessions to the South to get California into the Union. There was talk that the president might exercise the veto if Congress passed Clay's resolutions. Then on July 4 Taylor became ill. "Old Rough and Ready" died on July 9, after only sixteen months in office.

Count the number of states open to slavery and the number closed to slavery. How did the Compromise of 1850 affect the balance of power in Congress? Why did some southerners object to the compromise?

Fillmore Succeeds Taylor

The new president was fifty-year-old Millard Fillmore.

Fillmore was born in 1800 in a log cabin in the Finger Lakes region of western New York. His father was a poor backwoods farmer, and when young Millard was fifteen, the elder Fillmore bound him as an apprentice to a clothmaker. The youth, however, was intelligent and ambitious and spent spare moments attending a one-room country school. He soon fell in love with his pretty red-haired teacher, Abigail Powers, two years his senior. She helped him with his studies and a few years later became his wife. Fillmore, encouraged by Abigail, saved enough money to buy freedom from his apprenticeship. He then took a job teaching school. With savings from his meager teaching salary, he financed the study of law and at twenty-three gained admission to the bar. He went to Buffalo around 1830, became active in politics, and after a term in the New York legislature, won election in 1832 to

Library of Congress

Millard Fillmore was nominated for vice-president in 1848 to complement Zachary Taylor's southern, military background. How did Fillmore's background differ from Taylor's?

in accordance with the doctrine of "popular sovereignty" — that is, each territory would decide on the issue of slavery by voting. The compromise also provided more help for slaveowners in tracking down fugitives. At the same time, the slave trade disappeared in the District of Columbia. The dispute over the Texas boundary was resolved, and Congress took over the Texas debt.

The Compromise of 1850 kept the Union from blowing apart, but many northerners were angry. The trouble was the new Fugitive Slave Law. This inhuman measure compelled northerners to help slaveowners capture runaways and made possible the return to slavery of Negroes who for many years had lived in the North. Ralph Waldo Emerson caught a popular sentiment when he announced: "This filthy enactment was made in the nineteenth century, by people who could read and write. I will not obey it, by God!" The Fugitive Slave Law actually wrecked the political career of Millard Fillmore. So many Whigs arrayed against the president for having supported the legislation that the party's convention in 1852 refused him renomination. The Whigs turned instead to another military hero. Having won the White House with "Old Tippecanoe" and "Old Rough and Ready," they decided to run "Old Fuss and Feathers," General Winfield Scott.

the House of Representatives. After joining with the emerging Whig party, he lost his bid for reelection in 1834 but returned to Congress in 1837, serving until 1843. He lost a campaign for the governorship of New York, then resumed his law practice. In 1847 he won election as comptroller of the state and in 1848 was selected as the vice-presidential candidate to give balance to the Whig ticket.

Taylor had taken a low view of Clay's compromise proposals, but Fillmore did not. In the weeks after Taylor's death, Fillmore, using his patronage power, persuaded wavering Whigs, particularly in the House of Representatives, to endorse the compromise. Additional support came from holders of bonds of the old Texas republic, mostly northeastern businessmen who would benefit if Congress took over the Texas debt. The bond-holders put pressure on northeastern members of Congress to get behind the compromise resolutions. The outcome, in September 1850, was passage of the compromise. California entered the Union as a free state. New Mexico and Utah became federal territories

STUDY GUIDE: Whig party candidate Zachary Taylor was elected president in 1848. The major issue when he took office was whether the territory recently acquired from Mexico would be open to slavery. When Polk had asked Congress for a secret appropriation to end the war and purchase California, the Wilmot Proviso was added to the bill. The proviso, which stated that slavery would never exist in any land purchased from Mexico, did not pass Congress. Then gold was discovered in California. In 1850 Clay offered a compromise. Clay's compromise provided that California would enter the Union as a free state. To compensate the South, Congress would pass stronger laws to help slave-owners capture fugitive slaves. Residents in the rest of the territory acquired from Mexico would decide the slavery issue for themselves. Taylor died after sixteen months in office. He was succeeded by Millard Fillmore. Clay's compromise was passed in 1850. Northerners were angry over the Fugitive Slave Law, a consequence of the compromise.

Franklin Pierce was the "dark horse" candidate in the election of 1852. Although little known outside his home state of New Hampshire, he was elected over General Winfield Scott, a national hero. How can this be explained?

FRANKLIN PIERCE

In 1852 the Democrats balloted forty-eight times before settling on a presidential candidate, Franklin Pierce of New Hampshire. Largely because the Democrats seemed more committed to the Compromise of 1850 than did the Whigs—and a majority of Americans favored the compromise—Pierce the following autumn edged Scott in popular votes and overwhelmed him in the electoral college.

Franklin Pierce was born in 1804 at Hillsboro, New Hampshire. His father was a veteran of the War of Independence and a prominent Republican politician who eventually served two terms as governor of New Hampshire. The Pierces were prosperous and young Franklin received his early training at exclusive preparatory schools. When he was fifteen he enrolled at Bowdoin College in Maine where he became acquainted with such promising young men as Henry Wadsworth Longfellow and Nathaniel Haw-

thorne. (The friendship with Hawthorne endured and, when the famous writer died in 1864, Pierce was at his bedside.) Pierce was a handsome and personable young man who had a host of friends.

After graduating from Bowdoin he studied law, entered politics, and during his father's second term as governor won election to the New Hampshire legislature. He went to Washington as a member of the House of Representatives in 1833, served two terms, and in 1836, at the age of thirty-two, won a seat in the Senate. On Capitol Hill he became known as an unswerving apostle of Andrew Jackson and a foe of abolitionist agitation. Because his wife, a sickly woman, despised Washington and usually stayed at home in New Hampshire and because the family needed a larger income, Pierce resigned from the Senate in 1842 and resumed his law practice in Concord.

In 1845 Pierce rejected an offer to be attorney general in the cabinet of President Polk, but the following year, upon outbreak of the Mexican War, accepted appointment as a brigadier general of volunteers. Without military talent or experience, Pierce received his commission because he was a faithful Democrat. In Mexico he served under General Scott and compiled a respectable record. After the war he declined to return to politics and when queried about the presidency said that the office "would be utterly repugnant to my tastes and wishes." Still, when it appeared at the Democratic convention of 1852 that none of the "front-runners"—Stephen A. Douglas, Lewis Cass, and James Buchanan—could muster the two-thirds vote necessary to win the nomination, his friends promoted him as an ideal compromise. He was a northerner who had great sympathy for the South, always had been a staunch Democrat, and had a respectable war record. He was, moreover, a good orator, had not been an aggressive politician, and had few political enemies.

At first, it appeared that Pierce would establish his presidential reputation in foreign affairs. He continued efforts, begun by Fillmore, to break through the isolation of Japan. Accordingly, early in 1854 Commodore Matthew C. Perry steered a squadron of warships into Yedo (Tokyo) Bay. Acting with tact and firmness, he persuaded the Japanese to open their doors to American trade.

Slavery meanwhile had gone into eclipse as a political issue and Pierce hoped that things would remain that way. Such hope was vain. Slave-catchers roaming the northern countryside

Commodore Matthew Perry used tact and a respect for Japanese customs, as well as an occasional show of force, to persuade the Japanese to trade with the West. Here he is pictured exercising his troops before the emperor's commissioners.

Library of Congress

kept the question before the northern conscience. If that was not enough, there was the book by Harriet Beecher Stowe, *Uncle Tom's Cabin, or Life Among the Lowly,* published in 1852. Although it rested in part on the author's lively imagination (she never had visited the South), the book sold 300,000 copies the first year and hardened northerners against the South's slave system.

Still, it was not fugitive slaves or Uncle Tom that precipitated the next national crisis. It was a railroad.

A few Americans in the late 1840s had begun to talk of a railroad reaching across the western half of the continent, linking the Mississippi Valley with the Pacific. Then came admission of California to the Union, making such a railroad a national necessity. However, a transcontinental rail line would be too vast a project for private enterprise, unless subsidized by the federal government. Thus, by the time Pierce became president, the matter had captured the attention of Congress.

The Gadsden Purchase

The first question was location of the "transcontinental." When Congress in 1853 authorized surveys of the four most likely routes, it seemed that a decision was at hand. The odds favored a southern route—one leading from New Orleans across Texas to Yuma and San Diego. Why? Because the most influential man in the Pierce administration was Secretary of War Jefferson Davis of Mississippi, who wanted the southern route. When it became evident that a southern road would need to pass through territory in

northern Mexico, Davis persuaded Pierce to purchase the necessary land. Negotiated by James Gadsden of South Carolina, the Gadsden Purchase (1853) paid Mexico $10 million for 45,000 square miles of desert (the southern edge of present-day Arizona and New Mexico).

STUDY GUIDE: Democratic candidate Franklin Pierce was elected president in 1852. Admission of California to the Union made a transcontinental railroad necessary. A southern route was favored, but the road would have to pass through Mexican territory. The Gadsden Purchase of 1853 brought this land into the United States.

THE KANSAS-NEBRASKA BILL

Then into the picture strode Stephen A. Douglas, senator from Illinois. Known as "the Little Giant"—he stood just a bit over five feet in height—Douglas was one of the shrewdest and most persuasive men in Washington, and he wanted the transcontinental railroad to follow the central route, terminating perhaps in Chicago and, incidentally, also passing through areas where he had speculated in land. To achieve his end, Douglas needed first to persuade Davis and the southerners away from support of the southern route. Second, he needed to arrange to organize the Great Plains into federal territories —for a government to protect settlers and property was a precondition of any western railroad. Douglas saw that he could resolve both parts of the problem with one stroke. The territory he sought to organize lay north of the Missouri Compromise line and hence was closed to slavery under the legislation of 1820. He would offer a bill to organize the area without reference to slavery, leaving it to the people— "popular sovereignty"—to decide for themselves whether they wanted the "peculiar institution." President Pierce quickly fell in with Douglas's plan.

The Douglas calculation proved correct—insofar as it applied to the South. The opportunity to break the Missouri Compromise and open new territory to slavery excited the southerners and they supported the Illinois senator's Kansas-Nebraska bill to create two territories in the Great Plains, Kansas and Nebraska. Nebraska doubtless would receive most of its settlers from Iowa and become a free state; Kansas, lying west of Missouri, probably would become a slave state. But Douglas was badly mistaken in his assumption that the North, to gain the terminus of the railroad, would quietly accept repeal of the Missouri Compromise. The Kansas-Nebraska Bill touched off a violent reaction in the free states. Only by exerting heavy political pressure were Pierce and Douglas able to bring enough northern Democrats into line to secure passage of the legislation (May 1854).

The North continued to seethe and the Fugitive Slave Law became virtually unenforceable as northerners openly defied it. At the same time there were political stirrings. Antislavery Whigs decided that the time had come for new political arrangements and in 1854 several locales—including Ripon, Wisconsin, and Jackson, Michigan—organized into groups which in an astonishingly short time came together as the Republican party. The object of the new party was to prevent expansion of slavery. As the Republicans gathered steam, the Whig party literally fell apart. Other northerners meanwhile were organizing companies to encourage and aid antislavery people to migrate to Kansas and rescue the territory from the slavemongers. The outcome was almost civil war.

"Bleeding Kansas"

In 1855 Kansas attempted to carry out the mandate of "popular sovereignty," but results were chaos. In an election accompanied by fraud and violence, proslavery people gained control of the territorial legislature and enacted laws protecting slavery. Antislavery colonists denounced the legislature, drew up the Topeka constitution, and applied for admission to the Union as a free state. Confusion and bloodshed continued in "bleeding Kansas" until late in the 1850s when the antislavery forces gained the initiative and outlawed slavery in the territory. (In the first year of the Civil War, 1861, Kansas gained admission to the Union.)

STUDY GUIDE: Stephen A. Douglas wanted a central route for the transcontinental railroad. This central route would cut through the

This wood engraving of the Kansas constitutional convention appeared in *Leslie's* in 1855. The convention's unsuccessful attempt at Popular sovereignty further antagonized both antislavery and proslavery forces.

Library of Congress

Great Plains, which had to be organized into federal territories to get government protection. This land was closed to slavery under the Missouri Compromise. To gain southern support Douglas proposed to offer the land without reference to slavery, leaving the decision to the people: popular sovereignty. Douglas's Kansas-Nebraska Bill meant repeal of the Missouri Compromise. It touched off violent reaction in the free states. Antislavery Whigs organized a new Republican party. In 1855 Kansas enacted proslavery legislation. Antislavery settlers denounced the legislature and applied for admission to the Union as a free state.

NORTH-SOUTH TENSIONS INCREASE

During the struggle for Kansas, other developments increased tension between North and South, including the Ostend Manifesto. Three American envoys to European countries (including James Buchanan) met in the town of Ostend in Belgium and announced in October 1854 that the United States would have a right to annex the island of Cuba, a colony of Spain, if the revolutionary movement in the island came under Negro control. Should Negroes take over, Cuba would be "Africanized and become a second St. Domingo, with all its attendant horrors to the white race, and suffer the flames to extend to our own neighboring shores, seriously to endanger or actually to consume the fair fabric of our Union." Northerners were shocked. In their view the Ostend Manifesto seemed a crude attempt by the Pierce administration to add a new slave territory. The emerging Republican party of course capitalized on such sentiments, although Pierce denounced the manifesto.

Spring 1856 brought another incident that inflamed North-South relations. It occurred after Senator Charles Sumner of Massachusetts delivered a powerful address entitled "The Crime Against Kansas" in which he scalded assorted politicians, including Senator Andrew P. Butler of South Carolina. Three days later Representative Preston Brooks, a nephew of Butler, came upon Sumner as he sat at his desk in the Senate chamber. Using a cane, Brooks thrashed the Massachusetts senator until he slumped to the floor unconscious. Replicas of Brooks's cane "sold like hot cakes" in the South. In the North the scholarly Sumner (who did not return to his

place in the Senate for several years) became a hero and martyr.

The Election of 1856

A few days later the Democrats met at Cincinnati in national convention. President Pierce hoped for renomination, but his support of the Kansas-Nebraska bill had eroded his support in the North. Hence, after seventeen ballots, the party nominated James Buchanan for president. Buchanan, a Pennsylvanian, had strength in the North. He also had appeal in the South, for like Pierce he was a "doughface" — a northerner with southern sympathies. And he had endeared himself to southerners by signing the Ostend Manifesto. In their platform, the Democrats endorsed the Compromise of 1850 and the Kansas-Nebraska Act.

The new Republican party held its first national convention two weeks later in Philadelphia. With the zeal of crusaders the Republicans lashed out against slavery in federal territories, denounced the Ostend Manifesto, and urged admission of Kansas as a free state. Remembering the Whig party's success with such military heroes as Harrison and Taylor, they nominated the western explorer and soldier, Colonel John C. Frémont, "the Pathfinder of the West."

There was a third contestant in the election of 1856, the American or Know-Nothing party. This party originated in fear of the "Popish peril" — the idea that Catholic immigrants, mainly Irish and German, threatened American institutions. Anti-Catholics first came together in such secret societies as the Order of the Star-Spangled Banner and, when questioned by outsiders, responded: "I know nothing." The Know-Nothing societies organized the American party in 1855 and the following year nominated Millard Fillmore for president. Then the party ran into trouble. Southerners managed a proslavery platform, whereupon most northern members excused themselves and joined up with the Republicans. It should be noted that what remained of the Whig party — which was not much — also nominated Fillmore, giving the New Yorker the honor of being the last Whig candidate for president.

In the South the Republicans of course had no support and in the election Buchanan carried every state below the Mason-Dixon line except Maryland, which gave its eight electoral votes to

Fillmore. In the North the Democrats attacked the so-called Black Republicans and warned that Republican ideas would disrupt the Union. The Democratic appeal brought five free states to Buchanan's column, but Frémont, rousing northerners with the horror of "bleeding Kansas," carried the remaining eleven. Buchanan thus won in the electoral college, 174–114–8.

After the election the Know-Nothing party disappeared, but the Republican party remained and continued to grow. Unlike the Democratic party, which had strength in every state of the Union, the new party represented the ideas of one section. As they surveyed the political landscape, thoughtful men asked: what will the South do if this purely northern party ever gains control of the national government?

STUDY GUIDE: The Ostend Manifesto contributed to North-South tensions. It proposed that the United States would have a right to annex Cuba if the revolutionary movement on the island came under Negro control. Northerners viewed this as an attempt by Pierce's administration to add a new slave territory. In the election of 1856 Democratic candidate James Buchanan was elected president.

JAMES BUCHANAN

The eldest son in a family of eleven children, James Buchanan was born in 1791 in a log cabin near the town of Mercersburg in the mountains of south-central Pennsylvania. His parents were Scotch-Irish Presbyterians (the elder Buchanan had immigrated from Northern Ireland in 1783). An intelligent and enterprising man, Buchanan's father prospered as proprietor of a frontier trading post and a speculator in land. At the age of sixteen "Jimmie" Buchanan enrolled at Dickinson College in Carlisle, Pennsylvania, was expelled because of mischief and insubordination, but after pledging good behavior returned to the school. In 1809 he graduated at the head of his class. Deciding on a legal career, he studied for three years and in 1812 opened a law office. Then, in summer 1812, the country went to war with Great Britain. A staunch patriot, Buchanan volunteered for military service and saw brief combat during the British attack on Baltimore in 1814. After the war he resumed his law practice and became such an outstanding legal practi-

James Buchanan approved of the Dred Scott decision and "popular sovereignty" for Kansas.

tioner that before the age of thirty he had amassed a sizable fortune.

Such a gifted lawyer easily gravitated to politics and after two years in the Pennsylvania legislature he served five terms in Congress (1820-31). He started his political career as a moderate Federalist, moved into the Republican party and when the Republicans broke into factions in the latter 1820s he aligned himself with the Democratic (Jacksonian) wing of the party. In 1832 President Jackson showed his gratitude by appointing Buchanan minister to Russia.

Next the Pennsylvania legislature elected him to the Senate and in 1835 he began ten years of service in the upper chamber of Congress. He declined an offer to be attorney general in the cabinet of President Van Buren, but accepted appointment as secretary of state in the administration of President Polk. His outstanding accomplishment was negotiation of the treaty that ended the Oregon boundary dispute with Great Britain.

By the mid-1840s Buchanan had become one of the notables of the Democratic party and in 1848 and again in 1852 he unsuccessfully sought the party's presidential nomination. Frustrated, he retired to his estate near Lancaster, Pennsylvania. When Franklin Pierce took the presidential oath in 1853 it seemed that Buchanan's political career—he was sixty-two years old—was

[135]

at an end. Then Pierce asked him to serve as minister to Great Britain, a stroke of luck, for he was out of the country during the sound and fury over Kansas. In part because he carried no scars from that controversy James Buchanan received the Democratic presidential nomination in 1856.

When "Old Buck" took office as the fifteenth president in March 1857, the American nation was pulsating with activity. Railroads were darting out across the countryside, factories were springing up, the agricultural domain was becoming larger each day. By rail, wagon, and flatboat great numbers of people continued to move westward. A comparison of the federal censuses of 1850 and 1860 would reveal that every state in the Union was gaining population at the expense of its neighbor to the east and through the ports on the Atlantic seaboard immigrants from Europe were arriving in substantial numbers.

National politics, unfortunately, did not present such an optimistic picture. The nagging question of slavery in federal territories remained unresolved. Until somebody found a solution acceptable to both North and South the political fabric of the country would be in jeopardy. Still, when Buchanan was inaugurated he felt no worry about the great national problem, for he knew that the Supreme Court was about to hand down a decision which he believed would put the entire matter to rest. In his inaugural address he announced that such a decision was forthcoming, pledged personal support of the decision, and urged "all good citizens" to do likewise. Two days later, on March 6, 1857, the Supreme Court released its verdict in the case of *Dred Scott* v. *Sanford*.

The Dred Scott Decision

In 1834 a Negro slave, Dred Scott, had accompanied his master, an army surgeon, from Saint Louis, Missouri to Rock Island in Illinois, a free state where they lived two years. From Illinois the two men traveled to Wisconsin Territory, where slavery was prohibited under the Missouri Compromise of 1820. After two years they returned to Missouri. Seven years later, in 1845, Scott sued for his freedom on the ground of temporary residence in a free state and a free territory. The case reached the Supreme Court in the 1850s.

In the opinion customarily cited for the majority (in those days each justice handed down a

separate opinion), Chief Justice Roger B. Taney (pronounced "Tawney") declared that Scott, as a Negro, was not an American citizen and thus had no right to sue in a federal court. That judgment squelched Scott's case. But Taney, a native of Maryland who favored slavery, went further. He declared that Scott's residence in Wisconsin Territory had not altered his status, for the Missouri Compromise prohibiting slavery in federal territory north of the line 36° 30' had violated the Fifth Amendment to the Constitution. The amendment provided that no person "shall . . . be deprived . . . of property, without due process of law."

Taney, in short, had accepted the time-honored southern view that federal territories belonged to all the states and a citizen of any state had a right to settle in any territory and take with him all his personal property, including slaves. By this decision neither Congress nor a territorial legislature had authority to prohibit slavery in a federal territory. Therefore, Douglas's "middle way" of letting the people of a territory decide the question for themselves—"popular sovereignty"—also was eliminated.

Buchanan's confidence that most citizens would submit meekly to the logic of the Supreme Court proved ill-founded, for the North erupted. To northerners the Dred Scott decision was another example of the "slave conspiracy" that allegedly dominated the government in Washington. They saw, moreover, that, armed with this decision, the forces of slavery would establish their abominable institution all across the American West. When western slave states appeared, the slavery interests would thus have a stranglehold on Congress and probably the executive branch as well. Then who could tell what might happen? Probably the slavemongers would set about to eliminate prohibitions on bonded servitude in the northeastern states and thus make the entire country a giant slavocracy.

STUDY GUIDE: Soon after James Buchanan took office in 1857, the Dred Scott decision was announced. Scott, a Negro slave, sued for his freedom after having lived in a free state and a free territory. The Supreme Court declared that Scott was not an American citizen and had no right to sue in a federal court. Many Northerners were angered by the court's decision.

THE EMERGENCE OF LINCOLN

Fifteen months after the Dred Scott decision, in June 1858, Republicans in Illinois convened at Springfield to nominate a candidate to contest Stephen A. Douglas's seat in the Senate. Many orators paraded to the speaker's rostrum and flailed away against the evils of slavery and the Democratic party, but only one man made more than a fleeting impression on delegates. Predicting that the slavery issue would boil into a national crisis, he announced that " 'a house divided against itself cannot stand.' I believe this government cannot endure permanently half slave and half free. I do not expect the Union to be dissolved; I do not expect the house to fall; but I do expect it will cease to be divided. It will become all one thing, or all the other." Unknown outside Illinois, the speaker was Abraham Lincoln and the convention nominated him for senator.

In a biographical sketch in 1860 Lincoln wrote that "I was born Feb. 12, 1809, in Hardin County, Kentucky. My parents were both born in Virginia, of undistinguished families—second families, perhaps I should say. My mother, who died in my tenth year, was of a family of the name of Hanks. . . . My paternal grandfather, Abraham Lincoln, emigrated to Kentucky about 1781 or 1782, where a year or two later he was killed by Indians, not in battle, but by stealth, when he was laboring to open a farm in the forest. . . . My father, at the death of his father, was about six years of age, and he grew up literally without education. He removed from Kentucky to what is now Spencer county, Indiana, in my eighth year. . . . It was a wild region, with many bears and other wild animals still in the woods. There I grew up. There were some schools, so called; but no qualification was ever required of a teacher beyond *'readin, writin, and cipherin,'* to the Rule of Three. . . . Of course when I came of age I did not know much. . . . I could read, write, and cipher . . . but that was all." Of his physical appearance Lincoln wrote that "I am, in height, six feet, four inches, nearly; lean in flesh, weighing, on an average, one hundred and eighty pounds; dark complexion, with coarse black hair, and grey eyes—no other marks or brands recollected."

The log cabin in which Lincoln was born was a crude building. It had one room, a dirt floor, and a fireplace of logs held together with clay. At night the family bedded down on rough planks attached to the wall. Such surroundings would seem to indicate that Lincoln's father was a ne'er-do-well. This was not the case. Thomas Lincoln always owned horses, had good credit, and on one occasion acted as appraiser of an estate. That a short time after Abraham's birth he could pay $300 for a Kentucky farm was evidence of thrift and energy. Unfortunately the Lincolns, father and son, were sometimes at odds and the bond between them was never strong. After Abe achieved national prominence, it was easy for people to conclude that a father who could not get along with such a talented son must have been a "no account."

After the War of 1812, Thomas Lincoln, like many other Americans in those years, looked to the setting sun and in 1816 led his family down and across the Ohio to southwestern Indiana. Life was hard in the Hoosier wilderness. Clearing enough land to put in a crop was a back-breaking task, and during the first year the family lived in a lean-to fashioned from limbs. In 1818 an epidemic of "milk sickness" swept the region. Ignoring the risks, Nancy Hanks Lincoln, a typical woman of the American frontier—pious, long-suffering, illiterate—ministered to neighbors suffering the ravages of the disease, came down with it herself, and died. Her husband nailed together a coffin and he, their three children, and a handful of neighbors laid her to rest on a shaded hillside. The following year the elder Lincoln went back to Kentucky on business and returned with a new wife, a kindly and gentle widow, Sarah Bush Johnston, who brought her own three children and a wagonload of furniture to the Lincoln cabin. Young Abraham adored his stepmother and she returned his love. He was referring to her many years later when he said: "God bless my mother; all that I am or ever hope to be, I owe to her."

During the years in Indiana Abe Lincoln grew to manhood. Like most frontier youths he spent endless hours swinging an ax and trailing a plow. But unlike most boys of the wilderness he had a compulsion to learn and walked all over Spencer County in all kinds of weather borrowing and returning the books of neighbors. His stepmother (who, one may note, lived to see her son installed in the White House) later told the well-known story of young Abraham sprawled in front of the fireplace, ciphering on boards, then shaving away the markings with a knife so he could cipher some more. Still, it was not all work and study. Tall and muscular, Abe was a personable lad, had a special talent for wrestling, perhaps the favorite sport on the frontier, and delighted friends by mimicking people he had observed. He was also a robust teller of tall tales. Otherwise he was a gentle youth, showed unusual tenderness toward animals, and was always sensitive to the feelings of other people. He seldom attended church services but read the Bible and took a reverent view of religion.

Shortly after Abe turned twenty-one, in 1830, the Lincolns loaded their belongings on two wagons and moved two hundred miles across icy creeks and rivers to the banks of the Sangamon in central Illinois. A year later Abraham helped navigate a flatboat down the Mississippi to New Orleans—his second flatboat voyage to the Louisiana city. On his return he settled in the village of New Salem, twenty miles northwest of Springfield.

A short time later the Illinois countryside was taken up with excitement over the Black Hawk War, and young Lincoln signed up with the local militia. Although he did not smoke, drink, or use profanity, the men of his company, most of whom were tough-talking, elected him their captain (probably because of his warm personality and skill as a wrestler). He encountered none of Black Hawk's warriors but later wrote that he had fought many "bloody battles with the musquetoes." Returning to New Salem, he managed a mill, kept a store that went bankrupt, acted as village postmaster, and, as every schoolboy knows, did some rail-splitting. (At one point he paid for a pair of trousers by splitting 400 rails for each yard of cloth.) Although a jack-of-all-trades, Lincoln preferred to work with his mind, which led to his study of law. After gaining admission to the bar (1837), he moved to Springfield, established a reputation as a lawyer, and eventually accumulated a modest fortune.

Lincoln as a youth tended to avoid girls. There apparently is no truth in the time-honored story that at New Salem Lincoln fell in love with Ann Rutledge, the comely daughter of the village tavern-keeper, only to suffer a broken heart when Ann died of typhoid.

About 1840 Lincoln became acquainted with an intelligent and spirited young lady from Lexington, Kentucky, Mary Todd, who was visiting a sister in Springfield. Romance blossomed, but it was an on-again-off-again affair until autumn 1842 when the couple were married. Mrs. Lincoln proved quite unlike her even-tempered husband. Her anger rose quickly and when agitated she had a lashing tongue. Still, she calmed quickly and was not the nagging wife that writers have suggested. One should add that Lincoln's untidiness and casual ways about the house gave her some provocation. If erratic, she could be warm and gentle, was devoted to her husband, and eventually presented him with four sons ("dear codgers" he called them).

Lincoln in Politics

Meanwhile, Lincoln had gone into politics and in 1834 began eight years of unbroken service in the Illinois legislature. An admirer of Henry Clay, he aligned himself with the Whig party and consistently spoke out against the ideas of Andrew Jackson and the Democrats. Although his service in the legislature was not distinguished—his major accomplishment was helping to engineer movement of the state capital from Vandalia to Springfield—he nonetheless learned about the political arts of persuasion, compromise, and maneuver.

Lincoln had long kept an eye on Washington and in 1846 he achieved an ambition by winning a seat in Congress. His term coincided with the Mexican War and he attracted some publicity by introducing "spot resolutions" aimed at embarrassing President Polk by forcing an admission that Mexico, not the United States, had jurisdiction over the "spot" where the first blood of the war had been spilled. By previous arrangement with another Whig of his district, Lincoln did not seek reelection in 1848. It was just as well, for his stand against the war was not popular in Illinois and he probably would have lost. Back in Springfield he returned to his law practice but retained ties with Whig politicians in Illinois. In the 1850s he began to build a reputation—despite a high-pitched voice—as an orator. It seemed that his political fortunes were looking up, and indeed his law partner later wrote that "his ambition was a little engine that knew no rest." When the Whig party fell apart, Lincoln easily made the transition to the new Republican party. Then came the nomination, in 1858, to oppose Douglas for the Senate.

Lincoln's views were typically Republican. He favored a protective tariff, more liberal land policy, and a Pacific railway. But his main interest was slavery. With fervor (resulting, he said, from observations during his second flatboat trip to New Orleans) he proclaimed the party position against extension of slavery to federal territories. He was not, one should note, an abolitionist, not a champion of Negro equality. Few northerners were. He believed the black

man had a right to freedom but opposed Negro citizenship. In the campaign against Douglas, Lincoln said he did not favor making voters or jurors of Negroes, or qualifying them to hold public office or intermarry with whites. He said that in a racially mixed society one race had to have the superior position and "I as much as any other man am in favor of having the superior position assigned to the white race."

The Lincoln-Douglas Debates

As was common in the nineteenth century, the two senatorial candidates, Lincoln and Douglas, agreed to a series of debates and through summer and early autumn 1858 they moved across Illinois from town to town, setting forth their views. The central issue was slavery. Lincoln called human bondage a moral evil. He was willing to tolerate the abominable institution in the South but insisted that it must not spill over to the federal territories. Lincoln thus urged defiance of the Supreme Court's decision in the Dred Scott case. Douglas refused to discuss the morality of slavery, standing on the position that "if each state will only agree to mind its own business, and let its neighbors alone . . . this republic can exist forever divided into free and slave states."

Most voters in Illinois shared Douglas's sentiments of "live and let live." But what about

Abraham Lincoln and Stephen Douglas engaged in a series of debates during a campaign for election to the United States Senate in 1858. The debate shown here took place in Charleston, Illinois.

slavery in the territories? The Dred Scott decision had destroyed Douglas's pet idea of popular sovereignty, for according to the Supreme Court a territorial legislature could not prohibit slavery. Was Douglas willing to accept the decision and risk eventual control of national affairs by the "slave power"? Or like Lincoln would he repudiate the decision? Douglas seemed caught in a dilemma. The Scott decision had come from a Supreme Court dominated by Democrats and had support of the Democratic administration in Washington. If he spoke out against the decision and urged defiance, he would alienate himself from leaders of the party. This would ruin his chances of becoming the Democratic candidate for president in 1860. If he failed to stand against the decision, he risked loss of the election.

Seeing Douglas's difficulty, in the debate at Freeport Lincoln pressed his opponent with the question: "Can the people of a United States territory, in any lawful way . . . exclude slavery from its limits prior to the formation of a State constitution?" Douglas apparently had no choice but to grab one of the horns of the dilemma and speak out for or against the Dred Scott decision.

"The Little Giant," however, had anticipated the question and given it careful thought. His response became known as the Freeport Doctrine. The Senator explained: "It matters not what way the Supreme Court may hereafter decide as to the abstract question whether slavery may or may not go into a Territory under the Constitution, the people have the lawful means to introduce it or exclude it as they please, for the reason that slavery cannot exist a day or an hour anywhere, unless it is supported by local police regulations." In a word, slavery required legal protection. Only local legislatures had authority to establish such protection. Thus if the people of a territory opposed slavery, the territorial legislature, reflecting their wishes, could keep bonded servitude from the territory by refusing to enact laws for its protection.

The Freeport Doctrine satisfied many doubtful people in Illinois and the state legislature returned Douglas to the Senate. Still, Lincoln had established himself as a leader in the new Republican party. The skill and personal magnetism which he exhibited in the debates carried his reputation far beyond the borders of his home state.

STUDY GUIDE: During the Illinois senatorial campaign of 1858, Abraham Lincoln met Stephen A. Douglas in a series of debates. The central issue was slavery. In one of these debates, Douglas was forced to state his position on the Dred Scott decision. His reply—the Freeport Doctrine—was that slavery required legal protection and only local legislatures could establish such protection. Thus people could keep slavery out of their territory by refusing to enact laws for its protection.

THE CRISIS DEEPENS

Other events strained the fragile bond between North and South in the late 1850s. There was the increasing support in the South for repeal of the law which had prohibited the importation of slaves after January 1, 1808. In spite of the law, the foreign slave trade never had stopped, and in the 1850s slavers deposited many thousands of Africans on the shores of the United States. Much of the profit went to New England shipping interests.

The South was interested in striking down bar-

riers to the overseas trade in Negroes because the supply of slave laborers was not keeping pace with the extension of the cotton domain. There were not enough slaves to meet current needs of southern planters, much less a surplus to exploit the vast areas of the Great Plains and the Far West which had been opened to slave owners by the Kansas-Nebraska Act and the Dred Scott decision. If there was no evil attached to buying slaves in Virginia and transporting them to Louisiana—so reasoned William L. Yancey of Alabama—"why is it not right to buy them in Cuba, Brazil, or Africa?"

While the possibility of renewing the horrors of the overseas slave trade infuriated citizens of New England and the Middle West, southerners felt irritation over happenings in the North. In particular there was the North's continuing defiance of the Fugitive Slave Law. On numerous occasions abolitionist mobs roughed up federal marshals attempting to return fugitives to southern masters. The Underground Railroad stepped up its activity. Northern state legislatures across the North passed "personal liberty laws" preventing federal marshals from using local jails when transporting fugitives, directing state judges to take no part in enforcing the statute, and permitting jury trials and writs of habeas corpus for Negroes accused of being runaway slaves. A climax came when the Supreme Court of Wisconsin declared the Fugitive Slave Law unconstitutional and ordered release of a man convicted of harboring an escaped Negro. Chief Justice Taney was furious and assailed the Wisconsin decision, but through the North it brought feelings of satisfaction.

John Brown's Raid

Next came the affair of John Brown. A veteran abolitionist, Brown had assisted antislavery groups during the struggle in Kansas. He supervised the lynching of five proslavery Kansans (the "Pottawatomie massacre") in retaliation for the "sack of Lawrence" by proslavery elements and worked for the Underground Railroad in Missouri. Then, in 1859, he implemented his boldest action. He would put guns in the hands of slaves who in turn would use them to obtain their freedom. The key to the plan was guns and to secure weapons the fanatical Brown led eighteen men, five of them Negroes, against the federal arsenal at Harpers Ferry, Virginia.

It was mid-October 1859. Before Brown and his men could complete their mission, word of the raid swept the countryside and nearby militia units swarmed into Harpers Ferry, compelling the invaders to take refuge in the engine house of the armory. Before many hours had passed, more militiamen arrived and also a contingent of federal troops under command of Colonel Robert E. Lee. Brown and his men fought savagely and when Lee's men finally forced their way into the engine house only Brown and four of his men were alive.

A week later Brown went on trial at Charles Town, Virginia, and in December 1859 died on the gallows. But upon receiving sentence he had said: "Now, if it is deemed necessary that I should forfeit my life for the furtherance of the ends of justice, and mingle my blood further with the blood of my children and with the blood of millions in the slave country whose rights are disregarded by wicked, cruel, and unjust enactments, I say, let it be done." These words electrified millions of people across the northern half of the country.

A few months later the nation turned to the election of 1860. Meeting in Chicago, the Republicans repudiated John Brown and pledged not to interfere with slavery in the South. But they stood firm against slavery in the territories. They also reaffirmed the party's support of the old Whig principles of tariff protection and internal improvements at public expense and put themselves behind the idea of free homesteads on public land for settlers. When the time came to nominate a presidential candidate, the delegates, on the third ballot, named Abraham Lincoln. Republicans had no idea of the depth of Lincoln's character or the range of his talents. When they put him at the head of their ticket they were looking at other attributes: his oratorical skill, log-cabin birth, residence in a key state (Illinois), and lack of enemies from previous political wars.

The Democratic Party Splits

The Democrats met at Charleston and within a few days their party blew apart. The issue was slavery. Led by Jefferson Davis, southerners demanded a platform plank demanding congressional legislation to protect slavery in territories (thus undercutting Douglas's Freeport Doctrine). The South also wanted a declaration that slavery was not a moral evil. Northern Democrats recoiled, a senator from Ohio declaring: "Gentlemen of the South, you mistake us—you mistake us—we will not do it." Delegates of eight states

of the lower South then stalked from the convention, whereupon those who remained went to Baltimore and nominated Stephen A. Douglas for president. Because his Kansas-Nebraska Bill had failed to bring slavery to Kansas, and because his Freeport Doctrine offered a way to circumvent the Dred Scott decision, "the Little Giant" was not acceptable to the South. Southern Democrats held a separate convention and nominated John C. Breckinridge of Kentucky for the presidency.

There was a fourth presidential candidate in 1860, John Bell of Tennessee. Bell was the nominee of the National Constitutional Union party, hastily put together in 1860. Ignoring slavery, the new party announced that it stood for the Constitution, Union, and enforcement of the law (including of course the Fugitive Slave Law).

Since Breckinridge and Bell were assured of most votes below the Mason-Dixon line, Lincoln needed to sweep the North to win the election. If Douglas carried a few northern states, no candidate would muster a majority in the electoral college. In that event the election would pass to the House of Representatives, where the Democrats probably would be able to elect one of their men—a proslavery man, no doubt—to the presidency. The campaign in the North was heated. Douglas emphasized that Lincoln's election probably would drive the South from the Union. Republicans retorted that a Democratic victory would mean the carving of federal territories into slave states, ruining chances of northern laborers for free homesteads in the West. Republicans also reminded northern workers of frequent southern sneers about wage labor.

Republican tactics proved sound. Although Douglas was a close second in popular balloting, he carried only one state, Missouri. Lincoln won every free state, including the two states recently admitted to the Union, Minnesota (1858) and Oregon (1859). The result was a comfortable majority in the electoral college. Breckinridge carried all the cotton states plus North Carolina, Delaware, and Maryland. Bell won Virginia, Kentucky, and Tennessee.

SECESSION

Leaders of the lower South now prepared to take their states out of the Union; they would not tolerate a Republican president. The first move came, appropriately, in South Carolina, the state of Calhoun and the nullification crisis of 1832, for more than thirty years the center of state rights agitation. The South Carolina legislature summoned a convention which, on December 20, 1860, declared that "the union now subsisting between South Carolina and other States, under the name of 'The United States of America,' is hereby dissolved." In the next six weeks Alabama, Florida, Mississippi, Georgia, Louisiana, and Texas also adopted ordinances of secession. Delegates of the seven states then met at Montgomery, Alabama, and on February 8, 1861, approved a constitution for the Confederate States of America. The document gave wide latitude to the states (a handicap in the coming war with the North) and set up elaborate safeguards to prevent the general government from meddling with slavery. Next day the Confederate Congress elected Jefferson Davis president.

In Washington, President Buchanan wrung his hands and did nothing. By now seventy years old and wearied by the sectional crisis. "Old Buck" could not face up to the prospect of touching off a civil war by asserting federal authority in the lower South. If he remained quiet, perhaps passions would cool, a compromise appear, and the difficulty pass. In any event, the problem would be Lincoln's after March 4, 1861.

Buchanan hoped for compromise, and so did many other people. In the North and "border states" of the upper South the hope lingered into April 1861. The most important compromise proposal came in December 1860 from Senator John J. Crittenden of Kentucky. Crittenden's formula had three points: (1) a constitutional amendment forbidding the federal government to interfere with slavery in the southern states; (2) legislation to compensate owners of fugitive slaves not recovered; and (3) revival and extension to the Pacific of the old Missouri Compromise line as a dividing line between slavery and freedom in the West. Lincoln and the Repub-

licans had no objection to the first two points but rejected the third. Revival of the Missouri Compromise line would deny their cardinal principle of no slavery in federal territories. The "Crittenden compromise"—and all subsequent compromise proposals—failed.

Lincoln is Inaugurated

The debate still continued as Lincoln rode up Pennsylvania Avenue to the Capitol on March 4, 1861, and took the oath as sixteenth president of the United States. Although the sun shone brightly, a chilling wind whipped through the federal city, the atmosphere was solemn, and the scaffolding and derricks around the partially completed Capitol dome seemed symbolic of the disordered state of the Republic. The new president did not flinch at the national crisis. In his high-pitched voice he announced that secession was illegal and that he would carry out responsibilities assigned him by the Constitution.

Despite the brave words of his inaugural address, Lincoln moved cautiously in asserting federal authority in the lower South lest he drive states of the upper South—notably Virginia, Maryland, and Kentucky—into the arms of the Confederacy. He knew that in these latter states there was strong sentiment for the Union. He also knew that for more than a half-century they had absorbed the state rights ideas of the Kentucky and Virginia Resolutions of 1798 and would look critically on federal coercion of the lower South. If forced to make a choice, he feared, leaders of the upper South might display deeper attachment to state rights than to the Union.

FORT SUMTER

Still, Lincoln could not delay indefinitely and in early April 1861 he decided that the moment had come "to fish or cut bait." Forcing the issue was the situation at two federal posts, Fort Pickens at Pensacola and Fort Sumter in Charleston harbor. These were the only federal installations in the lower South that had not surrendered to the Confederates. The problem was simple. The two posts were nearly out of provisions, and if Lincoln did not dispatch supply ships, Pickens and Sumter would fall, federal prestige suffer a staggering blow, and Confederate independence be assured. If he sent the ships, the rebels probably would resist. That would mean civil war. The president determined to act. He learned on April 6 that it would not be possible to reprovision Fort Pickens, but after advising the governor of South Carolina of his intention ordered supply ships to Sumter.

Sumter was a formidable fort located on an island in Charleston harbor. If reprovisioned it might hold out indefinitely and threaten shipping in and out of the Confederacy's most important Atlantic port. Telegraph wires crackled between Charleston and the Confederate capital at Montgomery. Rebel leaders did not want war and hoped to secure independence peaceably. But they considered the federal presence at Sumter as intolerable.

Hence they instructed General P. G. T. Beauregard, their commander at Charleston, to bombard the federal garrison if Sumter's commander, Major Robert Anderson of Kentucky, refused to surrender. When Anderson refused to give up, Beauregard prepared for combat.

The Confederate attack began at 4:30 on the morning of April 12, 1861. The shelling continued—hour after hour into the night. His ammunition gone, Anderson accepted Beauregard's terms after thirty-four hours and on Sunday, April 14, ninety United States soldiers marched out of the fort.

The rebels had fired on the national flag and across the North the response was electric. Ralph Waldo Emerson wrote of the "whirlwind of patriotism" touched off by the action at Charleston and declared: "Now we have a country again. Sometimes gunpowder smells good." On April 15 Lincoln called for 75,000 volunteers to put down the rebellion and two days later announced a blockade of southern ports. But at Richmond, on April 17, a state convention decided that Lincoln had violated the constitutional right of states to secede peaceably and voted to take Virginia out of the Union. In the next few weeks Arkansas, Tennessee, and North Carolina also seceded.

There was some satisfaction in Washington in those hectic weeks when the mountainous sections of western Virginia refused to recognize the secession ordinances of the Richmond convention. At Wheeling in June 1861 a Union government was organized which eventually controlled fifty counties. Although Virginia sent troops to prevent the counties from forming a new state, the federal forces won. The western counties now were safe for the Union and two years later, in 1863, West Virginia became a state.

What of the other slave states, Delaware, Maryland, Kentucky, and Missouri?

Delaware never wavered. Linked economically with the free states, it rejected secession and responded to Lincoln's call for troops.

Maryland's position was more crucial, for if the Old Line state seceded, the federal capital would be isolated. There were legions of Confederate sympathizers in Maryland and four federal soldiers died on April 19, 1861 when a mob attacked the Sixth Massachusetts Regiment as it marched across Baltimore from one railroad station to another. To prevent a recurrence, Lincoln ordered federal troops to march around the city of Baltimore when going from one station to another. Several state and local officials were imprisoned. But by the end of 1861 the state was safe for the Union.

Equally important was Kentucky, bordering three free states and stretching along three-fifths of the Ohio River. As Lincoln explained, "I think to lose Kentucky is nearly . . . to lose the whole game." And at another time he said: "I hope I have God on my side, but I must have Kentucky."

Lincoln pledged that no federal troops would enter the state so long as it kept to an announced policy of neutrality. To allay fears of Kentucky slaveowners he emphasized that his objective in the war was preservation of the Union, not emancipation of slaves. His tactics worked, for the government at Frankfort stayed with the Union and twice as many Kentuckians eventually fought for the North as for the South.

In March 1861, two weeks after Lincoln's inauguration, Missouri's governor, Claiborne F. Jackson, an ardent southerner, sought to take the state into the Confederacy. Battles were fought but federal victories assured Union control of most of Missouri.

> STUDY GUIDE: Two federal installations in the South had not surrendered to the Confederates. One could not be reprovisioned, but Lincoln told the governor of South Carolina that he planned to send supplies to the other — Fort Sumter. If Fort Sumter stayed in federal hands, it could threaten shipping in and out of Charleston. Rebels bombarded it on April 12, 1861 when Sumter's commander refused to surrender. Lincoln called for volunteers to put down the rebellion. Four more states then seceded from the Union.

SUMMING UP THE CHAPTER

Names and Terms to Identify

abolitionists
The Liberator
Antonio López
  de Santa Anna
Battle of San Jacinto
"Fifty-four forty or fight!"
Sam Houston
George Bancroft
Bear Flag Revolt
Treaty of Guadalupe
  Hidalgo
"Old Rough and Ready"

Matthew C. Perry
Gadsden Purchase
"Bleeding Kansas"
popular sovereignty
Charles Sumner
Know-Nothing party
Freeport Doctrine
secession
Jefferson Davis
Crittenden
  Compromise

Study Questions and Points to Review

1. Some people thought Tyler should run a "caretaker" administration when he took the presidency on the death of Harrison. What was Tyler's attitude?

2. What was the purpose of the Webster-Ashburton agreement?

3. What impact did the cultivation of cotton have on slavery?

4. Define "manifest destiny."

5. Why was Polk considered a "dark horse" candidate?

6. What was the purpose of the Slidell Mission? Was the mission successful?

7. Why was the Free-Soil party organized? What part did the Free-Soilers play in the election of 1848?

8. What was the Wilmot Proviso?

9. Why did California enter the Union as a free state?

10. What was the Fugitive Slave Law and what were its results?

11. How did the Ostend Manifesto increase tension between the North and the South?

12. What was the central issue of the Lincoln-Douglas debates?

13. What was the purpose of John Brown's raid on Harpers Ferry?

14. Why did the Confederates fire on Fort Sumter? What was the result of this attack?

Topics for Discussion

1. When Tyler assumed the presidency, the Constitution had no provision for presidential succession if both president and vice-president died. What do you think would have happened if Tyler had been killed during his term in office?

2. What was the American Colonization Society? Do you think the Civil War could have been prevented if more people had supported that organization?

3. What arguments did those who favored slavery use to support it? What were the arguments used by abolitionists?

4. James K. Polk has been rated by historians as a "near-great" president. Do you agree or disagree with this rating? Give reasons for your answer.

5. Analyze the major points of the Compromise of 1850. How would you have reacted to this compromise if you had been living in 1850?

6. What do you think President Buchanan should have done to meet the secession crisis during the last months of his presidency?

Subjects for Reports or Essays

1. Assume that it is the year 1837 and you are a newspaper editor. Write an editorial supporting or opposing annexation of Texas.

2. Prepare a report on the Underground Railroad.

3. Write a brief biographical sketch on one of the following: Winfield Scott, Stephen A. Douglas, John C. Frémont, John Brown, William Garrison, Harriet Tubman, Harriet Beecher Stowe.

4. Prepare a class report on one of the following topics: (a) Nat Turner's Rebellion; (b) Discovery of gold in California; (c) John Brown's raid on Harpers Ferry; (d) Fort Sumter.

5. Read *Uncle Tom's Cabin*. Report on why you think this book was so popular when it first appeared. What do you think of Mrs. Stowe's portrayal of slavery?

6. After reading one of the books listed in the "Further Readings" section, report on it to the class.

Projects, Activities, and Skills

1. Using Atlas Map 14, locate: Mexico City, San Antonio, Monterrey, Monterey, Sonoma, Rio Grande, Buena Vista, Vera Cruz, Guadalupe Hidalgo, Cerro Gordo.

2. Refer to Atlas Map 10 and to Table 3 in the Appendix. How many square miles of area were added to the United States between 1840 and 1860? What was the percentage of increase in population between these years? Using Table 8 in the Appendix, describe the trend of immigration between 1840 and 1860. What areas contributed the most immigrants in this period?

3. Using Table 7 in the Appendix, describe United States foreign trade in the years between 1830 and 1860. Was the balance of trade favorable during most of the period?

4. The country's leading writers in the 1840s and 1850s were Ralph Waldo Emerson, Henry David Thoreau, Nathaniel Hawthorne, Herman Melville, Walt Whitman, Henry Wadsworth Longfellow, James Russell Lowell, William Gilmore Simms, John Pendleton Kennedy, and Edgar Allan Poe. Read selections from one of these authors. What do these writings reveal about the mood of the time? Support your conclusions with quotations.

5. Interview your friends and members of your family. Ask them: What were the causes of the Civil War? Compare findings with the class.

Further Readings

General

Antislavery: The Crusade for Freedom in America by Dwight L. Dumond. A study of the abolitionist movement.

The Civil War in the Making and *The Growth of Southern Nationalism, 1848-1861* by Avery O. Craven.

Early Negro Writing, 1760-1837 ed. by Dorothy Porter.

The Growth of Southern Civilization, 1790-1860 by Clement Eaton. Provides insights into the antebellum South.

The Irrepressible Conflict: 1850-1875 by Arthur C. Cole. A useful book on the coming of the Civil War.

Lincoln and the First Shot by Richard N. Current.

The Mexican War by Otis A. Singletary. Very readable.

Ordeal of the Union (8 vols.) by Allan Nevins. The first volume touches on the Mexican War.

The Peculiar Institution by Kenneth M. Stampp. A well-written indictment of slavery.

Prologue to Sumter by Philip V. Stern. A collection of source materials from John Brown's raid to the time of Sumter.

Race and Politics: Bleeding Kansas and the Coming of the Civil War by James A. Rawley.

Rehearsal for Conflict: The War with Mexico, 1846-1848 by A. H. Bill.

Slave Trading in the Old South by Frederick Bancroft. Good account of the domestic slave trade.

Slavery Defended: Views of the Old South ed. by Eric L. McKitrick. Contains source material.

Biography

Abraham Lincoln by Benjamin P. Thomas. The best of the many Lincoln biographies.

Harriet Tubman: Conductor on the Underground Railroad by Ann Petry.

John Tyler: Champion of the Old South by Oliver P. Chitwood.

The Raven by James Marquis. The life of Sam Houston.

Stephen A. Douglas: Defender of the Union by Gerald M. Capers. Covers the coming of the war.

William Lloyd Garrison and the Humanitarian Reformers by Russel B. Nye.

Fiction, Drama, Poetry, and Music

Abe Lincoln in Illinois by Robert E. Sherwood. Prize-winning play about Lincoln's early life.

American Ballads and Folk Songs by Allen Lomax and John A. Lomax. Good collection.

American Negro Poetry ed. by Arna Bontemps.

The Big Sky by Alfred B. Guthrie, Jr.

By the King's Command by Shirley Seifert. Life in early Texas.

The Confessions of Nat Turner by William Styron. Best-selling novel about a slave revolt.

Death Comes for the Archbishop by Willa Cather. Set in the New Mexico Territory.

John Brown's Body by Stephen Vincent Benét. Prize-winning epic poem.

Uncle Tom's Cabin by Harriet Beecher Stowe.

White and Negro Spirituals by George P. Jackson.

CHAPTER 5

CIVIL WAR

THE THUNDER OF GUNS in Charleston harbor signalled the start of the most devastating war in the history of the Western Hemisphere. In the next four years more than six hundred thousand American soldiers would die in the Civil War. No war since then has claimed so many American lives, not even World War I or World War II. The Civil War also cost the country more than $20 billion in arms and supplies between 1861 and 1865. The cost of rebuilding the nation in the years that followed was even higher.

The war would have other consequences. It would decide that one republic rather than two would exist in the territory marked out on maps of 1861 as "the United States of America." It would resolve the long dispute over the nature of the federal Union by putting to rest the old southern idea that the American republic was a loose partnership of sovereign states. Instead was established the principle, spelled out by John Marshall more than forty years before, that the United States was a union of people, one and indivisible.

The war would determine that a great democratic nation would follow Mexico, the South American republics, and the British Empire in abolishing human slavery within its borders. Finally, the war would have far-reaching economic results. It would disrupt the economy of the South while spurring that of the North. The outcome would be a further shifting of the nation's economic balance in favor of the northeastern quarter of the country.

THE OPPOSING SIDES

At the start of the Civil War, most European observers expected the Confederacy to succeed in establishing independence. To put down the southern rebellion federal armies would have to sweep across a hostile countryside and bring the Confederates to total defeat. Like the thirteen colonies in the 1770s, the South faced a less difficult task. It did not have to invade the enemy's territory or destroy his army. It merely had to hold the North at bay, prevent United States forces from wrecking the Confederate army and

government, and hold out until the North grew weary of the pain and expense and agreed to a settlement recognizing southern independence. From this strategy came tactical advantages. The South would have interior lines of communication which required no protection. Fighting a defensive war, the South would be able in many engagements to station soldiers behind thick breastworks and compel the enemy to charge across open fields.

The Confederacy appeared to have other advantages. There was unity. Except for the mountain areas of western Virginia and eastern Tennessee, most people of the South rallied behind the war. There was military leadership. Many of the best officers in the federal army in 1860-61 were southerners, and with the action at Sumter most offered their services to the Confederacy. Another asset—or so it seemed—was Jefferson Davis, one of the most able and experienced men in American public life. Then there was cotton. Rather than watch their textile mills gather rust, the British and French—according to Confederate calculation—would break the northern blockade and might even join the South to assure continuing access to cotton.

Most notable of the North's advantages was population—more than twenty million people in the loyal states to nine million (counting slaves) in the Confederacy. If the South's defensive strategy required fewer soldiers, the North's edge in manpower was nonetheless impressive. Equally striking were material resources. America's financial centers were in the Northeast—in Philadelphia, New York, Boston—and the federal government had credit at home and abroad. Confederate finances by comparison were shaky. Industrial power and transport favored the North. Ninety percent of the country's factories were in the North and these could turn out quantities of iron, textiles, leather goods, guns and ammunition, boots and field equipment. Having little industry, the South would have to look to Europe for many of the "sinews of war." The North had a fairly efficient network of railways, roads, and waterways; the South's system of transport was smaller, less integrated, and by

HEADLINE EVENTS

1861 Morrill Tariff Act
Fort Sumter fired on
Lincoln orders troops to put down rebellion
Union begins blockade of Confederate states
Britain announces its neutrality
First Battle of Bull Run
McClellan replaces McDowell as commander of Army of the Potomac
Trent affair

1862 Lincoln appoints Edwin M. Stanton secretary of war
Union forces capture Fort Henry and Fort Donelson
Monitor and *Virginia* battle
Battle of Shiloh
Peninsular campaign
Battle of Seven Pines
Congress abolishes slavery in District of Columbia
Confiscation Act
Seven Days' Battle
Lincoln discusses with Cabinet plans to free slaves in Confederate states
Farragut captures New Orleans, Baton Rouge, and Natchez
Congress abolishes slavery in federal territories
Homestead Act
Pacific Railway Act
First transcontinental telegraph
Department of Agriculture created
Morrill Land-Grant College Act
Second Battle of Bull Run
Newspapers publish plans for Emancipation Proclamation
Battle of Antietam
Lincoln warns Confederacy to surrender or he will proclaim their slaves free
Battle of Perryville
General Burnside replaces McClellan as commander of the Army of the Potomac
Union defeat at Fredericksburg
Battle of Murfreesboro

1863 Lincoln issues Emancipation Proclamation
General Hooker replaces Burnside as commander of Army of the Potomac
Federal conscription law enacted
National Banking Act
Battle of Chancellorsville
Recruitment of Negro soldiers begins
West Virginia enters the Union
Maximilian set up as emperor of Mexico by Napoleon III
Battle of Gettysburg
Grant captures Vicksburg
Port Hudson taken by Union forces
Draft riots in New York
Foreign minister Charles F. Adams warns British about Laird rams
Battle of Chickamauga
Lincoln delivers Gettysburg Address
Battles of Lookout Mountain and Missionary Ridge
Lincoln announces plan for reconstruction of southern states

1864 Grant given command of all armies of the United States
Lincoln defeats Wade-Davis Bill with pocket veto
Wilderness campaign
Kearsarge sinks the *Alabama*
Confederate power broken in Shenandoah Valley
Sherman takes Atlanta and begins march to the sea
Battle of Winchester
Nevada enters the Union
Lincoln reelected president
Battle of Nashville
Sherman occupies Savannah

1865 Grant takes Petersburg and Richmond
Lincoln inaugurated for second term
Lee surrenders to Grant at Appomattox Court House
Lincoln assassinated
Thirteenth Amendment ratified

1866 *Ex parte Milligan* case

comparison poorly equipped. Seapower was another northern advantage. Most officers of the United States Navy in 1860-61 were northerners, and in the division of armed forces at the start of the war the North held on to the bulk of the navy. Power on the sea also required merchant vessels and the northern merchant marine in 1861 was second in the world only to that of Great Britain.

Leaders of the North and South and foreign and domestic observers carefully weighed the advantages and disadvantages as the two sections slipped into war. But none of them added to the balance of the North the skills and determination of the tall man who lived at 1600 Pennsylvania Avenue, the White House. As matters turned out, he was one of the North's principal assets.

Lincoln's Contribution

Although Lincoln lacked military experience, he had no intention of being a figurehead as commander-in-chief of federal forces. Using the telegraph, he kept in constant touch with field armies. He pored over maps and reports. He made decisions about strategy. When he thought it necessary he changed generals. Indeed, for nearly two years, aided by Secretary of War Stanton, Lincoln was for all practical purposes the commanding general of the United States Army, until he appointed U. S. Grant to that position in 1864. Lincoln's performance as commander-in-chief was not brilliant, but it was very creditable.

Lincoln also was more than a commander. He brought a quiet dignity to the cause of the Union. While Jefferson Davis, 115 miles away in Richmond, appealed to class and sectional hatred to rally the Confederacy, Lincoln referred to "our late friends, now adversaries." He continually reminded northerners that one day southerners again would be their countrymen. As spelled out in the Gettysburg Address of 1863, the war, in Lincoln's view, was a struggle for democracy and freedom in the United States, a test to see "whether that nation, or any nation so conceived and so dedicated, can long endure." Here was an appeal that touched the hearts of millions of people from New England to the Great Plains — industrialists and farmers, factory hands and immigrants — persuading them that the cause of union was worth the awful sacrifices.

Some northerners in early 1861 wanted to let the southern states depart in peace. Still others

(including Secretary of State William H. Seward) talked of a foreign adventure which would make the country forget internal differences and unite against a common enemy. Amid the controversies in those weeks Lincoln never lost his composure, never lost sight of his purpose of honorably preserving the Union. And when Sumter was running out of supplies, he did not hesitate. Here indeed was, to a large extent, the story of the Civil War from the northern vantage. If Lincoln was able to persuade northerners that they were engaged in a noble crusade, he also had to keep their wills from weakening. The task was great, for periodically northern spirits would weaken. Whenever a northern attack failed or a federal army suffered heavy losses, defeatism would sweep the loyal states. But one man who never lost the vision of victory was the president. Without his steadfastness of purpose it is possible that the North would not have borne the agonies of 1861-65.

As a postscript it is interesting that between James K. Polk in 1849 and Theodore Roosevelt

Below, a Union guard makes a security check before allowing a passenger to board the Georgetown Ferry outside Washington, D.C. The ferry carried passengers across the Potomac River, which separated the capital city from Virginia, a Confederate state. Passes were used to keep Confederates from crossing into Washington. This photograph was taken in 1861 or 1862 by an assistant to Matthew Brady.

Library of Congress

in 1901 the United States produced only one outstanding president—and he just happened to be in the White House at the time the country faced its gravest crisis. Ponder the fate of the Union if Franklin Pierce or Benjamin Harrison had been at the helm in 1861-65. Equally remarkable, Americans in 1860-61 had no idea that Lincoln possessed qualities of greatness. They sized him up as little more than an inexperienced western politician who was an able orator, had few political enemies, and would remain faithful to the Republican platform. Few of them glimpsed his wisdom, patience, and courage.

STUDY GUIDE: As the Civil War began, Confederates had the advantage of fighting a defensive war. They also had unity and excellent military leadership. Population was one of the Union's biggest assets. The Union also had material resources. The federal government had good credit. Most factories were in the North, and there was an efficient transportation network and effective seapower. Lincoln was also one of the North's main assets.

STRATEGY OF THE WAR

How should the forces of the United States go about defeating the rebels? The most comprehensive plan came from the army's general in chief Winfield Scott, "Old Fuss and Feathers" of the Mexican War. A Virginian in his mid-seventies, hence too old for a field command, Scott had the finest military mind the country had produced. His idea was to blockade southern ports, cutting the rebels from outside support. Next he would run a line of fortified posts down the Mississippi, dividing the South in two. A land attack by the North would wait until the federal army had reached a peak of strength and efficiency and the blockade had weakened the enemy. At that point the United States would unleash the army and with superior manpower and resources squeeze the life from the Confederacy.

Requiring a long and expensive war and demanding great patience, Scott's plan had little appeal. Looking for a quick and cheap victory, most northerners in spring 1861 wanted federal armies to smash through to Richmond, the new Confederate capital. Capture of the seat of the southern government, they thought, would wreck morale and end the rebellion. For many days Horace Greeley's New York *Tribune* carried the banner: "FORWARD TO RICHMOND! FORWARD TO RICHMOND!"

Fearing that inaction would weaken northern morale, Lincoln at length succumbed to pressure and sanctioned an attack on Richmond. The plan was to move against Manassas Junction, a railroad center and crossroads thirty miles west and slightly south of Washington. After defeating a smaller Confederate force (commanded by P. G. T. Beauregard), the Union army would rush through the Manassas Gap in the Blue Ridge Mountains. Then it would overwhelm a second rebel army (under Joseph E. Johnston) in the Shenandoah Valley which until then would be kept occupied by a small federal force led by General Robert Patterson. After that would come a military promenade to Richmond and the war would be over.

Bull Run

To execute the plan, a federal army comprised mainly of volunteer regiments marched from the capital in early July 1861. Their commander was General Irvin McDowell. Accompanying the soldiers was a throng of correspondents, congressmen, and even some finely dressed ladies.

The Confederates had figured out what the federals were up to and loaded most of Johnston's force in the Shenandoah on trains—after it had made some menacing feints at Patterson. When the battle finally started on a plateau near a stream called Bull Run (a few miles from Manassas Junction), Confederate reinforcements were on the way.

July 21 was a Sunday, and at two o'clock in the morning Union officers awakened their men and moved them into position. The attack came a few hours later and within minutes confusion took command of the battle. Uniforms and flags of the two armies were similar and soon the entire area was enveloped in dust and smoke. As the regiments swayed back and forth, it seemed that the Union troops would carry the field, whereupon McDowell sent off a telegram to Washington announcing victory. Then came disaster. One segment of the rebel line, commanded by a bearded, sad-eyed general named Thomas J. Jackson, refused to give. Inspired, another Confederate leader shouted: "Look! There stands Jackson like a stone wall." At the same time rebel reinforcements from the Shenandoah began to arrive. Before the increasing Confederate pressure, Union forces fell back. They became entangled with the sightseers who had come out from Washington and soon were running—abandoning equipment, wounded comrades, and two congressmen.

Back in Washington the president, on receiving McDowell's victory message, had gone for a Sunday drive. When he returned to the White House, at about 6:30, Secretary of State William H. Seward, his voice trembling, conveyed the bad news. Showing no emotion, Lincoln called a cabinet meeting. Through the long night he and his advisers deliberated on what they should do in event of a Confederate attack on the defenseless federal capital. (Fear of an assault was unwarranted; the Confederates were almost as confused in victory as were the federals in defeat.)

While Lincoln met with his cabinet, terrified troops began to straggle into the city. Some fell down in the streets and went to sleep, others stumbled into barrooms and got drunk. The stream of defeated soldiers into the capital continued through the rain and heat of the next day.

McClellan Takes Command

The defeat at Bull Run shocked the North into realization that the war would be no walkover. A few days later, Lincoln gave command of the Army of the Potomac to thirty-four-year-old George B. McClellan.

A graduate of West Point, McClellan had served in the Mexican War and as an American military observer in Russia during the Crimean War. He had won acclaim for his leadership a few weeks before in the action in West Virginia. A vain man, he thought Lincoln a fool and on several occasions in months to come would treat the president crudely. Still, he had ability. He was a skilled tactician and after the war Robert E. Lee would call him his most talented opponent. McClellan was particularly good in training and organization. These were skills needed to restore the morale of soldiers beaten at Bull Run and to whip into shape the ill-trained volunteer regiments that troop trains were disgorging each day in Washington. After securing the capital against a possible Confederate assault, "Little Mac'" turned to the task of bringing order from the confusion. His performance, marked by patience and firmness, was brilliant.

For a while the country applauded but as summer turned to autumn the North became restive and began to yearn for a new stab at Richmond. Even Lincoln, listening daily to the sounds of bugles drifting across the Potomac from McClellan's encampment, seemed to catch the Richmond fever. No doubt he knew that northern morale needed a battlefield success, that the people would not long tolerate a "phony war." But McClellan refused to budge, arguing that the Confederates in northern Virginia outnumbered the Army of the Potomac and a new federal attack would bring another disaster—and probably end the war on Confederate terms. While McClellan exaggerated the strength of the enemy, he had a point in insisting that there should be no offensive until the army was prepared. Each day, moreover, the naval ring was tightening about southern ports and, as Scott had proposed, McClellan was building his army for a full-powered thrust against an enemy weakened by the blockade.

McClellan had his way and for the remainder of the year 1861 it was "all quiet along the Potomac."

STUDY GUIDE: Most northerners wanted federal forces to capture Richmond, the Confederate capital, and get the war over with quickly. Lincoln agreed to an attack on Richmond by way of Manassas Gap in the Blue Ridge Mountains. Confederates figured out federal strategy and were waiting at Bull Run. Rebel General Stonewall Jackson held the line until reinforcements arrived. As Union forces fell back, the North realized that the war would be no pushover. Lincoln gave command of the Army of the Potomac to George B. McClellan. McClellan brought organization and training to federal troops.

DIPLOMACY

Meanwhile, the diplomatic mechanism had been turning. Understanding that the outcome of the war might depend on foreign intervention—or the absence of it—both the United States and Confederate governments gave much attention to diplomacy.

At the start of the war the Confederates seemed to have the diplomatic advantage. Europe needed cotton and, it was widely believed, would do whatever was necessary to maintain the flow of cotton from Confederate states. Thus it clearly was to the interest of the governments in London and Paris that the American nation remain fractured. British shipping, for example, might replace New England rivals as the main carriers of the South's overseas trade. Finally, well-to-do classes in Europe, especially in Britain, felt a kinship with the planters of the American South. Still, the North was not without diplomatic leverage. Whatever the advantages of Confederate independence, European working classes could feel no sympathy for a government that was defending Negro slavery. There was also northern wheat, more important, it would turn out, than southern cotton, for Britain and France had accumulated surpluses of cotton before the action at Fort Sumter. Later they would find new sources of supply in Egypt, India, and Brazil.

Even before Fort Sumter, the Confederate government sent agents to England. The envoys failed to gain recognition of Confederate independence, but in May 1861 the government in London took note of hostilities in America and declared its intention to be neutral. This was a denial of the United States contention that the Confederates were waging an illegal rebellion. It was recognition of Confederate "belligerency." The British therefore would take no action against Confederate privateers as "pirates" and would not prevent British shipbuilders from constructing ships for the Confederate navy. In their anger over this development, Lincoln and Seward almost overlooked another British order, in June 1861, forbidding British port authorities to admit captured ships. Depriving privateers of the best markets for their booty virtually killed Confederate privateering. It also forced Confederate naval vessels to destroy captured federal ships and cargoes, depriving the Confederacy of a source of badly needed income.

The *Trent* Affair

An episode in autumn 1861 nearly drove Britain into the arms of the Confederacy. Two Confederate diplomats, James M. Mason and John Slidell, slipped through the federal blockade at Charleston and boarded the British steamer *Trent* at Havana—destination Europe. As the *Trent* moved to sea on the morning of November 8, the steam frigate U.S.S. *San Jacinto* ordered the *Trent* to stop and a detachment of American marines went aboard.

British ship or no, the marines took Mason and Slidell off the *Trent* and a few days later the two men were prisoners in the United States. Across the North there was wild applause and Captain Charles Wilkes of the *San Jacinto* received a promotion. To leaders in Washington, including President Lincoln, it seemed that the North had scored an important victory. In Britain, however, the reaction was different. Considering Wilkes's action an insult to their flag, the British demanded an apology and release of the prisoners. The American minister in London, Charles Francis Adams, saw the gravity of the situation and urged his government to make amends.

Fortunately the Atlantic cable had broken down, and some of the angry dispatches between London and Washington did not appear immediately in the newspapers, giving tempers on both sides of the Atlantic a chance to cool. At length Lincoln and many northerners saw the folly of antagonizing England. Following a four-hour meeting at the White House on Christmas Day, Secretary Seward informed the British minister that the men "will be cheerfully liberated." Thus passed the most serious diplomatic crisis of the war.

STUDY GUIDE: At the start of the war, the Confederacy seemed to have the diplomatic advantage. Europe needed cotton, and the Confederate states could supply it. But, more important, the North had wheat. Britain refused to recognize Confederate independence. In autumn 1861 war almost broke out between the North and Great Britain when the U.S.S. *San Jacinto* took two Confederate diplomats from the British steamer *Trent*. The prisoners were released after strong British protest.

INTERNAL POLITICS

Meanwhile, internal politics plagued Lincoln. A faction of the Republican party, the "Radicals," saw the war as a crusade against the "slave power." They demanded an immediate proclamation abolishing slavery and wanted a war to the bitter end to destroy the plantation aristocracy of the South. Whatever his private thoughts about a no-compromise stand against slavery, Lincoln understood that a declaration of "holy war" in 1861 would drive the border states into the Confederacy, alienate northern Democrats, and probably result in permanent dissolution of the Union. The presidential wisdom was lost on the Radicals who saw Lincoln's arguments as a sign of weakness.

Still, this Radical enthusiasm produced one noteworthy result: it brought as secretary of war in January 1862 a stocky little man with tangled whiskers and steel-rimmed spectacles, Edwin M. Stanton.

Lincoln's first secretary of war was Simon Cameron, a politician who had delivered Pennsylvania's votes to the Illinois candidate at the Republican convention in 1860. Smelling corruption, an investigating committee of the House of Representatives, dominated by Radicals, in December 1861 reported widespread graft in the awarding of war contracts. Whereupon Lincoln in a curt note informed Cameron that he was the new minister to Russia, then named Stanton as secretary of war. A Radical, Stanton had deplored Lincoln's "painful imbecility" and referred to the president as "the original gorilla" and "the Illinois Ape." The new secretary was crude, ill-mannered, abusive, and intemperate. He also was harsh, cruel, intolerant, and sly.

Fortunately Stanton had other qualities. He was intelligent, incorruptible, untiring, dedicated, resourceful, and efficient. When Lincoln wanted to pardon every man who had deserted the federal army, Stanton came down hard on the side of discipline. He badgered governors and congressmen, tongue-lashed barons of industry, and tore up bad contracts. He drove himself and his subordinates unmercifully. He seemed a man about to explode from pent-up energy, a man with a computer-like mind in that day before computers. He never wavered in his loyalty to the Union and Abraham Lincoln. The outcome was magnificent. Seldom in the years 1862-65 did United States soldiers lack weapons or ammunition. If Lincoln sometimes found the secretary irritable, he also recognized his immense talent, saying at one point: "Folks come up here and tell me that there are a great many men in the country who have all Stanton's excellent qualities without his defects. All I can say is, I haven't met 'em! I don't know 'em! I wish I did!"

STUDY GUIDE: Radical Republicans viewed the war as a crusade against slavery and wanted the plantation aristocracy of the South destroyed. In 1862 Edwin Stanton was appointed secretary of war. He was highly successful in mobilizing Union forces for war.

U. S. GRANT

While McClellan continued to drill his army along the banks of the Potomac, a new United States commander early in the year 1862 began to attract attention. His name was Grant.

The son of a tanner and farmer, Hiram Ulysses Grant was born in 1822 in a two-room house at Point Pleasant, Ohio, but before he was two years old the family moved to Georgetown in southwestern Ohio, where he grew up. As a boy "'Lyss" was shy and sensitive. These characteristics remained with him the rest of his life. He did not swear—not even an occasional "damn." He abhorred violence, despised game-hunting, and treated animals with compassion.

Grant's father determined that his eldest son should have "book learning," so "'Lyss" attended nearby schools and got the rudiments of an education. In 1838, the elder Grant managed an appointment for his son to the United States Military Academy at West Point, New York. Confronted with the glad news, Ulysses announced that he would not go to the academy. Jesse Grant replied that he would, and years later Ulysses wrote "I thought so too, if he did."

When he arrived at the academy in 1839 the youth found that the congressman who had made his appointment had sent in his name as Ulysses Simpson Grant. (Grant already had dropped his first name—to get away from the initials "H.U.G.") Academy officials turned aside his feeble protest that Simpson was not part of his name, and when classmates noted the initials "U.S." they began to call him "Uncle Sam" and eventually just "Sam." "Sam" he remained to fellow officers for the rest of his military career.

As a cadet Grant, short (five feet eight inches) and thickset, was no model. He despised the discipline of military life, put great hope in a bill that went before Congress at the time to abolish the academy, and on one occasion tried unsuccessfully to get himself expelled. Otherwise he was an average student, showed interest in mathematics, and upon graduation ranked twenty-first in a class of thirty-nine. But he was the outstanding horseman in the corps of cadets during his years at West Point, a matter of some annoyance to southern cadets who thought the country's best horsemen were from the South.

Three years after his graduation the United States went to war with Mexico. Grant disapproved of the war and later wrote that he had regarded it "as one of the most unjust ever waged by a stronger nation against a weaker nation." But he served with distinction as a regimental quartermaster under "Old Rough and Ready" Taylor whose casual manner and dress he made his own. In later stages of the war he served under Winfield Scott and won a citation for gallantry in the fighting before Mexico City. After the war he returned to Saint Louis and married Julia Dent, the sister of a West Point classmate.

As was inevitable for a professional army officer, Grant eventually had to be separated from his wife and in the early 1850s found himself on desolate frontier posts, first in the Pacific Northwest, then in California. Lonely and miserable, he sought refuge in liquor, and in 1854 his army superiors forced him to resign. In truth he was not a drunkard, and his difficulty with the army derived in part from a personality clash with a superior officer.

More discouragement followed. Building a crude house on land owned by his father-in-law, not far from Saint Louis, he tried farming, but bad weather and an economic recession which swept the country in the late 1850s turned the venture to failure. Next he became a partner in a real estate firm in Saint Louis. Another failure. It is interesting to note that his father-in-law had given him a slave which he might have sold for a thousand dollars. With that money Grant might have met many of his obligations; instead he gave the man his freedom. Broke and seemingly without any future, Grant, who now was the father of three children, asked his own father for a job. The elder Grant gave him one—in the family leather store at Galena, Illinois, where he worked as a clerk under younger brothers.

Grant Takes Command

When the Civil War broke out in 1861, Grant, thirty-nine, wrote the War Department offering his services. He received no reply. Then one day he was standing stoop-shouldered by a field watching a new militia captain trying to drill a company of volunteers. Exasperated, the captain asked Grant, whom he knew to be a former military man, if he would like to drill the company, whereupon the stubby storekeeper took his first step into the history of the Civil War.

Soon Grant's name came to the attention of the governor of Illinois who gave him minor administrative assignments at militia headquarters in Springfield. Refusing to promote himself for higher responsibility, Grant seemed destined to spend the war far from the spotlight

—until the governor appointed him colonel of an undisciplined volunteer regiment whose carousing and hooliganism had earned it the title "Governor Yates's Hellions." It was in mid-June 1861 when Grant, wearing a seedy civilian coat and a rumpled felt hat, rode into the regiment's encampment. The first day on the drill field the men jeered the new colonel. Grant did not retaliate but in his strange, quiet way asserted his authority and soon had the unit in fighting trim. In late summer the regiment performed well against rebels in Missouri and the following autumn Grant, his star now rising rapidly, was a brigadier general in command of United States forces at Cairo, Illinois.

STUDY GUIDE: Ulysses S. Grant, a West Point graduate, had resigned from the army in 1854. At the outbreak of the Civil War, he offered his services but received no reply. He then worked with volunteers and soon was in charge of a regiment. By autumn 1861 he was a brigadier general in command of federal forces in Illinois.

WAR IN THE WEST

Studying maps, federal military men saw that control of the Tennessee and Cumberland rivers would secure the federal position in Kentucky and deliver much of Tennessee to the Union. They also saw that two Confederate earthworks, Fort Henry on the Tennessee and Fort Donelson on the Cumberland, both just below the Kentucky border in Tennessee, commanded the rivers. To direct an operation against these forts the federal leadership turned to Grant.

Grant chomped his cigar and began to draw plans. Noting the formidable heights of the two forts, he planned a joint land-water attack with Andrew H. Foote, commander of seven armor-plated gunboats tied to piers at Saint Louis. The plan was successful. On February 2, 1862 Fort Henry surrendered. Two weeks later at Fort Donelson the Confederate General Simon Bolivar Buckner asked for terms. As a torchlight flickered in the early hours of February 16, Grant scrawled a note: "No terms except unconditional surrender can be accepted." Thinking Grant unchivalrous, Buckner nonetheless ordered his 15,000-man army to put down weapons. When the news flashed over northern telegraph wires, U. S. Grant became "Unconditional Surrender" Grant.

Shiloh

Grant soon crumbled the entire Confederate defense line in western Kentucky, and as Foote's gunboats churned up the Cumberland the rebels abandoned Nashville, capital of Tennessee. Then Grant's superior, General Henry W. Halleck, put a brake on the federal advance and withdrew Foote's gunboats for operations against Confederate positions on the Mississippi. Halleck's moves enabled Confederate forces facing Grant to regroup and concentrate at Corinth in northeastern Mississippi, twenty miles from a church named Shiloh.

Grant meanwhile had moved his 45,000-man Army of the Tennessee up the Tennessee River to Pittsburg Landing, a few miles north of the Mississippi border. Seeing an opportunity for surprise, the Confederate leader Albert Sidney Johnston quietly moved forward with more than 40,000 men. On Sunday morning, April 6, 1862, while most federal soldiers were still in their blankets, Johnston sent his army yelling and firing to the attack. In minutes the Union right wing collapsed.

Leisurely taking breakfast when the first shots broke the calm, Grant quickly saw the situation. Where other generals might have ordered a retreat to save as much of the army as possible, he determined to fight. Union lines finally braced, and by mid-afternoon the rebel attack ran out of steam. At that point Johnston, to rally his men for a final charge, rode forward, only to be killed by a federal bullet. Thus passed one of the Confederacy's best leaders, a more able man, some people have thought, than Robert E. Lee. The fighting continued that night. By dawn Grant had received reinforcements. With their aid Grant's forces fought on to victory. But the cost was great and Shiloh was the war's deadliest combat to date.

Grant came in for heavy criticism for being surprised at Shiloh. There were charges (not true) that he had been drunk. Editorials demanded his release. But Lincoln and Stanton never wavered. When a temperance delegation called at the White House and announced that it was unbecoming for a drunken general to command Christian soldiers, Lincoln playfully asked: "What brand does he drink? I'd like to send a barrel of it to the other generals."

On the Mississippi

By this time Halleck's campaign on the Mississippi was in gear and on the same day the Confederates withdrew from Shiloh (April 7, 1862) federal forces captured a rebel fortress in the bend of the Mississippi at the Kentucky-Tennessee border. Two months later Foote's gunboats scattered a Confederate flotilla at Memphis.

Meanwhile, Commodore David G. Farragut, a craggy old seaman from Tennessee, had moved federal gunboats from the Gulf of Mexico into the Mississippi and captured New Orleans. After depositing soldiers at New Orleans, Farragut continued up the Mississippi and in August 1862 Baton Rouge and Natchez surrendered. The federals now controlled the river from Saint Louis to the Gulf—except for the fortresses at Vicksburg ("the Gibraltar of the Mississippi") and Port Hudson, a few miles upstream from Baton Rouge. For almost another year Vicksburg and Port Hudson remained Confederate links with Arkansas, Missouri, and Texas.

STUDY GUIDE: To secure their position in Kentucky and gain much of Tennessee, federal forces needed control of the Tennessee and Cumberland rivers. Thus it was necessary to capture Forts Henry and Donelson. Grant took both forts by February 1862 and then crumbled the entire western Kentucky defense of the rebels.

Confederate forces led by General Albert S. Johnston regrouped and concentrated near Shiloh. Grant braced for battle. Johnston was killed in a deadly combat. Federal forces continued to gain control along the Mississippi. Commodore David Farragut captured New Orleans, Baton Rouge, and Natchez.

WAR IN THE EAST

While there was success for United States arms in the West in 1862, there were failures in the East. The man who contributed most to that lack of success was a Confederate general, Robert Edward Lee.

Robert E. Lee

Lee was born at Stratford, Virginia, in 1807, the son of "Light-Horse Harry" Lee, a cavalry officer in the War for Independence. Fifty-one at the time of Robert's birth, the elder Lee died eleven years later. His influence on his son had been slight. Instead the youthful Lee absorbed the traits of thrift, industry, and self-control from his mother, a member of the Virginia aristocracy. At the age of eighteen he entered West Point, where he was a model cadet and compiled a brilliant record. Two years after graduation he married Mary Ann Randolph Custis, a great-granddaughter of Martha Washington. The young couple moved into the Custis family home at Arlington Heights, a mansion just across the Potomac from the federal capital. Army life of course meant long separations from wife and children, the most difficult being the twenty-two months during the Mexican War when Lee served under General Scott and won praise for quiet efficiency and devotion to duty. Perhaps Lee's most pleasant years in the army were 1852-53 when he was superintendent of West Point. At the time of the secession crisis in 1860-61 he was stationed on the Texas frontier.

Devoted to the Union, Lee in January 1861 wrote his son that "I am not pleased with the course of the 'Cotton States,' as they term themselves." And as he traveled eastward after the secession of Texas he was confident that Virginia would not join the Confederacy. Then came the attack on Fort Sumter. While a convention at Richmond deliberated Virginia's response, in mid-April 1861, Lincoln offered Lee the field command of the United States Army. Lee declined, explaining that he could not take part in an invasion of the South. Next day he learned that the Virginia convention had voted for secession. What should he do? That evening while his wife entertained guests, he walked among the trees, gazed out across the Potomac, and paced the floor of his upstairs bedroom. After several hours he made his decision. He sat down and wrote a letter resigning from the federal army, then prepared to accept command of the military forces of Virginia.

The Peninsular Campaign

Impatient with McClellan's slowness, Lincoln ordered an attack on Richmond early in 1862. By what route? Lincoln preferred a frontal assault, one that would leave the Army of the Potomac wedged between the Confederates and the federal capital. McClellan favored flanking tactics. His idea was to float the army down the

Library of Congress

At the beginning of the Civil War, Abraham Lincoln offered General Robert E. Lee command of the Union Army. Why did Lee refuse?

Chesapeake and move on Richmond via the peninsula formed by the James and York rivers. "Little Mac's" tactics were sound, more so after March 9 when the federal ironclad *Monitor* — a raftlike vessel with revolving turret amidship — in a five-hour battle forced the Confederate ironclad *Virginia* (formerly the *Merrimac*) to return to Norfolk for repairs. After a month-long debate McClellan got his way. Still, Lincoln and Stanton insisted on keeping 50,000 federal troops in the vicinity of Washington and in western Virginia as insurance against a Confederate thrust northward. In May and June when Stonewall Jackson with only 17,000 men maneuvered up the Shenandoah Valley — one of the most brilliant and daring movements of the war — federal leaders refused to release any of the troops defending Washington to reinforce McClellan.

When the peninsular operation began in early April, McClellan, ever cautious, rejected a rapid movement up the peninsula toward Richmond. Instead he spent a month besieging Confederate positions at Yorktown. When Confederates abandoned Yorktown in early May, McClellan continued to inch forward. Then the rebel commander Joseph E. Johnston launched a counterpunch on May 31. Surprised, McClellan quickly recovered and the Battle of Seven Pines (or Fair Oaks) was a draw. During the fight Johnston was seriously wounded, and Lee became commander of all Confederate forces opposing McClellan.

Bad weather forced a lull in operations the first three weeks of June. Then Lee threw his army against McClellan. For all his deficiencies as an offensive commander, McClellan performed brilliantly in countering Lee's thrusts. The action raged for a week—the Seven Days' Battle. Supported by gunboats, the federal lines held, whereupon on July 2 Lee broke contact and withdrew his army to Richmond.

Morale in his army was good and McClellan asked permission to renew the attack—after he had regrouped. But Lincoln accepted the counsel of his new general-in-chief, "Old Brains" Halleck, and approved orders bringing the Army of the Potomac back to Washington.

The Confederacy's star seemed on the rise. While the federals had scored victories in the West, the rebels had saved their capital. Morale among rebel divisions was high, thousands of fresh volunteers were pouring into Richmond, and in Lee the Confederates had found a splendid military leader. Even the blockade was about to disappear—so the rebels thought—for under construction in England were ironclad "rams," whose underwater "piercers" would splinter the wooden hulls of federal cruisers. To top things off, two dashing cavalry officers, John Hunt Morgan and Nathan Bedford Forrest, were leading hit-and-run raids through central Kentucky. Before long the Bluegrass State would probably fall into the Confederacy.

The Second Battle of Bull Run

The last days of August 1862 brought the Second Battle of Bull Run.

A few weeks after ordering evacuation of the peninsula Halleck began to gather forces for a new strike at Richmond, this time via the direct route. In charge was General John S. Pope, a stern leader with a long black beard who had won acclaim in action along the Mississippi. When federal plans became clear—but before many of McClellan's divisions from the peninsula had joined Pope—Lee divided his army and sent Stonewall Jackson northward along the eastern slopes of the Blue Ridge Mountains. Swinging eastward Jackson easily captured a federal supply base at Manassas Junction. To catch the illustrious Jackson, Pope wheeled his army around and headed for the place to which Jackson had moved—the wooded area where United States and Confederate arms had clashed thirteen months before in the Battle of Bull Run.

Lee, meanwhile, followed Jackson's route northward with the main rebel force and on August 29, 1862, his men were in position. In two days the Second Battle of Bull Run was over. The outcome was Union disaster and

Soldiers who were wounded in battle were treated at makeshift field hospitals set up near the battlefront. Those who were most seriously wounded were taken to military hospitals behind the lines. The photograph below was made at a field hospital three days after a battle which took place June 27, 1862, at Savage Station, Virginia.

Library of Congress

This drawing shows Union scouts observing Lee's troops before the battle at Antietam. Although McClellan knew Lee's battle plans, how did he fail to defeat Lee?

Library of Congress

Pope's army streamed back toward the city of Washington.

Union fortunes had reached a low point, for previous victories in the West, however magnificent, could not balance the psychological consequences of disaster at the doorstep of the federal capital. Defeatism swept the North, and without Lincoln's grim resolve the attempt to preserve the Union might have collapsed in those dark days of late summer 1862.

Antietam

Less than a week later, September 4, Lee's Army of Northern Virginia, 40,000 strong, splashed across the Potomac into western Maryland, then moved north and west toward Hagerstown. Lee's objective was to cut railroads linking northeastern cities with the West, persuade Maryland to join the Confederacy, and by his presence in Union territory increase the northern feeling of defeatism.

Lincoln, at that point, relieved Pope and gave full authority to McClellan. In a few days "Little Mac" restored order from the shambles left by

Bull Run. Meanwhile Confederate troops under Jackson captured Harpers Ferry.

McClellan now had a rare bit of good luck. From the body of a slain Confederate messenger his men brought papers setting out Lee's entire plan of battle. It was clear that Lee had divided his army and was vulnerable to a well-executed attack. Next day McClellan cautiously moved his troops forward. McClellan's deliberate tactics, it turned out, gave Lee time to spin his army around, march southward, and take up positions at Sharpsburg along Antietam Creek. The delay also enabled Jackson to reach Lee before the battle. When the Union attack began on September 17, Lee was well entrenched. But after two days of the bloodiest fighting of the war, Lee was compelled to withdraw.

McClellan might have pursued the badly mauled Army of Northern Virginia. But, characteristically, he elected to stay put. In Washington the president was furious. McClellan—so Lincoln thought—had botched the attack at Antietam and then permitted Lee to escape. Exasperated, the president in early November 1862 relieved "Little Mac"—for the last time.

Tactically the battle at Antietam was a draw, but technically it was a Union victory with great consequences. It temporarily ended rebel dreams

[157]

of victory via a dramatic stroke into northern territory, shattered the illusion of Lee's invincibility, and gave new strength of purpose to the North. It caused the British to drop plans for recognizing Confederate independence. Most important, it gave Lincoln an opportunity to announce his Emancipation Proclamation.

STUDY GUIDE: Lincoln ordered an attack on Richmond early in 1862. McClellan wanted to move federal troops down the Chesapeake and approach Richmond from the peninsula. When the Confederates abandoned Yorktown, he inched forward. Then Confederate General Joseph E. Johnston launched a counterattack. General Robert E. Lee took command after Johnston was wounded. Lee thrust his army against McClellan and then withdrew to Richmond. McClellan was denied permission to renew the attack, and Richmond was spared. A few weeks later, Union forces began gathering for a more direct attack on Richmond. When federal plans became clear, Lee sent Stonewall Jackson northeast along the eastern slopes of the Blue Ridge Mountains. The Second Battle of Bull Run was a Union disaster. In September 1862 Confederates moved toward Hagerstown, Maryland. McClellan learned of Lee's battle plan. He allowed Lee to take up positions along Antietam Creek. Then he attacked. After two days of heavy fighting, Lee withdrew.

THE GREAT PROCLAMATION

Lincoln feared any action on slavery might drive border states to join the Confederacy, yet the urge to turn the war into a crusade against human bondage had gathered strength across the North. In response, Congress in spring–summer 1862 redeemed a Republican campaign pledge and abolished slavery in the District of Columbia, outlawed slavery in federal territories, and passed the Confiscation Act declaring that slaves "captured" by United States forces and slaves of convicted rebels were free.

By this time, Lincoln, believing Kentucky and Maryland reasonably safe for the Union, prepared to speak out against slavery. At a cabinet meeting in July 1862 he proposed a proclamation that all slaves in rebel territory would be free as of January 1, 1863. Noting the recent failure of McClellan's peninsular campaign, Secretary Seward warned that such a pronouncement at that time would appear a desperation tactic to rally northern spirits. Better to wait for a Union victory. Lincoln agreed. Then came Antietam. Five days after the battle Lincoln summoned the cabinet and told of a covenant he had made with God: to free the slaves as soon as United States arms drove the Confederates from Maryland. Next day newspapers published the preliminary Emancipation Proclamation: on New Year's Day 1863 all slaves in any state then in rebellion against the United States "shall be, then, thenceforward, and forever free."

In diplomacy the effects were exactly what Lincoln had hoped. European liberals and workingmen rejoiced, the northern cause became sacred, and Confederate hopes of intervention by Britian and France were dashed—for no government in London or Paris would dare line up with the southern "slave power" against forces committed to destruction of bonded servitude in America. The immediate practical result for the slaves was almost nothing. The proclamation did not apply to loyal slave states, New Orleans, or occupied parts of Virginia. Only in areas still

Black soldiers are helping slaves escape into the North across the Rappahannock River in Virginia in this 1862 photograph. About 186,000 black soldiers fought in the Civil War.

under Confederate control were slaves to be free, meaning that they would go right on being slaves until liberated by the United States Army. Still, Lincoln's proclamation made certain that if the North won the war slavery would disappear. In recognition of that fact, West Virginia, Maryland, Missouri, and Tennessee abolished slavery before the war ended. (The Thirteenth Amendment to the Constitution, the logical sequel to the proclamation, ended slavery in the other states, Delaware and Kentucky, in 1865.) There was, however, an intangible side to the proclamation. Negroes viewed it as a great expression of their aspiration for freedom. They focused on the words "henceforth shall be free." The dream they saw in emancipation made it for them, and eventually for mankind, a great historic document—expressing man's enduring search for freedom.

Criticism in the North

In the North, abolitionists of course cheered, but from other quarters came criticism of the president for diverting the noble purpose of the war, that is, to save the Union. Much noise also came from "Copperheads" (northerners who supported the South) who hoped to use the proclamation as an instrument for galvanizing northern opinion against the war. So sharp was the reaction in many areas of the North that a few weeks after the proclamation Lincoln's political opponents made gains in the congressional elections. As time passed, however, criticism diminished and northerners were taken up in the crusade for liberty as well as Union.

Perryville

It appeared, meanwhile, that the Confederates might regain the initiative in the West, for General Braxton Bragg had conceived an elaborate plan for driving from the mountains of east Tennessee northward to Louisville and Cincinnati. Bragg hoped to maneuver Generals Grant and Carlos Buell into battles that would break federal power in the West. Thus Bragg in August 1862 moved 40,000 men out of the Tennessee mountains and across the Cumberland, destination Louisville.

Bragg's movement was a signal for stirrings farther west. Rebel forces prepared to move against Grant, but after some fighting failed to break Union defenses. Thus an important part of Bragg's plan failed.

To the east Bragg had continued his northward march and in an attempt to rally Kentuckians to the Confederacy dispatched 10,000 men under General Edmund Kirby Smith in the direction of Lexington and Cincinnati. This expedition failed, too, whereupon Smith turned around to rejoin Bragg. When confronted by Union reinforcements, General Bragg had second thoughts about giving battle and withdrew his Confederate army toward the state capital at Frankfort.

Buell meanwhile proceeded northward to secure Louisville, then moved eastward to catch Bragg. The armies finally clashed on October 8, 1862, at Perryville. The Confederates actually were not beaten, but Bragg, overtaken with pessimism, marched southward to his base in east Tennessee. Because he failed to pursue the rebel army, General Buell lost his Union command and was replaced by General William S. Rosecrans.

Fredericksburg

The actions at Antietam and Perryville indicated that things were looking up for the North. Then came a new disaster.

On relieving McClellan in early November 1862, Lincoln gave command of the Army of the Potomac to General Ambrose E. Burnside. This was a mistake, for McClellan, in spite of all his shortcomings, had ability. Burnside did not. Burnside was a handsome West Pointer, whose peculiar style of whiskers, extending down in front of each ear, became known as "burnsides" and later as "sideburns." He had served in the Mexican War and at Antietam directed one of the critical attacks. He seemed a logical choice for higher command.

Cold and snow had settled over northern Virginia when Burnside, an amiable and well-intentioned fellow, took charge. Following Antietam spirits were high and recent volunteers had swelled the ranks of the Army of the Potomac to 113,000 men. Burnside's plan for getting to Richmond was to concentrate behind the Rappahannock opposite Fredericksburg, then storm forward. When the attack began, on December 13, 1862, Lee was ready and the Confederate army won a great victory inflicting horrible losses on federal troops.

A few weeks later Lincoln relieved Burnside and gave the Army of the Potomac to another hero of Antietam, Joseph ("Fighting Joe") Hooker.

The telegraph, observation balloons, and photography were useful in gathering intelligence and in deploying army units. This is a telegraph train setting up a line for use during the battle of Fredericksburg.

Library of Congress

STUDY GUIDE: In 1862 Congress outlawed slavery in federal territories and abolished it in the District of Columbia. After the Battle of Antietam, Lincoln announced the Emancipation Proclamation. In the western campaign, Confederate General Braxton Bragg moved men toward Louisville, Kentucky. The opposing armies met near Perrysville and the Confederates were driven southward. In November 1862 McClellan was replaced by General Ambrose Burnside. Burnside's plan for getting to Richmond failed and he was relieved by General Joseph Hooker a few weeks later.

BEHIND THE LINES

Only a fraction of the southern and northern populations in 1861-65 were fighting in the armies. The overwhelming majority of Americans lived the four years of war far from the sounds and horrors of the battlefield.

Recreation

Although war and politics were their principal concern, Americans in 1861-65 had time for literature, drama, and recreation. Henry Wadsworth Longfellow published *Tales of a Wayside Inn* in 1863 and James Russell Lowell amused wartime readers with his second series of *Biglow Papers*. John Greenleaf Whittier continued to compose poetry. Even in the South, more oppressed by the war then the North, such poets as Henry Timrod, Sidney Lanier, and Paul

Hamilton Hayne turned out creditable verse. The war years were a brilliant period for drama and Americans flocked to the theater in increasing numbers. There was also baseball, not a new game but one that had evoked only mild enthusiasm before the war. Now it became a standard pastime, particularly for men of the Union army.

Conscription

For political leaders in Washington and Richmond a major activity was meeting the problem of manpower requirements of the armies. When it became clear that the volunteer system was incapable of satisfying the need for men, the South and then the North turned to conscription. Particularly interesting was the federal conscription law (1863), which permitted an individual to pay $300 and avoid the draft by procuring a "substitute" who would go to the army in his stead. A "rich man's measure," the legislation touched off rioting in working-class sections of New York City in summer 1863 when officials drew the first names. To restore order, it was necessary to rush in federal troops.

Black Soldiers

Negroes offered a possible source of manpower and Lincoln, from the start of hostilities, wanted to recruit them for the federal army. Congress rejected the idea; this was a war to preserve the Union and was not considered to be the concern of Negroes. Then came the Emancipation Proclamation and thinking in the North began to change. Clearly Negroes deserved a chance to fight for the destruction of slavery. By spring 1863 the federal government established machinery for recruiting Negroes. By the end of the war, 186,000 black men had borne arms for the United States, 38,000 of whom had died (a mortality rate forty percent higher than that of white soldiers). The good morale of the black troops was reflected in their soldierly response on the battlefields.

In the view of the South, use of Negro troops by the North was an insult, and the Confederate Congress in May 1863 resolved that any white officer of Negro soldiers, if captured, should be executed. The Confederate secretary of war approved the killing of some Negro prisoners of war—as a warning to other Negroes. (In one notable affair Confederate soldiers refused to permit Negro soldiers to surrender and instead shot them down or burned them alive.) Then during the last gasps of the rebellion, in early 1865, General Lee urged recruitment of slave soldiers. Leaders in Richmond approved the necessary legislation. The measure came too late, however, to help the Confederacy.

Financing the War

Politicians also wrestled with matters of finance and in the North they met the problems effectively. The government in Washington raised more than $2 billion through bond issues. Lesser sums came from the tariff, income taxes, manufacturing taxes, licenses to physicians and dentists, and levies on "luxury" commodities. There were also the "greenbacks," paper money issued without backing of a gold reserve. Federal printing presses eventually cranked out $450 million in "temporary" greenback currency—a no-interest loan extracted by the government.

The fiscal problem in the South was beyond solution. At the start of the war the Confederacy netted about $1 million by seizing customs houses and the federal mint at New Orleans and took in a lesser sum by confiscating private debts which southerners owed northern creditors. But bond issues brought in little revenue, and Confederate currency depreciated as fast as printing presses could turn it out. More effective was a ten percent tax on farm produce, to be paid in kind. Livestock and grain received in this way helped feed Confederate armies; tobacco and cotton, sold by the government and in one in-

stance used as security for a European loan, produced badly needed cash.

Confederate political leaders had little opportunity to take up matters that did not bear on the war or organization of their infant government. Such was not the case in Washington. Congress, easily dominated by Republicans now that southern Democrats had departed, put on the statute books some of the most important measures of the nineteenth century. First came the Morrill Tariff (1861), a protectionist act that reversed the thirty-year trend of lowering import duties. It started a protectionist trend that would last for more than seventy years. The year 1862 brought the Homestead Act, providing that the government would virtually give public land to individuals who would live on it. The Morrill Land-Grant College Act (1862) granted each loyal state a large tract of public land, proceeds from the sale of which were to establish agricultural colleges. Under provisions of the measure sixty-nine "land-grant" colleges eventually appeared. The Pacific Railway Acts of 1862 and 1864 provided federal subsidies for construction of transcontinental railroads. The National Banking Act (1863-64) drove state bank notes out of existence and established a uniform national currency. Finally, three new states gained admission to the federal Union: Kansas (1861), West Virginia (1863), and Nevada (1864).

Disloyalty and Subversion

For leaders in both Washington and Richmond the problem of disloyalty and subversion commanded attention. In both the North and South there were many people who favored the other side. In the first months of the war Lincoln dealt arbitrarily with individuals in Maryland who he thought were obstructing United States military operations. Then in 1862 he announced that persons resisting conscription, discouraging enlistment in the federal army, or "guilty of any disloyal practice affording aid and comfort to rebels" would be subject to martial law, denied the writ of habeas corpus, and tried in military courts. These were harsh measures by a democratic government which purportedly was waging a crusade for human freedom. Under the proclamation, federal military authorities eventually confined about thirteen thousand individuals.

Whatever the possible consequences, open support of the Confederacy, obstruction of the war effort, and calculated encouragement of defeatism continued in the North, particularly in Ohio, Indiana, and Illinois. One of the best-remembered southern sympathizers or "Copperheads" in the North was Clement L. Vallandigham of Ohio who, after conviction by a military tribunal on a vague charge of making utterances that tended to "weaken the power of the government in its efforts to suppress an unlawful rebellion," was escorted to Confederate lines and banished from the North. Vallandigham did not long remain in the South. By way of Canada he returned to Ohio in 1864 and even helped draft the national platform of the Democratic party in that year!

There was wide criticism of Lincoln's treatment of civilians accused of subversion, and many critics accused him of turning the presidency into a dictatorship. After the war, in 1866, the Supreme Court, in the *ex parte Milligan* case, ruled that the president had indeed exceeded his authority, that the Constitution gave the chief executive no power to order military trials for civilians in districts where civil courts were open. As for the Confederacy, Jefferson Davis assailed Lincoln for his arbitrary acts. But when faced with northern sympathizers in the South, Davis too suspended habeas corpus and in general moved against subversion with a heavy hand.

Diplomacy

The central diplomatic question at the start of the war—and down to the latter part of 1863—was whether Britain and France might help the Confederacy secure independence. The British in spring 1861 recognized Confederate belligerency but on other points took positions that proved beneficial to the North and in late 1861 accepted a peaceful solution to the *Trent* crisis. Next came a diplomatic tug-of-war over Confederate vessels under construction in British shipyards (most famous of which would become the C.S.S. *Alabama)*. The law prevented British builders from turning out warships for belligerents, but the ships built for the Confederacy, displaying no armament, were supposedly merchantmen. Insisting that the vessels were intended to be commerce raiders, the United States minister in London, Charles Francis Adams, piled protest on protest. Adams was correct in his estimate, for after the vessels left Britain they took on cannon and before the war ended destroyed 250 northern merchant ships.

More serious was the crisis over the "rams." These were tiny steam-driven vessels armored with four and a half inches of iron plate and equipped with seven-foot wrought-iron "piercers" at the prow, three feet below the water line. The Confederates contracted with the British firm of William Laird and Sons for several of these vessels and with them expected to destroy the federal blockade of southern ports, maintained with antiquated wooden cruisers. As the rams neared completion in 1863, Adams and others concluded that their escape from Britain would mean the end of the blockade and achievement of Confederate independence. Despite assurances by the Foreign Office in London that no more Confederate warships would sail from Britain, Adams repeatedly reminded the British of the gravity of the situation and in September 1863 warned that escape of the rams would result in war with the United States. When it appeared that a crisis was at hand, the foreign secretary advised Adams that the government had seized the Laird vessels. A short time later the rams entered the service of the British navy.

One other important diplomatic episode of the war years was the attempt of the French emperor Napoleon III to take over Mexico.

When the Civil War disrupted the American Union, the emperor, a man of modest talent but large ambition, saw an opportunity to restore French grandeur in the New World. Bankrupt and torn by dissension, Mexico seemed a likely place for a new French adventure. So the emperor, along with Spain and Great Britain demanded payment on unpaid Mexican debts and put troops ashore in Mexico. Within a month Spain and Great Britain withdrew their forces, whereupon the French troops occupied Mexico City and in June 1863 set up a puppet government. Cued by Napoleon, the new regime promptly chose a young Austrian archduke, Maximilian, as emperor. Here of course was a flagrant violation of the Monroe Doctrine. Lincoln and Seward protested and determined to act as soon as they restored United States authority in the rebellious southern states. (Following an ultimatum by the United States and deployment of 50,000 American troops along the Mexican border, the French in 1867 withdrew from Mexico, whereupon Maximilian promptly lost his throne—and his life.)

Other Americans meanwhile concentrated on the business of arming, equipping, and feeding the northern and southern armies. Results in the North were spectacular. Hundreds of new factories appeared, many existing ones turned to war production, and as a consequence federal soldiers had good weapons, ammunition, uniforms, and boots. Northern agriculture made an equivalent record, turning out enough food for the civil and military populations and a surplus for sale overseas. Rapid mechanization of northern agriculture during the war was largely responsible for this achievement, but the Homestead Act, encouraging thousands of farmers to take up land on the Great Plains in the war years, was a factor.

Squeezed by the federal blockade, the South managed to increase industrial output, and the rebels lost no battles for want of arms or ammunition. Still, Confederate uniforms became more tattered as the war progressed, there were never enough tents or blankets, and by the end of the war many rebel soldiers were barefooted. Needless to say, the civilian population in the South suffered chronic shortages of manufactured articles. Food was another problem. By converting cotton lands to food crops the South had no trouble holding off starvation, but many south-erners, in and out of the army, survived on salt pork and dry corn.

Prisoners and Wounded

Behind the battle lines still other individuals guarded prisoners of war and tried to heal the wounded.

Life in military prisons, North and South, was grim. At Richmond's Libby Prison northern captives suffered from the cold and short rations. After the war stories of brutality and murder by Confederate guards were common. A worse hell-hole was the prison camp at Andersonville, Georgia, where 30,000 Union prisoners, crowded into crude and unsanitary barracks, endured disease and hunger. Prisoners accused

Thousands of soldiers, both Union and Confederate, died in prison during the war. The drawing below shows the Confederate prison at Andersonville, near Americus, Georgia. More than 13,000 soldiers died there. Today it is a national historic site.

Soldiers rest outside the hospital at a Signal Corps camp near Georgetown. After the first Battle of Bull Run, Lincoln feared an attack on Washington and heavily garrisoned the area. What advantage would the Confederates have gained by capturing Washington?

the commandant at Andersonville of being a sadist who systematically tortured and murdered captives and threw corpses to his dogs. In northern prisons many Confederate captives died of exposure and neglect by federal officers, some of whom saw themselves as avengers of the horrors of Libby and Andersonville.

The care of the wounded in the Civil War challenges the credulity of people a little more than a century later. Chronic shortages of anesthetics made many operations a torture that defies description. Those were the days before Louis Pasteur and his theories of disease transmission. Unsanitary techniques—the use of instruments and sponges in one operation after another without disinfecting and washing surgical instruments in cold water drawn from the nearest bucket often resulted in lockjaw and gangrene. One Civil War surgeon later estimated that "it was seven times safer to fight all through the three days of Gettysburg than to have an arm or leg cut off . . . with the septic surgery then practiced."

STUDY GUIDE: Most Americans spent the war years far from the battlefields. Manpower was a major problem. A federal conscription law allowing men to pay money to avoid service touched off draft riots in New York in 1863. After the Emancipation Proclamation, Negroes

were recruited. In the North money was raised through bond issues, tariff, taxes, and by printing paper money—greenbacks. In the South the financial problem was beyond solution.

During the war years Congress passed the Homestead Act, Morrill Land-Grant College Act, Pacific Railways Act, and the National Banking Act.

Confederate merchant ships were being built in British shipyards. The United States protested that these were actually commercial raiders. Confederates also contracted for Laird "rams" which the British seized before they reached the South. In Mexico Maximilian was set up as emperor by Napoleon III in violation of the Monroe Doctrine.

THE TURNING POINT OF THE WAR

The war, of course, continued. By spring 1863 "Fighting Joe" Hooker had restored the Army of the Potomac to fighting trim. The federal command developed new ideas for breaking through to Richmond, and President Lincoln came down from Washington to inspect Hooker's army and go over battle plans. He seemed cheered as column after column of United States troops passed in review. The new plans seemed sound. Taking advantage of numerical superiority, Hooker intended to divide his army and make a three-pronged attack.

Hooker's plan functioned smoothly in the opening stages, but Lee saw through Hooker's design, moved the bulk of his army to Chancellorsville, and in early May outmaneuvered and defeated the Union army in heavy fighting.

Chancellorsville had been Robert E. Lee's most brilliant victory. It had come at great cost, however, for during the night of May 2, men of a North Carolina regiment saw shadowy forms moving in the darkness and thought them to be Union skirmishers. Silently taking aim, the North Carolinians fired a volley. The forms fell. One of them was Stonewall Jackson. Hit twice, Jackson died a few days later. His death was a staggering loss to southern military leadership.

Gettysburg

Exhilarated by Chancellorsville, Lee now turned northward, to Pennsylvania, where another great victory might crack northern morale and win

Confederate independence. Along the Mississippi, moreover, a federal army under U. S. Grant was closing in on the Confederate fortress of Vicksburg. To offset the psychological effects of a great Union triumph in the West, should Vicksburg fall, the Confederacy would need a dramatic victory in the East. Jefferson Davis doubted the wisdom of Lee's venture but reluctantly gave his star general the signal to proceed. Thus in early June 1863 the Army of Northern Virginia, 76,000 strong, began to move off in a northerly direction, across the Blue Ridge Mountains, up the western edge of the Shenandoah Valley, across the Potomac, and through Hagerstown in Maryland.

Hooker was still in command of the Army of the Potomac, but he was soon replaced by General George C. Meade. A good disciplinarian, Meade was not apt to perform brilliant battlefield maneuvers. But he was cool-headed and not apt to do anything rash.

Lee meanwhile took up a strong defensive position at Cashtown, a few miles northwest of Gettysburg, and awaited a federal attack. A short distance to the south and east of Gettysburg, Meade had also moved to the defense. Then, on June 30 roving units of the two armies, quite by chance, collided near Gettysburg, whereupon the main units converged on the sleepy crossroads town as though drawn by a magnet. Fighting was sharp on July 1, and the Confederates had the better of the exchange. More important, the 80,000-man Army of the Potomac on that day took up positions along Cemetery Ridge, a limestone outcropping to the south of Gettysburg that stretched for three miles and formed a giant hook. A mile to the west, across open terrain, 75,000 Confederates dug in along Seminary Ridge.

Lee took the offensive the following day. He threw one column against the Union right at Culp's Hill (around the bend of the hook), another against the left at Round Top and Little Round Top. Possession of these rises would enable Confederate artillery to fire into the federal line. For a time it seemed that Lee's plan might work, but United States infantrymen, fighting with the fury of men possessed by demons, held the critical heights against the onrushing rebels. Here perhaps was the decisive action of the American Civil War.

Believing Meade had weakened the center of his line to guard his flanks, the next day Lee launched a mammoth gray wave of troops across open ground in order to break through the middle of the Union defense. He miscalculated. The federal center on the afternoon of July 3 bristled with muskets and artillery pieces. When the rebel columns—one of them an elite Virginia division commanded by General George Pickett—moved into the open, they came under a withering fire. A few Confederate soldiers made it inside federal lines, but they were soon killed or captured.

Union officers now expected an order to counterattack. Meade did not give it. Rebel survivors limped back to Seminary Ridge and on the night of July 4-5 the Army of Northern Virginia retreated southward. High water delayed Lee at the Potomac, and from Washington the president and Halleck appealed to Meade to strike a crushing blow at the rebel army. But Meade advanced deliberately, the Potomac subsided, and the Confederates got away.

Grant Takes Vicksburg

While the North on July 4, 1863, buzzed with excitement over the victory at Gettysburg, telegraph instruments began to click out news of another Union triumph. Grant had taken Vicksburg.

By the turn of the year 1863, several months had passed since Admiral Farragut moved his ships up the Mississippi. The Confederate flag continued to float over the fortresses at Vicksburg and Port Hudson, which stood atop high bluffs and were strongly fortified.

Concentrating on Vicksburg was General U. S. Grant. Unmoved by continued criticism over his surprise at Shiloh and false charges that he was a drunkard, Grant studied the problem of taking the fortress. When he finally thought through a plan, he explained it to his tall, firm-jawed subordinate, William Tecumseh Sherman. Sherman was aghast. Grant would march the Army of the Tennessee, now upstream from Vicksburg, down the west bank of the Mississippi to a point below Vicksburg, cross the river, and attack the fortress from the rear. As Sherman noted, there were difficulties because the federal troops would be outnumbered and could not be supplied.

Undaunted, Grant went ahead. The result was a campaign of unsurpassed brilliance in the Civil War, begun at the end of April 1863 when main units of the army crept along the Louisiana side of the Mississippi to a point twenty-five miles below Vicksburg. Grant crossed over into Mississippi without opposition, and quickly pinched off the enemy garrison at Grand Gulf. He then turned eastward and on May 1 his army overran a Confederate garrison at Port Gibson, eleven miles inland from the river. Continuing through broken and thickly wooded country in a northeasterly direction, on May 12 Grant's men struck at Raymond, thirty miles east of Vicksburg, and drove rebel defenders back. By this time Sherman, following in Grant's footsteps, had moved up and on May 14 defeated a Confederate force just west of Jackson, the capital of Mississippi. Sherman's troops then marched in and occupied the town. Control of Jackson, a railroad junction, would make it difficult for other Confederate regiments in Mississippi to reinforce Vicksburg.

Grant's army then moved to Vicksburg. In eighteen days Grant's army, heavily outnumbered and virtually cut off from its base of supply, had marched 150 miles through enemy territory, won five battles, driven the main rebel force inside Vicksburg, and blocked reinforcement of the fortress. After two unsuccessful attacks against the fortress, Grant put Vicksburg under siege. Their food gone, the Confederates surrendered seven weeks later. On July 9 Port Hudson, besieged by a United States force, also hoisted a white flag, whereupon Lincoln announced: "the Father of Waters flows unvexed to the sea."

On to Chattanooga

Several hundred miles to the east of Vicksburg, meanwhile, other important military engagements were shaping up.

After the Union victory at Perryville in autumn 1862, the Army of the Cumberland under Rosecrans had marched southward and taken up winter quarters at Nashville. Beaten but not broken at Perryville, General Bragg reorganized his southern army, then moved to Murfreesboro, thirty miles southeast of Nashville.

From Murfreesboro, Bragg waged a campaign of harassment against the federal troops until, in December 1862, General Rosecrans moved to the offensive. At length the armies of Bragg and Rosecrans were dug in along the Stone River near Murfreesboro.

On December 31 Bragg struck across the frozen battlefield. Then a gallant stand by divisions under General Philip Sheridan, a hero of Perryville, delayed the Confederate advance. Other troops under the brilliant General George H. Thomas of Virginia (who during the war

never lost a battle), stopped the rebels in their tracks. Still, it appeared that the Confederates were the victors at Murfreesboro (or Stone River) and Bragg expected the Army of the Cumberland to withdraw. Rosecrans was thinking of retreat, but not Thomas and Sheridan. They wanted to attack. And so on the cold morning of January 2, 1863, Bragg was astonished when his men failed to dislodge the federals. His forces weary and battered, Bragg led his army down the road to Chattanooga. Rosecrans did not follow.

The Army of the Cumberland remained at Murfreesboro for six months, until late June 1863. Then Rosecrans deliberately began to maneuver across the high pine barrens of southeast Tennessee toward Chattanooga, an important rail junction and the gateway to Atlanta. Without a battle he skillfully compelled Bragg in early September to abandon Chattanooga and withdraw into northern Georgia. But then Bragg prepared for a counterattack, whereupon Rosecrans took up positions along Chickamauga Creek, twelve miles below Chattanooga.

On September 19, the Confederates attacked, but Bragg's first thrusts faltered before the determination of the Army of the Cumberland. Then came the famous "jumbled order of Chickamauga"–an order by Rosecrans which became confused in transmission and caused the opening of a gaping hole in the center of the Union line. Pouring through the hole the rebels sent thousands of federal troops, and also their commander, Rosecrans, flying back to Chattanooga. But one federal commander remained in the thick of it: Thomas. With a reckless counterattack his corps finally stemmed the Confederate charge. Next, while awaiting a fresh rebel assault, Thomas personally located men and cannon. At length the rebel blow fell and wave after wave of gray-clad infantrymen rushed the heights. Each time Union musketry and artillery sent them reeling back down. As darkness fell, the rebels assembled for a final assault. Nearly out of ammunition, Thomas's men fixed bayonets and in the light of a harvest moon again threw the Confederates down the ridge. From that evening to the end of his life, George H. Thomas was "the Rock of Chickamauga."

Chickamauga was a rebel victory but a costly one. Still, Bragg had Rosecrans penned up in Chattanooga. To save the situation, Lincoln appointed Grant as supreme commander of United States armies in the West. Grant's first act as supreme commander was to relieve Rosecrans and place Thomas in command of the Army of the Cumberland.

Lookout Mountain and Missionary Ridge

Weakened by withdrawal of several thousand troops for duty elsewhere, Bragg's army nonetheless was entrenched on Lookout Mountain south and west of Chattanooga and on Missionary Ridge to the east. When Grant turned to the problem of dislodging Bragg, he decided that frontal attack was out of the question. Instead, a series of clever maneuvers led by Generals Sherman, Thomas, and Hooker dislodged the Confederates from their positions on Lookout Mountain and Missionary Ridge.

Exhilarated by the victories around Chattanooga, the federal Congress restored the rank of lieutenant-general, vacant since the time of George Washington, and in March 1864 Lincoln confirmed it on Grant. Then, after making Halleck chief of staff, the president appointed Grant as commander of all armies of the United States.

Atlanta

When Grant left for Washington, his faithful subordinate in the Shiloh and Vicksburg campaigns, Sherman, took over the western department. The new commander immediately fixed his gaze on Atlanta, a railroad junction and the center of the Confederacy's small munitions industry. For a drive on Atlanta, Sherman could muster 100,000 troops. Still, the obstacles were formidable. Separating Chattanooga and Atlanta, more than a hundred miles apart, was one mountain ridge after another. To guard the passes the rebel commander, Joseph E. Johnston (who had replaced Bragg), had more than 60,000 soldiers. To supply his army, moreover, Sherman was dependent on a fragile single-track railroad reaching down from Nashville.

Sherman, moved his men out of Chattanooga in the first week of May 1864. Employing tactics of speed and mobility, Sherman inevitably turned Johnston's flanks and forced the rebels to withdraw. Mountain ridges were crossed, towns fell before Sherman's relentless drive. By mid-July the federal army had crossed the Chattahoochee and was approaching the city of Atlanta. Unimpressed by Johnston's great skill in this masterful retreat, Jefferson Davis now changed commanders. To defend Atlanta he turned to John B. Hood, a one-armed Texan renowned for dash and courage.

Hood was not content to await a federal siege and on July 20, 1864, lashed out against Sherman's army. Unwisely he directed the main thrust against Thomas and, as usual, regiments under "the Rock of Chickamauga" held. The operation cost Hood 8,000 casualties and when the Confederates withdrew, Sherman's army drew in tighter around Atlanta. Two days later Hood tried again. Again the federals refused to yield, inflicted heavy casualties, and sent the rebels reeling back into Atlanta. Hood was still determined to attack and on July 28 struck Sherman's right flank. Failure number three.

By now siege guns were rumbling down the track from Chattanooga and through the month of August their deadly projectiles screamed and crashed into Atlanta. Impatient—and realizing that he was dangling deep in enemy territory at the end of a thin supply line—Sherman in late August pulled much of his army from the trenches and marched in a giant circuit around Atlanta to the south of the city. His aim was to cut Atlanta's lifeline, the railroad to Macon. When Sherman's men attacked, it was plain that Atlanta was finished and Hood with 35,000 soldiers marched out of the city in a northwesterly direction. Thereupon Sherman scrawled a message to Lincoln: "Atlanta is ours, and fairly won." It was September 1, 1864.

Wilderness Campaign

Victory dotted the path of United States armies of the western department in spring-summer 1864, but frustration continued to plague federal forces in northern Virginia.

Grant, as general-in-chief, determined to mobilize the North's superior manpower and resources and, if it came to that, wear out Lee's Army of Northern Virginia. He also planned to maintain steady pressure on Lee and thus prevent him from reinforcing Confederate armies in Georgia opposite Sherman.

Grant ordered the Army of the Potomac, 100,000 strong, to move on Lee via the tangled country, called the Wilderness, around Chancellorsville. Brimming with hope, on May 4, 1864—at the same time Sherman was moving out of Chattanooga toward Atlanta—the main striking force splashed across the Rapidan and entered the Wilderness. Then it happened. Lee lashed out at Grant's flank, and in two days of heavy fighting inflicted great losses on the federal army.

The Wilderness was a Confederate victory and Lee expected the federal army, as it always had done, to retire a safe distance and lick its wounds. But Grant was not Burnside or Hooker or Pope. He never paused. He continued to push his armies forward in spite of huge losses. His determination was summed up in a dispatch to Halleck on May 11 during the bloody combat at Spotsylvania: "We have now ended the sixth day of very heavy fighting. Our losses have been heavy, but so have those of the enemy. I propose to fight it out on this line if it takes all summer." And so he did.

The North was aghast. In a single month Grant lost (killed and wounded) more than fifty thousand men without so much as denting Confederate defenses. Newspapers referred to the stubby commander as "Butcher Grant" and demanded his removal.

United States forces had virtually destroyed resistance in the western half of the Confederacy. Sherman had advanced relentlessly toward Atlanta. Lee's losses, in proportion to the size of his army had been nearly as great as Grant's. But many northerners, forgetting or ignoring these facts, doubted that it would ever be possible to crush the southern rebellion. Only three men in the entire world—Lincoln, Grant, and Lee— seemed to realize that the Confederacy was sinking, that only loss of will by the North could save it.

Unmoved by criticism—he had become accustomed to verbal abuse—Grant slipped his army southward and eastward. He maneuvered with skill, and for a time Lee stumbled about in confusion, puzzled as to Grant's intention. Then Grant, after absorbing fearsome losses at Cold Harbor, a few miles from Richmond, by-passed the Confederate capital. He laid siege to Petersburg, an important railroad junction to the south.

In the Shenandoah Valley

Entrenched behind stout defenses at Petersburg, Lee decided to spare part of his army for a dramatic movement up the Shenandoah Valley toward the Potomac and Washington. To save their capital, the federals might lift the siege of Petersburg. Better still, if Washington should be captured, northerners—who were already discouraged by recent casualty lists and failure to subdue the Army of Northern Virginia—might be persuaded to make peace on the basis of Confederate independence.

Thus by the first week in July 1864 a 15,000-man force was marching up the Shenandoah Valley toward Washington. The early days of the campaign were successful and Confederate troops at one point came within sight of the federal capital. In addition, the southern commander, General Jubal Early, sent troops to make raids in Maryland and Pennsylvania.

Lincoln and Grant determined to do something about the Shenandoah Valley. First, it was necessary to deal with Early, still lurking just over the Potomac. Second, the time had come to eliminate the valley as a storehouse or granary for the Confederacy. To carry out their plans they turned to five-foot-two-inch Philip Sheridan, a veteran of Perryville and Murfreesboro, Chickamauga and Missionary Ridge.

After a month of maneuvers, Sheridan and Early came together on September 19, 1864, at Winchester, twenty-two miles west of Harpers Ferry. The battle was fierce, but after some confusion Sheridan won. News of the victory crackled over northern telegraph lines and Lincoln wired Sheridan: "God bless you." There was reason to rejoice—and people did rejoice. For things suddenly were looking up for the North. The previous month, August, Admiral Farragut had steered a fleet of United States sloops, gunboats, and monitors into Mobile Bay, and in the face of anchored mines or "torpedoes" shouted: "Damn the torpedoes, full speed ahead!" His ships then destroyed a Confederate naval force and supported a troop assault that captured Fort Morgan. Next, on September 1, had come the fall of Atlanta. And now Sheridan's magnificent triumph.

But Early was not finished. Below Strasburg, twenty miles southwest of Winchester, he regrouped. He thought his defenses impregnable. Sheridan thought otherwise and on the night of September 22 his men caught the Confederates by surprise and defeated them. Again the wires crackled and people rejoiced. In Atlanta and in the trenches around Petersburg federal guns roared salutes. Sheridan had no time to acknowledge cheers. Keeping an eye on Early, he set about to put the torch to the Shenandoah Valley. In the next few weeks his men moved back and forth over the rich farmland, burning and destroying (and also hanging rebel guerrillas caught harassing federal operations). Clearly the valley would offer no further food to the South in the present war.

Still, the Confederates refused to quit. On the morning of October 19 at Cedar Creek, a few miles northeast of Strasburg, Early's men came yelling and shouting through the thin federal picket line and within minutes routed Sheridan's sleepy soldiers. Sheridan rallied his fleeing troops. He galloped up and down the battle line, and to the superheated imaginations of the troops, "Little Phil" seemed a giant. When he gave the signal, like a great blue wave the Army of the Shenandoah swept forward. There was no stopping it. Confederate power in the Shenandoah was broken—permanently.

STUDY GUIDE: By spring 1863 General Hooker had restored the Army of the Potomac and proposed a three-pronged attack on the Confederates. Seeing through Hooker's plans, Lee moved most of his army to Chancellorsville and won his most brilliant victory. He then headed toward Pennsylvania. He hoped another victory there might crack Union morale and win Confederate independence. Hooker was replaced by General George Meade. The armies of Lee and Meade collided at Gettysburg. Thinking that Meade had weakened the center of his line to guard his flanks, Lee ordered a breakthrough of the middle of Union defenses. Lee miscalculated. His retreat from Gettysburg was the turning point of the war.

In the West Grant took Vicksburg. General Rosecrans and Union forces occupied Chattanooga in September 1863. Then at Chickamauga, Rosecrans lost control of his army and returned to Chattanooga. General George Thomas stemmed the rebel attack, but Rosecrans was trapped. Grant relieved Rosecrans and placed Thomas in charge of the Army of the Cumberland. In a series of bitter battles, the Confederates were defeated.

Grant was made commander of all armies in March 1864. He placed General William T. Sherman in charge of the war in the West. Sherman's goal was to send Confederate General Joseph Johnston retreating eastward. Sherman left Chattanooga in May 1864 and forced Johnston back through Georgia to Atlanta. Sherman took Atlanta by September.

In Virginia Grant was facing Lee. Grant's forces moved into the Wilderness near Chancellorsville in May 1864. Lee inflicted heavy losses on the Union army, but Grant continued pushing forward. Lee then sent General Jubal Early up the Shenandoah Valley toward Wash-

ington. Grant sent General Philip Sheridan to expel Early's forces. In September 1864 Sheridan won a victory at Winchester. Early regrouped, but Sheridan defeated him again. The Confederates refused to quit fighting, but by October their power in the Shenandoah Valley was broken.

THE ELECTION OF 1864

Only one other time in history—in the United States in 1812—had a government faced a general election in time of war. Lincoln, in 1864, believed that, in spite of the great national crisis the citizens should have the opportunity to speak. He said: "We cannot have free government without elections; and if the rebellion could force us to forego or postpone a national election, it might fairly claim to have already conquered and ruined us."

To attract "war Democrats" the Republicans temporarily changed their name and called their party the National Union party. They had good reason to do everything possible to widen their

In this photograph taken by Mathew Brady in 1864 Abraham Lincoln is shown with his son Tad. Lincoln's quiet determination helped bolster the sagging spirits of northerners during the bleakest days of the Civil War.

appeal, for by the time their national convention assembled at Baltimore (June 1864) Republican prospects did not appear bright. The victories at Gettysburg, Vicksburg, and Chattanooga by now were fading memories. The reality of the moment was Grant's fearsome losses and his inability to crack the Army of Northern Virginia.

At the convention Lincoln was renominated. For vice-president the party turned to a "war Democrat," Andrew Johnson of Tennessee, a strong Union man who since March 1862 had been military governor of his state. Then Lincoln, in July 1864, ran into trouble with the Radical wing of the Republican party. He failed to support a Radical measure, the Wade-Davis bill, setting out a stern federal policy toward the South after the war. Infuriated, the bill's authors published a denunciation of the president and Radicals toyed with the idea of calling a new Republican convention to reconsider Lincoln's nomination. While nothing came of this back-stairs intrigue, Lincoln, in the face of Republican disunity and a mood of despair in the North, wrote privately in August 1864 that "it seems exceedingly probable that this administration will not be re-elected."

The Democrats converged on Chicago for their convention. Honeycombed with Copperheads, a platform was adopted calling for an immediate end of hostilities and a peace settlement "on the basis of the federal Union of the States." After approving the platform, the delegates nominated George B. McClellan for president. "Little Mac" promptly repudiated the peace plank but fashioned a campaign strategy designed to capitalize on northern frustration and war-weariness.

During the summer and fall, however, the war news became good for the North. A few days before the Democratic convention, United States land and sea forces took Fort Morgan at Mobile. Three days after McClellan's nomination came the fall of Atlanta. After that came Sheridan's brilliant triumphs in the Shenandoah Valley. Northern spirits soared—and with them Lincoln's chances. Still, on election day, November 8, 1864, the president felt uncertain. Perhaps it was the weather. A cold rain and gusty winds lashed the federal capital that day. At seven o'clock in the evening Lincoln and his secretary made their way across the rain-soaked grounds of the White House to the War Department building to check returns. The scene was dreary: only a few people milling about, little puddles of water standing on the floor, the lonesome clatter of telegraph instruments. But the news was good. New York, Pennsylvania, Massachusetts, Indiana—were all going for Lincoln. When the final returns were in, the president had buried McClellan in an avalanche of electoral votes, 212-21.

STUDY GUIDE: In the election of 1864 the Republicans changed their name to the National Union party. Lincoln was renominated and Andrew Johnson, a "war Democrat," was his running mate for vice-president. Democrats nominated George McClellan. Lincoln won in an avalanche of electoral votes.

FROM ATLANTA TO THE SEA

When he abandoned Atlanta, the Confederate leader Hood did not give up hope of defeating General Sherman. If he could cut Sherman's line of communication—a fragile ribbon of iron stretching back to Nashville—he might starve the enemy into submission. Thus after reorganizing his battered regiments in northern Alabama he marched back into Georgia, moved across Tennessee and moved northward to Sherman's supply base, Nashville. Meanwhile, to counter Hood, 22,000 federal soldiers at Atlanta scrambled aboard trains and rolled northward toward the Tennessee capital. Their commander was George H. Thomas.

Sherman's Objectives

Hood believed an army could not operate without its base of supplies, but Sherman thought otherwise. He cut loose from Atlanta in mid-November 1864, and marched three hundred miles in a southeasterly direction to Savannah, feeding his army off the Georgia countryside. This was an easy proposition inasmuch as it was autumn and cribs were filled with corn, smokehouses with bacon and ham. His objective was to cut a path of destruction sixty miles wide which would eliminate an important source of rations for Lee's army, weaken the Confederate economy, and sever Virginia and the Carolinas from the lower South. He also hoped to weaken the southern will to resist by demonstrating that his army could go wherever it wished in the

South without paying heed to supply lines or Confederate military forces.

Sherman is remembered to the present day for his famous remark that "war is hell." He set fire to Atlanta and led 62,000 men southeastward toward the sea. There was little Confederate resistance as federal soldiers ripped up railroad tracks, put the torch to houses and crops, and destroyed wagons and bridges.

Incredible at it seems, Sherman's large army was out of touch with Washington for a full month. In those anxious weeks many rumors swept the North that the men were starving and at every crossroads were coming under murderous fire by Georgia marksmen. Then in December the army emerged at Savannah, made contact with the federal gunboat *Dandelion,* and with signal lanterns said: "Tell President Lincoln that General Sherman makes the American people a Christmas present of the city of Savannah. . . ." The march had cost Sherman fewer than four hundred men.

Nashville

While Sherman slashed his trail of destruction across Georgia in late November 1864, Hood was making his way northward with about 40,000 Confederate soldiers, many of them fresh recruits, to capture Nashville. At the Tennessee capital the northern commander Thomas had assembled a force of 50,000 men. After two weeks of heavy fighting, the North won. Thomas determined to pursue Hood's retreating army. The pursuit was relentless. Unable to get organized, Confederate soldiers were cut down by the hundreds; thousands of others surrendered. It was the only time in the war that an entire army met destruction. Thomas, "the Rock of Chickamauga," now had another nickname, "the Hammer of Nashville."

With the action at Nashville, the war in the West was over; no Confederate force existed west of the Appalachians that was capable of challenging the arms of the United States. This meant that Jefferson Davis's authority by the end of 1864 was confined to three states: Virginia, North Carolina, and South Carolina.

STUDY GUIDE: After General Sherman took Atlanta, he turned to Savannah. Cutting a sixty-mile wide path of destruction along three hundred miles, he emerged in Savannah in December. Meanwhile Confederate General Hood was heading northward toward Nashville to Sherman's supply base. Confederate forces met destruction, and the war in the West was over.

LAST DAYS OF THE CONFEDERACY

Only a miracle could save the Confederacy at the beginning of 1865. Food was scarce, the postal system had ceased to function, and factories were wheezing along on one cylinder. More than half the army had deserted. Confederate leaders nonetheless refused to admit defeat and Richmond continued to echo calls to greatness and a war to the last man. They made Robert E. Lee a veritable military dictator.

Sherman Turns to South Carolina

While Confederate leaders dreamed of eventual victory, General Sherman assembled his 60,000-man army at Savannah in mid-January 1865 and marched northward—toward South Carolina, the cradle of the Confederacy, the state most responsible in the northern view for the terrible destruction of the past four years. Sherman's men had carried a festive mood on their march through Georgia, but they were grim, even angry, as they approached South Carolina. Sherman wrote: "The whole army is burning with an insatiable desire for vengeance on South Carolina. I almost tremble for her fate, but I feel she deserves all that seems in store for her."

To counter Sherman, Lee assembled remnants of several Confederate forces, about 35,000 men in all, and placed them under the command of Joseph E. Johnston. But Sherman could not be stopped. Carrying muskets overhead, his men splashed through the cold swamps, captured the narrow causeways that crossed the lowlands, chopped trees and constructed corduroy roads for their wagon trains. And when they came to a town, village, or plantation, they applied the torch. Charleston fell to Sherman on February 18, 1865.

Delayed only slightly by icy rain and rebel counterjabs, Sherman pursued the Confederates into North Carolina. At length, on March 19, Johnston made his last stand in a densely wooded area near Bentonville (similar to the Wilderness in Virginia). The fight was fierce and the Confederates held on bravely. But it was no use. Sherman's army was too large and powerful.

The war in the Carolinas was over.

To Appomattox

In Virginia the war lingered on. Much had happened since summer 1864: Sheridan's campaign in the Shenandoah, Sherman's march to the sea, Thomas's smashing victory at Nashville, the federal onslaught in the Carolinas. But—if one consulted the maps—the situation in the vicinity of Petersburg and Richmond had changed little. The Army of Northern Virginia still occupied Petersburg, and United States forces under Grant continued their siege.

Battle maps were deceptive. Grant by March 1865 had a well-fed, well-shod army of 115,000 in the trenches around Petersburg. Plagued by desertion, Lee's tattered Army of Northern Virginia had dwindled to 54,000 men. Loss of the Shenandoah Valley, Georgia, and most of the Carolinas had removed its main source of rations. Clearly Lee, for all his tactical brilliance, could not hold Petersburg much longer; if he did not evacuate the city, Grant would surround him. The fall of Petersburg and its railroads would of course make Richmond indefensible.

In desperation Lee decided to take the offensive. His army attacked on March 25, penetrated the federal picket lines, ran into a wall of musket and mortar fire, and fell back. The action had cost Lee 6,000 men.

Grant now moved to the offensive and Petersburg fell on Sunday, April 2.

Even before Grant's attack, Lee had sent a message to Davis, delivered while the Confederate president was attending church, that the army must abandon Richmond and Petersburg. While the federals hammered at Petersburg's defenses on April 2, Lee organized the withdrawal and Davis prepared to remove the Confederate government farther south. That evening Davis, aboard a special train, clattered down the Richmond and Danville Railroad. Over the next five weeks, until his capture by federal cavalrymen at Irwinsville, Georgia, he tried vainly to rally the South to continued resistance. Lee abandoned Richmond and tried to get what was left of his army to the Blue Ridge Mountains. But by the evening of April 7, Sheridan's cavalry had worked around the Confederate army and taken up positions at Appomattox Court House, across

Union forces who marched into Richmond found that Lee's retreating army had burned the business district. Why had it been impossible for Lee's troops to hold the city any longer?

Lee's line of retreat. Lee was trapped. Still, he decided to launch one last stroke to try to break through Grant's lines. On Sunday morning, April 9 (Palm Sunday) the Confederates made a gallant but futile attack. At that point Lee told fellow officers: "There is nothing left for me but to go and see General Grant, and I had rather die a thousand deaths." With that he dispatched a messenger carrying a white flag to request a meeting with the United States general.

A War Ends

On that epochal Sunday morning at Appomattox Court House a stillness more awesome than an artillery barrage settled over the battle lines. Soldiers of both armies sensed that the war, for all practical purposes, was about to end. But they could not quite believe it. They had fought so long that they had come to feel the war must go on forever.

Lee and Grant meanwhile agreed to meet in the early afternoon in the parlor of Wilmer McLean's two-story brick house. At the appointed time Lee appeared wearing a full-dress uniform, embroidered belt, and buff gauntlets. A presentation sword dangled from his side. Mudsplattered, Grant rode up to the house about 1:30

P.M. He wore a private's blouse with the straps of a lieutenant general tacked to the shoulder (he later apologized for his appearance, explaining that the army had outrun his baggage train). He carried no side arms. When Grant strode into the parlor, Lee stood up and the two men shook hands. Grant at once noticed Lee's sword and made up his mind that he would not accept it. Still, if Lee offered it he did not want to refuse it, because then Lee would have to thank him. And that would hurt Lee's pride.

After the handshake Grant mentioned that he remembered Lee from the Mexican War and doubted, considering differences in their ranks and ages (Lee was fifteen years older than Grant), that Lee would remember him. More small talk. Then Lee, his emotions under severe stress, moved the conversation to the purpose of the meeting, the surrender of the Army of Northern Virginia. After some discussion Grant asked for his order book, took out a pencil, and scrawled his terms: officers and men paroled, arms and military equipment surrendered, officers to keep their side arms (his solution to the problem of Lee's sword) and also their horses. When he finished he carried the paper across the room to Lee.

Sitting at a table, Lee pushed aside some books and brass candlesticks, took his steel-rimmed spectacles from his pocket, and after wiping the lenses with a handkerchief began to read. To make insertions Grant handed him a pencil. The generous terms pleased Lee, who commented: "This will do much toward conciliating our people." He noted, however, that many Confederate enlisted men owned their horses and would be unable to put in a crop to carry their families through the next winter without them. Grant replied that he would issue an order allowing every Confederate soldier who claimed a horse or mule to take the animal home. Lee then mentioned that his men had barely eaten for several days, whereupon Grant ordered 25,000 rations delivered to Confederate lines.

The terms of surrender agreed upon and documents signed, Lee rose, shook hands with Grant, bowed to the other United States officers, and with his aide left the room. At the doorway he stopped, his gaze taking in the blooming Virginia countryside, and pounded his fist three times into the palm of his hand. After Lee had mounted his gray horse, Traveller, Grant, standing on the front steps of the house, raised his hat in parting salute. Lee lifted his hat in return, then rode away.

In a field to the front of the McLean house the Stars and Stripes billowed in the breeze.

STUDY GUIDE: Sherman began a march northward toward South Carolina in January 1865. Lee assembled his remaining forces under General Joseph Johnston to counter Sherman. But Sherman couldn't be stopped. In March Johnston made his last stand near Bentonville. The war in the Carolinas was ended. Grant took Petersburg, Virginia on April 2. Lee abandoned Richmond and tried to get his army to the Blue Ridge Mountains. Union forces took positions across his line of retreat. Lee surrendered at Appomattox Court House on April 9, 1865. With his surrender the Confederacy collapsed. Confederate President Jefferson Davis was captured five weeks later in Georgia.

SUMMING UP THE CHAPTER

Names and Terms to Identify

William H. Seward
George B. McClellan
David G. Farragut
Vicksburg
Antietam
Thirteenth Amendment
Perryville
Braxton Bragg
Copperheads
Joseph Hooker

"greenbacks"
Homestead Act of 1862
Clement L. Vallandigham
ex parte Milligan case
Maximilian
Andersonville
Chancellorsville
George C. Meade
Chickamauga
Appomattox

Study Questions and Points to Review

1. What were the consequences of the Civil War?

2. What advantages did the South have at the start of the Civil War? What were the advantages of the North?

3. What contribution did Lincoln make to the northern war effort?

4. What was Winfield Scott's strategy for defeating the South?

5. Who were the Radical Republicans?

6. What was the Morrill Tariff?

7. What was the Emancipation Proclamation? What did the Proclamation accomplish?

8. Why did Lee invade Pennsylvania in 1863?

9. Why did the Republican party temporarily change its name during the wartime election?

10. Who opposed Lincoln on the Democratic ticket in the election of 1864?

11. What was Sherman's objective in his march to the sea?

12. On Atlas Maps 15, 16, and 17, locate: Fort Henry, Shiloh, Fort Sumter, Fort Donelson, Port Hudson, Chickamauga, Chattanooga, Vicksburg, Atlanta, Nashville, Petersburg, Atlanta.

Topics for Discussion

1. When was the turning point of the war? Why?

2. What diplomatic advantage did the Confederacy have over the Union at the start of the Civil War? What do you think would have happened if Great Britain had sided with the Confederacy instead of maintaining a neutral attitude in the war?

3. Give your opinion on this statement: The Confederacy had better generals and more courageous soldiers in the Civil War.

Subjects for Reports or Essays

1. Assume it is autumn 1862. You are a northern newspaper editor and Lincoln has recently announced the Emancipation Proclamation. Write an editorial praising or criticizing the president for his action.

2. Write a short biography of one of the military leaders mentioned in this chapter.

3. Prepare a report for class presentation on one of the following topics: (a) The part women played in the Civil War; (b) Sherman's "March to the Sea"; (c) The Negro and the Civil War; (d) Military weaponry during the Civil War; (e) Hospital and medical facilities during the Civil War.

Projects, Activities, and Skills

1. Matthew Brady was an American photographer who took his camera onto the battlefield during the Civil War. His photographs of the Union armies have given us a vivid pictorial history of that war. Using reference materials, locate some of these photographs and report your impressions of them to the class.

2. Use a stamp collection to illustrate major events and persons of the Civil War era.

3. Listen to recordings of Civil War songs of the North and South. What does the music tell you about the sentiments of the northerners and southerners?

4. If you live near or have visited the site of a Civil War battle or a place that was important in that era, prepare a report on it for classroom use.

5. Arrange a classroom exhibit on the Civil War. Use pictures of important political and military leaders. Display models and illustrations of equipment and uniforms. Perhaps some members of the class can provide memorabilia of the war.

6. There are many excellent books on the Civil War. Some of them are listed in the "Further Readings" section. Choose one of these books on a phase of the war that most interests you and report on it to the class.

Further Readings

General

Army Life in a Black Regiment by T. W. Higginson. A fascinating account written in 1870.

The Blue and the Gray: The Civil War as Told by Participants ed. by Henry Steele Commager. A very interesting collection of contemporary accounts.

The Confederacy by Roland Charles.

The Emancipation Proclamation by John Hope Franklin. An outstanding study.

Glory Road: The Bloody Route from Fredericksburg to Gettysburg, Mr. Lincoln's Army, and *A Stillness at Appomattox* by Bruce Catton. A trilogy about the Army of the Potomac.

The Life of Billy Yank and *The Life of Johnny Reb* (2 vols.) by Bell I. Wiley. These two books tell what the war was like for the common soldier.

The Negro in the Civil War by Benjamin Quarles. A useful study.

Biography

Abraham Lincoln: The War Years (4 vols.) by Carl Sandburg.

Grant Moves South and *Grant Takes Command* by Bruce Catton.

The Personal Memoirs of U. S. Grant (2 vols.) by U. S. Grant. The outstanding memoir of the war.

R. E. Lee (4 vols.) by Douglas S. Freeman.

Sherman: Fighting Prophet by Lloyd Lewis.

Stanton: The Life and Times of Lincoln's Secretary by Benjamin P. Thomas and Harold M. Hyman.

Fiction

Andersonville by MacKinlay Kantor. A prize-winning novel based on the notorious Confederate prison.

The Crisis by Winston Churchill. A classic.

The Red Badge of Courage by Stephen Crane. Realistic story about a young soldier at Chancellorsville.

Pictorial History

The American Heritage Picture History of the Civil War by Bruce Catton.

Civil War in Pictures by F. Pratt.

Gardner's Photographic Sketch Book of the Civil War by A. Gardner.

Mr. Lincoln's Cameraman: Matthew B. Brady by R. Meredith. Contains photographs by the Civil War photographer.

CHAPTER 6

RECONSTRUCTION AND BLACKS

AT THE WHITE HOUSE on the evening of April 9, 1865, President Lincoln and his wife were entertaining guests in the Red Room when Secretary of War Stanton entered. Choked with emotion, he read a telegram he had just received from General Grant. It announced Lee's surrender of the Army of Northern Virginia. The only remaining rebel force of any consequence was that in North Carolina under Joseph E. Johnston and clearly it could not hold out much longer.

THE NATION CELEBRATES VICTORY

Only a handful of Washingtonians heard the glad news that night. Then at dawn the following day an awful rumble broke the morning calm. Buildings trembled, windowpanes shattered, but most people were not alarmed. They guessed that federal batteries were saluting, at last, Grant's final victory over Lee. Thousands of them dressed quickly, rushed into the streets, and snapped up newspapers bannering the reports from Appomattox Court House. Church bells rang out, locomotive whistles shrieked, and flags blossomed everywhere.

The thoughts of many people turned to the White House, and by early afternoon a throng had gathered around the presidential mansion. Tired but happy (he was thirty-five pounds underweight), Lincoln appeared briefly at a window. At his side his son Tad waved a captured Confederate flag. The president turned aside requests that he make a speech, but then Tad bolted onto the porch with his banner. The distinguished chief executive, to the amusement of the crowd, moved with obvious embarrassment to retrieve the boy. Now outside, clutching Tad's hand, Lincoln turned to the crowd and promised a speech the following evening. Then he expressed fondness for the southern war song "Dixie," now a prize of war, he said, and asked the Navy Band to play it.

Lincoln Pleads for Unity

Tuesday evening, April 11, was warm and humid, and a large crowd assembled on the front lawn of the White House, spilled over into Pennsylvania Avenue, and blocked traffic. At length a window of the mansion opened, curtains parted, and the tall, gaunt frame of the president came into view. His appearance signaled a thunderous ovation. Lincoln waved to the throng, then waited for silence. In a few moments the cheering faded. After adjusting his spectacles the president began to read his speech. Standing at his side, Mrs. Lincoln held a lamp over the pages. Everybody expected a rousing oration exalting the Union's glorious triumph over rebellion. Instead Lincoln turned to the problem of reconstructing the nation. He urged northerners to put aside passions of the past four years, purge themselves of thoughts of revenge, and get on with the business of "restoring the proper practical relations between these [southern] states and the Union." The audience was disappointed and people began to drift away before the speech ended. When the president finished, those who remained offered only polite applause.

The Radical Republicans, who wanted to hang Confederate leaders and punish the South for treason, were aghast. Despite his pocket veto of the Wade-Davis Bill in summer 1864, Radicals had thought, now that the war was over, they might win Lincoln over to a stern policy toward those slavemongers who had tried to tear the Union asunder.

Three days later, April 14, Good Friday, Lincoln went to his office at 7:00 A.M. After signing a few papers the president had a light breakfast with his family, returned to the office, and routinely received a stream of callers. In mid-morning he made a quick trip to the War Department to learn if any word had come in from General Sherman indicating that the small Confederate force in North Carolina was ready to surrender. No news. Back at the White House he had an interview with Grant and reiterated his hope that the North would consent to generous treatment of the prostrate South. Next came a cabinet meeting, a light lunch, and more work at the office, including the pardoning of a deserter from the federal army — "I think the boy

[175]

HEADLINE EVENTS

1864 Lincoln pocket vetoes Wade-Davis Bill
Lincoln reelected to presidency

1865 Lincoln inaugurated for second term
Freedmen's Bureau created
Lee surrenders at Appomattox Court House; Civil War ends
Lincoln addresses his countrymen for last time
Andrew Johnson assumes presidency upon assassination of Lincoln
Johnson issues amnesty proclamation
Southern states form new governments; enact black codes
Thirteenth Amendment ratified
Congress convenes; Radicals refuse membership to representatives of former Confederate States

1865-1866 Seward presses French to get out of Mexico

1866 Johnson vetoes bill to extend Freedmen's Bureau
Civil Rights Act
"Waving the bloody shirt"

1867 Nebraska enters the Union
First Reconstruction Act
Tenure of Office Act
Command of the Army Act
United States purchases Alaska from Russia for $7.2 million
United States gains Midway Island in Pacific

1868 Fourteenth Amendment ratified (only by northern states)
House of Representatives impeaches Johnson; Senate sits as jury

1869 Ulysses S. Grant inaugurated president

1870 Fifteenth Amendment ratified
Enforcement Act

1871 Ku Klux Klan Act

1873 Grant inaugurated for second term
Financial panic

1876 Disputed Hayes-Tilden election
Electoral commission rules that Hayes is president

1877 Hayes inaugurated president

can do us more good above ground than under ground," he observed — and revocation of the death sentence of a Confederate spy.

After receiving a few more callers he managed to slip away at five o'clock for a drive with Mrs. Lincoln. A matched pair of black horses drew the presidential carriage up past the Capitol and over to the Navy Yard. As they rode the couple talked of their future together. Perhaps they would tour Europe, then return to Springfield, where Lincoln might resume his law practice. Back at the White House again and more callers. Then dinner and another quick trip to the War Department.

At 8:15 the president and Mrs. Lincoln again climbed in the presidential carriage, this time to drive to Ford's Theatre to attend a performance of the popular comedy, *Our American Cousin*. Down the driveway they rolled, through the east gate, eastward on Pennsylvania Avenue. By now a misty fog had settled over the city, causing gaslights to put out an eerie glow. Sidewalks were nearly deserted. Only the rhythmic clatter of hoofbeats disturbed the evening calm.

A few minutes later the carriage pulled up in front of the theater. Act One of the play was in progress, but when the leading lady spied the Lincolns she stepped to the front of the stage and began to clap her hands. Everyone in the theater looked about, then stood up. As the presidential party moved down a side aisle, the band broke into "Hail to the Chief." Ushered to the flag-draped state box above and to the right of the stage, Lincoln acknowledged the ovation, then settled back in a haircloth rocking chair to the rear of the box. To get a better view of the stage, his White House guard took a seat near the front. The play was light and funny and Lincoln chuckled throughout. For a while he held Mrs. Lincoln's hand.

Lincoln Is Assassinated

During the third act a young man moved quietly down the side aisle, handed a note to the president's coachmen, and passed through a little door to the state box. The play was nearing its climax and the din of laughter filled the theater. A few moments later there was a muffled shot. A cloud of smoke drifted out from the shadows. The man, a mentally unbalanced actor, John Wilkes Booth, leaped down to the stage. From the presidential box came a scream. Dragging his left leg (broken in the leap), Booth waved a knife and shouted: *"Sic semper tyrannis"* —

"Thus always to tyrants"—the motto of the state of Virginia.

Confusion and panic seized the theater until, after some minutes, federal soldiers restored order. The soldiers also cleared a path and several men carried the limp form of the president across the street to a small stone house belonging to a tailor. Placed diagonally on a bed (because of his great length), Lincoln breathed heavily. Examining surgeons found that Booth's bullet had entered the back of the head and lodged near the right eye. Soon cabinet members, congressmen, and other officials gathered at the president's bedside. In a front room Mrs. Lincoln sobbed. Through the long night men talked in whispers, their words punctuated by the labored breathing of the sixteenth president. By morning a cold rain had begun to fall. Still a large, silent crowd kept a vigil in the street outside. Gradually the breathing became weaker. At 7:22 A.M., April 15, 1865, Abraham Lincoln died.

Andrew Johnson, President

The new president was Andrew Johnson.

Born in a shack at Raleigh, North Carolina, in 1808, Johnson, like Lincoln, grew up in poverty. But unlike Lincoln, who attended school for about a year, Johnson never spent a single day in a classroom. When he was three years old his father, a handyman, died, and when he was thirteen he was apprenticed to a tailor. Under terms of the apprenticeship he was to receive room, board, and clothing in exchange for his labor until he reached the age of twenty-one. Two years later young Andrew ran away, worked for a time as a journeyman tailor in South Carolina, then returned to Raleigh. Learning that the tailor who held his apprenticeship bond had posted a ten-dollar reward for his capture, he persuaded his mother and stepfather to migrate with him over the mountains to eastern Tennessee.

After a difficult trip in a two-wheeled cart drawn by a blind pony, the Johnsons settled in the village of Greeneville. There Andrew acquired a two-room house, tacked up a sign reading "A. Johnson, Tailor," and opened a shop. At nineteen the youthful tailor married Eliza McCardle, a kindly woman who by day read to her husband as he worked and in the evening taught him to write. From the union came five children, one of whom became a federal soldier in the Civil War and died in battle.

Library of Congress

This wood engraving of the assassination of Abraham Lincoln appeared in *Harper's* in 1865. After his death, what became of Lincoln's plans for Reconstruction?

Ambitious and industrious, Johnson prospered as a tailor (and to the present day remains the only craftsman ever to achieve the American presidency). He built a comfortable house in Greeneville, and bought some slaves. Through most of his life he made his own clothes and while governor of Tennessee, as a gesture of goodwill, presented the governor of Kentucky with a suit tailored by his own hand.

Johnson also took part in local debating forums and eventually attracted attention as an orator. Robust, even crude, his speaking style was effective, and this oratorical flair, inevitably perhaps, took him into politics. His platform was uncomplicated: he scorned the planter aristocracy of the South and championed the interests of the "common man." His appeal struck a chord with voters. Always running as a Democrat, he advanced steadily—from alderman, to mayor, to the state legislature, to the national House of Representatives. After five terms in Congress (1843-53), where he supported the Mexican War, voted for the Compromise of 1850, and became one of the initial advocates of a homestead law, he served two terms as governor of Tennessee (1853-57). Then he won election to the United States Senate.

Johnson was still in the Senate at the time of the secession crisis in 1860-61 and was the only one of twenty-two southern senators to stand up for the Union. When his state seceded he remained at his desk in Washington, although

Andrew Johnson succeeded Abraham Lincoln as president. Why didn't he support the Radical Republicans' tough reconstruction policies?

fellow southerners denounced him as a traitor and Confederate authorities seized his house and property back in Greeneville. In the North he stood out as a hero.

At Lincoln's request Johnson resigned his seat in the Senate in 1862 to become military governor of Tennessee, a large part of which by that time had been restored to federal control. Then came 1864, an election year. Having rechristened their party the National Union party, Republicans sought to appeal to "war Democrats." Who could better make such an appeal than the Democratic Unionist from the South, Andrew Johnson? Hence, Johnson received second place on the party's presidential ticket. In March 1865, just a month before Lincoln's murder, he took the oath as vice-president.

A rather handsome man, Johnson was solidly built, stood five feet, nine inches, had black hair, dark, piercing eyes, and a firm mouth. His expression usually appeared hard. He was intelligent, energetic, and had bulldog-like cour-

age. But he also lacked tact, spoke his mind bluntly, and had no talent for the kind of smooth maneuvering that had carried Lincoln through political tight spots. He was stubborn and reluctant to yield or compromise, even in the face of impossible odds. Complicating his problem when he entered the White House, he had no personal following in the South or North, and no prestige, like Lincoln, for having led the government in a war. He had broken with the Democrats and remained unaccepted by the Republicans; thus he had the support of no party organization.

STUDY GUIDE: As the North rejoiced in its victory over the Confederacy, President Lincoln turned to the problem of reconstructing the nation. The Radical Republicans wanted to punish the South severely. They opposed Lincoln's more moderate reconstruction plan. Lincoln's assassination brought Andrew Johnson to the presidency. Johnson lacked Lincoln's influence and political ability.

THE PROBLEM OF RECONSTRUCTION

The overwhelming problem confronting the seventeenth president was the same one that had commanded the attention of Lincoln in his last days: reconstruction.

Lincoln had begun to ponder the problem of rebuilding the fractured Union almost from the day the Confederates fired on Fort Sumter in April 1861. In his view the secession ordinances of southern states had no legal foundation (otherwise his attempt to restore federal authority in the South would have lacked justification), and thus the states never had ceased to be members of the federal Union. They were, as he later put it, in a state of suspended animation—out of their normal relationship with the rest of the country. A formula was needed which, upon restoration of federal authority, would enable the southern states to return to a normal relationship as quickly and easily as possible. Who had responsibility for drawing up a formula for reconstruction and directing its execution? In Lincoln's mind the answer was clear: the president.

Lincoln's ideas jelled slowly, and by the end of the year 1863 he determined to set out a program for reconstruction. The result was his Proclamation of Amnesty and Reconstruction offering pardons to former Confederates (except certain categories of military, diplomatic, and civil officers) who would take an oath to support "the Constitution of the United States and the Union of States thereunder." When persons in any state equal in number to one-tenth of the votes cast in that state in the presidential election of 1860 had taken the oath and established a government, the president would recognize that government. (There was not one provision in the "Lincoln plan" to promote or guarantee Negro participation in the politics of reconstructed states.)

Radical Opposition

Radical Republicans were appalled. They too had thought about reconstruction and had settled on a stern policy toward the South. Their motives were mixed. Many Radicals had long felt contempt for the pretensions of the South's planter class and now relished the thought of humiliating the fallen aristocrats. Others felt that southerners had committed treason by their rebellion and must suffer the consequences; anything less would be a betrayal of the scores of thousands of northern soldiers who had laid down their lives in 1861-65 to smother the Confederacy. Some Radicals had genuine feelings of compassion for the Negroes who had borne the awesome weight of the South's social system. They would have no part of a plan, such as Lincoln's, that failed to guarantee Negroes full privileges of American citizenship, and would instead leave them at the mercy of former masters.

The Radicals were aware that the kind of reconstruction sought by Lincoln, assuring white control of southern governments and probably no Negro participation in politics, would bring a resurgence of the Democratic party in the South and weaken the hold of the Republicans in Washington. Conversely, the program of the Radicals, which would disfranchise most former Confederates and guarantee suffrage to former slaves, would bring forth Republican regimes in southern states and cement Republican power in the national capital.

Weighing the problem further, Radicals began to evolve the idea that the southern states by their rebellion had forfeited all rights and privileges in the federal Union. Contrary to the thinking of Lincoln, the states of the Confederacy were not merely in a condition of "suspended animation," temporarily out of their normal relationship with the rest of the country. They had committed "state suicide." As constituted before 1861, they no longer existed. They were federal territories. As territories it would be necessary for them to draft new constitutions and apply for admission to the Union as states. Some Radicals even toyed with the idea of new boundaries for states of the South. Who would spell out conditions on which these territories would receive political organization? Who would approve their admission to the Union? Not the president. Under the federal Constitution those responsibilities belonged to Congress.

The Wade-Davis Bill

Carrying through on their logic, Radicals in Congress in summer 1864 won passage of the Wade-Davis Bill, setting forth their formula for reconstruction. Where the Lincoln plan would have allowed southern states to function under their old constitutions, the Wade-Davis Bill required that these states, on being occupied by federal forces, must draft new constitutions. Before a constitutional convention could convene, however, it would be necessary for a majority of the enrolled white male citizens of a state to take an oath to uphold the Constitution of the United States. Radicals thought such a formula would be "more democratic" than Lincoln's ten percent idea.

Next came provisions to make certain the new constitutions met Radical wishes. First, an individual, to be a delegate to a convention or to be eligible to vote for a delegate, had to take an ironclad oath that he had never voluntarily borne arms against the United States or in other ways aided and abetted the Confederate rebellion. This presumably would assure election of constitutional conventions weighted with southern Unionists sympathetic to Radical views. Second, the constitutions had to deny political rights to all high-ranking civil and military officers of the Confederacy, proclaim the abolition of slavery, and repudiate state and Confederate debts incurred in the rebellion against the United States. Third, constitutions, before they could go into effect, had to have approval of Congress, meaning that if they failed to pass muster with the Radicals the conventions would have to try again.

The Wade-Davis Bill did not become law. Lincoln killed it with a pocket veto. Radicals nonetheless were determined. A few weeks later they published "the Wade-Davis manifesto," a stinging rebuke to the president and a declaration of intent to impose their ideas on southern reconstruction.

But Lincoln was also determined. He presented his views to civil and military leaders, received representatives from areas of the South occupied by federal forces, and discussed reconstruction with members of Congress and his cabinet. He began to pardon individuals in the "excepted" categories—that is, high civil and military officers of the Confederacy. He also stepped up the pace of administering the loyalty oath in occupied areas. Ignoring laments of the Radicals, he went ahead with the business of implementing his "ten percent" plan of reconstruction (and by the time of his death had recognized state governments in Tennessee, Louisiana, Arkansas, and Virginia).

In his second inaugural address, in March 1865, he sounded the theme of generosity toward the South when he said: "With malice toward none, with charity for all, with firmness in the right, as God gives us to see the right, let us strive on to finish the work we are in; to bind up the nation's wounds. . . ." In his last public address, on April 11, 1865, Lincoln begged the North to put aside the passions of war and without rancor restore the southern states as quickly as possible to "their proper practical relation with the Union."

Then on April 15, 1865, Andrew Johnson became president.

Johnson's Policy of Reconstruction

Whatever Radicals may have felt about the death of Lincoln—and some of them thought it a godsend—they were delighted by Johnson's apparent views on reconstruction. During the political campaign of 1864 Johnson had declared that "the traitor has ceased to be a citizen, and in joining the rebellion has become a public enemy." Then, shortly after entering the White House, he told a Radical senator that "treason must be made infamous and traitors must be impoverished." Everybody of course knew that Johnson had built his political career on hatred of the South's planter aristocracy—which had been the heart and soul of the Confederacy.

Radicals and others misjudged the new president. Antiplanter, he was not antisouthern, and he felt no particular affection for Negroes. And

as an ideological descendant of Jefferson and Jackson, he believed in letting states manage their own affairs with a minimum of federal interference. Unlike Radicals (who upheld the tradition of Hamilton and Clay), he had scant sympathy for the idea of federal encouragement of business. Johnson also maintained a strong devotion to the memory of Abraham Lincoln. He put great faith in the policies of his predecessor.

Accordingly the seventeenth president picked up where Lincoln had left off and proceeded with a generous policy of reconstruction. Since Congress was not in session and could not convene without a presidential call until December 1865, he encountered no legislative obstacles. Like Lincoln, he proclaimed a general pardon to southerners who would pledge loyalty to the federal Constitution. However, he added to the "excepted" category "all persons . . . the estimated value of whose taxable property is over twenty thousand dollars," an indication that he had not forgotten his long-time hostility toward the South's elite.

Otherwise Johnson's plan of reconstruction was perhaps slightly more generous than Lincoln's, for there was no "ten percent" requirement. It directed the provisional governor of each state not already reconstructed under the Lincoln plan to call for elections to a constitutional convention under suffrage provisions that had existed before the war (hence no Negro voters). Only individuals who had been qualified voters before the war were eligible to be delegates to the convention (hence no Negro delegates).

When "that portion of the people . . . who are loyal,"—whites who had taken a loyalty oath—had written a constitution repealing secession ordinances, abolishing slavery, and repudiating state debts incurred to help the Confederacy, the president would admit that state into constitutional relations with the federal government. What about the civil liberties of former slaves? Like Lincoln, Johnson left that matter with the southern states.

Within a few months after Johnson became president, the remaining unreconstructed states —Mississippi, Georgia, Texas, Alabama, North Carolina, South Carolina, and Florida—were at work under the Johnson plan establishing civil government and charting their postwar social and economic orders. Watching events with an anxious eye, the president hoped that southern reconstruction would be accomplished before the Radical-dominated Thirty-ninth Congress assembled the following December.

STUDY GUIDE: Lincoln's Proclamation of Amnesty and Reconstruction had been designed to restore the southern states to the Union as quickly as possible. It did not contain harsh penalties. The Radical Republicans set forth a much harsher reconstruction proposal in the Wade-Davis Bill. Lincoln's pocket veto prevented the bill from becoming law. When Johnson became president, he continued Lincoln's generous policy of reconstruction.

CONFEDERATE RECONSTRUCTION

When the guns fell silent at Appomattox Court House, southerners, despite Lincoln's generous ideas on reconstruction, had expected that the government in Washington would treat them with a heavy hand. The war had been long and difficult, had claimed more than 350,000 northern lives, and in the northern view responsibility for the awful events of 1861-65 rested exclusively with the South. One could hardly expect the North to welcome the vanquished South back into the federal partnership with a fraternal embrace. Lincoln's death heightened southern pessimism. But then came Johnson's program of reconstruction. With a minimum of restrictions the federal government was permitting the former Confederates to reconstruct themselves. The effect was exhilarating. Putting aside any lingering bitterness, southerners by the tens of thousands pledged allegiance to the federal Constitution. High-ranking civil and military officers of the Confederacy, including Robert E. Lee, requested presidential clemency and Johnson by September 1865 was signing a hundred pardons each day for southerners in "excepted" categories.

A few dark spots still clouded the picture for southerners during summer and autumn 1865. One was the continued presence in southern cities and towns of United States soldiers, many of whom were former slaves. Southern whites believed this to be a calculated insult. In the words of the Alabama legislature, federal troops were a "constant source of irritation to the people." Even on this point Johnson seemed anxious to appease the South. He stepped up demobilization of the federal army, and by spring 1866 only a handful of soldiers remained in the former Confederacy.

The Freedmen's Bureau

The Freedmen's Bureau was established as the war was moving to a conclusion, in March 1865, as a temporary agency (to last one year) to help former slaves and to administer abandoned lands in the South. After Lee's surrender, the bureau shifted into high gear. Under the competent direction of General Oliver O. Howard, the bureau assisted white refugees as well as freedmen by supplying food and medical services. It helped resettle thousands of displaced persons, helped a few Negroes acquire land (most of it poor), and helped those freedmen get started in farming. It also supervised labor contracts involving freedmen and urged white employers to deal fairly with them. It established courts and boards which mediated disputes between white planters and black laborers and also settled many civil and criminal cases involving freedmen. It built hospitals and established or supervised elementary and secondary schools, vocational schools, and colleges. By 1870 some 250,000 Negroes, kept illiterate in slavery, were enrolled in 4,300 schools.

Whatever its good works, white southerners despised the Freedmen's Bureau. In particular they resented the bureau's educational program. Education, they thought, would "spoil" Negroes and divert them from the heavy, unskilled labor and domestic service that providence had ordained for them. Hence they ostracized, even intimidated, white teachers (many of whom were "Yankee girls" from New England) who had come south to help former slaves learn to read and write. Hooligans wrecked and burned many Negro schools.

To undermine the Freedmen's Bureau, white southerners complained of corruption and maladministration in the agency—and there was some of both, particularly the latter. President Johnson in 1866 sent out an investigating commission to check on the bureau, but investigators could find so little misconduct that they soon abandoned the search. The corruption they did uncover often took the form of secret arrangements between bureau agents and southern whites to take advantage of Negroes. Critical opinion in the South did influence President Johnson, and in February 1866 when Congress voted to extend the life of the bureau and in-

Museum of the Confederacy, Richmond, Va.

These jurors made up the first integrated panel called to duty in the United States. The grand jury selected from among them indicted Jefferson Davis in 1868 for treason. However, Jefferson was never tried. Why not?

crease its power, the president exercised his veto. Several months later, however, Congress passed the extension bill over the presidential veto.

Southern whites did not permit discontent over federal troops and the Freedmen's Bureau to delay the business of political reconstruction. They drafted new state constitutions, elected officials, and set up governments. Political rights for Negroes? They never considered the possibility. To undercut Radical Republicans of the North who, in Johnson's words, "are wild upon Negro franchise," the president urged token enfranchisement of former slaves. His appeal created not a ripple of interest. In the view of southern whites, the Negro was not—and never would be—capable of prudent political judgments; hence Negro participation in politics was absurd.

The outcome was rapid restoration of leaders of the Confederacy to positions of power. The Confederate vice-president, six Confederate cabinet officers, fifty-eight Confederate congressmen, four Confederate generals, and five colonels won election to the Thirty-ninth Congress. In the Louisiana legislature former Confederate officers wore their uniforms and across the South service in the "lost cause" of 1861-65 virtually became necessary for political success.

In control of the political machinery of the South, the former Confederates began the task of rebuilding their region. They set out to repair railroads, bridges, and public buildings, issued bonds, and voted pensions for Confederate veterans. Some state legislatures sought to attract northern capital by exempting new factories from taxation. Others built hospitals,

insane asylums, and prisons. And most turned attention to building the South's first system of free public education—for white children.

Black Codes

To fix the place of the Negro in the postwar society of the South, reconstructed state legislatures and local governments adopted laws and ordinances which became known as "black codes." The codes varied from state to state, but generally prevented Negroes from testifying against whites, forbade Negroes to bear arms, required Negroes to be off the streets by sundown, and prohibited Negroes from any kind of work except agricultural and domestic service. Intermarriage between Negroes and whites was punishable by long imprisonment. If a Negro failed to have a job, he was subject to arrest and a jail sentence as a vagrant. Some codes prohibited sale of alcoholic beverages to Negroes and others decreed punishment for Negroes who made "insulting gestures" to whites. The Mississippi code forbade Negroes to buy or rent farms. In Louisiana black farm laborers, in the first ten days of each January, had to sign contracts with planters that were binding for the rest of the year.

Violence and Terror

To control freed slaves, and also to assure a steady supply of cheap labor, white leaders in 1865-66 calmly tolerated a reign of terror against blacks in many parts of the South. There was a great deal of violence by poor whites who galloped about the countryside on horseback, usually at night, beating and murdering blacks.

For the poor whites this often was a matter of giving vent to old frustrations. Unable to afford slaves and embittered by their own low estate, they had long despised the Negro and yearned to "take him in hand" and "prove" their own superiority. Slaves, of course, had represented a large investment and masters were careful to protect them from the pent-up rage of poor whites. Then came emancipation and the black man's protection was gone.

Underlying this determination to keep the Negro "in his place" was a feeling of confidence that the federal government under the leadership of Lincoln and Johnson had committed itself to a policy of allowing whites of the South to order the affairs of the freedmen and would do nothing to disturb the system of white supremacy. Such confidence grew when President Johnson in a special message to the Senate in December 1865 spoke blandly of the "black codes" as "measures . . . to confer upon freedmen the privileges which are essential to their comfort, protection, and security."

By spring 1866 the reconstruction process was complete—or so it seemed. Civil government was functioning across the former Confederacy. The same men who had manipulated the power before and during the war were again in control. The Negro was in a subordinate position which was little improved over that of slavery. It was almost as though the Civil War had never taken place.

STUDY GUIDE: Most southerners had expected harsh terms. They expressed their pleasure with Johnson's program of reconstruction by pledging allegiance to the federal Constitution. However, they resented the presence of federal troops in the South and opposed the Freedmen's Bureau. Former leaders of the Confederacy gained control of the political machinery of the South. They denied political rights to Negroes.

REACTION IN THE NORTH

Meanwhile there were rumblings through the North.

While congressional Radicals had spoken out for stern treatment of the South, a majority of the northern people, taken up with their own problems of demobilization and reconversion, were willing in the months after Appomattox to go along with presidential reconstruction. There doubtless was something to say for a policy calculated to heal quickly the wounds of the recent war. But then disturbing reports began to filter out of the South. Everywhere, it seemed, southern whites were treating federal troops with sullen contempt. They were also creating, seemingly in a spirit of defiance, the cult of the "lost cause," a glorification of the rebellion.

At the same time, the very men who in 1861-65 had attempted to break up the Union were slipping back into the seats of political leadership. Next the North became aware of the determination of southern whites to oppress former slaves and deny them ordinary civil liberties. Northern whites, it was true, had never treated Negroes as equals and many states of the North, even after the Civil War, continued to restrict the political and social rights of black men. Still, they had not bound the Negro in a web of legislation designed to keep him as a second-class citizen. Northerners expected Negroes in the South, in light of their new status as freedmen, to receive at least as much consideration as black men had long enjoyed in the North. Instead the South was imposing "black codes." To millions of northerners it seemed that despite the Emancipation Proclamation and the Thirteenth Amendment to the Constitution (an amendment prohibiting slavery, ratified in December 1865) the South intended to reestablish slavery in a new guise.

Northerners were at first puzzled, even hurt by the behavior of former Confederates. Then as months passed and the trend of events in the South came into sharper focus their tempers began to rise. Refusing the North's hand of friendship was one thing. But had the South forgotten which side won the war? Many northerners shared the sentiments of the Chicago *Tribune* that the North would turn the state of Mississippi into a frog pond before permitting "black codes" to "disgrace one foot of soil in which the bones of our soldiers sleep and over which the flag of freedom waves."

The changing mood of the North naturally encouraged Radicals, who never for a moment had considered accepting presidential reconstruction as an accomplished fact—as Johnson hoped they might. Since Lee's surrender in April 1865, Radicals had counted the months and weeks until Congress would meet in December. They were determined to undo the work of Lincoln, Johnson, and the Confederates. By late autumn 1865, it seemed that northern opinion, apathetic or hostile to Radicalism the previous spring, was swinging behind Radical ideas and would provide the necessary political and moral support.

The Champions of Radicalism

Two men, Representative Thaddeus Stevens of Pennsylvania and Senator Charles Sumner of Massachusetts, had emerged as the leading champions of Radicalism. The more aggressive of the pair was Stevens, an angry, sarcastic old man.

Born and reared on the Vermont frontier, Stevens, after graduating from Dartmouth College, had migrated to southern Pennsylvania. He became one of the leading attorneys of the state and owner of a large if rather unprofitable ironworks. As a young man he had caught the spirit of the abolitionist crusade, deciding that slavery was "a curse, a shame, and a crime." He offered without fee his legal talent to many fugitive slaves and in 1838 refused to sign a new constitution for Pennsylvania (which he had helped draft) because it denied the vote to "men of color."

Like all abolitionists, Stevens developed an unyielding hatred of the planter aristocracy of the South and longed for the day when the southern gentry would be made to pay for its sins against blacks.

Stevens's abolitionist zeal did not weaken in the 1840s and 1850s. When he entered Congress in 1849 (as a Whig), he established a reputation as an uncompromising opponent of slavery. He helped organize the Republican party in Pennsylvania in the mid-1850s and when the secession crisis developed in 1860-61 hotly opposed any concessions to the South. Lincoln's and later Johnson's ideas of a conciliatory policy of reconstruction naturally roused his fury and he never flinched in his determination to impress the Radical stamp on the postwar South.

Charles Sumner was nineteen years younger than Stevens. While Stevens seemed to carry the marks of his backwoods origin, Sumner was urbane and polished, was not an angry man, and did not have a volcanic temper. A member of a wealthy Massachusetts family, he had graduated from Harvard, later lectured at the school, and for three years (1837-40) traveled about Europe. By the 1840s he had become inspired with a strong sense of humanitarianism, took part in a

movement to outlaw war, and then turned to abolitionism. He helped put together the Free-Soil party in 1848, entered the United States Senate in 1851, and revealed a unique talent for controlled invective and biting sarcasm in lashing out against the Fugitive Slave Law and the Kansas-Nebraska Bill. He joined the new Republican party in 1854 and in the Senate chamber in 1856, after delivering a speech entitled "The Crime Against Kansas," was beaten senseless by a senator from South Carolina (see Chapter 4). Injuries sustained in the assault kept him from his Senate desk for more than three years and made him a hero in many parts of the North.

When the Civil War broke out, Sumner became an ardent exponent of an emancipation decree and aligned himself with Radical Republicans. In 1862 he formulated the "state suicide" theory that the South, through its rebellion, had forfeited all rights under the Constitution. Unlike Stevens and other Radicals, however, he did not hold strong feelings of vindictiveness toward the Confederates. His central purpose during the period of reconstruction was to safeguard the civil liberties of freedmen and make certain that Negroes shared in the political life of the postwar South.

STUDY GUIDE: Northerners became angry when southern leaders passed "black codes" to limit the freedom of former slaves. As a result, Radical Republicans won wider support in the North for their tougher Reconstruction policy.

RADICALS VERSUS JOHNSON

Taking advantage of Article I, Section 5 of the Constitution, permitting Congress to judge the qualifications of its members, Radicals in Congress made their first move in December 1865 by refusing membership to representatives elected from former Confederate states. This assured Radicals of continuing control of Congress and made it likely that on at least some issues they would be able to muster the two-thirds vote necessary to override presidential vetoes.

Next Radicals created the Joint Committee of Fifteen, six senators and nine members of the House of Representatives, "to inquire into the condition of the States which formed the so-called Confederate States of America." The committee had a mandate to decide whether any southern states were entitled to representation in Congress. Until such time as the committee made its report Congress would accept no members from states of the late Confederacy. The outcome was one of the first full-scale inquiries in the history of the national legislature. Nearly one hundred and fifty witnesses paraded before the joint committee. Most of them testified to the alleged arrogance of whites and mistreatment of former slaves across the entire South. When the committee issued its report, in June 1866, it concluded that presidential reconstruction—returning control of the South to former Confederates—had been "madness and folly." The report called for adequate safeguards "before restoring the insurrectionary States to a participation in the direction of public affairs."

Congressional Radicals, meanwhile, had confronted Andrew Johnson for the first time in February 1866 when the president vetoed the bill to extend the Freedmen's Bureau. Unimpressed by the Radical argument that former slaves would need the social and educational services offered by the bureau for a long time to come, Johnson attacked the bill on the ground that it created too much patronage, required an oppressive tax burden, and called for military courts in time of peace. The bill, he said, was unnecessary, unwise, and unconstitutional.

The Civil Rights Bill of 1866

Next, in April 1866, Congress passed the Civil Rights Bill, necessitated by the Dred Scott Decision of 1857 that Negroes were not United States citizens. This bill extended citizenship to "all persons (except Indians, who were wards of the government) born in the United States and not subject to any foreign power . . . of every race and color, without regard to any previous condition of slavery or involuntary servitude." The bill also proclaimed the right of such citizens to make contracts, sue, hold real and personal property, and enjoy "full and equal benefit of all laws and proceedings for the security of person and property, as is enjoyed by white citizens." Condemning the legislation as an unwarranted intrusion on state rights, the president again exercised his veto. Stevens and Sumner rallied the forces of Radicalism, mustered the necessary two-thirds vote, and enacted the measure anyhow. Three months later Radicals overcame Johnson's veto of the Freedmen's Bureau Bill.

The Fourteenth Amendment

While Radicals were overriding Johnson's veto of the Civil Rights Bill, in spring 1866, Stevens, Sumner, and others began to worry lest the Supreme Court declare unconstitutional not only this legislation but other measures the Radicals had in mind. The result was the Fourteenth Amendment to the Constitution. The first section of the amendment repeated provisions of the Civil Rights Bill and forbade "any state to deprive any person of life, liberty, or property, without due process of law" or to "deny any person within its jurisdiction the equal protection of the laws."

The second section aimed to compel southern

This was the scene in the lobby of the House of Representatives during debate on the Civil Rights Bill of 1866. President Johnson vetoed the bill. Congressmen who supported it used all kinds of persuasion to enact the bill over his veto.

Library of Congress

states to guarantee Negro suffrage, although some Radicals uneasily noted that it would also apply to states in the North that still denied Negroes the right to vote. It provided that states denying male inhabitants the franchise would face a proportionate loss of representation in Congress and votes in the electoral college.

The third section rejected the pardons which Presidents Lincoln and Johnson had conferred on many civil and military officers of the Confederacy. It provided that only Congress, by a two-thirds vote, could pardon individuals who had broken an oath of allegiance to the United States to serve the Confederacy. The section also provided that (unless pardoned, of course) Confederates who had violated federal oaths were excluded from seats in Congress, the electoral college, and other federal offices.

The fourth section upheld the validity of the debt of the federal government while forbidding the federal government or the states to assume any debts incurred to aid the rebellion or make compensation for losses resulting from the emancipation of slaves.

On submitting the Fourteenth Amendment to the states (June 1866), congressional Radicals advised the South that ratification would open the way for prompt admission of southerners to membership in Congress. When Tennessee a few weeks later approved the amendment, its elected representatives received their seats in the House and Senate. All other states of the former Confederacy, however, rejected the amendment. Even in the North the amendment did not generate great enthusiasm. Few northerners shared the sentiments of Stevens and Sumner about Negroes, and many were reluctant to support a constitutional decree that would strike at political discrimination against Negroes in the North as well as the South. Hence, by the end of 1866 only a few northern states had gotten around to considering the amendment, and not until July 1868 had all of them approved, sometimes—as in Pennsylvania—after lengthy debate.

Northern Discontent Increases

Whatever their thoughts about the Fourteenth Amendment, northerners were becoming increasingly convinced that the Radicals were right. They believed that presidential reconstruction had failed, that it was necessary—as the editor of the New York *Tribune,* Horace Greeley, had written—to "plough the ground again and sow new seed." Reinforcing such conclusions were continuing reports of violence against freedmen, the most distressing of which came out of Memphis and New Orleans.

The outburst at Memphis, in spring 1866, resulted from tension between white policemen and Negro soldiers. After several incidents in which policemen and soldiers pushed one another about, white mobs joined the "peace officers" in a three-day assault on the city's Negro populace until federal soldiers restored order. Forty-six Negroes—men, women, and children—were dead. Several Negro churches and school buildings were smoldering rubble. White casualties: one man injured.

The affair at New Orleans took place on July 30, 1866, when Radicals began steps to disfranchise certain former Confederates and enfranchise some freedmen. A procession of Negroes cheered the Radicals and this was the spark that touched off angry whites. When the riot ended, more than thirty Negroes and four whites were dead.

Unaware of the dimension of the North's increasing hostility toward presidential reconstruction, President Johnson continued to think it possible to turn the Radical tide. The key to the struggle would be the congressional elections of autumn 1866. Radicals at that time controlled barely two-thirds of the votes in Congress, enough to override presidential vetoes on some issues, not on others. If Johnson could engineer defeat of only a handful of Radical representatives and senators, he could beat down Radical legislation with his veto. Stevens, Sumner, and their followers would be able to do nothing about it.

To achieve his purpose, in the summer of 1866 the president set about reviving the National Union coalition that had carried the Lincoln-Johnson ticket to victory in the election of 1864. It was no use. Only a few "moderate" Republicans were willing to follow his leadership. Most would-be National Unionists were Democrats. Johnson next determined to take his case against Radicalism to "the people" and in late August began an ill-starred "swing around the circle," a speaking campaign intended to undermine Radical candidates in the coming elections. By special train he traveled to Baltimore, Philadelphia, New York, Albany, Buffalo, Erie, Cleveland, Detroit, Chicago (where he dedicated a monument to Stephen A. Douglas),

Saint Louis, Indianapolis, Pittsburgh, Harrisburg, and back to Washington. At each city and at innumerable whistle-stops in between he attacked the Radicals, particularly Stevens, the Civil Rights Act, and the Fourteenth Amendment. His speeches were intolerant and bitter, careless and irresponsible. When challenged by hecklers, he snarled, cast aside presidential dignity, and exchanged verbal broadsides. It was a performance which did the cause of anti-Radicalism no good.

Northern Democrats took their cue from Johnson (who, for all practical purposes, had returned to the Democratic fold). Through the balance of the campaign they made race prejudice the cornerstone of their appeal. They accused Republicans of believing in racial equality and favoring intermarriage of whites and blacks. They charged that Republicans planned to encourage migration of cheap Negro labor from the South to industrial centers of the North. One pro-Johnson leader declared that it was a "settled policy" of Radicals to enforce their ideas with a regular army of black troops.

Centering much of their oratorical fire on Johnson, Radicals reminded voters that the president had been drunk at the time of his inauguration as vice-president (the result, it seems, of taking some whiskey when he was already ill). They inferred from this that he was a habitual drunkard although there was no evidence that he ordinarily drank to excess. They charged that Johnson kept a harem in the White House, had been involved in the plot to murder Lincoln, and was conspiring to turn over the federal government to former Confederates and northern "Copperheads."

"Waving the Bloody Shirt"

Then Republicans used the tactic of "waving the bloody shirt" – playing on passions aroused in the war by identifying the Republican party with the Union and patriotism, the Democratic with the Confederacy and treason.

Johnson's unpopularity, the North's increasing hostility toward the South, and the "bloody shirt" did not exhaust Republican advantages as the election of 1866 drew near. Republicans also had the support of northern business, particularly manufacturing and financial interests. The North was prosperous at that time, and businessmen naturally did not wish to see the electorate "rock the boat" by restoring the Democrats to power. Republicans, moreover,

had given industry and financiers what they wanted most: low taxes, a protective tariff, sound currency, and subsidies to western railroads. Democrats since the time of Jefferson and Jackson, on the other hand, had supported the interests of the farmer, opposed the protective tariff, and toyed with unorthodox fiscal ideas.

The welfare of business, then, had become bound up with the welfare of the Republican party – or so it seemed. Was there much likelihood that the Democrats in the foreseeable future might return to national power? As businessmen saw it, there was. If presidential reconstruction stood, the states of the former Confederacy would become strongholds of the Democratic party and eventually Congress would have to grant membership to their elected representatives. Should a handful of northern states then swing into the Democratic column, the Democrats again would have control in Washington. The probable outcome would be an attempt to set aside advantages which business had received under the Republicans. Hence the obvious course for businessmen was to support the Republican party, now dominated by Radicals, and encourage the Radicals in their determination to overturn presidential reconstruction. With former slaves enfranchised and former Confederates disfranchised, the South would be Republican and, as a result, Republican domination in the national capital would be assured for many years to come.

As election day approached, Republicans were confident. They were quite aware of their advantages and also knew that Johnson's "swing around the circle" and the Democrats' appeal to racism had not struck a responsive chord. Their confidence was justified. On election day they achieved a resounding victory. They gained control of every state legislature in the North and the Republican candidate won every northern gubernatorial contest. More important, the electorate assured Republican Radicals of majorities of more than two-thirds in both the Senate and House of Representatives. Johnson was now powerless to save presidential reconstruction; the voters had disarmed his only weapon, the veto.

STUDY GUIDE: Radical Republicans wanted to hold their control of Congress. They refused membership to representatives elected from the former Confederate states. Radical opposition to President Johnson increased when he vetoed the Freedmen's Bureau and Civil Rights bills. The Radicals gathered enough support to pass both bills. Radical pressure led to passage of the Fourteenth Amendment to the Constitution. This amendment guarantees equal rights to all citizens. In the congressional elections of 1866, the Radical Republicans won control of both houses of Congress. This ended presidential Reconstruction.

RADICALS TAKE CHARGE

Savoring their electoral victory, Radicals charted strategy over winter 1866-67. Their principal object, of course, was the undoing of "Confederate" reconstruction. But other thoughts had begun to seize the Radical mind: destruction of presidential power and, perhaps, removal of President Johnson.

The Reconstruction Bill of 1867

To get on with the business of reconstruction, Radical style, Congress passed the first Reconstruction Bill on March 2, 1867. The measure ended the Lincoln-Johnson governments in the South and divided the former Confederacy (Tennessee excepted) into five military districts. Each district was commanded by a general of the federal army. When necessary the district commander could remove civil officials, make arrests, try civilians in military courts, and use federal troops to keep order.

The legislation also charged district commanders with responsibility for setting in motion the new program of political reconstruction. First they were to enroll as voters all adult males, regardless of color—except those who were disfranchised for participation in the Confederate rebellion—and arrange for election of delegates to state conventions. Each convention would then draw up a new state constitution providing for Negro suffrage. After voters had ratified the constitution, they could elect a governor and state legislature. The first legislature was to ratify the Fourteenth Amendment. The new government, however, would be "provisional only, and in all respects subject to the authority of the United States" until Congress had approved the new constitution and the Fourteenth Amendment had become part of the federal Constitution.

RECONSTRUCTION OF THE SOUTHERN STATES

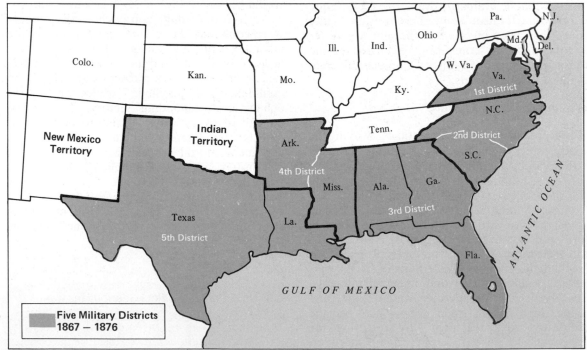

Five Military Districts 1867 – 1876

Thaddeus Stevens led the fight in the House of Representatives for passage of the Civil Rights Bill and the Reconstruction Acts. He was a prosecutor in the impeachment of Andrew Johnson. Although seriously ill, Stevens was carried to the proceedings each day.

Denouncing the Reconstruction Bill as unconstitutional, on the ground that the Constitution gave Congress no authority to fix voting requirements, President Johnson vetoed the bill. It was a futile gesture. Stevens and Sumner easily mustered the necessary two-thirds vote in the two houses of Congress and the bill became law without the presidential signature. Subsequent acts (late March and July 1867 and March 1868) also passed over Johnson's veto.

Attempts to Limit the President

Radicals also took steps to limit the power of the president. On the same day they pushed through the Reconstruction Bill, March 2, 1867, they managed passage of the Tenure of Office Act and Command of the Army Act. The first of these measures provided that the president could not remove members of his cabinet or other civil officeholders appointed with consent of the Senate without the Senate's approval. The legislation had two objectives. It would prevent the president from getting rid of Secretary of War Edwin M. Stanton, the lone member of the Johnson cabinet who favored Radicalism. It would also shield other Radical Republicans in federal jobs from the presidential wrath.

The Command of the Army Act provided that the president could issue military orders only through the "general of the army" (presently General Grant, who seemed increasingly friendly with Radicals). If the president did not approve of the way the general was executing—or not executing—his orders, there was not much he could do about it, for the legislation permitted removal of the general only with consent of the Senate. Thus Congress had restricted Johnson's control of the armed forces and, Radicals hoped, made certain that he would not issue orders to commanders of the new military districts in the South that might impede Radical reconstruction.

Johnson did not flinch. He assailed Radical attempts to limit the power of the presidency, issued orders (with Grant's approval) to commanders of southern military districts curtailing their power, and removed district commanders who displayed sympathies for Radicalism. He also spoke out against Negro suffrage and in his annual message of December 1867 declared that "of all the dangers which our nation has yet encountered, none are equal to those which must result from the success of the effort now making to Africanize the [southern] half of our country." In late 1867, at the time he uttered those words, Johnson had some reason for encouragement. In recent elections across the North the Democratic party had made a remarkable revival, outpolling the Republicans in Ohio, Connecticut, Pennsylvania, and New York. This seemed a repudiation of Radicalism. Even more encouraging, from Johnson's view, Ohio rejected a Negro suffrage amendment, New Jersey refused to delete "white" from its voting requirements, and Maryland approved legislation restricting the suffrage to Caucasians.

STUDY GUIDE: Over the president's veto, Congress passed the Reconstruction Bill of 1867. The South was divided into five military districts. Each district was placed under a commander and ruled like an occupied territory. In an effort to limit the power of the president, the Radicals also won passage of the Tenure of Office Act.

JOHNSON IMPEACHED

Any optimism the president may have felt was ill founded, for Radicals were ready to remove him from office. Their chances of success seemed bright.

Radicals had begun to think seriously of the possibility of getting rid of Johnson at the time of the campaign of 1866. The first step was to gather evidence that the president had committed "high crimes and misdemeanors." After examining the charges, the House of Representatives—acting under Article I, Section II, of the Constitution—would decide if the evidence warranted a trial. If the decision was affirmative, the Senate, sitting as a jury, would listen to the arguments for and against the president. If, as specified in Article I, Section III, two-thirds of the members present voted "guilty," the president would be removed from office.

By early 1867, Radicals were ready to act. They pushed through the House a resolution instructing the Judiciary Committee to "inquire into the conduct of Andrew Johnson." Aided by the Pinkerton detective agency, the committee examined the charges brought against the president: that he had illegally returned property to former Confederates, pardoned men who were still traitors at heart, abused the veto power, and been involved in the plot to murder Lincoln. Evidence was scant and by a vote of 5-4 the committee in June 1867 moved not to recommend impeachment.

Then came Johnson's maneuvers to undermine Radical reconstruction by curtailing the authority of commanders of southern military districts and removing district commanders who seemed in sympathy with Radicalism. Accordingly the Judiciary Committee reconsidered its earlier recommendation and in autumn 1867 voted 5-4 in favor of impeachment. The committee charged Johnson with "usurpation of power" and with attempting to reconstruct southern states "in accordance with his own will, in the interests of the great criminals who carried them [the states] into the rebellion." But many Radicals decided there was insufficient evidence and in December 1867 the House overwhelmingly rejected an impeachment resolution.

Johnson's reprieve was short-lived, for within three months his running dispute with the Radicals over the Tenure of Office Act reached a climax which gave new opportunity to those who wished to turn him out of the White House. Convinced that the Tenure of Office Act was unconstitutional, Johnson had removed Stanton from his position as secretary of war and replaced him with Grant in August 1867, while Congress was not in session. When Congress reconvened, he was sure the Senate, acting under the Tenure of Office measure, would refuse to sanction Stanton's removal.

Johnson's idea was to retain Grant as secretary of war anyhow and force the matter into the federal courts. Hopefully the courts would uphold his view that the Tenure of Office Act violated the Constitution. As expected, the Senate early in 1868 declined to approve the ouster of Stanton. But then Johnson's plan misfired. Somewhat confused and preferring not to be a political storm center, Grant surrendered his office to Stanton. Johnson was furious and accused Grant of treachery. He appointed another man as secretary of war. Stanton, who had as much determination as the president, barricaded himself in his quarters in the War Department, and refused to surrender his office.

The House Votes for Impeachment

At that point, in February 1868, Radicals charged that Johnson had violated the Tenure of Office Act and thus was guilty of "a high misdemeanor." The House of Representatives agreed and by a margin of 126-47 voted to impeach the president. Next—and the order of procedure was curious—the House began to gather evidence to support its judgment. A short time later the House adopted several articles of impeachment which charged the president with violating the Tenure of Office Act and also with attempting "to bring into disgrace, ridicule, hatred, contempt and reproach the Congress of the United States."

The president's trial before the Senate began in March 1868. As prescribed in the Constitution (Article I, Section III), Chief Justice Salmon P. Chase was the presiding officer, a stroke of luck for Johnson since Chase insisted on strict legal procedure. Managing the prosecution were five Radical members of the House, including Stevens, who, it turned out, became so ill and feeble during the trial that servants had to carry him to and from the sessions.

An Able Defense

Johnson, who was not present during the trial, placed his defense in the hands of four able attorneys. These men put forth strong arguments in his behalf. They noted that the real case against Johnson rested on politics. They argued that the Radicals disapproved of the president's policies, hence wanted him out of the way. They warned that the constitutional system of checks and balances would be severely weakened if a hostile Congress could intimidate a president by threatening him with removal. The defense also argued that the president had been within his rights to take action designed to test the constitutionality of the Tenure of Office Act. And then, in their most clever move, Johnson's attorneys pointed out that the Tenure of Office Act protected cabinet officers during the term of the president who had appointed them. Who had appointed Stanton? Lincoln. Thus Johnson had not violated the legislation at all.

Whatever the logic of the case in defense of Johnson, the outcome was by no means certain. Tension ran high in the capital as time drew near, in mid-May, for the vote. The city buzzed with speculation, gamblers quoted the latest odds, and doubtful senators came under merciless pressure to vote this way or that. Then came the day of the vote, May 16, 1868. The sky was overcast. By mid-morning a large crowd had gathered in Pennsylvania Avenue and slowly began to converge on Capitol Hill. While the crowd milled about, carriages clattered up to the Capitol and discharged the main participants in the drama — senators, representatives, the chief justice, and counselors.

Johnson Acquitted

A murmur went through the galleries when four men carried into the room the pain-ridden form of Senator James W. Grimes of Iowa. Radicals had hoped his illness would prevent Grimes from appearing. A Republican who sympathized with Johnson, he was sure to vote for acquittal. Then came the climactic moment. The clerk began to call the names of the senators. As he neared the end of the roll call, the issue remained in doubt. Now a hush fell over the chamber. The clerk had reached the name of Edmund G. Ross, Republican of Kansas, who had not indicated how he might vote and had come under more intensive pressure than any

Andrew Johnson is the only United States president ever to be impeached. Were Johnson's vetoes of Reconstruction acts the real reason for the trial?

other senator. He voted "not guilty." That did it. Johnson's acquittal on this count was assured. The final tabulation showed thirty-five senators voting "guilty," nineteen (twelve Democrats and seven Republicans) voting "not guilty," one vote less than the two-thirds necessary for conviction.

Within minutes a throng of people was making its way down Pennsylvania Avenue to the White House. The news brought tears to the eyes of the president, but he did not appear before the crowd. That night, after a band had serenaded him, he went briefly to a window and thanked the musicians.

The Radicals were not quite finished. After a vigorous effort to persuade just one dissenter of May 16 to change his vote, the Radicals prepared for a roll call on two other articles of impeachment. It came on May 26, but the outcome was exactly as before, 35-19 for conviction. With that the Radicals abandoned hope of getting rid of Johnson, whose term would expire in less than a year anyhow. The Senate adjourned, and Republicans turned attention to their national convention, which in a few weeks would nominate the party's presidential ticket for the election of 1868.

Johnson had kept his office, but his "victory" was hollow. He was a president without influence and in the remaining months of his term received little notice. For a time he entertained the wild hope that the Democrats would make him their presidential nominee and that on election day the following autumn voters would vindicate his stand against Radicalism. The hope was vain. Democrats decided that over the past four years Johnson had made too many enemies.

[191]

To head their ticket they named Horatio Seymour, governor of New York. The Republicans turned to General Grant, and in the election of November 1868 the Republican ticket won handily in the electoral college.

STUDY GUIDE: Determined to get rid of Johnson, the Radicals voted to impeach him. At the trial Johnson was acquitted. In the election of 1868 the Republican candidate, General Ulysses S. Grant, won the presidency.

FOREIGN AFFAIRS

Johnson left the White House on March 4, 1869 and prepared to return home to Tennessee. Looking back over his presidency, he had slight cause for satisfaction. His great purpose of a tolerant policy of reconstruction, calculated to appease southern whites and return former Confederates to power, had failed. Instead of peace and goodwill, as he had hoped, Reconstruction had brought turmoil and bitterness.

Still, in foreign affairs the seventeenth president could note some achievement. While he and the Radicals tugged over federal policy toward the late Confederacy, his secretary of state, William H. Seward, in 1865-66, had pressed the French emperor, Napoleon III, to get his troops out of Mexico where they were bolstering the puppet regime of Maximilian I (see Chapter 5). Because of the great expense and limited rewards of the venture, and also because of the complexities of European politics, in April 1866 the French gave way to Seward's pressure and announced plans for removing troops from Mexico. Maximilian insisted that he was now a Mexican, not an Austrian, and tried to hold his throne. It was no use. He fell into the hands of Mexican partisans and in June 1867 died before a firing squad.

"Seward's Folly"

Meanwhile Seward was negotiating with the Russians for purchase of Alaska. The Russians had held the giant territory for a century and a half and now figured that they would not be able to hold it in the event the Americans again caught the spirit of expansion. They were willing to sell. Seward saw the territory as a potential treasure house and thought it a bargain at the

Courtesy Alaska Travel Division

As Secretary of State under Lincoln, William H. Seward kept European nations from establishing diplomatic relations with the Confederacy. Under Johnson, Seward arranged to buy the Alaskan territory from Russia.

price the Russians were asking. Many of his countrymen, however, lacked his vision and ridiculed Alaska as "Seward's icebox," while deriding the treaty that he arranged with the Russian minister as "Seward's folly." With support of the Radical leader Charles Sumner, the secretary nonetheless got the treaty through the Senate. Then the deal nearly collapsed when the House of Representatives balked at appropriating $7.2 million to complete the "Alaska purchase." Only after the Russian minister, with Seward's connivance, bribed several congressmen did the appropriation bill pass.

That same year, 1867, an American naval officer planted the Stars and Stripes on the Midway Islands, a thousand miles west of the Hawaiian Islands in the Central Pacific, and Nebraska was admitted to the Union as the thirty-seventh state.

STUDY GUIDE: During Johnson's term in office, his Secretary of State, William Seward, got the French government to agree to end their military support of Maximillian I, the puppet ruler of Mexico. Another of Seward's accomplishments was to arrange with Russia for the purchase of Alaska.

THE SOUTH'S NEW ELECTORATE

Meanwhile commanders of southern military districts were proceeding in accordance with the Reconstruction Acts of 1867. They set about the business of discharging state governments established in 1865-66 under the plans of Lincoln and Johnson. The process of political restoration of the former Confederacy began anew. The first step was to enroll voters who would elect delegates to state constitutional conventions. It was a difficult task, accomplished mainly by federal soldiers and agents of the Freedmen's Bureau.

Under the Radical formula three groups would comprise the new southern electorate: Negroes, northerners who since Appomattox had settled in the South, and southern whites who were willing to take the "ironclad oath" that they had not voluntarily aided and abetted the Confederate rebellion.

Negroes

The first of these groups, the Negroes, for the most part were quite unprepared to assume the responsibility of voting because they had been kept illiterate during slavery and also in the brief period of "Confederate reconstruction." But many white frontiersmen who received the vote in the time of Andrew Jackson, and a great many immigrants who were being enrolled as voters by political "bosses" in Boston, New York, Philadelphia, and Baltimore were also illiterate. A former slave who won election as a delegate to the constitutional convention in South Carolina conceded the political inadequacies of Negroes: "I believe, my friends and fellow-citizens, we are not prepared for this suffrage. But we can learn. Give a man tools and let him commence to use them, and in time he will learn a trade. So it is with voting. We may not understand it at the start, but in time we shall learn to do our duty."[1] Yet even then, some blacks had managed to educate themselves or to attend school. John Hope Franklin in *Reconstruction: After the Civil War* has shown that a few blacks had attended college in the North or abroad. Some had earned positions of public office in the northern states, and others had become articulate spokesmen for blacks. These blacks provided effective leadership and carried out their political responsibilities with integrity and efficiency.

How did black people feel toward the white people who had held them in bondage for more than two centuries and abused them with the "black codes" and other acts of discrimination? Few blacks entertained ideas of "getting even" with former masters. On the contrary, blacks in constitutional conventions and later in state

[1] Quoted in John Hope Franklin, *Reconstruction After the Civil War*, copyright 1961 (Chicago: University of Chicago Press), p. 87.

A freedman, pictured in *Harper's,* campaigns for office. Many Negroes who held public office during Reconstruction were well qualified and well educated. Of the twenty-two black congressmen, ten had gone to college. Five were lawyers. Who are some of the black officeholders at the federal and state level today?

Library of Congress

legislatures spoke out regularly for removing political disabilities from whites who had supported the Confederacy. Nor did Negroes in the time of Radical Reconstruction make any large push for integrating southern society.

Carpetbaggers

The individual in the second category of voters — northerners who ventured South after the Civil War — became a "carpetbagger," a term once used to describe any suspicious-looking stranger but now defined as an unprincipled person of the North who after the Civil War swooped down on the South to cheat and exploit its people. A fair number of northerners did take up residence in the South in the years after Appomattox, but recent studies have shown that only a few had plunder and exploitation as their goals. Many so-called carpetbaggers had been federal soldiers who during the war found the southern climate to their liking and determined to settle down in the region. Ex-soldiers usually set up small businesses or went into farming.

Some northern industrialists and investors saw the South, crippled by the war, as a land of economic opportunity. Northerners of this type, using their technical know-how and capital, made important contributions to the physical restoration of the South and did much to foster diversification of the region's economy. "Carpetbag" businessmen in the latter 1860s, for example, established the foundations of the South's present-day iron and steel industry. Finally, many northerners — also labeled carpetbaggers — were teachers and ministers who journeyed southward after the war to meet educational and religious needs of freedmen.

While northerners-come-South had varying backgrounds and purposes, they were nonetheless united in allegiance to the Republican party. For one thing, most had been Republicans before venturing southward and saw no reason to change their politics. For another, they revered the memory of Abraham Lincoln and would have considered it a betrayal to turn away from Lincoln's party. As for businessmen, they sought governments in the South that would protect investments. Many had observed firsthand the lawlessness and violence which had reigned in parts of the region during "Confederate reconstruction," in 1865-66, and decided that the situation required Republican regimes supported by federal troops.

Businessmen, moreover, had become accustomed in the North to favors showered on them by the Republican party: tax exemptions, land grants, and favorable banking and insurance laws. They doubted that southern Democrats, traditionally oriented toward agriculture, would display much concern for the welfare of business. Other northerners in the South — teachers, ministers, and humanitarians — knew of course that the Democratic party had no interest in advancement of the freedmen. The only hope for the former slave was in the Republican party. Convinced therefore that their varied interests required a strong Republican organization in the South, carpetbaggers now faced the next question: how could they make the party a strong and enduring political instrument? Answer: by securing and holding the Negro vote. And so northerners in the South, whatever their private feelings (and many of them felt slight affection for Negroes), fully supported Radical ideas about enfranchising the freedmen.

Carpetbaggers came to provide much of the leadership in southern governments during the time of Radical Reconstruction. This was natural. Given their interests — a sympathetic business climate and the welfare of freedmen — they had a large stake in the politics of their adopted region and were anxious to control the governments. Because of the disfranchisement of former Confederates, moreover, they were the group best prepared by training and experience to assume political leadership in the southern states after the breakdown of presidential Reconstruction.

Scalawags

Then there were the southern whites — called "scalawags" by their white neighbors — who took positions in the constitutional conventions and state legislatures created under the Reconstruction Acts of 1867. A large percentage of these individuals had opposed secession in 1860-61 and during the war made no great attempt to conceal their sympathy for the Union. The result in many cases had been a good deal of abuse at the hands of Confederates. Many scalawags, on the other hand, were poor whites who long had resented the privileged position of the planter elite in southern society. Hence Radical Reconstruction offered Unionists and poor whites an opportunity to settle old scores.

Still, all scalawags were not wartime Unionists

or poverty-ridden whites. A few—including Robert E. Lee's able corps commander, General James A. Longstreet—simply decided that the vanquished must come to terms with the victors. They joined the Republican party, and took an active part in southern politics. Others were southern businessmen who liked such Republican economic policies as the protective tariff and federal appropriations for internal improvements. Finally, many former Whigs in the South gagged at the thought of uniting with their old enemies, the Democrats. These former Whigs saw Republicanism as the heir of Whiggery, and lined up with the Negroes and carpetbaggers.

Whatever their background, scalawags often felt uncomfortable in the Republican party. In particular they did not like the idea of dealing with Negro politicians on terms of equality. They also came under more intensive criticism by fellow southern whites than did Negroes and carpetbaggers. (One white called them "scaly, scabby runts in a herd of cattle.") As time passed, therefore, most of the scalawags strayed from the Republican party and found their way into the ranks of "the white man's party," the Democratic.

STUDY GUIDE: Under the Radical formula the new southern electorate was composed of Negroes, Northerners who had gone south after the war (carpetbaggers), and southern whites (scalawags) who had not aided the Confederate cause.

THE SOUTH UNDER CARPETBAG RULE

When agents had completed the task of enrolling an electorate in a state within a district, the federal military commander of the district called for election of delegates to a convention to draft a new state constitution. Who served as delegates? In Alabama, Georgia, and North Carolina a majority were scalawags. Carpetbaggers and scalawags—that is, whites—comprised a large majority in most states. In Louisiana, however, by agreement, half the delegates were Negroes, and in South Carolina blacks occupied 76 of 124 seats. Hence the notion, accepted by many generations of southern whites in the decades after the Reconstruction era, that Negroes dominated all conventions is largely a myth.

Liberal Constitutions

Even though they passed up a rare opportunity to experiment with unorthodox political structures (for example, the unicameral legislature or executive branch responsible to popular assembly), the constitutional conventions did draw up documents that were more liberal than those they replaced. All of them swept away property qualifications for voting and office-holding. They also provided for universal manhood suffrage—although of course there were restrictions on individuals who refused to vow that they had not voluntarily assisted the Confederacy. The constitutions of Virginia, North Carolina, and South Carolina did away with the old system of legislative apportionment that discriminated in favor of tidewater areas.

All the constitutions provided for free public education for both black and white children. Those of South Carolina and Louisiana forbade segregation in public schools. Some constitutions provided tax exemptions for poor people, others established agencies to assist poverty-ridden people. Most set up state-operated orphanages and institutions for the insane and for deafmutes. Abolition of imprisonment for debt, revision of tax systems (to eliminate advantages long enjoyed by the planter elite), and enlarged rights for women were other features of the new constitutions. Most constitutions reformed penal codes, reduced the number of capital crimes, and updated the judiciary. South Carolina's constitution granted residents of the state —for the first time—the right to get a divorce.

Whatever their merits, the new constitutions came under heavy criticism from southern whites. Planters and other well-to-do groups, calculating that much of the financial burden would fall on them, concentrated on the expense of such institutions as free public schools and mental hospitals. Others seethed over restrictions on the franchise for former Confederates and the provisions guaranteeing the vote to Negroes. Racially mixed schools were another sore point. Still, for most southern whites the constitutions were denounced mainly because carpetbaggers, scalawags, and Negroes (especially Negroes) had drafted them. Despite criticism, most of these constitutions remained in effect for many years after the return of former Confederates to power in the 1870s.

Whenever a state completed the business of drafting a constitution, the district military commander would arrange elections to choose state officials and a legislature. Elections completed, the state's new civil leaders would assemble and turn to their initial task, ratification of the Fourteenth Amendment to the Constitution. On approving the amendment the state was eligible under the Reconstruction Act of March 1867 to apply for readmission to the federal Union. A few states ran into delay, mainly because Radicals in Washington were dissatisfied with the suffrage provisions of their constitutions, but by 1870 civil governments were again humming in every state of the former Confederacy.

The Men Who Controlled the Governments

As one might expect, the composition of the new governments was about the same as that of the recent constitutional conventions. Carpetbaggers and scalawags held a majority of the positions. The idea, held by many succeeding generations of white people in America, that the years of Radical rule were a time of "Negro domination" is a myth. Even in South Carolina, where blacks exerted their greatest influence, whites occupied the governor's office and controlled the upper chamber of the legislature. In Mississippi, where the black population was larger than the white, Negroes never controlled any unit of the government. In other southern states, Negroes had even less authority.

The same pattern prevailed in southern delegations in Congress; during the time of Radical Reconstruction only twenty-two Negroes went to Washington to represent the former Confederate states in the national legislature. Most of the black men who served in the House and Senate at this time were men of education and political experience, and their conduct brought them praise. The prominent Republican leader James G. Blaine of Maine wrote that the black congressmen of both the House and Senate "were as a rule studious, earnest, ambitious men, whose public conduct . . . would be honorable to any race."

In the South the new governments faced large problems and responsibilities. First, they had to get on with the business of cleaning up the mess left by the war—railroads torn asunder, highways and bridges in disrepair, public buildings destroyed. Perhaps the most feverish activity came when legislatures turned to the problem of restoring the region's railroads. Charters were granted to new railroad companies and often the states underwrote the cost by endorsing railroad bonds and granting outright subsidies.

At the same time the legislatures took up the mandate given them in the new state constitutions for providing public schools and other institutions of social welfare. Some legislatures undertook to encourage northern industrialists to establish factories in the South and others sought to attract settlers from the North as well as Europe, sometimes offering homesteads on generous terms as an inducement. The new governments also reformed penal codes, revised formulas for tax assessment, and passed civil rights legislation. A civil rights law in Arkansas, for example, contained public accommodation provisions similar to those of the federal Civil Rights Act that would pass Congress a century later, in 1964.

Corruption in the Governments

The achievements were impressive and mark the bright side of the picture of Radical rule in the South. Unfortunately there was another side—a seamy side. For in the several years after 1867 fraud, influence peddling, and extravagance cast a long shadow over the political life of the South.

Corrupting forces had already begun their work in 1865-66 during the time of "Confederate" Reconstruction. In those years many politicians could not resist the temptation of seizing profitable opportunities where they found them. Carpetbaggers, scalawags, and Negroes, when they took over in 1867, displayed no inclination to return to political purity. And, one might add, when the former Confederates regained power across the South in the 1870s the reign of corruption continued.

What was the nature of the corruption that stained the record of virtually every Radical government? Subsidies and loans to railroad companies which put down flimsy tracks or no tracks at all was one of the most lucrative forms of cheating in the postwar South. Kickbacks from builders, printers, and others who received contracts, charters, and franchises from state governments were another. Bribes were used to enable lawbreakers to escape prosecution. Planters and industrialists paid bribes to evade taxes.

In his first year in office the Radical governor of Louisiana had an income of $100,000 (his official salary was only $8,000), the result of bribes and outright stealing from the state's public school fund. Another governor allegedly stole and sold supplies of the Freedmen's

Bureau, and still another admitted taking bribes amounting to $40,000. The legislature of South Carolina voted a thousand dollars to one of its leaders in gratitude for his faithful service — after he had lost that sum on a horse race. The same legislature bought fine wines, women's apparel, and — for unfortunate members — coffins, charging the purchases to "legislative expenses."

Corruption of course was not confined to the South in the time after the Civil War. A wave of corruption swept the rest of the country, from New York and Philadelphia to Washington, Saint Louis, and California.

This raises the interesting question: Why did America — South, North, and West — experience this breakdown of private and public morality in the years after the Civil War? The explanation probably is twofold. First, the war, like all major wars, upset the social organization of the country. When a country is at war, there is a dramatic change in the national life. People are wrenched from their normal routines and environments and faced with new situations, opportunities, and temptations. Time-honored restraints on personal conduct — family, church, neighbors — lose much of their effectiveness. The inevitable result, it seems, is a moral letdown. The end of the war brings no quick return to normal patterns of life. Hence, the moral letdown carries over into the postwar period.

After the Civil War, moreover, a second factor was at work — the rapid expansion of the national economy (see Chapter 7). Like wartime mobilization, this expansion, North and South, brought rapid social change, presented opportunities and temptations, and eroded old moral restraints. The outcome was the wave of corruption which caught up Radical leaders, planters, and businessmen of the late Confederate states, as well as politicians and barons of industry in the North. The same combination of wartime mobilization, followed by rapid economic expansion, produced similar periods of large-scale fraud and corruption in politics and business after American participation in World War I in 1917-18 and World War II in 1941-45.

STUDY GUIDE: The new state governments formed in the South under carpetbag rule made many improvements in social and economic life. Unfortunately their record was stained by fraud and corruption.

BREAKDOWN OF RADICAL RECONSTRUCTION

During the time of "Confederate" Reconstruction, in 1865-66, white men in the South unleashed a campaign of violence against former slaves and those institutions designed to assist blacks in the transition from bondage to freedom. The Freedmen's Bureau was, of course, attacked. But so was a northern-financed organization, the Union League, designed chiefly to instruct Negroes in their "rights and duties" as American citizens, particularly those pertaining to voting.

The Ku Klux Klan

Among individuals taking part in the campaign were a band of young ruffians of Pulaski, Tennessee, who several months after Lee's surrender formed themselves into an organization that soon became known as the Ku Klux Klan. To reinforce their power to frighten illiterate and superstitious Negroes — and also, no doubt, to bolster their own courage and give their evil activities an appearance of religious sanction — the Klansmen fashioned a weird and elaborate ritual and outfitted themselves in hooded white costumes. Often operating at night, they terrorized Negroes who gave the slightest hint that they considered themselves the social or political equals of whites. Other targets included agents of the Freedmen's Bureau and Union League, and anyone else who offered assistance to blacks. The principal weapons of the Klan included the blacksnake whip, rope, pistol, and knife.

Who were the Klansmen? In the beginning most were so-called poor whites, but eventually the organization attracted more "respectable" individuals, including General John B. Gordon, who had been with Lee at Appomattox Court House, and General Nathan Bedford Forrest, a hero of the Confederate cavalry service who became grand wizard of the Klan.

When in 1867 Radicals took over responsibility for Reconstruction, removed former Confederates from political offices, and installed carpetbaggers, scalawags, and Negroes in their places, the Klan and kindred organizations (such as the Knights of the White Camellia, White Line, White League, White Brotherhood) stepped up their activities. They concentrated on Negroes (and their white tutors) who were determined to exercise their right to vote and hold political office.

The attempts of the federal government to suppress the Ku Klux Klan were useless. Why did the Klan disappear as Southern whites regained control of their state governments? Does the Klan exist in states outside the South today?

The Fifteenth Amendment

Radicals feared that the tactics of intimidation might achieve their purpose and keep thousands of Negroes from the polls. This would permit newly reconstructed governments of southern states to slip back into Confederate hands. If that happened, they were sure, the legislatures would pass measures carefully designed to keep blacks away from the ballot box. Accordingly, in February 1869 Congress adopted the Fifteenth Amendment to the Constitution forbidding states to deny or abridge the right of citizens to exercise the franchise "on account of race, color, or previous condition of servitude." Over the next thirteen months legislatures of

three-fourths of the states registered approval, and in March 1870 the amendment went into effect.

Meanwhile, Radical governments in Tennessee Arkansas, and North Carolina passed "Ku Klux" laws providing stiff punishments for individuals convicted of participation in terrorist activities. Such measures achieved next to nothing. Then Radicals in the South turned to the federal government for support. The outcome, in May 1870, was the first of several measures passed by Congress to clamp down on the Klan and Klan-like organizations. Labeled an Enforcement Act (to enforce the Reconstruction statutes), the legislation of 1870 called for fine and imprisonment of any person convicted of obstructing qualified persons in their effort to vote. It authorized federal marshals to enforce the law. Because of the Klan's ability to frighten witnesses and keep them from testifying in court, the measure proved ineffectual. Accordingly, in February 1871 Congress passed a second Enforcement Act to strengthen the legislation of the previous spring. The new law authorized federal courts to appoint special supervisors to oversee elections. Any interference with the activities of these men would be a federal offense, punishable by fine and imprisonment.

Grant Fights the Terrorists

Following more reports of terrorism in the South, in a special message to Congress President Grant urged more extreme measures. In April 1871—over the protests of some northern members who saw the new legislation as an attack on civil liberties, Congress responded with the so-called Ku Klux Act, a temporary statute that would expire the following year. Declaring that activities of such organizations as the Klan amounted to "rebellion against the government of the United States," the law empowered the president to suspend the writ of habeas corpus and proclaim martial law to put them down. President Grant a few months later used the new law and ordered federal troops to suppress a wave of lawlessness and intimidation in South Carolina. But the reign of terror in the South did not stop. When the Ku Klux Act expired in 1872, it was clear that only large-scale intervention by the federal army could save what remained of Radical Reconstruction. Georgia, Virginia, Tennessee, and North Carolina already were back under "Confederate" control.

Before the Judiciary Committee of the House of Representatives in March 1871, a suffragette argues in favor of giving women the right to vote. How did women apply the new Fourteenth and Fifteenth Amendments to their fight for equality?

Library of Congress

There would be no such intervention, for by the year 1872 the spirit of idealism and anger which had helped bring about the Reconstruction Acts of 1867-68 was nearly exhausted. Concerned with problems of industrialization, railroad construction, and westward expansion, most northerners no longer were much interested in the fate of the freedmen or in punishing the rebels. True, northerners still responded to political orators who "waved the bloody shirt of rebellion" when assailing Democrats and celebrated the glories of "the Grand Army of the Republic" (the United States Army of 1861-65). Most, however, had become weary of the continuing unrest and violence in the South, longing for a return to national harmony, wanting to "live and let live."

It seemed that the only way to have peace in the country was to terminate the Radical experiment and permit the South's whites to return to power where they already had not done so. Other considerations of course were working against the Radicals. Unrest and terrorism in the South created a bad business climate. Many northern industrialists and financiers, wishing to make profits in the South, were anxious for a return of peace and stability. The easiest way to achieve peace and stability, they concluded, was to give control of the region back to the late rebels.

There was revulsion, too, in many quarters of the North over corruption and extravagance in Radical regimes of the South. Perhaps the Confederates would restore honesty to public administration. Finally, several of the leading proponents of Radicalism in 1865-68, notably Thaddeus Stevens, had died. Others, including Charles Sumner, had mellowed and no longer felt inclined to chastise the late enemies of the Republic. Consequently, by 1872 Radicalism was without strong and effective leadership.

Radicals Lose Control in the South

In the year 1873 Texas slipped from Radical control; in 1874, Alabama and Arkansas; and in 1875, Mississippi. By 1876 only in South Carolina, Florida, and Louisiana, where federal troops and local militia had managed to sustain them, did the Radicals retain a feeble grip. Then, in autumn 1876, came national and state elections. Amid rioting, disorders, and wrangling, the Democrats, made up largely of former Confederates, regained power in Florida. In Louisiana and South Carolina both the Radicals and Democrats claimed victory.

In the national election, the principal candidates for president were Samuel J. Tilden, Democrat, and Rutherford B. Hayes, Republican. The vote was close, but it appeared that Tilden had won—until Republican leaders challenged the count in four states and succeeded thereby in denying the Democratic candidate a majority in the electoral college (see Chapter 9). Who should be the nineteenth president, Tilden or Hayes? After weeks of debate, Congress referred the matter to a special electoral commission which in February 1877 ruled in favor of Hayes. But the commission's decision had come along strict party lines, the Republican majority of one on the commission proving decisive.

When Tilden's supporters erupted, there was worry in Republican ranks lest the Democrats try to prevent Hayes's inauguration. Republican leaders decided that the best way to assure Democratic consent was to strike a bargain with the powerful southern wing of the party. What did southern Democrats want most from a new administration in Washington? Among other things, they sought removal of the remaining federal troops in the South. Without the troops the deadlocks over control of the state houses in South Carolina and Louisiana were certain to end in Democratic victories. Republican leaders found the South's terms acceptable and Hayes quietly entered the White House in March 1877. A month later he removed the last federal soldiers from South Carolina and Louisiana. Without a struggle the "redeemers," as southern whites persisted in calling those politicians who restored white supremacy, took over the governments in Columbia and Baton Rouge.

STUDY GUIDE: Many southern white people opposed efforts to help the former slaves. Organizations such as the Ku Klux Klan launched campaigns of violence against black men and those who helped them. To assure all people the right to vote, Congress and three-fourths of the states approved the Fifteenth Amendment. New legislation was also passed to stop the activities of terrorist organizations. By the early 1870s most northerners were no longer interested in maintaining the Radical regimes in the South. Former Confederates won control of many state governments, and the last federal troops were removed from the South.

BLACKS AFTER RECONSTRUCTION

White-skinned southerners rejoiced at the passing of Radical Reconstruction. In New Orleans, artillery batteries bellowed and church bells pealed when the last of the federal troops left the city. Black southerners took a different view. They realized that the North had put aside the noble dream of forcing the South to keep the promise of the Declaration of Independence; they knew that final peace between the sections would come at their expense. And so it came to pass that the period of southern history which white men looked upon as one of redemption was the low point for the black man in the United States. It seemed worse, if that were possible, than the time of slavery.

The Economic Status

When pondering the problem of the Negro in the years after "redemption," one's thoughts usually turn to segregation, social ostracism, unequal justice, and political disabilities. While Negroes across the South faced all of these problems in varying degrees in the closing decades of the nineteenth century and into the twentieth, the most severe aspect of their plight was economic. In plain language, a great percentage of black people lived in stark poverty, often on the edge of starvation.

What was the reason for this? Why did emancipation leave the Negro in more severe economic straits than he had known in the days of slavery?

When the guns fell silent, the most overwhelming problem in the South was to restore the region's war-shattered economy. Since the southern economy rested on agriculture, this meant getting the farms and plantations back under cultivation. To achieve that end—to plow the earth, plant seed, harvest cotton, tobacco, and sugar—it was necessary to get Negroes back to the fields. But that required some doing, for the war had destroyed the system of slave labor. Most former slaves had fled from farms and plantations when the northern armies arrived. Hence it was necessary to work out new arrangements between white planters and black field hands. If the planters had held large cash reserves, such arrangements would have presented no difficulty; Negroes would have become wage laborers. Few planters, however, had much money.

To resolve the problem the Freedmen's Bureau helped planters and Negroes work out "sharecrop" arrangements. The planter would provide the "cropper" with land, implements, a mule, seed, and a miserable little house. The sharecropper or tenant would then cultivate the land and at the end of the harvest turn over to the planter one-third to one-half of his crop and keep the rest for himself. Many "poor whites" also entered sharecrop contracts. By the 1880s the sharecrop system had become the South's dominant socioeconomic institution—as the slavery-plantation system had been before the war.

Unfortunately it was not a happy system. The cropper, whether black or white, seldom could save enough money to become the owner of his own farm and usually had to work from sunup to sundown, seven days a week, to enable his family to subsist. The planter could not easily employ scientific methods of agriculture when relying on sharecrop labor. The usual outcome was poor yields accompanied by abuse of the soil.

The low returns of sharing crops did not exhaust the burdens of the tenant farmer, black or white. The "cropper" had to have groceries, clothing, and other supplies to carry him and his family through to harvest time. Having little cash, he usually had to borrow to make such purchases. The result was the appearance of the crop lien system. What this ordinarily meant was that the local merchant or storekeeper would advance supplies and household necessities to the sharecropper and, as security for the loan, would place a lien on the latter's share of the coming harvest. When the harvest season was over, the sharecropper often found that he had to turn over virtually the entire crop. First, the contracted share went to the owner of the land and then the remainder to the storekeeper (who in many instances also was the landowner) who had supplied him with credit.

Increasing the difficulties of the crop lien system was the sharecropper's vulnerability to dishonest or unfair treatment. Since the "cropper" had to have the shopkeeper's supplies, he had no choice but to accept prices and interest rates imposed by the shopkeeper, no matter how excessive. Then the sharecropper—especially the Negro—usually had little or no education. He had scant understanding of commercial transactions, and as a consequence was an easy mark for the dishonest shopkeeper when it came time to settle accounts. If the shopkeeper also owned the land, the "cropper's" plight was even more hopeless, for if he disputed the shopkeeper-landowner's figures the latter could expel him from the land. Seeking redress via legal action usually was futile if the sharecropper was a Negro. The black tenant could not hope to secure a fair hearing in white-controlled courts against a white landowner.

Improving Economic Conditions

What could the Negro sharecropper do to improve his economic condition? The answer was, not much. Perhaps the best means of escape from the oppressive system was for the Negro to purchase a piece of land and set himself up as an independent landowner. Unfortunately two factors worked against that possibility. First, it was virtually impossible for the "cropper" to save up enough money to purchase land. Second, if he could scrape together the funds, he was apt to find in many areas of the South that white landowners simply would not sell land to black farmers. As for bargaining between rival landlords to secure better sharecropping contracts, the landlords of many regions ended that possibility by getting together and agreeing precisely as to what terms they would offer "croppers"; they would not compete among themselves for sharecrop labor.

What about the industries of the so-called New South? Did they not present some opportunity to the Negro?

It is true that the South experienced considerable industrial growth in the decades after the Civil War. When one compares the "Old South" with the "New," he rather quickly notes the region's accent on the virtues of industrialization in the era that followed the war. It was quite a change from the old days when southern leaders railed against the evils of the factory system of the northeastern part of the country. Iron and coal deposits in Alabama and Tennessee, for example, produced a new steel industry, centered at Birmingham and Chattanooga. In South Carolina and Georgia, where labor was cheap, water power plentiful, and raw cotton nearby, textile mills became a familiar feature of the landscape. Tobacco processing plants appeared in North Carolina and Virginia, sugar refineries in Louisiana, and cottonseed-oil mills in Mississippi. At the same time thousands of miles of new railways appeared and up and down the tracks clattered freight cars carrying the raw materials and finished products of southern industry.

Who provided the labor for the South's new industry? Mainly white people from depressed rural areas. Industrialists, bowing to the prejudices of white workers who would not work side-by-side on terms of equality with black men, made a special point of excluding Negro labor. Unless of course the white laborers became restive and started to push for better wages, hours, and working conditions. If that happened, a company—as the Tennessee Coal and Iron Company did in the 1890s—could tap the great reservoir of black workers who would gladly work for subsistence wages in a factory to escape the grinding poverty of the farm. Usually, however, the mere threat to hire black workers in their place was enough to keep white factory hands "in line."

Black Artisans Suffer

At the same time, Negroes in the South lost the foothold they had held in slave days in such skilled trades as carpentry, shoemaking, painting, tailoring, and blacksmithing. On the plantations before the war masters often had trained slaves in many crafts to meet the ordinary needs of the plantation operation. After the war the South still needed skilled labor, and during the frenzied period of rebuilding the skilled worker could command good wages. White men did not stand aside and permit Negroes to reap a large part of the dividends. More than that, whites decided that Negroes should have none of the dividends. Whereupon the Negro artisan or craftsman virtually dropped from sight in the South, consigned by prejudice and hatred to a life as a dirt farmer or domestic servant.

Black Businessmen

A handful of black men across the South, especially toward the end of the nineteenth century, managed to set themselves up in business, usually by pooling savings with one another. They operated groceries, drugstores, bakeries, restaurants, and hotels, usually in neighborhoods that were predominantly Negro. A few operated shirt factories and lumber mills, and some even raised sufficient capital to go into banking. But most Negro commercial ventures were small operations that solicited business only from black patrons. Very few of them realized substantial returns and a great percentage failed in the face of white competition.

In considering the economic difficulties of the southern Negro after the Civil War one should in fairness note that this was not an easy period for a region which despite all its industrial growth remained predominantly agrarian. After an initial postwar boom that saw production of such staple crops as cotton, tobacco, and sugar move back to prewar levels, the region suffered a severe slump in prices following the nationwide Panic of 1873. This was the worst economic catastrophe the country had faced to that time.

Congress, meanwhile, under rigid Republican control for most of the period, steadily raised the tariff on foreign imports. This reduced overseas competition and enabled domestic manufacturers to charge southern planters (and consumers all across the country) higher prices for farm implements, shoes, clothing, and household furnishings. Natural disasters, particularly periodic floods and droughts, added to the burdens of southern agriculture. Then around 1892 a colorful little bug, the boll weevil, moved up from Mexico, crossed the Rio Grande, and left a trail of destruction that ran into millions of dollars as he moved eastward across the cotton states. And so if Negroes in the years after Reconstruction suffered acute economic distress — distress that was multiplied because of the color of their skins — it is also true that few white men, as had been the case in the days of slavery, achieved great wealth and led lives of ease at their expense.

STUDY GUIDE: In the decades after the Civil War Negroes suffered severe economic hardship. They did not benefit from the South's industrial growth during this period.

BLACKS IN SOUTHERN SOCIETY

In the years following the end of Reconstruction in the 1870s, few white people questioned the second-class status which blacks still held. However, there was not yet any large movement to legalize racial segregation, even though former Confederate leaders were regaining political power in the South. The "Jim Crow" laws — laws which made separation of blacks and whites legal — did not come until later.

In *The Strange Career of Jim Crow,* the historian C. Vann Woodward indicates that more than a decade passed before the first Jim Crow law appeared upon the law books of a Southern state. In those first years after Radical Reconstruction Negroes rode in integrated railway coaches, attended the theater without much restriction (if they could dredge up the price of admission), and patronized saloons and ice-cream parlors frequented by whites. Indeed, as Woodward points out, northern visitors in the South often were scandalized at the sight of Negro women suckling white infants, black and white children playing together, Negro servants enjoying friendly conversation with their employers. Even in politics there was no immediate move to disfranchise Negroes, and a scattering of Negroes in southern states continued to hold minor public office.

Still, one must take care not to overdraw this picture of easy intimacy and tranquillity between the races in the closing decades of the nineteenth century. Although extreme practices of segregation and disfranchisement had not become operative, southern whites never for an instant flirted with the idea that Negroes might one day become social or political equals. They never wavered in their conviction that the black man must stay "in his place." And already taking form were some of the social controls which whites would exercise over Negroes far into the twentieth century.

Economic Coercion and Jail

The most common means used to control blacks was economic coercion—the withholding of jobs or money. A black servant or sharecropper who seemed independent or outspoken among whites could be fired, and his or her employer could make it very hard to find other work. Blacks were told how to vote, and in those days voting records were not secret and could be checked.

Jail was another way of controlling blacks who strayed from the narrow path marked out for them by powerful whites. To make this latter method workable, state and local governments in southern states devised legal codes which could result in extended jail terms for individuals convicted, by all-white juries or white judges, of the most petty crimes. In Mississippi, for example, the theft of any property worth ten dollars or more could result in a prison sentence up to five years—and a Negro often received the maximum penalty. Confinement was only part of the punishment. All across the South in these years state governments devised schemes for leasing convicts to private individuals and corporations. The lessee would provide food, clothing, and shelter for the prisoner, put him to work, and pay the state a sum of money for his services. The prison lessee system had the advantage to the state of turning a financial burden—guarding and maintaining prisoners—into a source of revenue.

The system, however, bred horrors that dungeon-keepers of the Middle Ages might have conceived. In most states there were no limits on the hours or types of work that lessees could demand of convicts. Discipline was usually left to the discretion of the lessee, whose foremen often viewed convicts, particularly those of dark skin, as subhumans. If a prisoner died—even though abuse, malnutrition, or overwork might have been a principal cause—the courts seldom held a lessee responsible. Convicts, chained together in gangs, often dug coal in water-filled mines, cut roads through mosquito- and snake-infested swamplands, or toiled from dawn to dusk in unheated factories. Their quarters were usually incubators of disease, their food barely enough to sustain life. Sometimes, the death rate among convicts exceeded twenty-five percent annually. It is true that poor whites as well as blacks fell victim to the inhuman prison conditions of the post-Civil War South, but the greatest weight of the region's abominable penal system pressed down on the black man. Accordingly, the white man's justice terrorized the Negro. Aware of these fears, whites exploited them as a means of controlling troublesome or rebellious Negroes.

When economic coercion, jail, or the threat of jail failed to restrain Negroes—or when a black committed a particularly obnoxious offense to a white—the outcome might be more direct, often a whipping or, if whites were sufficiently aroused, a lynching. Reliable estimates indicate that between 1882 and 1901 more than one hundred and fifty lynchings occurred each year across the southern tier of states—one every two and a half days. Sometimes the victims were the most intelligent and energetic Negroes, individuals who were the potential leaders of their people. Some historians have guessed that between 1877 and the turn of the century, white terrorists murdered a whole generation of black leaders.

New Opportunities for Education

Although life in the economic and social climate of the post-Civil War South was indescribably difficult for the Negro, there was at least one bright spot—his new opportunities for securing an education. During the time of slavery it had been a calculated policy of white masters to keep slaves illiterate. Slaves who could read and write—so the reasoning went—were potential radical leaders who represented a threat to the slave system. During the period of "Confederate" Reconstruction, in 1865-66, white leaders continued to oppose Negro education. They feared that freedmen, armed with the ability to read and write, might get ideas about being something other than hewers of wood and drawers of water.

Then came Radical Reconstruction, and perhaps the most enduring achievement of Radicalism was establishment of Negro schools in virtually every southern community. When white "redeemers" returned to power in the South in the 1870s, one of their first ambitions was to reduce appropriations for public education. Such ambitions also struck hard at poor whites. Like their black neighbors, they had grasped the value of the systems of free public education set up by the Radicals, and they rallied to the defense of their schools. Redeemers responded to the agitation of poor whites. Also fearing a hostile reaction from the government in Washington, they decided it would not be smart to try to freeze out Negro schools.

Eventually, to be sure, there was considerable difference in distribution of school funds by southern boards of education. As a consequence Negro school facilities came to lag far behind those of neighboring white schools, and Negro teachers received lower wages than their white counterparts. For example, in Mississippi in 1895 the average monthly wage for white teachers was $33.04, compared with $21.53 for Negroes. In a short time, white and Negro schools became unequal as well as separate. Nevertheless, Negroes, believing education a necessity if they were to escape the indignities and oppression of the "New South," made its pursuit an essential goal. Despite the inconveniences and expense, most Negro parents made certain that their children learned as a minimum to read and write, add and subtract.

Assisting the development of Negro education in the South in these years were white philanthropists of the North. George Peabody, a merchant and financier, established the Peabody Education Fund "for the promotion and encouragement of intellectual, moral, or industrial education among the young people of the more destitute portions of the Southern and Southwestern States." He supported the fund to the amount of two and a half million dollars. John F. Slater, a New England textile manufacturer, set up a fund "for uplifting the lately emancipated population of the Southern states and their posterity, by conferring on them the blessings of Christian education." The main objective of Slater's foundation was the training of teachers for Negro elementary and secondary schools. Some foundations supplemented salaries of Negro teachers, bought books and equipment, and financed construction of school buildings. How did white citizens of the South feel about such northern philanthropy? Inasmuch as philanthropists showed no disposition to upset the

system of segregated education, southern whites seldom objected to their support of Negro schools and indeed usually welcomed it.

As for higher education, an array of Negro colleges and universities came into existence in the South in the decades after the Civil War. These included Howard, Fisk, Atlanta, and Tuskegee. Northern philanthropy played an important part in the appearance and maintenance of these institutions. But Negroes themselves, particularly students, worked to raise funds for their schools of higher learning. For example, a singing group of students from Fisk University traveled through America and Europe. Their performances, which featured spirituals and Negro work songs, raised $150,000, to help construction of Jubilee Hall, an attractive classroom building on Fisk's campus.

The quality of the new Negro colleges and universities—as with predominantly white institutions—varied. Constantly pressed for funds and dependent mainly on Negro instructors (who were products of inferior elementary and secondary schools of the South), it seems fair to say that most were below the standard of comparable white schools. In the twentieth century the gap widened. By midcentury the quality of Negro higher education became a matter of grave concern to leaders, Negro and white, who believed the black man would never achieve economic and social equality with his fellow Americans until he achieved equality in education.

STUDY GUIDE: Most southern white people accepted without question the view that Negroes would never be their social or political equals. Negroes were kept "in their place" by threatening them with loss of employment, violence, or prison. Radical Reconstruction widened educational opportunities for black people by establishing Negro schools in almost every southern community.

BLACK LEADERS EMERGE

In the closing decades of the nineteenth century, particularly after Radical Reconstruction had run its course, only a handful of black men were able to rise above the low environment to which prejudice and callousness had consigned them. Few were able to achieve national reputations or exert great influence in national affairs. One of those few was Frederick Douglass.

Frederick Douglass was born a slave in Maryland, but escaped to Massachusetts in 1838. He was a leading orator and writer of the antislavery movement in the 1840s. During the Civil War he organized two Negro regiments in Massachusetts. After the war he was an official in the government in the District of Columbia.

Frederick Douglass

Born in 1817 in his grandmother's cabin in Talbot County, Maryland, Douglass was the son of a slave woman and an unknown white man. During his formative years he lacked not only the care and affection of a father but that of his mother as well. She worked on a plantation twelve miles distant from the cabin where young Frederick spent his infancy and early boyhood with his grandmother. When the boy was seven, his master took him from his grandmother and assigned him to a nearby plantation where he endured considerable abuse and hardship, much of it from the slave woman directed to look after him.

When he was nine, Douglass had a stroke of luck. His master sent him to Baltimore to be a house servant of relatives. Soon after his arrival he heard his mistress reading aloud from the Bible and with some boldness asked her to teach him to read. A sweet and gentle woman, she taught him the alphabet and a few simple words. But then her husband learned what was going on and ordered her to stop the lessons, declaring: "If you teach him to read, he will want to know how to write, and with this accomplished, he will be running away with himself." But it was too late; the precocious young slave already had gotten "the hang" of reading and in secret worked to sharpen his skill. He also practiced writing. The more he learned, the more he yearned to be free and this yearning made him miserable, a matter of some concern to his mistress. "Poor lady," he later wrote, "she did not understand my trouble, and I could not tell her. Nature made us friends, but slavery made us enemies. . . . We were both victims of the same overshadowing evil — she as mistress, I as slave."

Then came misfortune. His master, the plantation owner, died and in settlement of the estate Douglass ended up back on the farm as a field hand. Next he was leased for a year to a "poor white" who frequently flogged his slaves. Back on his owner's plantation, in 1835 Douglass conspired with several fellow slaves to escape to the North, but one of them betrayed the scheme and Douglass landed in jail. Then his luck turned again. His master sent him to Baltimore and apprenticed him to a ship-caulker. Here he worked alongside youthful whites who continually taunted and abused him and one day gave him a fearful beating. Indignant at this assault on his slave, Douglass's master demanded a warrant for the arrest of the ruffians, only to hear the magistrate reply: "I am sorry, sir, but I cannot move in this matter except upon the oath of a white man." Still, life was looking up for the young slave. He learned the ship-caulking trade, turning over all wages to his master, of course, received a promise of emancipation at age twenty-five, and had freedom to come and go pretty much as he pleased.

Not content to await emancipation, in 1838

Douglass scraped together some money, disguised himself as a sailor, and took a passenger train to New York. A few days later he was joined by a free Negro woman whom he had known in Baltimore. They were married and settled in New Bedford, Massachusetts, where Douglass became a common laborer. Then in the year 1841 he attended a meeting of the Massachusetts Anti-Slavery Society and much to his embarrassment was asked to address the gathering. Although, as he later recalled, he "trembled in every limb," Douglass's words moved his listeners. They inspired the abolitionist leader William Lloyd Garrison, who followed him to the rostrum, to ask: "Have we been listening to a thing—a piece of property, or a man?"

From that moment, Douglass was an activist in the abolitionist crusade. Some abolitionist audiences doubted, however, that a man of such intelligence and eloquence could ever have been a slave.

Next Douglass published his *Narrative of the Life of Frederick Douglass* in 1845. Fearing that the book might lead to his re-enslavement (for legally he was still a fugitive), he went to Europe, where he remained for two years.

After his return home, Douglass established a new abolitionist journal, *North Star,* lectured, and took part in politics. He also became a confidant of the lonely fanatic, John Brown. After the failure of Brown's raid on the federal arsenal at Harpers Ferry in 1859 the governor of Virginia demanded Douglass's arrest. The outcome was another flight from the country, this time to Canada, then to England and Scotland.

When the Civil War broke out, Douglass was back in the United States, urging an emancipation proclamation long before Lincoln was ready to issue one. He also offered to recruit Negro soldiers before the North was willing to consider the idea. Later he assisted in recruiting the 54th and 55th Massachusetts colored regiments which won acclaim for courage. When he protested Confederate atrocities against captive black soldiers, President Lincoln summoned him to the White House. Describing his first meeting with the president, Douglass later wrote: "Long lines of care were already deeply written on Mr. Lincoln's brow, and his strong face lighted up as soon as my name was mentioned. As I approached and was introduced to him, he arose and extended his hand and bade me welcome. I at once felt that I was in the presence of an honest man—one whom I could love, honor, and trust without reserve or doubt."

By the time the war ended, Douglass was the best-known and most respected Negro in America. To black people he was a source of inspiration. He had something of the appearance of an Old Testament prophet with his strong physique, heavy brow, firm mouth, and long frizzly hair and beard etched with gray. In the Reconstruction era he urged the cause of full civil liberties for former slaves, but he had passed the peak of his energy and his leadership of the Negro people was essentially symbolic. Still, Douglass remained the titular leader of black Americans until his death. In recognition of his service to the country in the war Douglass received several federal appointments. He was marshal for four years and recorder of deeds for five years of the District of Columbia. From 1889 to 1891 Douglass was minister and consul general to Haiti. He was appointed by the president of Haiti to represent that country at the World's Columbian Exposition held in 1893.

Douglass died in 1895 at the age of seventy-eight. In Douglass's declining years a younger black American was achieving a reputation as an eloquent spokesman for the Negro cause. The name of this emerging young black leader was Booker T. Washington.

Booker T. Washington

Washington entered the world as a slave about 1856 in Franklin County, Virginia. Like Douglass, his father apparently was a white man, his mother a slave. As with most slaves, life was hard for young Booker and his family. His mother was the plantation cook and her duties prevented her from giving much attention to her children. The family lived in a crude one-room cabin (about fourteen feet by sixteen) which had a dirt floor and no glass windows. In his autobiography, *Up From Slavery,* Washington recalled that to the best of his knowledge he never slept in a bed until after the Civil War. He also recalled that even as a small boy he had had little time for play, for "I was occupied most of the time in cleaning the yards, carrying water to the men in the fields, or going to the mill."

The young slave was only eight or nine years old in 1865 when the Civil War came to an end and he and his family received their freedom. Walking most of the way, the family set out for Charleston, West Virginia, where they joined the husband of Booker's mother (the father of his half-brother), who previously had followed

Booker T. Washington (1856-1915) believed that Negroes could improve their lifestyle by becoming well educated. In 1881 he organized Tuskegee Institute, a college for Negroes, in Alabama. Washington also organized a national Negro Business League.

Charles Phelps Cushing

federal soldiers across the mountains to the new state. They finally settled at the town of Malden, a few miles from Charleston, where salt-mining was a booming industry, and soon Booker who was only ten years old was tending a salt furnace. It was at this time that the youth determined to become educated and with some success he began to teach himself to read and write. Then a school for Negroes opened in the vicinity. The school generated much enthusiasm and Washington later recalled that "a whole race was trying to go to school. Few were too young, and none too old, to make the attempt to learn. . . . The great ambition of the older people was to try to learn to read the Bible before they died." Young Washington worked out an arrangement whereby he arose at four o'clock in the morning, worked in the salt furnace until nine, attended classes, and worked two more hours at the salt furnace after school.

A few years later Washington, now working in a coal mine, overheard some men talking of Hampton Normal and Agricultural Institute, a school of higher learning for Negroes in Virginia. He later recalled that "not even Heaven presented more attractions for me at that time" than did Hampton Institute. And so in 1872 he packed his belongings in a satchel and set out for Hampton, some five hundred miles away. Arriving penniless, hungry, and dirty, he gained admission to Hampton after he had swept the recitation room (three times, he later wrote). "The sweeping of that room was my college examination," he recalled in his autobiography, "and never did any youth pass an examination for entrance into Harvard or Yale that gave him more genuine satisfaction."

His tuition was paid by a northern philanthropist, and he did janitorial work for his room and board. Washington spent three years at Hampton, learned the trade of brick mason, and graduated in 1875. After returning to Malden, where he taught school for three years, he went back to Hampton to deliver a graduation address. The speech made such an impression that the principal of the school, General Samuel C. Armstrong, made him his secretary. In 1881 Armstrong received a letter from two men in Tuskegee, Alabama—one a former slave-owner, the other a former slave. They asked him to recommend someone who could start a normal school, a school for the training of teachers, at Tuskegee, for which the Alabama legislature had voted a charter. Armstrong recommended Washington.

Soon Washington was on his way to Alabama and on July 4, 1881, he opened Tuskegee Institute "in a little shanty and church which had been secured for its accommodation." Under his care the school grew until by the time of his death in 1915 it had more than a hundred buildings, two thousand acres of land, and a faculty of nearly two hundred members.

When Washington went to Tuskegee he had already begun to formulate his belief that the biggest problem facing Negroes was that of carving out for themselves a place in a white-dominated society which was essentially hostile to them. To meet the problem he concluded, first, that Negroes must do nothing to antagonize the white community, meaning that they must respect the law, show proper deference to white leaders, and exert no pressure for social equality. They should develop habits of thrift, honesty, good manners, and industry.

Second, Washington felt that Negro education should concentrate on preparing blacks to perform more effectively and efficiently the tasks that white society had assigned them; that is, it should strive in the main to make them better farmers and domestic servants. (In his autobiography Washington lamented that in his first year at Tuskegee he found that Negro girls could locate the Sahara Desert or the capital of China on a map, but "could not locate the proper places for the knives and forks on an actual dinner table, or the places on which the bread and meat should be set.")

While conceding that such subjects as physics, mathematics, and history were worthy of study, Washington emphasized that "for years to come the education of the people of my race should be so directed that the greatest proportion of the mental strength of the masses will be brought to bear upon the everyday practical things of life, upon something that is needed to be done, and something which they will be permitted to do in the community in which they reside." Washington believed that full equality in American society could come only when the Negro won the respect of the white man and by his virtue and industry compelled the white man to purge himself of prejudices against the black race. Such a change in white attitudes he knew, unfortunately, would take many years, probably generations. In the meantime the Negro was to be patient and not turn away from the formula Washington had devised for securing the white man's respect.

Washington's message was well received by whites in the North and South. Whites in particular liked the emphasis on obedience of the white man's law and the appeal to blacks to be patient and stay "in their place." By the mid-1880s, as a consequence, Booker T. Washington was much in demand as a public speaker. He addressed colleges and universities (including Harvard) and state legislatures in all parts of the United States.

Perhaps his most influential speech came at the Cotton States and International Exposition at Atlanta in 1895 in which with force and eloquence he restated his ideas. With that address he established himself as the leading spokesman of black Americans, succeeding Frederick Douglass, who had recently died. Some Negroes, to be sure, challenged his leadership and hotly opposed his views, particularly his stress on industrial education. Washington, critics argued, aimed to make the Negro an "Uncle Tom" and his ideas, if universally accepted, would consign blacks to a permanent state of second-class citizenship or worse. Doubtless there was much to say for such criticism. Still, considering the climate of white opinion, in the North as well as the South — a climate permeated with the idea of Negro inferiority — there was also something to say for the view that Washington's program was the only one that held out any hope of improvement for the Negro in American society.

Booker T. Washington was deeply religious. He read from the Bible each day and sprinkled his speeches with quotations and allusions from Holy Writ. He was a very modest man, accepted honors bestowed on him in America and Europe with grace, and treated all people — leaders of government or illiterate cotton-pickers — with tact and dignity. He never betrayed any trace of cynicism or anger, only melancholy at the sad plight of his people. He never lost faith in the American dream and persisted in the belief that one day his people, too, would achieve the promise of the good life in America. He married three times, his first two wives preceding him in death. The most renowned of the eleven books he wrote was his autobiography, *Up From Slavery*. First published in 1901, it was eventually translated into eighteen languages.

STUDY GUIDE: The second half of the 1800s saw the emergence of two distinguished Negro leaders, Frederick Douglass and Booker T. Washington.

A TRAGIC TIME FOR BLACK AMERICANS

The decades after the Civil War were a tragic era for black Americans, the time when white America dashed the bright hopes which the Emancipation Proclamation had aroused. In the South, where the great majority of Negroes continued to live (for the migration of blacks from South to North, spurred by the two World Wars of the twentieth century, had not set in), they faced severe economic and social restrictions. If they "got out of line," they suffered vigilante justice. In the North the system of discrimination was not so highly developed or structured as in the South and the threat of physical violence did not hang perpetually over their heads. But menial labor, segregation, and contempt were the lot of most black people in the North as well as in the South.

Perhaps it was too much to expect white Americans—most of whom had little formal education and were not fully capable of grasping the implications of the Declaration of Independence and the American democratic ideal—to open their hearts at once to dark-skinned people who until very recently had been slaves. And one might even make an argument for the gradual transition of Negroes to first-class citizenship and full membership in the American democratic community. But what in looking back is so saddening is that white America showed no interest in a transition, gradual or otherwise. White Americans accepted as self-evident the idea that Negroes were the biological inferiors of whites—an idea utterly repudiated by modern science.

Then with twisted logic some white Americans moved to the conclusion that black men need not enjoy all the rights and privileges of American citizenship.

The vast majority of white Americans were decent, neighborly, God-fearing people. Most were only vaguely aware of the plight of the Negroes who lived across the tracks on the other side of town or in shacks throughout the countryside. And if they knew they could usually console themselves with the naïve notion that the Negroes were happy and had no real ambition to improve their surroundings.

As for violence and lynchings, most white people wished no harm to blacks. If asked they probably would have expressed strong disapproval of acts of bodily harm against Negroes, especially if such acts might result in death. But most white people failed to grasp the hard truth. They failed to see that by embracing the idea that one race was biologically inferior to another, and accepting the cruel system of discrimination, they were responsible for opening the door to intimidation and acts of brutality directed against blacks.

The prejudices and contempt of white neighbors shattered what little dignity many Negroes had left after the long generations of enslavement. Loss of dignity turned many individuals to self-hatred. Some black men despised themselves for being members of a group whose miserable state seemed to prove its inferiority—whose members, according to history books which lauded the achievements of such white men as Washington and Jefferson and Lincoln, had contributed nothing of consequence to the growth of America. (History books of that earlier era, concentrating on political and military developments, scarcely recognized that, from the time of the Jamestown colony, the sweat and toil of millions of Negro Americans had constituted a mighty contribution to the development of their country.)

Sociologists in recent years have provided endless proof of the unfortunate social consequences when individuals are stripped of pride and self-respect. The restrictions on the economic activity of Negroes sapped the ambition of millions of blacks, compelled them to resign themselves to lives as tenant farmers or domestic servants, and persuaded them that it was futile to try to "buck the system." They were convinced that the good life in America would always elude them.

Thus a culture of poverty and despair, with all its attendant evils, took shape in the form of black ghettos all over the United States. The hopes that were aroused by the end of the Civil War in 1865 had been quickly crushed. It would be a hundred years before federal laws would guarantee the right of black Americans to join a labor union, buy a meal at any public restaurant, or vote.

STUDY GUIDE: Black Americans had high hopes in the years following the Civil War, but most whites refused to accept them as equals. Whites remained indifferent to economic and social discrimination against blacks. The result was poverty, frustration, and despair in black communities across the country.

SUMMING UP THE CHAPTER

Names and Terms to Identify

"ten percent" plan of reconstruction	Command of the Army Act
Wade-Davis manifesto	Salmon P. Chase
"black codes"	"Seward's folly"
Thaddeus Stevens	carpetbagger
Charles Sumner	scalawag
Joint Committee of Fifteen	Union League
Fourteenth Amendment	Fifteenth Amendment
Horace Greeley	sharecropper
"waving the bloody shirt"	Tuskegee Institute
Tenure of Office Act	prison lessee system

Study Questions and Points to Review

1. What was the subject of Lincoln's victory speech? What was audience reaction to his speech?

2. What were Andrew Johnson's views on the secession crisis at the outbreak of the war?

3. What was one overwhelming problem that confronted Andrew Johnson when he became president?

4. What was Lincoln's formula for reconstruction? Why were Radical Republicans appalled by Lincoln's plan?

5. What was the Wade-Davis Bill? How was it defeated?

6. What effect did Johnson's plan of reconstruction have on southerners?

7. What were the provisions of the Civil Rights Bill of 1866?

8. How did Johnson hope to turn the tide of Radical opposition to presidential reconstruction?

9. What was Johnson's plan when he appointed Grant secretary of war? Did his plan work?

10. Why was the Ku Klux Klan organized? Who were the Klansmen? How did Congress clamp down on the Klan and similar organizations?

11. What problems occupied northerners to the extent that they were no longer much interested in the fate of the freedmen?

12. Be sure you understand the following terms used in this chapter: enfranchisement, mandate, manifesto, pocket veto, clemency, demagoguery, amnesty, demobilization, patronage, acquittal, kickbacks, philanthropists, vigilante justice. Divide the class into teams. The winning team is the group which can correctly define most words without using a dictionary.

Topics for Discussion

1. What qualities did Andrew Johnson bring to the presidency? What qualities necessary to the office of president did he lack?

2. What do you think were the strongest arguments for and against Radical views on reconstruction of the South?

3. Why was the Freedmen's Bureau established? Why were some white southerners opposed to the Bureau? Do you think Johnson had good reasons for vetoing legislation extending the Freedmen's Bureau? How would you evaluate the Freedmen's Bureau?

4. If you were a northerner in 1867-68, do you think you might have supported the Reconstruction legislation of these years? Give reasons for your answer.

5. What in your opinion were the main reasons for the breakdown of Radical reconstruction of the South?

6. What was the place of the Negro in the South in the Reconstruction era?

Subjects for Reports or Essays

1. It is April 12, 1865. You are a newspaper reporter. Last night you listened to President Lincoln deliver his victory speech in which he urged speedy reconciliation of the North and South. Write a newspaper article supporting or opposing the president's ideas.

2. Assume that you are a former Confederate and the year is 1866. In a letter to the editor of a northern newspaper write the strongest possible defense of the "black codes." Or, assume that you have no sympathy toward the "black codes," and write a letter criticizing the codes.

3. In a brief essay defend or challenge the ideas that former slaves should have received the right to vote immediately upon emancipation and that it was proper to disfranchise former Confederates.

4. Many Negroes challenged the leadership of Booker T. Washington and opposed his views. Prepare a report evaluating Washington and his views. State whether you agree or disagree with criticism he received.

5. Prepare a report for class presentation assessing the presidency of Andrew Johnson. Would you classify him as "great," "near-great," "average," "below average," or "failure"? Explain your classification.

6. On the basis of outside reading, write an essay on the role of the philanthropist in the development of Negro education after the Civil War.

Projects, Activities, and Skills

1. In his book *Profiles in Courage,* John F. Kennedy wrote a vivid account of the dramatic moment when Senator Edmund G. Ross cast his "not guilty" vote at the impeachment trial of Andrew Johnson. Read this account to the class. Discuss why you think Kennedy considered Ross's actions worthy of a profile in courage.

2. Prepare an in-depth report on the two black U.S. senators and the twenty black representatives who served in Congress during the Reconstruction era. Make a map of the South and show on it the states represented by these men. Find out about their educational backgrounds. How many were college graduates? How may were former slaves?

3. Listen to recordings of Negro spirituals and folk music. On the basis of outside reading prepare a report on the contributions which blacks have made to American folk music.

4. Arrange an illustrated exhibit on some of the black institutions of higher learning that were mentioned in this chapter. Include photographs of famous graduates.

5. Read again the author's description of Frederick O. Douglass on pages 205-206. Locate a twenty-five-cent U. S. postage stamp in the "prominent Americans" series, first issued in 1965. Do you agree with the author's description of Douglass? Tell why you think Douglass was selected for this series.

6. Several books about black Americans in the South during Reconstruction are listed in the "Further Readings" section. Read one of these selections and write a review of it.

Further Readings

General

America's Black Congressmen by Maurine Christopher.

The Day Lincoln was Shot by Jim Bishop. Fascinating account; easy to read.

The Era of Reconstruction: 1865-1877 by Kenneth M. Stampp. An important book on the subject.

The Framing of the Fourteenth Amendment by Joseph B. James. This is the best study of this constitutional amendment sponsored by Radicals.

From Slavery to Freedom: A History of American Negroes by John Hope Franklin.

A History of the Freedman's Bureau by George R. Bentley. An excellent work about a much-abused agency.

Invisible Empire: The Story of the Ku Klux Klan, 1866-1871 by Stanley F. Horn.

The Lincoln Nobody Knows by Richard N. Current. Presents Lincoln's views on Reconstruction.

The Negro in South Carolina During the Reconstruction and *The Negro in Tennessee, 1865-1880* by Alrutheus A. Taylor.

Negro Thought in America, 1880-1915: Racial Ideologies in the Age of Booker T. Washington by August Meier. The psychological effects of the decline of rights for black Americans is treated.

Origins of the New South, 1877-1913 by C. Vann Woodward.

Reconstruction After the Civil War by John Hope Franklin. This is one of the best general books on Reconstruction for high school readers.

Right to Vote: Politics and the Passage of the Fifteenth Amendment by William Gillette. This is the best study of this Radical-sponsored amendment to the Constitution.

The South During Reconstruction by Merton E. Coulter. Sets forth a traditional interpretation of Reconstruction.

The Strange Career of Jim Crow by Alrutheus A. Taylor. A well-written account of the beginnings of legalized racial segregation in the South.

The Struggle for Equality: Abolitionists and the Negro in the Civil War and Reconstruction by James M. McPherson.

Biography

Andrew Johnson: A Study in Courage by Lloyd P. Stryker.

Andrew Johnson and Reconstruction by Eric McKitrick. A revised approach to Reconstruction. This study repudiates the idea that Johnson was a hero and that Radical Reconstruction was a travesty of justice.

Andrew Johnson: President on Trial by Milton Lomask.

Booker T. Washington: Educator and Racial Interpreter by Basil J. Mathews.

Frederick Douglass by Benjamin Quarles. Interesting biography by the distinguished black historian.

Frederick Douglass by Booker T. Washington. Based on the memoirs of Douglass, listed below.

The Life and Times of Frederick Douglass by Frederick Douglass. Interesting memoirs of this important American.

Lincoln and the Negro by Benjamin Quarles.

Thaddeus Stevens: A Being Darkly Wise and Rudely Great by Ralph Korngold.

Up from Slavery by Booker T. Washington.

Fiction and Poetry

Friendly Persuasion by Jessamyn West. Gentle story of a Quaker family after the Civil War.

Gone With the Wind by Margaret Mitchell. Epic novel of the Civil War and Reconstruction told from a southern viewpoint.

O Captain! My Captain by Walt Whitman. This poem was written to commemorate Lincoln's death.

The Unvanquished by William Faulkner.

Americans who were alive between 1850 and 1900 saw the United States change from an agricultural nation to an industrial giant rich in iron ore, coal, and oil. Steel mills like the ones on the right rose up, and new cities began to grow around them.

Brown Brothers

3

INDUSTRY, ENTERPRISE, AND POLITICAL LIFE

CHAPTER 7

AN ERA OF ENTERPRISE

IN 1850, ON THE EVE OF its industrial revolution, America was a sprawling agrarian nation. Each year the lush agricultural land yielded a dazzling array of products—wheat, cotton, corn, livestock, tobacco—whose total value dwarfed that of the Republic's scattered factories, mills, and mines. To provide rapid efficient overland transportation, the country had fewer than twenty-five thousand miles of railways.

The cities were sleepy, unkempt, and by later standards quite small. By and large, the country was fairly prosperous. Outside the slave community there was little grinding poverty. The skilled worker enjoyed status and security; a few individuals had managed to become millionaires In world affairs the United States did not count for much in the politics of nations.

Then in the years 1861-65 came the Civil War. Men of the North and South needed guns and ammunition, uniforms and boots, tents and wagons. Americans in both sections, but especially in the North, responded with more and larger factories. After the war ended, the country did not turn its machines into plowshares but converted them to peacetime uses. Meanwhile businessmen who had experienced unprecedented prosperity during the war invested savings in new industry.

By the 1880s the accelerated expansion of industry was the central reality of American life. By the beginning of the twentieth century the United States had undergone an economic revolution and by the outbreak of World War I in Europe in 1914 it had become the mightiest industrial power in the world.

SOCIAL DARWINISM

In considering the growth of industry in America or any country, one normally begins by looking for the circumstances or events that encouraged industrialization. At the outset one can say an assortment of circumstances and events—or factors—contributed to the rapid growth of industry in America in the closing decades of the nineteenth century and the early part of the twentieth. One that has aroused great historical interest was the intellectual climate of the country in the generations after Appomattox. While it is hard to say with much precision to what extent this climate influenced industrialization, historians of our own time generally agree that it was important.

In America the time after the Civil War was a freebooting, no-holds-barred era for business, a period when competing enterprises seemed to wage a savage struggle for survival and prosperity. With or without this competition, other circumstances, including the country's vast mineral resources and its manpower, would have brought industrial expansion. But in the absence of such competition it might not have occurred so quickly. The intellectual climate encouraged businessmen to compete with little restraint and provided a sanction for business buccaneering. For the time after the Civil War was the great era of Social Darwinism.

Origins of Social Darwinism

What were the origins of Social Darwinism? There was a similarity between the ideas of Social Darwinists of the latter part of the nineteenth century and those of the Puritans of Massachusetts Bay Colony in the seventeenth century. Both, for example, exalted hard work and looked with scorn on leisure and time-wasting. Doubtless many people in the post-Civil War era who embraced the teachings of Social Darwinism found them easy to accept because they seemed not too unlike those that had come down from Puritan ancestors. Other individuals who are known to history as Social Darwinists had worked out ideas on social evolution before the famous works of the English naturalist Charles Darwin ever appeared.

Still, the published writings of Darwin, notably his books *The Origin of Species* (1859) and *The Descent of Man* (1871), provided the main stimulus and basis for the view of society called Social Darwinism. According to this view, human society, like the world of plants and animals described by Darwin, is constantly evolving (presumably changing for the better). Men, like

HEADLINE
EVENTS

1825 Erie Canal opens

1830s Faraday invents dynamo

Baltimore and Ohio railroad and Chesapeake and Ohio canal struggle for right of way

1837 Financial panic; canal empire collapses

1844 Telegraph line between Baltimore and Washington

1846 Howe patents sewing machine

1849 Department of Interior created

1852 Otis builds first successful passenger elevator

1853 Singer opens plant to manufacture sewing machines

mid 1850s Bessemer process introduced

Commercial possibilities of petroleum recognized

James Oliver introduces chilled plow

1856 Western Union Company organized

1859 Comstock Lode discovered

The Origin of Species (Darwin)

Drake strikes oil at Titusville, Pa.

1860 Winchester introduces repeating rifle

1860s Sholes introduces practical typewriter

1861-1865 Civil War

1862 First Pacific Railway Act

1863 Steel rails introduced

Union and Central Pacific railroads begin work on transcontinental railroad

1865 Block signal system introduced on railroads

late 1860s Open-hearth process used

1868 Janney patents automatic railway car coupler

1869 Westinghouse patents air brake

First transcontinental railroad completed at Promontory Point

1870 Construction begins on Pacific Northwest railroad

Standard Oil Company is chartered

1870-1890 Herbert Spencer spreads idea of Social Darwinism

1870s Remington begins marketing typewriters

1871 *The Descent of Man* (Darwin)

Closed electrical circuit used to activate railroad signals

1873 Financial panic

1876 Court decisions uphold states' rights to regulate public utilities

Congress gives rate differential to land-grant railroads to carry mail

Telephone introduced

1877 Edison makes first phonograph

Gasoline-powered vehicle built by George Selden

1879 Edison devises first practical light bulb

1880 Eastman patents roll film

1880s Railroads accept standard track gauge

Gasoline engines appear in Germany

1882 Seeley patents electric iron

Wheeler patents electric fan

1883 Second transcontinental railroad completed

Railroad time adopted

1887 Interstate Commerce Act

1890 Sherman Antitrust Act

1890s Duryea, Haynes, Olds, and Ford making successful motor cars

1892 Pneumatic tire appears

Railway Safety Appliance Act

Diesel engine invented

1893 Edison introduces Kinetoscope

Financial panic

1896 Hadaway patents electric stove

1901 United States Steel Corporation established

Spindletop pool tapped

1904 Mallet-type locomotive introduced in United States

1907 Electric washing machine introduced

1911 Kettering self-starter for motor car

1914 United States has become mightiest industrial nation in world

1918 Four standard time zones adopted

1941 "Big Boy," heaviest locomotive introduced on Union Pacific

National Portrait Gallery, London

The writings of the English naturalist Charles Darwin formed the basis of a view of society known as Social Darwinism. How would this view of a dynamic, changing society fit in with the mood of present-day America?

animals, are in a perpetual competition with one another to survive and dominate, and from this competition presumably comes a steady improvement in the quality of the human species and the condition of society.

For a clearer understanding of these ideas it is useful to compare Social Darwinists with the apostles of the Enlightenment of the eighteenth century—Thomas Jefferson, John Locke, and Benjamin Franklin. The Darwinists and the men of the Enlightenment shared an abiding and profound veneration for scientific fact. Their reading of scientific teaching, however, was different. The universe of the Enlightenment was a Newtonian universe (so called in honor of the English physicist Isaac Newton). It was static and harmonious, moving like a clock in the same path at the same speed. The universe of the Darwinist was in flux, was dynamic, always changing and evolving.

When Jefferson and Locke and their followers transferred their view of nature to the social order, natural law became natural rights. Just as the universe did not change, neither did the rights of life, liberty, and property. Equally important, man with his reason and intelligence could understand the well-ordered, unchanging universe. With understanding came the power to control his destiny, a critical point, for the Enlightenment of Jefferson and Locke allowed for

unlimited progress, and such optimism appealed to men of liberal spirit who wished to reform or change society.

The Darwinist took a different view. He saw nature, blind and turbulent, overwhelming man and society. Human intelligence and energy counted for little. Evolution, to be sure, implied progress, but social improvement would come slowly—in a "natural" way—and the individual or society could do little to hasten it.

The Darwinian view of society, or Social Darwinism, had a large following in the United States in the generations after the Civil War. The man most responsible for spreading it was an Englishman, Herbert Spencer. From about 1870 to 1890 Spencer and his ideas attracted wide attention as he traveled about the country, speaking on college campuses, before business groups, and at public gatherings. He influenced many notable people, including the writers Theodore Dreiser, Jack London, Hamlin Garland, and Edgar Lee Masters. Spencer's Darwinian ideas fell in admirably with the mood of America in that era of rapid and uncoordinated industrialization and urbanization. As the historian Richard Hofstadter has noted in *Social Darwinism in American Thought,* they were scientific and comprehensive, sufficiently broad and vague to appeal to a range of people. And they were not too technical; laymen as well as scholars could understand them.

Principles of Social Darwinism

What were the principles of Social Darwinism? Perhaps the most important was repudiation of government interference in society. Spencer taught that the social mechanism was like a sealed engine which worked best if one did not tinker with it. Society, he believed, should evolve in a natural way. Such ideas led the Social Darwinist to oppose government assistance to the poor; the poor obviously were unfit and hence, under the iron laws of nature, must bear the consequences. There was no room in the Social Darwinist system for government regulation of housing conditions or abolition of child labor.

Some Social Darwinists deplored free public education, sanitation regulations, and the federal postal system. Socialism of course was wrong. In a socialist society the community would control land, capital, and industry, and the government would supervise the economy to assure a wide distribution of wealth. According to the

Social Darwinist view, such practice would penalize and discourage the "superior" members of society—that is, the people of talent and energy—and thus slow down rather than accelerate social progress.

Social Darwinists, one should add, understood full well that society must pay for the absence of restraint that they advocated, that there would be ruthless competition and some people would get hurt. But they believed that in the long run their program would benefit society, just as the struggle for survival in biology improved the species of plants and animals. It would prove more expensive, they thought, to coddle the weak and unfit. William Graham Sumner of Yale, the sociologist and leading American proponent of Social Darwinism, wrote that the alternative to survival of the fittest in society was survival of the unfittest. To try to speed social progress, he contended, was futile and any attempt to do so would bring confusion and degeneration.

Effect of Social Darwinism on Business

What did wide acceptance of the ethic of Social Darwinism mean for American business? Most American workers and farmers had never heard of Herbert Spencer and only vaguely understood the biological theories of Darwin. Still, the ideas of Social Darwinism filtered down to them via newspaper editorials, books, and magazines, and it seems fair to say that a substantial part of the population was in rhythm with them.

Social Darwinism appeared to offer scientific support of the favorite idea of American businessmen in the time after the Civil War, laissez-faire—"hands-off," no government interference with the social and economic mechanism. It exalted hard work and suggested that laziness, inefficiency, and lack of ability were the causes of failure. Hence there was no reason why society should shed tears or waste time and energy on individuals and businesses that could not succeed. It gave sanction to ruthless struggling for success, "proved" that the successful members of society were the fittest members, and proclaimed that society should not try to restrain these individuals—the mainsprings of social improvement—but should praise, imitate, and encourage them.

In more practical terms, wide acceptance of Social Darwinism—especially among such influential members of society as leaders of business, newspaper editors, politicians, and spokesmen of religion—meant that during much of the period of industrial growth in America there was minimal clamor for restraint on the activities of business. Reflecting the national mood, the government in Washington, not to mention governments of most states, made no serious attempt to bring business under effective public control. This attitude permitted reckless exploitation of natural resources, cutthroat competition, hoodwinking of consumers, and intimidation of labor. But it also brought large profits and a rapid expansion of industry. The outcome was a dramatic improvement in the national standard of

AMERICAN BUSINESS ACTIVITY: 1850 — 1869

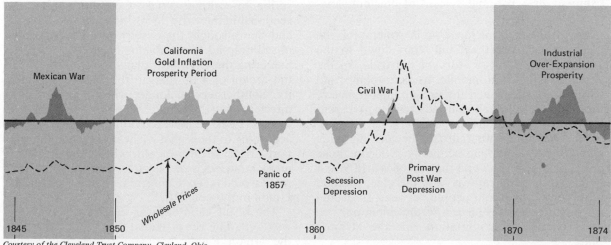

Mexican War

California Gold Inflation Prosperity Period

Civil War

Industrial Over-Expansion Prosperity

Wholesale Prices

Panic of 1857

Secession Depression

Primary Post War Depression

1845   1850   1860   1870   1874

Courtesy of the Cleveland Trust Company, Cleveland, Ohio

living—although, to be sure, the distribution of the fruits of the new prosperity was quite uneven.

STUDY GUIDE: American industry grew rapidly in the decades after the Civil War. The writings of the Englishman Charles Darwin provided the basis for a view of society called Social Darwinism. According to this philosophy, human society was constantly evolving, and men were in competition with one another to survive and dominate. This competition would lead to improvement not only for individuals but also for their society. Social Darwinism insisted that government should not interfere in this competitive struggle. This philosophy won wide acceptance in the post-Civil War American society. During this period men worked hard and competed fiercely for the profits of the new industrial nation.

TRANSPORTATION EXPANDS

In discussing the factors that contributed to the expansion of manufacturing enterprises and such industries as oil refining and meat-packing in the time after the Civil War, one must take special note of transportation. A transportation network serves as the veins and arteries of an industrial nation, carrying raw materials to centers of production and finished products to markets. Without it the industrial mechanism cannot spring to life; if it falters, the mechanism ceases to function. And so it was in America that an essential step for achieving industrialization was establishment of a national system of efficient, low-cost transportation.

The story of transportation in America in the half-century after the Civil War, down to the 1920s, was mainly a story of railroads. In the present day the automobile, truck, airplane, and barge have diminished the unique importance of the railroad, although railroads remain an essential part of the national transportation system. In the 1950s and 1960s railroads became an ailing giant of the American economy. Still, in those years between 1865 and the end of World War I (1918) the steam railway was the chief method of moving freight and people between cities and towns and came to have a virtual monopoly on long-distance transportation in the United States.

The Canal Empire Collapses

America's railroads developed slowly. In the early years equipment was crude and undependable, service poor, accidents frequent. No one thought about a national system of railroads; hence, the width between rails, or the gauge, varied wildly. Most commercial lines sought to accomplish nothing more than to promote the trade of cities along the Atlantic seaboard. Moreover, railroads appeared at a time when the country was taken up with enthusiasm for canals.

The great Erie Canal had opened in 1825 and all over the country men had visions of duplicating that magnificent triumph. While some men dreamed of waterways, others organized canal companies. In the 1830s when the Chesapeake and Ohio Canal and the Baltimore and Ohio Railroad struggled in the Maryland legislature for rights of way through a gorge of the Potomac, no one could be sure that the future did not belong to the canal. Then came the Panic of 1837, which at last resolved the question. Resting on a shaky financial foundation, the canal empire collapsed. The railroads survived the disaster and slowly extended their tiny, brittle rails to new regions.

A Transcontinental Railroad Is Sought

By the 1850s the railway age was almost at hand. People recognized that rail connections could mean prosperity for cities and states, even regions. Failure to secure service could mean ruin. The upshot was a furious competition for railroads. Towns and counties competed, sometimes offering tax exemptions and pledges to subscribe to railroad stock. Competition became sectional in the early 1850s when both the North and South sought the eastern terminus of a proposed railroad to the Pacific coast.

During the Civil War plans were made to turn the dream of a railroad to the Pacific into reality. Southerners no longer were in Congress to interfere with railroad schemes, so northern members passed laws providing a Pacific railway according to their own wishes. They had the support of President Lincoln, who recognized that mere knowledge of plans to construct the railroad would keep California on the side of the Union in the conflict.

The result, in 1862, was the first Pacific Railway Act. The act provided that two companies, the Union Pacific and Central Pacific, would build a railway connecting the northeastern states with California. The Union Pacific would build westward from the Missouri River, the Central Pacific eastward from Sacramento. Both companies would receive loans from the federal government, the loans varying according to the terrain crossed by the roads.

The act also provided for land grants. The two companies would receive ten alternate sections of public land—a section of land was 640 acres—for each mile of track put down. The railroads in turn could sell the land to cattlemen, farmers, miners, or speculators and thus meet construction costs and debt payments.

The loans and land grants benefited the railroad companies—and also the federal government. The government eventually loaned the Union Pacific and Central Pacific, as well as other railroads, $64 million. The government collected $63 million in principal and $104 million interest—a brilliant financial success. The government attached conditions to the land grants. All government traffic on land-grant railroads moved at a reduction of fifty percent from rates charged commercial shippers and travelers. Then in 1876 Congress decreed that compensation for handling mail would be twenty percent less for land-grant railroads than for others. (These rules existed until 1940. A fifty-percent rate reduction continued on military and naval personnel and cargo, bringing large savings to the government during World War II in 1941-45. At length, in 1946, Congress eliminated all rate differentials, but not before the railroads had paid the government many times over for their land grants.)

Construction Problems of the Transcontinental Railroad

Construction of the first transcontinental railroad moved slowly in the beginning, largely because the country was putting its energy and wealth into the Civil War. The Central Pacific broke ground in January 1863, the Union Pacific eleven months later, but serious work did not get under way until the end of the war.

The genius of the Union Pacific was General Grenville M. Dodge, a veteran of the Civil War who became chief engineer in 1866. Dodge commanded a small army of Irish immigrants, Civil War veterans, and even some ex-convicts. Occasionally the men had to lay aside picks and hammers and take up carbines to fight off Indians

who objected to the Union Pacific's invasion of the buffalo country.

Dodge's counterpart in the West was Charles Crocker, who had helped organize the Central Pacific Railroad several years earlier. Crocker's most pressing problem was labor. He needed thousands of workers to take on the difficult job of building the Central Pacific over the Sierras and across the deserts of Nevada and the Utah Territory beyond. To solve this problem, Crocker turned to the Chinese community.

Chinese immigrants had been arriving in California regularly for the last twenty years. By 1867 there were about 50,000 Chinese in California, many of them laborers. Crocker recruited thousands of Chinese immigrants as laborers on the Central Pacific Railroad. The work was hard, the hours were long, and the pay was low. Armed with simple tools—shovels, picks, and wheelbarrows—they slowly pushed the railway eastward.

A fair measure of dishonesty marked construction of the first transcontinental railroad. The device yielding the most loot was the construction company owned in part (secretly, of course) by directors of the railroad. In their capacities as railroad officers, the directors awarded their own construction companies extravagant contracts to build the railroads. Thus they enriched themselves at the expense of innocent stockholders of the railroad companies to whom they were legally and morally responsible.

The Crédit Mobilier Scandal

The most infamous construction company was the Crédit Mobilier, builder of the Union Pacific. Crédit Mobilier corruption eventually reached the national government in Washington when leaders of the company, fearing embarrassing investigations, distributed stock among influential politicians. Investigations came anyhow and the ensuing revelations shocked the country.

Meanwhile, Crédit Mobilier and its Central Pacific counterpart put down track at a furious pace. So haphazard was construction that much of the line required rebuilding within a short time. Haste resulted from the terms of the Pacific Railway Act, which designated no point for joining the Union Pacific and Central Pacific and made government subsidies dependent on miles of track laid. In the absence of an agreement on a meeting point, advance crews in early 1869 met in northern Utah but did not halt construction. They simply continued putting down crossties and rails and, as a consequence, the new transcontinental had several miles of parallel grading. At length the Congress had to intervene and named Promontory Point in the Utah Territory as the place where the two roads would join.

The Golden Spikes

On May 10, 1869, Promontory Point was the scene of one of the most celebrated events of the nineteenth century. About six hundred people gathered around as Presidents Leland Stanford of the Central Pacific and Thomas C. Durant of the Union Pacific drove two golden spikes into holes which had been bored in a crosstie made of California laurel. Telegraph wires were coiled around Stanford's hammer, and his blows activated a national circuit which sent news of the event throughout the country. Onlookers cheered, bands played, locomotive bells clanged and whistles bellowed. Newspapers printed extra editions; in Philadelphia the old Liberty Bell in Independence Hall tolled again; and in Washington a magnetic ball, released by the telegraphic signal, dropped from its pole on the Capitol dome.

Workers lay rails over solid oak ties in the process of building the Atchison, Topeka, and Santa Fe Railway, known as the Santa Fe. The line was founded in 1859 and became one of the most prosperous railroads in the nation. It has 21,500 miles of track from Chicago through the Gulf states to the Pacific coast. Is the railroad of today obsolete as a mode of transportation?

Santa Fe Railway Photo

Expansion Continues

Construction of the first transcontinental accounted for only a fraction of the country's railroad activity in the second half of the nineteenth century. The period 1865-1900 saw rail mileage in the United States increase to two hundred thousand miles. By 1916, the peak year of rail mileage, the United States had 254,000 miles of railway, more than all the nations of Europe combined.

The first transcontinental railroad had hardly been completed before other transcontinentals were moving out from the Middle West to the Pacific coast. First was the Northern Pacific. In 1864 Congress voted a charter and land grant for a line from Lake Superior along a northern route to the Pacific Northwest. Construction did not begin, however, until 1870 because the company had trouble raising money. Only when Jay Cooke, financial angel of the northern cause in the Civil War, assumed management of the road did investors show confidence. Then came misfortune. In September 1873 Cooke's financial empire collapsed and construction of the Northern Pacific stopped. More serious, Cooke's failure triggered a national financial panic which led in turn to a long, dismal economic depression which gripped the country for several years.

By the late 1870s the Northern Pacific, now under the management of receivers, was again inching westward. At this time a Bavarian immigrant and well-known Civil War news reporter, Henry Villard, became interested in the road. Villard, who had gained control of steamship and railroad properties in Oregon secured control of the Northern Pacific, and began to push construction. In September 1883, at a point west of Helena, Montana, with President Chester A. Arthur and former-President Grant looking on, the last rails went into place to complete the second transcontinental railroad.

Other Rail Lines Appear

Other rail lines appeared in the trans-Mississippi regions, including the Chicago and North Western, the Missouri-Kansas-Texas, the Chicago, Rock Island and Pacific, the Denver and Rio Grande, and the Chicago, Burlington, and Quincy. Along the old Santa Fe trail—from Atchison, Kansas, along the Arkansas River to Trinidad, Colorado, and over the Raton spur of the Rockies, through Apache and Navajo country, to Santa Fe and Albuquerque—ran a road whose tracks eventually would reach Chicago in the Middle West and Los Angeles and San Francisco in California. This was the Atchison, Topeka, and Santa Fe, destined to become one of the most prosperous railroads in the country. Until creation of the Penn Central system in 1968, it was the largest in the United States in terms of route mileage.

Leland Stanford, Collis P. Huntington, and other promoters of the Central Pacific, meanwhile, had not put aside their interest in railroading after the affair at Promontory Point. They built a line from San Francisco through the San Joaquin Valley to Los Angeles and across the Gadsden Purchase to El Paso. Their road was the Southern Pacific, second largest in the country in terms of mileage until appearance of the Penn Central. At El Paso the Southern Pacific joined the Texas and Pacific to link California with New Orleans, fulfilling the dreams of Jefferson Davis and the antebellum South.

Many of the new railroads were ill conceived, poorly engineered, and recklessly financed. Then came the line built by James J. Hill, the "empire builder." Hill's road was the Great Northern.

Hill had arrived in the frontier town of Saint Paul in Minnesota Territory in 1865 and over the next twenty years busied himself with merchandising and freighting. While on a business trip in connection with these enterprises—a trip to Winnipeg via dog sled in winter 1870—he made a contact which would greatly influence his subsequent career as a railroad builder as well as the development of the North American continent. Moving across the prairie he happened on a party headed by Donald Smith, an official of Hudson's Bay Company, the great fur-trading organization of Canada. Hill and Smith struck up a friendship which was instrumental in the eventual construction of two giant railroads, the Great Northern in the United States and the Canadian Pacific in Canada.

A few years later, in 1878, Hill began his railroad enterprise by securing control of the bankrupt Saint Paul and Pacific Company. Hill had to rely on private capital. With Smith's help he obtained much of the financial support he needed in Canada. Later, when Smith was building the Canadian Pacific, Hill returned the favor.

Hill built his railroad empire carefully. Financial management was conservative and construction moved slowly. Hill built branch lines to areas that would generate traffic for his road. He recruited people—immigrants as well as native Americans seeking new opportunity—selling them cheap passage in second-class cars and helping them find good land. He encouraged scientific agriculture, gave quality livestock to farmers, supported churches and schools. The result was that Hill's Great Northern Railroad did not reach Seattle until the year 1893. But unlike other transcontinentals it weathered all financial crises. In the depression years which followed the Panic of 1893, the Great Northern was one of the few railroads to continue dividend payments. By the turn of the century, Hill had gained control of his chief competitor, the Northern Pacific.

While the transcontinentals aroused popular enthusiasm and set off parades and celebrations, developments east of the Mississippi were no less important. It was in the post-Civil War period that Cornelius Vanderbilt, who had made a

In 1886 *Harper's* published this engraving of the interior of a railroad car under the title "The Modern Ship of the Plains." What effect did the opening of new rail lines have on immigration?

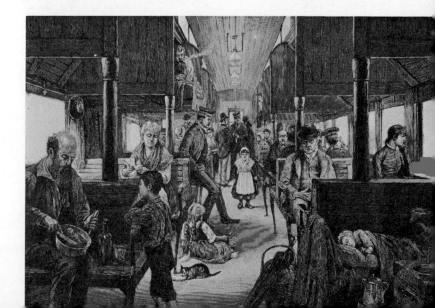

EXPANSION
OF INDUSTRY

During the late 1800s the growth of American industry transformed the nation. Businessmen with a talent for organization and efficiency created vast industrial empires. Large factories employed millions of Americans. Many men made fortunes from the industrial growth in America, and immigrants came to the United States in hopes that they too would share in the wealth.

1

Courtesy Ford Motor Company

2

Courtesy State of Minnesota

1

By using the assembly line method, the Ford Motor Company was able to produce large quantities of automobiles. Because production was efficient and inexpensive, the company was able to sell cars at low prices. After 1914 Henry Ford reduced the hours of the working day in his plant to eight hours. Ford's assembly line production became a model for many industries.

2

As American industry grew during the late 1800s, iron became a precious natural resource. Large deposits of iron ore were found in Minnesota, Michigan, Utah, and Alabama. The open pit mine shown here is located in Minnesota, within the rich Mesabi Range.

3

John D. Rockefeller became one of the wealthiest men in the United States by gaining control of the oil industry. This portrait was painted by Eastman Johnson when Rockefeller was a young man.

3

Courtesy The University of Chicago

4

The Vanderbilt family accumulated a vast fortune in the late 1800s. Their fortune enabled them to live in lavish style. George Washington Vanderbilt built the Biltmore House near Asheville, North Carolina, in the 1890s.

5

Iron ore that was mined in Minnesota and Michigan was transported to steel mills in Pittsburgh and Chicago. By 1900, the United States had become the largest steel producer in the world, and mills like the one shown in this painting produced millions of tons of steel each year.

4   Courtesy State of North Carolina

5   The Bettmann Archive

fortune in the ferrying business (and hence was known as "Commodore" Vanderbilt), moved into railroading and merged several small lines into the sprawling New York Central system.

At the same time the Pennsylvania Railroad, under the leadership of J. Edgar Thomson, became the greatest business organization in North America. When Thomson took over the road in 1874, the Pennsylvania consisted of a line from Philadelphia to Pittsburgh, an assortment of branches, and a line to Lake Erie. But with Thomson pulling the strings, the "Pennsy" came to rival the Vanderbilt lines and reached New York City, Washington, Saint Louis, Cincinnati, and Chicago. By the beginning of the twentieth century, it was transporting more freight and passengers than any railroad anywhere and had become known as "the Standard Railroad of the World." (The Penn Central, created in 1968, was the product of a merger of the New York Central and the Pennsylvania companies.) In these same years the Baltimore and Ohio and the Erie brought their rails to the Great Lakes and the Ohio Valley.

The closing decades of the nineteenth century also witnessed important railroad developments in the South. The region's meager rail network had met destruction in the Civil War, so a major task during the postwar years was restoration and expansion. By the end of the century the largest road below the Mason-Dixon line was the Southern. A newcomer, the Southern had come into existence in 1894 when the financier J. P. Morgan brought together several loosely controlled, poorly managed roads. Equally important was the Louisville and Nashville, which—under the astute management of Milton H. Smith—became a political as well as economic power in a half-dozen southern states. Competing for business along the Atlantic seaboard between the Chesapeake Bay area and Florida, their tracks running parallel at some points, were the Atlantic Coast Line and the Seaboard Air Line (merged in the 1960s into a single company, the Seaboard Coast Line).

Another major southern road was the Illinois Central, the first railroad to receive a federal land grant (by a congressional act of 1850). By 1900 the Illinois Central, its tracks reaching down from Chicago, was operating 2,300 miles of road below the Ohio River, connecting such points as Louisville, Memphis, and New Orleans. There were two roads whose operations centered in the Virginia–West Virginia coal country: the Norfolk and Western and the Chesapeake and Ohio. These lines attracted scant attention at first, but by the middle of the twentieth century, when other railroads were in decline, these two "coal roads" were among the healthiest in the country.

STUDY GUIDE: The industrialization of America depended on the establishment of a national system of efficient, low-cost transportation. The first Pacific Railway Act in 1862 provided loans and land grants for the Union Pacific and Central Pacific Railway companies to begin construction of a line connecting the northeastern states with California. By the close of the nineteenth century, railroads were expanding throughout the nation.

TOWARD A NATIONAL RAIL SYSTEM

When the railway age began, nobody seemed to think about a national rail system. Most railroads were only a few miles long, usually con-

This 1860 lithograph shows a view of the Illinois and Michigan Railroad central depot in Chicago. How did the increasing number of rail lines west of the Mississippi affect the growth of Chicago?

Library of Congress

necting neighboring towns or running from a mine to a nearby factory. Larger roads often sought to promote the commerce of a particular city. The Baltimore and Ohio, for example, was intended to restore to the port of Baltimore the traffic it was losing to New York because of the Erie Canal; the Pennsylvania sought the same end for Philadelphia. The outcome was a crazy-quilt national pattern of railroads.

Moreover, the width between rails varied from road to road, making interchange of cars impossible. Major cities often had no connecting tracks between different lines. To handle through shipments it was necessary to unload cargo from freight car to wagon, dispatch the wagon crosstown to another railroad, and unload the cargo from wagon to a new freight car. Similar maneuvering moved freight across rivers having no bridges. Such clumsy operations were slow and expensive. Also there was no standard time. Most towns observed sun time, so when it was noon in Chicago, it was 12:31 P.M. in Pittsburgh and 11:27 A.M. in Omaha. The passenger station at Buffalo had three clocks, each posting a different railroad time.

Only in the last decades of the nineteenth century did railroads in America take on the appearance of a national system. Much of the change can be attributed to the financiers and bankers who came to dominate railroad companies. These men had no sentimental attachment to small independent lines and could see that efficient operation on a national scale would bring greater return on investment. The consequence was a rapid merger of short lines into large systems. The Pennsylvania, for example, absorbed several hundred lesser companies before the beginning of the twentieth century.

Other bottlenecks to efficient operation also disappeared. Bridges eventually spanned rivers at all important points. New techniques came into use for interchanging traffic at terminals, including the railroad company whose sole function was shifting cars from road to road. Nearly all railroads accepted a standard gauge of track, four feet, eight and one-half inches. Perhaps the most dramatic change of gauge occurred on a 550-mile stretch of the Illinois Central. After careful preparation, all train operations on the division stopped at dawn on July 29, 1881. By three o'clock in the afternoon 3,000 workmen had shifted the gauge on the entire line. The roads resolved the time problem by arbitrarily establishing a system of standard time. In 1883 most communities quickly adopted railroad time,

although one editor protested that he would prefer to operate on "God's time—not Vanderbilt's." The four standard time zones used today were established by federal law in 1918.

As railroads increased in number, roads began to coordinate operations. They scheduled freight and passenger trains to connect with those of other roads and organized cooperative fast freight lines. Under this latter arrangement connecting roads formed an administrative pool in which each road contributed a share of equipment and offered shippers through bills of lading. While these operations sometimes worked a hardship on nonaffiliated lines, they saved time and money.

Technological Improvements Promote Efficiency

Important technical improvements promoted railroad efficiency in the second half of the nineteenth century. Steel rails—first used on the Pennsylvania in 1863—were more durable than those made of iron. By the turn of the century, the brittle iron rail was virtually a relic. Rails also became heavier, making operations smoother and safer. In the Civil War period rail often weighed less than thirty pounds per yard; by 1900 some roads were putting down rail weighing more than 120 pounds. There were advances in signaling. Collisions, both head-end and rear-end, were frequent in the early days of railroading, largely because of inadequate signaling systems. Then in 1865 the Camden and Amboy put into operation a block-signal system to keep trains separated by a prescribed interval, or "block" of distance. The Camden and Amboy system was operated manually—by hand—but in 1871 William Robinson devised a closed electric circuit to activate signals.

Meanwhile, the steam locomotive underwent major improvement. The steam injector, an engineering wonder by which steam from the locomotive put water into the boiler, began to appear around 1865. After proving that a ton of bituminous coal had the same heating capacity as one and a third cords of hardwood, the Pennsylvania in 1862 retired its last wood-burning freight locomotives. Other roads quickly followed. The smooth-running little 4-4-0 type locomotive (four-wheel leading truck, four driving wheels, and no trailing truck) became standard and in 1893 the New York Central's No. 999 reached the fantastic speed of 112.3 miles per hour. The period also saw development of larger locomo-

The grand opening of the nation's first transcontinental railroad was heralded in this Union Pacific poster. In May 1869 wildly celebrating crowds gathered at Promontory Point, in Utah Territory, for ceremonies marking completion of the line.

tives, some weighing more than 150 tons and having eight and ten driving wheels.

Then in 1904 the Baltimore and Ohio purchased the country's first Mallet-type locomotive (named for the Swiss designer Anatole Mallet). It was a giant machine with two sets of cylinders and driving wheels. Built for mountain service, this locomotive was slow but served as the model of many locomotives to come, including the famous "Big Boy" of the Union Pacific. Built in 1941, the "Big Boy" with tender weighed 1,207,000 pounds—the heaviest locomotive the world has seen.

Safety Is Promoted

Promoting safety as well as efficiency were the automatic coupler and air brake. A crude link-and-pin device originally provided coupling for railroad rolling stock, making the switching of cars slow and dangerous. The brakeman had to stand between the cars and guide the "link" of one coupler into the socket of the other and complete the coupling by dropping a "pin" into place. This was a risky business, and mangled hands and missing fingers became the trademark of railroad brakemen. Many inventors patented automatic coupling devices, but the first successful one was derived from a model whittled by a veteran of the Confederate Army, Eli H. Janney.

There was, in addition, the braking problem. Brakeman had always brought trains to a stop by scampering from car to car and twisting handbrakes. This, too, was slow and dangerous. The problem ended, in theory at least, when a New York inventor, George Westinghouse, developed a successful air brake after observing the use of compressed air in tunnel construction in France. In the Westinghouse system each car in the train had its own reservoir of air and the engineman set the brake by permitting air to escape. If the train broke in two, of course, air would be released and both sections would come to a halt. Westinghouse, only twenty-two years old, patented his brake in 1869.

Acceptance of the air brake and automatic coupler came slowly. Application of the devices to existing rolling stock was costly, and some railroad officers doubted their value. During an interview Cornelius Vanderbilt shouted to Westinghouse: "Do you pretend to tell me that you could stop trains with wind?" Consequently the Janney Car Coupling Company languished and and Westinghouse turned his great energies and talents elsewhere, first to developing railroad signaling devices, then to organizing the Westinghouse Electric Company. All railroads did not adopt the new coupling and braking systems until 1892 when Congress passed the Railroad Safety Appliance Act in the interest of safety.

There were other noteworthy technical developments, including the refrigerator car, a boon to the citrus fruit and meat-packing industries. Railroads also developed cars for special shipments —horizontal tank cars for oil and hopper cars for coal. Innovations in equipment, notably the Pullman sleeping car and the dining car, increased the comfort of passengers.

Cutthroat Competition with Canals

Railroad expansion and development were dealing a heavy blow to water transportation in America. In the 1840s and 1850s many water carriers, especially steamboat companies, had enjoyed prosperity and a popular approval akin to that which the present generation has accorded the jet airliner. When the Civil War began in 1861, nearly two thousand steamboats were operating on the Ohio-Mississippi river system. In the fifteen years after Appomattox, water carriers generally held their own. In 1880 a million tons of freight left Saint Louis by riverboat. Then came decline, the consequence of increased competition from railroads. In 1900 only 245,000 tons left Saint Louis via water. Despite a feverish attempt to meet railroad competition by reducing rates, the Erie Canal suffered a similar loss of traffic.

There were several reasons why water carriers were unable to compete with railroads. One was the abiding determination of railroads to destroy water competition. Vanderbilt's New York Central refused to handle the freight of any firm doing business with the Erie Canal. This was a fatal blow to the canal's New England traffic since New England's prosperity depended on continuing service by Vanderbilt's railroad empire. More important were the natural advan-

The growth of railroads dealt a heavy blow to water transportation in the 1800s. However, people continued to ship cotton, copper, and other goods which would not spoil. This photograph shows bales of cotton being rolled down the gangplank and onto the levee at Memphis, Tennessee around 1900.

tages of the railroad. The railroad was faster than the river steamer or canal boat and served a much larger area. With a minimum of expense railroad companies could put down track to tap new sources of revenue—factories, oil fields, mines, and wheat areas. Another factor was nature. Ice blocked the Upper Mississippi part of each year, periodic floods interfered with water traffic, and sometimes the rivers were too low for navigation. Water carriers in that era were also less progressive and resourceful than railroads. Damp and dirty cargo decks on lake and canal boats often resulted in damage to grain cargoes, while inadequate storage facilities at receiving points exposed freight to foul weather and thieves.

Still, water transportation was not finished and in transporting heavy, nonperishable goods it remained important. In the last years of the nineteenth century the forests of Wisconsin and Minnesota were yielding quantities of timber and rivers and streams provided the best means of conveying timber to mills. Coal was another commodity which could move economically by water—on huge barges propelled by powerful steamboats. Then there was iron ore. In the second half of the nineteenth century the country began to exploit the ore deposits of the Lake Superior region, with resultant prosperity for steamship companies operating on the Great Lakes.

STUDY GUIDE: At first most railroad lines were short and did not connect with other lines. This made it difficult to ship freight long distances. In the later 1800s short lines were merged into larger systems. Railroad operations became more efficient, partly as a result of technological improvements such as steel rails and better steam locomotives. Although water transportation declined in importance, it was still useful for transporting coal and iron ore.

CORRUPTION, ABUSES, REGULATION

Expansion, technical improvements, and nationalization in the latter part of the nineteenth century made the period a glorious chapter in the history of American railroads. There was also a dark side to the story. Punctuating the phenomenal growth of rail transport was a wave of corruption and discrimination which eventually produced a great public clamor for regulation.

The sensational Crédit Mobilier was only one of many instances of dishonesty associated with railroads in the post-Civil War era. In the South much activity of so-called carpetbaggers resulted in fortunes from reconstruction of the region's railroads. In the building of transcontinental roads construction companies fleeced stockholders. A congressional investigating committee late in the century estimated that five transcontinentals had cost $634 million; duplication would cost $286 million.

Much stock of such railroads was sheer "water," meaning that it bore little relation to the true value of the property. The result of this dishonesty often was high freight rates, for it was necessary to continue regular dividend payments and thus prevent railroad shares from losing value in the stock exchanges.

Stock Manipulation

Fraudulent manipulation of railroad stock was another characteristic of the new railway age and through such manipulation some sharp promoters managed to get rich. Among the more prominent names involved in these dishonest maneuvers were Daniel Drew, Jay Gould, and James Fisk. The railroad which fell victim to some of the largest and most daring stock operations was the Erie, whose difficulties began in 1854 when Drew, a former cattleman and steamship rival of Vanderbilt, turned his greedy attention to the road. During the next twenty years Drew and his group systematically enriched themselves at the expense of Erie stockholders and customers.

Possibly the most sensational episode involving the Erie occurred in 1866. It is worth recounting, for it illustrates the kind of business buccaneering that was possible in that era of rapid economic growth and Social Darwinism. It began when the Erie suddenly needed money and Drew agreed to lend a hand. As security, Erie directors went to their treasury vault and handed over to Drew a quantity of unissued Erie stock and $3 million in bonds which he could convert to Erie stock whenever he wished. Nobody outside the inner circle of the Erie management knew of these goings-on, so Drew began a "short selling" operation in Wall Street. That is, he made contracts at current prices for future delivery of Erie stock which he had not yet purchased.

When a speculator sells short, he is gambling that the price will fall before the date on which he must deliver the stock. The difference between the contract price and the price he pays on the delivery date is profit. As days went by, however, Erie stock, instead of falling, increased in price, indicating that Drew would have to buy stock for delivery at a higher price than that of the contracts. Rumors began to circulate on Wall Street that "Uncle Daniel" was cornered — and many speculators and observers doubtless felt delighted.

Then Drew played his ace. Converting his $3 million in bonds to Erie stock, he dumped this and other stock in the Wall Street market. The sudden influx of stock created panic among Erie shareholders, and many ordered brokers to sell their shares for whatever they would bring. As a consequence quotations on Erie stock plunged from 80 to 50. Drew now purchased the company's stock at the lower price to meet his contract obligations. The outcome was a profit to him of several million dollars. (In later manipulations Drew met financial ruin at the hands of one-time allies, Gould and Fisk, ending his days as a salesman of Bibles, hymnals, and sealskin coats.)

Establishing Rates

Shippers as well as stockholders often suffered in that era before transportation came under public regulation. Perhaps the principal abuse was in fixing freight rates. In the present day there are various theories of rate-making. For example, some railroad men believe the value of the commodity being shipped should determine the rate, meaning that the road should receive more for moving fine furniture than coal or lumber. Others contend that the rate should depend solely on what it costs the railroad to make the shipment. Considering the complexity of the subject, complete fairness probably is impossible.

In the post-Civil War years the railroads made little effort to treat shippers impartially. The prevailing theory for establishing rates was simplicity itself: charge all the traffic will bear. Where there was no alternate way for the shipper to move his goods, say, by another railroad or canal boat, freight rates were high. Where they faced competition, railroads often slashed rates far below the break-even point, making up the loss on sections of the line where no competition existed. For example, the rate for shipping grain

Passengers aboard the Pacific Railroad's *Hotel Express Train* could enjoy eating dinner in elegant dining cars as they traveled coast to coast in the 1870s. Later in the 1800s, many wealthy business leaders built their own private railroad cars and furnished them lavishly.

from Saint Paul to Chicago, where several roads competed for business, was about 12.5 cents per hundred pounds in the 1890s. But from Minnesota towns to Saint Paul, where railroads usually had no competition, the rate was twenty-five cents.

Railroads often charged less for shipping for the long haul from Chicago to Saint Louis, where, again, there was competition, than for short hauls from Chicago to intermediate points, where there was no competition. At one time the competition for passengers among roads operating between Chicago and Saint Louis became so intense that an individual could travel between the two cities for a dollar. To counter the destructive effects of such cutthroat competition, railroads became involved in a new evil: pooling. Roads operating between identical points, say, Saint Paul and Chicago or Saint Louis and Chicago, entered "gentlemen's agreements" to refrain from competition and maintain high rates. In some pools, railroads even agreed to prorate or divide profits. The result was high charges for shippers and passengers.

Other Abuses

There were other abuses. Railroads often made secret agreements with favored shippers whereby "Shipper A" would pay a higher rate for an identical shipment than "Shipper B." At times roads declined to publish rate schedules, leaving it to freight managers to determine the charge for each shipment. The manager would then size up each shipper to decide what he could or would pay and fix rates accordingly. This meant that rates for similar shipments sometimes varied widely. Another abuse was the rebate whereby railroads refunded to the favored shipper part of the rate he had paid.

Railroads had little affection for such rate-cutting gimmicks as secret agreements and rebates, but powerful shippers such as the Standard Oil Company, which sometimes had the option of using any of several lines, often forced them on the roads as a price for their business. John D. Rockefeller even compelled railroads to rebate to his Standard Oil Company a percentage of the freight charges paid by competing petroleum producers!

Farmers Suffer Mistreatment

Farmers on the Great Plains seemed to come in for special mistreatment. Since the Plains farmer seldom had any alternative to shipping his grain eastward via the nearest railroad, he usually had to pay the rate imposed by that road—and the rate tended to be high. As a condition for moving their grain, moreover, railroads often compelled farmers to use railroad-owned elevators and warehouses. These facilities controlled the grading of grain and frequently paid the farmer on the basis of low grading while selling the grain at eastern exchanges on the basis of high grading.

A railroad could also apply a transit rate when it feared the farmer might ship his grain to Saint Paul or some other point, then switch it to another road which might offer a lower rate for the remainder of the journey. Under terms of the transit rate, the road on which the shipment originated compelled the farmer to agree to use that road for the entire shipment. He was also forced to pay the rate in advance. Such a practice prevented farmers from taking advantage of rail competition which might exist on part of the route of shipment. The outcome, of course, was higher transportation costs.

In their competition for charters and sub-sidies—and to prevent troublesome regulation—railroads in the decades after the Civil War worked unceasingly to influence members of state legislatures and other individuals who had the power to mold popular opinion. They sought to influence legislators by maintaining elaborate lobbying organizations, by making regular contributions to political campaigns, and, more important, by giving bribes. No one will ever know the true extent of bribery, but historians of the period are unanimous that it was widespread. Another instrument for persuading legislators—and such people of influence as newspaper editors and clergymen—was the free pass, which permitted the holder to ride passenger trains without charge. In that era when the passenger train was the principal means of traveling long distances, and even from one neighboring town to another, a pass was a valuable commodity which over the years could save its owner a considerable sum of money.

A Movement Toward Public Regulation

At length a great many Americans became fed up with the high-handed and corrupt tactics of railroads, typified by William Vanderbilt's famous remark, given in an interview aboard his private railway car, that "the public be damned." And so in the difficult years following the Panic of 1873 they began to demand an end to railroad buccaneering. The upshot was a movement to bring railroads under public regulation.

The movement for control gathered steam when such states as Iowa, Wisconsin, Minnesota, Missouri, Nebraska, Massachusetts, and California outlawed rebates, free passes, and discrimination in rates and services. Railroads hotly contested the right of states to regulate their activities, arguing that such measures deprived them of their property without due process of law and hence violated the Fourteenth Amendment to the Constitution.

Then in 1876 the Supreme Court handed down decisions upholding the right of states to regulate private enterprises which in effect had become public utilities. The case of *Munn* v. *Illinois* was the outcome of a suit by warehouse owners challenging a regulatory statute of Illinois. In one of the most heralded rulings in history the Court declared that "when one devotes his property to a use in which the public has an interest, he, in effect, grants the public an interest in that use, and must submit to be controlled by the public for the common good." In

Peik v. *Chicago & North Western R.R.* and *Chicago, Burlington & Quincy R.R.* v. *Iowa* the Court ruled that states could fix maximum railroad and passenger rates.

The decisions of 1876 seemed a great victory for advocates of public regulation of railroads, but then in 1886 the Supreme Court handed down a new decision that dealt a heavy blow to attempts by states to curb railroad abuses. In the Wabash rate case the Court ruled that an Illinois law aimed at eliminating the practice of charging a higher rate for a short haul than for a long one infringed on the authority of Congress. The Court maintained that Congress had the exclusive right to regulate interstate commerce, that is, commerce originating in one state and terminating in another. States, under this ruling, could regulate only that commerce which originated and terminated within the borders of the state, or intrastate commerce. Most rail traffic was interstate in character, meaning that regulatory statutes passed by states were generally useless.

Interstate Commerce Act of 1887

It became apparent that only the national Congress in Washington could provide effective regulation of railroads. The outcome was the Interstate Commerce Act of 1887 which prohibited pools, rebates, and higher rates for short hauls than for long hauls by interstate carriers. The measure also stated that all rates should be "reasonable and just" and required railroads to publish their rates. The legislation of 1887 created the Interstate Commerce Commission to administer the law, not to enforce it. Responsibility for enforcement rested with the courts.

The railroads did not organize a campaign to defeat the interstate commerce legislation. By the mid-1880s they had come to favor the idea of some sort of federal regulation. Indeed most railroad leaders supported the bill when it came before Congress. What accounted for this turnabout of the railroads on the issue of public regulation? One reason was their weariness over cutthroat competition. The roads saw federal regulation as the only effective means of curbing the reckless rate-slashing that had depressed profits and driven many companies into bankruptcy. Moreover, the railroads hoped that the Interstate Commerce Commission might even become an agency for enforcing profit-maintaining pooling agreements by parallel lines.

In its early years the Interstate Commerce Act proved a disappointment. Ruling that it could not fix rates and virtually nullifying the long-haul–short-haul provision of the act, the federal courts in a series of decisions removed much of the authority of the ICC. In the period 1887-1905 sixteen cases involving ICC rulings were accepted by the Supreme Court and in fifteen the Court decided in favor of the roads. As for helping the railroads, as the roads had hoped, the legislation failed to prevent cutthroat competition, in part because Congress in 1890 passed the Sherman Antitrust Act outlawing secret rate-making among rival enterprises.

Still, the Interstate Commerce Act established the principle of federal regulation of business and opened the way for better legislation in the future.

Contributions of the Railroads

One should not permit railroad abuses and the controversy over regulation to obscure the important contributions of the railroads in the last decades of the nineteenth century. In the post-Civil War era railroads bound the country together and without them and the telegraph America would have remained a collection of rather isolated states and regions. Railroads made possible the astonishing growth of American industry, brought every hamlet within range of commodities produced in all sections of the country, and tended to equalize prices across the nation. They reduced costs of manufacturing, which in turn reduced consumer prices and increased the national standard of living. They increased land values. And, despite discrimination, there was a steady decline in freight rates in those years: in 1872 the average rate per ton-mile was two and one-half cents; by 1882 it was 1.24 and by 1898, about three-quarters of a cent.

This meant that America could exploit the economic principle of comparative advantage — the principle that each locality concentrates on producing what it can produce best and secures other needs from other areas. There are two requisites for putting the principle of comparative advantage into effect. One is the absence of trade barriers. The American Republic had had this from the beginning; there were no tariffs between the states of the federal Union. The United States was a gigantic free-trade area.

The other requisite is efficient, low-cost

transportation. The railroads in the latter part of the nineteenth century gave the country such transportation. Free domestic trade and low-cost transportation, then, combined with an abundance of natural and human resources, helped produce for Americans the highest level of prosperity ever experienced by any people in the history of the world.

STUDY GUIDE: The tremendous growth of rail transport was accompanied by widespread corruption. Dishonest railroad men charged excessive freight rates and cheated stockholders. They were unfair in their charges to farmers who depended on shipping crops by rail. In the years after the Panic of 1873 these corrupt practices led to a movement to bring railroads under public regulation. In a series of decisions the Supreme Court said that states had the right to regulate railroads within their borders. In an effort to regulate rail traffic between states, Congress passed the Interstate Commerce Act of 1887.

THE GROWTH OF INDUSTRY

After the Civil War, the westward movement (which never had stopped, even during the conflict) accelerated. But overshadowing that important development in the era after Appomattox was the continuing exploitation of the country's natural wealth, above and below the surface of the earth, and the spectacular expansion of manufacturing. Except for occasional pauses, as during the depressions of the 1870s and 1890s, the national industrial mechanism steadily enlarged, turning out increasing volumes of materials and manufactures. By the outbreak of the World War in Europe in 1914, the United States had eclipsed Great Britain, Germany, and France in output of iron, steel, and coal and had become the leading industrial country of the world.

Bases of Industrial Expansion

What made possible the phenomenal industrial growth in the nineteenth century? What spurred it on?

As noted earlier, the intellectual climate of the second half of the nineteenth century was typified by the ideas of Social Darwinism. This stimulated industrial expansion by giving sanction to "no-holds-barred" competition among businessmen and helping to prevent restraints on greed and exploitation.

Then there was transportation. Without efficient, low-cost transportation, which America secured in the second half of the nineteenth century, American industry could not have prospered and become powerful.

Natural Resources

Equally important were the abundant resources which nature had bestowed on America, particularly coal and iron. In an area centering in northeastern Pennsylvania the American nation had the largest deposits of anthracite coal in the world. In the Appalachian Mountain range, from Pennsylvania through West Virginia and eastern Kentucky to Alabama, it had an almost inexhaustible field of bituminous coal. There were also large bituminous coal deposits in the Mississippi Valley region, in western Kentucky, Missouri, Illinois, Iowa—and elsewhere.

At the onset of America's industrial age, these great coal riches were virtually untapped. In a land abounding with trees, people had given little thought to the possibility of firing stoves, furnaces, and locomotives with any fuel other than wood. But when men began to dream of great industrial empires, in the middle of the nineteenth century, they understood that the nation's diminishing timberlands could not meet the new requirements for fuel. So they looked to coal. As a consequence the national output of bituminous coal more than doubled in each of the four decades between 1850 and 1890. Production of anthracite coal in 1860 was ten times what it had been in the year 1840.

Iron was present in many states in the Union. When the industrial age began in the middle of the nineteenth century, Americans were only vaguely aware of the extent of the country's iron treasures. Then, after the Civil War, men began to find that deposits in the Lake Superior region, first discovered by government surveyors around 1844, ranged for hundreds of miles across northern Minnesota and the upper peninsula of Michigan. The Lake Superior deposits, which included the Mesabi range, eventually provided ninety percent of the ore that fed America's steel mills. Some of the Lake Superior ore, particularly in the Mesabi range, was near the surface of the earth and was extracted by giant steam shovels operating in huge

Prospectors found "black gold" when they struck oil at Spindletop. This photograph was made there in 1915.

pits. Other ore was deep inside the earth and required shaft mining. In the years after the Civil War important deposits of ore were discovered in Alabama and Utah.

Americans had other underground resources, including gold and silver. From the 1850s to the 1890s, when South Africa began to yield quantities of the yellow metal, the United States was the world leader in production of gold. After discovery of the fabulous Comstock Lode in Nevada in 1859, it became the leading producer of silver. The country also had rich deposits of zinc, lead, nickel, and copper.

And there was oil.

When white settlers first arrived in western Pennsylvania, they found that Indians of the region gathered petroleum from seepages, using it for medicine and, despite considerable smoke and stench, for illumination. Following the Indians' example, the whites also took to using the black liquid, particularly for treatment of colds, rheumatism, toothaches, and assorted maladies. About the middle of the nineteenth century, Samuel M. Kier, a druggist in Pittsburgh, developed a process for distilling petroleum and began to market his product as an illuminant.

In 1855 a report was issued on the commercial possibilities of petroleum by the scientist Benjamin Silliman, Jr., followed by experiments on its refining. Several small oil companies now appeared, and one of these leased some land near Titusville, Pennsylvania, hiring Edwin L. Drake

to supervise the drilling of a well. Drake hit oil in 1859 and before long the well was turning out twenty-five barrels a day. Soon oil prospectors were flocking to western Pennsylvania. Other wells came in, and by 1862 the United States was producing more than one hundred million gallons of petroleum per year. Most of it went into kerosene for lamps and various kinds of lubricants.

Within a few years new oil regions opened up, particularly in New York, Ohio, West Virginia, Kentucky, Tennessee, and California. Toward the end of the nineteenth century, men discovered quantities of oil in Wyoming, but the big strikes came around the turn of the twentieth century, and after, in Texas, Oklahoma, Kansas, Louisiana, and Illinois. The most spectacular came in 1901 along the Gulf Coast of Texas when oil men tapped the Spindletop pool. The following year, 1902, Spindletop yielded seventeen and a half million barrels of "black gold."

Agriculture

The country's agricultural domain was another resource that contributed to industrial growth. Southern cotton farms and plantations, for example, produced the fiber that fed New England's textile mills. Tobacco from Virginia, North Carolina, Kentucky, and Tennessee sustained the cigarette industry. Cattle and hogs were the foundation of the meat-packing industry. With the advent of the metal can such farm produce as corn, peas, and tomatoes became the basis of a large prepared-foods industry.

Other resources of great importance in America's industrial expansion—but ones which people often take for granted—were timber and water.

Despite the wanton destruction of millions of trees, the United States at the dawn of its industrial age still had countless acres of timberland. From these forests came material that supported numerous industries. The manufacture of furniture, office equipment, wagons, and railway cars —to say nothing of construction—depended on timber. Water was also essential to industrial growth, for quantities of water are necessary in most manufacturing. It takes, for example, about thirteen barrels of water to turn out one barrel of oil and about sixty-five thousand gallons to make a ton of steel. With its streams, rivers, and lakes the United States was richly endowed with this precious commodity.

A Need for Human Resources

America's industrialization required human as well as material resources, for it was necessary to have men to operate machines, dig coal and ore, and run locomotives and steamboats. During the great era of industrial expansion the country with a minimum of difficulty met industry's increasing appetite for labor. Part of the credit for this success rested with the high birth rate in the United States. In those days people tended to see a large family as an economic and social asset rather than a liability, and it was not unusual to find ten or twelve children in one household even in crowded cities. This natural growth in population helped provide workers for American industry.

Then there was immigration. In the second half of the nineteenth century and the first two decades of the twentieth immigrants arrived on America's shores in unprecedented numbers— from northern and western Europe, the Far East, southern and eastern Europe. Some immigrants had a little money when they arrived and were able to become shopkeepers in the cities or take up land in the Middle West, in California, or on the frontier. A few were skilled artisans. But millions of new arrivals, particularly the unskilled and penniless immigrants from Ireland and Italy, the Balkans and Poland, took what work they could find in the new mines and factories.

Finally, America's farms were a source of manpower for the country's industry. Between the Civil War and World War I agriculture in America enjoyed at best intermittent and uneven prosperity. During much of the era it was seriously depressed, in part because the mechanization of agriculture permitted fewer farmers to turn out increasing quantities of farm produce. The result was a labor surplus in American agriculture. Inevitably, given the demand for labor in industry, as well as the excitement of the city compared with the isolation of the farm, many farmers and sons of farmers packed belongings and went off to urban centers to seek employment in industry.

Industrialization, at least in a free-enterprise country, requires more from its human resources than mere physical strength. Men must make certain psychological contributions. For example, industrial growth in a country requires that at least some members of the population have unusual energy and drive, a willingness to risk the possessions and wealth of the moment against the possibility of a large return, perhaps great wealth, in the future. Without this entrepreneurial spirit, sustained industrial expansion is improbable.

Substantial numbers of Americans, for whatever reason—liberal government, free-enterprise tradition, or frontier heritage—were endowed with this spirit, and the result was a strong stimulus for the expansion of American industry. Americans, moreover, had no special attachment to the ideas and methods of their economic past and were perfectly willing to employ new techniques and devices. They readily accepted the economic advantages of the machine over skilled hand labor. Despite a few laments from craftsmen and romantics, the American industrial empire was built on a countless array of impersonal devices that whirred, hummed, clanked and screeched, but turned out a dazzling volume and untold varieties of materials and manufactured goods of the highest quality. In the view of numerous European visitors to America, acceptance of the machine by capital and labor was a key to the country's great industrial achievements.

Capital Requirements

Industrial growth requires an abundance of investment funds. Except for occasional periods of depression, such as in the mid-1870s, there was no shortage of such funds in America during the era of industrialization. During the Civil War, many businessmen realized large returns in meeting the military needs of the United States. When the conflict ended, they sought opportunities for investment of their new fortunes. Many of them inevitably turned to industry. Investment funds also came from overseas. America seemed to present untold opportunities for profit, and financiers and speculators in London, Paris, and Amsterdam were anxious to seize them. Considerable investment funds came from the "little people" of America—individuals with a few dollars which they were willing to risk in industrial ventures on the chance that they might gain a fortune later.

Technology and Science

Further stimulating industrial growth in America were the activities of countless scientists and inventors.

Among the most important technical advances in the era of industrialization were those in the field of power. Down to the middle of the nineteenth century the water wheel remained a principal source of power for America's factories and mills. Horses, mules, and oxen were the source of power for small vehicles. But then inventors and engineers began to fashion improvements in the reciprocating steam engine—really a locomotive with driving wheels lifted from the ground. The result was virtual disappearance of old-fashioned water wheels as a means of turning machines.

Other men developed the steam turbine, an engine in which steam under great pressure turned vanes on a spindle enclosed in a cylinder, hence doing away with the piston and flywheel of the reciprocating engine. Still others, notably Charles F. Brush, a young engineer in Ohio, perfected the dynamo, invented in England by Michael Faraday back in the 1830s. The dynamo, powered by a steam turbine or rushing water, generated electricity and sent it over copper wires to turn machines in urban factories, drive trolley cars up and down urban streets, and perform countless tasks in the urban home.

Then there was the internal combustion engine, an invention that took its origins from the development of gunpowder in China in the Middle Ages. The first efficient gasoline engines appeared in Germany in the 1880s, although as early as 1877 George B. Selden of Rochester, New York, had built a vehicle powered by a

Courtesy Wyoming Travel Commission

The abundance of iron ore deposits throughout the nation contributed to the growth of American industry. These wood-burning kilns date back to 1865. They once supplied the iron industry of Utah with the charcoal fuel needed in the smelting process.

gasoline engine. A few years later a German, Rudolf Diesel, developed the first successful "diesel" engine which burned a low-grade fuel oil and required no spark plugs. Diesel and gasoline engines are best known for their application to the horseless carriage, or motor car (and truck), but men of business also harnessed the internal combustion engine to the mill, factory, and mine.

The advent of new methods of delivering power to factories opened the way for improvements in machine technology. The outcome was a dramatic increase in America's industrial output. Advanced machines, for example, revolutionized the country's textile industry. Under the primitive conditions of early America the production of 500 yards of cotton sheeting required 5,605 hours of human labor. By the year 1900 cotton manufacturers, using new machines, could turn out 500 yards of sheeting with an expenditure of only 52 man-hours of labor. By the turn of the twentieth century, a single machine operated by one person could work 3,000 buttonholes a day, many times the number that the same individual could work by hand.

Inventions Create Industries

Other inventions created new industries and businesses which in turn provided jobs, increased the demand for steel and copper, generated traffic for railroads, and stimulated foreign trade. The telegraph—invented by Samuel F. B. Morse—came into practical use when Morse strung a wire along the tracks of the Baltimore and Ohio Railroad from Baltimore to Washington. In 1844 the wire crackled with the first long-distance telegraph message: "What hath God wrought!" By the time of the Civil War, a web of telegraph wires, most of them owned by the Western Union Company (organized in 1856), had brought instant communication to most parts of the country.

In 1846 Elias Howe invented a sewing machine and seven years later, in 1853, Isaac M. Singer opened a plant in New York City for manufacture of the machines. In 1852 Elisha G. Otis built the first successful passenger elevator, an invention which made the modern skyscraper possible. In 1855 James Oliver introduced the chilled plow—a plow with a hard iron surface. In 1860 Oliver F. Winchester test-fired the first repeating rifle. In the 1860s a Milwaukeean, Christopher Sholes, perfected the first practical typewriter, then sold his patent rights to E. Remington & Sons, who in the 1870s began to market typewriters.

Alexander Graham Bell's telephone produced its first distinguishable conversation in 1876, became the "hit" of the Philadelphia Exposition of that year, and soon began to be installed in America's homes and offices. In 1877 Thomas A. Edison made the first phonograph. In 1879, Edison devised the first practical electric light bulb and a year later erected the first factory for manufacturing the new bulbs. In 1880 George B. Eastman patented the first successful roll film and a few years later brought out the "Kodak" hand camera which led to popularization of photography. In 1882 Schuyler Skaats Wheeler built the first electric fan and in the

1880s and 1890s other inventors brought out the electric flatiron, electric range, electric sewing machine, and electric vacuum cleaner. The electric washing machine appeared in 1907.

Several developments, including John Carbutt's introduction of celluloid film, led in 1893 to invention of Edison's Kinetoscope, a box-like device for showing motion pictures—the viewer holding his face against the box and cranking a continuous roll of film as he peered inside at the "movies."

George B. Selden built the first horseless carriage in America in 1879, but not until the 1890s did such mechanics as Charles E. Duryea, Ransom E. Olds, Elwood Haynes, and Henry Ford put together successful motor cars. The pneumatic tire appeared in 1892 and in 1911 Charles F. Kettering perfected the self-starter.

Products of Better Quality Result

The development of many new industrial techniques increased efficiency, stepped up output, and resulted in products of better quality. Improved methods of preparing and preserving meat, for example, stimulated the meat-packing industry. The roller process of grinding wheat into flour obtained a more perfect separation, thus eliminating discoloration. A technique for producing steel was discovered almost simultaneously in the mid-1850s by a Kentucky ironmaster, William Kelly, and the Englishman Henry Bessemer. Known as the Bessemer process, it is a method for forcing compressed air through molten metal to burn out impurities. Late in the 1860s the open-hearth process appeared. Considerably slower than the Bessemer process, the open-hearth method permitted better control of the molten metal and hence produced

The camera was one invention which attracted a great deal of attention in the late 1800s. In 1878, before motion pictures were invented, an architect bet a friend that a galloping horse raises all four feet off the ground at the same time. Then he hired a photographer to prove it. The photographer set up a series of cameras at a racetrack, and this was the result.

Thomas Edison invented the first phonograph in 1877, and it soon became a popular form of entertainment. The records used on these early phonographs were wax cylinders which were turned by hand, and the sound was amplified by a large horn. The illustration at left is an engraving from an 1878 issue of *Harper's*.

Library of Congress

better steel. It was adaptable, moreover, to almost any kind of ore or scrap (and therefore became known as the "scavenger of the trade"). By the time of World War I most steel production in America was by open hearth.

Another source of stimulation for America's industrial growth in the decades after 1850 was the expansion of markets at home and abroad. In the United States, growing population increased the domestic demand for goods and services which in turn produced a continuing expansion of business. New inventions created their own special markets and stimulated industrial growth.

A Golden Era for International Trade

The second half of the nineteenth century and the first fourteen years of the twentieth were a "golden era" for international trade. World international commerce—that is, total exports and imports—amounted to $2.8 billion in 1840, $14.8 billion in 1880, and $40.4 billion in 1913. What accounted for this dazzling increase in world trade? First, the mechanization of industry, in Europe as well as America, resulted in such levels of production that domestic markets became saturated and businessmen looked beyond their own borders for places to sell surplus output.

Second, this was a time when the international political situation was relatively stable. Between the Crimean War, which ended in 1856, and World War I, begun in 1914, there was no general conflict involving several major powers to muddy the waters of international commerce.

Third, international trade flowed with relative ease, despite intense rivalry between the industrial nations and, after 1873, a steady increase in tariff duties by such countries as the United States, Germany, France, Austria, Belgium, Italy, and Russia.

Fourth, during these decades the economic

growth of most of the countries of Europe and North America expanded at a fairly steady rate. The international accounts of these countries remained well balanced, and the international monetary system, based on the gold standard, functioned smoothly. Except for a few brief depressions (in the mid-1870s and mid-1890s in America), the leading trading nations enjoyed economic stability and there was no serious wrenching of the mechanism of international trade. The United States fared very well in the competition for foreign markets, largely because it was able to turn out quantities of goods of high quality and low price. Between 1850 and 1900 its foreign trade enjoyed a sixfold increase. Growing markets overseas naturally encouraged the growth of America's industry.

As a result, American industry—and with it

The Brooklyn Bridge, with a span of 1,595 feet, was the longest suspension bridge in the world when it was opened to traffic in 1883.

Library of Congress

all sectors of the national economy—expanded rapidly in the long era after 1850.

STUDY GUIDE: Abundant natural resources, particularly coal, iron, and oil, contributed to the industrial growth of the United States. The manpower needed for industrialization was amply provided by the high native birth rate and the great influx of immigrants. The availability of capital was another factor that made industrial growth possible. American and foreign investors were eager to put money into industrial ventures in the hope of earning large profits. Scientists and inventors made important technical advances that further stimulated industrial growth. New industrial techniques increased efficiency and resulted in products of better quality. The expansion of markets at home and abroad also stimulated growth. The nations of the world were relatively stable, politically and economically, up to 1914, which resulted in a favorable climate for international trade.

THREE LEADERS OF BUSINESS

Who were some of the men who took prominent parts in the growth of American industry?

If the foregoing question were addressed to a cross section of present-day Americans, there is little doubt that the name most frequently given would be John D. Rockefeller.

John D. Rockefeller

During the second half of the nineteenth century, a number of shrewd businessmen waged a Darwinian struggle for supremacy in America's industrial jungle. The man who established a lasting reputation as the most talented and ruthless of these men was John D. Rockefeller.

Rockefeller was the founder of the Standard Oil empire. He was pale and lean in appearance, mild and unpretentious in manner. Yet he came to symbolize the robber barons of American business. Because he carried on the struggle for power with such superb skill, Rockefeller destroyed the dreams of many less able and less lucky men. As one commentator has said, every man who failed in the oil business had a tale of how Rockefeller had done him in.[1]

---

[1] Stuart Holbrook, *The Age of the Moguls,* copyright 1953 (New York: Doubleday & Co., Inc.), p. 134.

Born near the village of Moravia in western New York in 1839, Rockefeller did not spring from wealthy origins. His father had dabbled with modest success in a range of enterprises, including medicine. For a time he billed himself as "Dr. William A. Rockefeller, the Celebrated Cancer Specialist." ("Doc" Rockefeller was an "herbal doctor" who treated patients with remedies concocted from plants and herbs.)

From the elder Rockefeller young John learned alertness, aggressiveness, cleverness—and also honesty and dependability. William Rockefeller insisted on promptness and exactness in meeting business obligations. To instill these qualities in his sons, so he once told a neighbor, "I trade with the boys and skin 'em and I just beat 'em every time I can. I want to make 'em sharp."

Mrs. Rockefeller was pious, industrious, and thrifty, and from his mother John D. Rockefeller gained an abiding dedication to religion. For many years, even after he achieved wealth and prominence in business, he taught a Baptist Sunday school class. Later, when he began to give away chunks of his fortune, he bestowed large sums on religious and religious-affiliated institutions.

After graduating from high school in 1855 at age sixteen, young John spent three months at a business school in Cleveland where he learned bookkeeping and some basic principles of business practice. Next he searched the city of Cleveland for a position—not in a little establishment but in a large firm where he could increase his knowledge of big business. The search ended when he took a job as clerk and bookkeeper in the office of one of Cleveland's leading produce shippers. His salary was $3.50 a week.

Energetic and ambitious, by 1859 Rockefeller had saved several hundred dollars and was ready to venture out on his own. He and a friend established a partnership as commission merchants in such commodities as grain, hay, and meat. The two young men chose a good time to go into business. The production of grain and meat in the Middle West was increasing, and the demand for those commodities was large in cities along the Atlantic seaboard. And so the firm of Clark & Rockefeller prospered.

Then in 1861 came the Civil War. Federal armies needed the kinds of commodities handled by Clark & Rockefeller and the outcome was even larger returns for the firm. Rockefeller avoided active service in the army, a matter of some embarrassment in later years. He explained that "I wanted to go to the army and do my part. But it was simply out of the question. There was no one to take my place. We were a new business, and if I had not stayed it must have stopped —and with so many depending on it." To go off and fight for the Union in his stead he hired substitutes.

During the war Rockefeller met and married the attractive daughter of a prosperous Cleveland businessman. He also became interested in oil. He sensed that the infant petroleum industry, enjoying a boom in the wake of Edwin L. Drake's success in 1859 in drilling an oil well, had a promising future. However, after observing the violent ups and downs in the returns of companies engaged in the risky business of taking oil from the fields of western Pennsylvania, Rockefeller focused on oil refining. The refining end, he decided, presented equal opportunities for profit with fewer risks. In the year 1863 Rockefeller entered a partnership with a handful of men and began refining oil in the vicinity of Cleveland. Within a few months he had pushed the commission enterprise to the background and made oil his main interest. At the same time other refineries were springing up in western Pennsylvania, western New York, and northeastern Ohio.

To beat the competition, Rockefeller, who quickly emerged as the most able and energetic member of the partnership, concentrated on efficient operation. He kept close watch over the books, cut costs by having the firm make its own barrels, and introduced techniques which resulted in petroleum products of higher quality than competitors turned out. He also salvaged by-products of the refining process which other refiners threw away. (Avoidance of waste was an obsession with Rockefeller.) He turned the by-products into such marketable commodities as paraffin, petrolatum, and paving material. All the while he urged his partners to put their profits back in the business: "Don't buy new clothes and fast horses; let your wife wear her last year's bonnet."

Less than four years after Rockefeller entered the oil business, in 1866-67, a severe depression in prices hit the industry. Oil men simply had glutted the market with petroleum products. Scores of refineries went under, but Rockefeller kept his firm afloat, largely because of the efficiency of his operation. When the crisis passed, he was in a stronger position than before. Meanwhile, he had begun to employ another device to get an edge on his competitors—the railroad rebate. Several railroads operating between the Middle West and the East Coast sought Rockefeller's business. He advised them that to secure his business they would have to rebate to his firm part of the rate it paid for shipping petroleum products. Demanding rebates was a fairly standard business practice in that era, and Rockefeller saw nothing wrong in securing them if possible. His firm had become the largest oil refiner in the Cleveland area. He believed that since he could assure a high volume of carloadings on a regular basis, it was entirely proper that he should pay lower rail rates than small competitors.

In the late 1860s Rockefeller persuaded his partners to dissolve their partnership and reorganize their firm as a joint-stock corporation. By offering stock for sale, the company could tap new sources of capital for expansion. Thus in January 1870 a new corporation—the Standard Oil Company—received a charter from the state of Ohio. With Rockefeller as president, the new company quickly established its preeminence in the refining industry. Over the next decade, taking advantage of advanced techniques and equipment, its own efficiency, and even "drawbacks," (that is, rebates to Standard of part of the rates paid to railroads by Standard's competitors), it forced competitors to combine with Standard on Rockefeller's terms—or else face ruin.

Then, beginning in the late 1870s, Standard gained control of major pipelines, put down new lines, and thus further dominated the petroleum industry. By the 1880s the company's supreme position in the industry enabled it to virtually control both production and prices of oil. It had become the greatest monopoly in the country's history.

Rockefeller's estimated fortune by the mid-1890s was $200 million. In 1896 he retired from active control of the Standard Oil Company but, it turned out, his fortune had just begun to grow. At this time the motor car appeared—a wonderful new stimulus to the petroleum industry. The chief product of oil refiners in the past had been kerosene for illumination. Now it became gasoline. Over the next two decades the value of Rockefeller's vast holdings in Standard Oil increased dramatically, and his personal wealth more than quadrupled.

In those years around the turn of the century Rockefeller began to give away large parts of his fortune—perhaps $500 million in all. Over a period of several decades he gave more than $35 million to the University of Chicago. He established the Rockefeller Institute for Medical Research, the General Education Board, which granted some $176 million for "the promotion of education in the United States of America, without distinction of race, sex, or creed." He also set up the Rockefeller Foundation for control and treatment of disease throughout the world.

Rockefeller lived until 1937. He never became a beloved figure in the eyes of his countrymen. Few of them saw him as an industrial statesman who had brought order to a chaotic industry, fostered efficiency, and produced quality products. Most concluded that he had been a "robber baron." Still, his philanthropy reduced criticism and in 1924, in the twilight of his extraordinary career, he could say, "For years I was crucified. It is better now."

Andrew Carnegie

Like Rockefeller, Andrew Carnegie was a man of humble origins. Born at Dunfermline, Scotland, in 1835, he was the son of a handloom weaver who found it necessary to toil long hours to keep food on the family table. In spite of this early poverty, Carnegie always considered his youthful years as rich and rewarding, for his parents William and Margaret Carnegie loved books. They instilled in their two sons an abiding interest in pursuits of the mind.

During the 1840s the machine, cold and impersonal, arrived in Dunfermline and methodically demonstrated that it could turn out cloth of higher quality in greater quantities and at less cost than could local handloom weavers. As the family income dwindled in face of the relentless competition of the machine, the Carnegies began to read with increasing interest the letters from Mrs. Carnegie's sisters in America. Recent immigrants, young Andrew's aunts described the opportunities that awaited honest and industrious people in the New World.

The elder Carnegie came home one day and announced that he could get no more work. Whereupon the family sold household belongings, borrowed money from friends, and in spring 1848 departed for America. At New York the Carnegies transferred to a river steamer, made their way up the Hudson to Albany, and moved through the Erie Canal and along Lake Erie. Then they went overland to the small Scottish community of Allegheny, Pennsylvania, not far from Pittsburgh.

America did not resolve the problems of the Carnegies. Allegheny was a ramshackle town with muddy streets. It periodically felt the ravages of fire, flood, and cholera. William Carnegie, singing as he manipulated the treadles of a loom, was soon turning out cloth, but the market for his wares was poor. Accordingly the boy Andrew, only thirteen years old, went to work as a bobbin boy in a cotton mill for $1.20 a week. Day after day, even when the snow was piled deep in the town, the youth arrived at the mill at six o'clock in the morning and worked steadily until six in the evening. Fortunately his employer eventually recognized his energy and talent and promoted him to bill clerk.

To learn more about bookkeeping, Carnegie after about a year in Allegheny moved to Pittsburgh. To meet expenses, he secured a job as messenger boy for a telegraph company. Shortly he became a telegrapher. The youthful Carnegie meanwhile determined to do more than master his trades. He sought to improve his general education, developed a fondness for Shakespearean drama, and with five other boys organized a self-improvement society. The boys sharpened their wits by debates and discussions.

At the same time, Carnegie became an avid reader of books. There were few public libraries in those days, but happily a prosperous citizen of the area opened his personal library of 400 volumes to working boys on Saturday afternoons. Many years later Carnegie, who gave millions of dollars for construction of libraries across America, described his appreciation of those Saturdays: "Is it any wonder that I resolved, if ever surplus wealth came to me, I would use it imitating my benefactor?"

Carnegie's subsequent rise to wealth and power was rapid. While a telegrapher he caught the attention of Thomas A. Scott, superintendent of the Pittsburgh division of the Pennsylvania Railroad. Scott made Carnegie, then eighteen, his private secretary and personal telegrapher. During the Civil War, when Scott went off to Washington as assistant secretary of war in charge of military transport, Carnegie went with him. He brought the first military train into the capital, and personally loaded wounded soldiers aboard hospital trains after the Battle of Bull Run in July 1861.

During Carnegie's twelve years with the Pennsylvania Railroad, he learned a great deal about big business operations. Thanks in part to Scott's counsel, he invested his earnings in such profitable enterprises as a telegraph line, construction company, horse-trading concern, several oil

Courtesy of Carnegie-Mellon University

Andrew Carnegie rose from a poor immigrant to become one of the nation's wealthiest men. His efforts helped to make the United States the leading steel-producing country in the world by the end of the nineteenth century. Carnegie believed that the very rich had an obligation to use their wealth for the public good. Why do you agree or disagree?

companies, a grain elevator, bank, bridge-building company, locomotive works, and sleeping-car company. Carnegie also invested in iron and, of course, the Civil War gave a powerful stimulus to that industry. His investments were so profitable that in 1865 he left Scott and organized the Keystone Bridge Company, which supplied iron materials for the bridges of the Union Pacific and other railroads.

By the 1870s the infant steel industry had attracted his attention. He built his first iron works near Pittsburgh, and soon was recognized as the king of the iron producers. Thanks largely to Carnegie, the United States before the end of the nineteenth century had become the leading steel-producing country in the world.

What accounted for Carnegie's success? To begin with, he gambled his future on a promising industry, steel. At the time of the Civil War, wood, stone, and iron were still the basic materials of buildings, bridges, rails, locomotives, and farm implements. By the 1870s—the time

when Carnegie went heavily into the steel industry—Americans were learning how to produce high-quality steel at low cost and were becoming acquainted with its obvious advantages over other materials. Carnegie benefited from America's seemingly endless supplies of cheap but high-grade iron ore and coal. He also had an advantage in the availability of efficient, low-cost transportation and a reservoir of skilled labor. He also benefited from the federal government's protective tariff against foreign steel.

Carnegie was not a practical steel man and did not particularly enjoy going into his mills to watch sparks fly from Bessemer converters. He was not even much of a business manager—for he was bored by balance sheets and despised the ordinary routine of the office. However, he was unsurpassed as an organizer, manipulator, expediter, and salesman. He did not marry until he was fifty-one. For most of his life, his main interests were business and philanthropy.

Carnegie was a keen judge of talent, and he chose gifted men to help him. One of these was Henry Clay Frick. Frick had large holdings which represented a key part of the steel industry. Carnegie recognized Frick's assets and his skill in management, and the two men became partners. Frick acted as manager of the Carnegie Steel Company and was responsible for much of its expansion and success.

Carnegie insisted that everyone in his company work efficiently and strive continually to improve the company's performance. To urge his workers toward greater efforts, Carnegie devised a profit-sharing plan to reward employees. He also cultivated important people, and even persuaded President Benjamin Harrison to visit Pittsburgh. In business Carnegie was ruthless. When a power struggle developed between him and Frick for control of the company, Carnegie did not hesitate to sacrifice Frick's friendship.

Carnegie's shrewdness and ruthlessness advanced his interests in other ways. He made improvements in his plants during periods of economic depression when costs were low. He also took advantage of depressions to buy out faltering competitors. He managed to gain control of some of the best ore lands of the Lake Superior region. By utilizing the most modern techniques and machinery, he turned out better steel than did competitors. He pushed to the limit the advantages deriving from his top position in the industry (to secure rebates from railroads, for example).

Among Wall Street financiers Carnegie was

called an "industrial pirate." Still, he had strong views regarding the social responsibilities of the man whose talent and good luck had brought him great wealth. He wrote that rich men should follow the teaching of Jesus of Nazareth by selling earthly possessions and using the proceeds for the benefit of mankind. Accordingly he sold the Carnegie Steel Company in 1901 to J.P. Morgan, who was forming the United States Steel Corporation. Carnegie then devoted the remaining eighteen years of his life almost exclusively to philanthropy.

The sums of money which Carnegie gave away were staggering. He turned over more than $60 million to aid in construction of some three thousand libraries in the English-speaking world, many of which are operating today. He contributed more millions to colleges and universities, including the Carnegie Institute of Technology in Pittsburgh. He gave $10 million to a hero fund to recognize individuals who had performed heroic acts in time of peace and spent more than $6 million to install new pipe organs in nearly eight thousand churches.

He contributed $1.5 million in 1907 for construction of a peace palace at The Hague in the Netherlands and in 1910 gave $10 million to the Carnegie Endowment for International Peace. (He hoped this organization would lead to "the abolition of international war, the foulest blot upon our civilization.") He established the Carnegie Corporation of New York with $125 million to foster educational surveys, medical education, public health, economic research, legal education and reform, and scientific research. He gave $4 million for a relief and retirement fund for his employees and a similar amount for a fund for individuals who had helped him during his earlier years. In all, before his death in 1919, Carnegie gave away more than $350 million.

J. Pierpont Morgan

Unlike Rockefeller and Carnegie, J. Pierpont Morgan was born (in 1837) into a wealthy family at Hartford, Connecticut. His grandfather had accumulated a fortune in stagecoaching, hotels, and fire insurance. His father, a partner in a dry goods firm and later a banker, managed to increase the family's wealth. Also unlike Rockefeller and Carnegie, Morgan had the advantage of excellent schooling. He graduated in 1854 from Boston English High School where classmates knew him as "the richest boy in school." He then went to Europe, establishing himself as a superb student of mathematics during a brief period of enrollment at Göttingen University in Germany, and for a time he weighed the possibility of an academic career.

For all his wealth and intellectual ability, Morgan made few close friends. He seemed gruff, arrogant, cold, and unsociable—giving the appearance of an angry man.

At nineteen, in 1856, Morgan became a clerk in his father's banking firm. The following year his father obtained for him a junior clerkship in a leading banking house in New York. The youth soon demonstrated that his quick intelligence and skill in mathematics would enable him to take care of himself in the world of finance. When the New York firm in 1860 rejected the elder Morgan's plea that his son be made a partner, young Morgan, on the advice of his father, set up an office of his own to deal in securities and foreign exchange.

Then, in 1861, came the Civil War and, like many other successful businessmen, Morgan did not volunteer for service in the federal army. When Congress passed the Conscription Act of 1863, he hired a substitute to enter the army in his place. Some of his wartime ventures were highly profitable, particularly a shabby speculation in gold, which, despite the war emergency, was an attempt to bring a temporary depreciation in the value of the national currency. From this operation Morgan netted $80,000. During the war Morgan was also involved in a scandalous deal involving the sale of defective rifles to the federal army for a handsome profit. Later investigations indicated that Morgan, who had put up money to help finance the venture, had been unaware that the weapons were unfit for use.

Morgan fell in love with a young lady named Amelia Sturges, only to discover in spring 1861 that she was suffering from tuberculosis. By autumn 1861 she was gravely ill. But Morgan determined to marry her, even though she was too weak to stand alone during the wedding. After the ceremony Morgan took his bride to England and the Mediterranean, hoping that the climate would restore her to health. It was no use. She died a few months later. Morgan married again, in 1865, and from this marriage there were four children.

Many of Morgan's early ventures were speculative and only incidentally stimulated the growth of industry. His methods, moreover, were no different from those of other successful business leaders of the time; that is, he pressed every advantage to the limit and showed no mercy to those who stood in his way. He engaged in a particularly vicious battle with those industrial pirates Jay Gould and James Fisk for control of the Albany and Susquehanna Railroad in 1869. When he won this brawl, his reputation on Wall Street soared. A few years later his father dazzled the financial world by clearing $5 million on a transaction with the French government, completed in 1871 while the Germans were besieging Paris during the Franco-Prussian War.

By 1873 the Morgans, father and son, who always worked closely together, had established themselves as leaders of American finance. The younger man, backed by his father, was now ready to fight Jay Cooke, financial wizard of the Civil War, for control of the sale of government bonds. Morgan managed to break the Cooke monopoly on the bonds. When in autumn 1873 Jay Cooke and Company collapsed, bringing on the panic of 1873, J. P. Morgan was supreme in the field of finance in America.

Much of Morgan's early activity was in railroads. He recognized that in this era of feverish, even reckless, railroad construction many lines had appeared which had scant chance of prosperity. Some lacked good connections, others faced too much competition, and others carried excessive burdens of debt. So Morgan moved in with his financial resources. Often shoving aside practical railroad men (many of whom had no knowledge of efficient business techniques), he reorganized such lines as the Philadelphia and Reading, Baltimore and Ohio, Erie, and Chesapeake and Ohio. Placed on sound financial footing and compelled to eliminate duplication and waste, the roads were in stronger competitive positions after Morgan's intervention. But his crowning achievement in railroads came in 1893 when he combined a number of struggling lines into the vast Southern Railway system.

Morgan conducted similar operations in manufacturing. He organized the Federal Steel Company, National Tube Company, and American Bridge Company. But his greatest achievement came in 1901 when he put together the United States Steel Corporation, a billion-dollar creation based on his purchase of Carnegie Steel. U.S. Steel was a giant holding company which, with eleven major companies, controlled some 170 smaller businesses.

Morgan's maneuverings in railroads and other enterprises in the years after 1890 brought a new era in American industry. Leadership of industry passed from the builders and manipulators like Vanderbilt, Rockefeller, and Carnegie to bankers such as Morgan. There were several reasons for this transition. For many individuals the generation after the Civil War was one of great prosperity. Many people invested surplus earnings in savings banks, trust companies, and insurance companies, which in turn invested the funds in new business opportunities. At the same time leaders of industry began to see important advantages in bigness and hence sought to combine related companies. To secure the funds necessary for consolidation, they turned to bankers. But bankers refused to invest their money unless they attached some strings. To guard their investments and prevent waste and duplication they insisted on an ever-stronger voice in the control of the companies. The eventual result was banker domination of industry and—not to be overlooked—a continuation of the rapid expansion of industry.

Because he wielded so much economic power, and also because he was a "money changer" (and hence did not produce anything, or so people thought), Morgan became the object of heated criticism by ordinary Americans and politicians including Theodore Roosevelt. When in 1912-13 a subcommittee of the House of Representatives headed by Representative Arsène Pujo of Louisiana investigated the so-called money trust, much of its effort centered on J. P. Morgan & Company. Morgan himself was a star witness. In Morgan's view he had never abused the public interest with his great power. He saw himself as a public benefactor. He had compelled companies to root out waste and corruption and on two notable occasions, in 1895 and 1907, had stepped in during times of economic crisis and used his power and prestige to save the fiscal integrity of the United States government.

Stunned by the criticisms of the Pujo committee, Morgan went off to Europe, where he died in the spring of 1913.

STUDY GUIDE: Among the men who played a prominent role in the growth of American industry were John D. Rockefeller, Andrew Carnegie, and J. Pierpont Morgan. Energy, skill, and ambition, combined with ruthless business practices, led Rockefeller to establish the Standard Oil empire. Carnegie, a Scottish immigrant, made his fortune in steel manufacturing. He helped make the United States the leading steel-producing country in the world. Morgan's shrewd and often ruthless maneuverings in railroads and other enterprises helped him to become the most important financier in America in the late nineteenth century.

A FIERCELY COMPETITIVE PERIOD

Competition is at the heart of the American economic system and all supporters of the system are quick to praise its social benefits. Under the stress of competing for a share of limited markets, rival companies are compelled to produce goods and services of high quality for sale at the lowest price which will enable them to cover costs and realize a reasonable margin of profit. When competition is absent—so spokesmen of the American system contend—the quality of services and goods is apt to be low and prices high. There is truth in these arguments in favor of the system of competitive enterprise. Still, while competition often operates to the advantage of society as a whole, it sometimes seems to work to the disadvantage of competing companies. Most serious from the view of businessmen is the way in which competition tends to keep prices—and therefore profits—down.

The second half of the nineteenth century, particularly the years immediately following the Civil War, constituted the most fiercely competitive period in the history of American business. In that era there was plenty of capital seeking investment and plenty of opportunities—in railroads, oil, steel, mining, new manufactures—to invest it. Equally important, Americans had boundless confidence in their own ingenuity and unlimited faith that markets in their country and across the world could consume their output of goods and services. Hence they launched innumerable business ventures with little or no regard for competitors.

Later events, unfortunately, revealed that the optimism of many people had been rash. Disorder, uncertainty, and wild fluctuations in prices and profits—also waste and inefficiency—seemed to characterize much of American business. The culprit was unrestrained competition. In America too many enterprises—many of them of the "shoestring" variety—were competing too furiously for limited markets.

In the scramble for business and profits businessmen sometimes resorted to fraudulent advertising, price slashing, and other unfair trade practices. Also, with so many firms producing the same product or service there was wasteful duplication of equipment and jobs.

Accordingly, some businessmen began to search for ways to bring order to American business, combat the destructive effects of competition, and eliminate the waste and inefficiency that seemed inherent in the operations of fifty-mile railroads and small factories. Under the leadership of such individuals as John D. Rockefeller and J. P. Morgan, the period of unrestrained competition began to pass in the late 1870s. Small firms fell under control of large ones, and by the turn of the twentieth century a few major corporations dominated much of American business.

Industrial Mergers

The instrument employed most frequently to bring about combination was the merger. When several companies in an allied industry came together, as in the uniting of several railroads (a horizontal combination), the result usually was increased strength. The combined capital reserves of the companies permitted stabilization of operations; combined management meant reduced overhead; and coordinated production and marketing brought increased efficiency. When combinations were along vertical lines—that is, a combination like Carnegie Steel or, later, the Ford Motor Company, which controlled raw materials, transportation, manufacture, marketing, and finance—the result was enormous strength and independence.

Industrial Pools

Unlike the merger, the pool had one purpose: to restrain competition. The pool was a gentlemen's agreement between rival producers or railroad managers. Often the agreement involved only prices or rates. Members of the pool would simply get together and agree to maintain prices or rates at levels which would assure maximum profit for everyone; there would be no competitive reduction of prices or rates. Sometimes the agreement was more inclusive, and members of the pool agreed to a division of business. At other times they agreed to divide profits. The pool had weaknesses and proved an unsatisfactory instrument for promoting order and stability. As a gentlemen's agreement, it had no legal standing and therefore was unenforceable in court. Pools sometimes sought to counter this handicap by requiring members to deposit with the pool a sum of money as a guarantee of good faith; sometimes the pool imposed fines on members who violated pledges. Such devices, however, proved cumbersome and ineffective. The pool had no permanent organization, and whenever a member saw the prospect of larger profit by operating outside the pool he usually found the temptation to pull out irresistible. Withdrawal by one member often touched off other withdrawals and brought the pool's collapse.

Industrial Trusts

To get around the uncertainties of the pool, businessmen in the 1880s began to turn to a new device, the trust, the invention of a lawyer in the employ of John D. Rockefeller. Strictly speaking a trust existed when affiliated companies, say, several manufacturers of barbed wire, turned over their stocks and power to a board of trustees. Here was no gentlemen's agreement, for the trust was based on appropriate documents. Once a company forfeited its powers to the trust, it could not get them back. The term trust, rigidly defined, did not necessarily mean monopoly control of an industry; a trust might conceivably control only a small part of a given industry and thus competition would continue, perhaps between rival trusts.

As things worked out in the United States, however, most trusts did secure monopoly control over their industries. Standard Oil, reorganized as a trust in 1882, gained almost absolute control over oil refining. The American Sugar Refining Company dominated the sugar industry. Thus in the popular mind the term trust became synonymous with monopoly. A trust existed—or so people believed—when a corporation or combination had sufficient control of an industry to be able to control prices in that industry.

Because of their unique ability to bring stability, promote efficiency, and tailor production to market demands, trusts had the opportunity to become great instruments for furthering the general welfare. Unfortunately few of the individuals manipulating the trusts felt any strong social consciousness. They ignored the public interest, and frequently abused their enormous power. Railroads were forced to grant rebates, and small competitors were destroyed by cutting prices. (Of course when competition disappeared the trusts usually raised prices to new highs.) The savings resulting from increased efficiency were seldom passed on to consumers. The trusts usu-

ally intimidated labor, bribed public officials, and showed not the slightest concern for conservation of natural resources. Referring to the sugar trust, one observer wrote that the trustees "can close every refinery at will, close some and open others, . . . artificially limit the production of refined sugar, enhance the price to enrich themselves and their associates at the public expense, and depress the price when necessary to crush out and impoverish a foolhardy rival."

It was only natural that the public would not remain silent indefinitely in the face of such conditions. Before the decade of the 1880s had passed, newspaper editors and popular orators were issuing fiery denunciations of the trusts, accompanied by demands for their destruction. In response, some state legislatures wrote strict incorporation laws designed to regulate activities of companies chartered in their states. But a corporation chartered in one state—under the terms of the Constitution—may do business in any other state. A trust therefore could escape restrictions of states having rigid incorporation statutes by incorporating in such states as Delaware, New Jersey, and West Virginia where incorporation laws were lax. Thus if trusts were to come under any kind of regulation, the federal government would have to take the initiative.

Sherman Antitrust Act of 1890

By 1888 sentiment for federal antitrust legislation was so strong that both major political parties pledged in their national platforms of that year to work for trust control. The outcome was the Sherman Antitrust Act of 1890, one of the more important laws to emerge from Congress in the thirty years after the Civil War. The measure declared illegal every contract, combination in the form of trust, or conspiracy in restraint of trade or commerce. Any person who monopolized or attempted to monopolize any part of trade or commerce would be guilty of a misdemeanor.

The Sherman Act in its early years proved a weak instrument for curbing the power of big business combinations. First, the legislation created a legal tangle in its failure to define the terms "trust," "conspiracy," and "monopoly." Second, the administrations of Presidents Benjamin Harrison (1889-93), Grover Cleveland (1893-97), and William McKinley (1897-1901) showed slight interest in using the measure to bring big business under effective public regulation. Third, few cases involving alleged violation of the Sher-

Courtesy of The New-York Historical Society

This cartoon published in *Puck* magazine in 1890 was typical of many attacks leveled against big business monopolies during this period. Why did state legislation fail to regulate unfair business practices?

man Act ever came to court in those years, and those that did almost invariably resulted in verdicts favorable to business.

Perhaps the most incredible case involved the American Sugar Refining Company, which in the mid-1890s had come to control ninety-five percent of the sugar-refining capacity in America, when it purchased four competing plants in Pennsylvania. The Supreme Court ruled that the Sherman Act applied only to monopoly in restraint of trade and that mere purchase of sugar refineries or the refining of sugar was not commerce in the strict constitutional sense.

Despite the intent of the Sherman legislation, the decade of the 1890s witnessed a sharp increase in the number of trusts and combinations. At the time of the Sherman Act's passage in 1890 only 24 trusts had been formed. Ten years later there were 183 such combinations, 120 of which had appeared since 1897.

In the 1890s the Sherman Act did score a few notable victories—over labor unions. The government broke the Pullman strike of 1894 when the courts defined union actions as a conspiracy in restraint of interstate commerce and issued an injunction to stop the strikers. Then in the Danbury Hatters' case in 1908, the courts held unions financially responsible under the Sherman Act to the full amount of their individual property for losses of business resulting from an interstate boycott. Other judges questioned the legality of any labor organization; under the Sherman Act it was possible that unions were illegal combinations.

Still, whatever its shortcomings, the Sherman

Act, like the Interstate Commerce Act of 1887, established a precedent for government regulation of business, undercut the old laissez-faire and Social Darwinist notion that the federal government had no right to interfere in the affairs of business, and prepared a foundation for more energetic attempts later to bring big business under public regulation.

STUDY GUIDE: Many unfair trade practices developed as businessmen scrambled for profits. By the beginning of the twentieth century, a few major corporations dominated American business. Such business practices as mergers and the formation of pools and trusts brought numbers of smaller companies together for increased profits and efficiency. Sometimes, particularly in the case of trusts, they secured monopoly control over an industry. A monopoly could set its own prices in the industry it controlled. Trusts were widely criticized for abusing their enormous power and ignoring the public interest. Increased public demand for regulation of trusts led to passage of the Sherman Antitrust Act in 1890. The Sherman Antitrust Act was not very effective, but it did establish a guide for government regulation of big business.

SUMMING UP THE CHAPTER

Names and Terms to Identify

Pacific Railway Act	"watered" stock
Herbert Spencer	Daniel Drew
Grenville M. Dodge	"gentlemen's agreement"
Charles Crocker	John D. Rockefeller
Crédit Mobilier	Mesabi range
Promontory Point	George Eastman
Jay Cooke	Bessemer process
James J. Hill	Andrew Carnegie
Cornelius Vanderbilt	J. Pierpont Morgan
George Westinghouse	Danbury Hatters' case

Study Questions and Points to Review

1. In considering the growth of industry in America, what factor does the author mention as having aroused the most historical interest? Why?

2. What effect did Social Darwinism have on business?

3. Why was a transportation system essential in achieving industrialization?

4. What caused the canal empire to collapse?

5. What were the factors that led to the appearance of a national system of railroads?

6. Why was the Interstate Commerce Act of 1887 enacted? What organization was established as a result of this legislation?

7. What invention besides the railroad does the author mention as having bound the nation together?

8. Explain the principle of comparative advantage.

9. How did America's agricultural domain contribute to industrial growth?

10. Explain what is meant by the term "entrepreneurial spirit."

11. In what field were the most important technical advances made in the era of industrialization?

12. What factors contributed most to the tremendous increase in world trade in the second half of the nineteenth century and the years prior to World War I in the twentieth century?

13. Who are the three leaders of business described in detail in this chapter?

14. Be sure you understand the meaning of these terms used in this chapter: intimidation, exploitation, cut-throat competition, hoodwinking, innovations, laissez-faire, capital, merger, pool, trust, rebate, private enterprise, manipulations, lobbying, commodity, monopoly. Divide the class into teams. The winning team is the group which can correctly define the most words without using a dictionary.

Topics for Discussion

1. Give your opinion on this statement: Efficient, low-cost transportation is vital to an industrial country.

2. Discuss the question: Why did James J. Hill's Northern Pacific railroad manage to survive all financial crises?

3. Explain what happened to water transportation in the period from 1850 to 1900.

4. Describe briefly Social Darwinism. What were its main principles? Do you agree or disagree with the Social Darwinists? Give reasons for your answer.

5. Discuss the characteristics of business leaders in the second half of the nineteenth century. What were their aims, attitudes, tactics, strengths, weaknesses, and achievements? Explain why you consider these leaders generally a constructive or destructive force in American society.

6. In your opinion, what are the pitfalls of unrestrained competition?

7. The author described the second half of the nineteenth century and the first fourteen years of the twentieth century as a "golden era for international trade." What does he mean by this description?

8. The Sherman Antitrust Act of 1890 is considered one of the more important laws to emerge from Congress in the thirty years after the Civil War. Explain why you agree or disagree with this viewpoint.

Subjects for Reports or Essays

1. Assume it is the year 1885. You are a wheat farmer in the Midwest. Write a letter to your congressman explaining why you want federal regulation of railroads.

2. Prepare a report explaining either the Bessemer or open-hearth process of making steel. Use drawings or photographs to illustrate your report.

3. Write a brief report explaining what in your opinion was the most important invention of those mentioned in this chapter.

4. Imagine you are a Social Darwinist. It is the year 1890. The Sherman Antitrust Bill is pending in Congress. Write a letter to the editor of a newspaper stating your objections to this pending legislation.

5. On the basis of outside reading, prepare a report on one of the following topics: (a) building the first transcontinental railroad; (b) the Crédit Mobilier Scandal; (c) immigration during the second half of the nineteenth century; (d) the impact of Social Darwinism; (e) the consequences of rapid industrialization.

6. Read one of the books listed in the "Further Readings" section and report on it in class.

Projects, Activities, and Skills

1. Using Table 18 in the Appendix, make a chart comparing the industrial distribution of gainful workers for the years 1860 and 1900. Indicate which categories show the greatest and least increase.

2. On Atlas Map 24, trace the major transcontinental rail routes of the late 1800s and early 1900s. Use Table 30 in the Appendix to make a chart showing miles of railroad built from 1830 to 1925.

3. Prepare a bulletin board display showing locomotives, railroad cars, steamboats, and canal boats used in the United States in the second half of the nineteenth century.

4. Prepare a display of photographs and sketches of major inventions of the period from 1865 to 1910.

5. Using a large map of the United States and symbols of your own design, prepare a display showing the location of major resources and basic industries in the United States.

6. American folk music is rich in songs about the railroad. "Take This Hammer," "The Wabash Cannon Ball," "Casey Jones," and "John Henry" are just a few. Listen to recordings of some of the railroad songs. Learn what you can of the history of the songs. What do the words tell you about the workers?

Further Readings

General

Age of Excess: The United States from 1877 to 1914 by Ray Ginger.

American Railroads by John F. Stover. Excellent survey of the railroad industry in the United States.

Industry Comes of Age: Business, Labor, and Public Policy by Edward C. Kirkland. Excellent study of industrial growth in the United States.

The Robber Barons by Matthew Josephson. Describes the trickery and deceit connected with the building of the railroads.

Biography

The Book of Daniel Drew by Bouck White.

Commodore Vanderbilt: An Epic of the Steam Age by Wheaton J. Lane.

The Great Pierpont Morgan by Frederick Lewis Allen.

Grenville M. Dodge: Soldier, Politician, Railroad Pioneer by Stanley P. Hirshon.

Fiction

The Financier, The Titan, and *The Stoic* by Theodore Dreiser. A trilogy about the late 1800s.

Looking Backward: 2000-1887 by Edward Bellamy. Boston in the year 2000.

The Octopus by Frank Norris. A novel about the power struggle between wheat farmers and the railroad.

The Rise of Silas Lapham by William Dean Howells. A classic story about a businessman in the 1800s.

CHAPTER 8

INDUSTRIAL SOCIETY

THE SPECTACULAR EXPANSION OF INDUSTRY in America in the era after 1850 revolutionized the national economy. It changed the country from a comparatively relaxed agrarian republic which exercised little influence beyond its own shores into a thriving industrial power. It also produced important changes in American society — in the size and distribution of the national population, the way people earned their bread, what they thought, how they lived, played, and prayed, and what they wrote.

Industrial America's appetite for workers greatly increased the number of individuals who toiled in factories and mills, on railroads, in mines and packinghouses, and thus dramatically altered the composition of the country's labor force. The new industry, with its accent on big companies and machines, brought far-reaching changes in the status of the individual working-man. The demand for labor accelerated the movement of people from the Old World to the New and the half century after the Civil War marked the high point of immigration in America.

Jefferson had written many decades before that the handmaiden of the factory was the city and, accordingly, the expansion of industry stimulated a parallel growth of cities. The city — crowded and disordered, corrupt and exciting — produced a social and cultural revolution in America, a revolution which continues in the second half of the twentieth century. This revolution is so huge and complex that historians have barely begun to measure its dimensions and explain its consequences.

INDUSTRIAL GROWTH BRINGS PROBLEMS FOR WORKERS

"Big business" enterprise as we know it today did not exist in America during the middle of the nineteenth century. Where in our own time such companies as General Motors, Ford, and Westinghouse employ scores of thousands of workers, the largest firms in the country in 1850 employed only a few hundred. Most factories, shops, and mills had only a handful of people on the payroll. In the small companies of the mid-nineteenth century the workers were acquainted with the manager, who often was also the owner. Thus they found it fairly easy to reach agreements on wages, hours, and working conditions. Most factories and mills, moreover, were not highly mechanized, hence the worker often had an important bargaining tool, his skill, without which the firm could not prosper.

Ability to communicate directly with the employer and his skill were not the only points in the worker's favor when negotiating wages and working conditions. There was, in addition, the absence of competition for his job. Seldom were unemployed men standing at the company's gates to take over his bench at the first chance. In part this was because few men, for example, immigrants or depressed farmers, had the skill necessary to perform his job. In part this was because most farmers who were down on their luck and many immigrants instinctively turned their gaze westward where a great and fertile domain beckoned.

Thus the industrial worker in America had a reasonably "good deal" in 1850. True, he worked long hours. But long hours were an honored tradition in America. More important, the individual worker, by the standard of the day, usually enjoyed decent wages and a fair measure of job security. If he was a skilled worker — and a great many individuals were — he had a job that was interesting. When he completed a day's work he could look over his output and take pride in the knowledge that with his sharp eyes and deft hands he had produced something that bore the mark of his own personality and spirit.

Then, in the second half of the nineteenth century, came the rapid expansion — and also modernization — of American industry. The industrial revolution exposed the workingman in America to a range of problems and circumstances with which he found it difficult to cope.

Mechanization

The machine was basic to modern industry. It multiplied man's strength many times and enhanced his ability to exploit the bounty of nature, as in the iron ranges of the Lake Superior region.

HEADLINE EVENTS

1792	Shoemakers unite to improve working conditions and wages	**1882**	Chinese Exclusion Act
1820s	Local craftsmen form unions	**1883**	*Life on the Mississippi* (Twain)
1837	Financial panic; labor movement suffers	**1884**	*The Adventures of Huckleberry Finn* (Twain)
1840s-1850s	Potato famine in Ireland causes mass migration to New World	**1885**	Foran Act

1792   Shoemakers unite to improve working conditions and wages
1820s   Local craftsmen form unions
1837   Financial panic; labor movement suffers
1840s-1850s   Potato famine in Ireland causes mass migration to New World
1848   Revolutions in Germany
1850s   Know-Nothing party agitates riots and gains political following
1850   Taiping rebellion causes Chinese migration
1861-1865   Civil War
c. 1865   Elevated railways built in New York
1865   *Celebrated Jumping Frog of Calaveras County* (Twain)
1866   National Labor Union formed
1869   *Innocents Abroad* (Twain)
        Electric vote recorder (Edison)
        Knights of Labor founded
        National Colored Labor Union founded
1870   Department of Justice created
1870s-1880s   Economic distress in Europe causes increased migrations to U.S.
1871   *The Hoosier Schoolmaster* (Eggleston)
1872   Post Office Department created
        Roughing It (Twain)
1873   Financial panic
        Cable car introduced
1876   *The Adventures of Tom Sawyer* (Twain)
        Telephone introduced
1877   Edison exhibits phonograph
        Russo-Turkish War
        Series of railroad strikes
        Greenback party supported by unions
        The American (James)
1878-1879   Edison develops dynamo
1879   Edison perfects electric light bulb
        Daisy Miller (James)
1880   Edison patents incandescent lamp
1880-1920   "New" immigrants arrive from southern and eastern Italy
1881   Federation of Organized Trades and Labor Unions of the United States and Canada created
        The Portrait of a Lady (James)

1882   Chinese Exclusion Act
1883   *Life on the Mississippi* (Twain)
1884   *The Adventures of Huckleberry Finn* (Twain)
1885   Foran Act
        The Rise of Silas Lapham (Howells)
1886   Haymarket riot
        American Federation of Labor formed
1887-1888   First successful electric street railway in Virginia
1890s   Long distance telephone in operation
1891   *Main-Travelled Roads* (Garland)
        Immigration law excludes paupers
1892   Eight-hour day for government workers established
        Homestead walkout at Carnegie Steel
1893   *Maggie: A Girl of the Streets* (Crane)
1894   Pullman Strike
        Immigration Restriction League created
1895   *The Red Badge of Courage* (Crane)
1896   Rural free delivery of mail begins
        Cleveland vetoes legislation in literacy tests for immigrants
1897   Subway in Boston begins operation
1898   Erdman Act
1903   Immigration legislation
1905   International Workers of the World formed
1906   Gentlemen's Agreement
1907   Immigration legislation
1908   Employers' Liability Act
1909   NAACP founded
1911   Triangle Shirtwaist Factory fire
1915   La Follette Seamen's Act
1916   Adamson Act
1917-1918   United States in World War I
1917   Congress passes law requiring literacy test for immigrants
        Bolshevik revolution in Russia
1920   Wave of nativism causes anti-Semitism and anti-Catholicism
1921   Quota law excludes immigration of Orientals
1922   Quota legislation
1924   Permanent quota legislation passes
1930s   Congress of Industrial Organizations formed
1965   Quota system abolished

It greatly increased output and worked with a rhythm that human hands could not match. The machine did not tire; it could toil hour after hour, day after day with only an occasional pause for lubrication or maintenance. It could reproduce the most intricate designs with no detectable variations. So overwhelming were the advantages of the machine over the skilled craftsman in most manufacturing enterprises that by 1890 eighty percent of America's manufactures were machine-produced.

What did mechanization of industry mean to labor? By reducing unit costs of production, machinery opened the way for general improvements in the standard of living in America. While industrialists seldom passed on to consumers a generous share of the savings made possible by mechanization, lower production costs nonetheless usually brought some reduction in prices of consumer goods. Thus with the dollars in his pay envelope the workingman who operated a machine could buy better clothing for his family and a larger quantity of the commodities that made life in his household more pleasant. For many workers, moreover, particularly those in heavy industries, machines lightened the burden of labor.

Still, mechanization had disadvantages for the workingman. Machinery usually represented a large investment for the company, and profits required that machines run all day every day. The worker had to adjust to the schedule of the machines (by working the night shift, for example). The machine also brought technological unemployment, that is, unemployment when machines took over the work of men. Fortunately the expanding economy managed to absorb most individuals thrown out of work by machines, but the interval between discharge and reemployment was usually painful and constituted a great social waste.

By the turn of the century American industry had grown immensely. Mass production was needed to meet the demands of an expanding population. This 1905 photograph shows women working in an assembly-line procedure hand wrapping food products. Why do you think many assembly-line jobs like this were handled by women rather than men?

Courtesy H. J. Heinz Company

The effect of mechanization on the skilled worker frequently was shattering. The machine often required no experience or special ability to operate and could crank out an endless stream of high-quality products. This nullified the craftsman's main asset, his skill, and dragged him down to the same social and economic status as the unskilled worker. It also weakened his will and ability to be creative. Even for the unskilled worker toiling at a machine, doing a single simple task hour after hour, week after week, year after year, the machine age often was dull, monotonous, and frustrating. In the view of some observers, it made the worker almost a robot. Of course the automobile manufacturer Henry Ford retorted to the latter criticism of mechanization by saying: "Some of our tasks are exceedingly monotonous, but then, also, many minds are monotonous—many want to earn a living without thinking, and for these men a task which demands no brains is a boon."

Corporations

The emergence of the large corporation as employer did offer some advantages to labor. The corporation could obtain credit for expansion, exploit distant resources, and penetrate world markets. Hence, it had greater opportunities for prosperity than did the little firm, and the individual worker's prosperity in the age of industrialization, as in the present day, hinged on the prosperity of the employer.

Unfortunately with the advantages came disadvantages. There was a conspicuous loss of intimacy in labor-management relations as corporations became larger. The employee no longer called the manager by his first name. The manager no longer knew firsthand the problems of his workers. If a worker suffered an illness or accident, the manager might not hold the job open or even help the worker through his difficulty. When the worker had a grievance he could not take it directly to the manager, hence misunderstanding between management and labor came easily.

Even if they felt sympathy for workers, managers in a large corporation were almost powerless to do much to improve wages, hours, and working conditions. The managers were responsible to directors and directors to stockholders. Most stockholders were interested only in the size of dividend checks and seldom knew or cared about the conditions of labor. Managers felt compelled to concentrate on maximum production at minimum cost—and wages of workingmen were a "cost."

The large corporation had enormous power and could counter a strike by workers more effectively than a small firm. It could often carry the expense of an extended stoppage of operations and thus had the capacity to wait out strikers. It could import workers from other areas to take the place of strikers and purchase newspaper space to present its arguments in a dispute to the public. It could also make better use than small firms of such devices as the blacklist—a list of names of labor agitators not to be hired, which would circulate through departments of a company and from company to company; the yellow dog contract—requiring an employee to pledge that he would not join a union; and the lockout—a company closing its plant and depriving workers of employment if they were about to demand higher wages, shorter hours or improved conditions.

Transportation

Improved methods of transportation, like mechanization and the giant corporation, offered some advantages for labor. Nationalized transportation broadened the base of the economy, gave business access to distant resources and markets, and enabled Americans to exploit the economic principle of comparative advantage. Thus each part of the country could concentrate on turning out commodities which local conditions permitted it to produce most efficiently. The outcome was increased efficiency and lower production costs which—when savings were passed on to consumers—meant improvement in living standards for workers.

Unfortunately there were also disadvantages. The nationalizing of transportation—the result of the transformation of the country's rail system into an integrated network—made it possible for corporations to exploit cheap labor wherever they could find it. The outcome in many cases was nullification of gains which workers had made over the years because of conditions in their own areas. If they declined to accept the lower wages and longer hours that prevailed in other parts of the country, they faced the prospect of companies packing up and moving their operations to those regions.

The classic example of this phenomenon was in the textile industry. Over the decades textile workers of New England had managed to improve their conditions of labor, securing higher pay and shorter hours. Then toward the end of the nineteenth century improved transportation gave owners of textile mills the option of moving operations to the South, where workers would accept lower pay and longer hours. This development often meant that the New England worker had to sacrifice the gains he had made and accept wages, hours, and working conditions comparable to those of the South—or see his job move to the South.

Then there was the nationalizing of business.

The nationalizing of business changed the character of many labor disturbances, particularly strikes. In the days of small business a strike by workers of a firm seldom had much bearing on individuals and companies in other regions and states and attracted virtually no attention outside the immediate area of the strike. But the appearance of large corporations whose business reached out across the entire country created new circumstances. A strike against a corporation—such as the Homestead walkout at Carnegie Steel of 1892 or the Pullman strike of 1894—touched the interests of individuals and companies in every part of the country. They brought a national clamor that the strike be settled. As this clamor increased, the issues that caused the strike often received scant attention. Popular pressure usually was directed toward the workers—to get back on the job, whatever their grievances against the company. Such pressure was usually effective. In most major strikes of the latter part of the nineteenth and the first part of the twentieth centuries, the combined power of popular opinion and government coercion (for federal and state officials saw unfor-tunate political consequences to themselves if industrial unrest got out of hand) brought the strike to a conclusion on terms favorable to the corporations.

Agriculture

Another factor that weighed heavily on industrial labor, especially in the closing decades of the nineteenth century, was the decline in agricultural opportunity in America. The machine had produced this decline. Although America's growing population stimulated agricultural output, demanding increasing supplies of food, fiber, and tobacco, the machine could perform the work of many men more efficiently and more economically.

The upshot was technological unemployment on the farm. In the past the unemployed farmer had moved west, acquired some land, and begun a new farm operation. But that solution to his problem no longer seemed very promising. Why? It was the infernal machine again. Those men who remained on the land turned out greater volumes of farm produce than the market could easily absorb. The outcome was a continuing decline in farm prices and of course hard times for agriculture in general. Thus the unemployed farm workers felt little inclined to go to a new area to take up farming.

Distressed farmers, instead of going west to begin a new venture in agriculture, usually moved to cities in search of work in industry. Their presence often created labor surpluses and aggravated the labor situation.

Business and industry employed many different methods to defy strikers. This engraving printed in *Leslie's* in 1882 shows immigrants arriving in New York to take the places of striking workers. What do you think of this tactic?

Library of Congress

Immigrants

American labor also faced problems as a result of the influx of immigrants, especially in the forty years after 1880 when the "new" immigrants from southern and eastern Europe — Italy, the Balkans, Poland, Czechoslovakia, and Russia — began to arrive in large numbers.

Before 1880 perhaps ninety percent of America's immigrants had come from northern and western Europe — the British Isles, Germany, and the Scandinavian countries. Many of these immigrants, particularly the Germans and Scandinavians, arrived with enough money to move inland to the Middle West — the Ohio Valley, Missouri, Wisconsin, and Minnesota — where they took up land and became farmers.

Other earlier immigrants, notably the Irish, who came to the New World virtually penniless, caused difficulties for the native workingman, particularly in the 1840s and 1850s. However, the Civil War and Reconstruction created a need to operate factories and build railroads, thereby absorbing surplus manpower.

Thus one can say that, in general, the pre-1880 immigrants did not present an unduly serious or continuing problem for native laborers.

Beginning in the 1880s, the "new" immigrants began to arrive from southern and eastern Europe, and by the turn of the twentieth century the flow of migrants from that part of the world to America had reached floodtide. Most arrived in a state of near poverty and those who had managed to save a little money were discouraged from taking up farming by the declining opportunities in agriculture. Hence they crowded into industrial centers and accepted conditions of labor which native workingmen found intolerable.

Rugged Individualism Leads to Problems

Conditioned by the myth of frontier experience and the ideas of Puritanism and Social Darwinism, most Americans accepted with little hesitation the view that in their country at least each individual must stand or fall according to his own energy and talent. The pioneer, they believed, had been a rugged individual who had conquered a vast wilderness.

Moreover, the theology of Puritanism — and Puritanism remained an important force in American life through the nineteenth century — seemed to offer divine sanction to rugged individualism. After the Civil War, Social Dar-winism "proved" that rugged individualism was essential if the country was to achieve enduring prosperity. Most Americans believed it would be a violation of their hallowed frontier tradition, and also bad policy, to condone a "soft" collective approach to any social and economic difficulties.

From this position the typical American of the nineteenth century developed hostility toward labor unions, their leaders, and tactics. Many Americans indeed saw unions, strikes, boycotts, and the closed shop as unpatriotic, immoral, and illegal. Such ideas, which even permeated the ranks of workingmen, made it extremely difficult for labor organizers (or "agitators," as many people called them) to establish unions. And when, after long and painful effort, unions came into existence they found that their adversaries, the employers, almost invariably could count on support of popular opinion.

What did the foregoing problems mean for the workingman in America in the era of industrialization? Put simply, they meant that he often toiled long hours in unpleasant (even dangerous) surroundings for low pay. It was not unusual for railroad enginemen and trainmen to work sixty or seventy hours at a stretch. Textile workers commonly put in a thirteen-hour day. Many workingmen put in work weeks that ranged from eighty to one hundred hours. As far into the twentieth century as the 1920s, steelworkers normally worked twelve hours a day, seven days a week. Wages were often as low as the worker could or would accept, enabling him and his family to subsist, not much more. There were no paid vacations, no unemployment insurance, no security against sickness or accident, and no old-age retirement plans. As President John L. Lewis of the United Mine Workers later expressed it, the free-enterprise system in America in the age of industrial expansion seemed to rest on a test to see how little a worker could eat.

Factories often were unsanitary and lacked the most rudimentary safety devices. Many factories were firetraps, leading to disasters such as the 1911 fire at the Triangle Shirtwaist Company in New York. That fire claimed 143 persons, mostly young women who were garment workers. They perished because there were no outside fire escapes.

STUDY GUIDE: Before the industrial age most workers were skilled craftsmen employed by small companies. By the end of the nineteenth century most American manufactured goods were machine-produced by large companies and corporations. Mechanization did benefit the workingman in some ways. It lowered the price of consumer goods and offered greater economic opportunities than did the small company. However, it also brought serious problems. By taking over the work of many men, mechanization caused unemployment and made factory work dull and repetitious. As an employer, the corporation was an impersonal organization. Corporations were interested only in greater profits. Workers found themselves powerless to obtain better wages and working conditions.

Improved transportation facilities made it possible to locate a particular type of industry, such as textiles, in one part of the country. This increased efficiency and lowered production costs. It also made it easier for industries to exploit workers by threatening to move where cheaper labor was available. The growth of large nationwide businesses made it more difficult for workers to strike. A strike against one corporation could affect people and companies in every part of the country. Popular opinion and government coercion often forced a strike to be ended on terms favorable to the corporation.

Mechanization reduced agricultural opportunities. Fewer men were needed to farm the land. Machines were able to produce more crops than the market could absorb, resulting in lower farm prices and hard times for farmers. Many farmers moved to the cities in search of work in industry, creating labor surpluses. The flood of new immigrants after 1880 also competed with workers for jobs. Most Americans accepted the idea of "rugged individualism" expressed in Social Darwinism. They rejected government interference and opposed organizations such as unions to help solve the problems of the workingman.

ORGANIZATION OF LABOR

America was not a poor country. Factories were humming. New rail lines were spreading out across the country. Cities were mushrooming. Many people were enjoying prosperity and a few were accumulating great fortunes. But the workingman and his family often lived in a dingy tenement near a factory or rail yard and breathed air made foul by the fumes of smoke or chemicals. Frequently every member of the family, including the mother and small children, had to find employment to help meet family expenses. There was little time, money, or leisure for intellectual or cultural pursuits. Schooling for the children beyond two or three grades—if that—was out of the question. If a new machine, an accident, or illness put the head of the family out of work, the outcome might be utter disaster. Disease, early death from overwork, poor food, and exposure were ever present.

Collective Action Needed

Clearly something was amiss. Unfortunately leaders of business were seldom disposed to grant higher wages and shorter hours. If labor conditions were going to improve, it would be up to the workingman to engineer the improvement. As an individual, he was almost powerless to do anything, particularly when his employer was a large enterprise. Only through collective action—whatever the public at large might think of it—could he realize the promise of the good life in America.

Labor unions were not new to the American scene. As early as 1792 the shoemakers of Philadelphia came together to improve wages and working conditions. Soon the printers of New York and tailors of Baltimore also had organized unions. Because of a tendency of the courts to view the strike, closed shop, and boycott as criminal conspiracies, this early labor movement achieved little and in the depression that followed the War of 1812 it expired.

The movement was revived in the 1820s by local craftsmen—shoemakers, printers, and carpenters. Using the strike as their chief weapon, the unions of the 1820s and 1830s realized a few victories, including wide acceptance of the ten-hour day. But then the labor movement again fell victim to a depression, this one touched off by the Panic of 1837. The depression brought major unemployment and in such a climate labor organizations crumbled as workers competed furiously for available jobs.

Meanwhile, the courts continued to take a dim view of labor unions and their activities. By the late 1840s the country was again prosperous, whereupon organized labor began a comeback. In the mid-1850s several groups of craftsmen—typographers, stonecutters, and hat finishers—united in national federations. The Civil War broke out in 1861, and while the dislocation of

This drawing by Winslow Homer of New England factory life appeared in *Harper's* in 1868. Workers stream out at "bell-time," the close of the day. Among them is a group of young boys who toiled the same long hours as their elders.

Library of Congress

trade and the demands of the military in the first months of the war slowed organized labor, unions in the latter part of the war became stronger. By 1864-65 there were two hundred thousand union members in the country. The future looked bright for the trade-union movement.

During their moment of strength in 1866 several national unions federated into the National Labor Union. Under William Sylvis the National Labor Union set out to gain social reform through political action. It sought abolition of the convict-labor system, grants of public land to settlers only (no land to speculators), and an eight-hour day. It also supported the controversial proposal to expand the currency with greenback dollars unsupported by gold. Leaders of several national unions disagreed with Sylvis's ideas and withdrew support. As a result the National Labor Union expired in the early 1870s. It had achieved little, although it helped get a law limiting the hours of federal employees to eight per day.

Black Men in the Labor Movement

Where did the Negro worker fit into the labor movement in post-Civil War America? A few leaders such as Sylvis wanted to bring Negroes into unions. Thanks to Sylvis's efforts, nine Negro delegates attended the National Labor Union congress of 1869 and the congress resolved that the union "knows no North, no South, no East, no West, neither color nor sex."

Despite this grand-sounding statement of unity, the delegates to the National Labor Union congress recommended that separate labor organizations be formed locally for black workers.

Political issues also separated black and white workers at the time the National Labor Union congress met. Many white workers were supporting "greenbackism," the idea that the government should issue quantities of paper currency that were not backed by either gold or silver. The goal would be to reduce the value of the dollar, making it easier for poor people to repay debts. The proposal was not popular with the national Republican party—the party of Abraham Lincoln—and so it was not popular with blacks. Blacks continued to view the Republican party as their chief hope for economic and social progress. It was the party which had won their freedom and which they hoped would guarantee their right to vote, to send their children to school, and to homestead in the West. Because of this issue, and because of the hostility of white unions, a group of blacks organized the National Colored Labor Union in 1869. Unfortunately, the life of this organization was short.

Knights of Labor

The year 1873 brought one of the most severe financial panics in American history and produced a general depression which dealt a sharp

Federal troops were called in by President Grover Cleveland during the great railway strikes of 1894. This picture printed in *Harper's* in July 1894 shows the first meat train leaving the Chicago stockyards under escort of the United States Cavalry.

Library of Congress

blow to the trade-union movement. Under the stress of hard times, national unions disintegrated, employers set about to destroy local labor organizations, and unemployed workers gladly sacrificed previous gains for a little work. The eventual outcome was a wave of labor unrest, climaxed in 1877 by a series of railroad strikes touched off when the Baltimore and Ohio slashed wages. From the B & O the strike spread to other lines. When violence and looting got out of the control of local authorities, the federal government intervened with troops—and the troops broke the strikes.

These developments of 1873-77 had several effects on labor. They brought renewed interest by labor in politics, and unions gave heavy support to the Greenback party in 1877 and 1878. There was an increased interest among workingmen in socialism, resulting in the appearance of the Socialist Labor party. Then a labor organization called the Knights of Labor gained new strength.

Founded in 1869 by an obscure garmentmaker, Uriah Stephens, the Noble Order of the Knights of Labor was not a conventional union. It sought to organize all Americans who "earned their bread by the sweat of their brows"—not just skilled craftsmen. The aims of this unusual order were hazy at first, but as time passed they became more apparent: arbitration of labor disputes (instead of strikes), an eight-hour day for workingmen, abolition of the convict-labor sys-

tem, laws forbidding the importation of contract workers from overseas, industrial safety laws, restrictions on child labor, postal savings banks, and government ownership of railroads, telegraphs, and telephones.

Such proposals appealed to many workingmen—and also to some farmers and shopkeepers. Just as important in the early success of the Knights of Labor was its elaborate secrecy and ritual, the work of Stephens, who had received training for the ministry, was a Freemason, and had a smattering of the Greek language. Local organizations called meetings by mysterious symbols chalked on fences and sidewalks; members identified one another by secret grips, passwords, and countersigns. The order had special appeal to the great body of unskilled workers who moved easily from job to job, had no trade, and could not gain entry in the craft unions. Finally, by emphasizing the dignity of all labor, the Knights appealed to some of the most downtrodden elements of society, particularly Negroes, who at one point made up about ten percent of the order's membership.

Under Stephens's guidance the Knights of Labor grew slowly. Then came the depression of 1873-77, whereupon many restless workingmen, particularly those lacking skills, turned to the Knights. Next Terence V. Powderly replaced Stephens as general master workman. The son of Irish immigrants who had known poverty and hard work, Powderly was a vision-

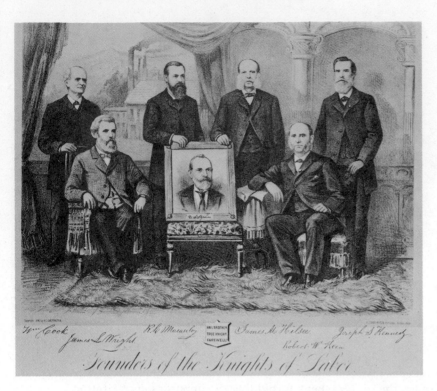

Founders of the Knights of Labor

Wm Cook   James L. Wright   R.C. Macaulay   James M. Hilsee   Joseph S Kennedy   Robert W. Keen

The Knights of Labor, a union founded in 1869, grew stronger after the Panic of 1873. The union's main founder, Uriah Stephens, is shown in the center of this lithograph, with the other founders around him. What event led to the decline of this union?

ary who sometimes hesitated when faced with difficult decisions. Still, he was a dynamic leader who preferred boycotts to strikes, opposed organization of workers according to crafts or skills, and favored the idea of joint political action by the Knights with organizations of farmers.

Membership in the Knights of Labor leaped from 19,000 in 1881 to 110,000 in 1885. Nor was this the end of the order's phenomenal growth. In spring 1885 members carried out a spontaneous and unauthorized strike against three of Jay Gould's railroads, the Missouri Pacific, Missouri-Kansas-Texas, and Wabash. Taken by surprise, Gould surrendered to the demands of the strikers. On the prestige of this victory, membership in the Knights of Labor boomed to 700,000. Then came disaster. Against the wishes of Powderly (who continued to abhor strikes), many local units of the order determined to strike on May 1, 1886, in support of the eight-hour day for all trades.

The Haymarket Square Riot

Things seemed to be going well, and there was some evidence that the strike was winning popular support for the eight-hour day. Then on May 4 several anarchists (men who believed that all government was evil) were addressing a group

of workers who had gathered in Haymarket Square in Chicago to protest alleged police brutality. Apparently fearing mob violence, policemen drew up and ordered the crowd to disperse. At that point somebody threw a bomb which exploded killing one officer and injuring several others. The country was horrified, and the result was a tremendous outcry against all protest movements, including those sanctioned by the Knights of Labor. Powderly condemned the Haymarket riot, but it was no use. Members of the Knights fell away in droves. At the same time another wildcat strike against the Gould railroads failed. Failure of the strike destroyed much of the luster the Knights had acquired the previous year. The decline continued, and by the end of the century the order had ceased to exist except in name.

The Knights of Labor still had made some progress. Its lobbying efforts in Washington helped secure passage of the Foran Act which imposed penalties on individuals importing contract workers from abroad. It also won abolition of the prison lessee system—the leasing of convicts by the state to private companies—in all states outside the South, thereby eliminating a source of cheap labor that competed with free workingmen. But perhaps its largest achievement was to provide fellowship and hope for thousands of unskilled workmen who were

[258]

scorned by other elements of society, including skilled craftsmen. The Knights of Labor pointed up the need for labor organizations along industrial lines in such giant industries as oil and rubber. This need, incidentally, was not effectively met by organized labor until the birth of the Congress of Industrial Organizations (CIO) in the 1930s.

Gompers and the AFL

Meanwhile, as the Knights of Labor was going into eclipse, a new organization appeared, the American Federation of Labor.

The end of the depression of the 1870s brought new life to the old national craft unions. A merger with the flourishing Knights of Labor was a possibility. But leaders of the craft organizations concluded that the Knights of Labor, with its battalions of unskilled workers, was not suitable to their purposes. In 1881 several of them met at Pittsburgh and formed the Federation of Organized Trades and Labor Unions of the United States and Canada. Growth of the new organization was slow, in part because of the opposition of Powderly and the Knights. The Knights wanted to divorce workingmen from loyalties to crafts and commit everyone to the objectives of all workers in all industries, skilled and unskilled alike.

About 1885, when the Knights of Labor began to make inroads on craft union membership, the Federation of Organized Trades called a meeting "to protect our respective organizations from the malicious work of an element who openly boast that trade unions must be destroyed." The outcome, in December 1886, was the creation of the AFL, a federation of craft unions (although some industrywide unions, notably the miners and brewers, would later gain admission). The AFL was not tightly knit, and the central organization had limited authority. Each national union in the federation, without consulting other members or the central organization, could make contracts with or call strikes against employers within its own jurisdiction. The purpose of the central organization was to help organize local unions and state federations, decide jurisdiction between member unions, prevent appearance of rival unions in the same trade, influence public opinion, secure favorable legislation, assist union members unemployed by strikes or lockouts, and try to keep the labor movement united.

The first head of the AFL—and president of the federation for every year except one (1895)

until his death in 1924—was Samuel Gompers.

A member of a Jewish family that had made its way to England from Holland, Gompers was born in the slums of London's East End in the year 1850. His father was a cigarmaker whose workshop was the family household and who barely earned enough to feed and clothe his family. Young Samuel grew up in the streets of the grimy and turbulent city, learned to read and write during the four years he attended school, and while still a boy was apprenticed to a cigarmaker.

Meanwhile, the family's economic situation went from bad to worse, whereupon the elder Gompers gathered together his family and their meager possessions and set sail for America. The family landed on lower Manhattan in summer 1863 at a time when New Yorkers were on the one hand celebrating the great Union victory at Gettysburg and on the other were trying to put down riots touched off by the move to conscript men for the federal army.

In America the youthful Gompers resumed the trade of cigarmaking and joined the Cigarmakers' Union. Since the craft of cigarmaking was almost automatic for the skilled worker and thus required little concentration, Gompers had ample opportunity to carry on discussions with fellow workers. Often one member of the group would read aloud while the others fashioned the cigars. It was in the heat and dust of the workshop that Gompers formed many of his ideas about society and the workingman's place in it. He also sharpened his mind by attending public lectures and participating in debating clubs.

At length it became apparent that Gompers had some essential qualities for inspiring and leading men. Most important, he was an effective public speaker, not because of any ability to manipulate words (in print his speeches appeared stiff and formal), but because of his fervor and oratorical style. In 1877—at the age of twenty-seven—he became president of the Cigarmakers' Union, helped organize the Federation of Organized Trades in 1881, and five years later became the first president of the AFL.

The central organization of the AFL had limited authority over individual unions and as president Gompers had little power on paper. Still, because of his ability to persuade and the prestige he managed to accumulate, Gompers asserted great influence over the unions of the AFL. Under his leadership the federation was the kingpin of the labor movement in America well into the twentieth century. He established local unions in trades that hitherto had been unorganized and central federations in cities where none had existed. He kept jurisdictional disputes between local craft unions to a minimum and resolved numerous disputes between AFL unions and management. He took care to keep the AFL free of affiliation with political parties, for he was convinced that organized labor could best secure its ends by compelling the major parties to compete for its support.

Gompers was by no definition a radical labor leader. Abhorring violence and staunchly faithful to the capitalist system, he was a "right-wing" unionist. Rather than turn American society upside down, perhaps by a socialist revolution, he sought such bread-and-butter gains for labor as the eight-hour day, higher wage scales, and employer liability for injuries sustained on the job. He fought unflinchingly to prevent the federation from evolving into a workingmen's political party and remained wary of alliances with politicians. He took no great interest in organizing the great body of unskilled workers in the giant industries, clinging instead to the old craft-union principle—which meant that the AFL never tried to represent more than a small fraction of the workingmen in America.

The Homestead Strike

The AFL faced important difficulties during the decades in which Gompers was its president. There was the disastrous strike in 1892 against the Carnegie steelworks at Homestead, Pennsylvania, by the Amalgamated Association of Iron, Steel, and Tin Workers. The association was the principal labor organization in the steel industry and one of the few industrial unions affiliated with the AFL. The strike was touched off when Henry Clay Frick, manager of the Homestead works, ordered a wage reduction. To break the strike, Frick dispatched Pinkerton detectives by barge along the Monongahela River to Homestead. When the Pinkertons attempted to land, a battle erupted which resulted in the death of nine strikers and three detectives.

The strikers won the battle, but the victory was temporary, for the Pennsylvania National Guard moved in and, by affording protection for strikebreakers, broke the strike. The outcome was annihilation of the Amalgamated Association and, for all practical purposes, the end of unionism in the steel industry for more than forty years. At the same time Gompers was failing in

In 1892 union men went on strike against the Carnegie steelworks at Homestead, Pennsylvania. This photograph shows strikers on watch for strikebreakers. Although the strike failed, it influenced the American labor movement. What do you think about the strike as a labor weapon? Would you participate in a strike if you were asked?

efforts to secure affiliation of the large unions, or "brotherhoods," of railroad-operating employees—engineers, firemen, conductors, and brakemen. The brotherhoods believed that their interests did not run parallel with those of other laboring groups and indeed found it impossible to unite with one another, let alone the AFL.

From the socialist wing of the labor movement —and also from anarchists, and other assorted radicals—Gompers and the AFL received a steady barrage of criticism because of the federation's toleration of capitalism and concentration on bread-and-butter gains. The most serious challenge to the AFL came in 1905 at Chicago when radicals formed the Industrial Workers of the World, the IWW, whose members became known as "Wobblies."

The new organization stated its position in the preamble of its constitution: "The working class and the employing class have nothing in common." It sought to unite all workers—skilled and unskilled, black and white, native American and foreign-born—in one giant union which planned to bring revolutionary changes in American society. To achieve its ends the IWW was willing to employ sabotage and violence as well as strikes and boycotts.

Because of its acceptance of strong-arm tactics, continuing internal squabbles, and the calling of strikes during the time of United States participation in World War I, the IWW had a checkered history. It never had a large membership and by the early 1920s had fallen into oblivion. But it attracted attention and during its brief and turbulent lifetime worked a serious hardship on other labor groups, including the AFL. Many Americans did not bother to examine distinctions between organizations and tended to cite policies and acts of the IWW as proof that all unions constituted a threat to the "American way of life."

Achievements of Labor

In the half-century before America's entry into World War I in 1917 many workingmen, especially those who were members of unions affiliated with the AFL achieved higher wages and shorter hours. Congress lent support to the movement for shorter hours by establishing the eight-hour day for government employees (1892) and, via the Adamson Act (1916), decreeing an eight-hour day for railroad employees. Many factories became safer and more sanitary. There was less competition from convict labor, and the Foran Act (1885) prohibited importation of contract workers from foreign countries.

The Erdman Act (1898) provided for arbitration of labor disputes involving interstate carriers. The Employers' Liability Act (1908) held railroads responsible for injuries sustained by employees in the line of duty. And the La Follette Seamen's Act (1915) regulated conditions of employment for maritime workers. In addition many states passed laws restricting female labor, and federal legislation in 1916 and 1919 barred from interstate commerce the products of child labor. Unfortunately, however, the Supreme Court ruled the latter measures unconstitutional.

Still, when compared with the magnitude of the problems, the achievements of labor during the long era between the Civil War and World War I seemed meager. For millions of workers, especially those in giant industries, wages were pitifully low and hours long. Most workingmen had no job security. There was little protection against illness or accident or a penniless old age. Vacation with pay was a dream. So was unemployment compensation. There was no guarantee of the right to organize and bargain collectively, and employers often resorted to intimidation, even violence, to prevent workingmen from establishing unions.

Between 1860 and 1890 daily working hours decreased while the average wage increased. However, the wage high in 1890 was the same as it had been in 1870. What caused the drop in wages in the 1870s?

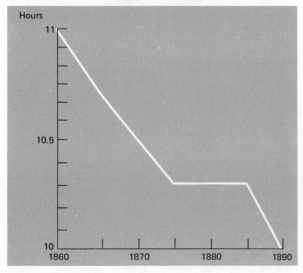

DAILY WORKING HOURS
1860 — 1890

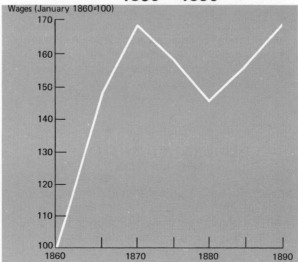

INDEX OF DAILY WAGES
1860 — 1890

Most workingmen in America during those years remained subject to the mercies of employers whom they did not know—employers whose first responsibility and interest was payment of dividends to stockholders. Unhappily, in that time of rugged individualism and Social Darwinism, generosity and benevolence, especially in the great industries, were rare commodites in the jungle of business in the United States.

STUDY GUIDE: Labor unions gained relatively little support until the middle of the nineteenth century. The Panic of 1873 led to a wave of labor unrest. This unrest was climaxed by a series of railroad strikes which were broken by the intervention of federal troops. Labor unions turned to political parties for help. They supported the Greenback and Socialist Labor parties.

During the 1880s the Knights of Labor became the leading union in the country. It declined in importance after the violence of the Haymarket riot in Chicago turned many Americans against unions.

A new labor organization, the American Federation of Labor (AFL), gained importance. Headed by Samuel Gompers, the AFL was a federation of craft unions which excluded unskilled workers. Gompers did not believe in violence and wanted to work for the betterment of the workingman within the capitalist system. Opposing this view in the early 1900s were the International Workers of the World, called "Wobblies." They believed violent means were necessary to bring revolutionary changes to American society. In the half century before World War I, a number of laws were passed which brought many gains for labor. Yet much remained to be done for the millions of workers, particularly the unskilled, who toiled long hours for poor pay with no job security.

IMMIGRATION CHANGES THE NATION

During the age of industrialization tens of millions of people from nearly every country in the world sought the promise of a better life in the United States. Some immigrants walked into the United States, from Canada and Mexico. A few swam across the Rio Grande. But the greatest number came by steamships and sailing vessels that had plowed their way westward across the Atlantic or eastward across the Pacific. On and on they came, year after year, decade after decade, like a great human wave. Whereas fewer than ten thousand immigrants entered the country in 1820, more than four hundred thousand arrived in 1854, nearly eight hundred thousand in 1882, and more than a million (or an average of better than three thousand per day) in each of the years 1905, 1906, 1907, 1910, 1913, and 1914. Historians and social scientists are still trying to assess the social consequences of that migration—the greatest movement of humanity in the history of the world.

The first immigrants to America were Indians who over many thousands of years trickled across the Bering Strait (or perhaps over a land bridge) from Siberia to Alaska. Their descendants fanned out across the width and breadth of North and South America. Then came Columbus's momentous voyage of 1492 and after that a migration of people from Europe to the New World. What brought these post-Columbian migrants to America? Most were drawn by the area's boundless economic opportunities. Others came in search of religious and political liberty. Some arrived in chains—as slaves. But whatever the reasons for their coming, those immigrants to the New World who sank roots in the present-day United States—white and black, brown and yellow—provided the foundation of a national population which in the second half of the twentieth century has exceeded two hundred million. In addition to populating a great territory that was virtually empty, those immigrants and their descendants transformed a tangled wilderness into the most prosperous and powerful nation in the world.

The Early Immigrants

Apart from 750,000 Afro-Americans and a scattering of Indians, Dutchmen, Germans, and Frenchmen, the overwhelming majority of the three and a half million people who lived within the borders of the United States at the end of the War for Independence, in 1783, came from the British Isles—England, Scotland, Wales, and Northern Ireland. And for the first thirty years after independence the composition of the national population remained relatively unchanged.

There were at least two reasons for this. First, because of an increasing moral sensitivity over the evils of the African slave trade (and a corresponding, if temporary, decline in the profits from slavery), the importation of blacks into the country declined sharply. Second, during the dreary years between 1792 and 1815, Europe was either gripped by general war or catching its breath while awaiting the next conflict. This was the era of the French Revolution and Napoleon. In the face of continuing crisis, European governments needed all the workers that they could find. So they made it difficult for Europeans to emigrate to America.

America's population did expand rapidly between independence and the end of the war—from 3,500,000 in 1783 to 8,500,000 in 1815. But this was mainly a result of the highest birth rate in the country's history. (For example, the birth rate among white Americans in 1800 was fifty-five live births per thousand persons; in 1975, the rate for all Americans was estimated at slightly less than fifteen per thousand.)

Then, in 1815, came the Battle of Waterloo in Belgium. There the combined forces of France's enemies—notably Britain and Prussia—crushed the imperial army of Napoleon. A short time later the former emperor was on his way to exile on the island of St. Helena in the South Atlantic, and peace settled over Europe. The flow of European immigrants began again.

The principal sources of this new migration were Ireland and Germany. Of the 5,000,000 immigrants who came to the United States between 1815 and 1860, about 2,000,000 were Irish and about 1,7000,000 were German. Some 750,000 others came from England, Scotland, Northern Ireland, and Wales. Still other immigrants were Swiss, Norwegian, Swedish, or Dutch.

Massive Irish Immigration

Several problems in Ireland prompted the Irish movement to the United States, a movement which over the next century brought more than 4,000,000 Irish men and women to America.

The first problem was that Ireland was overpopulated—it had more people than its economy could support. The Irish, most of whom were farmers, labored under an outdated and oppressive system of agriculture. They used tools and methods which had not improved since the Middle Ages. A large percentage of them tilled the land of absentee landlords (most of them English) who charged very high rents. The typical Irish peasant family—their income amounting to only a few pennies a day—lived in a one-room hut and subsisted on potatoes, a little milk, and occasionally some fish.

Adding to the hardships of the Irish was domination by the British. The British felt contempt for the Irish, denied them political privileges, and forced them to support the Church of England, even though most of them were Roman Catholics.

Irish migrants sailed to America in a steady stream in the 1820s and 1830s. Then in the late 1840s and 1850s the movement of the Irish to the New World swelled to a new high. A series of cold, damp summers caused a potato rot which destroyed almost the entire crop in Ireland. Famine and disease were widespread, and nearly a fourth of the population died. Only the lucky escaped to the United States.

Irish immigrants seldom found a paradise waiting for them in the United States. Few of them had had any schooling, and most arrived penniless. The large majority had been farmers in Ireland, but because of their recent unhappy experiences in agriculture, few had either the money or the desire to buy land and begin new farms. Many Irish immigrants took up picks and shovels and joined construction crews on the Erie Canal and other projects. Others found work in the mill towns of New England. They settled in New England in such large numbers that eventually they converted that former center of Puritanism into the most intensely Catholic region of the United States.

Most Irish immigrants had to work long and hard for low pay. They also faced another old problem: religious discrimination. Many Protestants who lived in New England were hostile to them because most of the Irish were Roman Catholics. Just as the British had wanted the Irish to support the Church of England, many Protestants were intolerant of Roman Catholics. For this reason, employers discriminated against Irish workers. Help-wanted advertisements often contained the notice, "No Irish need apply." The Irish were a chief target of criticism of immigrants in general and Catholics in particular from the 1830s to the 1850s. During this period they were accused of "polluting" American society with "foreign" ideas.

The Great German Immigration

Germans comprised the second largest group of migrants to the United States between independence and the Civil War.

A number of German immigrants had arrived in America in the seventeenth and eighteenth centuries, many of them settling in the valleys and towns of Pennsylvania. During the War for Independence there was another small influx of Germans, mostly soldiers hired by the British to help put down the American rebellion. After the war perhaps twelve thousand of these German mercenaries remained in America, built homes, and raised families. But it was not until after 1815 that Germans began to migrate to the New World in considerable numbers. A mere trickle at first, the movement of Germans to America increased in the 1830s and 1840s. Between 1815 and 1914 more than five million Germans crossed the Atlantic and settled in the United States.

What prompted the large migration of Germans to America after 1815?

Some Germans left the "old country" for political reasons. Early in the nineteenth century the ideas of the French Revolution—liberty, equality, and fraternity—found a considerable response among Germans who had tired of autocracy and feudalism. After Napoleon's downfall in 1815, however, the leaders of Europe set about to crush the remnants of liberalism on the Continent. Disillusioned, some German liberals sought refuge in America. Others remained and led liberal uprisings against the established order in 1830 and again in 1848. Such uprisings failed, and each produced a new exodus of liberals, many of whom found their way to America.

Those who came after the revolutions of 1848, known as the "Forty-eighters," included some unusually talented individuals. Still, the great number of immigrants from Germany did not travel to America in search of political liberty— or to escape German "militarism." The typical German immigrant was a farmer who came to America because the soil was rich and the price of land was low.

German immigrants usually arrived in America with a little cash, and only a few remained in port cities along the Atlantic seaboard. Most traveled via the Erie Canal and the Great Lakes to the interior. Some settled in such cities as Cincinnati, Louisville, Saint Louis, and Milwaukee. More often they took up land in the Ohio and Mississippi valleys, where they proved to be excellent farmers. German farmers used fertilizers, diversified crops, and emphasized dairying and livestock. Many German farmers were unusually thorough. When they found stumps on their land they removed them rather than work around them.

The German farmer was also conservative, seldom speculating on the chance that a railroad or canal might suddenly increase the value of his land. The Germans were a convivial people who enjoyed singing and dancing, parades, and picnics with beer, cheese, rye bread, and sausage. They also took an active interest in politics in the United States. In the years before 1850 they usually sided with the Democratic party— considering it the friend of the farmer and immigrant. But in the 1850s many Germans switched to the new Republican party, largely because of their hatred of slavery. The shift of Germans from the Democratic party to the Republican had great consequences, for it was the German vote in states of the old Northwest that helped tip the national balance for Abraham Lincoln in the critical election of 1860.

German immigrants, like the Irish, often were the victims of discrimination. Germans who were Catholic often encountered hostility in such cities as Cincinnati and Louisville. But they experienced much less difficulty than did Irish-Americans, largely because most of the Germans settled in the countryside, usually in areas inhabited by other Germans, and tended to keep to themselves. As a rule, they were slow to learn the English language and in general had limited contacts with other Americans. Hence the Germans, except the minority that lived in cities, had fewer opportunities for disagreement and conflict with other groups than did the English-speaking, urban-dwelling, and spirited Irish immigrants. Moreover, the German habits of thrift and industry often won the admiration of even the most hardened nativists— those who favored natural-born citizens over immigrants.

Immigration After 1860

America's Civil War of 1861-65 reduced but by no means stopped the movement of immigrants to such ports as Boston, New York, and Philadelphia. In that four-year period more than a half-million Irishmen, Germans, and other Europeans responded to the lure of the New World. With the end of the war the pace of immigration quickened. In the next half-century between 1865 and 1915 more than twenty-five million immigrants entered the country.

As in the pre-Civil War era, most immigrants in the three decades after 1860 came from northern and western Europe and, also as before, most came for economic reasons. In the 1870s and 1880s the grain farmers of the British Isles, Germany, and Sweden found their markets invaded by farmers of the United States, Canada, and Russia. The outcome was a farm depression in northern and western Europe which caused many families to move across the Atlantic to the New World.

Concurrent with the farm depression were other difficulties in northern and western Europe. In Sweden the timber industry experienced depression when shipbuilders turned from wood to iron as their basic construction material, while America's tariff on foreign iron cut into the profits of Swedish ironmasters. As a result many Swedish timber and ironworkers joined distressed farmers on the way to the United States. Germany's manufacturing industries suffered setbacks in the 1880s, which in turn produced an exodus to America of artisans, miners, ironworkers, and textile workers. Great Britain encountered similar difficulties in the 1880s and as a consequence many coal miners and ironworkers in England, Scotland, and Wales set sail for America.

While economic distress in northern and western Europe in the 1870s and 1880s compelled thousands of people to migrate, assorted groups in America were urging Europeans to make the move to the New World. Among these groups were such states as Wisconsin, Minnesota, and Iowa which sought Europeans who would take up unsettled land within their borders. To achieve their aims, they sent out smooth-talking agents and established bureaus which distributed maps and pamphlets.

Also seeking to attract immigrants were southern states which hoped to replace Negroes with cheap foreign labor. Because there was little good land for sale at low prices in the South, southern recruiting campaigns yielded few returns.

There were also offers from the land-grant railroads, which had received great tracts of western land from the federal government to subsidize construction of rail lines. If the roads were to meet their obligations and prosper, it was necessary to dispose quickly of this land to settlers. Like the states, land-grant railroads therefore dispatched agents to Europe and sometimes paid part of the immigrants' steamship passage to America and railroad fares across the continent to the West. In some instances the roads built immigrant housing, where settlers could stay without charge until they selected land, which the roads sold at moderate prices. Other railroad companies built churches and schools, and a few planted "lure" colonies of Germans and Scandinavians—to serve as magnets for immigrants of similar background.

Most Germans and Scandinavians, as before 1860, made their way to the interior of the country. Scores of thousands of them took up land, although, compared with previous times, larger numbers settled in urban areas—in Milwaukee, Saint Louis, Minneapolis, and Saint Paul. Immigrants from Ireland, like their predecessors, usually had little money and hence congregated in cities along the northeastern seaboard, taking what work they could find in the unskilled labor market. Several organizations sought to encourage Irish-Americans to spread to rural areas and take up farming. As in the past, however, the typical Irishman, conditioned by experience in the homeland to take a low view of agriculture, showed scant interest. As for migrants from other parts of the British Isles—Scotland, England, and Wales—there was little pattern to their settlement in America. Some went west and became farmers, others took up mining, and still others found work in manufacturing.

Beginning in the late 1880s immigration from northern and western Europe started to decline. By the beginning of the twentieth century, barely twenty percent of the new arrivals in America were coming from countries in that area of the Continent.

What brought this slowing of large-scale immigration from the north and west of Europe? First, there was a slowdown in birth rates in countries across northern and western Europe. This meant, as years passed, that fewer people were competing for available jobs. Accordingly wages and working conditions began to improve. Second, the rapid expansion of industry in such countries as Germany and Sweden in those years offered new sources of employment for displaced artisans, farmers, and woodsmen. Third, governments in such countries as Britain and Germany, understanding the importance of manpower in the developing international rivalries, looked with official disfavor on emigration. To reduce discontent at home and thus discourage people from leaving, Germany, and also Sweden, engineered social and economic reforms. Great Britain made no great effort to check emigration from the British Isles but encouraged migrants to settle in the British Empire—in Canada, Australia, New Zealand, or South Africa. Fourth, America lost much of its attraction for people of northern and western Europe. Most of the good cheap land in America was taken up by 1890, returns from farming in the New World were in decline, and mechanization of both industry and agriculture in the United States was creating a manpower surplus which in turn was depressing the standards of labor. Opportunities in America after the mid-1880s seemed no better than those in the homeland. So why leave?

Problems in Eastern and Southern Europe Bring New Immigrants

In the mid-1880s, as the movement of people to America from northern and western Europe began to decline, a new group of immigrants began to arrive. These so-called "new" immigrants came from southern and Eastern Europe — Italy, the Balkan countries, Poland, Czechoslovakia, Hungary, and Russia. By 1896, more immigrants were arriving each year from these countries than from northern and western Europe. By 1910, eighty percent of all new arrivals in the United States came from southern and Eastern Europe. These immigrants flocked to the cities of New England, New York, and New Jersey. Soon they spread out to the mining towns of Pennsylvania and Ohio and to industrial centers such as Pittsburgh, Cleveland, Chicago, Detroit, and Milwaukee.

The reasons for this new wave of immigrants were largely economic. Almost the entire region of southern and Eastern Europe was burdened by illiteracy and outdated agricultural methods. The area was vast and ridden with poverty. Under these circumstances, it would have been natural to expect a wave of immigrants from southern and Eastern Europe even before the 1880s. Before then, however, migrations out of the region had been limited by law. The governments which controlled most of the area wanted to keep their labor force, so they made laws to discourage emigration.

Then, in the latter part of the nineteenth century, there was a general relaxing of such restrictions. In Italy the relaxation grew out of a new liberal spirit which accompanied the movement of 1859-60 to unify the states and principalities of the Italian peninsula under a single government. In the Balkans relaxation followed the emancipation of Serbia, Bulgaria, and other national areas from Turkish control after the Russo-Turkish War of 1877.

In the Austro-Hungarian empire (which included Austria, Hungary, parts of present-day Poland, Rumania, and Yugoslavia, and all of Czechoslovakia) restrictions declined after a general political reorganization that followed the union of Austria and Hungary in 1867. In Russia and in areas of the Balkans that remained under Turkish control, authorities simply ceased to enforce prohibitions against emigration.

At the same time economic conditions in southern and eastern Europe became worse. In part this unhappy development resulted from the collapse of the old feudal system, with its maze of restrictions and obligations on the peasantry. At first the passing of feudalism seemed to promise a better life for the peasant. But there were difficulties. Most important, abolition of feudal arrangements led to splitting large estates into small independent farms. Apparently this was good for the peasant. As a free proprietor, he could manage his own affairs and receive all the returns from his labor. Unfortunately the peasant knew little of modern techniques, was too poor to buy modern equipment, and lacked knowledge of farm management. He usually found it impossible to cultivate his small holding efficiently. As a consequence, depression with all its attendant hardships settled over the agricultural regions of much of eastern and southern Europe. Whereupon many distressed farmers in Poland, Czechoslovakia, Hungary, and the Balkans began to seek new opportunity and quite often their search took them to America.

Immigrants from Italy

Southern Italy, the source of most migrants from the Italian peninsula to America, saw the worst of these troubles. Through the centuries that area had suffered many burdens, including a long political tradition of neglect and misrule. Economic conditions were made worse by primitive agricultural methods. Malaria sapped the strength of the people. But the heaviest weight on the region was an absentee landlord system akin to that of Ireland earlier in the nineteenth century. The system had the usual abuses: high rents, short leases, and unscientific methods. There was no interest in soil conservation.

Then came the elimination of feudal obligations, release of lands belonging to the Roman Catholic church, and the breaking up of large estates. As in eastern Europe, the outcome was increased inefficiency and more severe poverty.

Next southern Italy received two serious economic shocks. First came the sudden loss of the region's largest market for its subtropical fruit — the United States. Fruit previously imported by the United States came to be supplied by fruit growers in the American states of Florida and California. At the same time, France, wishing to encourage its own wine industry, put up prohibitive tariffs against foreign wines, thus depriving wine makers of southern Italy of what had once been their most profitable market.

As the economic situation worsened, large numbers of southern Italians looked westward, first to Latin America, where they expected to find a climate and culture more to their liking. But political turmoil and economic difficulties in Latin America soon diverted most Italian migrants toward the United States.

Immigrants from Russia, Canada, and Mexico

Migration to America from Russia was a different proposition. The major reason for exodus from the Russian empire was religious. Most immigrants from Russia were Mennonites, Jews, and Catholics.

The first to come were the Mennonites. Of German origin, these people had migrated to Russia near the end of the eighteenth century because of persecution in Germany and a guarantee of considerable independence in Russia. In the year 1871, however, the czar responded to a growing mood of Russian nationalism and withdrew special privileges from the Mennonites. Whereupon thousands of Mennonites from Russia traveled to America and took up land — much of it railroad land — where they attracted attention for their thrift and industry.

Far more numerous were the Russian Jews, who began streaming to the United States in the 1880s. In Russia, as in most areas of Europe, Jews had endured many centuries of discrimination. With the increase of Russian nationalism late in the nineteenth century, persecutions of Jews became nearly intolerable. The government enforced old restrictions and imposed new ones. These included laws that limited Jewish worship, excluded Jews from public office, denied them educational opportunities, and made it difficult for Jews to become physicians, lawyers, or teachers.

Around the beginning of the twentieth century, there was an increase in the emigration from the Russian empire of other minority groups, particularly Catholics from Poland and Lithuania. Like the Jews, these people were seeking an escape from oppression of one sort or another. During those same years there was also a small group of Portuguese who responded to the opportunity of America. Most Portuguese migrants found work in the factories of New England and the orchards of California. Encouraged by American Protestant missionaries, several thousand Armenian and Syrian Christians, victims of continuing persecution by Turks, found a sanctuary in the United States. Meanwhile many Canadians, attracted by economic opportunity and a more temperate climate, made their way across the Canadian-American border. Canadian immigrants of English origin blended so easily into the American population that most Americans were not even aware that they were immigrants. In the Southwest, large numbers of Mexicans moved into Texas and California. Unlike the Canadians, however, the Mexican immigrants often met a hostile reception in the United States.

Chinese and Japanese Immigrants

Large numbers of immigrants came from China and Japan. These new arrivals from the Far East had also encountered economic difficulty at home and were seeking opportunity in the New World. The Chinese, most of whom came from South China, began to arrive around 1850, following the economic paralysis and famine brought on by the Taiping rebellion. Over the next thirty years some three hundred thousand Chinese entered the United States, finding employment as construction workers, miners, laundrymen, butlers, cigarmakers, and farm laborers. Most of the Chinese — and also the Japanese — settled in California.

The Japanese moved eastward across the Pacific in the 1880s, after the emperor lifted a ban against Japanese emigration. In the beginning most Japanese migrants went to Hawaii as contract laborers on American sugar plantations. From there many moved on to the United States. Other Japanese migrated directly to the United States or entered the country via Mexico.

STUDY GUIDE: Until the late eighteenth century the majority of people living in the United States had come from the British Isles. After

1815 many new immigrants came from Ireland and Germany. A new wave of immigration from northern and western Europe took place after the Civil War. In the mid-1880s increasing numbers of people came from southern and eastern Europe. Many immigrants also came from China and Japan.

REACTIONS TO IMMIGRATION

Did the "new" immigrants from southern and eastern Europe find some sort of perfect solution to their problems when they arrived in America?

Like the Irish and some other immigrant groups (notably the Chinese) of previous decades, immigrants from Italy, the Balkans, Poland, and Russia seldom found a promised land in America. Few arrived with much in the way of money or skills, and they often fell victim to loan sharks, unscrupulous boardinghouse keepers, and shady employment agencies. Although a few managed to take up farming or become farm laborers in New England, the Middle West, and California, most gravitated to the slums or ghettos of large eastern and midwestern cities. There they crowded into ramshackle, rat-infested tenements.

To earn a living, some "new" immigrants became peddlers. Others were able to set up such enterprises as bakeries, restaurants, and grocery stores. But most—and this often included women and children—had to take what they could find in the unskilled labor market. They worked long hours for low pay in garment factories, packinghouses, steel mills, and coal mines, or as janitors and street cleaners. Usually the family income, even if every member had some sort of job, was not enough to provide adequate food, clothing, or medical services. The result was widespread malnutrition, disease, and often premature death.

Immigrants Are Socially Rejected

The "new" immigrants from southern and Eastern Europe also faced the problem of social isolation. Most of them could not speak English. Their traditions were not Anglo-Saxon, and they were not Protestants. These differences were viewed with suspicion by many Americans of northern and western European ancestry. Because of this cold reception, and also because customs in the United States seemed strange to them, the

Library of Congress

Some Americans did not approve of the flood of new immigrants. This view was expressed in an 1888 cartoon from *Leslie's*. The tall American, surrounded by odd-looking "foreigners," is portrayed as "The Last Yankee—A Possible Curiosity of the Twentieth Century." How would you feel if other people considered you odd and undesirable?

"new" immigrants, much like immigrants of other eras, moved into neighborhoods populated by other recent arrivals from the "old country."

In such neighborhoods they spoke their native tongues and indeed made a strong effort to create in America a tiny copy of the society and culture they had left behind. The center of these transplanted societies was usually the church or synagogue. Since the immigrant could not put up a house in the crowded city that looked like the one back in the homeland, he built and decorated a place of worship which enabled him, maybe once a week, maybe a few minutes every day, to return to the "old country."

Other centers of immigrant activity were fraternal organizations such as the Bohemian Slavonian Protective Association and the Polish National Alliance. Such societies often provided life insurance for immigrants and in other ways sought to help counter the heartache and loneliness of a forbidding New World. Equally important, they sought to preserve the culture and traditions of the homeland. For example, they sponsored amateur theatrical productions, songfests, and public celebrations of the national holidays of the homeland.

It was during those years of heavy immigration that the French sculptor Auguste Bartholdi designed the massive "Liberty Enlightening the World"—better known as the Statue of Liberty—for New York Harbor. Emblazoned on the base of the statue are lines from *The New Colossus,* a poem written by Emma Lazarus:

> . . .Give me your tired, your poor,
> Your huddled masses yearning to breathe free,
> The wretched refuse of your teeming shore.
> Send these, the homeless, tempest-tossed, to me:
> I lift my lamp beside the golden door.

For the immigrant safely within the United States, wrapping cigars by day and living in an unkempt tenement by night, ignored or reviled by older generations of Americans, the golden door often seemed to lose its luster.

End of the Immigrant Dream

By the 1880s, many people in the United States were beginning to talk about limiting the flow of foreigners to their shores. Such thoughts were not entirely new. Most of the original thirteen colonies had sought to limit the immigration of Catholics and Jews. In 1729, for example, the colony of Pennsylvania set about "to discourage the great importation and coming of numbers of foreigners and lewd, idle and ill-affected persons" who would endanger the "quiet and safety of the peaceable people."

The movement of large numbers of Roman Catholics from Ireland and Germany in the decades after 1815 prompted a new wave of hostility to immigrants. The climax came in the 1850s with the Know-Nothing movement which sought to protect American institutions from foreign, particularly Catholic, contamination.

As a result of Know-Nothing agitation, mobs shattered windows of Catholic churches in Boston, blew up a Catholic church in Dorchester, Massachusetts, harassed German picnickers, and killed some fifty German and Irish residents of Louisville in an infamous affair known as the "Bloody Monday" riot. Know-Nothings sought to carry their influence into national politics in 1856 when they nominated a presidential candidate, former-president Millard Fillmore. Fillmore carried only one state, Maryland, whereupon the Know-Nothing movement expired. (See Chapter 4.)

Most Americans in the 1860s and 1870s, however, recognizing that the country's industrial apparatus needed manpower, focused on the economic benefits of large-scale immigration. The outcome was an effort to stimulate rather than restrict immigration.

Discrimination Against Asians

At the same time Americans were trying to attract immigrants to the industrial northeast, anti-Chinese sentiment was growing on the West Coast. Chinese laborers who would work for very low wages had been encouraged to come to the United States while the transcontinental railroad was being built. But as California's labor force grew, many workers began to resent the Chinese laborers because they were competing with them for jobs. Acts of violence were aimed at the Chinese, and Californians pressured Congress to limit Chinese immigration. As a result, the United States persuaded China to accept a treaty giving the United States the right to suspend Chinese immigration. In 1882 Congress passed the Chinese Exclusion Act. This law banned immigration by Chinese laborers for ten years. It was extended several times, until the quota law of 1921 banned all Asian immigrants.

Nativist Groups Campaign Against Other Immigrants

By the 1880s and 1890s, hostility toward all immigrants, not just Asians, had surfaced. As in earlier times, Catholics often were principal targets of criticism by nativists, those who favored native-born citizens over immigrants. New organizations such as the American Protective Association dredged up and circulated the same biased stories which had been used by the Know-Nothings forty years earlier. The main goal of the nativists was to restrict immigration.

As a result of nativist pressure, Congress took some halting steps to restrict immigration—or at least to keep out "undesirable" foreigners. A bill in 1882 forbade immigration of convicts, lunatics, idiots, and other individuals apt to become public charges. Legislation in 1891 added paupers, polygamists, and persons suffering "loathsome" diseases to the excluded list. A similar law in 1903 extended the list of unacceptables to epileptics, prostitutes, professional beggars, and—as a result of the murder of President William McKinley by Leon Czolgosz—anarchists or individuals advocating assassination or violent overthrow of the government. Legislation in 1907 denied entry to imbeciles, victims of tuberculosis, and individuals who had committed crimes involving moral turpitude.

As the movement of immigrants from southern and eastern Europe accelerated at the end of the nineteenth century and into the first two decades of the twentieth, the pressure for curbs on immigration increased. The 1890s and early 1900s were the heyday of Anglo-Saxon supremacy, a period when many Americans believed that Darwinism had proved the superiority of British and American civilization. But immigrants from southern and eastern Europe were not Anglo-Saxons. Fearing that America's "superior" Anglo-Saxon civilization might suffer fatal contamination, nativists wanted to restrict the movement of "inferior" people from the south and east of Europe to the United States.

Literacy Tests Attempt to Restrict Immigration

To campaign for curbs on immigration, particularly from southern and eastern Europe, the Immigration Restriction League was organized in 1894. Over the next twenty years the league was a leader in the movement to persuade Congress to pass legislation stemming the flow of foreigners to America. What was a suitable method for keeping out immigrants, especially those from the south and east of Europe? Nativists knew that because of extreme poverty, peasants of southern and eastern Europe seldom had an opportunity to go to school and hence could not read or write. They hit upon the literacy test as a means of immigration restriction. A literacy test would appear to be aimed at guarding the country from an influx of ignorant and therefore undesirable people. The true purpose of halting migration from southern and eastern Europe would be obscure.

With the support of Senator Henry Cabot Lodge of Massachusetts, a measure passed Congress in 1896 to exclude any immigrant unable to read forty words of any language. President Grover Cleveland, a man of strong moral convictions, his term about to expire, vetoed the legislation on the ground that it betrayed the American tradition. Attempts to pass literacy test bills in 1898, 1902, and 1906 failed to get by Congress. But the future—an America virtually closed to immigration—was closer.

Nativists then scored a victory on the West Coast against the Japanese. Immigrants from Japan had begun to arrive about the time immigration from China ended, and what native Californians had said about the Chinese they now said about the Japanese. Anti-Japanese organizations appeared, but nativists had scant success against the Japanese until 1906 when the school board of San Francisco ordered Oriental children to attend segregated schools. Word of the order touched off a wave of anti-American demonstrations across Japan, which seriously embarrassed President Theodore Roosevelt's attempt to build better relations with Japan. The outcome was a compromise. Under heavy pressure from the White House, the school board withdrew the segregation order and the governments in Tokyo and Washington negotiated the so-called Gentlemen's Agreement whereby Japan promised to deny passports to laborers wishing to migrate to the United States.

Nativists meanwhile gathered sufficient support in Congress to secure passage of literacy test bills in 1912 and again in 1915, only to see them returned with veto messages by Presidents William Howard Taft and Woodrow Wilson. But World War I, which broke out in Europe in 1914 brought a wave of hatred of foreigners in America and in 1917 Congress passed a literacy test measure over Wilson's veto. The new law, it turned out, was a disappointment to nativists. Italian and Slavic peasants who wanted to come to America learned to read well enough to pass the literacy test. After the armistice of November 1918, large-scale immigration resumed. The proportion of new arrivals from southern and eastern Europe was the same as before passage of the literacy test legislation. More drastic measures seemed in order.

The "Red Scare" Limits Immigration

By 1920 the right psychological moment for more restrictive immigration legislation had arrived. The Bolshevik revolution in Russia in 1917 had produced a "red scare" in the United States, a period in which Americans feared that communist radicals were lurking everywhere, waiting for the chance to topple American society. It was not long before people noted that immigrants were active in the country's radical organizations. Americans by 1920 were also realizing that their crusade to make the world safe for democracy in 1917-18 had failed. There was as much selfish nationalism loose in the world as before the war, and, if anything, less democracy. The result was a new contempt for foreigners and their institutions. Then a sharp economic recession in 1920-21 brought wide unemployment in America, increasing organized labor's desire to curb the flow of foreign workingmen into the country. Finally, the 1920s saw a new outbreak of nativism which was manifested in anti-Semitism and anti-Catholicism and in a renewal of the idea of Anglo-Saxon superiority.

Quota System Established

In 1921 Congress passed legislation limiting the number of people of each nationality who could enter the country the following year to three percent of the number of foreign-born persons of that nationality living in the United States in 1910. With the support of the White House, it extended this measure in 1922 and in 1924 enacted permanent legislation. The act of 1924 had a dual purpose. It placed a ceiling on immigration by limiting the number of individuals who could enter the country annually to 150,000. It clearly aimed to discriminate against immigrants from southern and eastern Europe by establishing a quota for each nationality in proportion to its contribution to the American population in 1890. That year represented the period before most immigrants from southern and eastern Europe had arrived.

The Immigration and Nationality Act of 1965

With the immigration legislation of the 1920s the United States broke with the past. For more than three centuries America had welcomed newcomers, or at least admitted them without restriction, but then it virtually closed its doors. Restrictions based on nationality remained in effect until 1965, when an amendment to the Immigration and Nationality Act abolished the quota system entirely. This most recent law permits entry of 170,000 immigrants yearly from all countries outside the Western Hemisphere and 120,000 from countries inside the Western Hemisphere.

STUDY GUIDE: Most of the post-1880 immigrants were poor and unskilled. They worked and lived in crowded, unsanitary slums in large eastern and midwestern cities. Unable to speak English, they formed their own neighborhood groups.

Many Americans grew increasingly hostile to the new immigrants because of their different languages, customs, and religious beliefs. The Know-Nothing movement of the 1850s heaped attacks on Roman Catholics, while hostility to Orientals led to federal legislation limiting immigration from China. The movement to restrict all immigration grew stronger by the end of the nineteenth century. Public pressure led Congress to pass legislation requiring that immigrants be able to read. World War I and the Bolshevik Revolution in Russia deepened unfriendliness toward all foreigners. During the 1920s new legislation was passed restricting immigration, particularly from southern and eastern Europe.

CITIES

Thomas Jefferson had insisted that cities were the handmaidens of industry, that cities would multiply and become larger in direct proportion to the expansion of industry. He believed that if there were no restrictions upon industrialization American society would one day be essentially urban. And so it happened in the era of rapid industrial growth in America. For, like giant magnets, factories, mines, and refineries attracted an endless stream of people. And it was people who created the cities.

The growth of urban America accelerated dramatically in the closing decades of the nineteenth century. By 1880 New York City's population numbered a million, ten years later a milion and half (not counting Brooklyn, which at the time was considered separately in population surveys). Chicago's population soared from a half million in 1880 to a million in 1890 to a million and a half in 1900. In the decade of the

1880s the population of Minneapolis–Saint Paul trebled; that of Detroit, Milwaukee, Columbus, and Cleveland increased by sixty to eighty percent.

What did this phenomenal growth of cities mean? It meant that by the turn of the twentieth century the United States was well on the way to becoming a great urban republic.

Immigration—a Source of Urban Growth

Many of the new urban dwellers were immigrants who were attracted by the excitement as well as the educational and cultural opportunities of the city. For example, even though the large majority of Scandinavian immigrants had some money and preferred the agrarian way of life, nonetheless, some 70,000 Scandinavians were living and working in Chicago by 1890, another 50,000 in Minneapolis–Saint Paul. Most Germans also preferred life in the countryside, but in Milwaukee, Saint Louis, Louisville, and Cincinnati one commonly heard

This 1881 engraving from *Leslie's* shows New York City health officers vaccinating Russian and Polish immigrants on board the steamship *Victoria*. Why did vast numbers of Eastern Europeans emigrate to the United States after 1880? How would you feel upon arriving in a totally new environment?

Library of Congress

the German language and saw newspapers printed in German. Poles, Italians, Russians, Czechs, Greeks, Serbs, and other immigrants also settled in cities.

So great was the rush of immigrants to cities that by 1890 a fourth of Philadelphia's population and a third of Boston's were of foreign birth. In that same year, 1890, four out of five of the inhabitants of New York and Brooklyn were immigrants or the children of immigrants, and by the end of the nineteenth century greater New York could boast half as many Italians as Naples, twice as many Irishmen as Dublin, and two and half times as many Jews as Warsaw.

Farmers Move to the City

The other great source of migrants to urban America was rural America.

Many farm families moved to the city because of the loneliness and drabness of life in the countryside. Often it was the farm wife who applied the pressure that took the family to the urban area. As the writer Herbert Quick recorded, women of the farm "in many cases . . . were pining for neighbors, for domestic help, for pretty clothes, for schools, music, art, and the things tasted when the magazines came in." The farm woman also wished to escape rural drudgery. Toiling without the help of electricity —which in recent generations has revolutionized farm life—she often bore the heaviest burdens of the farm family.

The writer Hamlin Garland reported that when he wrote his *Main-Travelled Roads* he had intended to "tell the truth" about farm life in the Middle West. "But I didn't," he went on. "Even my youthful zeal faltered in the midst of a revelation of the lives led by the women on the farms of the middle border. Before the tragic futility of their suffering, my pen refused to shed its ink. Over the hidden chamber of their maternal agonies I drew the veil."

A more important stimulus for the movement from the countryside to cities was the declining economic returns of farming in the latter part of the nineteenth century. Through the decades after the Civil War, except for fleeting periods of prosperity, prices of wheat, cotton, and livestock steadily went down. Farm costs—what the farmer paid for barbed wire, seed, household wares—remained constant or even increased. The farmer therefore had to work harder, sometimes raising twice or three times the quantities

POPULATION DISTRIBUTION

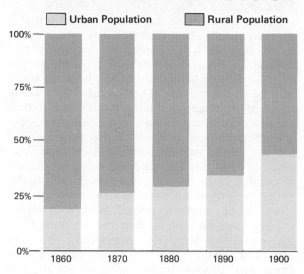

☐ Urban Population   ■ Rural Population

	1860	1870	1880	1890	1900

100%
75%
50%
25%
0%

This graph shows the decline in rural population in the last half of the nineteenth century. What factors led to the migration from farm to city?

The agricultural research of George Washington Carver was one of the bright spots in a picture of declining agricultural opportunity at the turn of the century. By developing many new products from such crops as peanuts, Carver convinced southern farmers that they could profitably grow other crops besides cotton.

of oats or barley as a decade before, simply to maintain his income. The burden often became intolerable.

Then in the closing decades of the nineteenth century the machine came to the farm, enabling the individual farmer to do the work of several hands in the past and creating a surplus of labor in rural America. Put simply, agriculture in those years could not adequately or decently support all the people living in the countryside. The only alternative, it seemed, was for large numbers of farm people to make their way to the city where, hopefully, the factories, mills, and shops would provide a measure of prosperity.

Traffic and Transportation

European travelers to the United States often complained that all American cities were alike. Such complaints were exaggerated, but it was true that a certain sameness characterized America's urban areas. Most, for example, had the checkerboard street pattern (not as picturesque as the winding thoroughfares of Vienna or Paris, but a good deal more convenient). Most also had the same kinds of shops arranged in about the same way, the same kinds of theaters, hotels, and public buildings.

American cities also shared common problems, one of which was traffic. Of New York one observer wrote that "the visitor is kept dodging, halting and shuffling to avoid the passing throng . . . The confusing rattle of 'busses and wagons over the granite pavements in Broadway almost drowns his own thoughts, and if he should desire to cross the street a thousand misgivings will assail him . . . although he sees scores of men and women constantly passing through the moving line of vehicles."

Cities never quite resolved the problems of congestion and haste on thoroughfares. But some did make headway against noise and discomfort caused by cobblestones, granite blocks, and wood blocks. After experimenting with various kinds of paving material, some cities settled on asphalt.

While their increasing populations prevented a completely satisfactory solution to the problem of mass transit, cities nonetheless managed some improvements. In an earlier era horse-drawn streetcars, omnibuses, and cabs had sufficed to move people about America's urban areas. But the new city of the industrial age required facilities that could carry great numbers of people for many miles along crowded streets at considerable speed.

The first attempt to solve the problem came shortly after the Civil War when New York erected an overhead, or elevated, railway. The "el," its web of steel girders protruding above the streets, directly through the heart of the city, was ugly and expensive. The small steam locomotives which powered the original four-car trains scattered hot lubricating oil and ashes on unwary pedestrians below. There was also the noise—the infernal, endless noise. Still, the elevated trains could whisk large numbers of people over congested streets and thus met the need for mass transit facilities in the expanding American city. New York steadily extended its elevated tracks and before the turn of the century Kansas City, Boston, and Chicago had similar facilities.

Less unsightly, noisy, and expensive than the elevated railway (and hence more popular in some cities in the late nineteenth century) was the cable car. Cable cars were introduced in 1873 as a solution to the problem of transit over San Francisco's hilly streets. Power came from a grappling device which connected the car with a steel cable moving in a trench between the tracks. Chicago, Philadelphia, and even New York installed cable systems in the 1880s.

Because the cable car had obvious limits in speed, capacity, and dependability, the electric street railway was introduced. Inventors had spoken of this possibility as far back as the 1830s, but talk achieved nothing because there was no cheap current. Then in the 1870s came the first practicable dynamo which could turn out low-cost electric power. After that the electric street railway was not long in coming. The first successful one appeared in Richmond, Virginia, in 1887-88. The outcome was a revolution in mass transit as cities and towns across the entire country sank rails into their streets and strung trolley wires overhead. With bells clanging and traction motors growling, the new electric streetcars went into operation. The cars were fast, comfortable, clean, and relatively inexpensive. Electric trains, replacing steam, also made elevated railways more tolerable.

The first urban mass transit systems in the United States were elevated railways, or "els." Below is a photograph taken in 1895 of an el which carried passengers through the Bowery, then a busy commercial section of New York City.

Finally there was the underground electric railway—the subway. Transplanted to America from Budapest and London, it was destined to become a symbol of the bustle of urban life. The narrow, winding streets of Boston, which made street railway operations slow and cumbersome, stimulated construction of America's first underground transit system. The first link in the system, only a mile and a half long, began operations in 1897. New York opened a more ambitious subway project in 1904.

Urban transport had another dimension, for most urban areas crossed rivers, streams, or inlets, making bridges necessary. New York's need was most acute, especially when business expansion began to force employees and executives to make their homes outside Manhattan. The first great bridge in the New York area was the Brooklyn Bridge, which was constructed under the direction of Colonel Washington A. Roebling. An invalid, Roebling supervised operations with field glasses while seated in a wheelchair on the roof of his house. Completed in 1883, the Brooklyn Bridge was the longest suspension bridge in the world. Its opening attracted President Chester A. Arthur and governors of several states. Other bridges, such as the Washington Bridge over the Harlem River, soon appeared in the New York area, and in the same period Pittsburgh bridged the Allegheny, Philadelphia the Schuylkill, and Saint Louis was con-

This engraving printed in *Harper's* in 1885 shows a street in Findlay, Ohio, lighted by natural gas. During the nineteenth century most cities depended on gas illumination. What inventions made possible the use of outdoor electric lighting on a large scale?

nected to East Saint Louis by the Eads Bridge over the Mississippi.

Communication and Illumination

Communication became more of a problem in urban America as cities became larger. As early as 1863, New York established free mail delivery within the city but the service was poor. In the words of one New Yorker: "You can send a letter to Boston, or Albany, or Chicago, with a tolerable certainty of its reaching its destination. But if you mail a missive from your office in Pine or William Street to your friend in Gramercy Park, or Lexington Avenue . . . the chances of its ever being heard from are slight."

Then came the telephone.

The telephone developed slowly after being exhibited at the Philadelphia Centennial Exposition in 1876. Part of the problem was excessive static in the original sets. There was also the difficulty of developing a central switchboard and, curiously, there was hostility by many people toward the telephone. Of this hostility one observer explained that "the dignity of talking consists in having a listener and there seems a kind of absurdity in addressing a piece of iron." Whatever the problems and prejudices, the telephone overcame them. By the end of the nineteenth century webs of wires suspended from poles crisscrossed every important city in a thoroughly ugly manner.

As cities became nerve centers of the country, it became necessary to improve long-distance communication. The telegraph had existed since the 1840s, but it had limits. The early telegraph could convey only one message at a time, and it took several hours to compose a brief message, deliver it to a telegraph office, and have it transmitted and delivered in a distant city. It took still more time to get answers to queries. Thus there was an open field for instant, long-distance communication. Seizing this opportunity were developers of the long-distance telephone. By the 1890s the telephone was ten times as popular as the telegraph as a means of communicating between cities. Perhaps the long-distance telephone received its most dramatic test during the presidential campaign of 1896 when Governor William McKinley of Ohio, the Republican candidate, successfully directed his campaign via telephone from his house in Canton.

There was also the problem of illumination.

Lack of satisfactory illumination often restricted urban factory and store operations to daylight hours, reduced the output of writers, artists, and scholars, and increased the hazard of any after-dark activity. For outdoor illumination cities through much of the nineteenth century depended on the dim glow of gas lamps. Indoors city dwellers relied on open-flame gas jets or kerosene lamps. The best hope of meeting the lighting problem seemed to rest with electricity, and for many years inventors turned thought and energy to development of electric illuminating devices.

Electric lighting on a large scale was not possible until a practical dynamo for generating electricity could be produced. Then, in the 1870s, Charles Brush and others resolved the dynamo problem. Inventors soon devised arc lamps which, amid a good deal of sputtering and hissing, provided brilliant outdoor illumination. But arc lights were unsuited for indoor lighting and inventors in Europe and America continued their efforts to produce a small, bright, safe, and inexpensive incandescent light. One of the inventors who attacked the problem was Thomas Edison.

Thomas Edison and His Inventions

While working for a railroad, as a boy, Edison had become acquainted with many telegraph operators, developed an interest in telegraphy, and shortly became a highly competent telegrapher. After several years as a telegrapher, during which time he moved from city to city, Edison decided to migrate to Boston. By the latter 1860s he had become fascinated by electrical equipment, and Boston at that time was the center for the manufacture of fine electrical equipment in America.

Things went well for Edison in Boston and in 1869 he secured a patent on his first invention, an electric vote recorder, a device for recording votes from an audience or legislative gathering. Next he moved to New York where he became a partner in an electrical engineering firm and in the period 1870-75 made several improvements on telegraphic equipment, one of which was refinement of the stock ticker. Edison was not a pure scientist, but a tireless trial-and-error experimenter whose genius lay in a rare ability to take the work and ideas of others, coordinate and improve them, and make them into something practical. By now both Edison's fortune—he received $40,000 from Western Union for his patent on the stock ticker—and reputation were growing. In the year 1876 he built a research laboratory at Menlo Park, New Jersey, gathered about him several other inventors, and in 1877 exhibited one of his most notable creations, the phonograph.

Edison, already widely referred to as "the wizard of Menlo Park," then announced that he would not try to perfect the phonograph, which he mistakenly regarded as a "mere toy." Instead he would turn his energies to the development of incandescent lighting. The entire country took note. When he indicated that he expected to succeed within a short time, leading scientists, who tended to look on him as an untutored upstart, hooted. In their view the problems involved in perfecting a multiple circuit for incandescent lights, not to mention those in developing the light itself, were insoluble.

Undaunted by critics, Edison drove himself and his associates unmercifully in the search for solutions to the problems of incandescent illumination. From his coworkers there was no grumbling, for Edison was a kindly man with a fine sense of humor who never failed to acknowledge the contributions of the "Menlo Park team."

Edison, like other inventors working on an incandescent light, understood that the central problem was to find a material for a filament which would resist intense heat and glow for hundreds of hours in a globe from which nearly all atmosphere had been removed — in a vacuum. But he also recognized that the problem of incandescent lighting was larger than finding a satisfactory filament. It would be necessary to develop a new dynamo to provide constant-voltage current in a multiple circuit and also to find a better method of pumping air from lamp globes so as to obtain a higher vacuum within the globes.

With minimal help from assistants, Edison developed the dynamo in 1878-79 and thus established the foundation for a multiple circuit of small, high-resistance lights. Meanwhile, his associates refined the method of extracting air from globes. During all this time Edison and his men were searching for a filament for the incandescent light. Edison already had decided that carbon was the ideal material for a filament, but the problem was to find a substance that, when carbonized, could withstand intense heat for an extended period. He and his associates experimented with numerous materials. Some glowed for a few minutes but invariably fizzled out. The problem looked hopeless.

Then on the night of October 21, 1879, Edison and his men inserted a carbonized cotton filament in a globe, pumped out the air, and turned on the current. They expected it to fizzle. But it glowed for thirteen and a half hours. Bursting with excitement, Edison and his men prepared other filaments of cotton thread, one of which glowed for forty hours. After this success Edison remarked quietly: "If it can burn that number of hours I know I can make it burn a hundred." To achieve a better incandescent light he dispatched agents to scour the world for a more durable material for a filament. After examining several thousand specimens, Edison found fibers of three types of bamboo and one of cane that suited his purpose. In later developments cellulose, platinum, and eventually tungsten were used for the filament.

In 1880 Edison patented his incandescent lamp. Within an astonishingly short time his invention had spread across the earth, lighting houses, offices, factories, thoroughfares, shops, streetcars, railway coaches, and mines. Edison's light, more than any other invention, transformed life in the urban world, making cities the world over synonymous with "the bright lights."

Water and Waste

Although the incandescent light revolutionized life in urban America, the steps taken to improve sewage and garbage disposal and to assure safe water supplies were at least as important. For as cities became more crowded, the danger of epidemics of typhoid and cholera — diseases closely related to impure water and filth — multiplied.

Many cities in the years after the Civil War had the beginnings of underground sewer systems, but such systems were not expanding rapidly enough. Hence sewage disposal was largely a matter of individual ingenuity. Factories and packinghouses, often located along streams and rivers, dumped their sewage into the streams. Most urban families relied on private vaults and cesspools. So inadequate were the means of getting rid of urban sewage that in 1879 a prominent sanitary engineer called sewage disposal "the great unanswered question of the day."

Garbage disposal presented similar difficulties. Cities along the Atlantic Ocean, such as New York and Boston, sometimes loaded garbage on barges, towed it several miles out to sea, and dumped it on the outgoing tide. Other communities often dumped garbage into the nearest river or stream or contracted with farmers who collected it and fed it to hogs. This sometimes resulted in diseased animals and, ultimately, the appearance of contaminated pork on American dinner tables. Problems of sewage and garbage disposal were closely related to that of assuring safe water supplies. This fact was only vaguely understood by urban leaders, whose main concern in the late nineteenth century was usually securing great quantities of water for their growing cities.

Urban Americans were slow to grasp the relatively new germ theory of disease — and prevention of disease was the critical reason why cities needed to improve sewage and garbage disposal and purify water systems. By the latter part of the nineteenth century, city dwellers were complaining about dirty water and the foul odors resulting from inadequate handling of sewage and garbage. Of the bad odors, a Chicago newspaper in 1880 commented: "The river stinks. The air stinks. People's clothing, permeated by the foul atmosphere stinks. . . . No other word expresses it so well as stink."

Other observers emphasized that inadequate sewage and garbage disposal was a hazard to health. One well-known crusader of the 1870s believed that "sewer gas" and other vapors produced by decaying filth were responsible for most communicable diseases! If cities were going to avoid epidemics, therefore, it was essential that they clean themselves up. He had reached the right conclusion, but for the wrong reasons.

By 1900, urban leaders were sufficiently aware of the germ theory that they began to act vigorously to improve methods of getting rid of sewage and garbage safely. They also took steps to guarantee their cities pure supplies of water, letting contracts to enlarge sewer systems, tightening sanitation codes, making garbage collection and disposal more efficient. New techniques of water filtration and purification went into effect. Although problems of pollution did not disappear, the outcome was a steady decline in urban death rates and, in general, American cities became more healthful places in which to live and bring up families.

Housing

America's cities shared many other problems —crowded schoolrooms, not enough parks and playgrounds, inadequate fire protection, increasing rates of crime and vice. But perhaps the most persistent and serious difficulty was lack of adequate housing. For millions of American urban dwellers incredibly bad housing was probably the worst aspect of life.

Unfortunately a majority of the people—including most immigrants—who streamed into America's cities in the decades after 1850 had no savings and were not regularly employed. They had hardly any prospects of moving up the economic ladder. Thus they could not hope to rent, much less buy, a nice little house in suburbia and had to take what they could find in the core of the urban areas. Many settled into damp, odor-ridden cellars and basements, but most crowded into tenements. Tenements were usually jerrybuilt wooden structures of four or five stories, perhaps thirty feet in width and reaching back from the street as much as 300 feet. Cut up into two-room apartments, a single tenement sometimes housed as many as 800 people. Such accommodations of course were hopelessly inadequate for most families.

There was no escape from tenement life for most working-class people in America's cities. Their lack of marketable crafts tied them to the kind of industrial and menial employment

which they could find only in cities. And their low wages, periodic unemployment, and perpetual indebtedness tied them to tenements.

As the country's urban population increased, the number of tenements increased. Because of its peculiar geography which restricted expansion, New York—built on islands and peninsulas—had more tenements than any other American city. By the closing decade of the nineteenth century, upward of a million and a half New Yorkers were living in tenements. And in one area of the city, covering five or six blocks, nearly 30,000 people were jammed. Probably no area of comparable size in the entire world was so crowded.

Immigrant families often converted apartments into "sweatshops" for the home manufacture of garments or cigars. Ventilation was poor and many of the earlier tenements had interior rooms which had neither windows nor air shafts. Tenements resembled ovens in the summer. In winter they seemed like ice boxes, for only paper-thin walls separated residents from the elements, central heating was usually a dream, and to find warmth families huddled around crude heating stoves. There was little privacy. Sanitation facilities were hopelessly inadequate. In cold weather they often froze, becoming completely useless.

In addition to being crowded and unsanitary, tenements were insect-ridden and rat-infested, and hence were veritable laboratories of disease. One section of New York became known as "lung block" because of the large number of deaths in the area from tuberculosis. The infant mortality rate almost defied belief. A writer in 1892 reported that in two New York alleys the death rate of children under five years of age had reached seventy-three percent.

Family life was next to impossible, for as a prominent sociologist reported in 1919, "home [life] is incompatible with huddling." The incidence of drunkenness, juvenile delinquency, prostitution, and crime in tenement sections was staggering.

Who owned the tenements? Usually the owners were businessmen, often the most respected individuals in their cities. They had their own comfortable residences far from the tenement sections and were interested only in maximum returns from their investments. To assure such returns they imposed excessive rents, knowing full well that most tenement dwellers had no place else to go, and kept improvements and repairs to a minimum. As for public regulation

This engraving was printed in *Harper's* in 1883. It shows New York tenement-house residents trying to find a breath of cool air on a sweltering summer night. What effect did mass immigration have on housing conditions in New York? Do conditions like this still exist today? Why?

of tenements, only a few laws and ordinances emerged to restrict tenement landlords and improve the lot of their tenants. More often than not these laws went unenforced.

The Protestant Religion and Urbanization

Among the more interesting aspects of the history of America's cities after the Civil War was the influence of urbanization on religion.

For churches in urban America the decades after 1865 presented serious challenges. To many working people, caught up in the struggle for survival in a strange urban jungle, religion, particularly as set out in Protestant churches in large cities, appeared irrelevant. Urban workers simply could not see beyond the problems of the present world—low wages, mounting debts, sickness, injury, unemployment—and grasp visions of heaven and hell.

Noted one clergyman in 1887: "Go into an ordinary church on Sunday morning and you see lawyers, physicians, merchants, and business men with their families . . . but the workingman and his household are not there." Another observer wrote that "to the mass of the working men Sunday . . . is a day for labor meetings, for excursions, for saloons, beer-gardens, base-ball games and carousals." Further evidence that Protestant churches were in deep trouble in cities came from figures showing the disappearance of many Protestant congregations in urban areas. For example, between 1868 and 1888 one area of New York gained two hundred and fifty thousand people but lost seventeen Protestant churches.

The relevance of religion in the new urban-industrial era was challenged by radical thinkers who were interested in social and political reform. For example, Karl Marx, the father of modern communism, maintained that religion was an opiate used by the "exploitive classes" to dull the senses of working people so that they would accept the trials of the present world in order to receive a reward of eternal bliss after death.

To win over working people and counter radical critics, some Protestant leaders determined to place less stress on otherworldliness and more on the problems of everyday life. The outcome was the "social gospel" movement. Social gospelers argued that the promise of an eternal reward in heaven must not interfere with achievement of a just society on earth. They emphasized that Christians had a sacred responsibility to assist in removing social and economic abuses. In the words of one spokesman of the social gospel: "If the church members were all doing as Jesus would do, could it remain true that armies of men would walk the streets for jobs, and hundreds of them curse the church, and thousands of them find in the saloon their best friend?"

The social gospel movement was not without influence. It aroused many urban progressives to a concerted attack on social evils. In 1908 it reached a high point with organization of the Federal Council of the Churches of Christ in America, which campaigned forcefully for elimination of factory hazards, abolition of child

[279]

Workingmen's indifference to churchgoing led many Protestant clergymen to play a more active role in improving the quality of city life. A leader in this "social gospel" movement was Dwight L. Moody, shown in this 1875 lithograph with his first Sunday School class of urban youths in Chicago.

Library of Congress

labor, reduction in hours of labor, and a six-day work week.

While the social gospel movement did not bring people rushing back to the churches, it at least demonstrated that some religious leaders were interested in the problems of ordinary people and no longer deserved the charge that they were opposed to reform.

Roman Catholicism and Urbanization

Like Protestantism, Roman Catholicism faced challenges in the era of industrialism and urbanization, but the migration of millions of Catholics from Ireland, Germany, Italy, and eastern Europe in this period brought an increase in the number of Catholics in America. Most of these Catholic immigrants gravitated to the cities of the Northeast and Middle West, and indeed the Catholic church in America became essentially an urban institution.

Because the Catholic church of the latter part of the nineteenth century was largely an immigrant church, many of its members saw their place of worship as a familiar sanctuary, a touch of home. Rich in ceremony, the Roman Catholic church (and also the Orthodox) had a special appeal to the lonely immigrant.

Unlike the leading Protestant churches of the city, many of whose members seemed to be

wealthy bankers and merchants, the Catholic church in urban America was from the beginning a workingman's institution.

The Roman Catholic church in America also had some men among its leaders who were interested in social reform. Most notable of these was James Cardinal Gibbons of Baltimore who recognized at an early date that religion must respond to the material needs of the laboring classes. Accordingly a social gospel movement (although it was not so called) appeared in the Catholic church before it began in the Protestant.

As a result of all the foregoing circumstances, the Catholic church was more successful than the Protestant in holding the support of its members among the working people of America.

The Jewish Faith and Urbanization

Jews, too, were influenced by the urbanization of society in the late 1800s. Earlier in the century there had been perhaps 150,000 Jews scattered throughout the United States. Most were recent immigrants from Germany and many had found prosperity as merchants, accountants, bookkeepers, lawyers, and teachers.

A fair percentage of the Jewish population in America placed some value on religious observance. But other Jewish Americans were sensitive to the intellectual currents of the day, including those which, on the basis of recent scientific discoveries, were attacking the old biblical beliefs. Such Jews often embraced Reform Judaism, which required less of the traditional customs and practices of the Jewish faith and tended to look upon the Bible chiefly as a source of moral and ethical ideas.

Then, beginning in the 1880s, large numbers of Jews from eastern Europe began to arrive in America. Most of these people were fleeing merciless persecution and discrimination. Over the next four decades upward of 2,000,000 Jews from eastern Europe entered the United States. Unlike the German Jews, who had spread over the country, the new immigrants tended to settle in cities and seek employment in industry.

The new arrivals, steeped in Jewish tradition, found Reform Judaism distasteful. To be sure, some Jewish immigrants from eastern Europe were political radicals who scorned all religion, including Judaism. But most of the new Jewish immigrants who clung to religion at all remained faithful to Orthodox Judaism with its time-honored customs and rituals.

In the next generation, some Jews of east European descent found their way into Conservative congregations, which retained many of the old traditions of Orthodoxy yet accepted a few of the changes of Reform Judaism. Others of that generation drifted away from religion. As the sociologist-historian Nathan Glazer has explained in his book *American Judaism,* many of the old Jewish customs and rituals seemed irrelevant or inconsequential in the new industrial-urban society. Even those who abandoned their religion, however, still generally continued to feel attachment to the Jewish community, generously supporting Jewish social and welfare organizations.

Women in an Urban Society

Another important aspect of urbanization was its effect on women, both economically and culturally. In rural America women had been part of an agrarian society, rearing children and managing a farm household. When they moved to the cities, some women took jobs in factories and packinghouses. Others who were more fortunate or better educated became salesladies in urban department stores, secretaries to urban businessmen, telephone operators, elementary school teachers.

The large-scale employment of women had several consequences. Wives who were contributing to the family income often felt less subservient to husbands. One result was a weakening of the husband's authority in the household. Other women, secure in their new economic independence, no longer felt bound to unhappy marriages, and the outcome was a sharp increase in the national divorce rate.

All urban women of course did not seek gainful employment. Some had a considerable amount of leisure and accordingly provided an expanding market for novels and for such periodicals as *Ladies Home Journal* and *Woman's Home Companion,* or became active in organizations such as the Daughters of the American Revolution, the Order of the Eastern Star, and the Women's Christian Temperance Union.

Children in the City

The activities of children of the city comprise another aspect of the story of urbanization in America. Many children had to sell newspapers, shine shoes, or work in factories to help their families scratch out an existence. Others, who were relatively free of restraint while their parents worked long hours away from home, became juvenile delinquents. Still others were able to take advantage of the unique cultural and educational opportunities of the city.

Advantages of City Life

It is so easy to concentrate so intently on the dark side of the story—tenements, noise, smoke, vice, political corruption—that one is apt to overlook the advantages of life in the expanding cities of America. And there were advantages.

Life in the city depended to a large extent on one's economic situation. If an individual had a secure position paying a decent wage he could live comfortably in the city and enjoy many things that were not available to Americans on the farm. For the unskilled workingman who could not find a steady job and whose entire family had to scour the city for whatever employment the individual members could find, the city was a hell-hole.

Compared with the farm and village, the city offered unmatched opportunities for schooling and vocational training. Cities had the resources, financial and organizational, that were necessary for the establishment and maintenance of

The mail-order catalog, vital to rural families, was less important in cities, where many stores awaited the shopper. This 1873 engraving from *Leslie's* shows fashionably gowned women using the elevator on opening day at Lord and Taylor's New York store.

schools. Because of the relative compactness of the city and its rapid transit systems, it was fairly easy for students, children and adults, to get to and from them. The city likewise offered other opportunities for intellectual and cultural advancement little known in rural America—libraries, museums, art galleries, theaters, good music, public lectures. And unlike the countryside, where isolation and loneliness were a heavy burden, the city offered numerous opportunities for recreation and conviviality.

Then there was health. The city had the best physicians, dentists, and hospitals. And one should not overlook the possibility of a balanced diet in the city. It is often thought that the farmer in America, if he had nothing else, had good food. This was not always true. Too many farm families subsisted on salt-pork and black-eyed peas. In the city it was different. Rapid transportation and improved methods of refrigeration provided urban residents with fresh meat, fish, vegetables, fruit, and dairy products.

Finally there were the conveniences of the city. Unlike the woman of the farm, the urban housewife who wanted a new dress did not have to rely on pictures in a mail-order catalog and then wait weeks for the merchandise. Instead she could go "downtown" to the department store, examine the merchandise for quality, make certain of the size, and complete the transaction all in a few hours. There also was home delivery of mail, unknown to the farm family until establishment of rural free delivery in 1896. Running water, eliminating the backbreaking toil of pumping and carrying water, was another convenience. And of course there was electricity. Almost unknown in rural America until the 1930s and 1940s, electricity provided illumination which brightened and enriched the world of the urban dweller.

Art and Literature

The history of urbanization in American society is more than a story of immigration, labor, and the growth of industry. Cities were the nerve centers of an expanding culture that expressed itself creatively in architecture, art, and literature.

The latter part of the nineteenth century was a period of Gothic revival. Ornate and ostentatious, the "psuedo-Gothic" or Victorian architecture of the time was characterized by jigsaw scrollwork, many gables, and long, narrow windows. Fortunately a few architects, notably Louis Sullivan, offered some relief from the showy emptiness of psuedo-Gothic by designing simple, functional buildings that seemed to harmonize with the American environment. As for painting, the period brought forth a few good landscape and portrait painters. Among the best of these were James McNeill Whistler (who, however, did most of his work in England) and Winslow Homer. Perhaps the outstanding American sculptor of the time was Daniel C. French who produced the great bronze statue of Abraham Lincoln for the Lincoln Memorial in Washington.

In literature the latter part of the nineteenth century was the era in which Samuel Langhorne Clemens, better known as Mark Twain, delighted readers around the world with his spirited and irrepressibly democratic writings. These included *The Celebrated Jumping Frog of Calaveras County* (1865), *Innocents Abroad* (1869), *Roughing It* (1872), *The Adventures of Tom Sawyer* (1876), *Life on the Mississippi* (1883), and *The Adventures of Huckleberry*

Finn (1884). During this same period, Louisa May Alcott published *Little Women* (1868–69) and other lively novels describing family life in Victorian America. Charles Waddell Chesnutt, the first black American novelist, published *The Conjure Woman* (1899), a series of stories about the everyday lives of slaves, and Bret Harte wrote colorful accounts of life in the American West.

Many writers of the late 1800s described life as it was in an effort to inform their readers. For example, Stephen Crane wrote *The Red Badge of Courage* (1895), a grimly realistic novel describing the experiences of a young soldier in the Civil War. In 1899 W. E. B. Du Bois published *The Philadelphia Negro,* the first important sociological study of a black community in the United States.

One of America's most important poets, Emily Dickinson, lived during this period, although most of her poetry was not published until many years after her death. Two of the most popular poets of the late 1800s were Eugene Field and James Whitcomb Riley. Paul Laurence Dunbar also won fame with his humorous poems and stories about the lives of blacks in the South.

Some American writers and artists lived in Europe. Henry James lived in London and produced sensitive novels contrasting the cultures and moral standards of the United States and Europe. Among James's outstanding works were *The American* (1877), *Daisy Miller* (1879), and *Portrait of a Lady* (1881). The painter Mary Cassatt lived and worked in France among the French impressionists, and earned acclaim for her pictures of women and children.

STUDY GUIDE: By the early 1900s America was on the verge of becoming a great urban republic. Great numbers of new city dwellers were immigrants. As agricultural prosperity declined, many farm people also made their way to the cities in search of jobs. The growing population of cities created serious problems. Steps had to be taken to improve public transportation, sewage, garbage disposal, and assure safe water supplies. One of the most serious problems was the lack of adequate housing. Thomas Edison's invention of the incandescent light helped to transform life in urban America. Despite the many disadvantages of the city, it did offer unique opportunities for employment as well as intellectual and cultural advancement. The late nineteenth century produced such celebrated writers as Mark Twain and Henry James.

SUMMING UP THE CHAPTER

Names and Terms to Identify

technological unemployment
blacklist
yellow dog contract
lockout
National Labor Union
Uriah Stephens
Knights of Labor
Terence V. Powderly
Haymarket riot
American Federation of
  Labor
La Follette Seamen's
  Act
Samuel Gompers
Wobblies
"new" immigrants
Chinese Exclusion Act
tenement
Winslow Homer
Homestead strike
Hamlin Garland
Henry James

Study Questions and Points to Review

1. What caused the decline in agricultural opportunity during the closing decades of the nineteenth century? How did this decline affect the rural population?

2. List three of the advantages of the machine over man.

3. How did mechanization of industry improve the standard of living in America?

4. What problem did American labor face as a result of the influx of immigrants in the four decades after 1880?

5. Why was it so difficult for labor organizers to establish unions during the nineteenth century?

6. What effect did the Panic of 1873 have on the trade union movement?

7. List three of the major labor acts passed in the half century prior to World War I. What were the provisions of each act?

8. In the development of the incandescent light, what was the central problem? Who resolved the problem? How?

9. Why did New York have more tenements than any other American city?

10. List five of the advantages of life in the city.

11. Be sure you understand the following terms used in this chapter: agrarian, "big business," mechanization, labor-management relations, strikes, unions, boycott, closed shop, agitators, arbitration, wildcat strike, absentee landlord, federation, "right wing," anarchist, sabotage, utopia, pauper, nativists, urbanization, sweatshop. Divide the class into teams. The winning team is the group which can correctly identify most words without using a dictionary.

Topics for Discussion

1. Why did farm families migrate to the cities starting in the late nineteenth century? Do you think they found what they sought? Explain your answer.

2. What was the philosophy of the social gospel movement? Evaluate the movement. Do you think the social gospelers accomplished their aims?

3. Name three methods of transportation that were used in urban areas to solve the problem of mass transit. Which method do you think was most successful? Which method do you think has created the greatest and least problems for our environment?

4. Explain the differences between craft unions and industrial unions. What are the advantages and disadvantages of each? Which type of union do you think better advances the interests of labor? Why?

5. What problems in Europe prompted migration to the United States? From which countries did most immigrants come before 1880? After 1880? How did native-born Americans receive the immigrants?

6. What prompted the rapid growth of cities in America after 1850? What problems were created because of this rapid urbanization? Do many of those problems exist today?

7. Grover Cleveland vetoed the legislation that would have excluded immigrants unable to read forty words of any language. Do you think he was justified in this action? Explain your answer.

Subjects for Reports or Essays

1. Conduct a poll in your class or neighborhood to determine local opinion on organized labor. Tabulate your results and prepare a report noting similarities and differences between current attitudes as revealed in your poll and attitudes of people in earlier periods.

2. Prepare a report on one of the following topics: (a) The immigrant and religion; (b) Black men in the labor movement; (c) Impact of the incandescent light on American life; (d) Post-Civil War urbanization in America; (e) Religion and urbanization.

3. The year is 1890. Assume you are a recent immigrant from Europe. Write a letter to a friend or relative in your native land describing your life in the United States.

4. Compile a list of immigrants and children of immigrants who have achieved prominence in America. For each person you list, give the land of origin and major accomplishment.

Projects, Activities, and Skills

1. Collect newspaper or magazine articles which favor or oppose positions taken by labor unions, and post them on your class bulletin board.

2. Using Table 20 in the Appendix, prepare a chart showing labor union membership for the period 1897 to 1915. Which unions show the greatest increase in membership? The least?

3. Using Table 8 in the Appendix, make a graph showing immigrants to America for the years 1820 through 1915.

4. Using a map of the United States and symbols of your own design, prepare a display showing the areas of the United States where immigrants of different nationalities preferred to settle.

Further Readings

General

American Cities: Their Historical and Social Development by Edwin Hoag. The development of the United States as reflected in the growth of its major cities.

American Labor by Henry Pelling. Covers 300 years of labor history in the United States.

A History of Urban America by Charles N. Glaab and A. Theodore Brown. Covers the period from colonial times to the present.

The Rise of the City, 1878-1898 by Arthur M. Schlesinger, Sr. An examination of the urbanization of the United States.

Strangers in the Land by John Higham. An excellent book on immigration.

The Uprooted by Oscar Handlin. A prize-winning study of the effects of immigration.

Biography

The Bending Cross: A Biography of Eugene Victor Debs by Ray Ginger.

Edison by Matthew Josephson.

The Making of an American by Jacob Riis. The autobiography of an immigrant.

The Path I Trod by Terence V. Powderly. The life of the leader of the Knights of Labor.

Fiction and Poetry

Maggie: A Girl of the Streets by Stephen Crane. This is considered America's first realistic novel.

Main-Travelled Roads by Hamlin Garland. Stories about Midwestern farm people.

The Rise of David Levinsky by Abraham Cahan. An immigrant wins wealth but not happiness.

Sister Carrie by Theodore Dreiser. A country girl in Chicago in the 1890s.

CHAPTER 9
POLITICS

AMERICA, IN EARLIER TIMES—particularly in the era of Hamilton and Jay, Jefferson and Madison—contributed much to the theory and art of government. However, the years after the Civil War were not a great period in America's political history. Perhaps Americans were so taken up with building railroads and developing western lands and industry that politics received only secondary attention. Perhaps the most energetic and talented people of the country preferred to seek the profits of business enterprise rather than the meager rewards of public service. Whatever the reasons, government at all levels—local, state, national—was weak, lethargic, and inefficient. Corruption seemed to be everywhere. Hamstrung by the arid ideas of laissez-faire and Social Darwinism, politicians seldom responded to appeals for reform. Instead they stood by while land was pillaged, laborers were oppressed, and consumers were cheated.

The top of the American political system is the presidency. And in those years after Appomattox the White House mirrored the shortcomings of politics across the width and breadth of the republic. Presidents of the era tended to be men of modest intellect, vision, and resourcefulness. They were often blind to the corruption and "influence-peddling" surrounding them. Essentially they were "party men" who were promoted to the presidency with the support of conservative financial and industrial interests. They were chosen in the belief that they were cautious in fiscal matters, would do nothing rash in foreign affairs, and would not flirt with any "radicals" who might entertain ideas of social and economic reform.

ELECTION OF 1868

The first presidential election after the Civil War took place in 1868. One might have expected the Republicans to look forward confidently to victory. Under the patient and determined leadership of Abraham Lincoln, they had guided the North to triumph in the war of 1861-65 and kept the federal Union together. Conversely, their Democratic opponents carried a taint of treason. Most Confederates had been prewar Democrats and during the war the Democratic party had been honeycombed with southern sympathizers or Copperheads.

Moreover, carpetbag regimes in the southern states had arranged to take away the vote of many white citizens who, if given the chance, would doubtless have voted Democratic. They had put on the voting lists tens of thousands of former slaves who were certain to mark their ballots for Republican candidates. However, the prospects of the Republican party in the preceding two or three years had suffered serious divisions, while the Democratic had experienced an amazing recovery. Hence, defeat for the Republicans in 1868 seemed quite within the realm of the possible.

What had happened? How had the Republicans lost the esteem built up in 1861-65? The answer lies in the political whirlwind built up in the years 1865-68 by controversies which were legacies of the war. Most notable of these problems were Reconstruction of the South and a knotty situation resulting from the federal government's issuance of several hundred million paper, or "greenback," dollars to meet the expense of putting down the Confederate rebellion.

The controversy over Reconstruction brought deep divisions in the Republican party. Supporters of a harsh policy toward the South, the so-called Radicals, gained the upper hand in the party's councils and, via their representatives in Congress, undid the Lincoln-Johnson program of generous treatment of the South. Many Republicans who disliked Radicalism drifted toward the Democratic party.

Reconstruction gave the Democrats a heaven-sent issue with which to rally their party, attract unhappy Republicans, and compel political independents of the North to forget that during the war the conduct of many northern Democrats had bordered on treason. Accordingly the Democratic party, which had become the advocate of leniency toward the South, and which

HEADLINE EVENTS

1865-1871 Tweed Ring active in New York
1867 Nebraska enters the Union
1868 Congress passes anticontraction bill
1869 Ulysses Grant inaugurated president
Grant signs legislation redeeming bonds for gold
Gold conspiracy
1870 Fenian Brotherhood broken up
1871 Treaty of Washington; *Alabama* dispute settled
1872 Crédit Mobilier scandal made public
1873 Grant inaugurated for second term
Grant signs "salary grab" legislation
Congress demonetizes silver; "the Crime of '73"
Economic panic
Spaniards seize *Virginius*
1875 Specie Resumption Act signed
1876 Disputed election of Hayes-Tilden
Greenback party appears
Colorado enters the Union
1877 Rutherford B. Hayes inaugurated president
Last federal troops withdrawn from South
1878 Bland-Allison Act
1879 Specie Resumption Act becomes effective
1881 James A. Garfield inaugurated president
Chester A. Arthur succeeds to presidency upon assassination of Garfield
1883 Pendleton Civil Service Reform Act
Mongrel Tariff Act
1885 Grover Cleveland inaugurated president
1887 Interstate Commerce Act
Dawes Act
1889 Benjamin Harrison inaugurated president
First Inter-American Conference
1885 Grover Cleveland inaugurated president
North Dakota enters the Union
South Dakota enters the Union
Montana enters the Union
Washington enters the Union
1890 Sherman Silver Purchase Act
Idaho enters the Union
Wyoming enters the Union
McKinley Tariff Act
Sherman Antitrust Act

could even claim to be the champion of the Reconstruction ideas of the great Lincoln, had experienced a remarkable renaissance.

The Greenback Issue

During the Civil War the federal government issued $450 million in "temporary" paper currency—a no-interest loan extracted by the government. Unsupported by gold—that is, one could not take a "greenback" dollar to a federal mint and secure a gold dollar in exchange—these famous green dollars went up and down in value. Sometimes they would purchase, in terms of gold, about seventy cents in goods and services, sometimes as little as forty cents. At the time Lee surrendered in spring 1865, some $400 million in greenback currency was still circulating. This situation gave rise to two issues of great political importance in the years 1865-68. First, with which kind of currency, gold dollars or greenbacks, should the government redeem bonds which it had sold during the war? And second, should the government reduce the volume of greenback currency in circulation or should it perhaps eliminate greenbacks altogether?

As for the bonds, their purchasers, in many cases eastern bankers, had usually purchased them with depreciated greenback currency. Now that the war was over, purchasers were pressing for redemption of both principal and interest in gold, which meant that bondholders hoped to make a killing. For example, a bond paid for in 1864 with greenback currency worth perhaps $40 in gold, if redeemed in gold, might by 1869 bring its owner $120 or more. The prospect of a bonanza for bondholders did not strike fire with individuals who did not own bonds, particularly farmers and workingmen, who would have to pay increased taxes if the government decided to redeem bonds in gold. In the view of most people who did not own bonds, the government should redeem bonds with greenbacks unless otherwise specified in the fine print of the bonds.

For bankers and other creditor groups—that is, the same people who held the bonds—reducing the volume of greenbacks seemed a great idea. A tightening of the money supply by reducing the number of dollars in circulation would cause the dollar to become more valuable. In other words, it would increase purchasing power. This would mean that dollars received in repayment of loans would purchase more goods and services than those lent a few years before. As with redemption of bonds in gold, the financial interests of the country stood to realize a windfall if the federal government withdrew quantities of greenbacks from circulation. Conversely, for debtor groups — and most farmers and workingmen had debts of one kind or another — the prospect of reduction of greenbacks was frightening. Debtors would have to repay obligations at face value. If the dollar became "dear," as it probably would if the government withdrew many greenbacks, prices and wages would fall. Debtors would thus find it much more difficult to raise the money to retire obligations than anticipated when they contracted them. If anything, debtors wanted more greenbacks, which would reduce the value of or cheapen the dollar, bring increases in prices and wages, and make repayment of debts easier.

With the approval of President Johnson, the Treasury Department in 1867 withdrew several million dollars in greenbacks. This step brought howls from debtors across the entire country. Whatever their private sentiments on contraction, members of Congress — Republican and Democratic alike — feared retaliation by their constituents, for the country had far more debtors than creditors. Accordingly, in early 1868 Congress passed an anticontraction bill which suspended the authority of the secretary of the treasury to reduce the volume of greenbacks in circulation. With that act, contraction of greenbacks temporarily ceased to be a political issue and had little bearing on the election of 1868.

The Bond Redemption Question

Although the contraction question slipped into the shadows, the matter of bond redemption remained front and center. When the political campaign of 1868 began to take shape, it was clear that the bonds would share the spotlight with Reconstruction as a central issue.

Where did the two parties stand on the bond redemption question? Their party having become a haven for businessmen and other economic conservatives, Republican leaders, despite the sentiments of Republican farmers and workingmen, stood for redeeming the bonds with gold. The leaders were persuasive, and delegates to the Republican national convention in Chicago in May 1868 dutifully praised Radical Reconstruction of the South and endorsed the leadership's ideas on the bonds.

Brown Brothers

At the Republican national convention of 1868, party leaders agreed that they needed a presidential candidate popular enough to make the public forget the issues of Reconstruction and greenbacks. In this drawing, a delegate nominates their choice — Ulysses S. Grant.

As for the Democrats, they were united in the belief that Radical Reconstruction should end and the South be returned to control of the former Confederates. But they had a hard time making up their minds on currency matters, for the Democratic party also had many businessmen in its ranks and was only slightly less conservative than the Republican. Only after extended debate did delegates to the party's national convention in New York, in July 1868, endorse the so-called Ohio idea. This plan proposed that the government should repay the national debt by redeeming the bonds with greenbacks, except of course when bonds specified repayment in gold.

The Republicans claimed that they were upholding the country's honor for, according to Republican logic, it would be a betrayal of the national integrity if bonds purchased with greenback currency were not redeemed with gold. The Democratic position, however, had wide popular appeal and increased the party's chances of winning the election.

Republican leaders understood that their party's position on Reconstruction and bond redemption was certain to alienate many voters. But the political history of the American republic offered ample evidence that a popular candidate for the presidency could bring people to forget a party's stand on issues. So the need of the Republicans in 1868 was to nominate a candidate to head the national ticket who would attract a great popular response. This presented no problem, for Ulysses S. Grant, the war hero of Vicksburg and Appomattox, was quite willing to lead the party. At the Republican national convention, Grant won the party's presidential nomination on the first ballot. Fresh out of heroes, the Democrats at length settled on Horatio Seymour as their presidential candidate. Who was Seymour? Many people asked that question in 1868. He was an undistinguished former governor of New York.

The campaign of 1868 was fierce. "Waving the bloody shirt," Republican orators reminded voters that men of the South who labeled themselves Democrats had authored the recent rebellion and that the infamous Copperheads of the North who had supported the South during the Civil War had also been Democrats. They hammered at the theme that a Democratic victory in the coming election would bring a return of former Confederates to power in the South. It was hardly necessary to add that such a turn of events would constitute a gross betrayal of the "boys in blue" who lay buried at Gettysburg and Chickamauga. Democrats countered—in an open appeal to racist sentiments which were only slightly less intense in the North than in the South—that Republicans sought social, political, and economic equality for American Negroes.

The effect of such appeals is hard to measure. On the issues of the campaign—Reconstruction and bond redemption—it is probable that a fair majority of the country's voters favored Democratic positions. But many northerners, recalling the sacrifices of the recent war and revering the memory of the martyred Republican president, Abraham Lincoln, could not bring themselves to vote for Democratic candidates, whatever the issues.

Grant himself did not take an active part in the campaign. He did not need to. In the view of millions of Americans, the general stood above politics. And therein rested much of his appeal. Caught up over the past decade in endless controversy and tension, much of it, they thought, the doing of stupid and grasping politicians, Americans by 1868 were sick and tired of politics. In Grant they thought they saw a man who was intelligent, resourceful, and generous, a man who somehow would lead the country out of tension and discord. They saw Grant as a man who would restore the tranquillity and unity that people fondly thought had prevailed in earlier generations.

On election day a majority of the country's voters marked their ballots for tranquillity, against professional politicians, for the memory of Lincoln—that is, they voted for Grant. And Grant won overwhelmingly in the electoral college. Still, even Grant could not compel a large part of the electorate to forget the issues. Out of more than five and half million votes cast, the general's popular margin over Seymour was only three hundred thousand. It seems fair to say that if disfranchisement of former Confederates, arranged by Radical Republicans over the previous two years, had not kept great numbers of southern whites from going to the polls, Seymour might have made it to the White House, in spite of his deficiencies.

STUDY GUIDE: In the years after the Civil War the American political system was weak, corrupt, and inefficient. By 1868, dislike for Radical Reconstruction had turned many voters away from the Republican party. The Republicans also lost support among farmers and workingmen. Republicans took the position that bonds sold during the war should be redeemed with gold. On this issue they sided with business interests who stood to lose money if the bonds were redeemed with cheap greenback currency. However, the immense popularity of the Republican candidate, General Ulysses S. Grant, hero of the Civil War, led the party to victory over the little known Democratic candidate, Horatio Seymour.

PRESIDENT GRANT FACES MANY PROBLEMS

What qualifications did Grant bring to the presidency when he took office in 1869?

Only forty-six years old at the time of his inauguration and thus a comparatively young occupant of the White House, Grant was alert and vigorous. He seemed to have a mind that was perceptive, orderly, and resolute. A kindly man, he got along well with people and was an effective public speaker. The prewar years when he had been accused of drinking too much had been lived down. He had dignity and integrity and despite his great military reputation had remained uncomplicated and unpretentious. Happily married, he was a dedicated husband and father. These of course were the qualities that had attracted voters in the election of 1868.

And they were not bad qualities for a president to have. If Grant had also possessed basic political skills, a sound knowledge of America's political mechanism, and a clear understanding of the problems pressing down on American society, he might have become a highly successful national leader.

Grant, however, remained a political innocent. Only recently had he begun to take an interest in politics. Before 1868 he had voted in only one presidential election, in 1856, when he cast a ballot for the Democratic candidate, James Buchanan. He had at best a misty comprehension of the federal Constitution, the responsibilities and powers of the presidency, and the relation between the executive and other branches of the national government.

Accustomed to military organization in which lines of authority and divisions of responsibility were clear and precise, Grant found the world of politics a jungle. People seemed to be going all ways at once and nobody knew for sure who was doing—or who was supposed to do—what. He found his new environment confusing. Because he was a good man who tended to believe that most other people also were good, particularly if they were his friends, Grant was an easy mark for clever politicians and privilege-seekers. Moreover, Grant had not the slightest wish to exercise strong presidential leadership. He saw his role as essentially administrative—to carry out the dictates of Congress. Or as Senator John Sherman of Ohio, the brother of the renowned General Sherman, put it: "The executive department of a republic like ours should be subordinate to the legislative department. The President should obey and enforce the laws, leaving to the people the duty of correcting errors committed by their representatives in Congress."

Crying out for solutions during the time of Grant's terms, 1869-77, were a host of problems —Reconstruction, the rampaging growth of industry, urban expansion, and immigration. Because of the great reservoir of prestige and goodwill he had accumulated, Grant had an unusual opportunity to attack the problems. (One must acknowledge, however, that the restrictions of laissez-faire and Social Darwinism would have inhibited even the most talented and determined president.)

Unfortunately Grant grasped only faintly, if at all, what was happening in American society. He just did not understand the problems. Even if he had understood, he lacked the political know-how and, equally serious, the will to lead. Therein lay much of the tragedy of the Grant presidency.

Of the national questions that did make their way to the presidential desk during Grant's terms, the foremost were Reconstruction, greenbacks, the tariff, and civil service reform.

Reconstruction

As for Reconstruction, Grant did not share the vindictiveness toward the South of other prominent Republicans and genuinely hoped for a hasty end to ill feelings between the sections. He expressed this view in his speech accepting the Republican nomination for president in summer 1868: "Let us have peace." But like most Republicans he sought to guarantee civil equality for former slaves and found that objective inconsistent with the goal of achieving sectional reunion. Such reunion could come, it seemed, only at the expense of the freedmen, that is, by turning southern politics back to the former Confederates. Accordingly Grant continued the Radical program of southern Reconstruction.

When southern whites reacted violently, he approved the Force and Ku Klux Acts, authorizing suppression of disturbances by military force and suspension of the writ of habeas corpus. When the violence continued, he used the powers given him by the new legislation. He did not hesitate to dispatch federal troops to maintain Republican, or carpetbag, governments in South Carolina, Arkansas, Alabama, Mississippi, and Louisiana.

The Greenback Issue

On the question of bond redemption, Grant stood by the Republican platform of 1868. As a consequence, one of his first acts on becoming president in 1869 was to sign legislation for redeeming the bonds with gold. On the question of contracting greenbacks, Grant, like other politicians of both parties, weighed the political mathematics of the situation, concluded that most voters were "pro-greenback," and then placed himself on their side. Indeed the Grant regime enlarged the volume of greenback currency in circulation.

Grant recognized, however, as did most Americans, that it was bad business for the country to circulate currency whose value went up and down in relation to gold. In effect the country had a first-class currency and a second-class currency. Near the end of his second term, in 1875, Grant supported the Specie Resumption Bill, which committed the government to exchange a dollar in gold for a greenback dollar. With this stroke, which became effective in 1879, the greenback dollar achieved parity with gold. When the holder of a greenback was secure in the knowledge that he could exchange his greenback for gold, he was perfectly willing to accept the greenback at "gold value" for his goods or services.

The Tariff Issue

On the tariff issue, Grant found himself caught up in ancient arguments over the merits of protection. As they had been for generations, farmers were the most vocal opponents of protection. They argued that high tariffs, which reduced foreign competition for American manufacturers, forced up retail prices for household goods, shoes, clothing, and farm implements. Because of the absence of foreign competition, farmers paid higher prices for American-made goods. In fact—so the argument went—they were paying a subsidy to domestic manufacturers. Or, to put it another way, the tariff took some of the farmer's profit and transferred it to the pocket of the manufacturer.

If agriculture had received some comparable advantage or compensation in return, tariff protection for industry might have been tolerable. But farmers, so far as they could see, got nothing from the tariff except the privilege of paying higher prices. Manufacturers disagreed. They argued that a large and healthy manufacturing apparatus would function to the benefit of all Americans, farmers included. If American manufacturing, still in its infancy, was to mature and become prosperous, however, it was necessary to protect it, via high tariffs on imports from overseas—especially from Europe.

Grant lined up with the manufacturers. Whether he was moved by their logic or the knowledge that they were heavy contributors to Republican campaign funds is an open question. Still, Grant could not completely ignore increasing popular sentiment against high tariffs and on the eve of the election of 1872 signed legislation which reduced rates on many imports as much as ten percent. His conversion to the idea of lower tariffs was short-lived, however, and soon

after the election he signed a bill restoring duties to former levels.

Civil Service

Regarding civil service reform, an increasingly outspoken element of the national population was urging elimination or at least modification of the "spoils system" of filling political jobs with the party faithful. In the view of civil service reformers, ability, integrity, and initiative should be the criteria for making appointments. The public servant who exhibited such qualities should be guaranteed against dismissal after the next election. Reformers looked hopefully to Grant for support, and in the year 1871 the president pledged a fair trial for a list of reforms proposed by a civil service commission. Unfortunately he failed to live up to his word and continued to fill government positions with Republicans who had proved their loyalty to the party.

STUDY GUIDE: Grant was totally lacking in basic political skill and knowledge. He failed to understand the great problems facing a growing industrial society. He continued the Radical program of Reconstruction and supported the Republican party positions on bond redemption and a high protective tariff. To win popular support, however, the Republicans put more greenback currency in circulation. Grant also supported the Specie Resumption Act, which made a greenback dollar equal in value to a dollar in gold. Grant failed to make good on his pledge to reform the civil service.

LIBERAL REPUBLICANISM AND THE GRANT SCANDALS

Partisan politics in America being what they were, Grant's response to Reconstruction, greenbacks, the tariff, and civil service reform was bound to feed the opposition Democratic party. As it turned out, the hostility which Grant and the Grant regime aroused was not confined to Democrats; many Republicans felt alienated by the eighteenth president and his policies. Accordingly the winds of revolt within the Republican party had reached gale proportions as 1872, an election year, approached. The outcome was the so-called Liberal Republican movement.

Liberal Republicanism began to take shape as soon as Grant's weaknesses as a political leader and his policies became apparent. Many disgruntled Republicans decided that Grant, whatever his personal virtues and past triumphs as a soldier, did not have and never would acquire the capacity to preside effectively over the national destiny. The president's stand on issues, particularly Reconstruction and civil service reform, did not help him. Most anti-Grant Republicans by 1870 had lost any sympathy they might ever have felt for Radicalism. In their view the Radical experiment had failed and indeed had made a bad situation worse. Hence the time had come to end Radical Reconstruction of the South and begin to restore sectional unity, whatever the cost to the freedmen. As for the civil service, most anti-Grant Republicans were obsessed with the idea of reform of the spoils system. These anti-Grant, Liberal Republicans were divided on the other issues of the day, particularly with respect to the tariff. But their differences seemed trivial when measured against the unifying hostility to Grant.

The anti-Grant Republicans came together in national convention at Cincinnati in spring 1872 and organized the Liberal Republican party. The meeting included some of the most respected and able men in American politics — Carl Schurz of Missouri, Chief Justice Salmon P. Chase, and Charles Francis Adams, Lincoln's ambassador to Great Britain. The new party seemed an oasis in the desert of American politics. But then weaknesses began to appear. Differences on such knotty issues as the tariff proved more divisive than expected and from the outset the party lacked cohesion. About all the members agreed on was that Radical Reconstruction was bad, civil service reform was good, and Grant was unfit for the presidency.

Compounding their difficulties, the Liberal Republicans passed over such illustrious political figures as Chase and Adams and handed the nomination to Horace Greeley, the editor of the New York *Tribune*. Greeley was a renowned newspaperman and had intellect, integrity, and ideals. But he had no political stature and little political know-how. His earlier support of such "far out" movements as spiritualism and vegetarianism also made him an easy target for opponents.

Seeing an opportunity to overturn Grant, the Democrats also endorsed Greeley in 1872. For a time there was hope that the coalition of liberal Republicans and Democrats could put the famous editor in the White House. But it was no use. Grant could appeal to the hallowed memory of Lincoln, while lesser Republican orators "waved the bloody shirt." The Grant organization, moreover, was lubricated by lavish contributions by manufacturing and banking interests. The result was a landslide victory for the president, who carried all but six states. Tired and disillusioned, Greeley died three weeks after the election.

Greeley's candidacy might have fared better in autumn 1872 if the electorate had caught a scent of the corruption that was permeating the upper levels of government during those years.

The Gold Conspiracy

In the first months of his presidency Grant had revealed his vulnerability to the powers of smooth-talking charlatans. Two prominent speculators, Jay Gould and James Fisk, both of whom had already established reputations for industrial piracy by their parts in the looting of the Erie Railroad, set about to make a killing in the gold market. To achieve their purpose they planned to corner the gold market and then withhold gold from sale. This move was sure to create panic among numerous speculators and brokers who had made contracts for the future delivery of gold in the expectation that in the meantime the price of gold would go down. (The difference between the contract price and the price they paid for the gold on the date of delivery would be profit.) Pressed to fulfill their contracts, the unfortunate speculators and brokers would have no choice but to buy the gold of Fisk and Gould. As the speculators and brokers scrambled to purchase the Gould-Fisk gold, the price would naturally go up and up — and the unsavory gentlemen Fisk and Gould would reap a fortune.

There was one possible stumbling block. The federal government owned a large reserve of gold which it tapped periodically to retire obligations. If the scheme of Gould and Fisk was to work, it would be necessary to make certain that when the price of gold began to climb, the government did not dump some of its gold in the market and thus force the price down. To guard themselves against that possibility, Gould and Fisk cast their eyes toward the president. When Grant visited New York, they entertained him lavishly while filling his head with the argument that any government interference with the gold market would delay the movement of crops to market and have a depressing effect on the entire economy. Meanwhile they also gave a piece of the action to Grant's brother-in-law, a small-time speculator. Next, as they began their maneuver, Gould and Fisk passed the word that they had influenced the president and that he would not authorize the Treasury Department to place federal gold on the market. Everything went perfectly. Gould and Fisk cornered the market. Panicky speculators and brokers rushed forward to buy gold from Fisk and Gould before the price went even higher.

At that point, in September 1869, Grant saw through the conspiracy. He directed the secretary of the treasury to put enough gold on the market to break the Fisk-Gould corner and send the price plunging. Still, numerous speculators and legitimate Wall Street brokers had already suffered irreparable harm. Moreover, Grant's reputation for competence, and also the dignity of the presidency, was tarnished. The affair was a "straw in the wind," a hint that corrupt men might be operating at high levels in the government. Unfortunately few Americans saw the "straw."

The Crédit Mobilier scandal during Grant's administration ended the political career of his vice-president, Schuyler Colfax. Colfax was accused of accepting bribes. Why did political corruption flourish in the post-Civil War era?

Crédit Mobilier Scandal

As the political campaign of 1872 was nearing its climax, the country began to piece together the shoddy tale of Crédit Mobilier. This was the construction company cleverly used by directors of the Union Pacific Railroad to fleece the railroad's stockholders. (See Chapter 7.) The Crédit Mobilier operation had got under way long before Grant became president, which perhaps explains why initial reports of the monstrous swindle did no damage to Grant's reelection campaign. After Grant entered the White House, in 1869, the Crédit Mobilier carried on and, nervous about the possibility of exposure by "do-gooders" in Washington, leaders of Crédit Mobilier brought members of Congress and officials of the Grant administration into the conspiracy by selling them stock in the company or giving it to them "on time."

The "Salary Grab"

While Americans were becoming increasingly aware of the dimensions of the Crédit Mobilier scandal, and at the same time increasingly suspicious of their leaders in Washington, Grant, in early 1873, signed the "salary grab." This

piece of legislation doubled the salary of the president and raised salaries of congressmen by fifty percent. If the pay increases seemed excessive, what really aroused the public was a provision of the measure making the raises for members of Congress effective for the past two years. Congress, so people calculated, had raided the Treasury by voting each of its members $5,000 of "back salary." In the face of a strong popular reaction, Congress quickly repealed the measure and restored old pay scales. But the affair gave further evidence of the greed and moral laxity that had pervaded Grant's administration.

A few days after the "salary grab," Grant rode up Pennsylvania Avenue to the Capitol and for the second time took the oath as president. Hardly had the sounds of the inaugural festivities died away before new scandals began to come to light. Grant's secretary of the navy had lined his pockets by selling naval contracts; his minister to England had become entangled in a mining swindle; and his minister to Brazil had defrauded the Brazilian government of $100,000 and then fled to Europe. His secretary of war had sold franchises for trading posts on Indian reservations; his own private secretary had assisted officials of the Treasury Department in swindling the government of millions of dollars in taxes on distilled liquors—the so-called

After the Panic of 1873, workers faced the prospect of unemployment or reduced wages. Railroad workers refused to accept a pay cut and a strike began in Martinsburg, West Virginia. Railway workers attacked non-striking "scab" workers. State troops were called, and finally President Hayes sent troops into three states. The defeated workers were forced to accept pay cuts. One hundred men died and over ten million dollars worth of property damage was done as a result of the strike.

Frank Leslie's Illustrated Newspaper, August 4, 1877.

Whiskey Ring scandal. The customs houses in New York and New Orleans, headed by Grant appointees, were corrupt.

Political corruption in the era after the Civil War was not confined to the national government. The bloody conflict of 1861-65, the bitterness of Reconstruction, and the confusions of the accelerating industrial-urban revolution had seriously weakened old ethical and moral restraints. These developments were reflected in politics—not just in Washington but in state capitals, cities, and hamlets across the entire republic. State leaders peddled their influence to railroads, prison lessees, and manufacturers. Municipal officials freely awarded franchises for trolley lines to the business interests that offered the officials the largest bribes. They bought up vacant land at low prices and then dramatically increased its value by connecting it with street-car tracks, sewers, and water lines.

The Tweed Ring affair—next to Crédit Mobilier the best-remembered scandal of the Grant years—had nothing to do with federal officials. It involved unsavory political operatives and businessmen in New York City. To place exclusive blame for the rampant political corruption of the day at the door of the White House, therefore, is unfair. No president could have prevented evil in that expansive time. Still, it is hard to escape the conclusion that Grant unwittingly contributed to the breakdown of public morality by trusting too much and failing to move hard and fast against wrongdoing in high places when its existence became apparent.

The postwar wave of extravagance and prosperity came momentarily to an end in autumn 1873 when financial panic hit the United States as well as the entire Western world. Confidence departed, corporations tumbled, banks closed, railroad construction ceased, and unemployment mounted. The outcome was a general economic depression. For the next four years hardship and misery stalked the nation, a sort of purging, or so it seemed, for the sins—national and personal—of the years before. Thus Grant departed the White House in 1877, leaving the twin legacies of corruption and economic distress. As a result, Grant has ranked near the bottom in any listing of the country's presidents—despite his success in preserving the government's credit during the depression, his support of specie resumption and achievements in foreign affairs.

STUDY GUIDE: Dissatisfaction with the incompetent Grant administration led to organization of a third party—the Liberal Republican party. The Liberal Republicans nominated newspaper publisher Horace Greeley for the presidency in 1872. The Democrats also nominated Greeley. But Grant easily won reelection.

Many scandals came to light during Grant's second administration. Grant himself was not involved in making profit from the gold conspiracy and dishonest operation of the Crédit Mobilier construction company. However these scandals pointed out his weakness and inability as president. Voters grew even more distrustful of their leaders after the "salary grab," when congressmen voted themselves excessive pay increases. Political corruption existed on every level of government. The Panic of 1873 caused a severe economic depression during the next four years.

FOREIGN AFFAIRS UNDER GRANT

The years 1869-77 brought successes in the field of diplomacy, and it is necessary to keep these in mind when making an assessment of the Grant presidency.

To head the State Department Grant had named a wealthy New York aristocrat, Hamilton Fish, as the secretary of state. Whatever Grant might have thought, Fish doubted his qualifications for the appointment, but at length accepted it—"with a heavy heart and with unnumbered misgivings."

A man of keen mind, integrity, and tact, Fish vastly underestimated his own ability. He soon established himself as the foremost member of the Grant cabinet and in the next few years made a record that ranks him among the outstanding secretaries of state in American history. Fortunately Grant recognized Fish's talents and had the good sense to let the secretary guide the administration on most questions of foreign policy.

The *Alabama* Claims

When Grant and Fish took office, the country's largest diplomatic problem centered on the so-called *Alabama* claims which dated from the Civil War. During the war several Confederate commerce raiders had been built in British ports. These vessels, most famous of which was the C.S.S. *Alabama*, took a heavy toll of northern commerce and, so northerners thought, helped prolong the war. Accordingly, at war's end the United States demanded that the government in London make restitution for the damages caused by the rebel raiders. In the years of Andrew Johnson's presidency, 1865-69, the British, with little ceremony, turned aside the American argument.

On taking over the State Department in 1869, Fish, fully supported by Grant, continued to press the *Alabama* claims. He maneuvered with tact and skill and then, in 1870, events in Europe reinforced his bargaining position. First, the Franco-Prussian War broke out and in a few weeks it was apparent that the French were headed for a humiliation at the hands of the new German Empire. In Britain the general public applauded the German victories, but the country's leaders felt misgivings. What if the triumphant Germans decided to expand their empire beyond the confines of Central Europe, say, to Africa, East Asia, or the western Pacific? In that event a collision between Germany and the British Empire would be hard to avoid. Meanwhile the Russians began to make unfriendly gestures toward the British while seemingly drawing closer to the Germans.

Feeling increasingly uneasy about their position in Europe, the leaders of Britain decided that, should they get involved in a war, they would not want their enemies to prey on Britain's overseas commerce with ships outfitted in the United States. Hence they had better erase the precedent they had established in 1861 by admitting they had misbehaved at the start of America's Civil War and by making appropriate restitution. While they were at it, it might be a good idea to go a few steps further in improving relations with the United States by negotiating removal of other points of friction with the Americans.

For its part, the United States made a contribution to better relations with Britain at this time by cracking down on the Fenian Brotherhood. This organization of Irish-Americans had entertained wild dreams of capturing Canada and holding it hostage until Britain granted independence to Ireland.

Their ranks filled with veterans of the Civil War who were outfitted in splendid uniforms of green and gold, the Fenians first attracted attention in 1866. A band of them moved on Canada via Maine, only to be intercepted and turned back by United States authorities. Unfortunately the administration of Andrew Johnson quailed before the outraged protests of Irish-Americans across the country. Hence federal authorities stood aside later that year when another group of Fenians crossed the Niagara River into Canada and engaged in inconclusive combat with Canadian militiamen. Nor did Johnson do much in subsequent years to stop Fenian raids across the Canadian border. But when the Fenians assembled in upper New York and Vermont, for their next major assault in 1870, Grant was president. Before they could move out, United States marshals arrested their leaders. With that the Fenian "armies" fell apart —to the relief of leaders in Washington and London.

Meanwhile, Fish continued to press the *Alabama* claims and by early 1871 negotiations were moving smoothly. They also were moving quietly, for Fish and his British counterparts understood that to reach acceptable compromises it was necessary to keep publicity to a minimum. Publicity would arouse emotions both in Britain and America and the force of popular opinion, carrying with it a threat of political reprisals if the home country's diplomats failed to achieve a victory, would severely reduce the chances of a settlement. At length, in spring 1871, this quiet diplomacy reaped its reward when negotiators signed the Treaty of Washington, then retired for a repast of strawberries and ice cream.

The Treaty of Washington

The Treaty of Washington was one of the most important diplomatic agreements in the history of the American Republic. In addition to resolving pesky problems of the moment, it cleared the way for a long period of cordial relations between the United States and Britain which with only minor interruptions has continued to the present day. The treaty provided that a five-man tribunal would meet at Geneva at the earliest possible date and arbitrate the *Alabama* dispute. The tribunal ultimately decided that Britain should pay $15.5 million to the United States, a sum that exceeded the actual damages caused by the Confederate commerce raiders.

The treaty also submitted to arbitration a long-standing Canadian-American dispute over fisheries. As a result, American fishermen secured almost unrestricted access to Canadian waters; Canadian fish and fish oil gained duty-free entry to the United States; and Canadian fishermen received the right to operate in American coastal waters down to the thirty-ninth parallel. The German emperor was asked to arbitrate a dispute over ownership of the San Juan Islands, between Vancouver Island and the present-day state of Washington, which resulted in the emperor awarding the islands to the United States. The treaty also opened to mutually free navigation the waterways bordering Canada and the United States and the American territory of Alaska, such as the Saint Lawrence, the Yukon, and the Great Lakes.

Santo Domingo

During the Grant administration an attempt was made to plant the Stars and Stripes in the Caribbean country of Santo Domingo—a bit of diplomatic maneuvering which Grant handled with little help from Fish.

Santo Domingo was a poverty-ridden country which had secured independence from Spain (1821), had been conquered by Haiti (1822), gained independence again (1844), requested annexation by Spain (1861), and became independent a third time (1865). The possibility of annexing Santo Domingo had caught the fancy of some Americans in the 1840s when people

began to talk seriously about a canal across the isthmus of Central America connecting the Atlantic and Pacific. Should the dream of an interocean canal come true, it would be important for the United States to have naval bases in the Caribbean both to protect and to advance American interests.

Upon conclusion of the Civil War in 1865, American leaders again looked to the Caribbean. One possible site for American bases was the Danish West Indies, known today as the Virgin Islands, and in 1867 Secretary of State William H. Seward negotiated purchase of the islands from Denmark for $7.5 million. But the Radical Republicans who controlled the Senate would not approve the necessary treaty since it was sponsored by Andrew Johnson.

Meanwhile, Seward sought to arrange the annexation of Santo Domingo. The leaders of Santo Domingo were quite willing to live under the Stars and Stripes. Perhaps American control would bring stability and prosperity to the country. And without doubt annexation by the United States would end forever the threat of conquest by the dreaded Haitians who occupied the western part of their island.

Seward's attempt to work out an annexation treaty came to nothing, but Grant, on entering the White House in 1869, determined to carry on. And more than the prospect of naval bases spurred the new president. Grant saw Santo Domingo as a place where large numbers of black Americans could settle and find prosperity. As he later wrote in his memoirs, "The island is upon our shores, is very fertile, and is capable of supporting fifteen millions of people"—meaning that it could absorb most of the black population of the United States.

Grant's idea was to organize the country into three or four all-Negro states which would become full-fledged members of the federal Union. In this way, he thought, he would achieve with one masterful stroke his goal of justice for black Americans—for in their own states they would enjoy self-determination as well as the protection of the Constitution. At the same time he would hasten the reunion of the former Confederacy and the rest of the Republic by eliminating, for all practical purposes, the knotty question of the place of the former slave in American society.

Encouraging Grant, unfortunately, and eventually bringing an odor of corruption to the entire Santo Domingo negotiation, was a small group of businessmen and speculators. Among these men was Grant's personal secretary, who calculated that annexation by the United States would open great opportunities in Santo Domingo. What the businessmen and speculators had in mind remains vague, but it seems they were thinking of some profitable exploitation of the country's human and material resources.

Grant's diplomacy appealed to leaders of Santo Domingo and a treaty of annexation emerged. Grant was elated, for of all the projects of his presidency none so captivated him as did the one for making Santo Domingo a sanctuary for America's former slaves. With this single maneuver, he hoped to resolve the entire problem of Reconstruction of the Union. Then came disappointment, the most bitter that Grant met as president. A group of senators caught a scent of corruption and opportunism in connection with the negotiation, and perhaps recognized that Grant's plan for resettling the freedmen in the Caribbean was hopelessly visionary. Led by the old Radical, Charles Sumner, they rallied against the treaty and kept it from securing consent of the Senate, as required by the Constitution.

Where was Hamilton Fish during the Santo Domingo affair? Obviously the secretary knew what was going on. But he considered Santo Domingo of secondary importance and possibly knew that the Senate was not apt to approve annexation. He thus permitted Santo Domingo to occupy Grant while he pressed the more serious business of negotiating differences with Great Britain and also dealt with delicate matters growing out of an uprising in Cuba against the imperial authority of Spain.

The Cuban Debate

Feeling weighted down by inefficient and arbitrary Spanish rule, Cuban patriots had revolted in 1868, the year before Grant moved into the White House. The response in the United States was immediate. Since their own successful rebellion against the British in 1775-83, Americans had rejoiced when any colonial people seemed to be following their example. So they applauded the Cuban revolt and in 1869 the House of Representatives voted a resolution of sympathy for the rebels.

Applause and sympathy were of no use, however, in pitched battles with Spanish soldiers and soon there was a move afoot in Congress to recognize Cuban belligerency. Such recognition would mean that in the American view the

Cubans were no longer rebels but bona fide belligerents fighting a foreign power. The consequence of this subtle distinction was that American citizens—who could not legally sell arms and ammunition to rebels carrying on an insurrection against a government friendly to the United States—would be able to ship guns and other war equipment to the Cubans.

At this point Secretary Fish entered the debate. He saw, first, that recognition of Cuban belligerency would arouse Spain against the United States. The outcome might be a war which the United States, both in military and psychological terms, was ill prepared to fight. Second, such a move by Congress would weaken if not destroy the American case in negotiations with Britain over the *Alabama* claims. The American position rested on the argument that British recognition of Confederate belligerency in 1861 had been premature and without legitimate cause. The British could now counter that in the case of Cuba, the United States had taken the same kind of action—and with no better reason than the British had back in 1861. Thus while Grant was maneuvering to annex Santo Domingo, the secretary of state quietly persuaded leaders in Congress to pass no new resolution on Cuba. As a result, he headed off a possible confrontation with Spain and kept alive America's claims against the British for the damages caused by Confederate commerce destroyers like the *Alabama*.

A few years later, in 1873, the Cuban rebellion produced a new crisis. On the high seas many miles from Cuban waters, the Spaniards seized a vessel flying the Stars and Stripes, the *Virginius,* hauled it to Havana, and shot to death fifty-three of the ship's passengers and crew. Quite obviously the ship had been on an expedition designed to help Cuba's rebels. Just as obvious was the fact that most of the men aboard the vessel, despite the Anglo-Saxon names which they gave to Spanish authorities, were Cubans, not Americans. Still, the Spaniards had attacked an American ship, and if Americans wanted war the Spaniards had given them a perfect excuse.

Secretary Fish and the State Department played it safe, waited for tempers to cool, then accepted a Spanish apology and also an indemnity for the non-American citizens whom the Spaniards had killed. With that the *Virginius* crisis passed and Fish could add another item to his list of accomplishments as secretary of state and Grant's chief advisor.

STUDY GUIDE: Grant's appointment of Hamilton Fish as secretary of state led to notable achievements in foreign affairs. Under Fish's guidance the United States and Britain signed the Treaty of Washington. This treaty settled the question of American claims against the British for damages caused by the British-built Confederate destroyer, *Alabama*. Grant's dream of annexing the Caribbean island of Santo Domingo as a haven for American Negroes was defeated by the Senate. Fish's diplomacy headed off a conflict with Spain over the issue of the Cuban rebellion.

Library of Congress

In his travels after leaving the presidency Ulysses S. Grant met Li Hung Chang, viceroy of China, in 1879. Grant hoped that foreign travel would restore his popularity, badly damaged by the scandals uncovered during his administration.

THE DISPUTED ELECTION OF 1876

In 1876 Americans, notwithstanding their preoccupation with the lingering economic depression, began to look to November when they would elect a host of political leaders, including a president and members of Congress. At that point, although the Liberal Republican movement which had divided their party in 1872 had disappeared, prospects for the Republicans did not appear bright. The Democrats could capitalize on the miseries of the depression, the so-called Grant scandals, and the increasing dissatisfaction over the attempt of Radical diehards to keep carpetbag regimes in power in the South. The Democrats had won a majority in the House of Representatives in the midterm elections of 1874, and there was nothing by early 1876 to indicate that they had lost their momentum. Indeed the Democratic party seemed substantially stronger by 1876, largely because the Radicals, despite their efforts to hold on, were steadily losing power in the former Confederacy. Since the elections of 1874, Alabama, Arkansas, and Mississippi had slipped from Radical control, leaving only South Carolina, Louisiana, and Florida in the carpetbag grip. It was certain that these newly redeemed states would return solid Democratic majorities in 1876.

Who would lead the two major parties in 1876?

President Grant had made it clear that he would not seek a third term in the White House. The leading contender for the Republican presidential nomination at the start of the year was Senator James G. Blaine, a spellbinding orator and loyal party man from Maine who was known among his followers as "the plumed knight." An intelligent man who knew his way around in the world of politics, Blaine probably would have

Library of Congress

This photograph of Ulysses S. Grant and his family was taken in 1885 shortly before Grant's death. Although dying of cancer, the former president was determined to complete his *Personal Memoirs* in order to provide financial security for his family. Mark Twain helped to make the publication a success. Grant had been the victim of bad investments and crooked bankers. By 1884 he was penniless.

[297]

James G. Blaine was the Republican presidential nominee in 1884. Blaine and his Democratic opponent, Grover Cleveland, hurled accusations at one another during a low-level campaign. The loss of what bloc of voters caused Blaine to lose the election?

made as good a president as any political figure of the time. But shortly before the Republican national convention there were disclosures linking Blaine with a shady railroad transaction. Delegates thus turned to Rutherford B. Hayes, the distinguished-looking governor of Ohio, and made him the Republican standard-bearer.

Relatively unknown in politics, Hayes had been a volunteer officer in the Civil War and three-term governor of his state. He favored civil service reform (and thus appealed to Liberal Republicans of 1872), was a conservative in fiscal matters (and thus appealed to businessmen), and had made no political enemies of any consequence. Above all, he had steered through the confusions and uncertainties of the Grant era. His reputation had emerged unblemished by any political scandal.

The Democrats in 1876 brought forth their best candidate since Stephen A. Douglas in 1860. He was Samuel J. Tilden, the governor of New York, who had earned national acclaim for his part in overthrowing the corrupt Tweed Ring of New York City. Like Hayes, he was an economic conservative, disliked the spoils system, and was incorruptible.

Whatever the integrity and high-mindedness of the presidential candidates, Tilden and Hayes, the campaign of 1876 quickly degenerated into a political brawl which brought credit to nobody. Hayes accused Tilden of unpatriotic behavior during the Civil War, claimed that "a Democratic victory will bring the Rebellion into power," and asserted that if the Democrats won the "poor colored men of the South will be in a more deplorable condition than they were in slavery." For his part, Tilden surrendered to the former Confederates, as well as to northerners who had tired of Radical Reconstruction, by making it clear that he would end attempts to guarantee first-class citizenship for former slaves.

Tilden the Victor?

When telegraph instruments tapped out voting returns on election night 1876, it appeared that Tilden had scored a substantial victory. His plurality in popular votes was 250,000 and he had broken the Republican hold in such northern states as New York, New Jersey, Connecticut, and Indiana. Apparently he had swept the South. But then alert Republican managers saw a glimmer of hope. Taking out pencil and paper, they calculated that if they could deprive Tilden of Oregon, South Carolina, Florida, and Louisiana, Hayes would win the presidency by one electoral vote, 185-184.

Republican leaders claimed that Hayes had won those four states. Democrats conceded nothing, and when conflicting sets of election returns came in from the disputed states nobody could be sure who would be the next president. Neither candidate had clear title to a majority of the votes of the electoral college—and the Constitution required such a majority.

In the next few weeks the controversy worked its way into Congress and the outcome was creation of an electoral commission to help decide the question of which man, Tilden or Hayes, should take the White House the following March. On the commission were seven Republicans, seven Democrats, and one member who supposedly was neutral. The neutral member, Justice Joseph P. Bradley of the Supreme Court, voted with the Republicans on every question and, accordingly, by a straight 8-7 vote the commission recommended that Hayes should receive the electoral votes of each disputed state.

The final decision, however, rested with Congress. For a time it seemed that Democratic

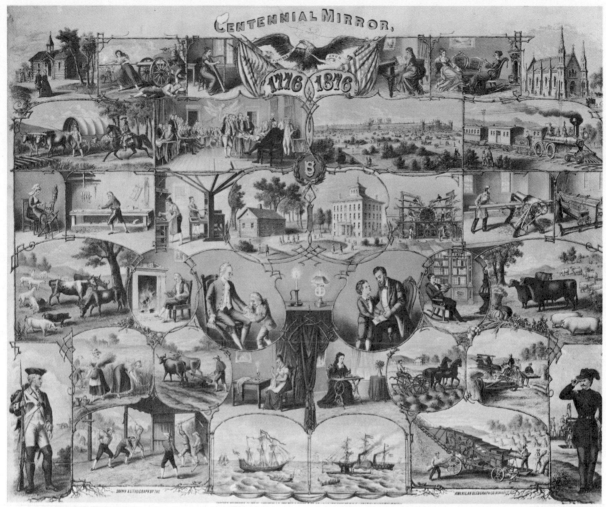

members might organize a filibuster to stall designation of Hayes as President Grant's successor. Then a bargain emerged. Democrats would accept Hayes as the new president and, on taking over the executive branch, Hayes, as commander-in-chief of the armed forces, would withdraw the last federal troops from the South. Removal of the troops would assure the end of Radical Reconstruction. Southern Democrats, according to the bargain, would also receive some control over federal patronage in the South, even during the Republican administration of Hayes, and Hayes would support a program to subsidize southern railroads. Following acceptance of these arrangements by Hayes and Republican and Democratic leaders in Congress, the Senate on March 2, 1877, only two days before expiration of Grant's term, announced that Hayes had bccn elected.

The nation celebrated its hundredth birthday in 1876 with a centennial exposition in Philadelphia. This lithograph, titled "Centennial Mirror," showed a panorama of scenes highlighting the nation's development.

Should Tilden rather than Hayes have entered the White House on March 4, 1877? The answer heard most often down through the years has been yes. Certainly for many years Democrats believed that the electoral commission which recommended Hayes's election acted contrary to the will of the electorate and helped to cheat their man of the presidency. In truth one cannot be sure that such an estimate was accurate. Oregon's vote no doubt rightfully belonged to Hayes. As for Louisiana, South Carolina, and Florida, it is true that carpetbag governments in those states threatened and intimidated white Democrats and used fraud to swing votes to

Hayes. Still, one must keep in mind that by 1876 all the other states of the late Confederacy had Democratic regimes, and those also used fraud threats and intimidation of Negroes to guarantee their states for Tilden. Thus it is not at all certain which man, Hayes or Tilden, would have won a fair and honest election in 1876.

STUDY GUIDE: In 1876 the Republican candidate Rutherford B. Hayes faced Democrat Samuel J. Tilden. Conflicting sets of election returns made it difficult to determine the winner. An electoral commission decided in favor of Hayes. Congress upheld this decision after Democrats agreed to swing their support to Hayes. In return for Democratic support federal troops were removed from the South.

RUTHERFORD B. HAYES

Rutherford Birchard Hayes was born in 1822 in the town of Delaware in central Ohio, the son of devout Puritans who had migrated westward from Vermont after the War of 1812. His father died before he was born, and hence he grew up with his mother and an uncle. The elder Hayes, an industrious and thrifty man, left an estate of $8,000, a substantial sum in the third decade of the nineteenth century. Consequently Mrs. Hayes was able to bring up her son in comfort and at the proper time send him off to college, first to Kenyon, a small college in Ohio, then to Harvard Law School.

On graduation from Harvard Law School in 1845 "Rud" Hayes returned to Ohio, practiced law for four years at Lower Sandusky (present-day Fremont) in the northern part of the state, then moved to Cincinnati. There he met and married Lucy Ware Webb, the daughter of a Cincinnati physician and a graduate of the Wesleyan Female College of Cincinnati. Mrs. Hayes became the first college-educated mistress of the White House in 1877. Eventually eight children were born, six of whom survived to adulthood.

In Cincinnati the young lawyer acquired a reputation as a civic leader, friend of abolitionists, and defender of runaway slaves. As a confirmed antislavery man, Hayes joined the new Republican party when it appeared in the mid-1850s. In 1858 he made his first venture into politics when the Cincinnati city council elected him city solicitor. But his political career had barely gotten

off the ground by the spring of 1861 when Confederates sent shells winging toward Fort Sumter.

Taken up in patriotic zeal, Hayes helped organize a volunteer infantry regiment, received a commission as major, and quickly revealed qualities of leadership. He also revealed courage. While leading troops up a mountain in Maryland, he was shot in the arm and in later engagements suffered at least four wounds and had several horses shot from under him. Because of his ability to lead and inspire men, and also because of his bravery, he received promotion to the rank of brigadier general in 1864.

Admirers back in Ohio meanwhile arranged his nomination for congressman, but when a supporter urged that he return to the district to campaign Hayes replied: "Thanks. I have other business just now. Any man who would leave the army at this time to electioneer for Congress ought to be scalped." Still, he won the election and finally took his seat in December 1865, several months after Lee's surrender.

In Congress Hayes deplored the generous Reconstruction policy laid out by President Johnson and thus easily lined up with Thaddeus Stevens and the Radical Republicans. Running as a Radical, he won reelection in 1866. Then in 1867 he resigned from Congress to seek the governorship of Ohio. He conducted a spirited campaign and was elected governor by 3,000 votes. As one might expect, his administration was free of scandal, conservative, and rather uninspired. He won reelection in 1869, chose not to seek a third term in 1871, and in 1872 campaigned for his old seat in Congress. This time the voters rejected him and in the wake of defeat he calculated that his political career had ended. But in 1875 Ohio Republicans again nominated him for governor and on election day he became the first man in Ohio's history to win the governorship three times. He did not complete his third term in the executive mansion at Columbus, for in 1876 the Republican national convention named him to head the party's presidential ticket and in March 1877 he entered the White House.

The Hayes Administration

No scandal tarnished the Hayes administration, and any lack of confidence in the honesty of the national leadership that Americans may have felt during the years of Grant's presidency was quickly dissipated. Hayes was probably the most devout man ever to occupy the White House. He and Mrs. Hayes usually began the day by leading the entire household of the presidential mansion in morning prayers and often ended the day by singing their favorite hymns. Mrs. Hayes, moreover, was the first "first lady" to decree that no wine or liquor would be available to quench the thirst of White House guests. In appreciation the Women's Christian Temperance Union presented her with a portrait of herself, which still hangs in the White House, but cynics called her "Lemonade Lucy" and accused the president of being henpecked by a domineering wife.

As president, Hayes (called "His Fraudulency" by embittered individuals who had supported Tilden in 1876) did moderately well. When historians in 1962 rated the men who had occupied the White House, he came out as an "average" president, fourteenth on the list of thirty-one. Perhaps his strongest claim to this relatively high ranking resulted from his determination to abide by a campaign statement that "he serves his party best who serves his country best." Accordingly Hayes chose subordinates and made appointments on the bases of talent and experience rather than unswerving allegiance to the Republican party. This was a refreshing turnabout from Grantism. The Hayes cabinet, for example, included four Liberal Republicans of 1872 and one ex-Confederate who had supported Tilden in 1876. Some historians have called this cabinet the best since Washington's.

In line with his hostility to the traditional spoils system, Hayes also made a noble effort to bring about civil service reform. His endeavors received little support in Congress, but he maneuvered as best he could without legislation. He tried to improve the civil service by making good appointments and removing incompetent political hacks. Such tactics naturally ran into opposition from Republican politicians. Opposition reached a climax when Hayes removed Chester A. Arthur from the post of collector for the port of New York. Arthur was a protégé of Senator Roscoe Conkling, one of the most powerful men in the Republican party.

Then there was Reconstruction. By the time of the inauguration of Hayes in March 1877, the only Republican, or carpetbag, regimes that remained were holding forth in South Carolina and Louisiana. These survived only because of the presence of United States soldiers. As president, Hayes immediately set about to keep his bargain with southern Democrats and

In the disputed presidential election of 1876 Congress made the final decision. Rutherford Hayes was the winner. What bargain did congressional Democrats accept in exchange for supporting Hayes over Tilden?

ordered withdrawal of the last federal troops from the South.

The Democrats quickly took over after the troops left Columbia and Baton Rouge. In a sense Hayes, a one-time Radical, was merely completing southern Reconstruction in accordance with the ideas of Presidents Lincoln and Johnson. His action was cruel to those black Americans whose cause he had championed as a young lawyer back in the 1850s. Nonetheless he claimed that he had taken the North and South a long stride down the road to reunion. Moreover, as if to placate the Negroes, he appointed Frederick Douglass as marshal of the District of Columbia.

The Money Question

Hayes encountered the money question on several fronts. First, there was the obligation im-

posed by the Specie Resumption Act of 1875 to build up the government's gold reserves so as to make possible, by 1879, the resumption of specie payment, that is, the free exchange of greenback dollars for gold. Hayes met the obligation by arranging the sale of gold bonds. On the first day of January 1879, therefore, the government was able to make specie payment. With this stroke, greenback dollars, which had fluctuated in value, became "as good as gold."

Second, there were continuing demands by debtor groups that the government enlarge the money supply by making new issues of greenback currency. Stimulating such demands was the economic depression touched off by the Panic of 1873 and still lingering when Hayes became president in 1877. Prices and wages had declined steeply. Compared with the period of prosperity which had gone before the depression, the dollar had greatly increased in value; that is, it was more difficult to acquire and would purchase more.

This 1877 engraving from *Leslie's* shows office-seekers in the lobby of the White House awaiting interviews with the new president, Rutherford Hayes. Hayes was opposed to the spoils system and tried to bring about civil service reform.

This development, as usual, weighed heavily on individuals who had borrowed during the time of high prices but had to repay debts at face value. Thus debtors wanted to expand the currency and, hopefully, reduce the value of the dollar. This in turn, would have the effect of scaling down debts. To promote currency expansion via paper money, the Greenback party appeared in 1876, gathered steam in the next two years, and in 1878 elected fifteen members to Congress. But President Hayes opposed the idea of new issues of paper money. So did a large majority of the people of the country, and greenbackism soon went into eclipse.

The idea of enlarging the money supply persisted however. As the Greenback party declined, debtors found a new remedy: free and unlimited coinage of silver at the ratio with gold of 16-to-1.

Debtors shortly learned that they had important allies in their campaign for "free silver"—the owners of silver mines in the western part of the United States. The reasons were fairly obvious. In recent years the market price of silver had declined sharply. For over a century, the market ratio between silver and gold had stood constant at about 15-to-1, that is, fifteen units of silver equaling one unit of gold. The government's coinage ratio, however, had been 16-to-1, meaning that it was more profitable for silver producers to sell their metal in the open market rather than to a federal mint.

Then, after 1850, came discovery of the great silver deposits in the American West, including the famous Comstock Lode in Nevada. These new silver mines yielded such quantities of the metal that by the early 1870s the market price began to slip. By 1873 the market ratio between silver and gold was about to pass 16-to-1, meaning that soon it would be more profitable for silver producers to sell to federal mints for conversion to silver dollars.

Anticipating that the country would soon be flooded with undervalued silver dollars, Congress in 1873 "demonetized" silver. That is, the government would no longer coin the white metal. Congress believed the old axiom that cheap money invariably drives other types of currency—in this instance, gold—from circulation.

For silver miners who wanted to sell their metal to the government at the old ratio of 16-to-1, here was a sad turn of events. The situation became even worse in the latter 1870s when the ratio in the market place was moving up to 17-to-1, 18-to-1, and higher. The legislation of 1873 demonetizing silver became "the Crime of '73." To debtors, who suddenly saw silver as a way to expand the money supply, the act of 1873 likewise became a crime.

Debtors, particularly farmers in the Midwest and South, realized that if they and the silver men could compel the government to resume purchase of silver at the old ratio, a huge amount of silver would come to the Treasury. If the Treasury turned the silver into money, the result would be a considerable expansion of the currency. The value of the dollar would come down, prices would go up, and the problem of debt repayment would ease. And so debtors and silver producers joined hands in a new and common cause: free

and unlimited coinage of silver at 16-to-1. Talk of increasing the money supply via greenbacks virtually disappeared. Here was a more subtle cause and one much more acceptable to those Americans who thought of paper dollars as a kind of fake currency and saw silver and gold as the only real money.

President Hayes, it turned out, had no more sympathy for unlimited silver coinage than he had for greenbackism. But in 1878, under heavy pressure from debtors and silver producers, Congress passed the Bland-Allison Act over Hayes's veto. This legislation directed the secretary of the treasury to purchase each month from two to four million dollars worth of silver at the market price and coin it into silver dollars at the ratio of 16-to-1. The measure proved disappointing to its supporters. While the government agreed to coin silver, it steadfastly refused to exchange a silver dollar for one of gold, but would exchange silver coins for gold only at the current market ratio. Like the pre-1879 greenbacks, then, the new silver dollars were not "as good as gold." The net result was that the Bland-Allison Act expanded the money supply only slightly, had no measurable effect on the value of the dollar (thus providing little relief for debtors), and brought scant profit to silver miners.

Then came a turn of events. The long economic depression of the 1870s began to pass. Foreign trade increased, prices and wages climbed, and unemployment decreased. As prosperity slowly returned, agitation for expansion of the currency, either with greenbacks or silver dollars, began to wane.

The upturn of the economy of course had political meaning. The political climate became more favorable for the Republicans, and leaders of the party of Lincoln looked forward to another victory in the election of 1880—provided they could overcome the disunity which had torn the party in recent years. The origin of this dissension bore only a vague relation to ideology or issues. It was essentially a conflict of the ambitions of party leaders. One group of patronage-seekers, whose members were called Half-Breeds, had gathered around the handsome senator from Maine, James G. Blaine. Another group, its members known as Stalwarts, was led by Senator Roscoe Conkling, a veteran spoilsman from New York.

Where did President Hayes fit into the Republican political equation as 1880 approached?

When he entered the White House in 1877, Hayes intimated that he would not be a candi-

AMERICAN BUSINESS ACTIVITY: 1870 – 1899

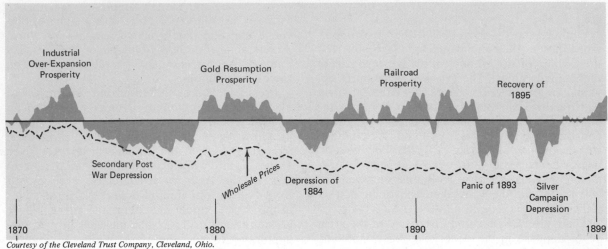

Industrial Over-Expansion Prosperity

Gold Resumption Prosperity

Railroad Prosperity

Recovery of 1895

Secondary Post War Depression

Wholesale Prices

Depression of 1884

Panic of 1893

Silver Campaign Depression

1870   1880   1890   1899

Courtesy of the Cleveland Trust Company, Cleveland, Ohio.

date for reelection in 1880 and indeed suggested a constitutional amendment restricting a president to a single six-year term. It really mattered little whether he wanted another four years in the presidency or not, for his hostility to the spoils system had alienated so many Republican professionals that his chances of renomination were gone. With Hayes removed from the picture, the leading contenders for the Republican presidential nomination in 1880 were Blaine, the Half-Breed champion, and former-President Ulysses S. Grant, Conkling's choice to carry the Stalwart standard.

> STUDY GUIDE: Hayes was honest and sought to bring about civil service reform. He took a hard position on the money question, despite pressure from debtors and silver producers. He opposed issuing more Greenback dollars and also free coinage of silver. Over his veto Congress passed the Bland-Allison Act permitting the government to coin silver. As 1880 approached, prosperity returned to the nation.

THE CAMPAIGN OF 1880

The Republicans assembled in national convention at Chicago in June 1880. The delegates deadlocked over the nomination of a presidential candidate. Blaine and Grant of course led the voting, but several "favorite sons" held the balance. Neither the Half-Breeds nor the Stalwarts

could strike a bargain with favorite sons to gain a clear majority. Orators harangued the delegates, the smoke in the convention hall became thicker, and tempers flared. But in roll call after roll call there was no significant change in the tally.

Sitting through these dreary proceedings was a well-known congressman from Ohio, James A. Garfield. The head of Ohio's delegation, Garfield was a Half-Breed and thus sympathetic to Blaine. However, he had dutifully supported Ohio's favorite son, Secretary of the Treasury John Sherman. Then it happened. After the thirty-third ballot, Wisconsin's delegation broke to Garfield, who had been placed in nomination earlier and on most roll calls had received a single vote. Stunned, Garfield stood up and sought to raise a point of order. Chairman George F. Hoar, senator from Massachusetts, rapped him down and called for a vote. Garfield showed strength on the thirty-fourth ballot, more votes came to him on the thirty-fifth, and on the thirty-sixth Blaine threw his support to the Ohioan, which assured his nomination.

Since Garfield was a Half-Breed and had won the nomination for president with the support of Blaine, the Republican convention, following time-honored political practice, nominated one of Conkling's Stalwart lieutenants, Chester A. Arthur of New York for the vice-presidency.

The Democrats were as divided in 1880 as were the Republicans. Much of the division was sectional. Many northern Democrats felt uneasy about cooperating with those southern members who had been in rebellion. Many southerners saw northern Democrats as being only slightly more desirable than Republican carpetbaggers. Moreover—and this had been a source of Democratic division since Thomas Jefferson had founded the party—the interests of urban Democrats of the North and agrarians of the South were not parallel.

Not all differences within the party were sectional, however; there were also divisions among Democrats of the same sections. For example, many former Whigs of the South, opposed to Abraham Lincoln's party, had come over to the Democratic party. These individuals were a constant source of irritation to southern Democrats, who could trace their political ancestry back to Jefferson and Jackson. Among northern Democrats there was friction between people who had managed the northern wing of the party for many decades and those who represented the interests of immigrants from Europe who in recent years had swelled Democratic ranks, particularly in northeastern cities.

The one man best equipped to smooth over differences and galvanize the Democratic party for victory was the presidential candidate of 1876, Samuel J. Tilden. But by 1880 Tilden was too old and too ill to run. The Democrats turned to General Winfield Scott Hancock of Pennsylvania. By nominating Hancock, who had won acclaim for leadership and daring while leading United States troops in the battle at Gettysburg, the Democrats confirmed their loyalty to the Union. In this way they hoped to undercut any plans the Republicans might have for "waving the bloody shirt." At the same time they avoided alienating the South, for Hancock, although a Yankee general, had won southern respect after the Civil War while serving as military commander of Louisiana. If Hancock had possessed political skill and experience, he might have made an excellent candidate. But he possessed neither.

Apart from a slight difference on the tariff (the Democrats favored a downward revision of tariff schedules), no serious issue separated the two major parties in the election of 1880. During the campaign Hancock threw away the tariff issue when he blandly announced that the tariff was "a local affair." Accordingly the parties ignored problems of 1880—such as the abuses of business monopolies, exploitation of natural resources, and the conditions of labor. Instead, they went back into the past to find reasons why they merited support of the electorate.

The efforts of President Rutherford Hayes to reform the civil service did not endear him to his fellow Republicans. This cartoon was published in *Puck* magazine in 1881. How does the new president, James Garfield, view the prospect of dealing with the problem placed on his doorstep by Hayes?

Republican orators, including Garfield, reminded voters that their party had saved the Union in 1861-65 and that most Confederates had been Democrats. They also accused Hancock of battlefield cowardice during the Civil War. For their part the Democrats recalled the Grant scandals and produced some vague evidence linking Garfield with the Crédit Mobilier fraud. The result of such tactics was a near standoff and on election night the returns gave Garfield such a scant plurality that the election of 1880 was one of the closest in history. Garfield, however, managed to carry most of the more populous states and as a consequence won in the electoral college by a comfortable margin, 214-155.

James A. Garfield

At the time Garfield won the presidency, the novels by the writer Horatio Alger—eventually more than a hundred of them appeared—were perhaps the most popular books in the country. Through most of the Alger stories ran one central theme: a poor boy of humble origins made his way up in the world by diligence and strength of character (and also good fortune, such as being on hand to rescue the boss's daughter from a runaway carriage, falling building, or raging river). As a man, the hero of the novel achieved eminence and power. Here (without the bit about saving a comely maiden) was the theme of Garfield's life. Indeed, the story of Garfield, with slight modification, could have provided the ingredients of an Alger novel.

The youngest of five children, James A. Garfield was born in Cuyahoga County, Ohio, in the year 1831. His birthplace was a crude single-room log cabin, and he was the last president who could claim such a "one hundred percent American" origin. His father and mother had migrated a few years before from New England to Ohio. While James was still an infant, his father died.

Mrs. Garfield found that her husband had left her deeply in debt. Determined to keep her family together, she sold fifty acres of the family farm and set about, with the help of her children, to cultivate the remaining thirty acres. Young James did chores around the farm, but nonetheless managed to attend school and developed a special fondness for reading.

When he was about sixteen, Garfield became a sailor on the Great Lakes. Then he was hired as a tow boy, driving the horses and mules that pulled boats up and down the Ohio Canal. His main ambition, though, was to get a college education. In 1848 his mother gave him seventeen dollars that she had scraped together, whereupon he set out for Geauga Seminary, an academy (roughly the equivalent of a present-day high school) at Chester, Ohio. Three years later he entered Hiram Eclectic Institute (later Hiram College), where he concentrated on Greek and Latin. Supported by a loan, he went on to Williams College in Massachusetts, where he earned high academic honors. On graduating from Williams in 1856, he returned to Hiram, became professor of Latin and Greek, and, after one year, at age twenty-six, president of the college. That same year, 1858, he married Lucretia Rudolph, who eventually presented him with seven children. Meanwhile, Garfield also served as a lay preacher in the Disciples of Christ sect and in the pulpit developed his skill as an orator.

Garfield was a young man bursting with ambition, and the leisurely life of a small college president did not provide a sufficient outlet for his energies. He took up the study of law and at length gained admission to the bar. He also developed an interest in politics and in 1859, running as a Republican, won election to the Ohio Senate. Two years later the Civil War broke out. Harboring no sympathy for the South, he joined a company that soon was attached to the Forty-second Ohio Volunteer Infantry, and when the time came to choose the unit's officers the men elected Garfield a lieutenant colonel.

At Middle Creek in eastern Kentucky Garfield led his troops to a minor victory over the Confederates and a short time later received promotion to brigadier general. At thirty-one, he was the youngest general officer in the federal army. Next he participated in the battles at Shiloh and Corinth, became chief of staff to General William Rosecrans of the Army of the Cumberland, and at Chickamauga, in September 1863, won a citation for delivering an important message after his horse was shot from under him.

In autumn 1862 Garfield's admirers back home arranged for his election to the House of Representatives. He resigned from the army after the action at Chickamauga, on the urging of President Lincoln, and took his seat in the lower chamber of Congress. Garfield was destined to serve in the House for the next seventeen years where he showed himself as a man of varied interests.

During the period of Reconstruction after the Civil War Representative Garfield from Ohio was an uncompromising Radical and voted for the impeachment of Andrew Johnson. Still, in 1876 he helped arrange the bargain with southern leaders that brought an end to the Radical experiment and delivered the presidency to Rutherford B. Hayes. He was an energetic worker in Congress, proved himself an effective orator, and in the time of the Hayes presidency, when Democrats controlled the House, served as Republican minority leader.

Despite a rather firm countenance, Garfield was a kindly and warmhearted man. His gentle and tolerant spirit, he hoped, would assure a peaceful and prosperous administration. Increasing his hope was an apparent continued decline of North-South bitterness.

Garfield's Assassination

Garfield sought a balanced adminstration and set about to reconcile the factions of the Republican party. His efforts came to grief. He soon found himself at odds with Conkling's Stalwarts, more so when it became apparent that Garfield was relying heavily on the advice of the Half-Breed leader, James G. Blaine, whom he had made secretary of state.

Meanwhile, a frustrated and angry Chicagoan, Charles J. Guiteau, was brooding over his failure to secure a diplomatic appointment from Garfield. A thirty-nine-year-old man with no particular diplomatic credentials, Guiteau had managed an interview with the president and had unsuccessfully pressed his appeal in a number of letters. On July 2, 1881, just four months after taking the presidential oath, Garfield prepared to travel to Massachusetts, where he planned to attend his college reunion. As he entered the Baltimore and Potomac station to board his train, Guiteau walked up behind him and fired two shots. One bullet grazed the president's arm, the other crashed into his back and fractured his spine. As Guiteau squeezed the trigger of his pistol he shouted: "I am a Stalwart! Arthur is now president!"

Within minutes, telegraph instruments were tapping out news that the president had been shot. But Garfield was not dead and across the nation there was hope that he might recover. To try to locate the bullet in Garfield's back physicians summoned the inventor Alexander Graham Bell, who rigged a device about the president's body. Results unfortunately were inconclusive and the bullet remained lodged. After lingering two months in the White House, the president was placed aboard a special train, which carried him to Eberton, New Jersey, a seaside town. For a time the salt-water breeze seemed to help. Then came an infection, followed by an internal hemorrhage. Garfield died on September 19, 1881.

Guiteau was captured and jailed moments after the shooting. He went on trial in mid-November 1881, pleading insanity. During the trial, he behaved like a madman, shouting and interrupting proceedings. The jury, after deliberating only one hour, adjudged him guilty of murder. Guiteau died on the gallows in a Washington jail in June 1882.

STUDY GUIDE: After bitter debate the Republicans nominated James Garfield for the presidency in 1880. The Democrats were also divided. They named Civil War hero General Winfield Scott Hancock. In one of the closest elections in history, Garfield won. A short time later he was assassinated by a disappointed office-seeker. Chester Arthur, the vice-president, succeeded Garfield as president.

ARTHUR SUCCEEDS GARFIELD AS PRESIDENT

The new president was Chester Alan Arthur, the man President Hayes had removed from the position of collector of the port of New York less than two years before.

Shortly after taking the oath as vice-president, on March 4, 1881, Arthur had broken with President Garfield. The cleavage came when the new president appointed one of Blaine's Half-Breeds to Arthur's old job of collector of customs at New York. Considering New York City to be Stalwart territory, Arthur and other Stalwarts were furious. Then came the shooting of Garfield. Many Americans were appalled that Arthur, a man with a reputation as an uncompromising spoilsman, might take over the White House. More than that, it seemed improper that Arthur, a Stalwart, should achieve the highest political office in the Republic as a consequence of the act of a disgruntled member of the Stalwart faction.

Aware of the delicacy of his position, Arthur claimed no executive authority during the weeks between the affair in the Baltimore and Potomac station and the death of Garfield. For all practical purposes, the country was without a president during that period. Arthur was at his home on Lexington Avenue in New York when he received the news of Garfield's death. There, at one-thirty in the morning of September 20, 1881, he took the presidential oath.

Born at Fairfield, Vermont, in 1830, Arthur was the son of a Baptist preacher who had migrated to the United States from Ireland. During his childhood the family moved from town to town, or, to be exact, from church to church, as was customary for minor Protestant clergymen in that era. By the time he was fifteen the family was residing in Schenectady, New York, and he enrolled there in Union College. He was an excellent student, earned a degree in three years, and was elected to the national honorary fraternity, Phi Beta Kappa, because of his high grades.

For a time after his graduation, Arthur alternated between the study of law and teaching school. Then in 1853 he moved to New York City where he became a member of a leading law firm. He soon established himself as a talented lawyer and won renown for his defense of fugitive slaves. As a man with strong abolitionist views, Arthur easily found his way into the new Republican party when it appeared in the mid-1850s. In 1856 he campaigned in New York for the Republican presidential candidate, John C. Frémont. Still, he had no ambition to run for public office and was never a candidate for anything until 1880 when he sought the vice-presidency on the Garfield ticket.

The prosperous young lawyer took a bride in 1859 and the couple eventually had two sons and a daughter. Meanwhile, he continued his behind-the-scenes political activities. In 1860 he threw his energy into the reelection campaign of New York's Republican governor. When the Civil War erupted in 1861, the governor appointed Arthur as acting quartermaster general of the state. His job was to provide equipment and arrange transportation for New York's volunteer regiments. He did his job well, but when a Democrat took over the governor's mansion in 1863 Arthur returned to his law practice.

Arthur continued his political endeavors, however, and before long was the chief assistant of Senator Roscoe Conkling, the boss of the Republican organization in New York. As a member of the Conkling machine, he worked for the election of Grant in the presidential campaign of 1868. In 1871 Grant rewarded him by making him collector of the port of New York. Controlling more than a thousand jobs, the collector at New York had great political power and Arthur dutifully used his position to advance the interests of the Conkling organization. Then, in 1879, federal investigators found evidence of corruption in the New York customs house. While none of it touched Arthur personally, President Hayes removed him from office. Next came his surprise nomination to the vice-presidency in 1880 and, on the death of Garfield, his elevation to the White House.

Six-feet-two-inches tall, Arthur was a man of dignity and manners. He was also an elegant individual who enjoyed fine food and drink, wore fashionable clothes, and found pleasure in elaborate social affairs. His wife died a year before he became president, but he nonetheless made the executive mansion a center of hospitality and gaiety during his presidency.

Although Arthur's political background indicated that he was nothing more than a party hack, the White House had a sobering effect, and the twenty-first president determined to make a good record. The consensus of many historians is that he achieved his purpose. He showed considerable courage in using his veto power against an expensive river and harbor ("pork barrel") bill and against a measure which violated a treaty with China by prohibiting Chinese immigration to the United States. Congress, however, overrode the latter veto. He prosecuted the "star-route" frauds which stemmed from contracts the Post Office Department had awarded to favored stage lines in the West. He approved an anti-polygamy bill which compelled the Mormon church to give up the practice of permitting plural marriage and opened the way for admission of Utah, in 1896, to the federal Union. He signed the measure that established four standard time zones for the entire country and thus eliminated the confusion resulting from the practice of each community operating on sun time.

Recognizing the country's naval weakness, Arthur began a program of replacing the navy's worm-eaten wooden vessels with new ships of steel. Then he made several suggestions that came to nothing but revealed a mind of considerable vision. One was a proposal for federal aid to education. Another was for legislation to take up the question of presidential disability and establish guidelines for the vice-president to assume executive authority if the president became unfit because of illness. He also proposed that the countries of the Western Hemisphere establish a uniform currency to facilitate trade and that they devise methods to prevent war in the hemisphere.

Civil Service Reform

Students of history, however, best remember President Arthur—the former lieutenant of the Conkling machine—as a champion of civil service reform. Reform of the spoils system had for many years been an ideal of liberal elements in American politics. Abraham Lincoln had expressed fear that the system was "going to ruin republican government" in America. Other presidents, their time taken up in seemingly endless interviews with office-seekers, had repeated Lincoln's lament. Nearly everybody agreed that the system opened the way for "influence peddling." Political appointees, recognizing that after the next election they might lose their jobs,

This 1884 drawing from *Harper's* shows President Chester Arthur on vacation in Newport, Rhode Island. As Garfield's successor, he entered the White House with the tarnished reputation of a party hack. What actions did he take in office that improved his image? Does changing one's image change one's character?

were tempted to "make hay" while they could.

During the 1870s, in the decade before Arthur took the White House, the drive for civil service reform quickened. It received endorsement of the Liberal Republicans of 1872 and, after 1877, of President Hayes. Support also came from newspaper editors and civil service leagues around the country. The murder of President Garfield by the disgruntled spoilsman gave reformers a new argument.

In the second year of Arthur's presidency, 1883, Congress responded to presidential persuasion and voter sentiment. It passed the Pendleton Civil Service Reform Act. This legislation created a bipartisan Civil Service Commission which was charged with the responsibility of providing "open competitive examinations for testing the fitness of applicants for the public service." The act also gave the president the power to extend the "classified list," that is, the authority to place more federal jobs under civil service.

Taking advantage of this last provision, Arthur and his successors extended the classified list — usually doing so just before leaving office so as to protect the jobs of their own political appointees. Between 1883 and 1917 the percentage of federal positions under the civil service system increased from thirteen to sixty. With enlargement of the federal government in subsequent decades, especially after 1933 (the year Franklin D. Roosevelt launched his New Deal program), the merit principle of the Pendleton Act became a central feature of government in the United States.

The Tariff Question

President Arthur also determined to look into the tariff question. Many people in America — observers of the national economy, politicians, ordinary citizens — were urging a reduction in import duties at the time Arthur assumed presidential responsibilities. Most conceded that there was a sound argument for protecting infant American industries, via high tariffs, from competition by European manufacturers. But by the 1880s many people were concluding that some industries enjoying tariff protection no longer were infants and that the time had come for them to stand on their own feet. They argued further that the absence of competition was enabling many American manufacturers to impose higher prices for their output than was necessary to assure legitimate profit. They thought, in other words, that the tariff was enabling manufacturers to realize excessive profits. In the end, of course American consumers paid the tab for these handsome profits. Tariff reformers were saying that it was time to give serious consideration to the interests of the millions of people in the country who purchased manufactured goods. A careful reduction of tariff schedules, they believed, would increase foreign competition for domestic manufacturers and force down prices of manufactured goods for consumers. Even with reduced tariffs American manufacturers would still be able to realize reasonable returns.

To study the question in greater detail, President Arthur appointed a tariff commission in 1882. Although every one of the nine members had favored high tariffs in the past, the commission recommended a general reduction in tariff schedules. The congressional response? Republicans in Congress succeeded in pushing through the so-called Mongrel Tariff Act of 1883, a measure which retained most of the evils of the old tariff.

The tariff legislation of 1883 brought little relief to American consumers. It nonetheless had historical importance, for it had the effect of dividing the Republican and Democratic parties on the tariff issue. Since the Civil War the two parties had differed only slightly on the tariff. But the measure of 1883 brought a sharp popular reaction, and the Republicans felt compelled to defend their handiwork. Democrats of course attacked. Consequently the Republican party established itself as the principal defender of tariff protection. The Democratic party became the chief advocate of lower tariff duties. Until the second half of the twentieth century, when Republicans joined Democrats in favoring lower trade barriers, the tariff was one of the issues that consistently separated the two parties.

While President Arthur may not have earned ranking as a "great" president, he certainly merited renomination by the Republican party in 1884. But he did not receive the chance to run for a second term. His support of civil service reform had alienated him from his old Stalwart allies without endearing him to the Half-Breeds. And so the Republican national convention in 1884 turned to "the plumed knight," James G. Blaine of Maine, nominating him for president. Arthur died within two years after he left the White House.

STUDY GUIDE: Chester Arthur was a competent president. His influence led Congress to pass the Pendleton Civil Service Reform Act. A Civil Service Commission composed of Democrats and Republicans was created to select well-qualified applicants for federal jobs. A commission appointed by President Arthur recommended that tariffs should be lowered. But Congress passed the Tariff Act of 1883 despite the recommendation. The Tariff Act of 1883 established the Republican party as the defender of tariff protection, while the Democrats took the opposing position. Opposition to civil service reform led the Republicans to bypass Arthur and nominate James G. Blaine for the presidency in 1884.

STATE POLITICS

Just as the national government in Washington displayed faint understanding or interest in the problems arising from the country's socio-economic revolution, so it was with most state governments. The history of the period points up a feature of American politics, namely, that the dividing line between state and national politics is thin. If state governments are slow to make reforms, there is not apt to be any reform impulse in Washington. Conversely, when state governments move to reform basic institutions, the spirit of the crusade usually finds its way to the national capital.

Politics for Profit

If state political leaders were not concentrating on the great social and economic problems of the day, what were they doing? The answer is not one that gives much credit to American politicians of that time. Most politicians at the state level were interested mainly in prying as much profit or advantage as they could from the political apparatus. Service in the public interest seldom crossed their minds.

The story of state politics at this time may not be very inspiring, but it is fascinating. The first requirement of the politician was to secure and hold office, and to achieve that end he had to appeal to voters. This presented no great problem, for the voters of most states were themselves taken up in the pell-mell economic growth of the country. Bent on sharing the profits of the industrial revolution, they were at best only vaguely aware of or interested in the problems resulting from economic and social changes. Thus the aspiring politician seldom had to come to grips with issues facing his state. He did not have to make elaborate promises that he would support reform when he reached the state capital. Normally he had to do nothing more than demonstrate that he had been a loyal Union soldier in the Civil War — or, in the South, that he had faithfully worn the gray uniform of the Confederacy — that no scandal had tarnished his reputation, that he was a God-fearing man and that he was an unswerving party member.

How did state politicians, once safely installed in office, turn a profit?

Several of them simply ran off with the funds of their states. One such scoundrel, James W. Tate, was treasurer of Kentucky and in 1888 departed for places unknown with an estimated

$250,000. A far more common enterprise was "influence peddling," that is, selling votes or favors to the highest bidder. If two railroad companies were competing for a charter to build a line between two points in the state, a member of the state legislature might sell his vote on the charter issue to the company offering the largest bribe.

A few reform-minded politicians occasionally raised their voices in an appeal to regulate business activities in the states. The unscrupulous operators—and state capitals in all parts of the country abounded with them—would then look to business interests to see how much it was worth to them to kill the reform. It often was worth a goodly sum.

Sometimes influence peddling was carried on in a more subtle fashion. For example, a company seeking political favor would offer its stock at considerable discount to key state officials. A company might also secretly advise state leaders of construction plans, thus enabling the latter to buy up land or in other ways make profitable investments in the area soon to be developed.

A Low Point in Politics

The history of state politics in this period offers only occasional bright spots. Sometimes the reform impulse surfaced in a state, resulting in a brief flurry of activity aimed at rooting out corruption and gearing the governmental mechanism to the public interest. This occurred in New York during the administrations of Governors Samuel J. Tilden and Grover Cleveland. Some states managed to build roads and bridges, somehow bumbling their way through to the twentieth century, when new forces in society brought improvement in the tone of state government.

Otherwise it is a dreary tale—one that knew no state or regional boundaries or party lines. Politics were pretty much the same in the North, South, and West, in states dominated by both Republicans and Democrats. State government in the closing decades of the nineteenth century was, for the most part, a paradise for incompetent and dishonest politicians, a hunting ground for seekers of special privilege.

Why was this so?

Voters failed to grasp the social and economic problems bearing down on their states in this age of rapid change. Most of them, moreover, were so taken up with the business of making ends meet or seizing new opportunities that they simply had little time for the affairs of their state governments—or, for that matter, government at any level. It was not easy for the voter to get a clear picture of what was happening at the state capital. There was no radio or television and most newspapers, metropolitan and rural, were mouthpieces for the interests of big business or assorted political factions.

The period after the Civil War also was a time when many of the old religious and moral restraints seemed to have become inoperative. Men got ahead in the best way they could, taking advantage of opportunities as they arose. The statehouse politician was no exception.

Finally, the last third of the nineteenth century was a time in America when the more intelligent and talented individuals tended to go into business, leaving politics to lesser men. Except for a few bosses at the top of the political organizations, the profits from influence peddling were small compared with the returns an energetic and resourceful person might realize in business. As a consequence, many political offices were filled by men of little ability who could not make the grade in other lines of enterprise. Such individuals, in addition to lacking understanding of what was happening in American society, were often easy marks for special-interest groups. The hacks and thieves in politics brought the prestige of political office, particularly at the state and local levels, to such a low point that honest men with good reputations did not care to or dare to go into politics. This consideration helped clear the way for the crooks and chiselers.

STUDY GUIDE: Statehouses throughout the nation were filled with corrupt, incompetent men in the latter part of the 1800s. Many of these politicians were more interested in personal profit than in public service. Voter indifference to politics made it easy for corrupt men to take charge.

LOCAL POLITICS

The story of local politics was essentially the same as that of politics at the state level. Like their counterparts in the state capitals, local politicians peddled their influence—to companies seeking streetcar franchises, to construction firms hoping for contracts to put down sewer or water lines, to racketeers who wished to avoid interference in their operations by the police or "do-gooders." They lied, cheated, and stole.

The most famous exhibit in this gallery of corrupt local politicians was William Marcy Tweed. As head of New York City's Democratic organization and superintendent of public works, "Boss" Tweed headed a ring which between 1865 and 1871 defrauded the city of countless millions of dollars and drove it to the verge of bankruptcy. The technique of the Tweed Ring was to allow contractors to overcharge the city—which was undergoing rapid expansion and development at the time. The contractors in turn would kick back a percentage of the profit to Tweed and his cohorts.

There were differences in the ways state and local politicians carried on their trade. To a large extent, these were the result of geography. The statehouse politician was more or less removed from his constituents and did not rub elbows every day with the voters to whom he owed his political influence. He was not easily accessible to them and not apt to enter their thoughts when a personal problem came up.

For the local politician, particularly in large cities, the situation was different. The voters in his district lived within a few city blocks instead of hundreds or perhaps thousands of square miles. The people whom he represented and to whom he owed his power lived in his neighborhood, called him by his first name and expected to be able to talk to him whenever they felt the urge. They thought that he should be ready to come to their aid whenever they needed a job or a loan. Local politics, especially in big cities, were more intimate than state politics. And, in spite of all the chiseling and influence-peddling, they were more democratic and more responsive to the needs of the people.

Local political leaders—particularly those in the great cities—were often so colorful that they have received considerable attention from students of American history. These politicians sometimes performed social services in behalf of the poor and downtrodden at a time when society as a whole—infected with the Social Darwinist idea that the poor were "unfit"—thought they ought to perish.

One such leader was George Washington Plunkitt, for many years a fixture in Tammany Hall. When the Society of Saint Tammany—so named for a legendary Delaware Indian chieftain—first appeared in 1789, it was a service and fraternal club. But as time passed, the Tammany clubhouse became a gathering place for Demo-cratic politicians. By the 1840s the club had evolved into an exclusively Democratic organization. By the 1850s it was the nerve center of Democratic politics in the city of New York.

Honest Graft

The son of Irish immigrants, Plunkitt advanced to the top of Tammany Hall in the last quarter of the nineteenth century by working hard and never swerving in his loyalty to the organization. The reporter William L. Riordon has told how Plunkitt eventually shared in the control of twelve thousand city jobs and an annual payroll of more than $12 million. Plunkitt once told Riordon that there were two kinds of graft: honest and dishonest. Plunkitt considered "dishonest graft" to be extorting bribes from racketeers, gamblers, and prostitutes. But "honest graft" was another matter.[1]

Perhaps the classic example of what Plunkitt called honest graft was this: he thought that city officials who learned that the city planned improvements in an underdeveloped part of town should be able to use that information to their own advantage by buying land before prices rose, then selling it at a profit. Plunkitt claimed that there were so many opportunities for this kind of "honest graft" that a politician would be a fool to take part in "dishonest graft."[2]

Leaders such as Plunkitt were not lazy men who sat around the Tammany clubhouse or city hall puffing on big cigars and counting their loot. Plunkitt was a politician day and night. Everybody in his district knew him, and he was continuously rendering service to the voters. Without complaint he would pull himself out of bed in the middle of the night and make his way to the police station to bail out a saloonkeeper of his district who had failed to close his bar at the legal time. He attended weddings, baptisms, and wakes. He never missed a church fair, and while there he bought chances on everything. If a slumlord was about to evict a poor family or a widow for failure to pay the rent, Plunkitt would turn up in court, obtain an extension of time, or perhaps pay a few weeks of the rent. In exchange for helping the people of his district, he expected their support on election day. "Honest graft" would provide his ultimate reward.

---

[1] William L. Riordon, "Honest and Dishonest Graft," *Plunkitt of Tammany Hall*, copyright 1963 (New York: E. P. Dutton & Co., Inc.), pp. 3-6.
[2] See note 1 above.

At his death in 1924, Plunkitt left an estate valued at more than a million dollars.

The Chicago Scene

Two other celebrated urban bosses were John J. ("Bathhouse John") Coughlin and Michael ("Hinky Dink") Kenna, leaders of the Democratic organization in the lusty first ward of Chicago from the 1890s through World War I. The first ward was filled with saloons (some of which belonged to Kenna), brothels, and gambling dens (and also Coughlin's bathhouses). Embracing much of the downtown area of the city, it was peopled by struggling working-class families and was made to order for the enterprising politician. The saloonkeepers, brothel operators, and gamblers needed protection from annoying city ordinances and prying "do-gooders." Directors of streetcar and construction companies were willing to pay big "commissions" for franchises and contracts aimed at bringing improvements to the area. The voters were pleased to exchange their votes for the numerous "social services" performed by energetic and resourceful politicians. Coughlin and Kenna, like Plunkitt, achieved fame and fortune.

STUDY GUIDE: During the 1870s and 1880s local politicians presented a sorry picture of greed and corruption. Among the most famous was Boss Tweed of New York, who headed a ring which cheated the city of millions of dollars.

THE CAMPAIGN OF 1884

Returning to the national political scene, the Republicans passed over President Arthur and named James G. Blaine as their presidential candidate in 1884. A veteran of many years in Congress, Blaine had supported Radical Reconstruction of the South and in the 1870s emerged as one of the leaders of the Republican party. He was a spellbinding orator with unusual personal magnetism. Still, he had inevitably become entangled in the controversies that wracked the party of Lincoln in the post-Civil War era and thus had plenty of political enemies. Certain business transactions of a dubious nature had also tarnished his reputation.

The Democrats in 1884 nominated Grover Cleveland, a man who four years earlier had

been unknown outside Erie County, New York. But after his election as mayor of Buffalo in 1881, Cleveland had won a national reputation. He reorganized the city's administration, purged incompetent appointees, and vetoed dubious ordinances. After his election as governor of New York in 1882, he clashed with "machine" politicians, particularly those of New York City's Tammany Hall. When placing Cleveland in nomination for the presidency at the Democratic national convention in 1884, General E. S. Bragg expressed a popular sentiment when he declared: "We love him for the enemies he has made."

The campaign of 1884 quickly descended to the lowest levels of political warfare, becoming perhaps the most bitter since the "Log Cabin" campaign of 1840 when William Henry Harrison battled Martin Van Buren. Democratic orators dragged out all the old charges that Blaine had been involved in shady dealings with unscrupulous businessmen.

The Republicans, not to be outdone, reminded voters that during the Civil War the Democratic candidate had dodged the dangers of war and hired a substitute to go off to the army in his stead. Then came an even more devastating charge, one that in most political campaigns would have spelled certain defeat. Republicans announced that some years before, Cleveland had fathered an illegitimate child. They began parading through streets and chanting:

> Ma! Ma! Where's my pa?
> Gone to the White House,
> Ha! Ha! Ha!

Cleveland turned this sensational disclosure to his own advantage. Contrary to their appeals that he issue an outraged denial, he directed his aides to "tell the truth." The truth was that Cleveland was guilty as charged. But to his credit he had not disowned the child and over the years had paid for its support. More important, his public admission added to his image as a man of courage and honesty.

During the campaign, moreover, Cleveland benefited from an unfortunate remark by a Blaine supporter. As part of a delegation calling on the Republican candidate, the Reverend Mr. Burchard, a Protestant clergyman, declared that the Democratic party was the party of "Rum, Romanism, and Rebellion"—liquor, Catholics, and former Confederates. When Blaine failed to disavow the statement, Irish Catholics in New

York rallied behind Cleveland. As a consequence, the Democratic candidate carried the Empire State by 1,149 votes. As in some previous elections, New York's big bloc of electoral votes determined the outcome, giving Cleveland his margin of victory in the electoral college (where the vote was 219-182).

STUDY GUIDE: After a bitter election campaign in 1884 the Democratic candidate, Grover Cleveland, defeated Republican James G. Blaine.

CLEVELAND'S FIRST ADMINISTRATION

Stephen Grover Cleveland (he dropped the "Stephen" while still a youth) was born in 1837 at Caldwell, New Jersey, the son of a Presbyterian minister and one of a family of nine children. While Grover was still an infant, his father took a pastorate in Fayetteville, New York, and later, after ten years, in Clinton, New York. Young Grover attended schools in those towns, but at the age of fourteen quit school to contribute to the support of the family. Running errands and clerking in a grocery store were his principal employment.

An ambitious and studious youth, Grover still had dreams of a higher education. Unfortunately his father died two years later. For the next two years Grover assisted his brother, a teacher at the New York Institution for the Blind. During this time he faithfully sent most of his small earnings to his mother. By the time he turned eighteen he had decided to migrate westward to seek his fortune. He set his sights on the bustling city of Cleveland, on the banks of Lake Erie. On his way to Cleveland, however, he stopped off at Buffalo to visit relatives. A prosperous uncle persuaded him that Buffalo offered as many opportunities as Cleveland and, to prove it, found him a job in a law office. Four years later, at twenty-two, Cleveland gained admission to the bar.

At this point, as the North-South controversy boiled to a climax, Cleveland began to take a strong interest in politics. His father, an outspoken antiabolitionist, had been inclined toward the Democratic party. So it seemed natural for the younger Cleveland to line up with the Democrats. When the war began in 1861, his allegiance to the Democratic party hardened. Cleveland was against the southern policy of the Republican president, Abraham Lincoln, and opposed the idea of trying to keep the South in the Union by force of arms. In 1862 he threw himself into the gubernatorial campaign in New York. When the Democratic candidate, Horatio Seymour, emerged victorious, Cleveland received appointment as assistant district attorney of Erie County. Because he opposed the war, and also because his mother and younger brothers and sisters needed his financial support, he put down $300 and hired a substitute when he was about to be drafted into the federal army.

At the age of twenty-eight, in 1865, Cleveland made his first campaign for elective office, running for district attorney of Erie County. He lost. Five years later, in 1870, he was elected sheriff of the county. Cleveland did not seek reelection when his term ended in 1873, returning instead to his law practice, where he remained for the next eight years.

Then, in 1881, reform groups in Buffalo, remembering his excellent record as sheriff, persuaded Cleveland to run for mayor. He won the election and within months had received acclaim for his reform activities. In 1882 New York Democrats nominated him for governor. Supported by reform-oriented Republicans, he swamped his Republican opponent and over the next two years reinforced his image as a man of integrity and an enemy of corruption. In 1884 the national Democratic party, which had not controlled the White House since the departure of James Buchanan in 1861, turned to "Grover the Good," governor of the most populous state of the Union.

A fat man (he weighed 260 pounds) Cleveland was not physically attractive, did not have much personal magnetism, and was an uninspiring orator. He was intelligent but not particularly imaginative. He had no special grasp of the great economic and social questions of the day, was not a political innovator, and was not moved by a reform impulse. His only important reform proposal during his first term in the White House was for a downward revision of the tariff.

Cleveland was a conservative, a defender of the existing state of affairs in American society. His principal assets as a national political leader were industry, integrity, and courage. He put in long days at his desk, often working into the early hours of the morning, going over every line of every measure approved by Congress. He exercised his veto power 413 times during his first

Grover Cleveland was a bachelor when he was elected to the presidency in 1884. Two years later he became the only president to be married in the White House. This drawing of the president's wedding was published in *Harper's* in June 1886.

term, mainly to stop private relief bills which he considered as nothing more than raids on the federal treasury. In the preceding ninety-six years, since Washington's inauguration in 1789, the twenty-one presidents of the United States had used the veto a total of only 132 times.

Cleveland, like Buchanan, came to the White House a bachelor. But unlike Buchanan, he did not remain single. In 1886 he became the only president to be married in the executive mansion. His bride was the twenty-one-year-old daughter of a former law partner. The president was forty-nine. The new Mrs. Cleveland was the youngest woman ever to be the first lady of the nation. Later she became the first presidential wife to give birth in the White House.

During his first term (1885-89), President Cleveland found that Democrats, denied White House patronage for twenty-four years, were hungry for the fruits of victory. Cleveland later said that the everlasting clatter of Democratic office-seekers had sometimes caused him to wish to resign. Eventually he struck a compromise with the spoilsmen of his party. He agreed to replace nearly all the Republican postmasters and about half of the other officials appointed by his Republican predecessors. But, as an advocate of the merit system in government, he

determined to protect the Civil Service Commission and extend the civil service list under the provisions of the Pendleton Act.

The GAR

Equally troublesome for the twenty-second president was the Grand Army of the Republic, the organization of veterans of the United States army during the Civil War. Sometimes called the "Grand Army of the Republican Party," the GAR was not apt under any circumstance to look with favor on a Democratic president, particularly one who had opposed the war of 1861-65 and avoided the draft. When Cleveland named a former Confederate general as his secretary of the interior, the GAR complained bitterly. Then Cleveland proposed that the federal government arrange the return of captured Confederate battle flags to the southern states. The GAR was furious.

More serious, however, was the president's

frequent use of the veto to kill private pension bills passed by Congress for Union veterans. He also angered the GAR by opposing its proposal for pensions for needy veterans suffering any physical disability, whether or not the disability was the result of military service. In 1887 the GAR lobbied through Congress the Dependent Pension Bill, a measure based on GAR ideas to help disabled veterans. Cleveland vetoed the bill, and this act weighed heavily against him in the election of 1888.

The Tariff

On the ancient and thorny question of the tariff, Cleveland made a major bid for reform. When Democratic advisers warned him to tread softly with the tariff—that is, leave the issue alone—the president responded, typically: "What is the use of being elected or reelected if you don't stand for something?" Hence he devoted his entire annual message to Congress in 1887 to the tariff. He believed the tariff, by

This wood engraving published in *Leslie's* in April 1887 shows an Easter tradition that has long been associated with the White House. On the grounds of the executive mansion children participate in egg rolling.

eliminating foreign competition, compelled American consumers to pay more for many manufactured items and thus was a tax paid by consumers for the benefit of industrialists. Cleveland declared that "our present tariff laws, the vicious, inequitable, and illogical source of unnecessary taxation, ought to be revised and amended." He scored the "infant industry" theory of tariff protectionists and saw the protective tariff as the companion of monopoly. For all his determination, Cleveland got nowhere with tariff reform.

Cleveland's Accomplishments

As his first term in the White House drew to a close, Cleveland could look back on several achievements. He had successfully frustrated

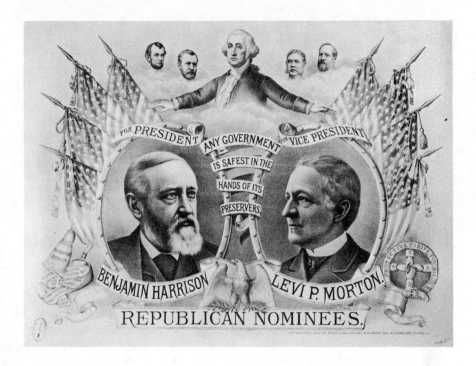

Benjamin Harrison, the Republican candidate, captured the presidency from Grover Cleveland in 1888. What helped Harrison to win the critical state of New York and swing the election to a Republican victory?

Library of Congress

the GAR's raids on the treasury and had extended the civil service list. His administration had exposed fraudulent practices by railroads, ranchers, squatters, and logging companies on Indian reservations. He had ordered western cattlemen to remove barbed-wire fences that illegally enclosed scores of thousands of acres of public land, recovered 81,000,000 acres of land when western railroads failed to honor the terms of their land grants, and vetoed assorted "pork-barrel" legislation.

Cleveland was the first president to take much interest in the problems of labor and in 1888 signed the bill creating the Department of Labor. Finally there was the Interstate Commerce Act of 1887, providing federal regulation of interstate carriers, and the Dawes Act of 1887, establishing a new federal Indian policy. Cleveland's part in the passage of these last two measures was small, but he had supported them and given them his signature.

STUDY GUIDE: Cleveland was a hard-working conservative president who favored civil service reform. His vetoes of pension bills brought him the opposition of the Grand Army of the Republic, an organization of Civil War veterans. Cleveland sought without success to lower the tariff.

THE CAMPAIGN OF 1888

During his term in office Grover Cleveland failed to capture the imagination of American voters. His stand on the tariff, moreover, set industrial interests against him, and his opposition to the spoils system soured many loyal Democrats.

On the other hand he had made a respectable record in the White House, especially when measured against the performances of his five Republican predecessors. Besides, he was the only Democrat in the country with a national reputation and thus the only Democrat who stood a chance of defeating the Republican presidential nominee in the election of 1888. With only a mild display of enthusiasm, therefore, the Democratic national convention of that year, meeting in Saint Louis, renominated him by acclamation.

The Republicans met in Chicago a short time later and went into deadlock. Benjamin Harrison of Indiana was not one of the contenders. Most delegates wanted to give the party's unsuccessful candidate of 1884, James G. Blaine, another chance, but Blaine, for reasons of health, had taken himself out of the contest. Still, Blaine retained his hold on the delegates and on learning of the deadlock sent a cable from Scotland curtly advising the convention: "Take Harrison." It seemed like a good idea. No

This engraving printed in *Leslie's* in 1889 shows voters using written ballots in a polling place. In 1888 a few states had adopted the Australian ballot system, in which voters marked their ballots in the privacy of a curtained booth. The first voting machine was used in New York in 1892.

Library of Congress

scandal had tarnished Harrison's reputation and in his rather undistinguished political career he had made no important enemies.

Unlike Cleveland, Harrison had made a good record in the Civil War, and he was the grandson of a former president, William Henry Harrison, which prompted Republicans to dub him "Young Tippecanoe" — a nickname that hardly fitted the undramatic, pious Ohioan-turned-Hoosier. And so on the eighth ballot the delegates "took" Harrison. After his victory in the November election, Harrison appointed Blaine as secretary of state, a move that caused some observers to doubt that the "plumed knight" had recommended Harrison's nomination solely for the welfare of the Republican party.

The campaign of 1888 was not as rough as that of 1884. Harrison was a bland individual and was not an easy target for traditional mudslinging, as Blaine had been in 1884. Harrison's followers decided it was not necessary to toss mud. They felt that if they said nothing that might work to Cleveland's advantage, Harrison would be assured of victory because President Cleveland had already made so many enemies — the GAR, Democratic spoilsmen, and industrialists who disliked his low tariff ideas.

In line with this strategy, Harrison spent most of his energy during the campaign delivering little speeches to delegations of Republicans who called on him at his house in Indianapolis. Meanwhile, Republican professional politicians, notably Senator Matthew S. Quay of Pennsylvania, shook down the country's manufacturing interests for financial contributions. As a result

the Republicans were able to put together an efficient, well-heeled organization.

As in previous elections, New York was the critical state in 1888. Cleveland sensed this from the start and knew he was in trouble because of the hostility of Democratic spoilsmen, particularly those affiliated with Tammany Hall. Then came the final blow. A former British subject, a member of the Republican party, cleverly inquired of the British minister in Washington how he should cast his vote in the presidential contest so as to serve the interests of Great Britain. The minister advised the man to vote for Cleveland. Two weeks before the election the Republicans gleefully published the letter. The outcome was devastating for the Democrats. In New York Irish-American voters — the very people who, following the "Rum, Romanism, and Rebellion" incident, had swung New York for Cleveland in 1884 — were aghast. Consumed as they were with hatred of Great Britain, they concluded that if Cleveland was good for the British he must be bad for the Irish. On election day, accordingly, New York went for Harrison. While returns from across the entire country gave Cleveland nearly one hundred thousand more popular votes than his Republican rival, Harrison carried the electoral college, 233-168.

STUDY GUIDE: Cleveland was renominated by the Democrats in the campaign of 1888. His Republican opponent was Benjamin Harrison, the grandson of William Henry Harrison. Cleveland lost the critical New York vote because Irish-Americans felt the English were support-

BENJAMIN HARRISON

Benjamin Harrison, born at North Bend, Ohio, in 1833, was, like Grover Cleveland, one of a family of nine children. The grandson of "Old Tippecanoe" Harrison, he was also the great-grandson of a signer of the Declaration of Independence. Young Ben spent his boyhood on his father's farm, which was just a few miles down the Ohio River from his grandfather's place. Relations between "Old Tip" and his grandchildren were warm, and it was a joyous occasion for seven-year-old Ben when his grandfather in 1840 won election to the presidency. Joy soon turned to sorrow, however, for the first President Harrison died after one month in office.

Meanwhile, Ben Harrison's father built a one-room schoolhouse for his children, isolated as they were in the country, and hired a teacher to drill them. When he was fourteen, Ben went to a preparatory school near Cincinnati, then entered Miami College in Oxford, Ohio. Graduating in 1852, ranking fourth in a class of sixteen, he decided to be a lawyer. He returned to Cincinnati, took a job in a law office, and gained admission to the bar. He also married Caroline Lavinia Scott, and later they had two children. In 1854 they moved to Indianapolis.

By the mid-1850s, Harrison was becoming active in politics. As the grandson of one of the country's most renowned Whigs, he easily gravitated to the new Republican party. On the eve of the Civil War, in 1860, he won election to the office of reporter of the supreme court of Indiana. He owed his triumph largely to his polished oratory. After the war erupted, Harrison organized the Seventieth Regiment, Indiana Volunteer Infantry in 1862. Riding with the army of the illustrious General Sherman, he led several charges against rebel fortifications, particularly in the Georgia campaign of 1864. Indeed he saw more combat in 1862-65 than "Old Tippecanoe" Harrison had experienced in a lifetime. At war's end he was a brigadier general.

Despite his absence from Indiana, Harrison in 1864 won reelection as reporter of the state supreme court. When peace came, he returned to that position. He declined renomination in 1868, resumed his legal career, and in a short time was one of the most prosperous lawyers in Indiana. He also became an influential voice in the state Republican party and in 1876, somewhat reluctantly, ran for governor. He lost that election, but four years later, in 1880, the state legislature elected him to the United States Senate.

Like most freshmen senators, Harrison had little opportunity to distinguish himself and in 1886 the legislature turned aside his bid for reelection. When his train steamed out of the national capital, he calculated that his political career had ended. Two years later he moved into the White House.

Harrison was a handsome man, always tastefully dressed. He stood only five feet six inches, however, and Democratic cartoonists liked to caricature him as a tiny fellow who was almost invisible under the giant beaver hat of "Old Tippecanoe" Harrison. Such an estimate was not entirely fair. If not very inspiring, Harrison was energetic and intelligent. He was also incorruptible and no scandal tarnished his presidency.

President and Mrs. Harrison were rather straitlaced people. There was a minimum of social activity, no gala parties, and a good deal of family prayer during their occupancy of the White House. Electricity came to the presidential mansion during the Harrison term but, fearing electrical shock, both the president and his wife were reluctant to manipulate light switches or bell buttons.

The second President Harrison was not without political principles, but his principles were not of the type that made for strong presidential leadership or advanced the cause of reform. Interpreting the Constitution in much the same way as had the framers of the document back in 1787, Harrison was careful not to interfere in the legislative process. He confined himself largely to executing the will of Congress.

Another of Harrison's principles was that the president was obliged to reward the party faithful with the spoils of victory. Accordingly he ignored a campaign statement that "only the interest of the public service should suggest removals from office." After his election he fired nearly every Democratic officeholder not covered by civil service. He also held up an order by President Cleveland extending civil service protection to railway mail workers until he could replace appointees with Republican regulars.

Perhaps the twenty-third president's only contribution to the civil service ideal—and it was an accident—was appointment of a young Republican from New York, Theodore Roosevelt, to the Civil Service Commission. Despite clashes with Harrison and other Republican leaders, including Roscoe Conkling, who spoke contemptuously of the "snivel service," Roosevelt bent his enormous energy toward making the commission, in his words, "a living force." So impressive was Roosevelt's performance that when Cleveland returned to the White House in 1893, he retained him.

Harrison and the Republican leadership in Congress did not forget the GAR. In 1890 legislation provided pensions for disabled Union veterans. Whether or not the veteran's disability had any connection with his military service was of no consequence. The cost to the taxpayers was considerable. The new legislation, which also provided small pensions for the widows and children of veterans, increased the annual outlay for veterans' benefits by fifty percent. Still, the GAR was not satisfied and continued to lobby for even more rewards for veterans and their families.

Meanwhile a return of hard times in the agricultural sector of the economy in the late 1880s had brought the so-called money question to the surface again. As in the past, debtor groups wanted the government to increase the money supply so as to scale down debts. Since the idea of unsupported paper currency was opposed by a great many Americans, the use of silver was urged as a basis for new issues of currency. Owners of western silver mines naturally were rendering strong support for such proposals.

Harrison and Republican leaders on Capitol Hill had little sympathy for debt-ridden farmers, but they were practical politicians who understood the need to appease voters. Moreover, the Republican leadership, much concerned about the welfare of the country's industrial establishment, saw an opportunity for a political "horse trade," that is, a silver measure in exchange for legislation to advance the interests of industry.

The Sherman Silver Purchase Act

In 1890 the president signed the Sherman Silver Purchase Act, a rather complicated measure which required the Treasury Department to purchase four and half million ounces of silver each month at the prevailing market price. On the basis of this silver, the government would issue new legal tender notes redeemable in gold or silver. The measure, it turned out, satisfied nobody except perhaps the silver miners. The new currency brought slight relief to debtors, but eastern financial interests, fearing that the influx of silver might drive the country off the gold standard, began to make their way to the treasury to exchange their paper dollars for gold. The result was a serious weakening of the federal gold reserve and with it declining confidence in the fiscal integrity of the federal government.

Then there was the tariff.

Republicans had won narrow control of Congress in the election of 1888 while campaigning for high tariff schedules, but President Cleveland, campaigning for low tariffs, had won a plurality of popular votes in the presidential contest. Because of the close division in Congress and the uncertainty of popular sentiment on the tariff, Republican leaders saw the possibility of defeat in the next national election on this sensitive issue. Speaker of the House Thomas B. Reed of Maine, known as "Czar" Reed, thereupon carried out maneuvers that to the present day must awe professional politicians.

Reed scanned the map of the Republic and noted that since 1867, when Nebraska gained admission, only one new state had entered the Union, Colorado in 1876. North of Colorado, however, was a tier of federal territories that had met the minimum requirements for statehood. Reed knew that voters in those territories were predominantly Republican. When the territories became states, they would increase Republican strength in Congress. The speaker went to work and in 1889 Washington, Montana, North Dakota, and South Dakota were ushered into the Union, followed in 1890 by Idaho and Wyoming.

Reed knew full well that many western Republicans did not favor the protective tariff. The West had no industries that needed to be guarded against foreign competition, and the region's prosperity depended in part on low prices for the output of eastern factories. Still, some western Republicans owned interests in silver mines and a great many more were debt-depressed farmers who wanted expansion of the national currency via silver.

It was this situation that presented the opportunity for a political deal. Friends of industry would support legislation sought by advocates of currency expansion on the basis of silver in exchange for the latter's support of a measure beneficial to industry. Hence, Reed had engineered the Sherman Silver Purchase Act, passed with the understanding that western members of Congress would support a tariff bill providing increased protection for eastern manufacturers.

The McKinley Tariff Act

The outcome was the McKinley Tariff Act of 1890, imposing the highest duties against foreign manufactures to that time. The act even offered protection to industries not yet existing in America, provided "responsible persons" demonstrated an intent to begin manufacture. To make the bill more agreeable to farmers—and here was another example of Reed's skill—the measure provided needless tariff protection for eggs, butter, potatoes, wheat, and barley. For the "man in the street" it also provided a "free breakfast table" by placing tea, coffee, and sugar on the free list.

While the "free breakfast table" had appeal, the idea of permitting sugar to enter the country without duty brought sharp debate. "Free sugar" had not come entirely from a wish to do something for the public. The main beneficiaries were American sugar refiners who depended on raw sugar from the Caribbean. Removal of the tariff on raw sugar would reduce the price paid by American refiners.

The prospect of Caribbean sugar entering the country duty-free brought howls of protest from Louisiana sugar planters. Reed and his friends were equal to this problem. They wrote into the bill a provision for a two-cents-per-pound bounty on raw sugar produced in the United States. Thus by a careful balancing of protection and subsidy they gave the refiners cheaper sugar and producers higher returns. The only loser was the public.

In spite of Reed's cleverness, dissatisfaction with the McKinley Act was widespread. There was general recognition that the measure would increase consumer prices. The congressional election campaign of 1890 was nearly over when the McKinley Act passed, and Democrats made a last-minute effort to capitalize on the dissatisfaction. Denouncing "Bill McKinley and the McKinley Bill," they concentrated on farmers, who generally saw that eggs and butter faced no serious foreign competition in the domestic market and that provisions of the legislation designed for their benefit were a sham. To re-

inforce their charge that Republicans favored "special interests," Democratic orators pointed to appropriations for pensions, rivers and harbors, and federal buildings.

For their part, Republicans tried to counter Democratic charges by pointing to the Sherman Antitrust Act which they had pushed through in 1890, a measure intended to eliminate the evils of business monopoly. They failed. The voters gave congressional Republicans the sharpest rebuke in the annals of American politics. Only holdover members permitted Republicans to retain control of the Senate. In the House of Representatives the balance shifted from a small Republican majority before the election to a whopping 235-88 margin in favor of the Democrats. Among the losers, incidentally, was Congressman McKinley.

Pan-Americanism

As his term drew to a close, Harrison could look back with some pride on his administration's record in foreign affairs. Serving his second term as secretary of state, James G. Blaine, with Harrison's support, had sought to promote "Pan-Americanism"—closer accord between the countries of the Western Hemisphere. With enthusiasm, Blaine and Harrison participated in the First Inter-American Conference, which met at Washington in 1889. The conference achieved few of its objectives, but out of it came a bureau known as the Pan-American Union. The Pan-American Union served as a clearinghouse for exchange of cultural, economic, and scientific information among the countries of the hemisphere. Blaine and Harrison also asserted American power in the Pacific, in Samoa and Hawaii. Before leaving the White House, the president sent the Senate a treaty for annexation of Hawaii.

In such manner did politics in America pass from 1868 to 1893. Those twenty-five years were no great period in American political history but were a time of lethargy and corruption, an era when politicians paid homage to the new captains of industry and ignored the worker and farmer. They were a time when second-rate men occupied the White House—men who were not even the leaders of their parties.

Still, the period after the Civil War was an important time in American politics. It saw the appearance of problems which only the federal government had the constitutional authority to handle. Gradually Americans began to understand that the old truths no longer applied, that it was a time to update political ideas. The outcome, in the 1890s and in the first two decades of the twentieth century, was a ferment which produced programs and legislation of enormous consequence.

STUDY GUIDE: By appointing loyal Republicans to many posts, Benjamin Harrison set back the cause of civil service reform. Depressed agricultural conditions led to renewed support for the silver issue. The result was the Sherman Silver Purchase Act of 1890, which seriously weakened the federal gold reserve. Western Republicans agreed to support the McKinley Tariff Act in exchange for eastern Republican support of the silver act. The new high tariff sharply increased consumer prices and caused widespread dissatisfaction. Many Republican congressmen were defeated as a result of the tariff policy.

United States participation in the First Inter-American Conference in 1889 brought closer accord between the countries of the Western Hemisphere.

SUMMING UP THE CHAPTER

Names and Terms to Identify

Horatio Seymour	Charles Guiteau
Specie Resumption Act	Pendleton Civil Service
Carl Schurz	Reform Act
Charles Francis Adams	Mongrel Tariff Act of 1883
Horace Greeley	George Washington
"salary grab"	Plunkitt
Hamilton Fish	Tammany Hall
Fenian Brotherhood	GAR
Treaty of Washington	Thomas B. Reed
James G. Blaine	"free breakfast table"
Bland-Allison Act	Pan-Americanism

Study Questions and Points to Review

1. How did the presidency in the post-Civil War era tend to mirror the shortcomings of politics across the nation?

2. How did the Republican party lose the esteem built up during the Lincoln administration?

3. In the years 1865-68 there was an issue that was second only to Reconstruction as a source of political controversy in America. What was this issue?

4. What four national questions confronted Grant during his administration?

5. What circumstances led up to the *Alabama* claims? What was the outcome of the claims?

6. Why was Grant interested in annexing Santo Domingo?

7. Who was Grant's major opponent in the election of 1872?

8. What was "the Crime of 1873"?

9. What was Cleveland's attitude toward the tariff?

10. What was the purpose of the Sherman Silver Purchase Act? Was it successful?

Topics for Discussion

1. Who were the presidential candidates in the election of 1868? What were the issues? What were the results?

2. Describe the diplomacy of President Grant and and Secretary of State Hamilton Fish. How would you evaluate Fish?

3. Evaluate the presidency of Rutherford B. Hayes.

4. Who were the Liberal Republicans? What is their importance in American history?

5. Discuss the candidates and the outcome of the presidential election of 1876. Is it fair to consider this a "stolen election"? Give reasons for your answer.

6. Defend or challenge the view that Grover Cleveland's first administration (1885-89) was an outstanding one in American history.

Subjects for Reports or Essays

1. Conduct a "presidential poll" in your classroom. Ask each student to classify Presidents Grant through Harrison as "great," "near great," "average," "below-average," or "failure." Tabulate your answers and report the findings to the class.

2. Write a brief essay defending or challenging the view that it would have been proper for the federal government to redeem its Civil War bonds with greenback currency.

3. Prepare a report to prove or disprove the following statement: The protective tariff was in the best interest of American society in the period from 1868 to 1893.

4. Using library materials, write a biographical sketch on one of the following: Carl Schurz, Thomas B. Reed, Roscoe Conkling, Horace Greeley, Hamilton Fish, James G. Blaine.

5. Prepare a report on the position of the "boss" in American politics.

6. Assume that it is November 1868. You are editor of a major newspaper. Write an editorial announcing your support either for Grant or for Seymour.

Projects, Activities, and Skills

1. Using reference materials in your library, make a chart showing tariff rates on dutiable imports from the 1828 Tariff of Abominations until the McKinley Tariff of 1890.

2. Gather information on the United States Civil Service Commission. Report on its history and structure. Include in your report job opportunities, salaries, and qualifications.

3. Report on any recent tariff developments.

4. Using Table 35 as a guide, memorize the names of all the presidents from Washington through Hayes.

5. Use Appendix Table 7 to make a graph showing the value of exports from 1790 to 1890.

6. Prepare an illustrated report on the story of money. Use a chart to show what happens to coins from the time the metal leaves the mines until the coins arrive in our banks. Consider also paper currency.

Further Readings

General

The American Commonwealth by James Bryce. An Englishman writes about American politics.

Boss Tweed's New York by Seymour J. Mandelbaum. The infamous Tweed Ring.

Bosses in Lusty Chicago: The Story of Bathhouse John and Hinky Dink by Lloyd Wendt and Herman Kogan. A lively account of Chicago's First Ward.

The Education of Henry Adams by Henry Adams. Contains source material on American politics from 1868 to 1900.

The Politicos, 1865-1896 by Matthew Josephson. The emphasis is on domination of government by politicians and bosses.

Biography

The Autobiography of Thomas Collier Platt by Thomas Collier Platt.

Bourbon Leader: Grover Cleveland and the Democratic Party by Horace S. Merrill.

Chester A. Arthur: A Quarter-Century of Machine Politics by George Frederick Howe.

Grover Cleveland: A Study in Courage by Allan Nevins. Prize-winning biography.

Hamilton Fish: The Inner History of the Grant Administration (2 vols.) by Allan Nevins.

My Memories of Eighty Years by Chauncey M. Depew.

Plunkitt of Tammany Hall by William L. Riordon.

Reminiscences of Carl Schurz by Carl Schurz.

Rutherford B. Hayes and His America by Harry Barnard. Based on Hayes's personal papers.

Fiction

Coniston by Winston Churchill. Politics in New England.

The Gilded Age by Mark Twain (Samuel L. Clemens) and C. D. Warner. Land speculation in the post-Civil War era.

The Honorable Peter Stirling by Paul L. Ford. Urban politics in the 1890s.

A Spoil of Office, Jason Edwards, and *A Member of the Third House* by Hamlin Garland. Political reform.

Pictorial History

This Fabulous Century, 1870-1900, Vol. 8, by the editors of Time-Life Books.

CHAPTER 10
THE WEST AND POPULISM

ONLY A FEW THOUSAND AMERICANS had migrated to the vast western territory when the Mexican War broke out in 1846. The largest number lived in the Mexican territory of California, mostly in the vicinity of San Francisco Bay and along the Sacramento River. Another pocket of white settlers was in the Oregon country. And still another was along the eastern rim of the Great Salt Lake in present-day Utah, where a handful of Mormons had established a colony.

Then in 1848 the United States, via the peace settlement with Mexico, acquired clear title to California. A mere two weeks earlier gold had been discovered near present-day Sacramento, an event that touched off a rush to California and swelled its population.

Miners did not confine their efforts to California, however. Within a short time, hundreds of leather-skinned men, lured by visions of wealth and luxury, were fanning over the western landscape in search of gold and silver. After the 1850s, cattlemen and then farmers closed in on that sprawling area. The resulting population increase was such that by the year 1890 the American frontier—or so the Census Bureau announced—had ceased to exist.

By the time the western frontier disappeared, a large majority of the West's inhabitants were farmers. For most of those sturdy people, the West proved not to be an easy road to wealth. It was a forbidding land of high winds, sparse rainfall, and assorted "varmints." Like the Indians who had occupied it for centuries, the West resisted the coming of the settlers.

High interest rates by banks, discrimination by railroads, and the protective tariff system complicated matters for western farmers. The result was a farm problem in the West which gave birth to one of the most celebrated protest movements in American history. The movement grew slowly at first, then in the 1890s burst forth as a full-blown political revolt—the so-called Populist revolt. It attracted not only men of the West but farmers of other sections, notably the South, who felt similarly frustrated by the deal which nature and America's society had given them.

THE MINING FRONTIER

A few white Americans had made their way to the western half of the continent by the mid-1840s. Most were farmers who had settled down to a relatively peaceful if sometimes difficult existence in the fertile valleys of central California and Oregon and on the plain bound by the Great Salt Lake and the Rockies. Others roamed through the mountains and along rivers and streams, trapping fur-bearing animals or trading with Indians.

Gold at Sutter's Sawmill

Then came an event that triggered a transformation of the American West. It occurred on January 24, 1848, when a carpenter from New Jersey named James Marshall was directing construction of a millrace for John A. Sutter's new sawmill in the Sacramento Valley of California. While inspecting a ditch which workmen had recently dug, Marshall observed some flecks of dull yellow metal. He took a closer look. Then he scooped up a sample of the earth, mounted a horse, and rode forty-eight miles to show his find to Sutter. He had discovered gold.

To make certain that workmen would stay on the job until completion of the sawmill, thereby giving Sutter time to strengthen his claim to the land, the two men, Marshall and Sutter, sought to keep the discovery a secret. It was no use. Word got out and before long hundreds of men were scouring the Sacramento Valley for gold. They found plenty of it.

The Gold Rush

By September 1848 news of the discovery at Sutter's sawmill had exploded across the eastern half of the American Republic. So plentiful were gold nuggets in the Sacramento Valley, according to some reports, that a man simply had to reach down, almost anywhere, and pick them up. Thousands of men dropped whatever they were doing, sold farms, tools, and household goods, and turned their gaze westward. To reach Cali-

HEADLINE
EVENTS

1637 Pequot massacre
1675 King Philip's War
1763 Pontiac's uprising
  Proclamation of 1763
1775 Lord Dunsmore's War
1794 Battle of Fallen Timbers
1803 Louisiana Purchase
1820s Most Indians east of Mississippi are forced
  to migrate westward
1820s Winnebago War
1832 Black Hawk's War
1832-1836 Creeks resist removal from their
  lands
1835-1840 Seminoles resist giving up their
  lands in Florida
1838 Trail of Tears
1845 Texas is annexed
1846 United States gains clear title to part of
  Oregon territory
  Mexican War begins
1848 United States gains clear title to California;
  gold discovered there
1849 Gold rush in California
1850 Compromise of 1850
  California enters the Union
1854 Kansas-Nebraska Act
1857 Butterfield stages begin operating
1858 Gold discovered near Pike's Peak
  Silver discovered in Nevada
1860-1861 Pony express operating
1860s Kit Carson leads troops against Indians in
  Southwest
1861-1865 Civil War
1862 Santee Sioux uprising
  Pacific Railway Act
1864 Second Pacific Railway Act
  Black Kettle's massacre
1867 Nebraska enters the Union
  Alaska purchased from Russia
  Patrons of Husbandry (Grange) formed
1869 First transcontinental railroad completed
late 1860s Cattle industry begins to expand
1870s Glidden fashions barbed wire
1874-1875 Red River War
1875 Civil Rights Act of 1875

1875-1876 Sioux War
1876 Greenback party appears
  Custer's last stand
  Colorado enters the Union
1882 Supreme Court rules Civil Rights Act of
  1875 is unconstitutional
1886 Geronimo surrenders
1887 Dawes Act
  Interstate Commerce Commission created
  End of open-range cattlemen's frontier
1889 Oklahoma territory opened to white settle-
  ment
  North Dakota enters the Union
  South Dakota enters the Union
  Montana enters the Union
  Washington enters the Union
late 1880s Ghost dances
1890 Sherman Antitrust Act
  Idaho enters the Union
  Wyoming enters the Union
  Sherman Silver Purchase Act
  American frontier ceases to exist
  Massacre at Wounded Knee
1890s Populist revolt
1892 Populist party (People's party) formed
1893 Financial panic
1894 Coxey's army marches on Washington
  Pullman strike
  Wilson-Gorman Tariff Act
1896 Utah enters the Union
  Gold discovered in the Yukon
  Plessy v. *Ferguson* ruling
  Rural free delivery of mail established by
  Congress
  Free silver a campaign issue
  Populist party falls apart after election
1896-1898 Gold rush to Klondike
1907 Oklahoma enters the Union
1910 Postal savings system authorized by Congress
1912 Alaska becomes a federal territory
1913 Sixteenth Amendment ratified
  Seventeenth Amendment ratified
  Federal Reserve Act
1916 Warehouse Act

fornia, most forty-niners, in the beginning at least, struck out across the Great Plains, usually in wagon trains. But tortuous mountain passes, burning deserts and hostile Indians took a fearsome toll of overland travelers. Eventually most gold-seekers traveled by sea. Many booked passage aboard giant sailing vessels and made the long voyage from Boston, New York, or Baltimore to California via the tip of South America. Others, notably midwesterners, drifted down the Ohio and Mississippi to New Orleans on flatboats and boarded ocean-going vessels for the Isthmus of Panama. There they trudged across the malaria-infested isthmus to the Pacific, and boarded other ships for the final leg of the trip to California.

Not all forty-niners were citizens of the United States. News of James Marshall's discovery had filtered across the Atlantic to the British Isles and the European continent and across the Pacific to Japan and China. As in America, it fired the imaginations of countless men, who took passage to California. In America these Europeans and Asiatics became part of a multiracial, multinational society that included Mexicans, Canadians, and American Indians, as well as some blacks from Massachusetts, Indiana, and Alabama.

Life on the mining frontier, whether in California or, later, in other parts of the West or Alaska, was primitive, rough, and often violent. Miners found shelter in tents or shacks made of whatever materials might be handy. Some pitched tents wherever they found themselves when darkness brought an end to the day's prospecting. Others made their way back to villages or

After gold was discovered in California in 1848, thousands rushed to the West Coast in hopes of striking it rich. These prospectors were photographed in 1852 as they panned for gold in the Auburn Ravine near Sacramento.

Courtesy California State Library

towns. To provide prospectors with food, tools, and personal gear, some men went into the retail and grocery business. In many cases these retailers were disillusioned ex-miners who realized that they were apt to accumulate more gold by supplying the material needs of prospectors than by scratching about the countryside with pick, shovel, and washbowl.

Other denizens of the mining towns set up different kinds of enterprises to relieve prospectors of any gold they might find—enterprises calculated to capitalize on the loneliness, frustration, and boredom of life on the mining frontier. In the gambling halls of many mining towns the faro game never stopped. Every mining town had its array of saloons and brothels. In such an environment brawls and shootings were frequent.

Political institutions on the mining frontier were nonexistent, at least in the beginning. To meet such problems as the size of claims or sanitation regulations, most mining camps and villages adopted the "town meeting" technique employed earlier in the New England colonies. To enforce the decrees of the town or mass meeting, the miners often established vigilance committees. These searched out alleged violators, brought the accused to quick and informal "trial," and without considering appeals hastily executed sentence—sometimes by stringing the individual found guilty to the nearest tree.

California a Free State

By 1849-50, California had become a national political issue which threatened to tear the federal Union apart (see Chapter 4). The heart of the issue was whether or not the region, recently acquired from Mexico, was to be open to slavery. It was an issue that could not long await resolution, for the influx of miners to California had swelled the population and made necessary the establishment of normal political institutions. At length Californians urged on by President Zachary Taylor took matters in their own hands, drew up a constitution (which prohibited slavery), elected a governor and legislature, and applied for admission to the Union as a state. Impassioned debate continued, but finally leaders in Congress pushed through the Compromise of 1850 which, among other things, admitted California as a free state.

The prospectors helped bring statehood to California, but they soon found that the supply of easily obtainable gold was exhausted. By the mid-1850s mining had become essentially a corporate enterprise. Only corporations, pooling the resources of many individuals, could afford the elaborate machinery necessary for exploiting veins of precious metal deep in the earth. Facing reality, some forty-niners quietly packed their belongings and headed back home. Others settled down to become farmers, merchants, or fishermen, providing a foundation for California's permanent population. But a few others dreamed of finding gold, perhaps in a little stream bed over the next mountain. These men continued to scratch about the California countryside or moved on with renewed hope when word arrived of a new strike in some other part of the West.

"Pike's Peak or Bust"

In 1858 a party of miners found gold near Pike's Peak in present-day Colorado. Veteran prospectors rushed overland from California, while "greenhorns" rolled across the plains in covered wagons, some of which displayed the slogan, "Pike's Peak or Bust." This rush was short-lived, and soon wagons were heading eastward bearing the slogan, "Busted, by God!"

Several months later prospectors uncovered a more promising lode in the vicinity of Central City, a few miles below Denver. At the same time that prospectors were scurrying about Colorado, other prospectors were discovering the fabulous Comstock Lode near Virginia City in the western part of present-day Nevada. Named for Henry T. P. Comstock, a member of an old Puritan family of Connecticut and a participant in the California gold rush, the lode yielded a considerable amount of gold and unprecedented quantities of silver.

Still other prospectors had begun to work in a northerly direction and in 1862 made a major strike at Benetsee Creek in present-day Montana. Two years later a party of four miners found a rich vein at Last Chance Gulch (present-day Helena, Montana). From Montana prospectors spilled into present-day Idaho, where they found gold in numerous places. They also discovered the yellow metal in west-central Wyoming and in 1874 came an important strike in the Black Hills region of present-day South Dakota. At length, in 1891-94 at Cripple Creek in Colorado came the last major gold and silver strike in the West (omitting Alaska). So fruitful were the "diggings" around Cripple Creek that the area's population mushroomed from fifty in the year 1890 to fifty thousand by 1900.

Rich silver and lead mines attracted thousands of persons to Leadville, Colorado. This engraving, published in 1879, shows prospectors crossing the mountains. The trip was hard; both people and animals died along the way.

What contribution did miners make to the conquest of the western frontier?

The miner who trudged across mountains, desert, and plains in an endless search for precious metal found out what was in that expanse of territory west of the ninety-eighth meridian. At the middle of the nineteenth century Americans, despite the expeditions of Lewis and Clark and Zebulon Pike, knew little about the West. On maps much of it was labeled simply as "the Great American Desert." In the next few years, however, prospectors wandered over virtually every inch of the western frontier. By word of mouth and in diaries or letters they reported their observations, thus familiarizing the rest of the country with that vast area.

Alaska

In 1867 the United States acquired the vast territory of Alaska. The Russians, claimants of Alaska from the early part of the eighteenth century down to 1867, and also a handful of Americans who had explored the area, knew there was gold in Alaska. But they had no evidence that it might be present in large quantities. After American acquisition of the territory, a few prospectors, lured by rumors that Alaskan Indians used gold nuggets as trinkets, made their way to Alaska and began to search streams and rivers for the yellow metal. These "sourdoughs"—so called because of the kind of pancakes they made with fermented dough—had little success in the beginning. Then in 1880 Joseph Juneau and another prospector made a rich strike in the vicinity of Gastineau Channel, one of Alaska's many salt-water inlets. The result was a rush to the area and eventually the appearance of a town which, appropriately, became known as Juneau

—the present-day capital of the state of Alaska.

To secure more orderly administration of the area, Alaska's miners appealed to leaders in Washington for legislation. In 1884 Congress proclaimed Alaska a federal district, extended federal regulations for staking claims, and authorized the president to dispatch federal officials to administer the district. Often to the chagrin of prospectors—who wanted the district run to facilitate mining enterprises—the early administrators sent from Washington devoted considerable attention to the aborigines of the area, particularly the Eskimos. Because of the wanton slaughter of whales and walrus, their principal sources of food, clothing, and shelter, Eskimos in the closing decades of the nineteenth century were facing extinction. Whereupon federal officials sought to remedy the problems of the Eskimos. A district governor saw a partial solution to those problems—reindeer. With support from the government in Washington, he taught the Eskimos to raise herds of domesticated reindeer. For many years these reindeer helped the Eskimos to survive.

As in California, the supply of easily obtainable gold in the Juneau area soon disappeared. Corporate mining interests moved in and prospectors moved out. Prospectors then moved across the Alaska border into Canada's Yukon Territory. And it was in the Yukon, in a stream called Rabbit Creek, that gold was discovered in August 1896. Soon sourdoughs from all over Alaska and the Yukon were flocking to the area and in winter 1896-97 the town of Dawson appeared at the junction of the Klondike and Yukon rivers.

Cut off from the rest of the world by snow and ice over the winter months, prospectors, their packs and sleds bulging with gold, began to make their way from Dawson to Skagway and Juneau in spring 1897. Within days the glorious news had traveled southward to the United States. As had happened in 1848-49 following the California discovery, the news ignited the imaginations of millions of people including Jack London and Robert W. Service. These two writers were destined to capture the drama and pathos of the Yukon gold rush in story and verse.

There are estimates that as many as one hundred thousand men and women, mostly from the United States, set out for Yukon Territory. Perhaps a third of them eventually made it to Dawson. Despite warnings by the United States and Canadian governments, some five thousand prospectors attempted to cross the mountain trail from Skagway to Dawson in the autumn and winter of 1897. Many perished in the severe cold which sometimes reached seventy degrees below zero.

Some prospectors made fortunes in the Klondike, but most did not. By 1898, the surface gold was nearly gone and, as usual, the mining industry became a corporate enterprise.

The gold rush of 1896-98 accelerated the development of Alaska, despite the fact that the biggest strikes were over the border in Canada. First, Alaska was the gateway and operational base for the Canadian fields, which meant that most of the profits from supplying the prospectors centered in Alaska. Second, many prospectors liked the "north country" and when the gold craze passed settled down in the area. Inevitably they tended to congregate along the seacoast in Alaska, rather than in the isolated Canadian interior. Alaska's population increased from 3,000 in 1890 to 30,000 in 1900.

The gold rush made Americans aware of Alaska and its potential for development. They learned that gold was only one of Alaska's natural treasures. The area abounded with salmon and timber, and had large deposits of coal and iron. To encourage Alaska's development, the United States government granted Alaskans an increasing voice in the administration of their government. In 1912 Alaska started on its way to statehood by becoming a federal territory.

One thing was certain: the sourdoughs who in 1890 put the spotlight on Alaska forever laid to rest the old notion that the Alaska purchase of 1867 had been "Seward's folly."

STUDY GUIDE: Before the 1840s only a small number of white Americans lived in the vast western territory. The discovery of gold in California in 1848 attracted thousands of new settlers. Life on the mining frontier without organized government was primitive and often violent. After bitter debate between proslavery and antislavery forces Congress, in the Compromise of 1850, admitted California to the Union as a free state. Prospectors in search of precious metals wandered over most of the western frontier. Some struck it rich in Colorado, Nevada, and other areas. Most men, however, settled down to less exciting occupations and provided the foundation for a permanent population in the West. Their experiences proved that settlement of the West would depend on the ability of the white man to solve the problems of transportation and Indian relations.

The influx of people as a result of the Alaska gold rush led Congress to make Alaska a federal district. The discovery of gold sometime later in the Canadian Yukon Territory brought a rush of prospectors to that area. Many came back from Alaska after the supply of easily obtainable gold had run out. The gold rush of 1896-98 helped to stimulate the development of Alaska, which became a federal territory in 1912.

THE TRANSPORTATION FRONTIER

Prospectors who scoured the western lands in search of precious metals helped to prove that settlement of the area could never take place on any large scale until the region was tied to the rest of the nation by efficient, low-cost transportation.

As early as 1845 the federal government had begun to ponder the problem, when Texas was annexed. In 1846 the country gained clear title to part of the Oregon Territory, where American settlers had already begun to stream. Two years later, by way of the peace settlement with Mexico, the United States acquired California and other southwestern lands. As a result, the problem of transportation began to receive increasing attention in the federal capital.

In the beginning, the government's concern centered on establishing regular mail delivery. National leaders understood that cheap, efficient postal service was essential to the development of a republic as sprawling as the United States. At length, after considerable negotiation with

several steamship companies, the government in Washington awarded contracts for transporting mail from New York to the West Coast by way of the Isthmus of Panama. Still, it took a minimum of thirty days for a letter to make its way from the East Coast to San Francisco by the sea route. Before long, Westerners, particularly Californians, were clamoring for overland service.

Stagecoaches Westward

Clearly, a transcontinental railroad was needed, but as Chapter 4 shows, all attempts to get on with a western rail line floundered on the rocks of sectional (North-South) politics. Accordingly the government turned to the idea of subsidizing a stagecoach line which would establish a link, at least for mail, passengers, and light express, between the Mississippi Valley and the Pacific. Even this proposition heated up the sectional controversy.

In 1857 the government awarded a contract, worth $600,000 a year, to John Butterfield and Associates to transport mail from Saint Louis to San Francisco over a 2,795-mile route. The route stretched from Saint Louis to Tipton, Missouri, southward to Fort Smith, Arkansas, and across present-day Oklahoma and Texas to El Paso. It continued westward over present-day New Mexico and Arizona to Fort Yuma, thence to Los Angeles and up the Pacific coast to San Francisco. The mail would travel aboard stagecoaches which also would carry passengers and light express, thus enlarging Butterfield's earnings.

Nearly a third of the route followed by But-

Westward expansion created the need to link the Pacific with the rest of the nation. In the late 1850s a government-subsidized stagecoach line was set up to carry mail and passengers. Why did early attempts to establish a transcontinental railroad fail?

terfield stages was in Arkansas and Texas. When those states seceded from the Union in 1861, authorities in Washington shifted the Butterfield route northward into territory that at least was under nominal control of the federal government. At the same time the government, hoping to improve western mail and passenger services and thus encourage California to remain loyal to the Union, raised Butterfield's annual compensation for handling mail to a million dollars. Still, the Butterfield firm found it hard to turn a profit and in 1866 sold out to the Wells Fargo interests. Wells Fargo continued the overland mail service until completion of the first transcontinental railroad in 1869.

The Pony Express

Meanwhile, other firms had sought a share of the western mail and express business, including Russell, Majors, and Waddell. This company, after 1855, had prospered as a freight carrier and in 1859-60 decided to enlarge its operations. One of the new enterprises of Russell, Majors, and Waddell was the fabled "pony express."

Behind the pony express was a belief that by moving mail between Missouri and California in half the time required by the Butterfield express the firm of Russell, Majors, and Waddell, despite the lack of a federal subsidy, could make a profit. The firm mapped a route beginning at

Saint Joseph, Missouri, where the pony express would make connection with a railroad from the East. The route went west to Fort Kearny, along the Platte River to Fort Laramie, through South Pass to Fort Bridger and Salt Lake City, across the salt flats and desert to Carson City, through the Sierra Nevadas to Sacramento, and along the Sacramento River to San Francisco. Over the winter of 1859-60, 190 stations were erected along that route. Roughly ten miles apart, the stations were places where riders changed horses and sometimes slept and where agents cared for the firm's five hundred horses.

Certainly the pony express, inaugurated in spring 1860, abounded with drama and excitement. Hunched down over its neck, the rider galloped his mount for ten or so miles to the next station where an agent stood waiting with a fresh horse. Without uttering a word the rider leaped to the ground, threw his mail pouch over the new horse, bolted into the saddle, and galloped away toward the next station. In the course of a day or night he would repeat this maneuver several times while completing his run of seventy or eighty miles. After taking some food and resting ten or twelve hours, he would be back astride a horse, moving in the opposite direction. Pony express riders, eighty of whom were constantly in the saddle, endured wind, snow, and blazing sun, as well as hostile Indians and white bandits.

The pony express succeeded in dramatically reducing the time of communication between the East and California. Where the Butterfield express required twenty or more days to deliver a letter from western Missouri to San Francisco, the pony express could do the job in ten. Unhappily, though, the pony express did not make a profit. Just as it was getting in gear, moreover, the federal government promised an annual subsidy of $40,000 to any firm that would run a telegraph line to the Pacific. By 1860, crews were raising poles and stringing wires, one working westward from Kansas City, the other eastward from San Francisco. The wires met in 1861 and instant communication between East and West heralded the end of the pony express.

Wagon Trains

As early as 1820, creaking covered wagons, pulled by teams of mules or oxen, had begun to move freight west at tremendous cost. For the most part these early freighting operations served a handful of men who earned a living by

Courtesy Wells Fargo Bank History Room

In 1866 the Wells Fargo Company took over operation of the overland mail service. This service continued until completion of the first transcontinental railroad in 1869. Shown here is a letter sent to California bearing the Wells Fargo printed frank.

trading with Indians or trapping fur-bearing animals. The Mexican settlements in present-day New Mexico were another source of business. From the early 1820s onward wagon trains filled with cutlery, tools, and brightly colored cloth ground down the Santa Fe Trail to Santa Fe. After the Mexican War, when the western territory of the United States nearly doubled, the appearance of new military posts and, later, of mining areas enlarged the opportunities of men interested in freighting.

A Railroad to California

Slow-moving and limited in carrying capacity, stagecoaches and covered wagons obviously could not meet the West's requirements for efficient, low-cost transportation. Railroads offered the only solution, and it was only a matter of time before the rails made their way westward. The Civil War, by removing southern opposition in Congress, opened the way for federal legislation providing the necessary subsidies for a railroad to California. The Pacific Railway Acts of 1862 and 1864 were the outcome.

Construction of the first transcontinental railroad began in 1865. The great project was completed in 1869 when railroad officials drove the famous gold spike into place at Promontory Point in Utah Territory. Other transcontinentals followed, and by the end of the nineteenth century the West was effectively linked with rail transportation. As railroad companies moved westward, so did settlers. It was to the rhythmic exhaust of the steam locomotive that the settlers completed their take-over of the West.

STUDY GUIDE: The gaining of Texas, California, and the Oregon Territory led Congress to seek efficient, low-cost transportation to the West for freight and passengers. A government-subsidized stagecoach service and wagon trains carrying freight proved slow-moving and unprofitable. The Pony Express provided faster mail delivery, but when the first telegraph line to the Pacific Coast was completed in 1861 it was no longer needed. The Civil War removed southern opposition in Congress, clearing the way for passage of legislation to subsidize building a railroad to California. By the close of the 1800s transcontinental railroads linked East and West.

INDIANS

The miners who trudged about the West also recognized that conquest of the region required elimination or pacification of the Indian tribes who ranged over the entire area. These western Indians were courageous and resourceful, sustained by a grim determination to prevent the white man from taking over their land. But the white man was also brave, resourceful, and determined. Equally important, he was reinforced by a superior technology and a degree of unity that Indian tribes, which often despised one another as much as they despised the white man, could never match. Hence the outcome was inevitable: the Indian never had a chance.

The story of the struggle between Indians and whites for that great western territory is not a pleasant chapter in American history. It is punctuated throughout by the tragedy of man's inhumanity to man.

White Man's Indifference

Most white men were callously indifferent, often hostile, to the Indians. And as a result of the white man's attitudes—indifference or hostility, or a combination of the two—he contributed to the decay of Indian cultures. The weakening of moorings with the traditions of their fathers and undermining of respect for self and tribe had a devastating effect on many individual Indians who could not or would not adjust to the ways of the white man. One can observe the consequences of this development in the saddening plight of many present-day American Indians who live in poverty-ridden surroundings where ignorance, malnutrition, and drunkenness are rampant, and where a newborn infant has a life expectancy of no more than forty years.

Chapter 1 shows that the colonists at Jamestown came in contact with Indians as soon as they landed in 1607. Despite some apprehension on the part of both Indians and whites, the two groups got along satisfactorily in the early years of the settlement. Upon the marriage in 1614 of John Rolfe and Pocahontas the white colonists were in virtual alliance with most Indians of the area. But when Pocahontas and her father, Powhatan, died, relations between whites and Indians deteriorated. In 1622 the Indians, alarmed by the steady expansion of the white colony, attacked the Virginia settlements. Beaten back by the whites, the Indians observed an uneasy truce until 1644 when they launched a new attack. Again the whites, because of superior organization, tighter unity, and better weapons, turned back the Indians. Thereafter Indians of the area were in steady retreat as whites relentlessly pushed the edge of settlement westward. For many years Indians tried to maintain or recapture their land on the Virginia frontier. But it was no use. All of Virginia was destined to fall to the white man.

In New England the little Pilgrim colony, founded at Plymouth in 1620, benefited from the guidance of a friendly Indian named Squanto, but the Puritans who arrived in the Massachusetts Bay area a decade later saw the Indians as agents of the devil. Denying that Indians had a legitimate claim to any of the land of New England, Puritans steadily enlarged the area of white settlement until, in 1637, the Pequot tribe of the Connecticut Valley determined to resist. For the Indians the resultant war was a disaster. The decisive action came near New Haven when Puritan militiamen, in the darkness of night, surrounded a Pequot encampment and, at dawn, attacked. When the engagement was over two Puritans and more than five hundred Indians were dead.

Frightened perhaps by the fate of the Pequots, other Indians in New England kept their peace over the next three decades. Then, in 1675, a fierce twenty-four-year-old warrior called King Philip determined to drive the Puritans into the sea. The ensuing war was brutal. Followers of King Philip killed white women and children and Puritans retaliated by offering bounties for the heads of Indians and selling captives into slavery. The outcome of course was predictable. Outnumbered, poorly armed, and loosely organized, the Indians never had a chance. The most devastating Indian conflict of the colonial period, King Philip's War marked the end of any serious Indian resistance to white expansion in New England.

Penn Seeks Equality

In New Netherland the Dutch revealed no special concern for the land claims of Indians and rather quickly pushed the Indians out of the Hudson Valley and New Jersey. The same course of events followed in the Carolina colonies far to the South. But in Pennsylvania the proprietor William Penn, in accord with Quaker ethics, purchased land from the Indians and in general sought to deal with them as brothers. Although compared with other English colonies, Pennsylvania treated Indians reasonably well, Penn's idea of Indian equality with the white man never quite worked out. As the edge of settlement inched westward from Philadelphia, the Indians were pushed off their lands.

Chapter 2 shows that Indians took an important part in the wars from 1689 to 1763 between England and France for control of North America. Because the French were more tolerant in their attitudes about racial differences than were the English, and also because the French were less interested in land for agriculture, the Indians more often than not allied with the men of New France. Still, the English, usually by taking advantage of tribal rivalries, were always able to find Indian support.

The Westward Push

So long as the French and English were waging their great contest and, accordingly, were competing for Indian assistance, the Indians were better able to hold on to their lands. Nonetheless the white man's wars sapped Indian strength and in New York and Pennsylvania, Maryland and Virginia, white farmers steadily brought more land under cultivation and pushed their settlements westward. Then came the year 1763 and the elimination of French power in North America. With disappearance of the French danger the English colonists moved westward. To avoid sharp clashes with Indians, the government in London drew the so-called Proclamation Line

in 1763, and forbade whites to settle beyond the Appalachian Mountains. Few whites paid any attention. Meanwhile the Ottawa chieftain, Pontiac, like King Philip nearly a century before, was attempting to rally Indians to drive the white man into the sea. Beaten at every turn, Pontiac's allies one by one, and finally Pontiac himself, in 1766, were forced to make peace as a matter of survival—on the white man's terms.

The story of Pontiac's uprising of course was not new. It was the old story of white farmers pressing in on Indian hunting grounds, Indians retaliating with flame and tomahawk, and whites methodically putting them to rout. Beaten and demoralized, the Indians always made their way to the peace table and signed agreements in which they surrendered land to whites. In the end, the Indians gathered women and children together and trudged off in the direction of the setting sun in search of new homes. And it was a story that would be repeated again. There was Lord Dunmore's War of 1775 which erupted when Shawnees, led by an able chief named Cornstalk, resisted white encroachment on Shawnee lands in the upper Ohio Valley. There was the war which resulted when tribes in present-day Ohio, encouraged by the British in Canada, resisted the coming of the white man in the decade after the War of Independence. That conflict was concluded by General Anthony Wayne's victory over the Indians at Fallen Timbers in 1795.

Despite Anthony Wayne's expedition and the action at Fallen Timbers, the new federal government in the 1790s was thinking in terms of "civilizing" the Indian by persuading him to accept the ways of the white man. Ultimately, so such leaders as George Washington hoped, the Indian would become an integral part of America's white society. Frontiersmen who knew Indians firsthand doubted that integration would ever work and did not help the process.

By the time Thomas Jefferson entered the White House in 1801, the government in Washington had begun to despair of converting Indians to white civilization. At the same time there was increasing worry about the danger of large-scale hostilities between the races as white pioneers pressed westward. A way to avoid collisions was to move the Indians farther westward. This proposition became more attractive after purchase of the Louisiana Territory from France in 1803. Jefferson and others reasoned that much of Louisiana consisted of mountains and plains which never would appeal to the white man and hence would provide a permanent refuge for the Indians.

Thus federal agents set about to separate Indians from ancestral lands and persuaded them to push westward beyond the Mississippi. These efforts of the white man were not always successful. Many Indian leaders—such as Tecumseh—resisted. Usually the white man, with his superior numbers and weapons, was the victor.

After the War of 1812, as the westward movement of farmers accelerated, the federal government stepped up the program of removing Indians from the eastern part of the country and resettling them in territory west of the Mississippi. President James Monroe, just before leaving the White House in 1825, wrote that the government in Washington, by separating the Indian from the white man—and thus assuring peace between them—was performing a great service for the Indians.

Some Tribes Resist

Relying on bribery and intimidation, agents of the federal government managed with minimum difficulty in the 1820s to persuade most Indians living east of the Mississippi, including the Chickasaws and Choctaws, to give up their lands and migrate westward. But some tribes, notably the Sauks, Foxes, and Winnebagos in the North and the Creeks, Seminoles, and Cherokees in the South, resisted.

Elements of the Fox and Sauk tribes led by the elderly Chief Black Hawk, after crossing the Mississippi into present-day Iowa, decided to return to former homelands. The outcome was the Black Hawk War which lasted about four months in the spring and summer of 1832 and brought expulsion of the Foxes and Sauks from northwestern Illinois and the lower part of present-day Wisconsin.

The Creeks finally signed a treaty ceding their lands in 1832. But the document contained no provision for removal, and most Creeks elected to remain on their ancestral domain. Badgered and cheated by whites, both government officials and those who wanted to take over their lands, the Creeks eventually became demoralized. A few retaliated ineffectually in the so-called Creek War, and at length, in 1836, most agreed to migrate westward. A large number perished along the way, including three hundred who went down aboard a dilapidated steamboat on the Mississippi.

The Seminoles in Florida put up a stiffer fight. Relying on guerrilla tactics and taking full advantage of their knowledge of the Florida swamplands, they held their own against white soldiers from 1835 to 1840. Eventually most Seminoles gave up and accepted movement to present-day Oklahoma. But some remained in the Florida swamplands and to the present day deny that they are subject to the authority of the government in Washington.

The Trail of Tears

In Georgia, the Cherokees had tried to adopt the ways of the white man and indeed, by white standards, had become the most civilized Indians of North America. Unfortunately few white men were impressed, and for many years the Cherokees endured harassment. At length, in 1835, the Cherokees accepted a treaty exchanging their ancestral domain in northern Georgia for a section of prairie in Oklahoma. Next, in 1838, came the migration westward over the "Trail of Tears," and the story of that movement is a sad page in the chronicle of American history.

It began with soldiers forcing Cherokees from their homes as though they were animals, for many members of the tribe, refusing to accept the treaty as binding, declined to leave peaceably. Others fled to North Carolina where the federal government eventually provided a reservation. The homeless Cherokees, assembled at bayonet point, began a tortuous journey to northeastern Oklahoma. The movement was poorly organized, rest and supply depots were in the wrong places, and warehouses were stocked with the wrong goods. Prodded by soldiers, the Cherokees—women and children as well as men, the sick and infirm as well as the healthy—were forced to travel many miles each day. The outcome was inevitable. Dysentery and malnutrition, exposure and exhaustion claimed 4,000 of the 11,500 Indians who set out on the migration.

Then there were the Winnebagos whose story is even more dreary—if that is possible—than that of the Cherokees.

In the 1820s the Winnebagos found their lands invaded by white men who sought to mine the lead that was found in the area. A brief fracas, the Winnebago War, ended like all such conflicts with the Indians beaten and yielding to the demands of the whites. A few years later, the Winnebagos, pressed by federal agents, reluctantly agreed to exchange lands in Wisconsin for a section of present-day Iowa. Federal bayonets were used to get the tribe to Iowa.

By the 1840s white farmers were closing in on Iowa and in 1846 the federal government moved the Winnebagos to northern Minnesota. The hostility of the Sioux tribes of the region, plus the poor soil and rigorous winters, demoralized the Winnebagos. Before long some were migrating back to Iowa and southern Wisconsin. Next the government removed them to a more hospitable area in southern Minnesota where the soil was rich and the climate more to their liking. But soon white farmers were pressing in and in 1862 the unfortunate Winnebagos were compelled to exchange their domain in Minnesota for a reservation in South Dakota. By this time the members of the tribe had become so dispirited that they required federal handouts in order to survive. Finally, later in the 1860s, the government once more moved the remaining Winnebagos to a reservation in Nebraska which they shared with the Omahas.

By the late 1840s an overwhelming percentage of Indian Americans were living west of the Mississippi River, most of them in that vast territory to the west of Iowa, Missouri, and Arkansas. The policy of removing the Indians from the East and settling them in the West seemed a success. True, there were few guarantees against further encroachment. Some observers agreed with the French visitor Alexis de Tocqueville, who predicted that whites, after exhausting possibilities in the East, would move in on the western Indians and drive them from one "final" location to another until "their only refuge is the grave."

Alexis de Tocqueville's prediction proved correct. There were thousands of square miles of desert and rock-cluttered mountain slopes in the West, but there were also great stretches of plains capable of producing wheat and barley and sustaining livestock, fertile valleys, and rich timberland. And hidden beneath sections of barren soil were mineral treasures of untold value. When the white man became aware of the opportunities, he invaded the West with slight regard for the welfare of Indians or promises made them by the government in Washington.

A Forbidden Land

In 1848 came the discovery of gold in the Sacramento Valley. Soon the Indians of the West could see trains of covered wagons inching over the plains and threading mountain passes as they made their way to California. Alarmed, the Indians often swooped down on the wagon trains and subjected the whites to flame and tomahawk.

Perhaps one hundred thousand Indians lived in central California at the time of the gold rush and, on the whole, they were a pitiful lot. In that era before irrigation and modern technology, California was a forbidding land. The Indians spent most of their energies moving about the countryside in a perpetual and desperate search for food.

For such people the coming of the white man might have been a blessing. It was not. Prospectors often scorned and cheated the Indian. Worse, they exposed him to such scourges as smallpox and venereal disease, also to "fire water"—whiskey. The result for the Indians of central and southern California was further degeneration—and death. Between 1850 and 1860, the Indian population of the region declined from 100,000 to 35,000.

The admission of California to the federal Union, in 1850, established the need for a railroad reaching from the Mississippi Valley to the Pacific. The outcome was the passage of the Kansas-Nebraska Bill in 1854, making Kansas and Nebraska federal territories. By approving the Kansas-Nebraska legislation Congress broke its promise to the Indians, who had been guaranteed that the area would remain their permanent homeland. Hardly had President Pierce approved the legislation before federal agents began to circulate through Kansas and Nebraska. They persuaded tribes, including the Pawnees, Delawares, and Miamis, to accept treaties which in 1854 alone reduced Indian landholdings in the area by ninety percent. Then, when Indians were slow to leave the land they had ceded, they received the same harsh treatment as had the Cherokees in Georgia.

Oklahoma Territory

Meanwhile, white settlers were streaming into Kansas. While the whites waged civil war over the question of slavery, they seemed to agree on the undesirability of having Indians as neighbors and began clamoring for removal of all Indians from the territory.

Where might the government resettle the Indians of the Kansas Territory? Present-day

Oklahoma seemed a likely place. True, Congress had set aside the latter area for the so-called Five Civilized Tribes, that is, the Cherokees, Creeks, Seminoles, Chickasaws, and Choctaws. But few men worried about the sanctity of treaties with Indian tribes.

Then came the Civil War and a fair number of Oklahoma's Indians, particularly the Chickasaws and Choctaws, lined up with the Confederacy. This was a natural step inasmuch as some Indians had Negro slaves, the Confederate states of Arkansas and Texas flanked the Indian domain, and the federal government, as soon as the war started, had withdrawn troops from the area.

Some of Oklahoma's Indians, however, particularly Cherokees and Creeks, joined Union ranks. In only one action in the entire war, at Pea Ridge in Arkansas, did Indians wearing the gray uniforms of the South take an important part. Still, the fiction that the Five Civilized Tribes had joined an alliance with the Confederacy opened the way, in 1866, for a treaty which compelled them to make room for Indians from Kansas and elsewhere on the plains. They were also compelled to permit railroad companies to run tracks across their land.

The time of the Civil War (1861-65), saw other important developments regarding Indians, especially the Santee Sioux. In 1862 in Minnesota, authorities with considerable difficulty, put down the Indians led by the warrior Little Crow. When the fighting ended, more than fifteen hundred Indians were prisoners and white Minnesotans were demanding that a large number of the captives should face the hangman. President Lincoln intervened and possibly saved the lives of many. Next, white authorities began to arrange removal of most remaining Indians from the state.

In the Southwest, groups of Apaches and Navajos took advantage of the federal government's distraction by the war against the South and unleashed a wave of attacks against prospectors, stagecoaches, and white settlements. Troops led by the legendary Kit Carson were swift to attack, and the results were predictable. The Indians were slaughtered and their crops and dwellings destroyed. As a result, the Indians agreed to settle down on reservations.

To the north, in the eastern part of present-day Colorado, there were stirrings among the Cheyennes and Arapahos who were forced in 1861 to live on a reservation between the Arkansas River and Sand Creek. The two tribes were both nomadic and had lived by following the buffalo herds. Soon they were straying off the reservations to raid mining camps, outlying farms, and stagecoaches.

At length, in summer 1864, the Indians refused orders of the territorial governor to stay on the reservation. All-out war followed, until the approach of autumn when the Indians, who viewed war as a warm-weather enterprise, began to think of peace. The chieftain Black Kettle, unable to get a peaceful agreement from the territorial governor, led seven hundred of his followers to Fort Lyon where he expected federal troops to protect them from the vengeance of the Colorado militia.

The federal commander made no promises to Black Kettle, and the militia commander ordered his troops to attack one night in late November of 1864. Black Kettle waved the Stars and Stripes, then a white flag. To no avail. The white men rushed forward, screaming, shooting, and burning. Women and children as well as men were savagely massacred. When the dust finally settled, 450 Indians were dead.

Many people in the eastern half of the nation were horrified. Then in summer 1865 came news of another massacre, this time of eighty-two federal soldiers. Seeking to protect the Bozeman Trail, a road to the Montana mining camps which cut across some of the Sioux tribes' best hunting grounds in present-day South Dakota and Wyoming, the soldiers had run into an Indian ambush. The outcome was pressure on the government in Washington to reassess federal Indian policy. Over the next dozen years assorted politicians, bureaucrats, and humanitarians searched for solutions to the "Indian problem" of the West.

Meanwhile federal agents, using the time-honored tactic of intimidation and bribery, persuaded numerous chieftains to accept new treaties designed to confine Indians to reservations. Persuading the young warriors to accept such restrictions was another matter. In summer 1868 roving bands of Cheyennes, Arapahos, Comanches, Kiowas, and Apaches, perhaps two thousand braves in all, began to cut a trail of death and destruction across southern Kansas.

When northerly winds began to howl across the plains, Indian operations, as usual, halted. But not those of the federal military commander of the area, General Philip H. Sheridan. After training his men in winter tactics, Sheridan mapped an elaborate offensive. Success of the operation was assured in late November 1868 when Colonel George A. Custer, in command of the main federal force, stumbled on a major Indian encampment in the Washita Valley in present-day Oklahoma. Carefully locating his men in the dead of night, Custer ordered an attack at dawn. In a furious hand-to-hand encounter the white soldiers overcame the Indians. By the following spring, most of the Indians were back on reservations.

But peace proved temporary. Indians of the southwest began attacks resulting in the Red River War of 1874-75, fought mainly in northern Texas. Again the white soldiers, now commanded by General William Tecumseh Sherman, employed winter tactics with deadly effectiveness. As in other campaigns against the Indians, white men benefited from superior organization, closer unity, and better weapons. Hence they convinced most southwestern Indians that, like it or not, they were going to have to stay on reservations and accept government by the white man.

To be sure, some warriors, notably Apaches, determined to keep up the fight. The best-known Apache leader was the fabled Geronimo, master of the tactic of strike and run. He was acquainted — or so it seemed — with every rock and crevice in the great Southwest and could function at peak efficiency in 110-degree heat. Geronimo terrorized the southwestern frontier, and also northern Mexico. Eventually, in 1886, he surrendered and, lest he escape and inflame the frontier once again, was dispatched finally to Fort Sill in Oklahoma Territory.

Although technically a prisoner of war, Geronimo led a relatively free and prosperous life in Oklahoma and in 1905 took a train to Washington where he attended the inauguration of President Theodore Roosevelt. In an interview with the president the old warrior appealed to him to "let me die in my own country." But Roosevelt explained to Geronimo that his return to Arizona could touch off a new wave of violence, hence he must remain at Fort Sill.

If the Red River War persuaded most Indians of the southern plains that it was futile to resist the white man, the Sioux War of 1875-76 persuaded most of those of the northern plains.

Except for a few spirited warriors who followed such leaders as Sitting Bull, Gall, and Crazy Horse, most Indians of the northern plains by the mid-1870s had agreed to lead peaceful lives on reservations marked out for them in the Dakotas, present-day Montana, and Wyoming. But life on the reservation did not suit the Indians, most of whom were members of Sioux tribes. For generations they had roamed the plains in pursuit of buffalo. To make matters worse, food and supplies sent to them by the federal government usually turned out to be of inferior quality.

Then, in 1875, word leaked out that gold had been discovered on the Sioux reservation in the Black Hills area of present-day South Dakota. Soldiers assigned to protect the reservation proved powerless to hold off the gold-hungry prospectors. Large numbers of braves, fed up with life on the reservation anyhow, began straying off the reservation to join up with Chief Sitting Bull.

Custer's Last Stand

Fearing a bloodbath, federal authorities ordered all Indians to be back on their reservations by the first day of February 1876, but many did not comply. This refusal suited the blue-clad soldiers of the United States Army, who had concluded that war was the only language which the Plains Indians understood. Confident of their own abilities, and generally disdainful of the Indians' willingness to stand and fight, they had no doubt about the outcome of any conflict.

While the Indians gathered supplies along the Big Horn River in the southern part of present-day Montana, the federal army set out. By June the army was beginning to close in on the Indians. In charge of one of the advanced columns was Colonel Custer, the hero of Washita. Custer either ignored or misunderstood his superior's orders and force-marched his regiment, the Seventh Cavalry, along the banks of the Little Big Horn River. On the afternoon of June 25 his scouts spotted an Indian village. Custer, leading a few hundred men, only part of his regiment, attacked. Unwittingly he had stumbled on the main Sioux encampment and within minutes his little band was surrounded by 2,500 Sioux warriors. Before the sun went down, Custer and all his men lay dead.

"Custer's last stand" was a signal for the Sioux and their allies to retreat in an easterly direction, toward the Tongue River. It was no use. By the end of October 1876, federal troops had managed to trap most of the warriors, although, to their immense disappointment, failed to capture the elusive Sitting Bull. With a few other braves, Sitting Bull escaped to Canada, where he stayed for the next several years until hunger

hunters. The Indians of the Great Plains had built their lives around the buffalo. They had nourished themselves on buffalo meat, clothed themselves and made tepees from buffalo hides.

At the middle of the nineteenth century perhaps fifteen million buffalo ranged across the plains, a seemingly inexhaustible supply. Then, after the Civil War, came the white man with his long-range rifle. Sharpshooters, including William F. ("Buffalo Bill") Cody, killed buffalo to provide fresh meat for construction gangs of the Union Pacific Railroad. Other white men thought it great sport to cut down the lumbering, nearsighted beasts. Next, a tannery in Pennsylvania learned to process buffalo hides into commercial leather and began to offer as much as three dollars for a single hide. With that, hunters swarmed over the plains and in some years in the early 1870s shot to death as many as three million of the great animals. Before the decade of the 1870s ended, all buffalo were gone on the southern plains, and by the mid-1880s only a couple of hundred remained in the northern plains. By the year 1904, the entire buffalo population of the West had slipped to thirty-four.

persuaded him and his comrades to return to the United States and surrender to federal authorities.

The Destruction of the Buffalo

Whatever the outcome of their battles with white soldiers, by the 1870s the Plains Indians could not continue the life they had known for so many generations. A central reason was the wanton destruction of the buffalo by white

The Last Indian Wars

On conclusion of the Sioux War in 1876 the sad drama of armed conflict between Indians and white men had about played out. Apart from the

In the twenty years after the Civil War, most of the Buffalo on the Great Plains were killed by white hunters with long-range rifles. How did this wanton destruction of the buffalo affect the life of the Plains Indians?

Harper's Weekly, August 2, 1884

Library of Congress

pursuit of Geronimo, which extended through the mid-1880s, only a few scenes remained. The most poignant perhaps took place in present-day Oregon, Idaho, and Montana and involved some of the most intelligent and civilized Indians in North America, the Nez Percés (so called because they decorated themselves with rings in their noses).

Like other Indians, the Nez Percés, who made their homes in the lush Snake River Valley, were compelled to sign treaties in which they surrendered large tracts of their domain. But whites were not satisfied and through the 1860s and 1870s pressed the tribe to give up even more land. Led by Chief Joseph, the Nez Percés refused to forfeit any more of the soil which held the bones of their ancestors. Then in 1877, came a confrontation between Indians and federal troops. Whereupon Chief Joseph and his people attempted to avoid capture by making their way to Canada.

Still, the attempt of the Nez Percés to avoid capture was doomed to fail. In October 1877, soldiers cornered Chief Joseph and his cold and hungry followers in western Montana. After their surrender the Nez Percés were carted off to present-day Oklahoma where they found little except disease and death. Later the government

Indians objected to having their lands taken by settlers. United States troops and the Sioux Indians fought bitterly in South Dakota. The last major battle took place in the Badlands in 1890. Uneasy peace was maintained afterwards. This photograph was taken in 1891 and shows an Indian camp in the Badlands near Pine Ridge, South Dakota.

returned them to reservations in Idaho and Washington.

The Dawes Act

In the late 1870s, white Americans in the East were becoming increasingly sensitive to the plight of the Indians in the West. Their concern reached new heights in 1881 with the appearance of Helen Hunt Jackson's book, *A Century of*

Chief Joseph of the Nez Percés became a hero after he refused to give up the traditional homeland of his people. He also was known for his intelligence, his military skill, and his nobility of character. This portrait was completed during his lifetime.

Library of Congress

This lithograph of a Sioux Indian chief was made from a drawing in 1901 by Frederic Remington, famous for his paintings of the West. By that date, most Sioux were living on reservations. Why did the Sioux tribes find it particularly hard to adapt to life on the reservation?

Dishonor, a biting indictment of the white man's treatment of the Indians. The result was pressure on Congress for some action on behalf of the Indians. In response Congress passed the Dawes Act in 1887. The essential idea of the Dawes legislation was to break up tribal relationships, convert the individual Indian into an independent farmer, and integrate him into the white man's society. To achieve these purposes the legislation authorized the president to divide tribal lands and give each head of a family 160 acres. To prevent whites from slick-talking unwary Indians out of their land, the law prohibited the Indian from disposing of his land for twenty-

By the time this photograph was taken in 1891, most Indian tribes had been settled on reservations. Shown here is a group of Indian chiefs and United States officials at the Pine Ridge reservation in South Dakota.

five years. All Indians who received land under terms of the legislation would become citizens of the United States and any reservation land remaining after the division would be sold, the proceeds going into a trust fund for educating Indian children.

The Dawes Act turned out to be less than a success. Most western Indians were not prepared by temperament or experience to become independent farmers. Hence they seldom found prosperity or happiness in their new lives. If anything, they became even more dependent on the federal government for the means of survival and more vulnerable to the tactics of unscrupulous people who were always trying to turn a profit at the expense of the Indian. The weakening of ties with ancestral traditions created a void in the life of the Indian which the white man's customs and traditions could not fill, and the result was further demoralization.

Some Indians resisted the government's attempt to convert them to the ways of the white man. In the late 1880s a number of them, particularly members of northern Sioux tribes, were caught up in a highly emotional movement which featured ghost dance rituals and looked for the appearance of a messiah or savior who would restore the Indian to his former dignity and power. A leader of the movement was Sitting Bull. When, in December 1890, the fabled Sioux

medicine man resisted arrest by Indian policemen he was killed. Two weeks later, when federal soldiers sought to disarm other Sioux, a fight broke out, resulting in the massacre at Wounded Knee in southwestern South Dakota. Two hundred Indians, including women and children, and twenty-nine soldiers died in this tragic affair, the last major armed conflict between Indians and whites in the United States.

STUDY GUIDE: The struggle between Indians and white men for the western territory is a tragic example of man's inhumanity to man. Despite their grim determination to hold onto their lands, the Indians never had a chance against the greater numbers and superior technology of the white man. After the Louisiana Purchase, the federal government began to move the eastern Indian tribes farther west. Some tribes, such as the Creeks and Seminoles, fiercely resisted attempts to resettle them. The forced migration to Oklahoma of the Georgia Cherokees over the "Trail of Tears" reveals the indifference and cruelty of many white men. By the 1840s the majority of Indians lived west of the Mississippi River. When white men began to move west in the middle of the nineteenth century, treaties with

INDIANS IN THE WEST 1850 – 1890

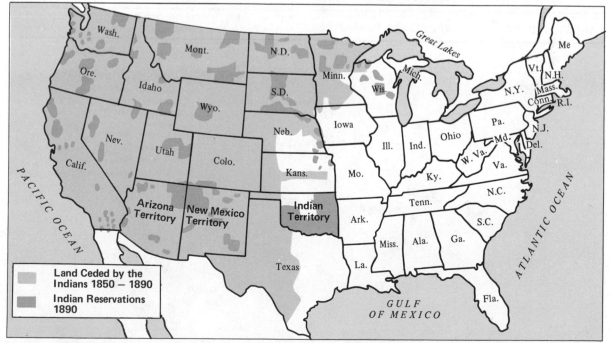

Land Ceded by the Indians 1850 – 1890

Indian Reservations 1890

Indians were disregarded and Indians were forced to resettle at the whim of Congress. The Indians fought a series of wars to preserve their land and way of life. Destruction of buffalo on the Plains by white hunters made it impossible for the Plains Indians to survive. Defeat in the Sioux War in 1876 brought an end to Indian resistance. Congress passed the Dawes Act in 1887 in an unsuccessful attempt to weaken tribal ties and make the Indian an independent farmer.

CATTLEMEN AND FARMERS

The enormous "open-range" cattle industry that flourished on the Great Plains from the end of the Civil War until the late 1880s started in southern Texas. After securing independence from Mexico, Texans rounded up the herds of stringy cattle that were wandering aimlessly over the area and crossbred them to produce beef more acceptable to the American taste. They began selling the cattle wherever they could find a market—in Texas, at New Orleans, in the gold fields of California and Colorado. Throughout the 1840s and 1850s, however, cattle-raising on the plains was an infant industry.

Texans Develop the Livestock Industry

Then, during the Civil War, Texans lost most of their markets for cattle. But the animals continued to reproduce, and when the war ended the herds were greatly enlarged. The war, moreover,

had depleted the cattle supply in the northeastern part of the Republic. Texans seized the opportunity and in spring 1866 began to drive herds northward toward Sedalia, Missouri. At Sedalia they arranged to load their animals in livestock cars of the Missouri Pacific Railroad for shipment eastward.

But the hilly route to Sedalia was ill suited for the long drive. The outcome was little or no profit. Then an enterprising meat dealer from Illinois built pens and loading chutes at Abilene on the Kansas Pacific Railroad. Immediately the long drive from southern Texas to Abilene, via the Chisholm Trail, became a success.

The "cowboys"—some of them black—who drove the herds northward have come to occupy an honored place in American folklore. However, any adventure that the cowboy experienced was slight when compared with the long hours of hard labor he had to endure. For weeks on end he would spend ten or twelve hours a day on horseback chasing strays and perhaps risking his life against Indians or angry farmers. He performed his work in blistering heat, driving rain, and bitter cold.

The business of moving cattle from Texas to railheads in Kansas by the long drive lasted only a few years. By the 1870s rail lines had inched into Texas, giving cattlemen there direct access to eastern markets.

Until the 1870s Texas cattlemen drove their herds north along the Chisholm Trail to the railroad town of Abilene, Kansas. This engraving published in *Leslie's* in 1871 shows cattle being driven up a ramp to be transported to market on the Kansas-Pacific Railway.

Texas cattlemen, meanwhile, discovered that Texas longhorns could survive quite well in more northerly latitudes. In the late 1860s and 1870s they began to fatten cattle on the luscious grasslands of the public domain in Kansas, Nebraska, Colorado, Wyoming, Montana, and the Dakotas. By the year 1880 it was almost impossible for one to travel longer than an hour anywhere on the Great Plains without catching sight of immense herds. In those years, the demand for western beef grew with the development of the refrigerator car and improved packing methods. The decline in cattle-raising in the eastern half of the country also sent market prices soaring. The result was a rush to the plains by would-be cattlemen, reminiscent of gold rushes a decade or so before. For many individuals the venture—at least for a time—proved highly profitable. For others, some of whom started with nothing more than a piece of the government land they had taken over and a few longhorns, it brought immense fortunes.

Cattlemen Unite

By the early 1880s many cattlemen, noting that pastures were wearing thin, concluded that the plains were falling victim to overgrazing. To protect pastures for their own herds, despite the fact that most of the land still belonged to the federal government, they started to string fences across the countryside. Many of them organized stock-growers' associations to control grazing and worked together to meet other common hazards, including rustlers, wolves, and prairie fires. It was no use. The great cattle boom was bound to end.

First, in the mid-1880s, the price of western beef began to fall because of glutted market conditions. Next, in 1885-86, came a severe winter in which large numbers of cattle on the plains died. The following summer brought a grass-withering drought which caused many cattlemen to panic and rush herds to market, where they further depressed prices. Then came the killing cold of 1886-87, perhaps the worst winter in the history of the West. In some parts of the northern plains the mercury plunged to fifty degrees below zero. With the brutal cold came heavy snowfalls. The outcome was death for millions of animals and bankruptcy for thousands of cattlemen.

While 1887 marked the end of the open-range cattlemen's frontier in the West, it did not end the cattle industry. Cattlemen who somehow

struggled through the perilous times went to work to put the industry on a more sensible economic foundation. They fenced the grassland (most of which they leased or bought from the government), carefully limited the size of herds, and began growing hay to assure survival of herds in time of drought or blizzard. As a consequence, prosperity eventually returned to the industry.

Cattlemen, meanwhile, had to face other problems. There were the sheepherders who invaded the plains early in the 1880s. Contending that sheep ruined pasturage by biting off grass close to the ground, cattlemen sought to turn back the sheepmen, sometimes with bullets. But the sheepmen continued to push into areas that cattlemen had considered their private domains.

The Farmer Moves Westward

A more serious problem for cattlemen, and sheepherders as well, was the dirt farmer who during and after the Civil War moved in on the Great Plains.

Down to the time of the Civil War, few farmers had ventured onto the plains. The absence of low-cost transportation in the region had made impossible a profitable agricultural operation. Indians occupied large areas of the plains. Finally, there was climate and geography. The farmer was accustomed to operating in the eastern half of the continent where rainfall always exceeded by a considerable margin the twenty inches annually considered a minimum for successful farming. Because of the heavy rainfall, trees were plentiful in the East.

The plains presented the farmer with new circumstances: they seldom received twenty inches of rainfall in a year, and there were few trees. This meant that the farmer had to devise ways of overcoming the shortage of water. He also needed equipment which would enable him to cultivate large tracts of land, for under the most favorable conditions the yield per acre would be low. Only by planting many acres could the farmer achieve a satisfactory return. Finally, he had to find substitutes for timber, particularly for fencing. He had to have fences to protect his crops from cattle that grazed the open range, but the cost of shipping in timber was prohibitive.

The problem of transportation was resolved in the 1860s and 1870s. During that time Indian resistance was practically ended. In those years railroad companies pushed their tracks across the Great Plains, and the federal government expelled Indians from much of the land they had held in the region.

Early in the 1870s, a farmer in Illinois, Joseph F. Glidden, fashioned barbed wire, and the fencing problem of the plains farmers was resolved. By the mid-1880s, Glidden, who rented a small factory and went into the barbed wire business, was turning out six hundred miles of barbed wire fencing every ten hours.

At first irrigation seemed the only solution to the problem of water shortage. Along the western edge of the plains, where farmers could divert water from streams rushing down from the Rocky Mountains, irrigation proved fairly successful. Elsewhere on the plains some farmers tapped subterranean pools with deep-drilled wells and brought water to the surface with pumps powered by windmills. But drilling wells was too costly an operation for most pioneer farmers. As a result, the ancient Middle Eastern technique of dry farming was employed. In dry farming the farmer sought to prevent moisture in the earth from evaporating through crevices by pulverizing surface soil and, in effect, blanketing the crevices with dust. The dust also attracted moisture up to the root systems of plants. Dry farming was adaptable only to cultivation of drought-resistant crops, such as spring and winter wheat. Still it enabled farmers to open vast areas in the semiarid region to agriculture.

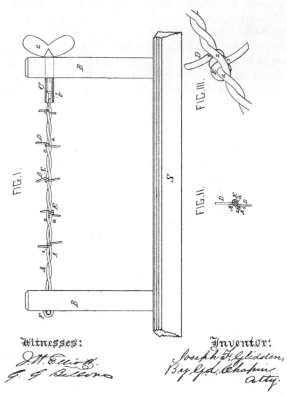

Courtesy American Patent Law Association

In 1874 Joseph F. Glidden received a patent for his invention of barbed-wire fencing. Shown here is the drawing submitted by Glidden to the Patent Office.

On the plains profitable farming depended on the cultivation of large fields. Until the late 1860s and 1870s, equipment that would make possible such operations did not exist. Then a range of implements and machines appeared, which resolved this aspect of the western farm problem. There were new plows specially adapted to the humus soils of the plains. Next appeared a plow on which a farmer could ride, then one that would cut two or three furrows at a time. There were new, more efficient planters, as

Land offices did a booming business in the decades after the Civil War as thousands of people headed west to acquire land from the federal government. This 1874 engraving from *Harper's* shows a Kansas land office.

Library of Congress

well as devices that speeded the tasks of mowing, raking, and baling hay. New machines, including the steam threshing machine and combine, appeared to speed the harvesting of crops.

This photograph was taken in 1887 in the vicinity of Coburg, Nebraska. It shows a pioneer family in front of their sod house. Why did farmers delay moving to the Great Plains down to the time of the Civil War? Why did they build sod houses?

Black Americans Settle the West

The movement of people to the plains accelerated as, one by one, barriers to settlement were overcome. The pioneers staked out farms in every part of the West, from the Canadian border to the Rio Grande, and in a third of a century they more than doubled the settled area of the United States. Texas, California, Oregon, Kansas, and Nevada were already in the Union when the great migration began. With settlement came political organization and the movement of the other territories toward statehood. Nebraska gained admission as a state in 1867, Colorado in 1876, North Dakota, South Dakota, Montana, and Washington in 1889, Idaho and Wyoming in 1890, and Utah in 1896.

Among those who moved toward the setting sun in the closing decades of the nineteenth century were a fair number of black Americans.

In 1879, following a crop failure in the South, a large migration of blacks to the Midwest got under way. Several thousand Negroes arrived in Kansas, Missouri, Iowa, and Nebraska. Some sought land; others hoped to find the equality that they believed was typical of the western frontier. For many such black people, the harsh winter of 1879-80 brought tragedy and disillusionment, for they lacked food, shelter, and clothing. In some towns they were met with hostility and were driven away. But in spite of setbacks, the black movement westward continued. In Oklahoma a number of all-black towns were established. One of these, Boley, founded in 1904, was publicized as "the largest and wealthiest Negro city in the world."

Some of the black men who helped to settle the West were adventurers—cowboys, cavalrymen, and explorers. Blacks were to be found on every western frontier from the gold rush in California in 1849 until the last gold strike in the Black Hills. Perhaps the best known black cowboy was Nat ("Deadwood Dick") Love, who was famed throughout the Dakota Territory for his skill in riding and marksmanship.

The Ending of the Western Movement

The climax of the westward movement during this era came in 1889. In that year the federal government opened present-day Oklahoma, or the Indian Territory as it was then called, to

THE WEST

The last frontier was settled between 1865 and 1890. The closing of the frontier brought about great changes in lifestyle for all Americans. The Indians of the West were defeated and confined on reservations. Western mining towns grew up overnight in areas where precious metals were found. Other towns became important as centers of transportation and trade serving ranchers. The diminishing supply of unclaimed land made it difficult for men to purchase new farms. During the 1890s a new political party was formed to deal with the problems that western farmers faced.

2   Courtesy Utah Travel Council

1   Rainier National Park Company, Tacoma, Washington   **3**   *The Bettmann Archive*

1

Many people were lured to the West by the magnificent character of the countryside. The beauty of the land contributed to the romance of the West. Mount Rainier in Washington State is shown here.

2

During the 1880s Frisco was a busy mining town. It was the site of the Horn Silver Mine, one of the richest silver mines in Utah. Today Frisco is a deserted ghost town with only a few decaying buildings.

3

The interior of a Mandan chief's tent is shown in this painting. The Mandan were one of the Plains peoples who occupied the grassland between the Mississippi and the Rockies. Like their neighbors, the Arikara and the Hidatsa, the Mandan were farmers who lived in permanent villages. In the late 1800s, white settlers claimed their land and created a reservation for them in North Dakota.

4

In the 1870s Dodge City, Kansas, was a large center for marketing and transporting cattle. Texas ranchers drove their cattle north to Dodge City because it was the nearest railroad depot. Cowboys liked to celebrate after the long ride from Texas, and cow towns like Dodge became wild and disorderly. This photograph shows Front Street, Dodge City, as it might have looked in the 1870s.

5

As crop prices fell in the 1890s, many western farmers joined the new People's Party and became Populists. William Jennings Bryan appealed to them when he ran for president in 1896 and 1900 because he proposed raising prices through the unlimited coinage of silver—"free silver." Bryan called the gold standard a cruel burden to people everywhere—a "cross of gold."

4   Courtesy State of Kansas Department of Economic Development

5   Library of Congress

white settlement. Although it was reserved for the Five Civilized Tribes, the Indian Territory had long attracted the envious gaze of white settlers. Throughout the 1870s and 1880s whites put heavy pressure on the government in Washington to set aside Indian claims to the entire territory. The white men contended that it was unfair to leave such a vast territory in the hands of a mere 75,000 Indians. They argued further that the Indians had done little to develop the area and claimed that white farmers could turn it into a paradise. At length, in 1889, federal agents persuaded Creeks and Seminoles for $4 million to surrender their title to a large portion of the territory, the so-called Oklahoma District. President Harrison announced that the district would be open to white settlement at noon on April 22, 1889.

Harrison's anouncement touched off a rush toward Indian Territory by farmers, speculators, and assorted adventurers. By April 22, perhaps one hundred thousand people were poised along the border of the district waiting for federal officers, precisely at noon, to fire pistols signaling that the district was open. Many men were on horseback, others sat anxiously in carriages, and a few were astride bicycles. Many others were crammed in or hanging from coaches of the Santa Fe Railroad, whose tracks crossed the district.

Finally, at high noon, federal officers along the border raised their pistols and fired. The scramble was on. Some people had entered the district sooner than April 22 and gave the future state of Oklahoma its nickname, the Sooner State. In less than twenty-four hours, homesteaders and speculators had staked out all the land of the district, nearly two million acres in all. The following year, 1890, Congress organized Oklahoma as a territory and again the area of white settlement enlarged—at Indian expense. In the year 1907 Oklahoma became a state.

STUDY GUIDE: The "open-range" cattle industry flourished on the Great Plains from the end of the Civil War until the late 1880s. Improved rail transportation gave cattlemen direct access to eastern markets. During the late 1880s overproduction and severe winter weather brought the cattle boom to an end, but a measure of prosperity was later restored. Cattlemen objected to the coming of sheepmen, whose flocks ruined their grazing land. Both sheepmen and cattlemen disliked the growing numbers of dirt farmers who moved to the Great Plains after the Civil War. Improved technology lessened some of the difficulties of farming on the Great Plains. Development of

CLOSING THE FRONTIER

First Transcontinental Railroad
Cattle Trails
States Admitted 1860 – 1900
Territories

efficient transportation and the end of Indian resistance convinced many eastern farmers to move west.

WESTERN FARM LIFE

For most of the pioneers life in the West did not turn out as they had planned. Instead of prosperity, most plains farmers found themselves confronted with knotty problems that added up to lives of hardship and poverty.

The difficult climate and geography of the Great Plains were a constant source of anxiety. Neither dry farming nor irrigation met the problem of sparse rainfall. The result was drought which baked the soil and prevented crops from sprouting; or, if they sprouted, from maturing. The plains also seemed a haven for insects, and each year assorted weevils and bugs destroyed part—sometimes much—of the farmer's labor.

The western farmer was also encountering the economic problems of rising costs and falling prices. He constantly had to pay more for his equipment, barbed wire, fertilizer, and seed; also for his family needs, such as clothing, furniture, and household wares. What caused rising costs? The protective tariff which guarded domestic manufacturers against foreign competition, enabling them to impose higher prices, had something to do with it. So did the trusts. Like the tariff, trusts tended to eliminate price-depressing competition.

Rising prices for the things the farmer needed might not have been a serious matter if the prices he received for his grain and livestock had increased correspondingly. Unfortunately that did not happen. Instead of following industrial prices upward in those years, farm prices went down. Wheat, for example, brought $1.45 a bushel in 1866, only forty-nine cents in 1894. Corn went from seventy-five cents a bushel in 1869 to twenty-eight cents in 1889.

What brought this sharp decline in prices? The increased efficiency of the American farmer. Increasing efficiency was mainly the consequence of the mechanization of agriculture, although application of new scientific methods and widespread use of fertilizers were also factors. The American farmer began to turn out more grain, cotton, and livestock than the domestic market could easily absorb. As a result, prices tumbled.

In the face of falling prices, the farmer desperately sought to maintain his income by stepping up production. This caused the market to become more glutted than ever and of course sent prices to even lower levels. It was a vicious circle. The farmer could not resolve the problem of surpluses by selling in the world market. The world market was also usually clogged, with resultant low prices, largely because of increased agricultural production in other countries.

There were other dimensions to the western farm problem, including the drabness, monotony, and loneliness of life on the plains. Numerous farm tasks that in the present day are done by electric- or gas-powered machines had to be done by hand. The farm wife spent long hours each day stoking and working over a coal- or wood-fired range that was hard to regulate and on hot days turned the kitchen into an inferno. To wash her clothes she built a fire under a large kettle or perhaps a hand-operated "washing machine" that agitated the clothing. She smoothed the garments with a flat-iron which she heated on the stove in the kitchen. The family had no easy access to emergency medical service, such as it was in the latter part of the nineteenth century.

It is true that several innovations reduced the drabness of farm life, on the plains and elsewhere, in the decades after the Civil War. There was, for example, the appearance of county and state fairs and, early in the twentieth century, the traveling Chautauqua. At fairs the farmer competed with neighbors in activities ranging from corn-husking to hog-calling, exchanged ideas, and bet on the horse races that in time became a central feature of most fairs. His wife exhibited pies and jams and visited with other farm wives. When the Chautauqua came to the county the farmer again enjoyed the company of other farmers and also watched a play, listened to brass bands, thrilled to the feats of acrobats and other performers, and absorbed the rhetoric of the leading orators of state and nation.

For many years the farmer had to travel to the nearest post office, which might be fifteen or twenty miles from his farm, to pick up his mail. Fortunately leaders of the country had long understood that development of the vast lands of the West required, among other things, frequent and efficient mail service. The result was the free delivery of mail to rural areas—RFD—voted by Congress in 1896.

Political problems were a source of frustration to the western farmer, as well as to farmers in other regions. Government did not seem to care about the plight of the farmer. This was an era of big business, of rapid industrial expansion. Politicians, both at the state and national levels, in both major parties, were tuned in to the needs and demands of the captains of business, not to those of farmers. It was businessmen who were creating new opportunities for prosperity. Hence businessmen rather than farmers attracted the interest of politicians.

STUDY GUIDE: Climate and geography made farming on the Great Plains a difficult occupation. Rising costs and falling prices because of overproduction kept profits low. Farm life was also lonely and monotonous. The farmer who lived in a period dominated by big business felt that the government did not care about his problems.

FARMERS UNITE

How could farmers meet their problems? In the view of many, their only solution lay in uniting in their own organizations or in joining parties dedicated to advancing the welfare of men of the soil. Thus, tens of thousands of farmers in the mid-1870s flocked to the new National Greenback party which sought to enlarge the country's money supply by massive issuance of paper currency unsupported by gold bullion.

Greenbackism

In the presidential election of 1876 — the Hayes-Tilden affair — the Greenback candidate, Peter Cooper, polled 81,000 votes. Over the next two years the National Greenback party evolved into the Greenback Labor party. In the congressional elections of 1878 the party received more than a million votes and sent fourteen members to Congress. Then a temporary improvement in farm prices caused many farmers to lose interest in greenbackism. Moreover, the idea of a currency not backed by precious metal offended large numbers of Americans. It was clear by 1880 that the central goal of the Greenbackers would never win sufficient popular support to be achieved. Hence the Greenback party quietly expired.

The Grange

More important as an instrument for advancing the interests of farmers was the National Grange of the Patrons of Husbandry or, simply, the Grange. A loosely knit organization, the Grange

appeared in the year 1867. Within a decade it had perhaps a million members, most of them in the West, South, and Middle West.

The initial purpose of the Grange was to relieve the drabness and monotony of farm life. By sponsoring picnics, square dances, and songfests it succeeded in bringing happiness into the lives of thousands of farm families. The Grange also acquainted farmers with new scientific techniques, sponsored lectures, and operated small lending libraries.

It was not long before the Grangers branched out into political activities, using the techniques of lobbying and threatening reprisals at the ballot box against politicians who did not support legislation favorable to farmers. The principal targets of the Grangers were railroads and warehouses which, they believed, were continually taking advantage of the dependence of farmers on their facilities by imposing excessive charges. The efforts of the Grange led several state legislatures to approve measures regulating the activities and rates of railroads and warehouses. Then, late in the 1870s, the Grange began to decline, in part because of a temporary improvement in farm prices, and also because of the failure of some ventures in cooperative manufacture and marketing of farm equipment. By the 1880s the Grange was little more than a social organization.

Farmers' Alliances

As the Grange went into eclipse, a number of organizations called "farmers' alliances" took up the agrarian protest. By the late 1880s most of these had joined into two large organizations, the Southern Alliance and the Northwestern Alliance. Like the Grange, the Alliances sponsored social affairs, held discussions and operated circulating libraries, and went heavily into cooperative manufacturing and marketing activities. But, also like the Grange, they are best remembered for their endeavors in politics.

More aggressive than the Grange, the Alliances proposed an elaborate program for advancing the general welfare of farmers. They wanted strict regulation and perhaps government ownership of railroads, abolition of national banks, and prohibition of "absentee landlordism." They wanted tax reforms, including a graduated federal income tax, and such political reforms as the secret ballot and direct election of United States senators. (At that time most voters had to mark their ballots in full view of their friends and

The Grange began in 1867 as a social organization for farmers but soon branched out into political activities. This engraving published in *Leslie's* in 1873 shows a Granger meeting in Illinois. Why was the plight of farmers ignored by government until this movement began?

neighbors—and also their employers and the local political chieftains—and state legislatures continued to elect members of the Senate.) Most important, at least in their view, the Alliances, like the Greenbackers of the 1870s, wanted to scale down the debts of farmers via currency expansion. They had no objection whatever to enlarging the money supply with unsupported paper or greenback dollars, but since most Americans thought money should have some metallic value the Alliances usually urged that the government should expand the currency by turning out unlimited quantities of silver dollars.

As membership in the Alliances swelled—the result of steadily worsening farm prices—leaders began to talk of consolidating the northwestern and southern organizations. Because of sectional antagonisms that dated back to the Civil War and before, there was no merger but the two organizations were in essential agreement on matters of tactics and programs. The year 1890 was an election year, and the Alliances determined to assert themselves in the various campaigns. In some areas of the South and Southwest, notably in Texas, the Southern Alliance gained control of Democratic organizations and nominated Alli-

ance men as Democrats. In the northern parts of the Great Plains and in the prairie regions to the east, the Northwestern Alliance did not try to penetrate the Republican and Democratic parties. Instead, it held local conventions, got its men on the ballots, and set out to elect them.

When returns came in on election day in November 1890, a wave of jubilation went through the ranks of the Alliances. Running as Democrats, Southern Alliance candidates had won governorships in four states, captured eight state legislatures, and secured forty-four seats in the national House of Representatives and three in the Senate. In Kansas the Northwestern Alliance had gained control of one house of the state legislature and sent five representatives and one senator to the federal Congress in Washington. In Nebraska and South Dakota the Northwestern Alliance also scored notable victories.

Leaders of the Alliances began to talk of a new

national political party, one that would represent the interests of farmers and men who toiled in factories and mines and on railroads. In 1891 delegates gathered in Cincinnati to consider forming a party. Discussions came to nothing, mostly because leaders of the Southern Alliance were hoping to enlarge their base within the established Democratic party.

By 1892 it seemed apparent that the forces of conservatism in the southern wing of the Democratic party would prevent any further encroachment by Alliance men. Therefore, in February 1892, delegates of the two Alliances met in Saint Louis and announced formation of the People's party, better known to history as the Populist party. The new party, delegates agreed, would hold its first national convention at Omaha the following July and challenge the Republicans and Democrats in the presidential election in the autumn.

STUDY GUIDE: To solve their problems, farmers formed their own organizations, such as the Grange. They also joined political parties, such as the National Greenback party, which seemed concerned about their welfare. The Grange lobbied successfully in several states for the passage of laws regulating railroad and warehouse rates. As the Grange grew less political and more social in the late 1880s, farmers' alliances took over the protest movement. Out of the various groups a new national political party was organized in 1892 — the Populists.

THE GROWTH OF POPULISM

Whether its analysis of America's farm problem was entirely accurate or not, the Populist party quickly gathered steam, particularly in the Great Plains states. When the party convened at Omaha in summer 1892, Americans witnessed a political meeting the likes of which they had never seen. The convention was more like an old-time revival than a political assembly.

The Populist Platform

Amid oratory, shouting, and hymn singing, delegates to the Omaha convention drafted a platform for the new party which resembled the program of the Farmers' Alliances. Populists wanted government ownership of railroads, prohibition of absentee landlordism, and, most of all, free and unlimited coinage of silver bullion at a ratio of 16-to-1 with gold.

Like the Alliances, the Populists also wanted direct election of senators, the Australian or secret ballot, and other reforms that, hopefully, would make government more responsive to the popular will. They wanted a graduated income tax and a subtreasury — a government agency which would store the farmer's crops until prices went up and at the same time grant him a cash loan on his crop.

The Populists attempted to enlist the support of urban laborers by proposing an eight-hour day for workingmen and restriction of the flow of immigrants to the United States. Immigrants competed with native workers and tended to bring a lowering of labor standards.

After approving a platform came the business of nominating a presidential ticket. To lead the party in its first national campaign delegates turned to Populism's elder statesman, James B. Weaver. A native of Ohio, Weaver had graduated from the Cincinnati Law School, been cited for gallantry while serving in the United States Army during the Civil War, and migrated to Iowa. A succesful lawyer, he became interested in politics, drifted into the Greenback party, and in 1880 polled more than three hundred thousand votes as the Greenback candidate for president. Between 1879 and 1887 he also served three terms in Congress.

The Republicans had assembled at Minneapolis the previous month and renominated Benjamin Harrison for the presidency. In 1890 the Republicans had taken a beating at the polls because of the McKinley tariff measure (see Chapter 9), but once again they made tariff protection the main plank of their platform.

The Democrats gathered at Chicago two weeks later and for the third consecutive time nominated Grover Cleveland as their standard-bearer. For the vice-presidency the Democrats turned to Adlai E. Stevenson of Illinois, the grandfather of the man their party would nominate for president in 1952 and 1956. Like the Republicans, the Democrats were indifferent to the grievances of farmers and sought to make the tariff — they favored lower duties — the central issue of the campaign.

Most of the campaign excitement came from Weaver, who worked strenuously to win farmers and workers to the Populist cause. The Iowan knew that he had no chance of winning the presidency in 1892, but he hoped that he could put the party on a firm foundation by making a good showing. Weaver quickly found that his most enthusiastic response came when he spoke about silver coinage. "Free silver," or so it seemed to many agrarians, somehow could resolve all the problems that in the 1890s were pressing down on America's farmers. Accordingly Weaver made the so-called money question the central theme of his campaign.

The Populist candidate's position presented difficulties for Grover Cleveland inasmuch as many western and southern Democrats had become enamored of Populist ideas on currency.

Characteristically Cleveland did not alter his own position. He made it clear that he had no sympathy for the radical monetary theories of Populism, that he was committed to the existing monetary system of the country which rested on the single gold standard. As a consequence, many eastern businessmen—terrified by the prospect of unlimited silver coinage—and many farmers, workingmen, and shopkeepers in the East who saw Populism as a threat from the West rallied to Cleveland's support.

Because of this support—and because Harrison was such a weak personality—Cleveland defeated his Republican opponent in the popular voting and won decisively in the electoral college. Weaver achieved his purpose of running a strong race. He polled a million popular votes and picked up twenty-two electoral votes. Encouraged by their showing in their first national campaign, Populists looked forward expectantly to 1896.

The Panic of 1893

Four months after the election, in March 1893, Grover Cleveland for the second time took the oath as president. Hardly had the New Yorker settled back into the routine of the White House when disaster overcame his administration. A financial panic—the Panic of 1893—struck the country and a general economic depression followed. Numerous corporations went bankrupt, banks closed, and farm prices sank to new lows. The ranks of the unemployed swelled.

Although he felt compassion for the depression's victims, President Cleveland believed that his first responsibility was to maintain the fiscal integrity of the national government. In the 1890s this meant he must maintain a substantial reserve of gold in the federal treasury. To achieve his purpose Cleveland set about to reduce federal spending. He also urged Con-

Brown Brothers

The issue was farm prices, and angry debates took place across the Midwest in the early 1890s over what might be done to raise them. Farmers felt that both Republicans and Democrats were indifferent to their problems, so many of them became Populists. This drawing records a debate between Populists and Republicans which took place within the Kansas legislature in 1893. What happened in 1893 which helped enlarge the Populist party?

gress to repeal the Sherman Silver Purchase Act of 1890 (see Chapter 9) which required the treasury to buy four and a half million ounces of silver each month. Since the treasury paid for the silver with new notes redeemable either in gold or silver, the Sherman measure had provided a means of enlarging the national money supply. This was a central objective of Populism. Hence, Populists and other farmers were outraged when Cleveland made his request. Their anger heightened when in autumn 1893 "goldbug" Democrats and Republicans in Congress combined to pass the repeal legislation.

Coxey's Army

As the months dragged by, the depression worsened. In the spring of 1894 some four hundred unemployed members of an "army" led by "General" Jacob S. Coxey of Ohio marched into Washington and demanded legislation establishing a massive road-building program to create jobs for the unemployed. Many frightened Americans saw "Coxey's army" as a beginning of revolution. There was widespread relief when federal officials arrested Coxey and two other

The Panic of 1893 was followed by a severe depression and widespread unemployment. Members of "Coxey's army" approach Washington in this 1894 photograph. They demanded legislation creating jobs for the unemployed. Why did many Americans fear "Coxey's army"?

leaders of the march for trespassing on the White House lawn and sent them to jail for twenty days. Deprived of leadership, hungry, and despairing of any favorable action by Congress, Coxey's followers quietly made their way back to their homes.

The Pullman Affair

Excitement over the Coxey affair had hardly subsided when the American Railway Union, led by Eugene V. Debs of Indiana, determined to show sympathy for five thousand workers whom the Pullman Company had fired for protesting a reduction in wages. The union decreed that its members would handle no trains that included Pullman cars. On the grounds that the American Railway Union was interfering with movement of mail, Cleveland's attorney general secured an injunction against the union, a step that in early July 1894 touched off mob violence. The president responded by ordering federal troops to Chicago, center of the violent activity. The result was further disorder. A few days later federal officials arrested Debs for violation of the injunction, and when the Hoosier labor leader received a six-month jail sentence the so-called Pullman strike collapsed.

Tariff Legislation

Cleveland's handling of Coxey and his use of federal troops against the Pullman strikers brought no applause from hard-pressed workingmen and farmers. But in that same year, 1894, the president took at least one step that heartened Populists. He urged a reduction in tariff duties and proposed that new tariff legislation should also include a provision for levying a tax of two percent on all incomes over $4,000 — which of course excluded most farmers.

The house responded with a bill along the lines of the president's proposal, but the Senate, while approving the income-tax provision, worked over the House's bill and raised import duties on most items. After a House-Senate conference, the House accepted the Senate's amendments, whereupon in August 1894 the two chambers approved the Wilson-Gorman Tariff Bill. Seeing that the bill would result in slight—almost meaningless—reduction of the tariff, Cleveland was furious and considered exercising his veto authority. Then, perhaps to save the income-tax provision, he decided to let the measure become law without his signature. Whatever satisfaction the president may have derived from the income tax, unfortunately, was short-lived, for the Supreme Court the following year ruled that such a tax was unconstitutional.

Gold Crisis

While his stand on the tariff gained Cleveland some support among farmers in 1894, he lost most of it in 1895. It all began with the dwindling federal gold reserve. Because of the depression, the government, despite the president's efforts to reduce expenses, was spending more money than it was taking in. By early 1895 the gold reserve had slipped to $40 million, a figure that most observers considered dangerously low. Unless the reserve was replenished, it appeared that the United States government faced possible bankruptcy.

Cleveland opened secret negotiations with a syndicate of New York financiers headed by J. P. Morgan, and the outcome was an arrangement by which the syndicate agreed to purchase a new issue of federal bonds. With the $65 million in gold that the transaction brought to the treasury, the government's credit and the gold monetary standard were saved. But farmers of the West and South — Democrats as well as Populists — who were suspicious of Wall Street, and J. P. Morgan in particular, were angry.

STUDY GUIDE: The Populists nominated James B. Weaver for the presidency in 1892. He ran on a platform urging free coinage of silver, government ownership of railroads, and direct election of senators. In 1892 the Republicans renominated Benjamin Harrison, while the Democrats chose Grover Cleveland as their candidate. Although Cleveland won, Weaver managed to poll a million votes. The Panic of 1893 caused great economic hardship for farmers. As a result, the Populist party gained strength. As the nation's gold reserves dwindled, many people, including Democrats, spoke out in favor of free coinage of silver.

THE FREE SILVER CAMPAIGN OF 1896

As farm prices continued to slump and agrarian distress became more acute, the Populist party naturally gathered strength. As it turned out, the ideas of Populism were gaining support at a faster pace than was the Populist organization. Across the South and West, many Democrats, while refusing to leave the Democratic party, were speaking out in favor of virtually all the planks of the Populist platform, especially the one calling for free and unlimited coinage of silver at 16-to-1. Indeed as the country prepared for the election of 1896, Populists faced the prospect that one of the major parties, the Democratic, might take over their program. If that happened, the Populist party was apt to disappear. On the other hand, such an event offered the best chance that the ideas of Populism might achieve fulfillment.

By 1896 large numbers of Democrats had been converted to Populist lines of thought. When the Democratic national convention opened at Chicago in July of that year, it was clear that "free silver" delegates were in control of the party's organization. Who would these delegates put forward as their choice for the presidential nomination? A good bet was William Jennings Bryan, a thirty-six-year-old orator-lawyer-politician from Nebraska.

Born and reared in Illinois, Bryan as a young attorney had migrated to Lincoln, Nebraska, where he soon became active in politics. He had a splendid speaking voice and felt genuine concern for the problems of the "common man," particularly the farmer. As a result, he attracted an enthusiastic following and won election to Congress in 1890 and 1892. Although he had earned a reputation as one of the outstanding orators on Capitol Hill, he lost his bid for a seat in the Senate in 1894, a year in which Republicans, taking advantage of depression-inspired frustration, defeated Democrats all across the country.

Bryan was an early convert to the ideas of Populism, but declined to abandon the Democratic party. By 1896 he had emerged as one of the most eloquent spokesmen of the party's "free silver" wing. Then came the Chicago convention and perhaps the climax of Bryan's career. During debate on the party platform he received the honor of offering the final argument in favor of free and unlimited coinage of silver. With a rare combination of dignity and passion he issued a powerful statement for agrarianism and the white metal.

As twenty thousand delegates and spectators shouted and stamped their feet, Bryan concluded: "You come to tell us that the great cities are in favor of the gold standard; we reply that the great cities rest upon our broad and fertile prairies. Burn down your cities and leave our farms, and your cities will spring up again as if by magic; but destroy our farms and the grass will grow in the streets of every city in the country. . . . Having behind us the producing masses of the nation and the world, supported by the commercial interests, the laboring interests and the toilers everywhere, we will answer their demand for a gold standard by saying to them: You shall not press down upon the brow of labor this crown of thorns, you shall not crucify mankind upon a cross of gold."

After adopting a platform that was a virtual carbon copy of the Populist program, Democratic delegates turned to the business of naming a presidential candidate. On the fifth ballot the vote went to Bryan. Infuriated, "goldbug" Democrats withdrew from the convention, organized the National Democratic party, and in September assembled at Indianapolis. They adopted a platform urging maintenance of the single gold monetary standard and nominated John M. Palmer of Illinois for president and the former Confederate general Simon Bolivar Buckner of Kentucky for vice-president.

The Populists assembled at Saint Louis two weeks after the regular Democratic convention and faced the question of whether or not to unite with the Democrats behind Bryan. If they joined the Democrats, there seemed a good chance that Bryan might win the White House and make the Populist program a success. Otherwise a Republican victory was certain, and few Republicans felt any kinship with Populism. But fusion with the Democrats would probably be the death knell of the Populist party.

Debate over what to do was vigorous, and such leaders of the party as Jacob S. Coxey hotly opposed fusion. Others, including James B. Weaver, were more interested in Populist ideas than in the Populist party and wanted to seize the opportunity presented by Democratic acceptance of the Populist program. These latter spokesmen prevailed and the convention endorsed Bryan. Then, in a show of independence, the delegates declined to nominate Bryan's Democratic running mate, Arthur Sewall of Maine, and instead nominated a Populist, Thomas E. Watson of Georgia, for the vice-presidency.

The Republicans had met at Saint Louis a few weeks before the Democratic convention and adopted a platform upholding the gold standard and the protective tariff. They also urged a more vigorous foreign policy for the United States and specifically called for annexation of the Hawaiian islands (see Chapter 11). For president the delegates nominated Governor William McKinley of Ohio, the man who had sponsored the tariff legislation which brought the Republican party to grief in the elections of 1890 (see Chapter 9). Like the Democrats, the Republicans had dissenters within their ranks, although not nearly so many as the Democrats. The outcome was organization of the National Silver Republicans, who met at Saint Louis in July and endorsed the Democratic presidential ticket.

Engineering McKinley's nomination and, after

PRESIDENTIAL ELECTION OF 1896

McKinley (Republican)
271 Electoral Votes

Bryan (Democrat, Populist)
176 Electoral Votes

the convention, directing his campaign, was Marcus Alonzo Hanna, a Cleveland industrialist who turned out to be one of the sharpest political operatives in the history of the American republic. Mark Hanna put together a smooth-running campaign organization and to lubricate it secured almost unlimited financial support from business leaders, who were terrified by Bryan. In truth the "silver-tongued orator" was a gentle spirit. He was a devout Presbyterian who did not smoke, drink, or swear and read from his Bible each day. Still eastern businessmen and conservatives viewed the God-fearing Nebraskan as a wild-eyed western radical, an enormous threat to the business-dominated society. So they financed McKinley's campaign and spared no effort to intimidate employees to vote against Bryan.

While McKinley waged a "front porch" campaign from his house in Canton, Ohio, receiving and giving little speeches to delegations who came to pay respect to the Republican standard-bearer, Bryan exhorted voters at hundreds of whistle stops and gave numerous formal addresses. He often evoked a hysterical response from his auditors, for he was perhaps the greatest stump speaker in the history of American politics.

It was no use. Bryan was strong in the West and South, but McKinley was dominant in the states of the Northeast. On election day the Republican candidate received the most popular votes and carried the electoral college, 271-176.

The Populist Party Falls Apart

After the election of 1896 the Populist party quickly fell apart. A few followers maintained a skeleton organization and nominated Populist candidates for the elections of 1900, 1904, and 1908. But most members drifted back to the parties, Republican and Democratic, to which they originally had given allegiance.

What brought the party's rapid decline? The obvious answer is that one of the major parties, namely, the Democratic party, had taken over its platform. Also, soon after the election the dreary depression began to pass. Within a year the country had returned to prosperity. Even farmers shared in the better times and, as their incomes inched upward, agrarians became less interested in protest.

The Populist party had never made the broad appeal necessary for success in national politics in America. Essentially a party of western and southern farmers, it was never able to establish links with workingmen, people of the urban middle class or farmers in the northeastern part of the nation. These latter groups tended to see the Populist party as a party of failures—hayseeds who were too lazy or incompetent to resolve their own problems. They also were inclined to view Populism's favorite idea, free silver, as a crackpot scheme.

Gains Made by Populism

Historians, in contrast, generally view the Populist party as a success. Not because of triumphs at the ballot box in the 1890s but because in the first two decades of the twentieth century so much of what Populists had sought came to pass. There was universal acceptance of the secret ballot. The Seventeenth Amendment to the Constitution provided for direct election of United States senators. Other reforms adopted by various states made government more responsive to the popular will.

Populist agitation on the currency question forced Americans to study monetary policy as never before, and the outcome was the monumental Federal Reserve Act of 1913. Populists had wanted a subtreasury program. In 1916 Congress passed the Warehouse Act which embodied the subtreasury principle. Populists wanted a graduated federal income tax. The way opened for such a tax with adoption of the Sixteenth Amendment in 1913. They wanted to borrow money from national banks on farm mortgages. This became possible via a provision in the Federal Reserve Act. They wanted postal savings banks. Congress authorized a postal savings system in 1910. They demanded strength for the Interstate Commerce Commission, created in 1887, and control of corporations in accord with the spirit of the Sherman Antitrust Act of 1890. Strength for the ICC and more effective regulation of business came in the years 1901-20 during the administrations of Presidents Theodore Roosevelt, William Howard Taft, and Woodrow Wilson.

Populism and Black Americans

Still, there was at least one terrible bleak consequence of the Populist revolt, and the victims were the country's black citizens.

In the South many white farmers who were

suffering acute economic distress responded enthusiastically to the appeal of Populism. Owners of large plantations, manufacturers, and others who clung to the conservative traditions of the "Old South," however, vehemently rejected Populist politics, remaining loyal to the Democratic party. White Populists, therefore, turned to black farmers for support. Large numbers of blacks accordingly signed up with the Populist party, and a few of them achieved positions of considerable responsibility in the party organization.

Unfortunately a deep hostility toward black men was embedded in the emotions of most white Populists, and it required a herculean effort on their part to suppress it in the name of mutual self-interest. This hostility gave planters, businessmen, and other conservative Democrats of the region their opportunity and they seized it. They assailed the Populist party as an instrument that eventually would deliver the South to the control of black men. For whites the idea of black supremacy raised fears and released all their pent-up hostility toward Negroes. The outcome was a serious weakening of the Populist party as large numbers of white Populists trooped back to the Democratic party, the guarantor of white supremacy.

One might logically conclude that with the collapse of Populism after the election of 1896 the fear of black supremacy in the South would have disappeared. It did not. Why? The agrarian revolt had opened serious wounds in the white community of the region. Cynical Democratic politicians and other white leaders concluded that the only sure way to achieve white solidarity was to arouse whites against blacks in the name of white supremacy.

First came nearly total disfranchisement of Negroes in the states of the old Confederacy. This was accomplished through instruments such as literacy tests (requiring blacks to interpret the state constitution to the satisfaction of white voting registrars) and the poll tax (requiring payment for the right to vote). Blacks thus lost any leverage on political leaders and policies which the ballot box might offer them. At the same time southern newspapers banned numerous stories of Negro crime or alleged crime calculated to raise white hatred of blacks to a new intensity.

Next came a fantastic array of laws and ordinances aimed at segregating the races — in a way that invariably discriminated against blacks and reinforced the idea of white supremacy.

Every southern state passed legislation requiring Jim Crow railway coaches and waiting rooms. There were laws prohibiting laborers of different races from working in the same room and requiring business firms to provide separate facilities. Segregation became the rule — usually the law — in schools, colleges, hospitals, mental institutions, and orphanages. Parks, theaters, and other places of amusement were compelled to observe strict segregation. Whites were not allowed to compete against blacks in sporting events, and ordinances required blacks to live in specified parts of towns. A sort of peak of absurdity was reached when North Carolina and Virginia prohibited members of any fraternal orders and societies which might admit both whites and blacks from addressing each other as brother.

Plessy v. Ferguson

Another major Supreme Court decision that affected Negroes was the *Plessy* v. *Ferguson* case of 1896. This ruling provided a legal foundation for racial segregation in public places on the basis of "separate but equal" facilities. It upheld a Louisiana law calling for separate accommodations for white and black railroad passengers. Justice John Marshall Harlan was the lone dissenter in this decision, claiming that the Constitution is colorblind.

Thus, the Populist revolt, which did so much that was needed, quite inadvertently provided the impetus for a new revival of racial hatred in the United States.

STUDY GUIDE: In 1896 the Democrats chose William Jennings Bryan as their presidential nominee and adopted a platform almost exactly like that of the Populists. The Populists also endorsed Bryan. William McKinley was the nominee of the Republicans, whose platform upheld the gold standard and the protective tariff. McKinley, strongly supported by eastern business interests, was elected. With the return of prosperity and the Democratic take-over of its platform, the Populist party disappeared after the election of 1896. However, the influence of populism led to the eventual passage of federal legislation in such areas as reform of the money system and control of big business. Unfortunately the Populist revolt also revived racial hatred in some parts of the United States.

SUMMING UP THE CHAPTER

Names and Terms to Identify

John A. Sutter	dry farming
"sourdoughs"	Nat Love
John Butterfield	Greenback party
Squanto	"free silver"
King Philip	James B. Weaver
Proclamation line of 1763	Coxey's army
Black Kettle	Eugene V. Debs
Geronimo	Marcus Alonzo Hanna
Chief Joseph	Seventeenth Amendment
ghost dances	John Marshall Harlan

Study Questions and Points to Review

1. According to the Census Bureau, by what year did the American frontier cease to exist?

2. The author mentions three factors besides the forbidding land and weather which complicated matters for western farmers. Name these three factors.

3. What was the name of the political revolt which burst forth in the 1890s as a result of the farm problem in the West.

4. Besides gold, what other natural treasures of Alaska did the prospectors discover?

5. Large-scale settlement of the West could not take place until what problem had been resolved?

6. How long did it take to construct the first transcontinental railroad?

7. What war broke out when elements of the Fox and Sac tribes decided to return to their former homelands?

8. Name the Five Civilized Tribes.

9. What animal was essential to the American Indian for food, clothing, and shelter?

10. Name the legislation which authorized the president to divide tribal lands and give each head of a family 160 acres.

11. What battle marked the last major armed conflict between Indians and whites in the United States?

12. What present-day state comprises what used to be called Indian Territory?

13. In the face of falling prices, how did the farmer seek to maintain his income? What was the result of his action?

14. Which political party sought unlimited coinage of silver in the election of 1892?

15. Name the Democratic candidate for president in the "free silver" campaign of 1896.

16. What happened to the Populist party after the election of 1896?

17. What two actions had resulted in nearly total disfranchisement of Negroes in the South?

18. Name the Supreme Court decision of 1896 which provided a legal foundation for racial segregation in public places on the basis of "separate but equal" facilities.

Topic for Discussion

1. Trace the history of the mining frontier in California. What were some of the main consequences of the "gold rush" to California?

2. What was the reasoning behind the pony express? To what extent was the pony express a success? Why did it disappear?

3. Give reasons why efficient, low-cost transportation was essential for conquest of the western frontier.

4. What in your opinion are the best arguments for and against the right of white men to occupy lands held for many centuries by the Indians?

5. Evaluate the policy of "Indian removal." What was the reasoning behind it? What were the consequence of the policy?

6. Do you think William Jennings Bryan might have made a good president? Why or why not?

7. How did the Populist revolt give impetus to racial discrimination and segregation in the South?

Subjects for Reports or Essays

1. Prepare a report on the meaning of the term *frontier*. Consider the word in the context of the western frontier, mining frontier, and transportation frontier, and as used in medical frontier and space frontier.

2. Using books in the library, prepare an essay on the gold rush in Alaska.

3. It is the year 1858. You have just completed a trip to California on the Butterfield stagecoach. Write a letter to a friend in the East describing your trip.

4. Write an essay setting forth your own evaluation of the white man's treatment of American Indians through the end of the nineteenth century.

5. Imagine you are a pioneer woman on the Great Plains. It is 1876. Write a letter to your sister in the East describing the joys and frustrations of your life in the West.

6. On the basis of library investigation, write a biographical sketch of one of the following people: James B. Weaver, William Jennings Bryan, Marcus Alonzo Hanna, Jacob Coxey.

Projects, Activities, and Skills

1. On Atlas Map 22 locate: Butterfield Overland Mail, Fort Smith, Fort Laramie, Salt Lake City; on Atlas Map 23 locate: Chisholm Trail, Little Bighorn, Pony Express, Sedalia, Virginia City; on Atlas Map 24 locate: Wounded Knee, Cripple Creek, Black Hills. Explain the significance of each as it relates to this chapter.

2. Using reference materials from the library, show on an outline map of the United States the major Indian reservations.

3. Read "The Law of the Yukon" by Robert W. Service. According to Service, what was the law of the Yukon?

4. Study a photograph of "The End of the Trail," the sculpture by James E. Fraser. What is your impression of the subject?

5. Prepare an exhibit on the mining frontier. Use a map to show the principal gold and silver fields. Collect sketches, prints, and photographs to illustrate the tools and techniques used by prospectors.

6. Prepare a display on the American Indians. On a map locate the areas occupied by the various peoples during the time covered in this chapter. Exhibit photographs or drawings of men and women of different Indian cultures. Display any examples of various Indian cultures that members of the class may own.

7. Listen to some early cowboy songs. What do the words to such songs as "Old Chisholm Trail" or "The Streets of Laredo" tell you about the times and the people?

8. Many of the events and people discussed in this unit have been commemorated on U.S. postage stamps. If you are a stamp collector, you might like to prepare a display of stamps about this era in American history.

Further Readings

General

American Indians by William T. Hagan. From Jamestown to the modern period.
The Battle of Little Bighorn by Mari Sandoz. A vivid account of Custer's defeat.
Bury My Heart at Wounded Knee: An Indian History of the American West by Dee Brown. The Sioux's story of the years 1860-90.
The Great Plains by Walter Prescott Webb. A classic work on farmers in the West.
The Populist Revolt: A History of the Farmer's Alliance and the People's Party by John D. Hicks.
The Sod-House Frontier, 1854-1890 by Everett S. Dick. Describes social conditions on the plains.
Transportation Frontier by Oscar O. Winther.

Westward Expansion: History of the American Frontier by Ray Allen Billington. Its bibliography has many titles on American Indians.

Biography

Geronimo: A Biography by Alexander B. Adams.
Ignatius Donnelley: The Portrait of a Politician by Martin Ridge.
McKinley, Bryan, and the People by Paul W. Glad.
Sutter: The Man and His Empire by James P. Zollinger.
Tom Watson, Agrarian Rebel by C. Vann Woodward.

Fiction and Music

Centennial by James A. Michener. Historical novel about an area near Denver.
Cimarron by Edna Ferber. Historical novel about the Oklahoma land rush.
Cowboy Songs and Other Frontier Ballads by Allen Lomax and John A. Lomax.
Giants in the Earth by Ole E. Rölvaag. A story about immigrants in the Dakota Territory.
Life on the Mississippi by Mark Twain (Samuel L. Clemens).
The Luck of Roaring Camp by Bret Harte. A short story about the West by a master of local color.
My Antonia and *O Pioneers!* by Willa Cather. Both novels depict life on the prairie.
Outcasts of Poker Flat by Bret Harte.
The Ox-Bow Incident by Walter van Tilburg Clark. An exciting novel set in the Far West.
Ramona by Helen Hunt Jackson. Sympathetic toward Indians; written in 1884.
The Track of the Cat by Walter van Tilburg Clark. A suspenseful novel set in the Far West.
When the Legends Die by Hal Borland. A Southwestern Indian boy seeks his identity in the early 1900s.

Pictorial History

Artists of the Old West by John C. Ewers.
A Pictorial History of the American Indian by Oliver La Farge.

In the early 1900s, the spirit of the United States was one of growing confidence. The American people took a new interest in Europe, Latin America, and Asia. At home, many worked for social reform, and women began to campaign for the right to vote.

▶

Library of Congress

THE NATION GROWS

4

SOME AMERICAN ARTISTS

In the late 1800s and early 1900s a number of important American artists made original contributions to artistic style. The artists represented here are considered to be of the realist school.

1

James Abbott McNeill Whistler was born in Lowell, Massachusetts, but he spent most of his life abroad. He studied art as a boy in Russia and later in Paris. Whistler was one of the most original American artists of the 1800s. His painting, *The White Girl*, was rejected by the Royal Academy in London in 1863. Later it won fame.

2

Thomas Eakins was an outstanding American artist. Eakins's realistic paintings reflect his scientific study of anatomy, perspective, light, and motion. He was also a master of character analysis, and this added an important dimension to his portraits. Eakins was born in Philadelphia, Pennsylvania. *The Biglin Brothers Racing* is considered one of his finest works.

1

National Gallery of Art, Washington, D.C.
Harris Whittemore Collection

2

National Gallery of Art, Washington, D.C., Gift of Mrs. Cornelius Vanderbilt Whitney

3

Henry O. Tanner, an American Negro artist, studied under Thomas Eakins in Philadelphia and later moved to Paris to study and work. He frequently painted Biblical subjects in a naturalistic style. *Portrait of the Artist's Mother* is shown here.

4

Winslow Homer won fame for his paintings of scenes at sea. Intensely dramatic, his paintings were intended more as symbols of life at sea than as individual portraits. The painting shown here is entitled *Breezing Up.* It was painted in 1876.

CHAPTER 11

AMERICA LOOKS OUTWARD

SHORTLY AFTER TEN O'CLOCK on the morning of March 4, 1897, president-elect William McKinley stepped into a carriage and made his way to the White House. A few moments after his arrival, President Grover Cleveland walked down the front steps of the executive mansion, shook hands with McKinley, and climbed into the carriage. The outgoing president was in good spirits, pleased at the prospect of putting aside the burdens of the presidency. He was also delighted that he was passing his authority to the conservative McKinley rather than to the "radical" William Jennings Bryan.

At the Capitol, on a special platform at the foot of the Senate steps, McKinley placed his hand on a large gilt-edged Bible and took the oath of office as president of the American Republic. Next came a long inaugural address in which McKinley pledged his administration to the principle of tariff protection and to a foreign policy aimed at preserving peace and America's national honor. "War should never be entered upon until every agency of peace has failed," he said, adding that "peace is preferable to war in almost every contingency."

WILLIAM McKINLEY

Born at Niles, Ohio, in 1843, William McKinley, Jr., was the seventh child in a family of nine children. His ancestors had been Scotch-Irish and English Puritans, and two of his great-grandfathers had fought on the American side in the War of Independence. His paternal grandfather, James McKinley, like many other Pennsylvanians in the opening years of the nineteenth century, migrated from Pennsylvania to northeastern Ohio. But unlike most such migrants James McKinley decided against farming, and became manager of a charcoal furnace. His son William also looked to industry for a livelihood.

At the time of the future President McKinley's birth, William McKinley, Sr., was operating a small pig iron foundry. Profits unfortunately were slim and when a depression hit the country in the late 1850s the McKinley family suffered serious financial distress. It is possible that this experience helped influence William McKinley, Jr., to advocate tariff protection. (Many small manufacturers such as his father blamed their difficulties on increased foreign competition resulting from federal legislation in 1857 lowering tariff barriers.)

The small town of Niles offered poor opportunities for education, so the elder McKinleys moved to Poland, Ohio, a larger town which had better schools. Young William was a serious student of better-than-average intelligence who displayed a special talent for oratory. On graduation from high school, he enrolled at Allegheny College in Pennsylvania, but illness and the family's financial difficulties limited his higher education to a single year.

In January 1861 "Bill" McKinley turned eighteen and three months later the Civil War began. Influenced by the wave of patriotism that swept northern Ohio, he enlisted as a private in the Twenty-third Ohio Volunteer Infantry and soon was in the field in western Virginia. He seemed to enjoy military life and won minor acclaim in the great battle at Antietam in 1862 when he drove a mule team through a hail of Confederate fire.

McKinley caught the attention of a major of the regiment, Rutherford B. Hayes, and a short time later received a commission as second lieutenant. His continuing friendship with Hayes, efficient service, and gallant behavior in the Shenandoah Valley campaign of 1864 brought him promotions to captain and then to major. Still, McKinley never felt any particular animosity toward the South, and without hesitation favored Lincoln's ideas on reconstruction. In political campaigns he seldom mentioned his military experiences.

After the war, McKinley decided to be a lawyer and read the law for two years in the office of a prominent attorney in Youngstown, Ohio. He gained admission to the bar and in 1867 opened a law office in Canton, Ohio. McKinley soon became active in Republican politics, and in 1869, largely because of his oratorical skills, won election as county prosecuting attorney. In 1871 he married Ida Saxton, the daughter of

HEADLINE
EVENTS

1850 Clayton-Bulwer Treaty
1867 Midway in the Pacific Ocean made United States possession
Alaska purchased from Russia
1889-1890 First Pan-American Conference
1891 Crisis in Chile when two American crewmen of *Baltimore* are killed in brawl
1893 Cleveland inaugurated for second term
1897 William McKinley inaugurated president
Dingley Tariff Act
1898 The de Lôme letter
Maine sinks in Havana harbor
Congress adopts resolution demanding Spain's withdrawal from Cuba
Teller Amendment
Congress declares war on Spain
Dewey wins Battle of Manila Bay
American army lands at Daiquiri, Cuba
El Caney captured
Battle of San Juan Hill
Spanish fleet destroyed
Hawaii annexed by United States
Puerto Rico invaded
Treaty of Paris
1899 Samoa partitioned between United States and Germany
Puerto Rico, Philippines, and Guam turned over to United States under terms of Treaty of Paris
Open Door policy in China announced
1899-1901 McKinley Commission studies location for American canal
1899-1902 Philippine Insurrection
1900 Boxer Rebellion
Currency Act
Hay-Pauncefote Treaty
Hawaii made United States territory
1901 Second Hay-Pauncefote Treaty
McKinley inaugurated for second term
Theodore Roosevelt succeeds to the presidency upon death of McKinley
Supreme Court rules on Insular Cases
1902 Philippines made unorganized territory by Congress

1903 Hay-Herrán Treaty
Panama declares its independence
Platt Amendment becomes part of treaty between United States and Cuba
United States and Britain settle Alaskan boundary dispute
1904 Hay–Bunau-Varilla Treaty
Roosevelt Corollary to Monroe Doctrine
1904-1905 Russo-Japanese War
1905 Roosevelt mediates Treaty of Portsmouth between Russia and Japan
United States takes over Dominican Republic's customs houses
Taft-Katsura Memorandum
1906 Roosevelt helps settle dispute between France and Germany over Morocco
1907-1908 Gentlemen's Agreement
1908 Root-Takahira Agreement
1908-1909 American fleet's goodwill cruise
1909 William Howard Taft inaugurated president
1909-1913 Era of "dollar diplomacy"
1910 Japan annexes Korea
1911-1913 Nicaragua is United States protectorate
1912 Alaska is given territorial status
1914 World War I breaks out in Europe
1915-1934 Haiti is a United States protectorate
1916-1917 United States intervention in Mexico
1917 United States enters World War I
United States purchases Danish West Indies; renames them Virgin Islands
Puerto Rico made federal territory; Puerto Ricans granted citizenship
Lansing-Ishii Agreement
1934 Platt Amendment repealed
1937 Statehood for Hawaii voted down
1941 United States returns customs houses to control of Dominican Republic
Japanese bomb Pearl Harbor
1942 Alcan Highway constructed
1946 Philippine Islands become independent
1952 Commonwealth of Puerto Rico created
1959 Alaska enters the Union
Hawaii enters the Union

Canton's leading banker. For a wedding gift the elder Saxton presented the newlyweds with one of the finest houses in Canton. It was from the front porch of this house that McKinley conducted his successful campaign for the presidency in 1896.

Within five years of their marriage the McKinleys lost two baby daughters and the tragedy shattered Ida McKinley's nervous system. She remained an invalid the rest of her life. William McKinley proved a devoted husband, making his wife's comfort and happiness the prime considerations in his life.

Despite the burden of his wife's broken health, McKinley remained active in politics. In 1876, while his friend Hayes was winning the White House, he won election to Congress. There over the next fourteen years he earned a reputation as one of the country's most forceful advocates of the protective tariff system. He sponsored the ill-starred McKinley Tariff Bill of 1890 and promptly lost his seat in Congress. But the following year Ohioans elected him governor, and he was reelected in 1893.

After Cleveland defeated Harrison in 1892, McKinley began to build a national following for the presidential campaign of 1896. He was supported by Mark Hanna and other wealthy industrialists. The climax came on March 4, 1897, when McKinley took the presidential oath.

Although diplomatic problems had begun to command increasing attention from American leaders, McKinley had never taken much interest in foreign affairs and expected to concentrate on domestic matters. Things did not work out as the president expected. Only two measures of much consequence that fell in the category of domestic affairs came forth during his years in the White House. The first of these was the Dingley Tariff Act of 1897, which raised import duties to an all-time high. Second was the Currency Act of 1900, which placed all forms of money issued by the United States on a parity with gold, established the gold content of the dollar at $20.67 an ounce, and established a gold reserve of $150 million to provide for the redemption of legal tender notes on demand.

However, McKinley is not remembered as a president who achieved important things in the domestic realm. His place in American history was established as a president who led the country in a successful war and presided over acquisition of an overseas empire.

William McKinley and his wife posed for this photograph in 1900. A year later the President was dead. What were McKinley's major accomplishments as president?

STUDY GUIDE: The Dingley Tariff and the Currency acts were the only major pieces of domestic legislation passed during McKinley's administration. Although he had expected to concentrate on domestic matters, McKinley found himself drawn into foreign affairs.

THE WEAKENING OF AMERICA'S ISOLATION

The generation after the Civil War was one of unparalleled activity in the United States. In those years Americans conquered their western frontier, built an industrial empire, and erected great cities. But so intense was their attention to internal matters that they virtually turned their backs on foreign affairs. Secretary of State William H. Seward complained in 1868 of the refusal of Americans "to entertain the higher but more remote questions of national extension and aggrandizement." In 1889 the editors of the New York *Sun* even went so far as to doubt the need of a diplomatic service. The editors called

Lawyers in New York City organized the Lawyers Sound Money Club to support McKinley and the Gold Standard. Groups like this one paraded down many American streets in the campaign of 1896. What election promise did McKinley keep?

the service "a costly humbug and sham," and suggested that "Congress should wipe out the whole service."

Americans were not much interested in the outer world, and leaders of the outer world showed little interest in America. They continued into the latter part of the nineteenth century to look on the United States as a second-rate country.

The Spirit of Empire

In the decade of the 1880s, however, the flags of England, France, the Netherlands, Belgium, Italy, and Germany were being placed at numerous points all over the globe. The feeling grew that such imperial activity was essential if a country was to receive recognition as a power of the first magnitude. Accordingly, Americans gradually became infected with the spirit of empire and renewed their interest in world affairs. Before another generation had passed, the Stars and Stripes waved over a string of overseas colonies. The United States, in the historical season after 1885, achieved the rank of a world power.

The intellectual climate of the country was one of the factors that sparked America's new interest in foreign affairs and overseas expansion. During the last third of the nineteenth century the ideas of Social Darwinism reached a peak of influence in the United States. In accord with Social Darwinism, great numbers of Americans concluded that the stronger and more intelligent members of society—that is, "the fittest"—were ordained by nature (or God) to achieve power and eminence. And so it was with races and nations. The ones that were collectively endowed with the highest measure of intelligence, strength, and energy would dominate those races and nations that were comparatively "unfit." This event would be dictated by an irrevocable law of nature.

Which people and nations of the world were the fittest? Many Americans were convinced that the Anglo-Saxons, that is, white people who traced their origins to northern and western Europe, were God's anointed. Therefore, in the phrase of the English poet Rudyard Kipling they felt that they must "take up the white man's burden."

Giving a special sanction to the notion of Anglo-Saxon supremacy were some of the country's best-known academicians and men of religion. The historian John Fiske wrote in 1885 that the Anglo-Saxon peoples were "manifestly destined" to dominate the world. He believed the great work of Anglo-Saxon domination had begun back in the seventeenth century when the English established colonies in North America. Fiske maintained that this process would continue until every corner of the world was Anglo-Saxon in language, religion, and political habits. The Reverend Josiah Strong, a Congregational clergyman, proclaimed Anglo-Saxon peoples had been given a divine commission to be their brothers' keepers.

Economics and Foreign Policies

What about economics — the search for materials, markets, and places for investment — as an inspiration for America's new world view?

In the closing decades of the nineteenth century, political leaders seemed particularly sensitive to appeals of businessmen who wanted the government in Washington to support trading and investment endeavors in Latin America and East Asia. Businessmen, for example, wanted the government to help them secure and maintain the same opportunities that were available to businessmen of such countries as Great Britain and Germany.

As for colonies, however, businessmen revealed little interest in their acquisition until the end of hostilities between the United States and Spain in summer 1898. Most raw materials which fed America's factories were available in the United States, and there was no visible threat to the flow of those materials which American industry brought in from abroad.

America's businessmen reasoned that natives in Africa's jungle or on Pacific islands were not apt to buy many items produced in the United States. Colonies, moreover, were costly to administer and required elaborate military and naval establishments. Also, the colonial powers often became involved in foreign complications, even war.

Whatever the influence of business, it seems in the last analysis that nationalism or patriotism was the principal force behind America's new stance in world affairs after the mid-1880s. Certainly it was a patriotic impulse, not a dream of profits, that moved Americans to give almost unstinting support in those years to a strong foreign policy.

Contributing to the new national spirit, of course, were the ideas of Social Darwinism, for these "proved" that the United States (as Americans had known all along) was a superior country. In the main, however, Social Darwinism probably provided justification for what Americans were determined to do anyhow, that is, secure the position of the United States as a major force in international affairs.

After 125 years of infancy and adolescence, the American nation was coming of age as the nineteenth century drew to a close. Americans had built a great industrial mechanism and conquered a sprawling frontier. They took immense pride in their material achievements and republican heritage and were quite aware of their nation's enormous potential for prosperity and influence. The result was a robust national spirit that would settle for nothing less than full membership in the club of world powers.

To gain such membership, Americans determined to flex their national muscles, take a leading part in world affairs, and acquire overseas possessions. In that era before the idea of imperialism fell into disrepute, an overseas empire was a symbol of national greatness, proof that a country had triumphed in the Darwinian struggle.

STUDY GUIDE: The United States was chiefly concerned with domestic affairs and took little interest in the outside world until the 1880s. Other nations considered the United States a second-rate power. After the mid-1880s the growth of nationalistic, patriotic feelings helped to create new interest in foreign affairs and overseas expansion. The ideas of Social Darwinism convinced many Americans that their country must seize the opportunity to become a world power.

BEGINNINGS OF THE NEW POLICY

The only overseas territories under the Stars and Stripes by the mid-1880s were Midway Island and Alaska. But in the closing years of the nineteenth century diplomacy and war brought additions to the American empire. Among these were American Samoa and Hawaii.

American Samoa

American interest in Samoa, a small group of islands lying 1,600 miles northeast of New Zealand, dated from the early part of the nineteenth century. At that time the government in Washington sent a small scientific expedition to the islands. Nothing came of this initial move.

In the 1870s, President Grant's attention was drawn to the advantages of the harbor of Pago Pago which could serve as an important way station for American traders doing business in the western Pacific and East Asia. The outcome of Grant's interest was a treaty giving the United States exclusive rights to Pago Pago. The treaty, however, failed to win the consent of the United States Senate.

In 1889, Great Britain, Germany, and the United States established a protectorate over

Samoa. This arrangement lasted only ten years. In 1899, the islands were partitioned between the United States and Germany. Britain received compensation elsewhere. While Germany received the largest land area under the treaty, the United States obtained Pago Pago.

Hawaii

The mid-Pacific archipelago of Hawaii had first been settled by Polynesians who had made their way eastward across the Pacific, moving gradually from island to island. Early European navigators, including Magellan and Drake, failed to sight Hawaii during their voyages about the Pacific. It was not until the 1770s that Captain James Cook of Great Britain happened on the islands. Accorded a friendly reception by the Hawaiians, the English unfortunately overstayed their welcome. The result was bickering and fighting between natives and sailors. During a brawl in 1779 Cook was killed.

Americans soon became interested in Hawaii, a natural outpost—or so it seemed to them—of North America. American trading vessels began calling at the islands. By the 1820s Christian missionaries from the United States were arriving in Hawaii. Pearl Harbor on the island of Oahu became a base for American whaling operations in the Pacific, and by midcentury American influence in the islands was considerable.

American leaders had become increasingly conscious of the strategic importance and economic potential of Hawaii. So had leaders of other countries, notably those of England and France. A central purpose of American diplomacy in the Pacific from the 1840s onward was prevention of non-American control of the islands. Because the Hawaiian monarchy was inefficient and corrupt, American leaders feared that the islands might be an easy mark for one of the imperial powers of Europe.

In 1875 a treaty was signed in which the Hawaiian monarchy promised to reduce concessions to non-American powers. The United States agreed to permit Hawaiian sugar growers to sell their product in America without paying tariff duties. Responding to appeals by American naval leaders who had come to view Hawaii as the key to a dominant position for the United States in the Pacific, the government in Washington a few years later compelled the Hawaiians to accept exclusive American control of Pearl Harbor as a naval base.

White islanders deposed Queen Liliuokalani in 1893 and set up the Republic of Hawaii. Judge Sanford B. Dole served as president until the U.S. annexed the islands in 1898. How important were economic motives in the overthrow of the queen?

In 1890 Congress voted American sugar growers a bounty of two cents per pound, a subsidy which permitted American growers to undersell Hawaiians in the United States market. The result was a severe economic depression in the islands. Most Hawaiian planters became convinced that the only solution to Hawaii's problems was annexation by the United States.

The uncertainties of Hawaiian politics also spurred the move for annexation. A corrupt dynasty nominally ruled the islands, although in 1887 the king, under threats, signed away much of his power.

In 1891 Queen Liliuokalani took the throne, determined to restore the monarchy's prerogatives. She was a fervent Hawaiian nationalist who resented American influence in the islands. When it appeared that a majority of the islanders were lining up behind her, the planters began to talk of overthrowing Liliuokalani's regime.

By the end of 1892 the planters determined to act. They organized a Committee of Public Safety and in mid-January 1893 demanded the queen's resignation. At the same time they ap-

Courtesy, Hawaii Visitors Bureau

Iolani Palace was originally the home of Hawaiian royalty. It was the seat of territorial government from annexation to statehood. The state legislature met in its downstairs galleries from 1959 to 1969, when it was replaced by a new capitol.

pealed for the "protection of the United States forces." This appeal found its mark with the American minister in Honolulu, John L. Stevens, who had urged annexation since his arrival in Hawaii in 1891.

The minister ordered marines from the cruiser *Boston,* anchored in Pearl Harbor, to come ashore. Supposedly the move was made to protect American property. In reality it was to intimidate the queen. Stevens also ordered the American flag hoisted over government buildings. Thirty hours later the minister announced recognition of the new Hawaiian provisional government, whereupon Liliuokalani yielded. Two weeks later Stevens proclaimed Hawaii an American protectorate.

Within two weeks officials of the new provisional government and representatives of the United States signed a treaty of annexation. Critics argued that the revolution in Hawaii had been "of sugar, by sugar, and for sugar," but the treaty had wide support across America. Before the treaty came to a vote, however, Grover Cleveland was inaugurated president in March 1893. Cleveland suspected that his country had committed a grave wrong against the Hawaiians and also believed that colonialism violated America's hallowed democratic tradition. He withdrew the treaty for reexamination, ordered the marines back to their ships, ordered the flag

hauled down in Hawaii, and called for an inquiry.

When his inquiry demonstrated improper actions by the United States, Cleveland was anxious to make amends. He leaned to the idea of restoring Liliuokalani. Given the temper of Hawaiian whites, however, that would have required armed intervention. Whatever the former queen's chances of restoration, they ended once and for all when she announced that if restored she would have the heads of those individuals who had helped to overthrow her.

Under the circumstances, Cleveland did nothing. But Hawaiian annexationists, still running the government in Honolulu, pressed on. After Japan defeated China in the war of 1895 and began to flex its muscles in the Pacific, the movement for annexation gained new support in the United States. In May 1898 — in the opening days of the Spanish-American War — an American naval squadron took Manila Bay. Americans suddenly saw Hawaii as a way station on the route to the Philippines. This seemed to put a new light on the matter, and in July 1898, President McKinley signed a joint resolution making Hawaii an American territory.

STUDY GUIDE: Samoa and Hawaii were among the important additions to the American overseas empire in the closing years of the nineteenth century.

NEW INTEREST IN LATIN AMERICA

American attention did not focus exclusively on the Pacific in the closing years of the nineteenth century. There was equal interest in areas to the south of the United States, although, in the beginning at least, few Americans thought of acquiring new territory in that particular part of the world.

In part this new interest in Latin America derived from the work of Secretary of State James G. Blaine who in the 1880s revived an old idea, first put forward by Henry Clay back in the 1820s. Calling for closer accord between countries of the Western Hemisphere, the idea was known as Pan-Americanism. Thanks to Blaine's efforts, the first Pan-American Conference met in Washington in 1889-90. Achievement fell short of hope, but the conference did provide a basis for future cooperation between nations of North and South America.

United States interest in Latin America eventually led to the Spanish-American War. Above, American troops charge El Caney, above Santiago, Cuba.

President McKinley watches the signing of the Peace Protocol ending the Spanish-American War. Representing Spain is Jules Cambon, the French Ambassador. U.S. Secretary of State William R. Day is on his right.

The Chilean Crisis

Less than two years later the United States had a minor crisis with Chile. The trouble originated in an awkward attempt by the United States to prevent an arms shipment to Chilean revolutionaries.

The revolutionaries won control of the government and were slow to forget the American stance in the civil strife. In October 1891, the commander of the cruiser *Baltimore,* anchored in Valparaiso harbor, granted shore leave to about a hundred seamen. At a bar a Chilean allegedly spat in the face of one of the *Baltimore* men, setting off a brawl in which two Americans died. News of the affair brought outrage across the United States. At a cabinet meeting, when Secretary Blaine defended the Chileans, President Benjamin Harrison solemnly reminded him: "Mr. Secretary, that insult was to the uniforms of the United States sailors." Harrison then sent a warlike message to Congress and dispatched the cruiser *Yorktown* to replace the *Baltimore.*

A wave of patriotism swept the country and most Americans seemed to share the sentiments of the New York *Sun* that "we must teach men . . . that we cannot be snapped at with impunity." The *Yorktown* meanwhile was making its way to Chile under the command of Robley D. Evans, who would soon be known throughout America as "Fighting Bob." When Evans arrived at Valparaiso, Chilean torpedo boats made several close passes at the *Yorktown.* Undaunted, Fighting Bob, as he later recalled, "gave orders that if one of them even scratched the paint of the *Yorktown,* to blow the boat out of the water." Fortunately the American gunboat went unscratched, tempers subsided, and the Chilean government made an appropriate apology for the attack on the *Baltimore*'s seamen.

The predicament with Chile was a tempest-in-a-teapot affair. It nonetheless showed the new American spirit in international relations and the low boiling point of American patriots when confronted with foreign insult, real or imagined. Unhappily it consumed some of the goodwill patiently built by statesmen of the Western Hemisphere during the Pan-American Conference.

Venezuelan Boundary Dispute

A more serious crisis developed a few years later, in 1895, out of a boundary dispute between Great Britain and Venezuela. Before it ended, the United States and Britain seemed near the brink of war. The difficulty resulted from failure to establish a boundary between Venezuela and British Guiana (present-day Guyana), which the British had acquired from the Dutch in 1814. For many years the matter of a precise boundary through the jungle seemed of small importance. Then, in the 1880s, gold was discovered in the area, and the location of the boundary became a matter of large importance. When the question of the boundary grew into a full-blown quarrel between Britain and Venezuela, President Cleveland, in 1887, offered to arbitrate, only to receive a stiff rebuff from the British.

The dispute dragged on into the 1890s. Thanks to clever Venezuelan propaganda it commanded increasing attention in the United States. The upshot was a congressional resolution in 1895 urging arbitration, whereupon Cleveland authorized his secretary of state, Richard Olney, to send a harsh note to Great Britain. Accusing the British of violating the Monroe Doctrine, he announced that the United States was "practically sovereign" in the Western Hemisphere "and its fiat is law upon the subjects to which it confines its interposition." Olney demanded that the British state whether or not they would submit the dispute to arbitration.

What prompted the Cleveland administration's firm position against the British on the Venezuelan question? Probably several considerations. First, the administration no doubt calculated that the British were violating at least the spirit of the Monroe Doctrine and believed it was in the interest of the United States to uphold the doctrine. Second, Cleveland doubtless was responding to the new national spirit in America which required that the country assert itself in world affairs, for he could well recall the fury of Americans when he shelved the Hawaiian annexation treaty two years earlier. Finally, it seems that Cleveland wished to support the expansion of American economic activity to the south of the United States. To do this it was necessary to check the spread of English influence in Latin America.

The British waited four months before replying to Olney's note. Then they reminded the United States that the "disputed frontier of Venezuela has nothing to do with any of the questions dealt with by President Monroe." The question in South America, they said, "is simply the determination of the frontier of a British possession which belonged to the throne of England long before the Republic of Venezuela came into existence."

"Mad clear through," Cleveland responded in December 1895 with a ringing message to Congress recommending that the United States fix the Venezuelan boundary and if necessary fight to maintain it. The message met wild enthusiasm in the country, for many Americans continued to equate all British policies and acts with the alleged tyranny of King George III in the 1770s. Other Americans hated the British as the principal guardians of the gold monetary standard. Several million Irish-Americans also despised the British for their own reasons. Then, some Americans were simply spoiling for a war against anybody. Such an individual was the youthful Theodore Roosevelt, who wrote: "Personally, I rather hope that the fight will come soon. The clamor of the peace faction has convinced me that this country needs a war."

The British government had second thoughts. From the vantage point of the whole British Empire, the Venezuelan boundary matter did not loom large. The British, moreover, were having trouble with the Dutch farmers, the Boers, in South Africa. Less than a month after Cleveland's message to Congress the German kaiser infuriated and alarmed the British by sending a congratulatory telegram to the Boer leader, Paul Kruger, following defeat of an unauthorized British raid on the Boers. With war pending in South Africa and an unfriendly Germany standing on the British flank in Europe, this clearly was no time to tangle with the United States. The result was an arbitration agreement between Britain and Venezuela over the boundary.

As for Americans, they had "twisted the British lion's tail," causing the world to take notice. With that satisfaction, most of them were willing to be friends with Britain and the threat of war passed.

STUDY GUIDE: The First Pan-American Conference in 1889 attempted to bring better relations between the United States and Latin American nations. A minor crisis with Chile strained Latin American relations. American involvement in a boundary dispute between Great Britain and Venezuela brought the United States to the brink of war with Britain. However, Great Britain and Venezuela agreed to a peaceful settlement of the dispute.

CUBA LIBRE!

While the affair in Venezuela was boiling, other events taking place to the south of the United States would have much greater consequences. Cuba was attempting to throw off Spanish rule.

By the early 1890s Cuba was enjoying a measure of prosperity, and it seemed that Spanish control was secure. Cuba's new prosperity, however, rested on free entry of Cuban sugar to the United States. When economic depression struck North America in 1893-94, Congress eliminated free entry for Cuban sugar. This congressional action shattered the Cuban economy. As despair settled over the island, Cuban nationalists raised the flag of revolt. Americans paid little attention. The quarrel over Venezuela seemed more interesting. Besides, Americans were suffering their own depression and were concentrating on the election of 1896.

By the time McKinley took the presidential oath in March 1897, however, American opinion regarding Cuba had begun to shift. Reports were filtering into the United States of the activities of General Valeriano Weyler. Sent from Spain in 1896 to pacify Cuba, Weyler sought to isolate rebels from their civilian support by herding vast numbers of Cubans into concentration camps. There is no evidence that he intended to harm inmates of the camps, but unfortunately the Spanish bureaucracy could not cope with problems of food and sanitation. Accordingly, upward of two hundred thousand Cubans died in those camps. News of the concentration camps produced shock and outrage in the United States, where Weyler became known as "Butcher" Weyler.

The "Yellow Sheets"

Meanwhile, competition among newspapers in the United States, particularly the big city dailies, became intense. In their search for increased circulation, editors resorted more and more to sensational reporting, lurid headlines, and exaggerated illustrations. Not content with reporting, the New York *Journal,* owned by William Randolph Hearst, contrived to manufacture news. Its editors directed a reporter to snatch a female rebel from a Spanish jail in Cuba and smuggle her to the United States. Hearst proclaimed that her only crime had been to defend her virtue against a Spanish officer. After the rescue, the *Journal* boasted in a front-page banner that it had secured the girl's freedom where the red tape of diplomacy had failed.

The de Lôme Letter

Rescue of a Cuban maiden was trivial compared with Hearst's exposé of February 9, 1898—a letter from the pen of Dupuy de Lôme, Spain's minister to the United States. Annoyed by references to the Cuban rebellion in President McKinley's state-of-the-union message of December 1897, de Lôme had written to a friend in Havana. In his letter he said that the president's remarks showed "once more . . . what McKinley is, weak and a bidder for the admiration of the crowd, besides being a common politician who tries to leave a door open behind him while keeping on good terms with the jingoes of his party."

Unfortunately somebody stole the letter from the desk of de Lôme's friend and delivered it to Hearst. De Lôme hastily resigned his post, and the Spanish government apologized for the minister's indiscretion. It was too late. The letter inflamed American opinion and took the United States a step nearer war.

"Remember the Maine!"

Less than a week after publication of the de Lôme letter, newsboys were shouting the grisly details of a disaster in Havana harbor. At 9:40 P.M., on February 15, 1898, a deafening explosion had ripped asunder the American battleship *Maine,* claiming the lives of 260 men.

The *Maine* had arrived at Havana several days before on a "courtesy call," although its true mission was to protect American lives and property in the event violence got out of hand in the Cuban capital. Then came the terrible evening of February 15. During the *Maine*'s death agony sailors from a nearby Spanish cruiser braved exploding ammunition to help rescue survivors of the blast. Spanish officials in Havana appeared genuinely sorry about the tragedy, ordered flags to half-mast, and assisted in a state funeral for the dead American seamen. In the United States, however, popular opinion jumped to the conclusion expressed in a private letter by Theodore Roosevelt: "The *Maine* was sunk by an act of dirty treachery on the part of the Spaniards."[1] As a consequence, the country was soon reverberating with the slogan: "Remember the *Maine!* To hell with Spain!"

---

[1] Quoted in Elting E. Morison, ed., *The Letters of Theodore Roosevelt,* Volume 1, copyright 1951 (Cambridge: Harvard University Press).

Large numbers of Americans wanted an immediate declaration of war on Spain, but President McKinley was determined to proceed with caution. His first step was to send a board of naval officers to Havana to investigate the *Maine* disaster. Unfortunately the water around the wreckage was muddy and the divers sent down to examine the *Maine's* hull had scant understanding of ship construction. Still, the board's report, published in late March 1898, stated that "the Maine was destroyed by the explosion of a submarine mine, which caused the partial explosion of two or more of the forward magazines." Who was to blame? The board disclosed that it had been "unable to obtain evidence fixing the responsibility for the destruction of the Maine upon any person or persons."

Whoever was responsible, the chief beneficiaries of the *Maine* disaster were Cuba's rebels.

Meanwhile the wheels of diplomacy continued to turn, and late in March 1898 the United States made two demands of Spain: an armistice in Cuba and an end to the concentration-camp program. Acceptance of these demands presumably would satisfy the United States and save the peace. Within two weeks the Spanish government yielded on both points. Diplomacy had scored a triumph, or so it seemed.

A War Spirit in America

Unfortunately a martial spirit was sweeping the United States and a great number of Americans would settle for nothing less than Spain's total withdrawal from Cuba. Otherwise they were for war. It seemed early in 1898 that many Americans wanted war more than they wanted a Spanish withdrawal.

The Democratic party's standard-bearer of 1896, William Jennings Bryan, thundered that "humanity demands that we shall act." Theodore Roosevelt, the assistant secretary of the navy in McKinley's administration and one of the country's most determined war hawks, genuinely feared war might elude the United States.

It is difficult to say what caused this war spirit in America. The period of the 1890s was a time when Americans felt inclined to flex their muscles. Hence, the prospect of war, particularly a "little" war with a second-rate power, had great appeal. There was also the humanitarian impulse. Ignoring the mistreatment of black men, Indians and ethnic minorities in the United States, many Americans were outraged when

EDITION FOR GREATER NEW YORK

NEW YORK JOURNAL
AND ADVERTISER.

NO. 5,571. *** Copyright, 1898, by W. R. Hearst.—NEW YORK, WEDNESDAY, FEBRUARY 16, 1898.—16 PAGES. PRICE ONE CENT In Greater New York | Elsewhere, and Jersey City. | TWO CENTS

MAINE BLOWN TO ATOMS IN HAVANA HARBOR;
OVER ONE HUNDRED OF HER CREW KILLED.

Three Million Dollar Battleship Destroyed by a Terrific and Mysterious Explosion While Her Men Are Sleeping.

THE FIRST BELIEF IS THAT A HIDDEN SPANISH MINE ANNIHILATED HER.

Captain Sigsbee Reports To Secretary Long That the Few Fragments Remaining are Ablaze, and Asks For Immediate Assistance from Key West.

BATTLE SHIP MAINE SAID TO HAVE BEEN DESTROYED BY AN EXPLOSION IN HAVANA HARBOR.

---

they pondered Spanish cruelties in Cuba. They felt obliged to lift the burden of Spanish colonialism from the Cubans, by force if necessary. Then some businessmen believed that continuation of the Cuban insurrection might bring radical leaders to power in Havana. Their policies would have an unsettling effect on the American economy.

Responding to the national sentiment for war, McKinley, on April 11, 1898—two days after learning of Spain's acceptance of his previous demands—asked Congress for authority to use force to end hostilities in Cuba. The message set off a bitter debate on Capitol Hill. Debate ended a week later when Congress adopted a joint resolution demanding Spain's withdrawal from Cuba. The resolution authorized the president to use force, if necessary, to secure that end. Proclaiming Cuba independent, Congress also

The day after the U.S.S. *Maine* exploded, Americans read wild headlines like these. No proof of a "hidden Spanish mine" was ever found. Why was the country so eager to believe that the Spanish were responsible? Do the news media today have even greater power to form public opinion?

pledged, via the so-called Teller Amendment (offered by Senator Henry M. Teller of Colorado), that the United States would not annex Cuba. This latter act of self-denial, which many Americans later regretted, presumably proved to the world, and to Americans themselves, that the only motive of the United States was to free Cuba from the Spanish. The Teller Amendment was a promise that the United States was not using the threat of war against Spain in order to claim Cuba, the choicest territory in the Caribbean, for itself. McKinley signed the resolution the next day.

Spain believed it had gone far enough in attempting to appease the United States on the Cuban question. The government in Madrid feared that revolution might follow acceptance of the American demand that Spain get out of Cuba and recognize the island's independence. The only choice was war, declared on April 24. The American Congress made its declaration the next day.

It doubtless was with a heavy heart that William McKinley took the United States to war in 1898, for he abhorred violence. But the national clamor for war was irresistible and only a dramatic recognition of Cuba's independence by Spain, it seems, could have spared the president his agonizing decision.

STUDY GUIDE: Efforts of Cuban rebels to free their island from Spanish rule attracted increasing attention in the United States. American big-city daily newspapers published sensational stories about Spanish atrocities in Cuba. These newspaper accounts aroused American sympathy for the Cuban rebels and hatred for Spain. This hatred was reinforced when a newspaper disclosed the contents of a letter written by Dupuy de Lôme, the Spanish minister to the United States. In his letter de Lôme criticized President McKinley. Hopes for peace grew dimmer after the sinking of the American battleship *Maine* in Havana Harbor. The cause of the *Maine* disaster remained a mystery, but Cuban rebels were quick to blame it on Spain. Diplomatic efforts failed, and the American public demanded war. McKinley regretfully agreed to declare war on Spain in 1898.

WAR AND PEACE WITH SPAIN

The first shells of the Spanish-American War burst halfway around the world from Cuba—at Manila Bay in the Philippines.

Dewey at Manila Bay

When Congress adopted the war resolution, the American Asiatic Squadron of six warships, under command of Commodore George Dewey, was moored at Hong Kong. In anticipation of war, Dewey had already painted his white vessels battle gray. On April 25 he received a cable from Washington to proceed to the Philippines and destroy a small fleet of Spanish warships in accordance with a plan designed earlier by Assistant Secretary of the Navy Theodore Roosevelt.

Guarding Manila Bay were formidable batteries on the island of Corregidor. For some unexplainable reason, however, the Spanish gunners did not open fire when Dewey nervously guided his vessels past them at midnight on April 30. Then, as the Americans approached Manila at dawn they found that the Spanish commander had withdrawn to a point several miles away. There, in shallow water—to give survivors a better chance—he had dropped anchor and was awaiting Dewey's onslaught.

When the American vessels drew within range of the Spaniards, Commodore Dewey, from the bridge of the flagship *Olympia,* gave his famous order: "You may fire when ready, Gridley." Thereupon the eight-inch guns of the Asiatic Squadron bellowed. For several hours, except during a pause for breakfast, the squadron steamed back and forth hurling shells at the Spanish vessels. The Spaniards answered, but with little effect. A few minutes past noon it was over. The Asiatic Squadron had blown ten Spanish ships from the water and taken the lives of nearly four hundred seamen. The only American death resulted from heat exhaustion. News of Dewey's victory at Manila Bay touched off a wild celebration across the United States, and the commodore became the hero of the hour.

Action in Cuba

While Dewey was churning toward Manila Bay, a tiny Spanish squadron of antiquated wooden-decked vessels under command of Admiral Cervera steamed away from the Cape Verde Islands, a few hundred miles off the west coast of Africa, destination, the Caribbean. The Spaniards knew that Cervera's squadron was on a suicide mission but, as in the Philippines, national honor compelled a show of resistance.

For a time there was no word on the whereabouts of the Spanish fleet. The result was alarm along the Atlantic coast of the United States that the Spaniards might be preparing to strike at American coastal cities. To relieve the anxiety of citizens, the Navy Department dispatched old monitors of Civil War design to offer as much protection as they could. Fortunately the Spaniards were entertaining no offensive ideas and instead sailed straight to the harbor of Santi-

Colonel Theodore Roosevelt posed atop San Juan Hill in 1898 with the First Volunteer Cavalry, the Rough Riders, after winning a hard-fought battle against the Spanish. Roosevelt later called the day the greatest of his life.

ago along the southeastern shore of Cuba, where they prepared to await the Americans. The flag ship *Cristóbal Colón* dropped anchor in full view at the mouth of the harbor, awnings were spread, and the commander permitted his men to lounge in the sun.

Where were the Americans? The Atlantic Fleet, commanded by Admiral William T. Sampson, and the Flying Squadron, comprising several cruisers and battleships, under Commodore Winfield Scott Schley, were thrashing about the western Atlantic and Caribbean trying to find the Spaniards. Days turned into weeks and across the United States millions of people breathlessly awaited word that Sampson or Schley had located Cervera's squadron. Americans were also keeping track of the voyage of the battleship *Oregon,* which was making its way from Bremerton, Washington, around the tip of South America to reinforce Sampson and Schley. On May 26, after sixty-eight days at sea, the *Oregon* lumbered into Key West. Then, two days later, Schley steamed by Santiago and spied his prey.

While the *Oregon* was being outfitted for combat, Schley pondered his next move. Caution seemed essential, for shore batteries guarded the mouth of the Santiago harbor—although, it turned out, one of the Spanish guns had been forged in the year 1688 and five others in 1724. After waiting several days, the commodore risked an attack, firing at the *Cristóbal Colón* through the harbor entrance. No hits were made. Next morning the *Cristóbal Colón* nonchalantly steamed out of sight inside the harbor and Schley stationed his vessels in a giant blockading arc. Then, a few days later, Admiral Sampson arrived and assumed command of naval operations around Santiago.

Meanwhile the army had lumbered into action and at Tampa, on the Gulf coast of Florida, was assembling a force to invade Cuba, commanded by General William R. Shafter.

Thousands of men, anxious to get in a blow at the Spaniards, answered President McKinley's call for volunteers. Within two weeks volunteer regiments were converging on Tampa. Lacking organization and discipline, the volunteers turned the Florida encampment into a madhouse. General Shafter, tortured by the heat and humidity, struggled as best he could to bring order to his command. But the War Department in Washington did not grasp the magnitude of his difficulties and repeatedly pressed him to get on with the invasion. Impatient with excuses, President McKinley finally, at the end of May, ordered Shafter to sail, ready or not. He was to land his army on the southeastern coast of Cuba. In cooperation with the navy they were to capture or destroy the Spanish garrison at Santiago and Admiral Cervera's little fleet in Santiago harbor.

Despairing of ever organizing his volunteers so as to make an orderly movement to the transports anchored in Tampa Bay, Shafter did an extraordinary thing. He passed the word that the expedition would sail at daybreak, and which regiments would go would be up to their own ingenuity.

The general's informal message set off a mad dash for the transports. A New York regiment commandeered a train that was heading toward the pier and held it at bayonet point until all the men were aboard. Theodore Roosevelt's Rough Riders, a volunteer regiment composed in part of cowboys from the West, captured the transport *Yucatan* and defended the gangplank against the Second Infantry and the Seventy-first New York.

After waiting for many days while Shafter and Admiral Sampson considered the question of where to attempt a landing, the 17,000-man American army scrambled ashore at Daiquiri on June 22, a few miles east of Santiago. The Spaniards did not contest the landing.

Battle of San Juan Hill

Two days later American units, including the Ninth and Tenth (Negro) Cavalry, began the movement toward Santiago. Spanish officers continued to display an amazing lack of initiative and imagination, and despite some sharp skirmishes the Americans pushed forward. Within a week the Americans had reached a point three miles from Santiago. But the campaign was not over. Between the Americans and the city was a ridge called San Juan Hill. Four miles to the north, on the flank, was the little town of El Caney, where an unknown number of Spanish soldiers were drawn up in a stone fort and blockhouses.

Utterly contemptuous of the "cowardly" Spaniards, the Americans were undaunted. On July 1 General Shafter, who had fallen victim to the heat and was directing the campaign from a cot in his tent, ordered an attack. The first objective was El Caney. At sunrise, some six thousand blue-clad Americans, shouting "Remember the *Maine*!" began the movement up the hill toward the little village. The Spanish defenders, numbering 500 men, put down a murderous fire, but Shafter's men continued the charge and after several hours routed the enemy.

While the action at El Caney still raged, eight thousand other American soldiers were storming the main Spanish force at San Juan Hill. One of several units involved was Theodore Roosevelt's Rough Riders, commanded by General Leonard Wood, not by Roosevelt. Although heavily outnumbered, the Spaniards were strongly entrenched and put up a fierce resistance, killing or wounding nearly a thousand of their enemies. But, as at El Caney, the Americans were not to be denied the victory. By four-thirty in the afternoon they had the hill. Theodore Roosevelt, who had galloped on horseback about the hill encouraging the Rough Riders who were on foot, would always consider this the greatest day of his life.

One of the units at San Juan Hill was a Negro regiment. Frank Knox of the Rough Riders (who many years later served as secretary of the navy) wrote home that, on separation from the Rough Riders, "I joined a troop of the Tenth Cavalry, colored, and for a time fought with them shoulder to shoulder. . . . I must say that I never saw braver men anywhere."

The Siege of Santiago

Taking El Caney and San Juan Hill was one thing; capturing Santiago was something else. The Spaniards still had a formidable army drawn up behind barbed-wire entanglements, which ringed the city. American commanders feared that their men, spread out in a thin line around Santiago, might be unable to stand up against a Spanish counterattack. Theodore Roosevelt, two days after his heroics at San Juan Hill, warned that "we are within measurable distance of a terrible military disaster."

A few miles off the coast, meanwhile, Sampson and Schley continued their blockade of Santiago harbor. Maintaining a blockade was dull, tedious business and the American seamen, after a month of it, had become tired and restless. Then on Sunday, July 3, 1898, as the Americans prepared for a routine inspection and the usual Sunday religious services, the Spanish fleet dashed out of the harbor. In minutes the American vessels were in pursuit. Before the day ended, a few burning hulks were all that remained of the sea power of Spain.

In the trenches around Santiago the American soldiers celebrated the great naval victory. But their commanders remained nervous, lest the Spaniards counterattack. Then in mid-July the commander of the Spanish garrison agreed to surrender to spare Santiago the miseries of a long siege.

The War Ends

In late July fresh United States troops went ashore on the island of Puerto Rico. The Spanish elected not to resist and the Puerto Rican campaign happily turned into a grand military promenade across the island.

And so into history passed "the splendid little war," as America's ambassador to Britain, John Hay, called it. From the perspective of the United States, the conflict had not been difficult. It produced hardly a campaign worthy of the name and fewer than four hundred Americans died in battle, although thirteen times that many died of diseases, most of them soldiers in Cuba who fell victim of yellow fever.

STUDY GUIDE: In the Spanish-American War Commodore Dewey defeated the Spanish fleet at Manila Bay in the Philippines. American forces invaded Cuba and won victories at El Caney, San Juan Hill, and Santiago Harbor. Spanish forces were heavily outnumbered and surrendered.

THE WAR'S EFFECT ON AMERICA

Although, as Theodore Roosevelt sadly admitted, it had not been much of a war, the "summer war" of 1898 nonetheless had an intoxicating effect on Americans. It heightened their national spirit, "proving" what they had long known—that they were a "great" people. It also set them to speculating on the opportunity to enlarge their overseas domain at the expense of the decaying empire of the Spaniards. By the time the war ended, most of them were determined to seize the opportunity.

Because of the Teller Amendment, the United States could not honorably raise the Stars and Stripes on Cuban soil. But Congress had made no pledge of self-denial regarding other Spanish territories. Especially attractive were the Philippines. American businessmen had come to see

Library of Congress

This political cartoon was drawn during the Senate debates over ratification of the Treaty of Paris. Uncle Sam is being measured for a new suit by President McKinley. Anti-Expansionists are trying unsuccessfully to get Uncle Sam to take a dose of anti-fat tonic.

the Philippine Islands as an excellent base for improving the American trading position in China. Protestant missionaries saw the islands as a place where they might carry the Christian message, although Spaniards had carried that message to the islands two centuries before. Thus, most Filipinos were already Christians, of the Roman Catholic faith.

The Treaty of Paris

At Paris, in October 1898, representatives of Spain and the United States, displaying much cordiality, drafted a peace treaty. Spain gave up all claims to Cuba and turned over to the United States Puerto Rico, the Philippines, and the island of Guam.

America's expansionist mood notwithstanding, the Treaty of Paris ran into sharp opposition when it came up for consideration in the United States Senate. The central issue of the debate was the Philippines. Few people were against taking Puerto Rico, which was not far from the United States, or Guam, which was so tiny as to seem unimportant.

But opponents of the treaty noted that the Philippine Islands were 8,000 miles west of San Francisco and would be difficult and costly to defend. They would involve the United States in Asian politics and might easily draw the country into some future war in the Far East. Opponents also pointed to problems that would arise from the attempt to integrate seven million brown-skinned Malays into the American social fabric. They contended that the federal Constitution "follows the flag" and thus the United States would be required to grant full citizenship to the Filipinos. This would mean that islanders might migrate to the United States without restriction and their products might enter the country without duty. And eventually the Philippines would have to receive the opportunity to become a state in the federal Union. Opponents of the Treaty of Paris argued finally that colonialism contradicted the American democratic tradition.

Supporters of the treaty, those people who looked kindly on the idea of a far-reaching American empire, responded vigorously. They asserted that as a sovereign country the United States had a right to acquire and govern territories. With the right to govern went the right to establish whatever kind of government seemed suitable. The government therefore was under no obligation to confer citizenship on the people of a territory, grant free entry to territorial products, or make provision for eventual statehood for the territory. In other words, the Constitution did not necessarily follow the flag.

The arguments of individuals who favored the treaty prevailed and in February 1899 the Senate consented to it—but by only one vote above the necessary two-thirds.

The United States had annexed an important overseas territory. It had also annexed a war. As in Cuba, there was a strong independence movement in the Philippines. Filipinos who had fought Spaniards were just as ready to fight Americans. Indeed they might have been more eager to fight Americans, for American leaders had sought and received cooperation from Filipino rebels in the war against Spain. True, the United States had made no promises to the Filipinos. But American leaders had permitted the Filipinos to believe that the United States would support their quest for independence.

Thus the Filipinos were furious over the Treaty of Paris and its provision that control of the Philippines would pass to the United States. Two days before the Senate ratification, hostilities broke out at Manila between American troops and insurgents led by the Philippine patriot Emilio Aguinaldo. The outcome for the United States was a longer and more expensive conflict than that with Spain. Known as the Philippine Insurrection, it did not end until July 1902. (See page 393.)

STUDY GUIDE: Victory over Spain heightened American feelings of nationalism and the desire for overseas territories. Under the terms of the Treaty of Paris, Spain turned over Guam, Puerto Rico, and the Philippines to the United States. Spain also gave up her claim to Cuba. Although the treaty finally won Senate approval, many Americans opposed the annexation of the Philippines. There was also opposition to the terms of the treaty in the Philippines. Some Filipinos continued to fight for independence for several years.

THE "BIG STICK" IN PANAMA

In September 1901, following the assassination of McKinley, Vice-President Theodore Roosevelt moved into the White House. The new president had once said: "I always have been fond of the West African proverb, 'Speak softly and carry a big stick, and you will go far.'" During his seven and a half years as president, he seemed to take the proverb seriously. At home he freely used his authority to bully or coerce coal operators, meat packers, and anyone else who in his view was harming the public interest. In diplomatic affairs he did not hesitate to throw the power of the United States in the international balance to intimidate foreign governments and secure his ends.

Roosevelt's most notable use of the "big stick" in diplomatic affairs came when he moved to redeem the Republican campaign pledge of 1900 to get on with the business of constructing a canal across the isthmus of Central America.

The de Lesseps Project

For generations Europeans and Americans had dreamed of a waterway across Central America. In the 1860s, upon completion of the Suez Canal linking the Mediterranean with the Red Sea, it seemed that a similar achievement in Central America must surely be at hand. The dream appeared near fulfillment a few years later when a French company headed by Ferdinand de Lesseps, chief engineer of the Suez project, acquired a franchise from the Colombian government. The French prepared to duplicate the Suez triumph by cutting a canal across Colombia's province of Panama.

Unfortunately the problems facing de Lesseps in Central America were not the same as those he had overcome in the Egyptian desert. The frightful expense of building a waterway through the Panamanian jungle, plus the ravages of yellow fever, brought the Central American venture to grief. By the 1890s, construction, about two-thirds completed, had come to a standstill.

The United States had kept a sharp watch on the activities of the de Lesseps organization. Over several decades American leaders had speculated on the advantages of such a waterway. Then the United States took possession of Hawaii and the Philippines. The country now had important territories in the Pacific which required naval protection. As the dramatic voyage of the *Oregon* around South America in spring 1898 had demonstrated, an isthmian canal was necessary to enable the navy to move quickly from one ocean to another. The alternative was to take on the expense of building and maintaining two large fleets, one for the Atlantic and another for the Pacific. A Central American canal would also make it easier — and more profitable — for businessmen in the eastern half of the nation to seize new trade opportunities offered by the presence of important United States territories in the Pacific.

So compelling seemed the arguments in favor of an isthmian canal that by the year 1900 the United States was determined to build and operate a canal across Central America.

The first obstacle to American construction of an isthmian canal was diplomatic. Back in 1850 the California gold rush had sparked interest in such a waterway. The United States and Great Britain, each fearing that the other might build a canal and operate it to its own advantage, had signed the Clayton-Bulwer Treaty. This treaty pledged that neither country would exercise exclusive control over or fortify an isthmian canal. The treaty was still in effect by 1900. But times had changed in the intervening half-century. The United States had become one of the leading nations of the world. Hence it would not accept restrictions imposed by the Clayton-Bulwer document in an area which it considered its special sphere of influence.

The Hay-Pauncefote Treaty

The outcome was negotiations between Secretary of State John Hay and the British ambassador in Washington, Lord Pauncefote. Those negotiations led to the Hay-Pauncefote Treaty (1900). The treaty provided that the United States could build and control but not fortify an isthmian canal. It also proclaimed that the United States, if it built a canal, would require ships of all nations to pay identical tolls for using the canal.

Things seemed to be proceeding smoothly. Then a hitch developed. Because of the non-fortification clause the treaty was not acceptable to the United States Senate, and for a time tempers flared in Washington and London. However, at that time the British were entangled in the Boer War in South Africa. They decided it was not smart to antagonize the Americans — who were about the only people in the world showing sympathy for the British cause in South Africa. The upshot was the second Hay-Pauncefote Treaty (1901), which authorized the United States to fortify as well as build and control a Central American canal. The second treaty retained the clause prohibiting any discrimination in tolls.

Panama and Nicaragua

The next question was: Where should an American canal be located, in Panama or Nicaragua? If it selected Panama, the United States would purchase the old de Lesseps franchise and begin construction where the French organization had left off. If it chose Nicaragua, it would start from scratch. To study the problem President McKinley had appointed a commission in 1899 and two months after his successor, Roosevelt, took office, in 1901, the commission made its report.

The report explained that Nicaragua had two principal advantages. In Nicaragua it would be possible to link several rivers and lakes to make a sea-level canal. A Panamanian canal, on the other hand, would require a series of expensive locks to lift ships up and over the isthmus. Second, Nicaragua was closer to the United States than was Panama. This meant that a canal across Nicaragua would result in lower shipping costs for American firms.

Panama's principal advantage was the work already accomplished by the French. If the New Panama Canal Company, a French firm that had taken over the bankrupt de Lesseps organization, would accept a reasonable price for its franchise, the final cost of a canal across Panama would be considerably less than that of a waterway across Nicaragua. The commission recognized that cost was a central consideration in this matter. Unfortunately the New Panama Canal Company was asking $109 million for its franchise, a price which the commission considered outrageous. The commission therefore recommended that the United States build its canal across Nicaragua.

The commission's recommendation sent a wave of panic through the New Panama Canal Company, for sale of its franchise to the United States offered the only chance of a return on its Panamanian venture. Accordingly, the New Panama Canal Company dramatically reduced the price of its franchise to $40 million, the value placed on it by the commission. Whereupon the new president, Theodore Roosevelt, persuaded the commission to reverse itself and recommend a Panamanian canal.

By this time the matter had already reached the halls of Congress. A few days before learning of the commission's revised recommendation, the House of Representatives had voted overwhelmingly in favor of the Nicaraguan route. The Senate, however, had not yet acted.

Seeing their opportunity, lobbyists for the New Panama Canal Company swung into action. They reminded Republican leaders in the Senate that the company had contributed $60,000 to the Republican campaign fund in 1900. Next they raised the fear that volcanoes in Nicaragua would endanger a canal in that country. Then, as luck would have it, the very volcano engraved on Nicaraguan postage stamps suddenly became active. A lobbyist immediately acquired ninety of the stamps and sent one to each senator, with a notation: "An official witness of the volcanic activity of Nicaragua."

Colombia Rejects Canal Treaty

A short time later the Senate amended the House resolution to make it call for a canal across Panama. When the House consented to the amendment, the measure went to Roosevelt, who gave it his signature in June 1902. The amended resolution authorized the president to secure the right to construct a Panamanian canal. However, in the event of unreasonable terms or prolonged delay in securing approval of the Colombian government, he was to seek a route across Nicaragua.

Purchase of the French concession did not automatically open the way for an American canal across the isthmus. Panama was a Colombian province; hence, the United States also had to make arrangements with the government in Bogotá. This seemed to present no problem. Recognizing that a canal would yield dividends

to Colombia, and quite incapable of financing such a venture itself, the Colombian government was anxious that the United States finish the work the French had begun.

In Washington, meanwhile, Secretary of State John Hay was aware of Colombia's position. To prod its leaders into a quick agreement with the United States, he threatened to open negotiations with Nicaragua. The scheme worked and in January 1903 Colombia signed the Hay-Herrán Treaty. This agreement provided that the United States would have a canal zone six miles wide across the isthmus and Colombia would receive an initial payment of $10 million and an annuity of $250,000.

The treaty promptly received the consent of the United States Senate. Not so in Colombia. Leaders in Bogotá wanted their government to receive more money. A large initial payment by the United States might have brought them to a quick agreement, but they also seemed to be looking ahead to autumn 1904, when the French concession in Panama would expire. Then the assets of the New Panama Canal Company would pass to the Colombian government. If they could delay the transaction for some fifteen months, the Colombians rather than stockholders of the French company would receive the $40 million which the United States was willing to pay for work already completed on the canal.

As a sovereign nation, Colombia was within its rights in rejecting the treaty. Still, President Roosevelt was furious and denounced the Colombians as "bandits" and "contemptible little creatures."

Independence for Panama

While the president fumed, there were rumblings in Panama. Once an independent country, in the middle of the nineteenth century Panama had voluntarily joined Colombia. But now Panamanians were dazzled by visions of prosperity if the canal went across their territory. They feared that the Americans, disgusted by the Colombian refusal, might return to the idea of building the waterway in Nicaragua. Thus Panama shared Roosevelt's feelings about Colombia's rejection of the Hay-Herrán Treaty. The result was an independence movement in Panama.

Supported by French money, Panamanian rebels put together a motley "army" consisting of five hundred bribed Colombian soldiers and more than four hundred members of the Panama

City fire department. Before hoisting the flag of revolt, the rebels would of course need some assurance of outside support from Roosevelt. Such a tiny, untrained force could not stand alone against the army of Colombia.

Accepted rules of international conduct forbade a country to aid a revolt against a friendly government. President Roosevelt nonetheless dispatched the cruiser *Nashville* to Panamanian waters. The day after the American warship's arrival, November 3, 1903, the Panamanians rebelled. The *Nashville* did not prevent the landing of a few hundred Colombian troops, ordered by leaders in Bogotá to counter the uprising. Still, the presence of the vessel encouraged the rebels, discouraged the Colombians, and thus helped assure success of the revolution.

The following day Panama proclaimed independence. Although international custom prescribed that a sovereign nation, such as Colombia, should have a reasonable time to put down a revolt in its territory, the United States waited only two days to recognize the new government of Panama. Next the leaders in Panama City appointed Philippe Bunau-Varilla, a French citizen who had been chief engineer of the old Panama Company, as Panamanian minister to the United States. Two weeks later, he and Hay signed the Hay – Bunau-Varilla Treaty giving the United States a canal zone ten miles wide across the isthmus. By this treaty Panama received the $10 million cash payment and $250,000 annuity originally intended for Colombia. Other provisions of the treaty made Panama a virtual protectorate of the United States.

Some Americans were appalled by Roosevelt's "cowboy diplomacy" in Central America. Most, however, shared the president's conviction that Colombia had no right to stand in the way of construction of a great highway of world commerce and hence had received precisely the kind of treatment it deserved. Reflecting the popular mood, the Senate in February 1904 overwhelmingly consented to the Hay–Bunau-Varilla Treaty.

STUDY GUIDE: Theodore Roosevelt used the power of the presidency to get what he wanted for the United States, even if it meant bullying other nations. One of his major goals was construction of a canal across Central America to connect the Atlantic and Pacific oceans. The Colombian government refused to approve the Hay-Herrán Treaty authorizing construction of a canal across Panama. Roosevelt supported the efforts of Panamanian rebels to win independence from Colombia. The United States was rewarded by Panama with the right to build a canal there. Roosevelt's highhanded diplomacy aroused bitter feelings in Latin America. He annoyed the British as well by urging legislation exempting American ships from paying canal tolls.

MORE OF THE "BIG STICK"

The venture in Panama was not the only intervention by the United States in Latin America in the early years of the twentieth century. At one time or another, successive presidents found themselves using the "big stick" in Cuba, the Dominican Republic, Nicaragua, Haiti, and Mexico.

When the United States went to war with Spain in 1898, it renounced any claim to Cuba. Disposing of the Cuban problem, it turned out, was not so simple as Congress had thought it would be. When hostilities ended and the Spaniards departed, the United States found Cuba hopelessly unprepared for self-government. Almost in desperation Congress established a protectorate over the island.

The Platt Amendment

The instrument for protection of Cuba was the Platt Amendment to the army appropriation bill of 1901. This amendment prohibited Cuba from entering into any treaty impairing its independence. It also sanctioned American naval bases on the island, including the one the navy had already established at Guantanamo Bay. Written into the Cuban constitution in 1901, the Platt Amendment became part of a treaty between Cuba and the United States in 1903. Until abrogated in 1934, it opened the way for American troops periodically to land in Cuba to preserve order and to protect American lives and property on the island.

The year 1905 brought United States intervention in another Latin American country, the Dominican Republic. The Dominican government had found itself unable to meet debt payments to foreign creditors. Touching off the intervention were rumors that Europe's powers were planning to land forces in the Dominican Republic to recover money owed their nationals.

If the Europeans did this, according to the logic of American diplomatists, the outcome could be an awkward, even dangerous, situation for the United States. Whatever its justification, European intervention could conceivably lead to an occupation of the country in clear violation of the Monroe Doctrine.

To forestall a possible crisis, American officials persuaded the Dominican president to invite the United States to take over the country's customs houses. The Americans then began to distribute part of the customs revenue to the Dominican government and part to the government's creditors. Although this arrangement brought comparative peace and prosperity to the country, Dominicans chafed at North American involvement in their affairs until at last, in 1941, the United States returned the customs houses to Dominican control.

Roosevelt Corollary to the Monroe Doctrine

Roosevelt had been weighing the possibility of United States intervention in the internal affairs of Latin American states for more than a year — since the winter of 1902-03 — when Britain and Germany prepared to coerce the Venezuelan dictator for nonpayment of debts. Fortunately the dictator agreed to submit the problem to arbitration at the last minute. However, the possibility of a European intervention in the Western Hemisphere and the difficulties it might create for the United States continued to haunt the president. Then came the financial breakdown of the Dominican Republic and rumors of intervention by Europe's powers. Therefore, in December 1904, six weeks before arranging to take over the Dominican customs houses, President Roosevelt justified his intervention in a letter to Secretary of State Elihu Root. The justification is known as the Roosevelt Corollary to the Monroe Doctrine.

Roosevelt wrote that "chronic wrongdoing, or an impotence which results in a general loosening of the ties of civilized society, may in America, or elsewhere, ultimately require intervention by some civilized nation, and in the Western Hemisphere, the adherence of the United States to the Monroe Doctrine may force the United States, however reluctantly, in flagrant cases of such wrongdoing or impotence, to the exercise of an international police power."

In other words, since the United States would not permit non-American powers to keep order and prevent "wrongdoing" in the Western Hemisphere, the United States had a moral obligation to do so. Nonpayment of foreign debts was in Roosevelt's view a form of wrongdoing (or perhaps a demonstration of impotence). Therefore the United States was obliged to see that Latin American republics paid such debts. To put it still another way, the United States could not permit Latin Americans to take shelter behind the Monroe Doctrine and thumb their noses at European creditors.

Roosevelt hoped that his appointment of the United States as the policeman of the Western Hemisphere would discourage disorder in Latin America. By the time he left the White House in 1909, however, trouble was brewing in Nicaragua. Before the year was out the country was torn by revolution.

Concerned about violence so near the Panama Canal, by then nearing completion, leaders in Washington kept a close watch on the Nicaraguan situation. In 1911, they coerced Nicaragua into becoming an American protectorate. As in the Dominican Republic, the United States took over the customs houses and from time to time over the next two decades American marines went ashore to put down uprisings. As in the Dominican Republic, American intervention was unappreciated by the local population and in 1933 the United States ended the protectorate.

Trouble in Haiti

Haiti was another trouble spot which also stood near the Panama lifeline. When matters got out of hand in 1915, President Woodrow Wilson dispatched troops and forced the government to accept a treaty making Haiti a protectorate of the United States. Still, several hundred Haitians died resisting American attempts to pacify the country. Although the American occupation eventually brought sanitation, roads, and schools, Haiti, like Cuba, the Dominican Republic, and Nicaragua, resented the intervention. In 1934 the United States ended the treaty of 1915.

Intervention in Mexico

Of greater importance was United States intervention in Mexico in the years 1914-16.

The Mexican ventures resulted from the revolutionary chaos that swept Mexico following the departure in 1911 of President Porfirio Diaz. Diaz's successor, Francisco Madero, lasted less than two years before he was assassinated and replaced by his star general, Victoriano Huerta. A few weeks after Huerta's accession to power in early 1913, Woodrow Wilson became president. Determined to uphold international morality (as he defined it, of course), Wilson recalled the United States ambassador from Mexico City and refused to extend recognition to the Huerta regime, which he described as a "government of butchers." In so acting, the new president was departing from time-honored American practice.

Until this time, the United States had not considered the morality of a government in deciding whether or not to extend recognition. If a government was in control of a country, as was Huerta's in Mexico, the United States always had recognized it as the legitimate government of the country and established diplomatic relations. What did Wilson hope to accomplish in this instance? Apart from putting the United States on the side of "morality," he hoped to isolate Huerta and bring about his fall. Things did not work out as Wilson hoped. Undaunted by the position of the United States, the Mexican leader managed to survive. Before the year 1913 was over he had established a military dictatorship.

Events finally came to a crisis in April 1914 when a boatload of seamen from an American naval vessel went ashore at the Mexican port of Tampico. They strayed into a restricted area and were arrested. While under arrest, they were paraded through the streets of the town. On learning of the incident, the local Mexican commander released the sailors and apologized to their commanding officer. A mere verbal apology was not enough for Admiral Henry T. Mayo of the American navy. He demanded that the Mexicans fire a twenty-one-gun salute to the Stars and Stripes, and President Wilson backed him up. The Mexicans rejected Mayo's demand.

As tempers on both sides became heated, American leaders learned that a German vessel was steaming toward Mexico with a cargo of ammunition for Huerta. American marines were immediately sent to occupy Veracruz, Mexico's principal port. After several months, Argentina, Brazil, and Chile mediated the dispute and the marines returned to their ships. But American occupation of Veracruz had weakened Huerta by cutting him off from overseas supplies. A short time later his enemies inside Mexico toppled him.

The new government of Mexico, headed by Venustiano Carranza, proved no more friendly to the United States than had that of Huerta. It set about to rid Mexico of United States influence. The new regime ran into difficulty, not from President Wilson but from Doroteo Arango, better known as Francisco ("Pancho") Villa, a rebel leader who had turned against Carranza. After failing to throw Carranza from power, Villa decided to discredit his former comrade by inciting a new American intervention. He brutally murdered sixteen young American engineers who had traveled to Mexico at Carranza's request to open a mine. No American intervention ensued. Next, in March 1916, Villa and his men made a raid across the United States border, burned the town of Columbus, New Mexico, and killed seventeen Americans. That did it.

President Wilson ordered Brigadier General John J. Pershing across the border with several thousand troops and for three hundred miles the Americans chased the elusive Mexican bandit. But as the United States edged toward the war in Europe—World War I—Wilson in February 1917 ordered Pershing and his men back to the United States. A month later the United States recognized the Carranza regime and sent an ambassador to Mexico City. Relations between the two countries thus began to thaw, but it took at least a generation to repair the damage brought by Wilson's meddling in Mexican affairs.

An Alaskan Boundary Dispute

On one notable occasion in those years the United States waved the "big stick" in a northerly direction, during a dispute with Britain and Canada over the Alaskan boundary.

This affair developed when discovery of gold in the Canadian Klondike in the 1890s brought to light uncertainties in a treaty of 1825. In that treaty Great Britain and Russia had fixed the boundary separating Alaska (owned by Russia) from Canada (which was British territory). Canadians now demanded a solution to the boundary problem that would leave them in control of several inlets along the Alaska panhandle and give free access to the gold fields by the sea. Determined to have a contiguous Alaska, the United States insisted on an interpretation of the boundary as it had existed for seventy-three years—one that would embrace all of Alaska's inlets.

The matter came to a showdown in 1903 when

the United States and Great Britain, with Canada's consent, signed a treaty to arbitrate the dispute. The arbitration tribunal consisted of three Americans, two Canadians, and one Briton. Determined not to sacrifice the American position in the argument, President Roosevelt named three Americans he knew would not yield to the Canadian view. Next the president displayed the "big stick" by letting the British member know that if the tribunal failed to adopt the American view the United States would arbitrarily run a line to its liking. The inference was that if the British and Canadians objected they would have to fight to uphold their view of the controversy. Whether Roosevelt's warning had much influence is hard to say. At any rate, the British delegate sided with the American delegates. By a vote of 4-2 the arbitration tribunal established the Alaskan boundary in accord with American wishes.

STUDY GUIDE: In the early years of the 1900s the United States often intervened in Latin American affairs. Cubans resented the Platt Amendment, which gave American forces the right to land in Cuba. In his corollary to the Monroe Doctrine, Roosevelt justified his intervention in the Dominican Republic by a new interpretation of the Monroe Doctrine. He upheld the right of the United States to function as an international police power to right any wrongdoing in the Western Hemisphere. Troubles in Haiti led Roosevelt to send troops there. The Haitian government was forced to accept a treaty making Haiti an American protectorate. Wilson's unfortunate meddling in Mexican affairs weakened relations between the two countries. Roosevelt's threats brought a settlement favorable to the United States of a dispute with Britain and Canada over the Alaskan boundary.

AMERICAN POLICY IN ASIA AND EUROPE

While the Western Hemisphere was the center of American diplomatic activity at the turn of the twentieth century, Asia and Europe nonetheless received considerable attention from leaders in Washington. Of particular importance were American policies toward China and Japan and efforts by Theodore Roosevelt to mediate international controversies.

The Open Door

With acquisition of the Philippine Islands, the United States had become a Far Eastern power charged with protecting a large and valuable territory. Meanwhile, there had been an increase in trade between the United States and the Far East, particularly with China. This commercial interest inspired the first important American maneuver in East Asia in the years after the Spanish war—the Open Door notes of John Hay, secretary of state under McKinley and Roosevelt.

In 1894, Japan and China had come to blows. The outcome was a thrashing for China, a giant, loosely knit nation presided over by the corrupt Manchu dynasty. The war with Japan exposed China's weakness, and in the next few years such powers as Russia, Germany, Great Britain, and France—as well as Japan—staked out "spheres of interest" in China. In their respective spheres each power extracted special concessions that compromised the sovereignty of the unhappy Chinese government. Each power, of course, administered its sphere to its own economic advantage. In American business circles there was alarm at such developments. What would happen to America's blossoming China trade if the powers adopted policies of commercial exclusion in their spheres? Although it was one of the powers playing the imperial game in China, Britain had similar misgivings. British leaders therefore proposed joint action with the United States to uphold the principle of equality of economic opportunity in China.

Recognizing that the traditional hostility which many Americans felt toward the British might wreck any joint attempt to meet the new China problem, American leaders declined the British overture. But then, in September 1899, Secretary Hay sent identical instructions to American ambassadors in Berlin, London, Saint Petersburg (present-day Leningrad), Paris, and Tokyo.

To safeguard American trade in China, the ambassadors were to seek assurances that the powers would not interfere with previous concessions granted by China to other nations. Within their spheres of interest they were not to discriminate in favor of their own nationals in the matter of harbor dues and railroad charges. To prevent collapse of the Chinese government, which depended on customs revenues, the ambassadors also were to ask for pledges that the powers would honor Chinese tariff laws and permit Chinese officials to collect the customs.

Hay's Open Door maneuver was clever, for it seemed to compel the powers to offer assurances that they would not take special advantages within their spheres. Refusal to give such assurances would amount to a confession that they were parties to the rape of China. Still, the powers in separate notes declined Hay's request.

The American secretary was not surprised. But he was not finished either. In March 1900 he boldly announced that the powers had given "final and definite" agreement to the Open Door idea. The powers now found themselves in a more awkward position than before. Silence would convey the impression that Hay had told the truth (which he clearly had not), that the powers had accepted the Open Door in China. A loud rebuke of the secretary would constitute a public admission that they were taking advantage of the unfortunate Chinese. All of them chose silence.

The Boxer Rebellion

A short time later, in spring 1900, a new crisis boiled up in China. An organization of Chinese patriots, the Boxers, led an uprising aimed at expelling the "foreign devils" from China. Like other Chinese, the Boxers were fed up with the way the imperial powers, including American businessmen and missionaries, were trampling on the rights and dignity of the people and government of China.

To achieve their purpose, the Boxers adopted the curious strategy of besieging the foreign legations in the national capital, Peking. Although the United States had no sphere of interest in China, the American legation came under attack along with those of Britain, Russia, Germany, and France. The government in Washington contributed 2,500 troops to an international expedition to break the siege.

While the international expedition, composed chiefly of Russian and Japanese soldiers, was slowly making its way to Peking, some 480 armed men inside the legations held off Boxer forces that numbered upward of twenty thousand men. In Europe and America there was little hope that the expedition would arrive in time, but day after dreary day — nearly sixty in all — the defenders, including some American marines, refused to budge. Then in early August 1900 the defenders, their numbers by now reduced to barely 250, caught the sound of distant gunfire. It was the international expedition.

Word that the siege had been broken and the legations saved signaled a wave of rejoicing in Europe and America.

Secretary Hay, meanwhile, feared that the European powers and Japan might seize the opportunity presented by the Boxer rebellion to detach large chunks of Chinese territory. Wasting little time, he issued the second Open Door notes in July 1900, at the height of the siege of the legations. The notes announced that the United States sought to "preserve Chinese territorial and administrative entity." Orally or in writing over the next few months the governments of Britain, France, Germany, Russia, and Italy agreed to the American policy.

Whether Hay's diplomacy influenced the decision of the powers to refrain from carving up China is hard to say. Probably not. Given the enormity of the problem — and also the expense — of trying to administer even a small part of China, a policy of outright colonialism likely had little appeal in the capitals of the powers.

The following year, 1901, the powers compelled the Chinese government to pay an indemnity of $333 million for damages done by the Boxers. The government in Washington later returned part of the share allotted to the United States. In appreciation, the Chinese government used most of the money to send Chinese students to the United States to study in American colleges and universities.

The Open Door notes marked only the beginning of American maneuvers in the Far East in the first years of the twentieth century. Of special importance was President Roosevelt's mediation of the Russo-Japanese War of 1904-05.

The Portsmouth Treaty

The Russo-Japanese War had begun when the Japanese directed a surprise attack on the Russian fleet at Port Arthur in Manchuria. After a successful but extremely expensive campaign on land, the Japanese climaxed the war by sinking thirty-two Russian ships in the Tsushima Strait.

Both Russia and Japan requested Roosevelt to mediate their dispute. The situation required tact, and the president proved equal to the task. At Portsmouth, New Hampshire, in September 1905, representatives of Russia and Japan agreed to peace.

The Treaty of Portsmouth brought Roosevelt the Nobel Peace Prize in 1906, but the Japanese were unhappy that they had not received larger concessions, including an indemnity. The result

"GOOD OFFICES"

This cartoon shows Theodore Roosevelt trying to mediate between Russia and Japan during the Russo-Japanese War. What was America's policy toward Japan in the years following the Treaty of Portsmouth?

was anti-American rioting in Tokyo. As relations with Japan worsened, the United States became fearful for the safety of the Philippines. This apprehension stemmed from the power Japan had displayed in the war against Russia. A short time after the ceremony at Portsmouth, Secretary of War William Howard Taft and the Japanese premier, Taro Katsura, made a secret agreement. Known as the Taft-Katsura Memorandum, the agreement recognized Japan's dominance in Korea in return for Japan's disavowal of "aggressive designs" on the Philippines.

Taft and Katsura had hardly completed their business when American-Japanese relations received a new shock. It came when the school board of San Francisco ordered Japanese-American schoolchildren, and also those of Korean and Chinese extraction, to attend segregated schools. Across the Pacific the people of Japan were furious at this insult to their kinsmen

in America, and a new wave of anti-Americanism swept the country. No less furious was President Roosevelt, but the school board did not change its order until Roosevelt and leaders of Japan made the so-called Gentlemen's Agreement (1907-08). By this agreement the government in Tokyo promised to deny passports to laborers wishing to migrate to the United States.

Still fearful that the Japanese might aim a strike at the Philippines, Roosevelt decided to send the American battle fleet around the world. Billed as a goodwill cruise, the voyage actually was a display of American naval power that hopefully would impress the Japanese.

To the surprise of the president, the government in Tokyo unexpectedly invited the fleet to visit Japan. Because of the need to improve relations, the president could not very well turn aside the invitation. But what if the Japanese, while the fleet was bottled up in Tokyo Bay, should seize the opportunity to blow up American naval power?

Recognizing the risks, the fleet dropped anchors at Yokohama in October 1908. The people of Japan were enthusiastic and friendly. They showered the American seamen with salutes, balls, and parades. The remainder of the voyage, via the Suez Canal, was an anticlimax and at length, in February 1909, the fleet steamed into Newport News.

To what extent the voyage of the American fleet impressed the Japanese is hard to say. Roosevelt elected not to rely entirely on this show of American power and endorsed the Root-Takahira Agreement, signed by Hay's successor as secretary of state, Elihu Root, and the Japanese ambassador Kogoro Takahira, in 1908. Although the terms were vague, the agreement indicated that the United States would not challenge Japan's recently enlarged position in Manchuria. In return, Japan would not challenge the United States in the Philippines, Hawaii, or Alaska.

In 1910 the Japanese annexed Korea. Then, in 1914, the World War broke out in Europe and, while the European powers battled, the Japanese had virtually a free hand to extend their power in East Asia. As a result, they tightened their hold in Manchuria and set about to weaken the government of China. Powerless to stop the Japanese, the United States did nothing more than offer feeble protests.

The United States entered the war in Europe in 1917. When Japan hinted that it might ally with America's enemy, Germany, the government in Washington felt compelled to appease the Japanese. The outcome was an agreement negotiated by Secretary of State Robert Lansing and a special Japanese envoy, Kikujiro Ishii. In the Lansing-Ishii Agreement of 1917, the United States recognized Japan's "special interests" in China.

The Philippines remained free of attack and during the war the Japanese did not side with Germany. But American policy in the years 1905-17 encouraged Japanese imperialism in East Asia.

"Dollar Diplomacy"

During the presidency of William Howard Taft (1909-13) the United States engaged in what historians refer to as "dollar diplomacy" in China and also in Latin America. In China the idea was to prevent further encroachment on Chinese sovereignty by the European powers and Japan while obtaining investment opportunities for American businessmen. A high point of the policy came when the United States in 1911 interfered with a scheme by European bankers to finance a new railroad in China. The results were disappointing. Taft and Secretary of State Philander C. Knox only succeeded in arousing the Europeans and Japanese against the United States. The subversion of China continued, and American businessmen realized few profits. The story of dollar diplomacy in Latin America was similar: profits were few and the policy annoyed the Latin Americans.

In the early years of the new century, the United States also took an interest in affairs in Europe. President Roosevelt won a measure of renown when he helped settle a dispute between France and Germany over the North African country of Morocco, a colony of France, in 1905.

Although the United States had no interests in Morocco, Roosevelt responded to the German kaiser's appeal that the president arrange an international conference to resolve the quarrel. With some reluctance he persuaded the British and French to meet the Germans at Algeciras in southern Spain. The outcome, in 1906, was an agreement that probably postponed the general war that came to Europe less than a decade later. The affair further established the United States as an influential power. Still, President Roosevelt came in for some criticism at home for violating the country's time-honored policy of isolation from foreign controversies in which no American interests were at stake.

STUDY GUIDE: Ownership of the Philippines and increased trade caused the United States to become more involved in Far Eastern affairs. Secretary of State John Hay persuaded the major powers to accept his Open Door policy, which gave the merchants of powerful nations equal opportunity to trade in China. Chinese patriots who wished to drive out Westerners started the Boxer Rebellion. American troops were part of an international expedition sent to China to put down the Boxer Rebellion. Theodore Roosevelt helped bring an end to the war between Japan and Russia in 1905. However the Japanese wanted payments from Russia after the war. Roosevelt did not support Japanese claims, and relations with Japan grew worse. American policy in the years 1905-17 encouraged Japanese imperialism. In 1907 Roosevelt helped to settle a dispute between France and Germany over the French colony of Morocco. During the Taft administration the United States engaged in "dollar diplomacy" in China and Latin America.

GOVERNING THE AMERICAN EMPIRE

Before 1898 the United States had only two overseas territories, Alaska and Midway Island. Midway was no more than a speck in the vast Pacific. Alaska, although its land area comprised more than a half-million square miles, had a population of fewer than 30,000.

Then, between 1898 and 1903, the United States acquired Hawaii, the Philippines, Puerto Rico, Guam, and American Samoa. It also gained control of the Canal Zone and purchased the Danish West Indies in 1917. Responsible for an empire that stretched halfway around the world and in which millions of people lived, the United States now had to face up to the problem of how to govern an imperial domain.

Administration of an Empire

One of the first questions requiring an answer was raised during debate over annexation of the Philippines in 1898-99: Did the federal Constitution "follow the flag"? The answer came in the year 1901 when the Supreme Court ruled in the Insular Cases that the Constitution followed the flag in the territories of the United States only when and to the extent that Congress wanted. The decision upheld the position of those sen-

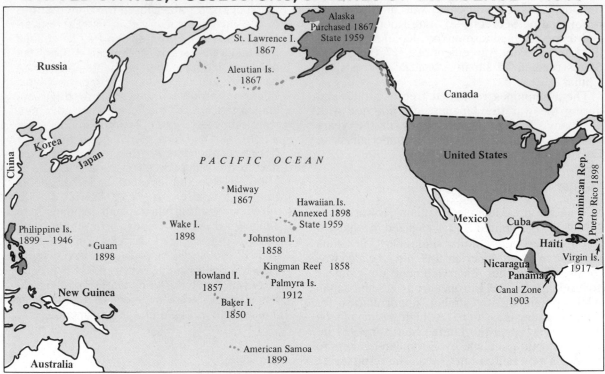

ators who in 1898-99 had argued that Congress had authority to restrict imports from American colonies, could deny American citizenship to inhabitants of colonies, and did not have to provide for colonies eventually to become states in the federal Union.

Still, Americans, proud of their tradition of having thrown off the shackles of colonialism, seemed uneasy in their new role of masters of colonial peoples. They scrupulously avoided the term "American Empire" and never established a colonial office or fashioned a consistent colonial policy. The result was a rather helter-skelter administration of their empire and a tendency to deal with each territory individually. Policies were drafted to meet specific problems as they arose, and, as a rule, colonial peoples managed their affairs with a minimum of interference from the United States. Such methods were often inefficient, but they were seldom oppressive.

Hawaii

In some ways the choicest jewel in America's imperial crown was the Hawaiian archipelago. Recognizing Hawaii's importance and its poten-tial for development, Congress in 1900 voted territorial status for the islands and United States citizenship for their people. The legislation also provided a popular assembly, although, as has always been customary in federal territories, the president in Washington appointed the territorial governor.

Over the years Hawaiians played an increasing part in the administration of the islands, and it seemed that Hawaii, like other federal territories in American history, was evolving toward statehood. Statehood, it turned out, was slow in coming. At length, in 1937, a bill to admit the islands to the federal Union came before Congress, only to run into several obstacles and fail to pass. A majority of Hawaii's population at that time had Republican sympathies. In 1937 Congress was controlled by the Democratic party. Thus many Democrats were reluctant to add to Republican strength by admitting a state that seemed certain to send Republican senators and representatives to Washington.

Many Americans opposed the idea of granting statehood to territory not connected with the other forty-eight states. They felt that all states of the Union should be joined physically as well

THE WORLD IN 1914

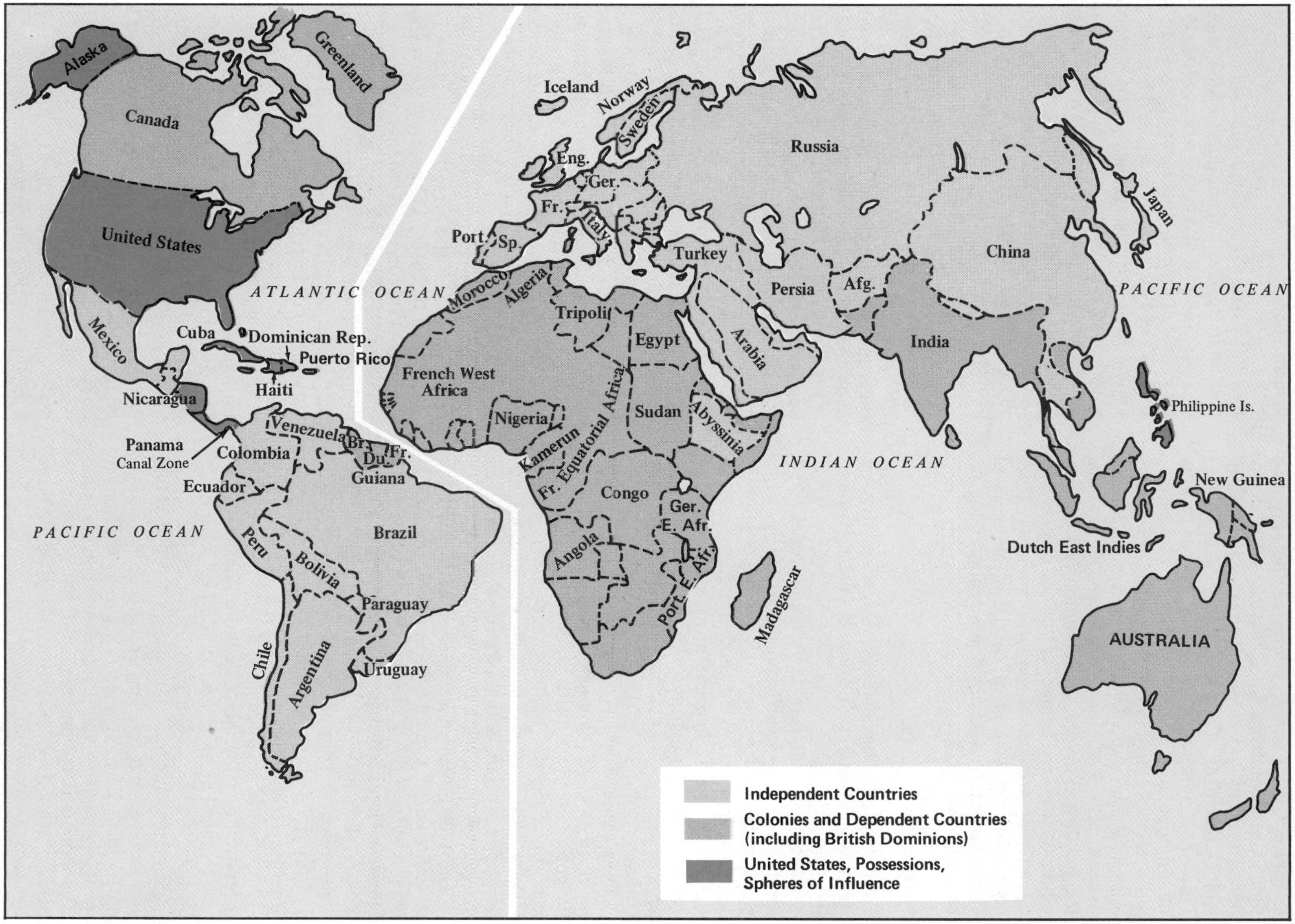

PACIFIC OCEAN

Japan

China

India

Afg.

Russia

Persia

Arabia

Turkey

INDIAN OCEAN

Madagascar

Sweden

Norway

Iceland

Abyssinia

Egypt

Sudan

Ger. E. Afr.

Congo

Port. E. Afr.

Eng.

Ger.

Italy

Fr.

Sp.

Tripoli

Fr. Equatorial Africa

Angola

Algeria

Morocco

Port.

Nigeria

Kamerun

French West Africa

Philippine Is.

New Guinea

Dutch East Indies

AUSTRALIA

Independent Countries

Colonies and Dependent Countries (including British Dominions)

United States, Possessions, Spheres of Influence

ATLANTIC OCEAN

Brazil

Paraguay

Uruguay

Venezuela

Br. Gu.

Du. Gu.

Fr. Guiana

Bolivia

Argentina

Colombia

Peru

Chile

Ecuador

Puerto Rico

Dominican Rep.

Haiti

Cuba

Greenland

Canada

United States

Alaska

Mexico

Nicaragua

Panama Canal Zone

PACIFIC OCEAN

as politically. Finally, white southerners and their representatives in Congress were determined to make no compromise with the idea of white supremacy. They took a jaundiced view of Hawaii's notions of racial equality and its racially mixed populations.

Fortunately the climate was different two decades later, in the 1950s. Memories of Japan's "sneak" attack on Hawaii in December 1941 and the revolution in overseas communications (particularly the appearance of the jet airliner) reduced the strength of earlier opponents. Over continuing opposition of southern members of Congress, Hawaii secured admission as the fiftieth state in 1959.

Alaska

To the north of Hawaii lay Alaska, a vast domain of majestic mountains and forests, rushing waters, and wildlife.

Although it had very few people, Alaska had strategic and economic importance. In 1912 Congress voted it territorial status. Like Hawaii, however, Alaska made slow progress toward statehood, largely because of its sparse population and doubts about the wisdom of admitting a geographically unattached territory to the Union.

Then came World War II. In the conflict with Japan in 1941-45, and also in the cold war with the communist world after 1945, Alaska assumed importance in the military calculations of the United States. New military installations appeared in Alaska, which of course generated an increase in the territory's civil population.

The War Department, in cooperation with the government of Canada, constructed the 1,523-mile Alaska, or Alcan Highway reaching from Dawson Creek, British Columbia, through the Yukon Territory to Fairbanks, Alaska. The highway carried supplies to military installations and provided an important link between Alaska and the United States.

Meanwhile, technological developments made it less difficult for men to endure Alaska's vastness, rugged terrain, and cold. The jet airliner brought Alaska within easy reach of the forty-eight states, making Alaska seem less forbidding and isolated and opening up new economic opportunities. The outcome was a steady movement of people to the "land of the midnight sun." The population went from 30,000 in 1900 to nearly 250,000 by 1960. In January 1959 Alaska became the forty-ninth state.

Puerto Rico

In 1900 Congress decided that America's new domain in the Caribbean, Puerto Rico, should be an "unorganized territory." According to congressional definition, this term meant that Puerto Ricans were citizens of the island but not of the United States. It further meant that Puerto Rico would have a government similar to that of the American colonies before the War of Independence. This arrangement lasted until 1917 when Congress made Puerto Rico a federal territory and conferred United States citizenship on its people.

Puerto Rico was making advances in education, sanitation, and trade. Then came the Great Depression of the 1930s. The world economic crisis was a devastating blow to the island's sugar industry. In 1936-37 riots and demonstrations rocked the territory. A special committee of the Puerto Rican legislature demanded in 1939 that islanders receive the right to elect their own governor and that leaders in Washington should begin to make provision for admission of Puerto Rico to statehood.

World War II brought a measure of prosperity to the island, and in 1947 Congress granted the committee's first demand, the right of Puerto Ricans to elect their governor. Three years later, in 1950, Congress authorized Puerto Rico to adopt a constitution. The constitution adopted in 1952 created the Commonwealth of Puerto Rico. Puerto Rico's people continued to be citizens of the United States. They and their products could move to the United States without restriction. The island's defense remained the responsibility of the armed forces of the United States, and the State Department in Washington supervised its foreign relations.

Puerto Rico had no voting representatives in Congress. But the government in San Juan, under the new constitution, conducted its internal affairs without interference from the mainland. Residents of the island paid no federal income taxes for, naturally, there could be no taxation without representation in the American system.

A new era in Puerto Rico's history had begun in 1948 when Luis Muñoz Marín became the first elected governor of the island. Over the next twenty years Muñoz and his Popular Democratic party labored to improve the quality of life on the island. Results were impressive. "Operation Bootstrap" attracted capital investment from abroad, mainly the United States and Canada, and that investment brought a dramatic increase in manufacturing and construction in Puerto Rico.

Much of the output of Puerto Rico's new industries came to the United States. Canada was the only country in the Western Hemisphere in the latter 1960s exporting more to the United States than Puerto Rico. Boosted by the jet airliner, Puerto Rico's tourist industry also boomed in the postwar era, making an important contribution to the island's prosperity. Because of its economic progress, Puerto Rico came to have the highest per capita income in Latin America. The island's government was able to clear slums, build schools, and inaugurate public health programs. Partly because of an exploding population that ate up much of the economic gain, Puerto Rico still had problems. The rate of unemployment hovered between eleven and thirteen percent. Also, gains in agriculture had not kept pace with those in industry.

A vocal minority of the people of Puerto Rico disliked the tie with the United States and longed for their island to be independent. The independence movement achieved notoriety in 1950 when two Puerto Rican nationalists tried unsuccessfully to shoot President Harry S. Truman. Four years later, in 1954, Puerto Rican nationalists entered the gallery of the House of Representatives in Washington, fired off pistols, and wounded five congressmen.

Most Puerto Ricans, however, taking their cue from Muñoz, liked the commonwealth arrangement. Under this system they enjoyed the protection of the United States but managed their own internal affairs and paid no federal income taxes. Then, in November 1968, Puerto Rican voters upset predictions. They ended Muñoz's twenty-year tenure and elected Luis A. Ferre, a millionaire industrialist and graduate of the Massachusetts Institute of Technology, as the island's governor. Believing that the benefits of statehood, economic and psychological, would outweigh the burden of federal taxes, Ferre advocated making Puerto Rico the fifty-first state of the federal Union. When he took office in January 1969, many observers were speculating that in the not-too-distant future the Stars and Stripes might take on another star.

The Virgin Islands

In the era before World War I, naval strategists felt that the United States needed a base in the Caribbean to protect the Panama Canal. Puerto Rico did not have a harbor that was considered adequate for this purpose. Then, during World War I, there was a fear that the Germans might seize islands belonging to other European nations. Therefore the United States purchased the Danish West Indies in 1917 and renamed them the Virgin Islands. Originally administered by the Navy Department, the islands passed to control of the Department of the Interior in 1931. (Other dependencies—Guam, Midway, American Samoa, and the Canal Zone—had similiar status.) The Great Depression struck hard at the islands, and in 1931 President Herbert Hoover called them "an effective poorhouse."

In 1933 Franklin D. Roosevelt, with his New Deal program, relieved some of the distress in the Virgin Islands. At the same time an increase in exportation of rum improved the economy of the islands. In 1936 Congress passed legislation providing for a territorial legislature for the Virgin Islands. The president, however, continued to appoint the governor until 1970, when, for the first time, the citizens elected the governor.

The Philippines

The most populous of America's overseas dependencies and the one farthest removed from the United States was the Philippines.

In the late nineteenth century, Filipino nationalists had fought Spaniards to gain independence. In 1898 they assisted the Americans in their operations against Spanish forces in the Philippines on the assumption that the United States would recognize the independence of the islands. The United States, however, elected to keep the Philippines.

Filipino nationalists were furious. Under the leadership of General Emilio Aguinaldo, who had served as provisional president during the struggle with Spain, they launched a guerrilla-type war. Their aim was to expel American authority. Before it ended in July 1902, the war claimed the lives of more than four thousand American soldiers and upward of twenty thousand Filipino guerrillas. Far more terrible was the toll of Filipino civilians: perhaps a quarter of a million dead of disease, pestilence and hunger as a consequence of the war.

The Philippine Insurrection appalled many Americans. As would happen in the 1960s during the war in Vietnam, many opponents of the war urged their countrymen to refuse to support the government in prosecution of the war.

From the time they annexed the Philippines, Americans indicated they did not consider their occupation of the islands as permanent. They seemed to agree that one day the Philippines would have independence. Still they declined for many years to face the question of precisely when they should grant independence. There was at least one good reason for American reluctance to get out of the Philippines. Given the imperial ambitions of some of the world's powers, notably Japan and Germany, the chances that the Philippines might long survive as an independent republic without protection of the United States did not appear bright. In 1902 Congress made the Philippines, like Puerto Rico, an unorganized territory and in 1906 affirmed America's intent of eventually withdrawing from the islands.

The Filipinos, like other peoples who fell under the control of the Americans in those years, received numerous benefits from the American presence, particularly in the areas of trade, education, and sanitation. Still, they continued to long for independence. They received a sympathetic hearing in the councils of the Democratic party, which had frowned on annexation of the islands in the first place. The Democratic platform of 1912 pledged independence upon establishment of a stable government in the Philippines. The Democratic-controlled Congress in 1916 wrote that pledge into law.

In his annual message on the state of the Union in 1920 President Wilson announced that the time had come to make the Philippines independent. Wilson, however, was nearing the end of his term and the Republican administration of President Warren G. Harding, which took office in 1921, saw otherwise. Over the next few years the United States ruled the islands with a rather heavy hand.

Then the Republicans had a change of heart. Before the 1920s ended they had joined the Democrats in urging independence for the Philippines. Several factors caused the change in Republican attitudes. The islands had not proved profitable for American business. They were also expensive and difficult to defend. And they enjoyed a privilege, namely, free entry of sugar into the United States, which American sugar growers wanted to terminate.

At length, in 1933, Congress passed legislation providing that the Philippines would become independent after a ten-year probationary period. Certain economic clauses of the measure, however, brought its rejection when it came before the legislature of the Philippines. A revised bill passed Congress in 1934 and this time received approval in the Philippines. The measure provided immediate commonwealth status for the Philippines and full independence in 1946.

The Commonwealth of the Philippines, headed by a former revolutionary leader, Manuel L. Quezon, came into existence in 1935. It appeared that Japanese occupation of the islands in 1942-45 would delay execution of the promised independence, but on July 4, 1946, the Stars and Stripes came down in Manila. The Republic of the Philippines joined the world's independent nations.

STUDY GUIDE: The Supreme Court ruled in 1901 that the Constitution went into effect in American territories only when and to the extent that Congress wanted. The United States never had a consistent colonial policy and handled each part of its empire on an individual basis. Congress voted territorial status to Hawaii and Alaska early in the twentieth century, but statehood was not achieved until 1959. Although some Puerto Ricans urge independence for their island, a movement has grown to seek statehood. The independence of the Philippines, first promised by the United States in 1906, was finally achieved in 1946.

SUMMING UP THE CHAPTER

Names and Terms to Identify

Currency Act of 1900	Winfield Scott Schley
Queen Liliuokalani	San Juan Hill
Robley D. Evans	John Hay
Richard Olney	Emilio Aguinaldo
"yellow sheets"	Ferdinand de Lesseps
Teller Amendment	Elihu Root
George Dewey	"dollar diplomacy"

Study Questions and Points to Review

1. Name the legislation of 1897 which raised import duties in America to an all-time high.

2. There were only two overseas territories under the Stars and Stripes by the mid-1800s. Name these two territories. Which two territories were added next?

3. What commodity did critics argue was the basis for the revolution in Hawaii in the 1890s?

4. Why was President Grant interested in Samoa?

5. What were the terms of the Treaty of Paris of 1898?

6. In what year was Hawaii made a territory of the United States?

7. How was Cuba affected by congressional action which eliminated free entry for Cuban sugar into the United States?

8. How did Cuba's rebels benefit from the *Maine* disaster?

9. Which country besides Panama was considered as a possible site for the canal?

10. What incident prompted President Wilson to send troops to Mexico?

11. What war was settled by the Treaty of Portsmouth?

Topics for Discussion

1. Why did Americans become interested in overseas expansion in the closing years of the nineteenth century?

2. Trace events leading to American annexation of Hawaii. Why was the United States interested in the islands? Do you think the United States had a legitimate or defensible reason for taking Hawaii?

3. Explain the Venezuelan boundary dispute of 1895. Do you think the British were violating the Monroe Doctrine? Was it proper for the United States to inject itself in the quarrel? Give reasons for your answers.

4. Explain what historians mean when they refer to the "big stick." Trace the high points of "big stick" diplomacy. What is your opinion of "big stick" diplomacy?

5. What was the Open Door policy? Would you consider it a monumental achievement in American diplomatic history? Why or why not?

6. Trace events leading to American acquisition of the Panama Canal Zone. What do you think of President Theodore Roosevelt's methods?

Subjects for Reports or Essays

1. Write an essay defending or challenging the idea that, given conditions in most parts of the world at the end of the nineteenth century, imperialism by Europe and America was in the interest of humanity.

2. Using books in the library, read accounts of the Battle of San Juan Hill. Prepare a report on the action and make a special point of assessing Theodore Roosevelt's part in it.

3. Do you agree or disagree with the idea that the federal Constitution should "follow the flag"? Write a report setting forth your views. Consider the Supreme Court's decision in the Insular Cases and make an evaluation of the Court's arguments.

Projects, Activities, and Skills

1. Use Atlas Map 26 to locate the following: Schley's naval blockade; Sampson's movements; Shafter's movements; Santiago; Havana; El Caney.

2. Prepare a travelogue for classroom presentation. Select one of the following destinations: Samoa, Hawaii, Philippine Islands, Puerto Rico, Alaska.

Further Readings

General

America's Colonial Experiment by Julius W. Pratt. The story of how America's overseas empire was administered.

Expansionists of 1898: The Acquisition of Hawaii and the Spanish Islands by Julius W. Pratt. Contains excellent analysis of America's foreign affairs.

Imperial Democracy by Ernest R. May. An excellent book covering the diplomacy of the war with Spain.

A Leap to Arms: The Cuban Campaign of 1898 by Jack Cameron Dierks.

The Splendid Little War by Frank Freidel. An exciting account of the Spanish-American War.

Biography

Autobiography by Theodore Roosevelt.

The Life and Times of Theodore Roosevelt by William H. Harbaugh.

The Rough Riders by Theodore Roosevelt.

Theodore Roosevelt and the Politics of Power by Wallace G. Chessman.

William McKinley and His America by H. Wayne Morgan.

Fiction, Essays, and Poetry

Hawaii by James Michener. A readable account of the Islands.

A Message to Garcia and Other Essays by Elbert Hubbard. The title essay was very popular in the early 1900s.

Unmanifest Destiny by Richard Hovey. A poet's protest against the conduct of the United States in the Spanish-American War.

Pictorial History

This Fabulous Century, 1900-1910, Vol. 1, by the editors of Time-Life Books.

CHAPTER 12

THE PROGRESSIVE ERA

THE TIME WAS A FEW MOMENTS before midnight, December 31, 1899. The place was America's largest city, New York. Although a blast of arctic air had swept over the northeastern part of the country, scores of thousands of people jammed New York's thoroughfares. At the stroke of midnight, a wild uproar broke loose. Horns bellowed, bells rang out, firecrackers exploded. Thousands of voices were raised in a grand, discordant chorus of shouts and cheers. New Yorkers were welcoming in the year 1900, the twentieth century, so most of them thought. On the beginning of the new century there was some disagreement. Some scholars insisted that the twentieth century would not begin until 1901, for, they pointed out, the first century had ended with the year 100, not 99, hence the nineteenth century obviously had to end with 1900, not 1899.

Not all New Yorkers, it was true, went in for noise and revelry. The financier J. P. Morgan sat quietly in the mahogany-paneled library of his brownstone mansion on Madison Avenue and played solitaire as 1900 came in.

In the national capital, Washington, the New Year's celebration had a special touch. President and Mrs. McKinley ushered in 1900, and the social season in Washington, with a glittering official reception for fifteen hundred dignitaries—the diplomatic corps, Supreme Court justices and their wives, senators, representatives, officers of the army and navy (including, naturally, Admiral Dewey), and veterans of the Mexican and Civil Wars. Their guests included such famous personalities as Alexander Graham Bell—and more than two thousand "ordinary" citizens.

THE "GOOD YEARS"

The writer Walter Lord in a popular book has labeled the period 1900-1914 as the "good years"[1] of American history. Why? Not because poverty, racism, and crime had suddenly disap-

peared or because the first years of the twentieth century were free of great tragedies. The period was good, Lord explains, because, "whatever the, trouble, people were sure they could fix it." However, they were not without their problems.

Tragedy and disaster, as well as prosperity and achievement, marked the "good years" in America. Black Americans continued to be objects of abuse and discrimination. Indeed, during these years the racial caste system in the southern states received its refinements. Immigrants continued to find misery and heartache in the mushrooming slums of urban America. And across the nation ten- and twelve-year-old children continued to work ten and twelve hours a day digging coal, making artificial flowers, rolling cigars, and operating spindles in cotton mills. The federal census of 1910 estimated that nearly two million children between the ages of ten and fifteen were gainfully employed in the United States, and a survey of 1913 indicated that twenty percent of the children of the country were making their own livings.

There were several great disasters during the "good years." In 1906, a devasting earthquake rocked San Francisco and set off fires that leveled great sections of the city. In 1912 the White Star liner *Titanic,* the largest ship the world had known, struck an iceberg in the North Atlantic on its maiden voyage from England to New York. The *Titanic,* which had been advertised as "unsinkable," carried more than fifteen hundred people, many of them Americans, to watery graves.

Economic Activity Accelerates

During the "good years" the people of the United States, having recovered after the depression of the 1890s and invigorated by the new status of their republic as a world power, built and hustled at a lively pace. They enjoyed the highest level of prosperity the country had yet known.

Statistics tell part of the story. The steel mills of the country belched forth 10,000,000 long

---

[1] Walter Lord, *The Good Years: From 1900 to the First World War,* copyright 1960 (New York: Harper & Brothers).

HEADLINE
EVENTS

1887 Interstate Commerce Act
1890 Sherman Antitrust Act
1890s Populist revolt
1893 Economic panic
      Duryea automobile appears
1894 Haynes automobile appears
      Pullman car strike
1898 Spanish-American War
1900 *Sister Carrie* (Dreiser)
1900s Ford produces first Model T car
1900-1905 Conquest of yellow fever
1901 William McKinley inaugurated for second
      term as president
      Theodore Roosevelt succeeds to presidency
      upon assassination of McKinley
1902 Muckraking articles begin appearing
      New York Central inaugurates *Twentieth
      Century Limited*
      National Reclamation Act
1903 Elkins Act
      Department of Commerce and Labor es-
      tablished
      Wright brothers make first successful air-
      plane flight
1904 *The Shame of the Cities* (Steffens)
      Louisiana Purchase Exposition, Saint Louis
      History of the Standard Oil Company
      (Tarbell)
1905 Theodore Roosevelt inaugurated president
      for second term
      Niagara movement organized
1906 Hepburn Act
      San Francisco earthquake
      The Jungle (Sinclair)
      Pure Food and Drug Act
      Federal meat inspection law
1907 Oklahoma enters the Union
      Economic panic
1908 White House Conservation Conference
      Inland Waterways Commission
      Aldrich-Vreeland Act
1909 William Howard Taft inaugurated president
      Perry reaches North Pole
      NAACP founded

      Payne-Aldrich Act
      Ballinger-Pinchot controversy
1910 Mann-Elkins Act
      Millikan measures charge of electron as
      definite constant
1911 National Progressive Republican League
      is founded
      Gyroscope (Sperry)
1912 New Mexico enters the Union
      Arizona enters the Union
      Titanic strikes iceberg and sinks
      Progressive party (Bull Moose party) ap-
      pears
      Postal savings banks, parcel post system
      created
      Theodore Roosevelt runs for president on
      Progressive ticket
1913 Woodrow Wilson inaugurated president;
      New Freedom administration
      O Pioneers! (Cather)
      Sixteenth Amendment ratified
      Seventeenth Amendment ratified
      Underwood-Simmons Act
      Department of Labor separate Cabinet de-
      partment
      Improved X-ray (Coolidge)
      Federal Reserve System created by Fed-
      eral Reserve Act
1914 Liquid rocket fuel (Goddard)
      Federal Trade Commission created
      Clayton Antitrust Act
      Panama Canal completed
      World War I breaks out in Europe
      Stevens Trade Commission Act
      Smith-Lever Act
1915 La Follette Seamen's Act
1916 Federal Farm Loan Act
      Warehouse Act
      Adamson Act
1917 Smith-Hughes Act
      Wilson inaugurated for second term
      United States enters World War I
1919 Eighteenth Amendment ratified
1920 Nineteenth Amendment ratified

AMERICAN BUSINESS ACTIVITY: 1900 — 1919

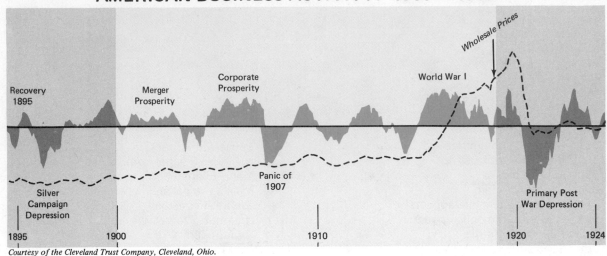

Recovery
1895

Merger
Prosperity

Corporate
Prosperity

World War I

Wholesale Prices

Silver
Campaign
Depression

Panic of
1907

Primary Post
War Depression

1895   1900   1910   1920   1924

Courtesy of the Cleveland Trust Company, Cleveland, Ohio.

tons of steel ingots and castings in 1900, 31,-000,000 in 1913. In the period 1900-14 railroads increased their route miles of track from 192,000 to 256,000. Central power stations in 1902 produced around six billion kilowatt hours of electricity. By 1912 they were producing over twenty-four billion. The total value of the country's exports in 1900 was $1.6 billion; in 1913 exports amounted to $2.6 billion.

The dramatic acceleration of economic activity naturally affected wages. The average annual income of the nonfarm laborer in the country moved from $490 in 1900 to $682 in 1914. With increased earnings many working-class families fulfilled the dream of home ownership. Accordingly, 421,000 new dwellings were started in nonfarm areas in 1914, as compared with 189,000 in 1900. Even the farmer, a victim of continuing hard times in the last third of the nineteenth century, shared in the prosperity of the "good years." A measure of his new affluence is reflected in the figures on farm implements. In 1900 the value of farm implements in the country was $750 million, in 1914, $1.7 billion.

Spurring the economic boom was an exploding national population. When Americans ushered in the year 1900, approximately 76,000,000 people were living in the United States. Swelled by the arrival of more than 13,000,000 immigrants, a birth rate that continued to be high, and a declining death rate, the population of the country by 1915 had soared past 100,-000,000.

The nation's cities felt the impact of the pop-ulation explosion and continued to receive a steady influx of new residents from rural areas. In the period 1900-10 urban centers were strained by a population increase of 38.8 percent. Meanwhile, considerable numbers of Americans continued to move west. As a consequence, three new states entered the federal Union during the "good years": Oklahoma in 1907 and New Mexico and Arizona in 1912.

The Motor Car

A significant development during the "good years" was the increasing popularity of the gasoline-powered motor car—the "horseless carriage." The motor car soon became a familiar part of the American landscape.

The motor car—for all practical purposes invented by Gottlieb Daimler and Karl Benz in Germany in 1885—made its appearance in the United States a few years later. In September 1893, a peculiar-looking vehicle with a one-cylinder engine, built by Charles E. and J. Frank Duryea, startled the people of Springfield, Massachusetts. Less than a year later, in 1894, a one-cylinder automobile put together by Elwood Haynes chugged about the streets of Kokomo, Indiana. Through the remainder of the 1890s many inventors and engineers experimented with the motor car and a few sought to produce it commercially. Still, only 8,000 automobiles were registered in the entire country by 1900. Not for long would this scarcity of cars continue. Over the next few years the automobile industry

Driving an automobile in the early 1900s was risky. Blow-outs, spark-plug troubles, and transmission failures were frequent. There were few service stations so every driver had to be his own mechanic.

"took off," despite the difficulties of motoring that resulted from a shortage of good roads, gasoline stations, and repair shops. Henry Ford turned out his first Model-T in 1908 and the General Motors Corporation was born that same year. In 1915 automobile registrations in the country passed 2.000,000. (By way of comparison, Americans in 1970 owned more than 100,000,000 cars and trucks.)

The year 1902 witnessed the inauguration by

Henry Ford pioneered the use of the assembly-line method of production. Here workers put together the 1913 Ford. There were some disadvantages to the early line. A customer could have any color car he wanted—as long as it was black.

the New York Central railway system of a luxury train, the Twentieth Century Limited, which could race passengers from New York to Chicago in the breathtaking time of twenty hours. During the "good years" the evangelist Billy Sunday, a former infielder for the Chicago White Sox, moved congregations by winding up like a baseball pitcher and exhorting listeners to "put it over the plate for Jesus." In 1904 throngs of people crowded to one of the most gala world's fairs in the history of the nation, the Louisiana Purchase Exposition in Saint Louis.

The first decade and a half of the twentieth century was a memorable period in the history of entertainment in America. It was a time when the social elite of the country gave lavish parties, sometimes costing as much as $100,000 for a single evening. During this period for the first time Americans in great numbers became captivated by professional sports, particularly baseball, which in those years boasted such performers as Ty Cobb, Honus Wagner, and Christy Mathewson. Automobile racing also began to attract excited audiences, first at the Vanderbilt Cup races in New York, then at a two-and-one-half-mile brick-surfaced oval at Indianapolis. The period was one during which a new medium of mass entertainment began to become popular—the motion picture. Early films were made in the East, but after 1912 Hollywood, California, became the center of the industry.

Crusaders for Righteousness

The "good years" had their share of crusaders. One was Frances Willard, whose special interest was prohibiting the production and sale of alcoholic beverages. Another was Susan B. Anthony, who with other feminists battled for "the emancipation" of women. Rejecting the status of women as second-class citizens, she fought for equal rights with men, demanding first of all the right to vote.

In those years Jane Addams, centering her operations at Hull House in Chicago, and other crusaders interested in "settlement" work tried to improve conditions of urban slum dwellers. They sought to explain the customs and habits of the New World to immigrants and to build the morale of the poor and uprooted people of urban America. Meanwhile a small band of crusaders led by Dr. W. E. B. Du Bois, a brilliant and highly educated Negro from Massachusetts, openly rejected Booker T. Washington's advice

that black Americans should passively accept their status as inferior citizens. In 1905, with other intellectuals, Du Bois organized the Niagara movement. In 1909 he became one of the original officers of the National Association for the Advancement of Colored People (NAACP), which based its platform on the earlier Niagara movement. The aim of the NAACP was to break down barriers of segregation, secure the right of Negroes to vote, and in other ways help the black man to obtain the civil liberties to which he was entitled. Over the next half-century Du Bois continued to labor for an integrated America in which blacks would enjoy equal opportunities and privileges with whites. (At length he concluded that his people would never achieve the promise of American life. In 1961, he migrated to Ghana and joined the Communist party. He became a citizen of Ghana and died there in 1963 at the age of ninety-five.)

Arts and Sciences

In addition to economic achievements, Americans marked the "good years" with some notable literary accomplishments. Theodore Dreiser brought a new realism to the novel and shocked many readers with his *Sister Carrie* in 1900. A few years later, in 1906, Upton Sinclair's *The Jungle* exposed the evils of the meat-packing industry, and Willa Cather's *O Pioneers!* published in 1913, explored the hardships of pioneer life on the Great Plains.

In science Thomas Hunt Morgan, using the fruit fly, made important studies in heredity, and Robert Millikan in 1910 announced that he had measured the charge of an electron as a definite constant. Several American scientists and inventors made refinements on the "wireless," or radio, recently invented in Europe. Others developed a synthetic fabric which they called rayon and perfected the first plastics. Elmer A. Sperry, an American, patented the gyroscope in 1911, and William D. Coolidge in 1913 developed a superior X-ray tube. In 1914 Robert H. Goddard patented the first liquid fuel rocket and a few years later demonstrated the lifting capabilities of rockets.

More memorable, however, were the first successful airplane flight by Wilbur and Orville Wright in 1903, Commander Robert E. Peary's dash over the ice to the North Pole in 1909, the conquest of yellow fever in 1900-05, and construction of the Panama Canal in 1907-14.

W. E. B. Du Bois was founder and editor of *Crisis* magazine, financed by the NAACP. It published art, articles, poetry, and fiction by and about Negroes. What attitude did Du Bois take toward Booker T. Washington?

The First Airplane Flight

The Wright brothers, who operated a bicycle shop in Dayton, Ohio, had thought about the possibility of building a "flying machine" for many years and in 1899 began to experiment with kites and gliders. In their shop they built a wind tunnel (which has hardly been improved upon to the present day) and tested various wing surfaces. Next they built an eight-horse-power gasoline motor weighing 180 pounds, rigged it to drive two propellers (which they also designed), and installed the entire mechanism in a two-winged contraption of struts, wires, and fabric. They called their conveyance, which weighed 650 pounds, "the whopper flying machine."

On December 11, 1903, everything was set. On a sandy beach near Kitty Hawk, North Carolina, the Wrights, helped by a few local

By 1913 women had taken their fight for equal rights to the streets. Here they march on the Capitol. The movement for equality began in 1848, but male voters defeated early constitutional amendments for giving women the vote.

E. Cady Stanton (right) and Lucretia Mott (top) convened the first women's rights convention in Seneca Falls, New York, in 1848. In 1869 the National Woman Suffrage Association was formed and Mrs. Stanton was elected president. Susan B. Anthony (bottom) was chairman of the executive committee.

John T. Daniels snapped this picture on Dec. 17, 1903, as pilot Orville Wright lifted the "whopper flying machine" aloft. Although the Wright brothers pioneered the aviation industry, they made very little money from their invention.

citizens, put down four fifteen-foot planks which served as a launching track. Who would have the honor of assuming a prone position in the middle of the lower wing and piloting the flying machine during its maiden flight? The brothers tossed a coin. Wilbur won. But in the first attempt the craft barely got off the ground, then stalled.

They made their second attempt six days later, on December 17, this time with Orville at the controls, wearing a starched collar, tie, and dark suit. "The whopper flying machine" again sputtered and bobbled down the crude runway. Jogging alongside, holding the lower right wing steady, was Wilbur, also clad in a suit and necktie. Then the craft took to the air. It reached an altitude of ten feet, soared along for twelve seconds, and settled to the earth 120 feet from the point of takeoff.

Man had entered a new era.

The North Pole

Commander Peary had spent two decades exploring Arctic regions and had become consumed by the dream of being the first man to stand "on the top of the world," the North Pole. After an unsuccessful attempt to reach the pole in 1906, he raised funds and outfitted his steamship, the *Roosevelt*. In early July 1908, cheered on by thousands of well-wishers, the *Roosevelt* sailed from New York. Accompanying Peary, as on previous trips, was Matthew A. Henson, his Negro assistant, who planted the American flag on the North Pole.

Peary set a northerly course to Labrador, and moved through Baffin Bay to Cape York on the northwestern coast of Greenland. He steered the *Roosevelt* through the ice-strewn channels to the west of Greenland, and in early September reached Cape Sheridan on the northern tip of Ellesmere Island. There he built a base camp of igloos, and dug in for the winter.

Over the long, brutal winter the commander studied charts, lectured his men, and supervised the preparation of equipment. Then, on February 28, 1909, whips cracked, dogs yelped, and the little caravan moved out over the polar ice. Sometimes the crews made twenty-five miles in a single day. Sometimes they were stalled for many hours while waiting for the ice to come together and make it possible for them to continue.

By April 2 Peary and his men were only 133 miles from the pole. To accompany him on the final dash the commander chose Henson, four Eskimos, and forty dogs. On April 6 the six men arrived at the North Pole and on the following day planted the Stars and Stripes and took possession of the pole in the name of the President of the United States.

Victory Over Yellow Fever

Yellow fever had claimed thousands of American soldiers in Cuba at the time of the Spanish-American War in 1898. For a number of years there had been periodic outbreaks of yellow fever in the United States, presumably originating in Cuba. When the United States took over the administration of Cuba, upon expulsion of the Spaniards, officials in Washington determined to do something about the disease. Accepting the prevailing view that filth resulting from poor sanitation practices was responsible for yellow fever's transmission, the army sent a physician, Major William Crawford Gorgas, to Havana to clean up the city. When he arrived, Gorgas met Dr. Carlos Finlay, a Cuban scientist-physician, who claimed that the Stegomyia mosquito rather than filth was the key to the yellow fever puzzle. What evidence did Finlay have? After all, there were eight hundred known species of mosquitoes. He had little evidence; mainly he had a hunch. Gorgas was not impressed and accordingly went ahead with the antifilth campaign which in a few months made Havana one of the cleanest cities in the world.

Then in 1900 a new epidemic of yellow fever struck Cuba's capital city. To investigate the situation, worried army officials sent a commission of four army surgeons headed by a Virginian named Walter Reed. On arriving in Havana, Reed listened to Finlay explain his mosquito theory and, like Gorgas, rejected it.

Then in July 1900 Reed learned that yellow fever had taken the life of an American soldier who had been confined for thirty-seven days in a stockade, where he had no contact with other victims of yellow fever. How had the soldier received the yellow fever virus? Probably from an insect, Reed guessed, most likely a mosquito.

Next Reed outlined a series of experiments involving yellow fever patients, mosquitoes, and individuals who presumably had no immunity to the disease. One of the latter was Dr. Jesse W. Lazear, an associate of Reed. Five days after coming down with the fever, Lazear died. To make certain that the disease could not be transmitted by other means, several volunteers slept for extended periods in the soiled pajamas and on the sheets of yellow fever patients. They suffered no ill effects.

Clearly Finlay's hunch had been correct; the Stegomyia mosquito was the carrier of yellow fever. How to get rid of the Stegomyia? That was fairly easy, for the Stegomyia normally lived only in houses—in the clean water of a pitcher or a water barrel or cistern. American and Cuban officials, under the direction of Major Gorgas, mounted a house-to-house campaign to eliminate water in pitchers and planters. They also put screens and films of oil over large deposits of water in the city. The results were amazing. In the year 1901 the city of Havana, for the first time in its history, had not a single case of yellow fever.

Two years later, in 1903, the United States acquired the Panama Canal Zone (see Chapter 11) and set about to construct the canal. In charge of sanitation, appropriately, was Gorgas (by now Colonel Gorgas).

Completion of the Panama Canal in 1914 gave the United States access to important sea routes and helped make the country a world power. Construction of the forty-mile channel began during Theodore Roosevelt's first term and ended during Woodrow Wilson's administration.

By this time it was known that the Anopheles mosquito was the carrier of malaria. Then came a shock. The admiral who headed the Isthmian Canal Commission did not believe that mosquitoes carried yellow fever and malaria. He ordered Gorgas to stamp out disease in the Canal Zone by eliminating filth. The outcome was predictable. A new epidemic of "yellow jack" struck the isthmus.

Blaming Gorgas for improper sanitation techniques the canal commission tried to dismiss him. President Roosevelt, on the advice of his friend and personal physician, Dr. Alexander Lambert, retained Gorgas to make war on mosquitoes. In 1905 the yellow fever epidemic in Panama ended.

Completion of the Panama Canal

The event that captured the public imagination most during the "good years" between 1900 and 1914 was the completion of the canal across the Isthmus of Panama. This engineering feat made it possible to move ships of the United States Navy quickly between the Atlantic and Pacific oceans. With this access to global sea routes and control of the canal, the United States became a major power among the nations of the world.

With yellow fever eliminated and malaria drastically reduced, construction of the canal in Panama was ready to swing into high gear.

As for the business of digging and blasting a forty-mile canal across the Panamanian isthmus, the first question to be resolved was: Should the waterway be a sea-level canal or a lock canal? Most engineers favored a lock canal. They pointed out that the Sault Sainte Marie Canal, a lock canal connecting Lake Superior and Lake Huron in North America, seemed as efficient as the Suez Canal, a sea-level waterway. A lock canal would also be much less expensive to build.

President Roosevelt and Congress approved plans for a lock canal. That decision made, serious work, directed mainly by civilians, got under way in 1907. But the pace was slow. This seemed to be largely because of faulty administration. Roosevelt then designated Lieutenant-Colonel George Washington Goethals of the army to be chief engineer of the project and chairman of the Isthmian Canal Commission. With Goethals in charge, the pace of construction quickened. At length, in 1914, the canal was ready for use. The waterway had cost $375 million.

STUDY GUIDE: Prosperity and achievement marked the years 1900-14 in America. The nation recovered from the severe depression of the 1890s. The motor car became a familiar part of the landscape, and the Wright brothers made their first successful airplane flight.

Even though times were generally good, many crusaders fought to right the wrongs in American society. Attention was focused on women's rights, prohibition, improvement of slum conditions, and opportunities for Negroes. One of the most memorable events of the era was Commander Robert Peary's successful attempt to reach the North Pole. Construction of the Panama Canal was completed, and the dread disease yellow fever was eliminated from the Canal Zone.

APPEARANCE OF THE PROGRESSIVES

The "good years" were also the time of the progressive movement—of "muckrakers" and "trustbusting" and the "Bull Moose" party. When examining the progressive movement, it is useful to take a look at progressivism's intellectual foundation.

In the generation after the Civil War the ideas and ethics of Social Darwinism guided the thought and behavior of great numbers of Americans. This meant that society permitted those who were the "fittest" to achieve as much wealth and power as possible while doing little to help the "weak" and "unfit."

Pragmatism

The physician-psychologist-philosopher William James rejected the grim inevitableness of Social Darwinism. A native of New York City, James had grown up in the 1840s and 1850s. In his home he was taught transcendentalist ideas: that man, by ignoring science and relying on his spiritual resources, could find truth and become the master of his destiny.

As an adult he had rejected the antiscientific ideas of the transcendentalists and indeed had been fully persuaded to Darwin's theory of biological evolution. However, he continued to treasure the transcendentalist idea that man, through his own inner resources, could perfect himself and his environment. What James was searching for was a view of life that held out hope of human perfectibility but was rigidly faithful to the findings of natural science. During his search he worked out a philosophy called pragmatism.

Pragmatism denied that man and his society had to evolve in the same mechanical way in which the world of plants and animals evolved. Using his intellectual and spiritual resources, man, according to pragmatism, could break in on the evolutionary process and, within limits, determine his own destiny. If an idea achieved its purpose—if it worked—it was a good idea. It did not matter whether or not the idea seemed logical or whether it fitted in with some theological or nationalist dogma or whether it was liberal or conservative, radical or reactionary.

While William James was the father of pragmatism, it was Lester Ward, a native of Joliet, Illinois, who penned the clearest and most comprehensive application of pragmatic ideas to the problems of society. Reared in poverty, a mill hand and minor government clerk for many years, and a self-taught sociologist, Ward, like James, recoiled at Social Darwinism. He believed that intellect and will set man apart from the rest of creation. Hence, the natural laws that provided for the survival of other animals and plants did not necessarily apply to humans.

Ward believed that environment transformed animals and plants, but man had the capacity to transform environment. He believed that man, with his intellectual powers, had been breaking in on nature's course and adapting his environment since the dawn of history. Civilization, Ward maintained, was the triumph of man over the blind forces of nature.

Ward believed that man, then, held his destiny in his hands. Man could not increase or diminish the powers of nature but he could direct them. How? Men acting individually could not accomplish much. The answer was through planning, organization, and collective action. To what agency would Ward entrust this great responsibility for mobilizing society for an assault on its problems? Answer: The government, which ideally was responsive to the needs of all its people.

Aims of the Progressives

Progressives were reformers who determined to bring an end to the era of laissez-faire — when the government had tended to keep hands off the social and economic mechanism in America. They wanted government, at local, state, and national levels, to take an active part in the social and economic life of the country and exercise some control over the course of the evolution of society.

Why did the Progressives want government to put its weight in the social balance? The answer was readily apparent.

By 1900 Americans had conquered a vast frontier, built a huge industrial empire, and were achieving status as a world power. Thoughtful citizens, however, were observing that many evils had accompanied the country's staggering material progress and rise to international prominence. The examples seemed endless. Americans had ravaged much of their landed heritage and, unhappily, no end appeared in sight to the rape of the land. The farmer had been a victim of chronic depression and hardship. Despite the Sherman Act of 1890 and the Interstate Commerce Act of 1887, business monopolies were forming at a rapid rate and railroads were still dealing high-handedly with the public interest. To enlarge profits, manufacturers, coal operators, cotton mill owners, and meatpackers had found it expedient to employ women and

children, pay starvation wages, and intimidate labor organizations.

Captains of business, often acclaimed as pillars of society, also were compelling workingmen to operate hazardous machines and toil in unsanitary, stench-ridden shops and plants. They crowded passengers into unsafe trains and steamships. They produced shoddy products, and sold meat and milk that were contaminated. Few laws prevented such practices. Meanwhile, much of the wealth of the country was gravitating into the hands of a privileged elite.

Progressives cited other ills in American society. The United States seemed unable to provide for its poor, aged, infirm, and insane. Prison conditions were generally abominable. Education was not of a uniformly high quality. Cities sprawled outward at an incredible pace

Frank Leslie's Illustrated Newspaper, January 28, 1888

In crowded city slums, landlords jammed families into single rooms in substandard tenements. Evictions were daily occurrences. In the early twentieth century who began to speak for the poor? Do conditions like this exist today? Why?

and could not solve such problems as paving and lighting streets, fire control, mass transportation, recreation, and the control of crime and vice. Finally, there was the twofold problem of corruption in government and the tendency of government at all levels to respond to the interest of manufacturers, railroad barons, and bankers rather than to the will and needs of ordinary people.

The Populists (see Chapter 10) had attacked many of the foregoing evils. Was not the progressive movement, then, perhaps a mere revival of the Populist revolt?

It is true that progressives took over much of the Populist platform. Most progressives, like Populists, were white, Anglo-Saxon Protestants of old-line native stock, and most former Populists fell in with progressivism. Still, there were important differences between progressivism and populism.

First, the impulse for the progressive movement came from a different source. Populism had sprung from the soil when angry farmers reacted against acute hardship. The progressive movement, on the other hand, originated mainly in the cities with intellectuals and well-to-do individuals, not from people who were downtrodden. The progressive movement, then, was not a movement from the slums or the farm.

The Populist revolt had been fired by the Panic of 1893 and reached its height during one of the worst depressions in the country's history. The progressive movement existed during the most prosperous era in American history to that time. The moods of the movements were different. Populists had been enraged, even desperate; progressives, if sometimes indignant, seldom were angry. The progressive program was larger and more inclusive than that of the Populists. Except for unlimited coinage of silver, progressives sought nearly everything that Populists had campaigned for—and a good deal more besides.

The progressive movement, unlike the Populist revolt, was not trumpeted into existence at state and national conventions by people who were fed up with existing conditions. It was not highly organized. It just happened. And most people who became progressives were not aware, at least in the beginning, that they had joined a "movement."

Progressives were Republicans and Democrats, Socialists and what-not, who had caught the reform spirit. Usually working within established political organizations, they sought to eradicate certain abuses in American society. In 1912 a Progressive party appeared, but it failed to attract even a majority of Americans who considered themselves progressives. Progressives did not comprise a group that was united in purpose. Some progressives favored this or that reform but not others, and on some basic points they differed quite sharply.

Early Progressive Politicians

The first politicians to fall in with the progressive movement were occupants of city halls. Such a man was Samuel M. ("Golden Rule") Jones, an eccentric reformer who was elected mayor of Toledo in 1897. He promptly deprived policemen of billy-clubs, established a free lodging house for tramps, set up free kindergartens, and built playgrounds. He also paid city employees a minimum of $1.50 a day (or fifty percent more than the prevailing wage for common labor.)

Other urban leaders, including Mayors Thomas L. Johnson of Cleveland, James D. Phelan of San Francisco, and Seth Low of New York, freed their cities from "boss" rule or control by state legislatures. Many of them labored for public ownership of transit and water systems, and electric power plants. The progressive urban leaders sought to improve public health and education, counter crime and vice, and ease conditions in slum areas.

From cities the progressive movement made its way to state capitals where power usually was in the hands of political "rings." The main concern of the typical state-house ring was to perpetuate its own power and profits. This meant protecting and advancing the interests of the railroads, manufacturers, meat-packers, millers, coal operators, and lumbermen whose "contributions" sustained the ring.

The most famous progressive at the state level was Robert Marion ("Fighting Bob") La Follette of Wisconsin. Elected governor in 1901, La Follette, a Republican, made the Badger State into what Theodore Roosevelt later called "the laboratory of democracy."

After gaining the upper hand on "machine" politicians in Madison, "Fighting Bob" engineered passage of laws that increased taxes on railroads and corporations, established a commission to oversee railroad rates, and brought banking in Wisconsin under public regulation. A civil service bill, a measure to restrict lobbying, a conservation and water power bill, and

THE PROGRESSIVE ERA

In the early 1900s journalists known as muck-rakers exposed hideous conditions in America's industrial cities. Public sympathy was aroused and social reform became a popular cause. Local, state, and federal governments began to deal with the problems of an industrial society.

1

Women and children who worked long hours in factories and mills had no protection from cruel or insensitive employers, and wages were very low. Such conditions led to a movement to form labor unions. This scene shows how many workers felt about their employers.

2

Living conditions for immigrants were particularly bad at the turn of the century. Adequate housing was not available and large numbers of immigrants were crowded into the poorest sections of the cities. This photograph shows the Lower East Side in New York City in 1898.

3

Popular music captured the mood of the social reformers during the progressive era. The song "No One Cares for Me" was a heartrending story of a poor orphan boy who sold newspapers for his living. Standing in the cold of winter he watched the Christmas festivities in a home of wealthy people.

4

"In the Heart of the City That Has No Heart" was a song warning that life in the city was cruel. Many songs of the time condemned city life and upheld the simple virtues of life "down on the farm."

1   *Bettmann Archive*

2   *Brown Brothers*

3   J. W. McDonald

4   J. W. McDonald

As governor of Wisconsin, Robert M. La Follette, Sr., began a series of progressive reforms. What were the measures that he steered through his state legislature?

a bill providing for direct primary elections were passed.

La Follette left the governor's mansion in 1906 to enter the United States Senate. From Washington he prodded the legislature in Madison to enact additional progressive measures, including a bill that made Wisconsin the first state to impose a tax on individual incomes. Meanwhile, governors in other states were attacking bossism in politics and the privileges of big business.

The Muckrakers

To achieve their goals, progressives obviously needed popular support. Beginning in 1902, articles exposing alleged evils in American society began to appear in such popular periodicals as *McClure's, Munsey's, Cosmopolitan,* and *Everybody's.* These articles focused public attention on social problems.

The authors of the articles became known as "muckrakers," a name given them by Theodore Roosevelt, who compared them with the character in *Pilgrim's Progress* "who could look no way but downward with the muckrake in his hands."

Most of the muckrakers were free-lance writers. Among the best remembered—and most honored—by history was Lincoln Steffens, who exposed corruption in urban America. His articles were later assembled and published in a classic book entitled *The Shame of the Cities.* Ida M. Tarbell also won renown for her scathing account of the history of the Standard Oil Company. Ray Stannard Baker explored antilabor activities of corporations, exposed abuses in the railroad industry, and made a pioneer study of racial attitudes in the country.

STUDY GUIDE: In opposition to the ideas of Social Darwinism was the philosophy of prag-

Progressives who wanted to reform society during the early 1900s pointed out that life was hard for many Americans. By 1913, twenty percent of the nation's children earned their own livings. This boy worked in the garment district of New York City.

matism. Pragmatism held that man's intellectual and spiritual resources could help him determine his own destiny. The progressive movement reflected this new philosophy. Progressive reformers looked to the government to help cure the social and economic ills of America. They opposed the Social Darwinist belief that government should keep hands off. Unlike the earlier Populist movement, the progressive movement had its origin in the cities, mainly among intellectuals and the well-to-do. It was also a wider movement in that it attracted people of all parties. The movement made its way out of the cities to state capitals. One of the leading progressives was Governor Robert La Follette of Wisconsin, who attacked the privileges of big business. Early in the 1900s a group of writers called "muckrakers" began to publish articles exposing the abuses and corruption in American society.

THE EMERGENCE OF ROOSEVELT

With the turn of the year 1900 Americans once again began to focus on the election of a president. Several minor parties contested the election of 1900. These included the Populist (or what remained of it) and the Social Democratic (which nominated Eugene V. Debs, renowned for his part in the Pullman strike of 1894). Attention centered, however, on the major parties, the Republican and Democratic.

The Election of 1900

The Republicans convened at Philadelphia in June and renominated William McKinley for the presidency. The vice-presidential nomination produced considerable excitement, for the name of Theodore Roosevelt was swirling about Philadelphia.

Elected governor of New York after his return from Cuba, Roosevelt was not much interested in the vice-presidency. He preferred instead a second term in the governor's mansion at Albany. But the Republican organization, or "machine" in New York, headed by Thomas C. ("Boss") Platt, disliked Roosevelt's reformist ideas. The machine decided that the best way to rid New York of the former Rough Rider was to get him elected vice-president.

Drumming up national support for the hero of San Juan Hill was not difficult. The delegates gave Roosevelt their enthusiastic endorsement as McKinley's running-mate. The Republican platform upheld the gold monetary standard and protective tariff, lauded the McKinley administration's foreign policy, and urged that the United States build and control a canal across the isthmus of Central America.

The Democrats gathered in Kansas City and again nominated William Jennings Bryan for president. Second place on the ticket went to Adlai E. Stevenson, the vice-president under Cleveland. The Democratic platform denounced the imperialist foreign policy of the Republican administration, assailed the Currency Act of 1900, and called for the free and unlimited coinage of silver.

The money question, which had dominated the campaign of 1896, was a dead issue by 1900. Bryan therefore made imperialism the central issue in his campaign for the White House. In his judgment the acquisition of colonies was in obvious conflict with the democratic tradition. He believed that voters were certain to respond to an antiimperialist appeal.

Bryan decided that the Philippines would be a prime illustration of the evils of the imperial policies of the Republicans. But millions of Americans did not care whether or not colonialism did violence to the American heritage. For that matter, Bryan and the Democrats were also vulnerable. They did not uphold the democratic ideal for black citizens across the South, where in those days the Democratic party reigned supreme. Theodore Roosevelt accused the Democrats of insincerity. He pointed out that they demanded self-government for "Malay bandits" while denying the right to vote of Negroes in the South. Roosevelt reminded voters of the bravery of black Americans during the fighting in Cuba. He suggested that Democrats should concentrate on "the wrongs of the men on whose breasts may be seen the scars gained as they fought for the flag."

On election day the McKinley-Roosevelt ticket won a clear majority of popular votes and defeated Bryan and Stevenson handily in the electoral college, 292-155. Four months later, in March 1901, McKinley and Roosevelt took their respective oaths. Then came tragedy.

McKinley Is Assassinated

In early September 1901 President and Mrs. McKinley traveled to the city of Buffalo to visit the Pan-American Exposition. On September 6 the president made his way to the exposition, where at the Temple of Music he would shake hands with his countrymen.

Among the excited throng was a mild-looking man of twenty-eight, Leon Czolgosz. Czolgosz, a Polish-American anarchist, carried a short-barreled .32 caliber Iver-Johnson revolver wrapped in a handkerchief. At seven minutes past four Czolgosz stood face to face before the president. McKinley extended his hand. Two shots cracked out. A thin veil of smoke rose. The president slumped into the arms of a friend. Soldiers and secret servicemen scrambled to seize Czolgosz. As McKinley settled onto a chair he allegedly said: "Don't let them hurt him." Next, his thoughts turning to the sickly Mrs. McKinley, the president whispered: "My wife—be careful . . . how you tell her—oh, be careful."

McKinley was rushed to a small hospital where surgeons probed unsuccessfully for the bullet. For a week the president struggled to survive. It was no use. He died on September 14.

After traveling to Buffalo the day after the shooting, Vice-President Roosevelt, to give the impression that McKinley would recover, rejoined his family which was vacationing in the Adirondacks in northeastern New York. On September 13, learning that the president was sinking, Roosevelt hurried back to Buffalo. That afternoon, in Buffalo, Roosevelt, after paying his respects to Mrs. McKinley, went to the house of Ansley Wilcox, thrust his right arm straight up in the air, and repeated the presidential oath. At forty-two he was the youngest chief executive in American history.

STUDY GUIDE: The assassination of President McKinley brought Vice-President Theodore Roosevelt to the White House. Roosevelt was a former governor of New York and hero of the Battle of San Juan Hill in the Spanish-American War.

THEODORE ROOSEVELT

Theodore Roosevelt and also his distant cousin, Franklin Delano Roosevelt, who became president in 1933, traced their ancestry in America to a Dutch farmer who had settled in New Amsterdam in 1649. Over the decades the Roosevelts had prospered as traders and mer-

Library of Congress

Theodore Roosevelt was the first president to add conservation to the list of national priorities. He named Gifford Pinchot, a conservationist, as head of the newly created Forest Service. What other efforts did Roosevelt make in behalf of conservation? What efforts is today's president making to conserve our country's natural resources and recreation areas?

chants and had added banking to the list of the family's enterprises. Like his younger relative, Franklin, Theodore Roosevelt took pride in his Dutch antecedents. Three of his grandparents, however, were of Scotch or English origin and the fourth, Cornelius Roosevelt, was by no means a "pure-bred" Dutchman.

Theodore Roosevelt's father, Theodore Roosevelt, Sr., was a wealthy banker; his mother was the daughter of a prosperous Georgia planter. Their first child, a daughter, was born in New York City where they lived for two years. Theodore Roosevelt arrived in 1858. Two years later, in 1860, Mrs. Roosevelt gave birth to another son, Elliott, who would be the father of Anna Eleanor Roosevelt, the future wife of Franklin D. Roosevelt and from 1933 to 1945 the first lady of the nation.

When the Civil War broke out in 1861, the elder Roosevelt, whose religious views inclined him toward pacifism, declined to enlist in the army despite strong Union sympathies. His decision was to remain a permanent embarrassment to his eldest son.

At an early age Roosevelt became a victim of severe attacks of asthma. When these attacks came, he usually turned to books and his assorted collections of rocks, insects, and mice. The family made the "grand tour" of Europe when Theodore was eleven. In spite of periodic asthma attacks the boy found the trip exciting. A few years later, in 1872-73, the family took another long overseas trip, this time to Egypt and the Holy Land.

Roosevelt's parents worried about their son's health, and his father eventually concluded that the boy himself would have to make a more determined effort to overcome his illness. He told his son that he had the mind but not the body and without the help of the body, the mind cannot go as far as it should. The boy responded that he would make his own body. And so he did. He worked out in a gymnasium, roamed the outdoors, and took up boxing. To correct faulty vision he began wearing eyeglasses.

As a boy, Roosevelt did his lessons under the watchful eyes of private tutors, then, in 1876, entered Harvard. By the time he went off to college he was strong and muscular, and asthma was no longer a serious problem. At Harvard he proved to be an industrious student and in 1880 graduated twenty-first in a class of 158.

While Roosevelt was still a student at Harvard, he suffered a severe shock: his forty-six-year-old father died of cancer. His loss was deeply felt, but he found consolation upon meeting Alice Hathaway Lee, an attractive lady two years his junior. Miss Lee and Roosevelt were married in 1880, then set out on a honeymoon in Europe.

Early Career

On their return home, the newlyweds settled in New York City and Roosevelt began to practice law. The legal profession failed to provide a satisfactory outlet for his energies and before long politics had become his central interest. Despite his wealthy upbringing, Roosevelt had no difficulty in getting on with saloonkeepers, ward-heelers, and other assorted types of individuals who ran politics in New York. In 1881, running as a Republican, he was elected to the state legislature. At Albany he quickly earned a reputation as a vigorous opponent of corruption.

The future looked bright for young Roosevelt. Then came fresh tragedy. After giving birth to a daughter, his wife Alice died. That same day, February 14, 1884, in the same house his mother also died.

Roosevelt's spirit was shattered. However, he completed the legislative term at Albany and campaigned for James G. Blaine in the presidential election of 1884. Then he went to seek a new life as a cattle rancher in the badlands of North Dakota Territory. For the next few years he concentrated on the strenuous life of a rancher and even became a deputy sheriff. However, he did not sever his eastern connections in those years and managed to spend a considerable amount of time in New York. Ill fortune unhappily continued to hound Roosevelt and in the terrible winter of 1886-87 he lost most of his cattle. As a result, he sold his ranch and gave up any ambition he might have had of becoming a cattle baron.

Roosevelt, meanwhile, had fallen in love with a former childhood acquaintance, Edith Carow, whom he married in London in 1886. He had also completed the construction of his many-gabled twelve-bedroom house, Sagamore Hill, at Oyster Bay on Long Island.

Roosevelt's interest in politics had not diminished and in 1886—just before the collapse of his cattle enterprise—he ran unsuccessfully for mayor of New York. He campaigned for Benjamin Harrison in the presidential campaign of 1888 and as a reward received appointment to the Civil Service Commission.

So effective was his work in that position that President Grover Cleveland, a Democrat, reappointed him in 1893. Then, in 1895, Roosevelt accepted appointment as president of the Board of Police Commissioners of New York City.

With characteristic energy, he attacked corruption in the police department and won acclaim for his nightly strolls in search of policemen not performing their duty. He irritated some New Yorkers with his strict enforcement of blue laws requiring saloons to be closed on Sunday. These citizens were not unhappy when President McKinley appointed Roosevelt assistant secretary of the navy in 1897.

Roosevelt, an effective orator, toured the country and spoke out in favor of a stronger navy. Then came the conflict over Cuba. Roosevelt was sure the Spaniards had blown up the battleship *Maine* in Havana harbor in February 1898 and was furious when President McKinley sought a peaceful solution to the Cuban problem. He rejoiced at the failure of the president's efforts. With the outbreak of war, Roosevelt helped form the famous Rough Rider regiment and fought in Cuba. From the heroics at San Juan Hill, he moved to the governorship of New York, the vice-presidency, and, finally, the White House. In 1904 he was elected president. He received more than 7,500,000 votes. The Democratic candidate, Alton B. Parker, drew 5,000,000 votes; the Socialist candidate, Eugene V. Debs, won 400,000 votes; and the Populist candidate, Thomas E. Watson, 100,000.

Theodore Roosevelt was a man of extraordinary intelligence. However, he repeatedly insisted that "character is far more important than intellect." He believed that the talented and well-born members of society have an obligation to help those who are less fortunate. By the standards of his day he was fairly tolerant of racial minorities and on occasion went out of his way to show consideration for the feelings of his black countrymen.

Roosevelt, next to Thomas Jefferson, was the most many-sided man ever to occupy the White House. He was a competent naturalist. He wrote more than thirty books. He herded cattle, climbed mountains, and explored the "River of Doubt" in Brazil.

Roosevelt was also a vain man. That vanity was displayed in his unseemly quest for the Congressional Medal of Honor after the charge up San Juan Hill and his assertion that "I took Panama." Intertwined with his vanity was the tendency to see every controversy as some sort of moral contest in which he stood forth as the champion of righteousness and anyone who disagreed with him was lacking in moral character or worse. Such a view enabled Roosevelt with clear conscience to ride roughshod over domestic politicians and foreign leaders who stood in his way.

Finally, Roosevelt's thirst for excitement and competition led to dubious attitudes about violence and combat. For example, he glorified war as offering the supreme opportunity for an individual to test his manliness.

STUDY GUIDE: Roosevelt came from a wealthy and prominent New York family. Possessing great energy and talent, he entered New York politics and won a reputation as a tireless foe of corruption.

THE ROUGH RIDER IN THE WHITE HOUSE

Down to the time he took over the presidency, Roosevelt had remained a regular Republican and taken only occasional excursions into reform efforts. Hardly had he settled into the executive mansion, however, when the progressive spirit began to infiltrate the national capital. He fell in with the budding progressive movement and, until he left the White House in 1909, gave the country its most liberal administration to that time.

Roosevelt never became a "fire-brand" type of progressive. Far from it. Much more cautious than his manner would indicate, Roosevelt opposed reform that seemed extreme and insisted that reform programs in no way threaten social stability.

Roosevelt, like other nonsocialist liberals, had not lost faith in the capitalist system. He was determined to assert the supremacy of the public interest over all segments of economic power in the country, but he also was determined to achieve his goals within the basic framework. Theodore Roosevelt sought to preserve the free-enterprise system by purging it of its abuses and compelling it to accommodate itself to the public interest.

Roosevelt and the Progressives

The first hint that the Rough Rider might be enlisting in the progressive movement came in December 1901, after he had been in office three months, when he sent his first state-of-the-union message to Congress. In this message he declared "there is a widespread conviction in the minds of the American people that the great corporations known as trusts are in certain of their features and tendencies hurtful to the general welfare." He called for establishment of a new cabinet position to be headed by a secretary of commerce and industries. He also advocated legislation authorizing the federal government to inspect the books and records of corporations engaged in interstate commerce.

Prompting Roosevelt's appeal for congressional action was the Northern Securities Company, created just a short time before by the financier J. P. Morgan. The Northern Securities Company sought to eliminate competition in the northeastern states by bringing together the Great Northern, Northern Pacific, Union Pacific, and Chicago, Burlington, and Quincy railway systems. Roosevelt thought this combination would be harmful to the public interest and a gross violation of the Sherman Antitrust Act of 1890. Congress did not agree with the new president and turned aside his request for legislation.

Roosevelt then directed Attorney General Philander C. Knox to prepare an antitrust suit against the Northern Securities Company. The case wended its way through the judicial mechanism for two years. In 1904, the Supreme Court, reversing its previous interpretations of the Sherman Act, ruled in favor of the government and ordered dissolution of the company. The decision was one of the most celebrated triumphs of President Roosevelt and the progressive movement.

Federal Regulation of Business

In 1903 Congress, responding to the increasing popularity of the president, established the Department of Commerce and Labor. Included in the new department was the Bureau of Corporations, which was to investigate and report on all corporations (except common carriers) engaging in interstate commerce. New legislation gave the federal government the necessary machinery for gathering information on the operations of big business. Encouraged the following year by the Northern Securities decision, the Roosevelt administration stepped up its campaign against business combinations. And by the time the Rough Rider gave up the presidency in 1909 his attorney general had instituted more than forty suits under the Sherman Act. The administration, it was true, overlooked some of the largest business combines and the president's reputation as a trustbuster was exaggerated. Still, Roosevelt made a start toward bringing business enterprise under a measure of federal regulation.

Roosevelt also set about to revitalize the Interstate Commerce Act of 1887, which had failed to provide much regulation. He persuaded Congress in 1903 to pass the Elkins Bill, which increased the power of the Interstate Commerce Commission to counter the practice whereby railroads granted rebates to preferred shippers.

Three years later, in 1906, he prevailed on Congress to approve the Hepburn Bill, which enlarged the ICC from five to seven members. The Hepburn Act took from the railroads and gave to the ICC the power to establish maximum railroad rates. The act also compelled railroads to

VOL. I   PHILADELPHIA, NOVEMBER, 1902   No. 1

Fable No. 1

Once upon a time there was a snake who supposed himself very powerful. This snake had a strong inherited fondness for frogs. His territory was encroached upon by the building of a railroad upon which there ran trains, that made his home very dangerous for both himself and his offspring. He fully realized the danger, and very foolishly decided to do away with it. Now, there lived near his home a very shrewd frog whom this snake could never swallow because this frog was always on the alert, carrying at all times in his mouth a bone, which would prevent his being swallowed by any snake. He was also a full-

Publications like *The Anti-Trust Monthly* helped consumers recognize shady business practices. They also urged buyers to demand legislation against monopolies. What was Roosevelt's policy toward trusts?

employ uniform methods of accounting. In addition, the Hepburn measure restricted the right of railroads to grant free passes and virtually prohibited railroads from carrying commodities produced by themselves or companies in which they had an interest. It broadened the ICC's jurisdiction to include express and sleeping-car companies, oil pipelines, ferries, and terminal facilities.

In his book *The Jungle* the writer Upton Sinclair charged that the meat-packing industry palmed off on unwary customers meat that was contaminated. Roosevelt was aghast at such charges and appointed a special investigating commission, which confirmed Sinclair's findings. Roosevelt then pushed through a federal meat inspection law. The same year he got through Congress the Pure Food and Drug law which forbade the manufacture, sale, or transportation of adulterated or fraudulently labeled foods and drugs in interstate commerce. These acts were not perfect and would require revision and refinement in years to come. Still, they offered some protection and established the precedent that the national government could protect the public's health against unscrupulous businessmen.

Then there was the president's action in the anthracite coal strike of 1902.

In May 1902, miners in the anthracite coal fields went out on strike. Month after month the strike dragged on, mainly because the coal operators refused to recognize the United Mine Workers as the bargaining agent for the striking miners.

By autumn 1902 many people were becoming alarmed that the strike would result in a serious coal shortage during the approaching winter. There was increasing pressure on President Roosevelt to intervene in the dispute. What kind of intervention? Few individuals who were urging Roosevelt to act were concerned over the plight of the miners. The prevailing sentiment was that the president should call out federal troops against the miners or use the Sherman Act.

Under the Sherman Act, the president could prosecute the union on the ground that it was a conspiracy in restraint of trade. Roosevelt, however, recognized that the miners had legitimate grievances over long hours and low wages. He summoned UMW president John Mitchell and representatives of the coal operators to confer with him at the White House. The meeting, on October 3, 1902, was stormy.

The White House meeting achieved nothing, but a short time later the president persuaded the UMW and the operators to accept arbitration of the dispute. The miners returned to work and early the following year the arbitration commission awarded them a wage increase of ten percent, reduced working hours, and eliminated some of the more flagrant abuses under which they had labored. For their part, the operators received permission to raise the price of coal by ten percent.

By his action in the strike, Roosevelt endeared himself to progressives, ended a work stoppage that threatened widespread hardship, and gave a boost to the labor movement in America. He also became the first president ever to intervene in a labor-management controversy in a way that benefited labor.

A Champion of Conservation

Progressives across the nation applauded Roosevelt's stand in the anthracite coal strike. They felt even greater elation when the twenty-sixth president emerged as a champion of conservation of natural resources. Roosevelt was the first occupant of the White House ever to show much interest in conservation. He withdrew from sale more than two hundred million acres of public land, much of it rich in timber and underground minerals. He persuaded Congress in 1902 to pass the National Reclamation Bill which set aside proceeds from public land sales in southwestern states to finance irrigation projects.

In 1908 he called the White House Conservation Conference which impressed upon the popular mind the importance of conserving natural resources. That same year he established the Inland Waterways Commission, which sought to preserve and develop the country's navigable rivers, lakes, and canals.

Problems of Black Americans

The most glaring shortcoming of the progressive movement in the early part of the twentieth century was probably its failure to take much interest in the problems of black citizens. This failure resulted in part from the unhappy fact that some progressives felt little affection and less compassion for their black countrymen. It resulted also from the view of some progressives that attempts to lift the burden of second-class citizenship from black Americans, in addition to being futile, would endanger other parts of the progressive program.

President Roosevelt was more helpful to blacks than were most white Americans at the time. During the Spanish-American War he had praised the courage of black soldiers and, while governor of New York, promoted legislation that banned racially segregated schools in the state. He boasted that "my children sit in the same school with colored children."

Shortly after taking the presidency he invited Booker T. Washington to the White House for lunch. Two years later Roosevelt appointed a prominent Negro, William D. Crum, to be collector of the port of Charleston. The *Colored American Magazine* called this appointment the black man's "greatest political triumph in twenty years."

Then came trouble. In response to problems arising from the movement of blacks from the countryside to cities an epidemic of racial violence took place in which white mobs used the hangman's noose, blacksnake whip, and torch against blacks and their property.

One outbreak of violence led to a national controversy because of President Roosevelt's response.

It happened in 1906 in Brownsville, Texas, where the first battalion of the army's all-black 25th Infantry Regiment was stationed. On the night of August 14, a group of 16 or 20 men rode through Brownsville on horseback, shooting at stores and homes. One Brownsville man was killed and another was wounded. Whites charged that the horsemen had been black soldiers. Roosevelt ordered an investigation.

Neither the army nor a county grand jury ever was able to identify the horsemen. Finally, the commander of the black soldiers demanded a confession. No one confessed. Roosevelt then signed a special order that discharged "without honor . . . and forever barred from re-enlistment" all 167 men stationed in the three companies. Several of the soldiers were near retirement, and six of them had won the Congressional Medal of Honor.

Some whites were pleased by the Rough Rider's firm action, but from the black press came a torrent of criticism. Roosevelt insisted that he had acted just as firmly with white soldiers in the past. He condemned lynching and called for better educational opportunities for blacks. He also appointed a black to a high federal post in Cincinnati, and threatened the Nashville, Chattanooga, and Saint Louis Railway with legal action to force it to offer facilities for black passengers. But the Brownsville episode had damaged Roosevelt's reputation among blacks, who never again viewed him as their special friend.

More than 66 years later, in 1972, the army officially cleared the names of the 167 black soldiers.

Roosevelt and the Economy

Some of President Roosevelt's actions and policies had little connection with the progressive movement. There was, for example, his response to a severe financial panic that struck the country in autumn 1907. To save a New York brokerage house whose collapse might trigger other failures and lead to a nationwide depression, Roosevelt permitted purchase of

In 1902 Theodore Roosevelt adopted "White House" as the official name of the president's home. He also had the building repaired, added the executive offices to the west wing, and rebuilt the east terrace.

the Tennessee Coal and Iron Company by the United States Steel Corporation. Many progressives were unhappy, but the president believed the national interest required this deviation from antitrust principles.

The following year, 1908, Roosevelt persuaded Congress to pass the Aldrich-Vreeland Bill authorizing banks to pump more currency into the economy, particularly in time of economic distress. The legislation also established the National Monetary Commission, which investigated the banking and currency systems of the United States and other countries. The commission's report influenced the shape of the Federal Reserve system, set up in 1913. During Roosevelt's administration the Army War College was established, the army's organization was reformed by creation of a general staff system, and the navy was upgraded.

Theodore Roosevelt — An Assessment

As president, Roosevelt provided strong, effective leadership. He also upheld the public interest against concentrated economic power. As the historian Arthur S. Link puts it, Roosevelt revitalized the presidency.[2] As Link observes, he was not able to dominate Congress as Woodrow Wilson would between 1913 and 1917 (or as Franklin D. Roosevelt would between 1933 and 1937). But he made himself a great popular spokesman. By appealing directly to the people, he often was able to bend Congress to his will.

In addition to rallying the people to his side, Roosevelt was a master politician who had a knack for compromise. He sometimes conceded smaller points in order to win important objectives. For his willingness to compromise, some progressives criticized him. But the twenty-sixth president was interested in results, not lost causes.

STUDY GUIDE: Theodore Roosevelt adopted the program of the progressive movement when he entered the White House. The Department of Commerce and Labor was established, and a start was made toward bringing business under a measure of federal regulation. Roosevelt used his influence to dissolve J.P. Morgan's Northern Securities Company. Legislation was passed to protect consumers from contaminated food and falsely labeled drugs. Roosevelt's tactful handling of the anthracite coal strike won him progressive support and helped the American labor movement. He also became the champion of conservation of America's natural resources. The progressive movement did not especially work to improve the conditions of Negroes.

WILLIAM HOWARD TAFT

In November 1904, Theodore Roosevelt pledged that he would not seek reelection in 1908. Few observers believed that Roosevelt—who would be only fifty years old in 1908—would keep the promise. Republicans and Democrats alike agreed that if he elected to seek a third term in the White House he would win an easy victory.

Roosevelt thoroughly enjoyed being president and admitted in 1907 that the prospect of another four years in the executive mansion appealed to him. But he also believed it would not be good for the Republic for one man to be chief execu-

[2] Arthur S. Link, *American Epoch: A History of the United States Since the 1890s,* copyright 1955 (New York: Alfred A. Knopf), pp. 93-95.

tive for more than two terms. He believed that any man could be corrupted if he kept power too long. So he did not yield to the temptation to break the two-term tradition, and before 1908 made it clear that he would not be a candidate for reelection.

Given his great popularity and his control over federal patronage, President Roosevelt was in a position, as election year 1908 approached, to dictate the presidential nominee of the GOP national convention. And Roosevelt had every intention of choosing the nominee. When he surveyed the list of possible successors, his first choice was Secretary of State Elihu Root of New York, whom he once called "without question the greatest living statesman." Root unfortunately had handicaps. While he had much experience and skill in diplomacy, he was a conservative who could not be counted on to continue Roosevelt's modest reform program.

Another possibility was Governor Charles Evans Hughes of New York, a man of iron will who had battled against corruption and who was a moderate progressive. However, Hughes had publicly rebuked Roosevelt over a federal appointment, which had infuriated Roosevelt. A third possibility was Secretary of War William Howard Taft, a genial man whose 300-pound weight and shaggy mustache made him a target of many jokes and a delight of cartoonists.

The father of "Big Bill" Taft was Alphonso Taft, a native of New England who had migrated westward to Cincinnati and had become a prosperous attorney. The elder Taft also became influential in Republican politics. He served as secretary of war in the cabinet of President Grant and was the country's minister to Russia and to Austria. William Howard Taft was born in Cincinnati in 1857. He had high intelligence and in school consistently ranked near the top of his class, in addition to being a good athlete. When he entered Yale in 1874, he heeded the advice of his father, kept athletic activities to a minimum, and instead concentrated on his studies. He graduated second in a class of 191. He then returned to his home town where he studied for two years at the Cincinnati Law School, received a law degree (this time graduating at the head of his class), and was admitted to the bar.

Early Career

William Howard Taft entered politics and, thanks to his father's influence, became prosecuting attorney of Hamilton County, Ohio in 1881. The following year he became a collector of internal revenue. He resigned in 1883, spent a few months with his parents in Vienna where his father was minister to Austria, then joined his father's law firm in Cincinnati.

In 1886 Taft married the daughter of a law partner of former-President Hayes. Mrs. Taft eventually gave birth to two sons, one of whom— Robert Alphonso Taft—became one of the most powerful members of the United States Senate in the late 1930s, 1940s, and early 1950s.

The year after his marriage, 1887, Taft received appointment as judge of the Ohio Superior Court, then won election to a five-year term. He resigned the judgeship in 1890 to accept President Harrison's appointment as solicitor general of the United States, in which position he established an enviable record. It was at this time that he became a friend of a youthful member of the Civil Service Commission—Theodore Roosevelt. In 1892 Harrison appointed Taft judge of the Sixth Circuit Court of Appeals. At the same time he served as a professor of law and dean of the law department at the University of Cincinnati.

The United States acquired the Philippines in 1898 and two years later President McKinley appointed Taft head of the United States Philippine Commission. The following year, 1901, Taft became the first civil governor of the islands, and did an outstanding job. He established a civil administration in which Filipinos would share responsibility. He oversaw construction of schools and roads, improvement of harbors, and completion of sanitation and other public health projects.

The result was a marked upgrading of the quality of life in the islands. Taft also took a tolerant, even affectionate, view of the Filipinos. He traveled to the interior of the islands and, despite the discomfort wrought by the heat and humidity, took part in native fiestas and dances. The Filipinos loved the governor and called him "Saint" Taft. A former rebel proclaimed that "Governor Taft turned a dying people to the light and life of modern liberties."

Taft's old friend, President Theodore Roosevelt, offered him a place on the Supreme Court. Taft long had dreamed of sitting on the high court, but he turned down Roosevelt's offer. First, he believed that his work in the Philippines was so important that he must stay on in the islands a while longer. Second, Mrs. Taft, who had visions of becoming the first lady, believed

Although William Howard Taft had difficulty getting along with the progressives in the Republican party, he did achieve some legislative successes. What Taft reform measures became law?

the Supreme Court would be an unlikely springboard to the White House. Then, in 1904, Roosevelt asked Taft to become secretary of war and, urged on by Mrs. Taft, he accepted.

Taft's friendship with the Rough Rider blossomed. The secretary of war was an amiable fellow, a good listener, and seemed in full accord with Roosevelt's type of progressivism. Because of his affection for Taft, and also because of Taft's good work in the Philippines and in the War Department, Roosevelt concluded that the Ohioan would be an ideal successor in the White House.

Taft's aging mother disagreed. She said: "I do not want my son to be president. His is a judicial mind, and he loves the law." Taft's ambitious wife had different ideas. She arranged an interview with Roosevelt and pressed her view that, whatever others might think, her husband was suited for the presidency. She prevailed and Taft, in typical good humor, agreed to be a candidate. Roosevelt used his influence on the GOP leaders, and at the Republican national convention in June 1908 Taft easily won the presidential nomination.

The Election of 1908

The election of 1908 proved a landslide. The Democrats, for the third time, nominated William Jennings Bryan on a platform that condemned monopolies and pledged reduction of tariff duties. But Taft, who also opposed monopolies and favored downward revision of the tariff, was carrying the mantle of Theodore Roosevelt, one of the most admired presidents. As a result, Taft received 7,600,000 popular votes to Bryan's 6,400,000 and trounced the Nebraskan in the electoral college by the vote of 321 to 162. To give Taft a chance to develop his own style in the White House and to avoid any criticism that Taft was a mere puppet, the Rough Rider, after Taft's inauguration, set out on a long expedition to Africa, to hunt big game.

Taft should have listened to his mother, for he was not temperamentally suited for the presidency. He was too good-natured; he enjoyed his food and sleep too much; he was not skilled or aggressive in dealing with Congress. His four years in the White House, 1909-13, turned into a nightmare. In his last months in office he confided to a friend that "each day I am a little bit happier in the knowledge that my successor's inauguration is that much nearer at hand." (Happily, this honest, public-spirited man found contentment in later years, for in 1921 President Warren G. Harding appointed him chief justice of the Supreme Court. Taft thus became the only individual to have held the two highest offices in the American government. He remained chief justice until shortly before his death in 1930.)

Trouble with the Progressives

Taft's miseries in the White House developed from his inability to get along with the progressive wing of his party. For by 1909 the GOP was dividing between conservatives and progressives.

Taft fell out with the progressives for two reasons. First, unlike Roosevelt, he did not have the energy and political skill to keep progressives happy while at the same time maintaining

satisfactory relations with the Republican "Old Guard." Second, Taft, for all the lip-service that he had given to progressive ideas, was essentially a conservative.

The first conflict between Taft and Republican progressives came in 1909 when progressives in the House of Representatives set about to trim the authority of their speaker, Joseph G. ("Uncle Joe") Cannon, of Illinois, an enemy of reform. Taft did not like Cannon, but decided that he must not alienate Republican conservatives by lining up against the speaker. Progressives were disappointed in the presidential stance and some concluded that they had been right in suspecting that Taft's progressivism was a veneer, that his views were those of the Old Guard.

A short time later Republican conservatives revised the tariff by passing the Payne-Aldrich Bill. This legislation raised duties on many imports and lowered them on only a few—a denial of the 1908 Republican platform. (Mr. Dooley, the Irish character created by political satirist Finley Peter Dunne, observed that curling stones, false teeth, canary-bird seed, hog bristles, and silkworm eggs were left on the free list. "Th' new Tariff Bill," he said, "put these familyar commodyties within th' reach iv all.")

President Taft had favored lower tariff duties and hence disliked the Payne-Aldrich Bill. Yet, he believed that most Republicans favored the measure and thus he should approve it. He feared a veto of the bill would arouse conservatives against him and endanger future programs. Taft finally signed the bill describing the Payne-Aldrich Act as the best tariff bill ever enacted by Republicans. Progressives were at once sad and angry.

The Ballinger-Pinchot Controversy

Next came the celebrated Ballinger-Pinchot controversy. Taft decided not to retain James R. Garfield, a son of former-President Garfield and a staunch conservationist, as secretary of the interior. Instead he named Richard Achilles Ballinger of Washington, an Old Guard Republican to head the Department of the Interior. Roosevelt's friend, Gifford Pinchot, the chief forester, was furious.

Pinchot was a Pennsylvania progressive for whom conservation of natural resources was almost a religion. He suspected that Ballinger was unfriendly to conservation. When the new secretary reopened to public sale valuable government lands in Wyoming and Montana, Pinchot was sure that Ballinger was dedicated to destruction of Roosevelt's conservation program.

In August 1909 Pinchot assailed Ballinger in a speech before the Spokane Conservation League. Then the chief forester provided information for a "muckrake" article, which appeared in *Collier's* in autumn 1909. The article charged that Ballinger had fraudulently transferred reserved coal lands in Alaska to a Morgan-Guggenheim syndicate. The charges rocked the Taft administration, and when Pinchot acknowledged that he had been supplying anti-Ballinger information to the press the president dismissed him.

Progressives erupted. Their fury heightened when a special committee of Congress issued a report that cleared the secretary of misconduct. The progressives claimed that the committee had been weighted in favor of Ballinger. Meanwhile, as the Ballinger-Pinchot controversy raged on, progressives in the House of Representatives, led by George W. Norris of Nebraska, reopened their campaign against Speaker Cannon. In March 1910, over Taft's opposition, they managed to curtail the speaker's power.

The break between Taft and the progressives was now complete. A fierce struggle developed for control of the Republican party between progressives and Taft and the Old Guard. Although federal patronage and financial support by business interests gave Taft some advantages in the contest, the progressives received a powerful assist in the summer of 1910. Theodore Roosevelt returned to the United States and quickly fell in with the anti-Taft rebellion. In early 1911, progressives, led by Senator La Follette, organized the National Progressive Republican League to promote "popular government and progressive legislation."

Republican progressives were less than fair in portraying "Big Bill" Taft as a reactionary politician and a friend of the "interests." Although his instincts were conservative, the Ohioan nonetheless presided over an administration that was fairly progressive and compared favorably with that of Theodore Roosevelt.

Taft's attorney general, for example, initiated ninety antitrust suits, or twice as many in four years as the Roosevelt administration had initiated in nearly eight. Moreover, the Taft administration did not concentrate on lesser business combinations. Instead it went after such industrial giants as General Electric, United States Steel, International Harvester, and Standard Oil. In 1910 Taft supported the Mann-Elkins Bill, which broadened the authority of the Interstate Commerce Commission by placing telephone, telegraph, wireless, and cable companies under the commission's jurisdiction. In 1912 he supported legislation establishing postal savings banks and a parcel post system. Other measures supported by Taft regulated safety in mines and on railroads, abolished phosphorous matches, created a federal Children's Bureau, and established employer liability for accidents suffered by workingmen when on jobs contracted for by the federal government. During Taft's administration the working hours of government employees were limited to eight per day.

Taft aided the progressive movement in other ways. Notwithstanding the attacks by Pinchot, he advanced conservation of natural resources. He withdrew oil lands from public sale, persuaded Congress to give him authority to reserve valuable coal lands, and set up the Bureau of Mines to conserve underground resources. The man appointed to replace Pinchot as chief forester was as dedicated to conservation as his predecessor had been.

Taft supported the Sixteenth Amendment to the Constitution, permitting a federal income tax. Without the income tax later social legislation could not have been financed. He also supported the Seventeenth Amendment providing for direct election of United States senators, also ratified in 1913.

STUDY GUIDE: In the election of 1908 Republican candidate William Howard Taft defeated Democrat William Jennings Bryan. Taft was unable to get along with the progressive wing of the Republican party. He refused to veto the Payne-Aldrich Bill raising tariffs and gave his support to House Speaker Cannon, a conservative Republican. The progressives turned against him. Their anger increased when he dismissed the ardent conservationist, Gifford Pinchot, as chief forester.

WOODROW WILSON

During the Taft administration a new personality appeared on the American political scene. Before the year 1911 this man had never held public office, but by 1912 increasing numbers of people were saying that he was "presidential timber." His name was Woodrow Wilson.

Born in 1856 in Staunton, Virginia, Thomas Woodrow Wilson was the third child and first son of Joseph R. and Jessie W. Wilson. His father was a respected Presbyterian minister and his mother, a native of England, was the daughter of a Presbyterian minister. When the boy was two years old, the family moved to Augusta, Georgia where his father became pastor of the First Presbyterian Church.

During the Civil War the elder Wilson supported the cause of the Confederacy. In later life Woodrow Wilson recalled seeing Robert E. Lee looking at wounded Confederate soldiers lying in his father's church when it was converted to a temporary hospital. Throughout his life Wilson took pride in the southern war effort, although he always insisted that because he loved the South he rejoiced "in the failure of the Confederacy." Five years after the war the Wilsons made their way to Columbia, South Carolina, where the elder Wilson became a professor of theology and also served as minister of a local Presbyterian church.

The disruption of southern life caused by the Civil War and Reconstruction delayed young Woodrow Wilson's start of formal schooling until he was nine years old, but he had a comfortable childhood. His father was financially secure and was accepted in the best social circles. The young "Tommie" Wilson enjoyed football and baseball and did not distinguish himself in school. Still he was not a frivolous boy.

Wilson had a strong religious faith, listened intently to his father's sermons, and read from the Bible and offered prayers every day. At an early age he concluded that God had provided men with an absolute standard of moral conduct to which they must adhere if they were to achieve order and prosperity. He held that belief until he died.

Like other boys, Wilson indulged in daydreaming. He dreamed of being an eloquent and admired political leader. To make his dreams come true, he set about to sharpen his skill as a speaker. He memorized speeches given by the world's statesmen and delivered them in woods or in empty chapels. He persuaded his friends to help him organize mock parliaments in which they could draw up laws and constitutions and develop the art of debate.

Putting aside dreams of political prominence, Wilson, at the age of sixteen, went off to Davidson College, a Presbyterian school near Charlotte, North Carolina, to prepare himself to become a minister. His ambition was to gain admission to the Presbyterian College of New Jersey (later Princeton University). Delayed partly because of illness, he finally enrolled in the school at Princeton in 1875. He was managing editor of the campus newspaper in his senior year and helped found the Liberal Debating Club.

Wilson had decided that he would not be a minister and instead returned to the idea of becoming a political figure. To that end he concentrated on the study of political science, history, and rhetoric. Upon graduation, he entered the law school at the University of Virginia. As he later explained: "The profession I chose was politics; the profession I entered was the law. I entered the one because I thought it would lead to the other." Wilson nonetheless found the law monotonous. Accordingly he spent much of his energy drilling in "the arts of persuasion" and soon established a reputation as an orator. When poor health struck him again, he returned home where he continued to study on his own, and in 1882 the University of Virginia awarded him a law degree. At the same time he received admission to the bar.

Early Career

"Fairly in love with speech-making" and convinced that "my *end* is a commanding influence in the councils (and counsels) of my country," Wilson began to practice law in Atlanta in 1882. A legal career, he calculated, would take him into politics. This, he hoped, would take him to those "councils," possibly the United States Senate. Soon, however, he was bored and depressed. After a while, he abandoned the law and gave up hope of being a statesman. Instead, he decided to make himself "an outside force in politics" through teaching and writing.

In 1883 he entered the graduate school of Johns Hopkins University in Baltimore, where he concentrated on history and political science. Three years later he received a Ph.D. degree. His doctoral dissertation, entitled *Congressional Government,* was published as a book and received favorable reviews. A central theme of the book was that the English parliamentary system was superior to the American system of government.

On completing his graduate studies, Wilson accepted a position as associate professor at a new women's college in Pennsylvania, Bryn Mawr. A short time later he married Ellen Axom, the daughter of a Presbyterian minister of Rome, Georgia. A kind and sensitive woman, the first Mrs. Wilson was a source of strength for her husband and eventually bore him three daughters. (Ellen Axom Wilson died in summer 1914. Loss of his wife was a heavy blow to Wilson and for a time his zest for living seemed to have disappeared. But then he met an attractive and charming widow, Edith Bolling Galt whom he married in 1915.)

After two years, Wilson left Bryn Mawr and in 1888 became a professor of history and politics at Wesleyan University in Middletown, Connecticut. Then came what Wilson later called "a crowning success." He received an appointment as professor of jurisprudence and political economy at Princeton. Over the next dozen years he lectured to thousands of Princeton students and wrote a five-volume *History of the American People*.

Wilson was chosen president of Princeton in 1902. There he inaugurated academic reforms that were eventually copied by nearly every college in the country. He recruited outstanding faculty members and raised academic standards. Within a few years Princeton rapidly became one of the most esteemed universities in the United States.

Then came trouble. Wilson set about to abolish private eating clubs and substitute college dining halls. The Princeton alumni, many of whom had fond memories of the old eating clubs, objected to the president's proposal. They began to grumble that Wilson was bringing too many changes. Other Americans who read of Wilson's stand, however, saw him as a champion of democracy and an opponent of snobbery.

Next came a controversy with the board of trustees over new reforms that he was urging. In spring 1910, Wilson spoke to the Princeton alumni at Pittsburgh, arguing that private universities were overly concerned with the wealthy class and neglected "opportunities to serve the people." The anger of the trustees reached a new peak.

Wilson Enters Politics

Wilson by now had attracted the attention of Democratic politicians. The Democratic party had not controlled the White House for nearly a decade and a half and badly needed fresh leadership. Accordingly several prominent Democrats advised Wilson in spring 1910 that they would like to make him president. As a first step, they advised him to seek the governorship of New Jersey. They assured him that the "boss" of the Democratic organization in New Jersey would engineer his nomination for governor by the Democratic state convention.

The proposal stirred his ambitions, and by summer 1910 Wilson was consumed with the idea of striking out on a political career. His previous writings, however, had revealed a hostility to organized labor and a contempt for immigrants. Therefore, despite his campaign against elitism at Princeton, progressive Democrats in New Jersey were not enthusiastic about Wilson's candidacy. But progressives could not prevent Wilson's nomination by the state convention.

In his acceptance speech, Wilson announced that, if elected, "I shall enter . . . office . . . with absolutely no pledges of any kind to prevent me from serving the people." He praised the platform which progressive delegates had drawn up. Thereafter, progressives began to revise their estimate of the professor-politician.

In the weeks that followed, Wilson resigned the presidency of Princeton and vigorously campaigned against his Republican opponent. In his speeches he sounded a good deal more progressive than he actually was. He won widespread applause when he apparently rejected the political machine that had arranged his nomination. He won the election in November by the second largest plurality in New Jersey's history.

The ballots had hardly been tabulated in New Jersey in November 1910 before the political boss James ("Sugar Jim") Smith wanted the Democratic state legislature to elect him to the United States Senate. He fully expected support of the governor-elect. But Wilson, faithful to the progressive principles which he had embraced before the election, declined to endorse Smith and instead campaigned for Smith's opponent who won. Progressive editors exulted that the "long-haired bookworm of a professor" had "licked the gang to a frazzle."

Next Wilson got through the legislature a far-reaching program of progressive reform: direct primary elections; a corrupt practices act; legislation giving cities the option to establish the commission form of government and permitting them to adopt the initiative, referendum, and recall. Other reforms included a measure giving the Public Service Commission power to set standards of rates and services; a pure food law; an act regulating the working conditions of women and children; and another providing for workmen's compensation.

Rise to Prominence

Wilson's spectacular rise to political prominence, his impressive record of achievement as governor, and his image of a man who would never compromise principle made him almost overnight a leading contender for the Democratic presidential nomination in 1912. From summer 1911 on he spent much of his time trying to gain support of the men, including Williams Jennings Bryan, for whose ideas he earlier had expressed disdain.

Democratic professional politicians felt little enthusiasm for Wilson. They considered him to be self-righteous and a man who could not be depended on to reward those who labored in his behalf. They favored the speaker of the House of Representatives, Beauchamp ("Champ") Clark of Missouri. Clark, although less progressive, from their viewpoint was a more reliable man.

As the Democratic national convention opened in 1912, Wilson's chances did not appear promising, and in the early balloting Clark opened a substantial lead. By the tenth ballot, Clark had mustered a majority of the votes. Wilson's advisers, observing that Clark was still short of the two-thirds vote required to nominate a Democratic candidate, urged him to stay in the contest. On the fourteenth ballot, William Jennings Bryan switched to Wilson, a dramatic move that stopped the drift to Clark. Meanwhile, Wilson was telling reporters that nobody was authorized to make any deals in his name. Perhaps he had forgotten to pass the word along to his managers in Baltimore. The managers began to drop hints to the Indiana delegates that their favorite-son candidate, Governor Thomas Riley Marshall, might gain Wilson's blessing for the vice-presidential nomination if they supported Wilson. On the next ballot Indiana voted for Wilson. Then Illinois and Alabama delegates flocked to Wilson. That finished Clark, and on the forty-sixth ballot Wilson was nominated. The vice-presidential nominee not unexpectedly was Governor Marshall of Indiana.

The Republican party meanwhile had blown apart. The division between President Taft and Republican progressives had become final in early 1910, and the Democrats won control of the House of Representatives and increased their strength in the Senate in the elections of autumn 1910.

Progressives at this point started plans to nominate "Fighting Bob" La Follette, the best-known progressive, for president. But other progressives, and many rank-and-file Republicans, began to press Theodore Roosevelt to challenge Taft for the nomination.

Roosevelt wavered, largely because he believed what he had said in the past: that it was undesirable for one man to hold the presidency for more than two terms. But at length the avalanche of appeals and also his own ambition persuaded him to change his mind. In February 1912 he told a reporter: "My hat is in the ring." Learning of the announcement, Taft was shocked. La Follette was furious.

STUDY GUIDE: Wilson, a college professor and later president of Princeton University, was a political unknown. His abilities attracted the attention of Democratic politicians, who helped him win the governorship of New Jersey.

THE CAMPAIGN OF 1912

Arriving in Chicago in mid-June 1912, a few days before the Republican national convention opened, Roosevelt exclaimed to his enthusiastic followers: "We fight in honest fashion for the good of mankind." It was evident that the Rough Rider, who had polled many more votes than had Taft in primary elections, was the favorite of a majority of Republican voters across the country. Roosevelt had enough delegates to put him within a hundred votes of a majority when the balloting for a presidential nominee began. (The Republicans, unlike the Democrats at that time, required that a candidate win only a majority in order to receive the nomination.)

There were problems, however. La Follette had forty-one votes committed to him and under no circumstances would he release them to Roosevelt. More serious, the credentials committee, under control of Taft forces, was in the process of rejecting Roosevelt's plea that 254 delegate seats claimed by individuals pledged to Taft should go to delegates favorable to Roosevelt.

The convention turned into one of the most disorderly political gatherings on record. Roosevelt partisans had a steamroller whistle which hooted whenever Taft supporters rose to speak. From the galleries battalions of Roosevelt backers chanted: "We want Teddy!" When it was clear that Taft would be nominated on the first ballot, 344 delegates who were pledged to the Rough Rider refused to cast votes. On announcement of Taft's nomination, they marched defiantly out of the convention.

Was Roosevelt cheated out of the nomination? The historical verdict is that he probably was. According to the historian William H. Harbaugh, at least twenty-five of Roosevelt's 254 challenges of Taft delegates were legitimate.[3] If the credentials committee had awarded those twenty-five seats to pro-Roosevelt delegates, so Harbaugh thinks, Roosevelt probably could have won over enough delegates from La Follette and Taft to win the nomination. Particularly important in Harbaugh's calculation were sixty black delegates who were pledged to Taft but who were under heavy pressure from more sophisticated blacks to switch to Roosevelt. (While not entirely free of racial prejudice, Roosevelt had shown himself to be more friendly to Negroes than had Taft.)

A few days later the Democrats assembled in Baltimore. They proceeded to adopt a progressive platform and nominated Wilson for president. In adopting progressivism, the Democrats virtually ended Roosevelt's hope that he might put together a third party made up of progressives from both parties.

Roosevelt nonetheless went ahead with plans for organizing a new party. Early in August 1912 delegates to the national convention of the Progressive party assembled in Chicago. The evening before the convention opened, Roosevelt arrived and exclaimed that he felt "as strong as a bull moose." From that moment on, the bull moose was the symbol of the Progressive party. Although they failed to win over Democratic progressives, or even large numbers of Republican progressives, Roosevelt's followers overflowed with zeal and enthusiasm. With unparalleled fervor they nominated Roosevelt for president and Governor Hiram Johnson of California for vice-president.

Roosevelt's nomination by the Bull Moose party made Wilson's election almost certain.

But the campaign of 1912 was not without drama. On October 14 a fanatic shot and wounded Roosevelt shortly before he was to make a speech. After the would-be assassin was wrestled to the ground by spectators, the Rough Rider, pale but fully conscious, ordered the man brought before him. "The poor creature," he muttered, then turned away.

[3] William H. Harbaugh, *Power and Responsibility: The Life and Times of Theodore Roosevelt,* copyright 1961 (New York: Farrar, Straus and Cudahy), pp. 435-36.

Library of Congress

The Wilsons posed for this photograph in 1912, the same year Wilson was elected president. From left are Margaret, Mrs. Ellen Wilson, Eleanor, Jessie, and Woodrow. How did Wilson rise from president of Princeton University to president of the United States in ten years?

Physicians examined Roosevelt's wound and insisted that he go at once to a hospital. Roosevelt instead proceeded to the hall where he was to speak. "I will make this speech or die," he said. He spoke in low tones: "I'll do the best I can, but there is a bullet in my body." A pause. "It is nothing. I am not hurt badly. I have a message to deliver and will deliver it as long as there is life in my body." While his audience looked on in horror, Roosevelt plodded through the speech. The Rough Rider then went to a hospital, where it was disclosed that the wound was not serious.

Roosevelt's display of courage thrilled Americans, but the running debate between Roosevelt and Wilson—both of whom virtually ignored Taft during the campaign—was much more important. For the two candidates, both of them progressives, spelled out their views of what a progressive administration should accomplish and their ideas varied widely. Roosevelt called his program the New Nationalism, Wilson's became known as the New Freedom.

The New Nationalism

Roosevelt's New Nationalism called on Americans to put aside the time-honored notion of Jefferson that a large and powerful federal bureaucracy in America would be a threat to the liberties of the people. Roosevelt also urged them to abandon the idea that the national government should keep its hands off the social and economic mechanism. American society in the second decade of the twentieth century was infinitely more complicated than it had been in Jefferson's day. Time had brought forth problems with which individuals could not easily cope except through help from the national government.

Roosevelt thought the time was past when the country should be permitted to bounce along with little or no guidance from the central authority in Washington. Therein lay the heart of the New Nationalism. Within the traditional framework of the free-enterprise system, the national government should take a continuing and active part in the social and economic life of the country so as to assure justice and equal opportunity for all parts of the national society.

What, specifically, was Roosevelt urging?

Foremost, he wanted progressives to abandon their assumption that monopoly was inherently evil. The old progressive argument had been that the monopolist in his greed for maximum profits could not resist the temptation to take advantage of consumers by charging exorbitant prices. To Roosevelt such notions were not necessarily accurate. There was no natural law that required monopolists to profiteer at public expense. Moreover, given the efficiency that bigness sometimes achieved, a monopoly conceivably could function so as to benefit the consumer. In any event, Roosevelt believed concentration and bigness in business were inevitable. Thus it was futile to try to break up all business combinations. The implication was that Roosevelt had little enthusiasm for the Sherman Antitrust Act of 1890.

In Roosevelt's view, the national government, instead of trying to destroy every big business combination, should oversee and police business. He felt that the government should make certain that businessmen used their great economic power in the interest of the general public. To that end he proposed a federal trade commission which would act as a watchdog on business. If the commission found any evidence of unfair trade practices, it would move quickly to bring the guilty before the courts.

Roosevelt's New Nationalism planned a broad program of social reform that would protect individuals, particularly working people, against some of the hazards of life in an urban-industrial society. He urged a minimum wage for female workers, a federal statute prohibiting child labor,

and a workmen's compensation act. He wanted the federal government to intervene in labor disputes and wanted to manipulate the tariff to assure fair wages for workers. He also favored an expanded federal health program.

The New Freedom

Wilson's New Freedom was progressive in that it aimed to assert the public interest over the private. Beyond that the New Freedom and the New Nationalism had few similarities. The New Freedom rejected Roosevelt's idea that social changes required a drastic new relationship between the national government and society. On the contrary, the New Freedom, which was strongly influenced by Louis D. Brandeis, later a Supreme Court justice, favored a restoration of the ideas of Thomas Jefferson. The Wilsonian program called for a decentralized, highly competitive society made up largely of farmers and small businessmen.

Wilson believed that the main function of the federal government should be to strike down the barriers to free competition and see that they remained down. He generally opposed social welfare legislation on the ground that it would stifle individual initiative, and would make many Americans wards of the state. He was also inclined to the view that it was undemocratic and hence unfair to tax the wealthy in order to uplift the poor or working people. Late in the campaign, it is true, Wilson expressed some interest in the social welfare ideas of the New Nationalism. Still he rejected Roosevelt's demand for a minimum wage for women workers and declined to speak out for a national child labor law.

The heart of Wilson's program was that the federal government should strike down all barriers to free competition in America. What were the barriers? One was the protective tariff. Wilson proposed to lower tariffs. Another was the banking and currency systems. Wilson would reorganize those systems. A third barrier was the large combinations of business, usually referred to as trusts. Unlike Roosevelt, Wilson believed there could be no such thing as a good trust that functioned in the public interest. Since trusts, by definition, were evil, they must be destroyed. To achieve such destruction, Wilson wanted to update the Sherman Antitrust Act by listing every conceivable way in which businessmen might restrain trade, then leave it to the courts to enforce the law.

Whether great numbers of voters in autumn 1912 understood the distinctions between the New Nationalism and the New Freedom is an open question. The election results were: 6,200,-000 for Wilson, 4,100,000 for Roosevelt, 3,400,-000 for Taft, and 900,000 for the perennial Socialist candidate, Eugene V. Debs of Indiana. Wilson swept the electoral college, winning 435 votes to 88 for Roosevelt to 8 for Taft. The Democrats also won control of both houses of Congress.

STUDY GUIDE: In 1912 Wilson was the Democratic presidential candidate. The Republican party was split between conservatives, who favored Taft, and progressives, who backed Roosevelt. When Taft won the Republican nomination, the Progressive wing formed a new party, the Progressive, or Bull Moose party. They nominated Theodore Roosevelt for the presidency. Roosevelt's program, the New Nationalism, called for the federal government to take an active part in providing for the social and economic well-being of the country.

Wilson's program, called the New Freedom, was progressive, but it rejected many aspects of Roosevelt's program. Wilson believed the federal government should strike down all barriers to free competition. But he did not favor social welfare legislation. The split in the Republican party made it possible for Wilson to win the presidency in 1912.

WILSON IN THE WHITE HOUSE

On entering the White House in March 1913, Wilson set out to put the ideas of the New Freedom into laws. Before the year ended Congress passed the Underwood-Simmons Act, which substantially lowered import duties. This marked the first successful attack on tariff protection in a half-century.

Next Wilson turned to the banking and currency systems. The outcome, also in 1913, was the Federal Reserve Act. This complicated measure aimed to weaken the control that giant financial institutions, particularly in New York, exercised over banking and therefore credit. By way of the new Federal Reserve Board, the measure increased the authority of the national government in fiscal affairs. Then the legislation gave greater elasticity to the currency by enabling banks to enlarge the money supply in times of economic distress.

During the winter of 1913-14, Wilson set his sights on monopolies and urged legislation that would update the Sherman Act. The outcome was the Clayton Antitrust Bill, introduced in Congress in early 1914, which aimed at monopoly practices not previously specified as illegal.

When he moved against monopolies, the twenty-eighth president met opposition from an unexpected source. Some progressives, notably those of the Bull Moose variety, advised him they did not think much of his plans for updating the Sherman Act. Like Roosevelt, they did not think big combinations of business were inherently evil and believed the trend toward bigness in business was irreversible. They thought that clever businessmen would find fresh ways to restrain trade that were not mentioned in the antitrust laws. They urged Wilson to support legislation designed to make certain that big businessmen operated in the public interest. They wanted Roosevelt's New Nationalism plan: a law elastic enough to enable the government to cope with all methods of restraining trade that might arise. Such a measure should outlaw in sweeping terms—but not attempt to specify—unfair trade practices and then leave it to a federal trade commission to oversee business activities and suppress unfair trade practices.

Creation of the Federal Trade Commission

Taken aback by criticisms of his antitrust proposal, Wilson reassessed his views and did a remarkable about-face. In late spring 1914 he made the Stevens Trade Commission Bill—a measure that embodied the thinking of his Bull Moose critics—the cornerstone of his program for regulating business. Although he had no objection to passage of the Clayton Bill, and indeed signed it into law in October 1914, Wilson lost interest in it. The most important provisions of the Clayton Act, from the perspective of history, were not the unfair trade practices listed. Its significant provisions were those which proclaimed that labor and agricultural organizations should not be considered as illegal combinations in restraint of trade under the antitrust laws. The act also restricted the use of the injunction in labor disputes and made strikes, peaceful picketing, and boycotts legal. Such provisions were hailed by organized labor as a "Magna Carta."

The Stevens Bill, with Wilson's powerful leadership in the late summer 1914, won ap-

This advertisement for the Pierce Arrow appeared in magazines in 1910. Owning an automobile showed the "arrogance of wealth" according to Woodrow Wilson. Do you think Wilson would have made that statement today?

proval of Congress. The measure outlawed, in general terms, unfair trade practices and created the Federal Trade Commission with power to move swiftly and directly against corporations engaging in such practices. The commission was empowered to issue cease-and-desist orders and, if such orders went unheeded, to bring a corporation to trial.

Further Reforms

Apart from support of the trade commission legislation, Wilson upheld the principles of the New Freedom spelled out in his campaign of 1912. The only other Bull Moose measures which he supported were the Smith-Lever Bill and the Seamen's Bill. The Smith-Lever Act provided grants-in-aid, on a matching basis, to states to establish agricultural extension systems. The Seamen's Bill, sponsored by Robert La Follette, aimed to improve working conditions of American seamen and strengthen maritime safety requirements. Wilson signed the former measure in spring 1914 and approved the latter in early 1915.

By autumn 1914 the president did not contemplate any further concessions to Bull Moose ideas and, indeed, thought his reformist period was over. He had achieved the main objectives of the New Freedom and henceforth reform would give way to readjustment. That is, in the next few years Americans would adapt themselves to the reforms of the previous eighteen months.

Wilson's estimate turned out to be premature, for two events took place whose consequences eventually would compel him to revise his thinking. First, in July-August 1914, World War I had broken out in Europe. Second, in the November 1914 elections the GOP made a remarkable comeback from the disaster of 1912. Republicans reduced the Democratic majority in the House of Representatives from seventy-

three to twenty-five and returned to power in such states as New York, Pennsylvania, Illinois, and New Jersey.

Preparedness Controversy

In response to the war in Europe, the country was rocked by a great debate over military preparedness. Like many peace-minded Americans, President Wilson feared that if the United States had the means to make war, it might be tempted to enter the European war. For this reason, he was against large-scale military preparedness by the United States.

Other influential Americans, notably Theodore Roosevelt, wanted to gird the United States against the day when events might draw it into the European conflict. Roosevelt denounced Wilson's policy of neutrality toward Europe's belligerents. The former chief executive wanted the United States to take a hard line against Germany. If such a policy took the country to war, so be it.

How did the preparedness controversy and Roosevelt's increasing hostility toward President Wilson influence the domestic political situation? Because of his attention to war issues, Roosevelt abandoned the Progressive party. Since his personality had been all that held Bull Moosers together, the party fell apart. Roosevelt reconciled himself with the Old Guard Republicans, many of whom were in rhythm with his ideas regarding preparedness and foreign policy. If many of the Bull Moose progressives followed the Rough Rider back into the GOP, the problems of the Democrats in the election of 1916 would be compounded.

The Campaign of 1916

The divisions in the Republican party which had given victory to Wilson and the Democrats in 1912 were healing. If the process continued, the GOP was sure to recapture both the White House and Congress. There simply were more Republicans than there were Democrats in the country at that time.

The task facing Wilson and the Democrats, if they were to stand any chance of winning the election of 1916, was obvious. They must lure into their party large numbers of former Bull Moose progressives. The only way they could accomplish that was to persuade Bull Moosers that the Democratic party alone held out hope of a dynamic program of economic and social reform. They must abandon the philosophy of the New Freedom which they had espoused in 1912 and embrace that of the New Nationalism.

Whatever his reputation as a man who never compromised principles, Wilson did not hesitate in the face of political reality. He set about to persuade former Bull Moosers that he was the champion of their brand of progressivism. The one-time followers of Roosevelt were skeptical. Then, in spring 1916, Bull Moosers and a few Democratic allies were laboring to win congressional approval of the Federal Farm Loan Bill, a measure for extending long-term credit to farmers on the basis of land and improvements. Seeing his opportunity, Wilson gave the legislation a presidential shove, whereupon it secured enactment. Bull Moosers were pleased.

When the political campaign of 1916 got underway, the Democrats met in Saint Louis and renominated Wilson and Marshall. The Republicans, meeting in Chicago, nominated the governor of New York, Charles Evans Hughes, a man of high intelligence and unsurpassed integrity. His views ranged somewhere between those of progressives and the Old Guard.

Spokesmen for Bull Moose progressives advised Wilson that two measures pending in Congress would provide a final test of his conversion to their type of progressivism: a child labor bill and a workmen's compensation bill. Now Wilson went to work, put pressure on Democrats in Congress, and in September 1916 both bills were passed. That same month Wilson also signed the Warehouse Act, a progressive measure designed to assist farmers in financing crops.

Large numbers of people who had supported Roosevelt and the New Nationalism in 1912 were now convinced that Wilson was their man.

Reinforcing the president's standing with Bull Moosers was the reminder that Wilson had "kept us out of war." The progressives felt certain that American entry into the war would shatter chances of further domestic reform — and were certain also that war would restore leaders of industry and finance to their former positions of influence. They were particularly susceptible to the appeal that Wilson was a champion of peace. The slogan "he kept us out of war" implied that the president, if reelected, would continue to stay clear of the European conflict.

Wilson in 1916 won a narrow victory over Hughes, 9,100,000 to 8,500,000. On election night, both Wilson and Hughes went to bed thinking that Hughes had been elected. Early

Woodrow Wilson was born in this house in Staunton, Virginia, in 1856. When he was two, his family moved to Augusta, Georgia. His earliest memories were of the Civil War. The Pierce Arrow was Wilson's car during his second term as president.

returns indicated that the Republican candidate had won a smashing victory in the Northeast and Middle West, losing only New Hampshire, Ohio, and Missouri. As expected, Wilson had dominated "the solid South." Then, in the early morning hours, telegraph instruments began to tap out the startling news that the president was running like a prairie fire in the western half of the country. When returns were finally tabulated,

In 1917 an amendment to the Constitution granting women the vote was submitted to Congress. It was passed by both houses and the necessary two-thirds of the states ratified it. In August 1920 the Nineteenth Amendment became effective. Why couldn't women vote prior to this time?

Wilson had carried every state from the Great Plains westward, except South Dakota and Oregon. Those western electoral votes, particularly the thirteen of California, gave Wilson his margin in the electoral college, 277-254.

Wilson's Second Term

In February 1917 President Wilson signed the Smith-Hughes Bill, a progressive measure which provided federal grants to states for promoting instruction in agriculture and the trades. Two years later, in spring 1919, Congress proposed the Nineteenth Amendment to the Constitution, guaranteeing women the right to vote. (This amendment received no encouragement from the White House, for Wilson took a dim view of women's participation in politics.) Women had long voted in a few states, particularly in the West, but not in the country as a whole. The Nineteenth Amendment was ratified in the summer of 1920.

Those who had rallied to Wilson in the hope that his reelection would keep the wheels of progressive reform turning, and would keep the country out of Europe's war, soon saw their hopes and dreams shattered. Within three months after the election—even before Wilson took the oath of office the second time—relations between the United States and Germany were ruptured. In April 1917 the United States entered World War I. (See next chapter.) As progressives had long feared, the war stifled the reform spirit. Not until Franklin D. Roosevelt became the president in 1933 would the progressive, liberal movement in America get up a fresh head of steam.

Whatever their disappointment in the years after 1916, progressives could look back over the previous fifteen or so years with satisfaction. In that period they had brought forth numerous reforms at the national, state, and local levels of government. Those reforms had strengthened democracy in America, enlarged the public's regulation of economic activities, and made some headway toward relieving the distress of society's victims. At the national level, Wilson certainly had presided over the most progressive administration in America to that time. Primarily because of those progressive accomplishments, most historians have rated Wilson as one of the top four or five chief executives in the history of the Republic (usually behind Lincoln, Washington, and Franklin D. Roosevelt).

Wilson and Black Americans

Like most white Americans of his time, Wilson never seriously questioned the assumption that white people were "superior" to those who were black or yellow. From that premise he moved easily to the conclusion that discrimination on the basis of color was not evil and, on the contrary, was, within limits, desirable.

Whatever his racial attitudes, Wilson nevertheless had sought black support during his first campaign of 1912. As a consequence, several leading spokesmen for black Americans, including W. E. B. Du Bois, urged Negroes who were at liberty to vote to mark their ballots for the southern-bred governor of New Jersey.

Wilson in 1913 first expressed sympathy for a plan, fashioned by white and black proponents of racial equality, for establishment of a National Race Commission to study race relations in America. Later he changed his mind, explaining that such a commission might provoke southern members of Congress and thus defeat his entire legislative program.

Because of the new president's southern connections, and his political indebtedness to southern whites, it was not long before white men from the South had more power in Washington than at any time since the Civil War. Some of Wilson's southern appointees, with consent of the president and his cabinet, immediately set about to segregate their departments. Accordingly, the Bureau of the Census, Post Office Department, and Bureau of Engraving, over the next several months, segregated workers in offices, shops, rest rooms, and restaurants. Negroes who objected were fired. Newly appointed federal officials in southern states took an even harder line. With approval of their superiors in Washington, they began to dismiss or demote black civil servants.

Such proceedings brought anguished complaints from black leaders and also from a number of northern and western progressives. Frank I. Cobb, the editor of the New York *World* who to this point had been a supporter of Wilson, declared: "It is a small, mean, petty discrimination and Mr. Wilson ought to have set his heel upon this presumptuous Jim-Crow government the moment it was established."[4] As for the president, he wrote in 1913 that "I would say that I do

---

[4] Quoted in Arthur S. Link, *Woodrow Wilson and the Progressive Era, 1910-1914,* copyright 1954 (New York: Harper & Row, Publishers, Inc.).

approve of the segregation that is being attempted in several of the departments." Still, the attacks on the racist practices of his administration jarred Wilson. The segregationist policy was reversed in the Treasury Department, and other departments of the national government ended plans to impose segregation on their government employees.

Blacks were not the only racial minority in America to suffer because of the racist attitudes of the Wilson administration. When the state legislature in California permitted discrimination against Japanese-Americans, there was no criticism from the White House that it was unjust and undemocratic. There was only a lame appeal that the legislators phrase the measure as inoffensively as possible so as to avoid touching off a new wave of anti-Americanism in the country of Japan.

Woodrow Wilson's great intellect notwithstanding, the twenty-eighth president, like most of his progressive contemporaries, failed to see that democracy's prosperity, indeed its survival, required that the promise of the democratic life be held out equally to all citizens, whatever their race or color. Not until after World War II would progressives (or liberals, as they came to be called) make a serious effort to come to grips with that truth.

STUDY GUIDE: Many of the goals of Wilson's New Freedom were reached during his first term. Major reforms were accomplished by the Underwood-Simmons Act lowering the tariff and the Federal Reserve Act reforming banking and currency systems. Wilson came to agree with Roosevelt and the progressives on how to control big business. He supported the Stevens Trade Commission Bill outlawing unfair trade practices.

When World War I broke out in Europe in 1914, Wilson was determined to keep America out of the conflict. Roosevelt urged that the country should made large-scale war preparations. Wilson opposed preparations for war. His stand against war and his support of social welfare legislation won him the support of many progressives. He narrowly defeated Republican candidate Charles Evans Hughes in the election of 1916. Although a few progressive measures were passed, Wilson increasingly turned his attention to the war in Europe. United States entry into World War I marked the end of the progressive era.

SUMMING UP THE CHAPTER

Names and Terms to Identify

Frances Willard	Leon Czolgosz
Jane Addams	Charles Evans Hughes
W. E. B. Du Bois	Mann-Elkins Bill
Wright Brothers	Seventeenth Amendment
Matthew A. Henson	New Nationalism
William C. Gorgas	New Freedom
Walter Reed	Federal Reserve Act of 1913
Lincoln Steffens	Smith-Lever Act

Study Questions and Points to Review

1. Name the organization that was established to break down barriers of segregation, secure rights of Negroes to vote, and in other ways help the black man to obtain his civil liberties.

2. Who was the first man to reach the North Pole?

3. Name the philosophy which taught that man, using his intellectual and spiritual resources, could break in on the evolutionary process and, within limits, determine his own destiny.

4. Who were the muckrakers?

5. Who opposed McKinley in the presidential election of 1900?

6. Name the author and title of the book that charged the meat-packing industry with palming off on unsuspecting customers meat that was contaminated.

7. How did Theodore Roosevelt bring about an end to the anthracite coal strike?

8. Theodore Roosevelt was considered a champion of conservation of natural resources. Name three things he did to advance conservation.

9. Why did Theodore Roosevelt decline a third term in the White House?

10. Who were the presidential candidates in the election of 1908? of 1912?

11. Which amendment of the United States Constitution guaranteed women the right to vote?

Topics for Discussion

1. Compare the ideas of Social Darwinism and pragmatism. How did pragmatism serve as an intellectual foundation for the progressive movement?

2. What were some of the principal problems in American society that progressives sought to change?

3. Compare the Populist revolt with the progressive movement.

4. Evaluate the status of black Americans in the years 1900-1917.

Subjects for Reports or Essays

1. The author Walter Lord has called the period 1900-1914 the "good years." Write an essay defending or challenging the idea that the years 1900-1914 merit such a title.

2. Recalling what you read in Chapter 10 on Theodore Roosevelt's foreign policies, and what you read in this chapter, write an essay defending or challenging the results of two presidential polls by historians which rate Roosevelt as one of the country's "near-great" chief executives.

3. Sample the writings of the muckrakers. Then, write your own evaluation of the muckrakers.

4. Assume it is November 1912. You are a newspaper editor. The presidential election is a few days away. Write an editorial endorsing one of the various candidates for president.

5. Write a brief report for classroom presentation on one of the following topics: (a) Peary's expedition to the North Pole; (b) the conquest of yellow fever; (c) the sinking of the *Titanic*; (d) the San Francisco earthquake; (e) Finley Peter Dunne's Mr. Dooley.

Projects, Activities, and Skills

1. Prepare a display on the invention and early development of the airplane. Exhibit models and photographs of early airplanes.

2. Arrange a classroom exhibit on Robert E. Peary's expedition to the North Pole. In your display use pictures of Peary, Matthew Henson, Peary's ship, and the equipment used. On a map trace Peary's progress from the time he left New York until he reached the pole.

3. Use a stamp collection to show how famous American women have been honored on U.S. postage stamps.

4. The years covered in this chapter — 1900-1914 — saw many significant changes and innovations in the newspaper. On the basis of outside reading, prepare a report on some of these changes. Consider the following in your discussion: the comic strip, magazine supplements, the Sunday edition, political cartoons, news photography, foreign language papers, feature columns, and the community weekly.

5. On an outline map of your state, shade in the following: national, state, and local parks, forests, grasslands, wildlife refuges, and public lands. Do you feel that a sufficient portion of the land in your state has been set aside for conservation of natural resources? What do you think is the greatest conservation problem in your state?

6. From magazines or other sources, make a portfolio of illustrations showing representative samples — for the years 1900-1914 — of one of the following: architecture, furniture, fashions, methods of travel.

Further Readings

General

Following the Color Line by Ray Stannard Baker. A contemporary account written in 1908 about black Americans in the Civil War.

The Good Years: From 1900 to the First World War by Walter Lord.

The Muckrakers ed. by Arthur Weinberg and Lila Weinberg. A useful collection of muckraking articles.

The Shame of the Cities by Lincoln Steffens. A classic muckraking work on municipal corruption.

Biography

The Life and Times of William Howard Taft: A Biography (2 vols.) by Henry F. Pringle.

A Negro Explorer at the North Pole by Matthew A. Henson. Henson's first-person account.

The North Pole by Robert E. Peary. Memoirs.

The Roosevelt Family of Sagamore Hill by Hermann Hagedorn.

Twenty Years at Hull House by Jane Addams. The story of one of the first settlement houses in the United States.

Woodrow Wilson and the Politics of Morality by John Morton Blum.

Woodrow Wilson and the Progressive Era: 1910-1917 by Arthur S. Link.

Fiction, Essays, and Music

The Fireside Book of Favorite American Songs by Margaret Bradford Boni and others.

The Jungle by Upton Sinclair. A classic novel about the meat-packing industry.

The Pit by Frank Norris. A business struggle provides suspense and drama.

A Tree Grows in Brooklyn by Betty Smith. The story of poverty in a Brooklyn tenement early in this century.

CHAPTER 13

WORLD WAR I

IF A POLLSTER on June 27, 1914, had asked a cross section of the American people to give the location of the city of Sarajevo, probably not one person in twenty-five could have given a correct answer. Six weeks later a large majority of Americans could have located Sarajevo and offered additional information about the city as well.

Sarajevo in 1914 was the capital of Bosnia, a part of present-day Yugoslavia, a province of the sprawling Austrian Empire. It was populated by Slavs who seethed under the rule of their Austrian masters. Bosnia was a hotbed of revolution, much of it inspired by neighboring Serbia. The Austrian government was sensitive to the unrest in the southeastern part of its empire and was considering granting considerable autonomy to the Balkan provinces. To demonstrate their good intentions, Austria's leaders also had arranged an official visit to Sarajevo by the heir apparent to the Austrian throne, Archduke Francis Ferdinand, and his wife, Sophie.

When he arrived at Sarajevo on Sunday morning, June 28, Francis Ferdinand was in high spirits. Throngs of people lined the narrow streets. Scattered among the crowd, however, were seven young Serbian revolutionary patriots. As the archduke's open automobile moved toward the town hall, one of the patriots hurled a bomb. Off target, the bomb exploded in the crowd and wounded several people. On arrival at the town hall, the archduke complained: "Mr. Mayor, I come to visit you and I am greeted with bombs." Soothed by his wife and determined to prove his royal courage, Francis Ferdinand continued the tour. A few minutes later his driver made a wrong turn and stopped. Whereupon another of the youthful patriots thrust his arm over the side of the automobile, and fired a pistol two times. One bullet struck Francis Ferdinand in the neck, the other hit Sophie in the abdomen. Within minutes the royal visitors were dead.

Americans and most Europeans read of the affair at Sarajevo in the next day's newspapers and tended to shrug it off as rather typical of political life in the turbulent Balkans. Even the capitals of Europe were relatively calm. Nobody realized that the young Serbian had fired the first shots in a conflict which over the next fifty-two months would claim the lives of upward of ten million soldiers and seamen and uncounted millions of civilians. The German kaiser, whose government was allied with that of Austria, was so little distressed that he continued plans for a summer cruise.

Europe's leaders obviously had not taken the pulse of the Austrian government. The Austrians were determined to use the royal murders as an excuse for punishing Serbia, which seemed to them to threaten the life of the Austrian empire. Their first move was to make certain that they had the support of their ally, Germany. The government in Berlin agreed to stand behind Austria's chastisement of Serbia.

Russia, however, had historic ambitions of its own in the Balkans, and the Russians were not prepared to tolerate an expansion of Austrian influence in the area.

WAR BEGINS

Austria declared war on Serbia in late July 1914. Russia began to mobilize its armies. Because of the Austro-German alliance, a Russian attack on Austria was certain to mean war between Russia and Germany.

War against Russia alone was not a matter of undue concern to the Germans; they and their Austrian allies probably could have won such a conflict. Russia, however, had an important ally to the west of Germany, namely, France. The French were still smarting over the humiliating defeat they had suffered in the Franco-Prussian War of 1870-71. Millions of Frenchmen in 1914 longed for the day when they might avenge the disaster of 1870-71 and recover their lost provinces of Alsace and Lorraine. Thus, if Russia and Germany came to blows, the French would probably join Russia in the conflict.

Accordingly, the German government in the last days of July 1914 demanded that the Russians stop mobilizing. When Russia refused, the

HEADLINE
EVENTS

1914 Archduke Francis Ferdinand assassinated
Austria declares war on Serbia
Russians mobilize for war
Germans declare war on Russia
France refuses German neutrality demand
Germans sweep through Belgium to attack France
Great Britain declares war on Germany
Wilson declares neutrality
French government abandons Paris
Germans defeat Russians at Tannenberg
Germans withdraw divisions from France to send to Tannenberg
French and British expeditionary forces dig in along Marne River
British declare North Sea a military area

1915 *Imperial Germany and the Industrial Revolution* (Veblen)
Germany announces waters around British Isles are war zone
Wilson warns Germany that U.S. will hold Germans accountable for any lives lost in war zone
Americans begin loaning money to Allies
German U-boat sinks *Lusitania*
U-boat sinks *Arabic*
U-boat torpedoes *Sussex*

1916 Battle of Verdun
Irish nationalists strike for independence from Great Britain
National Defense Act establishes Council of National Defense
Wilson again protests U-boat torpedoing
Germany pledges that submarines will not attack merchant ships without warning

1917 Germans announce they will resume unrestricted submarine warfare
Zimmermann telegram intercepted
United States breaks off diplomatic relations with Germany
Three merchant ships flying U.S. flag are torpedoed
Wilson asks for declaration of war
Congress declares war on German Empire

Committee on Public Information (Creel Committee)
French defeated at Chemin des Dames
Allies introduce convoy system
Pershing's American Expeditionary Force arrives in France
Selective Service Act
Espionage Act
First War Loan Act
Food Administration; Hoover appointed administrator
Fuel Administration established
First American battalions move into front lines
Italian army cracks at Caporetto
Bolshevik revolution in Russia

1918 Wilson announces Fourteen Points
Baruch heads War Industries Board
Treaty of Brest-Litovak
Germans launch offensive; attack British near Somme River
General Foch appointed supreme commander of British and French armies
Germans attack along Belgian-French frontier
War Labor Board created
Germans try to divert attention from Flanders by launching attack at Chemin des Dames
Sedition Act
Aisne-Marne offensive begins
U.S. divisions join Foch along Marne
Battle of Château-Thierry
Battle of Belleau Woods
Second Battle of the Marne
Allies and Americans send military forces to Murmansk and Archangel
American divisions attack Marne salient
Meuse-Argonne offensive begins
German resistance weakened
Prince Max of Baden tries to end war by diplomacy
Armistice signed

1920 American forces leave Siberia

Germans declared war on August 1. Germany, meanwhile, had demanded assurance of French neutrality in the event of a Russo-German war. The French rejected the German demands. Germany, in a higher state of military readiness than the other European powers, hit France with full force before the Russians could strike from the east. After knocking France from the war, in less than seven weeks, the Germans hoped to wheel their armies around and take on the Russians. To meet the exacting timetable, however, it was necessary for German armies to sweep into France across the countryside of Belgium in violation of a long-standing treaty guaranteeing Belgian neutrality. When the Germans moved across the Belgian frontier, Great Britain, which for many generations had held that it could not tolerate domination of Belgium by a major continental power, declared war on Germany.

The date was August 4, 1914.

STUDY GUIDE: Austria declared war on Serbia after the assassination of Archduke Francis Ferdinand and his wife. Russia mobilized in spite of Germany's demands to stop. France refused Germany's request to remain neutral. Germany invaded France through Belgium and violated Belgian neutrality. Thereupon Great Britain declared war on Germany.

AMERICA'S INITIAL RESPONSE

These events caught the United States by surprise. This was in part because American diplomatic representatives in Europe had failed to sense the crisis and had not kept leaders in Washington informed. During those fateful weeks after Sarajevo, for example, the American minister in Belgium was secluded at a country place where he was writing a novel about rural life in Ohio.

Wilson Proclaims Neutrality

The American leaders, like their counterparts in Europe, decided that the war would be short, probably over in a few weeks or months. In modern war—so it seemed in August 1914—new weapons of immense power, the mobility of armies, and improved communications had given the offense such superiority over the defense that an extended conflict was out of the question. The United States decided to maintain a stiff neutrality, for this clearly was one of those periodic European upheavals that President Washington in 1796 had warned Americans to avoid. As President Wilson proclaimed the country's neutrality, Americans felt relief, even a curious pride, that an ocean separated them from Europe's latest bloodletting. In the words of one newspaper: "Peace-loving citizens of this country will now rise up and tender a hearty vote of thanks to Columbus for having discovered America."

Attitude Toward France

More important than anti-German or pro-British sentiments was the American attitude toward France. Whatever they might feel about the British, Germans, Russians, or Austrians, a great many Americans could not turn their backs on France. It was very simple. The French had helped the Americans in the War of Independence. And many Americans sensed that their country might not have become what it was if the French had not rallied to the support of the thirteen colonies in the 1770s and 1780s.

In the early months of the war millions of Americans revised their opinions and became more favorable to the British and French. Many who had leaned toward the Germans at the start of the war became neutral or, more often, pro-Ally. Others who had tried to view the war impartially turned to outright support of the British and French. And those Americans who had lined up with the British and French at first became more solid in their support of the Allies.

Still, this was Europe's war and in 1914 most Americans despite their sympathies were determined to stand apart.

American leaders were determined to compel observance of their rights as neutrals, particularly on the seas. The idea that belligerent powers must not interfere with peaceful activities of non-belligerents was an American tradition. Since 1776 the United States had managed to persuade most major powers to accept American principles concerning the rights of neutral countries, including their right to free use of the seas. Still, when the first shots rang out in Europe in August 1914, America's rights as a neutral seemed to present no large problem. Many observers believed it would be a short war and that vessels carrying goods from America would not become a concern of military strategists.

A Long War

In August 1914, the Germans, fighting on two fronts, were about to score a dazzling victory. In the last days of the month, at Tannenberg in East Prussia, German armies under General Paul von Hindenburg administered a disastrous defeat to Russian forces bearing down on Germany from the east.

In the west, meanwhile, the kaiser's forces had swept through Belgium and fixed their sights on Paris. In the first days of September the French government abandoned the capital. Then, just before the action at Tannenberg, the German chief of staff, fearful that the Russians might crack German defenses, withdrew divisions from France and dispatched them to the Eastern Front. The divisions arrived at Tannenberg after the great battle was over.

At the same time, several thousand French soldiers rushed to the battlefront, some of them arriving in taxicabs seized in Paris by a French general. Along with a small but spirited British force, they dug in along the Marne River fifty miles northeast of Paris. In the second and third weeks of September 1914, in one of the epic battles of history, they brought the German advance to a halt.

In the next few weeks one fact became clear: the defense had tipped the scales heavily against the offense. The opposing armies settled down into trenches, and the dream of a short war vanished. It would be a long war of position, designed to wear the other side out. The Western Front would consume millions of men and inestimable quantities of arms, ammunition, and supplies. While the new circumstances presented serious problems for the Germans, they seemed even more ominous for the British and French, who could not match Germany's industrial and agricultural capacity. Still, there was hope for the Allies, for the British navy ruled the Atlantic sea lanes to a great arsenal, the United States.

"Neutral" U.S. Sends Arms to Britain and France

Before the close of the year 1914, sea lanes of the North Atlantic were churning with hundreds of merchant vessels carrying thousands of tons of munitions and supplies to Britain and France. For the United States, suffering an economic recession when the war broke out, the new trade seemed fortunate. By the summer of 1915 the country was basking in prosperity. The Germans found it impossible to obtain arms and supplies in North America because of British control of the sea. They protested sale of war materials to Britain and France, claiming that Americans were not maintaining neutrality. The American view, resting on law and international precedent, was that private American citizens had a right to trade with belligerents if they wished, and nothing obliged them to avoid discriminating between belligerents.

What about loans to belligerents?

If it wished to remain neutral, the government of the United States could neither sell arms nor lend money to belligerents. But private citizens of the United States could do both. At the beginning of the war the Wilson administration urged Americans not to lend money to Europe's warring powers. Then the administration quietly relaxed the policy. In summer 1915, the policy was abandoned completely. It was obvious that loans were necessary for continued Allied purchases in America and hence for maintaining the current high level of prosperity.

From that point on, American citizens loaned billions of dollars to the Allies. Did this activity compromise American neutrality? It is hard to say. Certainly Americans who had a financial stake in an Allied victory were not apt to be neutral in thought. Still, there is no evidence that financial interests, as millions of Americans later came to believe, influenced President Wilson's policy or helped to take the United States to war, in 1917, on the side of the Allies.

STUDY GUIDE: When World War I began, President Wilson was determined to keep the United States neutral. As the war continued, American sympathy for Britain and France grew stronger. Instead of the short war America had foreseen, the Great War turned into a long conflict fought in trenches along the Western Front. Despite German protests, American businessmen sold vast quantities of war materials and loaned billions of dollars to Britain and France.

AMERICA'S NEUTRALITY CHALLENGED

The commerce on the seas made it inevitable that neutral rights would become an issue. It was also inevitable that Great Britain, wishing to

FIRST WORLD WAR

When war broke out in Europe in 1914 many Americans felt that the United States should make every effort to remain neutral. Isolationist, antiwar feeling was strong. However, once the United States declared war, most of the public patriotically upheld the country's stand.

3   Courtesy Philadelphia Free Library, Prints and Pictures

1   J. W. McDonald

2   J. W. McDonald

1

Sentiment against the war was expressed in the popular song "I Didn't Raise My Boy To Be a Soldier."

2

The song "I'm Glad to Be the Mother of a Soldier Boy" was written in answer to those who opposed the war.

3

This navy recruitment poster was drawn in 1917 by Howard Chandler Christy. Christy was a well-known American illustrator and painter. His illustrations appeared in various New York magazines. Christy's painting *Signing of the Constitution* is in the Capitol building in Washington, D.C.

press its sea advantage, would encounter difficulty with the United States.

The first test came in November 1914 when the British proclaimed the North Sea a military area. They began to plant mines in clear violation of traditional ideas about freedom of the seas. A neutral vessel had to stop at a British port for instructions on how to sail safely past the mines. While in port the British could search the ship for contraband and delay the voyage for weeks or months. The British also arbitrarily redefined contraband. Contraband previously had consisted of materials having direct military use, meaning that food, medicine, and materials for civilian consumption could flow freely to belligerent ports. But recognizing that the old idea of contraband was antiquated in this new era of total war, and wishing to capitalize on their sea power, the British lengthened the contraband list. By 1915 the list included almost everything that a neutral might wish to ship to Germany.

The British made other departures from traditional rules. Their navy took unprecedented liberties with the right of visit and search. Old rules permitted belligerent ships to stop neutral merchantmen and search for contraband, but the British claimed—correctly—that the present war had created exceptional conditions. It was impossible, they noted, to search a modern vessel in a few hours. While a British cruiser was bobbing alongside a neutral merchantman, it would make an easy target for an enemy submarine. So the British hauled neutral ships to British ports for visit and search, a procedure that sometimes delayed neutral merchantmen for months. There also was the matter of British blockading procedure, patently illegal under existing international law. Instead of locating warships near enemy ports—in accord with conventional rules—the British stationed their cruisers in the sea lanes hundreds of miles from port, where they intercepted neutral commerce. Then sometimes the British opened American mail in search of contraband, and at other times their merchantmen flew the Stars and Stripes as a disguise.

Reaction to British Policies

How did the United States respond to British violations of its rights as a neutral? The Wilson administration protested, but the protests were friendly and carried no threats.

Economic considerations help to explain America's patience in dealing with the British.

Any sort of clash with Britain would have threatened commerce with the Allies and would have weakened the American economy. More important, the government in Washington, in spite of the president's appeal for neutrality, favored the cause of the Allies. Wilson did not necessarily want the Allies to crush the Germans. Indeed he continuously sought a mediated settlement of the war, a "peace without victory," as he described it in January 1917. Still, if it was to be a war to the bitter end, he certainly did not want the Germans to win. Hence, Wilson did not propose, by insisting too strongly on his country's rights as a neutral, to deprive the Allies of advantages on the sea. Equally, he did not want the United States to get into war against the Allies.

Relations with Germany

Despite widespread outrage in the United States over Germany's treatment of Belgium, diplomatic relations between the governments in Washington and Berlin were without incident in the early months of the war. Then came an abrupt change. In February 1915 the Germans announced that the waters around the British Isles were a war zone and that their submarines would attempt to sink enemy merchantmen on sight. They added that inasmuch as the British sometimes tried to protect their vessels by flying neutral flags they could not guarantee the safety of neutral ships.

Like the British military area in the North Sea, the war zone ran roughshod over time-honored ideas about freedom of the seas. Unrestricted submarine warfare also ran directly against the old idea that a belligerent warship must not destroy an enemy merchantman without first making certain of its identity and providing for the safety of passengers and crew. Since some British merchant vessels were armed with concealed deck guns, the Germans considered it foolhardy to expose their U-boats, of which they had only a handful, by giving the traditional warning.

How did leaders in Washington respond? While President Wilson issued mild protests against British activity in the North Sea, he declared that his government would hold Germany to strict accountability for American lives and ships lost in the so-called war zone. Inconsistent? Yes, for there was scant difference in striking a mine, fixed silently beneath the ocean's surface, or being struck by a torpedo launched from a submarine. And Germany had as much right as did Britain to depart from conventional rules. Still, one must not judge Wilson's policy solely on the basis of its consistency or even the president's frequent pronouncements about international morality. His purpose in preventing Germany from winning the war must be considered, too. Then one must keep in mind that there was small likelihood that American merchantmen would run afoul of British mines, for few vessels flying the Stars and Stripes had reason to operate in the North Sea. The chances of damage and death in the war zone, where numerous American ships were active, seemed large and hence a stronger protest seemed in order.

The *Lusitania*

Among the ships plying in and out of Germany's war zone was the British passenger liner *Lusitania,* swiftest in the transatlantic service. Because the Germans had been unable to sink any ships traveling faster than fourteen knots, the British concluded that this great vessel was immune from attack. Even if torpedoed the *Lusitania*'s watertight compartments presumably would prevent the ship from going down. Such assurances comforted nearly two hundred Americans on May 1, 1915, as they filed up the *Lusitania*'s gangplank. They were sailing in defiance of advertisements placed in New York newspapers by the German government reminding them that Britain was at war and that they traveled on the liner at their own risk. So confident was the *Lusitania*'s captain about the invulnerability of his ship that he ignored instructions to conduct boat drills. As the liner neared the southern coast of Ireland, he ordered a reduction in speed.

Scanning the waters off Ireland on May 7, 1915, was the periscope of a German U-20, a far-ranging submarine with only a few torpedoes left which was preparing to return to Germany.

In the ship's log the U-20's commander recorded: "Four funnels and two masts of a steamer. . . . Ship is made out to be large passenger steamer. . . . Clean bow shot at a distance of 700 meters. . . . Torpedo hits starboard side right behind the bridge. An unusually heavy explosion takes place with a very strong explosion cloud (cloud reaches far beyond front funnel). The explosion of the torpedo must have been followed by a second one (boiler or coal or powder?). . . . The ship stops immediately and heels over to starboard very quickly, immersing simul-taneously at the bow . . . the name *Lusitania* becomes visible in golden letters."

The U-boat captain's terse account failed to capture the human drama aboard the stricken liner. Hundreds of terror-crazed people battled rushing water, crashing metal, and each other in a mad struggle for survival. Their struggle lasted only eighteen minutes. When the *Lusitania* slid beneath the waves, it took 1,198 people to watery graves. Of the dead, 128 were Americans.

Reaction to the *Lusitania* Affair

News of the *Lusitania* tragedy produced an electric reaction in the United States. Even more than the invasion of Belgium the previous summer, it outraged American opinion and moved the country against Germany. It made no difference that the liner had carried 4,200 cases of rifle cartridges which the British intended to use to kill German soldiers on the Western Front, or that the German government had warned Americans to stay off the ship. The *Lusitania* had carried no defensive armament and nothing had prevented the U-20 from rising to the suface of the sea and giving the conventional warning before sinking the liner.

President Wilson shared the country's shock and outrage. For weeks the transatlantic wires cracked with diplomatic communications between Washington and Berlin. Some of the president's advisers urged war, but Wilson was a

In 1915 when a German U-boat sank the British liner S.S. *Lusitania* killing 1,198 passengers, Americans pressed Wilson for action. How did he handle the situation?

peaceful man. Moreover, he recognized that despite their fury most Americans desperately wanted to stay clear of hostilities. Wilson struck a responsive chord in a speech at Philadelphia three days after the *Lusitania* disaster when he asserted: "There is such a thing as a man being too proud to fight. There is such a thing as a nation being so right that it does not need to convince others by force that it is right."

Still, the president pressed Germany for a disavowal of the *Lusitania* sinking and assurance that there would be no repetition. When his messages became warlike, his secretary of state, William Jennings Bryan, who conscientiously had tried to be neutral, resigned from the cabinet. The new secretary was Robert Lansing, who looked with sympathy on the prospect that the United States might one day enter the war on the side of the Allies.

The Germans defended the attack on the *Lusitania* as an act of just self-defense. They also hoped—in the words of the American ambassador in Berlin—that people in the United States would "get excited about baseball or a new scandal and forget" the *Lusitania* affair. Accordingly they stalled, and Americans lost interest.

In August 1915, a U-boat sank another British liner, the *Arabic*. Two Americans were killed. Fearing the *Arabic* sinking would help pro-Allied war hawks, Germany apologized in October 1915 for the *Arabic* incident. Moreover, the German government promised an indemnity and announced that U-boat commanders were under orders to sink no more liners without providing for the safety of passengers and crew. The *Arabic* pledge was a victory for Wilsonian diplomacy, although the president had put American prestige on the line on the issue of unrestricted submarine warfare. What if the Germans had a change of heart and unleashed their U-boats? Could the United States as a great power back away from its *Lusitania-Arabic* stand?

The American position against the submarines was reinforced in the spring of 1916 when a U-boat torpedoed the French channel steamer *Sussex*. The Wilson government protested, and again the Germans backed down, pledging that submarines would not attack merchant vessels without warning—provided the United States would compel other belligerents to observe the "laws of humanity." In other words, if the United States did not force the British to relax their starvation blockade of Germany, the government in Berlin would not feel bound by the

Sussex pledge. Despite this condition the Germans placed on their agreement, the pledge brought a dramatic reduction in tension between the United States and Germany. Relations between the two countries remained placid till February 1917.

Now it was the Allies' turn to try American patience.

STUDY GUIDE: America's rights as a neutral nation were violated on the high seas by the British. Through blockades and stop-and-search tactics, Britain interfered with American merchant shipping. Although the United States protested, sympathy for the Allied cause kept Wilson from taking a hard line. When Germany began unrestricted submarine warfare, Wilson protested more strongly. Protest turned to outrage when a German submarine sank the passenger liner, *Lusitania*, killing over a thousand people. A German pledge not to attack merchant vessels without warning eased tensions.

AMERICA MOVES TOWARD WAR

The world's attention in spring 1916 was fixed on the ancient French fortress of Verdun, where two great armies stood locked in the deadliest combat of World War I (more than a half-million would die in "the Hell of Verdun"). Irish nationalists decided the time was ripe to strike a blow for independence from Great Britain. Incensed at this stab in the back at a time when they were fighting for their lives on the Western Front, the British put down the rebellion with needless ferocity. Their action aroused a storm of anti-British feeling in the United States.

In July 1916, the English issued a blacklist of eighty-five persons and firms in the United States suspected of doing business with Germany. British subjects were forbidden to have dealings with persons or businesses on the blacklist. Americans were furious, for as neutrals they had as much right to trade with Germany as with the Allies. Even the New York *Times,* strongly pro-Ally, called the blacklist the "most tactless, foolish, and unnecessary act of the British Government during the war." President Wilson shared the national irritation and wrote that "I am, I must admit, about at the end of my patience with Great Britain and the Allies."

Wilson was further annoyed by the cold response of the Allies to his efforts in the summer and autumn of 1916 to end the war by mediation. The president thought his proposals fair to all belligerents, and the Germans seemed to show some interest, but they may only have been trying to win favor with Wilson. However, after their success in halting the attacks on Verdun in June 1916, the French had begun to entertain hopes of victory. Hence France showed little interest in Wilson's proposals. Then, the British, in early July 1916, launched a massive offensive along the Somme—an action in which the British introduced the mechanized tank. The outcome was a disaster. The Germans cut down the British. If the British had sat down to talk peace with the Germans after the Somme tragedy they would have been negotiating from a position of weakness. Not until their military position had improved would Britons consider Wilson's proposals for peace via mediation.

The harsh treatment of the Irish, the blacklist, and the refusal to mediate disgusted Wilson. Still, the president never lost sight of his view that a German victory would run counter to American interests. Thus he refused to threaten any strong action that might weaken the Allied position against the Germans. He simply hoped that the war might soon end in a negotiated settlement—a "peace without victory." If such a peace could not be arranged, Wilson hoped for an Allied triumph.

Then, in early 1917, came a sudden turn in America's relations with Germany.

Submarine Warfare Resumes

After the failure at Verdun, the Germans, in August 1916, gave command of their entire army to Field Marshal Paul von Hindenburg and his brilliant subordinate, General Erich Ludendorff. Toward the end of the year 1916 the two men made an inspection of the Western Front. They found tired and demoralized soldiers, equipment and fortifications in disrepair. They decided that some dramatic action was needed to tilt the military balance in favor of the German army. What was needed? Resumption of unrestricted submarine warfare.

Hindenburg, Ludendorff, and other leaders fully understood that such a drastic step would probably bring the United States into the war. America's regular army, however, was small, and it would require many months to draft and train civilian soldiers and shuttle them to France. Meanwhile—in six months, according to the

German estimate—the unleashed submarine, by severing the New World lifeline of the Allies, would bring Britain and France to their knees. Accordingly, the military consequences of United States entry in the war would be zero.

It was a desperate gamble and there were impassioned protests from German civil leaders. But Imperial Germany decided to take the risk. Unrestricted submarine warfare would resume on the first day of February 1917.

A Revolution in Russia

As matters turned out, this decision was one of the monumental blunders of history, for Russia was on the verge of collapse. And Russia's eventual departure from the war would dramatically tip the military balance on the Western Front in favor of the Germans.

The people of Russia were sick and tired of the war, which had taken a terrible toll of Russian men and money. Many were fed up with the corrupt and inefficient regime of Czar Nicholas II. The result in March 1917 was a revolutionary upheaval which toppled the czarist government and brought to power leaders who hoped to bring liberal democracy to Russia.

The new provisional government sought to keep Russia in the war, but another political group in the country, the Bolsheviks, wanted peace at almost any price. Committed to the idea of establishing a "dictatorship of the proletariat," the Bolsheviks were awaiting an opportunity to overthrow the provisional government. The Germans in spring 1917 then made their second momentous decision of the year—and, in the view of many historians, their second monumental blunder.

The German government contacted the brilliant Bolshevist theoretician Nikolai Lenin, who since 1914 had been living in exile in Switzerland, and arranged to transport him to Russia. With Lenin and the Bolsheviks in control in Russia, the Germans calculated, the Eastern Front would collapse. Guided and inspired by Lenin, the Bolsheviks, in November 1917, overthrew the provisional government and set up a Communist dictatorship. The new Communist government immediately arranged Russia's departure from the war. Peace between Germany and Russia became final in March 1918 via the Treaty of Brest-Litovsk.

As the war with Russia came to an end, the Germans moved hundreds of thousands of soldiers and great quantities of equipment to the Western Front. By the spring of 1918 their forces were clearly superior to the combined armies of Britain and France. Only the arrival of more than two million troops from America in spring-summer 1918, dramatically tilted the military balance to the Allies.

However, the Germans had not grasped soon enough the situation inside Russia. Accordingly, the order to resume unrestricted submarine warfare had already gone into effect on February 1, 1917.

Wilson Faces Germany's Challenge

How did the United States respond to the German order?

For several agonizing days President Wilson wondered if it might not be possible to endure Germany's latest challenge. Woodrow Wilson was a peaceful man who instinctively recoiled at the prospect of acting in a way that would move the United States toward Europe's terrible war. He could not help but recall, moreover, that he had just won reelection based on a campaign slogan that "he kept us out of war."

Nevertheless, Wilson concluded that he could not honorably continue to deal with Germany in light of its resumption of unrestricted submarine warfare. On February 3, 1917, he went before Congress. While professing America's friendship for the people of Germany, Wilson announced that the United States had severed diplomatic relations with the German government. He also warned that if Germany's submarine campaign claimed American ships or lives, "I shall take the liberty of coming again before Congress, to ask that authority be given me to use any means that may be necessary for the protection of our seamen and our people." More precisely, U-boat attacks on American merchantmen or unarmed passenger liners might bring the United States into the war on the side of the Allies.

Over the next few weeks there were no U-boat attacks on passenger liners or American merchantmen. President Wilson, and also a great majority of his countrymen, hoped against hope that the Germans might act with restraint. Still, the pressure on the president to enter the war against Germany was increasing. Some of the pressure was economic, for shipowners, wary of submarines, were canceling sailings and thus causing goods to pile up on wharves of eastern seaports. Much of it came from war hawks, such as Theodore Roosevelt, who believed that Great Britain and France were defending the values of Western civilization. They wanted Wilson to throw America in the balance on the side of the Allies.

The Zimmermann Telegram

At last, late in February 1917, America's fragile peace began to break apart. First there was destruction of the British liner *Laconia* by a U-boat. Among the victims were three Americans. At the time he was absorbing the details of the *Laconia* tragedy, President Wilson received another shock: British authorities handed him an intercepted dispatch, the famous Zimmermann telegram.

Drafted by the German foreign secretary, Alfred Zimmermann, the telegram advised Germany's minister in Mexico City that in event of war with the United States he was to seek an alliance with Mexico. If the Mexicans would become allied with Germany, and if the combined German-Mexican arms emerged victorious in the war, Mexico was to receive "the lost territories in Texas, New Mexico, and Arizona."

Incredible though the proposal was, one could argue that Germany had as much right as the next country to seek allies. Wilson nonetheless was outraged. Fearful that he might set off a national clamor for war, Wilson did not release the Zimmermann note immediately. A few days later he placed before Congress a request for broad authority "to protect our ships and our people in their legitimate and peaceful pursuits on the seas." With such authority he planned to order guns installed on American merchant vessels. Once armed the merchant vessels hopefully could defend themselves against attacks by German submarines.

In Congress, however, were a number of senators and representatives who believed that the United States should go to great lengths to avoid involvement. They were even willing to sacrifice some time-honored notions about freedom of the seas—notions which they thought were out-of-date anyhow. Charging that Wilson was seeking authority to wage undeclared naval war against Germany—and possibly even full-scale war—these pacifist members of Congress attacked the presidential request.

To arouse public support Wilson then released the Zimmermann telegram to the press on March

1, 1917. The country's initial response to the message was disbelief, then anger, but the president's tactic failed to achieve its immediate purpose. Members of the Senate who were opposed to intervention filibustered against the legislation wanted by Wilson. These determined pacifist senators became known to history by the president's description of them: "a little group of willful men."

Congress Declares War

The pace of events now quickened. Without congressional authority Wilson ordered the arming of American merchantmen. Next came news that on March 18 U-boats had torpedoed three merchant vessels flying the Stars and Stripes. Seizing their opportunity, war hawks increased their appeals for hostilities. But, strangely, the events of March 18 seemed to bring a renewed sentiment for peace.

President Wilson spent much of the next two weeks secluded in the White House. He received the disturbing news that Germany's submarine campaign was succeeding beyond expectation and that the icy waters of the North Atlantic were swallowing thousands of tons of Allied shipping. He also learned that Allied credit was near collapse. It appeared that only American intervention in the war (opening the way for the government in Washington to lend money to the Allies) could save Allied finances. And he learned that the morale of the British and French was weakening.

Wilson summoned Congress into special session and on the evening of April 2 made his way up Pennsylvania Avenue to the Capitol. He solemnly entered the chamber of the House of Representatives where all members of Congress, justices of the Supreme Court, and other dignitaries were assembled. Announcing "the world must be made safe for democracy," Wilson asked Congress to declare war on the German Empire. Thunderous applause greeted the request. Across the nation millions of people who for more than two and a half years had prayed for peace were thrilled when they read the president's words.

The war resolution did not pass immediately, for the "willful men" organized another filibuster. After four days, however, the congressional pacifists gave way before the national sentiment for war. The filibuster ended and the war resolution passed overwhelmingly (373-50 in the House, 82-6 in the Senate). Wilson signed it on April 6, 1917. The United States was at war.

STUDY GUIDE: In 1917 the Germans began unrestricted submarine warfare again. They hoped to break the battlefield stalemate and defeat the Allies. Wilson broke off diplomatic relations with Germany, but he resisted pressure to declare war. Hostility to Germany increased after the interception of the Zimmermann telegram. In this telegram the Germans urged a German-Mexican alliance if the United States entered the war. German submarines torpedoed three American ships in March 1917. Wilson grew more uneasy when it became evident that the Allied powers were on the verge of financial collapse. Finally he real-

On April 2, 1917, Woodrow Wilson called a special session of Congress and asked for a declaration of war. What recent events had convinced Wilson this was necessary?

Library of Congress

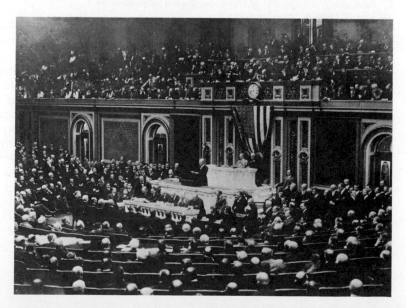

ized there was no alternative. In April 1917 he asked Congress for a declaration of war on Germany.

OVER HERE

Mobilizing a great country for war was a many-sided and complicated business.

The possibility that the country might become involved in the war had occupied Americans almost from the time of the battle along the Marne in September 1914. In those early days a small minority of citizens, including Theodore Roosevelt, a few members of Congress, and fol-

Opponents spoke out vigorously against Wilson's modest war preparedness program. The neutralist William Jennings Bryan resigned as secretary of war over the issue. When America finally entered the war, it was unready. In what areas of national defense was Wilson's program inadequate?

The New-York Historical Society

A Challenge Accepted

To all whom it may concern:

Whereas, President Wilson, speaking recently in St. Louis, challenged those who differ with him as to the immediate need for unusual naval and military preparations to "hire large halls" and state their case to the public, and

Whereas, the various militarist organizations masquerading as "defense" societies and falsely claiming that they alone can speak for American patriotism are deliberately creating a widespread condition of hysteria as to the safety of this country and the danger of foreign invasion, and

Whereas, this reckless propaganda of militarism and jingo-imperialism if allowed to go on unchecked will inevitably lead to the destruction of the principles of liberty and freedom upon which the hope of American Democracy is based;

We hereby announce that

We have accepted the President's challenge and have hired the largest halls in New York, April 6; Buffalo, April 7; Cleveland, April 8; Detroit, April 9; Chicago, April 10; Minneapolis, April 11; Des Moines, April 12; Kansas City, April 13; St. Louis, April 14; Cincinnati, April 15; and Pittsburgh, April 16; where the following American Citizens, who have volunteered their services, will set forth

THE TRUTH ABOUT "PREPAREDNESS"

STEPHEN S. WISE
WASHINGTON GLADDEN
SCOTT NEARING
MARTIN HARDIN
JAMES H. MAURER
HERBERT BIGELOW

GEN. ISAAC R. SHERWOOD
AMOS PINCHOT
A. A. BERLE
ARTHUR L. WEATHERLEY
JOHN HAYNES HOLMES
JOHN A. McSPARRAN

Signed: ANTI "PREPAREDNESS" COMMITTEE
Munsey Building, Washington, D. C.

lowers of a preparedness organization urged that the United States strengthen its military forces.

Like other men of peace in the country, President Wilson was inclined to the pacifist view that a strong military establishment was likely to lead to war. He felt that a country whose military muscles were bulging was not apt to spend much time seeking negotiated settlements of international differences. Advocates of preparedness replied with a logic similar to that used in the present nuclear age. They argued that military power, enabling a government to retaliate quickly to hostile acts by a foreign state, was a way to prevent war rather than a factor apt to draw the government into war.

Wilson's Preparedness Program

After the German "war zone" pronouncement—during the *Lusitania* crisis of spring-summer 1915—President Wilson felt compelled to make concessions to the preparedness view. He was aware that the country's military weakness was hindering his attempt to put diplomatic pressure on Germany. Accordingly, the president, in autumn 1915, asked for legislation that would substantially increase the size of the army and in other ways add to the country's military strength.

Wilson's proposals ran into vigorous opposition. Americans who wanted Germany to win the war knew full well that if the United States ever became a belligerent in the conflict it would be on the side of Germany's enemies. Preparedness, they believed, would move the United States toward belligerency. Hence they opposed preparedness.

More serious was the opposition of many progressives, both of the Republican and Democratic variety. In the progressive view the war was utterly senseless. Its only beneficiaries were heartless arms manufacturers and international bankers. Some progressives had decided that munitions makers and bankers, in league with bloodthirsty militarists, had probably arranged the war for their own profit. It was easy for progressives to conclude that the preparedness movement was a plot by manufacturers and bankers to line their own pockets at the taxpayers' expense. Progressives feared, moreover, that if the United States went to war, their liberal reform movement would be the first casualty. (History would confirm their fear, for once in the war the chief concern of the country became victory, and the domestic reform movement collapsed.)

Wilson went on a speaking tour to rally support for his preparedness program, which was modest and would not come close to putting the country on a war footing. He marched at the head of a preparedness parade in Washington and held numerous conferences with congressional leaders. At length, in June 1916, Congress passed the National Defense Act. Ridiculed by Theodore Roosevelt, the measure among other provisions added a little muscle to the army—over a five-year period. Two months later, a more important law provided for a three-year naval building program.

Such measures fell far short of preparing America for war. When Congress voted for war in April 1917 the regular army had fewer than 130,000 officers and men. The army, moreover, had not yet adopted a standard machine gun, although the machine gun had become the dominant battlefield weapon on the Western Front. American factories had given little thought to turning out artillery pieces, tanks, or warplanes. And American military leaders had barely begun to weigh the problem of war with Germany.

The Draft

The most explosive question was: How could the army in a short time swell its ranks to at least three million men? Boiled down, it was a question of whether the government should rely on volunteers or put a draft system into effect. Debate was heated. Many Americans believed it was a violation of a young man's right to liberty, stated by the Declaration of Independence and guaranteed by the federal Constitution, to compel him to serve in the army.

Other Americans recalled the terrible draft riots of 1863—when the federal government set about to conscript young men for service in the Civil War. They predicted that similar rioting would greet any attempt to conscript men for the present war. Those favoring conscription countered that every young American had a sacred obligation to fight for his country if necessary. They argued that it was undemocratic and unpatriotic to rely on volunteers while permitting other young men to enjoy the safety and prosperity of the home front. An enthusiastic supporter of the draft, Theodore Roosevelt declared: "I would have the son of the multimillionaire and the son of the immigrant who came in steerage

Attention!

ALL MALES between the ages of 21 and 30 years, both inclusive, must personally appear at the polling place in the Election District in which they reside, on

TUESDAY, JUNE 5th, 1917

between the hours of 7 A.M. and 9 P.M. and

Register

in accordance with the President's Proclamation.

Any male person, between these ages, who fails to register on June 5th, 1917, will be subject to imprisonment in jail or other penal institution for a term of one year.

NO EXCUSE FOR FAILURE TO REGISTER WILL BE ACCEPTED

NON-RESIDENTS must apply personally for registration, at the office of the County Clerk, at Kingston, N. Y., AT ONCE, in order that their registration cards may be in the hands of the Registration Board of their home district before June 5, 1917

Employers of males between these ages are earnestly requested to assist in the enforcement of the President's Proclamation.

Signed,

BOARD OF REGISTRATION
of Ulster County
E. T. SHULTIS, Sheriff
C. K. LOUGHRAN, County Clerk
Dr. FRANK JOHNSTON, Medical Officer

The New-York Historical Society

Congress passed a Selective Service Act on May 18, 1917. All men between the ages of 21 and 30 were eligible for the draft and had to register. This is a draft notice from Ulster County, New York. What were the opposing views on the draft? How do you *feel* about today's draft laws? What do you *think* about them?

sleep under the same dog-tent and eat the same grub."

The European powers had already demonstrated that the volunteer system could not meet the enormous manpower requirements of the Western Front. There was no alternative to conscription. Faced with the realities of the situation, most senators and representatives voted for conscription. In May 1917, six weeks after declaring war, Congress passed the Selective Service Act. By the time the war ended a year and a half later, more than twenty-four million men between the ages of eighteen and forty-five had registered for the draft and almost three million had been called to military service. There was hardly a ripple of disturbance.

Passage of the Selective Service measure left President Wilson with another delicate problem: the old Rough Rider, Theodore Roosevelt. Roosevelt wanted to recruit, train, and lead to the fighting front a division of horse riflemen. Although failing in health, Roosevelt was full of spirit and had dreams of repeating his heroics at San Juan Hill. After turning aside several requests, Wilson at length granted Roosevelt an interview to discuss the matter. The two men met at the White House and in Roosevelt's view had a "bully time."

The prospect of a Roosevelt division had the fervent support of French leaders who had visions of a dramatic upsurge of morale in the trenches when the Rough Rider arrived. Wilson had to treat the appeal cautiously because of Roosevelt's great popularity. However, he never gave serious thought to the idea of permitting Roosevelt to raise a division. He had several reasons. First, Roosevelt was an amateur in military affairs. He was not qualified for the command he sought. Second, Roosevelt would have found it difficult, probably impossible, to contain his dynamic personality. This might have confronted Wilson with the unrewarding task of removing the popular former president for failure to obey orders. Finally, there was politics. Both major parties were looking forward to the election of 1920. Roosevelt, who then would be only sixty-two, seemed a likely Republican candidate for the presidency. If permitted to go to France and polish his reputation as a military hero, the Rough Rider, should he become the GOP standard-bearer in 1920, would be unbeatable.

Financing the War

Raising and training an army was only one of many problems facing the country. The nation's great material resources had to be harnessed if American was to make an effective contribution to the war. To do this would require sweeping aside time-honored ideas about free enterprise.

Accordingly Congress invested Wilson with greater control over the national economy than any president had known to that time. He received authority to take over industries, requisition supplies, fix priorities, and control distribution. When the railroads of the country nearly collapsed under the burden of war he received authority, in December 1917, to operate the railroads. The result was the nearest approach to a socialized state that the United States had experienced.

Financial experts decided that borrowing would have to be the principal means of meeting the war's monetary requirements. This, of course, would mean that future generations would have to pay much of the debt incurred to make the world safe for democracy. Two weeks after declaring war, Congress passed the first War Loan Act, authorizing the Treasury Department to issue $7 billion in notes and bonds. The legislation stipulated that the bonds should be sold through popular subscription, thus giving all Americans an opportunity to invest in the democratic crusade.

In the course of the war, the Treasury conducted four Liberty Loan drives. To publicize Liberty bonds and to urge people to buy them, it

Help him to help U.S.!

Help the Horse to Save the Soldier

THE AMERICAN RED STAR ANIMAL RELIE[F]
National Headquarters, Albany, N.Y.

Courtesy, Philadelphia Free Library Prints and Pictures

Artist James Montgomery Flagg used himself as the model for Uncle Sam. Flagg's best-known work is Uncle Sam pointing his finger and saying "I Want YOU." The recruiting poster was used again during World War II.

[444]

resorted to parades, patriotic posters, newspaper advertisements, and rallies. From the sale of bonds and employment of other devices for borrowing, the Treasury raised $23 billion. Taxes, mainly on corporate and individual incomes, yielded another $10.5 billion. One should note that corporations and people who received high incomes paid the lion's share of the national tax bill during the war. This was mainly because the Wilson administration, strongly supported by progressives, was determined that the old saying about poor men fighting but rich men profiting in war would not apply in this conflict. Despite a few well-publicized exceptions, Americans in high-income groups profited quite modestly from the war and many did not profit at all. The incomes of workingmen and farmers enjoyed a higher percentage of increase during the war than did those of individuals in high-income categories.

Mobilizing Industry

Then there was the problem of mobilizing American industry.

Congress, by way of the National Defense Act of 1916, had established a Council of National Defense. By April 1917, the council had made an inventory of American industry and had created a board to control the purchase and supply of munitions. Still, the pace of industrial mobilization was slow in the months after the declaration of war. The Council of National Defense therefore created a new agency in summer 1917, the War Industries Board. The mission of the board was to allocate raw materials, control production, and in other ways gear the national industrial plant for war.

Unhappily the War Industries Board floundered for many months, mainly because of poor leadership. Finally, in early 1918, President Wilson appointed Bernard M. Baruch, a Wall Street financier, to head the board. Baruch became an economic czar and within a few months the board had the national industrial mechanism humming smoothly and efficiently.

The board imposed severe controls over materials, enforced efficiency, and eliminated waste. It reduced the kinds of automobile tires manufactured in America from almost three hundred to nine, told elevator operators how many stops they could make, and regulated the size of packages to make more efficient use of boxcar space. It fixed priorities, controlled production, and

resolved labor-management disputes. Often the board stimulated production by allowing a wide margin of profit, although in most cases excess-profits taxes recovered much of the return.

There were some disappointments. For all his genius, Baruch was unable to build an aircraft industry between the time he took over the War Industries Board and the end of the war—barely eight months. As a consequence, only a handful of American-built planes reached the fighting front. Then American soldiers had to depend on machine guns manufactured by the country's European allies. And most ships and locomotives ordered by the government to meet the needs of war were not delivered until after the shooting had stopped.

Still, the achievement of American industry was magnificent. In later years German military leaders, looking back on the war, believed it had been decisive, depriving Germany of victory.

No less impressive than the achievements of the War Industries Board—and no less important—were those of the Food Administration.

Hoover and the Food Administration

When Americans entered the war in spring 1917, they faced a dual problem: the necessity to take care of their own food requirements and at the same time to increase dramatically food shipments to their allies in Europe. Shortages of food had become severe in Great Britain, France, and Italy. If not overcome, these shortages threatened to undermine the entire Allied war effort. To meet the problem, the United States would have to step up the output of food and at the same time reduce domestic consumption of food. And this had to be done in a matter of a few months.

To supervise the national food program President Wilson turned to Herbert C. Hoover. Hoover was a wealthy mining engineer who had earned an international reputation as a humanitarian and administrator. He had organized an emergency relief agency that had saved thousands of Belgians from starvation after Germany occupied their country in 1914. A few months later, Wilson created the Food Administration with Hoover as the administrator. To stimulate wheat production Hoover announced that the Food Administration would pay far more than the current market price for all the wheat farmers could produce. He utilized the same tactic to increase hog production. At the same time he persuaded millions of Americans, particularly in cities and small towns, to raise their own carrots, cabbage, and lettuce in small "war gardens." In the cities the gardens were planted wherever there was space—in vacant lots, in backyards, in window boxes, and in schoolyards.

To reduce the domestic consumption of food, Hoover relied on voluntary cooperation and appealed to his countrymen to observe "Wheatless Mondays," "Meatless Tuesdays," and "Porkless Thursdays." He urged restaurants and hotels to cut down the wheat products on their menus and persuaded bakeries to use substitutes for wheat and sugar. Posters were tacked up announcing that "Food Will Win the War!" To help conserve the grain supply, the sale and consumption of intoxicating liquors was temporarily prohibited.

The Food Administration's program of conserving food—called "Hooverizing"—had great popular support. Violations aroused the fury of a patriotic citizenry. The editors of a popular magazine caught the national mood when they wrote: "Do not permit your child to take a bite or two from an apple and throw the rest away; nowadays even children must be taught to be patriotic to the core."

Hoover's program was a smashing success. Food production soared and food consumption in the country declined. By the end of the war, the United States was exporting nearly three times as much food to Allied countries as it had in prewar days. Hoover's reputation as a man of efficiency took on new luster. His successful work as food administrator helped him toward the White House, a goal Hoover finally achieved in 1929.

The Fuel Administration established in summer 1917, set about to increase coal production, mainly by encouraging operators (via promises of high prices) to sink shafts in marginal coal lands. The Fuel Administration also sought to save coal by encouraging Americans to observe "Fuelless Mondays," accept daylight saving time, and keep electric signs and displays darkened. The War Labor Board, set up in the spring of 1918, intervened in labor-management disputes and sought to move workers to areas where there were labor shortages. In general the board tried to increase labor's productivity while preventing the exploitation of labor. During the war, as a result, the wages of working men actually went up, hours went down, and the membership rolls of labor unions swelled.

A War Consciousness

The aspect of wartime mobilization that most distressed President Wilson was the conscious shaping of American thought through propaganda. War had come to America only after a long period of hesitation and deliberation. A propaganda campaign seemed necessary to convert the apathy of people to enthusiasm. Such a campaign would aim at establishing the idea that the Germans were brutes and that Americans and their allies were moved only by the highest ideals. The manipulation of popular thought to acceptance of such conclusions ran counter to all of Wilson's cherished principles. He was a man who had always been dedicated to intellectual honesty and independence of thought. Still, a government-directed campaign to rally the nation behind the war seemed essential.

A few days after signing the war resolution, Wilson created the Committee on Public Information and named George Creel, a liberal newspaperman from Denver, as its director. The principal objective of the Creel Committee was to arouse a war consciousness among the population. But the committee also had a second function: to prevent publication or spread of information and ideas that might give aid and comfort to the enemy.

Censorship thus became a secondary function of Creel's committee. Most newspapermen accepted voluntary censorship. However, Creel did use his authority to stop propaganda by radical labor organizations urging workingmen to boycott the war effort. A few books, notably Thorstein Veblen's *Imperial Germany and the Industrial Revolution,* which presented the Germans as reasonable and decent people, were also casualties of Creel's censorship authority.

More important were the efforts of Creel's committee to rally popular support for the war. The committee enlisted the talents of numerous artists to paint pictures and design posters for Liberty Loan drives and to urge young men to join the armed services. The most famous poster was of Uncle Sam pointing his finger and saying: "I want *YOU* for the United States Army." To produce films depicting German barbarism the committee turned to the country's budding motion picture industry.

To "prove" that the German nation had always been depraved and that Germany's will to power had caused the war, the committee recruited some of America's best college history professors. These men wrote pamphlets and articles, which later, in calmer times, caused the authors considerable embarrassment.

Anti-German Attitude

The success of Creel's propaganda campaign is hard to estimate. But if one is to judge by the anti-German hysteria, it was a howling success. Many colleges and high schools stopped teaching German; universities revoked honorary degrees previously awarded to distinguished Germans; German-American citizens endured continuing intimidation and harassment.

Statues of the German hero of America's War of Independence, Baron von Steuben, came down and libraries stopped circulating books on German topics. Sauerkraut became "liberty cabbage." German measles turned into "liberty measles." Beer, considered a German beverage, came under attack. The city of Cincinnati banned pretzels, another German treat, from lunch counters and saloons.

German-Americans were not the only victims of wartime hysteria. Socialists and other opponents of the war came under patriotic attack. Senator Robert M. La Follette of Wisconsin, the great progressive leader who had voted against the war resolution, was burned in effigy in Madison, the capital of his home state. Then there were the slackers—people who failed or refused to do what fellow citizens thought they ought to do in support of the war effort. For example, the farmer who declined to buy the quota of Liberty bonds set for him by a local committee might find a yellow poster tacked to his gate and yellow paint splattered across his house.

The Espionage Act and the Sedition Act

Superheated patriotism became public law when Congress passed the Espionage Act (June 1917) and the Sedition Act (May 1918). The first of these measures forbade an individual to make any false statements which might interfere with America's war effort. There were heavy penalties for anyone convicted of promoting disloyalty or obstructing recruitment of men for the armed forces. The Sedition Act was designed to punish persons who made statements that brought into "contempt, scorn, contumely, or disrepute" the American form of government, the federal Constitution, the Stars and Stripes, or the armed forces.

Under the espionage and sedition legislation the government prosecuted more than two thousand people and nearly half were convicted. Federal authorities suppressed such Socialist organs as the *American Socialist,* the *Masses,* and the Milwaukee *Leader.* For a time they even suspended publication of *The Nation* when that periodical criticized police behavior during a roundup of so-called slackers in New York City.

The most celebrated case involving the espionage and sedition measures, however, involved the Socialist leader Eugene V. Debs. In a speech before the Socialist national convention in Ohio in June 1918 Debs announced his revulsion toward the war. Arrested and brought to trial, Debs was sentenced to ten years in prison. While an inmate of the federal penitentiary at Atlanta, he ran for president on the Socialist ticket in 1920 and polled nearly a million votes.

Observing that America was fighting to save democracy in Europe in 1917-18, many students of history have been critical of restrictions on democracy at home. It cannot be denied that in the name of patriotism and national security private citizens and government officials committed many excesses which do not add luster to the story of America's past.

As for President Wilson, he accepted the view that if it was right to compel young men to fight and die for their country, then it was equally right to punish individuals who obstructed the war effort or gave aid and comfort to the enemy.

STUDY GUIDE: Before America entered the war, Wilson had not favored a program of military preparedness. When Germany began submarine warfare, Wilson decided legislation was needed to increase the nation's military strength. Despite opposition from Progressives in Congress, the National Defense Act was passed. After war was declared, Congress passed the Selective Service Act to draft men into the armed services. Wilson was given wide powers by Congress to mobilize the nation's economy for war. To help finance the war, Congress passed the War Loan Act authorizing the Treasury Department to issue millions of dollars in notes and bonds. The War Industries Board and Food Administration proved effective in gearing the nation's industrial and agricultural resources for war. A Committee on Public Information was created to rally popular support for the war. Its propaganda campaigns created anti-German feelings across the nation. Some personal liberties

ON THE SEA

When the Germans unharnessed their submarines in early 1917 they expected that within six or eight months the Allied governments would be compelled to ask for a peace settlement—on Germany's terms—even if the United States entered the war. That calculation, however, proved wrong. German U-boats failed to defeat the Allies. For that failure—and it was a critical failure—the American navy, in a more advanced state of readiness than was the army, deserved much credit.

In spring 1917, the U-boat campaign was succeeding beyond the wildest dreams of Germany's leaders. Concentrated in the waters around the British Isles, submarines were sinking Allied merchantmen at a rate of several each day. So serious was the situation that the First Sea Lord of the British Admiralty, John Jellicoe, told Rear Admiral William S. Sims of the United States Navy that "it is impossible for us to go on with the war if losses like this continue. . . . They will win, unless we can stop these losses—and stop them soon."

Sims asked: "Is there no solution for the problem?"

Almost without emotion, Jellicoe answered: "Absolutely none that we can see now."

What the Allies and their new associates, the Americans (the United States never became an Allied power, but remained an Associated power), needed were new techniques for countering the submarine.

The Convoy System

The British practice had been to concentrate warships in waters around the home islands, directing each vessel to roam about a prescribed area of the sea in search of submarines. Although this method of countering U-boats had been a colossal failure, the Admiralty was contemplating no changes. A few young officers in the Royal Navy, however, believed there was a better way to deal with the submarines. They suggested dispatching merchantmen in groups accompanied by warships as convoys. Across the open sea, where the vastness of the ocean provided a great measure of protection, only one or two cruisers would escort the merchant vessels. Then, perhaps three hundred miles west or south of the British Isles, an entire squadron of destroyers, cruisers, and submarine chasers would form around the convoy and shepherd it through waters where the danger of submarine attack was greatest. The Admiralty thought poorly of the convoy idea. Zigzagging through the ocean, merchant vessels would not be able to stay in formation, they argued, and simultaneous arrival of a convoy of ships would jam port facilities.

Fortunately Admiral Sims was receptive to new ideas, and he liked the arguments for the convoy system. Sims convinced the British prime minister, David Lloyd George, of the system's merits and Lloyd George put pressure on the Admiralty to run a convoy on an experimental basis. Routed from Gibraltar to England in May 1917, the first convoy came through without a scratch. Within a few months one convoy after another was sailing in and out of British waters. Almost overnight, even though the Germans were putting more U-boats in operation, Allied shipping losses began to decline sharply.

The convoy was the most important Anglo-American innovation in the sea war, but the Allied and Associated powers also sought to counter the U-boat in other ways. Improved mechanical devices for picking up underwater sounds of submarines were used and more powerful depth charges were developed. Planes dropped bombs on German submarine pens along the North Sea and Adriatic, but had little effect. Other planes flew out over coastal waters to spot submarines for destroyers and sub-chasers. So successful were the planes in their spotting mission that submarine commanders tended to stay away from waters that were under aerial surveillance.

The Mine Barrage

Perhaps the most ambitious tactic for countering the submarine was the so-called mine barrage, or belt. In winter 1917-18 the British stretched such a barrage of mines across the narrow Strait of Dover. The result was a virtual end to submarine activity in that area. Next the American and British navies, over Admiral Sims's objection, set about stringing a similar barrage from the northern tip of Scotland to the coast of Norway.

The objective was to block the mouth of the North Sea against submarines. Estimates of the effectiveness of the North Sea barrage vary. Some writers have concluded that it was of virtually no consequence in the war at sea. Others think that the presence of the mine belt had an ill effect on the morale and hence the efficiency of submarine crews. A third mine barrage, in the Adriatic, proved completely ineffectual.

Results of the fight against submarines were heartening. From a high of 880,000 tons in April 1917, Allied shipping losses declined to half that figure by December 1917 and after April 1918 never exceeded 200,000 tons in a single month. Equally impressive, American and British troop transports, heavily escorted by warships, ferried more than two million soldiers to Europe in 1917-18 without loss of a single vessel.

Such results were decisive. The British and American navies had reversed the trend of the war at sea.

STUDY GUIDE: Germany's use of unrestricted submarine warfare failed to defeat the Allies. The Allied powers used convoys of ships to escort merchant vessels and shield them from attack. This sharply reduced their shipping losses. German submarine activity was further discouraged by Allied use of mines and airplanes.

OVER THERE

When the United States entered the war on April 6, 1917, the Western Front stretched from a point a few miles west of the town of Ostend on the North Sea across the western tip of Belgium in a southerly direction for 130 miles. It then turned eastward near Soissons in northern France and meandered another 100 miles to a point a few miles east of Verdun. From there it extended southward for twenty-five miles to Saint-Mihiel, then another twenty-five miles in an easterly direction. Finally it wandered in a south-southeasterly direction across Lorraine and Alsace to the Swiss border. It was a front that had changed only slightly since autumn 1914.

At this time, however, the French and British were starting an offensive along the northern part of the front. It was their hope to break the long stalemate. Anticipating Allied movements, the Germans had made a strategic with-drawal which shortened and straightened their line. General Robert Nivelle, the French commander, proceeded with the attack despite British objections. It was a disaster. In a diversionary move, the British attacked first. The Germans hardly flinched and kept their troops in place. When Nivelle unleashed the main attack on April 16 at Chemin des Dames, along the Aisne River, German artillerymen, machine gunners, and riflemen mowed down French soldiers by the thousands.

Allied troops staggered back to their trenches. Frightened, frustrated, and angry, many French soldiers rioted. Others threw down their weapons and deserted the trenches. Similar feelings of anger and frustration gripped the civilian population of France. To save the situation, leaders in Paris turned to the hero of Verdun, General Henri Philippe Pétain. To restore discipline in the army, Pétain came down hard against the mutineers and deserters and ordered many of them shot. At the same time he set out to restore morale by showing concern for the welfare of the troops (for example, by taking a special interest in the quality of their food) and assuring them that there would be no more suicidal attacks.

Before long, order had returned in the French trenches. The presence of Pétain, moreover, heartened the civilian population, although discouragement plagued the French nation for many months to come.

Pershing Sizes up the Situation

Meanwhile, in late May 1917, six weeks after America's entry in the war, General John J. Pershing, who would lead the American Expeditionary Force—the AEF—and a staff of 190 officers and men left New York. Their destination was France. Their purpose was to lay the foundation for the eventual arrival of a large American army. After a stop in England, Pershing—known in America as "Black Jack" because he had served with a black cavalry regiment in the Spanish-American war—was enthusiastically received in Paris. Next Pershing and his staff officers toured the Western Front, conferred with Pétain, and met with the leader of the British Expeditionary Force, Field Marshal Sir Douglas Haig. At the time Haig was masterminding a new British offensive effort near Ypres in Belgium. The Briton had a poor opinion of the fighting qualities of the French, but immediately took a liking to Pershing. He confided to his diary: "I was much struck with his quiet gentlemanly bearing—so unusual for an American."

How did Pershing size up the military situation on the Western Front? Pershing sensed that the British offensive at Ypres was not going anywhere. He saw further that the French were drained physically and spiritually as a result of the recent disaster at Chemin des Dames. He knew that it would be many months before they could make another large offensive effort. As for the Germans, it did not seem likely that they would try an offensive push in the near future. They had not yet recovered from the psychological consequences of their last attempt to crash through Allied defenses at Verdun in 1916. Moreover, they still had a large army stationed along the Eastern Front. Therefore, they would have a hard time mustering the superiority in manpower and weapons necessary for a large offensive action in the West.

Pershing reached two conclusions. First, the war was apt to remain deadlocked for a long time to come, which meant there would be no peace before a large American force could arrive. Second, given the weakness of the French, a much larger American army would be required than leaders in Washington had planned to send to the Western Front. The country's political and military chiefs were disturbed by Pershing's second conclusion but decided to meet his manpower requests.

The Doughboys Arrive in France

The first soldiers of the AEF landed in France in late June 1917. They were a mere handful of men and it would be nearly a year before soldiers from the United States would begin to arrive in large numbers. However, it seemed a good idea to get some American troops to the battle area as quickly as possible. The presence of some "doughboys"—as American soldiers came to be called—would heighten war enthusiasm in the United States and, more important, bolster the spirits of Allied troops. The plan appeared to work. On America's Independence Day, July 4, a battalion of the First United States Infantry Division touched off a wild display of enthusiasm by Parisians when it marched smartly down the Champs-Élysées. The French people, wearied and frustrated by nearly three years of war, began to think that victory might be possible.

While doughboys were lifting Allied morale, Pershing was debating with French and British military leaders over the best way to use American forces. Allied leaders wanted the Americans to become reserves, to be integrated among British and French units. Pershing was determined that American divisions should remain intact. In his judgment any breakup of American units would weaken the confidence of American soldiers, prevent officers in the AEF from securing important experience in staff responsibilities, and undermine the national pride of civilians back home. The American general carried his point, whereupon American troops began training, under French supervision, to learn the techniques of trench warfare.

On October 21, 1917, the first American battalions moved into the front lines, along a quiet sector near the town of Toul in northeastern France. For nearly a fortnight there was little activity. Then, on the evening of November 2, the Germans unleashed an artillery barrage. Next a small German raiding party stormed into the American trenches. The raiders killed three

Courtesy, The Smithsonian Institution

At 40 John J. Pershing was still a lieutenant. While serving in the Philippines, he was finally promoted to the rank of captain. But President Theodore Roosevelt was so impressed by Pershing that he made him a brigadier general over 862 senior officers.

men – the first Americans to die in action on the Western Front – and carried off eleven prisoners.

British Setbacks

While American soldiers were receiving their baptism of fire, the military picture suddenly turned very dark for the Allied powers.

First, as Pershing had anticipated, the British offensive in the marshlands of Flanders, near Ypres, had floundered. Sir Douglas Haig, however, had refused to give up his dream of a breakthrough. During the summer and early autumn of 1917 he kept sending British soldiers forward. Torrential rains, mud, and stubborn German resistance continually foiled operations. When ice settled over the Belgian countryside in mid-November even Sir Douglas had to admit that the campaign was a failure. The net result of the action: the British had advanced 9,000 yards – and lost 245,000 men.

While the British soldiers were struggling in the rain and mud around Ypres, the Germans, in September and October 1917, moved several divisions southward. Their aim was to reinforce their Austrian allies who were preparing an assault against the Italians at Caporetto in the northwestern corner of present-day Yugoslavia. When the attack came, on October 24, the Italian army cracked. Some 275,000 Italian soldiers surrendered and the remainder set off in headlong flight across the Italian frontier. (A volunteer ambulance driver with the Italian army was a young American writer, Ernest Hemingway, who would later use the Caporetto campaign as a setting for his novel *A Farewell to Arms*.)

While Austrians and Germans poured onto the plain of northeastern Italy, the British and French, in desperation, moved several divisions from the Western Front to stem the enemy tide in Italy. Fortunately the Germans felt compelled to withdraw most of their troops from the Italian front. The attack ran out of momentum, and the crisis passed. Still, the Caporetto disaster revealed Allied weaknesses, encouraged the Germans, and caused many Frenchmen, Britons, and Italians to wonder anew if victory was possible.

Trouble in Russia

Then, in November 1917, came the greatest disaster of all. In Russia the Bolsheviks, led by Lenin, took control of the government and im-mediately moved to take their country out of the war. At this point, however, the Germans made another of their fateful decisions of World War I. Instead of dealing generously with the Russians, reaching a quick settlement and wheeling their entire army in the east to the Western Front, they determined to impose a conqueror's peace. Their aim was to leave Germany in control of great slices of Russian territory.

Despite their longing for peace, the Soviet leaders rejected such arrangements. The result was protracted negotiations at Brest-Litovsk, on the western border of present-day Russia, which delayed movement of German forces to the Western Front. Powerless to do otherwise, the Soviets eventually in March 1918 had to accept Germany's terms. However, to guard their conquests the Germans had to keep a million soldiers in the east. If those troops, or most of them, had been available for service on the Western Front in spring-summer 1918, the Germans might have pierced Allied defenses, stormed to Paris, and forced a peace settlement favorable to themselves. Failing that, they might have prevented the Allies from taking the offensive after mid-July 1918 and brought about a peace that was more satisfactory to them than the one they later had to accept.

The German Offensive

By mid-March 1918 the Germans had transferred enough divisions from the east to give them nearly 325,000 more men in the trenches of the Western Front than the Allies and the Americans had. With that edge in manpower, the German general staff planned offensive actions which it hoped would carry Germany to victory.

The first blow fell against the British near the Somme River in northwestern France. The Germans opened the attack at 4:50 A.M., March 21, with an artillery barrage in which many German guns fired shells containing mustard gas. Five hours later the artillery fire was lifted and through the fog and smoke the infantry moved forward. Outnumbered and outgunned, the British fell back.

It appeared that the Germans might capture Amiens, a hub of Allied communications in northwestern France. As the Germans continued to press forward, the British and French military and political leaders met on March 26. At Sir Douglas Haig's suggestion, they named General Ferdinand Foch of France the supreme com-

American tanks press the attack on the Germans in the Argonne Forest in 1918. Allies wanted to destroy the Sedan-Mézières Railroad, a main supply route for the Germans. How long did the war last after the Allies won the battle?

U.S. Signal Corps Photo in National Archives

mander of British and French armies. For the first time in the war, incredible as it seems in retrospect, the Allies had unity of command. A few days later Allied resistance stiffened, the German attack began to run out of steam, and the threat to Amiens passed. By April 5 the battle was over. The Germans had sustained heavy losses of their own but had shattered an entire British army, taken 90,000 prisoners, and advanced as much as thirty-five miles.

Four days after the Somme offensive ground to a halt, on April 9, the Germans launched a new attack along the Belgian-French frontier in the vicinity of the Lys River, some fifty miles north of the Somme. Once again, the British were on the receiving end. Using mustard gas and high explosives, German troops forced the British back again. The British were forced to sacrifice the little bit of land they had purchased at such a ghastly price the previous year in the Ypres campaign.

German soldiers, however, did not display the same dash and iron discipline as in the past. Some units threw away precious time when they paused to enjoy captured rations—an indication that the starvation blockade of the British navy had begun to have serious consequences for German soldiers as well as civilians. Moreover, the British, their backs to the English Channel, fought like demons and compelled the Germans to pay a heavy price for their gains. At last, on April 29, the Germans ended the attack. The Germans had pushed the British back as much as ten miles and captured more territory than had the Allies in the entire war to date. German casualties (killed, wounded, and captured) came to 281,000 as opposed to 561,000 for the Allies.

Still, the Germans had failed to break through Allied defenses. And the Americans were beginning to stream into France in increasing numbers.

In the first weeks of May the Germans began to prepare a new strike at the British in the lowlands of Flanders in Belgium and northwestern France. If they could break through in that area, they believed, they could turn the Allied flank and win the war. But they needed to be careful. If the Allies sensed a new attack in Flanders, they were sure to rush reinforcements to the area which likely would undo German plans. So the Germans decided to divert Allied attention away from Flanders. They opened the new campaign with an attack against French positions at Chemin des Dames, along the Aisne River, where the French had met disaster in their disastrous offensive of spring 1917.

On May 27 came the artillery barrage—high explosives and gas. Next the foot soldiers went "over the top," worked their way through barbed-wire entanglements, and advanced toward the French trenches. The French had not anticipated the attack and fell back in confusion across the Aisne, with the Germans in hot pursuit. By the second day the Germans had advanced twenty miles and were pressing toward the Marne. Dazzled by this unexpected success against the French, the German high command scuttled the plan for an attack against the British in Flanders. Instead they poured men and weapons into the battle area around Chemin des Dames.

A bad case of jitters seized the French capital. What if the Germans should make a clean breakthrough at the Marne and send their columns racing down the road to Paris? The political leaders of France made preparations for abandoning the capital. Pershing warned the War Department in Washington that if the military situation continued to deteriorate "a ministry favoring peace" might take over the French government. In the face of such dreadful possibilities, Pershing temporarily abandoned his resolve to keep the American army intact. He turned over five United States divisions to Foch for service along the Marne.

Belleau Wood

The first Americans to start toward the battle area were members of the Third Infantry Division. The road from Paris to the Marne was clogged with civilian refugees and with dazed French soldiers. By May 31 the Americans had begun to take positions along the Marne at Château-Thierry. Joining the French units that were still in the fight, the Third Division helped prevent the Germans from crossing the Marne at that point. Not far behind the Third Division was the Second United States Infantry Division, to which was attached a brigade of American marines. By June 2 the Second had

dug in along a line below an old hunting preserve, Belleau Wood, a few miles west of Château-Thierry.

German divisions by this time were overextended, troops were weary, and there was really no chance of a breakthrough to Paris. But Allied and American commanders had no way of knowing that. When German divisions occupied Belleau Wood, the Americans prepared to dislodge them. Spearheaded by the marines, the first attack came on June 5. As the Germans put down a murderous rifle and machine-gun fire, the marines charged across fields of wheat dotted with poppies. The marines took a hill that day — at a cost of over a thousand casualties. But that was only the beginning. For nearly three weeks the battle raged, and in those terrible days the marine brigade lost more than five thousand men, army units more than three thousand.

At last, on June 25, the Americans claimed control of Belleau Wood — an area of about one square mile. The German attack had already run

With the coming of World War I, the airplane developed rapidly. In 1914, planes traveled about 75 miles an hour. By 1917 their speed was up to 150 miles an hour. The flight ceiling went from 10,000 feet to 24,000 feet.

U.S. Signal Corps Photo in National Archives

The all-black 369th Infantry of the 93rd Division was the first American regiment to see action. They spent 191 days in the trenches and were the first to cross the Rhine. The French government awarded the regiment the Croix de Guerre and singled out 171 enlisted men and officers for individual honors.

U.S. Signal Corps Photo in National Archives

out of steam, so that, in tactical terms, Belleau Wood had minor importance. Of greater importance was the performance of American troops, both marines and soldiers. Inexperienced at first, the Americans quickly learned how to handle themselves on the battlefield. Equally striking was their dash and courage. Describing the new American troops, a German intelligence officer wrote: "The spirit of the troops is fresh and one of reckless confidence." For the Germans this was extremely bad news.

The Germans, in spite of Belleau Wood, had scored impressive gains with their offensive along the Aisne. They had pushed their enemies back as much as forty miles, captured 40,000 prisoners, and taken 650 guns. And they were standing on the right bank of the Marne River, only forty-five miles from Paris.

A fortnight later German divisions, their ranks by now filled out with men over forty and boys under twenty, began to form east and west of Reims. The Germans hoped to force the Allies to concentrate forces for the defense of Paris, whereupon they would launch a decisive assault against the British in Flanders.

Fortunately the Allies and the Americans had learned from prisoners the precise moment when the attack would begin. They directed their own artillery to pound German positions one hour before the Germans loosed their preparatory barrage. Caught in the open at assembly points, German soldiers fell by the hundreds as Allied shells screamed down on them. Still, on the morning of July 15 the Germans charged forward—for the last time, it turned out, in World War I.

East of Reims, French and American units—including the Forty-second ("Rainbow") Division—stopped the Germans almost in their tracks. West of Reims, the Second Battle of the Marne was going differently. French units were falling back and before long the Germans had crossed the Marne.

Then the Germans ran into trouble. Its flanks exposed by the French retreat, the Third United States Infantry Division was holding its ground. There the German attack floundered. By noon of the second day, July 16, it was clear to German leaders, particularly General Ludendorff that victory in the war was beyond their reach. Fresh American soldiers pouring into France had tilted the military balance irrevocably against the German Empire.

The Allies Take the Offensive

General Foch (soon to be named a marshal) concluded that German strength was almost at an end and started a counteroffensive. On July 17, the First and Second United States

Infantry Divisions and the First French Moroccan Division assembled in the Compiègne Forest east of Soissons.

The objective of the three divisions was the highway that ran along the western edge of the Marne salient, between Soissons and Château-Thierry. Torrential rains drenched the American and Moroccan soldiers, but the rain and leaden skies masked their movements from the Germans. On the morning of July 18, under sunny skies, the three divisions attacked. Elsewhere along the salient other French and American divisions also moved forward. Over the next few weeks fresh American divisions, and also French divisions (which suddenly had taken on a magnificent fighting spirit), continued to press forward. By the first week of August the Marne salient had disappeared.

As the Franco-American counteroffensive was running out of steam, the British attacked to the east of Amiens on August 8. Totally surprised, the Germans fell back. By August 11 the Battle of Amiens was over. Amiens was important, mainly because of the wave of defeat it touched off in the German high command. The kaiser recognized that continuation of the war would mean certain defeat for his empire. He instructed his foreign secretary to end the war via diplomacy.

In early August, meanwhile, General Pershing

The Volunteer Motor Corps from Staten Island, New York, practices ambulance technique. In World War I the American Red Cross equipped and shipped overseas 54 base hospitals.

at last realized his dream: nearly all American units in France had come together and operated as the First United States Army. The initial objective of the First Army was the Saint-Mihiel salient in Lorraine, a thorn in the side of France since September 1914. On September 12, 1918, the attack began. The Germans, however, had already decided to withdraw. Resistance, therefore, was comparatively light, and by the second day the salient had dissolved.

Early in September, as the First Army was moving into position around Saint-Mihiel, Marshal Foch had begun new moves against the Germans along the entire line from Flanders to Lorraine. The First Army, after pinching off the Saint-Mihiel salient, moved some forty miles northwest. There it prepared to attack the Germans along a line extending from the Meuse River westward through the large Argonne Forest.

By the last week in September, more than six hundred thousand doughboys were in position and ready to attack. Among the American fighting men were Captain Harry S. Truman (an artilleryman in a division made up of National Guardsmen from Missouri and Kansas), Brigadier General Douglas MacArthur (who was commander of a brigade of the Forty-second Division), Lieutenant Colonel George S. Patton, Jr., and Corporal Alvin C. York (a former conscientious objector from Tennessee who, in one dramatic action, would kill twenty-eight Germans, take over a hundred prisoners, and bring in thirty-five machine guns).

The attack along the Meuse-Argonne line opened at dawn on September 26 and lasted until November 1. The Germans put up fierce resistance. At heavy cost the Americans inched their way forward through fog, gas, and a hail of machine-gun bullets and artillery shells. During this brutal action one battalion of 554 men, mostly from New York, was cut off and surrounded by the Germans. The New Yorkers bravely held off the enemy, but when relief at last appeared only 194 members of the "Lost Battalion" were able to walk away.

As October drew to a close, the last Germans were cleared from the Argonne. At this point, as the government in Berlin prepared for peace, German resistance weakened. Over the next several days American units chased the enemy northward to the eventual armistice line. In the Meuse-Argonne campaign more than twenty-six thousand Americans had died—roughly half the United States' combat deaths in the entire war.

STUDY GUIDE: Before America entered the war, the Allies were weakened by heavy losses and repeated failures to overcome the powerful German army. Even more discouraging to the Allied cause was Russia's withdrawal from the war. This made it possible for the Germans to move troops from the Eastern Front to battle lines in France and Belgium. The arrival of American troops, led by General John Pershing, provided the additional manpower needed to keep the Germans from winning the war. An American victory at the Battle of Belleau Wood bolstered Allied morale. German troops were defeated along the Marne and at Amiens. The German high command realized the end was near. In the Meuse-Argonne offensive American forces suffered heavy losses, but the Germans were forced to retreat.

BLACK AMERICANS AND THE WAR

When the United States joined forces with the Allied cause in 1917, most black citizens rallied to support of the national war effort. The editor of the black periodical the *Crisis,* W. E. B. DuBois, expressed the sentiments of most black Americans in spring 1917 when he wrote: "Our country is at war. . . . If this is *OUR* country, then it is *OUR* war. We must fight it with every ounce of blood and treasure."[1]

Although, with the possible exception of Indians, Negroes made up the most economically depressed segment of the national population, they bought perhaps a quarter of a billion dollars of Liberty bonds. Since many Negroes were farmers and cooks, black Americans were called on via the Food Administration's program to increase the production of food and limit its consumption. The Food Administration appointed a number of blacks to positions of responsibility in its organization.

A Northward Movement

More important, at least in long-range consequences, was the movement to the North during the war of perhaps a third of a million Negroes from the South. The decline in immigration resulting from the war, induction of several million men into the armed forces, and a sharp increase in industrial production needed for the war effort created a labor shortage in northern urban-industrial centers. Blacks went northward despite appeals by white southerners that they not leave—and thus deprive whites of cheap farm labor and domestic servants. By the thousands they found work in munitions factories and shipyards, in mines and steel mills, on railroads and in automobile plants.

These black migrants did not find a "promised land" in the North. They did enjoy higher living standards—and were less frequently intimidated and were bound by fewer formal restrictions than in the South. But they still found that they were victims of prejudice and discrimination. They had to find housing in segregated ghetto areas, were denied entry to many hotels and restaurants, and often had to send their children to segregated and almost inevitably inferior schools. There was also scattered racial violence in northern cities during the war. The worst incident occurred in East Saint Louis, Illinois, where forty Negroes died in riots that resulted when a factory set out to hire black workmen to meet a government contract.

---

[1] Edward M. Coffman, *The War to End All Wars,* copyright 1968 (New York: Oxford University Press), p. 69.

In the Armed Forces

How did black Americans fare in the armed forces? The marines refused to accept black men into their corps and the navy used its handful of blacks (fewer than six thousand) to perform menial tasks. The army took a different view. Blacks had served the army well in the Civil War, the Indian wars of the West, the Spanish-American War, and the Philippine Insurrection. When America entered the war, there were about twenty thousand Negroes in the regular army and national guard. Although army recruiters in the early months of the war turned away thousands of black men who sought to volunteer, the selective service system—or draft—ushered some 367,000 black Americans into the army.

Wearing the uniform of the army did not mean the end of discrimination and abuse for the black man. Most Negroes were assigned to segregated or all-black units—although the highest officers in such units usually were white. These units customarily received the worst the army had to offer in equipment, clothing, and rations. On military posts black soldiers encountered the familiar "white only" signs tacked to certain buildings and facilities. White enlisted men often refused to salute black officers. On one occasion, at Camp Lee, Virginia, a white sentry paced around a group of whites holding a prayer meeting—to keep out any brother Christians of black skin who might wish to join in.

Assignment of black units to training camps in the South brought vigorous protests from white southerners. A few nasty incidents took place, the worst in Houston, Texas, in September 1917 when a riot broke out between white civilians and black soldiers. Seventeen whites died in the Houston affair. After hasty trials that ran roughshod over conventional rules of legal procedure, thirteen black soldiers were hanged for murder and mutiny.

Ironically the black soldier who was making his contribution to the crusade for democracy and freedom received better treatment from French civilians and soldiers than from his white countrymen. The French seemed devoid of racial prejudice. Ignoring appeals of some ranking white Americans that they not "spoil" the blacks, the French treated Negro soldiers with dignity and consideration—treated them as equals.

Black doughboys began arriving in France in

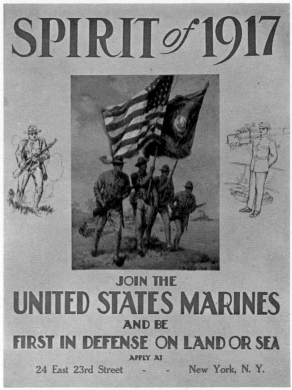

Each branch of the armed services advertised for recruits in World War I. The marines were among the first troops to land in Europe and they fought brilliantly at Soissons, Saint-Mihiel, and Belleau Wood. Blacks, however, were not allowed in the corps. Why not?

summer 1917 and by the time the war ended, some sixteen months later, about two hundred thousand black Americans had served in Europe. Because of the low esteem in which white officers held them, and also because the illiteracy rate was high among black Americans, most of these men—perhaps one hundred and fifty thousand—were used to unload ships and for other types of labor battalions. But four all-black infantry regiments in the Ninety-third Division saw much combat on the Western Front. The four regiments, fighting mainly under French command, performed well, suffered casualties comparable to those of white American units, and received many decorations. One of the regiments, the 369th, won the name "Hell Fighters" from the Germans.

White American officers in the battle zone found it hard to purge themselves of their prejudice toward black Americans. They ignored the excellent performance of most black combat units under their command.

STUDY GUIDE: Most black Americans rallied to support the war effort. As the nation's industries mobilized for war, many black people moved from the South to the North to seek work in factories. Thousands of black Americans served in the armed forces, where segregation and discrimination were common.

THE RUSSIAN INTERVENTION

One aspect of World War I which has continued to intrigue historians was the Allied and American intervention in Russia. This is a complicated piece of history which is very difficult to unravel. In broad outline it began in spring 1918, shortly after the Russians left the war via the Treaty of Brest-Litovsk. It did not end until Japan—an Allied power—withdrew its last troops from Siberia in the year 1922. Interventionist operations centered around Murmansk and Archangel, in the extreme northwest of Russia, and Vladivostok, on the east coast of Siberia.

What prompted the Allies and the Americans to send military forces to Russia in 1918?

Motives were mixed. The British and French hoped to restore the Eastern Front. Russia's withdrawal from the war had enabled the Germans to move many divisions to the battle line in France and Belgium. The British and French had wild ideas of persuading units of the Russian army to get back in the fight against Germany and thus relieve some of the pressure on the Western Front.

Equally important in the view of British and French leaders were huge stockpiles of armaments and supplies which they previously had sent to Russia. These were standing almost unguarded at Archangel, Murmansk, and Vladivostok. If return of the arms and supplies to Britain and France was out of the question, the British and French at least wanted to prevent them from falling into German hands.

A third consideration—and one that seemed to capture the fancy of some Americans—was the fate of forty thousand Czechs. These men had fought alongside the Russians against the Germans and Austrians to help liberate the Czech homeland from the Austrian Empire. When Russia left the war, the Czechs, to continue their struggle for Czech independence, had sought and received permission to make their way across Siberia to Vladivostok. From there they would sail around the world to France and the Western Front. By spring 1918, the Czechs were strung out along the Trans-Siberian Railroad, on their way to Vladivostok. Abruptly the Soviet government, pressed by the Germans, ordered the Czechs arrested and imprisoned. The Czechs determined to resist, and it was in large measure to help rescue them that the United States consented to participate in the Siberian phase of the intervention.

Were the Allies and Americans toying with the idea of overthrowing the infant Bolshevik, or Communist, regime in Russia when they decided to intervene in that country?

For the Americans, the answer is a firm no. Russia's departure from the war had not disturbed Americans as it had Britons and Frenchmen. Besides, Americans in 1918 knew little about bolshevism and did not see it as a great threat to Western civilization. Many Americans, moreover, felt that any kind of government, even one led by Lenin, was an improvement over the autocratic tyranny which the czars had imposed on Russia for centuries.

The British and French had stronger views about the dangers of bolshevism, or communism. It is probable that some leaders in London and Paris saw an Allied and American intervention leading to bigger things, namely, to an overthrow of Lenin and his govenment. Still, in spring 1918 the Germans were taking the offensive on the Western Front. Given the danger that the Germans might break through and win the war, British and French leaders were in no position to give much thought or energy to plans for ridding the world of bolshevism.

After the armistice of November 1918, it is true, the British and French sent armies to southwestern Russia. And the French in particular set about assisting anti-Bolshevist Russians in their counterrevolution against the Soviets. But, drained by the recent war with Germany, neither the British nor the French could muster much enthusiasm for an adventure inside Russia. Accordingly, the British evacuated their soldiers from the southwest of Russia in 1919 and the French did likewise the following year.

Wilson's View

President Wilson thought poorly of the whole idea of sending troops to Murmansk and Archangel. Believing it a misuse of manpower which was needed in the fight against the Germans on the Western Front, he grudgingly agreed to send three American battalions to northwestern Russia in summer 1918. Wilson made it clear, moreover, that the exclusive mission of American soldiers in the operation was to protect supplies and prevent them from falling to the Germans. Doughboys were not to advance to the interior of Russia.

The intervention at Murmansk and Archangel did not amount to much. Bad weather had damaged the supplies stockpiled in the area and much of the material had been stolen. It was immediately apparent that there was no chance of restoring the Eastern Front. A few skirmishes took place—against Soviet troops. But in military terms these were trivial. The entire intervention cost the Allies and Americans fewer than five hundred lives. The real slaughter came after Allied and American soldiers departed. After their departure the Soviets shot down perhaps thirty thousand of their countrymen who had allegedly collaborated with the foreign interventionists.

President Wilson had only slightly more enthusiasm for the venture in Siberia. Weather and thieves had claimed most of the supplies at Vladivostok. However, to help the escaping Czechs (who were becoming involved in the civil war shaping up inside Russia and would not leave the country until 1920), he agreed to send seven thousand troops to Siberia. After landing at Vladivostok in late summer 1918, the Americans spent most of their time guarding sections of the Trans-Siberian Railroad. They met the Soviets in only two minor skirmishes. American troops remained in Siberia until 1920, however. The reason for their comparatively long stay on Russian soil? To keep an eye on the Japanese, who had sixty thousand soldiers in the area and seemed to be dreaming of extending their empire into Siberia.

STUDY GUIDE: After Russia withdrew from the war, Wilson reluctantly allowed American troops to go with other Allied military forces to Russia. The Allies hoped to persuade some Russian troops to continue fighting the Germans. They also wanted to reclaim supplies left on Russian territory. Another goal was to rescue Czech troops imprisoned by the new Soviet government. Nothing much was accomplished by these Allied moves. However some Americans stayed in Russia until 1920 in order to observe Japanese soldiers in the area.

ARMISTICE

On the Western Front it was clear by early October in 1918 that before long the Germans would be expelled from Belgium, France, and Luxembourg. Then they would be faced with the prospect of defending their own homeland against the onrushing Allies and Americans.

German military and political leaders, their spirits shattered, determined to end the war by diplomacy as quickly as possible. Their first step, on October 4th, was to arrange appointment of Prince Max of Baden as chancellor of the German government. The Germans hoped that Prince Max, a political liberal, might receive special consideration from President Wilson. Wilson in turn might prevail on Allied leaders to deal leniently with the Germans. On his second day in office Prince Max dispatched a cable to Wilson requesting an armistice. By making the cable public, the American president might have engineered a total collapse of German resistance on the Western Front. Instead he kept it secret—even from his counterparts in London and Paris.

The Fourteen Points

On October 8 the president cabled Max for a clarification. Did the Germans subscribe to the Fourteen Points, the peace program he had outlined the previous January?

To demonstrate that the United States sought a peace settlement assuring justice and dignity to all nations and did not seek to humiliate its enemies, Wilson had announced the Fourteen Points in January 1918. When Wilson made them public, they were intended to encourage the war efforts of the Allies and Americans and weaken resistance inside the territories of Germany and its allies, notably Austria and Turkey. He hoped they would attract support of men of liberal spirit the world over. Among other things, the Fourteen Points urged abolition of secret diplomacy; freedom of the seas in war and peace; removal of economic barriers among nations; reduction of armaments; return of Alsace and Lorraine to France; independence for Poland; dismemberment of the Austrian Empire; and creation of new independent states in Eastern Europe. Best remembered, of course, was Point Fourteen, the one calling for "a general association"—or League—"of nations."

Prince Max replied on October 12 that Germany accepted the Fourteen Points as a basis for peace and assumed that America's associates, Great Britain, France, and Italy, also accepted them. As a matter of fact, they did not accept the Fourteen Points. When leaders in London and Paris learned, via leaks from Washington and Berlin, that Wilson was negotiating with the Germans on the basis of his personal peace program, the British and French leaders were furious.

The Wilson-Max negotiations then hit a snag. First, there was a report that German machine gunners had killed other Germans when they tried to surrender to American infantrymen. Next came news that a German U-boat had sunk another unarmed passenger liner killing many women and children. A new and powerful wave of anti-German sentiment swept the United States. Sharing the popular outrage, Wilson cabled Prince Max on October 14 that Allied and American military leaders would fix the terms of any armistice. In the days that followed, Max tried to win Wilson over, but the president, on October 24, cabled Max that the United States could not negotiate with the present rulers of Germany. The implication for Germany was clear: remove the kaiser and it still might be possible to arrange a peace treaty on the basis of President Wilson's Fourteen Points.

As German leaders agonized over the president's latest message, the situation for Germany went from bad to worse. German defenses on the Western Front began to crumble, Turkey left the war on October 30, Austria quit on November 3. Also on November 3 German sailors mutinied, killed some of their officers, and forced their ships to return to port. Meanwhile, the home front began to collapse and the Socialist party on November 7 announced that unless the kaiser abdicated the following day it would join other hostile groups in launching a revolution in Germany.

By the time the Socialists issued their ultimatum, the end of the war was in sight. Pressed by Wilson, Allied leaders grudgingly consented to make peace on the basis of the Fourteen Points. However they insisted that Wilson first agree to compromise his position on freedom of the seas and promise not to stand in the way of requiring Germany to pay reparations to the Allies. Wilson finally yielded to the pressure of the Allied negotiators and the way was clear for Marshal Foch to arrange an armistice with the Germans.

Terms of the Armistice

A German armistice commission met with Foch on November 8 in his private railway coach, parked on a siding in Compiègne Forest. The terms of an armistice were that the Germans must withdraw their army to the left bank of the Rhine, turn over stores of supplies and equipment to the Allies and Americans, and liberate prisoners of war and deported inhabitants of occupied countries. They must also surrender their submarines and battle fleet and scrap the Treaty of Brest-Litovsk, as well as a similar treaty with Rumania. As for the Allies and Americans, they could requisition such German property as their armies of occupation might require and could continue to maintain their naval blockade around Germany pending a final peace settlement.

The Germans gasped when they read these stiff terms. But they had to accept them. Finally Foch decreed that German delegates would make their way to this same spot on the morning of November 11 to sign the armistice documents. All hostilities would end promptly at 11 A.M. on that day—the eleventh hour of the eleventh day of the eleventh month.

Within Germany revolutionaries were threatening to overthrow Kaiser Wilhelm II. Before dawn on November 10, Wilhelm boarded his royal train and fled to Holland. For the next twenty-three years, until his death during World War II, the kaiser lived in exile in the Netherlands, a lonely and rather pitiful relic of a bygone era.

The final scene of the drama of 1914-18 was played out the next day, November 11. As dawn broke over the French countryside, German delegates passed through Allied lines and were taken by Allied officers to Compiègne Forest. The Germans solemnly entered Foch's railway coach and signed their names to the armistice documents.

World War I belonged to history. It had claimed the lives of nearly ten million human beings.

STUDY GUIDE: With his empire on the verge of collapse, the German kaiser was forced to step down from his throne. Faced with defeat, the German high command had no choice but to accept the harsh terms of the Allied peace settlement. Wilson consented to these terms. However, he hoped to create conditions that would assure a peaceful postwar world.

SUMMING UP THE CHAPTER

Names and Terms to Identify

Sarajevo
Paul von Hindenburg
Bolsheviks
Treaty of Brest-Litovsk
Alfred Zimmermann
National Defense Act of 1916
War Loan Act
War Industries Board
Bernard M. Baruch
Food Administration

George Creel
slackers
"liberty cabbage"
Espionage Act of 1917
Sedition Act
Douglas Haig
doughboys
Ferdinand Foch
Belleau Wood
Prince Max of Baden

Study Questions and Points to Review

1. Name the royal couple whose assassination led to a declaration of war on Serbia by Austria. Why did Austria use the royal murders to punish the Serbians?

2. Why was the United States patient in dealing with British violations of its rights as a neutral?

3. Why were the British confident that the *Lusitania* was immune from German attack?

4. What effect did the sinking of the *Lusitania* have on the American people?

5. Why did William Jennings Bryan, Wilson's secretary of state, resign from the cabinet?

6. What was the subject of the Zimmermann message?

7. Why has Germany's decision to resume unrestricted submarine warfare been considered one of the monumental blunders of history?

8. When did the United States enter World War I?

9. Why was Wilson against the idea of permitting Theodore Roosevelt to raise a division of horse riflemen?

10. What was the principal objective of the Creel Committee?

11. Why did Pershing want to keep the American divisions in Europe intact?

12. What was the significance of the Battle of Amiens?

13. Name the peace program Woodrow Wilson announced in January 1918.

14. When was the armistice signed?

Topics for Discussion

1. In 1914 President Wilson pleaded for Americans to be neutral in thought as well as actions. What do you think he meant?

2. Discuss the progress made by Germany against the Allies up to the time the United States entered the war. How effective were German submarines against Allied shipping?

3. The author lists two monumental blunders made by Germany: The resumption of unrestricted submarine warfare when Russia was on the verge of collapse, and the sending of Nikolai Lenin to Russia. Evaluate these actions and give your opinion on how they affected the outcome of the war.

4. Why did the United States declare war on Germany? Do you think the United States could have stayed out of World War I? Give reasons for your answer.

5. Discuss the steps involved in mobilizing the United States for war. How do you account for the great success in getting ready for war so quickly?

6. What events in autumn 1917 indicated a sharp turn in the war in favor of Germany and its allies?

7. Evaluate the contribution of American forces in stopping the German offensives in June and July 1918.

8. Give your evaluation of America's participation in the intervention in Russia by Allied and Associated powers.

9. Describe the diplomatic fencing between the German and American governments in October 1918.

Subjects for Reports or Essays

1. On the basis of outside reading, write an evaluation of President Wilson's policy toward the European belligerents in 1914-17.

2. Write an essay making the strongest possible case for Germany's unrestricted use of the submarine.

3. After examining conflicting interpretations that historians have advanced, write an essay setting forth your own views on why the United States entered World War I in 1917.

4. Assume it is January 1918. You are an American citizen of German ancestry. Write a letter to a friend in a neutral country commenting on the acts of harassment against German-Americans.

5. Using books in the library, prepare a report on one of the following topics: (a) the black American and World War I; (b) the role of women in World War I; (c) the weapons and military strategy of World War I; (d) the home front; (e) propaganda and public opinion during World War I.

6. Interview as many people as you can find who can recall the years 1917-18. Ask them to describe their recollections of the war years. Report your findings to the class.

Projects, Activities, and Skills

1. Prepare an illustrated report on the German U-boat of World War I. What was its size, range, and speed? How many men were in its crew? How deep could it go, and how long could it stay submerged? How many torpedoes could it carry? Where were its bases?

2. Prepare a classroom report on the *Lusitania* and its last voyage. Use photographs and maps to illustrate your report.

3. On Atlas Map 27, locate the following and explain their strategic importance: the British blockade, German U-boat activity, Caporetto, Sarajevo, Brest-Litovsk.

4. Listen to some of the popular songs of the World War I era. What do the words tell you about the spirit of the times?

5. Prepare an illustrated report on the aircraft of World War I. What were some of the important planes? What were their capabilities? How were they used? How important was the airplane in World War I?

6. On the basis of outside reading, report on the role of war censorship in the United States and the effect of the Creel Committee. Compare newspaper coverage of World War I and the Spanish-American War.

Further Readings

General

America at War: 1917-18 (vol. 2) by Frederic L. Paxson. An account of America's "home front."
America Goes to War by Charles C. Tansill.
From Slavery to Freedom: A History of American Negroes by John Hope Franklin. Describes the contributions of black Americans to the victory over Germany in World War I.
The Great Departure: The United States in World War I, 1914-20 by Daniel M. Smith.
The Guns of August by Barbara Tuchman. A best-selling account of the first days of the war.
The Long Fuse: An Interpretation of the Origins of World War I by Lawrence Lafore.
The War to End All Wars: The American Experience in World War I by Edward M. Coffman. Covers the airplane's contribution and also considers the problems of black American soldiers.
Wilson the Diplomatist: A Look at His Major Foreign Policies by Arthur S. Link.
World War I: An Outline History by Hanson W. Baldwin.
The Zimmermann Telegram by Barbara Tuchman. Argues that this event was the catalyst in taking the United States to war.

Biography

Admiral Sims and the Modern American Navy by E. Elting Morison.
Memoirs of World War I by William Mitchell.
The War Memoirs of Robert Lansing by Robert Lansing.

Fiction and Drama

All Quiet on the Western Front by Erich Maria Remarque. A European novel expressing the futility of war.
A Farewell to Arms by Ernest Hemingway. A novel about an ambulance driver on the Italian front.
In the Company of Eagles by Ernest K. Gann. A French pilot avenges his friend's death.
One of Ours by Willa Cather. A prize-winning novel about a young American in the war.
What Price Glory? by Maxwell Anderson and Laurence Stallings. A realistic drama that portrays the ugliness of war.

Pictorial History

This Fabulous Century, 1910-1920, Vol. 2, by the editors of Time-Life Books.

World War I was followed by a period of peace and plenty. Then came 1929, and the beginning of the Great Depression. Millions of unemployed workers overcame their pride and stood in long lines for bread or soup given away by churches and other charities.

Franklin D. Roosevelt Library

5
BETWEEN
TWO WORLD WARS

CHAPTER 14

NORMALCY

ON THE MORNING OF NOVEMBER 11, 1918, telegraph wires crackled the happy news of the armistice across the length and breadth of the United States. Newspapers bannered the news in "extra" editions.

Word that the fighting had stopped and doughboys would soon be on their way home touched off a wild celebration. Factory and locomotive whistles screeched, and foghorns bellowed. In cities and towns enthusiastic citizens built huge bonfires and held spontaneous parades. All across the country men and boys snake-danced, whistled, and shouted and well-dressed ladies, their hemlines a daring six inches above the ground, rang cowbells and waved flags. People hugged and kissed total strangers.

Celebrating at the White House in Washington was more restrained. In mid-morning President Wilson scribbled a message to his countrymen: "The armistice was signed this morning. It will now be our fortunate duty to assist by example, by sober, friendly counsel, and by material aid in the establishment of just democracy throughout the world."

WILSON AND THE PEACEMAKERS

The words of the president did not sound a new theme but only expressed ideas which Wilson had voiced repeatedly over the previous nineteen months. In his war message to Congress, April 2, 1917, he first told Americans that they should embark on a great crusade to bring democracy and self-determination to peoples across the entire world.

Wilson had known from the outset that achievement of such exalted goals would not be easy. Through diplomatic channels, he had learned as early as 1915 that America's allies, including Britain and France, had ideas about a peace settlement that were quite different.

In addition to defeating Germany, the Allied powers hoped to win some dividends, or spoils from the war, notably certain territories under the flags of Germany and its allies. To arrange for this postwar distribution of the fruits of victory the Allies, beginning in 1915, had negotiated

a battery of secret treaties. If honored those treaties would violate Wilson's precious principles, particularly the one about self-determination: the right of the people of a nation to choose their own form of government and manage their affairs without outside interference.

Wilson nevertheless pressed on with his ideas about a peace settlement in which there would be no conquerors and no vanquished—a "peace without victory." In January 1918, on the heels of the Bolshevik Revolution in Russia and serious Allied setbacks on the battlefield, he announced his famous Fourteen Points, a program for peace. The cynical old French premier Georges Clemenceau said the Fourteen Points bored him, that "even God Almighty has only ten." But the American president's peace program fired the imagination of people around the world. European Catholics put pictures of Wilson alongside images of saints, a translated volume of Wilson's speeches became a "best-seller" in China, and leaflets telling of the Fourteen Points circulated in the Austrian Empire. Poles, Czechs, and Bosnians were aroused by the promise of liberation.

A Democratic Defeat

Ten months after he had proclaimed the Fourteen Points, a few days before the armistice, President Wilson's prestige suffered a devastating blow. The president's Democratic party went down to defeat in the congressional elections of 1918. And it went down after Wilson had made the election into a vote of confidence for himself.

The president had good reason for wanting a national vote of confidence in autumn 1918: peace negotiations would soon be underway and his own bargaining position would be increased if he had the support of a majority of his countrymen. In the closing weeks of the campaign he appealed to the voters: "If you have approved of my leadership and wish me to continue to be your unembarrassed spokesman in affairs at home and abroad, I earnestly beg that you will express yourselves unmistakably to that effect by returning a Democratic majority to both

HEADLINE
EVENTS

1874 Woman's Christian Temperance Union established

1876 Prohibition party runs first candidate for president

1893 Anti-Saloon League established

1911 National Urban League founded

1913 Webb-Kenyon Act

1915 New Ku Klux Klan organized

1915-1918 Series of secret treaties negotiated between Allies

1916 Child Labor Act

1917 United States enters World War I
Bolshevik revolution; Communist regime established in Russia

1918 Wilson announces Fourteen Points
Sweeping Republican victory in election of 1918
Armistice signed; World War ends

1918-1920 Big red scare; fear of bolshevism

1919 Eighteenth Amendment ratified
Volstead Act
Peace Conference opens in Paris
Lodge issues "Round Robin" statement
Wilson makes second trip to Paris
Lodge delays vote on Versailles Treaty and adds reservations to it
Wilson appeals to people to explain America's membership in League
Wilson suffers paralytic stroke
United Mine Workers seek socialized coal industry
Wilson orders that resolution-laden treaty be voted down
Winesburg, Ohio (Anderson)
Wave of strikes

1920 Nineteenth Amendment ratified
Commercial radio bradcasting begins
Explosion on Wall Street
Main Street (Lewis)
This Side of Paradise (Fitzgerald)
Senate refuses to ratify resolution-laden Treaty of Versailles
Sacco-Vanzetti case
League of Nations organized
Blackstone Clique selects Harding as Republican presidential candidate

1920s Era of speakeasies, bootleg racketeers, and Prohibition

1921 William Howard Taft appointed Chief Justice of the Supreme Court
Legislation imposes restrictions on immigration
Warren G. Harding inaugurated president
Treaty restores peace between U.S. and Germany, Austria, and Hungary
Washington Conference for Limitation of Armaments

1922 Fordney-McCumber Act
Babbitt (Lewis)

1923 Warren Harding dies; Calvin Coolidge succeeds to the presidency

1924 Teapot Dome Scandal
Immigration further restricted
Soldiers' Bonus Act
Progressive party nominates Robert La Follette for president
Coolidge elected president
Indians granted citizenship

1925 Coolidge inaugurated president for second term
Scopes "monkey trial"
The Great Gatsby (Fitzgerald)

1926 *The Sun Also Rises* (Hemingway)
Richard Byrd flies over North Pole

1927 Charles A. Lindbergh makes first solo nonstop flight across Atlantic
Advisory Committee finds Sacco and Vanzetti guilty
Coolidge vetoes McNary-Haugen bill and Muscle Shoals bill
The Jazz Singer, first talking movie starring Al Jolson

1928 Kellogg-Briand Pact
Iron lung (Drinker.Shaw)
Herbert Hoover defeats Al Smith for the presidency

1929 *The Sound and the Fury* (Faulkner)
Herbert Hoover inaugurated president
A Farewell to Arms (Hemingway)
Stock market crash
The Great Depression begins

the Senate and the House of Representatives."

The president's appeal proved unfortunate. Despite his role as commander in chief in a successful war, Wilson's popularity had slipped since his reelection in 1916, largely because of widespread resentment over wartime controls and taxes. Moreover, the split in the Republican party was healing. That split had given Wilson and the Democrats their triumphs in the elections of 1912 and 1916.

The outcome on election day 1918 was a sweeping Republican victory. How did European leaders view the verdict of the American electorate? In their estimate, Wilson had received a vote of "no confidence." Because of the way Europe's parliamentary systems functioned, any one of them would have been compelled to resign if given a similar defeat by the voters. Reinforcing the assessment of Europe's leaders were the words of such "Wilson-haters" in America as Theodore Roosevelt, who after the election announced: "Mr. Wilson and his Fourteen Points and his four supplementary points and his five complementary points and all his utterances every which way have ceased to have any shadow of right to be accepted as expressive of the will of the American people."

The Peace Conference

Wilson, meanwhile, had made plans to travel to Paris as head of the American delegation to the peace conference.

Some historians believe the president would have done better to remain in Washington far removed from the angry debates over territories promised in the secret treaties. Remaining in the White House, Wilson would not have been subjected to the pressures of Paris and the persuasive powers of Prime Minister David Lloyd George of Britain and Premier Georges Clemenceau, "the Tiger" of France. Hence, he might have held out more effectively for a peace settlement along the line of his Fourteen Points. At home, moreover, the president could have kept his finger on the country's political pulse and perhaps prevented the collision in the Senate that eventually defeated much of his work at Paris.

However, Wilson was enormously popular among the people of Europe. He also had great persuasive abilities. Thus there was something to the argument that the president's presence at the peace conference would make more likely the acceptance of a liberal and generous settlement.

Wilson felt he had a responsibility to humanity and to the brave Americans who had given their lives in the recent crusade for democracy. He believed that this responsibility required his attendance at the peace table. And so a few days after the armistice, he made public his plans to travel to Paris.

Next Wilson announced the delegates who would assist him during the peace negotiations: Secretary of State Lansing, the president's personal adviser Edward M. House, General Tasker H. Bliss of the army, and a career diplomat, Henry White. Capable though they were, not one of those men had any influence with the leaders of the Republican party, whose support was crucial. Only the Republican-controlled Senate would have the power to approve the treaty.

Under the circumstances, Wilson should have searched the Senate for a prominent Republican or two to serve on the peace delegation. A logical choice would have been Senator Henry Cabot Lodge of Massachusetts. In the Republican-controlled Senate, Lodge was slated to be chairman of the Foreign Relations Committee. This committee would scrutinize any treaty which might emerge from the Paris conference. If Lodge had helped draft the treaty he would be more sympathetic during committee hearings.

Unhappily Wilson and Lodge despised one another, so Lodge's membership on the peace delegation was out of the question. Still, there were other Republicans whom Wilson might have considered, such as former-President Taft, Charles Evans Hughes, or Elihu Root. All were men of ability who were favorable to Wilson's peace program, including the League of Nations. Unfortunately the president, for all his idealism, displayed a narrow partisanship and refused to bid for Republican support.

His delegation chosen, Wilson, accompanied by numerous technical assistants, sailed from New York on December 4, 1918. The president's mood was optimistic. When he landed in France nine days later, he met a tumultuous reception and his optimism increased. A Paris newspaper proclaimed that "never has a king, never an emperor received such a welcome."

Still, most of the people who cheered the American president also hated Germans. They were determined to have revenge for the evils which in their estimate the Germans had visited on them in the previous four years. Thus they were not in total sympathy with Wilson's ideas about peace. Wilson, it seems clear in retrospect, was asking too much of the people of the

President Woodrow Wilson (center) receives a royal welcome at Dover, England, in 1918 before going to Paris to attend the peace conference. Would Wilson have done better to remain at home and let his delegation handle the difficult peace negotiations?

Allied countries. The war had been too long, too terrible, and too costly for them to accept Wilson's pious formula for a "peace without victory."

When the peace conference opened in mid-January 1919, an atmosphere of tension filled the French capital. Lloyd George later told the British Parliament: "I am doubtful whether any body of men with a difficult task have worked under greater difficulties—stones crackling on the roof and crashing through windows, and sometimes wild men screaming through the keyholes."

The main objective of the Allied negotiators was to gain for themselves the spoils which they had promised each other in their secret treaties. They intended to force Germany to pay heavy reparations for war damages and make certain that German military power would never rise again. President Wilson thought in terms of a settlement that would leave no open wounds which might lead to another major war. On the question of territorial adjustment, he insisted on self-determination. He also sought creation of a League of Nations to settle international disputes amicably and punish peace-breakers. On the matter of reparations, he understood Allied feelings. However, like a few other farsighted men at Paris, he realized that such reparations would open the way for future trouble in Europe.

The League of Nations

In the first weeks of the conference, while his popularity in Europe was at a peak, Wilson achieved his most striking triumph at Paris. He overcame the opposition of European negotia-

tors, who wanted to draft a peace settlement first and then talk about a League of Nations. He persuaded the conference to adopt a charter for the League and incorporate it in the peace treaties. The president had feared that if consideration of the League was delayed until other problems were resolved the delegates might never develop a "general association of nations."

Because his presence was essential in Washington when the session of Congress ended on March 4, Wilson returned to the United States in mid-February 1919. Savoring his triumph on the League question, the president was full of enthusiasm. His joy was ill-founded. Across the United States opposition to the idea of United States membership in a world organization was gathering.

A few hours before Congress adjourned, Senator Lodge read the famous "Round Robin" statement that consideration of a League of Nations should await a peace treaty with Germany. The statement carried the signatures of thirty-seven Republicans who would be members of the Senate in the new Congress. This was more than enough to prevent ratification of a treaty providing for American entry in Wilson's "general association of nations." Wilson was disturbed, but he remained confident that most Americans favored the League. He felt sure they would put sufficient pressure on the senators to compel them to consent to American membership in the new international organization.

In mid-March 1919 the president returned to Paris, where the task of hammering out a peace settlement continued. Drained by an attack of

Courtesy French Government Tourist Office

The treaty of peace with Germany was signed at the Palace of Versailles, near Paris, in June 1919. Why did Wilson accept the peace treaty after Allied refusal to include most of his Fourteen Points in the final settlement?

influenza, Wilson became edgy and irritable. At one point he became so frustrated that he threatened to quit the conference. Part of his frustration was a result of his inability to convert the European leaders to his thinking. Consumed by an obsession for spoils, security, and revenge, they hacked away at Wilson's Fourteen Points. They ignored "open covenants openly arrived at." Instead they determined the fate of Europe behind closed doors. They ran roughshod over self-determination and threw freedom of the seas to the scrap heap. They insisted that Germany admit guilt for the war and agree to payment of heavy indemnities. They demanded that Germany dismantle its army and navy and pledge never again to become a first-rate military power. Wilson feared lest the Europeans have a change of heart and junk the League of Nations, which he saw as the only hope for peace in the world. Accordingly, he swallowed his frustration and, to save the League, sadly accepted defeat on most of his fourteen-point program.

On June 28, 1919, the treaty of peace with Germany was signed at the Palace of Versailles outside Paris. The Germans felt betrayed. They had put down their arms on November 11, 1918 in the belief that peace would rest on President Wilson's Fourteen Points. Now they faced a conqueror's settlement. Especially disturbing was the "war guilt" clause of the treaty, a gross

distortion of history in Germany's view and also in the view of many later historians in America. To show its contempt for the settlement, the government in Berlin sent two minor officials to Versailles to sign the treaty.

President Wilson departed for home on the next day, reasonably satisfied with the outcome of the conference. He told reporters: "I think that we have made a better peace than I should have expected when I came here to Paris."

STUDY GUIDE: Wilson's ideas about a peace settlement differed sharply from those of the Allies. Before the war ended, Wilson announced his Fourteen Points calling for justice for all nations. Wilson urged the creation of a League of Nations to prevent future wars. The Allies were eager to seek revenge on an enemy who had cost them great suffering. They negotiated secret treaties which violated Wilson's proposal to let all nations choose their own political destiny.

The Democrats were defeated in the congressional elections of 1918. This defeat was a blow to Wilson's prestige and cast doubt on public support of his leadership.

Wilson himself headed the American delegation to the Paris peace conference in the hope of influencing a liberal and generous settlement. He convinced the Allies to adopt a charter for the League and incorporate it into the treaty. However, Congress refused to consider a League until the signing of a peace treaty with Germany. In order to keep the League in the treaty, Wilson was forced to accept a final peace settlement with harsh terms for Germany. The terms of the treaty bore little resemblance to the principles contained in his Fourteen Points.

THE TREATY OF VERSAILLES

In important particulars the Treaty of Versailles did not mirror Wilson's ideas. Firmly embedded in the treaty, however, were provisions for the League of Nations. In the president's view, the sacrifice of a few principles was a small price to pay for a world organization with power to mediate disputes and prevent war.

The "heart" of the League covenant, or constitution, as Wilson explained, was Article X. This article pledged members of the world organization "to respect and preserve as against external aggression the territorial integrity and existing political independence" of all other members. The covenant contained no promise that members would enforce the pledge by going to war. However Article XVI bound them to punish an aggressor by imposing a total blockade in trade, finance, and communication. A key to the League's chances of success was the support of the United States, by now the most powerful country in the world. President Wilson foresaw no problems. Popular opinion in America would not permit opposition senators to scuttle his handiwork.

Wilson's optimism was exaggerated. Some Americans saw the League as a superstate that would compromise American sovereignty and constitute a betrayal of the national heritage. Former-Senator Albert J. Beveridge of Indiana caught this sentiment when he described the League as the work of "amiable old male grannies who, over their afternoon tea, are planning to denationalize America and denationalize the Nation's manhood."

Others believed the League was the kind of "entangling alliance" that George Washington had warned against in his famous Farewell Address of 1796. They believed the League would drag the United States into foreign conflicts that were none of its concern. Some critics saw the League variously as a "cat's paw" of the British Empire, the Roman Catholic church, and Wall Street. Others raised the specter of a League dominated by Negroid and Oriental races. Some Americans simply thought the League idea was too visionary. They preferred to trust in international law and the traditional balance of power to keep the peace.

Many people in the United States were indifferent to the League, but they despised certain treaty provisions or the man, Wilson, whose vision had created it. German-Americans were furious because the Treaty of Versailles dealt harshly with Germany. Italian-Americans were angry because Wilson had turned aside Italy's demand for larger pieces of Austrian territory including the city of Fiume. Irish-Americans at rallies hissed the name of Wilson because the peace conference had declined to take up the question of Irish independence.

Some Americans, particularly Republican political leaders, felt contempt for Wilson. Finally there was a fear in Republican circles that the president planned to seek a third term in the impending election of 1920. Despite the Republican comeback in the elections of 1918, the president would be hard to beat in 1920 if he could tack the League of Nations to a banner of achievements that already included successful leadership in the late war.

Lodge's Tactics

Leader of the Republican opposition in the Senate was Henry Cabot Lodge, chairman of the Foreign Relations Committee. Lodge had been in the Senate for many years but had accomplished little. His modest record of achievement on Capitol Hill had resulted from a restricted imagination, a cool personality, and a narrow partisanship rather than from lack of intellect. Often at odds with Wilson, Lodge felt an intense hatred for the president. By 1919 that hatred inevitably carried over to the League of Nations.

The Massachusetts senator, to be sure, had other objections to America's membership in the League. Like many others, he viewed the League as a supergovernment which would compromise American sovereignty and take America into foreign quarrels and wars in which no American interests were at stake.

The Treaty of Versailles, complete with its provisions for American membership in the League, went to the Senate and then to the Foreign Relations Committee in July 1919. Lodge like Wilson, reasoned that a majority of the people probably favored the League. To give pro-League sentiment time to abate, he adopted the strategy of delaying a vote on the treaty as long as possible. He also devised the tactic of attaching amendments, or "reservations" to the treaty. Consideration of reservations took still more time. And if the Senate adopted the reservations, Lodge calculated, Wilson might then oppose the treaty. Blame for America's refusal to join the League would then shift to him.

Most of Lodge's reservations were harmless, but there was one which was sure to incur the wrath of the president. It declared that the United States would assume no obligation under Article X of the League covenant to guarantee the territory or independence of other members. Instead, Congress would decide in each instance what, if any, action the United States might take in the event of aggression. This reservation would prevent the United States from reacting promptly and automatically to trouble. And Wilson knew that prompt action by members was necessary if the League was to be an effective agency for enforcing peace.

EUROPE AND THE MIDDLE EAST AFTER WORLD WAR I

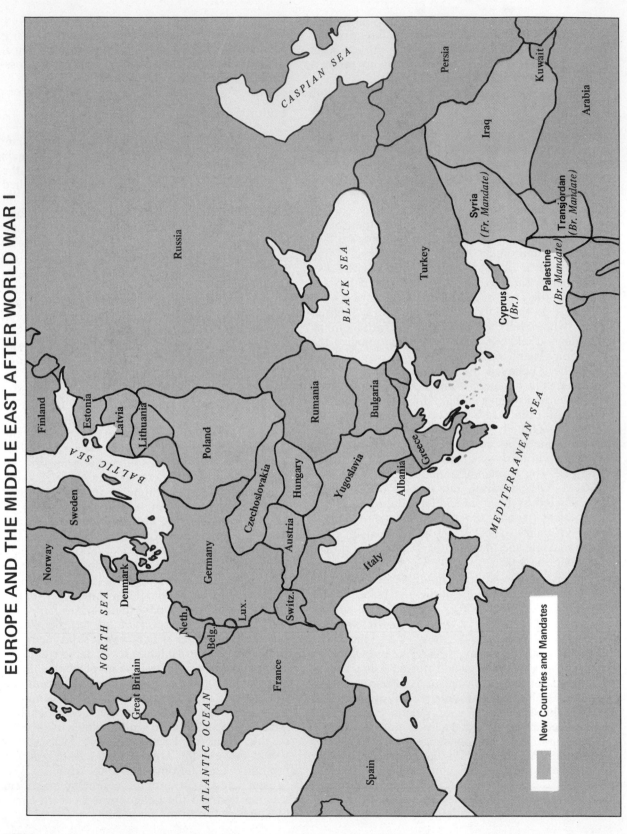

CASPIAN SEA

Persia

Kuwait

Arabia

Iraq

Syria
(Fr. Mandate)

Transjordan
(Br. Mandate)

Palestine
(Br. Mandate)

Turkey

Cyprus
(Br.)

BLACK SEA

Russia

MEDITERRANEAN SEA

Rumania

Bulgaria

Greece

Yugoslavia

Albania

Finland

Estonia

Latvia

Lithuania

Poland

Czechoslovakia

Hungary

Austria

Italy

BALTIC SEA

Sweden

Norway

Denmark

Germany

Neth.

Belg.

Lux.

Switz.

France

NORTH SEA

Great Britain

ATLANTIC OCEAN

Spain

New Countries and Mandates

Wilson Appeals to the People

As his patience wore thin, Wilson, in late summer 1919, determined to take his case directly to the people. He would make a long train trip around the country and personally explain the case for American membership in the League without the reservations. The president's physicians warned against such a tour. But the president insisted and made it plain that he was willing to die for his cause.

In the Middle West the president met a cordial response as he warned that America needed the League to avoid a repetition of the recent sacrifices on the Western Front. Failure to make the League work, he said, would open the way for new wars in Europe which inevitably would require intervention by the United States. As the train passed westward, crowds became larger and more demonstrative.

By the time the train reached the Pacific Coast, the trip had become a triumphal procession. Republican leaders sent two of their best western orators, Senator William E. Borah of Idaho and Senator Hiram Johnson of California to trail Wilson as a "truth squad." After touring California, the president's special train turned back eastward and on September 25, Wilson addressed a great throng at Pueblo, Colorado. People wept as they listened to the president say: "It always seems to make it difficult for me to say anything, my fellow citizens, when I think of my clients in this case. My clients are the children; my clients are the next generation."

That evening the exhausted president collapsed. With shades drawn his train sped back to Washington. A few days later he suffered a paralytic stroke and for weeks was near death. For many months, until the end of his presidency in March 1921, he lay almost secluded in the White House, an invalid in a wheelchair, protected against the outer world by his devoted wife.

Although rumors circulated that Wilson was insane, the president's mental faculties remained unimpaired. His central thought in those awful months was that there should be no compromise on the League: the United States must enter the new international organization without Lodge's reservations. When the Foreign Relations Committee in autumn 1919 reported the Treaty of Versailles with fourteen reservations, Wilson issued instructions from his sickbed that Democrats in the Senate should vote against it. Most

Senate Democrats followed the president's instructions. As a result, the treaty with reservations was easily defeated.

Democrats now recognized that there was no chance of getting the United States into the League without reservations. Many of them concluded that it would be better to have the country in the world organization on Lodge's terms than on the outside. They urged Wilson to compromise. Continuing to believe the country was with him, the president refused. The treaty, with the reservations phrased differently, went before the Senate again in March 1920. Again Wilson directed fellow Democrats to vote "no."

The Treaty Defeated

This time some Democratic senators ignored the president and voted for the reservation-laden treaty. To no avail. The final tally was short of the two-thirds majority necessary for ratification. Even if the Senate had consented to the treaty in 1920, it seems probable that Wilson would have withheld his signature.

So it was that the United States, which had cooperated so magnificently in winning World War I, refused to cooperate in guaranteeing the peace. In retrospect it seems unfortunate that Wilson refused to sanction America's entry in the League even with Lodge's reservations. For it is plain that absence of the United States severely handicapped the international organization's ability to function quickly and effectively in the world community.

Still, Wilson was correct that the only way the League could keep the peace was by responding promptly and automatically to aggression whenever and wherever it occurred. Proof came in the 1930s when the leading members of the League reserved for themselves the right to decide whether and to what extent they would act under Articles X and XVI of the League covenant. In other words they adopted for themselves the same kinds of reservations that Lodge had proposed for the United States. The saddening consequence was that when aggression occurred the League debated and delayed and in the end did little. The unhappy truth, of course, was that Wilson was at least a generation ahead of his time. People, in Europe as well as America, were not ready to take a hard stand against aggression unless their own national interests were threatened.

STUDY GUIDE: Senate opposition to the Versailles treaty, especially to the League of Nations, was led by Henry Cabot Lodge. Lodge tried to delay a vote on the treaty until popular enthusiasm for it had died down. He also attached a number of reservations to the treaty, which he knew would be unacceptable to Wilson. To win public support for the League, Wilson undertook an exhausting cross-country speaking tour. He suffered a paralytic stroke which left him bedridden until his term of office ended. Lodge continued to press for reservations that would limit American participation in the League. Wilson refused to compromise, and the Senate never mustered enough votes to ratify the treaty. Thus the United States never joined the League of Nations.

THE ELECTION OF 1920

Woodrow Wilson's refusal to compromise on the League reservations rested in part on the president's determination to make the presidential election of 1920 a great national referendum on the question of American entry in the League of Nations. Wilson believed that a majority of his countrymen favored American membership in the new world organization on his terms and would vote accordingly. The Democratic national convention, which met in San Francisco in June, therefore, adopted a platform endorsing the Treaty of Versailles and the League of Nations. After forty-four wearisome ballots, the delegates nominated Ohio's Governor James M. Cox, a moderate progressive, for president. Cox in turn selected President Wilson's promising young assistant secretary of the navy, Franklin Delano Roosevelt of New York, to be his running mate. Wilson was not considered for a third term because of illness. He remained an invalid until his death in 1924.

The Republicans had met at Chicago three weeks before. The GOP platform promised an increase in the tariff, tax reductions, and legislation to restrict the flow of immigrants into the United States. It also condemned President Wilson's League of Nations but favored "agreement among nations to preserve the peace of the world."

Who would be the Republican candidate for president?

Theodore Roosevelt had died in January 1919, and most of his followers rallied around General Leonard Wood, who in 1898 had commanded the Rough Riders in Cuba. Wood was the front-runner for the GOP presidential nomination. Closely behind was Governor Frank O. Lowden of Illinois, a champion of farm and business interests of the Middle West. Other possibilities included Senator Hiram Johnson of California, a leading progressive; Herbert Hoover, who had recently announced that he was a Republican rather than a Democrat; and a relatively obscure senator from Ohio, Warren G. Harding.

A sharp-eyed political operative named Harry M. Daugherty was trying to arouse the interest of delegates in Senator Harding because, he later explained, Harding "looked like a President." Daugherty foresaw that the convention would deadlock and predicted that party leaders would compromise on Harding.

The Blackstone Clique

Balloting for the Republican presidential nominee began on the afternoon of Friday, June 11. After several roll calls, neither Wood nor Lowden had succeeded in putting together a majority. After adjournment that evening, Republican leaders, most of them senators, gathered in the Blackstone Hotel and agreed on Harding as their candidate. Why Harding? Because he was a conservative who would not drive Republican progressives from the party, had made few political enemies, and was a pliable man who would respect the wishes of Republicans in Congress.

When balloting resumed the following day, the deadlock between Wood and Lowden continued. Finally, on the tenth ballot Harding received the nomination. The "Blackstone clique" tried to dictate a vice-presidential candidate, only to be rebuffed by the delegates. In an interesting show of independence the delegates nominated Governor Calvin Coolidge of Massachusetts.

The Harding Campaign

Harding conducted his campaign from the front porch of his house in Marion, Ohio. There he received visiting delegations, smiled at visiting celebrities and welcomed his running mate, Calvin Coolidge, who made the inevitable pilgrimage to Marion. In his speeches Harding emphasized that what America needed was "not heroism but healing, not nostrums but normalcy, not revolution but restoration, not agitation but adjustment . . . not submergence in internationality but sustainment in triumphant nationality." The candidate's vision of the country's requirements did not leave much room for American membership in the League of Nations. However, pro-League Republicans, including Charles Evans Hughes and Elihu Root, indicated that a Harding victory would open the way for the United States to join the world organization with the Lodge reservations.

Whatever its intellectual deficiencies, Harding's campaign found a mark with voters. People particularly liked the part about "returning to normalcy." By 1920, Americans were sick and tired of being exhorted to reach for higher rungs on the ladder of Wilsonian idealism. They wanted to forget about the ills of American society and the need for reform; they wanted to forget about crusades for democracy and grand schemes for world cooperation to keep the peace. They wanted to concentrate on their own individual problems and interests. They wanted to be left alone. They wanted a rest.

That was precisely what Harding promised them. Accordingly, when the voters went to the polls on November 2, 1920, they gave Harding and Coolidge 16,000,000 votes. Cox and Roosevelt received only 9,000,000. The Republican margin in the electoral college was 404-127. Not since the year 1860, when Stephen A. Douglas had carried the banner of his hopelessly divided party, had a Democratic presidential ticket gone down to a defeat of such magnitude. By carrying Tennessee, Harding even cracked the "solid South." The Republicans naturally widened their control of both houses of Congress.

STUDY GUIDE: The Democrats nominated James M. Cox for president in 1920. Republican leaders were unable to agree on a presidential candidate. Finally in a "smoke-filled room" in a Chicago hotel they decided on Senator Warren Harding. Americans eager for a "return to normalcy" elected Harding.

THE INTOLERANT 1920s

The election of 1920 is one of those events which historians frequently cite as marking the end of one era and the beginning of a new one. Harding's victory over Cox symbolized the triumph of the forces of political reaction and fervent nationalism over those of domestic progressivism and international idealism. One indication of the changing times was the rising tide of intolerance in America.

This new spirit of intolerance had begun to manifest itself during the time of World War I. It was a spirit which accompanied the great surge of patriotism that developed during the war. Its principal targets were Americans of German descent and a handful of socialists and other pacifists who openly criticized the national war effort. The resulting abuse and harassment of German-Americans and war critics comprise some of the sad pages in the history of the country's democratic crusade of 1917-18. But then the war ended and the doughboys came marching home. One might have expected the campaign against individuals who were deemed to be less than "one-hundred-percent Americans" to grind to a halt. It did not. In the months and years after the armistice of November 11, 1918, superpatriots turned attention to political radicals, socialists, and labor agitators.

Organized Labor

What factors accounted for postwar America's "big red scare," which led to a drive against the country's leftists, real and alleged?

One was the new power of organized labor. This was an outgrowth of the government's policy of encouraging collective bargaining between labor and management so as to prevent any disruption of the flow of supplies and equipment to the war front. Then came the end of the war, and the country went back to a peacetime economy. This process of reconversion was unfortunately accompanied by widespread dislocations, confusions, and shortages, which sent prices spiraling upward. Wages did not keep pace and workingmen, caught in a wage-price squeeze, became restless. The result was a wave of strikes across the nation. Men and women walked off their jobs in shipyards and shoe factories, telephone offices and subways. In Boston the police went out on strike. This prompted Calvin Coolidge, governor of Massachusetts at the time, to make his celebrated comment that "there is no right to strike against the public safety by anybody, anywhere, anytime." That comment brought Coolidge the Republican vice-

1

THE
1920s

The 1920s were a period of change. Young people of the "roaring '20" revolted against prewar standards. Girls wore skirts that came above their knees. Jazz bands captured the spirit of the times. The "return to normalcy" was, for many people, a retreat into isolation from the world. The spirit of reform seemed almost forgotten. Some Americans made fortunes on paper in a rising stock market and ignored the fact that others lived in poverty.

1

The Treaty of Versailles which ended World War I was signed in the Hall of Mirrors at Versailles near Paris, France. The end of the war marked the beginning of a new era in American life.

2

Woodrow Wilson was awarded the Nobel prize for peace for his part in forming proposals to maintain world peace after World War I.

3

Prohibition prevented the legal sale of alcoholic beverages, so people drank illegally in clubs called "speak-easies." The painting *Interior of a Speakeasy* was made by American artist Ben Shahn.

2

3

4

4

Both Members of This Club is a painting by American artist George Bellows. Bellows lived in New York City and attended many professional prize fights. Boxing reached its height of popularity in the United States in the 1920s.

5

Rudolph Valentino was an extremely popular romantic actor in the silent motion pictures during the 1920s. Two of his films were *The Sheik* and *Blood and Sand.*

6

Clara Bow starred in silent films during the 1920s. She quickly gained popularity and was called the "It Girl" by her promoters. She became the sex symbol of the day.

5   The Museum of Modern Art, Film Stills Archives

6   The Museum of Modern Art, Film Stills Archives

presidental nomination in 1920. With the strikes came violence which brought many injuries, a few deaths, and much property damage.

To the strike wave and its attendant violence a great percentage of the American population reacted with predictable outrage. In part the outrage was a result of the inconvenience which always accompanies labor disruptions. In part it was a result of hardship and financial losses endured by stockholders, businessmen, and others whose livelihoods depended on industries or companies tied up by strikes. And in part it was a result of the public attitude toward the labor movement.

Many Americans had long taken a dim view of organized labor. In their judgment unions were conspiracies, labor leaders were agitators trying to upset the American tradition of the rugged individual, and strikes were acts of subversion. The fact that some bearded radicals of East European origin were connected with the labor movement in the United States merely reinforced the notion that organized labor was un-American.

During the strike wave of 1919 some workingmen made it clear that they would not rest content with an increase in wages and reduction in hours. They would settle for nothing less than a brand-new industrial order. In that new order the government, as an agency of all the people, would exercise control rather than "fat-cat" capitalists such as the Rockefellers, Morgans, and Du Ponts. The United Mine Workers at their convention in September 1919, for example, came out for nationalization or socialization of the coal industry. When a delegate rose up in opposition to this resolution he was booed and shouted down with cries: "Coal operator! Throw him out!"

Such displays sent a chill down the spines of millions of Americans. Many were inclined to view wild talk about nationalizing industry as coming straight out of Moscow. As a matter of fact, the Bolsheviks, who in 1917 had established their Communist regime in Russia, did exercise some influence on the labor movement in America in the postwar period. The Bolsheviks had overthrown the czar and ended one of the most oppressive autocracies in the world. They were taking dramatic steps to improve the conditions of the ordinary people of Russia. That their dictatorship of the proletariat had the capacity to be as oppressive and autocratic as the czardom it had displaced was not yet apparent to outside observers.

The Fear of Bolshevism

At the same time that newspapers were bannering news of labor unrest, the fear of bolshevism in America received dramatic reinforcement. First, in spring 1919, a crude bomb turned up in a package delivered to the office of Ole Hanson, the mayor of Seattle who had barnstormed the country in an effort to arouse Americans to the danger of red subversion. The bomb intended for Hanson did not go off, but the very next day a maid suffered serious injuries when she opened a bomb-laden package which had been mailed to Senator Thomas R. Hardwick of Georgia. Hardwick had spoken out for legislation to restrict immigration in the United States on the ground that it offered a good way to keep out Bolsheviks. Reading of the tragedy which had befallen Senator Hardwick's maid, an alert postal worker in New York the following day discovered sixteen packages that had been addressed to prominent business leaders and public officials. Because of insufficient postage the packages had not been delivered. All contained bombs. Then a month later a bomb exploded at the front door of the residence of Attorney General A. Mitchell Palmer in Washington.

While Americans seethed at these apparent examples of Bolshevist treachery, striking workers tied up the steel industry. Few people noted that many steelworkers were bearing the burden of a seven-day work week and a twelve-hour day. What they did notice was that William Z. Foster was one of the strike leaders. A capable man who would later run for president on the ticket of the American Communist party, Foster was a known radical. Accordingly, the steel strike became, in the language of the country's "red-baiters," a part of the Bolshevist conspiracy. Next, in September 1919, came the demand of the United Mine Workers that the government socialize the coal industry.

A National Campaign Against Leftists

The stage was now set for a national campaign against the country's leftists. Eager to provide leadership for such a drive was Attorney General Palmer.

Palmer's first act was to secure an injunction against leaders of the mine workers' union so as to head off a threatened strike in the coal industry. Although the war had been over for nearly a year, the attorney general rested the case for an injunction on a wartime law that forbade interference with production of coal. The miners went on strike anyhow. Next Palmer determined to get rid of Communist leaders in the country. That the alleged Communist leaders had violated no statutes did not bother Palmer. With no regard for their legal rights or concern for their families, he sent federal agents after the red leaders. Before long, a number of them were put on a ship dubbed "the Soviet ark" by America's superpatriots, destination, the Soviet Union.

So favorable was the public response to the move against Communist leaders that Palmer decided to broaden his activities. Taking advantage of a wartime sedition law that authorized deportation of aliens who advocated overthrow of the government, the attorney general prepared to rid the country of all foreign-born Communists. On New Year's Day 1920, Palmer's agents swooped down on Communist meeting places in cities across the entire country, arrested six thousand alleged Communists, and seized records, literature, and anything else that might serve as evidence in a court of law. In most instances, the accused individuals were detained illegally and eventually tried on the basis of the most flimsy evidence, including pictures taken from the walls of their meeting places. Fortunately the courts revealed a greater respect for the rules of jurisprudence than did the attorney general. Most of the accused were released. Where was the president? Why did he not lift a hand for reason and tolerance? Wilson was sick, confined to the White House, and concerned only with the struggle over the League of Nations.

Other Americans had also taken up red-baiting. The renowned evangelist Billy Sunday declared that "if I had my way with these ornery wild-eyed Socialists and I.W.W.'s, I would stand them up before a firing squad and save space on our ships." A group of Protestant clergymen called for deportation of all Bolsheviks. The state legislature of New York expelled five duly elected members who happened to be members of the Socialist party. Prominent liberal periodicals, including *The Nation* and *The New Republic,* were branded as "revolutionary," as were such distinguished reformers as Rabbi Stephen S. Wise, Norman Thomas, and Jane Addams. To avoid the wrath of the red-baiters, of course, many Americans took extreme care to say or do nothing that might be considered radical.

It appeared by late summer 1920 that "the big red scare" was about to run its course. Then at midday on September 16, a horse-drawn wagon stopped in front of the Wall Street office of J. P. Morgan & Company. The driver climbed down from the seat and casually walked away. A few moments later, the wagon was the center of a thunderous explosion. Buildings shook, glass shattered, smoke billowed up to the sky. And in the street and adjacent offices thirty people lay dead or dying. (J. P. Morgan was out of the country at the time.) For years, police and detectives combed the evidence without result. But everybody was certain of one thing: here was another foul deed by the Bolsheviks. And in that one blinding moment of the explosion in Wall Street red-baiting was shifted back into high gear.

The Sacco-Vanzetti Case

The following year, 1921, brought a new episode in "the big red scare" when the names of Sacco and Vanzetti captured the country's attention.

The celebrated case of Sacco and Vanzetti began in April 1920–several months before the Wall Street explosion–with the murder of a paymaster and his guard at South Braintree, Massachusetts. Shortly after the slaying two Italian immigrants, Nicola Sacco and Bartolomeo Vanzetti, both reputed to be anarchists, were arrested and charged with the crime. A jury found the two men guilty and a judge sentenced them to death.

The case attracted little attention in the United States at the time. But political radicals in Europe and Latin America believed Sacco and Vanzetti were being persecuted for their radicalism. In their countries they conducted several violent demonstrations on behalf of the two men. During one demonstration a bomb exploded, killing twenty people. Such events caused some Americans to become interested in the Sacco-Vanzetti case. Before long, liberals in the country were in almost unanimous agreement that foreign radicals were correct. Sacco and Vanzetti had indeed been tried and convicted because of the radicalism they avowed, rather than the presence of hard evidence that they had committed the murder at South Braintree. The liberals had a point. During the trial Judge Webster Thayer publicly expressed contempt for anarchism and then permitted the state's attorney to make the radicalism of the accused men the focus of his case. Liberals were also much moved by the quiet demeanor of Sacco and Vanzetti, particularly the latter, an intelligent and sensitive man who seemed incapable of a payroll murder.

Compix Photo

Niccola Sacco and Bartolomeo Vanzetti arrive for their trial on robbery and murder charges. Why did foreign radicals and American liberals believe the two aliens were tried for their radicalism rather than an actual crime?

Despite protests, rallies, and demonstrations, the verdict of the original trial stood, and one appeal after another for a new trial was denied. Then in 1927, seven years after the trial, the governor of Massachusetts, who was considering a pardon for the two men, appointed a blue-ribbon advisory committee. The committee included the presidents of Harvard and the Massachusetts Institute of Technology. He asked them to review the evidence of the case. The committee reported that the facts indicated Sacco and Vanzetti had committed the crime, whereupon the governor put aside thoughts of a pardon and allowed the two men to die in the electric chair.

Were Sacco and Vanzetti guilty? Later studies have indicated that Sacco, at least, probably was. Did they receive a fair trial? By generally accepted rules of law, they did not. Whatever the facts surrounding the murder and trial, the case of the two immigrant-radicals stands out as a reminder of how honorable persons such as Judge Thayer can mishandle solemn responsibilities when swept up in popular hysteria.

Immigration Restrictions

There were other aspects of America's "red scare," including the federal legislation of 1921 and 1924 that imposed sharp restrictions on im-

migration in the United States. These laws ended the long era in which foreigners could enter the country almost at will.

For several decades "one-hundred-percent Americans" had been seeking restrictive legislation as the flow of immigrants from Southern and Eastern Europe increased. America's involvement in Europe's war and the spirit of superheated nationalism it aroused strengthened the position of those who wished to make America a preserve for "regular Americans." Finally, after the war, during the red scare, advocates of immigration restriction noted that a high percentage of the radicals in the country were immigrants. So they argued that an effective way to strike at the terrible Bolsheviks was to scrap the ancient policy of free immigration. For Americans taken up with the fear of bolshevism such an argument had great appeal. The outcome was increased pressure for restriction. At length, in 1921 and 1924, Congress acted.

Communists, real and alleged, were not the only victims of the dark side of the American personality which surfaced in the era of normalcy. Negroes, Jews, and Catholics–people who for one reason or another could not quite qualify as "regular Americans"–also became targets of intolerance and abuse.

Disillusioned Negroes

Negroes had given strong support to the national war effort in 1917-18, in part no doubt because they hoped the war might bring them full membership in America's democratic society. Then the war ended and the illusions of black Americans were shattered. Rather than heralding a great new advance of democracy in America, the war touched off a sharp reaction.

In the South, where most blacks continued to live, whites seemed more insensitive than ever to the claims of Negroes. In northern cities, to which many Negroes had migrated in the war years to meet labor shortages, blacks in the postwar era often found themselves elbowed out of their new jobs to make way for white doughboys returning from the battle front. Some Negroes returned to the South, but many others remained and took what work they could find, frequently as janitors, street cleaners, or garbage collectors. When his working day finally ended, the black man in the urban North returned to the black ghetto, likely as not to a dilapidated, rat-infested slum dwelling. While the system of segregation and discrimination was less apparent in the North than in the South and not subject to a maze of statutes and ordinances, the black northerner was not allowed to forget that he was a member of a presumably "inferior" race.

Anti-Semitism and Catholic-baiting

Jews felt the wrath of some Americans for a number of reasons. First, they were non-Christians, members of a "race" that had rejected and eventually had been held responsible for the death of Jesus of Nazareth. Second, Jews were thought to be clannish; that is, they tended to associate with and marry other Jews. (It did not occur to anti-Semites that such fraternal behavior might have been a natural closing of ranks in the face of discrimination and abuse.)

Third, Jews, in the estimate of many patriotic Americans, were a people of divided loyalties, who felt as deeply committed to "international Jewry" as to the United States. Fourth, some of the country's political radicals–anarchists, socialists, communists–were Jews of East European origin.

The manifestations of anti-Semitism in America in the 1920s were legion. Employers refused to hire Jews, landlords refused to rent apartments and houses to Jewish tenants, neighborhoods and towns adopted convenants excluding Jews. Some private schools closed their doors to Jewish girls and boys, and authorities at Harvard debated the desirability of limiting the number of Jews who might enroll as undergraduates. Perhaps the country's best-known anti-Semite was the automobile manufacturer Henry Ford. Ford used the columns of his newspaper, the Dearborn *Independent,* to blame Jews for nearly every ill that had ever befallen American society and to charge that Jews were involved in a great international conspiracy to dominate the world.

Catholic-baiting was an old story in North America. From the time of the first English settlers, intolerance of Catholicism–or "popery," as Protestants frequently called it–had been a force in American life. During the nineteenth century the country had endured epidemics of anti-Catholicism. Thus the hostility and abuse directed against Catholics after World War I was merely a new breaking out of an old disease.

The arguments used to justify attacks on Catholics in the age of "normalcy" varied little from those of previous times. "Regular Americans" contended that Catholics had divided loyalties; that is, they felt at least as much devotion to the pope in Rome as to the Stars and Stripes in America. They were clannish, as was evidenced by their insistence on educating their children in church-operated parochial schools rather than in little red schoolhouses. Catholics also clung to a range of religious customs and practices that offended the sensibilities of many Protestant Christians. They abstained from meat on Friday and venerated the Virgin Mary, erected crosses atop their churches and confessed their sins to priests whom they addressed as "Father."

The Ku Klux Klan

Into this misty environment of hate, suspicion, and fear appeared the Ku Klux Klan. The aim of the Klan was "to unite white male persons, native-born Gentile citizens of the United States of America, who owe no allegiance of any nature to any foreign government, nation, institution, sect, ruler, person, or people; whose morals are good, whose reputations and vocations are exemplary . . . to cultivate and promote patriotism toward our Civil Government; to exemplify a practical benevolence; to shield the sanctity of the home and the chastity of womanhood; to maintain forever white supremacy, to teach and faithfully inculcate a high spiritual philosophy through an exalted ritualism, and by a practical devotion to conserve, protect, and maintain the distinctive institutions, rights, privileges, principles, traditions and ideals of a pure Americanism." So declared the order's constitution.

The original Ku Klux Klan appeared in the South after the Civil War. It aimed at terrorizing Negroes and "keeping them in their place," particularly away from the voting booth. Following the restoration of former Confederates to absolute control of the southern political mechanism, the Klan lost its reason for existence and died away. But then, in 1915, a Georgian named William Joseph Simmons organized a fraternal order intended to promote patriotism and preserve "the southern way of life." Dusting off the pages of southern history, he dubbed his organization the Ku Klux Klan. In its early days the new Klan attracted little attention and few members. Then came the war, the era of normalcy, and the outpouring of hostility for things and people thought by "regular" citizens to be un-American.

The moment of opportunity for the Klan had arrived.

In the South, black Americans were the main targets of the Klan. Klan members believed that they were biologically superior to blacks, and they tried to prevent black men and women from becoming first-class citizens. By frightening and threatening blacks, the Klan tried to prevent them from protesting segregation or from objecting to trials by all-white juries.

Usually the Klan was able to achieve its aim of intimidating Negroes without resorting to violence. A huge flaming cross glowing in the night on a hillside or a parade of Klansmen, wearing their robes—of white, scarlet, blue, yellow, or green, depending on the member's position in the order—was enough to frighten most black people. If such "peaceful" means were not sufficient, the Klan was quite willing to use other, more violent methods.

In the northern states, particularly in small towns where Negroes were almost nonexistent, Catholics and Jews were the chief targets of the Klan. Unlike in the South, the Klan in the North seldom whipped or lynched its "enemies." Instead it burned crosses, paraded, and organized boycotts against Catholic and Jewish merchants. It also circulated inflammatory literature charging Catholics and Jews with the most offensive crimes and outrages. It sought to defeat Catholic and Jewish candidates for public office and tried to secure laws prohibiting parochial schools. The Klan also sought to place its own members in positions of power and influence. As a result, the order gained control of the political mechanisms of many towns and cities across the Middle West. In Ohio and Indiana the Klan took over the state governments for brief periods.

In addition to providing a convenient instrument for harassing Negroes, Catholics, and Jews as well as immigrants and Bolsheviks, the Klan had other appeals. The rituals, secrecy, and bizarre costumes seemed to satisfy a need for pomp, mystery, and excitement lacking in otherwise dull lives. The Klan at its peak in the mid-1920s had perhaps four and a half million members. It was a big business. To join the order an individual had to pay a ten-dollar enrollment fee, part of which went to the Klansman credited with recruiting the new member, part of which went to assorted King Kleagles and Grand Goblins. Another part finally made its way to the national headquarters in Atlanta, to the Imperial Wizard, Colonel Simmons.

There is no precise way to measure the extent of the power and activities of the Ku Klux Klan. As time passed, increasing numbers of Americans became sickened by the misdeeds perpetrated by the Klan in the name of Americanism. Even some Klansmen, while they did not become friends and defenders of Negroes, Catholics, and Jews, concluded that the methods of the KKK were not the best way to promote the interests of Anglo-Saxon Protestant America. By 1930, therefore, the Klan had nearly disappeared in the North and in the South was no more than a shadow of its former self.

STUDY GUIDE: During the 1920s conservative forces and a spirit of nationalism prevailed in America. A rising tide of intolerance swept the nation, directed against organized labor and political radicals. Under special attack were the Bolsheviks, who had established a Communist government in Russia and were trying to enter the American labor movement. Feelings against radicals in America were reflected in the Sacco-Vanzetti case. Sacco and Vanzetti were Italian immigrants, said to be anarchists. They were charged with murder in Massachusetts and sentenced to death. Many liberals charged that hysteria had prevented the two men from getting a fair trial.

Suspicion of all foreigners influenced the passage of federal legislation on restricting immigration. Many minority groups, especially Jews, Catholics, and Negroes, suffered from intolerant attitudes during the twenties. The Ku Klux Klan was particularly active during this period.

THE "ROARING" 1920s

The era of normalcy—the time of the "big red scare" and the Ku Klux Klan—was also the time of national Prohibition, Al Capone, and the "monkey trial" at Dayton, Tennessee.

For the better part of a century assorted organizations and individuals had sought restrictions on the right of citizens to produce, distribute, and consume alcoholic beverages. In the beginning, in the 1820s and 1830s, the movement for "temperance" met little success. Then in the 1850s it picked up momentum. By the outbreak of the Civil War in 1861, several northeastern and midwestern states had become "dry" by adopting prohibition statutes.

During the Civil War the work of the temperance forces was undone as one state after another repealed legislation prohibiting production and sale of liquor. But the temperance movement refused to die, largely because the era after the Civil War seemed to offer greater proof than ever of the evils of strong drink. As pointed out by advocates of temperance, liquor was inevitably the handmaiden of gambling and prostitution. And distillers and brewers were considered sources of support for some of the more corrupt political "bosses" in the country.

Religious Groups Clamor for Prohibition

The largest Protestant denominations in the United States had agreed by the second half of the nineteenth century that it was a sin to drink liquor. Thus churchgoing Protestants were mainstays of the temperance movement. Particularly active in the drive were the Methodists, who had an unusual awareness of social problems. The movement for temperance indeed became a Protestant crusade. The Woman's Christian Temperance Union (WCTU), founded by Frances E. Willard in 1874, and the Anti-Saloon League, founded in 1893, were essentially religious organizations.

To achieve their ends the temperance forces issued propaganda to show the evils of liquor. They organized parades and discussion groups, sponsored rallies and public lectures. They campaigned for candidates of the Prohibition party, which ran its first candidate for president in 1876. They studied Democratic and Republican candidates for political office and gave their blessing to those who had spoken out against liquor. They lobbied in state capitals for statewide prohibition laws and, failing that, for local-option statutes — laws giving towns and counties the option to vote themselves "dry." Some of the more militant temperance leaders tried more direct methods. Most renowned of the "hardliners" was Carry Nation. A six-foot, 190-pound woman from Kansas, Mrs. Nation was arrested some thirty times around the turn of the century for attacking saloons with a hatchet and otherwise disturbing the peace.

Slowly but steadily the temperance forces achieved their objectives. They succeeded because they were more zealous than were their opponents. Equally important, they were far better organized. By the time the United States entered World War I, in 1917, they had prevailed upon two-thirds of the states of the federal Union to adopt prohibition statutes and several others to approve local-option measures. As a result, fully three-fourths of the national population resided in counties that were legally "dry." Nor was their success limited to the states. The Anti-Saloon lobby prevailed upon Congress in 1913 to approve the Webb-Kenyon Bill prohibiting transportation of alcoholic beverages into "dry" states. They also persuaded leaders on Capitol Hill to consider an amendment to the federal Constitution outlawing strong drink nationally. A resolution embracing such an amendment received a majority vote in Congress in 1916, but failed to receive the necessary two-thirds.

The Eighteenth Amendment

When, in April 1917, the United States entered the war, the stage was set for the temperance forces to score their greatest triumph.

Before the war, the advocates of prohibition had rested their argument on the alleged sinfulness of drinking with the heartache and misfortune that liquor brought to individuals, their families, and their communities. But now their arguments took on a new dimension. Prohibition became a matter of patriotism. Temperance advocates stated that the country could save a great deal of grain if it discontinued production of beer and whiskey. Temperance advocates noted that to be efficient a man must be sober. They observed that beer was the German national beverage and that most of the leading brewers in America and many of the distillers were of German origin.

In December 1917 Congress gave the necessary two-thirds vote to a proposed amendment providing that "after one year from the ratification of this article the manufacture, sale, and transportation of intoxicating liquors within, the importation thereof into, or the exportation thereof from the United States and all territory subject to the jurisdiction thereof for beverage purposes is hereby prohibited." Thirteen months later, in January 1919, the Eighteenth Amendment, after receiving approval of three-fourths of the states, was added to the Constitution. To provide an enforcement apparatus for the new amendment, in autumn 1919 Congress passed the Volstead Act over President Wilson's veto. The legislation defined intoxicating liquor as any beverage containing more than one-half of one percent of alcohol and placed the administration of the law under the Bureau of Internal Revenue.

The Eighteenth Amendment closed the corner saloon. It caused great breweries in Milwaukee, Saint Louis, and other cities to turn to production of "near beer"—a brew containing no more alcohol than was permitted by the Volstead Act. Distilleries in central Kentucky and elsewhere became idle and deserted. But it did not quench the thirst of tens of millions of Americans for alcoholic drink. National Prohibtion was born of the same spirit of idealism and self-sacrifice that had caused Americans during the war to thrill to President Wilson's plan for a League of Nations. It became effective, in 1920, at the very moment when Americans were deciding they had had enough of idealism and self-sacrifice and wanted to return to normalcy. Hence they refused to obey the Eighteenth Amendment just as they had refused to accept the League and voted for Harding.

Violation of the Prohibition amendment was easy enough. When no federal inspectors were around breweries turning out "near beer" could increase the alcoholic content of their product. Industrial alcohol, which could provide the base for a variety of homemade beverages, was readily obtainable. Pharmacies, which could sell alcohol when prescribed by physicians, were another source of the forbidden spirits. For only a few dollars an ingenious individual could purchase the equipment and set up a still in his cellar. Many Americans had been making their own wine and "home brew" for years and went on making them after adoption of the Eighteenth Amendment. Then enormous quantities of whiskey, wine and beer were smuggled into the country from Canada, Europe, the West Indies, and Mexico.

Speakeasies—illegal bars, saloons, and night clubs—sprang into existence and flourished in nearly every town and city. In garages, cellars, and closets people who otherwise were law-abiding citizens turned out quantities of homemade beer and whiskey. The hip flask became a badge of distinction, and rumrunners made fortunes smuggling liquor into the country. In the great cities racketeers fought it out with tommy guns for control of vast empires of bootleg liquor.

Under the Eighteenth Amendment, underworld figures instantly saw an opportunity for enormous profits. Thirsty Americans wanted beer and whiskey. They, the mobsters, would supply it. They could smuggle it in from foreign sources, hijack it, buy it from independent bootleggers, or make it themselves. How would they distribute their products? Selling to anyone on the street would be too cumbersome and risky. Sales to speakeasies was the solution. The largest opportunities lay in the great cities where hundreds and even thousands of illegal bars and saloons were confined in relatively small areas. Concentration on these outlets would simplify the problems of administration and distribution and would mean that the mob would have to deal with only one political administration and police force.

Organized Crime Supplies Liquor

One of the first Prohibition mobsters was a shabby Chicagoan named Johnny Torrio. But Torrio learned quickly that other underworld figures in Chicago had similar ideas. He decided to eliminate the competition and imported from New York a youthful thug, Alphonse Capone. In addition to persuading other mobs to stay out of Torrio's territory, Capone made certain that proprietors of speakeasies did not accept the products of any suppliers other than Torrio.

Capone was immensely successful and within a short time took over the entire operation. He eliminated most competitors and when new gangs appeared to challenge his empire he dispatched his henchmen to take care of the rivals, usually in a hail of bullets.

Capone, known as "Scarface Al," lived his role as undisputed kingpin of the country's bootleg racketeers to the hilt. He moved about Chicago in an armor-plated automobile convoyed by other cars filled with armed thugs. He threw lavish parties at his winter estate in Florida. During the 1920s he had no serious disputes with the law, in part because he kept himself removed from actual operations of his rackets, in part because he listened to the counsel of expert lawyers. In addition, he always had a battery of local politicians and policemen in his employ. It was an incredible performance, and one that captivated readers of newspapers and magazines. Capone became something of a folk hero, which of course says a great deal about the state of America in the era of normalcy. But the law finally caught up with him in the 1930s—not for murder, bribery, or extortion, but for income-tax evasion.

Despite wholesale violation of the Eighteenth Amendment and the activities of racketeers like Al Capone, evangelical Protestants—or "fundamentalists"—insisted throughout the 1920s that the "noble experiment" of national Prohibition was a rousing success. The verdict of history does not bear them out. Prohibition was a disaster, for the country and also for the fundamentalists whose influence declined as bootleggers, rumrunners, and racketeers made a mockery of their bright predictions.

Darwinism Debated

The breakdown of Prohibition was not the only disaster endured by fundamentalist Protestants in the era of normalcy. There was the unhappy quarrel over whether or not the Bible was literally true—biblical literalism.

The controversy over biblical literalism was not new in the 1920s. For centuries some men interested in science had questioned the idea that the Bible was the literal word of God. The appearance of Charles Darwin's books on evolution in the second half of the nineteenth century resulted in a long debate on the subject, which threatened to wreck Protestantism in America. Protestantism survived the initial crisis of Darwinism. Some Protestant groups rejected all points in the Bible that seemed to conflict with science. Replying to critics that the Bible was not meant to be understood, others merely ignored Darwin and the findings of natural science.

After the World War the old controversy over interpreting the Bible flared anew. Encouraged by the "big red scare"—which equated bolshevism with atheism—fundamentalist Protestants tried to persuade state legislatures, particularly in the South, to pass laws prohibiting the teaching of biological evolution in public schools and colleges.

Those who opposed the teaching of the theory of evolution made little headway in the beginning. But then, in the early 1920s, they captured the attention of "the Great Commoner," William Jennings Bryan. Before long, their campaign was operating under a full head of steam.

Bryan was an ideal leader of the forces of fundamentalism. Three times a candidate for president and a former secretary of state, he had a national, indeed an international, reputation. He was perhaps the greatest orator of his generation. He was a man of great courage, unmatched faith in evangelical Christianity, and bewilderingly ignorant of the teachings of natural science. He had devoted a lifetime to championing the interests, hopes, and dreams of the God-fearing people of rural America.

Spurred by the eloquence of Bryan and the zeal of fundamentalists, opponents of evolutionism won wide support across the country's "Bible Belt." In March 1925, the legislature of Tennessee approved a law stating that "it shall be unlawful for any teacher in any of the universities, normals and all other public schools of the State, which are supported in whole or in part by the public school funds of the State, to teach any theory that denies the story of the Divine creation of man as taught in the Bible, and to teach instead that man has descended from a lower order of animals."

The American Civil Liberties Union viewed the law as a denial of the freedom of teachers to teach the truth as they saw it—a denial of academic freedom. The ACLU, in other words, considered the law as an attempt by the legislature in Nashville to compel teachers to teach mythology and superstition rather than scientific fact. The Union immediately offered free legal counsel to any teacher in Tennessee who would dare to challenge the antievolution statute.

A short time later, in Dayton, Tennessee, some thirty-five miles northeast of Chattanooga, three men discussed the law. One of the men was John Thomas Scopes, a modest, well-mannered young graduate of the University of Kentucky who taught biology at Central High School in Dayton. All three men agreed that the measure was deplorable. They talked further. Why not test the law? The American Civil Liberties Union would pay legal expenses. A trial would attract attention, put Dayton on the map, and add some interest to their lives. And so Scopes, in part for the fun of it, agreed to give his biology class an evolutionist lecture. One of his companions would then file a complaint with local authorities. Scopes gave the lecture, the companion complained, and the police arrested Scopes. A grand jury returned an indictment and a trial was scheduled for the following July.

To defend Scopes the ACLU, sparing no expense, retained the country's best-known attorney, Clarence Darrow—a craggy liberal who was an avowed religious skeptic—and two other prominent civil liberty lawyers. To assist the prosecution the World's Christian Fundamentals Association brought in William Jennings Bryan.

As the time of the trial approached, Dayton was like a combination of a carnival and a great revival meeting. Tents sprang up and "hellfire-and-damnation" preachers exhorted listeners to be steadfast in their faith in the Bible. Other men vended hot dogs and lemonade. And a few enterprising booksellers hawked volumes on biology which presumably explained the peculiar theory of evolution. Hundreds of newspapermen, photographers, and telegraph operators converged on Dayton from every corner of the nation.

The "Monkey Trial"

It was hot and humid in Dayton when the trial began. In the courtroom the main participants peeled off their suit jackets and presented arguments in shirt-sleeves. Continually interrupting proceedings were photographers and movie cameramen who moved about the courtroom, shifted furniture, and climbed on tables. Present in the courtroom also was a strange black instrument, a radio microphone, the property of Station WGN in Chicago, which was offering its listeners live coverage of the celebrated "monkey trial."

The issue to be decided was whether or not Scopes had violated the law. There was no question that he had. But the defense was determined to put the law itself on trial, to establish the scientific validity of the theory of evolution, and to demonstrate that evolution and Christianity were not irreconcilable. Bryan, however, charged that Darrow's sole purpose was "to slur at the Bible."

Then, on the afternoon of July 20, in a surprise move, the defense asked to put Bryan on the stand. A member of the prosecution's staff testifying as a witness for the defense? It was incredible. Why such an irregular request? Well, Mr. Bryan was a self-proclaimed expert on the Bible and presumably could answer questions that the defense wished to ask about the meaning of the sacred book. Would Mr. Bryan consent to take the stand? Of course he would.

Because of the heat and also because of the crowds, the judge had moved the trial outdoors. And so on a crude platform before a great throng of onlookers, Darrow set about cross-examining the Great Commoner.

Why was he questioning the champion of fundamentalism? Roared Darrow: "To show up Fundamentalism . . . to prevent bigots and ignoramuses from controlling the educational system of the United States." Purple with rage, Bryan jumped to his feet, shook his fist, and rasped: "To protect the word of God against the greatest atheist and agnostic in the United States!" In more restrained moments Darrow asked the witness about the date of creation. Although scientists estimated the earth to be hundreds of millions of years old, Bryan calmly responded that God had created the world in 4004 B.C. Darrow asked if Bryan seriously believed that the first woman had been created from the rib of the first man and that the diversity of languages in the world derived from the collapse of the tower of Babel. Bryan did believe. Darrow asked if Bryan honestly believed that Jonah had survived for three days in the belly of a whale and that Joshua actually had made the sun stand still. Bryan believed.

The hopes of fundamentalists had run high when the Scopes trial began. But in the view of many people the encounter of July 20 reduced fundamentalist theological ideas—and those of William Jennings Bryan—to intellectual rubble. In the last minutes of Darrow's interrogation, Bryan's own followers began to laugh at his answers. For Bryan, a good and kindly man, a man of the people as well as a man of God, this must have been the saddest moment of his life. In retrospect the humiliation of the Great Commoner takes on a special sadness, for Bryan was nearing the end of his long and honorable career. Weakened by the strain of the trial, he died in Dayton one week later.

Scopes was found guilty of violating the law and fined one hundred dollars. Later the supreme court of Tennessee, citing a legal technicality, set aside the judgment against him. This move prevented evolutionists from appealing the conviction and testing the constitutionality of the law. The antievolutionists continued their campaign against Darwinism, persuading three more southern states to outlaw the teaching of biological evolution in the public schools. The downfall at Dayton and the death of Bryan, however, had taken the steam out of their movement. By the end of the 1920s, it was little more than a memory.

STUDY GUIDE: American involvement in World War I helped temperance leaders to influence congressional passage of the Eighteenth Amendment. This amendment prohibited the sale, transportation, and manufacture of alcoholic beverages throughout the nation. However, Prohibition failed to prevent people from obtaining liquor, either by making it or by smuggling it in from abroad. In the great cities racketeers such as Chicago's Al Capone fought for control of vast empires selling "bootleg" alcohol.

The Scopes "monkey trial" in Tennessee

brought together two famous men, William Jennings Bryan and Clarence Darrow. Darrow defended Scopes, whose teaching of Darwin's theory of evolution in a public school violated a Tennessee law. Bryan represented Protestant fundamentalists who accepted literally the story of Creation as told in the Bible. Through their influence laws had been passed in many southern states prohibiting the teaching of biological evolution. Scopes was found guilty of violating the law, but the highly emotional trial was a humiliation for Bryan and the fundamentalist cause.

Compix Photo

Senator Warren G. Harding takes his front porch campaign to the women voters of Marion, Ohio. The presidential election of 1920 was the first in which women could vote.

THE "GOLDEN" 1920s

The decade after the armistice of 1918 was a time of intolerance, gangsterism, and religious strife. But it was also for many Americans a time of prosperity, happiness, and achievement, a veritable "golden era."

The Economic Boom

War had touched off an economic boom in America and the economic mechanism, except for a brief slowdown over winter 1918-19, continued to thrive. The federal policy of huge loans to the Allied governments in the postwar period was partly responsible for the absence of any sharp break in prosperity when the country shifted from war to peace. The Allied governments used much of the loans to buy grain, cotton, and manufactures in the United States. Another factor was the resumption of private construction when the federal government lifted wartime restrictions on building materials. But then, in 1920-21, the boom ended, largely because the government in Washington drastically reduced loans to foreign countries. The outcome was a severe economic depression.

The depression passed quickly with a return of confidence among leaders of business. By 1922 prices, employment, and profits were moving up and by 1923 prosperity was back in the saddle. Dark spots remained in the economic picture, however, for agriculture, mining, and textiles did not share fully in the good times of the period. Moreover, large numbers of Americans, such as sharecroppers in the rural South and urban families depending on incomes from menial labor, endured severe privation. The gains of the great middle class, if steady, were

less than spectacular. In other words, the principal beneficiaries of the rampaging prosperity of the 1920s were the handful of people—perhaps five percent of the total population—at the top of the economic pyramid.

Still, the years after 1922 were among the most prosperous in the history of the nation, and in each year the economy performed better than in the preceding one. Between 1923 and 1929, the gross national product—that is, the total national output of goods and services—increased twenty-three percent, from $78.8 billion to $97.1 billion. Corporate profits in that period increased sixty-five percent from $4.7 billion to $7.6 billion.

The Automobile

Many Americans took advantage of their rising affluence to purchase automobiles. Indeed the age of normalcy was the time when the motor car triumphed over the horse and buggy, took dead aim on the steam passenger train, and added a new dimension to the lives of the people of the United States.

The rich displayed their wealth by purchasing a Duesenberg (which might cost upward of $20,000) or a Stutz or a Pierce-Arrow. Great numbers of middle-class Americans purchased an Essex, Ford, or Chevrolet.

Automobiles became faster, more comfortable, and more dependable. The open touring car with its folding canvas top gave way to the closed car with its rigid top, full-sized doors, and windows that could be tightly closed to keep out dust, cold, and moisture. As automobiles became more numerous, state, local, and federal authorities improved roads and highways and built

AMERICAN BUSINESS ACTIVITY: 1920 — 1929

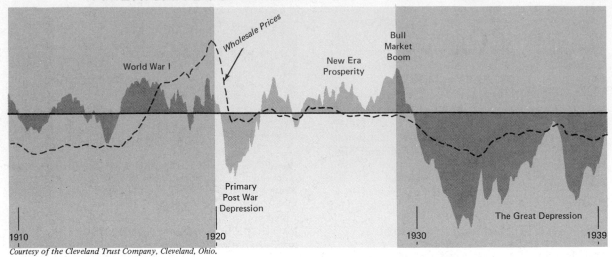

World War I

Wholesale Prices

New Era Prosperity

Bull Market Boom

Primary Post War Depression

The Great Depression

1910   1920   1930   1939

Courtesy of the Cleveland Trust Company, Cleveland, Ohio.

hundreds of thousands of miles of new ones. The consequences were enormous. Automobiles provided jobs for millions of people—in auto manufacturing, repair, sales, financing, production and sale of gasoline and oil, tires, road construction, and steel making. The automobile explosion also gave a new mobility to the people of America and revolutionized society. Rural isolation virtually disappeared. A trip to relatives forty miles away, which had required all day to make in a horse-drawn wagon or buggy, could now be made in a little more than an hour. Delivery trucks, taxis, and passenger cars whizzing up and down main thoroughfares and side streets dramatically speeded the tempo of life in the nation's cities.

The Radio

Many Americans bought radio receiving sets and regularly tuned in broadcasts—jazz music, news reports, political conventions, baseball games—originating from new transmitting stations. These stations were springing up because of the popular enthusiasm generated in 1920 when KDKA in Pittsburgh, the country's first commercial broadcasting station, broadcast returns of the Harding-Cox election. (One can measure the popular acceptance of radio with the inevitable statistics: Americans in 1922 spent $60 million on radio receiving sets; in 1929, $842.5 million, an increase of 1,400 percent.)

Movies and Sports

Americans went to the movies in increasing numbers. They thrilled to the performances of Rudolph Valentino and Greta Garbo and laughed (after 1928) at the antics of Walt Disney's animated cartoon characters. Near the end of the decade they crowded into movie houses to witness the first major "talking picture," *The Jazz Singer,* starring Al Jolson. This was the time when vaudeville, with its array of dancers, jugglers, and comics, made its last stand in America.

People wagered on the great thoroughbred racehorses, Man O'War and Twenty Grand. Sports fans bought tickets to cheer such heroes as Babe Ruth and Walter Johnson in baseball, Red Grange in football, Jack Dempsey and Gene Tunney in boxing, Bobby Jones in golf, and Bill Tilden in tennis. Americans spent hundreds of thousands of dollars on the tile pieces necessary for playing Mah-Jongg, a game imported from China. They bought books and magazines in record numbers, went to county fairs and gasped at the stunts of parachutists and wing walkers, and, when they felt daring themselves, paid a couple of dollars to take a short ride in an open-cockpit biplane.

Ballyhoo

It was in the "golden" twenties that somebody coined the word "ballyhoo," the exaggerated publicity associated with the period. There were

Listening to the radio was enough of a novelty in the early 1920s to merit a picture showing Senator Robert La Follette, Sr., of Wisconsin tuning in his receiving set. By 1929, millions of his fellow Americans owned their own radio receiving sets.

Courtesy State Historical Society of Wisconsin

publicity seekers sitting on flagpoles and widely publicized marathon dance contests. The funeral of Rudolph Valentino in New York in 1926 (which press agents cleverly turned into a near riot) secured reams of free publicity for the dead actor's films. And newspapers seemed filled with sensational accounts of murder trials, rescues, and channel swims.

The 1920s were the era of "flaming youth." It was a time when some youngsters, taken up with the new and exciting ideas of the Austrian psychiatrist Sigmund Freud, shocked their elders by flouting conventional standards of morality, particularly with respect to card playing, drinking, smoking, and sex.

Closely related with these changing attitudes, was the new position of women in American society. Encouraged by approval of the Nineteenth Amendment to the Constitution, which proclaimed that they were the political equals of males, some women in the 1920s set out to further the process of emancipation. Not only did they drink and smoke cigarettes in public, they also bobbed their hair, wore lipstick, and dressed in knee-length skirts (a shocking departure from the time a few years before when no self-respecting woman dared show more than her ankles).

Science and Technology

Notwithstanding the ballyhoo and accent on pleasure, the 1920s had some solid achievements.

Medical researchers developed new and faster-acting anesthetics and a mechanical "iron lung" for people whose chests had been paralyzed by polio. Two inventors, John Daniel Rust and Mack Donald Rust, produced a mechanical cotton picker. Applications of science and technology to mining, manufacturing, transportation, and communication resulted in a steady improvement in the quality of the output of American industry.

The Arts

American literature, theater, and music came of age during the 1920s and began to win international acclaim. The 1920s were a golden age for the creative arts in America.

In music the ragtime songs that had become more and more popular after 1900 were blended with Negro blues and spirituals and rhythms from Africa to make a new kind of music called jazz. No one knows where jazz began, but it reached a kind of perfection among black musicians in New Orleans and spread to Kansas City, Chicago, San Francisco, and New York. Early in the 1920s jazz became a craze throughout the United States and was beginning to excite admiration in Europe. Performers such as Louis Armstrong, Thomas ("Fats") Waller, King Oliver, Ferdinand Joseph ("Jelly Roll") Morton, Bessie Smith, and orchestra leaders such as Edward Kennedy ("Duke") Ellington, Cab Calloway, Paul Whiteman, Noble Sissle, and Fletcher Henderson have become legendary in

[487]

the history of American music. Jazz music also provided the themes for formal compositions in George Gershwin's "Rhapsody in Blue" and "Concerto in F."

The 1920s were a period that has never since been equaled in the American theater. In the peak year, 1927, 268 different productions were presented on Broadway and in the theaters of New York City. Touring companies carried the most successful Broadway plays to large cities throughout the nation. Outstanding among the theatrical triumphs of the 1920s was the production of *Showboat,* based on the novel by Edna Ferber, with music by Jerome Kern and Oscar Hammerstein II. In the same decade Eugene O'Neill was awarded the Pulitzer prize three times for drama. Other distinguished playwrights included Robert E. Sherwood, Elmer Rice, Maxwell Anderson, George S. Kaufman, and Marc Connelly.

Brilliantly staged revues produced by Florenz Ziegfeld, George White, and others presented such popular performers as Fannie Brice, Will Rogers, Al Jolson, and Eddie Cantor.

A Search for Meaning

World War I not only changed the map of Europe. It also marked a break with traditional values for many young men and women. Disillusioned with life in America and seeking new points of view and new means of expression, some stayed on in Paris after the war. Others left America to join them. These expatriates were called the "lost generation." A number of them were encouraged by the American poet Gertrude Stein, who had lived in Paris for many years. Among the American writers who lived and worked in Paris were others who also gained wide recognition: Ernest Hemingway, William Faulkner, Katherine Anne Porter, F. Scott Fitzgerald, T. S. Eliot, Thornton Wilder, John Dos Passos, e. e. cummings, and William Carlos Williams.

American writers and poets in the United States were also examining the world around them, some with affection, others with dissatisfaction. Outstanding among them were Robert Frost, Archibald MacLeish, Stephen Vincent Benét, Theodore Dreiser, Edna St. Vincent Millay, and Sinclair Lewis.

Greenwich Village in New York provided a setting for part of the renaissance of American writing at home just as the Left Bank in Paris

did for the works of expatriates. New American magazines, produced chiefly in New York, set high standards for sharp social observation and sophisticated humor. The *American Mercury,* founded by H. L. Mencken and George Jean Nathan, Harold Ross's *New Yorker,* and others such as *Vanity Fair* and the old *Life* gained wide circulation and shaped American tastes. The writers who met at the Round Table in New York's Hotel Algonquin became famous for their wit and sharp, often cynical, humor: Alexander Woollcott, Robert Benchley, James Thurber, Dorothy Parker, Moss Hart, Edna Ferber, Franklin P. Adams, and Heywood Broun.

The Harlem Renaissance

In another part of New York a renaissance was also taking place. Negro writers in Harlem were publishing novels, stories, and poems that expressed a revival of interest in the black heritage. The works of James Weldon Johnson, Claude McKay, W. E. B. Du Bois, Countee Cullen, and Langston Hughes set the pace for Negro writers of the Harlem Renaissance in the 1920s.

Lindbergh Crosses the Atlantic

The most glorious achievement—and assuredly the most ballyhooed—occurred in May 1927. A quiet-spoken young aviator, Charles A. Lindbergh piloted his single-engine aircraft, *Spirit of St. Louis,* from New York to Paris to win a $25,000 prize. Newsmen dubbed him "the flying fool" and "Lucky Lindy," and he became a national idol.

Considering the feats of astronauts, some young Americans of the present day may look back on Lindbergh's solo flight across the Atlantic in spring 1927 and yawn. Movies of the *Spirit of St. Louis* pitching and splashing down the muddy runway of Roosevelt Field show a far less imposing scene than does a giant rocket spewing vapor as the gantry pulls away before blast-off.

Still, consider a few comparisons. Lindbergh had to find his own financial backing. He helped design and build his aircraft. He made all the plans for his flight. And when his little Ryan monoplane took to the air he was on his own. He was the Lone Eagle. For more than thirty-three hours he flew alone over the North Atlantic until

The nation thrilled to the daring exploit of Charles A. Lindbergh in 1927. He made the first nonstop solo flight across the Atlantic to France in his monoplane, *Spirit of St. Louis.* Lindbergh's feat aroused greater interest in aviation.

Minnesota Historical Society

he touched down at Le Bourget Air Field near Paris.

Americans of 1927 recognized Lindbergh's daring and the dimension of his accomplishment. City after city across the country accorded him ovations for more than a year after his flight, and his success gave a tremendous impetus to aviation. As Lindbergh wrote "when the *Spirit of St. Louis* flew to Paris, aviation was shouldering its way from the stage of invention onto the stage of usefulness."

STUDY GUIDE: The 1920s were prosperous years. Increasing numbers of Americans were able to buy automobiles. People seemed intent on having a good time. The film industry grew rapidly, and people flocked to the movies. Radio broadcasting caught the public's attention and the radio industry expanded. Women, having recently won the vote, became more independent. There were great achievements in the field of literature. Writers such as Lewis,

Commercial aviation came of age in the decade after World War I. In 1929 the Boeing 80-A, known as the "Pioneer Pullman of the Air," went into service. It boasted a heated cabin and could carry eighteen passengers.

Courtesy The Boeing Company

Hemingway and Faulkner gained world-wide recognition. Charles Lindbergh's solo flight across the Atlantic was perhaps the most thrilling event of the decade.

WARREN G. HARDING

The era of normalcy was the time of Harding and Coolidge.

Born on a farm in Morrow County, Ohio, in 1865, Warren Gamaliel Harding became the twenty-ninth president of the United States. In the estimate of many historians he was the worst chief executive in the country's history. He was the first of eight children born to George and Phoebe Harding. The elder Harding was a man who never quite found the prosperity and contentment he sought. He was a farmer at the time his son was born, but after a short course in medicine, he became a country doctor.

Young Warren attended Ohio Central College in Iberia, Ohio, where he played an alto horn and edited the college yearbook. Upon graduation in 1883, he took a position as a country school teacher. But Harding's first love was newspaper work. As a lad he had learned the printing trade, so after a short time he quit teaching and became a reporter for a newspaper in Marion, Ohio.

During the presidential campaign of 1884, Harding spoke out in favor of James G. Blaine, the Republican candidate. His employer, a Democrat, fired him. Whereupon Harding, a determined and energetic young man of nineteen, persuaded two friends to join him in purchasing a bankrupt newspaper, the Marion *Star*. Soon he became sole owner of the paper, turning it into a profitable enterprise. At the age of twenty-five he married. Mrs. Harding was energetic, ambitious, and domineering. She had much to do with Harding's eventual rise to national prominence.

An unswerving Republican, Harding was beginning to dabble in politics and in 1892 made his first campaign for public office. He ran for county auditor and lost. The defeat proved no serious setback, and over the next few years Harding became influential in the councils of the Republican party in Ohio. He was also learning the political trade and in 1899 won election to the state senate.

In the capitol at Columbus Harding did not make a distinguished legislative record. However, he won the thanks of Republicans throughout Ohio when he mediated differences between two warring factions of the GOP. As a reward for this service, he received the Republican nomination for lieutenant governor in 1903 and the following autumn won the election. Then Harding's luck turned sour. He gained the Republican nomination for governor in 1909, only to go down to a crushing defeat. He was a victim of quarrels which were splitting the GOP into conservative and progressive wings across the entire country.

Harding, it turned out, was not finished. A stalwart supporter of conservative Republicans, he received the honor, at the Republican national convention in 1912, of nominating his fellow Ohioan, President Taft, for a second term in the White House. Then came fresh disappointment. In the autumn election Taft trailed both Woodrow Wilson and Theodore Roosevelt. Harding thus concluded that his own political career was at an end.

Mrs. Harding and a sharp-witted small-town lawyer named Harry M. Daugherty, who was a close friend of Harding, thought otherwise. They persuaded him in 1914 to seek the Republican nomination for the United States Senate. Harding won the nomination as well as the autumn election and in 1915 entered the Senate. He won no acclaim for legislative ability, but he followed the Republican leadership, proved a likeable fellow, and got along with his colleagues.

Despite his dull performance in the Senate Harding continued to move up in the Republican party. He delivered the keynote address at the party's national convention in 1916, then received his party's nomination for president in 1920. Riding the postwar reaction against Wilsonian idealism, he easily defeated the Democratic candidate, James M. Cox, a fellow Ohioan, in the autumn election.

The Harding Administration

Except for the treaty of 1921, formally restoring peace between the United States and Germany, and the Washington Conference for the Limitation of Armaments of 1921-22 the achievements of the Harding adminstration in foreign affairs were few. In domestic affairs the Harding administration established a system for preparing the federal budget. It supported a measure by which the federal government extended aid to states for the promotion of the health and welfare of expectant mothers and infants. And it pressed the steel industry to eliminate the twelve-hour day for workingmen.

Otherwise the administration concentrated on reducing federal spending, advancing the interests of business, and keeping organized labor in check. To achieve such ends, Congress was persuaded to repeal the excess-profits tax, reduce inheritance taxes, and raise the tariff to an all-time high by the Fordney-McCumber Act of 1922. The Department of Commerce, presided over by Herbert Hoover, became the clearinghouse for a range of business activities. But the Federal Trade Commission was weakened by filling it with appointees from the ranks of big business. Meanwhile, Attorney General Daugherty ignored the antitrust laws—except when it was possible to use them to break the power of organized labor (as when he used a sweeping injunction to break a strike against the Bethlehem Steel Company).

The administration had an important ally, the Supreme Court, which was particularly helpful in the drive to keep labor "in its place." The Court upheld yellow-dog contracts, permitted suits against unions under the antitrust laws, and declared boycotts organized by labor groups to be illegal. It also declared unconstitutional the Child Labor Act of 1916 and nullified the minimum wage for women.

When recalling the Harding administration in later years, some Americans remembered all-night poker parties in the White House during which the president and his cronies gambled, drank bootleg booze, and puffed cigars. Many more remembered the administration's scandals. For operating out of "the Little Green House" on K Street in Washington, members of Harding's "Ohio gang" did a booming business. To crooks and chiselers they sold immunities from federal prosecution and for handsome fees arranged government appointments as well as pardons and paroles for convicts.

Of particular renown was the Teapot Dome scandal. In this notorious affair Secretary of the Interior Albert Fall accepted an estimated $400,000 for arranging transfer of valuable naval oil reserves at Teapot Dome in Wyoming and Elk Hills in California to private oil companies headed by E. L. Doheny and Harry F. Sinclair. Meanwhile, the head of the Veterans' Bureau, Charles R. Forbes, assisted by dishonest subordinates, was defrauding the government of

Library of Congress

During the presidential election of 1920 Warren G. Harding promised a "return to normalcy" and won an overwhelming victory. If Harding had exercised stronger leadership, would so much corruption have taken place during his administration?

millions of dollars. Forbes and his cronies received kickbacks for overpaying contractors who were supplying materials for building veterans' hospitals. Other irregularities occurred in connection with payment of claims to German companies whose property in America had been seized during World War I.

To the present day nobody has unearthed evidence that President Harding was party to the thievery in his administration. Apparently he had no inkling during his first two years in the White House that some of his favorite subordinates and poker cronies were betraying his trust and robbing their countrymen. Eventually, however, word began to reach him that things were not as they should be. During a trip to Alaska and the Pacific Coast in June-July 1923, he learned even more. The disclosures cracked his spirit.

Looking wan and depressed, the president sailed down the Alaska-Canada coast to Seattle, where he was stricken, probably with a mild heart attack, although his physician diagnosed the malady as indigestion. A few days later he arrived in San Francisco and once again fell ill, this time with pneumonia. Lying in bed and listening while Mrs. Harding read to him he died August 2, 1923.

STUDY GUIDE: Harding was a man with limited ability who played politics according to the party rules. His administration reflected the big-business sympathies of the Republican party. Numerous scandals rocked the Harding administration. One of the worst was the Teapot Dome affair in which the Secretary of the Interior accepted a bribe to transfer valuable naval oil reserves to private oil companies Harding died in office shortly after learning of these scandals.

CALVIN COOLIDGE

The new president was Calvin Coolidge, a sharp-featured, frugal, God-fearing Yankee from Massachusetts.

Calvin Coolidge was born at Plymouth Notch, Vermont, on July 4, 1872, one of two children of Virginia and John C. Coolidge.

Young Calvin attended Black River Academy at Ludlow, Vermont, twelve miles from Plymouth Notch, spent a term at Saint Johnsbury Academy, and entered Amherst College, Massachusetts, where he took special interest in debating and public speaking. An average student, he graduated from Amherst in 1895, then took a job as a clerk in a law firm in nearby Northampton. He was admitted to the bar in 1897, opened his own law office in Northampton, and began to take an interest in politics. Like most natives of Vermont, he was a "rock-ribbed" Republican. He moved up the political ladder slowly, one rung at a time, serving in such minor elective offices as city councilman and city solicitor.

In 1905 Coolidge married Grace Goodhue, a teacher at a school for the deaf in Northampton. Charming and intelligent, Mrs. Coolidge was a continual source of strength and encouragement for her husband. During her White House years she was one of the most popular first ladies in the history of the nation. She gave birth to two sons, one of whom died in 1924.

Coolidge was active in politics and in the years after his marriage enjoyed an unbroken string of elective triumphs. He served in the lower house of the state legislature in Boston (1907-8), was mayor of Northampton (1910-11), state senator (1912-15), and lieutenant governor (1916-18). He won election as governor of Massachusetts in 1918 and earned a national reputation during the Boston police strike of 1919 when he spoke out forcefully against the strikers and ordered the state militia to the city to keep order. In 1920 Coolidge won the GOP nomination for vice-president. With Harding, Coolidge was swept to victory in the election the following November.

Coolidge Becomes President

Never an insider in the Harding administration, Coolidge as vice-president patiently presided over the Senate and otherwise attracted little attention. Then, during the night of August 3, 1923, while he was visiting his father in Vermont, a telegraph messenger rapped at the door of the house. The messenger advised Coolidge that Harding was dead. Coolidge dressed and in the eerie glow of a kerosene lamp put his hand on the family Bible. After his father (who was a notary public), he repeated the presidential oath. The formalities over, the thirtieth president went back to bed and slept soundly until morning.

The Election of 1924

Less than a year later, in June 1924, delegates to the Republican national convention in Cleveland enthusiastically nominated Coolidge for a full four-year term in the White House. They urged Americans to "keep cool with Coolidge." For vice-president they turned to Charles Gates Dawes, a prominent banker of Chicago.

The Democrats gathered in New York two weeks later. Their convention nearly blew apart when the time came to nominate a presidential candidate. Delegates from the populous Northeast were determined to nominate Governor Alfred E. Smith of New York. Smith was an avowed "wet" on the Prohibition question and also happened to be a Roman Catholic. Delegates from areas where "dry" sentiment was strong and the Ku Klux Klan was a power quailed at the prospect of a "wet" and a Catholic heading the Democratic ticket. At length on the one hundred and third ballot, the weary delegates nominated John W. Davis, a conservative lawyer from West Virginia.

There was a third party in the field in 1924, the Progressive party. It was put together by former Bull Moosers and other assorted liberals to try to bring new life to the defunct progressive movement. Meeting in Cleveland in July, the Progressives nominated Senator Robert M. La Follette of Wisconsin for president.

The corruption of the Harding administration was by now generally known and logically should have been a heavy liability for the Republican ticket in 1924. However, Coolidge polled more votes than did Davis and La Follette combined (15,000,000 to 8,000,000 to 4,000,000 respectively). He won the electoral college in a landslide.

For many years after his retirement from the White House in 1929, great numbers of Americans looked back on Coolidge as an ideal president. Why this admiration for the thirtieth president? Certainly Coolidge's standing with his countrymen did not rest on a zeal for reform, a record of legislative achievement, or diplomatic triumph.

The Coolidge Administration

Nothing was more remote from Coolidge's mind than reform. Only two measures of much consequence emerged from Congress during his years in the White House. One was the McNary-Haugen Bill, a complicated measure designed to improve farm income in the country. The other was a bill for government operation of hydroelectric and other facilities at Muscle Shoals, Alabama. Coolidge vetoed both of them.

The high point of the Coolidge years came in 1928 when the United States signed the Kellogg-Briand Pact outlawing war (see Chapter 16). In searching for the root of Coolidge's popularity, one inevitably turns to the economic climate of the times. The economy was humming in the period of the Coolidge presidency and nothing does more to enhance a presidential reputation than prosperity. Fortunately for Coolidge's reputation, he departed the White House months before the great stock market collapse of October 1929. His successor, Herbert Hoover, reaped the ill will which the passing of prosperity inevitably generated.

Many Americans genuinely liked the Yankee president. They were pleased during his White House years when he posed for cameramen in the elaborate feathered headdress of the Sioux nation or pitched hay on a horse-drawn wagon in

Library of Congress

"Keeping cool with Coolidge" was an expression that accurately mirrored the uneventful administration of Calvin Coolidge. Considering the lack of achievement of his administration, why did so many Americans consider Coolidge an ideal president?

Vermont or fished for trout while neatly attired in a business suit. They were pleased too that nearly every tourist in Washington could file by and shake hands with the president. They delighted in his practice of saying nothing but "yes" and "no" during interviews and referred to him affectionately as "Silent Cal." This habit became the subject of many jokes concerning Coolidge's economy with words. (There was, for example, the story of the young lady who sat next to him at a dinner and told him that she had made a wager that in the course of the evening she could compel him to say three words. Looking straight ahead, the president responded: "You lose.")

By 1927 Americans were wondering whether President Coolidge might seek another full term in the White House. Then, while on vacation in the Black Hills, in August 1927, the president handed reporters a statement: "I do not choose to run for President in 1928." The statement was ambiguous and seemed to leave the door open to a draft by the Republican national convention the following summer. Some students of history believe that Coolidge indeed hoped to be renominated. Still, he did nothing to encourage a draft.

The Conventions of 1928

Most Republicans took Coolidge at his word that he did not want to run again. Delegates to the GOP national convention met in Kansas City in June 1928. They approved a platform endorsing Prohibition, the protective tariff, and a complicated program for stimulating agriculture. Then, on the first ballot Herbert Hoover was nominated for president. For the vice-presidency Senator Charles Curtis of Kansas was nominated.

The Democrats convened in Houston two weeks later. They adopted a platform urging "economic equality for agriculture and other industries," assorted reforms for labor, and enforcement of the Prohibition laws. On the first ballot, they nominated "the Happy Warrior," Governor Alfred E. Smith of New York, for president. It was the first time in the country's history that a major party had nominated a presidential candidate who had spent his entire life in the city, with no visible roots in the countryside. In addition to being an urbanite, "Al" Smith was a Catholic, a "wet" who openly favored repeal of the Eighteenth Amendment, and a champion of the millions of immigrants who lived in the great cities. His own forebears had migrated to America from Ireland in the nineteenth century. For vice-president the Houston convention named Senator Joseph T. Robinson of Arkansas.

The campaign of 1928 turned out to be one of the most notorious in the history of the nation. This was not because of anything Hoover and Smith said but because of the nature and ferocity of the attacks on Smith. Many of those who assailed Smith feared what might happen if a Catholic, a "wet," and a friend of immigrants took over the White House. And their fear seemed to increase when Smith appeared on the campaign trail in a brown derby, chomping on a cigar, and speaking with the accent of the East Side of New York.

Smith's greatest handicap was not his religion, urban origins, or stand on Prohibition. It was his opponent, Herbert Hoover, one of the most respected men in America. Hoover was an intelligent and industrious individual who had been born in a two-room house in rural Iowa. He had gone on to achieve riches and reputation. He had saved millions of lives by administering relief projects in strife-torn parts of the world, had served as secretary of commerce under Harding and Coolidge, and was one of the architects of the rampaging prosperity of the 1920s.

Hoover appealed to the agrarian tradition that millions of Americans, despite the growth of cities, still treasured. A Tennessee editor summed up the feelings of many white Anglo-Saxon Protestants in the country. He wrote that Smith's appeal was "to the aliens, who feel that the older America, the America of the Anglo-Saxon stock, is a hateful thing which must be overturned and humiliated; to the northern Negroes, who lust for social equality and racial dominance; to the Catholics who have been made to believe that they are entitled to the White House, and to the Jews who likewise are to be instilled with the feeling that this is the time for God's chosen people to chastise America. . . . As great as have been my doubts about Hoover, he is sprung from American soil and stock."

Under the circumstances, the outcome of the election was apparent long before election day. On November 6, 1928, voters trooped to the polls and gave Hoover a resounding victory. Hoover won 21,000,000 votes to Smith's 15,000,000. He shattered the solid South by capturing Virginia, Texas, Tennessee, North Carolina, and Florida, and carried the electoral college, 444-87.

On March 4, 1929, Herbert Hoover took the oath of office. The era of normalcy was nearly over.

STUDY GUIDE: Harding was succeeded in office by Calvin Coolidge, who won the presidency in his own right in 1924. Although no important legislation was passed during his administration, Coolidge was an extremely popular president. This popularity rested to some extent on the prosperity of the country. Like Harding, Coolidge sided with big-business interests and frowned on some activities of organized labor.

Herbert Hoover won the presidential election of 1928. In a bitter, hard-fought campaign he defeated the Democratic candidate, Governor Al Smith of New York. Hoover appealed to those voters who valued America's agrarian traditions.

SUMMING UP THE CHAPTER

Names and Terms to Identify

Georges Clemenceau	speakeasy
David Lloyd George	Al Capone
James M. Cox	"monkey trial"
A. Mitchell Palmer	John Thomas Scopes
Nicola Sacco	Harry M. Daugherty
Bartolomeo Vanzetti	Albert Fall
Webster Thayer	John W. Davis
WCTU	Alfred E. Smith
Eighteenth Amendment	Charles G. Dawes
Volstead Act	ballyhoo

Study Questions and Points to Review

1. What dividends, or spoils of war, did the Allied powers hope to win as part of the peace settlement after World War I? How had they attempted to arrange them?

2. What did Wilson mean by the term "a peace without victory"?

3. Define self-determination.

4. How had Wilson's prestige suffered a blow after the Fourteen Points had been proclaimed?

5. Why has Wilson's choice of delegates to assist him in the peace negotiations been considered unfortunate?

6. Who would have been a logical choice as a prominent Republican to serve on the peace delegation? Why did Wilson not choose him?

7. What was Wilson's attitude on the matter of reparations which the Allies sought?

8. What was the subject of Lodge's "Round Robin" statement?

9. Wilson considered Article X the "heart" of the League covenant. What was the subject of this article?

10. Several objections to the League of Nations were raised by Americans. Give two of these objections.

11. What strategy did Lodge use to delay voting on the treaty? Why did he use this tactic?

12. Which of Lodge's reservations incurred the anger of the president?

13. Who were the Democratic candidates for president and vice-president in the election of 1920?

14. Why did the Sacco-Vanzetti case in the beginning attract more attention in Europe and Latin America than it did in the United States?

15. Name the defense attorney and the prominent man who assisted the prosecution in the Scopes trial.

16. What was the verdict in the Scopes trial?

17. When did Lindbergh cross the Atlantic? How long did his flight take?

18. What was the Teapot Dome scandal?

19. What was Al Smith's greatest handicap in the election of 1928?

Subjects for Reports or Essays

1. In material in the library, read what historians have to say about Woodrow Wilson's Fourteen Points. Then prepare a report on the president's fourteen-point program for peace.

2. On the basis of outside reading, including the book *The Roots of American Communism* by Theodore Draper, write a report on the actual strength and influence of communism in the United States in the years of the "big red scare."

3. Interview "senior citizens" in your family or community concerning enforcement and violation of Prohibition in the age of normalcy. Write a newspaper story on the basis of the interviews.

4. From sources in your library write a brief biographical sketch of Henry Cabot Lodge.

5. Prepare a report, complete with graphs and charts, on the state of the American economy in the decade after World War I. Explain the reasons for the ups and downs in the economy, the general prosperity after 1922, and the assorted "dark spots" in the economic picture. You will find the following Appendix tables useful in compiling your report: 10, 12, 17, 18, 20, 22, 23, 25, 29.

6. Consider American literature in the age of normalcy. Why do you suppose the period produced so much rich and exciting literature?

Topics for Discussion

1. Evaluate Woodrow Wilson's decision to attend the Paris Peace Conference at the end of World War I, the membership of his peace commission, and his willingness to compromise on other parts of his peace program so as to secure European support for the League of Nations.

2. What were the main peace-keeping features of the League of Nations? What were the arguments for and against American membership in the League without reservations? Do you think the United States should have entered the League on Wilson's terms? If that was impossible, should the United States have joined the League with the Lodge reservations? Explain your answers to these questions.

3. On the basis of what you have learned in Chapters 12 and 13, as well as the present chapter, defend or challenge the view of many historians that Woodrow Wilson merits ranking as a "great" president.

4. Explain the causes of the "big red scare." What were some of the manifestations of the country's fear of Bolshevism?

5. Why did the Ku Klux Klan gain new influence in the 1920s? How did it seek to assert influence? What success did it have?

6. Why were Prohibition laws virtually impossible to enforce? How were they violated? Why did they give rise to widespread racketeering?

7. Discuss the automobile's development in the time after World War I. What was its impact on American society? Consult Appendix Table 31, "Motor Vehicles—Factory Sales and Registrations: 1900 to 1970."

Projects, Activities, and Skills

1. As a class project prepare an exhibit on the 1920s. Include pictures of leading personalities and events of the period. Display books by the leading authors, models of automobiles, locomotives, and airplanes, examples of architecture, art, and fashions, data on the economy, and information on the presidential elections of 1920, 1924, and 1928. You might also include mementos, pictures, and information pertaining to your own state or home town during the age of normalcy.

2. Prepare an exhibit on automotive developments in the 1920s. Display models and pictures of the automobiles of that era. Include a report on the impact of the automobile on American life in that period.

3. Gather photographs and write brief biographical sketches of some of the celebrities of the 1920s: Babe Ruth, Red Grange, Charles A. Lindbergh, Rudolph Valentino, Greta Garbo, and others.

4. Read a novel or several short stories that were written during the 1920s. Prepare a report on what the material you have read tells you about the age of normalcy.

5. Prepare an illustrated report on Charles A. Lindbergh's flight across the Atlantic Ocean. Display pictures of his plane, his flying gear, and his equipment.

6. Prepare a report for class presentation on jazz music in the 1920s. Include in your report accounts of the top jazzmen, the influence of jazz music on the rest of the world, and, if possible, samples of recordings of some of the people you discuss.

Further Readings

General

Dry Decade by Charles Merz. A colorful account of the Prohibition era.
The Great Crusade and After: 1914-1928 by Preston Slosson. A useful study which focuses on social history.

Only Yesterday by Frederick Lewis Allen. Written by a perceptive journalist just after the period ended, this book is one of the best and is definitely the most readable.
The Perils of Prosperity, 1914-32 by William E. Leuchtenburg. An outstanding survey.
Red Scare: A Study in National Hysteria, 1919-1920 by Robert K. Murray. This is the standard work on the subject.
Republican Ascendency, 1921-1933 by John D. Hicks. An excellent book on the politics of this period.
Tragedy in Dedham: The Story of the Sacco-Vanzetti Case by Francis Russell.
The Twenties: Fords, Flappers and Fanatics ed. by George E. Mowry. A good collection of documents from the 1920s.
Woodrow Wilson and the Great Betrayal by Thomas A. Bailey. The story of the failure of the Treaty of Versailles in the Senate.

Biography

A. Mitchell Palmer: Politician by Stanley Coben.
Al Smith and His America by Oscar Handlin.
Center of the Storm: Memoirs of John T. Scopes by John T. Scopes and James Presley. The memoirs of the biology teacher tried for teaching Darwinism.
The Spirit of St. Louis by Charles A. Lindbergh.
The Story of My Life by Clarence Darrow. Memoirs of Scopes's lawyer.

Fiction and Drama

Arrowsmith, Babbit, and *Main Street* by Sinclair Lewis. Three novels about America in the 1920s.
The Great Gatsby and *This Side of Paradise* by F. Scott Fitzgerald. Two literary classics of the post-World War I period.
Inherit the Wind by Jerome Lawrence and Robert E. Lee. Drama about the Scopes "monkey trial."
The Sun Also Rises by Ernest Hemingway. A novel about the "lost generation"—the Americans who lived in Europe after the war.
Winterset by Maxwell Anderson. A drama based on the Sacco-Vanzetti case.

Pictorial History

The Lawless Decade: A Pictorial History of the Roaring Twenties by Paul Sann. Covers the period from 1918 to 1933.
This Fabulous Century, 1920-1930, Vol. 3, by the editors of Time-Life Books.

CHAPTER 15

DEPRESSION AND THE NEW DEAL

AFTER PLODDING THROUGH his inaugural address on March 4, 1929, Herbert Clark Hoover accepted the congratulations of various dignitaries and was whisked to the White House for lunch. Hoover then moved to a nearby reviewing stand where he watched a two-hour inaugural parade. Although Hoover's first address as president had moved few of his countrymen, most Americans felt serene in the conviction that the destiny of the Republic was in good hands. Nearly everyone agreed that the new president was a man of high intelligence, experience, and integrity. More than that, he seemed typical of the "American dream," a Horatio Alger whose energy and resourcefulness had taken him "from rags to riches."

HERBERT HOOVER

Hoover was born in 1874 in a tiny frame house at West Branch, Iowa. He was the son of devout Quaker parents. His father, a blacksmith, died when young Herbert was six years old, his mother when he was eight. At the age of ten he went to Oregon to live with an aunt and uncle. While still a teen-ager, Hoover decided to be an engineer. In 1891 he enrolled in the new Leland Stanford Junior University in California.

On graduating from Stanford in 1895, Hoover took a position with the United States Geological Survey, then went to San Francisco where he worked in the office of a prominent mine operator. Then he spent a year in Australia managing a gold-mining operation. In 1898 Hoover, back in the United States, married his college sweetheart, Lou Henry (who eventually would give birth to two sons). The day after the wedding Hoover and his bride boarded a steamship for China, where the young engineer supervised harbor improvements and port and railway construction, prospected for gold, and investigated anthracite coal deposits.

When the Boxer Rebellion (see Chapter 11) broke out in 1900, Hoover and his wife were stranded in Tientsin. As he would do in the future, he organized food and clothing relief for the embattled foreign colony and also for

Chinese refugees. Over the next several years, Hoover was continuously on the move from one country to another—to Burma, to China, to Russia—opening mines and organizing mining syndicates. He achieved a reputation as one of the world's foremost mining engineers and accumulated a fortune estimated at $4 million.

When World War I broke out in 1914, Hoover was in London. Because of his business connections in many countries, he was asked to direct massive relief operations for the Belgians. He accepted the assignment, which he performed magnificently. Before long he was receiving world acclaim as a humanitarian. After America entered the war, in 1917, President Wilson appointed Hoover head of the United States Food Administration. This resulted in another notable performance.

When the war ended, Congress established the American Relief Administration. Almost automatically, Hoover became chief of the new agency. The agency helped ward off starvation and chaos, and also bolshevism in Europe after the armistice. Climaxing Hoover's postwar relief activities was his response in 1921 to an appeal to help relieve a famine that was sweeping Russia. Remaining in the United States (where he was secretary of commerce in the Harding administration), he organized a drive for funds. By 1923 he had channeled $30 million for relief to the Soviet Union. Soviet leaders praised Hoover. Without his efforts, the famine might have toppled the new and shaky Soviet regime.

In 1919 Hoover's name was mentioned in connection with the pending presidential election of 1920. Mildly interested, Hoover allowed a small group of Republicans to launch a low-key campaign for his nomination. Hoover's candidacy sparked little interest, but after the election, President-elect Harding appointed him secretary of commerce. Hoover would hold that office until his own entry into the White House in 1929.

As head of the Department of Commerce, Hoover urged better housing for Americans and organized safety conferences to consider steps

THE
1930s

The Depression forced drastic changes in the American way of life. When the economy collapsed, millions of people lost their jobs, and starvation became a real threat. As president, Franklin D. Roosevelt took extreme measures to bolster the economy. His New Deal policies gave a great amount of power to government agencies. Some people felt that Roosevelt's policies would threaten the American capitalist economy and democratic government. Other people applauded Roosevelt's response to the national emergency.

1   Franklin D. Roosevelt Library, Hyde Park, New York

2   Franklin D. Roosevelt Library, Hyde Park, New York

3

Nebraska State Historical Society

4

Cincinnati Art Museum and Associated American Artists, New York

1

At the left is a photographic portrait of President Roosevelt, who was elected president four times.

2

When Franklin Roosevelt ran for a third term, he broke a long-standing tradition. Supporters of Wendell Willkie displayed buttons and banners in 1940 protesting Roosevelt's candidacy.

3

During the 1930s many government projects provided jobs for the unemployed.

4

During the 1930s a number of people criticized the establishment for its failure to cope with the problems facing the country. Satire was one means of protest. Grant Wood's painting, *Daughters of Revolution*, provided a commentary on those members of society who felt themselves to be superior to others because of their ancestry.

5

City and farm workers expressed their protest against injustices and inequality in the song "Goin' Down the Road."

5 Goin' Down the Road

I'm lookin' for a job with honest pay,
I'm lookin' for a job with honest pay,
I'm lookin' for a job with honest pay,
   Lord, Lord,
And I ain't gonna be treated this-a-way.

Forty cents an hour won't pay my rent,
Forty cents an hour won't pay my rent,
Forty cents an hour won't pay my rent,
   Lord, Lord,
And I ain't gonna be treated this-a-way.

I can't live on cornbread and beans,
I can't live on cornbread and beans,
I can't live on cornbread and beans,
   Lord, Lord,
And I ain't gonna be treated this-a-way.

I'm goin' down the road feelin' bad,
I'm goin' down the road feelin' bad,
I'm goin' down the road feelin' bad,
   Lord, Lord,
And I ain't gonna be treated this-a-way.

to reduce traffic accidents. He took an interest in aviation, still an infant industry in the 1920s, and persuaded Congress to authorize the aeronautics branch in the Department of Commerce. He also became interested in radio, another new industry and prevailed upon Congress to establish the radio division in his department. In 1927, Hoover was the first man to have his image transmitted by a new if primitive technological marvel, television.

Hoover favored industrial peace via collective bargaining and helped persuade Congress to establish the National Railway Mediation Board to resolve labor disputes in the railroad industry. He also spoke out for a child labor amendment to the Constitution, urged private unemployment insurance, and suggested ways to remedy the ills of the coal industry. He fought foreign monopolies that tried to exclude American businessmen from overseas opportunities and directed the Bureau of Foreign and Domestic Commerce to advance the interests of American business in foreign countries. When asked, he offered counsel to businessmen and made the Department of Commerce a clearinghouse of information between segments of business. He encouraged businessmen to cooperate with one another, by organizing "trade associations." These bound companies in related industries to avoid unfair trade practices and, in some instances, established machinery for controlling production and maintaining minimum prices.

Hoover was shy and felt ill at ease in large crowds or among strangers. He was not a spellbinding orator. Still, most Americans approved his policies, which favored business. They viewed him as a chief architect of the prosperity which much of the nation was enjoying in that era of Republican ascendancy. Accordingly, he became one of the most popular men in the country and by the mid-1920s had fixed his sights on the presidency.

Republican professionals were not warmly disposed toward Hoover's ambitions. They feared they would be unable to dominate him if he made it to the White House.

By the time delegates to the GOP national convention assembled in Kansas City in June 1928, the Hoover steamroller had crushed all opposition. On the first ballot Hoover won the nomination. He was clearly the choice of the Republican rank and file across the country. Charles Curtis was his running mate for the vice-presidency. In the autumn election Hoover triumphed over the Democratic candidate, Alfred E. Smith, and was installed in the White House in March of 1929.

STUDY GUIDE: Herbert Hoover's integrity and years of successful public service helped him to win the Republican nomination in 1928.

BACKGROUND TO THE DEPRESSION

On accepting the Republican nomination for president in 1928, Herbert Hoover announced that the day might be at hand when poverty would be banished from the United States. While Hoover uttered those optimistic words, serious weaknesses were afflicting the national economy. Most glaring, perhaps, was agriculture, which was depressed and burdened each year by more commodities than markets could easily consume. Similarly, two major industries, coal and textiles, were ailing.

Another weakness was the distribution of income. A very small percentage of the national population—about five percent—was receiving a whopping one-third of all personal income in the country. That comparatively small economic elite was a principal source of the investment funds necessary to keep the wheels of business turning. It was also a major source of consumer spending. Anything that struck hard at the prosperity of that group, forcing it to curtail investment and spending, would have a devastating effect on the entire economy.

Corporate profits were increasing at a much faster pace than were earnings of working people. Encouraged by rising profits, business was continuing to expand. Because he could get credit without much difficulty by making installment purchases, the average American was continuing to purchase the stepped-up output of industry. Still, it was inevitable that one day he would reach a point where his fairly static income would no longer be able to carry additional installment loan payments. At that point, he would have to reduce his buying. If great numbers of average people reached that point at the same time, the entire economy was sure to feel a severe pinch.

The economy of the United States in the 1920s suffered other weaknesses, including a fragile corporate structure and an equally shaky banking structure. The principal corporate weakness was the new empire of holding companies that

HEADLINE
EVENTS

1924 Indians born in the United States are given full citizenship

1929 Hoover inaugurated president
Agricultural Marketing Act
Federal Farm Board created
Stock market crash

1930 Smoot-Howley Tariff Act

1930-1936 *U.S.A.* (Dos Passos trilogy)

1930s Technicolor movies appear

1932 Reconstruction Finance Corporation
"Bonus March" on Washington
Glass-Steagall Banking Act
Empire State Building completed
Tobacco Road (Caldwell)

1933 Franklin D. Roosevelt inaugurated president
Emergency Banking Act
Civilian Conservation Corps created
Commodity Credit Corporation
Electric Home and Farm Authority
Agricultural Adjustment Act creates AAA
Federal Emergency Relief Act creates FERA
Sale of Securities Act
TVA created
World Economic Conference meets in London
Home Owners Loan Act creates HOLC
Glass-Steagall Banking Act creates FDIC
National Industrial Recovery Act creates NRA, PWA
Twentieth Amendment ratified
Twenty-first Amendment ratified; repeals Eighteenth Amendment
Civil Works Administration created
Subsistence Homestead Act
Frances Perkins becomes first woman to hold Cabinet position

1934 Gold Reserve Act
Trade Agreements Act
Securities and Exchange Act
Congress creates Federal Communication Commission, Federal Housing Administration

National Resources Planning Board
Export-Import Bank established
Railroad Retirement Act
Wheeler-Howard Indian Reorganization Act

1935 President's Reemployment Act (Blanket Code)
Rural Electric Administration formed
Work Relief Act
Supreme Court declares NIRA unconstitutional
Wagner Labor Relations Act
Social Security Act
Banking Act of 1935
Revenue Act
WPA created; NYA created
Public Utilities Holding Company Act
Studs Lonigan (Farrell)
Wheeler-Rayburn Holding Company Act

1936 Supreme Court declares AAA unconstitutional
Soldiers' Bonus Act
Soil Conservation and Domestic Allotment Act
Flood Control Act
Absalom, Absalom! (Faulkner)

1937 Roosevelt's second inauguration
Supreme Court "packing" episode
Farm Tenancy and Rural Rehabilitation Act
Hindenburg crashes at Lakehurst, N.J.
United States Housing Authority created by Wagner-Steagall Act

1938 Second Agricultural Adjustment Act
Du Pont manufactures nylon bristles
Fair Labor Standards Act (Wages and Hours Act) becomes effective
CIO separates from AFL

1939 Reorganization Act
Du Pont manufactures nylon yarn
Fiberglass patent issued
Grapes of Wrath (Steinbeck)
World War II begins in Europe

1940 *Native Son* (Wright)
For Whom the Bell Tolls (Hemingway)

UNEMPLOYMENT 1925–1945

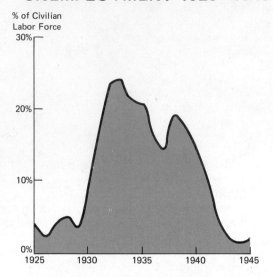

% of Civilian Labor Force

had appeared since World War I. Such companies controlled large segments of the utility, railroad, and entertainment businesses. The weakening of a single operating company in a holding-company complex could trigger a series of failures that would have drastic repercussions for great numbers of investors and workers.

A central weakness of the banking structure was the large number of small, poorly managed banks. When a bank failed, as happened with surprising frequency in the prosperous 1920s, people who had deposits in other banks in the vicinity became nervous and many withdrew their money. The result was a chain reaction which sometimes brought a rash of failures and weakened the mechanism of credit over a wide area.

Herbert Hoover determined to attack at least one of the foregoing weaknesses, the depression in agriculture. He urged farmers to organize voluntary cooperatives and withdraw marginal land from cultivation. His object was to reduce output of price-depressing surpluses. Hoover supported the Smoot-Hawley Tariff Bill, which in 1930 received congressional approval. This act raised import barriers against foreign agricultural produce. The Hoover administration also sponsored the Agricultural Marketing Act of 1929, a complicated measure which established stabilization corporations to purchase surplus farm commodities in the open market. It was hoped that this would push farm prices up. Unfortunately, Hoover's policies failed, and agriculture continued to suffer.

Reckless Speculation

While the president was wrestling with the farm problem many of his countrymen—perhaps a million of them—were recklessly speculating in corporate stocks.

The expectation of the stock-market speculator was that tomorrow, and next week, and next month the prices of stocks on the exchanges would go up. After all, they had risen

AMERICAN BUSINESS ACTIVITY: 1930 – 1939

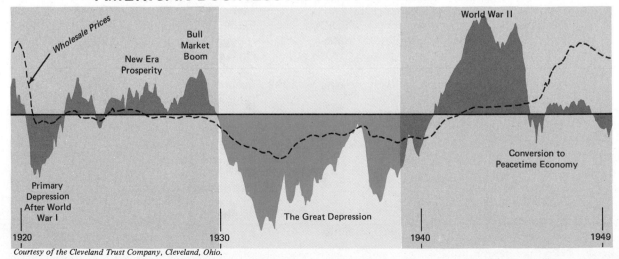

Courtesy of the Cleveland Trust Company, Cleveland, Ohio.

last month, last week, and yesterday. The speculator was not interested in dividend payments. He expected to hold his stocks for a few weeks or months, during which time, hopefully, the prices would increase. Then, at an appropriate moment, he would sell his stocks and realize a tidy profit.

Of course every speculator knew that the market could not continue its upward movement indefinitely. At some point stock prices were inevitably going to fall, and at that moment every speculator would want to unload his securities to save what he could. Why, then, did speculation continue unchecked? Because every speculator calculated that he would jump in the market, make his killing, and get out before the inevitable day of reckoning arrived.

Speculation was encouraged because banks were willing to lend large sums to speculators. Speculators could buy stocks by putting up only part of the purchase price in cash and borrowing the balance from their brokers—buying on margin. The market boomed through the spring and summer of 1929. Observers noted signs, however, that economic activity in the country was slackening, in part because many people had reached the end of their ability to make installment purchases. Speculators could not have cared less.

On September 3, 1929, the "great bull market" of the 1920s reached its peak. Next, in mid-October stock prices began to sag. Finally, on the morning of October 24—"black Thursday"—brokers were deluged by orders from owners of stock to sell. Prices plunged.

Over the next month stock prices declined an average of forty percent. Over the next three years the listed value of stocks plunged from $89 billion to $15 billion.

Who were the people wiped out or staggered by the stock market crash? A great percentage of them were members of the economic elite —people who were responsible for much of the investment and a large share of the consumer spending in the country. Thus when the stock market collapsed, the economic mechanism suddenly lost much of its energy. Meanwhile, some of the other weaknesses of the economy came into play. Most important, giant holding companies wobbled and fell. Banks began to collapse.

At the same time, workingmen, clerks, and farmers cut back spending to save for the proverbial rainy day that seemed about to come. As a result the economy slowed down another notch. The number of people out of work increased. And people who found themselves added to unemployment rolls had to curtail spending. When consumer spending slackened, factories had to trim production. More unemployment. More retrenchment. And so it went. Down, down, down.

By the summer of 1930 the situation had become extremely serious, and by the end of the year desperate. Could things possibly get worse? They could, and did. Month after month the economic slowdown continued. The grim year 1931 gave way to 1932 with no improvement. "Hard times" were getting worse. Of Americans over fourteen years of age only 1,550,000 were unemployed in 1929. By 1932 the figure had climbed to 12,060,000.

STUDY GUIDE: The stock market "crash" of 1929 brought on a severe depression. The economy had shown earlier signs of weakness. Agriculture had been in a depressed state for some time. Too many small, poorly managed banks made the nation's banking system shaky. Businesses and corporations were poorly organized, so that the failure of one company could trigger a series of failures. Reckless speculation in the stock market was a major cause of the "crash." A small percentage of the population received most of the nation's income. When this investor class lost its money, the entire economy suffered.

THE DEPRESSION AND SOCIETY

For most Americans the Great Depression resulted in severe reduction of personal incomes. Millions of breadwinners received furlough or dismissal notices and could not find new employment. By 1932, the chief sources of support for more than one-fourth of the national population were unemployed. Unemployment insurance? It was almost unheard of in the United States in the early 1930s.

Many people survived because of the generosity of relatives who had saved a little money or managed to hang on to jobs. Periodic gifts of food from relatives down on the farm helped many unemployed urban families. Others, less fortunate, turned to soup kitchens and bread lines which appeared in cities and towns. For other necessities, including clothing, shoes, and

A sign of the times was the disturbing number of stores "to rent." Thousands of small businesses failed during the depression, contributing to growing unemployment.

coal, they relied on private charity and local welfare agencies.

Because they were unable to pay rent, many families moved in with relatives or accepted the charity of landlords who carried delinquent tenants. Others settled into cardboard and tar-paper shacks in "Hoovervilles" that sprang up on unoccupied land on the fringes of cities and towns. They lived without running water, bathroom facilities, electricity, cooking ranges, refrigeration, or mattresses. Other families broke apart as fathers left them—their morale shattered by their inability to provide support for loved ones. Sons, hoping that a distant city or another part of the country might yield a job, scrambled aboard passing freight trains and set out in search of work.

In their despair some unemployed people became thieves. Others begged. And tens of thousands sold apples on the streets. Wives took in laundry, rented spare rooms, and cooked for boarders. Families spaded the back yard and cultivated carrots, cabbages, and potatoes. Some built coops and raised chickens. Many families canned quantities of food in the family kitchen.

During the depression a substantial majority of the country's workers were employed. Still, figures on employment were misleading. Many people who were employed were working only one or two days a week. Sometimes such employment was a result of the generosity of workingmen who, because of the seniority system, had held their jobs. Some of these men agreed to lay off one day a week to provide work for individuals of less seniority. The net result of underemployment was a severe loss of income as compared with the 1920s.

Wages Decline

Employers, faced with falling revenues, had to trim labor costs. This meant, in addition to dismissing some employees, reducing wages of those who were retained. Hence, most workers who remained fully employed saw their earnings decline one-third and more.

Offsetting the decline in wages was a corresponding decline in prices. Eggs often sold for less than a dime a dozen, milk for seven cents a quart, ground beef for twelve cents a pound. A new Plymouth, Ford, or Chevrolet sold for $500.

In spite of rock-bottom prices, most Americans who were working full time, as well as those who were unemployed or underemployed, felt compelled to cut back spending. They postponed purchases of electric appliances and furniture, gave up the luxury of dining out, and abandoned dreams of acquiring diamond rings, watches, fur coats, and fine china. Hundreds of thousands of people had telephones disconnected. Millions of couples put off having babies, and uncounted marriages were delayed. Great numbers of intelligent, ambitious high school graduates gave up hopes of going to college. Families resorted to home remedies and treatments instead of consulting physicians.

Americans in the depression found that there was one demand on the family income that had not declined: the debts they had contracted at the high price levels of the 1920s to purchase houses, cars, furniture, and household appliances. Indeed repayment of debts—at face value—presented one of the most devastating and demoralizing problems of the depression. Obviously the man who was out of work altogether could not meet his obligations. But even the man who was working full time often found it impossible to keep up installment loan or mortgage payments because of his severe loss of income.

Many Americans inevitably became angry. That anger deepened when they contemplated the ironies of the depression: hunger in a land where storage bins were bulging with grain; people shivering for want of warm clothing and blankets while warehouses groaned under the weight of surplus cotton and wool; factories standing idle when people were needing the products of industry. How did Americans show their anger? In many cities they organized parades and demonstrations that sometimes got out of control and resulted in injuries as well as broken windows. In Oklahoma City, in early 1931, hungry and jobless men and women raided a grocery store.

Angry farmers organized "farm committees." On occasion, brandishing shotguns and clubs, they prevented foreclosure sales of farms, livestock, and implements of bankrupt neighbors. The National Farm Holiday Association centered operations in Iowa, but was also active in Minnesota and Nebraska. It sought to bring about an increase in farm prices by preventing food from going to cities. Members of the association blocked roads by chopping down telegraph poles. They stopped trucks transporting farm produce and ordered drivers to turn around and go back where they had come from.

The "Bonus March" on Washington

In 1932 veterans of World War I demanded immediate payment of a bonus that Congress had voted in 1925, payable in 1945. A "Bonus March" was held in Washington, D. C. Arriving in trucks, aboard freight trains, and on foot, about twenty thousand veterans settled in abandoned federal buildings on Pennsylvania Avenue and in a shantytown that sprang up near the city. They milled about Capitol Hill, many carrying signs reading "Cheered in '17, Jeered in '32." Rabble-rousing was virtually nonexistent and only a tiny fraction of the bonus marchers revealed any revolutionary impulses. When Congress rejected the bill for immediate payment of the bonus, in July 1932, many of the veterans set out for home. Others, having nothing better to do, ambled back to the evacuated buildings or to their shantytown. Then, two weeks later, President Hoover, fearing some sort of violent rampage, directed the capital police to evict squatters from the buildings along Pennsylvania Avenue.

The police moved out on the morning of July 28, 1932. For a time everything was peaceful. Then somebody hurled a brick. Shots rang out. Two bonus marchers fell dead. Hoover, mean-while, had directed General Douglas MacArthur to have federal troops in readiness. When he learned of the clash between marchers and police MacArthur sent troops and several tanks down Pennsylvania Avenue. The veterans cheered. But then chaos erupted, and within moments bayonets were flashing. Tear gas was used to scatter the veterans. Fortunately nobody was killed. Next the soldiers moved to the shanties and set them afire. Millions of Americans were aghast.

Other Movements

While some people vented frustration and anger by riots, demonstrations, and bonus marches, others sought social action. One attempt was revolutionary politics. During the 1930s many Americans became alarmed at increasing socialist and communist influence in the country. Such alarm was exaggerated. Proof came in the presidential election of 1932 when barely a million out of forty-four million voters marked ballots for socialist or communist candidates. (Socialist and communist candidates did even worse in 1936, winning only 267,000 votes out of more than forty-five million.)

Then there were the movements led by the Reverend Charles E. Coughlin, Dr. Francis E. Townsend, and Huey P. Long, Jr.

Father Coughlin of Royal Oak, Michigan, was a spellbinding radio orator. Each week he reached millions of Americans with his message that bankers were at the root of the world's economic ills. As time passed, the radio priest became increasingly attracted by the idea of the "corporate state," such as the one Benito Mussolini had established in Italy. Father Coughlin's flirtation with fascism disenchanted many of his followers, and in the latter 1930s his influence declined.

Doctor Townsend, a physician from Long Beach, California, became the prophet of millions of senior citizens in the 1930s. He proposed that all Americans over age sixty should receive a monthly pension of $200, provided that they would accept no gainful employment and would spend the money within thirty days. Congress feared that millions of elderly voters might retaliate at the ballot box. However, it accepted the verdict of economists that the Townsend plan was utterly uneconomic and eventually rejected it.

Huey Long of Louisiana proclaimed that

wealth should be shared and every man should be a king. He assaulted "the interests," — oil companies, railroads, and utilities. In 1928 he was elected governor of Louisiana. As governor, Long set out to "soak the rich" and provide innumerable benefits, including hospitals, bridges, and free textbooks, for the people. By fair means and foul, including intimidation and kidnapping, the "Kingfish," as he called himself, achieved many of his goals. He established himself as a veritable dictator of Louisiana and, through assorted payoffs, became a rich man.

Surveying his success in Louisiana, Long began to dream bigger dreams. Perhaps he could duplicate his Louisiana triumph on a national scale. In 1932 he entered the United States Senate. Soon "Share Our Wealth" clubs were springing up all over the country. By the end of 1934 it was clear that the "Kingfish" had a considerable national following. Long was a Democrat, but he had broken with the Democratic president, Franklin D. Roosevelt. He thought that he would win the White House, if not in 1936, in 1940. Then on September 8, 1935, Long was assassinated in Baton Rouge by an opponent.

Achievements of the Depression Era

The age of the Great Depression witnessed some notable achievements in science, technology, literature, and transportation. Working in quiet, antiseptic laboratories that contrasted starkly with the outer world of slums and unemployment, men of science experimented with a range of antibiotic drugs which in subsequent decades would provide physicians with a powerful new weapon in the war against infection. Other scientists and inventors developed polaroid glass and the FM radio. E. I. Du Pont de Nemours & Company began commercial production of nylon toothbrush bristles in 1938 and the following year began manufacturing nylon yarn. A patent for fiber-glass techniques was issued in 1939. In 1932 the Empire State Building in New York City, the world's tallest skyscraper, was completed.

Some of the most significant novels of the period treated social themes and seemed particularly relevant in the depression. There was James T. Farrell's trilogy entitled *Studs Lonigan* (1935), a study of the difficulties of Irish-Americans in Chicago; Erskine Caldwell's *Tobacco Road* (1932); John Dos Passos's trilogy entitled

U.S.A. (1930-36); John Steinbeck's remarkable portrait of depression-shattered farmers, *The Grapes of Wrath* (1939); and Richard Wright's stirring account of life in a black ghetto, *Native Son* (1940).

Although the depression had brought many of them to bankruptcy, railroads introduced an impressive array of streamlined passenger trains, some of them powered by diesel-electric locomotives. Most heralded were the Union Pacific's *M-10001,* the Milwaukee Road's *Hiawathas,* and the Burlington route's *Zephyrs.* It was in the mid-1930s that the Douglas company brought forth the first modern airliner, the rugged and dependable DC-3, a twin-engined craft that would still be serving commercial carriers around the world more than thirty years later.

For entertainment great numbers of Americans, scraping up a few pennies here and there, went to the movies, which seldom betrayed the slightest hint that outside the theater an economic crisis was gripping the country. It was in the 1930s that technicolor movies appeared and Hollywood turned out its all-time classic, *Gone with the Wind* (1939), starring Clark Gable and Vivian Leigh. Most families had radios and spent many hours each week listening to such comedians as Jack Benny, Fred Allen, and Bob Hope, the newscaster Lowell Thomas, and the music of popular bands such as those of Paul Whiteman and Benny Goodman.

Americans also read books. Lending libraries reported a substantial increase in the number of borrowers. Most readers sought to escape the problems of the depression. The mysteries of Erle Stanley Gardner and Ellery Queen were at the top of the best-seller lists every year. Of novels that won literary acclaim, Pearl Buck's *The Good Earth* about China and John Steinbeck's *The Grapes of Wrath* about the displaced farmers of the "dust bowl" were among the most popular.

In the world of sports, a high point came in 1932 when Los Angeles hosted the Olympic games. But it was the old reliables — major league baseball, college football, professional boxing, and thoroughbred racing — which aroused the greatest enthusiasm. Especially popular were baseball, which highlighted such stars as Lou Gehrig, "Dizzy" Dean, "Lefty" Grove, Carl Hubbell, and Jimmy Foxx, and boxing, which boasted such outstanding performers as Henry Armstrong, Lou Ambers, Barney Ross, and the incomparable Brown Bomber, Joe Louis, world heavyweight champion.

The Twenty-first Amendment

At the start of the depression many people continued to consume bootleg liquor and patronize speakeasies. It was clear that a large percentage of the nation had given up on the "noble experiment" of Prohibition. In early 1933 Congress presented to the states the Twenty-first Amendment to the Constitution, which repealed the Eighteenth Amendment. The new amendment received approval of the required number of states and was proclaimed ratified in December 1933. Saloons returned and speakeasies disappeared or became legitimate.

STUDY GUIDE: The Great Depression brought hard times to millions of Americans. Banks failed, unemployment rose, and factory production decreased. Many people showed their anger and frustration by organizing demonstrations. On a "Bonus March" to Washington, World War I veterans demanded immediate payment of a bonus Congress had voted them. Hoover was widely criticized for sending in troops to break up the demonstration. Some people turned to radical politics, such as communism, to try to find a way out of their troubles.

HOOVER AND THE DEPRESSION

What should the federal government do to counter the depression? As President Hoover sized up the situation, the answer to that question was fairly clear. Like chief executives during previous recessions and depressions, he decided that his main responsibility was to maintain the fiscal integrity of the federal government. That meant he should remain calm, reduce expenses, balance the federal budget, and wait for prosperity to return of its own accord.

Still, as the economic picture darkened, the president felt compelled to act. He called periodic meetings of leaders of industry and finance, chiefs of labor unions, and heads of farm organizations. The meetings were widely publicized. Their purpose was to convey the appearance that the government and leaders of business, labor, and agriculture were mobilizing for a concerted assault on the crisis. This, it was hoped, would restore the confidence of the individual who was thinking of withdrawing his savings from a bank, of the corporation that was pondering a cutback of its labor force, of the loan company that was hesitating to provide funds for a new construction project.

Hoover also approved a modest program of public works. Under this program the government planned or completed several hundred public buildings, constructed more than thirty thousand miles of federal highways, and began construction of Boulder Dam on the Colorado River. The Federal Farm Board extended aid to depressed farmers, and the administration sought to deal with farm surpluses through the purchasing activities of stabilization corporations.

In 1932 Hoover approved legislation creating the Reconstruction Finance Corporation. A great federal lending agency, the RFC loaned funds to state and city governments. These loans enabled many states and cities to meet payroll obligations or to launch public works projects of their own. Two examples are the Golden Gate Bridge in San Francisco and the Los Angeles Aqueduct. More important, the RFC made loans to railroads, banks, agricultural agencies, and manufacturing concerns.

On one point, however, the president did not change: he would not approve a program of federal relief for the unemployed. His position was that relief was a responsibility of local and state governments, churches, and private agencies. He believed that relief in the form of a dole would destroy individual initiative and the moral fiber of those who received it. He also feared that a massive program of federal relief would bankrupt the federal government and bring the downfall of the Republic.

Such a view was not shared by many of Hoover's countrymen. They reminded the president of his part in relieving the suffering of starving Belgians, Hungarians, and Russians during and after World War I. They criticized him for not doing the same for hungry Americans during the depression. Hoover, of course, cared deeply about human suffering. Still, he believed that on the matter of relief his hands were tied. Above all, he must not take the government into bankruptcy.

Under the circumstances Hoover's popularity inevitably waned. The president and a few key advisers—especially Secretary of the Treasury Andrew W. Mellon—became targets for depression-inspired attacks and satire. The tent and shack villages of the unemployed were called "Hoovervilles," old newspapers became "Hoover blankets," and jack rabbits became "Hoover hogs."

Hooverville, U.S.A., was an all-too-common place name bitterly given to the groups of shacks in which many of the unemployed and homeless lived during the depression. This "community" of shanties sprang up on a vacant lot in Lower Manhattan.

Courtesy Franklin D. Roosevelt Library, Hyde Park, N.Y.

Some public officials did not share the president's unhappy fate. On the contrary, the reputation of one man enlarged dramatically in the years after the crash of 1929: Franklin Delano Roosevelt, the governor of New York.

STUDY GUIDE: Hoover was not in favor of using the power of the federal government to aid economic recovery. He did, however, approve a modest program of public works. His administration also extended aid to depressed farmers and created the Reconstruction Finance Corporation to loan funds to city and state governments. Hoover refused to approve a program of federal relief for the unemployed. This turned many voters against him.

FRANKLIN DELANO ROOSEVELT

Franklin Roosevelt was born in 1882 in a mansion on his father's estate overlooking the Hudson River at Hyde Park, New York. He was the son of James and Sarah Delano Roosevelt. His father, of Dutch and English ancestry, had a fortune which rested largely on assorted ventures in railroading. At the time of his son's birth, the elder Roosevelt was fifty-four years old. An aging and rather sickly man, he never exercised much influence on the youth. He died when Franklin was eighteen.

Sarah Delano Roosevelt was only twenty-eight when her son and only child entered the world. A tall, handsome woman of a socially elite family, she had been educated abroad and traveled around the world. Mrs. Roosevelt would live (until 1941) to see her son achieve world prominence. She was an intelligent and strong-willed woman, for whom her son felt a deep and abiding attachment.

As a youth, Roosevelt lived the life of an American "blue blood." He was attended by servants, traveled in Europe, and his early schooling came from governesses and private tutors. At the age of fourteen he entered Groton, a preparatory school in Massachusetts, and, upon graduation, enrolled at Harvard University.

The year after his graduation from Harvard, in 1905, Roosevelt married a distant cousin, Anna Eleanor Roosevelt, a shy and sensitive girl of nineteen who was the niece of President Theodore Roosevelt. After a honeymoon in Europe, Roosevelt attended Columbia University Law School. Legal studies bored him and he never earned a law degree, although he was able, in 1907, to pass the bar examination.

Early Career

While working in a Wall Street law firm Roosevelt became active in Democratic politics. In 1910 he won election as state senator. In 1912 he worked for the election of Woodrow Wilson, despite the fact that Wilson's chief opponent in the presidential sweepstakes was his distant cousin Theodore Roosevelt. Grateful for his support, Wilson appointed Franklin Roosevelt assistant secretary of the navy in 1913. In the Navy Department Franklin Roosevelt proved energetic and effective. After the war, he threw himself into Wilson's crusade for American membership in the League of Nations. Then, in 1920, he ran unsuccessfully for the vice-presidency.

After the election of 1920 Roosevelt resumed the practice of law and also involved himself in several business ventures. In August 1921, he suffered a chill, which was followed by a high fever and, finally, paralysis from the waist down. Physicians diagnosed his illness as poliomyelitis. Roosevelt never walked normally again.

Roosevelt's mother wanted him to forget public life, but his wife, Eleanor, quietly urged him to challenge his handicap. At the Democratic national convention of 1924 he evoked a hysterical response when, supported by crutches, he gave his famous speech nominating Alfred E. Smith for president. Four years later, in 1928 he again nominated Smith, who this time won the endorsement of the Democratic convention. Smith immediately began to press Roosevelt to run for governor of New York State.

Smith calculated that Roosevelt's personal magnetism and his family name would increase the chances of carrying New York in the presidential contest. Foreseeing a Republican tide in the election, Roosevelt consented reluctantly to run. Thanks to a strenuous campaign, the magic of the Roosevelt name, and a split in Republican ranks in New York, he won a narrow victory, although Smith lost the state to Hoover.

As governor, Roosevelt earned a reputation as an energetic and imaginative chief executive. Most notably he won passage of an old-age pension program and several measures that benefited labor.

When the Great Depression began Roosevelt organized an emergency committee on unemployment. He proposed a compulsory program of unemployment insurance for New York and in summer 1931 created the Temporary Emergency Relief Administration. This emergency relief organization spent $20 million to help desperate New Yorkers through the winter of 1931-32. Carefully drawing attention to his record, particularly his steps to relieve depression distress, Roosevelt waged a successful campaign for reelection in autumn 1930.

Roosevelt was uninterested in grand social and economic theory. He was a practical man who was concerned with tangible projects, such as construction of great bridges and dams, reclamation of soil and forests, and the stringing of electric power lines across the countryside.

To the extent that he wanted to preserve the traditional system of political democracy and free enterprise, Franklin Roosevelt was a conservative, like his relative Theodore Roosevelt before him. To the extent that he was willing to endorse changes within the traditional framework, he was a liberal or progressive.

Roosevelt was cheerful, buoyant, and optimistic. He was totally convinced that intelligent and resourceful men and women could resolve the country's problems. Gifted with a rich, smooth voice, he had a rare ability to communicate. Roosevelt also loved politics and, as time passed, most Americans, whatever their political allegiances, came to consider him a master political craftsman.

The Election of 1932

When the Democratic national convention opened in Chicago in June 1932, Roosevelt's chances of winning the two-thirds vote required for nomination seemed doubtful. Then John Nance Garner of Texas, the conservative speaker of the House of Representatives, agreed to throw his support to Roosevelt. In return Roosevelt pledged that if nominated he would ask the convention to make Garner his vice-presidential running mate.

With Garner's support, Roosevelt secured the nomination on the fourth ballot. The Texan was duly nominated for second place on the presidential ticket. Next, Roosevelt demonstrated his characteristic flair for the dramatic. He put aside the tradition that a presidential nominee should think it over for a couple of weeks and then notify the national chairman of the party of his acceptance of the nomination. Instead he flew to Chicago to tell delegates in person that he would be their nominee. As delegates roared approval, Roosevelt announced: "I pledge you, I pledge myself, to a new deal for the American people."

The Republicans had convened in Chicago two weeks before the Democrats. The delegates concluded that dropping the Republican president would destroy whatever chances they might have of victory in the autumn election.

John Nance Garner of Texas was speaker of the House of Representatives in 1932. Franklin D. Roosevelt sought the presidential nomination of the Democratic party that year.. Garner agreed to support FDR in return for his pledge to make the Texan his vice-presidential running mate.

Therefore they renominated President Hoover and Vice-President Curtis.

Cautiously confident of victory, Roosevelt said nothing on the campaign trail that was profound and little that was controversial. In only one speech did he indicate that if elected he might organize a bold attack on the depression. Otherwise his campaign statements sounded conservative. He spoke out for reduced federal spending and a balanced budget—or made vague statements. The strategy worked perfectly. On election day Americans gave Roosevelt and Garner almost twenty-three million votes to less than sixteen million for Hoover and Curtis. The Democratic ticket carried the electoral college by a vote of 472-59. As a result of the election, moreover, Roosevelt was assured of heavy Democratic majorities in both houses of Congress.

For most Americans, including Hoover and Roosevelt, the period seemed endless between the election on November 8, 1932 and FDR's inauguration as president on March 4, 1933. Before the period expired, however, the country

learned that future "waiting periods" would not be so long. On February 6, 1933, the Twentieth Amendment to the Constitution received ratification. Among the amendment's provisions was one that moved the inauguration of presidents and vice-presidents from March 4 to January 20.

Meanwhile, the depression tightened its grip on the country. Factories that had been wheezing along on one cylinder cut back production, and retail trade declined. Unemployment by some estimates approached fifteen million. In the White House, Hoover was trying manfully to deal with the crisis. To that end he repeatedly sought the president-elect's endorsement of various plans he had in mind. Roosevelt realized that such endorsement would bind him to Hoover's policies and ideas. Thus he politely declined all of these overtures. During the long wait Roosevelt remained buoyant and calm— even when, on February 15, 1933, he narrowly missed death in an attempted assassination.

STUDY GUIDE: Born into a wealthy New York family, Franklin Delano Roosevelt overcame the handicap of polio to become governor of New York. He launched many programs to relieve depression distress in New York. His record there made him the leading Democratic presidential candidate in 1932.

Roosevelt won the presidency by a wide margin over Hoover in 1932. Both houses of Congress also gained heavy Democratic majorities. Roosevelt avoided approval of Hoover's proposals in the months before his inauguration.

THE NEW DEAL

At his inauguration, March 4, 1933, Roosevelt repeated the presidential oath after Chief Justice Charles Evans Hughes. Then he began his inaugural address. In a high and clear voice, he electrified his countrymen when he announced: "First of all, let me assert my firm belief that the only thing we have to fear is fear itself."

Reviving Credit

Brave words had their place, but something more was required if the United States was to make an early exit from the Great Depression. The government must come to grips with the crisis of fear that had brought banking activity in the country to a virtual standstill. Banks were the principal source of credit and without credit the national economy was like an engine without fuel.

Two days after taking office, Roosevelt used authority provided by a law enacted during World War I to meet the banking crisis. He ordered all banks in the country to stop all activities except the making of change for four days—a "bank holiday." At the same time he summoned Congress into special session. On the first day of the special session, March 9, the national legislature rammed through the Emergency Banking Act in eight hours. The new legislation permitted the Reconstruction Finance Corporation to buy the preferred stock of banks and in that way give distressed banks an injection of fresh capital. It also validated the "bank holiday" and set up procedures for reopening banks.

The emergency banking legislation divided banks into four categories. In the first category were those that were fully sound, with assets equal to deposits. Such banks could resume unrestricted payments to depositors at once. Surprisingly, half of the nation's banks, with ninety percent of the banking resources, were in the first category. In the second category were banks—about one-fourth of the total—that were in a less satisfactory condition. Banks in that category could reopen and pay out a percentage of their deposits. In the third category were banks whose assets were so exhausted that they could make no payments from old deposits but might reopen and accept new deposits. In the fourth category were about a thousand banks

Library of Congress

". . . the only thing we have to fear is fear itself," were the stirring words of President Franklin D. Roosevelt in his 1933 inaugural address. What immediate steps did FDR's new administration take to remove the climate of fear that gripped the nation's banking community?

in such poor condition that they were not permitted to reopen. These made up about five percent of the banks of the country.

To explain what the government was doing and urge people to put aside fears and return their money to banks, President Roosevelt spoke to the nation via radio on March 12, 1933. This was the first of his celebrated "fireside chats." The chief executive's tones were soothing, his words simple and direct. And the results were astonishing. Within three weeks more than a billion dollars had flowed back to the banks.

While taking steps to strengthen the country's

This scene was photographed in June 1932 at the Millbury Savings Bank, in Massachusetts. It was repeated in many banks throughout the nation as depositors rushed to withdraw savings before the bank collapsed. Were the moves made by President Hoover adequate to restore confidence in the faltering American economy?

Courtesy Franklin D. Roosevelt Library, Hyde Park, N.Y.

banks, the New Deal administration set about to stimulate the flow of credit in other ways. Most important, it dramatically enlarged the activities of the Reconstruction Finance Corporation. Guided by Jesse Jones, the RFC established several subsidiaries. The Commodity Credit Corporation was set up to support farm prices. The Electric Home and Farm Authority financed purchases of electrical appliances, particularly in rural areas. The Export-Import Bank sought to stimulate America's foreign trade.

The RFC also financed public works programs, drainage, levee, and irrigation projects, and school construction. It loaned vast sums to railroads, insurance companies, credit unions, building and loan associations, livestock credit corporations, airlines, and natural gas companies. The RFC became a powerful instrument of state capitalism. It became the largest single investor in the national economy and the biggest bank in the country. Nearly all of its investments proved sound and of the billions of dollars it loaned, nearly every cent was repaid.

While trying to revive credit, the New Dealers also sought to help individuals and businesses that were weighted down with debts they had contracted in more prosperous times. For example, they sponsored changes in bankruptcy laws. These changes helped those who were not able to pay their debts to come to an understanding with creditors quickly and at small legal cost.

The problem of indebtedness was more severe for the country's farmers than for any other group. To meet the problem of farm indebtedness the New Deal administration in its first two years passed four major laws to help farmers retain or recover their properties. After 1935 foreclosures—the taking of farms for nonpayment of debts—in rural America virtually came to an end.

In small-town and urban America many people who had gone into debt to build or buy houses faced loss of their properties through foreclosure. During the last year of the Hoover administration more than two-hundred fifty thousand families had lost their homes. Early in 1933 foreclosures were taking place at a rate of more than a thousand a day. To meet the problem, in April 1933, President Roosevelt asked Congress to establish the Home Owners' Loan Corporation. Swinging into operation quickly, the HOLC bought mortgages from holders who were about to begin foreclosure proceedings. It also put up money for taxes and financed repairs. Finally it rewrote mortgages to enable distressed home

owners to retire mortgage obligations over long periods of time at low rates of interest. As a consequence of such activities, hundreds of thousands of families managed to keep their homes.

STUDY GUIDE: Promptly after his inauguration, Roosevelt summoned Congress into special session. An Emergency Banking Act was passed to strengthen the nation's banking system. The activities of the Reconstruction Finance Corporation were enlarged to stimulate the flow of credit. Other legislation provided loans to help debt-ridden farmers, businessmen, and home owners.

DEVALUATION AND THE TARIFF

Essential to the New Deal's recovery program were policies designed to reverse the trend of deflation and bring about inflation. New Dealers sought to restore and maintain price levels that had prevailed in the country in the 1920s.

Prices of goods and services had declined sharply, and so had corporate and personal incomes. Despite the fall of price-income levels, businessmen, farmers, and workers who had borrowed money in the 1920s were obliged to repay debts at face value. Tens of millions of businessmen, farmers, and working people whose incomes were drastically reduced could not repay their debts.

To illustrate, suppose a man in 1929 had been earning fifty dollars a week. Setting aside ten of those dollars to make payments on a car would probably have caused little strain. Then came the depression. The man's income probably sank to fifteen or twenty dollars a week. How could the man keep up the ten-dollar weekly payment? Probably he could not. More than that, how could he and millions of his countrymen make the new purchases and investments that were needed to get the economy moving again? They could not until they got out from under their burdens of debt. And they would be unable to lift the burdens until incomes went up. Incomes would not go up until prices went up. Hence it was necessary to reverse the trend if the country was to get out of the depression.

The first step to restore prices was made possible as the result of a provision of the Emergency Banking Act. This act gave the president authority over gold for the duration of the economic crisis. Using that authority, in April 1933, President Roosevelt ordered all persons to deliver to the Federal Reserve or member banks all of their gold coins, gold bullion, and gold certificates. Then he took the United States off the international gold monetary standard by forbidding the export of gold. The dollar had previously been pegged by the American government's pledge to exchange dollars for gold at a rate of $20.67 an ounce. Going off the gold standard meant that it would find a lower level in the world's currency market. Thus, by taking the United States off gold, Roosevelt devalued the dollar. As a result the foreigner would receive more dollars in exchange for the same number of units of his native currency than in the past. The devalued dollar would make American goods more attractive to foreigners and hence would stimulate foreign purchases in the United States. Stepped-up foreign purchasing would stimulate the American economy which would in turn push prices and wages upward.

In the weeks that followed devaluation, the pace of economic activity in America quickened. The commodity price index jumped, and unemployment figures revealed a slight decline. President Roosevelt accordingly lost interest in the World Economic Conference which was scheduled to take place in London beginning in June 1933.

The declared aim of the conference was to stabilize the world's currencies and thereby stimulate international trade. Noting the apparent results of the recent devaluation of the dollar, Roosevelt concluded that further devaluation might accomplish even better results. Thus he did not want to stabilize the American currency, at least not yet. And so, shortly after the World Economic Conference opened, Roosevelt issued his famous "bombshell message" in which he made it plain that the United States had no interest in the conference. Inasmuch as cooperation by the United States, the leading economic power of the world, was necessary for its success, the conference adjourned a short time later.

Then in late summer of 1933, the pace of economic activity in America slackened. Prices slipped and unemployment increased. Roosevelt then embarked on a positive program of dollar depreciation, as opposed to the indirect method of devaluation used previously. This was perhaps the most inexplicable scheme ever sanctioned by the New Deal administration. The idea

was originated by George F. Warren, a professor of farm management at Cornell University. Warren proposed to raise the price that the United States government would pay for gold. The outcome, according to Warren's calculations, would be further depreciation of the dollar. This, in turn, would stimulate foreign purchases in the United States and push prices and wages in America to higher levels.

The price which the government would pay for gold in December 1933 passed thirty-four dollars an ounce. At that point Roosevelt prepared to terminate the gold-buying experiment and stabilize the dollar in terms of gold. Thus he prevailed on Congress, in January 1934, to approve the Gold Reserve Bill. The gold reserve legislation directed Federal Reserve banks to turn over to the Treasury (in exchange for gold certificates) the gold coins which they had been holding since Roosevelt ordered them turned in the previous April. It provided that the gold coins be melted into gold bars. If it chose to do so, the government could release these gold bars to balance foreign accounts. (Imbalances would arise if more dollars were spent or invested overseas than were taken in from overseas.)

The day after enactment of the measure, January 31, 1934, Roosevelt, by executive order, officially devalued the dollar to 59.06 percent of its former weight in terms of gold. This meant that the government would pay thirty-five dollars an ounce for gold. Availability of gold to balance foreign accounts was all that kept the United States from being on an out-and-out paper money basis.

The Tariff Question

The aim of devaluation of the dollar was to stimulate America's overseas commerce which, by accelerating the pace of economic activity in the country, would push prices and wages upward and reduce unemployment. With this in mind, New Dealers naturally sought additional ways to increase foreign trade. Accordingly they created, in 1934, the Export-Import Bank, a subsidiary of the Reconstruction Finance Corporation. The bank financed the movement of goods in international trade and extended credit to countries wishing to do business in the United States. More important, New Dealers set out to reduce or get around existing tariff barriers.

When discussing the tariff question in the Roosevelt administration, attention inevitably settles on the secretary of state, Cordell Hull. A former representative and senator from Tennessee, Hull for many years had been a champion of liberal trade. Therefore, by definition, he was an enemy of the protective tariff. He believed liberal trade would assure prosperity and peace among the nations of the world.

Roosevelt did not share Hull's view of the blessings that would flow to mankind as a result of elimination or reduction of tariff barriers. Still, he thought the arguments in favor of liberal trade outweighed those of protectionists. In March 1934, he asked Congress for authority to make tariff concessions to governments which made equivalent concessions to the United States. This was the principle of reciprocal trade agreements. (As matters turned out, Roosevelt, influenced by Hull, did not insist on equivalent concessions. Using the most-favored-nation principle, he granted concessions to all nations which did not discriminate in trade policy against the United States.) Despite vigorous opposition by Republicans, the Trade Agreements Bill won congressional approval.

Under previous legislation the average duty on commodities imported into the United States had reached fifty-three percent of the value of the commodity. Under the New Deal's trade agreements program, tariff barriers were dramatically beaten down. The average duty by 1951 was less than fifteen percent, by 1961 less than ten percent. During the 1930s, however, the program seemed to give only a minimal lift to the country's overseas commerce. Thus it did little to restore prices and wages.

STUDY GUIDE: To restore prices to their pre-Depression levels, Roosevelt took the nation off the gold standard. This action reduced the value of the dollar. Roosevelt hoped that increased foreign purchases as a result of devaluation would stimulate the American economy and push prices and wages upward. In other efforts to increase foreign trade, New Dealers created the Export-Import Bank and moved to reduce existing tariff barriers.

THE NRA

Stimulation of foreign trade by devaluation of the dollar and reduction of tariffs was one aspect of the New Deal program to raise prices and wages. Another was mobilization of American industry. The instrument for such mobilization was the National Recovery Administration, established by the National Industrial Recovery Act of June 1933.

At the heart of the NRA program were codes of fair competition—a separate code for each industry, drawn up by representatives of industries themselves. Each firm in an industry covered by a code, when the code received the president's signature, was subject to prosecution and penalties if it refused to comply. Most codes prohibited unfair trade practices, including deceptive advertising, imitation of trademarks, making sale of one product contingent on sale of another, and securing business by "cutthroat" price cutting. The central purpose of the codes, however, was to restrict competition and bring output into line with demand. That was what New Dealers were talking about when they spoke of mobilizing industry. The idea was to cut back industrial production and make commodities relatively scarce.

Scarcity, New Dealers hoped, would generate competition among consumers and push prices, and with them wages, upward. To that end most codes, in one way or another, provided for controls on production. Some codes, for example, established production quotas for each component of an industry; some fixed limits on the hours that machines could be operated; some prohibited construction of new production facilities; others prohibited operation of machinery or equipment that had previously been idle.

How did leaders of organized labor look on the NRA, whose codes sanctioned a practice, restraint of business competition, over which workingmen and their spokesmen had fought for generations?

Section 7

New Dealers had anticipated a possible reaction on the part of labor. Therefore they included in the industrial recovery legislation a section which in labor's view more than compensated for accepting restraints on business competition. Section 7 provided that every NRA code must guarantee that employees had a right to organize and bargain collectively through representatives of their own choosing. Moreover, employees should be free from interference, restraint, or coercion by employers in the designation of such representatives or in other concerted activities for the purpose of collective bargaining.

The section also provided that no employee and no one seeking employment should be required as a condition of employment to join any company union or to refrain from joining a labor organization of his own choosing. Section 7 also contained provisions guaranteeing the right of self-organization of workers and collective bargaining in industries in which there were no NRA codes. The right of labor unions to organize and bargain collectively was assured first by Section 7 and, after 1935, by the National Labor Relations Act. As a consequence, labor unions saw their membership rolls enlarged from 2,858,000 in 1933 to 7,218,000 in 1937 to 10,489,000 in 1941.

Since industry codes could not be drafted overnight, Roosevelt urged employers, pending completion of codes for their respective industries, to sign the President's Reemployment Act. This act was popularly called the "blanket code." Acceptance of the blanket code, which pertained chiefly to labor, would hasten the benefits intended for labor under the NRA program, notably better wages.

Within a few months over two million employers with sixteen million employees signed the blanket code. They thus became eligible to display the official emblem of the NRA, a blue eagle spread out above the caption: "We do our part." These employers agreed to hire no workers under sixteen years of age. They promised to pay clerical and service workers minimum wages ranging from twelve dollars in small towns to fifteen dollars in large cities for a maximum of forty hours of work per week. Factory operators agreed to pay workers in most cases a minimum of forty cents an hour for a maximum of thirty-five hours of work each week.

Signers of the President's Reemployment Act agreed to do business only with firms that had signed the blanket or industry codes. This meant that the NRA sought to organize a nationwide boycott against employers operating outside the NRA system. Reinforcing the boycott was a presidential order requiring federal agencies to do business only with firms that had agreed to comply with the blanket or industry codes.

At first the NRA met with great popular enthusiasm, much of it drummed up by an unparalleled publicity campaign. However, the NRA was soon the target of much criticism.

Critics, including some university professors, attacked the agency's commitment to the idea of raising prices by making commodities scarce. These critics observed that the ultimate aim of the New Deal was to restore Americans to standards of living that had existed before the depression. This goal seemed to require increased production of electrical appliances, clothing, automobiles, and furniture.

New Dealers countered that the first requirement for achieving recovery — within the framework of the free enterprise system — was to stop the downward spiral of prices and wages. Only by bringing production into line with demand, by limiting production, could the downward spiral be stopped. At the same time it was limiting production, the government would act to increase the demand for industry's output — by stimulating foreign trade, for example. Gradually, restrictions on output would be relaxed and the country would return to full production. Such arguments impressed few critics.

More hostile and persistent was the criticism of small businessmen, who argued that the national recovery program was rigged in favor of big business. Such criticism came mainly from the difficulty encountered by small businessmen in meeting minimum wage standards set by the NRA. This raised the question: If they could not pay decent wages, did small businessmen have a right to exist? In the estimate of many Americans in the 1930s, the answer was a resounding no.

In a decision resulting from the case of *Schecter Poultry Corporation* v. *United States*, involving a code of the live poultry industry, the Supreme Court ruled in May 1935 that the National Industrial Recovery Act was in conflict with the Constitution. Because of the criticisms generated by the national recovery program, the Roosevelt administration made no attempt to rewrite the legislation to meet objections of the Supreme Court. Instead the NRA was permitted to expire.

Contributions of the NRA

As an instrument for countering the depression, the NRA apparently had minimal value. And insofar as it held down production, the agency was an obstacle to restoration of living standards that had prevailed in the 1920s. The NRA established on a national basis the principle of maximum hours and minimum wages for labor. In so doing, it dealt a heavy blow to the kind of business competition which labor leader John L. Lewis described as resting on a test to see how little a worker could eat. It virtually abolished child labor in the United States, undermined sweatshops, and transformed the position of labor by making collective bargaining a national policy. It stamped out a range of unfair trade practices and established new standards of economic decency in America. As a consequence, in a little more than a year, it registered a host of achievements that had dominated the dreams of progressive reformers for half a century.

STUDY GUIDE: The National Recovery Administration was created to bring output into line with demand. Codes were drawn up to cut back industrial production. It was hoped that scarcity of commodities would raise prices and wages. To win support from organized labor for this measure, the NRA assured unions the right to organize and bargain collectively.

FARM PROGRAMS

The New Dealers also set in motion a program which they hoped would restore prices and incomes in agriculture. The need to do something for agriculture seemed urgent. In the years after 1929 farm prices in the United States had declined more than fifty percent.

The Agricultural Adjustment Act

The central personality in the New Deal's farm program was the secretary of agriculture, Henry A. Wallace of Iowa. He thought the problem in agriculture — overproduction which pushed down prices — was not unlike that in industry. What was needed was to curtail the output of such commodities as corn, livestock, cotton, tobacco, eggs, and butter. Farmers therefore ought to make their produce relatively scarce. To that end, New Dealers persuaded Congress, in spring 1933, to approve the Agricultural Adjustment Bill. The measure established a new agency, the Agricultural Adjustment Administration.

The agricultural adjustment legislation provided several techniques for creating a degree of scarcity which in turn would push prices upward and add to the income of farmers. The government, for example, could lease land from farmers and take it out of cultivation. But the heart of the New Deal's program was the domestic allotment plan — payment of cash subsidies to farmers in return for pledges to restrict output.

The halls of Congress echoed with laments by conservative Republicans that the Agricultural Adjustment Act was "more bolshevistic than any law or regulation existing in Soviet Russia." But in spring of 1933 the domestic allotment program moved into gear. Then came disturbing news. A bumper crop was threatening to push the price of cotton to a new low.

The result was the cotton plow-up of summer 1933. Holding out the lure of cash subsidies, and also the prospect of higher prices for cotton that ultimately went to market, the AAA persuaded a million cotton farmers to plow under ten million acres of cotton plants. This was between one-fourth and one-half of the potential crop of 1933.

Observing that millions of their countrymen were in need of clothing, blankets, and mattresses, many Americans were aghast at the cotton plow-up. But in spite of criticisms and laments, the price of cotton moved up steadily. By 1936 it was nearly double what it had been in 1933.

Surplus Problems

Corn was also plagued by troublesome surpluses and, since most corn found its way to market in the form of pork, Wallace proposed a large cutback in hog breeding. But when statistics revealed that 1933 promised to be a year of "bumper" hog output, the secretary directed the AAA to purchase and slaughter six million little pigs. Critics contended that so long as there were hungry people in the world there could be no such phenomenon as a surplus of food. They insisted that it was a sin against God and man to embark on a program of destruction of food. Hog prices went from $3.34 a hundredweight in 1932 to $4.14 in 1934 to $8.65 in 1935 to $9.50 in 1937.

Surpluses were also ruining hundreds of thousands of farmers who depended on wheat for their livelihood. To meet the problem the AAA for a time considered a plow-up of wheat. However, it settled on a program of subsidy payments in return for pledges by farmers that they would cut back the planting of wheat. Then nature took a hand.

Over the winter of 1933-34 rain and snow were unusually light on the Great Plains, the breadbasket of the United States. The earth became dry and hard. Thus rain that fell the following spring could not be absorbed. Then came summer. Week after week, skies remained cloudless. Next the winds began to blow. From

Drought and dust storms turned the Great Plains into a wasteland during the early 1930s. Crops were destroyed and farms in the "dust bowl" were abandoned. How were prices of farm products affected by these conditions?

the Dakotas to Texas great clouds of dust—the topsoil of the plains—billowed up to the sky, turned daylight into darkness, then began to blow eastward, across the Mississippi, over the Appalachians, and out to the Atlantic. The drought and dust storms turned vast sections of the plains into desert and introduced the term "dust bowl" to the language. They also brought a cutback in wheat production that was far greater than the AAA could have engineered by its domestic allotment program. As a consequence, wheat became scarce and the price per bushel went from thirty-eight cents in 1932 to eighty-four cents in 1934 to ninety-six cents in 1937.

As other agricultural products became scarce, prices rose. Corn, rice, and Irish potatoes all became more costly. The average price of all farm products rose two-thirds from 1932 to 1936.

Soil Conservation and Domestic Allotment Act

In early 1936 the Supreme Court declared that central parts of the Agricultural Adjustment Act were unconstitutional. The Roosevelt administration proposed new legislation by which, in a revised form, it hoped to continue promoting scarcity in agriculture. The outcome was the Soil Conservation and Domestic Allotment Act.

While the act was a measure to encourage soil conservation, it was essentially intended to control surpluses of the great money crops and keep prices and farm income moving steadily upward.

Under the new legislation farmers received cash payments for shifting acreage from soil-depleting crops—cotton and tobacco—to soil-conserving crops—alfalfa and red clover. This change would strengthen the soil. Equally important, so the administration calculated, it would also bring a reduction in output of basic crops.

The Soil Conservation and Domestic Allotment Act proved a frail instrument for restricting output of wheat, corn, and tobacco. Accordingly, the problem of large surpluses again began to trouble the country's farmers. As surpluses enlarged, prices began to drop; and as prices went down, so did farm income. The Roosevelt administration, now in its second term, persuaded Congress, in early 1938, to approve the second Agricultural Adjustment Bill. The new legislation was a long and complicated measure. Drawing on both the Agricultural Adjustment Act of 1933 and the Soil Conservation and Domestic Allotment Act, it sought by various forms of subsidy and coercion to persuade farmers to cut back production. The second agricultural adjustment legislation, however, brought no great improvement to agriculture in America. On the contrary, surpluses continued to increase. By 1939 the country seemed threatened with a severe break in farm prices. Then, in September 1939, World War II broke out in Europe. Surpluses were absorbed, and by 1941 the country's farmers were enjoying a boom.

Sharecropping

The New Deal's farm program brought a notable increase in farm prices and incomes, at least between 1933 and 1938. It improved the soil and helped to restore the morale of millions of farmers. However, it did increase the difficulties of millions of tenant farmers, particularly sharecroppers.

Essentially a southern phenomenon, the sharecrop system had started in the South in the decades after the Civil War. By the time of the Great Depression, the system held in its clutches some three million men, women, and children. Somewhat more than half of these sharecroppers were black. Usually illiterate and hopelessly in debt, sharecroppers were often cheated by dishonest landlords, moneylenders, and merchants. To try to make ends meet, the entire family customarily worked in the fields from dawn to dusk. Many sharecropper families existed under conditions of almost unbelievable poverty with only the barest food, clothing, and housing to sustain life.

The New Deal unfortunately brought little improvement in the life style of sharecroppers. It worsened conditions of great numbers of them. First, the bulk of the cash payments under the domestic allotment program went to the owners of the land. The only benefit of consequence to the sharecropper was the increase in prices which he might get on his share of the smaller crop. More serious, New Deal programs resulted in expulsion of uncounted sharecroppers and other tenants from the land. Many landlords used AAA benefit payments to buy tractors, which in turn enabled them to cut back the number of agricutural workers required for their operations.

As great tracts of land were converted from production of money crops to soil-conserving crops, large numbers of sharecroppers and other tenants were not needed. Some sharecroppers went off to the cities in search of work, swelling the pool of unskilled labor in urban areas. Others, particularly those from Arkansas and Oklahoma made their way in a bewildering array of jalopies to California. These were the Arkies and Okies who were immortalized in John Steinbeck's novel *The Grapes of Wrath*. In California they hoped to find prosperity as wage laborers in the vineyards, orchards, and lettuce and cotton fields. Instead they found little except weariness, pain, and a level of poverty that was often worse than they had known before.

New Dealers were deeply moved by the problems of tenant farmers and migrant workers. They did what they could to lighten the burden of victims of their programs, for example, by establishing camps along the Pacific Coast for migrants. Still, so they reasoned, there was a heavy overconcentration of manpower in America's farm belt, particularly in the cotton states. If agriculture was to prosper, it seemed clear that the number of people who lived by farming must be balanced with the demand for farm commodities. Just as it seemed necessary to reduce agricultural output and prevent commodities from crowding markets, so it seemed essential that surplus farmers had to be removed from the land. An extremely harsh medicine, to be sure, but one that New Dealers considered absolutely necessary if agriculture in America was to recover.

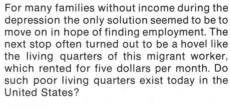

For many families without income during the depression the only solution seemed to be to move on in hope of finding employment. The next stop often turned out to be a hovel like the living quarters of this migrant worker, which rented for five dollars per month. Do such poor living quarters exist today in the United States?

USDA photo

STUDY GUIDE: BY creating a scarcity of farm products, the New Deal also hoped to restore prices and incomes for farmers. The Agricultural Adjustment Administration paid cash subsidies to farmers who promised to limit production. After the AAA was declared unconstitutional, revised legislation was passed to encourage soil preservation as well as to cut back production. The New Deal farm program increased farm prices and income, but it brought even harder times to sharecroppers and tenant farmers.

SPENDING AND RELIEF

To promote national recovery, New Dealers also tried to stimulate economic activity by large-scale federal spending. New Dealers also gave much thought to another concern: relief for the unemployed. Unlike their Republican predecessors they believed the federal government had a responsibility to guarantee a minimum of economic security for all citizens. This meant providing money for the basic necessities of those who were destitute. New Dealers determined to accomplish two goals at one time by spending large sums of federal money in such a way that it would stimulate recovery while providing relief for the unemployed. One New Deal agency designed to achieve this dual function was the Public Works Administration, established under Title II of the National Industrial Recovery Act of June 1933.

Public Works Administration

The chief of the PWA was Roosevelt's secretary of the interior, Harold L. Ickes, a native of Chicago and former Bull Moose Republican. Ickes was a crusader for liberal reform. The PWA got off to a slow start, in part because great public works projects required time-consuming planning, engineering surveys, and cost estimates. Then to guard against corruption, Ickes personally went over every PWA contract and kept an eye on all PWA operations. The result was further delay.

While it failed to make an early contribution to recovery, the PWA nonetheless accomplished a great deal. The agency granted or loaned some $6 billion for construction or improvement of courthouses, city halls, jails, schools, sewage systems, water systems, tunnels, public housing, power distribution facilities, bridges, subways, roads, highways, hospitals, hospital facilities, and buildings for colleges and universities.

The PWA was also responsible for flood control projects, dams, railway electrification, railroad passenger stations, aircraft carriers, cruisers, destroyers, submarines, army posts, military airports, and military and naval aircraft.

Work-Relief Program

To provide relief for the destitute, in the spring of 1933 President Roosevelt persuaded Congress to create the Federal Emergency Relief Administration. To direct the new agency he appointed Harry Hopkins, who had directed relief activities in New York when Roosevelt was governor. Through the FERA the government provided a handout to Americans who were out of work. But Hopkins did not like that approach. He wanted a "work-relief" program in which a man or woman would receive a check in return for labor performed in the public interest. By giving a person something useful to do and offering him a check for his labor, work-relief would sidestep the demoralizing effects of the dole. On the contrary, he thought, it would bolster the self-respect of those who received payment for work.

At length Hopkins aroused the interest of the president in work-relief. In autumn 1933 Roosevelt issued an order establishing the Civil Works Administration. The results were astounding. Supported by a small underpaid staff of people who shared his zeal, Hopkins in two months put more than four million Americans to work. Laboring in every county and town in the nation, CWA employees built or improved roads, highways, sewers, parks, playgrounds, athletic fields, swimming pools, schools, and airports. They taught school children and illiterate adults, exterminated insect pests, raked leaves, and dug ditches. Hopkins also put artists and writers on the CWA payroll. When critics spoke out against relief payments to individuals engaged in such "frivolous enterprises" as art and literature, Hopkins replied, "They've got to eat just like other people."

Largely because of the strain on the federal budget, Roosevelt announced in March 1934 that the CWA—which had consumed nearly a billion dollars in a few months—would expire as soon as current projects were completed. The passing of the agency, in mid-summer 1934, left the FERA as the only federal agency providing relief on a grand scale.

The WPA

In November 1934, the New Deal won a rousing endorsement at the polls. Instead of losing strength in Congress—the usual fate of America's majority party at the time of midterm elections—the Democrats picked up ten seats in the House of Representatives and, almost incredibly, ten in the Senate.

Republicans had made the New Deal's spend-

This photograph taken in Chicago in 1934 during the height of the depression captures the feeling of desperation shared by millions of unemployed workers. How did Roosevelt differ from Hoover in his views on federal relief for the unemployed?

ing and relief programs an issue during the electoral campaign. The outcome of the balloting seemed a vote of confidence for the administration's relief activities. As a consequence, in spring 1935 Congress appropriated $4.8 billion for relief purposes. To dispose of a great chunk of that appropriation, Roosevelt created the Works Progress Division and named Hopkins as its head. The new agency, which Hopkins promptly renamed the Works Progress Administration—the WPA—had authority to "recommend and carry on small useful projects designed to assure a maximum of employment in all localities."

Moving quickly and boldly, Hopkins soon initiated an incredible array of WPA projects. His methods and projects, however, generated a great deal of criticism. The Chicago, *Daily Tribune* declared in 1936 that "Mr. Hopkins is a bull-headed man whose high place in the New Deal was won by his ability to waste more money in quicker time on more absurd undertakings than any other mischievous wit in Washington could think of."[1]

In all, the WPA undertook a quarter of a million projects in every county, city, and town in the United States. The projects ranged from highway construction and the extermination of rats to the playing of the world's greatest symphonies.[2]

Such projects consumed great sums of money, which taxpayers had to put up. Still, funds expended on WPA helped the country move out of the depression. The WPA provided work and income, and thus the necessities of life, for enormous numbers of people. The agency employed more than eight million people between 1935 and 1941. Counting dependents of employees, WPA earnings directly benefited between twenty-five and thirty million Americans.

A lesser agency for providing relief was the National Youth Administration, created in 1935. The NYA had two purposes. It was to administer a work-relief, training, and employment program for persons between ages sixteen and twenty-five who were not full-time students in school or college. As a general rule, these were members of families that depended on relief. Second, the NYA was to provide part-

---

[1] From the *Chicago Daily Tribune* as quoted in Robert E. Sherwood, *Roosevelt and Hopkins: An Intimate History,* rev. ed., copyright 1950 (New York: Harper & Row Publishers, Inc.), p. 81.
[2] From Donald S. Howard, *The WPA and Federal Relief Policy,* copyright 1943 (New York: Russell Sage Foundation, Publishers).

time employment for needy high school, college, and graduate students to help them remain in school. To accomplish the first purpose, the NYA sponsored work-relief enterprises, made apprentice agreements with private employers, and organized vocational training, guidance, and placement services. In all, some 2,600,000 young people were eventually involved in such projects. To achieve the second purpose, the NYA provided assistance for several hundred thousand high school, college, and graduate students. Students worked as filing clerks, secretaries, and laboratory, teaching, and library assistants.

The CCC

The Civilian Conservation Corps was established in March 1933 to get unemployed young men off the streets and into useful and healthful work in the countryside. To qualify for CCC, a young man had to be between the ages of seventeen and twenty-five and unmarried (unless he was a veteran of the armed forces). He also had to pass a physical examination, and, at the time the program started, be a member of a family that was on relief.

If accepted as a CCC volunteer, a young man agreed to serve a minimum of six months. Then he was shipped off to one of more than thirteen hundred army-style camps which dotted the landscape from Maine to California. At the camp, which was administered by the regular army, he was subjected, in a mild sort of way, to army-style discipline. In return for his labor he received subsistence, medical care, and a wage of thirty dollars per month, twenty-two of which had to go to his family or other dependents.

Within three months of its formation the CCC was supervising activities of three hundred thousand young men. The corpsmen planted trees, built reservoirs, dug ditches, built bridges, constructed emergency roads, dug fish ponds, built fire towers, fought pine-twig blight and Dutch elm disease, constructed airplane landing fields, cleared beaches and camping grounds, and restored historic battlefields. In the evening, many of the young men attended classes. Those who were illiterate received instruction in reading and writing. Others learned trades and skills by attending vocational training classes.

In the estimate of most Americans the CCC turned out to be one of the New Deal administration's most fortunate inventions. A Gallup poll in 1936 recorded that three out of five Americans opposed the AAA, but more than four out of five favored the CCC. The Civilian Conservation Corps performed countless tasks aimed at conserving and restoring the country's physical resources. It also took great numbers of demoralized and potentially troublesome young men out of slum neighborhoods and off freight trains and provided them with steady and healthful work, regular rest, wholesome food, expert medical care, and gave them the experience of developing a kinship with the country's forests, streams, and mountains. Many of them acquired the rudiments of an education or a skill or trade. In all, more than two and a half million young men passed through CCC camps.

Enormously proud of the CCC, President Roosevelt hoped to make it a permanent agency of the federal government. But then came World War II. And young men who otherwise might have marched off to mountains and forests with shovels and axes on their shoulders instead marched off to distant battlefields. By the time the war ended, in 1945, Roosevelt was dead and the CCC was nothing more than a memory.

STUDY GUIDE: The New Deal tried large-scale federal spending to stimulate economic activity and provide financial assistance for the unemployed. Numerous agencies were established, notably the Works Progress Administration, to provide jobs for millions of the unemployed. The National Youth Administration and Civilian Conservation Corps gave special attention to the needs of young people. In the congressional elections of 1934 the New Deal won a rousing vote of confidence by gaining strength in both houses of Congress.

CONSERVATION, ELECTRICITY, AND TVA

Although its first objective was to provide work-relief for unemployed young men, the CCC owed its widespread popularity in no small measure to its efforts to preserve and restore the physical bases of American civilization. Many New Dealers looked upon conservation of natural resources as almost a religion. Because of conservationist sentiments—which were shared by the president—New Dealers seldom missed an opportunity to make conservation one of the aims of their programs. They were not haltered by indifference or commitments to private groups, as had been many of their Republican predecessors in the 1920s. Much of the work of the AAA, the WPA, and the CCC was directed toward preservation of soil, water, and trees.

Other agencies of the New Deal were designed exclusively to promote conservation. One was the Soil Erosion Service, set up in 1933 by Harold Ickes to conduct soil-erosion surveys and carry out preventive measures. This agency was reestablished in 1935 as the Soil Conservation Service under the Soil Conservation Act. By this act the federal government accepted soil conservation as a national responsibility.

Following the lead of the federal government, many states then set up their own conservation districts, which increased the effectiveness of the federal program. To coordinate conservation activities the New Deal administration meanwhile had established the National Resources Planning Board in 1934.

The Tennessee Valley Authority was designed in part to restore and conserve the physical resources of the basin of the Tennessee River. But the TVA was much more than a conservation project.

Six hundred and fifty miles in length from its source in the Great Smoky Mountains to Paducah, Kentucky, where it emptied into the Ohio, the Tennessee River drained an area of forty thousand square miles. Because of severe soil erosion and frequent flooding resulting from mistreatment of the land and cutting of trees by ill-informed pioneers and logging companies, the area was one of acute poverty. Its per capita income by 1933 was only one-half the national average.

Some people early in the twentieth century concluded that the key to prosperity for the Tennessee Valley area was hydroelectric power. Then, during World War I, the federal government built the mighty Wilson Dam on the Tennessee River to produce electricity to power nitrate plants at Muscle Shoals, Alabama.

But after the war, Republican administrations in Washington fell under the influence of lobbyists for private utilities companies and felt inhibited by the view that government production of power was socialistic. They refused to operate the facility at Wilson Dam. Hence the rushing, foaming water of the Tennessee splashed uselessly through the dam's spillways.

Whereupon Senator George W. Norris entered the controversy over Wilson Dam. A Republican progressive of Nebraska, Norris believed that private utilities companies were overcharging the public. He argued that government operation of the hydroelectric station at Wilson Dam would offer a yardstick for measuring the fairness of rates of private companies. In 1928 and again in 1931 Norris managed to secure congressional ap-

One of the New Deal's most ambitious programs was the Tennessee Valley Authority. Its goals were to produce electricity and to conserve natural resources. This map shows the location of dams in the TVA system in the early 1970s, nearly 40 years after the TVA was organized. Why did some conservatives oppose creation of the TVA in the 1930s?

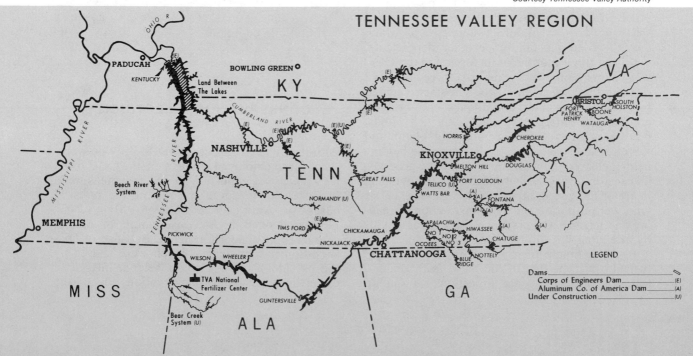

proval of bills providing for government production of hydroelectric power on the Tennessee River. Both times he saw his dreams dashed by presidential vetoes.

When Franklin Roosevelt entered the White House, Norris had an ally. Roosevelt wanted to take steps to prevent erosion and floods and promote the navigability of streams in the Tennessee Valley as well as to produce hydroelectric power. He wanted to carry out a vast experiment in social reconstruction. In April 1933, Roosevelt prevailed on Congress to pass legislation creating the Tennessee Valley Authority. Republican conservatives protested that the scheme smacked of communism.

Under the TVA's direction, farmers and local and federal agencies (including the CCC) set out millions of trees. Within a few years they turned barren hillsides into masses of green. The agency encouraged farmers to conserve soil by planting clover and alfalfa, terracing hillside land, and employing the contour method of plowing. More notable, over a ten-year period the TVA built twenty-one dams. The TVA's dams comprised the largest engineering project the world had seen to that time. The dams virtually eliminated flooding on the Tennessee and helped control the floodwaters on the lower reaches of the Ohio and Mississippi Rivers. They also provided a nine-foot channel for the Tennessee River between Knoxville and Paducah. As a consequence, the river, which in 1933 had carried only twenty million ton-miles of freight, carried one hundred million ton-miles in 1941. By 1956 it carried two billion ton-miles. And the dams housed giant turbines which, when propelled by rushing water, produced electricity.

The consequences of the TVA's power program were impressive. At the time of the agency's beginning only two farms in a hundred in the Tennessee Valley enjoyed the benefits of electricity. Ten years later twenty farms in a hundred were hooked up to electric power lines. By the early 1950s ninety in a hundred had electricity. Attracted by low-cost power, numerous industries moved into the area and stimulated the economy.

The TVA inspired a revolutionary change in the marketing of electric power which benefited consumers of electricity in every part of the nation. The private utilities industry had believed that a high-rate–low-consumption approach to power distribution would yield the most dividends to stockholders. The TVA, however, operated on a low-rate–high-consumption

USDA photo

In order to bring electricity to remote areas, the Rural Electrification Administration was formed in 1935. The REA loaned money to farmers' cooperatives which wanted to distribute electricity, and by the early 1970s, ninety-eight percent of the country's farms were served by electric power. Above, employees of a cooperative in North Carolina are shown installing new power lines in the early 1960s.

philosophy. Nobody could quarrel with the social desirability of the TVA approach. But surprisingly, the low-rate–high-consumption approach also yielded greater profits. Private utilities companies got the message. The result was a general lowering of rates and an increased consumption of electricity all over the country.

Whatever its achievements, the TVA faced a running challenge by private utilities companies until 1937 when the Supreme Court upheld the agency's right to produce and sell electricity in competition with private firms. At that point some power companies in the Tennessee Valley sold plants and transmission lines to TVA. Others, adopting the agency's low-rate–high-consumption philosophy of distribution, determined to compete with TVA. Most of them prospered. In the years 1933-53 the power capacity of private utilities in the valley increased two hundred percent as compared with an increase of only ninety-one percent for private utilities in the rest of the country.

The TVA was not the New Deal's only experiment in public power. At the same time that such dams as Norris and Fontana were going up in the Tennessee Valley, similar facilities were being built in other parts of the nation. There was Bonneville on the Columbia, Fort Peck on the Missouri, and Grand Coulee, also on the Columbia. By 1936 twenty major dams were under construction in seventeen western states.

New Dealers, meanwhile, were laboring to extend electricity to all of rural America. In 1933, ninety percent of the country's farms were without electricity. Private power companies had not considered it profitable to stretch power lines into the countryside.

In 1935 Roosevelt established the Rural Electrification Administration to get electricity to the farmers. At first the REA sought to lend funds to private utilities companies for extension of power lines to rural areas. When private firms showed little interest, the agency began to organize and lend to farm cooperatives which would buy or generate electricity and distribute to members. Overcoming vigorous opposition by private companies, by 1950 the REA was providing, or by its existence had persuaded private firms to provide, electricity to ninety percent of the farms in the nation.

STUDY GUIDE: The New Deal actively promoted conservation of natural resources through such agencies as the National Resources Planning Board. Congress created the Tennessee Valley Authority to produce hydroelectricity and to improve the Tennessee Valley by preventing soil erosion and floods. Conservative Republicans opposed the TVA. They considered it socialistic and a threat to private enterprise. The TVA helped to improve the Tennessee Valley and brought the benefits of electricity to farmers living in the area. It also lowered electric rates. A Rural Electrification Commission brought electricity to ninety percent of the nation's farmers.

REFORM

Economic recovery and relief for the needy were central features of the New Deal programs. With its recovery and relief programs, the government accepted responsibility for the economic security of the people, which was perhaps the most essential reform in the Roosevelt administration. Other aspects of the New Deal, however, had reform as their central purpose.

Labor Conditions

New Dealers set about reforming the conditions of labor in America. Wages were low, hours long, and working conditions often unsatisfactory. Workers usually lacked any job security or protection against the hazards of illness, accident, or unemployment. In most industries, vacation with pay was only a dream.

Most working men and women had no effective means of improving conditions. In most industries in the early 1930s there was no means of airing grievances or bargaining collectively. Conceivably the government could have stepped in and become an arbiter between employers and workers. But New Dealers quickly concluded that a better way to create a new labor-management relationship was for the government to guarantee working people the right to organize and bargain collectively. Then the workers, through their unions, could secure their own victories.

The first opportunity to encourage expansion of organized labor came in spring 1933 when New Dealers included Section 7 in the National Industrial Recovery Act. Section 7 guaranteed workers the right to organize and bargain collectively through unions of their own choosing.

Early in 1935 Senator Robert F. Wagner of New York introduced legislation to strengthen organized labor. Under the Wagner Bill the National Labor Relations Board (created the previous year) would have the power to order elections in a plant or business firm to see if workers wanted a union and, if so, which union. If a majority of workers in the plant or firm chose a particular union, that union would become the exclusive bargaining agent of all the workers, whether all had wanted the union or not. The NLRB would also have authority to define and prohibit unfair labor practices and enforce decisions through machinery patterned after that of the Federal Trade Commission.

Debate over the Wagner legislation was superheated, and for a time the president maintained a policy of hands off. Then, in April 1935, the Supreme Court nullified much of the National Industrial Recovery Act. In so doing it made

Section 7 ineffective. At this point Roosevelt began to press for passage of the Wagner Bill. The presidential push proved decisive, and in July 1935 the measure became law.

In 1938 the New Deal administration sponsored another piece of legislation of importance to labor—the Fair Labor Standards Act, sometimes called the Wages and Hours Act. The legislation established a maximum work week of forty-four hours for workers engaged in interstate commerce or in production of commodities entering interstate commerce and a minimum wage of twenty-five cents an hour. Increased wages for the lowest-paid workers in the country tended to push up wage scales for those whose wages were above the minimum.

Membership rolls of labor unions swelled as a result of the New Deal's labor program. The outcome was higher wages, shorter hours, greater security, safer and more sanitary working conditions, and more fringe benefits for the country's workers. The program also touched off a bitter internal quarrel which divided the ranks of organized labor.

Concerned mainly with the interests of crafts workers, the American Federation of Labor had never tried seriously to organize the great body of unskilled and semiskilled workers in the giant industries. As a result, industrial workers had been neglected. Such AFL chieftains as John L. Lewis, Sidney Hillman, and David Dubinsky recognized that the New Deal measure offered a unique opportunity to organize and improve the lot of workers in the big industries. Faithful to the principle of organizing workers according to their crafts or trades, most leaders of the AFL scorned the idea of establishing huge industrial unions. Lewis and his followers thereupon created the Committee for Industrial Organizations later renamed the Congress of Industrial Organizations. In defiance of the AFL, the CIO set about organizing industrial unions.

Industrial workers flocked to the CIO. Early in 1937 the new labor organization won its first great victory when it secured contracts from the United States Steel Corporation and its subsidiaries. But the high point of CIO activity came when automobile workers occupied plants first of the General Motors Corporation and then of the Chrysler Corporation in the famous sit-down strikes of 1936-37.

Although sit-down strikes were illegal, they proved successful, largely because of heavy pressure put on the companies by the New Deal administration in Washington. Added to this pressure was the reluctance of Governor Frank Murphy of Michigan to use the National Guard to evict the strikers. Meanwhile, the CIO was organizing workers in other industries, including rubber and textiles. By 1941 total membership of the CIO had eclipsed that of the AFL.

Stock Exchanges and Banks

While they were engineering labor reforms, New Dealers were also acting to bring stock exchanges and banks under effective public control. In 1932-33 the Senate Committee on Banking and Currency, under direction of its chief counsel, Ferdinand Pecora, had disclosed shocking practices by titans of finance. The committee found that financial adventurers had organized pools and sold stocks back and forth among the members to make it appear that the stocks were active. Next they would raise prices of the stocks, whereupon unsuspecting investors, thinking the securities were moving up on their own merits, would step in to purchase. Members of the pools would then unload their overvalued stocks and "shear the sheep."

To counter such practices, President Roosevelt persuaded Congress, in May 1933, to approve the Sale of Securities Bill. This act required sellers of securities to file detailed and accurate information regarding the securities with an agency of the federal government.

Another abuse disclosed by the Pecora committee resulted from the affiliation of investment banking companies with commercial banks. These banks, instead of giving honest advice to depositors, had often referred depositors to their own investment affiliates, sometimes with disastrous results. To curb this abuse the Glass-Steagall Bill (often called the Banking Act of 1933) was passed in June 1933. This act prohibited commercial banks in the Federal Reserve system from having investment affiliates. A firm had to sell securities or accept deposits; it could not do both. The Glass-Steagall Act also restricted use of Federal Reserve bank credit for stock market speculation and established the Federal Deposit Insurance Corporation to guarantee deposits in savings banks.

In 1934 Roosevelt signed the Securities and Exchange Act, which provided for federal regulation of securities exchanges. The act also established the Securities and Exchange Commission to serve as a watchdog on exchanges.

To head the SEC the president turned to

Joseph P. Kennedy, a stock market speculator who had engaged in some of the practices exposed by Pecora's inquiry. Liberals were aghast, but Kennedy did an effective job during his brief tenure. Most important, perhaps, he persuaded the financial community, which had deplored the New Deal's securities legislation, to make its peace with the SEC.

Another piece of reform legislation in money and banking was passed in August 1935, the Banking Act of 1935. The main purpose of this act was to reconstruct the Federal Reserve System and bring increased government control over money and banking in America. The central provision of the legislation gave the Federal Reserve Board—the representative of the general public—rather than Federal Reserve banks control over open-market operations. In open-market operations the Federal Reserve system bought and sold government securities so as to influence reserves of member banks. In that way it enlarged or contracted the base of the money supply.

Marriner Eccles, chairman of the Federal Reserve Board from 1936 to 1948, believed that open-market operations were the most important single instrument of control over the volume and cost of credit. As a result of the Banking Act of 1935 that instrument began to serve the public interest rather than the interests of private banks.

Holding Companies and Taxes

Another New Deal reform sought to break up utility holding companies. There was at the time a widely held view that public utility holding companies had long gouged the public, prevented public regulation of their operations, and corrupted politicians. In 1935 President Roosevelt proposed legislation that included a death sentence for utility holding companies. To counter the measure, holding company lobbyists organized a campaign of propaganda and pressure, but Roosevelt eventually gained the substance of what he wanted. When approved in August 1935, the Wheeler-Rayburn Holding Company Act gave the Securities and Exchange Commission supervisory control over financial operations of holding companies. The act also required destruction over a five-year period of the largest utilities empires.

Another major goal of New Dealers was redistribution of the national income, to be accomplished by revising the tax structure. Thus

in June 1935, President Roosevelt asked Congress to increase taxes on inheritances, impose gift taxes, increase levies on very great individual net incomes, and establish a new graduated corporate income tax.

Variously labeled as a "soak the rich" and "soak the successful" scheme, the legislation came under unparalleled attack by the right wing of American politics. At length Congress scuttled the inheritance tax provision and virtually eliminated the corporate income levy. When approved in August 1935, the Revenue Act increased estate, gift, and capital stock taxes, levied an excess-profits tax, and raised the surtax on incomes above $50,000 to the highest point in history.

The immediate results of the wealth-tax legislation proved disappointing to New Dealers. The percentage of the disposable national income received by the highest income groups remained essentially unchanged over the next several years. But then, during America's participation in World War II from 1941 to 1945, the revised tax structure brought a considerable redistribution of the national income. For example, the most prosperous one percent of the population in 1929 had received 19.08 percent of the disposable income; in 1935, 12.74 percent. In 1944 it received 6.61 percent. The most prosperous five percent had received 33.81 percent of the disposable national income in 1929 and 27.89 percent in 1935. It received 15.75 percent in 1944.

Housing

To make a start on the staggering problem of inadequate housing, the New Deal administration established the Housing Division of the PWA in summer 1933 to clear slums and build low-rent dwellings. However, the accomplishments of the division were minimal. Then, in 1937, Roosevelt signed the Wagner-Steagall Act creating the United States Housing Authority, which superseded the Housing Division. Essentially a lending agency, by the early 1940s the USHA had assisted in construction of 130,000 dwellings. Thus it could claim to have done more to clear slums than any other agency in the history of the United States. Of course it barely made a start in shrinking the total slum area of America's cities.

In 1933 the New Deal administration set up the Subsistence Homestead Division to construct small rural communities where destitute people could find shelter, engage in handicrafts or light manufacturing, and raise some of their food. By 1935 twenty homestead communities were under construction. Fearing the communities might be an entering wedge for communism, conservatives in the country launched an unrelenting attack on the homestead program. Some New Dealers, moreover, viewed the entire homestead idea as a silly dream. Residents of the communities never looked upon the homesteads as anything more than places where they could ride out the depression until circumstances permitted them to return to their real homes. As a consequence, the homestead communities failed to become a permanent part of the American landscape.

Social Security Legislation

The Social Security Act of 1935 was the most heralded and important of the New Deal's reform measures. Although unemployment and old-age insurance laws had been common in European countries for many decades, the idea of social security had sparked little interest in the United States. Most Americans had a deep commitment to the pioneer tradition of the self-reliant individual. But the Great Depression caused large numbers of people in the United States to weigh the merits of a national social security program.

In 1934 several measures went before Congress to provide unemployment compensation and old-age insurance. One was enacted—the Railroad Retirement Bill setting up a pension program for retired railroad workers. President Roosevelt, however, thought Congress should consider social security as a single package. He appointed a special committee to examine the question. The committee was headed by Secretary of Labor Frances Perkins, who in 1933 had become the first woman to serve in a presidential cabinet. After extensive study the committee concluded that each state was the best judge of its own unemployment problems. It recommended that a federal unemployment insurance program should be administered by the states. The committee further suggested that inasmuch as great numbers of workers in the course of a lifetime moved from state to state, an old-age insurance program should be administered by the national government in Washington. In August 1935 the Social Security Bill passed both houses with overwhelming majorities in spite of criticism that it smacked of communism.

To provide for unemployment compensation, the legislation permitted the national government to collect a three percent payroll tax from all employers in each state. It would then return to the state ninety percent of the money for distribution in accordance with the state's unemployment insurance laws. The legislation imposed certain regulations on state and local unemployment agencies. They could not refuse unemployment benefits to a worker because he would not take a job in a nonunion plant or where there was a labor dispute or for which wages and hours were less satisfactory than was ordinary for that type of labor. Otherwise each state was at liberty to set up whatever requirements it wished.

Regarding old-age pensions, the social security legislation provided that annuity payments would go to workers in included classes who, with their employers, had contributed a percentage tax on wages (by 1948, three percent for each). At age sixty-five the worker, if he quit work, would receive an annuity as long as he lived. The amount of the annuity would depend on the individual's earnings, but in no case (under the original legislation) would it be less than ten dollars a month or more than eighty-five. The measure also provided that the federal government would grant funds to states on a fifty-fifty matching basis for old-age pensions for people who were not covered by the annuity program. Such pensions could not exceed forty dollars a month.

Other features of the Social Security Act provided for federal grants to states, usually on a matching basis, for other social services. These included care of needy dependent children, health care for mothers and children in poverty-ridden areas, medical, surgical, and corrective services for crippled children, aid to homeless and neglected children, vocational training for the physically disabled, aid to the needy blind, and public health services.

The social security legislation of 1935 was not perfect. Because it left so much authority in the hands of the states, for example, the unemployment insurance program did not always distribute its benefits as New Dealers had hoped. Old-age pensions, especially for individuals not covered by the annuity program, were far below what was required for elderly citizens to maintain a decent standard of living. Still, the Social Security Act marked a radical departure from the past. More than any other piece of New

Deal legislation, it committed the United States to the principle of the democratic welfare state.

Social Security makes available to the wage earner many benefits, including an old-age pension. How did the Social Security Act of 1935 mark a break with the pioneer tradition of the self-reliant man? Do you think that Social Security is necessary?

STUDY GUIDE: To strengthen organized labor and improve working conditions, Congress passed the Wagner Act and other legislation setting maximum working hours. The Securities and Exchange Act created a commission to bring stock exchanges and banks under public regulation. The Federal Reserve System was reorganized under the Banking Act of 1935. A federal housing authority made a start at solving the problems of inadequate housing across the country. The most well-known New Deal reform measure was the Social Security Act of 1935. It provided unemployment compenstion and old-age pensions for workers, as well as other benefits.

INDIANS AND BLACKS

How did Indians and black Americans fare during the time of the Great Depression and New Deal?

New Deal Indian Policy

Life had never been easy for America's Indians, who in the 1930s numbered about three hundred thirty thousand (or less than two-tenths of one percent of the national population). For many years they had been deprived of their farmland and hunting grounds, cooped up on bleak and generally barren reservations, virtual wards of the white man's government. Indians had lost much of the spirit and dignity which had made them objects of awe and respect of many whites.

Most Indians lived in abject poverty and misery. The coming of the Great Depression had worsened their conditions of existence only slightly. From time to time the government in Washington had sought to do something for them. For example, an act of Congress in 1924 had compensated Pueblos for lands they had lost to white men. Another measure that same year admitted all Indians born in the United States to full citizenship. But the Indians had never received more than the leftover attention of leaders in the national capital.

When Roosevelt entered the White House in 1933, he did not have much time to devote to the special problems of a comparative handful of Indians. Still, in small ways the new president sought to inaugurate a "new deal" for his Indian countrymen. As a consequence, Indians participated in New Deal programs, including the CCC, WPA, and NYA. More notable, Roosevelt supported the Wheeler-Howard Indian Reorganization Act of 1934. This act provided a larger measure of self-government for Indians and safeguards for their civil liberties, resettled landless Indians, and promoted conservation of Indian lands. Meanwhile, Indians were aided by a particularly active commissioner of Indian affairs, John Collier. Collier organized livestock cooperatives in Indian communities, encouraged arts and crafts and other tribal activities, promoted education on Indian reservations, and sought to restore Indian pride.

Despite these efforts, the overall effect of the New Deal's Indian policy was minimal, and Indian Americans continued to languish. In the 1970s humanitarians were still searching for solutions to the problems confronting America's Indians.

Black Americans and the Depression

Although poverty had long been a way of life for most Negroes, the Great Depression fell hard on America's fourteen million black citizens. A large percentage of the country's Negroes worked on the farms of the South. After the crash of 1929, when prices of farm commodities fell to new lows, black farmers found themselves particularly hard-pressed. Blacks were the first to be let go when employers in cities had to trim labor forces. Well-to-do whites, when compelled

to trim expenses, often began by dismissing black domestic servants.

The depression brought no weakening of racial prejudices. The year 1931 produced one of the most saddening episodes in the history of race relations in America, the "Scottsboro affair." Following a rumble between youthful black and white vagrants aboard a freight train, an all-white jury in Scottsboro, Alabama, found several of the black youths guilty of rape. The decision was based on highly dubious testimony by white girls who had also been aboard the train. The youths were sentenced to death. The following year, 1932, the Supreme Court threw out the conviction, whereupon authorities in Scottsboro arranged a new trial. Although one of the girls denied her previous testimony and admitted the story of rape was a lie, a second all-white jury also found the Scottsboro boys guilty as charged. (Eventually they were freed.)

Few Negroes felt much enthusiasm over the election of Franklin D. Roosevelt. His record seemed to indicate that he had no special interest in the rights of black Americans. The initial estimate of blacks proved wrong. At the side of the new president, moreover, was his wife Eleanor, a woman whose feeling for humanity was genuine and who made the rights of black

Among the people hardest hit by the depression were the nation's blacks. Their despair is captured in this painting, *They Were Poor,* by Jacob Lawrence, who lived in Harlem, New York, during the depression. This is one of sixty paintings in a series Lawrence called *The Migration of the Negro, 1940-41.*

Americans a special object of her enormous energies. Mrs. Roosevelt continually pressed for fair treatment for black Americans in New Deal programs. She kept Walter White, executive secretary of the National Association for the Advancement of Colored People, informed of her husband's views. From time to time she arranged conferences between White and the president. In 1939 when the Daughters of the American Revolution denied use of Constitution Hall in Washington to the Negro contralto Marian Anderson, Mrs. Roosevelt publicly criticized the organization and withdrew her membership.

Another individual who exercised great influence on Roosevelt with respect to Negroes was Harold L. Ickes, the secretary of the interior and chief of the PWA. A former president of the NAACP, Ickes became the president's informal "secretary of Negro relations." He ushered into the New Deal administration such intelligent and energetic blacks as Robert C. Weaver, who thirty years later would become the first black man to serve in a presidential cabinet, Ralph Bunche, who would become a leading personage in the United Nations, and Thurgood Marshall, who in the 1960s would become the first Negro to receive appointment to the Supreme Court.

The New Deal administration's record of service for black Americans was mixed. Because of the AAA's program of acreage restriction, many black tenant farmers in the South were expelled from the countryside and had to make new lives in the alien surroundings of urban America. Meanwhile, to retain the goodwill and cooperation of the white population in the Tennessee Valley, the administration in Washington permitted the TVA to discriminate against Negroes in some of its activities. President Roosevelt, while lashing out against lynching of Negroes, did not act to secure congressional approval of bills against lynching that came before Congress in the 1930s. He also refused to do anything more than speak out against the poll tax, a device widely used in the South to prevent blacks from voting.

On the other hand, New Dealers insisted that black Americans should share fairly in the federal government's great relief programs. Local officials, notably in the South, sometimes compromised directives of leaders in Washington that there was to be no discrimination in the administration of relief. But Negroes in large numbers were on the rolls of the FERA, worked on the WPA, and comprised about ten percent of the youths who volunteered for the CCC.

Despite these weaknesses, most black Americans were aware that the New Deal administration had been the first since the time of Reconstruction to show genuine interest in their problems. In the belief that the New Deal's relief activities had saved many of them from starvation, many black people came to revere Franklin Roosevelt. As a result, most Negroes who were able to vote, mainly outside the South, left the Republican party of the Great Emancipator, Abraham Lincoln, and joined the Democratic party of Franklin Roosevelt.

Changing Attitudes Toward Blacks

Some observers of the historical scene in the 1930s have detected a change in the attitudes of many whites toward blacks. At the start of the decade a great many whites seemed to view blacks, at best, as ineffectual, happy dolts. Such a view prevailed in comic strips, plays, movies, and radio scripts. Although by the end of the

decade the idea of Negro stupidity had not disappeared from movie screens and the radio, it seemed less commonplace than a few years before.

More important, some whites were beginning to see that their black countrymen had aspirations and feelings not unlike their own. The acceptance of Negroes to membership in CIO unions and the popularity among white readers of Richard Wright's novel *Native Son* (1940) seemed to indicate changing white attitudes toward blacks.

Another indicator was the response of whites when blacks were the victims of outrageous incidents. For example, the Nazi dictator Adolf Hitler, at the Olympic games in Berlin in 1936, snubbed Jesse Owens, the great Negro sprinter and broad jumper of the United States, and refused to award him his gold medals personally. Many whites in America were incensed. When the German heavyweight boxer Max Schmelling made derogatory remarks about black American champion Joe Louis on the eve of their title bout in 1937, there were sparks in the United States. Most white Americans were delighted when the "Brown Bomber" annihilated "Herr Max" in the first round. When Marian Anderson was denied the use of Constitution Hall in Washington, D. C., many Americans were affronted. A predominately white audience of 75,000 people was on hand when Harold Ickes made the Lincoln Memorial available for Miss Anderson's concert on Easter Sunday 1939.

Still, the black man who, day in and day out, had to struggle through life in the 1930s, probably could sense little letup in the racism of white Americans. The manifestations of that continuing racism were everywhere—in segregated schools and neighborhoods, black ghettos, discrimination in hiring and wages, unequal administration of justice, denial of the vote. Most craft unions of the AFL and the railroad brotherhoods continued to prohibit blacks from membership. Organized baseball continued to reject black players, one of whom Leroy ("Satchel") Paige was conceded to be one of the finest pitchers in the nation. Thus the black man down on the farm or in the ghetto had good reason to believe that things had not changed much between 1930 and 1940.

STUDY GUIDE: Some efforts were made to help the Indians, but they continued to face serious difficulties. President Roosevelt did not actively press for increased civil rights. However, his New Deal relief programs helped thousands of black Americans and won him wide support in the black community.

DECLINE OF THE NEW DEAL

Although the Supreme Court had struck down their industrial recovery and agricultural adjustment programs, New Dealers in the spring of 1936 could look back over the previous twelve months with much satisfaction. In that year prices and wages had inched upward. The New Deal had set in motion a huge program of work-relief. And, most important, it had brought forth a range of reforms.

The Campaign of 1936

Against a background of satisfaction and optimism, delegates to the Democratic national convention assembled in Philadelphia in June 1936. Amid unrestrained enthusiasm they renominated Roosevelt and Garner. They also abolished the century-old two-thirds rule for choosing presidential and vice-presidential candidates. Instead, they restored the simple majority rule. Southern Democrats would soon lament the death of the two-thirds rule. Its passing deprived them of the ability to veto candidates not favored by the southern wing of the party, for example, those who seemed friendly to black causes. The Republicans had convened earlier in the month at Cleveland. After adopting an anti-New Deal platform, they nominated Governor Alfred M. Landon of Kansas for president and Colonel Frank Knox, former Rough Rider and a Chicago newspaper publisher, for vice-president.

Before the Roosevelt-Landon contest could get underway, a new factor appeared in the national political equation. This was the Union party, fashioned by assorted radicals who despised Roosevelt and the New Deal. The candidate of the new party was Representative William Lemke, a Republican progressive of North Dakota. His aim was to put together a coalition of the followers of the Reverend Charles E. Coughlin and Dr. Francis E. Townsend, as well as those of the late Huey P. Long (who were now led by a rabble-rousing preacher, the Reverend Gerald L. K. Smith).

For a time the Democrats thought the Union party might attract millions of voters who normally marked ballots for Democratic candidates. A few pessimists feared the Unionists might even enable Landon to topple Roosevelt. Led by people of diverse interests and ideas, who had little in common beyond their hatred of Roosevelt, the Union party, however, began to fall apart as soon as it was put together. Moreover, the crude attacks on Roosevelt by Coughlin, who called the president a communist and "anti-God," disenchanted many potential followers. By election day the Union party was a shambles and constituted a threat to nobody.

Roosevelt, however, had forged a coalition of workers, farmers, southerners, Catholics, Negroes, Jews, and ethnic groups. He was unbeatable in 1936. On election day he polled 27,751,000 votes to 16,681,000 for Landon to 882,000 for Lemke. Carrying every state except Maine and Vermont, Roosevelt won in the electoral college by 523-8. The Roosevelt avalanche likewise assured the Democrats unprecedented majorities in the new Congress: 77-19 in the Senate, 328-107 in the House. The New Deal had reached high tide.

Packing the Supreme Court

Encouraged by his electoral triumph, President Roosevelt decided that the time was ripe to do something about the Supreme Court. In addition to the National Industrial Recovery Act and the Agricultural Adjustment Act, the Court had declared several lesser New Deal measures unconstitutional. The president suspected that, unless its composition was changed, the Court would soon strike down the Wagner Labor Relations Act and the Social Security Act.

Shortly after taking the presidential oath for the second time, in early 1937, Roosevelt sent Congress a message in which he contended that federal court dockets were congested because many judges were elderly and infirm. To meet the alleged problem, he asked for authority to appoint additional judges. Most important, he wanted authority to enlarge the membership of the Supreme Court from nine to a maximum of fifteen if justices, after reaching age seventy, declined to retire.

New Supreme Court Plan Criticized

The presidential story about increasing the efficiency of the federal judiciary fooled no-

"To Furnish The Supreme Court Practical Assistance."

THIS ACT SHALL TAKE EFFECT ON THE 30TH DAY AFTER THE DATE OF ITS ENACTMENT.

CONGRESS

Roosevelt attempted to pack the Supreme Court with judges sympathetic to New Deal policies. This editorial cartoon published in the Washington *Post* reflected the widespread criticism of FDR's move. Why did the "court-packing" scheme finally prove unnecessary? Are Supreme Court justices still appointed on a political basis?

body. Roosevelt was clearly seeking, via appointment of new justices who shared his views, to convert the Supreme Court's pro-New Deal minority into a majority. The result was an unparalleled attack directed at the White House. Roosevelt's Republican and conservative critics claimed that he was trying to pack the Supreme Court with New Deal lackeys. The same critics argued that the presidential scheme would destroy the "checks and balances" which the founding fathers had written into the federal Constitution. Even liberals who deplored the recent decisions of the "horse and buggy court" did not wish to see the independence of the Court weakened. They feared creation of a precedent which would enable a president, whenever he felt the urge, to change the composition of the Court.

While debate over the "court packing" scheme boiled, other events weakened Roosevelt's position. First, Justice Owen Roberts, who previously had voted with the anti-New Deal faction suddenly converted to the pro-New Deal faction. As a consequence, in March-May 1937, the court upheld a battery of New Deal measures, including the Wagner and Social Security acts, most of them by a vote of 5-4.

Then, in mid-May Justice Willis Van Devanter, an opponent of the New Deal, announced his retirement. Van Devanter's retirement meant that the new pro-New Deal majority on the Court would be 6-3 when Roosevelt appointed a new justice. The new justice was Hugo Black of Alabama, who remained a member of the court until 1971. Despite the change in the Court's composition, Roosevelt stubbornly and foolishly continued to fight for his reorganization bill. In July, after 168 days, he was finally compelled to admit defeat. Over the next two and a half years, however, four more justices left the bench. Their replacements were men in rhythm with the New Deal. As a result, people began to talk about the "Roosevelt court."

The New Deal Loses Support

The attempt to pack the Supreme Court persuaded large numbers of Americans that ultra-conservatives were right, that the president was indeed power-hungry. As a result, it turned them to opposition of the New Deal.

Other developments also weakened Roosevelt's hold — and, by definition, the New Deal's hold — on the affections of the country. First, there was the president's open sympathy with the CIO's sit-down strikes which were capturing headlines in 1937. In the estimate of many Americans, the sit-downs were nothing short of an attack on the rights of private property and seemed a beginning of some sort of violent revolution. A president who approved such an attack, so the argument went, was a menace to the traditional institutions and values of the nation.

Next, in summer 1937, a sharp recession struck the national economy. It resulted when Roosevelt attempted to balance the budget by ordering a cutback in federal spending. This cutback dramatically slowed the process of "priming the pump." Prices tumbled, the industrial mechanism slowed down, and unemployment increased. Much of the economic recovery achieved since 1935 was nullified by the dreary recession which dragged on into 1938. The recession removed some of the luster that the president and the New Deal had taken on as a result of the slow but steady improvement in the state of the economy.

The Roosevelt "Purge"

Finally, in the summer of 1938, Roosevelt set out to engineer the defeat in Democratic primary elections of several prominent Democratic conservatives. These candidates included Senators Walter George of Georgia, Millard Tydings of Maryland, and E. D. ("Cotton Ed") Smith of South Carolina, who had become opponents of the New Deal. Dubbed a purge, and thus calling up a comparison with Adolf Hitler's extermination of ranking Nazis in 1934, the presidential meddling backfired completely. Virtually every Democratic conservative whom Roosevelt opposed emerged triumphant, and across the nation the idea that the president had dictatorial ambitions won new converts.

Roosevelt's loss of popularity and the resultant diminishing of his political strength caused a serious cracking of the unity of the Democratic party. It also helped cement an alliance — the so-called conservative coalition — between Republican conservatives of the North and West and Democratic conservatives of the South. This alliance would prevent, after 1938, any additional New Deal legislation of importance. (It also would dominate Congress and prevent any far-reaching liberal reform until 1964-65 under President Lyndon B. Johnson.) And so, while the Supreme Court became willing to approve New Deal measures, Congress, dominated by the conservative coalition, would pass few measures for it to consider.

Whatever their ability to prevent passage of new legislation, congressional conservatives did not have the political muscle to roll back what the New Deal had done since 1933. Thus the major New Deal measures remained on the statute books.

STUDY GUIDE: Franklin D. Roosevelt won a landslide reelection victory in 1936. He was angry that the Supreme Court had declared some of his New Deal legislation to be unconstitutional. Roosevelt tried to pack the court with new justices who shared his views. He failed in this attempt. He also attempted to engineer the defeat of Democratic conservatives in Congress, but failed. As a result of these moves, he was widely criticized for being power-hungry and lost much support. An economic recession in 1937 and support for union "sitdown strikes" also hurt his popularity. An alliance between Democratic and Republican conservatives in Congress after 1938 prevented the passage of any additional major New Deal legislation.

EVALUATION OF THE NEW DEAL

How does one evaluate FDR's New Deal?

While its program and policies failed to produce full recovery from the Great Depression, the New Deal nonetheless stimulated the na-

By 1932, more than one-fourth of the persons who supported themselves or their families were out of work. Above is a bread line in Manhattan in 1932. What New Deal programs provided relief to the unemployed during the 1930s?

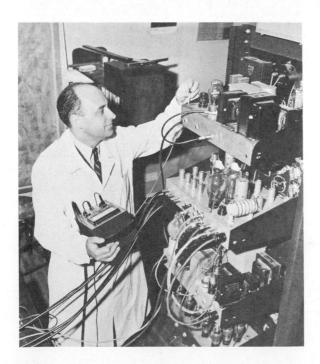

The beginnings of atomic research were undertaken during the 1930s. Shown here in his laboratory is Enrico Fermi, Italian-born physicist who came to the United States to work in 1938.

[534]

tional economy. Except for the recession of 1937-38, the result was a steady improvement in the country's economy from 1933 down to 1941 when World War II brought total recovery.

The New Deal provided a great deal of relief to unemployed victims of the depression and tided many desperate Americans through the dark years of the 1930s. It restored confidence in the institution of banking, revived credit, and helped millions of farmers and home owners to retain their properties. It brought forth new standards of business decency, virtually eliminated child labor in the country, increased the bargaining power of labor, and improved working conditions in industries. It prepared the way for a more equitable distribution of the national income and brought banks, securities exchanges, and private utilities under more effective public regulation. The New Deal dramatically reduced America's tariff barriers and reformed the national monetary system. It helped salvage the natural resources of the country, greatly expanded the use of electricity, and provided a new measure of security for the unemployed, the aged, and the handicapped.

Most important, the New Deal established the principle that the federal government has a responsibility to provide minimal economic security for all of its citizens.

At the same time the New Deal encouraged growth of the federal bureaucracy (from 588,000 employees in 1931 to 1,370,000 in 1941). It created administrative confusion, was often wasteful, and increased the national debt (from $20 billion in 1932 to $43 billion in 1940). It imposed new restrictions on the activities of businessmen and farmers and at some points conflicted with the federal Constitution. It failed to meet the problems of the city and inadequate housing in the country and did virtually nothing to break down the wall of discrimination and segregation which limited the freedom and opportunity of black Americans.

The New Deal, then, was something about which honest and intelligent people could differ. From the perspective of both conservatives and liberals, one could find serious shortcomings. On the other hand, New Dealers, taking note of political, economic, and psychological realities in the 1930s, could make a strong case in its defense.

STUDY GUIDE: People differ on the merits of the New Deal. Those who favor it claim that it

stimulated the national economy after the depression and it placed responsibility on the federal government to provide some economic security for the people. But opponents claim that the New Deal created a huge federal bureaucracy, it was wasteful, and it brought administrative confusion. Moreover, it did little to fight discrimination.

SUMMING UP THE CHAPTER

Names and Terms to Identify

Charles Curtis	Cordell Hull
Smoot-Hawley Act	"blanket code"
Charles E. Coughlin	Henry A. Wallace
Huey Long	Harold L. Ickes
Twenty-first Amendment	George W. Norris
Reconstruction Finance	Rural Electrification
Corporation	Administration
John Nance Garner	Robert F. Wagner
New Deal	Pecora Committee
"bank holiday"	Joseph P. Kennedy
Gold Reserve Bill	Frances Perkins

Study Questions and Points to Review

1. What position did Herbert Hoover hold in the Harding administration?

2. Why were Republican professional politicians unenthusiastic over Hoover's presidential ambitions?

3. How did Hoover plan to attack the depression in agriculture? Was his policy successful?

4. What was the purpose of the Bonus March on Washington? Who were the participants?

5. When did Prohibition end?

6. As chief executive what did Hoover feel was his main responsibility in countering the depression?

7. Why did Hoover refuse to approve a program of federal relief for the unemployed?

8. Who was Franklin Roosevelt's Republican opponent in the presidential election of 1932?

9. What provision did the Twentieth Amendment make for the inauguration of the president and vice-president?

10. As part of the New Deal's recovery program it was essential to the nation's economy to bring about inflation. Why?

11. What happened to tariff barriers as a result of the New Deal trade agreements program?

12. In the years after 1929, by what percent had farm prices in the United States decreased?

13. What was the reason for the cotton plow-up of 1933?

14. What did Section 7 of the National Industrial Recovery Act guarantee to workers?

15. How was labor union membership affected by the New Deal's labor program?

16. Who besides the aged were provided for in the Social Security Act?

17. How did Roosevelt seek to inaugurate a "new deal" for the American Indians?

18. How did most black Americans react to the New Deal administration?

19. Why did Roosevelt want to enlarge membership of the Supreme Court?

Topics for Discussion

1. Review the prepresidential career of Herbert Hoover. How, in your judgment, did Hoover's life and activities before he entered the White House shape his ideas and attitudes as president?

2. What caused the great stock market crash of 1929? What was the connection between the collapse of stock prices and the subsequent economic depression?

3. Explain how the New Deal administration set about to revive credit and meet problems of indebtedness.

4. Explain how the New Deal administration sought to stimulate prices by devaluing the dollar and lowering the tariff.

5. What were the objectives of the National Recovery Administration? How did the NRA propose to achieve its objectives? What problems beset it? What happened to it? What were its achievements?

6. What were the objectives of the New Deal's agricultural adjustment program? How was the program to achieve its objectives? What problems beset the program? What were the accomplishments of agricultural adjustment?

7. Describe and compare the activities and accomplishments of the Federal Emergency Relief Administration, Civil Works Administration, Public Works Administration, Works Progress Administration, National Youth Administration, and Civilian Conservation Corps.

8. What were the origins of the Tennessee Valley Authority? Why was it criticized? What were its goals? How did it go about achieving them? What were its accomplishments?

9. Explain why the New Deal lost momentum in the time after the election of 1936.

Subjects for Reports or Essays

1. Gather information and write your own account and analysis of the Bonus March of spring-summer 1932. Compare that march with protest demonstrations which have occurred during your lifetime.

2. Write a biographical sketch of one of the following: The Reverend Charles E. Coughlin; Dr. Francis E. Townsend; Huey P. Long, Jr.

3. Read and write a brief note on one of the outstanding novels of the depression era: John Steinbeck's *Grapes of Wrath* or Richard Wright's *Native Son.*

4. Using materials in the library, write a biographical sketch and assessment of Eleanor Roosevelt.

5. Gather information and write a report on one of the following topics: (a) the banking crisis and "bank holiday" of 1933; (b) the NRA; (c) the dust storms; (d) sharecroppers; (e) the TVA.

6. Prepare a report on a Rural Electric Membership Corporation cooperative in your county or area. When was it organized? What precisely does it do? How many farms does it serve? How was it financed? What are the electric rates? What do its members think of it?

Projects, Activities, and Skills

1. You are a newspaper reporter. Write a feature story on the Great Depression. Interview people in your family or community who remember the depression. Ask them about their most vivid recollections of the period of "hard times."

2. Using material from the library, make a study of the literature, art, movies, and music of the 1930s. What do these sources tell you about Americans and life in America during the Great Depression?

3. Compile a report on the projects and activities in your community or county accomplished by the Civil Works Administration, Public Works Administration, Works Progress Administration, National Youth Administration, and Civilian Conservation Corps.

4. Prepare an exhibit on the Tennessee Valley Authority. On a map of the valley locate the major TVA installations. Display photographs of some of the dams and steam plants and diagrams showing how the hydroelectric power stations operate. Include in your exhibit statistics showing development of the valley—for example, consumption of electricity—since the advent of TVA.

5. Describe some of the major scientific, technological, and literary achievements of the depression era. Use pictures to illustrate your account.

6. Using Tables 20 and 21 in the Appendix, make a chart showing how labor union membership increased during the New Deal.

7. Examine Appendix Tables 9, 10, and 11 on expenditures of the federal government. What do the tables tell you about government expenditures during wartime? During depressions?

Further Readings

General

The Age of Roosevelt (3 vols.): *The Crisis of the Old Order, The Coming of the New Deal,* and *The Politics of Upheaval* by Arthur M. Schlesinger, Jr. This brilliantly written trilogy contains a wealth of information.

Franklin D. Roosevelt and the New Deal, 1932 1940 and *The Perils of Prosperity: 1914-32* by William E. Leuchtenburg.

The Great Crash, 1929 by John Kenneth Galbraith.

The Great Depression ed. by David Shannon. Useful collection of source materials.

Hard Times: An Oral History of the Great Depression in America by Studs Terkel. Interesting personal recollections of the depression era.

Just Around the Corner: A Highly Selective History of the Thirties by Robert Bendiner. An amusing and witty book.

The Lean Years: A History of the American Worker, 1920-1933 by Irving Bernstein. A useful account.

Since Yesterday: The Nineteen-Thirties in America by Frederick Lewis Allen.

TVA and the Power Fight: 1933-1939 by Thomas K. McCraw.

Biography

The Autobiography of a Curmudgeon by Harold K. Ickes.

Herbert Hoover and the Great Depression by Warren Harris.

Minister of Relief: Harry Hopkins and the Depression by Searle F. Charles.

Roosevelt and Hopkins: An Intimate History by Robert E. Sherwood.

The Roosevelt I Knew by Frances Perkins.

Roosevelt: The Lion and the Fox by James M. Burns.

This I Remember by Eleanor Roosevelt.

Fiction and Drama

All the King's Men by Robert Penn Warren. This novel is an account of a political career much like that of Huey Long's.

Another Part of the House by Winston M. Estes. The story of a family's troubles during the Great Depression.

The Grapes of Wrath by John Steinbeck. A poignant novel about migrant farm workers in the 1930s.

Sunrise at Campobello by Dore Schary. A dramatization of Roosevelt's battle with polio.

Pictorial History

The Lawless Decade: A Pictorial History of the Thirties by James D. Horan.

This Fabulous Century, 1930-1940, Vol. 4, by the editors of Time-Life Books.

CHAPTER 16
THE ROAD TO PEARL HARBOR

DURING THE POLITICAL CAMPAIGN of 1920 the Republican candidate for president, Senator Warren G. Harding of Ohio, promised a "return to normalcy." Nobody was quite sure what this pledge meant; Harding probably was not even certain himself. Following Harding's inauguration on March 4, 1921, the meaning of "return to normalcy" became apparent. In the domestic sphere there would be no resurgence of the progressive movement. In foreign affairs, "normalcy" meant an end to high-sounding rhetoric about making the world safe for democracy. Instead, the country would mind its own business and avoid the world's conflicts. What about the League of Nations? Harding announced that the League issue was "as dead as slavery."

Why did Americans in the years after World War I turn their backs on world responsibility? Such a question defies a precise answer, but one can note several factors that contributed to the isolationist mood.

ISOLATION — AN OLD TRADITION

Isolation was an old habit, imbedded in the American tradition. The tradition found its origins in several sources, including geography. From its birth the United States had enjoyed a security unique in the history of modern nations. The Atlantic and Pacific oceans served as giant barriers against aggression from Europe or Asia, and the country's neighbors in the Western Hemisphere were too weak to pose a threat. Another source of American isolation was economic. The North American continent offered such rewards that Americans inevitably turned to the business of exploiting their own empire.

Like Thomas Jefferson, most Americans saw the Old World as corrupt and autocratic, the opposite of democratic America. They wanted their country to be as little like Europe as possible. They remembered the counsel of their first president, George Washington, who in his Farewell Address of 1796 warned of "the insidious wiles of foreign influence." Washington had urged "as little political connection as possible" with foreign countries and noted the

advantages of "our detached and distant situation." Americans, it was true, had deviated from the isolationist tradition. They had established a far-flung empire and taken part in World War I. But by 1921 the soldiers had returned and victory parades had ended. The old habit of looking inward reasserted itself.

Reinforcing the isolationist mood was widespread disappointment over the results of America's participation in the recent war. America's leaders had oversold the war to the people. Instead of presenting American participation as a matter of national interest, distasteful but necessary, they had portrayed the war as a crusade for democracy. Yet at the peace conference and in the postwar world there seemed as much selfish nationalism as before the war and, if anything, less democracy. Americans became disgusted with themselves for having been so foolish as to become party to Europe's war. They concluded that Washington and Jefferson had been right: Europe was hopelessly corrupt. Americans felt they should have as little as possible to do with it.

During the war most Americans had accepted the view that the Germans were the aggressors. After all, they had fired the first shots on the Western Front. But in the 1920s some historians concluded that the guilt for the war was not entirely Germany's. The outcome was a deepening of America's disillusionment with the recent war.

By the 1920s war had lost its glamour. It was so ghastly that it defied the imagination. Reinforcing the new image of war was Erich Maria Remarque's grim novel *All Quiet on the Western Front*. Tens of thousands read the book, millions saw the motion picture. The cost of postwar bonuses for the veterans of 1917-18 also helped turn Americans against war. Then there were the war's permanent victims, men who had taken shrapnel and gas, living reminders of the reality of war.

Groups and Individuals for Peace

Lest the average American weaken in his determination to stay out of war, a host of peace organizations sought to keep him aware of the

HEADLINE
EVENTS

1899-1900 Open Door Policy
1917 U.S. purchases Virgin Islands from Denmark
1917-1918 U.S. in World War I
1919 League of Nations is created
1920 Permanent Court of International Justice (World Court)
1921-1922 Washington Naval Conference
1921-1931 U.S. participates in over forty League conferences
1922 World War Foreign Debt Commission
Reparations Commission
1924 Dawes Plan
1927 Geneva meeting of U.S., Britain, and Japan
1928 Clark Memorandum
Kellogg-Briand Pact
1929 *All Quiet on the Western Front* (Remarque)
1930 Young Plan
London Naval Conference
1931 Mudken Incident
Japan seizes Manchuria
1931-1932 Stimson Doctrine
1932 World Disarmament Conference
1933 Roosevelt announces Good Neighbor Policy in inaugural address
Montevideo Conference; Hull repudiates Roosevelt Corollary
Hitler appointed chancellor of Germany; Nazi party takes control
1934 Platt Amendment cancelled
Marines withdrawn from Haiti
1934-1936 Nye Committee investigates munitions trade and neutrality
1935 Neutrality Act
1936 Hitler moves troops into Rhineland
Italy completes conquest of Ethiopia
Inter-American Conference at Buenos Aires
Civil war breaks out in Spain
Hay–Bunau-Varilla Treaty of 1903 is modified
1936-1937 U.S. passes additional neutrality legislation
1937 Incident at Marco Polo Bridge near Peiping, China

Roosevelt issues "quarantine speech"
Japanese take Nanking, China
Panay incident
Hitler has established a dictatorship in Germany
1938 Munich Agreement; Sudetenland is ceded to Germany
Hitler seizes Austria
1939 Hitler takes Czechoslovakia
Roosevelt urges repeal of arms embargo clause of neutrality law
Russia sends army into Finland
Hitler invades Poland
Russians attack Poland; Poland divided between Germany and Russia
Congress repeals arms embargo and authorizes danger zones
1939-1940 Phony War
1940 Hitler occupies Denmark, Norway, Netherlands, Belgium, and France
Evacuation of Allied troops from Dunkirk in France
Tripartite Pact creates Rome-Berlin-Tokyo Axis
Destroyer Deal
Roosevelt defeats Wendell Willkie for presidency
U.S. places embargo on scrap metal to Japan; later on iron and steel
1941 Lend-Lease Act
Hitler takes control of Yugoslavia and Greece
Robin Moor sinks in South Atlantic
Roosevelt confers with Churchill (Argentina Conference); Atlantic Charter is by-product of meeting
Greer episode
Kearny is torpedoed by Germans
Reuben James sunk by U-boats
Japanese occupy southern Indo-China
Japanese bomb Pearl Harbor
Congress declares war on Japan
Germany and Italy declare war on the United States

The Permanent Court of International Justice, or World Court, was an agency of the League of Nations headquartered in The Hague, Netherlands. Why were American isolationists opposed to United States membership in the World Court?

futility and horror of war. These organizations included the American Committee for the Cause and Cure of War, the National Council for Prevention of War, the Women's International League for Peace and Freedom, SOS (Stop Organized Slaughter), and the Veterans of Future Wars. The Veterans of Future Wars was a college organization that demanded bonuses in advance for the young men who would die in the next war.

These peace groups received support from some of the country's best-known intellectuals, including the historian Charles A. Beard. In 1935 Beard wrote: "We tried once to right European wrongs, to make the world safe for democracy. . . . [Isolation] may be no better, for aught anyone actually knows. But we nearly burnt our house down with one experiment; so it seems not wholly irrational to try another line."[1]

---

[1] Charles A. Beard, "Heat and Light on Neutrality," *The New Republic,* Volume LXXXVI, February 12, 1936.

Finally, the postwar era produced a spirit of superheated patriotism in America. Probably the new spirit of nationalism derived in part from disillusion over the war. But whatever the origin, it gave strength to the isolationist movement. Representative Maury Maverick of Texas exhibited this mixture of patriotism and isolationism in 1935 when he announced: "In our Revolution against the British, Lafayette came over here, and Baron von Steuben, also a foreigner, came to train our Revolutionary troops, and we were glad to have them; but we don't like foreigners any more."

STUDY GUIDE: Americans were disappointed that they had gotten involved in Europe's war, for there seemed to be as much selfish nationalism in Europe in the postwar era as before. War lost its glamour by the 1920s. Books and films such as *All Quiet on the Western Front* reminded people of the horror of war.

SEARCHING FOR PEACE

During the 1920s Americans found that they could not entirely bury their heads in the sand. They recognized that disorder in other parts of the world was of some concern to the United States. So, while rejecting membership in the League of Nations, they cooperated in less risky ventures designed to advance peace. Peace was what Americans wanted. Isolation was a means to secure peace. It was not an end. If other means could achieve peace, they were willing to compromise isolation. Thus Americans supported disarmament and took a leading part in the Washington Conference of 1921-22. They also helped to negotiate a pact outlawing war.

The Washington Conference

The Washington Conference evolved out of concern in the United States and Great Britain over the expansionist tendencies of the Japanese and the enormous expense of maintaining powerful navies. As a result of such concern, the governments of the two countries agreed in summer 1921 to summon a conference of the leading nations to meet at Washington and try to resolve the problems. Most countries receiving invitations accepted readily, but in Tokyo the response was less than enthusiastic. At length, the Japanese agreed, and in November 1921 Secretary of State Charles Evans Hughes opened the conference.

The central problem before the conference was the ambition of Japan, a problem that had been developing for many years. In the second half of the nineteenth century Japan had taken itself from the Middle Ages to the modern era. Throwing off the restrictions of feudalism, it had made contact with the outer world, built factories and railways. It also put together a strong military establishment and in 1895 waged a successful war against China. By the opening of the twentieth century the Japanese were asserting themselves throughout the Far East.

The United States began to fear for its recent acquisition, the Philippines, almost at Japan's doorstep. The result was a series of agreements in which the United States purchased security for its holdings in the Far East by recognizing Japan's special position in Korea, Manchuria, and China. Increasing Japanese influence was also partly responsible for the Open Door policy, which the United States proclaimed in 1899-1900.

While the European powers and America were distracted by World War I, the Japanese tried to elbow their way to new concessions in China. They met limited success, but after the war they demanded and received, by the Treaty of Versailles, all of Germany's islands north of the equator as well as the former German leasehold in the Chinese province of Shantung. After the Allied intervention in Russia in 1918, the Japanese refused to withdraw their troops from Russian territory. At the same time a dispute arose between the United States and Japan over the island of Yap, a cable station between Guam and the Philippines. The United States government viewed these events with alarm.

Complicating the Far Eastern problem was the alliance of 1902 between Japan and Great Britain. Alliance of the two island empires had seemed a good idea in 1902, but by 1921 the British were having second thoughts. Their dominions of Canada, Australia, and New Zealand saw the prospect of a war between Japan and the United States in which Britain would be bound to Japan. Distressed, the dominions urged Britain to end the alliance. The United States was also distressed. Since the War of 1812, American security had depended in part on the British navy, and it worried American leaders to think of going to war with Japan and finding the British navy on the enemy's side.

To resolve the Far Eastern problem the Washington Conference brought forth three major treaties. The Four-Power Treaty (United States, Great Britain, Japan, and France) ended the Anglo-Japanese alliance. The United States could now breathe easier; it need not fear battle with the British navy in the event of war with Japan. Japan was not altogether happy about ending the alliance. A Japanese delegate lamented: "We have discarded whiskey and accepted water." The four powers also agreed to respect each other's island possessions in the Pacific, and, in case of controversy, promised to try to negotiate a settlement. For the United States this part of the treaty offered increased security for the Philippines.

The Nine-Power Treaty (the above four, plus Belgium, China, Italy, the Netherlands, and Portugal) was an agreement concerning the Open Door policy. The nine nations agreed to equal commercial rights in China and promised to refrain from taking advantage of conditions in China to seek special privileges. As a result, American commerce in China seemed safer.

A third major treaty negotiated at the Washington Conference was the Five-Power Treaty (United States, Great Britain, Japan, France, and Italy). This treaty provided for limitation of naval arms, the outstanding accomplishment of the conference.

Clamor for Disarmament

Disarmament had captured the popular imagination. After World War I most people concluded that disarmament was the surest and least complicated way to peace. How could countries wage war if they had no guns or ammunition? People also believed that when arsenals were bulging, nations were less apt to seek peaceful solutions to international problems. Armaments were also expensive and thus increased taxes.

At the start of the 1921-22 conference Secretary Hughes dramatically proposed that the powers either scrap or abandon plans for building sixty-six capital ships (battleships and aircraft carriers) totaling almost two million tons. A British observer said that Hughes sank "in thirty-five minutes more ships than all the admirals of the world have sunk in a cycle of centuries." After several weeks of negotiation, the powers accepted Hughes's recommendations. The United States, Great Britain, Japan,

France, and Italy agreed to reduce their strength in capital ships and maintain their navies at a ratio of 5:5:3:1.75:1.75. With only a few exceptions, they would build no new capital ships for ten years and then replace only vessels that were twenty years old.

Here was a large victory for naval disarmament. But was it a victory for American interests in the Far East? Consider the tonnage ratios between the United States, Britain, and Japan. At first glance they appear to favor Britain and the United States. The British navy, however, had responsibilities in every ocean of the world. The United States fleet had to protect American interests in the Atlantic, Pacific, and Caribbean. While the Japanese navy would have three capital ships to five each for Great Britain and the United States, its domain was much smaller —the western Pacific. The implication was clear. Japan would have naval superiority in its chosen area: its price for giving up the alliance with Britain.

There was another little-noted provision of the Five-Power Treaty. The United States and Britain agreed to erect no new fortifications or naval bases in the western Pacific. For the United States that meant no expansion of defenses in the Philippines or Guam. The Japanese could build fortifications as they saw fit.

It is clear that Japan made concessions to American interests at the Washington Conference. But most Japanese concessions were promises. In the Four-Power and Nine-Power treaties the Japanese pledged observance of the Open Door in China and respect for American territories in the western Pacific. The only act in connection with these pledges was withdrawal from Shantung. On the other hand, the other powers, including the United States, made important concessions to Japan. They granted the Japanese naval supremacy in the Far Pacific. And the United States and Britain promised not to expand their defenses. In light of later developments, it seems clear that Japan emerged the winner at Washington.

Nobody in 1922 could predict the future, and for several years the Washington Conference received acclaim in America as a monumental diplomatic achievement. The naval race in capital ships ended, and nearly everyone except naval officers and shipbuilders praised this result. At the same time tensions lessened in the Far East. The Japanese expansionists temporarily went into eclipse, and it appeared Japan was evolving toward a Western-style democracy.

The Five-Power Treaty did not satisfy popular wishes for naval disarmament. The treaty limited only capital ships. The powers could build as many smaller vessels—cruisers, destroyers, submarines—as they wished. And build they did.

Another Attempt at Disarmament

In 1927, at the prompting of President Coolidge, representatives of the United States, Britain, and Japan met at Geneva to draft a treaty limiting lighter ships. Disagreement developed between the United States and British delegations. The Americans proposed extension of the 5:5:3 ratios, but the British, because of their worldwide commitments, insisted that their figure should be larger. The conference collapsed. The interesting point here is that the British and Americans saw themselves as possible enemies in the "next war."

Agitation for a new naval disarmament treaty continued. The result was the London Naval Conference of 1930. This conference drafted the London Naval Treaty, signed by the United States, Great Britain, and Japan, and in part by France and Italy. The five powers agreed to extend the holiday on new capital ship construction to 1936. Then the United States, Britain, and Japan agreed to limit smaller ships. They accepted a 5:5:3 ratio for heavy cruisers, 10:10:7 for light cruisers and destroyers, and 10:10:10 for submarines.

Japan Shatters the Peace

If advocates of disarmament received the London Naval Treaty enthusiastically, their enthusiasm was short-lived. In the following year, 1931, Japan shattered the peace by seizing the Chinese province of Manchuria in violation of the Nine-Power Treaty of 1922. It was clear that Japanese pledges meant nothing when they ran counter to Japanese ambition. Clearly, too, after a decade of moderation Japan was hoping to dominate East Asia. Imperialism was hardly consistent with disarmament, so Japan's action in 1931 signaled the end of naval limitation.

There was, meanwhile, one last effort in the 1930s for disarmament, this time in land armaments. While less expensive than navies, armies were an equal threat to peace. Thus in 1932 the World Disarmament Conference met at Geneva. President Herbert Hoover tried to duplicate Secretary Hughes's success of 1921 by dramatically calling for scrapping of offensive weapons. When this proposal failed, he suggested reducing world arms by nearly a third. The conference responded sluggishly. Despite hopes of people everywhere, the conference, which dragged on until 1934, achieved nothing. Japanese aggression in East Asia, the rising nationalism of Fascist Italy, the dread of bolshevism, and revival of German power brought an end to the great disarmament efforts of the 1920s and early 1930s.

Was Disarmament Possible?

What can one say about those noble dreams of disarmament? Were they unrealistic?

Perhaps disarmament dreams two generations ago were unreal. Some statesmen thought they were. Secretary of State Henry L. Stimson (1929-33) privately called Hoover's ideas for the World Disarmament Conference a scheme from *Alice in Wonderland*. Unlike many spokesmen for disarmament, he thought armaments were the result of international tension and insecurity rather than the cause of war. Only by removing the tensions did he believe the world could achieve disarmament.

Taking part in the world's quest for disarmament in the 1920s and 1930s was not the only American departure from pure isolation. The United States cooperated with the League of Nations. Republican administrations of the years 1921-33, however, would not consider taking the United States into the League as a regular member. Political considerations, as well as the isolationist impulse, prevented that.

Still, Americans—Republicans, Democrats, isolationists—longed for peace. And the League offered some hope of adjusting international differences. Why not cooperate when expedient? The United States, moreover, could not ignore that the League one day might take action against American interests. Thus the United States maintained five permanent officials at Geneva to represent American interests at the League. And from 1921 to 1931 the United States participated in more than forty League conferences, many of which sought to secure peace.

There was also the Permanent Court of International Justice, commonly called the World Court. Organized by the League in 1920, the court functioned separately and invited non-League countries to join on terms of equality.

The purpose of the court was to settle disputes between countries according to international law. A former American secretary of state, Elihu Root, a Republican, had helped draft the charter of the World Court.

Each Republican administration of the post-World War I period, as well as the succeeding Roosevelt administration, sought to gain Senate approval of membership in the World Court. But at this point the more fervent isolationists drew the line. Cooperation with the League was one thing; membership in a League agency was another. Isolationists feared that membership in the World Court might open the way for the United States to join the League—through the back door.

More important, what if the World Court handed down decisions contrary to American interests? As a concession, the proposal for American membership was modified to prevent any case involving the United States from going before the court without American consent. With this proviso it seemed that the court could not possibly damage American interests. Opponents still remained adamant. Even President Roosevelt, for all his popularity, could not persuade the Senate to approve American membership.

Kellogg-Briand Pact

Unquestionably the most celebrated attempt to preserve peace in the years after World War I came in 1927-28 when sixty-two governments signed or adhered to the Pact of Paris. Commonly called the Kellogg-Briand Pact, this agreement outlawed war.

The idea was not new. People had talked about outlawing war for a long time. In 1927, the French foreign minister, Aristide Briand, proposed a treaty between the United States and France renouncing war. The proposal received a boost when Charles A. Lindbergh's historic solo flight from New York to Paris brought a new outpouring of Franco-American friendship.

The government in Washington was not enthusiastic about Briand's idea. The United States wanted no entangling alliances and feared that a treaty such as Briand proposed might create an awkward bond between America and France. But popular opinion favored the idea of a treaty renouncing war. Briand, who actually hoped that a bilateral treaty with the United States would help guarantee France against any attack by Germany, had cleverly mobilized American peace organizations behind his proposal. American leaders could not afford to offend popular sentiment by rejecting Briand's proposal outright. But they could be just as clever as the Frenchman. When Secretary of State Frank B. Kellogg replied in December 1927 to Briand's proposal he asked: why should the treaty bind only the United States and France? Might not a major contribution to peace result if all the principal countries of the world renounced war as an instrument of national policy?

Kellogg's proposal appealed to popular opinion even more than did Briand's. Briand was not interested but as a man of peace—a winner of the Nobel Peace Prize—he could not easily turn aside the American proposal. After a period of diplomatic maneuver, representatives of fifteen countries gathered at Paris and in August 1928 signed the Kellogg-Briand Pact. All the contracting parties condemned war as a solution to international controversies and renounced war as an instrument of policy. They also reserved the right to defend themselves if attacked. Eventually sixty-two nations joined this high-sounding agreement which cynics later termed "solemn ballyhoo" and "an international kiss." In January 1929 the Unites States Senate consented to the pact, 81-1.

The weakness of the Kellogg Pact was obvious. It had no provisions for punishing nations waging aggressive war. Some individuals wanted to strengthen the pact by having the nations pledge economic sanctions against violators. American isolationists would have no part of such ideas. The means of enforcing the Kellogg Pact, then, was popular opinion, which likely would vary from country to country.

The War Debts

There were other matters that forced the United States from the path of pure isolation. Most important was the reparations-war debts question.

Failure of the wartime Allies to repay their war debts to the United States government—and indeed their well-known desire to avoid repayment—had stimulated isolationism in America. The Allies had borrowed about $10 billion from the government in Washington. At the time they borrowed the money there was no hint that they might consider the loans as different from ordinary loans. The loans were contracts. In the years 1914-18, however, the economies of the Allied countries had suffered. The Allies had stretched their gold reserves to purchase munitions. In the postwar period they found it next to impossible to repair the damages of war and have something left to pay the United States. The American protective tariff also made it difficult for Europeans to earn dollars with which to repay the United States government by selling products in the United States.

Germany was the source from which the Allies, particularly the French, had expected to obtain money for paying war debts. The Treaty of Versailles stated that Germany had started the war and must pay reparations to the Allies. But Germany's economy had also suffered in the war. Like the Allies, the Germans found it nearly impossible to rebuild and have a surplus for payment to other governments. The Allies insisted that if Germany did not pay reparations, the United States should not demand full payment on the war debts. The United States refused to admit any connection between reparations and war debts. The Allies must repay, regardless of what Germany did.

Even so, the United States consented to scaling down the war debts. In 1922 Congress created the World War Foreign Debt Commission. Between 1923 and 1926 the commission negotiated settlements with thirteen governments. These settlements canceled much of the debt by reducing the interest. Simultaneously a Reparations Commission, created by the Paris Peace Conference, established a committee headed by the Chicago banker Charles G. Dawes to study reparations problems. From this study came the Dawes Plan of 1924.

The Dawes Plan provided an international loan to Germany and reduction in the amount of Germany's annual reparations payments. But Germany's total obligation remained unchanged. For a time the Germans met payments faithfully, thanks to loans from the United States. Then a committee, headed by the New York financier Owen D. Young, began a new study of the reparations problem. In 1930 the Germans and their creditors agreed to the Young Plan. This plan reduced Germany's reparations obligation from about $33 billion of principal (plus interest) to about $9 billion of principal (and $17 billion of interest).

Soon after adoption of the Young Plan the Great Depression struck Europe. Further payment of war debts or reparations seemed impossible, whereupon President Hoover proposed a one-year moratorium on such payment. Congress consented, but it expected resumption of debt payments the next year. Expectation was in vain. Payment on reparations and war debts ended with the Hoover moratorium, except that Finland, which had a small debt to the United States and an export surplus providing it with dollars, paid in full.

STUDY GUIDE: Most Americans were committed to isolationism during the 1920s and 1930s. But the United States cooperated with other nations in attempts to seek a lasting peace. The United States participated with Britain, Japan, and France in the Washington Conference. The United States was uneasy about Japan's growing military strength and ambition to acquire new territory. Out of the conference came several important treaties: an Anglo-Japanese alliance was ended; America's Open Door policy in China was accepted; and the major powers agreed to limit naval armaments. The joint agreement to reduce naval strength was hailed as a major achievement. Disarmament had become a popular cause after World War I. Many people believed that nations would not go to war so quickly if they lacked arms and munitions. The five major powers attended the London Naval Conference of 1930 and agreed to further naval disarmament proposals which later proved ineffective. Japan's ambitions in East Asia violated the Nine-Power Treaty and signaled the end of naval limitation. A World Disarmament Conference held during the 1930s failed to reduce the world's supply of land armaments.

Although never a regular member, the United States sent representatives to meetings of the League of Nations. In an effort to preserve peace, sixty-two nations signed the Kellogg-Briand Pact outlawing war. The pact was ineffective because it contained no provisions for punishing nations who violated the pact.

Economic troubles made it difficult for the Allied nations to pay war debts owed to the United States. For similar reasons Germany could not pay war reparations to the Allies. The United States agreed to reduce Allied war debts. The Dawes and Young plans reduced the amount of German reparations and made payment easier.

THE WEAKENING OF PEACE

As the decade of the twenties ended, Americans, when they found a moment to ponder the world situation, inclined toward optimism. No major war was in progress—only disturbing turmoil and revolutions in South America and China. Even without American support, the League of Nations seemed to be working effectively. Disarmament had met some success. Having received the endorsement of eight other countries, the Open Door was no longer just American policy. The world's powers had outlawed war.

Such optimism was ill-founded. The coming decade would prove an unhappy one for liberty, democracy, and peace—ideals dear to Americans. Through bloody purges and the virtual enslavement of the Russian people, the Soviets would stabilize their system. Italian fascism, since 1922 concerned mainly with domestic improvements, would become militant. A totalitarian regime would displace moderate government in Japan. Republicanism would expire in Germany.

During the 1930s all the noble dreams of the years since 1917 would be reduced to ashes. The world would become unsafe for democracy, arsenals would bulge with more munitions than ever, and the peace settlement of Paris would disintegrate. The treaties of the Washington Conference would suffer repudiation, the League of Nations would prove powerless to keep peace, the Kellogg Pact would become a butt of jokes. By the end of the decade the world would burst into flame for the second time within a generation.

Most historians mark the year 1931 as the beginning of the era of World War II. Events of that year set the world on its slide into global conflict. Instigator of these events was the ancient but now streamlined empire of Japan.

The Japanese had pledged in the Nine-Power Treaty to respect the territorial integrity of China. By signing the Kellogg-Briand Pact, they had renounced war as an instrument of policy. Japan was also a member of the League of Nations and thus pledged to peace. But the Japanese in 1931-32 ignored their commitments and swallowed Chinese Manchuria.

Since the Russo-Japanese War of 1904-05, the Japanese had controlled a leasehold in southern Manchuria. Guaranteed by treaty with China, the leasehold produced lumber, coal, iron, and soybeans. Hence, it had assumed great importance in the Japanese economy.

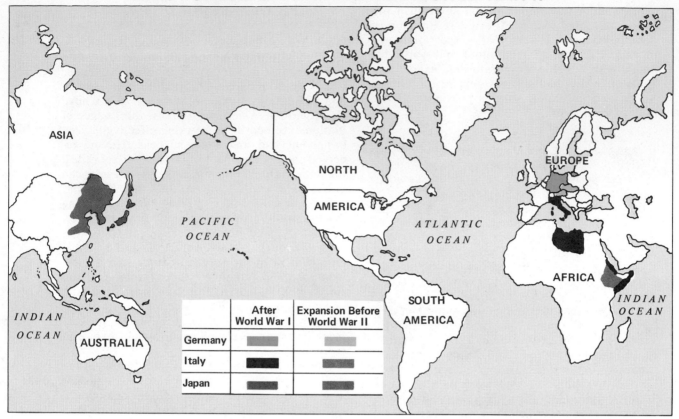

	After World War I	Expansion Before World War II
Germany		
Italy		
Japan		

Then the late 1920s the Chinese, led by General Chiang Kai-shek, determined to rid themselves of the Japanese. The leaders of China saw that the binding thread of the leasehold was the Japanese-owned South Manchuria Railway. They also saw that the railroad's prosperity depended on traffic originating outside the leasehold, in Chinese territory. So the obvious way to get rid of the railroad—and the Japanese—was to draw away the line's Chinese traffic. Accordingly, Chiang Kai-shek prevailed on the Chinese warlord in Manchuria to put together a system of rail lines to circumvent and eventually destroy the South Manchuria Railway.

Such maneuvers by the Chinese would have been risky at any time, but were especially so in the late twenties and early thirties. The Great Depression struck Japan in 1930, and in a single year export of raw silk fell by fifty percent. As economic difficulties multiplied, the Manchurian leasehold took on greater importance. There was, moreover, the problem of the Russians, the ancient rivals of the Japanese. The Russians were stirring in northern Manchuria, reviving

Germany, Italy, and Japan were determined to satisfy their territorial ambitions even before the outbreak of World War II. Trace the extension of their political power on this map.

memories of the battles of 1904-05 and also raising the threat of Communist expansion in East Asia.

Despite their anger at the Chinese and the economic plight at home, civil authorities in Tokyo took a cautious view of the situation in Manchuria. Not so the officers of the Japanese army in Manchuria. They believed the time had come to act. The army had little sympathy for the liberal ideas of Japan's political leaders and accused the civil government of being "soft" on China. The soldiers also had dreams of a great Japanese empire that would stretch across the Far East, including China, and Southeast Asia.

The Mukden Incident

Without consulting civil authorities in Tokyo, young army officers manufactured an incident near the city of Mukden. They claimed that on the night of September 18, 1931, the Chinese set off an explosive charge that ripped away thirty-one inches of track on the South Manchuria Railway. Unable to explain how the Mukden Express had passed over the line twenty minutes later, the Japanese said the train had miraculously jumped the gap.

Following the Mukden incident there was considerable sympathy for Japan in the United States and Europe. The Japanese over the past decade had behaved themselves. They had drawn back from imperialism, accepted naval disarmament, and signed the Kellogg Pact. The Chinese had also given the Japanese a great deal of provocation. But as the Japanese army moved out of the leasehold, allegedly in pursuit of Chinese bandits, the outer world became alarmed. The government in Tokyo was powerless to stop the militarists. The army's action was popular, and the government could not afford to appear less patriotic than the soldiers.

When Japan's plan became clear—occupation of all of Manchuria—the League of Nations took up the question. Here was the first serious threat to peace since creation of the world organization in 1919. How the League responded would have significant bearing on its future as a keeper of the peace. Under the League covenant, members were obliged to impose economic sanctions against an aggressor. Unfortunately the League was unable to act. Its leading members, Great Britain and France, seeing a parallel between Japan's difficulties in the leasehold and problems within their own empires, were unwilling to support strong action. Without cooperation of the United States, moreover, sanctions would achieve nothing. All the League could do in autumn 1931 was express hope that Japan would order its troops back to the leasehold. When that failed, the League merely dispatched to Manchuria an investigating commission.

The Stimson Doctrine

The American government was not a member of the League, but nothing prevented it from acting against Japan. Action might have serious consequences, however, since the Japanese depended on American cotton and oil.

Secretary of State Henry L. Stimson recognized the possibilities of the situation. Several times he suggested that the United States ought to consider economic sanctions against the

United Press International Photo from Compix

By early 1932, Japanese forces had occupied all of Manchuria. In 1933 Japanese soldiers began to invade Jehol Province to the south. Here, on March 23, they prepare to seize Chengte, the capital of Jehol. The city lies only a few miles north of the Great Wall of China.

Japanese. Such a step might instill courage in the members of the League, and joint action by the United States and the League might give pause to Japan. President Hoover vetoed the idea. A peaceful man, Hoover did not believe any important American interest was at stake in Manchuria. He suspected that strong action by the United States would mean war with Japan—a senseless war over issues that did not concern the United States. And the shrunken American military establishment was utterly unprepared to fight a war. For the president the overwhelming problem of the United States in 1931-32 was the economic crisis at home, the Great Depression.

The most that Hoover would authorize was the Stimson Doctrine. This pronouncement by the secretary of state declared that the United States would not recognize any situation or treaty brought about in violation of American rights. Since Japanese aggression had violated the Nine-Power Treaty, which required respect for the territory of China, the United States would not recognize the Japanese conquest of Manchuria.

By not recognizing the conquest of Manchuria, Americans advertised to the world that they condemned Japan's aggression. Leaders in Washington hoped other countries would do likewise—that the force of moral pressure might compel the Japanese to return to the leasehold. Unhappily the other powers were reluctant to join in. Hence the Stimson Doctrine did not stop the Japanese; they soon set up the puppet kingdom of Manchukuo in Manchuria. The doctrine merely aroused the Japanese against the United States and, some historians have thought, lit the fuse that exploded at Pearl Harbor ten years later.

Many historians who have studied the Manchurian crisis and recent American diplomacy have criticized Secretary Stimson's policy. In general they have concluded that the United States should have set aside self-righteous ideas about international morality and recognized the Japanese as a bulwark against Communist expansion in East Asia. They reason that a "realistic" policy would have prevented the costly Pacific war of 1941-45, saved China from the Communists, and headed off such difficulties in Southeast Asia as the Vietnamese conflict of the 1960s and 1970s.

Defenders of Stimson say he saw that China would one day be the dominant power of the Far East. Population and geography assured this. Stimson believed that giving in to Japan's aggression might result in loss of China's friendship and perhaps turn China into a militant giant. In the light of what has happened in East Asia since World War II, who is to say that Stimson did not have a clearer view of reality than have his critics?

Rise of Adolf Hitler

While Japan was devouring Manchuria, trouble brewed in the struggling German Republic. Created in the last days of World War I, the Republic lacked the support of any democratic tradition. Then the Republic faced the insoluble problem of recovery from the war and reparations payments. Next came the Great Depression of the early 1930s.

In addition to the economic crisis there were psychological problems in Germany—humiliation over defeat in the war and bitterness over what the Germans thought were the unfair terms of the Treaty of Versailles, especially the provision blaming Germany for the outbreak of war in 1914. Such a situation offered an opportunity for a patriot-agitator, Adolf Hitler, and his brown-shirted followers, the Nazis. Hitler blamed Germany's woes on Jews, Communists, republican degeneracy, and the Treaty of Versailles. He reminded Germans that the Republic had signed the treaty of peace with the Allies.

By late 1932 the Republic was about to collapse, and the Communists and Nazis were preparing for a "no-holds-barred" struggle for Germany's political wreckage. To head off the Communists, the president of the Republic, Paul von Hindenburg, a general of World War I, appointed Hitler as chancellor in January 1933. A few weeks later Hitler's Nazi party, polling just forty-four percent of the votes, won a national election and took control of the government.

Hitler had gained power by republican means, but he immediately set out to destroy republicanism in Germany. He succeeded with breathtaking speed, and by 1937 had established the Nazi dictatorship. All the while he proclaimed, amid enthusiastic approval of many Germans, that Germany must have *lebensraum*—living room. It must have territory into which the growing German population might expand, territory which would provide food, raw materials, and markets for a great industrial nation. Clearly Hitler expected to find his living room in Eastern Europe, and it was also clear that he would soon lead Germany to challenge the Treaty of Versailles.

The first challenge came in March 1935 when Hitler renounced those articles of the treaty providing for German disarmament. He openly began to create the most powerful military machine the world had seen. Next, early in 1936, he ordered German troops into the Rhineland, which had been proclaimed a demilitarized zone by the Versailles settlement. When Europe's democracies, notably France and Great Britain, let Hitler get away with these violations of the 1919 treaty, it was soon clear that they merely encouraged him to new adventures.

The martial spirit was also loose in Benito Mussolini's Italy. Late in 1934 the Italians provoked a quarrel with the East African kingdom of Ethiopia. Through the spring and summer of 1935 the League of Nations desperately tried to mediate the crisis, but Italy was bent on conquest. Conquest of Ethiopia would give Italy a large overseas territory and avenge a humiliating defeat Ethiopia had inflicted on Italy in 1896. Then such a conquest—Italians seemed to think—would restore some of the grandeur of ancient Rome.

The Italians launched their attack in October of 1935. The Ethiopians, commanded by their emperor, Haile Selassie, fought courageously, but Italy secured its conquest in spring 1936.

Adolf Hitler reviews a military parade in Nuremberg in 1937. Between 1932 and 1937, he was able to establish a Nazi dictatorship in the former German Republic. What conditions made it possible for him to take control?

American Reaction to European Problems

Americans reacted with alarm to these rumblings in Europe. They feared the world was slipping dangerously near the brink of a new general war, and they wanted no part of another world war. Americans had suffered disillusion following failure of World War I to make the world safe for democracy. By the mid-1930s the country was in the grip of the Great Depression. Many Americans had concluded that the crash of 1929 and the subsequent depression had resulted from the economic boom of 1914-18. They reasoned that bust invariably follows boom. War brings boom. So to avoid another bust, avoid war.

Most Americans believed that conflicts in Europe, Asia, and Africa did not concern the United States. They continued to believe it possible to isolate America from the wars of the Old World, rejecting the idea that war in one part of the world constitutes a threat to the peace of the other parts. They believed that nazism, fascism, and all the other Old World "isms" were evidence of a new breaking out of the Old World's habit of bloodshed and disorder. Let the Old World devour itself, but let America live, they said.

Americans in the 1930s reached other conclusions regarding their country's part in world affairs. They decided that if the United States had not become an arsenal for the Allies in 1914-17 it would not have become an object of German military strategy. If this had not occurred, the United States would not have entered the World War. By this time millions of Americans agreed with Senator Homer T. Bone of Washington who, in 1935, declared that "the Great War was utter social insanity, and was a crazy war, and we had no business in it at all."

Economic as well as political isolation, then, was necessary for peace. Foreign powers, moreover, might show less desire for war if they knew that America, the greatest industrial country in the world, would close its armament factories to belligerents.

Passage of Neutrality Act

Isolationist ideas gathered increased support as Italy prepared to attack Ethiopia. Congress responded in August 1935 by passing the Neutral-

In 1919 Benito Mussolini organized a political party known as Fascists. Within three years, he was powerful enough to become premier of Italy. Here he addresses a crowd of followers in the cathedral square at the Italian town of Pistoia.

ity Act. The legislation provided that upon out-break of war anywhere in the world the United States would embargo munitions shipments to all belligerents, victims and aggressors alike. In the war about to break out in East Africa, ill-equipped Ethiopia would receive the same treatment as its attacker, Italy.

The Neutrality Act did not cover food, medical supplies, scrap metal, trucks, gun cotton, and oil—articles as important in modern war as guns, bullets, and warplanes. Some observers noticed this weakness, but others pointed to the bad effect a total embargo against belligerents would have on American overseas trade and hence on efforts to recover from the depression.

The Neutrality Act was passed against the wishes of President Roosevelt and Secretary of State Cordell Hull. Roosevelt and Hull were not "internationalists" or advocates of collective security in the present-day sense. In public statements the president sometimes sounded like an isolationist. But the two men wanted to retain the executive's traditonal freedom of maneuver in foreign affairs. They did not wish to have their hands tied in a developing crisis by previous acts of Congress. If it seemed desirable, they wanted to be able to cooperate in collective measures to keep the peace and punish aggression—perhaps in cooperation with the League of Nations. Thus, in 1935 Roosevelt sought legislation that would, upon outbreak of foreign war, permit him several alternatives: to do nothing, proclaim an embargo against all belligerents, or designate the aggressor and embargo shipments to him while keeping open the lines of trade to the victim.

Isolationists Oppose Embargoes

This idea of "discriminatory" or "punitive" embargoes was opposed by isolationists. Like President Hoover in 1931-32, they believed that such measures—embargoes against aggressors—were acts of war that would invite retaliation and involve the United States in conflicts in which it had no interest.

They argued further that in a developing international crisis it was often impossible to be sure who was the aggressor. If the president tried to name the aggressor, he was apt to make a mistake that would have tragic consequences. To reinforce this argument, isolationists noted that in 1914 most Americans had been sure the Germans were the aggressors while scholars now viewed the matter differently.

Recognizing that most Americans accepted the isolationist logic, and not wishing to weaken his domestic program, the president reluctantly signed the Neutrality Act of 1935, and also two measures that succeeded it in 1936 and 1937. As the editors of *Collier's Weekly* noted, "The same Congress which voted almost unlimited discretion to the President in domestic matters took from the President practically all discretion in foreign affairs."

The Neutrality Act of 1935, a temporary measure, was scheduled to expire in February 1936. When the expiration date drew near, isolationists campaigned for a new bill. President Roosevelt hoped for a measure that would allow him some flexibility upon outbreak of a foreign war, but his hopes were in vain. At length Congress passed a bill retaining the arms embargo of the 1935 legislation, and added a new provision prohibiting Americans from lending money to belligerents. This amendment was a response to the belief that the United States had become financially linked with the Allies in 1914-17. The result had been pressure to intervene in the war when it appeared the Germans might win. Such ideas received wide publicity, but little proof, from the hearings of the so-called Nye Committee. A special Senate committee, it was headed by Senator Gerald P. Nye of North Dakota and from 1934 to 1936 investigated the munitions trade and neutrality. As a result of its disclosures, many Americans concluded that financial considerations had been the leading cause of America's entry in the World War in 1917.

The Neutrality Act of 1936 expired in 1937, whereupon Congress passed a third neutrality measure in May 1937. Like its predecessor, it prohibited munitions shipments and loans to belligerents. The act also made it unlawful for American citizens to travel on belligerent-owned ships. Thus there would be no repetition of the 1915 crisis over loss of American lives when a German submarine sank the British liner *Lusitania*. To make the law apply to conflicts such as the Spanish Civil War, then in progress, the 1937 law applied to civil strife as well as international war.

Profit-conscious Americans still declined to go the full way with economic isolation. There was nothing in the legislation to prevent belligerents from purchasing nonmilitary commodities in the United States. However, the law provided that the president could designate items which the belligerent would have to pay for in cash and carry away in his own ships—a "cash and carry" principle. If a belligerent had to carry goods away from American ports in his own ships, American ships would not run the risk of being attacked by the other belligerent. If the belligerent paid cash, there would be no nagging debt problem after the war.

The Spanish Civil War

When the third Neutrality Act was passed, the world's storm center was Spain, where one of history's most barbaric civil wars had broken out in 1936. Its land unproductive and its people divided into many factions, Spain had been in turmoil for years. When a republican government replaced the corrupt and ineffectual monarchy in 1931, the situation got worse. Leaders of the republic tried to engineer separation of church and state and also seemed to be setting Spain on the road to socialism. Such moves aroused the Catholic hierarchy and political conservatives, and the upshot was a rebellion in 1936 led by General Francisco Franco.

While Americans only vaguely understood the complexities of the Spanish situation, many were not long in taking sides. Political liberals generally supported the Republicans, or Loyalists, seeing them as defenders of democracy. Then the dictators Hitler and Mussolini rallied to the side of Franco, sending air squadrons that devastated towns and cities under Loyalist control. Liberals in America became more vehement in their support of the Republicans. Catholics and conservatives, on the other hand, sided with Franco, especially after the Soviets began to assist the Loyalists. In their view the followers of Franco were waging a holy war against atheism and communism. This view received reinforcement when a few American Communists joined the Lincoln Brigade and went off to Spain to fight for the republic.

The American government moved cautiously, most reluctant to take a stand when opinion in the country was so divided. After Europe's powers agreed in summer 1936 to keep clear of the Spanish conflict, leaders in Washington announced that the United States would do likewise. To make such a policy effective, Congress in early 1937 voted an arms embargo against both sides in Spain. A few months later Congress passed the Neutrality Act of 1937 which had a provision forbidding arms shipments to combatants in civil wars.

The American policy, it turned out, worked to the advantage of Franco and the rebels. Liberals protested, but President Roosevelt refused any changes. The debate on Spanish policy became academic when Franco early in 1939 captured the last Loyalist strongholds.

Did the United States take the proper position in the Spanish Civil War? Liberals to the present day have persisted in the view that the American policy of 1936-39 permitted destruction of democracy in Spain. After leaving the White House in 1953, former-President Harry S. Truman wrote in his memoirs that Republican Spain had been lost because of the embargo. The historian Julius W. Pratt, in his study of Cordell Hull (*The American Secretaries of State and Their Diplomacy*), takes a different view. Pratt says that lifting the embargo for the Loyalists would not have changed the outcome of the war, unless such action had been followed up by positive assistance, which would probably have involved the United States in hostilities with Germany. Noting the increasing Communist influence as the war progressed, Pratt also thinks that if the Loyalists had won, Spain would have become a satellite of the Soviet Union. He feels that Spain ruled by Franco has been preferable to a Communist Spain.

The Far East

While world attention was fixed on Spain, an incident at the Marco Polo Bridge, a railway junction near Peiping in North China, brought a new crisis in East Asia.

The situation in the Far East had been reasonably quiet for several years. The League of Nations commission investigating the Manchurian incident had condemned Japan's aggression. Prodded by Secretary Stimson, the League early in 1933 adopted the commission report. This prompted the Japanese to stalk out of the League. A few weeks later Japanese forces moved into North China, but representatives of the Chinese and Japanese governments accepted a truce in spring 1933. A relative calm then settled over East Asia as the Japanese turned to the business of consolidating their position in Manchukuo. While they continued to dream of gaining control over China, leaders in Tokyo decided to achieve their ends by "peaceful" means—subversion and bribery.

The incident at the Marco Polo Bridge in July 1937 was a confusing affair in which Japanese and Chinese soldiers exchanged a few shots and the Japanese shelled a Chinese town. Whatever caused the incident, and nobody to the present day apparently knows precisely how it started, Japanese authorities determined to use it as a pretext for launching a new military adventure in China. Within a few days reinforcements were rolling into North China from Manchukuo. With comparative ease Japanese forces scattered Chinese defenders and established control over the Peiping-Tientsin area.

Meanwhile, in August 1937, fighting broke out at Shanghai, China's largest port. After holding out for more than two months against the Japanese, the Chinese forces began to retreat up the Yangtze River. Combat was fierce, and the world looked on in horror as the Japanese tried to shatter the Chinese spirit by unleashing their bombing planes against the civil population. Chiang Kai-shek's capital, Nanking, fell in December 1937. Japanese soldiers gave themselves over to an orgy of looting and murder, the infamous "rape of Nanking."

Roosevelt's "Quarantine" Speech

Despite shock at Japanese brutalities, the people of the United States considered the war in China as none of their business. President Roosevelt and Secretary Hull did not agree. The president seemed to be trying to shake the country from its isolationist position when he gave his sensational "quarantine" speech at Chicago in October of 1937.

Deploring the new outbreak of "international lawlessness" in East Asia, Roosevelt proposed that peaceful peoples should quarantine aggressors. He explained that "when an epidemic of physical disease starts to spread, the community approves and joins in a quarantine of the patients in order to protect the health of the community against the spread of the disease. . . . War is a contagion, whether it be declared or undeclared."

These were noble sentiments, but they failed to strike fire in America. Roosevelt complained privately that "it's a terrible thing to look over your shoulder when you are trying to lead—and to find no one there."

The following month, November 1937, the League of Nations sponsored an international conference at Brussels, Belgium, to consider the China problem. The meeting came to nothing, largely because American delegates, their hands tied by isolationism at home, were in no position to consider measures to punish Japan. The conference ended soon after it started with a mild rebuke of Japan as a violator of the Nine-Power Treaty.

The *Panay* Incident

A few weeks later Americans felt momentary shock when they learned of the *Panay* incident. To protect American lives and property in China, the United States had for many decades maintained a naval squadron on the Yangtze. As Japanese and Chinese armies struggled up the river toward Nanking in December 1937, the gunboat U.S.S. *Panay* sought to perform its protective mission and at the same time to stay out of the way of the combatants. To escape Japanese artillery fire the vessel left its anchorage near Nanking on December 11 and moved up the river. It was joined by three American tankers. The next day the four ships dropped anchor twenty-seven miles upstream from Nanking, and the *Panay* sent a radio message to inform the Japanese of the new location.

It was a bright day and the *Panay*'s awnings bore freshly painted American flags. In the early afternoon a squadron of Japanese bombing planes roared overhead and a few seconds later began a bombing run. In a few moments the first bomb crashed down on the *Panay*. The action continued for a half-hour, until the gunboat rolled over and went down in fifty feet of water. The tankers also were settling to the bottom. Three Americans were dead, many injured.

In the United States the response was one of fury. Japanese leaders were quick to apologize for the outrage and offer an indemnity, explaining that the pilots had mistaken the American vessels for Chinese. Skeptical, the State Department accepted the Japanese explanation. Within a few weeks the *Panay* affair was forgotten—and Americans remained as wedded as ever to the policy of isolation.

The Japanese, meanwhile, continued their conquest in China. By 1939 they had captured most of the country's coastal areas and river valleys.

Hitler Takes Austria and Czechoslovakia

A few weeks after the *Panay* episode Hitler shattered the calm that seemed to have settled over Europe (Spain excepted). After several weeks of threatening its leaders, he seized the neighboring state of Austria early in 1938. Next he began making impossible demands on Czechoslovakia.

In autumn 1938, following negotiations at Munich, Britain and France tried to appease Hitler by forcing the Czechs to cede to Germany the Sudetenland, a German-speaking border territory. Appeasement proved fruitless. In March 1939 the German chancellor jarred Europe and the world by breaking the Munich arrangement and taking the rest of Czechoslovakia.

Americans observed these events closely. It hurt to see democracies fall under the Nazi dictatorship, especially Czechoslovakia. The most democratic state in Eastern Europe, Czechoslovakia was a young republic, one of the happier results of the World War, and a democracy that had borrowed much of its democratic faith from America.

American Reaction to War in Europe

President Roosevelt was disturbed by events in Europe and in April 1939 addressed a sensational appeal to Hitler and Mussolini. He asked for pledges that they would not attack any one of thirty European and Near Eastern countries for a period of ten years. He also suggested an international conference to deal with disarmament and international trade. Europe's democracies responded enthusiastically, but the dictators came forth with insolent rejections.

Roosevelt openly sympathized with the countries threatened by aggression. If the dictators attacked, he hoped to place the moral and material resources of the United States on the side of their victims. In May 1939 he urged repeal of the arms embargo clause of the neutrality law. Repeal would place the arms factories of the United States at the disposal of the democracies, just as in 1914-18, for there was no doubt that Britain would again control the seas in the event of a general war. The United States, as in the previous war, would become an arsenal for one group of belligerents.

Such a prospect distressed much of the American citizenry, still taken up with the isolationist idea that American intervention in World War I had been a colossal mistake. The policy Roosevelt was proposing, people thought, would bring a repetition of the events of 1914-17. One

side would depend on American assistance. The other side would retaliate. Ships would sink, people would die. The United States would protest. There would be diplomatic wrangling. Propagandists would stir emotions. Rationality would vanish. The United States would reach a point at which it must fight or retreat. It would fight.

Roosevelt saw that events might follow such a course. He hoped the United States might avoid war, but he thought the United States could not sit by and watch democracy perish. The possibility of retaliation by the dictators was a danger the United States must face.

Presidential logic moved few isolationists. The climax came in July 1939 when senators of both political parties gathered at the White House for an evening conference with Roosevelt, Hull, and Vice-President John Nance Garner. Hull set out to explain the administration argument for repeal of the arms embargo. The old isolationist champion, Senator Borah, interrupted: "I do not believe there is going to be any war in Europe." Hull then invited Borah to the State Department to read the dispatches coming in each day from Europe indicating the contrary. Roared Borah: "I don't give a damn about your dispatches." Tears welled in the secretary's eyes. Garner then turned to Roosevelt: "Well, Captain, we may as well face the facts. You haven't got the votes, and that's all there is to it."

Good Neighbor Policy

As the world situation deteriorated, Roosevelt sought to enlist on his side the republics of the Western Hemisphere. His device, announced in his inaugural address of 1933, was the Good Neighbor policy.

In his address of March 4, 1933, Roosevelt said: "In the field of world policy I would dedicate this nation to the policy of the good neighbor." Although he intended this policy for the entire world, it came to mean United States relations with Latin America. Relations with Latin America had long been unsatisfactory, a legacy of United States intervention dating back to the turn of the century. The Good Neighbor policy sought to make Latin Americans forget the past, persuade them that they had nothing to fear from the "Colossus of the North," persuade them to look on the United States as a friend — "a good neighbor."

The government in Washington had begun to

move toward good neighborliness in Latin America shortly after the end of World War I. When the shooting stopped in November 1918, Germany, long considered a threat to North American interests in the New World, lay beaten. More important, the United States emerged from Europe's conflict as the world's foremost power and now seemed quite capable of taking care of its interests in the Western Hemisphere, including the Panama Canal. Making its position even more secure were new bases in the Virgin Islands, which the government in Washington had purchased from Denmark in 1917. World War I also brought changes in the world's view of imperialism. As a consequence, the possession of colonies, interference in affairs of friendly states, and coercion of weak nations by the powerful came under continuing attack, particularly in democratic countries. Responding to these changes, the United States, in the era of normalcy, put aside the "big stick" and began to fashion a fresh policy in Latin America.

Despite considerable provocation, the North American giant refrained from a new intervention in Mexico in the 1920s. The difficulty during this period stemmed from the Mexican constitution of 1917, which claimed that all of the country's mineral resources were the property of the Mexican government. Such a claim threatened the interests of North Americans who had invested in Mexican lands, especially oil.

Fortunately the governments in Mexico City and Washington approached the problem with restraint. Dwight W. Morrow was appointed United States ambassador to Mexico in 1927. An intelligent and sensitive diplomat, Morrow dealt tactfully with the Mexicans. The leaders of Mexico, for their part, promised to satisfy legitimate claims of North American investors.

The Clark Memorandum

Next the United States, in 1930, published the so-called Clark memorandum, drawn up in 1928 by Undersecretary of State J. Reuben Clark. This document seemed to repudiate Theodore Roosevelt's "corollary" to the Monroe Doctrine, by which the United States might intervene in the affairs of Latin America's republics under certain circumstances. Nothing the United States might have done could have brought greater satisfaction to Latin Americans than the Clark memorandum. Nothing grated

Latin Americans quite so much as the assumption of the United States that it was the policeman of the Western Hemisphere, with a special right to intervene in the affairs of its sister republics.

Still, the Clark memorandum was vague. Moreover, it was a statement or policy by the administration of President Hoover and hence was not necessarily permanent. Did Franklin Roosevelt support the Clark memorandum? In 1933, during the Montevideo Conference, a meeting of representatives of all governments in the hemisphere in the capital of Uruguay, the Latin Americans received their answer. In tones that were loud and clear, Secretary Hull, the chief United States delegate to the conference, spoke out in favor of a pact declaring that no American state had the right to intervene in the internal or external affairs of another. There was no longer doubt that the United States repudiated the Roosevelt Corollary.

The United States soon matched Hull's words with deeds. Disorders in Cuba, arising from economic difficulties and the arbitrary rule of the dictator Gerardo Machado, annoyed the United States, but Franklin Roosevelt held his peace and landed no troops in Cuba. In 1934 the United States cancelled the Platt Amendment, which the United States had forced on Cuba after the Spanish-American War. The amendment compromised Cuban sovereignty and had opened the door to American intervention. The United States, also in 1934, withdrew the last marines from Haiti, and in 1936 signed a treaty with Panama moderating the terms of the Hay–Bunau-Varilla Treaty (1903). Lending support to the Good Neighbor policy were the reciprocal trade treaties of 1934 and thereafter.

As the world situation worsened, the Roosevelt administration sought to broaden the Good Neighbor policy. Its aim was to promote hemispheric solidarity, to make the Western Hemisphere a bastion against aggressors of Europe and Asia, and to commit every country in the hemisphere to that principle of the Monroe Doctrine regarding resistance to outside attack. In 1936 Roosevelt, as a "traveling salesman of peace," sailed to Buenos Aires to address a special Inter-American Conference on this subject. While no agreement resulted, the president received an enthusiastic reception, a preview of the later wartime cooperation of nearly all nations of the Western Hemisphere.

The Good Neighbor policy was an important step toward accord between the United States and its sister republics of the New World. It marked a reversal of the policy whereby the United States was the self-appointed policeman of the area. It failed to remove all of Latin America's enmity toward the United States, but under the circumstances it achieved as much as was then possible. During World War II the United States had the support of most of its neighbors to the south. With a few exceptions, this support continued into the postwar era.

STUDY GUIDE: Japanese aggression in 1931 marked the beginning of the era leading to World War II. Japanese officers staged an incident at Mukden which was used as an excuse to seize Chinese Manchuria. Neither the League of Nations nor the United States took strong action against Japanese aggression. Serious economic difficulties and bitterness over the humiliating terms of the Versailles Treaty helped to topple the German republic. By 1937 Adolf Hitler and his Nazi party had established a dictatorship. Hitler sent German troops into the Rhineland and openly began to build a powerful military mechanism, in violation of the Versailles Treaty. Under dictator Benito Mussolini, Italy seized the East African kingdom of Ethiopia. Americans were alarmed by all these acts of aggression, but determined to avoid war. During the 1930s Congress passed a series of neutrality acts banning loans and shipment of munitions to belligerent countries.

In 1936 a rebellion led by General Francisco Franco brought civil war to Spain. Hitler and Mussolini gave armed support to Franco, which caused severe destruction to Loyalist-controlled Spanish towns. Although American sympathies were with the Republicans, the United States remained neutral and voted an arms embargo against both sides in Spain. Franco's forces won.

Japanese aggression in China prompted Roosevelt's speech urging all nations to "quarantine" aggressive nations. The Brussels Conference in 1937 failed to halt Japanese aggression in China. After Hitler seized Austria and Czechoslovakia, Roosevelt tried unsuccessfully to get peace pledges from Hitler and Mussolini. Isolationists in the United States rejected the president's plea for repeal of the arms embargo clause of the Neutrality Act. Roosevelt's Good Neighbor Policy toward the countries of Latin America brought improved relations and cooperation between the United States and its neighbors to the South.

FAREWELL TO ISOLATION

Despite Senator Borah's confidence that no war was imminent in Europe, by the summer of 1939 Adolf Hitler was making preparations for his next conquest, Poland. His tactic was a standard one of aggressors: make impossible demands on the intended victim, and when the victim refuses to yield, attack.

A gallant nation with a tragic history, Poland had the support of the two great democracies of the West, France and Great Britain. But so had Czechoslovakia. Taking note of the Czech experience, Hitler was sure the two West European powers would not act vigorously to prevent his aggression.

Of greater concern was Poland's eastern neighbor, the Soviet Union. Would the Russians sit by while Germany devoured Poland? To prevent a two-front war involving Russia, in late August 1939 Hitler negotiated a pact with the Soviets. Each party pledged not to attack the other and also by a secret agreement decided to divide Poland and the rest of Eastern Europe into German and Soviet "spheres of interest." Hitler then launched his attack on September 1, 1939, on the preposterous pretext that Poland had invaded Germany.

This time the democracies of Western Europe knew that force was the only language Hitler understood; appeasement was futile. Great Britain and France honored previous commitments to Poland and on September 3 declared war on Germany.

The Russians attacked Poland from the east on September 17. Eleven days later Germany and the Soviet Union arranged a division of Poland.

Except for Communists and a handful of Nazi supporters, Americans overwhelmingly sympathized with the Poles, more so after Hitler hurled his bombing planes against Polish cities in an attempt to terrorize the civilian population. Still, the isolationist impulse in the United States remained strong. This was Europe's tragedy; it did not concern America. So thought a majority of Americans, but not their president.

Congress Repeals Arms Embargo

Two weeks after Hitler's invasion, Roosevelt summoned Congress to a special session. In a

In 1939 Hitler reviewed his troops in Warsaw.

dramatic and emotion-laden speech he requested repeal of the arms embargo provision of the neutrality law. He sought to enable the Allies to obtain in the United States the munitions to resist the Nazis. As a concession to isolationists he proposed designation of certain "danger zones," the waters around Europe, into which Americans could not travel or sail their ships. The provision would reduce the risk of losses of American lives and ships as a result of belligerent action, which had been the chief objective of the neutrality legislation.

There followed a debate which some historians have called one of the most momentous in American history. It lasted six weeks. The issue was clear. To preserve their own peace, Americans could insulate themselves from Europe's war—at the risk of destruction of democracy in Europe. Or they could risk their own peace by placing their factories and arsenals at the disposal of the democracies. Debate ended in early November 1939. Responding to shifting popular opinion, alarmed at the sweep of Hitler's armies across Poland, Congress repealed the arms embargo and authorized danger zones. Purchasers of munitions, however, would have to operate on a cash-and-carry basis. America still hoped to stay out of the war.

Repeal of the arms embargo did not end debate over American policy toward belligerents, but most people agreed that the United States must prepare against the possibility of its involvement in the war. The nation began to bolster its armed strength, stepping up production of guns, tanks, and planes. The army and navy raised their manpower. The United States would be ready if war came—so Americans thought.

The Phony War

While formally at war with Germany, the British and French had not clashed with Hitler's armies by the time the Germans and Soviets completed their conquest of Poland. And neither the Germans nor the Western Allies showed any disposition to break the calm that now settled over Europe. The result was the Phony War of winter 1939-40.

Hitler indeed had no ambition in Western Europe and hoped for peace. But the British and French, confident that Hitler's forces could not breach the French defense system, the famous Maginot Line, rejected Nazi overtures.

Meanwhile, fighting had broken out in Finland. Fearing that the nonaggression pact with Germany might fall through one day, the Russians in the autumn of 1939 made territorial demands on Finland designed to increase the security of the Soviet Union. When the Finns rejected the demands, the Soviets in late November of 1939 sent the Red Army across the Finnish frontier. As Americans cheered, the Finns put up heroic resistance, inflicting several humiliating defeats on the Russians. Inevitably, however, the Soviets overwhelmed the Finns with superior numbers, and the winter war of 1939-40 ended in March 1940. Finland kept its independence but lost part of its territory and had to make military and economic concessions.

Hitler's Armies Strike

In April 1940, the Phony War ended as Hitler's armies in lightning strokes occupied Denmark and Norway. Next they swept into the Netherlands, Belgium, and Luxembourg, then into France. They astounded the world by easily maneuvering around the Maginot Line and shattering French defenses. In one of the most heroic episodes of the war the British, in May, evacuated three hundred thousand soldiers from the beaches of Dunkirk in northern France. But Nazi divisions were already hammering toward Paris. Hitler received unnecessary help from the Italian dictator, Mussolini, who declared war on the British and French and attacked France in the south.

French resistance had collapsed by mid-June. On June 22, 1940, French leaders surrendered in the same railway carriage in which the Germans had signed the armistice of November 11, 1918. Three months later representatives of Germany, Italy, and Japan met in Berlin to sign

On June 14, 1940, the German army entered Paris. Eight days later, France surrendered. Here German troops march through the Arc de Triomphe. General Charles de Gaulle escaped to London and established the Free French movement. French men and women who stayed behind formed resistance groups.

United Press International Photo from Compix

the Tripartite Pact creating the so-called Rome-Berlin-Tokyo Axis.

Churchill Asks for U.S. Aid

Hitler's victories in western Europe meanwhile had brought changes in Great Britain. The result was a new prime minister, Winston Churchill. The new British leader had no intention of giving in to the Nazis, but he knew that Britain standing alone could not resist Nazi pressure indefinitely. So he turned to the United States for help. Roosevelt responded in June 1940 by arranging for transfer to Britain of surplus stocks of guns, ammunition, and planes owned by the United States government. Such action was not neutral. International law prohibited a neutral government from providing arms to belligerents. And in accord with the neutrality law, Roosevelt had proclaimed America's neutrality on the outbreak of war in September 1939.

The subtleties of international law did not bother Roosevelt. He tried to get around them by ordering the government's munitions sold to private companies which, in turn, sold them to Britain. In his view, time was short. The Germans were massing forces in the west of France for a cross-Channel invasion of the British Isles, and it seemed they might strike at any time. Some of Roosevelt's advisers, including the ambassador to Britain, Joseph P. Kennedy, did not think the British could fight off the Germans. American support would probably be too late. America's arms might even fall to the Germans. Better to concentrate on building a "fortress America," they counseled.

Roosevelt, however, was determined to do what he could to save Britain. In the summer of 1940 the "pipeline" from the United States to the British Isles began to do service. To keep it operating, the Roosevelt administration arranged to step up the manufacture of munitions in the United States. (One should add that the Nazis were unable to wrest control of the skies over Britain and the English Channel; as a result the invasion of Britain never came off.)

The Destroyer Deal

Churchill had also asked for American destroyers, to help guard the English Channel and protect convoys bringing precious supplies to Britain from overseas. Roosevelt wrestled with the question of a destroyer transfer for many weeks. The United States had surplus vessels, but would the Germans retaliate against a transfer by attacking the United States? Moreover, Roosevelt at that time was campaigning for reelection. If the transfer stirred a popular reaction, the upshot might be a Republican victory at the polls in November.

At length the president decided that a destroyer transfer would not rouse the Germans to war against the United States. As for the election, he would take his chances. In September of 1940 he completed the "destroyer deal" in which he transferred to Britain fifty antique destroyers—"four-stackers" of World War I vintage. At the same time the British granted the United States the right to build naval and air bases in British territory in the Western Hemisphere—Newfoundland, the Bahamas, Bermuda, Jamaica, Saint Lucia, Antigua, Trinidad, and British Guiana.

It turned out that the destroyer deal provoked little criticism. Most Americans—even isolationists—saw the exchange of a bunch of old ships for a string of bases as a sharp bargain. The only serious reaction resulted from the way the president made the transfer, by executive agreement without the advice and consent of Congress.

Thus the destroyers, called "more precious than rubies" by Churchill, steamed out of American ports for Britain. British seamen were appalled at their inefficiency, and the ships were not very effective against the Germans. Still, it is possible that by thrashing about in the Atlantic they gave some pause to leaders in Berlin. More important, they sealed the alliance between the United States and Britain, inspiring the British historian Philip Goodhart two decades later to call them "fifty ships that saved the world."

The Presidential Election of 1940

While the country buzzed over the destroyer deal, the election campaign was reaching a climax. At Philadelphia the previous June the Republicans had nominated a "dark horse" for president, Wendell L. Willkie of Indiana. A successful corporation lawyer and former head of a private power combine, Willkie was intelligent and energetic. He was also a friendly man, with a booming bass voice and an unruly shock of hair that gave him unusual appeal. On the great questions of the day he stood surprisingly close to Roosevelt, favoring continued support of the British and endorsing the basic principles of the New Deal.

At the beginning of the campaign the main issue was Roosevelt's violation of the two-term tradition. Billboard pictures of Willkie carried the caption: "Third term means dictatorship." Then, as polls showed Willkie running behind, Republican managers persuaded the candidate to attack Roosevelt as a man whose policies would take the United States into Europe's war. Labeling Roosevelt a warmonger was unfair. But so were the tactics Roosevelt used in retaliation. The president presented Willkie as a "head-in-the-sand" isolationist who would do nothing while Hitler stamped out democracy in Europe. Lumping Willkie with such Republican isolationists as Congressmen Joseph W. Martin, Jr., Hamilton Fish, and Bruce Barton, he delighted Democratic audiences by intoning the catchy phrase: "Martin, Barton, and Fish."

The tactics of Willkie and Roosevelt probably had slight bearing on the outcome. If his luster had diminished since 1936 (as a result of the "court-packing" episode and the "purge" attempt of 1938), Roosevelt was still the idol of millions. He was the man who had brought relief to victims of the Great Depression, the man who had challenged the "economic royalists." Willkie, for all his personal magnetism, could not shake from the memories of many Americans the fact that the Republicans had been in power in 1929, the year the great economic catastrophe had struck. Accordingly, Roosevelt defeated Willkie in the popular balloting, 27,000,000 to 22,000,000, and overwhelmed him in the electoral college, 449-82.

Lend-Lease

The Roosevelt administration wanted to help the British; it also wanted to avoid a postwar debt problem. So it conceived a plan which, according to Roosevelt, would eliminate that "silly, foolish old dollar sign." Instead of lending money, the United States, as Roosevelt explained in a dramatic press conference in December 1940, would lend war equipment. When the war ended, the borrowers would return the equipment. The president compared the procedure with lending a garden hose to a neighbor to put out a fire that otherwise might spread to one's own house.

Roosevelt recognized that under this so-called Lend-Lease plan the United States would be giving equipment to the Allies. As Senator Robert A. Taft of Ohio said: "Lending war equipment is a good deal like lending chewing gun. You don't want it back." Roosevelt was undisturbed. He calculated that at this point the British were fighting democracy's fight against the Axis tyranny. No Americans were dying in the battle. Americans should be grateful that their role was that of paying the bill.

In congressional hearing on the Lend-Lease Bill—which bore the interesting legislative number H.R. 1776—isolationists heaped scorn on the proposal. They called it another step on the road to war. Senator Burton K. Wheeler of Montana crudely compared the measure with the cotton "plow-up" of 1933. He branded it the "New Deal's 'triple A' foreign policy—to plow under every fourth American boy."

Lend-Lease also had its advocates, none of whom was more outspoken than the man Roosevelt had beaten in the recent election, Wendell Willkie. When a congressman reminded Willkie of some of his more virulent campaign attacks on Roosevelt's foreign policies, Willkie replied that "in moments of oratory in campaigns we all expand a little bit." A majority of Americans, it turned out, favored Lend-Lease, and in March 1941 both houses of Congress passed H.R. 1776 by large majorities.

Isolationist Position on Lend-Lease

Isolationists were correct in their assertion that Lend-Lease was a long step toward American involvement in the European war. This became more apparent when passage of H.R. 1776 raised the question: Was the United States going to stand by while German submarines sent Lend-Lease cargoes to the bottom of the Atlantic? Unfortunately the British did not have enough warships to provide adequate protection. The only solution, it seemed, was to use the American navy to escort Lend-Lease convoys. But the inevitable result would be clashes with German submarines and cruisers, and eventually war.

Roosevelt understood the need to protect Lend-Lease cargoes but also realized he must move cautiously lest he touch off a new wave of isolationism in the country. As an ingenious compromise he announced a "neutrality patrol" by American planes and ships in the western Atlantic. The patrol would not defend Lend-Lease convoys, but was to "observe and report" belligerent movements and thus keep war from "our front doors." The objective, of course, was to flash the location of German U-boats, alerting merchantmen to veer away and inviting British cruisers and destroyers to attack. To widen the patrol, Roosevelt soon signed an agreement with the Danish government bringing Greenland into "our sphere of cooperative hemispheric defense." From Greenland he turned to Iceland, and the government of Iceland in July 1941 accepted American "protection."

To supply American troops on Iceland, it was necessary to operate convoys between the island and the United States. This raised the question: Why not allow British ships carrying Lend-Lease cargoes to join the convoys for protection as far as Iceland? The Royal Navy could then escort the Lend-Lease ships on the last leg of the voyage to Britain. Still fearing an isolationist outburst, President Roosevelt wavered, but in September 1941 he finally issued the necessary order.

The War in Europe Intensifies

Meanwhile, Hitler found that he was unable to crush the British by massive air attacks. So he turned to the south and east. His armies in North Africa, commanded by the renowned "Desert Fox," General Erwin Rommel, had sent the British retreating toward the Egyptian border and were threatening the Suez Canal. In April 1941 Hitler sent his armies crashing into the Balkans, and after three weeks of fierce fighting the Germans were in control of Yugoslavia and Greece.

Before the world could catch its breath after these spectacular victories, the dictator wheeled his forces around and in June 1941 began the invasion of the Soviet Union. At the same time German submarines were prowling the Atlantic, sending millions of tons of shipping and hundreds of seamen to the ocean bottom. One U-boat victim was the merchantman *Robin Moor,* sunk in the South Atlantic, the first American ship to go down in World War II. If Hitler succeeded in defeating Russia—and it seemed in summer-autumn 1941 that he might do just that—it would be very difficult for the British to hold out, unless the United States joined the fight.

While Hitler focused on Russia, Roosevelt in midsummer 1941 thought it would be a good idea to have an informal exchange of views with Prime Minister Churchill. Arrangements were made for the two men to have a shipboard rendezvous off the coast of Newfoundland near Argentia. Presumably on a fishing cruise, the president sailed from New London on August 3, 1941, aboard the yacht *Potomac.* At sea he transferred to the cruiser *Augusta* for the trip to Newfoundland. Churchill crossed the choppy North Atlantic aboard the H.M.S. *Prince of Wales,* a new battleship that was the pride of the Royal Navy.

Atlantic Charter

The problem of defeating Germany dominated the discussions, but posterity remembers the Atlantic Conference for an almost incidental by-product of the meeting—a joint declaration of Anglo-American war aims known as the Atlantic Charter. The charter announced that neither the United States nor Great Britain sought new territory, that the two powers favored self-determination for all people and an equitable distribution of the world's wealth. It stated their determination to destroy nazism and

A meeting between President Roosevelt and Prime Minister Winston Churchill of Britain took place in August 1941 off the coast of Newfoundland aboard the U.S.S. *Augusta*. What did the two world leaders hope to achieve in their joint declaration known as the Atlantic Charter?

Official U.S. Navy photo

to seek an international organization in the postwar era to guarantee peace. The British saw the document as a means of identifying the United States more closely with the war. Roosevelt hoped the charter would rally people in occupied countries to defiance of the Nazis. Ringing with noble sentiments, the charter also distracted Americans from the main business—discussion of war plans—and undercut isolationist criticism of the meeting.

On returning home, Roosevelt assured the country that he had made no commitments which brought the United States any nearer the European war. That was not quite true, for during the Atlantic Conference the president had promised the British he would issue an order permitting British merchantmen to join American convoys between the United States and Iceland. Such an order would of course sharply increase the chances of an armed clash with Germany.

Despite his pledge to the British, Roosevelt found it difficult to issue the convoy order, lest he touch off an isolationist reaction. Then came the *Greer* episode.

The *Greer* Affair

An old "four-stacker," the destroyer U.S.S. *Greer* was carrying passengers and mail to Iceland on September 4, 1941, when it made contact with a German submarine. A radio message summoned a British plane which dropped bombs and depth charges. The U-boat commander turned on the *Greer* and ordered the firing of two torpedoes, both of which missed. The *Greer* answered with depth charges, which also were off target. Then it broke contact and steamed on to Iceland.

The *Greer* affair was Roosevelt's opportunity, and a few evenings later he delivered a radio address that was beamed across the world. Declining to mention that the *Greer* had provoked the submarine, he announced: "I tell you the blunt fact that the German submarine fired first upon this American destroyer without warning, and with deliberate design to sink her." He declared that "when you see a rattlesnake poised to strike, you do not wait until he has struck before you crush him." Roosevelt then proclaimed that American ships and planes "will no longer wait until Axis submarines lurking under water, or Axis raiders on the surface of the sea, strike their deadly blow—first." They would shoot on sight. The President next turned to convoy escort. Explaining that the United States fleet had the duty of "maintaining the American policy of freedom of the seas," he said that American ships and planes "will protect all merchant ships—not only American ships but ships of any flag—engaged in commerce in our defensive waters."

Having taken the country to the edge of war with Germany, Roosevelt in the next few weeks fixed his attention on the Neutrality Act. He asked Congress to repeal "crippling provisions" that prohibited the arming of American merchantmen and prevented American ships from entering "danger zones." Seeing them as steps to war, isolationists recoiled at such proposals.

Then came news on October 17 that German torpedoes had hit the destroyer U.S.S. *Kearny,* killing eleven American seamen. (The *Kearny* had projected itself into a battle between British and German vessels.) Infuriated, the House of Representatives voted to abolish the prohibition on arming merchant ships.

Two weeks after the *Kearny* affair a German U-boat sank the U.S.S. *Reuben James,* on convoy duty near Iceland. More than a hundred seamen went down with the vessel, the first American warship lost in World War II. The next week the congressional debate over revision of the Neutrality Act came to a climax. While the closeness of the vote proved that the isolationist spirit was still strong, the Senate on November 7 voted 50-37 for repeal of remaining restrictions. Six days later, by a vote of 212-194, the House did likewise.

The United States had in truth declared naval war on the Germans, and any knowledgeable person could see that total war would not be far behind. As Senator Wheeler said: "You cannot shoot your way a little bit into war any more than you can go a little bit over Niagara Falls." But before a break could come with Germany the United States entered the war via the "back door"—the Pacific.

STUDY GUIDE: After Hitler invaded Poland, Britain and France declared war on Germany. Most Americans still wanted to remain neutral. Over isolationist objections, Roosevelt influenced Congress to repeal the arms embargo in order to provide military aid to the Allies. By 1940 Hitler's armies occupied Scandinavia, the Low Countries, and France. Hitler's "Axis" alliance with Italy was broadened to include Japan.

With Britain standing alone against the Axis powers, Prime Minister Winston Churchill turned to the United States for help. Roosevelt arranged for the transfer of surplus war materials and destroyers to Britain. Congress passed a Lend-Lease Bill authorizing the loan of war equipment to the Allied nations. With each step the United States departed further from its position of neutrality.

After Hitler invaded North Africa, the Balkans, and the Soviet Union, Churchill met with Roosevelt at the Atlantic Conference to discuss the problem of defeating Germany. Out of the conference came the Atlantic Charter. This charter promised to build a peaceful world after nazism was destroyed. German submarine activity brought the United States closer to war with Germany.

DAY OF INFAMY

The situation in Asia became more ominous in spring 1940 when Hitler ended the Phony War and sent his armies westward into the Low Countries and France. Fighting for their lives in Europe, the British, French, and Dutch were in no position to protect colonies in Southeast Asia—Burma, Malaya, Indo-China, the Dutch East Indies.

For the Japanese here was an opportunity too good to let pass. The result in summer 1940 was pressure on the British, French, and Dutch to grant Japan special privileges in their Asian territories. A special target was French Indo-China, where the Japanese demanded the right to station troops and build airfields, allegedly to facilitate the war against the Chinese. The French government at Vichy—located in the part of France which Hitler had left unoccupied—toyed with the idea of resisting the Japanese. Then they gave way to reality, and in September 1940 opened the northern part of the colony to Japanese forces.

Later that same month the Japanese strengthened their position in East Asia by joining the Axis alliance with Germany and Italy. Japan was to have supremacy in the Far East, Germany and Italy were to be supreme in Europe, and each pledged to support any of the others that came under attack.

In response to these Japanese moves, the government in Washington proclaimed an embargo on shipment of scrap metal to Japan in autumn 1940. Later that year Roosevelt widened the embargo to include such commodities as iron ore and steel. At the same time he arranged a loan to Chiang Kai-shek and promised the Chinese fifty modern fighter planes.

The Japanese early in 1941 sent a new ambassador to Washington, Admiral Kichisaburo Nomura, considered a friend of the United States. For the next nine months Nomura conferred regularly with Secretary of State Hull, but the talks got nowhere. In his memoirs Hull recalled that conversations with Nomura always seemed "to come to a certain point and then start going around and around in the same circle." The problem was simple. Nomura could not pledge that Japan would discontinue its empire-building. Hull could not pledge that the United States would stand by while the Japanese swallowed East Asia.

Fearing that their old enemy Russia might take advantage of their distraction in Southeast Asia to threaten the northern flank of their empire, the Japanese were making overtures to Moscow, looking to a nonagression pact. The Russians suspected that Hitler was about to scrap the Nazi-Soviet treaty of 1939 and send his armies into the Soviet Union. To cope with the Germans they would need all the strength they could muster. Hence a neutrality agreement with Japan, securing their eastern frontier, had great appeal to leaders in Moscow. The result was a Soviet-Japanese nonaggression pact, signed in spring 1941.

It came as a surprise in Tokyo when the Germans two months later invaded the Soviet Union. Although the Axis alliance was defensive, meaning that Japan was under no obligation to help Germany, some Japanese nonetheless wanted to discard the recent nonaggression pact with Russia and rally to the support of the Nazis. Most Japanese leaders saw the situation differently. In their view, a war against the Russians in Siberia would yield little profit. It would be better, they concluded, to keep up the pressure in Southeast Asia, a treasure house of rice, rubber, tin, oil, bauxite, and manganese. In line with such thinking, the government in Tokyo ordered Japanese forces to occupy the southern part of Indo-China in July 1941.

Response to Japanese Aggression

American cryptanalysts having broken Japan's secret diplomatic code, leaders in Washington knew what the Japanese were planning and had time to prepare a response. Thus when Japanese transports entered the harbor at Saigon in Indo-China, the president issued an order "freezing" Japanese assets in the United States. This meant that only a license issued from Washington would release "frozen" Japanese dollars to pay for transactions in the United States. If the Japanese went forward with plans in Southeast Asia, the president could retaliate by refusing licenses. Should he choose, he could in this way stop all commerce between the United States and Japan.

Since the Japanese economy depended on trade with America—and since American oil was the lifeblood of the Japanese military machine—Roosevelt calculated that the threat of an economic boycott might persuade leaders in Tokyo to second thoughts about their adventure in Southeast Asia. Of course it could also drive them to war with the United States.

The Japanese went on with the business of consolidating their position in Indo-China, and over the next few weeks Roosevelt stopped nearly all trade between the United States and Japan. The British and Dutch joined the boycott, making Japan's economic isolation almost complete.

The freezing order and subsequent embargo came as a shock to leaders in Tokyo. They had expected some response from Washington to the move in Indo-China—perhaps a new moral pronouncement about aggression, maybe even the addition of a few items to the existing embargo list. But nothing so severe as this. As Roosevelt had anticipated, the embargo placed a severe strain on the Japanese economy. Particularly serious was stoppage of the flow of oil, for Japanese oil reserves could meet domestic and military needs for little more than a year. Contrary to Roosevelt's hope, however, the embargo did not cause Japanese leaders to draw back. Instead they increased their pressure on Southeast Asia, especially the oil-rich Netherlands Indies.

Hoping that the United States might lift its economic sanctions and at the same time accept Japan's "new order" in East Asia, the Tokyo government, meanwhile, tried diplomacy. The prime minister, Prince Fumimaro Konoye, tried in August and September 1941 to arrange a meeting with President Roosevelt somewhere in the Pacific. Certain that Japan's militarists would not permit any substantial concessions, Roosevelt rejected the idea.

Japanese Strategy

Japanese military chieftains were convinced by early September that war was the only solution to Japan's problems with the United States. Taking their view to the emperor, they compared Japan with a patient suffering a critical illness. Drastic surgery might bring death, but it offered the only chance of saving the patient's life. The emperor still hoped for peace, and the military men agreed to give the diplomats a few more weeks to work out a settlement.

Japanese generals and admirals nonetheless went ahead with preparations for war. They calculated that the chief obstacles to their plans in Southeast Asia were the American B-17 bombers in the Philippines and British ships and planes at Singapore. To destroy the B-17s Japanese aircraft based on Formosa would make a surprise attack and catch the "flying fortresses" on the ground. As for Singapore, the Japanese needed to capture the base. But that presented no great difficulty. Since the big guns at the installation pointed out to sea, Japanese soldiers would land far up the Malay peninsula and attack from the rear.

Conquering Southeast Asia was one thing, defending it, another. A first step would be to knock out the American Pacific Fleet based in Hawaii. Since American attention would be fixed on Japanese maneuvers in Southeast Asia, the fleet ought to be an easy target for a surprise air attack launched from carriers. With the American fleet destroyed and out of action, the Japanese would entrench themselves in the Marianas, Carolines, Gilberts, Marshalls, Bismarcks, Solomons, and Philippines. Thus they would establish a defensive perimeter stretching from the Kuriles through the Central Pacific and eastward to the gates of India. Bristling with guns, ships, and planes, the perimeter would be impregnable. Eventually the Americans, also struggling against Hitler, would grow weary of the struggle in the Pacific and accept a settlement recognizing Japanese dominance in East Asia.

While Japanese militarists pored over maps and charts, Japanese diplomats continued to seek a peaceful settlement. They found that in return for lifting the trade embargo the United States demanded pledges of an early Japanese withdrawal from China and Southeast Asia. The Japanese countered that they could consider such a withdrawal only after "satisfactory" conclusion of the "China incident" (the expression which the Japanese used when referring to the war in China). To that end the Japanese insisted that the United States force Chiang Kai-shek to accept Tokyo's terms for ending the "incident"—terms that would make China a Japanese vassal. American leaders were in no mood for such one-sided bargains.

Japan Prepares for War

It was clear by mid-October 1941 that the Americans would not yield to diplomacy, so the militarists of Japan set their plans in motion. At the same time Prime Minister Konoye's cabinet resigned and General Hideki Tojo replaced Konoye. Three weeks later Tojo and his militant associates held a five-hour meeting with the emperor. Out of respect for the emperor's continuing hope for peace, they agreed to play the diplomatic game a while longer. But if the Americans did not give way by November 25, the cabinet would ask the emperor's permission for war. Sure that the Americans would stand firm, the Japanese militants scheduled the stroke against the United States for December 8, Tokyo time.

While the diplomatic game continued, Japanese warships returned to home ports. Stevedores loaded most of the ships with equipment for tropical operations, but thirty-three vessels— carriers, battleships, cruisers, destroyers, and tankers—took on winter gear. On November 18 the thirty-three ships, one by one, moved out of their ports, steamed far out to sea, then swung northward toward the Kurile Islands. At Tankan Bay in the Kuriles shivering seamen loaded the ships with fuel and supplies. By November 26 everything was set and the task force slipped into the icy waters of the North Pacific, destination, Pearl Harbor.

Thanks to "Magic," a decoding device, leaders in Washington knew of the November 25 deadline. When there was no settlement by that date, they knew that the Japanese would soon strike in Southeast Asia. But they did not know that American bases in Hawaii and the Philippines would be the objects of the Japanese attack. They reasoned that it was more likely the Japanese would aim their first blow at the British and Dutch outposts in the southeastern part of Asia.

Sure that the chance of settlement had passed, Secretary Hull nonetheless decided to make a final offer, if for no other reason than to prove to history that the United States had "gone the last mile" in the search for peace. On November 27 he handed Japanese envoys a "ten-point" proposal which restated principles that the Japanese had rejected many times in the past. It was certain to draw a rejection. That same day a "final alert" went to commanders in the Pacific. The message to Admiral Husband E. Kimmel at Pearl Harbor said: "This dispatch is to be considered a war warning. Negotiations with Japan looking toward stabilization of conditions in the Pacific have ceased and an aggressive move by Japan is expected within the next few days."

"Climb Mount Niitaka"

Maintaining radio silence, using high-grade fuel to keep smoke to a minimum, and throwing nothing overboard, the Pearl Harbor striking force steamed on undetected. Then on December 1 Japanese leaders went before the emperor and submitted their decision for war. To strengthen their case they explained that Germany and Italy, although not bound by the Axis alliance to help Japan if it attacked another power, had promised to follow Japan to war with the United States. The emperor said nothing, but silence in such matters amounted to approval. That same day a message went out to the task force: "Climb Mount Niitaka." This was the signal to proceed with the raid on Hawaii.

In Washington the first days of December passed quietly as leaders of the United States waited for the Japanese to strike. "Magic" having given no hint of a Pearl Harbor raid, the attention of America's leaders was fixed on the western Pacific and Southeast Asia. A Japanese task force was moving around the tip of Indo-China into the Gulf of Siam, indicating an assault on Malaya or Siam. Large Japanese troop concentrations in Formosa and the Carolines suggested an attack on the Netherlands Indies or perhaps the Philippines. American leaders reasoned that the Japanese probably would not hit the Philippines, on the chance that Congress might not declare war if United States territory was not attacked. Indeed the central question pressing on President Roosevelt in those days was whether the country would rally to war against Japan if American bases did not come under attack.

Out in the Pacific the task force under Admiral Chuichi Nagumo steamed on, passing nine hundred miles north of Midway on December 3. A few hours later the Japanese fleet veered to the southeast. Then on December 6 final preparations were made for the strike at Hawaii. On that day ship captains summoned all men to the top decks and explained the mission. There were speeches and cheers. Some seamen wept. Up the mast of the flagship *Akagi* went the flag that had flown over the Japanese flagship during destruction of the Russian fleet in the Tsushima Strait in 1905. Nagumo now gave the order for full speed ahead. Radio operators anxiously monitored Honolulu's commercial stations for any sign that the Americans had been alerted.

That evening in Washington, "Magic" decoded the first thirteen parts of Japan's fourteen-part reply to Hull's "ten-point" proposal of November 27. Reading the message, President Roosevelt said: "This means war."

Next morning, December 7, 1941, the president received the fourteenth part of the Japanese note. It announced that because of "the attitudes of the American government" there was no chance of a negotiated settlement of differences.

Later that morning "Magic" decoded another message. Marked "Urgent—Very Important," it directed Nomura to submit Japan's reply to the "ten-point" proposal promptly at one o'clock that afternoon. Perhaps something was going to break in the Pacific at that hour. There was some delay in getting this latest bit of intelligence to the army's chief of staff, General George C. Marshall, who was on his usual Sunday-morning horseback ride. But when he read the intercept Marshall decided on a new alert to San Francisco, the Canal Zone, Hawaii, and the Philippines. Radio operators quickly got through to San Francisco, the Canal Zone, and the Philippines, but there was no response from Hawaii. Unaware of the urgency of Marshall's message, the signal officer in charge of the army's message center then sent the warning to Hawaii by Western Union.

Pearl Harbor Attacked

It was near dawn in the mid-Pacific. Aboard the Japanese task force there was frenzied activity. Airplane engines were screaming, mechanics were making last-minute adjustments. At 6:00 A.M. the carriers nosed into the wind, and a few moments later the first planes roared down flight decks. Pearl Harbor lay 230 miles to the south and slightly west.

At 7:55 A.M. the Japanese planes droned over Pearl Harbor. There was no antiaircraft fire. No interceptor planes took to the air. The American Pacific Fleet was spread out below as if it were on parade. A few moments later a young Hawaiian of Japanese origin, riding a motorcycle, heard explosions from the direction of Pearl Harbor. Headed toward the army base, he carried in his pouch the communication dispatched two hours earlier by General Marshall.

As news poured into the United States from the Pacific, people were thunderstruck. So fixed were most Americans on the war in Europe that they were only vaguely aware that matters had come to a crisis with the Japanese. They were even more shocked when they learned the extent of the disaster, the most terrible in the annals

of the American army and navy: six battleships destroyed or disabled, many lesser vessels sunk, most planes at the army's air base immobilized, nearly three thousand Americans killed.

Then came more bad news. Seven hours after the Pearl Harbor raid the Japanese had attacked the Philippines — and their planes had wiped out the squadron of B-17s.

Declaration of War

At noon the following day, December 8, 1941, President Roosevelt, dressed in formal morning attire and accompanied by his son James, went to the Capitol. At 12:30 P.M. he entered the chamber of the House of Representatives, where senators, representatives, members of the cabinet and Supreme Court, diplomats, and other dignitaries were assembled. A tremendous ovation greeted the president, and across the

The American naval base at Pearl Harbor in Hawaii was the target of a surprise Japanese air attack on December 7, 1941. It was the greatest disaster in American naval history. Shown here is the U.S.S. *Shaw* burning in Pearl Harbor. Could better preparedness by the United States have prevented this disaster?

nation there was a hush as millions of Americans gathered around radios to hear his words.

Alone at the rostrum, Roosevelt opened a black notebook, then began: "Yesterday, December 7, 1941 — a date which will live in infamy — the United States was suddenly and deliberately attacked by naval and air forces of the empire of Japan." Less than a half hour later the Senate unanimously voted for war. The House a few minutes later did likewise, although there was one dissenting vote, that of Jeannette Rankin of Montana, a lifelong pacifist who had also voted against war in 1917. A few hours later at the White House the president, now in a

Wearing a black armband in mourning for the American dead at Pearl Harbor and the Philippines, F.D.R. signs the declaration of war against Japan on December 8, 1941. Were Americans more united in supporting this declaration of war than they had been at the beginning of World War I?

Courtesy Franklin D. Roosevelt Library, Hyde Park, N.Y.

business suit, a mourning band around his left arm for the dead at Pearl Harbor and the Philippines, signed the war resolution.

Four days later Germany and Italy honored their commitment to Japan and declared war on the United States, whereupon the American government recognized a state of war with those countries.

STUDY GUIDE: Continued Japanese aggression in Asia led the United States to place an embargo on shipment of metals to Japan. When the Japanese moved to occupy Indo-China, President Roosevelt stopped nearly all trade with Japan, as did Britain and Holland.

This new embargo included oil which Japan needed desperately to run its huge war machine. Japanese assets in America were also frozen. Japanese military leaders urged war with the United States although diplomats continued to seek a peaceful settlement, even up until the attack on Pearl Harbor. It soon became clear that the United States would never yield to Japanese territorial ambitions in Asia. In December 1941 the Japanese launched an air attack against the American naval base at Pearl Harbor in Hawaii. The United States promptly declared war on Japan. Germany and Italy, Japan's allies, then declared war on the United States.

SUMMING UP THE CHAPTER

Names and Terms to Identify

Four-Power Treaty
Nine-Power Treaty
Five-Power Treaty
Henry L. Stimson
World Court
Aristide Briand
Frank B. Kellogg
Charles G. Dawes
Young Plan
Mukden Incident

lebensraum
Nye Committee
Francisco Franco
U.S.S. *Panay*
Montevideo Conference
Wendell L. Willkie
Atlantic Charter
U.S.S. *Kearny*
Pearl Harbor
Jeannette Rankin

Study Questions and Points to Review

1. What was the purpose of the Permanent Court of International Justice?

2. Why did the United States lack enthusiasm about Briand's proposal?

3. What was the weakness of the Kellogg-Briand Pact?

4. What was the Dawes Plan?

5. What incident did the Japanese use as an attempt to justify conquest of Manchuria?

6. Why have many historians criticized Stimson's policy?

7. What were the provisions of the Neutrality Act of 1935?

8. The outbreak of "international lawlessness" in what part of the world prompted Franklin Roosevelt to deliver his "quarantine" speech?

9. For what reason did the United States maintain a naval squadron on the Yangtze River in China?

10. What document, drawn up in 1929, seemed to repudiate the Roosevelt Corollary to the Monroe Doctrine?

11. When did the United States cancel the Platt Amendment?

12. What action did Franklin Roosevelt take as a result of the attacks on Poland?

13. What three nations were involved in the Tripartite Pact?

14. When he sought to aid Britain in 1940 how did Roosevelt try to get around the international law which prohibits a neutral government from providing arms to a belligerent?

15. What two consequences did Roosevelt have to consider when he was contemplating transferring destroyers to Britain in 1940? What was his decision?

16. What was the main political issue at the beginning of the presidential campaign of 1940?

17. What was the purpose of Roosevelt's "neutrality patrol"?

18. When did the United States declare war on Japan?

Topics for Discussion

1. Why did the people of the United States turn away from world responsibilities and turn toward isolationism in the 1920s and 1930s?

2. What were the achievements of the Washington Conference of 1921-22? Do you consider the conference a milestone in American diplomatic history?

3. Consider the post-World War I war debt-reparations problem. Do you think the United States should have agreed to cancellation of the war debts? If so, on what terms? Explain your answer.

4. Trace the origins of the Pact of Paris or Kellogg-Briand Pact. Give your evaluation of the pact.

5. Discuss the American response to the Manchurian crisis of 1931-33. What is your opinion of the Stimson Doctrine?

6. Explain and evaluate United States policy toward the Spanish Civil War.

7. Describe America's response to the outbreak of hostilities in China in 1937. To the "quarantine" speech. To the *Panay* incident. What do these responses tell you about the views of most Americans toward foreign affairs in 1937?

8. Evaluate American relations with Japan in 1940-41.

Subjects for Reports or Essays

1. Write an essay setting forth your ideas on why the United States did or did not take the best stand with regard to the war-debt question. If you think American policy was misguided, explain what in your view the policy should have been.

2. After reading further on the subject, write an essay evaluating United States policy toward the Spanish Civil War.

3. What do you think of the 1930s isolationist argument that war in Europe and Asia did not concern the United States? What do you think would have been the consequences of an Axis victory in Europe and the Far East? Would such a victory have done serious harm to American interests? As things turned out, do you think it might have been better for the United States to have kept free of the war, even at risk of an Axis victory? Set forth your ideas in an essay.

4. A criticism of Roosevelt's policy before Pearl Harbor is that he left initiative with the Axis powers, that he should have worked to take the United States into war many months before Pearl Harbor (see Stimson's memoirs). What do you think are the strongest arguments for and against such criticism? State your views in an essay.

5. In the library, examine available books on the subject of the Pearl Harbor attack. Why do you think Pearl Harbor was asleep on December 7, 1941? Give your answer in a brief essay.

Projects, Activities, and Skills

1. Assume it is summer 1922 and you are a newspaper editor. Write an editorial commenting on the Washington Conference and its treaties.

2. Take a poll of members of your family, teachers, and friends. Ask them to explain the meaning of the Good Neighbor policy. Ask them how the United States manifested its good neighborliness. Ask for an evaluation of the policy. Report your findings.

3. Using Atlas Map 21 locate Mukden, Manchuria, and the site of the *Panay* incident in China. Prepare a brief report for class presentation on each of these incidents.

4. As a class project prepare a display on Pearl Harbor. On a map of the Pacific trace the route of the Japanese task force. On a map of Oahu show the disposition of ships at Pearl Harbor, the locations of other installations, the route of the Japanese planes in making the attack. Use illustrations and models of ships and planes involved in the attack, and photographs of individuals such as Yamamoto, Nagumo and Kimmel. Show one of the film documentaries of the raid that are available. Play a recording of President Roosevelt's "Day of Infamy" speech.

Further Readings

General

America First: The Battle Against Intervention, 1940-41 by Wayne S. Cole. A good study of the antiwar movement in the last years before Pearl Harbor.

American Diplomacy, 1900-1950 by George F. Kennan. A small masterpiece by a historian and diplomat.

Back Door to War by Charles C. Tansill. Argues that Roosevelt maneuvered the U.S. into war.

The Challenge to Isolation: The World Crisis of 1937-40 and *American Foreign Policy* (2 vols.) by William L. Langer and Everett S. Gleason. This is the outstanding study of American foreign relations from the time of the *Panay* affair to Pearl Harbor.

Day of Infamy by Walter Lord. A thrilling account of the raid on Pearl Harbor.

The End of Glory: An Interpretation of the Origins of World War II by Laurence Lafore.

The Reluctant Belligerent: American Entry into the Second World War by Robert A. Divine. Surveys American policy from 1933 to Pearl Harbor and is particularly good for the period 1939-41.

This is Pearl! by Walter Millis. This is one of the first—and one of the most readable—books on the coming of the Japanese-American war.

The United States and the Far Eastern Crisis of 1933-1938 by Dorothy Borg. Covers America's relations with Japan in the mid-1930s.

Biography

Hitler: A Study in Tyranny by Alan Bullock. An excellent book on Hitler's rise to power.

President Roosevelt and the Coming of the War, 1941: A Study in Appearances and Realities by Charles A. Beard.

Turmoil and Tradition: A Study of the Life and Times of Henry L. Stimson by Elting E. Morison.

Fiction, Drama, and Poetry

Dunkirk by Robert Nathan. A ballad about the evacuation of Dunkirk in the summer of 1940.

I Forgot for a Moment by Edna St. Vincent Millay. Writing in July of 1940, the poet recalls prewar Europe.

The Moon is Down by John Steinbeck. A novel set in a German-occupied country early in the war.

There Shall Be No Night by Robert E. Sherwood. A prize-winning play about a Finnish doctor at the outset of the war.

Watch on the Rhine by Lillian Hellman. A play about a refugee from Hitler's tyranny who alerts Americans to the dangers of Nazism.

More than eight million Americans served in World War II. Those who returned home safely found many uncertainties facing them in the years that followed. The major issues were unemployment, the uses of atomic energy, civil rights, and the cold war. ▶

Wide World

WORLD WAR II AND THE AFTERMATH

CHAPTER 17

WORLD WAR II

FOR THE SECOND TIME in a generation, the United States was at war in Europe. When the war started, most Americans, unaware of recent military technology, assumed it would fall into a pattern similar to that of World War I. They thought it would be a conflict in which the defense would have the upper hand, a war of artillery barrages and infantry charges carried on mainly by foot soldiers operating from trenches and underground fortifications.

But then startling news came from the battle zone. Adolf Hitler's *Panzer* divisions were clanking across the plains of Poland with astonishing ease and scattering the antiquated units of the Polish army like frightened sheep.

By mechanizing the battlefield the Germans introduced a new type of warfare. Their swift armored divisions, spearheaded by tanks and bound together by electronic communications, became the central striking force. Gasoline became as critical in military calculations as bullets and numbers of soldiers. And the infantry became secondary in importance to the armor.

In the first days of hostilities, people across the world gasped in horror as Hitler sent his *Stuka* dive-bombers shrieking down on Poland's capital city, Warsaw. Targets of the *Stukas* were houses, public buildings, streets, utilities, transit lines, and people. The purpose was to create panic and despair among the enemy's population.

World War II differed from previous wars in other respects. Most notable was the introduction of a range of new weapons and devices throughout the war. Earlier conflicts had seldom witnessed the appearance of new weapons after the first shellburst. Soldiers usually had returned to peacetime pursuits lugging the same guns and equipment with which they had entered battle.

A BATTLE OF THE DRAWING BOARDS

In World War II scientists and technicians in Allied and Axis countries waged a "battle of drawing boards." Fighting men continually employed and adapted to new weapons and techniques. There was radar, the device that helped the British Royal Air Force to win the battle of Britain against Hitler's *Luftwaffe* in 1939-40.

German scientists invented a magnetic marine mine and perfected the snorkel submarine. The British countered with new mine-sweeping devices and submarine detectors. American engineers meanwhile improved the navy's torpedoes, which were decidedly inferior to Japanese torpedoes at the start of the war, and developed the "jeep" aircraft carrier, a small carrier. This carrier proved invaluable during the stages of the war which took place in the Pacific.

At the same time other American technologists worked on a tank that would match tanks of Hitler's *Wehrmacht*. Before the war ended they brought forth the powerful Pershing and Patton tanks. American engineers also produced the B-29 Superfortress, which was unleashed on Japan, the P-47 Thunderbolt and P-51 Mustang fighter planes, which provided long-range cover for strategic bombers, and the proximity fuse, which would detonate an antiaircraft shell if it passed fairly close to a hostile plane.

Toward the end of the war the Germans introduced the deadly V-1 and V-2 rockets and a jet fighter plane. If perfected a few years sooner these weapons might have altered the course of the war. Then, in the summer of 1945, came the most important and fearsome scientific and technical achievement of the war—the atomic bomb.

In the years 1941-45 American scientists and engineers placed an impressive array of new weapons and equipment at the disposal of America's fighting men, but the United States was poorly prepared for war when the Japanese raided Pearl Harbor in December 1941. The war had broken out in Europe twenty-seven months before, in September 1939. After the fall of France in June 1940, America's leaders knew that sooner or later the United States was apt to become a belligerent. At the Atlantic Conference of August 1941, four months before Pearl Harbor, President Roosevelt and Prime Minister Churchill discussed the strategy that the United States and Great Britain would employ to defeat the Axis powers when—not if—America entered the war. Before Pearl Harbor, Americans had enlarged their army and navy, stepped up the output of war equipment, and enacted the first peacetime draft legislation in

HEADLINE EVENTS

1939 Physicists outline fear of nuclear weapons to Navy Department
Einstein writes to Roosevelt urging crash program to develop atomic weapon
Manhattan Project gets under way

1939-1940 Battle of Britain

1940 Fall of France

1941 Germans attack Soviet Union
Atlantic Conference
Japanese attack Pearl Harbor

1942 War Production Board begins operation
Japanese take Singapore and control Indonesia
Japanese-Americans removed to internment camps
Bataan death march
Wainwright surrenders at Corregidor
Battle of the Coral Sea
Battle of Midway
Assault on Guadalcanal begins
Operation Torch begins
British attack Rommel at El Alamein
Allies establish control of Guadalcanal
Scientists learn to control atomic chain reaction

1943 Casablanca Conference
Afrika Korps surrenders
Allies land in Sicily
Victor Emmanuel III has Mussolini imprisoned
Italy unconditionally quits the war
Allied troops land in Italy
Allies take Naples
Nazis seize Rome
Mid-Pacific drive gets underway
Marines land at Tarawa and other Gilbert Islands
Cairo Conference
Teheran Conference

1944 American Sixth Corps lands at Anzio
Marines and soldiers land on Kwajalein
Germans evacuate Monte Cassino
American troops enter Rome
Operation Overlord, invasion of Normandy
Germans begin using V-1 buzz bombs

Russians begin offensive; regain Minsk
Russians enter Poland
American forces land on Guam
Roosevelt, MacArthur, and Nimitz meet at Pearl Harbor
Sansapor, Morotai, Palau, Ulithi, and Ngulu taken; route to Philippines
Germans begin using V-2 rockets
Invasion of southern France
French reclaim Paris
Finland and Rumania agree to armistice
Russian troops enter Yugoslavia
Battle of Leyte Gulf
Americans enter Germany
Battle of the Bulge

1945 Allies land at Lingayen Gulf
Allies regain ground lost in Battle of the Bulge
Russians take Warsaw
Roosevelt inaugurated for fourth term
U.S. troops enter Manila
Anglo-Americans move toward Rhine
Yalta Conference
Marines land at Iwo Jima
Russians enter Danzig
Americans invade Okinawa
Nazi death camps discovered
Battle of Berlin
Roosevelt dies; Truman assumes the presidency
San Francisco Conference; Charter for UN written
Americans and Russians meet at Elbe
Mussolini shot by Italian partisans
Hitler commits suicide in Berlin
Germany surrenders unconditionally
Okinawa falls to Allies
Potsdam Conference
First test of nuclear weapons at Alamagordo, New Mexico
Atomic bomb dropped on Hiroshima
Russia declares war on Japan
Atomic bomb dropped on Nagasaki
Japan surrenders unconditionally
Dumbarton Oaks Conference

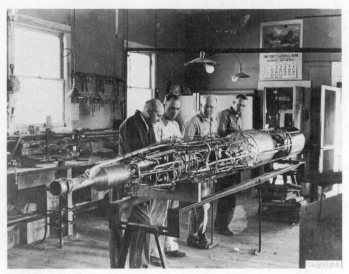

Photo by Anthony Stewart, © National Geographic Society,
Courtesy Esther C. Goddard

Dr. Robert Goddard (left) inspects the fuel pumps on one of his 1940 test rockets. Goddard is called the father of modern rocketry. His tests laid the groundwork for intercontinental missiles, satellites, and manned space flights.

their history. But mobilization efforts before December 1941 seemed almost halfhearted. Production of consumer goods actually increased in summer 1941.

STUDY GUIDE: In World War II scientists of Allied and Axis nations developed a variety of new weapons. The United States was not prepared in the early years of the war. However, by 1945 a powerful war machine had been built up in America. The Germans introduced rockets and a jet fighter plane toward the end of the war. In 1945 the first atomic bombs were dropped by American bombers on Japanese cities. The atomic bomb helped bring World War II to a sudden end.

WARTIME STRATEGY

Several years before the raid on Pearl Harbor, American leaders began pondering the possibility that the United States might become engaged in war with Germany and Japan at the same time. They concluded that in the event of a two-theater war the United States should concentrate on one enemy at a time.

Which enemy? Almost automatically they settled on Germany. They feared that if given enough time German science and technology might produce weapons of devastating power.

Germany would be a much more dangerous enemy than Japan. Coupled with respect for German technology was a false notion that the Japanese would use inferior materials and makeshift methods in putting together their war mechanism. This notion was created by the cheap toys and trinkets marked "made in Japan" which for years had flooded United States markets.

By the time of the Pearl Harbor assault, in December 1941, the Germans had already established themselves as masters of most of Europe and had pushed Russian armies to the gates of Moscow. If the Germans could consolidate the territories they had already conquered, force the Soviets to terms, and strangle the British, they would have such immense power that it would be impossible to defeat them. Hitler would achieve his dream of dominance in world affairs. In East Asia and the Western Pacific the Japanese had made great conquests. But they still had far to go before fulfilling their dream of "a new order" in that part of the world. Thus the time element seemed less critical in the Pacific than in Europe.

Anglo-American Plan for Defeating Germany

What should be the strategy for defeating Germany?

The British plan was to move deliberately, weakening Germany for a prolonged period before mounting a full-powered strike against Hitler's empire. The British wanted to impose a naval blockade around Axis territory, conduct bombing raids against strategic points inside Germany, and carry on a propaganda campaign coupled with support of resistance groups in German-occupied countries. British, American, and Canadian forces meanwhile would "close the ring" about Germany by striking and capturing key points on the perimeter of Axis territory. Finally, unless Hitler sought peace beforehand, the Anglo-Americans would launch a massive amphibious assault against the German *Reich*.

American military leaders viewed the British proposal for defeating Hitler as a strategy of weakness. They wanted to begin immediate preparations for a massive strike across the English Channel into Northern France. Most of them hoped to launch such an assault before the end of 1942 and at the latest in 1943. The British, however, refused to consider a cross-Channel movement for 1942 and held out little encouragement that they would support one in 1943. Without British cooperation a cross-Channel maneuver was out of the question.

The British refused to act hastily in getting Anglo-American forces ashore in France. Why? Because, for one thing, they remembered World War I, when more than nine hundred thousand British troops had perished, most of them in trenches and on battlegrounds in Belgium and France. In World War II every responsible British leader was determined to avoid a repetition of the horror of 1914-18. If possible they wanted to avoid a cross-Channel invasion altogether, hoping that tactics of "closing the ring" somehow might bring the Germans to defeat. Failing that, they were bent on delaying an invasion until Anglo-American forces were decidedly superior to those of their enemies.

The British argument for delaying a cross-Channel invasion went beyond the terrible memories of 1914-18. The British believed that if the Germans drove an Anglo-American invasion back into the sea, a wave of defeatism and despair would seize the people of Britain and America. This would prevent a second attempt. Therefore, everything should be done to guarantee the success of that invasion effort. Specifically, efforts should be made to weaken Germany before the invasion by blockading German ports, bombing German factories and communications, and harassing the German perimeter. Furthermore, the invasion should not be tried until the North Atlantic lifeline between America and Britain—still a target of German U-boats—had been secured. British leaders also wanted to delay an invasion until the United States had trained enough qualified soldiers and American factories and shipyards had produced enough equipment. British leaders wanted the sheer weight of the invasion force to be so immense that German defenses on the beaches of France could not withstand it.

STUDY GUIDE: Hitler's conquest of much of Western Europe convinced American military strategists of the necessity to defeat Germany before taking on Japan. British military leaders favored a plan of weakening Germany by using blockades and bombing raids before launching a cross-Channel invasion. The Americans favored an immediate invasion of the European continent, but they could not proceed without British cooperation.

WAR IN EUROPE

Unable to move without British cooperation, American military men put aside thoughts of an invasion in 1942. Still it seemed unwise to do nothing more than launch bombing raids from England and poke around the perimeter of the Axis empire. A failure to engage German ground forces in serious combat might weaken the British and American will to fight and lend support to German propaganda claims that the Anglo-Americans were "paper tigers."

A more important consideration was the USSR. Hitler, frustrated in his attempts to defeat Great Britain, had invaded the Soviet Union in June 1941, hoping to take its rich agricultural and mineral resources. Three million men strong, Hitler's armies operated on a front that stretched from the Baltic to the Black Sea. Spearheaded by tanks, the Germans moved forward in the summer and autumn of 1941 with astonishing speed. One by one, important Soviet cities such as Minsk, Kiev, Smolensk, Orel, and Odessa had fallen. By the end of November 1941 the Germans were only a few miles from Moscow. Marking the path of the Nazi conquest were ruins of hundreds of burned-out villages and towns, a ravaged countryside, and the bones of hundreds of thousands of Russian soldiers and civilians.

German losses were heavy—more than twenty percent of the army had been killed, wounded, or captured by the end of November. On the day before Japan's raid on Pearl Harbor, Soviet armies near Moscow, led by Marshal Georgi K. Zhukov, mounted a counterattack that threw the Germans back several miles and punctured the myth of German invincibility. But the Soviets at the start of 1942 still remained in grave jeopardy. They were clamoring for Britain and the United States to do something in the western part of the European theater to ease German pressure on the eastern front. The Soviet clamor increased in spring and summer 1942 when the Germans organized a new offensive that humiliated the Russians at Kharkov, completed the conquest of the Crimea by taking Sebastopol, and sent armies rushing toward the great industrial center on the Volga, Stalingrad.

The Invasion of North Africa

The Americans in particular were anxious to respond to Soviet appeals. (The British were inclined to be somewhat less sympathetic than were the Americans to the plight of the Russians. They recalled that Stalin's deal with Hitler in August 1939 had helped bring on the war in the first place and that the Soviets had done nothing for them when they alone faced Hitler.) And both American and British leaders were anxious to avoid the charge that they were carrying on a phony war.

The outcome was Operation Torch, the Anglo-American amphibious landings in Morocco and Algeria in North Africa in November 1942.

Operation Torch—the brainchild of Prime Minister Churchill—would help "close the ring" around the Axis empire. According to Churchill's plan, Allied armies would advance eastward from Morocco and Algeria and westward from Egypt. Caught between the converging Allied armies, hopefully, would be the celebrated *Afrika Korps* of the German "Desert Fox," Field Marshal Erwin Rommel.

Directed by a comparatively unknown lieutenant general, Dwight D. Eisenhower, Torch was no easy venture. There was danger that German submarines prowling the Atlantic and Mediterranean might attack the task force ferrying men and equipment to the beaches of Morocco and Algeria. General Francisco Franco of Spain, presumably an ally of Hitler, might also close the Gibraltar strait. Of even greater concern to Anglo-American leaders was the possibility that French forces in North Africa—under orders of the Vichy regime in unoccupied France—might resist the Anglo-American landings.

Fortunately the submarine threat failed to materialize, and Spain elected to do nothing rash at Gibraltar. The French offered scattered resistance, but the second man in the Vichy regime, Admiral Jean Darlan, happened to be in Algiers when the invading force appeared. And Darlan, promised by the Allies that he would become the political chief of North Africa, directed French forces to hold their fire. As a result, very little Anglo-American blood was shed on the landing beaches of Morocco and Algeria.

In October 1942, a few weeks before the landings in Morocco and Algeria, the British Eighth Army commanded by Lieutenant General Bernard L. Montgomery, struck German and Italian forces under Rommel at El Alamein in Egypt. Heavily outgunned, the "Desert Fox" soon was falling back. Over the next eighty days he directed one of the longest retreats in the history of warfare—1,750 miles, or roughly the distance from Moscow to Paris. At length, in Tunisia, Rommel clashed with Allied armies advancing eastward from Algeria.

The Americans had their first serious taste of combat in North Africa in February 1943 when Rommel hurled his armor at the American Second Corps. Still inexperienced in battle, the Americans reeled for a few days. Then, led by two men who would emerge from the war as two of America's most renowned commanders—Major General George S. Patton, Jr., and Brigadier General Omar N. Bradley—the GIs caught their balance and quickly learned the arts of camouflage and digging in. In less than two weeks they recovered lost ground and were pushing Rommel's soldiers back.

In early spring 1943 the great Allied pincers closed in North Africa. The armies under Eisenhower which had advanced eastward from Algeria linked up with Montgomery's Eighth Army which had chased Rommel all the way across the desert from Egypt. The "Desert Fox" was now bottled up against the sea in northern Tunisia. Furious at the turn of events in North Africa, Hitler made no attempt to evacuate the *Afrika Korps*. Instead, after ordering Rommel back to Germany, he stood by in May 1943 while 275,000 capable German and Italian soldiers surrendered.

The success in North Africa was only one of three major triumphs by the Allied powers in early 1943. In the Western Pacific marines and soldiers of the United States, after six months of brutal jungle fighting, breached the Japanese defensive perimeter by clearing the emperor's forces from the island of Guadalcanal. More important, the Soviets defeated a German army at Stalingrad.

Battle of Stalingrad

The first German blows against Stalingrad came from the air, in the summer of 1942, when the *Luftwaffe* rained hundreds of thousands of bombs on the city. In August the German Sixth Army, reinforced by unenthusiastic divisions of Hungarians, Rumanians, and Italians, reached Stalingrad and quickly surrounded the city except for the Volga waterfront. Next the Sixth Army moved inside the city. Nourished by a thin supply line of boats and barges that moved back and forth across the Volga in the face of continual assaults by German artillery and aircraft, the Russians put up heroic resistance. Still, because they had superiority in firepower, the Germans relentlessly pushed the Russians back. By the end of September, German forces were in control of the southern and central sections of Stalingrad.

Then, suddenly, in late November 1942, the tide of battle turned. Following a carefully concealed buildup of forces, the Soviets unleashed a two-pronged counteroffensive from points northwest and south of Stalingrad. On both fronts the Soviets toppled German and Rumanian divisions which had been guarding the flanks of the Sixth Army inside the city. After four days the two Soviet columns joined together fifty miles west of Stalingrad. The German Sixth Army was encircled. Finally, on January 31, 1943, German forces in Stalingrad surrendered. Hitler's great dream of subduing Russia had turned to ashes.

Submarine Warfare

While the North African campaign was moving to a climax, in the spring of 1943, the Anglo-Americans had begun to get the upper hand in their war in the Atlantic against German submarines. Operating in wolf packs, which enabled them to break through the defenses of convoys, new and improved U-boats over the winter of 1942-43 had taken a heavy toll of Allied shipping.

Then, in spring 1943, the Anglo-Americans, using new detection devices, long-range bombing planes, and escort aircraft carriers, stepped up the war against submarines. In the period May-December 1943 they sank 186 U-boats. Allied shipping losses dwindled as a consequence, and the path was cleared for assembling a giant amphibious force in the south of England to make a cross-Channel strike into France.

The Italian Campaign

To divert German divisions from the Russian front and avoid the phony war charge, Anglo-American leaders meanwhile planned an invasion of the large Mediterranean island of Sicily. In July 1943 the American Seventh Army under Patton and the British Eighth Army under Montgomery landed on five beaches along the southern coast of Sicily. Caught off guard, German and Italian defenders quickly retreated to the northern half of the island. After five weeks of fighting little more than a delaying action the Axis abandoned Sicily to the Allies.

The action in Sicily—clearly a prelude to an Allied assault on the Italian peninsula—con- vinced most Italians that fighting was useless. Whereupon King Victor Emmanuel III in late July 1943 stripped the dictator Mussolini of power and had him imprisoned. In early September 1943, after several weeks of haggling with the Allies over terms, the new Italian regime announced that Italy unconditionally had quit the war. The immediate effect of the Italian surrender, however, seemed slight, for during the preceding month the Germans had rushed reinforcements to Italy and had virtually taken over administration of the country. They also began making feverish preparations to resist the Allied invasion.

Meanwhile, in North Africa and Sicily, Allied forces under the overall command of Eisenhower assembled for the assault on Italy. The first Allied troops to land in Italy were elements of the British Fifth Army under Montgomery. On September 3, they passed unopposed from Sicily to the toe of the Italian boot. The main blow, however, fell a week later on September 9 when the American Fifth Army under Lieutenant General Mark W. Clark waded onto beaches near Salerno, fifty miles below Naples.

To achieve surprise the Allies had decided not to "soften up" the landing zone with a preliminary bombardment from the sea and air. However, the resourceful German commander in Italy, Field Marshal Albert Kesselring, anticipating an assault at Salerno, had prepared strong defenses with tanks, machine guns, mines, and barbed wire. Braving heavy casualties, the Americans refused to be pushed into the sea. At length, on October 1, men of the Fifth Army trudged wearily into Naples, which gave the Allies an excellent port and an air base.

Anglo-American armies now were entrenched along a line that stretched across Italy from the Volturno River on the Tyrrhenian Sea to Termoli on the Adriatic. All territory below that line was under Allied control. At that point the Allies might have ceased operations in Italy, for occupation of Sicily and the lower part of the Italian boot guaranteed their ability to control the Mediterranean and contain the Germans in that part of the European theater. But, urged on by Churchill, who had a peculiar fascination for operations against Europe's "soft underbelly," they elected to stay on the offensive in Italy.

The result was not altogether satisfactory. Occupying numerous mountain peaks, which gave them a clear view of the Allies, and assisted by rain, snow, and mud, which continually hampered Allied offensive maneuvers, Kesselring's

German armies over winter 1943-44 meted out heavy punishment and effectively stalled Allied advances.

To break the stalemate that had settled over the battle line north of Naples, the Allied high command decided to strike behind the German main line of resistance at Anzio, a resort center on the Tyrrhenian Sea south of Rome. Once established on the Anzio beachhead, Allied troops would strike inland and create such confusion that the Germans would be compelled to make a general retreat.

In January 1944 the American Sixth Corps went ashore at Anzio. Caught by surprise, the Germans reacted quickly. Soon the invaders were on the defensive, pinned down inside the Anzio beachhead and subjected to murderous artillery and machine-gun fire and aerial bombardment.

While the GIs at Anzio grimly held out, fighting continued north of Naples. By the spring of 1944 the action was centered around the ancient Benedictine monastery atop Monte Cassino, a mountain which dominated the main inland road from Naples to Rome. The German-occupied monastery was turned to rubble by Allied shells and bombs. In May, German resistance weakened and Allied soldiers captured what remained of the monastery, terminating one of the epic battles of World War II.

After seizing Monte Cassino, Allied forces pressed forward. The troops on Anzio finally broke through German defenses. On June 4, 1944, two days before the great cross-Channel invasion of France, American troops entered Rome and were greeted with unrestrained enthusiasm by the city's residents. It had taken eight months and hundreds of thousands of casualties to travel the one hundred miles from Naples to the Eternal City.

After taking Rome, the Allies continued the push up the Italian boot and were still pushing, at great expense, when the war in Europe finally ended in May 1945. The Italian campaign had engaged great numbers of Allied troops and huge quantities of equipment that might have been used to better advantage in Northern Europe.

Soviet Victories

In February 1943, the Soviets recaptured Kursk, Rostov, and Kharkov. Then in March 1943, the Germans recaptured Kharkov and began a major counteroffensive against Kursk. The German counteroffensive was launched in July 1943.

Before long the area around Kursk was a raging inferno. Few actions in World War II were so fierce. The Soviets held on to Kursk. Within three weeks they broke the German attack and retook all land captured by the Germans in the first stages of their offensive. A short time later the Soviets captured Orel, Kharkov, and Smolensk. In October 1943, Soviet soldiers forced their way across the Dnieper River and marched triumphantly into Kiev in November. At the same time other contingents of the Red Army attacked German forces besieging Leningrad.

Advancing German armies had cut off Leningrad—an important industrial center and port on the Gulf of Finland—from the rest of the country in August 1941. However, the Red Army garrison assigned to defend the city refused to surrender. The people of Leningrad were continually harassed by German shells and bombs. Although they were often without food, electricity, heat or water, they refused to yield. In early 1942 a thin supply line was established across Lake Ladoga, and in early 1943 a rail link was forged with the outer world. Still, the German siege continued. During the siege an estimated one million Leningraders died of starvation and disease resulting from exposure and malnutrition. Then in January 1944 the Red Army routed the Germans around Leningrad and ended one of the most agonizing and heroic chapters of World War II.

Next, in March 1944, the Soviets unleashed a massive spring offensive in the Ukraine, and in early April their armies crossed into Rumania. In May they recaptured Sebastopol and cleared the Germans from the Crimea. A week after the Americans entered Rome, the Soviets opened an offensive against Finland, which had thrown in with Germany.

Operation Overlord

Meanwhile, in 1943-44, the Americans and British, in the south of England, slowly assembled a giant force for the long-delayed invasion across the English Channel into Northern France. In command of the build-up was General Eisenhower, who had been shifted from the Mediterranean theater in late 1943. The British continued to look with apprehension on the cross-Channel project, code-named Operation Overlord. It was no use. Inasmuch as U-boats had been virtually cleared from the North Atlantic and American factories were producing incredible quantities of munitions and equip-

Many Nisei, Japanese-Americans, volunteered for duty in World War II. Here members of the 100th Infantry have captured some German storm troopers near Orciano, Italy, July 15, 1944. Why did the American government intern Japanese-Americans during the war?

U.S. Army Photograph

ment, British objections to an early invasion of the Continent were weakened. Once the target date for Overlord was set, however, the British — despite their misgivings — gave the operation unstinting support.

To prepare the way for the tanks and foot soldiers when the great Anglo-American force sailed across the Channel, bombing planes of the United States Army Air Force and Britain's Royal Air Force accelerated operations against Hitler's "Fortress Europe."

Early in the war the British had begun to send scattered bombing planes over German-held territory, mainly to harass the Germans and keep up their own spirits. In August 1940, two months after the fall of France, a squadron of RAF planes bombed Berlin with little effect. When Hitler attacked the Soviet Union in June 1941, he felt compelled to commit most of the *Luftwaffe* to the Eastern front, whereupon the British stepped up their bombing activities. The British attacked submarine pens, docks, power stations, railroads, bridges, and dams. Then, in the spring of 1942, putting as many as a thousand planes in the air at once, they carried out the first Allied saturation raids against major Axis cities.

America became a belligerent in December 1941, and by early 1942, American airmen were on their way to England to organize the Eighth Air Force. In cooperation with the RAF, they carried out strategic bombing operations against Hitler's "Fortress Europe." The commander of the Eighth Air Force, after spring 1942, was Major General Carl A. ("Tooey") Spaatz.

In anticipation of Operation Overlord, bombing raids were stepped up on targets far behind the enemy's main line of ground resistance — usually industrial centers. In summer 1943, for example, the Eighth Air Force by day and the RAF by night made a succession of raids that battered refineries and docks at Hamburg, Germany's principal seaport. During the attacks great sections of the city were set ablaze and thousands of civilians were killed.

By 1944, strategic bombers crisscrossed the *Reich* on an around-the-clock basis.

By early 1945, Allied strategic bombers had dealt severe blows to German industry and communications. If Hitler's ground forces had held out much longer they would have found themselves without the weapons, equipment, and supplies necessary to continue the fight.

Although strategic raids on industrial centers yielded fewer dividends before 1945 than American and British airmen had expected, tactical air power — airplanes functioning in direct support of ground operations — succeeded magnificently. In the weeks before Operation Overlord twin-engined medium bombers and Flying Fortresses devastated roads and bridges in Northern France, cleared invasion beaches, harassed German troop movements, hammered

B-17s bomb the light metal alloy works at Solingen, Germany during World War II. Weather conditions were consistently bad over the continent. But radar, then a new device, enabled the Allies to bomb pre-selected sites accurately.

fortifications, and struck at supply depots and staging areas. At the same time Allied fighter planes drove the German *Luftwaffe* from the skies of Northern France and enabled General Eisenhower, on the eve of the Normandy invasion to reassure his soldiers: "If you see fighting aircraft over you, they will be ours."

During and after the cross-Channel invasion, Allied airmen and soldiers developed a respect for each other and learned to coordinate battlefield operations. The airplane, flying in close support of tanks and infantrymen, became, as it long had been for the Germans, an important weapon in ground warfare.

Meanwhile, in spring 1944, the great invasion force, which included nearly three million Allied troops, began to make final preparations. Radiomen sent out a stream of fake messages to confuse the Germans. Bombing planes hit targets far removed from the Normandy beaches selected for the assault. At the same time GIs checked their gear, talked in subdued tones, and contemplated the battle that soon would be upon them. Some wrote letters home. Others prayed.

The scheduled invasion date was June 4, 1944, but high winds and heavy seas forced a postponement until June 6. Through the night of

June 4-5 rain and wind continued to churn the waters of the English Channel. Then, at 4:15 A.M. on June 5, Eisenhower, after reading forecasts of clearing weather and weighing the consequences of delay, announced: "O.K. We'll go."

The Normandy Invasion

The first Allied troops were airborne soldiers —three divisions or about eighteen thousand men in all—who made their way into France by gliders and parachutes. Their mission was to disrupt communications, blow up bridges, and distract the Germans from the main battle area— the beaches. Unfortunately the airborne movement was not a great success. Many soldiers died when gliders crashed and parachutes brought men down in flooded areas.

The main assault force embarked from nearly a dozen points along the south coast of England. Never in the history of warfare had such a massive amphibious operation been attempted. As dawn broke over the French countryside, German soldiers, peeping out from concrete pillboxes, surveyed the great Allied armada in open-mouthed amazement. Loudspeakers on the transports barked out the order: "Away all boats."

As the landing craft started toward the beaches, more than seven hundred Allied warships drew into position and pointed their guns toward Hitler's Atlantic Wall. With a succession of flashes and a long, deafening rumble, the Allied navies commenced a bombardment which hopefully would eliminate German resistance. Overhead, the roar of thousands of Allied airplanes added to the din. Then, at roughly 6:20 A.M., amphibious tanks, assault troops, and underwater demolition engineers approached the beaches and began clearing fifty-yard paths through German obstacles and mine fields to the landing sites. Finally, shortly before 7:00 o'clock, the main bodies of troops began to arrive.

At Utah Beach, an American objective, the German response was negligible and the invasion proceeded smoothly. A similar story was repeated at Gold and Sword beaches, where the British splashed ashore, and at Juno Beach, where the Canadians quickly knocked out German defenders. But at Omaha Beach, an American target, the Germans, entrenched behind cliffs on the flanks of the four-mile beach,

General Dwight D. Eisenhower talks with members of the 502nd Airborne Division before they embark for Operation Overlord. The airborne were the first Allied troops to invade France, June 6, 1944. What were their special orders?

had managed to survive the naval bombardment. When GIs began piling out of the landing craft they ran head-on into a hail of bullets and shells. In the confusion some of the landing craft at Omaha discharged their men in deep water and many soldiers drowned before having a chance to fire a shot. Despite heavy casualties the Americans pressed relentlessly forward.

By nightfall of June 6, it was clear that Operation Overlord had succeeded. Nearly 150,000 Allied troops were ashore in Normandy, and already had captured eighty square miles of French countryside.

German Rockets Hit Britain

For war-weary people in Britain and America the Normandy invasion was a triumph. The sense of triumph, however, was dimmed by an incredible new weapon unveiled by the Germans just a week after Operation Overlord—the V-1 buzz bomb.

The V-1 was a small pilotless airplane powered by a rocket engine. Used to reopen the battle of Britain rather than against Allied armies in Normandy, the V-1s traveled at a speed of only 360 miles per hour and many were knocked from the skies by the RAF and by antiaircraft guns. A more sophisticated and formidable weapon was the V-2, a true rocket. The V-2s, introduced in August 1944, were unstoppable, but only five hundred of the deadly missiles ever made it to London.

While the V-1s and V-2s terrorized civilian populations, they did minimal damage. They did not break British morale any more than had the great air raids of 1939-40.

Some German military men recognized that buzz bombs and rockets could not save Germany from defeat. Contemplating the catastrophe in Normandy and the rash of disasters in Russia, they began in early summer 1944 to urge Hitler to seek a peace settlement. The dictator turned aside such appeals and instead ordered his troops to fight to the death. Whereupon a group of ranking officers conspired to murder him but failed.

The Liberation of Paris

The Anglo-Americans meanwhile were setting into motion a new amphibious assault against the Germans, aimed at the Mediterranean coast of France. The object of the operation was to secure the flank of Allied armies when they broke out of Normandy and launched their drive toward Germany.

The invasion came off in mid-August 1944. After overcoming minimal resistance, American and French troops rolled up the Rhone Valley. By mid-September 1944 a junction was made with forces which had broken out of Normandy and reached a point just north of Switzerland. Except for its northeastern corner, France was now free of the Germans.

Allied armies to the north were fighting their way southward and eastward from Normandy. This raised a question: When would Paris be liberated? General Eisenhower was in no hurry to take over the French capital. He believed that Paris had little strategic value, and he did not wish to assume responsibility for feeding four million Parisians.

Eisenhower directed the French underground inside Paris to make no armed movements against the Germans. His directive was ignored. Urged on by General Charles de Gaulle, who since 1940 had commanded Free French forces based in England, the underground sparked an uprising that quickly gained enthusiastic support among Parisians.

As a result, Eisenhower felt compelled to divert Allied units—including a French armored division—to the French capital city. Next, de Gaulle made a triumphal entry into Paris, acting independently of American and British leaders. He established himself as the undisputed leader of France.

On securing Paris, in late August 1944, Allied armies moved north and east. They occupied the coast of the English Channel as far as Ostend, Belgium, captured the great Belgian port of Antwerp, and made a junction with American and French forces moving up from the Mediterranean. In October they captured their first German city, Aachen, just over the border from Belgium. Then they took aim on the strongholds of Metz and Strasbourg—both of which would fall into their hands in late November.

Then came frustration.

To open the sea lane to Antwerp, eliminate rocket launching sites, and secure a bridgehead on the Rhine—near Arnheim in the Netherlands—General Eisenhower authorized Field Marshal Montgomery to attack the Germans north and east of Antwerp. Gains were minimal, and to some Americans the entire operation seemed a costly setback. The Allies did not succeed in opening Antwerp until mid-November. Next, American troops made an attack through the Hürtgen Forest. Again the Germans resisted fiercely and the outcome was an Allied defeat with heavy casualties.

Battle of the Bulge

In early December 1944, as winter settled over Northern Europe, the pace of battle on the Western front slackened. But then came a full-scale disaster for the Allies, or so it seemed.

Aware that he somehow must regain the initiative if he was to survive, in late September 1944 Hitler began to mass soldiers and stockpile supplies and equipment for a counteroffensive in the West. On December 12, he explained his plan to division commanders. Three great German armies would strike westward through the Ardennes Forest in Luxembourg and Belgium, drive across the Meuse, and recapture Antwerp. Hitler believed that this fresh display of German power would shatter Allied morale and cause the Allies to sue for peace. The division commanders were dumfounded. *Der Führer* must be mad. Still, he was *Der Führer* and they prepared to go through with the operation.

Because the Germans had carefully and cleverly concealed their build-up, the Allies had no inkling that their enemies were up to something big. On the contrary, Allied manpower on the eighty-five-mile ghost front in the Ardennes sector had been reduced and many inexperienced troops had been brought up. Then, as snow fell across the Ardennes, preventing Allied aerial reconnaissance, the Germans drew into position. At 5:30 A.M., December 16, they sprang forward.

Spearheading the German attack were large numbers of new Tiger tanks, whose thick armor and eighty-eight millimeter guns made them far superior to any American tanks in the area. Surprised, Allied troops—nearly all of them Americans—reeled back in disarray. At one point, eight thousand of them put down weapons and allowed themselves to become captives, an American surrender eclipsed in size only by that on the Bataan peninsula in the Philippines in early 1942. The Allied main line of resistance disintegrated, and the Battle of the Bulge became an indeterminate number of small unit engagements. Many civilians were killed in a murderous crossfire. Snow and bitter cold added to the misery of the battle for soldiers and civilians alike.

In its first stages, then, the Ardennes campaign went according to German plan. By Christmas Day, the Germans had created a bulge in the Allied line more than fifty miles deep. At one point, however—at the Belgium town of Bastogne—they met frustration. Surrounded and cut off from aerial reinforcement by foul weather, American troops at Bastogne fought with unparalleled fury.

Then the Germans ran out of steam. As the skies cleared, Allied aircraft began to provide close air support for armored and infantry units and to parachute supplies to the men inside Bastogne. At the same time, Field Marshal Montgomery and his British forces squeezed the bulge from the north while General Bradley and the Americans did likewise from the south. To break the Bastogne encirclement, General Patton stormed through the bulge with tanks.

Thus the tide of the battle turned, and by mid-January 1945 the Allies had regained nearly all of the ground lost in the first days of the German attack.

The Eastern Front

On the Eastern front meanwhile, the Soviets had continued to press forward with only occasional pauses. In the latter part of June 1944, three weeks after the Anglo-American invasion of Northern France, the Soviets began a major offensive. Taking 100,000 German prisoners, they gained the city of Minsk. In mid-July troops of the Red Army crossed the border into Poland. In August the Soviets launched an offensive in Bessarabia and Rumania which within a few days took them into Bucharest and Ploesti. In September they declared war on Bulgaria, a German ally, and in that same month compelled the governments of Finland and Rumania to agree to armistice terms. At the end of September troops of the Red Army entered Yugoslavia. A few weeks later they and Yugoslav partisans under command of Marshal Tito (Josip Broz) entered Belgrade, the Yugoslav capital city.

While the Anglo-Americans were clearing out the last pockets of resistance in the bulge in Belgium and Luxembourg, the Soviets in early 1945 cranked up a new offensive in Poland. As a result, they soon captured Warsaw. A week later the Soviets took the Hungarian capital, Budapest, and the Polish town of Poznan, half way between Warsaw and Berlin. In March they entered the Baltic port of Danzig and crossed the border into Austria.

The Wehrmacht Begins to Crumble

The Anglo-Americans spent a month regrouping after the Battle of the Bulge. Then, in late February 1945, they began to press toward the Rhine. By the first week in March they had captured Cologne and driven the Germans to the east bank of the Rhine.

Now came a remarkable stroke of fortune. Allied forces learned from a captured German soldier that the great bridge spanning the Rhine at Remagen was prepared for demolition and would be destroyed in forty-five minutes. Armored units dashed to seize the bridge and disarm the explosive charges before they went off. They succeeded. Thus the Allies breached Hitler's last natural defensive barrier in the West. Over the next few weeks American, British, Canadian, and French units slashed through German defenses and completed giant encirclements. Allied forces advanced on all fronts from the North Sea to the Swiss frontier and in Italy, where German defenses had finally begun to come apart. Of special importance was occupation of the Ruhr, Germany's industrial heartland.

Hammered on all sides and despairing of stopping the relentless advance of their enemies, German soldiers began to surrender in droves. At the same time heavy bombers were pulverizing German cities in around-the-clock raids. The end of the war in Europe was clearly in sight.

Discovery of German Atrocities

Then, in their moment of triumph, the Allies were chilled by discovery of Nazi concentration camps at such places as Buchenwald, Dachau, and Belsen—captured by American and British units—and Auschwitz in Poland—taken by the Soviets.

When Allied soldiers stumbled on the camps they could scarcely believe their eyes. First they encountered hollow-eyed prisoners, walking skeletons who had survived their ordeal mainly because Allied armies had taken the camps with such speed that the Germans had not been able to dispose of all inmates. Next they came upon the remains of those who had not survived and whose corpses had not been burned, buried in huge pits which had been covered with a thin layer of earth. Then they found gas chambers where Germans—after stripping their victims of clothing, shoes, jewelry and spectacles—had murdered them. Finally they found crematories where the bodies of inmates had been burned to ashes.

General Eisenhower requested that newsmen and photographers be flown to Germany at once to survey the scene for themselves. The resultant reports and pictures stunned people all across the globe.

What were the camps and the gas chambers and the crematories all about?

Hitler had a deep hatred of Jews, and he was using mass murder to destroy them. In Germany and in occupied countries, his secret police methodically rounded up Jews, herded them aboard freight cars like cattle, and dispatched them to the camps. Elderly people, infants, and many women who did manage to survive the trip often were put to death at once. Those who were able to work were organized into forced labor battalions where they remained until they died, usually within nine months. Those who became sick and unable to work were liquidated. Even in death the victims of Hitler's program of genocide made a final contribution to the *Third Reich*—their shorn hair was used to stuff mattresses, gold was extracted from their teeth, and their bones and ashes were used to make soap and fertilizer.

In all, nearly six million Jews perished in concentration camps—half of them at Auschwitz. The Germans also enslaved great numbers of non-Jews from occupied countries, particularly Russia. A high percentage of them— victims of malnutrition, disease, overwork and abuse—did not survive.

While the world pondered the horrors of Nazi death camps, and while some of Hitler's underlings, against the will of the dictator, tried frantically to work out an armistice with the Anglo-Americans, the war in Europe moved to a climax. The focal point became the German capital city, Berlin.

Allies Debate the Capture of Berlin

Who would take Berlin? The question had been an object of heated discussion between leaders of Britain and the United States for several weeks.

Prime Minister Churchill argued that capture of the seat of Nazi power by the Western Allies would have great symbolic importance. When the time came to work out a peace settlement, he thought, the victory would strengthen the Anglo-American hand over that of the Russians. Thus Churchill wanted to mount a full-powered drive which, if all went well, would enable British and American forces to beat the Soviets to the city.

Such logic was lost on General Eisenhower. In his judgment Berlin had no particular military value. A drive on Berlin would divert Anglo-American forces from more important military targets. Eisenhower felt that the dubious honor of being first in the German capital might cost the Western Allies as many as one hundred thousand casualties.

The general was aware that the Soviets were determined to capture Berlin. They had suffered much more in the war than had either the British or the Americans. They would look upon it as a monumental insult if the Anglo-Americans raced in and snatched the city from them. The government in Washington accepted Eisenhower's arguments. And so the Soviets, in mid-April 1945, launched an offensive against Berlin. As Eisenhower had anticipated, the battle for Berlin did not turn out to be easy. The Germans, though outgunned and outmanned, resisted fiercely. Before the last shot was fired 150,000 Soviet soldiers had been killed or wounded.

Victory in Europe

While the battle for Berlin raged, American and Soviet troops, in late April 1945, met near Torgau, on the Elbe River some seventy miles south of Berlin. The following day, across the Alps in Northern Italy, Mussolini, who had been liberated by German soldiers shortly after his imprisonment in 1943, was captured by Italian partisans. He was shot and his body was strung up for public display in front of a gasoline station in Milan. Two days later, April 30, came Hitler's turn to die. While Russian shells rained down about his bomb-proof bunker in Berlin, the dictator took his own life. A week later Admiral Karl Doenitz whom Hitler had named as his successor arranged for Germany's unconditional surrender. The surrender document was signed in a schoolhouse at Rheims in France, which was the headquarters of General Eisenhower. To symbolize Allied unity in Soviet-occupied Berlin, the surrender ceremony was repeated the following day, May 8, VE (Victory in Europe) Day.

STUDY GUIDE: After Hitler's invasion of Russia, Soviet leaders asked for Anglo-American aid. The result was the highly successful Operation Torch. British and American armies landed in Morocco and Algeria and overcame Rommel's *Afrika Korps.* The Allies won another major victory in Stalingrad, where Russian defeat of German troops ended Hitler's dream of defeating Russia.

The Allies overcame the threat of German submarine warfare through use of improved detection devices, bombers, and convoys. Anglo-American forces invaded Sicily in preparation for an assault on the Italian peninsula. Italy promptly withdrew from the war, but German forces in Italy resisted the Allied invasion. Hard-won victories at Naples and Monte Cassino finally carried Allied forces on to Rome. The Germans, meanwhile, were suffering defeats in Russia. The siege of Leningrad failed, and German forces retreated from Sebastopol and the Crimea.

In anticipation of a cross-Channel invasion, the Allies launched a program of strategic bombing of Germany. In June 1944 Operation Overlord succeeded and the Allies invaded the European continent. Thousands of Allied troops landed on the French coast.
German losses did not sway Hitler in his determination to fight to the death. Anglo-American forces overcame German resistance in most of France. In an effort to regain the offensive, Hitler launched his Ardennes campaign in late 1944. The bitterly fought Battle of the Bulge resulted in heavy casualties for Allied forces, but the Germans were finally turned back.

On the Eastern Front the Soviet army overcame resistance in Rumania, Yugoslavia, Poland, and Hungary. Anglo-American armies swept through Germany and occupied the Ruhr, Germany's industrial center. Thousands of German soldiers surrendered. The capital city of Berlin surrendered to Russian forces after putting up stiff resistance. With defeat at hand, Hitler committed suicide. The war in Europe was over.

WAR IN THE PACIFIC

While American fighting men were waging war on the desert of North Africa, clawing their way up the Italian boot, and storming Hitler's "Fortress Europe," great numbers of their countrymen were locked in equally grim and vicious combat with a different enemy half-way around the world.

At the outset of the Pacific war, the United States sought merely to contain the Japanese until Hitler's empire in Europe could be destroyed. Then it would be possible to turn full attention to the Pacific theater. The Japanese, on the other hand, had a great dream. After eliminating the American Pacific Fleet at Pearl Harbor and the big B-17 bombers in the Philippines, they would send their armies swarming through Southeast Asia—the Philippines, Thailand, Burma, Malaya and the Netherland Indies—a treasurehouse of oil, rubber, tin, iron ore, manganese, and rice. These resources, which added to those of Manchuria, Korea, and the coastal area of China already under Japanese control, would make the Japanese empire enduringly prosperous and powerful.

At the same time the Japanese would sweep across the Western Pacific and erect a giant defensive barrier stretching from the Kurile Islands north of Japan eastward to Attu and Kiska in the Aleutians. Their line of defense would go down through Wake, the Marshall and Gilbert islands in the Central Pacific, westward through the Solomon and Bismarck islands, across New Guinea to the Netherland Indies, and up Malaya and Burma to the border of India.

The Japanese had set their grand scheme in motion in early December 1941 by the aerial strikes at Pearl Harbor and at Clark Field in the Philippines. Two days later they took the American island of Guam in the Marianas and two weeks later captured Wake Island. On the same day that Japan attacked Pearl Harbor and Clark Field, Japanese forces prepared to drive from Saigon in French Indo-China against Thailand and the British colony of Malaya. The Thais quickly surrendered in the face of certain defeat. The British, however, were determined to fight any Japanese amphibious landings along the east coast of the Malay peninsula. They dispatched six warships from Singapore. Finding that the British ships were operating without aerial cover, Japanese bombers and torpedo planes on December 11, 1941 sank the *Prince of Wales* and *Repulse*—two of the most powerful vessels in the Royal Navy.

In spite of losing these warships, the British hoped that they might be able to hold Singapore, the strategic center of Southeast Asia. Over the years they had built up Singapore's defenses.

Unfortunately most plans for defending the base had rested on the assumption that any attack would come from the sea, not from the tangled jungle to the north. Hence most of the big guns of the fortress pointed toward the sea. The Japanese, of course, struck through the jungle. In February 1942 Japanese soldiers swarmed over makeshift British defenses and captured Singapore.

While bearing down on Singapore, in December 1941–February 1942, Japanese amphibious forces jumped from island to island in the Netherlands Indies—present-day Indonesia. The high point of their campaign to win control of the great archipelago came in late February 1942 when a Japanese fleet destroyed a squadron of Australian, British, Dutch, and American vessels in the Java Sea between the islands of Borneo and Java. Allied naval power in the area thus eliminated, the Japanese had only to mop up isolated groups of Allied forces to complete their conquest of the islands. At the same time the Japanese expelled the small group of Allied forces from Burma.

Fall of the Philippines

While the contests in Malaya and the Netherlands Indies were taking place, Americans in the months after Pearl Harbor focused their attention on the grim and brutal struggle in the Philippines.

The Japanese invasion of the Philippines came just before Christmas 1941, when Japanese amphibious forces went ashore on Luzon, the largest island of the Philippines. General Douglas MacArthur, having personally trained and organized much of the army in the Philippines, was confident that the Japanese would be repulsed. The general's confidence soon turned to despair. Although numerically superior, the American-Filipino army proved no match for the Japanese. Within a few weeks the emperor's soldiers captured Manila and drove American and Filipino forces to the Bataan peninsula, thirty miles across the bay from Manila.

In the mountainous and jungle terrain of Bataan, the Americans and Filipinos fought furiously, expecting reinforcements from the United States. No reinforcements came. While taking a heavy toll of Japanese soldiers, the outgunned American and Filipino regiments fell back from one defense line to another. Then, when Allied defeat appeared imminent, President Roosevelt ordered General MacArthur to

make his way to Australia. Upon arrival at Darwin, Australia, the general uttered his famous pledge: "I shall return."

By early April 1942 GIs on the peninsula and their Filipino comrades had reached the end of their endurance, whereupon most of them surrendered. A handful of American and Filipino soldiers, however, led by Lieutenant General Jonathan M. Wainwright—whom Roosevelt had appointed to succeed MacArthur—managed to escape to Corregidor, a fortress a few miles off the tip of Bataan. They continued to hold out until May 6, when Wainwright was forced to surrender.

The defeat in the Philippines saddened the people of the United States. Then when news began to trickle out of the islands of the "Bataan death march," sadness turned to cold fury.

The "death march" occurred when the Japanese set out to transfer 70,000 American and Filipino prisoners to a railroad center some fifty-five miles to the north. From there the POWs would move by train to Camp O'Donnell for internment. Japanese commanding officers had made no provisions for handling the prisoners. The outcome was utter confusion. The Japanese were unable to supply adequate food and medical care to the prisoners. Even worse was the problem of transportation. A shortage of motorized vehicles meant that half of the prisoners, already weakened by hunger and disease, had to walk from the tip of Bataan to the railroad center. Thousands encountered no serious mistreatment. But for many the march turned into a nightmare. Japanese soldiers acting without orders shot, stabbed, kicked, and clubbed large numbers of the captives whom they were assigned to guard. Because of such abuse, and because of malaria, wounds, and sheer exhaustion, perhaps 16,000 Americans and Filipinos died before they could reach Camp O'Donnell.

During those agonizing months between the attack on Pearl Harbor and surrender in the Philippines, one event lifted the spirits of the people of the United States. That event was a spectacular but ineffectual air raid on Tokyo in April 1942 by a squadron of B-25 bombers under command of Lieutenant Colonel James H. Doolittle.

From the American point of view, the situation in the Pacific in the spring of 1942 was not as dark as it might have been. During the Pearl Harbor raid the Japanese had failed to destroy the navy's fuel storage tanks or sink a single aircraft carrier. This meant that the United States had plenty of fuel oil and six big flattops — *Enterprise, Hornet, Lexington, Saratoga, Wasp,* and *Yorktown* — with which to conduct naval operations in the Pacific. Almost as important, the Americans still had "Magic," the decoding device which enabled them to tune in to many top-level Japanese conversations and thus anticipate Japanese moves in the war.

The Japanese, overconfident after their recent triumphs, were preparing to embark on a new campaign of conquest instead of consolidating and defending territories which they had already taken. They planned to move out across the Coral Sea, capture New Caledonia, the Fiji Islands and Samoa, thus gaining control of the sea lane that linked the United States with New Zealand and Australia. They also planned to take key islands at the tip of the Aleutian chain in Alaska. And, most important, they set their sights on Midway Island in the Central Pacific, from which they could blast the naval base at Pearl Harbor, only a thousand miles away. If, as a result, they could compel the American fleet to operate from bases in California, the Japanese would drastically reduce the range and effectiveness of American naval power.

Battle of the Coral Sea

In early May 1942 the Japanese dispatched troop transports toward the southeastern coast of New Guinea, where Japanese soldiers were to go ashore and capture Port Moresby. Next, imperial soldiers would move across the Coral Sea to take New Caledonia and then proceed to the Fijis and Samoa. For the first time since Pearl Harbor, however, Japanese plans went wrong. Because the Americans were able to decode intercepted messages, they knew what the Japanese were planning. To head off the Japanese fleet, they sent a task force into the Coral Sea east of New Guinea, spearheaded by the carriers *Lexington* and *Yorktown.* On May 7-8 — only hours after Wainwright's surrender at Corregidor — a fierce but unique battle took place: opposing ships did not sight or shoot at one another. Instead the battle was one of planes versus planes and planes versus ships.

The outcome of the Battle of the Coral Sea was a standoff, or even a Japanese victory, inasmuch as American losses were slightly larger than those of the enemy. The chief American casualty was the aircraft carrier *Lexington.*

Strategically, however, the action was a triumph for the Americans because it compelled the Japanese to turn back their troop transports and cancel the assault on Port Moresby. As a result, the threat to New Caledonia, the Fijis, and Samoa was ended, at least for the time being. The action in the Coral Sea demonstrated that the Japanese could be stopped. It proved that Americans were a match for the Japanese and thus reinforced American morale. It also reassured Australians who wondered if their country might be on the list of Japanese targets.

The Battle of Midway

Hardly pausing after the Coral Sea encounter, the Japanese turned their attention to Midway, the tiny atoll in the Central Pacific which they hoped to use as a base to blast Pearl Harbor. In charge of the Midway operation was Admiral Isoroku Yamamoto, architect of the Pearl Harbor raid. To achieve surprise at Midway, he dispatched a diversionary force toward the Aleutian Islands. Then, in late May 1942, with Yamamoto in command, a huge fleet led by four aircraft carriers steamed from Japan toward Midway. Thanks to decoded messages the Americans knew Japanese plans. Admiral Chester W. Nimitz of the American Pacific Fleet strengthened Midway's defenses with the carriers *Enterprise, Hornet,* and *Yorktown.*

The Battle of Midway, one of the most crucial actions of World War II, began on the morning of June 4, 1942 when Japanese planes sped toward Midway. After dropping bombs on the island, Japanese airmen spotted the American naval force, including the three flattops, and radioed the news back to their commander. Here was an opportunity to render the American navy a defeat from which it would take years to recover. The planes were ordered to return to their carriers to refuel and rearm with a special type of bomb designed for use against ships.

Then it happened.

While Japanese planes were returning to their carriers, American dive bombers and torpedo planes began racing from the flight decks of the *Enterprise, Hornet,* and *Yorktown* in search of targets. Low clouds hanging over the Central Pacific obstructed their vision. But suddenly an opening appeared in the cloud formations. Spread out below were four Japanese carriers. Within a few minutes, three of the Japanese carriers were smoking wrecks.

Despite loss of the three carriers, the Japanese kept up the fight. Later in the day they managed to destroy the American carrier *Yorktown*. Then planes from the *Enterprise* bagged the fourth and last Japanese flattop, whereupon Admiral Yamamoto, shaken by the monstrous disaster, led the remnants of the great Japanese task force westward across the Pacific to the home islands.

The Tide of Battle Changes

The tide of battle in the Pacific turned at the Battle of Midway in June of 1942. After that Allied victory, the Japanese, who had maintained the initiative in the war, were on the defensive.

In spite of the losses at Midway, the Japanese still had a powerful defensive perimeter which stretched for thousands of miles in a giant arc from Attu and Kiska in the Aleutians to the frontier of India. Breaking through it would not be easy.

When American military and naval leaders scanned maps of the Western Pacific in the weeks after Midway, they concluded that the keystone of Japanese defenses was a string of bases in the Solomon and Bismarck islands which they dubbed "the Bismarck barrier." Before the Americans and their allies—mainly the Australians and New Zealanders—could drive the Japanese back toward their home islands, it would be necessary to breach that barrier. Where would the Allies organize an assault against Japanese positions in the Solomons and Bismarcks? Principally in Australia and to a lesser extent on Espiritu Santo, an island in the New Hebrides which at that time was a forward base for Allied operations in the area of the Coral Sea.

The Battle of Guadalcanal

Then came disturbing news. The Japanese were constructing an airfield on the island of Guadalcanal in the Solomons. From this air base they could send long-range bombing planes against Espiritu Santo and ravage the supply route from the United States to Australia. A hurried decision was made to expel the Japanese from Guadalcanal. This operation, if successful, would remove the threat to Espiritu Santo and the Australian supply line. It would also provide the Allies with an important forward base from which they could breach the Bismarck barrier.

The assault on Guadalcanal came at dawn on August 7, 1942. After a three-hour naval bombardment, troops of the First Marine Division waded onto the beaches of Guadalcanal and three neighboring islands. Japanese resistance was negligible. The marines quickly captured the air strip which the Japanese had been building and renamed it Henderson Field. For the next several weeks combat on the island remained at a low level. Then, in early September, the Japanese decided to eliminate the Allied threat to their defensive perimeter. They began to pour reinforcements into the Guadalcanal jungle. The outcome was a ferocious campaign which turned into one of the epic actions of World War II.

Snakes, scorpions, mosquitoes, hidden Japanese snipers, malaria, dysentery, 115-degree temperatures, torrential showers and the rotten odor of decaying vegetation all gave the struggle in the jungle of Guadalcanal added terror and misery. But it was the massive naval clashes in the waters around the island that determined Guadalcanal's future.

The naval struggle near Guadalcanal started out badly for the Allies. On August 9, two days after the marines had gone ashore, a Japanese task force slipped by Allied ships and surprised a squadron of American and Australian vessels near Savo Island. The Japanese sank one Australian and three American heavy cruisers with no loss to themselves. Other sea engagements followed over the next two months. Losses on both sides were very heavy. Among the American ships that went down were the carriers *Wasp* and *Hornet*.

Then Admiral Nimitz gave command of Allied forces around Guadalcanal to Vice-Admiral William F. ("Bull") Halsey, Jr. A short time later came the climactic naval battle of Guadalcanal.

The Japanese had sent a task force toward the island to bombard Allied installations. Before the fleet could take up firing positions, however, it was intercepted by Allied ships and planes on November 13, 1942. The clash that followed was confusing and murderous. The Americans lost four destroyers and two cruisers. The Japanese lost two destroyers and a battleship. The Japanese ships, however, had failed to accomplish their mission. Henderson Field and other important installations had been spared a crippling attack. A few hours later, planes from the carrier *Enterprise* spotted a convoy of Japanese transports carrying troops toward Guadalcanal.

Planes from both the *Enterprise* and Henderson Field swooped down on the transports, and sank seven of them. Only 4,000 of the 10,000 Japanese troops ever made it to the island.

By the end of November 1942 Allied naval supremacy around Guadalcanal had been established. Japanese soldiers in the jungle, more or less cut off from outside support, steadily lost ground. In January of 1943, Japanese transports, under cover of darkness, slipped to the northwestern tip of Guadalcanal and evacuated their remaining soldiers. For the first time, the Japanese had lost a major encounter on land.

New Guinea

A few hundred miles west of Guadalcanal, meanwhile, in the swamps of eastern New Guinea, American and Australian army troops had been waging an equally grim campaign against the Japanese. The GIs and Aussies had been sent to New Guinea by General MacArthur in September 1942 to stop Japanese units which were within thirty miles of Port Moresby. Capture of Port Moresby would give the Japanese a forward base from which to attack Australia and the supply route linking Australia and the United States. The Japanese advance was stopped, then slowly the enemy troops were pushed northward. By January 1943 the Japanese were cleared from southeastern New Guinea.

Still, the Japanese did not abandon hope of returning to the offensive in New Guinea. Accordingly, under stormy skies in late February 1943, they dispatched a convoy of eight transports and eight destroyers from Rabaul, their great fortress on New Britain in the Bismarcks. The American and Australian air forces, aided by clear weather, sank all eight of the enemy transports and four of the destroyers in the resultant Battle of the Bismarck Sea. As a consequence, the Allies were able to retain the initiative in New Guinea.

Casablanca Conference

While the struggles on Guadalcanal and in southeastern New Guinea were coming to an end, the Allies were using barely fifteen percent of their manpower and materials in the Pacific theater. Although fully committed to the "beat Hitler first" strategy, American leaders did not want to lose the initiative in the Western Pacific.

They pressed their view at the Casablanca Conference of President Roosevelt, Prime Minister Churchill, and other leaders of the United States and Great Britain in North Africa in January 1943.

The outcome was a compromise. The Americans agreed to postpone the projected cross-Channel operation until 1944, and the British permitted offensive operations in the Western Pacific. Defeat of Germany nonetheless was to remain the main target of the two powers.

Allies Plan Japanese Defeat

With the go-ahead for new offensive operations in the Pacific, Allied planners, mainly American, pushed ahead with plans for defeating Japan. It was commonly believed that the Japanese would not agree to an unconditional surrender until their power to resist had been completely broken. Hence it would be necessary to fight them all the way to Japan and then occupy their home islands. Therefore the big question was: how should the Allies get to Japan?

The planners concluded that Allied forces might reach Japan by four possible routes. First, by proceeding from the Indian Ocean by way of Singapore, Malaya, French Indo-China, southeast China, and the island of Formosa. A second possibility was a movement on Japan by way of Alaska and the Aleutian Islands. For a variety of reasons, planners discarded both of these routes.

The third route—favored by General MacArthur—would take Allied forces from the Bismarcks across New Guinea, through Mindanao and Luzon in the Philippines, and on to Japan. Navy men argued that such a movement would be roundabout and open to devastating flank attacks by Japanese forces based in the Carolines and Marianas. Instead they favored a fourth approach—straight across the mid-Pacific from the Gilberts and Marshalls to the Carolines and Marianas, on to Formosa and the east coast of China, for a final assault on the Japanese home islands. MacArthur objected. He believed that it would prove terribly costly to slice through the defenses that the Japanese had constructed on the islands and atolls of the mid-Pacific.

The eventual outcome was a compromise between routes three and four. Allied forces under MacArthur would advance along the New Guinea-Mindanao axis while the navy's amphibious forces under Admiral Nimitz would move westward through the mid-Pacific.

China's Role in the Pacific

Where did Chiang Kai-shek and the Chinese, who had been fighting the Japanese off and on since 1931, fit into Allied plans for defeat of Japan?

American leaders had hoped that the Chinese might become an effective force in the war against Japan and that Chiang might emerge with enough prestige and power to become a pillar of stability in postwar East Asia. To help Chiang, President Roosevelt, shortly after Pearl Harbor, turned to Major General Joseph W. ("Vinegar Joe") Stilwell. Stilwell had just taken up his new assignment when the Japanese moved into Burma and cut the only overland supply route to China—the Burma Road, which ran from India to the interior of China. After taking his battered Allied army out of Burma to India, Stilwell helped organize an aerial supply line over the Himalayas from India to China. Then he tried to persuade Chiang Kai-shek to reorganize the ineffectual Chinese army. However, with only a handful of American soldiers committed to the China-Burma-India area, the Chinese were never able to apply any considerable pressure on the Japanese. On the contrary, the Japanese, in 1943, organized an offensive which took their armies deeper into China.

Allied Planning Reaps Dividends

To put the compromise plan into effect required replacement of the destroyed aircraft carriers. Not until arrival of new and bigger carriers, notably the *Essex*, would the Allies again be able to take the offensive. Thus, in the first half of 1943, a relative quiet settled over the Pacific theater. The only engagements of any consequence were the successful Allied assaults on the islands of Attu and Kiska in the Aleutians, which the Japanese had occupied at the time of the Midway operation.

MacArthur and Nimitz meanwhile were assembling forces for their dual offensives. MacArthur was the first to swing into action. In June 1943 army troops, ferried and supported by a navy task force commanded by Halsey, took the island of New Georgia in the Central Solomons. New Georgia gave the Allies another base from which their planes could strike Japanese strong points, particularly Rabaul, the great fortress on the island of New Britain. In the next two months Allied forces made their way across the Solomons. In September 1943, American and Australian soldiers, moving by sea, swept to the north coast of New Guinea, captured Salamaua and Lae, and secured the eastern tip of the huge island.

American leaders decided to leapfrog the fortress of Rabaul. They elected to attack other strategic points where Japanese defenses were less imposing, leaving Rabaul to be subjected to aerial bombardment and a naval blockade. Accordingly, in March 1944, American troops, overcoming fierce resistance, captured the Admiralty Islands north of New Guinea.

Meanwhile, in late autumn 1943, Admiral Nimitz's drive across the mid-Pacific had gotten underway. The first objectives of the mid-Pacific offensive were Makin and Tarawa, tiny atolls in the Gilbert Islands.

On November 20, 1943 army troops quickly overcame the few hundred Japanese defenders on Makin. Tarawa proved more difficult. The Japanese had constructed strong fortifications of steel and concrete, but four days of fierce combat eliminated Japanese resistance.

Nimitz now turned to the Marshall Islands northwest of the Gilberts. Through December 1943 he sent American planes on a steady stream of bombing raids against Japanese positions. In January 1944, he dispatched a great fleet—which included twelve aircraft carriers—toward the islands. On January 31, after leapfrogging several strongly fortified islands, American troops stormed and took Kwajalein.

The following day marines went ashore on two neighboring islands. Because of highly effective preliminary naval bombardment, the attackers met less resistance than had been anticipated. Two weeks later they assaulted the atoll of Eniwetok, west of Kwajalein. Enemy resistance was sharp but was quickly overcome.

The day before the assault on Eniwetok, a navy task force staged a massive raid on Truk, a Japanese-held atoll in the Carolines lying north of Rabaul and southwest of Eniwetok. Truk—sometimes called the "Gibraltar of the Pacific"—was one of Japan's principal air and naval bases in the Western Pacific. The attack was a smashing success. The Japanese, whose morale was severely shaken by the attack, virtually abandoned Truk as a naval base.

Nimitz's next objective was Japanese-held islands in the Marianas—Saipan, Guam, and

Tinian, west of Eniwetok. For several months new long-range B-29 Superfortresses struck at targets in the Marianas. In early June 1944 — while GIs in Europe were hitting the beaches of Normandy — a fleet of 535 vessels and 127,000 marines and soldiers set sail for the Marianas. On June 15, troops went ashore at Saipan. The action was difficult, and the island was not firmly in American hands until July 9.

Battle of the Philippine Sea

Meanwhile, four hundred miles west of Saipan a great naval action had taken place — the Battle of the Philippine Sea.

For many months Japanese naval leaders had hoped to lure the American Pacific Fleet into a showdown engagement. They saw their opportunity when news began to trickle in to Japanese headquarters that American troops, supported by a huge naval task force, were fighting their way ashore at Saipan. Within hours of the American landing at Saipan, a Japanese carrier force set out for the Philippine Sea.

Aware of the Japanese fleet and confident that it was headed in his direction, Admiral Raymond A. Spruance alerted the task force supporting the Saipan operation. When a huge squadron of Japanese aircraft roared in its direction on June 19, 1944, the American fleet was ready. The result was disaster for the Japanese. Shipboard antiaircraft guns and American fighter planes devastated Japanese air groups and rendered Japanese naval air power a blow from which it never recovered.

A month later American marines and soldiers, after mopping up on Saipan, landed on Guam. The Japanese offered the usual fierce resistance. But after three weeks the island was firmly under American control. On July 25 other American forces landed on Tinian, less than four miles from Saipan. Supported by airplanes, which for the first time dropped napalm on enemy positions, they routed the Japanese after a week of hard fighting.

The Marianas victories in June-August 1944 were perhaps, next to Midway, the most crucial actions in the Pacific war to that time. Japanese leaders began to realize that victory for Japan was impossible and that total destruction of the Japanese empire was probably inevitable. From their new base in Saipan submarines of the United States would be able to step up attacks on Japanese shipping. And from air strips on

Saipan, Tinian, and Guam B-29 Superfortresses would bomb the Japanese home islands. In the meantime, the Allies would move closer from island to island. Still, the Japanese, like the Germans, were of no mind to surrender. Instead the leaders of Japan sought to gird their citizens for the ordeal ahead by ousting the ministry of General Tojo, which they blamed for recent military disasters.

Allies Move into the Philippines

To the south of the Marianas the forces of General MacArthur also had been active.

After securing the Admiralty Islands, in March 1944, MacArthur turned his attention to New Guinea. On April 22 American soldiers supported by land-based and carrier-based aircraft and naval gunfire, went ashore on the north coast of the huge island. Within a month the Americans had established bases for the continuing movement up the New Guinea–Mindanao axis. In mid-May 1944 American soldiers took the island of Wadke just off the coast of New Guinea. After Wadke, the Americans took the big island of Biak, although it took GIs two months to eliminate enemy resistance. Whatever the expense, Biak gave the Allies another excellent base for the movement on the Philippines.

At great cost of human life, MacArthur and Nimitz took a series of islands — Sansapor, Morotai, Palau, Ulithi, Ngulu — setting the stage for the invasion of the Philippines. In mid-October a huge amphibious force moved toward Leyte. On the morning of October 20, after naval guns and bombing planes had shelled the landing zones, army troops splashed onto beaches along Leyte's northeast coast, meeting little opposition. Later that day General MacArthur waded through the surf onto a beach, went before a truck-mounted radio microphone, and announced: "People of the Philippines. I have returned."

The Battle of Leyte Gulf

Main elements of the American Pacific fleet now moved into the waters around Leyte. The Japanese determined to engage American ships in another showdown battle which might stall the Allied advance toward the Japanese home islands. Virtually the entire remaining Japanese navy headed for Leyte — leading to what became the greatest naval action in history, the Battle of Leyte Gulf, October 23-27, 1944. The Japanese cleverly divided their fleet into three parts. Japanese pilots using *Kamikaze* tactics crashed their planes loaded with explosives on the decks of American warships. But the result was overwhelming defeat for the Japanese navy.

The Allies Take Luzon

Fighting in the jungle and valleys of the island of Leyte continued well into 1945. While the battle continued to rage on Leyte, the United States took another step toward Luzon. In mid-December a convoy, after running a gauntlet of *Kamikaze* attacks, unloaded American army troops on the beaches of Mindoro, a large island south of Luzon. Opposition was minimal.

On January 9, 1945 army troops—their convoy again subjected to murderous *Kamikaze* attacks—waded onto the beaches of Lingayen Gulf on the northeast coast of Luzon. The landings were fairly easy. Within a short time GIs had secured a beachhead and built fields for airplanes which would support their drive southward through the jungle toward their principal objective, Manila. As anticipated, Japanese resistance stiffened when the Americans, supported by Filipino guerrillas, pushed inland.

At the end of January, American soldiers landed at other points on Luzon and began to advance toward Manila. At length, in early February, the Americans reached the outskirts of the city, but the Japanese who were inside determined to fight to the bitter end. The result was brutal house-to-house combat which lasted until early March and left the city devastated. While the battle inside Manila continued, other American forces, after a heavy naval and aerial bombardment, rooted the Japanese out of the caves and tunnels of Corregidor. Next came the task of clearing Manila Bay of several hundred sunken Japanese ships and getting port facilities in shape to support the final Allied lunge toward Japan.

The battle for Luzon did not finally end until the imperial government in Tokyo surrendered in August 1945.

By February 1945 it was clear that the war in Europe would probably be over before summer. The outlook in the Pacific did not appear so promising. The Americans and their allies had swept the Japanese from most of their island bastions in the Western Pacific and nearly blasted their navy from the sea and their air forces from the sky. But the Japanese still retained a formidable army and a rugged homeland which offered unlimited opportunities for defense. Moreover, the Japanese had a fanatical determination to resist an invasion of their home islands. Totally unaware that scientists and engineers in America were perfecting a nuclear weapon of unimaginable power, most American military and naval leaders estimated that it would take another eighteen months after defeat of Germany to subdue Japan.

In February 1945, then, the war in the Pacific seemed far from over.

Iwo Jima

To further weaken Japanese resistance and hasten the end of hostilities, Major General Curtis E. LeMay dispatched large formations of B-29 Superfortresses from bases on Saipan, Tinian, and Guam in the Marianas against targets in Japan. The Marianas-based bombing campaign, however, encountered difficulties. First, Japanese aircraft, based on the tiny volcanic island of Iwo Jima, were intercepting B-29s as they made their way to Japan. Second, because the south coast of Japan lay 1,400 miles from the Marianas, it was not possible for fighter planes to escort the big B-29s over the enemy homeland. Third, again because of the distance separating the Marianas and Japan, crippled B-29s often had been unable to make it back to base hence had gone down in the sea.

The solution seemed obvious: drive the Japanese from Iwo Jima, which lay halfway between the Marianas and Japan. Japanese airfields on Iwo Jima would then become bases from which American fighter planes could escort B-29s over Japanese targets and as landing fields where crippled B-29s could touch down for repairs before flying back to the Marianas. And so, on February 19, 1945, after the most intensive bombardment of any invasion target in the Pacific war, marines went ashore on the south coast of Iwo Jima.

Meeting almost no opposition on the beaches, the marines moved inland. They met a hail of fire. On the third day they cleared the enemy from Mount Suribachi on the southwest end of the island.

After pushing the Japanese from the western half of the island the marines restored Iwo Jima's principal airfield. While the battle raged

Official U.S. Navy Photo

Marines raised the flag on Mt. Suribachi, Iwo Jima, February 23, 1945, but the Japanese held the island for another month. Why was the capture of Iwo Jima so important to Allied strategy?

on the rugged eastern half of the island, damaged B-29s began to use the facility. By mid-March 1945, organized resistance on Iwo Jima came to an end.

The Okinawa Campaign

Attention now turned to Okinawa, an island in the Ryukyu chain only 350 miles Southwest of Japan. Okinawa had been selected as a substitute for Formosa as the final jumping-off point for the invasion of the Japanese home islands.

In late March 1945, under the command of Admiral Spruance, a giant American invasion force started out from Eniwetok, Ulithi, Saipan, and Leyte and converged on Okinawa. Before hitting Okinawa, however, soldiers and marines took several adjacent islets, and GIs destroyed several hundred Japanese suicide boats. Next, on April 1, Easter Sunday, after warships and planes had pounded the landing zones, army troops went ashore on the west coast of Okinawa, twenty miles above the southern tip of the island.

In accordance with the Japanese defense plan, GIs who hit Okinawa's beaches on April 1 met no opposition and over the next few days established a beachhead. Then, suddenly, on April 6, the Japanese launched a massive suicide attack from the air. Two hundred *Kamikazes*

screamed down on the American fleet. In five hours they sank six ships and damaged eighteen others. But the attack fell short of its goal and did not turn the tide of the campaign in favor of the Japanese.

The *Kamikaze* assault of April 6 caused slight interference with the operations of ground forces on Okinawa, now swollen by the arrival of additional soldiers and marines. The northern part of the island was easily occupied. The southern part was a different matter. When American troops began to push southward from their beachhead, they encountered the bulk of the Japanese army, still entrenched in pillboxes, tunnels, and caves on the southernmost part of the island. But American troops, taking advantage of their superior numbers and firepower, broke the stalemate and slowly expelled the Japanese from their positions.

Offshore, meanwhile, the *Kamikaze* attacks continued against American ships—and British vessels which joined the Okinawa campaign after the surrender of Germany in early May 1945. So heavy was the toll of Allied naval tonnage that the government in Washington, fearing a popular outcry, refused to disclose publicly how devastating the suicide attacks had been. In all, thirty-two ships—thirty of them American—went down in the waters off Okinawa, and sixty-one suffered heavy damage.

Finally, their food and ammunition nearly gone, the Japanese reached the end of their ability to resist in June of 1945. A few thousand of them surrendered. Others, including two ranking generals, committed *hara-kiri*. The battle for Okinawa had claimed the lives of more than sixty thousand Japanese soldiers, perhaps forty thousand civilian inhabitants of the island, and more than twelve thousand Americans.

Plans for the Invasion of Japan

With the capture of Okinawa, preparations for an invasion of the Japanese home islands were accelerated. The recent casualties on Iwo Jima and Okinawa indicated that an invasion of Japan would be the most bloody operation of the war. Some leaders estimated that conquest of the Japanese homeland could cost the lives of a quarter-million to a half-million Americans— more American lives than had been lost in the entire war in Europe and the Pacific up to that time. In the face of such prospects American leaders desperately hoped that the Japanese might accept an unconditional surrender before America's soldiers and marines hit the beaches of Japan.

In the weeks after the Okinawa campaign, the Japanese took a terrible pounding. B-29s, operating from Okinawa and the Marianas, and carrier-based aircraft turned Japanese cities into roaring infernos. Other planes isolated the home islands by sinking the ferry boats which linked one island with another. Allied battleships and cruisers moved unopposed up and down the Japanese coast, shelling harbors, railways, and other strategic targets. At the same time American submarines, which already had sent millions of tons of Japanese shipping to the bottom of the sea, mopped up the remnants of the enemy's merchant marine.

The loss of Okinawa and the stepped-up air and naval campaign against their home islands persuaded some Japanese leaders, including Emperor Hirohito, that the time had come to seek an end to the war. The Japanese government hoped that the Soviet Union, with which Japan was not yet at war, might act as an intermediary. It indicated to the Russian government in Moscow that Japan might be willing to accept a negotiated settlement of the war in the Pacific.

The Soviets brushed aside the Japanese overtures. If the Pacific conflict ended before the Soviets could enter it, they might be deprived of concessions in Manchuria and elsewhere which the Americans and British had promised them as compensation for joining the war against Japan after defeating Germany. (Thanks to the decoding device "Magic" the Americans were fully aware of the nature of the communications between Tokyo and Moscow.)

From July 17 to August 2, 1945, President Truman, Prime Minister Churchill—replaced during the meeting by Clement Attlee—and Premier Stalin met at Potsdam, near Berlin, to discuss postwar administration of Europe. The leaders of the "Big Three" powers also talked about Japan. On July 26, representatives of China joined with two of the "Big Three"—England and the United States—in issuing the Potsdam Declaration, calling for Japan's unconditional surrender.

Unfortunately the declaration did not include a statement drafted by the American secretary of war, Henry L. Stimson, that the Allies might be willing to accept a constitutional monarchy headed by the present emperor as the postwar government of Japan. Assuming that the Potsdam declaration meant that the Allies planned to oust the emperor, the prime minister in Tokyo announced rejection of the declaration on July 28.

STUDY GUIDE: Japanese leaders hoped to conquer all of Southeast Asia and set up a giant defensive barrier across the Western Pacific. After conquering the British fortress of Singapore, the Japanese wiped out Allied naval power in the Java Sea and took over the Netherlands Indies. The Japanese invaded the Philippines, forcing American and Filipino forces to retreat. In vicious fighting on Bataan and Corregidor American troops were forced to surrender. Japan's hope of conquering New Caledonia, the Fiji Islands, and Samoa was defeated, thanks to American knowledge of the Japanese secret code. American forces won a victory over the great Japanese task force at Midway Island in the Central Pacific. Then the Japanese were forced to retreat at Guadalcanal after fierce fighting on land and sea. Meanwhile American and Australian forces were fighting to remove the Japanese from New Guinea. They won a great victory in the battle of the Bismarck Sea, removing the threat of a new Japanese attack on New Guinea.

At the Casablanca Conference Franklin Roosevelt persuaded Churchill that the Allies, mainly Americans, should undertake new offensive operations in the Pacific.

After a lull in the Pacific theater in early 1943, American forces swung into action across the Solomon Islands and also captured the Admiralty Islands. In a drive to knock out Japanese defenses in the mid-Pacific, American forces fought their way to victories in the Marshall, Gilbert, Marianas, and Caroline islands. After the Japanese fleet met disaster at the Battle of the Philippine Sea, American troops secured their position on Saipan and Guam. With these new bases, the Americans could step up attacks on Japanese shipping.

In a campaign to get back the Philippines, American forces cleared Japanese troops from parts of New Guinea and built bases. Enemy resistance was wiped out after bitter fighting on Wadke and Biak islands. In late 1944 a huge amphibious force invaded the Philippines at Leyte and fought a series of battles against the much weaker Japanese fleet. The Japanese put up stiff resistance at Leyte and Luzon.

In early 1945 victory in the Pacific still seemed far off to American military leaders.

To obtain a base on Iwo Jima, American marines fought a fierce battle and suffered heavy losses. At Okinawa Japanese suicide planes inflicted heavy losses on American ships before Japan acknowledged defeat.

American military leaders, afraid of heavy American casualties, faced the grim prospect of invading the Japanese home islands. The Potsdam declaration announced Allied intentions to accept nothing less than Japan's unconditional surrender. This made the Japanese determined to fight till the death.

THE ATOMIC BOMB

Rejection of the Potsdam declaration signaled final preparations for the most fateful air strike in history—the atomic raid on Hiroshima in southwestern Japan.

In 1896 a French scientist discovered radioactivity in uranium ore. Next, in 1905, a brilliant physicist in Germany, Albert Einstein, published his theory of relativity, which indicated that the tiny invisible atom contained within itself enormous stores of energy. Over the next three decades physicists sought to release the power of the atom. Then, in early 1939, the world scientific community was startled by the news that a German nuclear physicist had succeeded in ripping open a uranium atom.

In America nuclear physicists were deeply alarmed. They understood that nuclear fission held out the possibility of an explosive device of unimaginable power. What would be the fate of the world if the Nazis continued their experiments and succeeded in producing a nuclear weapon? Accordingly, in March 1939, two physicists—one of whom was Enrico Fermi, an Italian who had migrated to the United States to escape the tyranny of Mussolini—traveled to Washington and outlined their fears to officials in the Navy Department. They received nothing more than a polite hearing.

In the summer of 1939, two other scientists called at the summer home of Albert Einstein on Long Island. Several years before, Einstein had fled Hitler's persecution of Jews in Germany and had become an American citizen. The scientists wanted Einstein to send a personal appeal to President Roosevelt urging the chief executive to authorize a crash program to develop an atomic weapon. Einstein finally agreed to sign a letter which would be delivered to the president.

The task of delivering Einstein's letter to Roosevelt fell to Alexander Sachs, a friend of one of the scientists who had contacted Einstein. In October 1939, a few weeks after the Germans had invaded Poland, Sachs was able to arrange a meeting with the president. At first Roosevelt seemed only slightly impressed. But then Sachs reminded the president that the American inventor Robert Fulton had tried to persuade

(From left) Albert Michelson, Albert Einstein, and Robert Millikan confer in 1931. All three were winners of the Nobel prize for their scientific contributions. The work of Michelson and Millikan confirmed Einstein's theory of relativity. How did Einstein encourage the U.S. to develop an atom bomb?

California Institute of Technology Photo

Napoleon to build a fleet of steamboats to mount an amphibious assault against the British Isles. He suggested that the course of history might have been much different if Bonaparte had not dismissed Fulton as a dreamer. At that point Roosevelt directed his secretary to get an atomic bomb project underway.

For more than two years after the Sachs-Roosevelt meeting, the atomic research program seemed to move slowly. Then, in late summer 1942, Secretary of War Stimson placed Brigadier General Leslie R. Groves in charge of the project.

The Manhattan Project

Over the next three years General Groves applied his special organizational talents to the atomic program—the Manhattan project. Meanwhile a galaxy of scientists and mathematicians—including Vannevar Bush, James B. Conant, Hans Bethe, James Franck, Niels Bohr, George B. Kistiakowsky, J. Robert Oppenheimer, Isidore Rabi, Ernest O. Lawrence, and Arthur and Karl Compton—wrestled with the scientific problems connected with the production of a nuclear bomb. An initial problem which required a solution was that of starting, controlling, and stopping a chain reaction. The solution came in early December 1942 when a group of scientists led by Fermi produced such a reaction under the grandstand of Stagg Field at the University of Chicago.

Production of atomic weapons was as much an industrial task as a scientific one. An incredible array of equipment—as well as an army of engineers, technicians, and workers—was required to turn out the basic materials of the weapons. Factories and laboratories in Oregon, California, Wisconsin, Illinois, Michigan, New York, and Tennessee were involved. At the peak of the project, half a million people were employed in production of atomic materials. By the summer of 1945 that vast scientific-industrial establishment, at a cost of $2 billion, had brought forth less than one hundred pounds of atomic materials—enough for a test device and three bombs.

Los Alamos, New Mexico was selected as a site for construction of a laboratory where atomic bombs would be designed and assembled. To head the design-assembly operation, Groves turned to Robert Oppenheimer, one of the project's most brilliant nuclear physicists.

Security arrangements at Los Alamos, where work got underway in 1943, were extremely severe. Telephones and conference rooms were monitored. Scientists and engineers and their families at the installation were virtually cut off from the outside world. When a member of the Los Alamos team left the installation he was kept under constant surveillance by security agents. Because of such precautions—and similar precautions at other Manhattan project installations—not more than a handful of people in the country ever knew that scientists and engineers were building a super weapon. Axis agents never gathered more than a smattering of information on the huge atomic energy program.

So tight were security precautions that Harry Truman, even when he became vice-president in January 1945, was not told of the purpose of the Manhattan project. He remained in the dark until he moved to the White House in April 1945 on the death of Roosevelt. After his first cabinet meeting, when everyone else had left the room, Secretary Stimson told the new president that there was something he ought to know about. Stimson then explained that scientists and engineers in America were trying to develop an explosive device of incredible power.

Meanwhile, through the years 1943 and 1944, the men of the Manhattan project worked at an intense pace. They were spurred by fear that the Germans might be first to make a nuclear weapon. In late 1944 they were reassured when Allied intelligence agents reported that Hitler never had taken much interest in atomic energy and thus there was no chance that the Germans would turn out a nuclear weapon in the present war. Still, they did not relax and by summer 1945 were ready for a crucial test of their work. At a remote bombing range on the reservation of the Alamogordo Air Base in New Mexico, a plutonium device was attached to the top of a 100-foot tower. At 5:30 A.M. on July 16, it was touched off.

The result was stupefying. First came a searing flash which was visible for 250 miles. It enveloped the test area and nearby mountain range in a dazzling glow of gold, orange, violet, gray, and blue which was many times brighter than the light of the midday sun. At the same time a column of white smoke and debris jetted upward, then billowed into a huge cloud. The column and cloud, which eventually reached an altitude of 40,000 feet, looked like a giant mushroom. Thirty seconds after the explosion those who were present for the test felt a blast of hot air; then they heard a deafening roar. To mislead Axis spies who might have heard reports of a great blast in the desert, project officials immediately put out a "cover" story that an ammunition magazine had exploded in a remote area of the Alamogordo Air Base reservation.

While scientists and engineers were perfecting an atomic bomb, several select B-29 crews were organized in the summer of 1944. They began training under Colonel Paul W. Tibbets, Jr.—the only member of the group who knew the purpose of the training program. Pilots and bombardiers were puzzled when they practiced dropping a single dummy bomb over the wastelands of Utah. At length they were sent to Tinian where they continued their training. On July 16, 1945—the same day that scientists proved the feasibility of atomic weapons with the nuclear explosion in New Mexico—a huge crate was hoisted aboard the cruiser *Indianapolis*. Within a few hours the vessel was racing toward Tinian. The crate, which contained casings for atomic bombs, was deposited on Tinian Island on July 26. Other materials for the bombs arrived by air.

Before the Alamogordo test, some scientists on the Manhattan project had urged the president to order some sort of demonstration of the bomb to give the Japanese a chance to see what it could do. Astounded by the bomb's fearsome power and made aware that its use would result in total devastation of their cities, they might agree to surrender.

The idea of a demonstration unfortunately presented difficulties. What if the demonstration bomb failed to go off? The Japanese might conclude that America's talk of a super weapon was a bluff and be reinforced in their determination to resist. What if the Japanese responded by moving American prisoners of war to Japan's cities and then defied the Americans to bomb their own people? There was also the matter of using up precious atomic materials in a demonstration. Producing such materials was a time-consuming process and in August 1945 the United States had materials for only three bombs. If the Japanese refused to ask for peace after a demonstration, the United States would have only two bombs with which to carry out its threat to devastate Japan's cities.

Hiroshima and Nagasaki

In the early hours of the morning of August 6, 1945 a B-29 roared down an airstrip on Tinian, slowly took to the air, and headed toward south-

western Japan. It carried a single uranium bomb. The primary target of the mission was Hiroshima. When advance weather planes reported clear weather at Hiroshima the target was confirmed.

Over Hiroshima, the eighth largest city in Japan, the bomb bay doors of the B-29 swung open and the bomb, which had been armed en route, was released. The aircraft was traveling 328 miles per hour at an altitude of 31,600 feet. The pilot banked the plane sharply to the left, then, a few seconds later, it shook violently as it received shock waves from the blast. A blinding flash lighted the Japanese sky and a great cloud, like a giant mushroom, slowly rose from the earth. Below, in the rubble and heat and smoke, 70,000 people were dead or dying.

Because the bomb had virtually destroyed Hiroshima, leaders in Tokyo were unable to tell immediately what had happened. Even when they learned the extent of the disaster few of them were prepared to consider unconditional surrender. Some officials in Tokyo surmised—correctly—that the Americans had no large stockpile of bombs of the type which had hit Hiroshima. Others simply preferred destruction to surrender, especially if the Americans refused to consent to retention of the emperor in postwar Japan.

Two days after the raid, Japan's leaders received news which, in their estimate, was at least as distressing as that which had come out of Hiroshima. After months of moving men and equipment from Europe across the wastelands of Siberia, the Soviet Union declared war on Japan and launched an attack against Japanese armies in Manchuria. The prospect of an invasion of their home lands by Communist hordes from Russia caused leaders of Japan to shudder.

Still, Japanese leaders made no decision to surrender. On August 9, the Americans, fearing that impending bad weather might cause a long delay, sent a B-29 from Tinian toward the city of Kokura. In the B-29's bomb bay was a plutonium bomb. When weather planes reported bad weather at Kokura, the B-29 headed for the secondary target, Nagasaki. A few hours later Nagasaki was a smoldering ruin.

Events now were moving toward a climax. Just before midnight on August 9, leaders of Japan—including the emperor—met in the air raid shelter in Tokyo which adjoined the imperial library. Some diehards continued to prefer national destruction to surrender, but in light of the Soviet entry into the war and the Nagasaki raid, advocates of peace had gained the upper hand. After all others had given their views, the emperor, his voice shaking with emotion, stated that the government should ask for peace on the basis of retention of the empire.

The following day the Tokyo government, through the neutral governments of Sweden and Switzerland, sent its surrender terms to the Allies. The American response hinted that the emperor might be permitted to keep his throne. On August 14, the government in Tokyo advised the Allies that it was willing to sign surrender documents. The following day at noon, the emperor of Japan began a radio broadcast which was heard in every hamlet in the land: "We have resolved to pave the way for a grand peace for all the generations to come by enduring the unendurable and suffering what is insufferable."

On September 2, 1945 aboard the *Missouri* in Tokyo Bay, two representatives of the Japanese emperor signed the documents proclaiming Japan's surrender. When the Japanese had finished, representatives of the Allied countries put their signatures to the documents. The climax came when General MacArthur moved to the table, picked up a pen, and with trembling hand signed his name.

STUDY GUIDE: The Manhattan Project was a top-secret federal atomic research program begun in the early years of the war. The first atomic bomb was successfully tested in the New Mexican desert in July 1945. The successful development of the atomic bomb led to the American decision to drop a bomb on Japan. It was hoped that this would end the war quickly and avoid an American invasion of the Japanese home islands. American atomic raids on Hiroshima and Nagasaki inflicted widespread death and destruction and led to the Japanese surrender.

THE HOME FRONT

Between 1941 and 1945, more than in any other conflict in their history, Americans were engaged in total war. In one way or another, nearly the entire population and most of the physical resources of the nation were marshalled against the country's enemies.

The accomplishments of the national indus-

trial mechanism were enormous. To meet the requirements of war, Americans increased the output of iron ore, coal, steel, and oil. They shored up their depression-weary railroad network, put down new rail and signal systems, and built hundreds of new locomotives. They revitalized their shipbuilding industry. They discontinued or drastically cut back production of most consumer goods, retooled factories — which previously had brought forth automobiles, refrigerators, and washing machines — to manufacture howitzers and tanks. With billions of dollars of government capital they built new factories which in turn cranked out the tools of war. They operated their mines, steel mills, oil refineries, and factories on a twenty-four-hour schedule.

Despite a decrease in the number of individuals engaged in agriculture, America's farms dramatically stepped up output of most commodities.

The State of the Economy

Responsible in part for the economic achievements at home was a battery of federal agencies which met most of the problems arising from the effort to gear the national economy for war. The War Manpower Commission, for example, concentrated on solving labor shortages whenever such shortages threatened to slow operations in vital industries or in agriculture. The Office of Price Administration labored, with a fair measure of success, to keep a lid on prices and rents. The Office of Defense Transportation tried to keep the national transportation network functioning smoothly. Most important of all was the War Production Board, headed by Donald M. Nelson, who previously had been an executive of Sears, Roebuck and Company. Swinging into action in January 1942, a few weeks after Pearl Harbor, the WPB set about mobilizing the country's vast economic resources.

The chief overseer of the national economic effort during the war was President Roosevelt. The president approved battle plans which required greater quantities of equipment and supplies than industrial leaders and bureaucrats thought it possible to produce. The result was enormous production, which assured battlefield success.

It required enormous outlays of money to feed, clothe, equip, transport, and pay the more than twelve million men and women who filled the ranks of the country's armed forces. Between 1940 and 1946 the United States spent $360 billion for defense and war purposes. Where did the money come from? Part of the funds came from taxes. The government collected $155.8 billion in taxes between 1941 and 1945. Still, Congress, perhaps more responsive to the wishes of voters than was the executive branch, never was willing to go as far as the Roosevelt administration wished in voting tax increases. The administration wanted, through taxation, to pay for the war as it was fought; Congress preferred passing along much of the expense of the war to future generations. In any event, the government was forced to borrow, mainly through war bonds, to meet the major share of the war's costs. As a consequence the national debt went from $43 billion in 1940 to $269 billion in 1946.

The Joint Chiefs of Staff

Working closely with civilian leaders of the country and coordinating activities of the home front and theaters of military and naval operations in Europe and the Pacific were the Joint Chiefs of Staff. The joint chiefs were: Admiral William D. Leahy, the chief of staff for the president; General George C. Marshall, the army's chief of staff; Admiral Ernest J. King, chief of naval operations; and General Henry H. ("Hap") Arnold, the commanding general of the army's air forces. The chairman and key member of the JCS was General Marshall.

The Consequences of Mobilization

Apart from the enormous production of war materials and the atomic bomb, the greatest happening on the home front in the years 1941-45 was the advent of a rampaging prosperity. Spurred by war contracts, business in America boomed. Unemployment virtually disappeared and, despite high taxes and inflation, the American worker could not recall when his pockets had bulged with so much money. Even the farmer prospered in these war years, and for a time the country lived in the blissful absence of a farm problem.

National mobilization had other consequences. It stimulated large movements of people. By August 1945, the distribution of population in the United States was considerably changed from what it had been in December

Americans at home contributed to the war effort by accepting food rationing and price and wage controls. They cultivated victory gardens and did without many consumer items. They also bought war bonds. Why did the government finance the war by issuing war bonds instead of raising taxes?

1941. Military installations, shipyards, and aircraft factories in 1941-45 acted as giant magnets which drew people westward to Texas, California, and Washington. More important was the movement of people—many of them black—from rural areas in the Middle West and South to urban industrial centers in the Northeast.

These population shifts raised important social and economic problems. Most notable was that of the position of the black American in an urban-industrial society. The movement of population tilted the time-honored political balances. For example, it enlarged the political influence of the industrial states of the Northeast, and also such states as California and Texas. It also gave Negroes (who were not denied the vote in the North and West as they always had been in the lower South) a new opportunity to exercise political power.

During World War II such items as automobiles, gasoline, shoes, sugar, and meat were rationed. Books of ration stamps were issued to individuals to purchase rationed items.

Total war brought changes in the everyday lives of the people. Particularly troublesome were shortages of food, gasoline, and shoes. To make sure that every citizen received a fair share, the government issued ration books containing stamps which were essential when buying meat, butter, sugar, coffee, canned foods, gasoline, and shoes. The motorist, for example, received only enough ration stamps to purchase five gallons of gasoline per week. Cameras, alarm clocks, and even hairpins disappeared from store shelves. More serious, no automobiles were manufactured for civilian use in 1942-45. Almost as acute was the shortage of tires. Unable to buy new tires, most motorists had to have old ones recapped with synthetic rubber which often refused to stay cemented to old casings. When the family refrigerator, range or vacuum cleaner stopped working, it was very difficult to get a replacement.

These shortages made an unforgettable impression on Americans who served on the home front. For years to come they would recall, often with a trace of nostalgia, how they sat around the kitchen table carefully budgeting the family's ration stamps, struggled along with a dilapidated car, and helped to meet food shortages by having a "victory garden" in the back yard.

Still, Americans at home in 1941-45 were not entirely preoccupied with news from combat areas, production, and the shortage of meat and automobiles. Millions of them flocked—sometimes two or three times each week—to movie theaters. Virtually every American household had a radio and most families listened to it several hours each week. Spectator sports enjoyed a golden era during the war. College football stadiums spilled over with fans; horse racing enthusiasts wagered record sums; and boxing fans took great interest whenever the "Brown Bomber," Private Joe Louis of the army, defended his world heavyweight title. But it was major league baseball which enjoyed the greatest boom.

Hostility against Japanese-Americans

World War II did not bring a repetition of the anti-German hysteria of 1917-18, and German-Americans were seldom objects of abuse. The situation unfortunately was different for 126,000 Japanese-Americans, most of whom lived in California. Many of them were nisei—men and women who had been born and educated in the United States after their parents immigrated to America from Japan. Many of their parents had been United States citizens for many years.

Then came the raid on Pearl Harbor. In their anger over Japan's sneak attack, most Americans recoiled against all things Japanese. Japanese-Americans were the victims of this new hysteria. Reinforcing the hostility were wild fears, particularly along the Pacific Coast, that Japan might follow up the raid on Hawaii by attacking the mainland. Large numbers of people easily jumped to the conclusion that Japanese-Americans would support any Japanese raiders or invaders. There was little or no evidence that most Japanese-Americans even felt much sympathy for the government of Tokyo. But frightened citizens, newspaper editors, and other leaders of opinion demanded that the federal government evacuate all Japanese-Americans to internment camps in isolated areas in the interior of the country.

Responding to pressure from the West Coast and in the War Department, in February 1942 President Roosevelt authorized removal of Japanese-Americans to internment camps. This decision, in the words of Justice Frank Murphy of the Supreme Court, constituted "one of the most sweeping and complete deprivations of constitutional rights in the history of this nation."

Pending preparation of camps, Japanese-Americans were herded into uncomfortable assembly areas which were surrounded by barbed wire and guarded by helmeted sentries. Angry and hurt over such mistreatment, some Japanese-Americans renounced their American citizenship. Others determined to prove their loyalty to the United States on the field of battle, whereupon hundreds of Nisei entered the army and fought bravely in Italy and the South Pacific.

Negroes in the War Years

As in previous wars, black Americans seemed as willing as their white countrymen to fight under the Stars and Stripes. And a few months after Pearl Harbor, in spring 1942, the navy—which had previously accepted enlistment of only a handful of Negroes, mainly as cooks and stewards—announced that blacks would be recruited for general service. For the first time they would be permitted to become noncommissioned officers. By 1944 the navy had advanced to the point where it was willing to commission blacks as officers. Even the marine corps, which had never knowingly admitted a

Negro, felt compelled to accept black recruits for segregated units. As in the past, the army had no qualms about recruiting blacks—for all-black units—and Secretary of War Stimson insisted that Negroes should have equal opportunities with whites to attend officer candidate schools. Then, toward the end of the war, on an experimental basis, the army integrated a few combat units in Europe. Twenty-five hundred Negro troops ably fought beside white soldiers with the First Army on the east banks of the Rhine River.

In all, more than a half-million black Americans served overseas in World War II. A large percentage of them were assigned to port battalions, truck companies, and engineer construction battalions. Others saw combat service in tank, artillery, and engineer combat units. Many thousands of others fought in the all-black Ninety-second Infantry Division, which saw action in North Africa and Italy, and the Ninety-third Infantry Division, which was engaged in operations in the Solomons and Philippines in the South Pacific. Still other Negro Americans—eighty of whom received the Distinguished Flying Cross—flew in the all-black Ninety-ninth Pursuit Squadron and the 332nd Fighter Group. Black airmen shot down more than a hundred Axis planes.

In spite of their patriotic response, black Americans in 1941-45 found little relaxation of the racist attitude of many of their white countrymen. The Red Cross carefully separated the blood of white and black donors in its blood banks. In Kentucky three black women wearing the uniform of the Women's Army Corps were beaten by local policemen when they did not promptly obey an order to move to a "colored" waiting room in a railroad station. Eating establishments in several southern communities denied service to black GIs. On military and naval bases Negroes encountered segregated post exchanges, movie theaters, and white-only officers' clubs and barber shops.

Racial tensions flared into riots on several occasions. The most serious riot came in June 1943 in Detroit, whose population had swelled by the arrival of more than four hundred thousand Negroes from the South since Pearl Harbor. The riot set off a spree of killing and looting. Local and state police, assisted by federal troops sent to the city by President Roosevelt, finally restored order—but not before twenty-five Negroes and nine whites had died.

Fortunately the story of race relations in

U.S. Army Photograph

Over 1,000,000 black men and women enlisted in the armed forces during World War II. The famous 92nd Division of World War I was reactivated and fought in Italy. Members of the Third Battalion, 370th Regiment, advance through the vineyards around Cascina, Italy, September, 1944.

America included some accomplishments in the war years. The most notable was the economic advancement of many black Americans. Negroes swarmed into northern factories and shipyards, where they became skilled workers. Some even achieved supervisory status. By the year 1944 black workers comprised more than eight percent of the personnel in the country's war industries. Many were able to enjoy a higher standard of living than they had ever dreamed of, but prejudice and discrimination by their white countrymen compelled them to live in ghetto neighborhoods.

Assisting black working people during the war was the Fair Employment Practices Commission (FEPC), created in June 1941—several months before Pearl Harbor. The FEPC was established by President Roosevelt as part of an agreement with the distinguished black leader A. Philip Randolph. The commission was created to head off a proposed march on Washington by fifty thousand Negroes in protest against being excluded from employment in defense industries. Throughout the war the FEPC fought discriminatory employment practices with a fair measure of success and sought to enforce antidiscrimination clauses in federal contracts.

There were other encouraging developments. Lynching, long a device for maintaining white control of society in the South, declined during the war. There were new attempts among whites and blacks to achieve better harmony. In 1944, in Atlanta, a distinguished group of Negroes and whites organized the Southern Regional Council to combat prejudice and misunderstanding. And most important perhaps, increasing numbers of white Americans came to realize that abuse and discrimination against black Americans were utterly intolerable in the United States. Likewise increasing numbers of Negroes vowed that they would no longer accept the insults of the past. If they were good enough to fight and die for their country they were good enough to enjoy the blessings of first-class citizenship.

Wartime Politics

Perhaps the most notable political happening of the war years was the comeback of the Republican party. Wartime prosperity blunted memories of the great economic collapse of 1929, which had occurred during a Republican administration. Wartime taxes and shortages,

Roosevelt's success in winning the labor vote is reflected in this CIO endorsement of the president and his economic policies. How did FDR manage to win over organized labor?

we'll do it again!

Our President says we can have full employment and production in peace. He has confidence in us. We have confidence in him.

ROOSEVELT
for full production
for full employment

moreover, caused resentment against the Democratic party, which was in power. In such circumstances the Republicans gained strength. In the midterm elections of 1942 they won forty-six seats in the House of Representatives from the Democrats.

Encouraged by this good showing, the Republican party looked forward with optimism to the presidential election of 1944. At its national convention in Chicago, the party nominated the youthful governor of New York, Thomas E. Dewey, for president. A man of ability and fairly liberal views, Dewey had won an enviable reputation in the politics of New York. In the campaign of 1944 he convinced many voters that the Democratic administration in Washington was old and tired. Still, Dewey was running against the greatest campaigner in American history, Franklin Roosevelt, who had been nominated for a fourth term at the Democratic national convention, also held in Chicago. In the popular balloting on election day Dewey ran well, winning 22,006,000 votes to 25,602,000 for Roosevelt. In the electoral college, on the other hand, he lost by a landslide, 99-432.

As matters turned out, the most important political happening in 1944 was the nomination of Senator Harry S. Truman of Missouri for the vice-presidency. The conservative wing of the Democratic party never had approved of Henry A. Wallace, the ultraliberal whom Roosevelt had selected as his running mate in 1940. In 1944 conservatives were threatening to drag their feet in the autumn campaign if Wallace was on the ticket again.

Roosevelt, exhausted and distracted by the war, took little interest in the vice-presidential contest until it appeared that the party might blow apart on the issue. At that point he decided that Truman should be the second man on the Democratic ticket. Probably nobody was more surprised by the decision than was Truman. Truman had arrived at the convention with every intention of nominating James F. Byrnes of South Carolina. Only when he heard by telephone from Roosevelt would he believe that he was the president's choice.

Roosevelt was only sixty-two years old when he won reelection, but the burdens of depression and war had been heavy and his health was failing. Through the year 1944 he frequently was absent from the White House and was functioning as a part-time president. Why then did he seek reelection? Apparently because he had come to believe the Democratic slogan that it would be a mistake for the country to "swap horses in the middle of the stream"—to change leaders during a war which was going extremely well. Roosevelt made a gallant attempt during the campaign to prove his vigor, parading, for example, for several hours through the streets of New York City in a heavy rainstorm.

After the election, Roosevelt more or less dropped from public view. Then, in February 1945 he returned from a summit meeting with Prime Minister Churchill and Premier Stalin at Yalta in the Crimea, and observers were shocked by his sagging appearance. Reporting on the Yalta meeting to a joint session of Congress, he referred, for the first time in his public career, to his physical infirmity when he apologized for remaining seated during the speech.

In early April 1945, as the war in Europe was swirling to a conclusion, Roosevelt boarded a special train of the Southern Railway for the Little White House at Warm Springs, Georgia. He hoped that the sunshine and soothing waters of the springs would revive him for the coming San Francisco conference, where his dream of a United Nations would achieve fulfillment. But, while sitting for a portrait on the afternoon of April 12, he complained of a severe headache and lost consciousness. A short time later the president was dead of a massive cerebral hemorrhage.

STUDY GUIDE: The nation's industrial and agricultural complexes achieved remarkable results in stepping up production for the war effort. The American economy boomed during the war. Large population shifts occurred within the United States. Many people, especially southern Negroes, moved to urban centers in the Northeast to work in defense plants, while California and other western states drew many workers. Food and gasoline shortages were common during the war. Japanese-Americans suffered discrimination, particularly on the West Coast, and were held in internment camps. Black Americans faced discrimination and segregation in the armed services. Full employment on the home front helped some Negroes to advance economically. Some federal efforts were made to end job discrimination.

In 1944 Roosevelt won a fourth term by defeating the Republican presidential candidate, Governor Thomas Dewey of New York. Roosevelt's health was failing from carrying the burdens of war, and he died in April 1945. Vice-President Harry S. Truman became president.

WARTIME DIPLOMACY

Leaders of the United States in 1941-45 sought to avoid a repetition of the mistakes which the victorious powers had made after the armistice of November 1918. American leaders were determined that after World War II all nations would heed the ideas of Woodrow Wilson and accept the principles of "universalism."

How, under the Wilsonian or "universalist" system, would peace be preserved in the postwar world?

United States diplomats believed that the time had come to put aside the balance-of-power concept and place responsibility for peace in the hands of a new international organization. This is what Wilson had hoped the League of Nations would do. The new organization would respond promptly, automatically, and effectively to international disturbances in any corner of the world.

Leaders in the Kremlin had goals in the war which ran roughshod over the American view that each nation in the world should have a right to shape its own destiny without outside interference. They were determined to incorporate the Baltic states—Latvia, Estonia, and Lithuania—into the Soviet Union and to exercise control over such countries as Poland, Rumania, and Hungary. They were determined to regain and keep the concessions which they had received in Eastern Europe as the result of their infamous deal with Hitler in August 1939. As for American ideas of an international peace-keeping organization—a United Nations—the Soviets could not have cared less. However, they consented, with no enthusiasm, to assist in the creation of such an organization.

Several international conferences of Allied leaders were held during World War II to determine policies. In the conferences Americans, Britons, Russians, and Chinese weighed questions of strategy for pressing on with the war and for postwar political and territorial arrangements. (See table on pages 604-605.)

From late August to early October 1944, at Dumbarton Oaks near Washington, D.C., representatives of the United States, Great Britain,

WORLD
WAR   II

SAVE FREEDOM OF WORSHIP

EACH ACCORDING TO THE DICTATES OF HIS OWN CONSCIENCE

NORMAN ROCKWELL

BUY WAR BONDS

1   Library of Congress

2   Courtesy Franklin D. Roosevelt Library. Hyde Park, New York   3   Courtesy of the Office of the Secretary of Defense

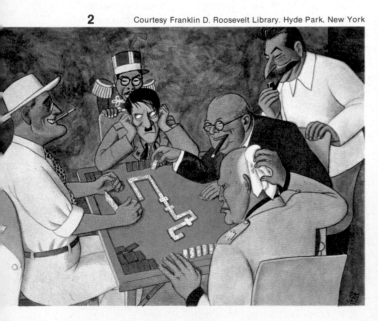

1

Norman Rockwell, an American artist, painted *Four Freedoms* posters to promote the sale of United States bonds to finance the war. *Freedom of Worship* is shown here.

2

Doble-Nueve is the title of this cartoon, which was given to President Roosevelt by a Cuban artist. It shows Roosevelt, Hitler, Churchill, and Mussolini playing dominoes while Hirohito and Stalin watch. Churchill is about to win the game by playing a double nine. The cartoon was made in Havana in 1944.

3

In February 1945 leaders of the Big Three allied nations met at Yalta on the coast of the Black Sea. President Roosevelt represented the United States, Prime Minister Churchill represented Great Britain, and Premier Stalin came from Russia. The three men met to discuss plans for the postwar world.

5 US Navy Photo

4

The United States dropped an atomic bomb on Hiroshima, Japan's eighth largest city, on August 6, 1945. This photograph records the result. More than 70,000 persons died almost instantly. American leaders hoped that the bomb would force Japan to surrender and end the war.

5

The United States dropped a second atomic bomb on Nagasaki on August 9. The next day the Japanese opened negotiations for peace. The Japanese officially surrendered on board the U.S.S. *Missouri* on September 2, 1945. General Douglas MacArthur signed for the Allies and General Yoshijiro Umeza signed for Japan.

4 *U.S. Air Force*

INTERNATIONAL CONFERENCES HELD DURING WORLD WAR II

Date	Location	Participants	Purpose
Aug. 1941	Atlantic Ocean	Roosevelt Churchill	Stated the principles of the Atlantic Charter.
Dec. 1941	Washington, D.C.	Roosevelt Churchill	Reaffirmed that Germany was principal enemy, thus Germany's defeat should receive priority. Accepted United Nations.
Aug. 1942	Moscow	Churchill W. A. Harriman	Told Stalin that Western powers would not be able to open a second front on the European continent in 1942.
Jan. 1943	Casablanca	Roosevelt Churchill	Reached compromise on Anglo-American invasion of Europe and an operation in the Pacific.
May 1943	Washington (Trident Conference)	Roosevelt Churchill	Agreed that in spring 1944 Anglo-American forces would cross English Channel and make a full-scale invasion of Northern France.
Aug. 1943	Quebec (Quadrant Conference)	Roosevelt Churchill	Reaffirm plans for cross-Channel operation in spring 1944. Agreed to supplementary invasion of France via the Mediterranean, and approved increased military and naval operations in Western Pacific.
Oct. 1943	Moscow (Conference of Foreign Ministers)	C. Hull A. Eden V. M. Molotov	Discussed future status of Poland; established committee to fashion policy for postwar Germany; agreed that peace-loving states should set up international organization—a United Nations—at earliest possible date.
Nov. 1943	Cairo (First Cairo Conference)	Roosevelt Churchill Chiang Kai-shek	Considered war in Pacific. Declaration of Cairo; pledged to continue war in Pacific until Japan surrendered unconditionally; restore Manchuria, Formosa, and Pescadores to China; bring about independence of Korea.
Nov. 1943	Teheran	Roosevelt Churchill Stalin	Concentrated on invasion of France. Talked also about structure of a postwar international organization to keep the peace. Stalin reaffirmed his promise to enter war against Japan after the defeat of Germany. In vague way Churchill and Roosevelt agreed that Soviets should receive some concessions—perhaps in Manchuria—for joining war in Far East.
Dec. 1943	Cairo (Second Cairo Conference)	Roosevelt Churchill I. Inönü	Affirmation of friendship between Turkey and United States, Great Britain, and Soviet Union. Decision that Eisenhower should be supreme commander of coming cross-Channel invasion.
July 1944	Bretton Woods (United Nations Monetary and Financial Conference)	Representatives of forty-four nations	Established an International Monetary Fund of $8.8 billion to stabilize national currencies and foster world trade. Also set up the International Bank for Reconstruction and Development to extend loans to nations requiring large-scale economic assistance.

Date	Location	Participants	Purpose
Aug.-Oct. 1944	Dumbarton Oaks	Representatives of United States, Britain, Soviet, China	Drew up plans for permanent postwar international organization. Dumbarton Oaks Plan placed responsibility for keeping peace with Security Council dominated by major powers. Plan served as basis for Charter of the United Nations.
Sept. 1944	Quebec (Second Quebec Conference)	Roosevelt Churchill	Considered war strategy and postwar status of Germany. Gave tentative approval to Morgenthau Plan — later rejected by FDR — stripping Germany of industrial capacity and reducing it to agrarian nation.
Oct. 1944	Moscow (Second Moscow Conference)	Churchill Stalin	Agreed that after war Rumania, Bulgaria, Hungary and part of Yugoslavia would be in Soviet sphere of influence; Greece and part of Yugoslavia in British sphere. After war Soviet should receive large part of Eastern Poland. Poland should receive compensation at expense of Germany. Roosevelt — not party to these arrangements — considered them not binding on the United States.
Feb. 1945	Yalta	Roosevelt Churchill Stalin	Discussed boundaries for Poland, Russian entry into war on Japan, and UN organization.
July-Aug. 1945	Potsdam	Truman Stalin Churchill (replaced by Attlee)	Agreements on occupation and administration of German territory. Russia renews pledge to go to war with Japan.

the Soviet Union, and China drew up a formula for a permanent postwar international organization. By placing primary responsibility for keeping peace with a security council dominated by the major powers the Dumbarton Oaks plan provided for a stronger international agency than had the covenant of the old League of Nations. The organization was weak, however, since permanent members of the security council would have the power to veto any action proposed by the council — a defect which had not burdened the League. The plan served as a basis for the Charter of the United Nations, which was approved the following spring (1945) at San Francisco.

The Yalta Conference

In February 1945 the wartime "Big Three" — Roosevelt, Churchill, and Stalin — held the most controversial of the international conferences of 1941-45 at Yalta in the Crimea. After the war many critics in the United States accused Roosevelt and Churchill (mainly Roosevelt) of having "sold Eastern Europe and Chiang Kai-shek down the river" to communism at Yalta.

During the Yalta conversations, Roosevelt and Churchill tentatively agreed to new boundaries for Poland. They insisted, however, that a final decision on Poland's postwar boundaries must await a general peace conference — a conference which was never held.

Presumably the Poles would cede to the Soviets all of their territory east of the so-called Curzon Line. This line, drawn by Britain's Lord Curzon during World War I, represented — or so Curzon thought — an appropriate dividing line between Poland and Russia. The line was ignored after the war when a permanent boundary between the two countries was worked out. Everyone at Yalta took pains to point out that the population of the Polish lands east of the Curzon line was predominantly Russian, not Polish. It was tentatively agreed that Poland would receive a comparable tract of territory from Germany as compensation for its lost eastern territory. Poland, in effect, was moved seventy-five to one hundred miles westward.

There was little that Roosevelt and Churchill could do except to agree, even tentatively, to such border revisions. Soviet armies were in Poland, those of the United States and Great Britain were not. Moreover, Roosevelt and Churchill had hoped that by agreeing with Stalin on the boundary question he might allow the Poles to establish their own government. Also, Roosevelt, and to some degree Churchill, wanted Stalin's support for a postwar international organization. Roosevelt thought that to break with Stalin over Polish border arrangements might ruin any dream of an effective international union. Clearly the new world organization would have no chance of success if it did not secure cooperation of all major powers.

Stalin promised "free and unfettered elections" in Poland and other nations of Eastern Europe. He also insisted that the Lublin Committee, comprised of Polish Communists—rather than the Polish government in exile in London—should provide the basis for a provisional government in Poland until elections could take place. This amounted to placing a Soviet-dominated government in power since members of the Lublin Committee were simply puppets of the Soviet Union.

Stalin also wanted an Anglo-American commitment that after the war Germany would be broken up into several small states. Roosevelt and Churchill were convinced that such action would produce economic weakness and political instability in Central Europe which would work to Soviet advantage. So, despite Stalin's pressure, Roosevelt and Churchill held firm.

At Yalta the British and Americans wanted to make final arrangements for getting the Soviets into the war against Japan as soon as possible after the defeat of Germany. A short time before the Yalta meeting Stalin had spelled out the concessions that he expected in return for joining the war against Japan.

He wanted a continuation of the Soviet-sponsored Communist regime in Outer Mongolia. He wanted restoration to Russia of privileges lost as a result of the Russo-Japanese war of 1904-05: return of the southern half of Sakhalin Island; internationalization of the port of Dairen in Manchuria, which meant that Soviet goods would pass through the port without duty; restoration of Port Arthur as a Russian naval base; and joint Sino-Soviet control of the Chinese Eastern and South Manchuria railways.

At Yalta President Roosevelt agreed to the Soviet terms for Soviet entry into the war

UNITED NATIONS/McCreary

Representatives of 49 countries signed the UN Charter in June, 1945. Above, a delegate from Ethiopia signs.

against Japan. Still, Roosevelt insisted that agreement by Chiang Kai-shek's government in China was also necessary. Chiang of course had little choice other than to accept the Yalta agreement. Thus, in August 1945, he ratified a treaty which formally granted the Yalta concessions to the Soviet Union.

Chiang Kai-shek believed that the terms of the treaty were more favorable to China than they would have been if the Soviets had entered the war without any prior agreements. In the years that followed, however, the tide of history ran against Chiang. By 1950 the Communists under Mao Tse-tung had routed him from the mainland of China and driven him to the island of Formosa. From many quarters in America came the charge that the Yalta agreement, by establishing the Soviets in Manchuria where they could easily reinforce Mao's forces, had opened the way for Chiang's defeat. These charges are considered in Chapter 18.

The United Nations

In April 1945, two months after the Yalta meeting, delegates from forty-nine countries arrived in San Francisco for a conference which, hopefully, would bring forth a charter for the new international organization—the United Nations. Although Americans were still mourning the sudden death of President Roosevelt, delegates began deliberations on April 25, using the Dumbarton Oaks plan as a base.

Before long representatives of the Soviet Union and the United States were locked in a dispute which seemed on the verge of blowing the conference apart. The dispute revolved around use of the veto by permanent members of the new organization's Security Council. The Soviets wanted to be able to use the veto to prevent the council from discussing an issue. The Americans were determined that the council should be free to discuss anything, that the veto should be exercised only to prevent the council from taking action. At length President Truman appealed to Premier Stalin, who instructed the Soviet delegation at San Francisco to yield to the American view on the veto question. Thereafter the conference proceeded fairly smoothly and on June 25, 1945, delegates unanimously approved the Charter of the United Nations.

The Charter of the UN established a structure for world cooperation, not one for effective world government. The delegates at San Francisco in 1945 were not prepared to sacrifice national sovereignty to an international organization. Like the League of Nations, therefore, the UN would lack financial independence and an ability to enforce its decisions—two handicaps which history had shown would doom almost any political organization to impotence.

The future of the UN would rest on the resolve and cooperation of the "great powers"— the United States and the Soviet Union. To the extent that the two superpowers were willing to carry out the will of the UN—that is, to the extent that their interests in the world ran parallel —the international organization would succeed. Unfortunately, even as delegates were approving the charter a cold war was taking shape between the UN's two most powerful members.

The United Nations in years to come would be able to perform important tasks aimed at relieving suffering and promoting health and the general welfare in poorer countries. And it would provide a channel of diplomatic communication and a forum from which nations, particularly smaller ones, could reach a world audience. But as a peace-keeping agency it would seem to flounder in a sea of Soviet vetoes.

The Potsdam Conference

The last of the great wartime conferences of 1941-45 took place at Potsdam, near Berlin, from July 17 to August 2, 1945. During the Potsdam meeting the new president, Harry S. Truman, headed the American delegation.

Several months before the Potsdam Conference—a few weeks after the meeting at Yalta—

the "grand alliance" began to weaken. It became increasingly clear in Washington and London that the Soviets had no intention of honoring their pledges regarding democracy and self-determination in Eastern Europe. Shortly before his death President Roosevelt expressed annoyance mixed with sadness when discussing Soviet behavior.

Truman had hardly settled into the presidential chair before he became aware of Soviet deceit, and a few days before the opening of the San Francisco conference he "dressed down" the Soviet foreign minister, Molotov. Startled by the president's remarks, Molotov exclaimed: "I have never been talked to like that in my life." Shot back Truman: "Carry out your agreements and you won't get talked to like that."

Meanwhile the British prime minister, Churchill, was becoming increasingly suspicious of the Soviets. In May 1945, a few days after Germany's surrender, he sent a long telegram to Truman in which he outlined his suspicions. He urged that Anglo-American armies continue occupying territory in Central Europe which, at Yalta, had been assigned to the Soviet zone of occupation. He felt that this was the only way to make sure that the Soviets were going to carry out their promises in Eastern Europe.

Truman chose not to follow Churchill's advice. He agreed with those State Department members who believed that the Western powers must try at least a while longer to get along with the Soviets. The president, to demonstrate America's goodwill, and also to establish a climate of friendship and trust for the upcoming Potsdam meeting, ordered American troops to withdraw to the American zone of occupation. The British had no choice except to retire to their own occupation zone.

During the conference at Potsdam the Americans and the British continued to tread softly in their dealings with the Soviets. As a result the Potsdam meeting was a friendly affair. But the Anglo-Americans also gave up one of their few remaining bargaining points. Without demanding a corresponding concession or some guarantee that the Soviets would live up to pledges regarding Eastern Europe, they agreed to transfer to the Soviet Union fifteen percent of the capital equipment in western zones of occupation in Germany.

Otherwise the leaders of the "Big Three" at Potsdam agreed to the establishment of a Council of Foreign Ministers which was to draft treaties with Austria, Hungary, Bulgaria, Ru-

mania, and Finland, settle outstanding territorial questions, and work out a peace arrangement with a central German government whenever such a government came into existence. They agreed that Germany should be disarmed, "denazified," and democratized. They also agreed that during the Allied occupation Germany should be treated as a single economic unit and that the German economy should be decentralized to eliminate the concentration of economic power which long had prevailed in Germany. Agriculture and "peaceful" industries were to be encouraged in Germany. The "Big Three" consented to procedures for bringing Axis war criminals to trial and agreed that Germany should pay reparations for losses inflicted on the Allies. The transfer of capital equipment in Western Germany to the Soviet Union was part of the reparations.

Finally, on July 26, the Potsdam Declaration was issued, demanding Japan's unconditional surrender.

Churchill, Truman, and Stalin appear friendly at Potsdam. However, Churchill and Truman were angered by Stalin's reluctance to aid them in the Pacific war. Stalin opposed their plans to return self-government to conquered European countries.

STUDY GUIDE: Although the United States had not been on good terms with the Soviet Union, Americans accepted the necessity of helping the Russians to defeat Germany. United States goals were very different from those of the Soviet Union. American leaders wanted each nation after the war to be able to shape its own destiny without interference. The Soviet leaders hoped to exercise postwar control over Eastern Europe. The United States and Britain took great pains in dealing with the Russians to avoid a separate Soviet-Nazi peace arrangement. The United States was committed to the idea that the Axis powers must be totally beaten and surrender unconditionally.

Numerous international conferences of heads of state were held during the war to shape wartime and postwar policy. Churchill and Roosevelt conferred on Anglo-American strategy. In 1943 at the Teheran Conference Roosevelt had his first meeting with Premier Stalin of the Soviet Union. Plans were drawn up for a permanent postwar international organization, the United Nations, at the Dumbarton Oaks Conference in 1944. The most controversial of the international conferences took place at Yalta in February 1945, attended by Churchill, Stalin, and Roosevelt. Stalin won concessions in Poland and also in East Asia in exchange for entering the war against Japan. In April 1945 delegates from forty-nine countries met in San Francisco to set up the Charter of the United Nations. The last great wartime conference took place in Germany at Potsdam, with President Truman heading the American delegation. The American alliance with the Soviets was already beginning to weaken because even at the early date Russian plans for domination of the Eastern European countries had become clear.

SUMMING UP THE CHAPTER

Names and Terms to Identify

Operation Torch	Joseph W. Stilwell
Erwin Rommel	*Kamikaze*
Bernard L. Montgomery	Henry L. Stimson
Albert Kesselring	Enrico Fermi
Operation Overlord	Manhattan project
Omaha Beach	Nisei
Auschwitz	FEPC
Jonathan M. Wainwright	Thomas E. Dewey
Chester W. Nimitz	Dumbarton Oaks Plan

Study Questions and Points to Review

1. How did the Germans introduce a new type of warfare in World War II?

2. Why did American leaders feel that Germany was a much more dangerous enemy than Japan?

3. What was British strategy for defeating Ger-

The map below shows the division between Communist and non-Communist countries that came to exist after World War II. The Soviet sphere of influence extended on all sides of the Soviet Union.

COMMUNIST COUNTRIES IN THE POSTWAR ERA, 1945-1965

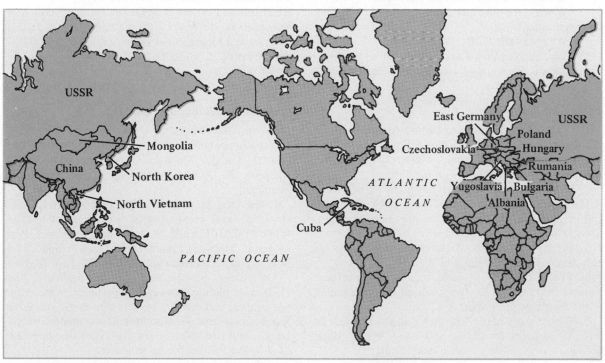

many? How did American military leaders view British strategy?

4. What caused the Italian regime to unconditionally quit the war in September 1943?

5. When did the cross-Channel invasion of Normandy take place?

6. What two new weapons did the Germans introduce shortly after the Normandy invasion?

7. Why was Eisenhower in no hurry to liberate the city of Paris?

8. How many Jews perished in Nazi concentration camps?

9. What was the United States plan for the war against Japan at the outset of the Pacific war?

10. What situation prompted General Douglas MacArthur to pledge: "I shall return"?

11. What was the "Bataan death march"?

12. What was unique about the Battle of the Coral Sea? Why was the battle a strategic triumph for the Americans?

13. Why is the Battle of Midway considered one of the most crucial actions of World War II?

14. What decision was made at the Casablanca Conference which had large bearing on the Pacific war?

15. Name the declaration which called for the Japanese to accept unconditional surrender or face utter destruction. What was Japanese reaction to it? Why?

16. What was an initial problem requiring solution before an atomic bomb could be produced?

17. When were the atom bombs dropped on Japan? On what cities?

18. Why was the FEPC created?

19. What conference was considered the most controversial of the wartime international conferences? Why?

Topics for Discussion

1. What was the reasoning behind America's "beat Germany first" strategy in World War II? How did the British propose to bring the Germans to defeat? What were American views on the subject?

2. Explain the reasons for the invasion of North Africa, Sicily, and Italy in 1942 and 1943. Trace the campaigns of these areas. Evaluate military operations in the Mediterranean.

3. Evaluate the Anglo-American strategic bombing campaign against Germany in World War II.

4. Trace the Anglo-American thrust into northern Europe in 1944-45. What accounted for the setback in the Battle of the Bulge?

5. Where did Chiang Kai-shek and the Chinese fit into Allied plans for defeat of Japan? Assess Allied activities in the China-Burma-India theater.

6. Why were Japanese-Americans interned during World War II? Try to project yourself into the climate of fear and anger of early 1942. Offer your own evaluation of the decision to remove Japanese to internment camps. What do you think might have been the attitude of those who were interned?

7. Consider the arguments for and against aid to the Soviet Union in 1941. Do you think the leaders of the United States showed good judgment in their dealings with the Soviets in the early stages of the war?

Subjects for Reports or Essays

1. Gather material from your school or local library and write an essay on the siege of Leningrad.

2. In a written report present your views on this statement: The United States should not have dropped atomic bombs on Hiroshima and Nagasaki in August 1945?

3. Write a brief biographical sketch of one of the following: General Douglas MacArthur, Admiral Ernest J. King, General George S. Patton, General Joseph W. Stilwell, Admiral William F. Halsey, Jr., Field Marshal Sir Bernard L. Montgomery, Field Marshal Erwin Rommel.

4. Assume it is November 1941. You are a newspaper editor. Write an editorial supporting or opposing lend-lease aid to the Soviet Union.

5. Using books found in your library, prepare a class report on one of the following topics: (a) Operation Overlord; (b) the Manhattan project; (c) the black American and World War II; (d) the contribution of women to World War II; (e) the home front.

6. Write a biographical sketch of one of the following: Winston Churchill, Josef Stalin, Franklin D. Roosevelt.

Projects, Activities, and Skills

1. On Atlas Maps 28 and 29, trace America's military campaigns in the European theater in World War II. Locate: Morocco, Casablanca, Ploesti, El Alamein, the Ardennes Forest, Berlin, Stalingrad, Leningrad.

2. On Atlas Maps 30 and 31, trace America's military and naval campaigns in the Pacific theater in World War II. Locate: Wake Island, Coral Sea, Port Moresby, Midway, Guadalcanal, Truk, Saipan, Iwo Jima, Okinawa, Hiroshima, Nagasaki.

3. Prepare a bulletin board display on World War II. Include photographs and biographical sketches of top political and military leaders. On maps locate the major military and naval actions. Using models, photographs, and souvenirs, show the types of equipment used by the fighting forces in the war.

4. Interview relatives and friends who served in the armed forces during World War II. Find out where they served and what they did during the war. Compare findings in class. Interview other relatives and friends who recall the wartime years 1941-45. Ask them to describe their recollections of the "home front."

5. Gather a collection of recordings of songs that were popular during World War II. After listening to the songs, report on what the music tells of the wartime mood of the country. Compare these songs with songs that were popular during World War I.

6. Prepare an illustrated report on weapons used during World War II. What were some of the important planes, ships, tanks, and small arms? What were their capabilities?

Further Readings

General

Between War and Peace: The Potsdam Conference and *Churchill, Roosevelt, and Stalin: The War They Waged and the Peace They Fought* by Herbert Feis. Two excellent studies of American diplomacy in World War II.
The Great Betrayal: The Evacuation of the Japanese-Americans During World War II by Audrie Girdner and Anne Loftis.
Guadalcanal Diary by Richard Tregaskis.
Hiroshima by John Hersey. Eyewitness accounts of what it was like when the bomb exploded.
Is Paris Burning? by Larry Collins and Dominique LaPierre. Describes the liberation of Paris.
The Last Battle by Cornelius Ryan. Describes the fall of Berlin.
The Longest Day by Cornelius Ryan. An account of D-Day, the Normandy invasion.
The Man Who Never Was: A True Story of Counterespionage by Ewen Montagu.

The Rise and Fall of the Third Reich: A History of Nazi Germany by William L. Shirer.
The Second World War (6 vols.) by Winston Churchill.

Biography

Anne Frank: Diary of a Young Girl by Anne Frank.
Atoms in the Family: My Life with Enrico Fermi by Laura Fermi.
George C. Marshall: Ordeal and Hope, 1939-1943 by Forrest C. Pogue.
Stalin: A Political Biography by Isaac Deutscher.
The Stilwell Papers by Joseph W. Stilwell.

Fiction, Drama, and Poetry

The Bridge Over the River Kwai by Pierre Boulle. Japanese prisoners build a bridge.
Burma Rifles by Frank Bonham.
The Caine Mutiny by Herman Wouk. A novel about American officers on a mine-sweeper who rebel against their inept, neurotic captain.
The Eve of St. Mark by Maxwell Anderson. A play about the courage of soldiers in war.
The Murder of Lidice by Edna St. Vincent Millay. A poem about a Czech village destroyed by war.

Pictorial History

The American Heritage Picture History of World War II by C. L. Sulzberger.
The Decline and Fall of Nazi Germany and Imperial Japan: A Pictorial History of the Final Days of World War II by H. Dollinger. An account of the last hundred days.
This Fabulous Century, 1940-1950, Vol. 5, by the editors of Time-Life Books.

CHAPTER 18

AFTER THE WAR

WHEN HISTORIANS RANKED the country's presidents in a poll in 1962, they placed Truman in ninth position and called him a "near-great" president. Even Republicans, who had few kind things to say about Truman in 1945-53, have tended to revise their opinion of the thirty-third president. Senator Barry M. Goldwater, for example, who at that time was hoping to win the White House, declared in 1963 that "the more I think about it, the more I think Harry Truman will go down in history as one of the greater presidents." He added that "what we need are leaders like Truman."

HARRY S. TRUMAN

Harry S. Truman's forebears plowed the earth and harvested crops in New England, New York, Maryland, Virginia, South Carolina, Kentucky, and Missouri. He was born in a little frame house in the village of Lamar in western Missouri in the year 1884. His father was a farmer and trader in livestock. After moving from place to place, the Trumans finally settled in the town of Independence, near Kansas City, and it was there that the youth grew to manhood. From livestock dealing and operating a farm outside the town, returns were good, and the Truman family lived comfortably.

At the age of ten the young Truman endured a severe case of diphtheria which weakened his eyes and ended his dream of going to West Point or Annapolis. Poor eyesight forced him to find refuge in books and music rather than the rough-and-tumble activities of most boys. On graduating from high school, just after the turn of the century, he moved from job to job until he finally settled down as a bank clerk. Following a series of financial reverses, his father and mother moved to the farm of Mrs. Truman's father near Grandview. In 1906 Harry joined his parents, deciding he would rather be a farmer than a bank clerk.

Early Career

Over the next decade, while many future colleagues in politics were attending college, Truman farmed. He also became active in poli-

tics, and received appointment as postmaster of Grandview. As an active Democrat, he traveled regularly to Kansas City to attend meetings of the Democratic organization in Jackson County —headed by the notorious Thomas J. ("Boss") Pendergast.

Truman was also active in the National Guard and in the spring of 1918 found himself on a troop transport headed for France. As captain of a field artillery battery, he saw brief but sharp combat in the Meuse-Argonne campaign in September-October 1918. On returning home he married his childhood sweetheart, Elizabeth Virginia ("Bess") Wallace. Next he and his former sergeant opened a clothing store in Kansas City, only to see their venture overwhelmed in the economic recession of 1922. Refusing bankruptcy, Truman eventually paid back all of his creditors.

Just before the clothing store failed, Truman received an invitation from the Pendergast political machine to run for county judge (county commissioner) of eastern Jackson County. Pendergast was fighting off a challenge to his control of the Democratic party in the county. Apparently he thought Truman, who had not been active with the Pendergast organization and who had a reputation for honesty, could strengthen his position. Truman accepted the nomination and won the election. In part because he had incurred the hostility of the Ku Klux Klan, he lost his bid for reelection in 1924. However, he returned to the courthouse in Jackson County in 1927. Over the next seven years he won acclaim for efficiency, industry, and honesty.

In 1934 Pendergast wanted to bolster his position in the state politics of Missouri. He settled on Truman to run for the United States Senate. No scandal had marred Truman's reputation. And his loyalty to the organization was beyond question. Truman won the Democratic nomination and walked to an easy victory in the election in November.

As do most freshman senators, Truman made no great impression. Then came disaster—or so it seemed. Tom Pendergast was convicted of accepting an enormous bribe to "fix" the state insurance commission and was sentenced in 1938 to prison. Truman declined to turn his back

HEADLINE
EVENTS

1941 Atlantic Charter

1942 United States and Great Britain establish War Crimes Commission

1943 Congress passes legislation to provide education and special training for disabled veterans

1944 Servicemen's Readjustment Act (GI Bill of Rights)

1945 Yalta Conference

Roosevelt dies; Truman succeeds to the presidency

War in Europe ends

War in Japan ends

Truman asks Congress for atomic energy policy

McMahon bill proposed; atomic energy commission of civilians

General Motors strike

General Marshall sent to China to urge coalition government

1945-1946 Trials of Nazi war criminals in Nuremberg

1946 Full Employment Act

Truman asks Congress to make Fair Employment Practices Commission a permanent agency

Civil Rights Commission appointed by Truman to study discrimination

Churchill delivers "Iron Curtain" speech in Fulton, Missouri

Legislative Reorganization Act

Truman seizes railroads

Truman asks for extension of Office of Price Administration

Atomic Energy Act; Atomic Energy Commission created

Truman announces Truman Doctrine

Twenty-second Amendment

Taft-Hartley Act

Marshall Plan (European Recovery program) announced

Treaty of Dunkirk between Britain and France

Presidential Succession Act

National Security Act creates National Military Establishment, Joint Chiefs of Staff, CIA, and National Security Council

Armed Forces merged under Secretary of Defense

Jackie Robinson becomes first Negro to play in major league baseball

Treaty of Rio de Janeiro (Rio Pact)

Truman seeks antiinflation legislation

Hoover Commission created to study executive reorganization

1947 *To Secure These Rights* (Report of Civil Rights Commission)

Brussels Pact between Britain, France, and Benelux countries

Berlin blockade; Berlin airlift begins

Congress provides funds for European recovery (Economic Cooperation Act); Economic Cooperation Administration

Ninth International Conference of American States; charter accepted for Organization of American States (OAS)

Independence of Israel declared

Truman calls special session of Congress to ask for wide authority to control profits, credits, and prices

Truman defeats Dewey for presidency

1949 Truman inaugurated president

Point Four program proposed in Truman's inaugural address

Reorganization Act

North Atlantic Treaty signed; NATO is created

Federal Republic of Germany created

National Military Establishment renamed Department of Defense

Soviets explode atomic bomb

Chiang Kai-shek establishes Free China government on Taiwan (Formosa); People's Republic controls mainland

1949-1950 Alger Hiss trial

1950-1953 Korean War

1951 Twenty-second Amendment

1955 Salk introduces polio vaccine

1965 *Autobiography of Malcolm X* (Malcolm X)

1967 Twenty-fifth Amendment ratified

on "the boss" and said that Pendergast had never asked him to do a dishonest deed.

With Pendergast in jail Truman's political career seemed to be ended. Few observers gave him much chance to win reelection in 1940. But Truman refused to concede defeat. He drove about Missouri rounding up support and was helped by several Democratic senators who spoke on his behalf. As a result, he won by a narrow margin in the Democratic primary and then, riding the coattails of President Roosevelt, defeated his Republican opponent handily in the November election.

As Truman began his second term in the Senate early in 1941, the country was stepping up its preparation for war. Catching a scent of profiteering and corruption in the national mobilization program, he persuaded the Senate to permit him to head a special investigating committee to look into the matter. The Truman Committee worked hard, lashed out at greed and self-seeking, and won recognition for reducing profiteering in defense industries. Still, most Americans in 1943 would have had trouble identifying Senator Truman.

Then came the year 1944. The Democratic party was badly split in the summer of 1944 over the nomination of Vice-President Henry A. Wallace, an uncompromising liberal. Many Democrats, responding to the conservative mood of the country, would have nothing to do with Wallace. At length Harry Truman, generally considered a "moderate," emerged as the compromise choice for vice-president on the Democratic ticket.

Truman Becomes President

Carried into office as Roosevelt's running mate, Truman took the oath as vice-president in January 1945. He then withdrew to the shadows and received little attention for the next three months. Then came the afternoon of April 12. Called to the White House, Truman was ushered to Mrs. Roosevelt's study on the second floor. When he entered, Mrs. Roosevelt stepped forward, put her arm around his shoulder, and quietly told him the president was dead. That evening at seven o'clock, in the Cabinet Room of the White House, Truman took the oath as the thirty-third president of the United States.

Most Americans had sympathy for this "average" man who faced the seemingly impossible task of succeeding Roosevelt. Truman, it turned out, was not as average as he appeared. He had a good mind and often astonished scholars with the breadth and depth of his knowledge. He hated pretense, felt compassion for society's underdogs, and had no patience with religious or racial intolerance. Truman also understood his own limitations and was willing to seek expert advice. He was a keen student of history and government and realized that some of the most successful presidents were those who had as-

Harry S. Truman is sworn in as the thirty-second president of the United States before members of his family and the cabinet. What were some of the problems Truman faced as president?

Compix

serted the powers of office. He knew further that they had not hesitated to make difficult decisions. As a reminder he kept on his desk a little sign reading, "The buck stops here." A mark of Truman the president was his willingness to take bold decisive action.

STUDY GUIDE: After working as a bank clerk and a farmer, Harry S. Truman became active in Missouri politics and won a seat in the U.S. Senate. He was a compromise choice for Democratic vice-presidential candidate in 1944. The little-known Truman became head of state a year later when Roosevelt died.

Walker-Missouri Tourism Commission

The Truman Library in Independence, Missouri, was dedicated in 1957. It is part of the National Archives. The library houses Truman's official papers.

DEMOBILIZATION AND RECONVERSION

Less than a month after Truman became president, the war in Europe ended. Although military men reckoned that it might take another eighteen months to subdue Japan, the White House was under pressure for limited demobilization. In response, the government approved discharge of a few veterans of the European campaigns and permitted some industries to return to nonmilitary production.

When the Japanese surrendered in August 1945, the pressure for demobilization became irresistible. By the end of September, the army was releasing 14,200 men per day. Then, in January 1946, Truman ordered a slowdown in demobilization because of Soviet maneuvers in Europe. The result was a national howl of protest. In such circumstances resistance was impossible and nine months after V-J Day the army's manpower had dwindled from 8,000,000 to 1,800,000.

As the cold war between the Soviet Union and the Western democracies took form, the president became more alarmed over the country's military weakness. He persuaded Congress in the spring of 1947 to extend the draft. He was defeated, however, when he proposed universal military training for all young men. The Communist take-over in Czechoslovakia early in 1948 sobered some people. In summer of that year Congress passed a new Selective Service Act requiring all men between the ages of eighteen and twenty-five to register for military service. In the area of national defense most congressmen nonetheless remained primarily interested in economy. At length Truman joined the economizers. The savings so realized enabled him to boast of a large budgetary surplus in 1949, but the country's armed strength reached a postwar low. On the eve of the Korean War, which broke out in June 1950, the army's manpower was down to six hundred thousand.

How should the country treat the veterans of World War II?

Long before World War II ended, Congress had passed legislation providing veterans with an impressive array of benefits. First, in 1943, came a measure providing education and special training for disabled veterans. In 1944 President Roosevelt signed the Servicemen's Readjustment Act, the famous GI Bill of Rights. This law provided for new veterans' hospitals, the physical and mental rehabilitation of the war's victims, a placement agency to help ex-servicemen and women find jobs, unemployment com-

World War II soldiers wore this insignia on their uniforms after being mustered out. They were allowed a period of time in which to replace their uniforms with civilian clothes.

pensation for veterans who could not find work, and low-interest loans to enable veterans to buy or improve houses, farms, or businesses.

The most heralded provision of the bill was one that helped veterans continue their education. Depending on length of service, the veteran could receive free tuition, books, and subsistence for job training or attendance of college. When the schooling provision of the act expired in 1956, nearly eight million veterans had received training or education. It had cost more than $14 billion, but most Americans considered it one of the best investments in the history of the nation.

As the United States took apart its great war machine and set about rewarding veterans, the country also wrestled with the complexities of converting the national economy from war to peace.

Employment

Many Americans faced the future with foreboding after World War II. How could the econ-

U.S. Army Photograph

Returning from overseas, a member of the 87th Infantry Division walks down the gangplank at Newport News, Virginia. Millions of men were mustered out of the armed forces at the end of World War II. What legislative action did Truman support to prevent a sudden increase in unemployment?

omy absorb the twelve million men and women who had served the armed forces? Would there be a depression?

Some Americans were not pessimistic. They believed that the country, craving consumer goods and bulging with savings accumulated during the prosperous years of war, would have no difficulty in shifting economic gears. They thought the economy did not have to alternate through periods of boom and bust. Through carefully controlled investment and spending, the federal government could guarantee prosperity. Accepting this logic, in September 1945 President Truman urged a "full-employment" bill proclaiming the principle that it was the responsibility of the federal government to promote maximum employment. Conservatives were aghast. They insisted that private enterprise alone should assume responsibility for the country's economic welfare. Although a conservative tide was running strong in postwar America, Congress in early 1946 passed the Full Employment Act. The measure created the Council of Economic Advisers to study the economy, advise the president, and assist in preparing an annual economic report to Congress. In the event that the economy revealed signs of weakness, the president was to recommend legislation to assure maximum employment.

As matters turned out, there was no depression, unemployment remained low, and most Americans forgot about the employment legislation of 1946. Still, the Full Employment Act was something of a landmark in American history. It imposed on the federal government the statutory responsibility to look after the national economic welfare and required it to take direct action to keep the economy prosperous.

Labor Problems

Despite planning, reconversion ran into snags. One snag was the unrest that seized the country's working people at the end of the war.

Emphasizing that labor had made few wage demands during the war, unions insisted on raises in pay. As a result, relations between labor and management deteriorated. In November 1945 workers at General Motors went on strike. Other strikes followed and over the winter of 1945-46 more than a million workers in such industries as steel and automobile manufacturing were off the job.

Then in spring 1946 President John L. Lewis of the United Mine Workers began demanding fringe benefits as well as a pay increase for miners. When coal operators refused Lewis's demands, the miners left the pits. Threatened with a shutdown of industries dependent on coal, President Truman seized the mines. In the end, however, Lewis achieved most of his goals. Several months later, in autumn 1946, Lewis made new demands. When he called another strike in defiance of a federal injunction, the government (which was still operating the mines) cited him for contempt. Miners stayed on the job, but several months later, after the mines had been returned to owners, Lewis won a new contract that met most of his demands.

The country, meanwhile, faced an equally serious threat. Railroad workers were considering a strike. As the threat of a walkout grew, President Truman seized the railroads in May 1946. He proposed a compromise settlement of the dispute, which the carriers and eighteen rail unions accepted. But two of the largest unions would not yield and ordered a strike. Furious, Truman threatened that unless the strikers returned to their jobs he would order them drafted and charge the army with running trains. Whereupon the striking unions terminated their walkout.

The labor picture brightened in 1947 and for the next few years labor-management relations were fairly tranquil. Wages went up, but management passed the cost to consumers. More important, innovations found their way into labor contracts. Wages became linked with the cost of living; when prices went up or down (usually up), wages followed. Other contracts provided company pensions to supplement Social Security when a worker retired, medical benefits for union members, and company-sponsored life insurance plans.

Further complicating reconversion was a collision between the president and the conservative coalition of northern Republicans and southern Democrats who ruled Congress.

The Fair Deal

Congressional conservatives were pleased with the new president when he entered the White House in 1945, for he had not been an uncompromising New Dealer in the Senate. Conservative illusions were shattered, however, when Truman sent his first domestic message to Con-

gress. More liberal than anything Roosevelt had ever dared to propose, the Truman program—eventually known as the Fair Deal—called for extension of Social Security, national health insurance, increase in the minimum wage, war against urban slums, new regional development projects patterned after TVA, a full-employment bill, and reorganization of the national government.

Truman's message also called for an extension of wartime economic controls, particularly those on prices. Conservatives were furious. They wanted to dismantle the elaborate system of controls. And apparently they mirrored the views of most people in the country. The war was over and Americans wanted to spend the savings accumulated in 1941-45. Business of course was anxious to satisfy the national hunger for automobiles, refrigerators, and washing machines. And it hoped for maximum profit from the "seller's" market.

In summer 1946 Truman asked Congress for an indefinite extension of the Office of Price Administration. This agency had been created during the war to hold a lid on inflation. Congress agreed to renew OPA, but so weakened its authority that the president vetoed the legislation. OPA controls ended two days later and within two weeks the country experienced the sharpest increase of inflation since 1942. Almost in desperation, Congress late in July 1946 voted a new bill to control rents and prices. Truman signed the bill but warned that it would prove ineffective. The president was right; the cost of living continued to inch upward.

Economic controls were an issue in the November 1946 elections. Most people were weary of wartime restrictions, and the issue worked to Republican advantage. The Republicans had other assets, including labor unrest and Truman's rising unpopularity. Many voters simply were concluding that the president was "too small" for his office. The outcome of the campaign was a Democratic disaster. On election day the Republicans, for the first time since 1928, won both houses of Congress, reduced Democratic margins in northern cities, and ousted several Democratic governors.

Interpreting the election as a rejection of his position on inflation, Truman set about ending economic controls. When prices continued to soar, he called Congress into special session in autumn 1947 and asked for antiinflation legislation. The resulting bill was ineffective.

Then came 1948, a presidential election year.

When the two major parties met in national conventions in 1948, both went on record as favoring measures to control prices. Both parties also advocated legislation that would advance civil rights, extend Social Security, and promote public housing.

Truman then made perhaps the cleverest move of his political career. He called the Republican-controlled Congress into special session in late July 1948 and asked for wide authority to control profits, credits, and prices—and also legislation which would advance civil rights, extend Social Security, and promote public housing. All that resulted was a hopelessly weak antiinflation measure.

By this time Truman was campaigning for his reelection. Over the next few weeks he crisscrossed the country, telling millions of voters that the Republicans had already failed on their promise to control inflation and also on various other pledges. On election day Truman scored a stunning upset victory over his Republican opponent, Thomas E. Dewey, and analysts found part of the explanation in his stand for controls. By autumn 1948 the country had become concerned over continuing inflation.

The reconversion story had other dimensions. With presidential approval, in November 1945 Congress reduced taxes nearly $6 billion. Many war plants built by the government were sold to corporations at low but probably fair prices. These plants represented a $17 billion investment that accounted for twenty percent of the country's industrial capacity.

Perhaps the most important fact of reconversion was the continued expansion of wartime prosperity. There was virtually no unemployment, and in the five years after the war national income went from $181 billion to $241 billion. Even the farmer shared in the rampaging prosperity.

The pent-up demand for consumer goods at the war's end was largely responsible for the boom. Important also was a continuation of heavy spending by the federal government—for relief and reconstruction in war-ravaged countries and to meet the challenge of the cold war between the Soviet Union and its satellites and the democracies of Western Europe and America.

Demobilization and reconversion presented fewer troublesome problems than Americans anticipated. The civilian economy absorbed twelve million servicemen and women with hardly a ripple of distress. There was no depression, as many Americans had feared, nor was there runaway inflation. There were strikes, shortages, price increases, and a black market. But reconversion came off with amazing speed and must rank as one of the great economic triumphs of American's history.

STUDY GUIDE: Truman wanted to slow down demobilization after the war, but popular pressure led to a rapid dismantling of the nation's military establishment. As the "cold war" developed between the Soviet Union and Western democracies, Congress was persuaded to enact new draft legislation. However, efforts to economize drastically reduced American armed strength.

Legislation provided many benefits for World War II veterans. The Full Employment Act was passed to help keep people working as the national economy was converted from war to peacetime production. A period of labor unrest, with numerous strikes, followed the war.

Congressional conservatives turned against Truman because of his "Fair Deal" program to extend social welfare benefits. They also opposed his call for extension of wartime economic controls to prevent inflation. Inflation soared, which provided Truman with a winning campaign issue in 1948. The economy continued to prosper after the war.

ATOMIC ENERGY

While converting the national economy from war to peace, Americans turned to other matters. One of the foremost was the controversial question of controlling the awesome power that had been unleashed at Hiroshima and Nagasaki.

Control of atomic energy entered public debate shortly after Japan's surrender, in August 1945, when President Truman asked Congress to fashion an atomic energy policy. He stated that nuclear power required an absolute government monopoly over fissionable materials. However, the president left open an important question: who should direct the atomic energy program, the military or a civil agency?

Observing that military control had worked well during the war, army and navy leaders wanted a continuation of military control. They feared that idealism about peace might influence a civil agency to drop the country's nuclear guard. The White House had no objection to military control. Accordingly, a bill went before Congress in October 1945 that would leave control of atomic energy in military hands.

Educators and religious leaders, scientists and political liberals erupted. Filled with a Jeffersonian distrust of generals and admirals, these people saw military control of atomic power as a danger to peace and democracy. Late in 1945 Senator Brien McMahon, Democrat of Connecticut, introduced a bill providing for an atomic control commission composed entirely of civilians. The McMahon Bill touched off a debate that continued into the following summer. President Truman spoke out in favor of McMahon's ideas. The most vocal opponents of provisions in the McMahon Bill were members of the House Un-American Activities Committee, who feared a civilian commission would be an easy mark for Communist infiltration.

After months of argument, Senator Arthur H. Vandenberg, Republican of Michigan, proposed a "military liaison board" to advise and consult with a civilian commission. Vandenberg's compromise assured passage of the bill, and in August 1946 President Truman signed the Atomic Energy Act.

The measure established a government monopoly over atomic materials and created an Atomic Energy Commission of five civilian members. The law gave the president exclusive authority to order use of atomic weapons and prohibited passing of atomic information to foreign governments, even friendly ones.

One aim of the legislation was to provide for peaceful use of the atom. Shortly after passage of the act, the AEC established several programs and divisions to work with private business and educational institutions in turning atomic energy to medical and industrial uses. Medical schools and hospitals received radioactive materials for cancer research and treatment, and in time the AEC approved contracts with private power companies to build nuclear reactors for generating electricity.

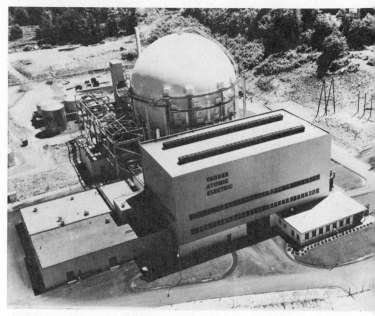

Courtesy Yankee Atomic Electric Company

Private power companies contracted with the Atomic Energy Commission to build nuclear reactors and sell electric power. What were the reasons behind the congressional debate over control of atomic energy?

GOVERNMENTAL REORGANIZATION

Reorganization—or reform—in the national government was another question that attracted considerable attention in the years after the war.

In the time of the New Deal and World War II, the federal government had trebled in size. But growth had come without coordination, and the result was much duplication and inefficiency. President Truman, in his Fair Deal message of September 1945, asked for authority to streamline the executive bureaucracy.

Some governmental reorganization had been underway before Truman spoke out. Early in 1945 Congress appointed a special investigating committee on congressional organization and procedure. The committee made several recommendations. The result was the Legislative Reorganization Act of 1946. This act reduced the number of congressional committees, took away some of the power of committee chairmen, established a permanent Legislative Reference Service to assist committees, and required lobbyists to register with Congress and disclose sums spent to influence legislation. Unfortunately the act overlooked some of the largest obstacles to legislative effectiveness—

STUDY GUIDE: The question of whether the control of atomic energy should be in the hands of a military or civil agency led to heated public debate. The Atomic Energy Act of 1946 established governmental control over atomic materials and created a civilian commission. Programs were established for peaceful use of the atom.

This is the Senate wing of the Capitol building. For many years, lawmakers discussed the need for streamlining congressional activities. What were the provisions of the Legislative Reorganization Act of 1946?

the Senate filibuster, the seniority system, and the power of the House Rules Committee. By the 1970s criticism of congressional organization and procedures was as sharp as ever.

In 1947 Congress authorized the president to appoint a commission to study executive reorganization. Truman appointed former-President Herbert Hoover to direct the investigation. The study group soon became known as the Hoover Commission.

Over the next eighteen months the Hoover Commission studied the complicated executive machinery. The commission found inadequate staffing, out-of-date accounting procedures, waste and duplication. The Hoover Commission recommended a reduction in the number of federal departments and agencies from sixty-five to twenty-three, establishment of a department of public welfare to consolidate federal activities in public health, education, and social welfare, and reorganization of the Post Office.

Responding to the Hoover recommendations, Congress in June 1949 passed the Reorganization Act authorizing the president to submit plans for executive reorganization. The presidential plans would go into effect automatically unless Congress specifically disapproved. In 1949-50 Truman submitted thirty-six reorganization plans, and Congress permitted all to go into effect except the one providing for a department of public welfare. (The conservative coalition feared that approval of a department of public welfare might imply acceptance of Truman's controversial plan for national health insurance.)

Most of Truman's changes reduced the number of agencies and bureaus, coordinated activities of others, improved administrative and budget practices, and tightened presidential authority. When Truman left office in 1953, more than half the Hoover Commission's recommendations had gone into effect.

Presidential Succession

Related to reorganization was the matter of presidential succession. The Constitution of 1787 provided no guide for the succession after the vice-president, and for nearly a century the question had remained unsettled. At length, following the death of President Cleveland's vice-president, Congress, in 1886, established the succession from the vice-president to the cabinet according to the dates cabinet posts were created. This meant that the secretary of state was next in line for the presidency after the vice-president.

Truman felt that the office of the president should be filled by an elective officer. Hence he proposed new legislation that would give the speaker of the House of Representatives and the president pro tempore of the Senate precedence over members of the cabinet in the presidential succession. He reasoned that next to the president and vice-president the speaker was the elected official most directly responsible to the people, for he owed his position to the voters of his district and the other representatives of the people, that is, to the other members of the House.

In June 1947 Congress passed the Presidential Succession Act embracing Truman's ideas. The measure failed, however, to provide a way to determine presidential disability and procedure for running the executive branch should the president become incapacitated. (This had happened on three notable occasions in American history: in 1881 when President Garfield was shot, in 1901 when President McKinley was the victim of a similar tragedy, and in 1919 when a stroke felled President Wilson.) Following two serious illnesses of President Eisenhower in the 1950s, such shortcomings attracted wide attention, although it was soon apparent that the problem had no easy solution.

When President John F. Kennedy was assassinated in 1963, Vice-President Lyndon B. Johnson moved to the White House, and the aging Speaker of the House John W. McCormack of Massachusetts became next in line for the presidency. Many Americans viewed the prospect of a McCormack presidency with displeasure and mounted an attack on the succession formula of the 1947 legislation. They also insisted that the country come to grips with the problem of presidential disability.

The result was the Twenty-fifth Amendment to the Constitution, finally ratified in February 1967. The amendment provides that in case the vice-president moves up to the presidency or if he dies or resigns—that is, if the vice-presidency becomes vacant—the president will nominate a vice-president who will take office when confirmed by a majority of both houses of Congress. Thus, unless the president and vice-president should die or be incapacitated at the same time, there will always be a vice-president in the wings ready to move to the White House if necessary. The Twenty-fifth Amendment provides that if the president declares in writing that he is disabled, the vice-president will become acting president. If the vice-president and a majority of the cabinet "or such other body as Congress may by law provide" declares in writing that the president is disabled, the vice-president becomes the acting president. The president can return to office if he declares in writing that no disability exists, unless the vice-president and a majority of the cabinet "or other body" declare otherwise. In the latter case, Congress shall determine the issue by a two-thirds vote of both houses.

The Twenty-second Amendment

After President Roosevelt's death in 1945, a movement quickly gathered for a constitutional amendment limiting the president to two four-year terms. In large measure the movement took origin in conservative dislike of Roosevelt and his New Deal. For an amendment would seem a repudiation of the man Americans had elected president four times. Still, many Americans saw danger in having one man at the top too long and concluded that an amendment would be a good idea.

When Republicans won control of Congress in the elections of 1946, one of their first objectives was an amendment. In March 1947 the Eightieth Congress adopted a resolution limiting the president to two terms, the incumbent, President Truman, excepted. If a president came to office because of the death of a president, he could seek two full terms if (like President Lyndon B. Johnson in the 1960s) he had served less than two years of an unfinished term. If he had served more than two years of the dead president's term, he could seek only one full term. Submitted to the states, the Twenty-second Amendment received ratification in 1951.

Military Reorganization

The disaster at Pearl Harbor had resulted in part from faulty military organization. In the years 1941-45 competition between branches of the armed forces had increased the cost of the war, at times even interfering with combat operations. Every proposal for unification of the services had aroused sharp opposition, particularly from the navy. Admirals feared that the army, being larger than the navy, would dominate a unified armed service. This might result in elimination of the Marine Corps and discrimination against sea-based air power.

President Truman was appalled by interservice rivalry and duplication. In August 1945 he ordered the army and navy to study the question of how they could better coordinate their activities. The key man in the study was Secretary of the Navy James V. Forrestal, a Republican. With the support of the president, Forrestal pushed discussions which resulted in the National Security Act of July 1947.

The National Security Act eliminated the War Department, establishing in its place the Departments of the Army and the Air Force. The secretaries of the two new departments, however, did not have cabinet status, as had the secretary of war in the past. Under the legislation the secretary of the navy also lost his cabinet rank.

To promote unification the measure created a new agency, the National Military Establishment (renamed the Department of Defense in 1949), headed by a secretary of defense. The secretary of defense was a member of the presidential cabinet, and the secretaries of the army, navy, and air force were answerable to him. The legislation also formalized the institution of the Joint Chiefs of Staff, directing them to work together to prepare defense plans and consider problems of strategy.

The National Security Act also established two other institutions, the Central Intelligence Agency and the National Security Council.

The CIA assumed responsibility for collecting and evaluating intelligence data. This task had been performed rather haphazardly by several agencies, sometimes with disastrous results (as on the eve of the Pearl Harbor raid). The argument for having a large central agency to perform basic intelligence tasks appeared unassailable, and it seemed in the decade after 1947 that the CIA was meeting its responsibilities with competence. When it later became known that the CIA had secretly engaged in other kinds of activities—for example, assisting in overthrowing or undermining governments unfriendly to the United States—the agency came under heavy criticism.

The National Security Council at the present time includes five statutory members—the president, the vice-president, secretary of state, secretary of defense, and director of the Office of Emergency Planning—and advisory members including the director of the CIA and chairman of the Joint Chiefs of Staff. Its main purpose is to establish an official apparatus for coordinating the thinking of the State Department and the Department of Defense on major foreign policy questions.

STUDY GUIDE: The Legislative Reorganization Act of 1946 brought reforms in congressional organization and procedure. As a result of the Hoover Commission recommendations, the Reorganization Act of 1949 led to reforms in the executive branch of government. Truman supported passage of the Presidential Succession Act of 1947. It provided that the next person in line for the presidency after the vice-president was the Speaker of the House. Failure of the measure to provide a way to determine when a president was not able to serve led to passage of the Twenty-fifth Amendment to the Constitution. Passage of the Twenty-second Amendment had limited a president to two terms in office.

In order to streamline defense and reduce competition between the different military services, many leaders wanted to unify the armed services. The National Security Act of 1947 was an effort in this direction.

LABOR

Waves of strikes after World War II resulted in a sharp popular reaction against the country's labor unions, whose membership rolls at that time included fifteen million men and women. Talk was common that labor had become too powerful, and with excessive power had come irresponsibility. Some people thought the root of the trouble was the Wagner Act of 1935. The time had come, such individuals concluded, to clip labor's wings.

The elections of 1946 brought a resounding Republican victory and sharpened the antilabor mood in the country. The new Eightieth Congress passed the Taft-Hartley Bill of June 1947, over President Truman's veto. The measure outlawed the closed shop (an agreement requiring a person to join a union before he could get a job), secondary boycotts, and the "check off" (an agreement requiring the employer to deduct union dues from pay envelopes). It forbade strikes against the federal government so there could be no strike if the government seized an industry. Union contributions to political campaigns were outlawed.

The act also made unions liable to damage suits, required them to make annual statements of their finances, and compelled union leaders to take oaths that they were not Communists. It required that a union give a sixty-day notice in advance of a strike. If the work stoppage would affect an entire industry or imperil the national health or safety, the "cooling-off" period could be extended to eighty days. In the extra twenty days the National Labor Relations Board could poll employees by secret ballot to determine if they wished to strike or accept management's final offer of settlement.

Organized labor denounced the Taft-Hartley Act as a "slave labor bill." Particularly threatening was the clause forbidding strikes against the federal government, which would enable the government to break any strike merely by seizing the industry. Labor leaders felt that this threatened the existence of unions.

Since businessmen could make contributions to political campaigns, labor thought it unfair that it no longer could open union treasuries to help elect labor's friends. The cooling-off period before a strike would deprive labor of the weapon of surprise and enable industries to stockpile materials before strikes. The provision for polling workers by secret ballot seemed an attempt to weaken the authority of union leaders.

Senator Robert A. Taft from Ohio was known as Mr. Republican because of his influence on his party. He co-authored the Taft-Hartley Act and supported federal aid to housing, education, and medical care. In 1940, 1948, and 1952 he was a leading candidate for his party's nomination for president.

The clause requiring heads of unions to swear that they were not Communists seemed to single out labor leaders as persons of doubtful loyalty. This infuriated labor.

Ironically, the Taft-Hartly Act temporarily strengthened the labor movement—contrary to the intent of its authors. In their hostility to the legislation, the American Federation of Labor and the Congress of Industrial Organizations put aside feuds of the past, closed ranks, and in 1955 merged into the AFL-CIO.

STUDY GUIDE: As a result of labor strikes after the war, many people felt unions had become too powerful. The result was passage of the Taft-Hartley Act regulating union activities and severely limiting the right of unions to strike. Opposition to this act helped to bring together the previously feuding AFL and CIO. The American labor movement, as a result, was strengthened. Truman's campaign promise to repeal the act helped him to win reelection in 1948.

CIVIL RIGHTS

The country's black population was beginning to assume a more aggressive posture in the post-war era. Negroes grew increasingly fed up with their role as second-class citizens or worse. They were determined to push back the walls of prejudice and discrimination to achieve the dignity and equality of opportunity that the Declaration of Independence, Atlantic Charter, and Charter of the United Nations said were rightfully theirs. Black leaders knew that the struggle would not be easy, for they well understood the grip that racism had on so many of their white countrymen. Still, they saw reason for cautious optimism. After the nightmare of nazism, they calculated, how could anybody cling to the notion that particular races or national groups had special rights over others? In the war, black Americans had rallied to the national standard and many had died in the struggle.

Black leaders could cite practical reasons for optimism. During the war, and also during the economic boom that followed, large numbers of Negroes had left the South and migrated to the urban industrial centers of the North and West. These blacks after meeting residence requirements moved easily on to the voting rolls of northern and western cities.

Before long, professional politicians of the North and West as well as black leaders were becoming aware that if blacks voted more or less in a bloc, they could exercise great influence at all levels of American politics—local, state, and national. In 1948 the public relations director of the National Association for the Advancement of Colored People, Henry Lee Moon, brought out a book entitled *Balance of Power.* Moon argued that black voters, by swinging certain pivotal states, could be the decisive factor in close presidential elections. Black leaders naturally hoped that the new voting strength would compel white politicians to take note of Negro problems and bring forth legislation and policies that would hack away at the barriers of discrimination. Political power would offer new hopes to blacks.

In the cold war competition with the Soviet Union the United States sought to present itself as a beacon of freedom, justice, and equal opportunity. But discrimination in the country made a mockery of such claims, providing grist for Communist propaganda mills. Seeing the problem, black leaders hoped that white Americans would put aside discriminatory practices. By welcoming the black man to full membership in the democratic community, white Americans could spike the Soviet propaganda charges.

Fortunately black Americans found allies in their struggle for civil equality. Some of their white countrymen became conscious of the fact that discrimination did not square with hallowed American democratic principles. They agreed with blacks that the time had come for America to honor its ideals. A substantial percentage of the people in this group were political liberals— most were northern and western Democrats— who saw the movement for civil equality as a logical extension of the twentieth-century progressive tradition. Blacks also received important assistance from a few church spokesmen who at long last began to see racial prejudice as a violation of their principle of brotherly love.

Some labor unions, particularly those affiliated with the CIO, were another source of support for blacks. Some labor leaders, for example Walter Reuther of the United Automobile Workers, shared the view that racial discrimination was morally wrong and that labor had an obligation to assist in campaigns to eliminate such discrimination. They believed that discrimination against one segment of the working population weakened labor standards generally. Thus, a part of organized labor urged equal treatment of all citizens, black as well as white.

Truman and Civil Rights

The most influential friend of black Americans in those years was the occupant of the White House, Harry Truman.

Like millions of other white Americans, Truman had taken racial discrimination for granted. Still, Truman was a "liberal" or "progressive," who almost by definition had strong sympathy for society's underdogs.

Like other liberals, Truman came to realize that discrimination because of race in democratic America was intolerable. As president, Truman was keenly aware that racist practices were a heavy burden for America in its relations with other countries, particularly with those emerging in Asia and Africa. Finally, Truman was a perceptive politician. He clearly understood the new electoral arithmetic resulting from the mass migration of Negroes from the South to the urban-industrial centers of the North and West. Supporting the aspirations of blacks might cost the Democratic party many votes in the "solid

South," but Truman knew that the balance of political power in America lay in the North and West. In those sections the black vote was becoming increasingly important.

Truman moved boldly in the area of civil rights. He took his first important step in 1946 when he asked Congress to make the Fair Employment Practices Commission, established by Roosevelt during the war, a permanent agency. Southern Democrats had been stopped in their opposition to FEPC during the war, when it had seemed necessary to make some concessions to Negroes to assure their unswerving support of the national war effort. In the postwar period, however, southern Democrats on Capitol Hill, with the help of northern Republicans, easily shot down the president's proposal. Later that same year Truman appointed a special Civil Rights Commission to study the problem of discrimination in America and recommend procedures for protecting the civil rights of all citizens. Composed of distinguished whites and blacks, some of them southerners, the commission issued a report in 1947 entitled *To Secure These Rights.* This report exposed racial segregation in the country and urged a systematic national program to root out racial injustice.

The president also appointed another committee to examine discrimination in higher education. This committee recommended elimination of inequalities in educational opportunities and abandonment of all types of discrimination in higher education. Reinforced by the reports of these committees, Truman appealed to Congress in February 1948 for legislation that would establish a permanent federal civil rights commission and a permanent FEPC. He asked for elimination of racial segregation in schools, transportation, and facilities serving the general public, such as restaurants and theaters. He proposed that Congress should make lynching a federal crime. As the president had expected, his proposals ran up against the conservative coalition and got nowhere.

A few months later, in July 1948, Democrats assembled in national convention in Philadelphia and civil rights became a raging issue. A band of liberal delegates headed by the youthful mayor of Minneapolis, Hubert H. Humphrey, determined to commit the Democratic party to far-ranging civil rights legislation. The zeal of this group captivated many northern and western delegates. At the same time, "bosses" of Democratic organizations in big northern and western cities, calculating that the party would lose the White House anyhow, decided that a strong civil rights plank would at least persuade most black voters to mark their ballots for the Democratic candidates in local elections.

Although delegates of Alabama and Mississippi left the convention, the liberal plank won approval of a majority of delegates. And in the ensuing campaign Truman gave it unflagging support. Truman became the first presidential candidate in American history to appeal openly for the black vote as he campaigned in such Negro ghettos as New York's Harlem and Chicago's South Side. His tactics worked. On election day black Americans voted overwhelmingly for him and other Democrats. As a result, Truman carried such states as Ohio, Illinois, Wisconsin, Minnesota, and California by narrow margins. The electoral votes of those states put him over the top in his contest with the Republican candidate, Governor Thomas E. Dewey of New York.

Through his second term, 1949-53, President Truman tried to redeem his party's civil rights pledges. The conservative coalition of Congress defeated Truman's legislative proposals, so he was forced to use other ways of making progress in civil rights. His achievements were considerable. He strengthened the Civil Rights Section of the Justice Department and directed the attorney general to assist private parties in civil rights cases. He appointed the first black governor of the Virgin Islands, promoted two blacks to federal judgeships, and directed that no defense contract should go to a firm practicing discrimination in employment. He moved against racial discrimination in federal agencies and directed that segregation should end in the armed forces. Truman broke social taboos when he invited blacks to attend the inaugural reception and ball in January 1949.

The Status of Black Americans in the Postwar Period

In the years after World War II, black Americans made modest strides in their struggle to achieve the promise of the good life in America, particularly in the North and West. Especially notable were gains in the economic sphere. Employment opportunities for blacks increased in some industries, including electronics, automobiles, and chemicals. Many black workingmen secured equality in wages and seniority rights, and increasing numbers of them achieved super-

visory status. Retailing firms began to hire black clerks, bookkeepers, and buyers; colleges appointed a few black faculty members; and the number of blacks entering the medical and legal profession slowly increased.

Outside the economic realm, larger hotels in the national capital began to accept black guests, and blacks were admitted to the city's public parks and swimming pools. Here and there across the country religious congregations integrated memberships. Archbishop Joseph E. Ritter ordered desegregation of the large Catholic school system of Saint Louis. Some city and town councils passed ordinances aimed at rooting out discrimination on account of race. A federal judge in 1947 ordered the Democratic party of South Carolina to permit Negroes to vote in its primary elections.

Most dramatic perhaps was desegregation of the "national pastime," major league baseball, when Jack Roosevelt ("Jackie") Robinson be-

Cicero, Illinois, was just one of the cities that experienced racial clashes in the 1940s. What factors heightened tensions between whites and blacks during and after World War II?

Tuskegee Institute

One of the few southern colleges open to blacks in the 1940s was Tuskegee Institute, where George Washington Carver once taught. The institute's School of Education building is shown in this recent photograph.

came first baseman of the Brooklyn Dodgers in 1947. Robinson opened the way for other black players, including Willie Mays, who joined the New York Giants in 1951.

The walls of racial prejudice and discrimination, of course, did not come tumbling down in the years after the war. Most blacks who lived in towns or cities, whether in the North or South, still lived in almost exclusively black, and usually ramshackle, neighborhoods. They often fell victims of slum landlords and loan sharks, the numbers racket and narcotics.

The black ghettos of Boston's Roxbury district and New York's Harlem were veritable prisons from which few blacks ever escaped. Malcolm Little, a Negro from Lansing, Michigan, lived in both during the 1940s and did escape. He became a black militant, and shortly before his death in early 1965 described his activities and observations in a remarkable memoir entitled *The Autobiography of Malcolm X*.

Racial prejudice and discrimination had other dimensions. All over the South, where the black man's situation hardly changed at all, and to a large extent in the North, black children continued to attend segregated and usually inferior schools. The doors of most white colleges and state universities in the South remained closed to blacks. White employers as a general rule continued to discriminate against blacks in hiring. A great percentage of the blacks who were listed in official statistics as having jobs were sweeping streets, collecting garbage, and cleaning rest rooms in hotels and public buildings.

Discrimination in wages and lack of opportunities for promotion also continued to plague most black workingmen.

Thus in the years after World War II the black American made some headway toward the goal of equal participation in the life of his country. But the advance was slow and painful. When the 1940s gave way to the 1950s, he was still far behind in civil rights and economic opportunity.

STUDY GUIDE: The Negro's search for civil equality after World War II was aided by some of his white countrymen. Among the first to help were labor leaders and politicians who saw the significance of the black vote in winning elections. President Truman urged passage of civil rights legislation. Although his efforts were opposed by congressional conservatives, Truman succeeded in breaking down some of the barriers.

ELSEWHERE ON THE AMERICAN SCENE

The postwar years saw the continuing growth of the national population, the result essentially of a "baby boom" which had begun in 1941-45 and did not subside when the guns fell silent. Census figures reveal that in 1950 there were 150,697,361 Americans (compared with 131,669,275 in 1940).

Statistics also reveal that in the postwar era

Americans continued to move away from rural areas to towns and cities. Whereas at the turn of the twentieth century only forty percent of the national population lived in urban areas, the number by 1950 had climbed to nearly sixty-five percent—and would continue to climb in the 1950s and 1960s. One of the chief reasons for this rural exodus was the continuing mechanization of agriculture. By 1950, for example, American farmers owned more than three and a half million tractors (compared with about a thousand in 1910) and more than seven hundred thousand grain combines (compared with perhaps a thousand in 1910).

By 1950 ninety percent of the country's farms had electricity. The New Deal's rural electrification program brought new labor-saving devices to the farm, including the milking machine and electric water pump. With mechanized equipment, farmers were able to increase production while reducing their manpower. Farmers and farm laborers who were displaced by machines found their way to towns and cities, where they swelled the urban population.

Growth of the Suburbs

More striking was the movement from the center of urban areas to the suburbs.

Suburbs were not a new phenomenon. From the time the first towns in America evolved into cities, there was a craving on the part of some urban dwellers to escape to the edge of the urban sprawl where they could find more fresh air, space, and tranquillity. The village of Brooklyn, for example, in the early nineteenth century became a suburb where prosperous New Yorkers

got away from the noise, confusion, and congestion of Manhattan. The increasing popularity of motor cars in the 1920s accelerated the movement to "suburbia." Efficient transportation was essential to life in the suburbs, as most suburbanites continued to find employment in the central city. But then came the Great Depression of the 1930s and the movement to the suburbs declined sharply. During World War II, the migration to the suburbs nearly halted altogether.

When the shooting stopped in August 1945, the pockets of many Americans were bulging with savings accumulated during the war. Within the next year or so automobiles again became plentiful. The exodus to the suburbs resumed, and by the late 1940s the movement of people out of central cities had become a flood.

The flight of people to the suburbs had serious consequences for cities. As affluent or prosperous white families moved out, poor white and black families, often from rural areas, moved in. The new city dwellers usually lacked incomes sufficient to maintain the same living standards as those people they had replaced. More often than not, they were also the products of cultural backgrounds that made it difficult for them to adjust to the complexities of the kind of life in the city.

The inevitable result was rapid decay of the inner core of city after city across the nation. Decay, of course, meant a decline in property values, which in turn meant a decline in tax revenues. On the other hand, the expense of city administration continued to climb. These problems of urban America would reach epidemic proportions by the 1960s and 1970s.

Suburban housing developments like this one sprang up all over America in the late 1940s. What were the consequences of this flight from the city to suburb? Is it still continuing?

Compix

Problems in Education

The continuing population explosion meant that increasing numbers of children were of school age. This created shortages of teachers and classrooms. Population growth however, was not the only reason for crowded schools, particularly at the secondary level. After 1945 the percentage of children staying in school steadily grew. In part this was because of the decline in economic opportunities for people without education or skill, which meant that a high school diploma was increasingly required for well-paying jobs. School dropouts, however, remained a problem and continued to evoke much discussion throughout the 1960s. Colleges and universities also experienced a population explosion in the late 1940s. One reason was the great number of veterans who took advantage of the educational opportunities of the GI Bill of Rights.

Religious Revival

For several decades before World War II, religion had seemed in retreat. This was partly because of continuing assaults by critics who saw religion as a bundle of superstitions and by political radicals who saw it as an opiate that conditioned people to accept injustice, oppression, and poverty.

Then came the war. In America and elsewhere, many people thought the bestiality of Hitler and his Nazi henchmen had been an almost inevitable consequence of casting aside the restraints and values of religion. Next came the cold war, and Americans pondered accounts of oppression and brutality in areas of the world dominated by the Soviet Union. Why did the Soviets have so little respect for human dignity? Because they opposed religious teachings, or so thought many Americans. Then the fear of atomic annihilation in the years after Hiroshima and Nagasaki doubtless turned the thoughts of some Americans to religion.

The outcome was a religious revival which reached a peak in the 1950s. Membership rolls of the country's churches and synagogues swelled, attendance at religious services increased, collection baskets overflowed. Christians and Jews supported a range of charitable, relief, and mission programs with unflagging dedication. New church buildings and parochial (mostly Catholic) schools were built. New sects appeared, including the Church of the Nazarene, the Churches of God, and the Pentecostal Assemblies. Colleges and universities with religious affiliations flourished. The "crusades" of a youthful Baptist minister from North Carolina, the Reverend Billy Graham, drew capacity crowds, and the books and radio talks of Monsignor Fulton J. Sheen commanded wide audiences.

To be sure, some observers, perhaps noting a steady increase in national rates of crime, divorce, and alcoholism, doubted the quality and depth of the religious commitment of many. Still, the statistical evidence of renewed interest in religion in America was striking.

Scientific Achievement

Most Americans retained a strong interest in science and its power to contribute mightily to the happiness and well-being of humanity. Therefore they offered no objection to continuation of large federal subsidies to support scientific research in the postwar period. Whatever the sources of support—for scientists also received support from industry and private foundation—scientific inquiry produced impressive results in the era after the war. Synthetic yarns produced more durable fabric; synthetic rubber provided safer tires. New plastics provided the raw material for a host of industries; research in electronics opened the way for improved television equipment. Research in medicine resulted in new antibiotic drugs, new techniques for combating cancer, and improved surgical methods.

Leisure Time

The prosperity of the postwar era meant that many Americans could afford a bewildering range of activities in their leisure time. Some of them traveled—in new, more streamlined automobiles or on trains. A train trip in those years could be a memorable experience. The railroads, confident that rail travel in America had a bright future, reequipped their feature trains—the *Twentieth Century Limited, Super Chief, Empire Builder, Orange Blossom Special*—with luxurious coaches, diners, and sleeping cars. When in a hurry the traveler might take an airliner. Air travel became safer. It also became faster and more comfortable, particularly with the introduction of such planes as the Douglas DC-6, whose four piston-driven engines could propel it along at more than 250 miles an hour.

In nonworking hours Americans flocked to

neighborhood bars and downtown night clubs, bowling alleys, and golf courses. They hunted and fished, spending record sums of money on guns and shells, fishing rods and lures. For several summers after the war they played softball with an enthusiasm not displayed before or since.

Some Americans spent part of their leisure time reading, attending plays, and listening to music. They read such standby magazines as *Life, Look, Saturday Evening Post, Collier's,* and *Good Housekeeping.* Or they might choose from a range of magazines focusing on murder cases, Hollywood gossip, or romance. As for books, Americans had little to read in the way of notable new works. There was no literary flowering, such as had occurred in the era after World War I. Perhaps the most important novel of the period was Norman Mailer's terrifying account of men in battle, *The Naked and the Dead,* published in 1948.

As in literature, there was little in drama after the war that was noteworthy, although such playwrights as William Inge, Tennessee Williams, and Arthur Miller turned out works that drew acclaim. Serious music seemed to fare better, and some critics detected a new maturity in the music being written and performed on concert stages in the country. Americans took a new interest in choral music, opera, and ballet. It was musical comedy, however, that enjoyed greatest popularity in the years after the war. Audiences flocked to such hits as *Annie Get Your Gun, Kiss Me Kate, Brigadoon, Carousel, South Pacific,* and *The King and I.* The great majority of Americans enjoyed the singing of Bing Crosby and Jo Stafford, the sounds of such name bands as that of Sammy Kaye, and the country rhythms of Clyde ("Red") Foley and Eddy Arnold. The movies, however, remained the number one diversion of Americans in the years after the war. Millions of people crowded into theaters two and three times a week to enjoy the performances of such stars as Clark Gable, Gary Cooper, Rita Hayworth, and Ingrid Bergman.

Major league baseball, featuring such superplayers as Ted Williams, Stan Musial, Joe DiMaggio, and Bob Feller, continued to attract the most attention. Professional football had not yet begun to rival baseball as a sports attraction, but it steadily gained in popularity. In football most of the headlines continued to go to the collegians, who lured hundreds of thousands of fans into vast stadiums. Other superperformers

Courtesy the National Foundation

Dr. Jonas Salk examines a live tissue culture of polio virus from which polio vaccine is made. His work, along with the later findings of Dr. Albert Sabin, all but eliminated the disease in the mid-1950s.

in the world of sports were "Sugar Ray" Robinson in boxing, Ben Hogan in golf, Jack Kramer in tennis, and George Mikan in basketball.

Then there was television. Television was not a new device. The first television images had been transmitted as early as the 1920s, when commercial radio broadcasting was still in its infancy and before "talking" films had appeared. Experiments with television continued through the 1930s. After the war, refinement of techniques and equipment brought pictures of improved quality and also reduced costs. The way thus opened for telecasting on a large scale.

The early screens were small, and the black and white pictures were often fuzzy. It took time, moreover, for producers, directors, and performers to adjust to the new medium. Still, the people of the country responded enthusiastically, especially when television brought into their living rooms the World Series and an array of singers, comedians, and other performers. So rapid was the growth of television's popularity that by the early 1950s manufacturers were pressed to meet the demand for receiving sets.

By 1950, sociologists and psychologists had not begun to weigh seriously the larger consequences of television, but it was soon clear that television was influencing the leisure-time habits of millions of people. Instead of flipping on the radio, they switched on the TV. As a result, the

big-name radio shows one by one left the air, sometimes to be transformed, not always successfully, into television programs. Radio increasingly became the preserve of "disc jockeys" and sportscasters. And the movie industry especially felt an impact. Television was soon spelling ruin for thousands of movie houses across the country, particularly the small neighborhood variety (although expansion of automobile ownership after the war widened the popularity of the "drive-in" movie).

Development of airplanes during World War II greatly improved their speed and weight limits. After the war the improvements made commercial air travel faster and cheaper than ever before. Here a DC-6 flies over Long Island, New York.

STUDY GUIDE: The national population continued to grow dramatically after the war. Large numbers of Americans moved away from rural areas and headed toward towns and cities, especially to the suburbs. The flight to the suburbs contributed to the decay of the inner cities. More students began to seek a higher education, and schools became

crowded. A religious revival during the 1950s increased church membership. The prosperity of the postwar era permitted increasing numbers of Americans to buy cars and television sets and to pursue a variety of costly leisure-time activities.

WORLD AFFAIRS

The postwar era in American foreign relations began on September 2, 1945. On that day representatives of the Japanese emperor signed surrender documents bringing World War II formally to a close.

The world of September 1945 was not, of

course, the same as that which had existed in December 1941 when Japanese bombs fell on Pearl Harbor. Global war had brought many changes.

There were changes in weapons. During the war scientists and technicians had developed an array of devices that overturned time-honored military and diplomatic equations. One such device was the long-range bombing plane. Unlike the planes at the start of the war, the new bombers could travel thousands of miles with tons of bombs. On drawing boards were even larger planes, powered by jet engines. There was the rocket-powered missile, invented by the Germans and used with devastating effect against Britain in the last year of the European war. Of overwhelming significance was the atomic bomb. Nuclear energy held limitless promise for promoting the welfare and comfort of humanity. It also gave mankind the means of self-destruction.

World War II had turned much of Europe—the traditional bastion of Western Civilization—to rubble. In addition to being in ruins, most of the European nations were virtually defenseless.

The war had produced ferment in that vast territory reaching from the western shore of Africa to the South China Sea. Most people in Africa, the Indian subcontinent, and Southeast Asia had never known political independence, but times were changing. Some of these peoples had fallen under Axis control during the war when Great Britain, France, and the Netherlands could not provide adequate defense. Hence their respect for prewar colonial masters had dwindled. Many also knew something of the Atlantic Charter and Charter of the United Nations which proclaimed that all people had a right to a choice of government, dignity, and equal opportunity. Such developments, combined with the weakness of Europe's "powers" at the end of the war, prevented restoration of the old colonial order. As a result, over the next three decades, scores of new nations—in Africa, the Middle East, Central Asia, and Southeast Asia—were created. Most of these emerging states lacked the material resources essential for prosperity and knew little about modern technology. They were plagued by disunity and lacked traditions of stability. Like Europe, they were weak and defenseless.

The war had likewise produced ferment in areas outside the prewar colonial domain—in Latin America, the Middle East, and East Asia. Although ruled by their countrymen, millions of people in these areas continued to suffer the twin evils of feudalism and poverty. Their governments were often corrupt and inefficient, had little interest in the general welfare, and were concerned mainly with protecting the privileges of a wealthy elite. Still, people in those lands had caught the spirit of the new gospel of human rights. They began to feel a new determination to achieve the promise of the good life of the twentieth century.

The war had produced a new superpower, the Soviet Union. When the Germans invaded Russia in June 1941, the Soviet Union hardly seemed a power of the first magnitude. Over the previous century—in the Crimean War, the Russo-Japanese War, World War I, the Russo-Polish War, the Russo-Finnish War—the Russians had suffered a long string of battlefield defeats. At first Hitler's armies routed Russian defenders and pushed to the gates of Moscow. But then the German attack stalled, and early in 1943 came the great Soviet victory at Stalingrad. By the end of 1943 the Soviets took the offensive and expelled the Germans from Russian soil in 1944. When fighting stopped in May 1945, the Red Army was occupying half of Europe. The victories of Russian armies naturally enhanced the power and prestige of the Soviet state. They also gave new strength and confidence to the world Communist movement. Guided by a curious mixture of Russian nationalism and Marxism-Leninism, the Soviets determined to expand the influence of both the Soviet state and the Communist movement. The most tempting objective was Western Europe. But the Soviets turned also to the emerging nations and those countries afflicted with feudalism and poverty.

The people of the United States and their leaders comprehended only dimly the changes that global war had brought. Americans did not fully grasp the strategic implications of the technical developments of the war period. They understood even less clearly the war's social and political consequences. They did not appreciate the seriousness of Europe's plight and did not clearly comprehend the ambitions of the Soviet Union. Americans failed almost completely to see that the war had aroused half the world to an awareness of its poverty and weakness.

In September 1945, Americans serenely thought they could turn their tanks and battleships into automobiles and washing machines and slip back into their old peacetime routine. If any disturbance appeared in the world, the new international organization, the United Nations, could take care of it, or so Americans thought.

Americans of 1945 had miscalculated. The world had not adopted America's ideas about democracy and self-determination of peoples. The old aggressive spirit that had given birth to the expansionist dreams of Nazi Germany, Fascist Italy, and imperial Japan was far from dead. And, unhappily, the UN would soon prove no more effective in keeping peace than the League of Nations had been. Before long, Americans would learn that their principles and ideals were no more secure in the postwar period than they had been in the time of Hitler and Tojo. In place of hot war, they would soon find themselves confronted with a cold war. Whatever their hopes about putting aside international responsibilities and returning to the business of peace, Americans would find it impossible. They could not relax behind the UN and more or less ignore trouble in other parts of the world.

War Criminals

On one point most Americans had very strong sentiments: the Axis war criminals must be punished.

In pressing for trials of "war criminals," thoughtful Americans wanted to demonstrate to the whole world how people can become parties to the most vile sins against humanity if they permit themselves to fall under the control of evil men. Americans also wanted to win universal recognition for a principle: that political and military leaders who engineer acts of aggression against other states or individuals are personally responsible for such acts and may not escape punishment later by contending that they had simply been carrying out orders of the state. In the view of Americans, the cause of justice required acceptance of this principle. They hoped, moreover, that the principle, if endorsed by most nations of the world, might in the future give pause to political and military leaders whose governments seemed bent on violating international standards of decency and morality.

Before the United States became a belligerent in World War II, President Roosevelt and Prime Minister Churchill warned the Germans that they would be held accountable for their "war crimes." When the fighting ended the Allies moved quickly to apprehend all suspected war criminals who were alive and could be found.

Still, there were problems. What, for example, should the Allies do about Italian leaders who had helped arrange the plundering of Ethiopia in 1935-36 and later supported Mussolini's de-cision to throw Italy in with the Nazis? In the course of the war the Italians had changed sides and by 1945 were friends of the Allies. Considering the Allied wish to nurture that friendship, it did not seem wise to parade before the world the sins committed by the Italian nation during its Fascist period. Moreover, the Italians had fought without much enthusiasm and nobody in 1945 feared a resurgence of Italian military power. The Allies therefore chose to ignore Italy's "war crimes," and no Italian was brought before Allied military courts.

A more serious problem was the question of the propriety, even the legality, of bringing alleged war criminals to trial at all. Under rules of law accepted in the United States, Great Britain, and many other countries of the world, an individual could not be held accountable for violating laws for which statutes, penalties, and means of enforcement had not existed at the time the acts were committed. An individual, in a word, might not be tried under laws established *ex post facto*. Statutes, penalties, and means of enforcement covering most of the alleged crimes for which Axis leaders were to be tried had not existed, either in international law or the laws of the Axis nations, at the time the crimes took place.

Many people felt that the trials would be a sham. Prime Minister Churchill for example saw no need for the trappings of legal procedure. He suggested that it might be a good idea to take Axis leaders out some morning and shoot them without preliminaries.

Whatever the problems, when the shooting stopped, the Allies pressed on with plans to bring Axis leaders, and many minor functionaries, to trial. The crimes committed by the Axis, particularly the Germans, had been too enormous and too heinous to overlook. The Allies believed, moreover, that it was necessary to demonstrate to potential aggressors and mass murderers of the future that their crimes would catch up with them, that they could not escape punishment as individuals by hiding behind the cloak of the state.

Over the next several years, the Allies would bring several thousand alleged war criminals to trial in Europe and Japan. And civil courts in the Federal Republic of Germany (or West Germany) would continue for more than two decades to administer justice to such individuals. The main events of the war crimes trials, however, took place in Nuremberg in Germany and in Tokyo, Japan. A number of war criminals were sentenced to death or imprisonment. Some of the accused were acquitted.

Advent of the Cold War

While the courts at Nuremberg and Tokyo were grinding out verdicts on the Axis war criminals, the wartime Grand Alliance was disintegrating.

During World War II the United States dreamed of a postwar world in which there would be no spheres of influence where the "great" powers would have special privileges. With the world organized on such a universalist principle, each country would order its own society and manage its own affairs without external interference. Peace and stability would be guaranteed by a world organization having the united backing of the leading powers, notably the United States, Great Britain, and the Soviet Union.

To appease the United States and thus keep the Grand Alliance working, the Russians gave lip service to these ideals until the end of the war. They endorsed the Atlantic Charter of 1941 and at the Yalta Conference in February 1945 pledged self-determination for the countries of Eastern Europe.

The Soviets felt no attachment to universalist principles. They wanted to dominate Eastern Europe to prevent a repetition of the German use of Eastern Europe as a springboard for invasion of the Soviet Union. Acceptance of universalism, moreover, would prevent the Soviets from fulfilling historic ambitions of Russian nationalism—control over the Balkans, for example—not to mention the ambitions of the international Communist movement. Under such circumstances, from the Soviet perspective, it would be unthinkable for the Russians to permit application of universalist principles in areas where the Red Army was entrenched and the power of decision thus assured to leaders in the Kremlin.

Leaders in Washington knew that the Soviets did not share America's enthusiasm for universalist ideas. But in the view of President Roosevelt, Secretary Hull, and other American advocates of universalism, the only alternative to universalism was a return to the old balance-of-power politics which down through the centuries had led countries to one war after another. If universalism seemed tinged with a heady idealism, it also appeared to American leaders to offer the only realistic way to prevent war and assure humanity's survival. American leaders hoped they might persuade the Russians—by dealing with them considerately, even generously—to give up suspicions of the West, abandon dreams of extending their power, and put trust in a world organization.

As the war in Europe drew to a close, leaders in Washington recognized that the Russians were bent on controlling countries on their borders from the Gulf of Finland to the Caspian Sea. When the Red Army in 1944 moved into the Baltic states of Estonia, Latvia, and Lithuania, the three states were quickly made a part of the Soviet Union. Two weeks after the Yalta Conference of February 1945 the Soviets arranged the removal of a coalition government of Communist and democratic parties in Rumania. The coalition was replaced by a regime clearly dominated by Communists. A few months later the Soviets intervened in a similar fashion in Bulgaria.

Then there was Poland, whose independence Britain and France had gone to war to preserve in 1939, and whose independence had become an obsession with many Americans. Against the wishes of the United States and Britain, and doubtless contrary to the will of the Polish people, the Soviets insisted at Yalta that the Communist-dominated Lublin regime should serve as the basis for a provisional government in Poland until "free and unfettered elections" brought establishment of a permanent government. The Soviets, it turned out, had no intention of honoring their Yalta commitments on Poland. They used the bayonets of the Red Army to reinforce the Lublin regime, and by autumn 1945 it was evident that the Soviets were converting Poland into a Russian satellite. The Poles, whose entire history had been punctuated by tragedy, would not have the right to determine their own destiny.

The Soviets did not consider important or even desirable the control of Finland (lest they drive Sweden into the arms of America and Britain). Greece was occupied by British forces, and Yugoslavia had its own Communist regime under Josip Broz (better known as Marshal Tito). Aside from these countries, the only country in Eastern Europe that appeared to be having any substantial success in resisting the Soviets was Czechoslovakia. Still, the Russians were active in that country, too. Perceptive observers could see that it was likely to be only a matter of time before the flame of Czech independence flickered out.

The Soviets, meanwhile, tried in 1945-46 to

compel Turkey to accept joint control with the Soviet Union of the Bosporus and the Dardanelles. But the Turks, who had maintained neutrality in the recent war, turned aside Soviet threats with the support of the United States and Britain.

Equally serious was Soviet behavior in Iran. To forestall Nazi activity in that country, the Soviets and British had occupied Iran in 1941. Later, to help secure the principal lend-lease lifeline to Russia (which passed from the Persian Gulf across Iran to the Soviet Union), the United States sent a small contingent of troops to the country. The Allies agreed to remove the troops within six months after the end of the war.

Great Britain and the United States honored their pledge to remove troops from Iran, but the Russians strengthened their forces in Iran and organized a Communist revolt in the northern part of the country. Only when the United States and Britain threatened to use force to defend Iran did the Russians, in late March 1946, remove their troops.

Soviet moves notwithstanding, Americans continued to dream of a universalist world. They continued to hope that the Russians would see the light and accept the universalist faith.

In early March 1946 Winston Churchill, speaking on the campus of Westminster College in Fulton, Missouri, announced that "an Iron Curtain has descended across the European Continent." He urged that the United States and Great Britain come together in a political and military alliance to counter the Communist threat to Western civilization. Most Americans responded negatively—many of them angrily—to these ideas.

However, the faith in universalism and the UN was beginning to weaken by late 1946. In early 1947 events in Greece and Turkey caused Americans to abandon the dream of securing Soviet support for a universalist world. The United States set about trying to prevent any further expansion of Communist power.

The cold war had begun.

Greece, Turkey, and the Truman Doctrine

The moment of truth for Americans came on February 21, 1947. On that day the British embassy in Washington sent American officials two notes announcing that the British government, drained by the recent war and edging toward bankruptcy, could no longer bolster the existing regimes in Greece and Turkey. Both countries were under heavy pressure from Soviet-supported Communist insurgents and seemed on the verge of collapse. American leaders were stunned. Without external reinforcement, the governments of Greece and Turkey would amost certainly give way to the Communists. This in turn—so American leaders calculated—might have consequences too terrible to contemplate.

Flanked by two Communist countries—Yugoslavia and Greece—Italy, which had the largest Communist party in Europe west of the Iron Curtain, would find it difficult to resist the Communist tide. If Italy fell, its northern neighbor, France, which also had a large Communist party, would likely not be far behind. If France went Communist, the victory of communism in Europe would be assured. Nor was that all. If the Communists won control of Turkey, it would be next to impossible to keep Iran out of the Communist orbit. Turkey likewise would make a perfect springboard for the spread of Soviet influence through the entire Middle East and across North Africa.

President Truman determined to act. He went before a joint session of Congress on March 12, 1947 and issued a dramatic appeal for funds with which to halt the spread of communism in the Eastern Mediterranean. To reinforce the non-Communist government of Greece, and also that of Turkey, Truman asked for an emergency appropriation of $400 million.

Truman, however, went an important step further in his address of March 12. He declared that every country of the world must choose between two alternative ways of life:

> One way of life is based upon the will of the majority, and is distinguished by free institutions, representative government, free elections, guarantees of individual liberty, freedom of speech and religion, and freedom from political oppression.
>
> The second way of life is based upon the will of a minority forcibly imposed upon the majority. It relies upon terror and oppression, a controlled press and radio, fixed elections, and the suppression of personal freedoms.
>
> I believe that it must be the policy of the United States to support free peoples who are resisting attempted subjugations by armed minorities or by outside pressure.[1]

---

[1] *Public Papers of the Presidents of the United States: Harry S. Truman; Containing the Public Messages, Speeches, and Statements of the Presidents, January 1 to December 31, 1947,* 1963 (Washington, D.C.: U.S. Government Printing Office).

With these words Truman announced an American policy of global resistance to the spread of communism. The policy became known as the Truman Doctrine. The fundamental principle of the Truman Doctrine was that the United States should attempt to hold back or "contain" the spread of Soviet power.

Most Americans applauded President Truman's resolve to "save" Greece and Turkey from communism. A few citizens, however, complained that the governments in Greece and Turkey were neither liberal nor democratic. The Truman administration responded that whatever the shortcomings of the existing governments, there was reason to hope that in time Greece and Turkey might achieve the democratic ideal. Under the Communists there would be no chance of democracy ever coming to the two countries.

Other critics complained that the president was bypassing the United Nations. To this complaint Senator Arthur H. Vandenberg, Republican of Michigan—who had much to do with shaping and implementing the foreign policies of the Truman administration—retorted that Greece could collapse fifty times before the UN could hope to meet the problem.

There were those who wondered why the United States was determined to hold back communism in the Eastern Mediterranean while at the same time urging General Chiang Kaishek, the leader of Nationalist China, to collaborate with Mao Tse-tung and the Chinese Communists. Officials in the State Department could only respond that the United States with a relatively small outlay of money might save Greece and Turkey from the Communists and head off a chain of unhappy consequences in Europe, the Middle East, and Africa. A similar outlay would have little effect in China; only a massive expenditure of funds could do much for Chiang.

Debate ended in May 1947 when the Eightieth Congress voted the president's request of March 12. Almost overnight military and economic assistance began to flow to Greece and Turkey.

In Greece an American military mission headed by General James A. Van Fleet took an important part in the campaign against Communist guerrillas. Under his direction, Greek troops, using American weapons and equipment, slowly gained the initiative.

A shift in international politics also gave non-Communist elements in Greece another important assist. Yugoslavia, Greece's Communist neighbor to the north, determined to resist dictation from Moscow. The result was a falling-out between the Soviets and Yugoslav Communists, led by Marshal Tito. Cut off from the Communist world, and fearing for their survival, the Yugoslavs looked westward. To improve their standing in the eyes of the United States and Britain, the Yugoslavs sealed the border between Greece and Yugoslavia, thus cutting off the movement of supplies and equipment to Greek Communists via Yugoslavia. American economic support, meanwhile, was putting Greece and Turkey on a surer economic footing. By the end of 1949, the Communist threat to Greece and Turkey had passed. The Truman Doctrine had chalked up its first success.

The Marshall Plan

In 1947 the State Department was preparing to announce a bold new program to implement the Truman Doctrine and prevent further expansion

General George C. Marshall, as secretary of state, put into effect the European Recovery Program, or Marshall Plan. He was also instrumental in forming the North Atlantic Treaty Organization. What were the two goals of the Marshall Plan?

of Soviet-Communist power in Europe. The program became known as the Marshall Plan.

Europe was in desperate condition at the end of the war. Cities had been turned to rubble, factories demolished, railways ripped up, canals clogged, farmland scorched. Food and clothing were scarce. Tens of millions of people were wandering about, homeless and jobless. Inflation was rampant, black markets were flourishing. For a time the United Nations Relief and Rehabilitation Administration helped many Europeans to ward off starvation, but the UN's resources were limited. It could not provide what Europe needed most, a massive injection of capital that would start economic wheels turning and enable Europeans to bring about their own reconstruction.

Americans had been so preoccupied with their own problems of reconversion that they failed to grasp the seriousness of Europe's difficulties. They failed to see that Europe was edging toward a total economic and political collapse. Even leaders of the national government in Washington seemed to grasp only vaguely the grim realities of Europe's condition.

Then came the terrible winter of 1946-47. Snow, ice, and wind lashed across Europe, stalling transport facilities, bringing industrial production to a standstill in many areas, dramatically increasing the level of personal suffering.

In January 1947, the United States had a new secretary of state. James F. Byrnes, the secretary since 1945, had resigned and President Truman appointed General George C. Marshall to succeed him. When he assumed his new responsibilities, Marshall learned that people in and out of the State Department were hard at work fashioning a plan for a large American effort to assist in the regeneration of Europe. In the view of these people, Europeans were nearing the end of their patience. Unless a measure of prosperity returned to their lives in the near future, Europeans were almost certain to look to the Communists for solutions to their problems. This would mean a vast increase in Soviet power. It also would have serious consequences for the American economy, for after the postwar boom ran its course, Americans would need a healthy Europe.

Secretary Marshall accepted the idea of trying to rescue Europe. In a commencement address at Harvard University on June 5, 1947, he announced the plan that would bear his name — the Marshall Plan. The plan, he said, was aimed against hunger and poverty, desperation and chaos and not against the Soviet Union or communism. The secretary defined his offer of aid to Europe as including "everything up to the Urals." This meant that the Soviet empire was at liberty to take part in the program and receive American assistance.

Although the invitation was genuine, we know today that Marshall and the State Department were hopeful that the Soviet Union and its satellites would not join in. By inviting the Soviet empire to take part in the program, American officials hoped to present to the world an image of American goodwill and generosity. They also hoped to spike any charges from the Kremlin that the United States was taking an aggressive stance against the Soviet Union.

For a time the Soviets seemed to waver, and American leaders squirmed for fear that the Russians might agree to go along with the plan. If the Russians were involved in the program of European reconstruction, Congress might refuse to appropriate the necessary funds.

The anxiety of American leaders heightened in June 1947 when Foreign Minister Molotov turned up at Paris to discuss Marshall's proposal with representatives of Britain and France. However, Molotov did not remain in Paris very long. Denouncing the Marshall proposal as a clever capitalist scheme to subjugate Europe, the Russians ducked back behind the Iron Curtain and forbade their Eastern European satellites to participate in the American-sponsored program. Then the Soviets announced the Molotov Plan for regenerating Eastern Europe. The Molotov Plan achieved virtually nothing.

Ironing out details of a huge international program of economic assistance took time. President Truman urged Americans to conserve food so that the country could make larger shipments to Europe. At the same time a special session of Congress passed legislation providing $540 million of emergency foreign aid. Most of this money went to Italy, France, and Austria. Drafting of the Marshall program was nearing completion, and in December 1947 Truman asked Congress for $17 billion to be distributed to the countries of Western Europe over the next four years.

In early 1948 Congress got down to the business of weighing Truman's request. It was clear at once that the Marshall Plan had strong support. There was, to be sure, some opposition, mainly from the extreme left wing of American politics. The former vice-president, Henry A. Wallace, saw the program as an open attack on the Soviet Union and branded it the "Martial Plan." His charges took on a sour ring in February 1948 when Czech Communists, with the help of the Soviets, established a hard-core Communist regime in Prague and took Czechoslovakia behind the Iron Curtain.

Spurred by Communist take-over of Czechoslovakia, in April 1948 Congress passed the Economic Cooperation Act, the legislation that launched the Marshall Plan. The measure provided that over the next four years Congress would appropriate a total of $17 billion for European recovery. (Because of Europe's rapid recovery only $12 billion was ultimately expended.) As a balm for the "China-firsters" who wanted more assistance to Chiang Kai-shek and his Nationalist regime, Congress at the same time appropriated $400 million for economic and military assistance to China.

The Economic Cooperation Administration (ECA) was the agency set up to direct the European Recovery Program (ERP) as the Marshall Plan was officially designated. It quickly swung into action, and over the next four years Europe was provided with a massive injection of capital. Great Britain received $2.8 billion; France, $2.6 billion; West Germany, $1.3 billion; Italy more than a billion; the Netherlands, nearly a billion.

The Results of the Marshall Plan

The most striking results of the European Recovery Program were seen in the growth of industrial production. West European industrial output by the year 1950 was up forty-five percent over 1947. And by 1952 West European industry was producing at a rate 200 percent higher than in 1938, the last year before the war. Because workingmen did not seem to receive a fair share of the fruits of the Marshall Plan boom, millions of them continued to support Communist parties, particularly in France and Italy. But the dramatic economic upturn sharply reduced the threat of Communist take-overs in the countries of Western Europe. Any strain on the economy of the United States was not noticeable. Americans spent more for liquor between 1948 and 1952 than they expended in Marshall Plan assistance.

The Marshall program came to an end at the time of the Korean War (1950-53). The original legislation provided that no Marshall Plan money was to go for military supplies or equipment. The war in Korea indicated that Communists had shifted from cold war tactics and were planning to achieve their objectives by open warfare. This caused the United States in 1951 to advise West European governments that most American assistance in the future would have to be for military purposes. And so by the year 1953 more than eighty percent of America's aid to Europe was being ticketed for programs designed to give the countries of Western Europe increased military muscle.

Crisis in Germany

While the legislation creating the European Recovery Program was awaiting President Truman's signature, a major crisis boiled up in Germany.

The origins of the Berlin—or, more accurately, the German—crisis of 1948-49 reached back into the closing period of World War II, when Soviet, American, and British leaders fashioned arrangements for the postwar occupation of Germany. With a minimum of quibbling, the Allies agreed that at the end of the war they would divide Germany into four occupational zones—one for France, as well as one each for the "big three" powers. According to the terms of the agreement, Berlin would be a hundred miles inside the Soviet zone of occupation. But western leaders believed that Berlin, as the capital of Germany, had special symbolic importance. Thus they divided the city into four sectors with each of the four nations controlling one section.

Failing to foresee a postwar breakdown of Allied unity, Anglo-American leaders did not secure guarantees of access to Berlin by rail or highway, although later they obtained a written agreement assuring them freedom of movement to and from the city via specified air corridors. Interestingly, nobody in 1944-45 seemed to envision that such a curious arrangement—a tiny island of Anglo-American-French control in the middle of the Soviet zone of occupation—clearly contained the seeds of future trouble.

The trouble began on April 1, 1948 when the Soviets started to halt motor and rail traffic that moved across their zone of occupation to Berlin. Partial at first, the "Berlin blockade" became total in June 1948. Although the blockade was aimed at driving the Americans, British, and French from Berlin, the real issue was the future place of the western part of Germany in world affairs.

The Russians were determined to prevent

revitalization of Germany—unless they could make all of Germany into a Communist satellite. A strong and prosperous Germany with its vast human and material resources—particularly those in the western zones of occupation—as part of the Soviet empire would virtually assure a Communist conquest of Europe. And the Russians in the years after 1945 were unquestionably dreaming of and planning for a Red take-over of West Germany.

A prosperous Germany that was either independent or allied with the Western powers was intolerable from the Soviet view. The reasons are fairly obvious. Having suffered so terribly at the hands of Germany in 1914-18, and again in 1941-45, the Russians had an overwhelming fear of the Germans. They determined that Germany must never again emerge as a first-rate power—unless it became a puppet of the Kremlin. A strong, unaligned Germany awaiting appearance of a new Hitler, or worse, a potent Germany lined up with the Western powers, would be a nightmarish threat to the Soviet Union.

More than dreams of a Communist take-over went into the mixture that produced postwar Soviet attitudes toward Germany. There was hatred. The Russians remembered their countrymen—perhaps fifteen million of them—who had perished during Hitler's assault on the Soviet Union. Accordingly, they insisted that Germany must now pay, to the extent that it was possible, for the destruction it had inflicted on the Soviet Union.

While American and British leaders could never accept the idea of a Communist Germany, they could understand Soviet fears of a German military power. Given Germany's state of total physical and moral collapse, however, it seemed unthinkable to Americans and Britons that Germany might ever again launch a blow at the Russians, especially since the Soviet Union was now a "superpower." American and British leaders, therefore, were quite willing to underwrite guarantees of Soviet security against any future German attack. Well aware of the devastation inside Russia, American and British leaders also accepted the Soviet demand that Germany should pay heavy reparations.

Reparations

The issue of reparations came to present serious problems, and proved to be one of the main rocks on which Anglo-American–Soviet co-operation in Germany eventually foundered. Put simply, the Americans and British, unlike the Russians, were not willing to let the Germans starve in order to make reparations payments to the Soviet Union.

This is not to say that Anglo-American leaders were bubbling with a spirit of "forgive and forget" toward Germany. But they recognized that Germany could not possibly achieve reconstruction and therefore internal stability if compelled to meet the enormous reparations payments demanded by the Soviets. American and British leaders believed that stability of Germany was essential if the Western powers were going to prevent the Soviet Communists from conquering all of Europe.

If Germany was forced to meet the Soviet reparations bill, the United States and Britain would have to pump massive relief into Germany. This meant that the Western powers would indirectly be picking up the bill for Germany's reparations payments to the Soviet Union. The United States and Britain had not ravaged Russia in the war. As a matter of fact, they were rather inclined to the view that the Soviets themselves were largely to blame for their own plight since they had collaborated with Hitler in 1939-41. Leaders in Washington and London were therefore not disposed to commit their governments to accepting the cost of Russian reconstruction. They also had other reasons for this attitude. Even before the war in Europe ended, the Soviets had begun to rally Communist clans in Western countries to resume the world revolution. The Soviets seemed determined to turn Eastern Europe into a giant satellite in clear violation of the will of the people of Eastern Europe, not to mention solemn Soviet promises made during the war. In violation of agreements with the United States and Britain, the Soviets had also stopped the flow of food from their zone in East Germany to western zones of occupation.

By summer 1946, the United States and Britain had concluded that there was no chance in the near future for working out a satisfactory agreement with the Soviets on such matters as German reparations or Germany's eventual political composition. On the point of Germany's political future, the Soviets were already well along with the business of building their zone of occupation in East Germany into a Communist satellite. They clearly had no intention of permitting reunification of the German nation on a basis of free elections.

Adding Frost to the Cold War

The existence of a cold war between the former wartime allies was becoming increasingly apparent. In the emerging confrontation with the Soviet Union, the Western powers wanted support of a strong and prosperous West Germany. To secure such support the United States and Britain set out to win over the West Germans. They promised the West Germans primary responsibility for managing their own affairs, pledging that Anglo-American armed forces would guarantee West German security. They also announced that they did not accept the Oder-Neisse line as a permanent frontier between Germany and Poland.

In accord with the new policy — proclaimed by Secretary of State Byrnes in a speech at Stuttgart in September 1946 — the United States and Great Britain in early 1947 merged their zones of occupation into a single zone — West Germany. (France brought its zone into the merger later on.) They proceeded to give Germans extensive administrative responsibilities. At the same time the Western powers, notably the United States, prepared to reinforce the West German economy and, as a result, included West Germany in the Marshall Plan. Next the United States and Britain engineered a sweeping reform of the West German currency, a step that was essential to West German regeneration.

These Anglo-American moves in West Germany in 1946-47 sent shock waves through the Kremlin. The prospect of a revitalized West Germany dependent on and closely allied with the Western powers was an extremely serious matter for the Soviets. West Germany was a heavy weight in the European power balance, and it would be a severe setback to the Soviets if that weight dropped firmly at the western end of the scale. The Soviet dream of making West Germany a Soviet-Communist satellite depended on withdrawal of Anglo-American military forces from West Germany, continuing economic chaos in West Germany, and a loss of confidence by the West Germans in Anglo-American promises of help and protection.

The Berlin Blockade

Sizing up the situation, the Soviets decided that serious problems required serious responses. What they must do, they concluded, was to engineer a crisis with the Western powers — a crisis from which the Western powers could not emerge triumphant but one over which they would be most reluctant to go to war. According to the Soviet plan, the Anglo-Americans would have two choices. One, they could terminate the crisis by making concessions. They might agree, for example, to withdraw their troops from West Germany and scuttle plans for reinforcing the West German economy. Or, two, they could accept defeat.

Acceptance of defeat, of course, would destroy the confidence of the West Germans in their new Anglo-American friends. It would put the West Germans and other West Europeans on notice that the Western powers, mainly the United States, were long on promises but, when a crisis came, short on deeds.

Where might the Soviets throw down a challenge to the Anglo-Americans? Berlin was an obvious place. By closing the land access routes from West Germany to the Anglo-American-French sectors of Berlin, they could easily stir up a crisis with the Western powers. But West Berlin was of little or no strategic importance to the Western powers. The Soviets calculated that the Anglo-Americans would not be disposed to touch off a war to retain their position in the former German capital. They would either make concessions to get the access routes to Berlin reopened or concede West Berlin to the Soviets.

Claiming that the Anglo-American currency reform in the Western zones of occupation violated wartime agreements on the administration of Germany, the Soviets began to harass traffic on land routes to Berlin. Eventually, in June 1948, they closed the West's land access routes to Berlin. The Western powers, however, did not follow the script which the Kremlin had drafted. They believed that the future of democracy in Europe, and perhaps in the entire world, required a firm stand in Berlin. Therefore, the United States, Britain, and France determined not to give way before the Soviet blockade.

To save Berlin — and at the same time avoid an armed clash with the Russians — the Western powers hit on the idea of a massive airlift of supplies to West Berlin. It was clear that the Russians did not want the crisis to erupt into a war. And the Western powers still had a written pledge from the Soviets guaranteeing them access to Berlin via certain air corridors. The Western powers reckoned that the Soviets would not run the risk of shooting down transport planes shuttling supplies to West Berlin.

Beginning in June 1948, hundreds of planes swung into action, flying food, coal, and many

During the Berlin airlift operation, planes like these C-47s at Tempelhof Airfield unloaded millions of tons of food and machinery. How did the airlift, or Operation Vittles, thwart Russian strategy?

Official U.S. Air Force Photo

other supplies to West Berlin's two million inhabitants. Month after month the planes maintained an aerial lifeline to the harassed Western sectors of the city—at enormous cost to the Western governments. Finally, after 321 days, the Soviets admitted that they were losing in this dangerous game. In May 1949 they reopened the land routes.

For the Soviets the entire affair was a disaster. The courageous and clever response to the Soviet challenge produced a wave of pro-Western enthusiasm throughout Europe. Instead of losing confidence in the United States and Great Britain, West Europeans (including the West Germans) had their faith renewed that the Anglo-Americans were determined to prevent any new Soviet thrust westward. As for West Berliners, they thrilled to the sight and sound of hundreds of giant planes circling above Tempelhof airdrome. Despite hardship, their morale increased through the dreary months of the crisis.

The Soviet defeat had other results. The Berlin blockade of 1948-49 spurred the Western powers to get on with plans to create an independent West German state. In September 1949 the Federal Republic of Germany, its capital in the old Rhineland city of Bonn, came into existence. Equally serious from the Soviet viewpoint, the Berlin crisis helped to bring forth the very kind

of Western military alliance which since the end of the war the Soviets had been hoping to prevent. In 1949 the western powers established the North Atlantic Treaty Organization (NATO).

North Atlantic Treaty Organization

A military alliance of West European and North American countries had been in the making for some time before the Soviets closed the land access routes to West Berlin. The first step had come in early 1947 when Britain and France signed the Treaty of Dunkirk pledging the two countries to united action if either was threatened by another power. A year later—on the heels of the Communist take-over of Czechoslovakia—Britain, France, and the Benelux countries (Belgium, the Netherlands, and Luxembourg) signed the Brussels Pact, a fifty-year military alliance binding each signatory to assist the other in case of an attack by an outside power.

It seemed clear that West Europeans would need a feeling of security from aggression from the East before they would throw themselves wholeheartedly into the European Recovery Program (Marshall Plan) then taking shape. Therefore American leaders expressed delight with the Dunkirk Treaty and the Brussels Pact. A few days after the signing of the Brussels

Pact, President Truman lauded the alliance and announced that he was sure the United States would help the signers carry out the aims of the pact. Obviously the president was preparing the way for eventual American membership in the alliance. American participation, as everyone understood, was required if any West European military alliance was to prevent Soviet aggression.

Knowing the American tradition against entangling alliances, many Americans felt misgivings about joining a military pact with the West European democracies. The brutal Communist coup in Czechoslovakia in 1948 caused thoughtful Americans to conclude that ideas about foreign involvement born at the end of the eighteenth century were not necessarily valid in the middle of the twentieth century. Then came the Soviet blockade of West Berlin, a crude power play which virtually destroyed opposition in America to membership in a European alliance system. When the Berlin blockade became total, Senator Vandenberg introduced a resolution in the Senate calling for American association with regional and collective arrangements based on continuous self-help and mutual aid—a polite way of saying that the United States should associate itself with the nations of the Brussels Pact. The resolution received overwhelming approval.

The Vandenberg resolution opened the way for negotiations which led to the North Atlantic Treaty, signed in April 1949 by Belgium, Canada, Denmark, France, Great Britain, Iceland, Italy, Luxembourg, the Netherlands, Norway, Portugal, and the United States. (Greece and Turkey entered the alliance in 1952, West Germany in 1955.) In the United States the treaty met only scattered opposition. (One of the opponents was Republican Senator Robert Taft of Ohio, who argued that the treaty violated the spirit of the UN, ran counter to time-honored American tradition, and might provoke the Soviet Union to hostile action.) In July 1949 the treaty won consent of the Senate by a vote of 82-13.

The heart of the North Atlantic Treaty was Article 5. This article announced: "The Parties agree that an armed attack against one or more of them in Europe or North America shall be considered an attack against them all; and consequently they agree that, if such an armed attack occurs, each of them, in exercise of the right of individual or collective self-defense recognized by Article 51 of the Charter of the United Nations, will assist the Party or Parties so attacked by taking forthwith, individually and in concert with the other Parties, such action as it deems necessary, including the use of armed force, to restore and maintain the security of the North Atlantic area."

The treaty did not provide that in the event of an attack on one member the other members of the alliance would automatically declare war. Each would take "such action as it deems necessary." Such wording seemed necessary to assure American membership in the alliance, for the federal Constitution of the United States provides that only Congress has the authority to declare war. If the treaty had required an automatic declaration of war by all members after an attack on one of them, opponents of the alliance in America might have defeated the treaty on the ground that the terms of United States membership were unconstitutional. Still, every member understood that the United States, whose nuclear power provided the military muscle of the alliance, was fully committed to go to war if one of the members came under attack. To guarantee its commitment the United States was prepared to station American troops in Europe, a circumstance that would assure American involvement in the conflict.

Latin America

During the later part of the 1940s, the principal battleground between America's democratic ideas and Soviet communism was Europe. But as the cold war began to take shape, American leaders sensed that the United States was involved in a global struggle and hence must take strong measures to prevent the spread of communism to countries far removed from Europe.

While there was no immediate threat of a Soviet-inspired military attack on Latin America, the United States nonetheless thought it desirable to bind the countries of the Western Hemisphere into some sort of military alliance. The United States had sought for many years to extend the Monroe Doctrine by committing all countries of the Western Hemisphere to resist any non-American threat to any one of them. The outcome was negotiations leading to the Treaty of Rio de Janeiro of 1947. The treaty provided that an attack on one American nation would be considered an attack on all and that all states must cooperate by contributing troops or supplies. The Rio Pact, not the North Atlantic Treaty, was the first entangling alliance which the

United States had joined since ending its pact with France in 1800. But since an outside attack on the hemisphere seemed highly unlikely, the Rio arrangement brought no controversy and little interest in the United States.

The poverty and unrest of Latin America made it a fertile ground for Communist ideas — especially open to subversion and guerrilla tactics, by which the Communists might achieve their aims. The United States saw that the Rio Pact did not really meet the problem of how to keep communism out of the Western Hemisphere. At the Ninth International Conference of American States, meeting at Bogotá, Colombia, in spring 1948, the United States pressed for a collective system of meeting such problems as Communist subversion.

As if to underscore the need for such a system, a revolt broke out in Bogotá as the conference was getting underway. This revolt was, in part, the result of Communist activity. In the span of a few days several hundred people died and large parts of the city were wrecked. When order returned, the delegates accepted a charter for an Organization of American States (OAS). The charter was not an anti-Communist document and, indeed, asserted that no state or group of states had the right to intervene directly or indirectly, for any reason, in the internal or external affairs of another. Still, Americans hoped that the procedures which the charter outlined for collective action to meet political and economic problems of the hemisphere might help to counter Communist activities.

Latin Americans were only mildly interested in the Rio Pact and the OAS. What they wanted was massive economic assistance, perhaps a "little Marshall Plan" for their part of the world. Then came disappointment. Thinking that its principal challenges were in Europe and Asia, and believing its resources limited, the United States advised the Latins that they would have to depend on their own resources and investment of private funds by North American and European capitalists. The result was a new wave of Latin American resentment toward the United States, an increase in old complaints about "Yankee imperialism," and a quiet spreading of Communist influence in the area, notably in Brazil, Chile, and Cuba.

Point Four Program

Many thoughtful Americans, including President Truman, did not believe the United States could afford to ignore altogether the underdeveloped countries of the world. A principal reason was that most Americans thought the poverty of those countries provided seedbeds for communism. Truman's response was the Point Four program, announced in his inaugural address of January 1949. A smaller, world edition of the Marshall Plan, Point Four would seek to check communism in poverty-ridden countries by helping them achieve prosperity and stability. Because of the demands on American resources, particularly in Western Europe, the main export under Point Four was to be American scientific and technical know-how. More than a year went by before Congress got around to acting, and the first appropriation was only $35 million. This was very small considering the dimension of the problem of poverty in the world.

In the first two years of the Point Four program, thirty Latin American, African, and Asian countries received assistance, most of which went to improve health, agriculture, and transportation. Although Congress quadrupled Point Four's appropriation in 1952, the program unfortunately remained more a promise than a fulfillment. The United States did not feel it had the funds to underwrite the economy of every poor country in the world. As the cold war dragged into the 1950s, moreover, Congress and the executive branch came under increasing pressure to earmark most foreign aid for military supplies and hardware.

Yugoslavia

By the time the 1940s were drawing to a close, Americans had some reason for satisfaction with the results of the new "containment" policy, at least in Europe, the Middle East, and the Western Hemisphere. They had prevented the spread of Soviet-Communist power in Iran and the Eastern Mediterranean. The Marshall Plan, Berlin airlift, and NATO had apparently stopped any Soviet plans for immediate further expansion westward in Europe. And the gains of communism in Latin America seemed minimal. But then a completely unforeseen challenge arose — an opportunity to help roll back the Iron Curtain in Southeastern Europe. It came when Marshal Tito of Yugoslavia broke with the Kremlin.

Tito, although a dedicated Communist, had never seen eye-to-eye with the Soviets. During the war he had quarreled with Stalin over matters of strategy and treatment of Yugoslavia. The essential cause of the rupture with the

Soviet Union was Stalin's determination to make Yugoslavia into a Soviet satellite. To achieve his ends the Soviet dictator sought to undermine Tito by penetrating the Yugoslav Communist party, the police, and the army.

Aware of what was going on, Tito was furious. Since the Soviets had no troops in Yugoslavia, and the party, army, and police were completely loyal to him, Tito was able to turn back Stalin's challenge. Then in 1948 Stalin accused Tito of putting his own ambitions above the well-being of the world Communist movement and in effect expelled him from the movement.

Leaders in the United States did not quite know what to make of the Soviet-Yugoslav shouting match. Up to that time open defiance of the Soviet Union by any Communist state had seemed unthinkable. Early in 1949, American leaders concluded that it was in the interest of the United States and the non-Communist world for Tito to succeed in establishing his independence from Moscow. They began to take steps to help the Yugoslavs overcome the consequences of being cut off from trade with the Soviet Union and its satellites. For his part, Tito knew that his survival depended upon assistance from the West. He therefore set about to improve his standing with the Western powers. He closed the border between Yugoslavia and Greece, cutting off Communist rebels in Greece from outside support. He made conciliatory gestures toward Italy, Austria, and Great Britain and turned to the United States for economic help, mainly in the form of grants and loans.

The people of the United States were not unanimous in support of the government's new policy toward Yugoslavia. It seemed to some Americans that it was illogical to try to keep Tito's Communist regime afloat in Yugoslavia while engaged in a global crusade against communism.

American leaders realized that they faced the problem of choosing between the lesser of two evils: a Communist regime headed by Tito—independent of the Kremlin—or a Communist regime under firm control of the Soviet Union. The advantages of an independent Communist government in Yugoslavia were clear. If Yugoslavia could keep its independence, the Iron Curtain would be pushed back to the middle of the Balkan peninsula. Tito's army had thirty-three divisions which might be available to the West, and there was a chance that Tito's defiance of the Soviet Union, if successful, might provoke unrest in other parts of the

Kremlin's satellite empire. (As matters turned out, in the wake of the Titoist revolt, Stalin ordered purges in the satellite countries. The purges removed possible rebels from positions of influence in satellite parties. When, some years later, in spite of such measures, satellite states seemed bent on independence—Hungary in 1956 and Czechoslovakia in 1968—the Soviets sent in Communist troops to reassert the Kremlin's authority.)

Relations between Yugoslavia and the United States were stiff and proper. Each government rested its policy toward the other on cold-blooded self-interest. Tito made it clear that he was not willing to exchange his communism for Western support, and the United States never suggested that he do so. American officials sometimes reminded Tito that American aid depended on the whims of Congress. Thus it might be a good idea to show consideration toward political prisoners and religion. Sometimes Tito seemed to heed such gentle prods, but he declined to compromise his Communist beliefs and continued to rule Yugoslavia with a strong hand.

Up to the year 1955 the United States had loaned or mostly granted more than $1 billion to Yugoslavia. One cannot say for sure that the American assistance—and the promise of more help to come—saved Tito, but it helped. American support did not assure permanent friendship between the United States and Yugoslavia. After the death of Stalin in 1953, Tito and leaders in the Kremlin smoothed over some of their differences, and in the latter 1950s relations between the United States and Yugoslavia cooled. Still, Yugoslavia did not become a Soviet satellite. Accordingly, the policy toward Yugoslavia and the Titoist revolt must rank as a major achievement of the Truman presidency.

China

After World War II American policies were concentrated on containing Soviet power and Communist influence in Europe, the Eastern Mediterranean, and the Middle East. At the same time followers of philosopher-politician Mao Tse-tung were achieving for communism its greatest victory since the Bolshevik Revolution in Russia—the take-over of China, the most populous country in the world. The climax came in December 1949 when General Chiang Kai-shek, China's leader for more than twenty years, led a million and a half of his more dedicated followers across the Formosa Strait to

After World War II, the Nationalist and Communist alliance in China fell apart. Chiang Kai-shek was unable to keep his position as leader. These peasants in Honan Province are refugees from the civil war.

the island of Taiwan (Formosa). There, without much regard for the wishes of the islanders, Chiang established his Free China government.

Even before Chiang's retreat to Taiwan, the United States had debated over America's responsibility for the inability of the Nationalists to hold back the Communist tide in China. Reflecting one view was a thirty-one-year-old Democratic congressman from Boston, John F. Kennedy. In February 1949 Kennedy charged that wrongheaded policies fashioned in the White House and State Department had opened the way for communism in China. In Kennedy's view, American concessions to the Soviets during the Yalta Conference had strengthened China's Communists at the expense of Chiang Kai-shek, and in the years after 1945 the United States had not given as much support to Chiang as it should have.

On the other side was the voice of Secretary of State Dean G. Acheson, who succeeded Secretary Marshall in January 1949. According to Acheson, in a speech given in January 1950, a month after Chiang's fall, the United States had provided large-scale military and economic assistance to Chiang. Because of deep-rooted corruption in his regime, however, and his failure to redeem pledges of social and economic reform, Chiang's popular support melted away. The Communists, Acheson said, had merely

mounted a great national spirit of dissatisfaction and ridden it to victory and power. Which argument did Americans in 1949-50 accept? Most of them seemed to agree with the critics of the Roosevelt-Truman policies toward China. Like Kennedy they believed that the United States had "sold Chiang Kai-shek down the river" to the Communists.

In assessing these policies toward China, one ought to take at least a brief look at China's history over the previous half century.

By the year 1900 the Manchu dynasty was tottering, after several centuries of nominal control over China. In 1911-12 it collapsed. Among the groups competing for power in post-Manchu China was the Kuomintang, or Nationalist party, headed by Dr. Sun Yat-sen, a man of high intelligence and considerable personal magnetism. Sun had limited success — until 1923 when agents of the new Communist regime in Russia offered to help organize his army and party. Sun accepted Soviet assistance and within two years the rejuvenated Kuomintang was ready to strike for control of the country.

Then came misfortune. Sun died in 1925, whereupon leadership passed to his chief general, Chiang Kai-shek. Although he had studied in Moscow and seemed to entertain Communist sympathies, Chiang soon clashed with the Communists. In 1927 he expelled the Communists from the Nationalist party. Meanwhile Nationalist armies were bringing vast territories under Chiang's authority. By 1928 the Nationalists had gained control of much of China.

Chiang v. Mao

Chinese Communists had little strength for several years until Mao Tse-tung took command of their movement in the early 1930s. Contrary to Marxist dogma, Mao set about organizing China's peasantry rather than the urban proletariat. The result was a dramatic increase of Communist influence. Alarmed, Chiang determined in 1934 to crush the Communists and, in a series of violent clashes, soundly thrashed them. Down but not out, the Communists retreated and in an epic "long march" thousands of Mao's followers escaped to remote northwestern areas where they rebuilt their forces for the revolution which they saw in the future.

Then came the year 1937 and Japan's attack on China. While Chiang's forces were pinned down or in retreat before the Japanese, the Communists, in the name of Chinese patriotism, returned to northeastern China. There they threw themselves into the fight against the Japanese aggressors. At the same time they brought large areas of North China under their control. By the end of World War II in 1945, perhaps a quarter of China's population was taking orders from Mao.

After 1937, most Americans saw Chiang Kai-shek as a hero who was defending his country against a cruel and merciless aggressor. Officials in the State Department, however, had never entertained a high opinion of the Nationalist leader. Before 1937 they doubted that he had the capacity to engineer China's regeneration. After Japan's attack they doubted that he would ever be able to expel the invaders. Following Pearl Harbor and America's entry into the war, the estimate of the State Department's China experts did not change. They continued to think poorly of Chiang.

Chiang did nothing in 1941-45 to persuade officials to change State Department views. Throughout the war American leaders continually hoped that Chiang would apply greater pressure against Japanese armies in China. Strong Chinese action never came. The American commander in the China-Burma-India theater, General Joseph W. ("Vinegar Joe") Stilwell, cited the low morale of Chiang's army and corruption in the Nationalist regime. He urged sweeping reforms in the army and government. Chiang failed to respond.

President Roosevelt and such military chieftains as Generals Marshall and MacArthur determined to bring the Soviet Union into the Pacific war as soon as the Grand Alliance had beaten Hitler in Europe. As a lure for the Soviets, the United States agreed at Yalta that the Soviets, as part of a postwar settlement, should receive certain concessions in Chinese Manchuria (see Chapter 17). The Soviets probably would have jumped into the Far Eastern war upon conclusion of fighting in Europe without an invitation. This would have given them control of Manchuria when Japan surrendered. Hence it seems academic to debate the influence of Yalta on the postwar history of China.

Soviet armies were entrenched in Manchuria when the Pacific war ended in August 1945. The question remains: To what extent were those Soviet forces responsible for the eventual Communist triumph in China? The Soviets doubtless helped Mao and his followers to consolidate their authority in Manchuria and also turned over to the Communists large stocks of captured Japanese arms and ammunition. Otherwise, Soviet support of Mao was minimal. The Soviets, remembering ancient rivalries with China, had mingled feelings about their Chinese comrades and were not entirely sure that a Communist victory in China would be in the Russian national interest. On the other hand, the Chinese Communists would have been the dominant group in Manchuria at the end of the war in any circumstances and probably could have secured control of the province without Soviet assistance.

China: 1945-1950

When the war in the Pacific came to its sudden conclusion in August 1945, leaders of the United States saw that there would be a race between followers of Chiang and Mao for control of areas which the Japanese would evacuate in China. To help Chiang win, American planes airlifted Nationalist soldiers to many strategic points and United States officials directed the emperor of Japan to order his armies in China to surrender only to the Nationalists. At the same time American leaders released to Chiang large quantities of United States military equipment and agreed to continue channeling financial aid to the Nationalist regime. Between 1945 and 1949 the United States provided Chiang's government with some $2 billion in grants and credits.

Still, when fighting broke out between Nationalists and Communists in autumn 1945, American leaders had scant hope that Chiang would win. They urged Chiang to form a coalition government with Mao. To arrange a peace settlement and bring about a coalition government of Communists and non-Communists, President Truman sent General George C. Marshall to China as a special ambassador in December, 1945.

For a time the chances of the Marshall mission appeared bright. The Nationalists and Communists agreed in January 1946 to a ceasefire. But the following spring Communists violated the truce, and civil war raged off and on for the rest of the year. A coalition government was never achieved. General Marshall returned to the United States in January 1947, his mission a failure.

Chiang's reputation was slipping, in part because of popular outrage over graft in connection with relief supplies sent to China by the United Nations. The Communists exploited the dishonesty and inefficiency in Chiang's regime. Then, as Mao's fortunes continued to rise, in 1947 Chiang launched his American-equipped armies against the Communists in Manchuria. Largely with old Japanese armaments, the Communists repelled the attack and took the offensive. By the end of 1948 they had cleared the Nationalists from northeastern China. At the same time the economy of Nationalist-controlled China collapsed. Fearing that the end was near, Chiang refused to risk his government's $300 million gold reserve to bolster the wildly inflating Nationalist currency. Nationalist soldiers began to flock to the Communist side, and some of Chiang's generals surrendered entire armies. With captured or surrendered American equipment, the Communists pressed forward on all fronts. By spring 1949 it was plain that Chiang was finished. He fled to Taiwan the following December.

Palestine

During the late 1940s important events were also occurring in the Middle East, in Palestine, where Jews were trying to establish a Jewish nation state over the strong objection of Arabs. Few people in the United States during that period saw the Palestine question as having any great bearing on the cold war. By the 1950s and 1960s, however, it became apparent that America's Palestinian policy in the Truman years had great importance for relationships with the Soviet Union.

The origins of the modern problem in Palestine go back to Old Testament times when Arab and Jewish societies appeared in that arid land along the eastern rim of the Mediterranean. Both Jews and Arabs claimed to descend from the prophet Abraham. The two groups lived in comparative peace until the eighth century B.C. when the dispersion of Jews through the ancient world took place. Jewish communities reappeared in Palestine in the fifth century B.C. But after the Arabs took over, in the seventh century A.D., the Jewish communities in Palestine disappeared.

The Jews scattered across Europe and many thousands of them eventually found their way to the New World. Intelligent, resourceful, and energetic, they sometimes found prosperity. They also often met discrimination and persecution at the hands of their Christian neighbors.

Late in the nineteenth century a movement known as Zionism appeared in Eastern Europe. Its aim was to return Jews to their ancestral homeland in Palestine, by that time part of the Turkish (Ottoman) empire. With a land and nation of their own, it was hoped that Jews could find peace and dignity. Zionists began migrating in small numbers to Palestine in the 1880s. During World War I Turkey sided with the Germans, and before long it was clear that the Turkish empire would soon collapse. Zionists were quick to see the possibilities of the situation. And when the British and French agreed that after the war Great Britain would take over Palestine, Zionists began to press for restoration of the country as a Jewish national home.

British leaders were sympathetic toward Zionist ambitions. The outcome was the Balfour Declaration of 1917, given by Foreign Secretary Arthur James Balfour, that Britain would "view with favor the establishment in Palestine of a national home for the Jewish people." But the declaration added that "nothing shall be done which may prejudice the civil and religious rights of the existing non-Jewish communities in Palestine." In 1920, the League of Nations made Palestine a mandate of the British, who immediately set out to redeem the Balfour pledge by opening the country to Jewish immigrants.

Angry over failure of the Paris Peace Conference (1919) to grant independence to Palestine, Palestinian Arabs resented the increase in the Jewish population. The outcome was terrorist attacks on Jews—to which the Jews retaliated. In spite of the difficulties of life in Palestine, Jews continued to migrate to the country. The migration accelerated after Hitler began his campaign of persecution of Jews in Germany.

During World War II, Palestine received little attention and the movement of Jews to the country virtually stopped. After the war, the Zionist movement again gathered steam. The sickening revelation of Nazi death camps—where perhaps six million Jews were murdered—brought an outpouring of sympathy for Jews which in turn gave reinforcement to Zionism. Jews in the United States, who hitherto had taken scant interest in the movement, suddenly saw Zionism as a sacred cause and became the movement's chief source of financial support.

The Palestine question meanwhile had become an international problem. The central issues were the number of Jews who might be permitted to migrate to Palestine and the political future of the country. Under heavy pressure by Jews in the United States, in 1946 President Truman favored allowing a hundred thousand Jewish immigrants to enter Palestine, a figure that infuriated the Arabs. As for political organization, the British mandate continued while assorted groups and individuals tried to draft a workable plan for partitioning Palestine between Jews and Arabs.

By the end of 1946 the British had reached the end of their patience in Palestine. Zionists were smuggling in Jewish refugees from Europe in defiance of British immigration quotas. Jews and Arabs were murdering one another. Nobody had developed a formula for the political future of the area which promised peace. Administering Palestine, moreover, was expensive, and the British no longer could afford the expense.

The Partition of Palestine

In early 1947 the British decided to get out of Palestine. They turned over to the United Nations the task of working out a Palestine policy. In autumn 1947 the United Nations approved a plan for partitioning the country, whereupon the British announced that they would withdraw their troops from Palestine at midnight on May 16, 1948.

The UN plan for Palestine, which received votes of delegates from both the United States and the Soviet Union, provided for independent Arab and Jewish states. The two states, however, were to function as a single economic unit and the city of Jerusalem was to have a special status designed to protect the rights and interests of both Jews and Arabs. The response of Arabs and Jews to the plan? Viewing as totally repugnant the idea of an independent Jewish state in what they believed was Arab territory, Arabs were furious. And delegates from Arab countries expressed their contempt for the partition arrangement by stalking out of the chamber of the General Assembly. Jews, on the other hand, were exuberant.

But then Jews became nervous. Clearly execution of the partition arrangement was going to touch off hostilities between Jews and Arabs. And in the face of such a prospect, and also because of increasing recognition that support of Jewish ambitions in Palestine was having a serious effect on America's relations with Arab countries, the government in Washington seemed to be wavering in its support of the partition plan. Indeed, it appeared that the United States might be reconsidering the whole idea of partition. And given its status as the premier of the world, the United States was in a position to compel the UN to set aside the recent resolution for partition and adopt a different scheme. A different arrangement for Palestine almost certainly would puncture the dream of an independent Jewish nation-state in that country.

Zionists in the Middle East and Jews in the United States wanted to head off any shift in American policy toward Palestine. They literally bombarded the White House with letters, postcards, and telegrams urging the government in Washington to continue its support of the UN partition plan and give its blessing to a Jewish nation-state in the Middle East. At length the Zionist campaign, which gave no heed to larger American interests in the Middle East, annoyed the president. For a time he refused to confer with Zionist representatives.

Officials in the State Department were deeply troubled by Zionist pressure. Their reason was simple. If the United States sponsored the creation of Israel, it would risk alienating the entire Arab world. And Arab nations had a population of a hundred million, territory stretching from West Africa to the Persian Gulf, and resources that included seemingly endless pools of oil.

In view of the cold war which existed between the United States and its allies and the nations of the Communist bloc, some members of the State Department believed that this was not a good time to take positions which were certain to arouse Arabs against America. Some officials also wondered how anyone could argue that Zionists had a right to carve out a fully independent nation in territory which had been an Arab preserve for more than a thousand years. In line with these views, officials in the State Department worked out a new American policy for Palestine in early 1948. This policy proposed to set aside the UN partition plan and establish a temporary trusteeship for the country, managed by the United States, Great Britain, and France. During the period of trusteeship, hopefully, Arab-Jewish passions would cool, the political future of Palestine would be reconsidered, and perhaps a formula satisfactory to all sides would be worked out. With consent of Secretary Marshall (but not President Truman) the new State Department proposal was made public. If approved, it would nullify, for the time being at least, the idea of an independent Jewish state.

Friends of Zionism erupted. Still, it was the president who in the last analysis determined policy. Whatever his annoyance with Zionists in America, Truman turned down the State De-

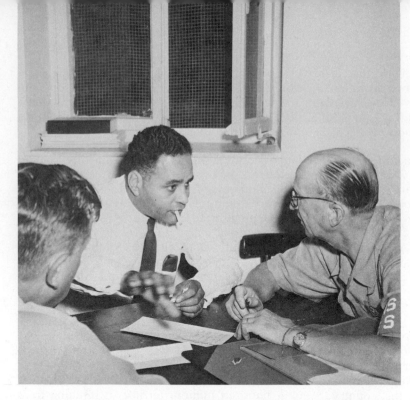

Dr. Ralph Bunche (center) and General A. Lundstrom, Chief Military Observer (right), confer at Haifa, Palestine, in 1948. Dr. Bunche became UN Acting Mediator after the Chief Mediator was assassinated. He received the 1950 Nobel Peace Prize for negotiating an armistice between Israel and the Arabs.

Official United Nations Photo

partment plan to revise the American stand with respect to Palestine. He elected to support the creation of Israel. So when Zionists declared the independence of Israel on May 14, 1948, the United States almost immediately recognized the new state.

Arab-Israeli War

After Israel's declaration of independence, war broke out between the new Jewish state and its Arab neighbors. In the year-long war the Israelis humbled their Arab opponents. When at last the UN arranged an uneasy truce, the Israelis had enlarged their territory by fifty percent. More than seven hundred thousand Arabs fled to neighboring Arab states, particularly Jordan and Egypt. The Arabs claimed that the Israelis forced them out. The Israelis claimed that the Arabs, in fright or out of hatred for Jews, simply abandoned their homes. Whatever the truth, the refugees remained a problem. Most of them lived in squalid camps maintained by the UN and supported mainly by funds from the United States.

In the years following the Arab-Israeli war of 1948-49 the Arabs continued to seethe. They directed much of their anger toward Great Britain and the United States, the foreign powers most responsible, they thought, for the presence of the Jews in their homeland. Although the

United States in subsequent years tried to appease the Arabs, mainly by its foreign-aid programs, Arabs continued to see the government in Washington as the guardian of their enemy, Israel. This situation worked to the advantage of America's cold war opponent, the Soviet Union, in the competition for influence in the Middle East.

STUDY GUIDE: Global war had brought many changes. New weapons, particularly the atomic bomb, gave mankind the means of self-destruction. The war helped to produce a new "superpower," the Soviet Union, intent on expanding the influence of communism. Most Americans failed to realize that the world was not the same place it had been before the war. New tensions leading to a "cold war" would make it impossible to put aside international responsibilities.

The Allied powers pressed for trials of Axis war criminals. In addition to punishing the criminals for their misdeeds, many people hoped to further the cause of justice by proving that individuals are responsible for their acts even if carried out on orders of the state. Many doubts were raised about the legality of the trials. Several thousand war criminals were brought to trial in Europe and Japan, notably at Nuremberg and Tokyo.

Russian ambitions in Eastern Europe doomed the Allied hope for a peaceful postwar world based on the universalist principle of the self-determination of nations. Soviet armies of occupation tightened Communist control over the Baltic states, Rumania, and Poland. Attempts were also made to enlarge Russian influence in the Middle East.

To halt the threat of a Communist take-over in Greece and Turkey, the United States sent military and economic assistance to the two struggling nations. In the historic Truman Doctrine, the president upheld the principle that the United States should attempt to prevent the spread of Soviet power and international communism.

In 1947 the United States announced the European Recovery Program, or Marshall Plan. Its purpose was to help carry out the Truman Doctrine and to put Europe back on its feet economically. Congress voted billions of dollars to finance this international program of economic assistance. Its success was measured by a dramatic upturn in the economies of Western European nations.

The Soviet Union was eager to bring West Germany into the Communist orbit. In an effort to win concessions toward this end, the Soviets closed land access routes from West Germany to the Anglo-American-French sectors of Berlin. The Western powers determined not to give way before the Soviet "blockade." To save Berlin, and yet avoid an armed clash with the Russians, the Western Powers began a massive airlift of supplies to West Berlin. The Berlin airlift was such a spectacular success that the Russians finally admitted failure and reopened the land routes.

The Communist threat in Eastern Europe, especially the take-over of Czechoslovakia, led the major European nations to form military alliances. After the Berlin blockade, the United States joined with the European nations in forming the North Atlantic Treaty Organization. Under the terms of the treaty, the United States committed itself to go to war if one of the member nations came under attack.

To prevent the threat of a Communist attack or subversion in Latin America, the United States and other countries of the Western Hemisphere signed the Treaty of Rio de Janeiro and also formed the Organization of American States. To check communism in poverty-ridden countries, Truman announced his "Point Four program" in 1949. Scientific and technical aid was given to many Asian, African, and Latin American countries under this program.

Stalin's determination to make Yugoslavia into a Soviet satellite led that country's head of state, Marshal Tito, to break with the Soviet Union. Tito wanted to preserve Yugoslavia as an independent Communist nation. Yugoslavia received aid from the United States to fight off Soviet domination.

Mao Tse-tung and his followers succeeded in establishing a Communist government in China in 1949. Chiang Kai-shek, Chinese Nationalist leader for more than twenty years, set up a "Free China" government on the island of Taiwan. Over the years the United States had given massive aid to Chiang, but corruption and inefficiency in his government helped contribute to his downfall.

The Zionist desire to restore Palestine as a Jewish national home met with sympathy from the British, who had been given Palestine as a mandate after World War I. After World War II the British gave up their mandate in Palestine and turned its affairs over to the United Nations. When the UN divided the country into two parts, the Jews determined to turn their part into the independent state of Israel. Israel's declaration of independence led to war between the new state and its Arab neighbors. The Israeli victory further increased Arab hostility. United States support of Israel angered the Arabs, who were then drawn more closely into the Soviet sphere of influence.

THE ELECTION OF 1948

One could hardly find a political "expert" who was not predicting an overwhelming Republican victory in the 1948 election. The Republicans had won smashing victories in the elections of 1946 and nothing had happened in the meantime to indicate a change in the political climate. Large numbers of Americans were in disagreement with the president by 1948. Many plainly disliked him, and many others felt that he was not big enough for the presidential job. Moreover, Truman's Democratic party was in disarray. The administration's strong position against Soviet expansion had alienated the extreme left wing of the party. The president's outspoken advocacy of equal rights for racial minorities, notably Negroes, had alienated many white southerners in the party.

Chances for the Democrats seemed so poor in spring 1948 that many of the party faithful wished the president would step aside, hopefully in favor of the popular General Dwight D. Eisenhower. Eisenhower's political affiliations were not known at the time, and he refused to take an active part in partisan politics, Democratic or Republican. Nonetheless, Truman determined to seek reelection.

When Republicans gathered at their Philadelphia convention in June 1948, battle lines quickly formed between liberal and conservative wings of the party. The champion of the conservatives was Senator Taft of Ohio, but the majority of the delegates favored the more liberal Governor Thomas E. Dewey of New York, the party's standard-bearer in 1944. For vice-president the convention turned to Governor Earl Warren of California, also a member of the party's liberal wing.

The Democrats gathered a few weeks later in the same city, Philadelphia. They fought over a civil rights plank and renominated Truman for the presidency, with Senator Alben W. Barkley of Kentucky, a colorful and popular figure, as his running mate.

Third Parties

Unlike the situation in most presidential elections, in 1948 the Republicans and Democrats were not to have the field virtually to themselves. Two new "third" parties made determined bids for votes.

One new party was the States' Rights, or Dixiecrat party. It was composed mainly of white southerners who objected to the civil rights plank of the Democratic platform. Its candidate was Governor J. Strom Thurmond of South Carolina.

The other new entry was the Progressive party, put together by the former vice-president, Henry A. Wallace. As a strong advocate of programs of social welfare and civil rights, Wallace had the support of many ultraliberals, Negroes, and workingmen in the country, most of whom normally voted Democratic. Wallace had also taken a vigorous stand against containment, not because he was a Communist sympathizer but because he believed such policies were apt to provoke a new global war. As a result, the country's Communists rallied to his standard. Consequently the Progressive party became increasingly identified in the popular mind with communism.

The Campaign and Election

Although the odds were against his reelection, President Truman determined that he would not go down without a fight. He called a special session of the Republican-controlled Congress to consider his proposals for a more liberal approach to inflation, price controls, civil rights, and public housing. Truman wanted strict price controls and strong federal programs to promote civil rights and public housing. Republicans, too, at their recent national convention, had gone on record as favoring more liberal policies in those areas. The Congressional session lasted only twelve days and it failed to produce any important legislation. The president only grinned at this lack of action.

Truman was now ready for his slugging match with Dewey. He addressed throngs of people at whistle-stops in every part of the country. In peppery language he assailed the "do-nothing" Eightieth Congress. He persuaded listeners that he, like many of them, was an "underdog" who was fighting the exploiters of the common man.

While Truman was swinging out at Republicans on the campaign trail, Governor Dewey was speaking in broad generalities, making few concrete pledges, taking care to say nothing that was offensive or controversial. His campaign tactics rested on a careful calculation of the realities of the existing political situation in America. He needed to secure the support of many voters who normally voted for the Democrats. He also needed full support of both the conservative and liberal wings of the Republican party. Therefore Dewey avoided taking any firm positions on the controversial issues of the day.

As the campaign ground to its conclusion, political observers saw no reason to change their estimate of the outcome of the election: Dewey would win easily. But on election day, to the astonishment of everybody (including, probably, Truman) Truman received 24,000,000 popular votes to nearly 22,000,000 for Dewey. Thurmond and Wallace each received a little more than a million.

Why did Truman win? His veto of the Taft-Hartley Bill in 1947 brought him the vote of organized labor in 1948. His support of civil rights guaranteed him the black vote. His unflinching support of continuing subsidization of agriculture brought the votes of millions of farmers. And his stand for price controls gained the votes of countless middle- and lower-income

Senator Alben Barkley addresses the 1948 Democratic Convention in Philadelphia. The convention was the scene of bitter fighting over the civil rights plank in the party platform. Delegates from Mississippi and Alabama finally walked out.

Acme Photo from Compix

Harry S. Truman holds the Chicago *Tribune* aloft to well-wishers at Union Station, St. Louis. The headline credits Thomas Dewey with winning the 1948 presidential election. What circumstances made it appear doubtful that Truman would be reelected?

Wide World Photo

people. Added to these factors was the president's clever presentation of himself as an underdog.

STUDY GUIDE: Few people gave Truman much chance of reelection in 1948. Truman had lost popularity, and two new parties appeared: the anticivil rights Dixiecrats, and the Progressives. The Republicans nominated Thomas Dewey. Truman's record in domestic politics helped him to win an upset victory.

THE END OF THE 1940s

Truman in his second term hoped to concentrate on affairs at home. In his view this meant reviving the twentieth-century progressive movement. The president wanted to redeem the pledges of the Democratic platform of 1948 regarding civil rights and public housing. He wanted to repeal the Taft-Hartley labor law, secure passage of an elaborate program of national health insurance, and put into operation a new and complicated program for agriculture.

Most of the president's dreams for domestic reform were not destined for fulfillment. The old conservative coalition of southern Democrats and northern Republicans continued to hold the power on Capitol Hill.

Even if there had been no conservative coalition in Congress, it is doubtful that Truman could have achieved much in the domestic realm during his second term. The people of the country were not greatly interested in the president's ideas regarding domestic reform.

Popular apathy was not the only ally of the conservative coalition. As the decade of the 1940s came to a close, the people of the United States suffered a series of psychological shocks which took away any zeal for domestic reform.

First came the realization in early 1949 that Chiang Kai-shek was finished in China, that the Communists were going to take over the most populous country in the world. Americans had a sentimental attachment to the people of China. They had seen themselves as the special guardians and benefactors of China — and fondly thought that the Chinese entertained equally warm feelings for Americans.

Now China was falling into the orbit of communism, about to become an enemy of the United States. It was a catastrophe beyond measure and left Americans at once bewildered, sad, angry, and frightened. Could it be that Marx and Lenin had been right, that communism indeed was "the wave of the future"?

Next came the sensational trial of Alger Hiss, who had held responsible positions in the New Deal administration of Franklin Roosevelt and in the State Department. Hiss had been accused by a self-confessed former Soviet agent, Whittaker Chambers, of having passed secret government documents to a Soviet spy ring. Although numerous intellectuals and other liberals vouched for his integrity and loyalty, the evidence against Hiss was impressive. In early 1950 a jury found him guilty of having perjured himself when he denied under oath that he had passed the documents. Could it be that Communists were working inside the American government, boring from within to bring about the collapse of the American system? To Americans in 1949 this was a chilling question.

In September 1949, Americans learned that the Soviets had exploded an atomic bomb. They had known that eventually Soviet scientists and engineers would unlock the secrets of atomic weapons. But American scientists had predicted this would not happen until the mid-1950s or even the 1960s. The Soviets instead had gotten the bomb within four years — ending America's nuclear monopoly and absolute security against an attack by the Soviet-Communist empire.

Finally, early in 1950, came the revelation that the Soviets had not mastered the mysteries of atomic weaponry by themselves. Clever spies, the most important of whom was a British physicist of German birth, Dr. Klaus Fuchs, had penetrated the American nuclear establishment, stolen secrets of the bomb, and passed them to Soviet agents.

What was happening? Was America, threatened from without, betrayed from within, about to collapse?

It was on this note of anxiety and fear, frustration and anger, that President Truman's dreams of domestic reform expired. It was on this note that the decade of the 1950s began.

STUDY GUIDE: Truman's hopes for further domestic reforms during his second term were never realized. The fall of China, revelations of Communist spies in government, and Russia's explosion of the atom bomb were viewed as threats to American security.

SUMMING UP THE CHAPTER

Names and Terms to Identify

Servicemen's Readjustment Act

Fair Deal

Arthur H. Vandenberg

Hoover Commission

National Security Act

Taft-Hartley Act

Malcolm X

Marshal Tito

George C. Marshall

European Recovery Program

Berlin blockade

Rio Pact

Organization of American States

Point Four

Dean G. Acheson

Alger Hiss

Alben W. Barkley

Study Questions and Points to Review

1. When and under what circumstance did Harry S. Truman become president?

2. What action did President Truman take when railroad unions ordered a strike in 1946?

3. What was the Atomic Energy Act of 1946?

4. Name the legislation that was introduced to streamline governmental organization and procedure. What three obstacles to legislative effectiveness did the act overlook?

5. According to the Presidential Succession Act of 1947, what elective officer would be next in line to the president after the vice-president?

6. What provision did the Twenty-fifth Amendment make if the vice-presidency becomes vacant?

7. According to the Twenty-second Amendment, a president can seek only one full term if he has served more than how many years of a dead president's term?

8. What cabinet position was abolished by the National Security Act of 1947? What cabinet post was established?

9. Name the organization established by the National Security Act which is responsible for collecting and evaluating intelligence data.

10. What was organized labor's reaction to the Taft-Hartley Act? How did the act temporarily strengthen the labor movement?

11. What serious consequence for the cities did the post-World War II flight of people to the suburbs have?

12. For what principle did Americans want to win universal recognition by bringing war criminals to trial?

13. What action did the Allies take against war criminals in Italy?

14. What universalist principle did the United States hope to see practiced in the post-World War II era? Was the United States able to secure Soviet support for this principle?

15. What plan was introduced to implement the Truman Doctrine and prevent further expansion of Soviet-Communist power in Europe?

16. Name the nations that were involved in the Brussels Pact. What was the purpose of the pact?

17. According to Dean Acheson, why did Chiang lose China?

18. What was the aim of the Zionist movement?

Topics for Discussion

1. Trace the background of Harry S. Truman. What assets and liabilities, strengths and weaknesses did Truman bring to the presidency?

2. Defend or challenge President Truman's contention that the Eightieth Congress was one of the worst Congresses in history.

3. Discuss the civil rights question in the post-1945 period. How would you assess the headway made in those years in assuring civil equality for all Americans?

4. Excluding civil rights, what were some of the main developments in American society in the years after World War II? Keep in mind such things as population growths and shifts, how Americans spent their leisure time, their literature and music.

5. Discuss the European Recovery Program (Marshall Plan). Offer your evaluation of that program.

6. Explain the Berlin crisis of 1948-49. What were the results of the crisis? What do you think of the way in which President Truman responded to it?

7. Discuss the origins of the North Atlantic Treaty Organization. What were the pros and cons of American membership in the alliance? Do you think American membership was a good idea? Why or why not?

Subjects for Reports or Essays

1. Read the report *To Secure These Rights*. Also examine other material that will give you insight into the problems of black Americans in the post-World War II era. Write an essay giving your evaluation of the status of Negroes during those years.

2. On the basis of books or other library material, write a biographical sketch of one of the following: George C. Marshall, Marshal Tito, Malcolm X, Harry S. Truman, Alger Hiss, J. Strom Thurmond.

3. Prepare a report for class presentation on one of the following topics: (a) the cold war; (b) the Nuremberg "war crimes" trials; (c) peacetime uses of atomic energy; (d) black Americans in the post-World War II era; (e) the Zionist movement.

4. Prepare a report on the North Atlantic Treaty Organization. Locate the NATO countries on a map. Give some of the vital statistics of each country at the time the treaty was announced. Include: popula-

tion, size of military forces, national income, principal resources and industries.

5. Write an essay defending or challenging the following statement: In terms of international morality and American national interest, President Truman took the proper course in his dealing with the problem of Palestine in the years 1945-48.

Projects, Activities, and Skills

1. In a poll in 1962 prominent students of history called Harry S. Truman a "near great" president. Take your own poll among parents, relatives, neighbors, and others who recall the Truman administration. Ask them to classify Truman in one of the following categories: great, near-great, average, below average, failure. Ask them to give reasons for their estimates of Truman as a president. Prepare a report of your findings for class presentation.

2. On a map of Europe locate the countries that became Soviet satellites in the years after World War II.

3. Prepare a list of the hit songs of the years 1945-49. Locate recordings of some of these songs and play them in class. Also read selections from some of the popular literature of that period, and if possible examine some of the popular magazines. What do they tell you of this era?

4. Gather photographs and write brief biographical sketches of some of the celebrities of the post-World War II era who were mentioned in this chapter.

5. Check census figures for the years 1930, 1940, and 1950. On a graph, chart the shifts in population for the nation, your state, your county, and your city or town. List the ten states that gained the most people and the ten that gained the least (or perhaps lost population) in the twenty-year period. Prepare a brief report suggesting some reasons why some states showed greater population growth than did others.

6. Compile an illustrated report on one of the following topics as it relates to the period covered in this chapter: (a) the impact of television; (b) increased leisure time; (c) growth of the suburbs; (d) post-World War II religious revival. Where possible, use charts, magazine clippings, photographs, or other materials.

7. Prepare a report on trends in American education. Explain the reason for increased college enrollment in the post-World War II era.

Further Readings

General

American Foreign Policy Since World War II by John W. Spanier. A good general work that takes up the diplomacy of the period.

The Crucial Decade—And After by Eric F. Goldman. A general account of the period after World War II.
NATO and American Security ed. by Klaus Knorr. A very helpful book about the North Atlantic Treaty.
The Negro Pilgrimage in America by Eric C. Lincoln.
Nuremberg Diary by G. M. Gilbert. A firsthand account of the war crimes trials in Germany.
The Price of Power: America Since 1945 by Herbert Agar. A short, interesting analysis of American policy.
Shirt-Sleeve Diplomacy by Jonathan Bingham. The Point Four program.

Biography

Decision in Germany by Lucius D. Clay. Memoirs of the American army commander in Germany at the time of the Berlin crisis of 1948-49.
George C. Marshall by Robert H. Ferrell.
Plain Speaking by Merle Miller. A lively series of interviews with Harry S. Truman in which Truman looks back on his administration; highly readable.
The Taft Story by William S. White.

Fiction and Drama

A Bell for Adano by John Hersey. The story of the American occupation of an Italian village.
Exodus by Leon Uris. A best-selling epic novel about the founding of Israel.
The Hidden Flower by Pearl S. Buck. A novel about a Japanese bride who encounters prejudice from her American in-laws.
The Long Way Home by Margot Benary-Isbert. The story of an East German boy and an ex-soldier who saved his life.
The Mouse That Roared by Leonard Wibberley. A humorous story about a tiny European country which declares war on the United States in order to qualify for foreign aid.
On the Beach by Nevil Shute. A novel about the last survivors of an atomic war.
Teahouse of the August Moon by John Patrick. A romantic comedy based on Vern Sneider's novel about the American occupation of Okinawa.

Pictorial History

Ebony Pictorial History of Black America, Vol. 2, by the editors of *Ebony*.

CHAPTER 19

THE 1950s

THE DECADE OF THE 1950s began with a feeling of uneasiness in the United States. There had been three major shocks since 1948: the explosion of an atomic bomb by the Soviets; the Communist Chinese victory over the forces of Chiang Kai-shek; and the trial of Alger Hiss. It was just the right moment for an anti-Communist crusade — and the leader was Senator Joseph McCarthy.

McCarthy had entered politics eleven years before, in 1939, when he was elected circuit court judge in Wisconsin. In 1942 he left his judge's bench to join the marines, and served as an intelligence officer in the South Pacific. In 1944 McCarthy resigned from the marines to campaign for the Republican nomination for the Senate in Wisconsin.

McCarthy lost the election in 1944 but made a second bid in 1946. In the Republican primary election he narrowly defeated the incumbent senator, Robert M. La Follette, Jr. In November he easily defeated his Democratic opponent. As a freshman senator, McCarthy's chief distinction was to become known as "the Pepsi-Cola kid" because of his campaign, on behalf of soft-drink companies, to end wartime controls on the distribution of sugar.

By 1950 McCarthy was beginning to look toward the year 1952 when he would seek re-election. He needed an issue that would appeal to the voters of Wisconsin and hit upon the threat of the world Communist movement and its capacity for penetrating democratic governments. Although to this point McCarthy had never intimated that the federal bureaucracy in America might be harboring subversives, he now announced: "the government is full of Communists." With that pronouncement McCarthy became the self-appointed leader of an anti-Communist crusade that would tarnish the history of the American Republic and make the term "McCarthyism" a household word.

McCARTHYISM

Senator McCarthy opened his campaign against Communist subversion in February 1950, when he addressed a group of Republican women in Wheeling, West Virginia, and announced that the State Department was riddled with Communists.

The senator's next speech, a few days later, was in Salt Lake City. In this address he charged that there were fifty-seven card-carrying Communists in the State Department.

After the speech at Salt Lake City, the senator began to attract headlines, and a popular clamor arose for him to identify the traitors — to name names. On February 20, 1950, McCarthy presented his "cases" against alleged Communists before the Senate. Shuffling papers about, jumping from one "case" to the other, he proved nothing.

Two days after McCarthy's presentation, the Senate passed a resolution to investigate the senator's charges. Responsibility for the investigation was given to a subcommittee of the Senate Foreign Relations Committee, headed by Senator Millard Tydings of Maryland, a conservative Democrat. Hearings began in March 1950. McCarthy's first case was that of a woman lawyer from New York who, it turned out, had never worked for the State Department or any other agency of the federal government. And so it went. When Tydings demanded that McCarthy produce evidence, he responded that the evidence was locked up in the files of the State Department. When Tydings got permission to examine the files, McCarthy charged that the files were phony.

At length, in mid-March 1950, McCarthy announced that he would stake everything on a single case. McCarthy then offered the names of four alleged Communists in the State Department — two of whom had never been in the department — and not a shred of evidence.

A few days later McCarthy again announced his willingness to stake everything on a single case. At a press conference he declared that he was about to name the top Soviet espionage agent in America. Finally on the day of the great revelation McCarthy pointed the finger of guilt at Owen Lattimore, a name completely unknown to most Americans.

Lattimore, whom McCarthy branded as "Alger Hiss's boss in the espionage ring in the State Department," was a professor of political

HEADLINE EVENTS

1950 McCarthy charges that State Department is riddled with Communists
North Korean troops invade South Korea; Korean War begins
Truman commits American air, naval, and ground forces to Korean War
Displaced Persons Act
UN forces driven into Pusan perimeter
MacArthur sends forces to Inchon
UN General Assembly authorizes UN command to invade North Korea
Chinese advances send UN forces reeling
Kefauver Committee investigates organized crime in America

1951 Eisenhower takes supreme command of NATO forces in Europe
UN forces open counteroffensive in Korea
Communists driven from below thirty-eighth parallel
Truman relieves MacArthur of command; Ridgway given command
Peace negotiations begin but fighting continues
Eisenhower resigns NATO command to campaign for presidency
ANZUS Pact signed

1952 McCarran-Walter Immigration and Nationality Act
Peace talks break off pending "constructive proposals" by Communists

1953 Dwight D. Eisenhower is inaugurated president
Peace talks resume
Stalin dies; new leadership takes over in Kremlin
Refugee Relief Act
Submerged Lands Act
Korean War ends
Soviets explode hydrogen bomb
Department of Health, Education, and Welfare is established

1954 Navy launches first nuclear-powered submarine, *Nautilus*
Army-McCarthy hearings
Air force academy created at Colorado Springs, Colorado
Saint Lawrence Seaway project bill authorized
Brown v. *Board of Education of Topeka* ruling by Supreme Court outlaws segregation in public schools
Geneva Agreement signed
Atomic Energy Act
Agricultural Act
Manila Pact; SEATO created

1955 Formosa Resolution
Summit Conference in Geneva; Eisenhower presents "open skies" proposal
Housing Act
Blacks begin a bus boycott in Montgomery, Ala.; Dr. Martin Luther King, Jr., gains national prominence
AFL and CIO merge

1956 Federal Highway Act
Soil Bank Bill signed
Eisenhower resolution in UN General Assembly demands cease-fire in Egypt

1957 Eisenhower Doctrine announced
Civil Rights Act
Integration crisis in Little Rock
Soviet Union launches *Sputnik I*
Southern Christian Leadership Conference organized

1958 *Explorer I* is launched
NASA is established
National Defense Education Act
Labor Reporting Act
Eisenhower sends marines to Lebanon

1958-1961 NASA launches five deep-space probes

1959 Alaska enters the Union
Hawaii enters the Union
Project Mercury announced
Landrum-Griffin Labor-Management Reporting and Disclosure Act
Khrushchev and Eisenhower meet at Camp David

1960 U-2 plane shot down in Russia; Summit conference in Paris ends abruptly
NASA launches *Echo I*
Civil Rights Act of 1960
Kerr-Mills Bill approved by Congress

Compix

In a 1952 speech in Chicago, Senator Joseph McCarthy charged that presidential candidate Adlai Stevenson associated with Communists. The letter he holds supposedly documents Stevenson's contacts with Communist groups. What helped McCarthy gain public attention?

science at Johns Hopkins University in Baltimore. He specialized in Far Eastern affairs and was one of the country's foremost experts in that field. Although he had looked sympathetically on Asian Communists, Lattimore was not a Communist according to the evidence. Moreover, he had never been an employee of the State Department. Even McCarthy eventually conceded that he had not been a spy. The most that could be said of Lattimore was that he had tended to see problems in East Asia from a perspective similar to that of the Communists. Officials in the State Department who were responsible for Far Eastern affairs had read his works and possibly been influenced by them. However, McCarthy's original accusation that Lattimore was the country's top spy and traitor was without substance.

Upon the conclusion of its inquiry, the Tydings subcommittee issued its report in July 1950, declaring that the senator's charges were groundless. However, the two Republican members of the subcommittee, Bourke Hickenlooper of Iowa and Henry Cabot Lodge, Jr., of Massachusetts, disagreed. They contended that the investigation had not been sufficiently broad to free the State Department of the charge that it was infiltrated with Communists. Despite this minority report, Democratic leaders felt confident that McCarthy was well on the road back to oblivion.

The Democrats were wrong. The election campaigns of 1950 were about to get under way, and Senator Tydings was running for another six-year term. McCarthy turned his energies to the task of defeating Tydings and received heavy

financial support from well-to-do conservatives, particularly oil men of the Southwest. His chief tactic was to present the conservative, aristocratic Tydings as one who was "soft" on communism. McCarthy's staff circulated a photograph showing Tydings in friendly chitchat with the former American Communist leader Earl Browder. Voters did not know that the photograph was a fraud—a composite which had been cleverly manufactured in McCarthy's office. In any event, the outcome was defeat for Tydings. Senator Scott Lucas of Illinois, the Democratic majority leader in the Senate, who had incurred McCarthy's wrath, also lost in 1950.

The destruction of the political careers of Tydings and Lucas was not lost on politicians of both major parties. Democrats awakened to the reality that McCarthy was very much alive and kicking. Many Republicans—including Senator Taft and Senator-elect Nixon, who had previously taken a dim view of McCarthy—suddenly saw the senator from Wisconsin as a priceless Republican asset. Other Republicans, however, were appalled at McCarthy and his tactics. A group of GOP senators—Margaret Chase Smith of Maine, Irving Ives of New York, Edward Thye of Minnesota, George Aiken of Vermont, Robert Hendrickson of New Jersey, and Wayne Morse of Oregon—drew up a "declaration of conscience" in which they disowned their colleague from Wisconsin.

McCarthy meanwhile continued to search for headlines. A favorite tactic was to tell reporters he was on the trail of something really big—or was about to bring forth a mystery witness. Such statements would get headlines in the newspapers the following day. But the big story seldom materialized and the mystery witness invariably failed to appear.

Nobody was invulnerable to McCarthy's attacks. This was demonstrated in June 1951 when McCarthy attacked General George C. Marshall, who by this time was secretary of defense in the Truman administration. What caught popular attention was McCarthy's assertion that Marshall had been an instrument of Soviet policy. Marshall of course was one of the most respected men in America. He had been one of the architects of America's military victories in the war of 1941-45. Twice he had come out of retirement to serve, first, in 1947, as secretary of state, then, in 1950, as secretary of defense. But McCarthy managed to create enough doubts about Marshall in enough minds that the latter's usefulness as a public servant was destroyed. Accordingly the general resigned and quietly retired—for the last time.

The triumph of McCarthy seemed complete. He became the delight of Republican organizations. At the Republican national convention of 1952 McCarthy enjoyed the spotlight, and a wild demonstration followed his introduction. And in the campaign that followed McCarthy took an active part, describing the Democratic candidate for president, Adlai E. Stevenson of Illinois, as a friend of traitors.

The scourge of "McCarthyism" unfortunately was not confined to Capitol Hill and in the early 1950s spread across the width and breadth of the nation. Many Americans became consumed with fear that Communists and "fellow travelers" were subverting American institutions and bringing about the collapse of the "American system."

STUDY GUIDE: Beginning in 1950 Republican Senator Joseph McCarthy charged that many Communists were employed by the State Department. His charges were investigated but found to be groundless.

McCarthy attacked Senators Tydings and Lucas and caused their defeat. He accused Secretary of Defense George C. Marshall of being an instrument of Soviet policy. Again, investigations showed there was no basis for McCarthy's charges. However, Marshall's usefulness as a public servant was destroyed.

McCarthyism spread across the nation. Some Americans feared that communism was destroying the American system by "boring from within."

WAR IN KOREA

While Communist infiltration was being investigated in the United States, events were taking place in East Asia that would have profound consequences. The Communist regime in North Korea was quietly assembling military forces above the thirty-eighth parallel in Korea for a thrust against the non-Communist republic of South Korea. On the morning of June 25, 1950, North Korean guns flashed and ninety thousand Communist soldiers plunged southward over mountain passes and through river valleys. The Korean War had begun.

Korea is a peninsula of rugged mountain ranges that juts from the Asian mainland southward into the sea. It always had been a poor country. Still, it boasted a rich cultural and intellectual tradition. Despite its precarious location—between China, Russia, and Japan—Korea managed to keep its independence from the fourteenth century onward. It also managed to isolate itself from the "corrupting" influences of the outer world and hence became known as the "hermit kingdom."

After Commodore Perry of the United States opened the door of Japan in the 1850s, the Japanese and the powers of the West set about to open up Korea. The Koreans resisted, but eventually accepted a treaty which opened diplomatic relations with Japan and cleared the way for other countries to have normal diplomatic intercourse with Korea.

In the decades that followed, the Japanese sought to enlarge their influence in Korea. This brought conflict with the Chinese, and in 1895 Japan declared war on China. After routing the Chinese, the Japanese established their supremacy in Korea. Then the Russians became active in Korea in the late 1890s. A showdown came in February 1904 when the Japanese launched a "sneak" attack against the Russian naval base at Port Arthur in southern Manchuria. In the ensuing war the Japanese humbled the Russians. The government in Tokyo established a protectorate over Korea and five years later, in 1910, annexed the country, making it part of the Japanese empire.

Koreans Seek Independence

The Japanese built roads and power stations and in other ways strengthened the Korean economy. Still, they ruled Korea with a heavy hand and incurred the hatred of the Korean people. The outcome was the creation of underground organizations that looked to the day when Korea again might be independent. Among the many Koreans who were active in such organizations was a man named Syngman Rhee. Through long years of imprisonment and exile Rhee never lost sight of the dream of independence. When the Japanese empire crumbled at the end of World War II, he and countless other Koreans thought their great dream was coming true.

And the dream was coming true—but only partially. At the Cairo Conference of 1943 leaders of the United States and Britain pledged that after the war Korea would be free and independent. Stalin agreed to that pledge. At the Potsdam Conference in July 1945, leaders of the United States, Great Britain, and the Soviet

Union agreed that when the war came to an end Soviet troops would accept the surrender of Japanese forces in Korea north of the thirty-eighth parallel; American forces would do likewise south of that line. There was no indication that the parallel might become any kind of permanent boundary. On the contrary, it was assumed that Soviet and American troops would withdraw and leave administration of the country to the Koreans.

Things did not work out as the British and Americans had planned. As soon as the Soviets arrived in Korea, in August 1945, they cut roads, railways, and power lines at the thirty-eighth parallel, and stopped all movement of people and goods between the two parts of the country. They set up a Communist government at Pyongyang. The new regime set about to turn North Korea, whose population was nine million, into a Soviet satellite.

Below the parallel, meanwhile, the twenty-one million people of South Korea were encountering confusion and hardship. Much of their difficulty was the result of being cut off from coal and electricity from the north. The United States protested Soviet behavior in the north and continued to solicit Soviet support for a single Korean government based on free elections. The Soviets showed not the slightest interest, whereupon the United States turned over the Korean problem to the United Nations in 1947.

The UN promptly recommended general elections for Korea and sent a commission to supervise such elections. When the Soviets refused to admit the commission to the northern part of Korea, the commission went ahead with elections in the south. In the summer of 1948 Syngman Rhee, by now an elderly man, became the first president of the Republic of Korea. In 1949 the United States withdrew its forces from the peninsula. The Communists attacked South Korea on June 25, 1950.

Republican critics contended that a speech by Secretary of State Acheson in January 1950 had persuaded the Communists that the United States would not resist an attack on South Korea. In his address Acheson explained that America's "defensive perimeter" in the Far East ran from the Aleutians to Japan, from Japan to the Ryukus, and thence to the Philippines. It is possible that the Communists interpreted his remarks to mean that the United States would not defend the other side of the line. Some American leaders believed that the Soviets were testing the will of the United States. They also suspected that the attack was designed to distract the United States in East Asia while the Soviets were preparing for some new adventure in Europe.

The United States Intervenes

The Communists had picked the wrong moment to test the will of American leadership. Distressed by the Communist victory in China and furious over Senator McCarthy's charges, President Truman was in a fighting mood in early summer 1950. On June 27, when he learned that South Korean soldiers were retreating and that the South Korean capital, Seoul, was about to fall, the president committed American air and naval forces to the war. A few days later he committed American ground forces to the defense of South Korea.

The president's decision to intervene in Korea was not merely the result of frustration. Like most Americans, he believed the Communists were trying to bring the entire world to communism. As a student of history, Truman recalled the failure of the peaceful countries of the world to counter the aggression of Japan, Italy, and Germany before World War II. In the president's view, if non-Communist countries turned their backs on the South Koreans, the Communist aggressors would mount new attacks. It would be cheaper in the long run to have it out with the Communists in Korea.

Truman believed that the future of the United Nations would depend on its response to the Communist aggression in Korea. If the United Nations failed to meet the threat, he felt that it would doubtless pass into oblivion in much the same way as had the League of Nations back in the 1930s.

There were other considerations. In 1947 the president had announced the Truman Doctrine of global resistance to Communist expansion. Now the Communists were putting the much-heralded doctrine to the test.

There was also the matter of the freedom and independence of the people of South Korea. Like many other Americans, President Truman was wedded to the principle of universalism — the idea that it was the responsibility of all countries of the world to help maintain the independence of all other countries. Thus he firmly believed the United States had a moral obligation to turn back aggressors who would destroy the independence of the infant South Korean republic.

KOREA

The UN Acts

The government in Washington requested a meeting of the Security Council of the United Nations to consider the Korean situation. Trygve Lie of Norway, secretary general of the United Nations, honored the American request and scheduled a meeting. But when the Security Council met on June 26, the Soviet Union was not present. The Soviets were boycotting the UN over refusal to admit the People's Republic of China to membership. Thus the Soviets were not on hand to exercise their veto. As a result, the Security Council voted unanimously in favor of a resolution ordering a cease-fire in Korea and a return of North Korean troops to positions above the thirty-eighth parallel.

When the North Koreans ignored the resolution, the Council recommended that members of the UN should "furnish such assistance to

the Republic of Korea as may be necessary to repel the armed attack and restore international peace and security in the area." In response, forty-two countries, including Canada, Great Britain, France, India, the Philippines, Thailand, Ethiopia, Turkey, Belgium, Australia, the Netherlands, South Africa, Colombia, and Luxembourg, contributed combat and supporting units. However, American and South Korean troops carried at least ninety-five percent of the operational burden.

MacArthur Directs UN Military Operations

The supreme commander of UN forces for the military operation in Korea was General Douglas MacArthur. After World War II, MacArthur had guided the remarkably successful Allied occupation of Japan. Dealing with the Japanese generously but firmly, MacArthur had engineered a political and social revolution and helped restore the war-torn Japanese economy to prosperity. In the process he won for the United States the friendship of its late enemy.

To meet the North Korean challenge Mac-Arthur had some eighty thousand American troops stationed in nearby Japan. Unfortunately these troops were not members of battle-ready organizations. The understrength American divisions began falling back as soon as they arrived at the front, and the North Koreans swept southward. By early August the North Koreans had driven the UN force, mainly Americans and South Koreans, inside a 140-mile perimeter at Pusan on the southeastern tip of the peninsula.

By the beginning of September the steady flow of fresh American troops and the reorganization of the South Korean army had given the UN command a large numerical superiority over the North Koreans. Moreover, new American equipment, notably powerful Patton tanks, was beginning to pour into Korea. At the same time aircraft carriers of the American navy and also the great battleship *Missouri* were reinforcing UN defenses. Despite repeated assaults by the North Koreans, UN forces refused to give any more ground.

Then, in mid-September 1950, General Mac-Arthur sent an amphibious force around the tip of the Korean peninsula into the Yellow Sea. Its destination was Inchon. MacArthur's plan was to attack North Korean lines of communication across the middle of the Korean peninsula. At the same time American and South Korean

Official U.S. Navy photo

In June President Harry S. Truman ordered American forces to help defend South Korea against invading North Korean Communist troops. Shown here are American troops landing at Inchon in September 1950, under the leadership of General Douglas MacArthur, commander of UN forces in Korea.

divisions would break out of the Pusan perimeter and push the North Koreans back toward the north.

The Inchon landing came off flawlessly and, at the same time, UN troops slugged their way out of the Pusan perimeter. Almost in a matter of hours the North Koreans were in pell-mell retreat. On September 26 MacArthur announced that "Seoul, the capital of the Republic of Korea, is again in friendly hands."

A few days later the UN command reported that it had eliminated all North Korean resistance below the thirty-eighth parallel. Now the question arose: Should UN forces, having cleared Communist armies from South Korea, pursue the North Koreans northward, crush the regime in Pyongyang, and hold democratic elections for the reunification of the Korean nation? In the UN there was some opposition to the idea of pushing the war beyond the thirty-eighth parallel, but the majority of delegates thought it would be foolish to leave Korea a divided nation. In the view of most delegates the UN had a golden opportunity to unite Korea by force and establish a democratic government.

Chinese Intervention

A serious matter in the estimate of some UN delegates was whether China might intervene in the war. China's involvement conceivably could escalate the Korean conflict into World War III. On this point assurances came from Washington that America's Central Intelligence Agency and General MacArthur's command were confident that the Chinese would not intervene if the UN carried the war to North Korea. Accordingly, on October 7, 1950, the General Assembly of the world organization voted 47-5 (with eight ab-

stentions) to authorize the UN command to invade North Korea.

UN forces plunged across the parallel and swept up the east and west coasts of North Korea. Within two weeks they sent the North Korean government packing from Pyongyang. During the advance South Korean troops were widely greeted by the North Korean people as liberators.

Rumors continued to circulate that the Chinese were preparing to enter the Korean War. President Truman met with General MacArthur on Wake Island in mid-October. The general reassured the president that the Chinese would not intervene and that the war would soon be over. But even as Truman was flying back to Washington, Chinese forces were beginning to trickle across the Yalu River into North Korea.

To reassure the Chinese that the UN command had no aggressive designs against China, President Truman pledged that there would be no invasion of China. Specifically Truman ordered MacArthur not to send American bombing planes against the Yalu River bridges, over which Chinese troops and supplies were streaming into North Korea. Totally unsympathetic with the idea of "limited warfare," MacArthur fumed when he received the president's instructions. He considered resigning his command.

Then came disaster. Chinese soldiers stormed forward on November 25, 1950. With an advantage in manpower and also the element of surprise, the Chinese sent UN forces reeling. By this time winter had begun to settle over Korea's mountainous terrain, and bitterly cold weather added to the distress of UN soldiers.

The UN troops in the west sector, thanks largely to the UN's command of the skies, were able to thwart Chinese plans to drive them into the sea. They made their way down the west coast of the Korean peninsula. The troops in the east sector were able to retreat to the port of Hungnam, from which the navy evacuated them southward by sea.

By New Year's Day 1951, Chinese armies were pressing across the thirty-eighth parallel with 485,000 men. To hold them back, General Matthew B. Ridgway, commander of UN field operations in Korea, had 385,000 soldiers. Ridgway's men continued to fall back, and a short time later Seoul again came under Communist control. By that time, however, the Chinese were dangling at the end of a long supply line. UN airpower was hammering them day and night. The cold weather and an epidemic of typhus were decimating their regiments. Some forty miles below Seoul their offensive ran out of steam.

At that point Ridgway, a veteran of the Normandy invasion of 1944, determined to take the offensive. UN forces slowly ground their way forward. In the process their superior firepower enabled them to exact a fearsome toll of Chinese soldiers. In March 1951 UN troops recaptured Seoul and by early April had virtually expelled Communist forces from all territory below the thirty-eighth parallel.

MacArthur Is Dismissed

Relations between Truman and MacArthur had been difficult for many months. Truman felt MacArthur's assurances that the Chinese would not intervene in Korea had played an important part in the decision the previous October to press the war into North Korea. That decision had led to the disastrous retreat from the Yalu. For his part, MacArthur believed the president's restrictions on operations — no bombing of the Yalu bridges, for example — had enabled the Chinese to unleash their devastating blows.

MacArthur continued in early 1951 to press for authority to enlarge the war against the Chinese. He wanted to impose a naval blockade around China's ports and use Chiang Kai-shek's Nationalist troops for raids against Communist installations on the Chinese mainland. Above all, he wanted to send American aircraft against Chinese bases and airfields in Manchuria.

President Truman and his advisers did not agree. They believed that enlargement of the war in East Asia could trigger a third world war. The Truman administration determined, if at all possible, to keep the war limited to the Korean peninsula.

MacArthur would not yield. Confident that he, rather than the president, reflected the popular will, he began openly to criticize administration strategy in Korea — despite a presidential order directing all officials to refrain from public discussion of military policy. A climax came when the general dispatched a letter to the Republican leader in the House of Representatives, Joseph W. Martin, Jr., of Massachusetts. In his letter MacArthur scalded Truman's policy and announced that "there is no substitute for victory." A few days later he issued another unauthorized statement in which he attacked "the inhibitions which now restrict the activity of United Nations forces."

Compix

General Douglas MacArthur and Harry S. Truman appear friendly during their 1951 meeting on Wake Island. The following April Truman relieved MacArthur as commander of Far East forces.

MacArthur's insubordination left Truman no choice. On April 11, 1951, without first notifying MacArthur, he called a midnight press conference and announced that he had relieved the general of his command. General Ridgway was named as MacArthur's replacement. Later the president explained that "if I allowed him to defy the civil authorities I myself would be violating my oath to uphold and defend the Constitution."

MacArthur's dismissal — and the way in which the president had handled it — touched off a storm of protest across America. A few days later, the general arrived in the United States for the first time in sixteen years and met a hero's welcome. Hundreds of thousands of people in San Francisco, Chicago, and New York lined the streets to cheer MacArthur. Congressional supporters arranged for the general to address a joint session of Congress. On April 19, MacArthur, in a rich baritone voice charged with emotion and with rare eloquence, defended his ideas.

Still, it was Truman who eventually carried the argument. Americans admired MacArthur as a military leader. They also decided, upon reflection, that they did not want to risk atomic war by following his strategic ideas. Most Americans came around to the view that MacArthur had been insubordinate and that the president had done the proper thing in insisting on civilian control of military policy.

Armistice Negotiations Begin

While the MacArthur controversy was boiling in America, the Chinese sought to return to the offensive in Korea. They ran up against a wall of fire and steel. Shaken by the failure of their latest attack, and also by their enormous casualties, the Communists let it be known that they were willing to consider a cease-fire. President Truman, still riding out the disturbance set off in America by his dismissal of MacArthur, was more than ready to seek a battlefield truce in Korea. Thus, in July 1951, the UN command accepted a Communist invitation to send a negotiating team to the village of Kaesong, just south of the thirty-eighth parallel, to work out an armistice.

Clearly the Communists were not seriously searching for an armistice, but were taking advantage of the battlefield lull to build up their military forces. Still, because a war-weary world desperately wanted the talks to succeed, UN negotiators let themselves be objects of endless insults and harangues — until mid-August 1951. At that time, apparently ready to return to the offensive on the battlefield, the Communists manufactured a bombing "incident" at Kaesong which brought a suspension of talks.

The new Communist offensive was broken up by the Eighth Army almost before it got started. The Eighth Army by this time was one of the finest fighting machines ever assembled by the United States. Then the UN turned to the attack, pushed the Communists back along the east-central sector of the front, and straightened UN lines.

In the wake of these new setbacks — and heavy casualties — the Communists were again ready to talk about a truce. In mid-October 1951 the armistice talks resumed, this time at Panmunjom, a few miles east of Kaesong. Progress was slow, and the discussions were repeatedly punctuated by insults. By early spring 1952, however, all major issues were resolved except one: return of prisoners of war. The Communists insisted that both sides should return all prisoners, against their wills if necessary. Having discovered that nearly half of the Communist prisoners — or about fifty-five thousand men — did not want to return to their Communist homelands, the UN command argued that prisoners should be free to choose for themselves whether or not they would be returned. As a result of this issue the war dragged on for another fifteen months.

The war in Korea continued through the spring, summer, and autumn of 1952. Each side was reluctantly willing to make peace on the basis of a Korea divided roughly along the thirty-eighth parallel. Neither was inclined to accept the casualties that would result if it mounted a new offensive. Hence, the war became stalemated. Because of the absence of large-scale offensive action, the world's attention was riveted on the tent village of Panmunjom where men continued to talk of an armistice. In early October 1952 the UN broke off the talks pending presentation of "constructive proposals" by the Communists. Talks would not resume until April 1953.

Meanwhile, some fighting went on, and American soldiers died at a rate of about forty or fifty per week. For many soldiers it seemed a war without purpose. There was no grand military objective which promised an end to the fighting. And American troops could not easily grasp the explanation that there were important political reasons for the endless patrols, artillery and mortar duels, attacks and counterattacks for a few barren hills.

Back home in the United States, people were similarly frustrated. Many had lost their stomach for the war after China's entry into the conflict and the disastrous retreat from North Korea. A large percentage — perhaps a substantial majority — of Americans never really grasped the president's idea that by fighting a "small" war in Korea the United States and the UN might head off a "big" war later on. They did not see that the future of the UN depended on facing up to aggression in Korea. They did not seem to feel that the faith in American commitments in other parts of the world required a firm American stand in Korea, that the independence of the Republic of Korea and its 21,000,000 people was important to the United States. What touched the people of the United States during this dreary period were the casualty lists from Korea, the price increases that the war had caused, and the interruption in the normal tempo of American life.

It was against this background of frustration with the Korean War that the people of the United States prepared for the national election campaign of 1952.

STUDY GUIDE: After World War II, the Soviets set up a Communist government in Korea north of the thirty-eighth parallel. The

United States wanted a single Korean government based on free elections. The Soviets refused to let a United Nations commission supervise elections. Elections were held only in the south. In 1948, the Republic of South Korea elected Syngman Rhee its first president.

On June 25, 1950, North Korean Communist soldiers attacked South Korea. President Truman sent American forces to support the South Koreans. The United Nations also pledged assistance. General Douglas MacArthur was named commander of UN forces in Korea. Early in the war there were many North Korean victories. Eventually UN forces took the offensive and regained the South Korean capital of Seoul. They drove into North Korea, and in autumn 1950 approached the Yalu River. But then the People's Republic of China sent troops into North Korea. UN forces were driven back below the thirty-eighth parallel.

On April 11, 1951 Truman relieved MacArthur of his command. The general had wanted to bomb Manchuria. Truman was determined to limit the war to Korea.

Peace negotiations began in July 1951. Armistice talks were deadlocked over the issue of return of prisoners of war. The war dragged on for another fifteen months.

THE ELECTION OF 1952

The Republicans, who had not controlled the White House for twenty years, set about to capitalize on the country's feelings about the war. They argued that if President Truman had not taken a "soft" line toward communism in Asia before June 1950, the Communists would not have tried aggression in Korea and there would have been no Korean War. Republicans, therefore, labeled the Korean conflict "Mr. Truman's war."

The war was not the only issue. Senator McCarthy was still bellowing about communism in the federal government. Millions of Americans believed his charges that the Democrats had permitted large numbers of Communists to secure positions of influence in the government.

Political corruption was another card in the Republican deck. Back in 1949 a Senate subcommittee had established that President Truman's military aide, General Harry Vaughan, had accepted gifts from individuals who had contracts with the federal government. A year before the election, in 1951, a Senate subcommittee on banking found that officials of the Reconstruction Finance Corporation had accepted gifts from individuals who were seeking loans from the federal agency. Later that year the Ways and Means Committee of the House of Representatives investigated the Bureau of Internal Revenue and charged that agents of the bureau had accepted bribes from persons suspected of income-tax evasion. As a result two ranking members of the Truman administration later received prison terms for aiding a tax dodger.

In 1950-51 a special Senate committee investigated organized crime in America. Headed by Estes Kefauver, a liberal Democrat from Tennessee, the committee held hearings, many of them televised, which revealed that Democratic "machines" in several large cities had close connections with racketeers.

Well before delegates began to assemble for the GOP national convention, the Republican slogan for the election campaign of 1952 had taken form: "Korea, corruption, and communism." Before the convention met at Chicago in July the list of possible candidates had narrowed to two: Senator Robert A. Taft of Ohio and General Dwight D. Eisenhower.

Known as "Mr. Republican," Taft was the idol of the conservative wing of the GOP, whose base was the Middle West. The son of former-President William Howard Taft, he had carried the Republican standard in political wars for many years. Large numbers of Republicans believed he had earned a chance to try for the White House.

Many liberal or moderate Republicans, most in the East and Far West, cringed at the prospect of Taft becoming the party's presidential nominee. In their view he would try to lead the country back to the "dark ages" of the 1920s. They remembered Taft as a prewar isolationist and feared that he would try to take the country back to isolation from international commitments.

The Republicans Choose Eisenhower

Liberal and "victory-first" Republicans, seeking an alternative to Taft, centered their attention on General Eisenhower. He had never participated in politics and was devoted to maintaining America's commitments across the world. He seemed to take a fairly liberal view of domestic problems and had personal charm and magnetism.

Few people knew for sure whether Eisenhower considered himself a Democrat or a Republican. Various Democratic and Republican leaders dreamed of persuading the popular general to enter the presidential race in 1952 because he seemed an unbeatable candidate. Such dreams did not diminish when Eisenhower, at the request of President Truman, left the country in early 1951 to take supreme command of NATO forces in Europe.

Through the summer of 1951 prominent Republicans paraded to Eisenhower's headquarters in Paris to urge him to seek the GOP presidential nomination the following year. Then, in September 1951, Senator Henry Cabot Lodge, Jr., of Massachusetts, called on Eisenhower and emphasized that a Republican victory in 1952 was essential to preservation of the two-party political system in America. Lodge argued that a Republican victory was also necessary to reverse certain Democratic policies which both men considered dangerous to the well-being of the nation. These included accumulation of political power in Washington, a steady extension of the "welfare state" principle, and continual deficit financing. Furthermore, Lodge contended that Eisenhower was needed to prevent the selection of Taft and thus make certain that the United States would not return to isolation.

Lodge's eloquence touched Eisenhower, and for the first time the general said he would weigh the possibility of running for president. The pressure now began to build. "Citizens for Eisenhower" groups sprang into existence, and early in 1952 the general announced publicly for the first time that he was a Republican. With that pronouncement he became eligible for the Republican primary election in New Hampshire. On March 11, 1952, Republicans of the Granite State gave Eisenhower a resounding victory over Taft. Other primary triumphs followed. In June the general resigned his NATO command and returned home to campaign actively for the nomination.

Taft still had strong support in the GOP organization. As the Chicago convention approached, he seemed to have a fifty-fifty chance of stopping the Eisenhower bandwagon. Then came disappointment for Taft. At the convention he lost a bruising contest over the seating of delegates from southern states. The outcome was a first-ballot victory for Eisenhower.

Eisenhower broke tradition by submitting a list of vice-presidential candidates to the convention. The delegates chose Senator Richard M. Nixon, the junior senator from California. Nixon was young (thirty-nine), thus balancing Eisenhower's rather advanced years (sixty-two). He was a conservative and thus would offset Eisenhower's apparent liberalism. He had built an imposing record as an anti-Communist and would therefore appeal to those Republicans who admired Senator McCarthy. He was an uncompromising partisan and would balance to some extent Eisenhower's image as a nonpartisan politician. And he came from California, one of the most populous states in the Union.

Stevenson Nominated by Democrats

Democratic prospects did not appear bright, particularly after the Republicans nominated Eisenhower. Nobody, including Truman, thought he could repeat the miracle of 1948. In late March 1952 Truman announced that he would not seek another term.

At the time Truman took himself out of the race, the front-runner was Senator Estes Kefauver of Tennessee, who had won much acclaim for his investigations of organized crime. Kefauver entered the various presidential primaries and won most primary elections. However he failed to muster enough delegates to carry the Democratic convention which met in Chicago.

The Democratic nomination of 1952 went to Governor Adlai E. Stevenson of Illinois, the grandson of President Grover Cleveland's second vice-president. A man of high intelligence and sophistication Stevenson had held several federal offices. After 1949 he had compiled a good record as governor of Illinois. To appease the southern wing of the party, the Democratic convention accepted Stevenson's suggestion and nominated Senator John J. Sparkman of Alabama for the vice-presidency.

The Campaign

In the campaign, Republicans lashed out at alleged corruption in the Truman administration and charged the Democrats with taking a soft line toward Communist subversion. They blamed the Democrats for the fall of Chiang Kai-shek and for policies in East Asia which had led to the war in Korea. Republicans scalded the president for having taken the United States into the Korean War without first seeking the consent of Congress. They described the containment policy as "negative, futile, and immoral," and promised to inaugurate new programs aimed at liberating peoples who lived behind the Communist "Iron Curtain".

Governor Stevenson, hardly known outside Illinois before his nomination for president, established himself as a man of eloquence and wit. Those qualities, coupled with his obvious grasp of national and world problems, won for him a devoted following. The Stevenson campaign reached a level of intelligent discussion and honesty seldom matched in the history of American politics. The governor's approach, however, failed to captivate millions of people on Main Street and down on the farm.

Stevenson's greatest handicap in the campaign was the popularity of his opponent, General Eisenhower. Known affectionately as "Ike," the general was more than a war hero. He radiated warmth, sincerity, integrity, and kindness. He had remained unspoiled by the honors heaped on him. It did not matter that he lacked eloquence and spoke haltingly, or that the intellectual content of his addresses was often thin. He appealed to the heart, and Americans instinctively trusted him. The Democratic hopes of victory faded when Eisenhower and Taft had a private meeting in which they resolved their differences, whereupon Taft rallied his followers behind the general.

Then, in September, Democratic hopes soared when the Republican vice-presidential candidate, Nixon, was accused of benefiting from a special fund collected by several millionaires in California. Nixon went before a national television audience and successfully defended his conduct in an emotion-packed address.

In the closing stages of the campaign, the general dramatically announced that, if elected, he would go to Korea. This prospect aroused the hopes of many voters that Eisenhower might bring an end to the war.

Republican Victory

On election day, November 4, 1952, the twenty-year drought for the Republicans ended with a landslide victory for Eisenhower and Nixon— 34,000,000 to 27,000,000 in the popular balloting, 442-89 in the electoral college. By carrying Virginia, Texas, Florida, and Tennessee, the Republican ticket even broke the "solid South." The outcome was more an Eisenhower victory than a Republican victory, for in the new Congress the GOP would control the House of Representatives by only eight seats, the Senate by one.

STUDY GUIDE: Democrats had controlled the White House for twenty years. Hoping to win the 1952 election, Republicans used the Korean War and corruption in government as campaign issues.

President Truman announced that he would not run for reelection. The Democrats chose Adlai E. Stevenson, governor of Illinois, as their candidate. Republicans turned to General Dwight D. Eisenhower as their candidate.

On election day, Eisenhower won a landslide victory. Democrats still remained powerful. The GOP won control of the House by only eight seats. In the Senate they had control by only one seat.

DWIGHT D. EISENHOWER

Dwight D. Eisenhower was born in Denison, Texas, in 1890, the third of seven sons born to David J. and Ida Elizabeth Eisenhower. His parents traced their ancestry back to Germany and Switzerland by way of Pennsylvania. At the time of Dwight's birth the Eisenhowers had recently migrated to Texas, following failure of a general store which the elder Eisenhower had managed at Hope, Kansas. Unable to find prosperity or contentment in Texas, the family, in 1892, was on its way back to Kansas, to Abilene.

Life for young Dwight was not easy—but not unduly harsh either. During summer vacations and at other times he had to work in a creamery and in the family garden, but unlike a large percentage of boys of his generation, managed to complete high school. He was a good student, and his favorite subject was history.

Early Career

Lacking the necessary funds for college, Eisenhower hit on the idea of applying for admission to the United States Naval Academy at Annapolis. The examination for the naval academy, it turned out, was also applicable for admission to the military academy at West Point. A short

"I Like Ike" was a sentiment shared by 34 million Americans who cast their presidential votes for Dwight D. Eisenhower in 1952. Did the World War II general's promise to end the Korean War help him win a landslide victory?

time after taking the examination he received an appointment to the latter institution.

When Eisenhower arrived at West Point in 1911, it seemed that he would establish a reputation as a football halfback, for he had already proved his ability in the sport while in high school. A knee injury during his sophomore year ended his career in football, whereupon he became a cheerleader. As a scholar at West Point, Eisenhower was about average. He was a man who preferred action — football, fishing, military maneuvers. When he graduated in 1915, he ranked sixty-first in a class of 168.

Commissioned a second lieutenant, in summer 1915 Eisenhower was assigned to Fort Sam Houston in Texas. There he met and married Mamie Geneva Doud, the daughter of a prominent businessman from Denver. Mrs. Eisenhower later presented her husband with two sons, one of whom died in infancy.

The United States entered World War I in 1917, and Lieutenant Eisenhower, much to his disappointment, did not receive a combat assignment. Instead he served during the war as an instructor at various military camps in the United States. After the war he did a tour of duty in the Panama Canal Zone and in 1932 became an aide to the army's chief of staff, General

Douglas MacArthur. Eisenhower was at General MacArthur's side later that same year when the "Bonus Expeditionary Force" was broken up in and around the national capital. Two years later, in 1934, Eisenhower went with MacArthur to the Philippines to help build a Filipino army. When he returned to the United States, he had achieved the rank of lieutenant colonel.

World War II broke out in Europe in 1939, and the United States began to build up its armed strength. Then came Eisenhower's first opportunity, the army's big maneuvers in Louisiana in summer 1941. He did so well in Louisiana that he won a promotion to brigadier general.

After Pearl Harbor, because of his experience in the Philippines, Eisenhower was summoned to Washington to help plan strategy for the Pacific war. He demonstrated such organizational ability and tact in reconciling differing opinions that General George C. Marshall, the army's chief of staff, named him chief of the Operations Division of the War Department. In this capacity he began to develop strategic plans for an eventual Allied invasion of Nazi-controlled Europe. In summer 1942 Marshall advanced Eisenhower over more than three hundred and fifty senior officers and made him commanding general of the European Theater of Operations (ETO).

Eisenhower's first major success was execution of the Allied invasion of North Africa in autumn 1942. For the first time the newspaper reading public in America became aware of a general named Eisenhower. In summer 1943 Eisenhower commanded the successful invasions of Sicily and Italy. Following this success President Roosevelt decided that he should command the cross-channel attack on Hitler's empire. After that he commanded the Allied armies pressing in on Hitler's *Reich* from the west.

After the German surrender in May 1945 grateful people the world over acclaimed Eisenhower as one of the war's greatest heroes, and governments showered him with honors. Then, late in 1945, President Truman recalled him from Europe and made him chief of staff of the army. Over the next two years Eisenhower supervised the army's demobilization and wrote his memoir of the war. Published in 1948, *Crusade in Europe* was an instant best-seller, offering a moving account of the military efforts in the war.

Eisenhower rejected all appeals that he enter politics, and in 1948 he left the army to take over the presidency of Columbia University. In 1951 President Truman asked him to return to the army, go to Europe, and turn NATO into an effective military instrument. From that position he went on to the White House.

Eisenhower Tackles the Korean War

The major problem confronting President Eisenhower was the war in Korea.

The new president determined to bring the war to a conclusion. His only choice was to put new pressure on the Communists.

Eisenhower dropped the word quietly via diplomatic channels that if the stalemate in Korea was not soon broken, the North Korean and Chinese Communists would feel the full brunt of America's military might—perhaps nuclear weapons. Almost at once the Communists became more pliable. In late February 1953 they agreed to exchange sick and wounded prisoners. The following month Josef Stalin, the Soviet dictator, died. Hardly was he in his grave before Communists in Korea agreed to resume the talks at Panmunjom.

In June 1952 the Communists accepted the UN position on return of prisoners, removing the last major obstacle to a truce. President Syngman Rhee protested the failure to guarantee a unified Korea by free elections. But on July 27, 1953, negotiators at Panmunjom, Communist and UN, ended a war in which more than thirty-three thousand Americans had died.

What had been the consequences of America's intervention in the Korean war?

Most important perhaps, the infant South Korea republic had been saved and its 21,000,000 people were given an opportunity to develop a free and democratic society. The prestige of the United Nations had been salvaged, giving the organization additional time to evolve into an effective instrument for keeping the peace. For the time being at least, the power of communism had been contained in East Asia, freeing Japan, the most important non-Communist nation in the area, of any immediate threat to its security. Finally, the integrity of the United States as a power ready to redeem its commitments was reinforced.

At the Panmunjom peace table Maj. Gen. B. M. Bryan (second from left), the senior member of the UN Military Armistice Commission, confronts Maj. Gen. Lee Sang Cho (second from right), the chief Communist delegate. After negotiating for two years, both sides agreed on a truce to end the Korean War in July 1953.

U.S. Army Photograph

Eisenhower and Senator McCarthy

By the time Eisenhower set out to seek the presidency, he had come to feel contempt for Senator McCarthy's tactics. Eisenhower especially deplored McCarthy's accusations which cast doubts upon the loyalty and integrity of General George C. Marshall. However, many Republican leaders saw the senator as an important asset to the party.

Eisenhower realized that he must not compromise his own integrity by appearing to endorse the senator's "witch hunt" tactics. Accordingly, when planning for a campaign in Wisconsin, Eisenhower decided to praise General Marshall —which, of course, amounted to a rebuke to McCarthy. Key advisers urged him to cut out the paragraph and, pressed to make a hasty decision, Eisenhower gave in. He deleted the words of praise for Marshall and permitted McCarthy, running for reelection to the Senate, to share the spotlight with him during his movements about Wisconsin.

McCarthy seemed to have increased prestige and influence when he returned victorious to Washington in early 1953. In an effort to attract more attention and retain his influence as a "Red hunter," he went after the Voice of America, a federal agency, claiming that there was subversive literature in overseas libraries maintained by the agency. Whereupon President Eisenhower expressed disdain for "book burners" and those who would impose "thought control."

The president was under heavy pressure from political advisers to walk softly where McCarthy was concerned. He was reluctant, in his own words, "to get in the gutter with that guy." In Eisenhower's view, patience was the best course. He believed that if "given enough rope" McCarthy would probably "hang" himself.

McCarthy meanwhile continued his attacks. When Eisenhower nominated Charles E. Bohlen, a career diplomat who had served under Roosevelt and Truman, to be ambassador to the Soviet Union, the senator called Bohlen a "security risk." The Senate, however, confirmed Bohlen by an overwhelming vote.

McCarthy hit the headlines in late 1953 when he accused the army of being lax toward Communists. The Eisenhower administration finally determined to stand up and fight. Its tactic was to focus attention on two of McCarthy's young aides, Roy Cohn and G. David Schine, who had traveled about Europe in search of subversion in America's overseas libraries. Schine had been drafted into the army as a private. Cohn, as chief counsel for McCarthy's subcommittee, demanded preferential treatment for Schine. McCarthy charged that the army was using smear tactics in these revelations.

The upshot was the so-called Army-McCarthy hearings of spring 1954. A subcommittee of the Senate Permanent Investigating Committee conducted the inquiry, which went on for five weeks before television cameras. The hearings themselves were inconclusive, but from that point, the senator's influence declined.

Several months later a special Senate committee headed by Arthur V. Watkins, Republican of Utah, investigated McCarthy's behavior and recommended that he be censured for conduct that tended to bring the Senate into disrepute. In December 1954 the Senate voted 67-22 to censure McCarthy.

The censure resolution demolished McCarthy. The senator did not attend the Republican national convention at San Francisco in 1956 and took little part in the campaign of that year. The campaign of 1956 produced little talk about alleged Communists in government, an indication that the era of McCarthyism was about over. The last major acts of the drama had been played out in 1954 when the Atomic Energy Commission fired J. Robert Oppenheimer, a nuclear physicist who had helped produce the atomic bomb, on the ground that he was a "security risk." Next, Congress passed the Communist Control Act, depriving the American Communist party of rights, privileges, and immunities normally extended to legal bodies.

As for McCarthy, his health began to fail, and in the spring of 1957 he died.

STUDY GUIDE: Dwight D. Eisenhower spent his early days in Kansas. He began his military career after graduation from West Point in 1915. His ability and tact earned him appointment as commanding general of the European Theater of Operations in World War II. He was acclaimed one of the war's greatest heroes. In 1951, Truman asked Eisenhower to serve as supreme commander of NATO forces in Europe.

Eisenhower's two major problems when he took office were the war in Korea and McCarthy. In June 1953 the Communists accepted the UN position on Korean war prisoners. A truce agreement ended the fighting on July 27, 1953.

When McCarthy accused the army of being soft toward communism, the Eisenhower administration began to fight back. The result was the Army-McCarthy hearings of 1954. After the hearings McCarthy's influence declined. The Senate passed an official vote of disapproval against McCarthy in 1954.

EISENHOWER THE CONSERVATIVE

When Dwight D. Eisenhower set out to capture the presidency in 1952, most observers considered him a "liberal Republican." Such an assumption seemed reasonable, for it was the liberal wing of the GOP which had persuaded the general to enter the presidential sweepstakes.

Eisenhower, who had learned a good deal about the "outer world" and its problems during his military career, surely qualified as a liberal Republican in international affairs. He was a "globalist" who believed the United States must continue to provide leadership and protection for the non-Communist world.

On domestic matters, Eisenhower's ideas were not so clearly defined. During his years in the army he had never felt compelled to give much thought to the social and economic problems faced by civilians. Still, as one writer has observed, Eisenhower started from a conservative base. This meant that he would be deeply concerned about fiscal integrity and wary of enlarging the authority of the national government. He had abiding faith in the free-enterprise system and no interest in becoming a new champion of the welfare state. (On the other hand, he had no notions about trying to repeal welfare state legislation enacted in the era of the New

This is the Westchester-Kaiser Homes
subdivision outside Los Angeles. During the 1950's, the movement to the
suburbs increased. Federal Housing
Authority regulations regarding down
payments and mortgages were relaxed, making it easier to finance a
home.

Compix

President Eisenhower's support influenced passage of the Federal Highway
Act in 1956. Billions of dollars were
spent to improve the nation's highways. Shown here is an overpass being constructed in Nevada over the
Southern Pacific Railroad and Hum-
boldt River on Route I-80 east of Elko.

U.S. Department of Transportation
Federal Highway Administration

AMERICAN BUSINESS ACTIVITY: 1940 — 1959

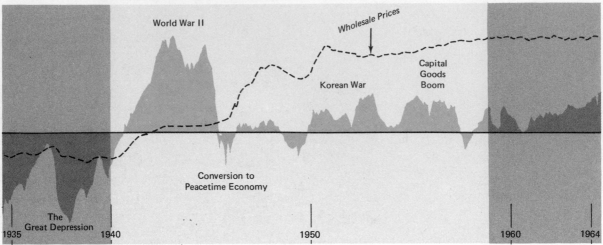

World War II

Wholesale Prices

Korean War

Capital Goods Boom

Conversion to Peacetime Economy

The Great Depression

1935   1940   1950   1960   1964

Courtesy of the Cleveland Trust Company, Cleveland, Ohio.

Deal.) As time passed, Eisenhower became more confirmed in his conservatism although he never veered away from his "liberal" approach to world affairs.

Fiscal Affairs

As a conservative in fiscal affairs, President Eisenhower determined to reduce spending, balance the federal budget, and curb inflation. In his judgment the most serious sin of the Democratic administrations had been their irresponsibility in managing federal finances.

As for balancing the budget, there was no way to avoid interest payments on the national debt, and previous laws required that millions of dollars be earmarked for veterans' benefits. What about foreign aid and defense? Eisenhower resisted the idea of economy at the expense of assisting America's friends overseas. Defense, of course, was the largest single item in the national budget and, in the continuing cold war situation, it was hard to do much trimming in that area. The administration did try to save some money by concentrating on nuclear weapons, which in their destructive capacity were less expensive than conventional weapons.

Complicating the business of balancing the budget was the pressure, particularly from business, to reduce taxes. As a result of such pressure, the administration in 1954 approved a large cut in taxes, particularly for business. The tax cut did generate increased economic activity which, in 1956, produced more tax revenue for the government and made possible a modest budgetary surplus, the first since 1948.

In sum, Eisenhower had limited success in reducing spending and balancing the federal budget. He did manage to bring the budget into balance three times during his eight years in the White House, but his deficits heavily outweighed his surpluses.

On the issue of inflation, the Eisenhower administration hoped to hold the lid on prices by reducing federal spending and pursuing a policy of "tight money." This meant raising the interest rate on new issues of government bonds, which in turn should attract investment funds into the Treasury, thus making it harder for private borrowers to obtain loans. When the federal government pumped less money into the economy — as a result of reduced spending — and when there was less money available to borrow, so the theory went, economic activity would slacken. Then the economy would cool and prices would become stable.

If the theory was sound, it was difficult to execute. The president found it hard to reduce federal spending. The big tax cut of 1954 worked against the attempt to control inflation by leaving individuals and businesses with more money to spend and invest. When recessions hit in 1953-54 and 1957-58 the Republican administration, haunted by memories of the economic crash of 1929, relaxed the "tight money" policy in order to warm up the economy.

Whatever the difficulties, the Eisenhower administration did not do badly in checking inflation. During Eisenhower's first three years in the White House, price indexes remained fairly stable. Prices went up three percent in 1956, but over the final four years of Eisenhower's presidency the rate of inflation was about one percent per year.

The Farm Problem

President Eisenhower also revealed his conservatism in his approach to the farm problem in America. It was the same old problem of declining farm income that resulted when farmers turned out more agricultural produce than their markets could profitably absorb. Markets continued to be glutted and farm income continued to lag.

There was also the "surplus." Under Democratic subsidy programs the federal government became the owner of surplus crops, which then had to be stored. The cost of storing surplus wheat, corn, and cotton in government bins was frightfully expensive, and taxpayers were grumbling. The presence of the surplus in a world in which hundreds of millions of people were ill-fed and ill-clad gnawed at the American conscience. Why did not the United States simply give away its surplus as a form of foreign aid? There were two principal arguments against this policy. First, dumping the surplus in poor countries might disrupt local economies. Second, if poor countries became dependent on "handouts" from America, they probably would not take the steps necessary to reform and improve their own agricultural practices. Dumping the surplus conceivably could do more harm than good.

The idea of subsidizing farmers violated conservative principles about competition and free enterprise. On the other hand, conservatives had long supported the protective tariff for industry, which, in its way, also was a subsidy. Most conservatives, including President Eisenhower's secretary of agriculture, Ezra Taft Benson, thought the time had come to cut back subsidies. They wanted to prepare the farmer for the day when he could no longer depend on federal supports. The result was the Agricultural Act of 1954, which introduced a system of flexible price supports for farmers designed to reduce subsidies. Farmers disliked the act. Many of them showed their displeasure at the polls on election day 1954, a development which helped return both the Senate and House of Representatives to Democratic control.

Farm income continued to slip, and in 1956

Photo by Larry S. Wiggins, Wichita, Kansas

Farm income continued to decline during the Eisenhower years. A midwestern farmer expresses his disagreement with the president's farm policies in this aerial photograph. Why did farmers oppose the Agricultural Act of 1954?

the Democrats passed a bill that would return agriculture to the pre-1954 level of subsidies. President Eisenhower vetoed the measure. Then, as farm income declined still further, the president, later in 1956, approved the Soil Bank Bill, introduced by Senator Hubert H. Humphrey of Minnesota. Under this legislation, the government made payments to farmers who reduced the number of acres they normally planted in six basic crops. There were also payments to farmers who agreed to use part of their land for conservation purposes.

These programs were not very successful. Farm income continued to lag. Many small farmers sold their farms and journeyed to the city or became tenants of larger operators. Moreover, surpluses continued to mount.

The Labor Problem

During his campaign Eisenhower drew applause from organized labor when he spoke in favor of softening some provisions of the Taft-Hartley Act. He received still more applause when he appointed Martin Durkin, a Democrat and president of the plumbers' union, as secretary of labor. In his first months in office Durkin worked out nineteen amendments to the Taft-Hartley law. These proposed amendments provoked a thunderclap from Republican conservatives, and Eisenhower declined to give them

Compix

AFL-CIO President George Meany, left, and Vice-President Walter Reuther greet delegates to the 1956 convention of the newly merged organization. The CIO had split from the AFL in the 1930s because it wanted to enroll both skilled and unskilled workers.

any sort of push. Durkin resigned. Eisenhower's "honeymoon" with labor was over. From that point on labor leaders viewed him as a conservative on labor questions. When he ran for reelection in 1956, they campaigned for his defeat.

Despite labor's estimate of Eisenhower, the 1950s were a period of considerable advancement for the labor movement. Wages increased steadily, and millions of workers came to enjoy new fringe benefits such as supplementary unemployment benefit programs. Congress also enacted legislation increasing federal minimum wage standards. A noteworthy event took place in 1955, when the American Federation of Labor headed by George Meany and the Congress of Industrial Organizations headed by Walter Reuther, patched their long-standing differences and merged into the AFL-CIO, with fifteen million members.

There was also a dark side to the labor picture during the Eisenhower years. The economic recessions of 1953-54 and 1957-58 brought hardship to many working people. Then, in the late 1950s, evidence of corruption in certain labor organizations came to light. For example, a special Senate Rackets Committee headed by

Senator John McClellan, Democrat of Arkansas, established that Dave Beck, head of the International Brotherhood of Teamsters, had misappropriated union funds.

A new wave of antilabor sentiment spread across the country. As a result, the Labor Reporting Act of 1958 was passed, requiring unions to account publicly for their welfare and pension funds. The Landrum-Griffin Labor-Management Reporting and Disclosure Act of 1959 provided additional safeguards for union funds. It guaranteed members the right to elect leaders by secret ballot and strengthened the Taft-Hartley Act's provisions regarding secondary boycotts and illegal picketing.

Oil and Gas

While conservatives did not always approve Eisenhower's position on labor, they had little cause for complaint when assessing his policies regarding offshore oil.

Offshore oil resources — that is, mineral resources lying beneath that part of the ocean floor which is adjacent to coastal states — had been a subject of political debate for a decade and a half. The submerged lands off the coasts of several states — notably California, Texas, and Louisiana — contained fabulous deposits of oil. Beginning in the 1930s, these states issued leases to oil companies to drill in those areas. The revenue from these leases fattened state treasuries. Political liberals, however, contended that state boundaries ended at the water's edge and that offshore lands were the property of all the people. Thus liberals insisted that revenues should go to the national government. President Truman in 1945 proclaimed that all offshore lands were the preserve of the entire republic. In 1947 the Supreme Court upheld this position. The coastal states increased their lobbying activities, and in 1952 Congress passed legislation transferring title of submerged lands to the states. But Truman vetoed the bill.

During the political campaign of 1952, General Eisenhower spoke in favor of state ownership of offshore lands. As president, he signed the Submerged Lands Act in 1953. That act gave coastal states title to land and resources beneath navigable waters three miles out to sea — except for Texas and Louisiana, both of which received title to lands ten miles off their coasts. This windfall to the states was valued at between $10 billion and $60 billion. Eisenhower also signed a companion measure, the Outer Continental Shelf Act. This act proclaimed that the federal government had jurisdiction over the seabed and subsoil of the continental shelf that was adjacent to the property of the states. Thus the federal government retained eighty percent of the mineral resources in submerged lands off the coast of the United States.

President Eisenhower favored exempting natural gas going into interstate pipelines from rate regulation by the Federal Power Commission. When an exemption bill passed Congress, it appeared that the president would sign. Just before final passage of the measure, Senator Francis P. Case, Republican of South Dakota, disclosed that a gas industry lawyer had contributed $2,500 to his campaign fund, apparently expecting that the senator would vote for the natural gas bill. Denouncing the contribution as a bribe, Case returned the money and voted against the bill. Whereupon Eisenhower announced that he favored the purpose of the bill but was shocked by the "arrogant" behavior of certain private persons. He vetoed the legislation.

Public v. Private Power

Perhaps the sharpest expression of Eisenhower's conservatism appeared in the president's position on public power versus private power. He opposed all public power development programs except in those rare cases in which private companies or local authorities could not meet an area's need for power.

The greatest public power project in the country was the Tennessee Valley Authority. Early in his administration Eisenhower branded TVA as an example of "creeping socialism." In the president's words, new TVA projects financed by the federal government would require "taxing the whole country to provide cheap power to the Tennessee Valley and allow it to siphon off industry from other areas." Eisenhower's opposition to expanding TVA's facilities opened the way for the first scandal of his administration.

The Atomic Energy Commission, whose plants in the area drew power from TVA, expanded operations and thus placed new demands on the valley authority. Inasmuch as Eisenhower opposed enlarging TVA's facilities, the administration decided it could meet the problem by eliminating the city of Memphis from TVA's area of responsibility. The AEC then granted a contract to Edgar H. Dixon and Eugene A. Yates, executives of two private utilities com-

panies, to build a new generating plant which would provide the city with electricity. Relieved of responsibilities at Memphis, TVA could meet the needs of the expanding atomic energy plants.

Most liberals and many Democrats saw the Dixon-Yates deal as a crude maneuver to weaken TVA. Fearing a sharp increase in electric rates, Memphis citizens also were furious. Accordingly, the city decided to build its own generating plant. At that point the government canceled the Dixon-Yates contract and prepared to pay compensation for expenses already incurred.

Then the Democrats disclosed that the government's consultant on the Dixon-Yates contract was also vice-president of the corporation which had acted as financial agent for Dixon-Yates. Here was a clear-cut case of conflict of interest. The Eisenhower administration swallowed the medicine and declared that the conflict of interest had voided the contract. The administration refused to compensate Dixon-Yates for expenditures already made when the project was canceled.

Then there was Hell's Canyon.

Hell's Canyon—a deep gorge on the Snake River along the Idaho-Oregon boundary—was one of the last and best remaining hydroelectric power sites in the country. The Truman administration had fashioned plans for constructing a high-level dam in the canyon to provide cheap public power and facilitate irrigation projects over a wide area. But the Eisenhower administration prevailed on the Federal Power Commission, in 1955, to grant a license to the Idaho Power Company to build three low-level dams in the region. This move undercut the Hell's Canyon project. Liberals and other advocates of public power erupted. Eisenhower stood by his guns, and the decision in favor of the Idaho Power Company stood.

Another round in the continuing battle over public versus private power occurred in 1954 when President Eisenhower asked for amendments to the Atomic Energy law. The amendments would authorize the AEC to issue licenses to private power companies wishing to build atomic reactors for production of electricity. Since the country's atomic energy program had been financed by taxes paid by all Americans, liberals wanted to retain the federal monopoly over the country's atomic resources. But Congress incorporated most of Eisenhower's requests in the Atomic Energy Act of 1954. The act of 1954 provided also for release of information about atomic weapons to America's allies and information about peaceful uses of atomic energy to friendly countries.

STUDY GUIDE: Eisenhower was conservative in domestic affairs. To balance the budget, cuts were made in defense spending. Tax cuts in 1954 eventually brought increased economic activity. The Eisenhower administration was fairly successful in checking inflation. But farmers had troubles. They produced too much and created surpluses that could not be sold. Farm incomes lagged.

The labor movement advanced during Eisenhower's administration. The AFL and CIO merged. Wages increased steadily. And millions of workers enjoyed new fringe benefits.

The Submerged Lands Act of 1953 gave most coastal states title to land and resources under water along their coasts. The Outer Continental Shelf Act gave the federal government control of the continental shelf outside the states' property.

Eisenhower believed the federal government should do less and private industry should do more in developing water power. He ordered the Atomic Energy Commission to negotiate with the Dixon-Yates group to build a plant to supply power to Memphis, Tennessee. The government canceled the Dixon-Yates contract when Democrats charged conflict of interest.

The Atomic Energy Act of 1954 permitted private companies to receive licenses to build nuclear reactors. It also provided for release of atomic information to America's allies.

EISENHOWER THE LIBERAL

While President Eisenhower's actions on domestic affairs were essentially conservative, he did some things that bore a moderately liberal stamp. For example, in 1953 he persuaded Congress to establish the Department of Health, Education, and Welfare. In the late 1940s the Hoover Commission and President Truman had recommended such a department. Congressional conservatives prevented passage of the legislation to avoid endorsement of Truman's controversial health insurance scheme. Confident that Eisenhower would support no far-out social welfare programs, Congress permitted HEW to come into existence.

Social Security and Housing

Although Eisenhower had no plans for dramatic innovations in the area of social and economic welfare, he was willing to support legislation to improve existing programs or meet specific problems. Eisenhower signed three bills that refined the Social Security system, enlarged benefits, and brought more than ten million additional Americans, including farmers, clergymen, and physicians, under Social Security.

Steering a moderate course, in 1955 the president recommended and Congress approved the Housing Act of 1955. This act provided a modest program of public housing construction and liberalized terms for loans for private housing construction insured by the Federal Housing Administration. The act empowered the FHA to insure loans for the renovation of older dwellings which helped stimulate the "urban renewal" movement of the 1960s.

Health Services

To improve the country's health services, Eisenhower was willing to proceed farther and faster than conservatives in his party wanted. A special Commission on Health Needs of the Nation urged a federal health insurance program to help Americans meet increasing medical costs. But the American Medical Association denounced the commission's proposal on the ground that it would bring socialized medicine to America. The proposal languished. In 1954 the president proposed a federally financed "re-insurance" fund to encourage private and nonprofit health insurance organizations to offer broader protection. The AMA once again won support of enough members of Congress to assure defeat of the proposal.

In the latter part of the Eisenhower presidency a debate boiled up over the question of federal medical assistance to the country's "senior citizens," usually defined as people over age sixty-five. Liberals pointed to the rapidly expanding size of the elderly population and noted the high cost of medical insurance and hospitalization. They proposed to help the elderly by providing medical insurance under the Social Security system. In effect, a wage earner would guard himself against heavy medical expenses in his declining years by paying increased Social

Security taxes during his more productive years. The American Medical Association once again raised the fear of socialized medicine and won support of enough members of Congress to assure defeat of the "medicare" proposal.

Still, the Eisenhower administration recognized that medical costs were a severe problem for elderly citizens. Hence the administration gave its blessing to the Kerr-Mills Bill, approved by Congress in summer 1960. Under this law the federal government granted funds to states for elderly citizens who could not afford adequate medical care. To qualify for assistance, however, a "senior citizen" had to sign a statement that he was nearly destitute, a humiliating act for many people, which kept large numbers from seeking help. Another weakness of the Kerr-Mills program was that it offered no help to elderly men and women who had managed to accumulate some savings but who faced the threat of being bankrupted by a long illness.

Education

On federal aid to education President Eisenhower took a position which might be described as moderately liberal. The high birth rate during the 1940s had caused a shortage of both teachers and classrooms. In the view of many observers only the federal government could solve the problem. But there was a hitch. According to conservative objections, a program of federal aid to education would lead to federal dictation in such matters as curriculum and teaching standards. White southerners feared that federal aid, sooner or later, would require elimination of racially segregated schools.

President Eisenhower believed a measure of federal aid to education was essential, but he was reluctant to do anything that smacked of federal interference in local school affairs. In 1953 he persuaded Congress to authorize federal grants to help build schools in "impacted areas" where defense industry and military installations had brought an abnormal growth of population. Two years later the president proposed massive grants for school construction in so-called hardship areas of the country. Opposed by conservative Republicans and southern Democrats, the measure died in Congress. The following year, 1956, the president asked Congress for authority to grant $1.25 billion for school construction over a five-year period and authority to provide another $750 million to schools through government purchase of school bonds. Conservative Republicans and southern Democrats again defeated the presidential request. In 1957, a similar bill failed for similar reasons.

Meanwhile, there was considerable talk about federal support for higher education. Study groups reported that there was danger of a serious shortage of physicians, scientists, and engineers. To prevent such a shortage from occurring, the groups recommended that the government assist young people and enlarge college faculties, classrooms, and dormitories.

In October 1957 the Soviet Union launched *Sputnik I,* the world's first space satellite. It was clear that the Soviets were far ahead of Americans in space science and technology. For Americans, this revelation was humiliating. It was also alarming. Science and technology, so Americans thought, were the keys to survival in the nuclear age.

A result of the post-*Sputnik* hysteria was the National Defense Education Act approved by Congress in September 1958. The legislation provided low-interest loans for deserving college and university students. If the borrower agreed to teach in elementary and secondary schools for five years after graduation, he would have to pay back only fifty percent of his loan. For students preparing to be college teachers the measure included a fellowship program. To encourage scientific and foreign language instruction at the secondary level, it appropriated $280 million for laboratories and textbooks. A smaller sum was included to advance foreign-language instruction in colleges. The National Defense Education Act, a compromise, did not come close to meeting the problems of American education. Still, in the view of many Americans it was a step in the right direction.

Immigration

President Eisenhower displayed his moderately liberal side on the question of immigration.

The need for reform of immigration laws had long been discussed. President Truman wanted to remove some of the restrictions of the immigration laws of the 1920s. In late 1945 he issued a presidential directive authorizing admission of forty-two thousand persons displaced by World War II. In 1948 Congress passed the Displaced Persons Bill, admitting over two hundred thousand displaced European adults and three thousand orphans. A second Displaced Persons Bill was passed in 1950 admitting another four hundred fifteen thousand displaced persons and orphans. As Truman was preparing to leave the presidency, in 1952, Congress passed the McCarran-Walter Immigration and Nationality Bill. This measure removed the ban on immigrants from East Asia and the Pacific, but it retained the discriminatory quota system. As a result of "McCarthyism," the McCarran-Walter Bill contained provisions for keeping out and deporting immigrants who might be "subversive." Displeased with the old quota features and the provision regarding undefined "subversive activities," President Truman vetoed the legislation. But Congress passed the bill over the presidential veto.

In early 1953 President Eisenhower urged abolition of discriminatory clauses in existing immigration laws. Congress passed the Refugee Relief Bill the following summer. This provided for admission of some two hundred thousand people fleeing communism and additional displaced persons. In 1956 Congress rejected Eisenhower's proposal to amend the McCarran-Walter Act. After the Hungarian revolt against Stalinism, in November 1956, the president issued a special directive permitting over twenty-one thousand Hungarian refugees to enter the country. The following year, 1957, Eisenhower made a new proposal for immigration reform. Congress did not accept all the president's suggestions, but it did approve admission of an additional sixty thousand immigrants annually. The measure granted entry to orphans adopted by American citizens and authorized admission of fifty diplomats who had defected from Communist countries. It also permitted entry of fifteen hundred scientists and technicians who might be of help in America's infant missile program.

International Trade

Political liberals felt only modest enthusiasm for Eisenhower's policies regarding social welfare and immigration, but they had no reason to complain about his views on foreign trade. For regarding foreign trade the president's stand was that of a four-square liberal.

President Eisenhower was anxious to do what he could to assure the prosperity of business. But he was no protectionist. Like many other advocates of liberal international trade policies, he believed that trade barriers were impediments to world peace. Whatever the advantages that tariff protection might hold out to American businessmen (and to some workers and farmers as well), peace must receive first priority. Eisenhower therefore made no concessions to protectionism and four times during his administration supported legislation to extend the reciprocal trade program.

Other Matters

Like all chief executives, Eisenhower naturally made decisions and supported legislation and programs that one could not easily classify as either conservative or liberal. In 1954 he approved a bill authorizing establishment of the Air Force Academy, finally located, in 1958, near Colorado Springs, Colorado. In 1956 he approved a bill appropriating $760 million for the Upper Colorado River Irrigation and Reclamation Project. He signed, in 1958 and 1959 respectively, the measures approving admission of Alaska and Hawaii as states in the federal Union.

The Saint Lawrence Seaway received the strong backing of Eisenhower. By the 1950s, a seaway seemed imperative because iron ore deposits in the Lake Superior region were approaching exhaustion. Midwestern states needed to gain access, by cheap water transport, to new sources of ore in Labrador and elsewhere. Moreover, Canada had begun to indicate that it might "go it alone" with a seaway project. A Canadian-owned and operated seaway of course might function to the disadvantage of the United States. Thus Eisenhower, against the opposition of eastern seaports and railroads, came out in favor of a bill authorizing joint construction with Canada of a Saint Lawrence seaway. Such a bill passed Congress in 1954.

Finally, there was the interstate highway program.

The need to improve the national highways was obvious. Great stretches of highways were continuously clogged with automobiles, trucks, and buses. Many roads were hazardous. At Eisenhower's urging and after much wrangling and many compromises, in 1956 Congress passed the Federal Highway Act. The act authorized expenditure of $27.5 billion to construct nearly forty-two thousand miles of modern four- to eight-lane interstate highways over a period of sixteen years. Another $5.1 billion was authorized for improvement of existing highways and roads. States would do the building and improving. The federal government would bear ninety percent of the expense. To provide part of the funds, Congress passed the Highway Revenue Act, which raised federal taxes on fuel, tires, buses, trucks, and trailers.

STUDY GUIDE: Eisenhower's administration did some things that were moderately liberal. In 1953 the Department of Health, Education, and Welfare was created. The Housing Act of 1955 provided for a public housing program. The Kerr-Mills Bill, passed in 1960, granted funds for medical care for senior citizens. Eisenhower secured grants for building schools in crowded areas. To increase aid to education, the National Defense Education Act was passed in 1958. A federal highway program was authorized with the Federal Highway Act of 1956.

During his administration, Eisenhower continued the reciprocal trade program.

CIVIL RIGHTS

During his long military career, Eisenhower appears to have accepted casually the army's system of racial segregation and discrimination, as did most other professional officers and a great part of the civilian population. But during the campaign of 1952 he indicated support for the civil rights views of Republican liberals. Two weeks after entering the White House, in February 1953, in his State-of-the-Union message he spoke eloquently of the need to eliminate discrimination in America and announced that "I propose to use whatever authority exists in the office of the President to end segregation in the District of Columbia, including the federal government, and any segregation in the armed forces."

Eisenhower's civil rights program soon began to bear fruit. Schools on military bases and Veterans Administration hospitals were desegregated. Beginning in 1954, all federal contracts included specific clauses prohibiting contractors from practicing segregation and discrimination. The president met with owners of movie houses in the District of Columbia and persuaded them to terminate segregationist practices. Hotels and restaurants in Washington, previously "white only," responded to Eisenhower's gentle appeals and opened their doors to blacks. In June 1953 the Supreme Court ruled that restaurants in the District of Columbia

New York State Department of Commerce Photo

In 1954 President Eisenhower gave strong support to a congressional bill authorizing joint construction with Canada of a Saint Lawrence seaway. Shown here are oceangoing vessels passing through the Eisenhower Lock of the seaway, which was officially opened in 1959.

could not refuse to serve Negroes. Administration emissaries persuaded the Capitol Transit Company to end policies of discrimination in employment.

Brown v. Board of Education

At the end of the Civil War and after the abolition of slavery, large numbers of black Americans had for the first time begun attending schools. In the South, where ninety percent of the black population lived, a system of racially segregated schools came into existence. Eventually seventeen southern and border states adopted laws requiring that schools within their boundaries be segregated.

Observing the inferiority of "colored" schools and aware that white-enforced segregation gave black children a feeling that they were inferior to whites, critics argued that such state laws were unconstitutional. But the Supreme Court, in 1896, handed down its famous decision in the case of *Plessy* v. *Ferguson*. In that case the Court ruled that state laws requiring segregated public facilities – railway coaches, waiting rooms, parks, schools – did not violate the Fourteenth Amendment provided that such facilities were "separate but equal." Unfortunately in many states the facilities, particularly schools, were more separate than equal in quality.

In the 1930s and 1940s black leaders began to hack away at the system of segregated schools. In a few states, including Missouri, Oklahoma, and Kentucky, they made some headway in cracking the barriers that had prevented blacks from entering colleges, universities, and professional schools. Into the 1950s, however, the system of racial segregation remained strong in elementary and secondary schools in many states, particularly those of the South. And the result was a flurry of lawsuits challenging the logic of the *Plessy* decision. Then on May 17, 1954, came the unanimous decision of the Supreme Court in the case of *Brown* v. *Board of Education of Topeka*. The practice of segregation in public schools, the decision stated, was in violation of the Constitution. The Court's opinion was written by Chief Justice Earl Warren, whom President Eisenhower had appointed to the court in 1953. It matters not, Warren argued, that separate schools might be equal in quality. For "separate educational facilities are inherently unequal." Therefore, the justices asserted those in segregated public schools were "deprived of the equal protection of laws guaranteed by the Fourteenth Amendment." (In 1954-56 the Supreme Court also voided segregation in tax-supported graduate schools, tax-supported colleges and universities, public housing projects, public parks and playgrounds, and on golf courses and interstate buses.)

The Court did not immediately offer a plan for ending segregation in public schools, but in May 1955 it directed federal district courts to assume responsibility for enforcing its desegregation decision. "While giving weight to . . . public and private considerations," the justices declared, "the [district] courts will require a prompt and reasonable start toward full compliance with our May 17, 1954 ruling . . . [and] the district court . . . [will] enter such orders and decrees . . . as are necessary and proper to admit to public schools on a racially nondiscriminatory basis with all deliberate speed the parties to these cases."

How did the country respond to the *Brown* decision?

In the North and West many black children attended all-black schools. But school segregation in the North and West usually resulted from the practice of drawing school district boundaries in accordance with segregated residence patterns. Since most black children lived in all-black neighborhoods, they naturally attended all-black schools. The result was *de facto* segregation – segregation because of circumstances, not because of law. It appeared that the Brown decision had no bearing on *de facto* segregation in the North and West. The decision seemed to be aimed against schools that were segregated as a result of state laws and local ordinances, and such laws and ordinances hardly existed in the North and West. Thus most northerners and westerners did not feel that the decision affected them.

In the South the response was different. Most southern schools were segregated because of laws and ordinances that required blacks and whites to attend separate schools. This was *de jure* segregation – segregation by law. The Brown decision directly affected southern schools.

A few liberal whites hailed the decision as a step toward eliminating the worst blight on society. Other whites – notably in such states as Delaware, Maryland, West Virginia, Kentucky, Missouri, and Oklahoma – recognized that integrated schools were inevitable and reluctantly prepared to comply with the high court's ruling.

In some states the response was angry and bitter. The legislature of Georgia resurrected the doctrine of nullification which the Civil War supposedly had buried forever, declaring that the *Brown* decision was "null, void and of no effect within the state." The government of Virginia set about to transform the state's public schools into state-supported "private" schools. (Subsequent judgments by the federal courts prevented Virginia from abolishing its public schools and using public money to support non-public schools.) Meanwhile the Ku Klux Klan was making a comeback. More important than the Klan – whose tactics of terrorism appalled many whites – were the white citizens councils which sprang up all across the South, with the support of most public officials and politicians of the region.

Determined to maintain the system of white supremacy in the South, the citizens councils usually avoided violence. Instead, they relied

Arkansas Gazette

on economic pressure. If a white businessman seemed soft on segregation, the local citizens council would direct whites to boycott his place of business and perhaps persuade the local bank to deny him further credit. If a black man indicated his intention to enroll his children in the local white school, the council might arrange to have him dismissed from his job and his mortgage foreclosed.

As a result of white opposition to the *Brown* decision, by 1960 only token integration of public schools had occurred in Arkansas, Florida, Louisiana, North Carolina, Tennessee, Texas, and Virginia. There was none at all in Alabama, Georgia, Mississippi, and South Carolina.

President Eisenhower declined publicly to pass judgment on the *Brown* decision. His refusal to endorse the Supreme Court's decision brought him heavy criticism from advocates of civil rights. His critics argued that he was a man of unprecedented prestige and popularity in America. They insisted that if he had spoken out in favor of the decision, he might have undercut much of the opposition that developed to it. As a consequence, they argued, desegregation of public schools would have proceeded more rapidly than it did.

A Crisis in Little Rock

When an integration crisis erupted at Little Rock, Arkansas, in 1957, President Eisenhower acted forcefully.

The Little Rock affair began in early Septem-

President Eisenhower sent federal troops to Little Rock, Arkansas, to end a school integration crisis in 1957. Despite this forceful action, why was he criticized by civil rights leaders?

ber 1957, when nine black students prepared to enroll in Little Rock's Central High School. Governor Orval Faubus reacted by calling out the Arkansas national guard. He sent armed troops to the school to keep blacks from entering. But a federal court order demanded that Faubus remove the troops. Faubus obeyed, and the black students entered the school. Then rioting broke out.

President Eisenhower swung into action. In a national radio and television address he denounced "the disgraceful occurrence" at Little Rock and issued a proclamation directing all persons "to cease and desist therefrom" their opposition to federal court orders and mobs to "disperse forthwith." He did not take this opportunity to make a statement in behalf of civil rights for racial minorities. His wrath was directed against those individuals who would resort to violence to upset orders of a federal court.

When large numbers of segregationists again gathered outside Central High School, in apparent violation of the presidential directive, the president dispatched a thousand army paratroopers to the scene. As soldiers patrolled inside and outside the building, the nine black students were able to enter the school and attend classes. Faubus denounced the "military occupation" of Arkansas. At length the situation calmed, and in early December 1957 most troops left Central High School.

The Civil Rights Act of 1957

Meanwhile, in September 1957 President Eisenhower signed the Civil Rights Act of 1957. This was the first civil rights legislation enacted by the federal government since the year 1875.

On the theory that local and state politicians, needing black votes, would take steps to eliminate disabilities against black Americans, Eisenhower sent a civil rights bill to Congress in 1956. The measure's primary purpose was to undercut some of the regulations and tactics used by whites to prevent black citizens from voting. The bill passed the House but, like other civil rights proposals before it, was defeated by a determined southern opposition in the Senate.

The administration proposed a similar bill the following year, 1957, and once again the legislation sailed through the House. In the Senate the Republican minority leader, William E. Knowland of California, assisted by Vice-President Nixon, steered the bill around the hostile Judiciary Committee headed by James O. Eastland of Mississippi. The Democratic majority leader, Lyndon B. Johnson of Texas, persuaded southern members not to organize a filibuster when it reached the Senate floor. As a result, the bill passed. It provided for a permanent Civil Rights Commission and appointment of an assistant attorney general to supervise the civil rights activities of the Justice Department. Equally important, or so it seemed in 1957, it authorized the federal government to issue court injunctions in cases in which citizens had been denied the right to vote.

The Civil Rights Act of 1957 failed to do much to break down barriers which prevented black citizens from voting. In 1959 the Civil Rights Commission reported that a vast majority of blacks in the southern states were being deprived of the vote by "the creation of legal impediments, administrative obstacles, and positive discouragement engendered by fears of economic reprisal and physical harm." In Mississippi, the commission discovered that only five percent of the state's blacks of voting age were registered to vote. To meet the problem, the commission urged new legislation authorizing the president to appoint special electoral registrars who would have authority to register all qualified Negroes as voters. The commission's recommendation

was not accepted by the Eisenhower administration.

The Civil Rights Act of 1960

Still, the administration concluded that further voting rights legislation was necessary. The outcome was a proposal which emerged as the Civil Rights Act of 1960. The new law provided that, if the Justice Department won a suit to require local officials to register blacks as voters, it could then ask a federal court to make a further finding that blacks had been prevented from voting because of discrimination. If the court agreed with the Justice Department's contention, it would appoint referees. If they found that voting discrimination persisted, the referees could put qualified black citizens on the voting rolls. In addition, because of recent acts of violence in which school and church buildings had been bombed and burned, the act of 1960 also made it a federal offense to transport explosives across state lines for illegal purposes.

During debate on the measure Senator John Sparkman of Alabama boasted that "the effects of the legislation will be negligible." Events proved the senator correct. Throughout the early 1960s white southerners continued to prevent large numbers of blacks from registering and voting. Yet one might argue that, whatever their deficiencies, the Civil Rights Acts of 1957 and 1960 were essential first steps before the more effective legislation of the mid-1960s could be passed.

The Advent of Martin Luther King, Jr.

During those years of court judgments, civil rights bills, and reaction by defenders of white supremacy, a youthful black clergyman of the South came into prominence. He was determined to lead his people out of the bondage of discrimination and second-class citizenship and into a promised land of dignity and equal opportunity.

Martin Luther King, Jr., was a kind and gentle man. He was the most honored and most influential -- and perhaps the most hated -- black man in America for more than a decade, until April 1968 when he was assassinated.

Born on January 15, 1929, in Atlanta, Martin Luther King, Jr., was the son of a Baptist clergyman. His father, the son of a sharecropper, had run away from home as a boy, worked his way through high school and attended Morehouse

College in Atlanta. During the 1920s the elder King had been deeply influenced by the ideas of Marcus Garvey. A Jamaican who believed that Negroes would never receive justice in America's white-dominated society, Garvey urged black Americans to return to Africa. The elder King became active in local movements to counter discrimination and injustice against his fellow blacks. The mother of Martin Luther King, Jr., a former schoolteacher, was the daughter of a clergyman who was one of Atlanta's most influential and prosperous Negroes.

Although the Great Depression was a hard blow to most black Americans, the King family was never destitute.

Life with his brothers and sisters was happy, secure, and reasonably comfortable for Martin Luther King, Jr. Like all black Americans, however, he came face to face with the racist attitudes of his white countrymen at an early age.

In school Martin Luther King, Jr., was a good student, skipping two grades. At age fifteen, in 1944, he enrolled in Morehouse College, where he continued to win praise from his superiors. "Turned off" by the emotionalism he had witnessed in Negro churches—emotionalism which he equated with antiintellectualism—he did not intend to enter the ministry. But then he came under the influence of the president of Morehouse and a professor of philosophy, both of whom were ordained ministers and men of outstanding intellectual qualities. King concluded, therefore, that the life of a clergyman could be intellectually satisfying.

King had been active in the NAACP since entering Morehouse. Like his father he wanted to work for the improvement of his fellow blacks and concluded that the ministry offered a good vehicle for doing so. In 1947, he was ordained in his father's church.

King received his A.B. degree from Morehouse in spring 1948 and the following September entered Crozer Theological Seminary in Chester, Pennsylvania, where he was one of six Negroes in a student body of a hundred. At Crozer he did "straight A" work, won an award as the school's outstanding student, and was elected president of the senior class. He received his Bachelor of Divinity degree in 1951.

At least as important as his academic achievements at Crozer was the new enthusiasm King acquired for the ideas of Mohandas K. Gandhi. The renowned leader of India's movement for independence from Great Britain, Gandhi had urged his followers to use tactics of nonviolence,

Compix

Organizing the Montgomery bus boycott and then the Southern Christian Leadership Conference propelled Martin Luther King into national and ultimately international prominence.

civil disobedience, and passive resistance. Doubtful at first that Gandhi's methods would work in the black man's struggle for civil equality in America, King eventually became immersed in Gandhi's writings.

Taking advantage of a fellowship, the young clergyman entered Boston University where he began work toward a Ph.D. degree. While studying in Boston, he met Coretta Scott, a talented singer from Alabama, who was studying music in Boston. They were married in 1953 in Heiberger, Alabama. A year later, in 1954, while writing his doctoral dissertation (he received his Ph.D. in 1955), King accepted a position as pastor of the Dexter Avenue Baptist Church in Montgomery, Alabama. On assuming his new position, King took a strong interest in the racial problems of his church members. He organized a social and political action committee to help them meet problems and urged members to try to become registered voters and to take part in activities of the NAACP.

The Montgomery Bus Boycott

Then, on the afternoon of December 1, 1955, a black woman in Montgomery, Mrs. Rosa Parks, tired after a day of work in a downtown department store, had aching feet. The result was a train of events that would propel Martin Luther King, Jr., to world prominence.

The first day of December 1955 was a warm one in Montgomery. When Mrs. Parks, a small, soft-spoken woman, boarded the Cleveland Avenue bus she was tired and her feet were hurting. Observing a familiar practice, she moved to the rear of the bus, normally reserved for Negroes, and sat down. On this day the bus was full of Christmas shoppers, and four white passengers were standing in the aisle. The driver of the bus made his way to the rear of the vehicle and ordered Mrs. Parks and three other blacks to surrender their seats. Mrs. Parks refused to move and thus, according to a Montgomery ordinance, was guilty of disturbing the peace. The driver then summoned the police, who arrested Mrs. Parks and took her to a police station.

When she boarded the Cleveland Avenue bus, Rosa Parks, a former secretary of the local NAACP chapter, had not planned a show of defiance. She decided, on impulse, to keep her seat. As she later explained her behavior, "My feet hurt." There was no commotion. No black passengers on the bus rallied to her defense, and when the police arrived she went away peaceably. Still, word of the affair quickly circulated among Montgomery's black residents. By nightfall frustration and anger, the result of generations of discrimination, were boiling to the surface. Telephone wires crackled and at length black leaders of Montgomery, including King and the Reverend Ralph David Abernathy, decided that Negroes should stage a one-day bus boycott to show their indignation.

The date set for the boycott was December 5. King and other leaders hoped that sixty percent of the black people of the city would honor the boycott. Instead more than ninety-nine percent of Montgomery's blacks declined to ride the buses. Elated, black leaders hastily decided to continue the boycott indefinitely. On the same day they created an organization called the Montgomery Improvement Association to direct the boycott and elected King as president. That evening, at a mass rally at the Holt Street Baptist Church, Martin Luther King, Jr., delivered his first major address as a civil rights leader. Urging his listeners to love their enemies,

King told them that they must protest without violence, courageously and with dignity. Looking to the future, he saw a day when historians would say: "There lived a great people – a black people – who injected new meaning and dignity into the veins of civilization."

The boycott continued month after month. To provide transportation for black citizens, the Montgomery Improvement Association organized a huge car pool. King, meanwhile, was facing harassment. For driving thirty miles an hour in a twenty-five-mile-an-hour zone he was arrested and jailed. Then, on January 30, 1956, while he was addressing a rally, a bomb was hurled on the front porch of his house.

In mid-November, the Supreme Court in Washington upheld a lower court's judgment that Alabama's state and local laws requiring segregation on buses were unconstitutional. After receiving a formal order from the court, city authorities of Montgomery ordered the buses desegregated on December 21. Thus ended the boycott, which had lasted 382 days.

The Nonviolent Crusade

The events in Montgomery made Martin Luther King, Jr., the best-known and most influential black man in America. Black leaders of the South were so impressed by his tactics and the support given them by Montgomery's black citizens that leaders from ten southern states met in Atlanta in January, 1957. They organized the Southern Christian Leadership Conference (SCLC) to launch a civil rights campaign for blacks. They agreed that the SCLC would use methods like those used in Montgomery. They chose King to lead this new civil rights group.

As the unchallenged leader of the nonviolent crusade for Negro rights, King was constantly on the move. In the year 1957 he traveled thousands of miles, made 208 speeches, and attended the independence celebration of the new republic of Ghana, the first African colony to gain independence. Then, in 1959, he achieved a dream of several years when he visited India, the homeland of Gandhi. Meanwhile, he found time to write his first book, *Stride Toward Freedom,* published in 1958.

As the decade of the 1950s was drawing to a close, King decided the moment had come to accelerate the nonviolent crusade for equal rights for black Americans. His decision resulted in part from his observation that the influence of Elijah Muhammad's Black Muslim movement –

a movement that scorned tactics of love and passive resistance – was increasing. King wanted to head off the black nationalists by further demonstrating the effectiveness of nonviolence. To lead the stepped-up struggle, he decided he must leave the Dexter Avenue church in Montgomery and return to Atlanta, headquarters of the SCLC. In early 1960 he returned to the city of his birth where he assumed closer direction of the SCLC, and also served with his father as a pastor of the Ebenezer Baptist Church.

Louis E. Lomax, a black journalist, was often a sharp critic of King. Lomax contended that King was a poor administrator and not a true intellectual. But he saw King as a man who had a unique ability to express the frustrations and weariness of the typical black American. In *The Negro Revolt,* published in 1962, Lomax wrote: "King is the foremost interpreter of the Negro's tiredness in terms which the mass Negro can understand and respond to. This is the magic about King's many speaking engagements; in some instinctive way he helps Negroes understand how they themselves feel and why they feel as they do; and he is the first Negro minister I have ever heard who can reduce the Negro problem to a spiritual matter and yet inspire the people to seek a solution on this side of the Jordan, not in the life beyond death."[1]

Martin Luther King, Jr., was more than a voice possessing the ability to express the hopes and aspirations of black Americans. He was a man of conviction and courage, gentleness and love. He was a man who captured the hearts of millions of his countrymen, white as well as black.

STUDY GUIDE: Eisenhower ended segregation in schools on military bases and in Veterans Administration hospitals. He also worked to end discrimination in the District of Columbia. The 1954 Supreme Court decision in the case of *Brown* v. *Board of Education of Topeka* ruled that segregation in public schools was in violation of the Constitution.

In 1957 an integration crisis erupted in Little Rock, Arkansas. Eisenhower sent troops to restore order.

In September 1957 Eisenhower signed the Civil Rights Act of 1957. But further voting rights legislation was necessary. The outcome was the Civil Rights Act of 1960.

In December 1955 Mrs. Rosa Parks, a Negro, was arrested when she refused to give up her seat to a white person on a Montgomery, Alabama, bus. Blacks staged a boycott in protest. The Montgomery boycott brought Martin Luther King, Jr., to national attention. King headed the Southern Christian Leadership Conference which was founded in 1957.

DEFENSE AND OUTER SPACE

Officials in Washington during the 1950s were taken up with the uncertainties of the continuing cold war. Realizing that the Soviets were rapidly catching up with the United States in nuclear technology, they gave increasing attention to the problems of military defense.

The central cog in America's military mechanism continued to be the nuclear warhead. In the beginning of the 1950s that warhead was a bomb which giant jet-powered bombing planes could deliver to any spot on the face of the earth. The bomb's power was increasing steadily and dramatically. On November 1, 1952, the first hydrogen bomb was detonated by the United States. Less than a year later, in August 1953, the Soviets exploded a similar device.

A few scientists in America were working to develop a long-range ballistic missile capable of carrying nuclear warheads across oceans and continents to enemy targets. They were working with minimum support from the national government. The federal budget of 1953 provided only a million dollars for development of ballistic missiles. Dwight D. Eisenhower later pointed out in his memoirs that this was less money than the government was spending each year to support the price of peanuts.

In the closing stages of World War II, the Germans had displayed the potential of rocket-powered warheads. After the war several German scientists who had helped design and build the V-1 and V-2 rockets, including Wernher Von Braun, were brought to America. But most American military men doubted that long-range ballistic missiles would become practicable in the near future.

Then, in 1953-54, American intelligence experts began to assemble data indicating that the Soviets, who had also obtained the services of

---

[1] Louis E. Lomax, *The Negro Revolt,* copyright 1962 (New York: Harper & Row, Publishers, Inc.), p. 91.

some of Hitler's rocket experts, might soon have an operational ballistic missile system.

In 1955 President Eisenhower directed the Defense Department to give top priority to the ballistic missile programs. Within three years the United States was well on the way toward producing its own operational ballistic missile system. At the same time the navy, which in 1954 had launched the first nuclear-powered submarine, the *Nautilus*, developed the technique for launching nuclear warheads from Polaris submarines. Director of the navy's Polaris program was Admiral Hyman Rickover.

American scientists and engineers during the 1950s were also fashioning techniques and hardware that would enable the United States to place artificial satellites in orbit around the earth. This American effort was in part a response to intelligence information that the Soviets were planning to use rockets as launch vehicles for artificial satellites. A one-sided space triumph would give the Soviets a tremendous boost in world prestige and might persuade many people in developing nations that Soviet claims about the superiority of the Communist system were true. More important, satellites might eventually become space-borne launching pads for intercontinental ballistic missiles armed with nuclear warheads.

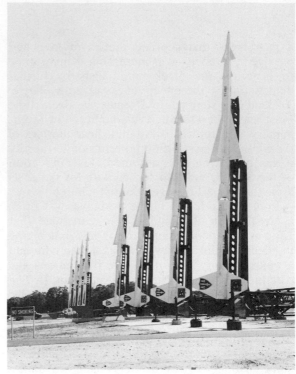

The growth of Soviet technology led President Eisenhower to give top priority in 1955 to the development of a long-range ballistic missiles program. Shown here are Nike guided missiles raised to their vertical firing positions at a Nike launching site in Lorton, Virginia.

The First Satellites

On October 4, 1957, Soviet scientists launched the world's first artificial satellite, *Sputnik I*. A month later, in early November 1957, the Soviets shot *Sputnik II* into orbit. This time their satellite, an eleven-hundred-pound vehicle — an incredibly heavy satellite in that era — carried a dog named Laika. Within a few weeks, America attempted to send a tiny navy satellite into orbit aboard its Vanguard rocket. The outcome, witnessed on television by millions of viewers, was a dramatic fizzle. Then, on the night of January 31, 1958, the army ignited one of its Jupiter-C rockets and sent the first American satellite, *Explorer I*, into orbit. *Explorer I* was much smaller than the *Sputniks*, for the Soviets had developed launch vehicles with much greater thrust than those developed by the United States. Still, the "beep, beep" emitted by the tiny radio transmitter aboard *Explorer I* lifted the morale of the American people. The satellite proved that the Soviets were not going to be without competition in their quest for superiority in outer space.

National Aeronautics and Space Administration

Later in 1958, a civilian agency, the National Aeronautics and Space Administration (NASA), was established. NASA's first spectacular came in December 1958 when one of the air force's Atlas rockets orbited a satellite. Less than two years later, in August 1960, NASA launched *Echo I,* a spherical balloon one hundred feet in diameter. As it orbited the earth, it reflected radio messages back to earth. Meanwhile, between autumn 1958 and early 1961, NASA launched five deep probes into outer space, one of which sent a satellite into orbit around the sun.

As the Soviet Union and the United States sent up their first satellites, scientists, engineers, and people in the streets began to speculate on the possibility of putting men in orbit and bringing them safely back to earth. In 1959 NASA released the names of seven military test pilots who would begin training as astronauts for America's man-in-space program, dubbed Project Mercury.

The original astronauts, whose names would become household words in those early days of space exploration, were Malcolm Scott Carpenter, Leroy Gordon Cooper, John H. Glenn, Jr., Virgil I. ("Gus") Grissom, Walter M. Schirra, Jr., Alan B. Shepard, Jr., and Donald K. Slayton.

Conventional Forces

Most Americans seemed to support the ballistic missile and satellite programs. Some, nonetheless, feared that the president was placing too much emphasis on nuclear weapons and not enough on so-called conventional forces—infantry regiments, tank battalions, tactical air squadrons.

That Eisenhower had favored nuclear weapons systems at the expense of conventional forces was beyond dispute. As soon as the Korean War ended in summer 1953, the administration began to dismantle much of the conventional military mechanism. It set about building a fearsome arsenal of nuclear warheads, strategic bombing planes, and, near the end of the decade, ballistic missiles. The central idea was to build a nuclear force so powerful that no aggressor would be able to knock out all of America's nuclear retaliatory force. After any attack the United States would have enough nuclear power left to destroy the aggressor. According to such calculations, America's great nuclear force should provide an effective deterrent to war.

As for limited, or "brush-fire" wars, such as the one in Korea, the Eisenhower administration intimated that, so far as the United States was concerned, such wars were a thing of the past. In the future aggressors would run the risk of a nuclear response, "massive retaliation," by the United States.

A central advantage of this new defense position was obvious: it made possible a reduction in military spending. Nuclear forces, relative to their destructive capacity, were less expensive to assemble and maintain than were conventional forces.

The argument against cutting back the country's conventional military forces turned on the problem of "brush-fire" wars. Nuclear weapons were so devastating that the United States would be extremely reluctant to use them except in a major war. This meant that the United States, lacking large conventional forces, was virtually powerless to fight small limited wars. Hence, there was nothing to prevent the Communists from nibbling away at the non-Communist world

by limited military action at countless points across the globe. Insofar as limited wars were concerned, "massive retaliation" was nothing more than a hollow slogan. So argued Eisenhower's critics. General Maxwell D. Taylor, one of the critics, noted that between 1945 and 1959 the world had endured eighteen armed conflicts, including the Korean War. Nuclear weapons were not used in any of them. Taylor contended that in the foreseeable future the chances were much greater for limited wars than for full-scale nuclear wars.

President Eisenhower stood by his military policies. He argued that a healthy economy, based on reduced federal spending for defense, was as important to America's survival as was military power. With his military prestige, Eisenhower had his way. The result was a weakness in America's strength in conventional forces which was not overcome until after 1961 when John F. Kennedy and Robert S. McNamara took over the responsibility of providing for the nation's defense.

Later in the 1960s, great numbers of Americans became disenchanted with the country's interventions in the "brush-fire" war in Vietnam —carried on with the conventional forces built up under Kennedy, McNamara, and Lyndon B. Johnson. Some critics began to suggest that it might be well to return to Eisenhower's "new look" military posture. If the country's conventional forces were small and weak, they said, there would be no temptation to project the United States into another frustrating limited war.

STUDY GUIDE: President Eisenhower encouraged the ballistic missile programs. During his administration the navy launched the first nuclear-powered submarine, the *Nautilus*.

In October 1957 the Soviets launched the first space sattelite, *Sputnik I*. In January 1958 the army successfully launched *Explorer I*. Later that year the National Aeronautics and Space Administration was created. Between 1958 and 1961 five deep probes into outer space were launched. In 1959 NASA announced the man-in-space program, Project Mercury.

Eisenhower favored nuclear weapons over conventional arms. The idea was to build a nuclear force so powerful that it would deter any aggressor. Consequently America's strength in conventional weapons was weakened. This weakness was not overcome until after 1961 during the Kennedy administration.

EISENHOWER AND EUROPE

In the election campaign of 1952 the Republicans had attacked the foreign policies of President Truman and his secretary of state, Dean G. Acheson. GOP orators maintained that the Truman-Acheson policy of trying to "contain" Soviet-Communist power in Europe within its current boundaries was a negative approach. Republican spokesmen contended that containment was an immoral policy because it recognized the legitimacy or at least the permanency of the Soviet conquest of Eastern Europe during and after World War II. The United States, they said, should not be content with containing Soviet-Communist power. It should pursue policies designed to "roll back the Iron Curtain" and liberate the "captive peoples" of Eastern Europe.

In late January 1953, Eisenhower's secretary of state, John Foster Dulles, declared support for Republican ideas about taking an aggressive stance against the Communists. He promised the "captive peoples" of Eastern Europe that "you can count on us."

The policy of "liberating captive peoples" was little more than a pious hope. The Republican administration was not prepared to do anything drastic to give substance to the policy. This was demonstrated first in June 1953 when anti-Soviet riots and strikes broke out in cities and towns across East Germany. President Eisenhower announced that the United States planned no physical intervention in Eastern Europe. Additional proof came in autumn 1956 when Hungarian "freedom fighters" revolted against Sovietism. The United States did nothing more than wish them good luck.

A Spirit of Conciliation

After the death of the Soviet dictator Stalin, on March 5, 1953, Republican leaders were trying to size up the new leadership in the Kremlin, a five-member group of the Council of Ministers headed by Georgi M. Malenkov. The first signs were encouraging. The North Koreans got down to the business of serious armistice negotiations,

with the result that the Korean War ended. At the same time, Malenkov was taking a more conciliatory stand toward America and the West than Stalin had in recent times. He insisted that the Soviet Union was eager for peace.

Still, America's leaders chose to hedge their bets. They continued to build up the country's nuclear striking force, more so after August 1953 when Malenkov announced that Soviet scientists had exploded a hydrogen bomb. They also sought to strengthen the defense of Western Europe. To that end, in September 1953, the United States reached an agreement with the Spanish dictator, General Francisco Franco. The United States was allowed to build and maintain military bases in Spain for at least ten years in return for $226 million in economic and military aid. A year later, in 1954, the North African state of Libya granted the United States long-term rights to an air base near Tripoli in exchange for economic assistance.

More important, the Eisenhower administration continued the effort begun under Truman to bring West Germany into the defense system of Western Europe. As in the time of Truman, they had difficulty with France.

The French had felt the dreadful effects of German military power three times (1870-71, 1914-18, 1939-45) and were edgy at the prospect of German remilitarization. Still the United States urged the establishment of a European Defense Community (EDC). Under the EDC formula, West Germany would enter NATO and put together several army divisions to be integrated into a multinational Western European defense force. After two years' debate the French rejected this plan—partly out of fear that the Americans and British might decide to remove most of their forces from Western Europe.

After the French rejection of EDC, the British prime minister, Sir Anthony Eden, unveiled a new and complicated proposal—a Western European Union (WEU). The WEU proposal included long-term commitments by the United States and Great Britain to maintain troops in Western Europe. These troops would presumably inhibit any dangerous West German ambitions. The French approved the plan in late December 1954.

Early in 1955 West Germany received recognition as a sovereign state. It entered NATO and prepared to contribute twelve divisions to the Western defense system. The agreement bringing Germany into NATO also provided that West Germany, without consent of WEU or NATO, could not manufacture atomic, biological, or chemical weapons or long-range bombing planes. It also compelled West Germany to pledge that it would never "have recourse to force to achieve the reunification of Germany or the modification of the present boundaries" of the Federal Republic.

The new masters in the Kremlin, in 1953-55, continued to display a spirit of caution and conciliation. They agreed to a peace treaty which reestablished Austria as an independent state. In the treaty the "big four" powers (Britain, France, the Soviet Union, and the United States) pledged to respect Austria's independence and territory. Since the end of the war Austria had been jointly occupied by armies of the Western Allies and the Soviet Union.

In the light of this new spirit of conciliation President Eisenhower made a dramatic proposal in December 1953. He called for establishment of an international agency under the United Nations to which the nuclear powers would turn over atomic material "to serve the peaceful uses of mankind." The Soviets showed little interest in this "atoms for peace" idea and nothing substantial came of it.

At the same time, the president urged the Soviets to work out a disarmament agreement with the United States. The United States since 1946, when it had offered the Baruch Plan for atomic control to the first session of the UN, had tried off and on for some disarmament agreement. The Americans had insisted that any disarmament agreement must be accompanied by a program to inspect military facilities to make certain the nations were honoring the agreement. The Soviets, however, had refused to consider any kind of inspection. The new Eisenhower proposal was unsuccessful, too.

A Summit Conference at Geneva

Some world leaders thought the softening of Soviet policy indicated that it might be an opportune time for a summit conference between Western leaders and the new leadership in the Kremlin – now headed by Nikolai Bulganin and Nikita S. Khrushchev. The initial reaction of President Eisenhower and Secretary Dulles was negative.

Then the president changed his mind. Contemplating the unimaginable consequences of a nuclear war, he concluded that if a summit conference had any chance of promoting peace it

OKEH! DROP THE GUNS!'

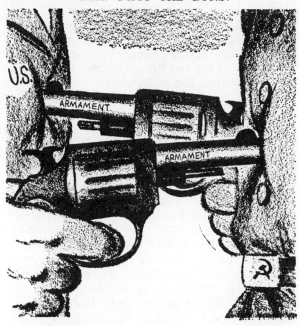

Don Hesse in the St. Louis Globe-Democrat

This editorial cartoon points up one of the main difficulties of disarmament plans: no nation wants to make the first move to give up its weapons. Did the development of the atomic bomb, with its unprecedented destructive power, help the cause of disarmament? What have recent disarmament conferences accomplished?

would be worth the effort. Moreover, the new British prime minister, Eden, who had replaced Sir Winston Churchill, would soon face a general election. Eisenhower believed the publicity and prestige that Eden would gain as a result of a summit conference would improve the Conservative party's chances of victory. Eisenhower agreed to a summit conference, and in July 1955 Eisenhower, Eden, Bulganin, Khrushchev, and Premier Edgar Fauré of France met in Geneva, Switzerland.

An atmosphere of friendliness prevailed during the five-day conference. The agenda provided that the conferees would focus on the unification of Germany, disarmament, and establishment of a general security system for all of Europe. Rather quickly, though, it became clear that the issues dividing the Western powers and the Soviet Union would not yield to good fellowship and informal conversation.

The Western powers stood firm on the principle that reunification of Germany could come only as a result of free elections throughout East and West Germany. Knowing that free elections would mean the loss of East Germany as a Soviet satellite, the Soviets refused the Western formula. The old controversy about inspection of military facilities prevented any headway on the problem of disarmament. As for a general European security system, the Soviets insisted that the United States and Britain remove their armed forces from the European continent. This condition was totally unacceptable to the Western powers.

As the meeting was about to close, President Eisenhower sent a wave of excitement across the world when he made a dramatic "open skies" proposal. Under the president's plan the major powers would supply each other with "a complete blueprint" of their military establishments and allow unlimited inspection of their territories by "unarmed peaceful planes." If its territory was under constant aerial surveillance one nation could not easily assemble forces for a surprise attack on any of the others. Eisenhower's proposal received so much favorable publicity that the Soviets did not dare reject it. They permitted the proposal to be a topic of diplomatic discussion for two years, until 1957, before the Soviets announced that they would have nothing to do with it.

Despite failure to reach any substantial agreements, President Eisenhower announced that "a new spirit of conciliation and cooperation" had been present. In subsequent months Americans read and heard a good deal about the "spirit of Geneva." They interpreted the phrase to mean that Soviet leaders were turning away from the tactics of terror and repression at home and intimidation and imperialism in foreign affairs.

The new "spirit" received dramatic reinforcement in February 1956 during the Communist party Congress. Nikita Khrushchev, who emerged as the leading member of the Soviet hierarchy, assailed the ruthlessness of Stalin and accused him of many errors in the conduct of Soviet foreign policy. Khrushchev declared, "We want to be friends and to cooperate with the United States in the effort for peace and security."

Khrushchev's words shocked the Communist parties in Western countries and nearly destroyed the American Communist party, for Western Communists had never faltered in their belief that Stalin was some sort of messiah. The Soviet leader's words sent a new wave of hope across non-Communist countries, particularly the United States. It seemed that Khrushchev had officially ended the principles of Stalinism and pledged the Soviet Union to a policy of peaceful competition and co-existence.

The Communists Tighten Their Grip

The Communist grip soon tightened again. In October-November 1956, Hungarians rose up in violent protest against the harsh and oppressive policies of the Communist regime in Budapest. When Hungary's "freedom fighters" refused to be intimidated by Soviet tanks, the Russians turned their guns on the rebels and extinguished the uprising in a sea of blood. Hungary was returned to the status of a docile satellite of the Kremlin.

Two years later, in November 1958, the Soviets provoked a new crisis in Berlin when Nikita Khrushchev issued an ultimatum demanding a radical change in the status of Berlin. He offered two alternatives. First, Berlin could be unified and handed over to the government of East Germany. Or, second, the Western sectors of Berlin, but not the Soviet Eastern sector, would be turned into an international free city. Khrushchev offered no guarantee that the East German Communists would keep their hands off a free city of West Berlin. He said the West would have to accept one of the alternatives by May 1959. Otherwise he would at that time turn over control of the access routes to West Berlin to the government of East Germany —which none of the Western powers recognized. Khrushchev was betting that the Western powers would not risk a nuclear war to maintain their position in West Berlin. The ability of the Communists to jam radar signals would prevent a repetition of the 1948-49 Berlin airlift.

President Eisenhower declared that the United States would not be party to any agreements which would turn West Berlin over to "hostile domination." The president was determined to show that the United States would honor its commitments under the North Atlantic Treaty. Eisenhower did not think this tough American position would lead to a nuclear war. Still, if war was required to maintain the Western position in Berlin, the president apparently was prepared to have it.

Weeks and months went by and neither the United States nor the Soviet Union showed any disposition to back down on the Berlin issue. It seemed as though a nuclear time bomb was ticking away. As Khrushchev's deadline for Western acceptance of one of his alternatives drew near, people across the world wondered if the two superpowers really would permit the bomb to explode. On the day of his deadline, May 27, 1959, Khrushchev did nothing. Thus the Berlin crisis of 1958-59 passed without incident.

Khrushchev's Visit

Then relations between the Kremlin and the West underwent another of their intermittent thaws.

A slight warming of relations had been evident even before the passing of Khrushchev's famous deadline, in early 1959, when the United States and the Soviet Union agreed to enlarge the cultural exchanges between the two countries. The Soviets set up an impressive exhibit in New York City showing aspects of life in the Soviet Union.

A few months later the curtain went up on an American exposition in Moscow. Vice-President Nixon officially opened the American display in summer 1959. While inspecting a model kitchen, the vice-president found himself engaged in an animated debate with Chairman Khrushchev on the relative merits of capitalism and communism. As the thaw continued, President Eisenhower invited Khrushchev to travel to the United States, tour the country, and meet informally with him to talk over Soviet-American problems. Khrushchev accepted.

Khrushchev arrived in Washington, D.C., in mid-September 1959. He was greeted by the president, taken on a sightseeing trip around Washington in a helicopter, and honored at a state dinner. Next he went on a ten-day tour about the United States. Climaxing the visit was a two-day meeting between Khrushchev and Eisenhower at Camp David, Maryland. The two leaders talked amicably and Khrushchev formally canceled his ultimatum on the Berlin question. Both men agreed that peaceful co-existence was necessary. Both intimated that it might be a good idea for leaders of the major powers to hold another summit conference to try to settle their differences. Finally the Soviet leader repeated an invitation to President Eisenhower to visit the Soviet Union in the coming year.

The Khrushchev visit apparently was a smashing success, and the public began to note repeated references to "the spirit of Camp David." Presumably the meeting between Eisenhower and Khrushchev signaled a new relaxation of world tensions and perhaps an end to the cold war. To take advantage of this new mood of friendliness, in December 1959, President Eisenhower and other Western leaders invited Chair-

Wide World

East-West relations improved after Khrushchev visited the United States to meet with Eisenhower.

man Khrushchev to meet with them at a new summit conference at Paris in May 1960.

STUDY GUIDE: Eisenhower continued to support NATO. But the United States also urged creation of a European Defense Community which would allow Germany to enter NATO. France refused to approve the EDC plan. Britain's prime minister Anthony Eden introduced a new proposal and a Western European Union was formed. France approved this plan. In 1955 the Federal Republic of Germany (West Germany) entered NATO.

Stalin died six weeks after Eisenhower took office. Eventually Bulganin and Khrushchev emerged as Kremlin leaders. Relations with the USSR became easier. Austria was re-established as an independent state. In 1953 Eisenhower offered his "atoms for peace" proposal. Nothing really came of it.

Soviet policy grew more flexible in 1955. In July a summit conference took place. At the meeting in Geneva Eisenhower presented his "open skies" proposal. It was discussed by the Soviets for two years but finally dropped.

In autumn 1956, Hungarians revolted against harsh Communist policies. The Soviets crushed the rebellion. Two years later the Soviets created a crisis in Berlin when Khrushchev demanded a drastic change in the status of the divided city. Eisenhower

[691]

took a firm stand and the crisis passed without incident.

In 1959 Soviet-American relations warmed up. A cultural exchange program was enlarged. Khrushchev visited the United States.

EISENHOWER AND THE MIDDLE EAST

The decade of the fifties found America increasingly involved in the affairs of the Middle East.

Arabs across North Africa and the Middle East remained furious over the part played by the United States in the birth of Israel. The government in Washington tried to calm the fires of anti-Americanism in the Arab world by proclaiming neutrality in the Arab-Israeli feud and providing economic and military assistance to Arab countries. However, the United States insisted on Israel's right to exist and hence in the Arab view was pro-Zionist — and anti-Arab.

The decline of British power in the Middle East was a burden for the United States. For nearly a century the British brought a measure of stability to the area. But after the war, the British did not have sufficient strength to maintain their dominant position in the Middle East. Many Arabs, notably the Egyptians, who had long chafed under British colonialism, were putting heavy pressure on the British by the early 1950s to get out of the area altogether and leave control with the Arabs. Despite their weakness, the British were not inclined to leave. For one thing, the Suez Canal was the lifeline between Britain's home islands and East Asia and the Southwestern Pacific where the British had important interests. The British also had strong interests in the oil resources of the Middle East, particularly in Iraq and the Arabian peninsula, which seemed to require a continuing British presence.

Unless the United States was prepared to risk a rise in Soviet-Communist influence in the Middle East, it had to try to fill the power vacuum being created by Britain's declining influence there. American presence in the Middle East was expensive; it also meant that the United States fell heir to the charges of colonialism which the Arabs had previously directed at Britain.

Britain's decline placed the United States in a delicate position with the British. Britain was America's chief ally in NATO. And lest it weaken the Western defense alliance, the United

Compix

As secretary of state under Eisenhower, John Foster Dulles was the principal formulator of American foreign policy.

States could not easily take positions in the Middle East that seemed contrary to British interests in the area.

As British influence declined in the early 1950s, American leaders became increasingly concerned over the possibility of a Soviet-Communist move into the Middle East. Surprisingly, since their retreat from Iran in 1946 and the success of the Truman Doctrine in Turkey in 1947-49, the Soviets had made no serious attempt to enlarge their influence in the Middle East. The Arab peoples of the area were impoverished and were ruled mainly by incompetent and corrupt governments — a classic seedbed for Communist ideas. To head off any Soviet-Communist penetration of the Middle East, leaders in Washington tried two approaches.

First, the United States increased economic and technical assistance aimed at developing Middle Eastern agricultural and mineral resources and improving general living standards. But this made little impact.

Second, the United States considered the possibility of bringing countries of the area into a military alliance similar to NATO. But when Secretary Dulles toured the area in spring 1953, he concluded that the countries of the Middle

East were too weak and disorganized to sustain an alliance on the NATO model. Some of the countries, it turned out, thought otherwise. In 1954 Turkey and Pakistan signed the Baghdad Pact, a defensive alliance aimed against possible aggression by the Soviet Union. The following year, 1955, Britain, Iraq, and Iran joined the alliance, which became known as the Middle East Treaty Organization (METO). The United States declined to join but was delighted with this new barrier to "contain" Soviet-Communist power and pledged support. Washington feared that a dramatic American move in the Middle East would arouse Egypt. The outcome would be an eruption of anti-Americanism. Such a development might be a serious matter, for Egypt straddled the Suez Canal and was located near the center of the Arab world. American leaders considered the goodwill and friendship of Egypt particularly important.

Egypt

In the late 1940s Egypt had limped along under the rule of King Farouk, a luxury-loving monarch who ignored the plight of his long-suffering people. In 1952 some army officers, including Lieutenant Colonel Gamal Abdul Nasser, overthrew Farouk. Two years later, in 1954, Nasser emerged as the undisputed leader of the military government. He became dictator of Egypt, although in 1956 he assumed the title of president.

Nasser's goal was to bring unity to the quarreling Arab peoples and enable them to make a

National Geographic Photographer George F. Mobley, Courtesy U.S. Capitol Historical Society

During most of the 1940s and 1950s Sam Rayburn of Texas was speaker of the United States House of Representatives. A lifelong Democrat, he served in this position for seventeen years, longer than any other man in congressional history. Elected to Congress for the first time in 1912, Rayburn served for forty-nine consecutive years.

Establishment of the United States Air Force Academy won the support of President Eisenhower in 1954. The academy was located near Colorado Springs, Colorado and graduated its first class in 1959.

Courtesy United States Air Force Academy

concerted assault on their common problems: poverty, ignorance, and their common enemy — Israel. The nerve center of this unified Arab world would be Egypt, and Nasser would be its leader.

The United States presented an obstacle to Nasser's ambitions, for the government in Washington would not permit destruction of Israel. To avoid a situation that might compel the United States to come to the rescue of Israel, American leaders had restricted the flow of arms to the Middle East.

On the other hand, the United States was the richest country in the world, interested in providing aid to "developing" countries. Hence it was an important source of the kind of economic and technical assistance that Egypt and the other Arab countries desperately needed. So, the United States in the early 1950s seemed willing to take a tolerant view of Egypt and make available economic and technical aid. However, American aid would depend on Nasser's showing no signs of executing his threats against Israel, doing nothing to interfere with the free flow of traffic through the Suez Canal, and doing nothing to upset American business activities in the Middle East.

In 1955 relations between the United States and Egypt began to turn sour. First came a sharp decline in the world price of cotton, a heavy blow to Egypt, whose economy depended largely on the sale of cotton in the world market. Nasser was quick to blame the United States for the hardship resulting from Egypt's dwindling income from cotton. He based his accusation on a rumor that the United States had dumped quantities of surplus American cotton in the market.

The Soviets, who were upset by the METO military alliance, decided to build a base of influence in Egypt by buying Egyptian cotton in exchange for Soviet armaments. The United States appealed to the Soviets in the name of the "spirit of Geneva" not to go through with the arms-for-cotton deal. It was to no avail.

The Aswan Dam Project

A short time later Nasser announced plans for constructing a huge dam and hydroelectric power station at Aswan, on the Nile River some eight hundred miles upstream from Cairo. In addition to providing cheap electricity, the dam at Aswan would enable Egypt, by irrigation, to increase by fifty percent the square miles of land under cultivation. Instead of two crops per year, Egyptian farmers would be able to plant and harvest three. The dictator-president turned to the West for support. Despite Nasser's dealings with the Soviets, in late 1955 the United States and Britain agreed to lend Egypt part of the money for the Aswan Dam enterprise.

Nasser's subsequent behavior became increasingly irritating to the Western powers. The Egyptian leader encouraged Arab terrorists to make raids against Israel and encouraged rebels in Algeria to step up activities against French authorities. He seemed to be drawing closer to the Soviets by recognizing the Communist regime of Mao in China. As a consequence, the United States and Britain stalled on their pledge of support for the Aswan project. To press the Americans and British, the Egyptians advised officials in Washington that if the Aswan funds were not soon forthcoming, they would get the money from the Soviet Union. Whereupon, in July 1956, with strong support in Congress, Secretary Dulles told the Egyptians that the United States had changed its mind and would not support the Aswan Dam project. A short time later the British made a similar announcement.

Denouncing the United States, praising the Soviet Union, and declaring that Egypt would never "beg for a loan," Nasser dramatically took over the Suez Canal a short time later. He proclaimed the canal a property of the Egyptian government and announced that income from operation of the canal would go for the Aswan Dam project. Their national spirit stirred by the bold action of their leader, most people of Egypt were happy. The British and French, who were the chief users of the waterway and the principal stockholders in the Suez Canal Company, were furious. The Americans, who owned and operated a canal in Panama, feared that the Egyptian dictator-president had established a dangerous precedent.

War in the Middle East

Israel, of course, was interested in developments regarding Egypt in the summer and autumn of 1956. Seeing Egypt as a perpetual threat, the Israelis doubtless hoped the British and French would follow through on their threats to rid the Middle East of the Egyptian upstart, Nasser. It is difficult to assess the extent to which the Israelis were coordinating plans and activities with the British and French. But in autumn 1956 the Israelis began to mobilize their military forces.

Then came the closing days of October 1956. The people of the United States were focusing attention on the second Eisenhower-Stevenson presidential contest and the Soviets were putting down the anti-Communist rebellion in Hungary. It seemed to the Israelis, and also to the British and French, that the time was opportune to liquidate the regime of Nasser. On October 29 the Israelis sent their armed forces plunging across the Gaza Strip into Egypt. In a dazzling display of speed, power, and maneuver the Israeli army routed the Egyptians and swept across the Sinai peninsula to the east bank of the Suez Canal.

The government in Washington acted immediately, fearing the Israeli-Egyptian war might escalate into World War III. A resolution was introduced in the Security Council of the United Nations urging all members to avoid use of force in Egypt and demanding that Israel withdraw its armies from Egyptian territory. Exercising their veto power, the British and French killed the resolution. On the following day, British and French bombing planes roared over Cairo and transports unloaded thousands of soldiers on Egyptian soil.

Screams of protest rolled in from Arab states, countries (such as India and Indonesia) that recently had thrown off the yoke of colonialism, and from the Communist world—in spite of the repression of Hungary. What the governments in London, Paris, and Tel Aviv had not expected was an equally hostile response from the United States.

Eisenhower made it clear that he deplored the aggressive behavior of America's friends and had a resolution introduced into the UN General Assembly demanding an immediate cease-fire in Egypt. The resolution won overwhelming approval.

The governments of Britain and France yielded and on November 6 gave up the military adventure in Egypt. The Israelis did likewise. By the end of 1956, the last British and French troops had departed. In March 1957 the Israelis, under heavy pressure by the United States, withdrew the last of their forces from Sinai.

The action of the United States saved Nasser without permanently increasing American prestige in the Arab world. It put a crack in NATO from which the alliance never fully recovered. It also drove an ill and bitter Anthony Eden from power in Britain.

United Nations

Emergency troops were sent to Egypt by the UN in 1956 to make sure that Britain, France, and Israel were honoring their promises to withdraw their forces. These UN troops are occupying former Israeli positions on the Sinai Peninsula as the Israelis withdraw. How did the invasion of Egypt affect relations within NATO?

As time passed, America's problems in the Middle East became increasingly explosive. Some people began to wonder if it would have been better to have allowed the Anglo-French-Israeli forces to eliminate Nasser and the base for Soviet-Communist influence that he provided.

The Eisenhower Doctrine

Most Americans were proud of the moral stand taken by their government in the Suez crisis. They were pleased at the praise which peoples around the world were lavishing on them and their leaders. Then, in January 1957, their president announced a new "doctrine"—the Eisenhower Doctrine. And again Americans—or most of them—were delighted.

The Eisenhower Doctrine was the consequence of a dramatic increase in Soviet activity in the Middle East following the Suez crisis and the ill-starred attack on Egypt. Its purpose was to prevent Communists from taking over any governments in the Middle East. To that end, the United States would provide economic and military assistance to countries of the Middle East. In case any Middle Eastern country came under attack by the forces of "international communism" the United States might intervene with military forces. A short time later Congress overwhelmingly endorsed the Eisenhower Doctrine and voted $200 million for economic and military assistance to countries of the Middle East.

The Eisenhower Doctrine did not bring peace

or stability to the Middle East. In Egypt and Syria the doctrine was officially denounced as a plot to promote Western colonialism in the Middle East. In the spring of 1957 anti-Western elements in Jordan nearly toppled the government of King Hussein. A short time later a pro-Communist faction took over the government of Syria. The following year, 1958, Syria joined Egypt and Yemen and formed the United Arab Republic. The head of the UAR, of course, was Colonel Nasser.

While Nasser was celebrating the birth of the UAR, in July 1958, a new crisis boiled up in the Middle East. Anti-Western conspirators in Iraq overthrew and murdered King Faisal, the country's youthful pro-Western monarch. It appeared that the Soviets would soon have a new center of influence in Iraq and that Iraq might join the UAR.

Trouble in Lebanon and Jordan

In Lebanon and Jordan pro-Nasser elements were active. Both President Camille Chamoun of Lebanon and King Hussein of Jordan feared a take-over by anti-Western forces, as had occurred in Iraq. Chamoun turned to the United States and Hussein to Britain. President Eisenhower sent several thousand marines and soldiers to help stabilize the situation in Lebanon and the British sent a force of paratroopers to Jordan. Eisenhower explained that American interests and peace in the world required an independent Lebanon.

Other countries did not agree with the Anglo-American actions. From Sweden, India, and Japan came protests that the intervention was unwarranted. Premier Khrushchev denounced the Anglo-American aggression and intimated that the Soviet Union might feel compelled to make a counterintervention. The governments in Washington and London, however, had no inclination to press their intervention beyond Lebanon and Jordan. As a result, the danger of large-scale hostilities receded.

The United States had placed the issue before the United Nations, and at length an agreement emerged. The Arab states, including the UAR, pledged noninterference in each other's affairs. The secretary-general of the UN promised to send observers to Lebanon and Jordan, and the United States and Britain withdrew their troops.

The preservation of the independence of Lebanon and Jordan seemed a magnificent achievement of the Eisenhower Doctrine. Some observers later called the Lebanese intervention one of Eisenhower's most successful moves in foreign affairs.

The Middle East at the Close of the 1950s

America's problems in the Middle East did not disappear. Nasser announced in late 1958 that the Soviets had granted a loan of $100 million to Egypt for the Aswan Dam project. Iraq pulled out of the Baghdad Pact and the Central Treaty Organization (CENTO), which replaced METO. The new regime in Iraq kept both the Soviets and the UAR at arm's length and established satisfactory relations with the United States. Of course, the feud between the Arabs and Israelis continued. Still, as the 1950s came to a close, the situation in the Middle East, from the vantage point of the United States, did not appear critical.

STUDY GUIDE: Arabs were angry over the part the United States played in the creation of Israel. To soothe their feelings and to prevent the spread of Soviet influence the United States provided economic and military aid to Arab nations.

Egyptian president Nasser sought to unify the Arab people to overthrow Israel. The United States then restricted the flow of arms to the Middle East. However, America did offer economic and technical aid to Egypt.

Nasser asked for American aid in building the Aswan Dam. Meanwhile, Egyptian terrorists were raiding Israel. The United States and Britain withdrew their support of the Aswan project. Nasser then seized the Suez Canal. He announced that money from its operation would go for the Aswan project.

The Israelis saw Egypt as a continuous threat. In October 1956 the Israeli army swept across the Sinai Peninsula to the east bank of the Suez Canal. Britain and France sent troops onto Egyptian soil. Arab states protested. The United States introduced a resolution into the UN Security Council demanding an immediate cease-fire in Egypt. The military venture in Egypt ended in November 1956.

Eisenhower announced the Eisenhower Doctrine in January 1957. This doctrine stated that the United States would provide economic and military assistance to countries of the Middle East to prevent Communists from taking over the governments. Egypt and Syria denounced the doctrine.

In Lebanon and Jordan, anti-Western forces were active. Eisenhower sent troops to Lebanon. The British sent forces to Jordan. The troops were withdrawn when the United Nations sent observers. The independence of the two nations was preserved.

THE FAR EAST

Like the Middle East, the Far East was a source of unending trouble for American policymakers in the 1950s. From time to time it appeared that the Far East might be the starting point for World War III.

When World War II ended in 1945, a fierce contest for authority developed in most of the countries of the Far East. In the Philippines — which received independence from the United States in 1946 — the non-Communists kept the upper hand. In China the Communists triumphed. In Korea the outcome was a partitioning of the country between Communists and non-Communists. In Southeast Asia the British,

French, and Dutch hoped to restore their prewar colonial order. They were opposed by various national groups that were bent on independence. In Burma and Indonesia the nationalists had triumphed and established independent states by 1950. In French Indo-China — present-day Vietnam, Laos, and Cambodia — the struggle was continuing and the outcome was in doubt.

Rapid political change, with its confusion and instability, together with grinding poverty, made East Asia a fertile ground for Communist ideas. The area seemed to be a prime target for outside Communist aggression. Or so thought American leaders, more so after the onset of the Cold War in Europe and the triumph of Mao Tse-tung and his Communist faction in China.

Then, in summer 1950, came the Communist invasion of South Korea, and the worst of American fears seemed to be confirmed: if internal subversion and civil war (as in China) would not achieve their objectives, the Communists were willing to resort to overt aggression.

As a consequence of the Korean affair, the government in Washington set about strengthening non-Communist defenses in the Western Pacific. It made its first step in Japan in the latter part of 1950 by opening formal peace

By 1955 Communism had secured its hold on much of the Far East. The Nationalist Chinese under pro-American Chiang Kai-shek had fled to Formosa and nearby smaller islands. Korea and Vietnam were divided into Communist and non-Communist sectors and an uneasy peace marked the rest of Indochina.

FAR EAST IN 1955

- U. S. S. R.
- Sakhalin
- Manchuria
- Mongolian People's Republic
- North Korea
- Japan
- Sinkiang
- South Korea
- *PACIFIC OCEAN*
- Afghanistan
- West Pakistan
- Tibet
- People's Republic of China
- Ryuku Is.
- Matsu
- Pescadores
- Quemoy
- Taiwan (Formosa)
- Nationalist China
- Nepal
- Hong Kong
- Republic of the Philippines
- India
- E. Pak.
- Burma
- Laos
- North Vietnam
- *BAY OF BENGAL*
- Thailand
- South Vietnam
- ■ Communist Countries
- Cambodia

negotiations with the democratic government in Tokyo. The outcome was a treaty that officially ended the state of war between the two countries. Forty-eight other countries that had been enemies of Japan likewise accepted the treaty. Signed in September 1951, the treaty recognized Japan's sovereignty and provided for an end to the Allied occupation of the country.

On the heels of the peace treaty came a security pact between the two governments which gave the United States the right to maintain army, navy, and air bases on Japanese soil. The purpose of the American forces was "to deter armed attack on Japan" and to put down any disturbances inside Japan that Communist governments might cause. At the same time the United States negotiated a mutual defense treaty with the Philippine republic and the ANZUS defense treaty with Australia and New Zealand. Both treaties were signed in 1951 during the presidency of Truman.

The "China Problem"

While dealing with other problems in Asia, the United States was also trying to work out a policy for dealing with the "China problem." When Chiang Kai-shek and his Nationalist followers fled the Chinese mainland in 1949 and took up residence on the island of Taiwan, or Formosa, the first impulse of the government in Washington was to leave him to his fate. This seemed to mean an eventual take-over by Mao Tse-tung and the Communists. President Truman announced in January 1950 that the United States would not dispatch armed forces to defend Formosa. The United States would not offer military assistance to Chiang and had no wish to establish military bases in territory still under Chiang's control.

A short time later Secretary of State Acheson outlined America's "defense perimeter" in the Far East in his celebrated speech of early 1950. Acheson reinforced Truman's statement. He indicated that Formosa—like Korea—was on the other side of the line which the United States was prepared to defend. As for Mao Tse-tung's Communist regime in Peking, the Truman administration did not grant it diplomatic recognition and indeed took a dim view of China's new leadership.

Many people in the United States clung to the belief that there was still a chance for a counterrevolution in China. Accordingly large numbers of Americans protested the Truman-Acheson policy of withholding further support from Chiang Kai-shek. They portrayed Chiang as a legitimate Chinese hero who had bravely fought first against the Japanese and then the Communists. The Truman-Acheson policy, they contended, was like throwing a friend and faithful ally to the wolves.

Then, in 1950, during the Korean War, China's Communist leaders sent thousands of soldiers into Korea. This brought about a hardening of the Washington government's anti-Maoist sentiments and a corresponding softening of attitudes toward Chiang Kai-shek. After the United States negotiated a peace treaty with Japan and mutual defense treaties with the Philippines, New Zealand, and Australia, it seemed only logical to look to Formosa as another possible defense against Communist expansion. Truman nonetheless moved cautiously. He did not set about negotiating an alliance with Chiang. He merely ordered the American Seventh Fleet to patrol the Formosa Straits and prevent any amphibious attack on Chiang's island from the mainland.

Truman also directed the fleet to prevent Chiang from attacking the mainland. If Chiang seized the opportunity presented by Mao's activity in Korea to launch an invasion of the mainland, the third global war of the twentieth century might be at hand.

Restraint of Chiang Kai-shek was a policy that offended many Americans, particularly Republicans, who had always taken a warmer view of Chiang than had Democrats. During the election campaign of 1952 Republicans maintained that containment of communism was a negative policy. They talked of "liberating captive peoples" and wanted to "unleash Chiang Kai-shek."

After winning the election, President Eisenhower advised Congress in February 1953 that the Seventh Fleet would "no longer be employed to shield Communist China." Eisenhower, in a word, was "unleashing" Chiang. But Eisenhower made it plain to Chiang that the United States would not support any Nationalist military adventure against the forces of Mao.

The principal danger was that the Chinese Communists might mount an amphibious assault against Formosa. To guard against that possibility, and also to bring Chiang Kai-shek's fortress into America's Western Pacific defense system, the United States and Chiang's government signed a mutual defense treaty in 1954. The United States promised it would help Chiang resist any Communist attack on Formosa or the Pescadores—but not Quemoy and Matsu, the tiny Nationalist-held islands within sight of the Communist-controlled mainland. For his part Chiang granted the United States the right to establish army, navy, and air bases in territory under his control. He promised not to undertake any military operations without consent of the government in Washington.

In early 1955 China's Communists began aiming threats in the direction of some of the smaller Nationalist-held islands, particularly Quemoy and Matsu. The latter two islands had no strategic importance. Still, being so close to the mainland, their occupation by Nationalist soldiers was an embarrassment to the Communists and a source of pride for the Nationalists. When it appeared that the Communists might back up words with action, President Eisenhower warned that the United States was prepared to resist any attack on the little islands. He asked Congress for a resolution authorizing him to use force to defend Formosa, the Pescadores, and "such related positions and territories . . . now in friendly hands," namely, Quemoy and Matsu. By an overwhelming vote, Congress approved the Formosa Resolution.

According to later assertions by Secretary Dulles, the United States and Red China now stood on "the brink of war." However, the Chinese Communists did not attack the Nationalist outposts, and the crisis of 1955 over Quemoy and Matsu subsided.

Three years later, in the summer of 1958, Chinese Communists on the mainland began to fire a continuing barrage of shells upon Quemoy and Matsu. Premier Chou En-lai of China intimated that the bombardment was the prelude to an invasion. President Eisenhower, acting on the Formosa Resolution sent American ships to the waters around the two islands. He also stepped up the flow of supplies and equipment to Chiang Kai-shek. After a short time the crisis passed and the two islands were shelled only rarely.

The Eisenhower administration continued the policy of refusing to grant diplomatic recognition to the Communist regime in Peking. Leaders in Washington throughout the 1950s talked at length about the immorality of doing business with the "gangsters" in Peking. The real reason for refusing recognition was the hope that Mao's government might collapse. If the United States recognized Mao's regime, the government in Washington could not easily support anti-Communist groups in China when an opportunity appeared for overthrowing the Communists.

For similar reasons the Eisenhower administration throughout the 1950s used its influence to prevent the admission of the People's Republic of China to membership in the United Nations. American leaders made the Peking government's admission to the UN a moral issue. The United States argued that the Chinese had waged war against the UN in Korea (although the Chinese saw their enemy in Korea as the United States, not the UN). American representatives also pointed out that China had repeatedly condemned the UN, and they quoted aggressive statements which had been made by Mao. The one act of aggression by China in the 1950s was the take-over of Tibet, a huge, thinly populated territory which, in the Chinese view, was a historic part of China.

America's reasons for keeping the Peking government out of the UN were really more practical. If the People's Republic of China became a member of the world organization, the American case for refusing to have diplomatic relations with the Peking regime would be seriously compromised. Acceptance of Red China in the UN might prevent the United States from assisting in the destruction of that government if an opportunity arose.

Before the 1950s came to a close, there was increasing opposition to the refusal to recognize Mao's government and to keeping it out of the UN. Critics of the policy insisted that there was no chance that Mao's government might be toppled by an internal upheaval. And Chiang Kai-shek's army was much too small to make a successful attack on the mainland. Critics contended, moreover, that there were compelling arguments for establishing diplomatic relations with the Peking government and bringing it into the UN. For one thing, the United States was encouraging China's isolation and delaying the day when the Chinese would try to make some accommodation with the rest of the world. Second, the policy gave the Soviet Union an opportunity to act as China's protector and benefactor in the face of American hostility. If the Chinese were brought into the family of nations, however, it might be possible to drive a wedge between the Soviets and the Chinese. Finally, critics argued, it was dangerous for the United States to have no direct contact with the most populous country in the world. The absence of diplomatic relations could lead to misunderstandings and miscalculations, such as had occurred during the Korean War.

In spite of these opposition arguments, America's Far Eastern policy through the years of the Eisenhower presidency was based upon nonrecognition of Red China and prevention of Red China's entry into the UN.

Southeast Asia

Throughout the 1950s American leaders continued to believe that Southeast Asia was an area of major importance in international political calculations. It was a vast area of two hundred million people. It was so rich in rubber, oil, tin, manganese, and rice that the Japanese had considered it a "treasure-house." American leaders continued through the 1950s to believe that America's interests in the world required that Southeast Asia not fall under domination of the Communists.

Communists were active, however, in Southeast Asia in the 1950s, notably in Malaya and Vietnam. Malaya was still a British colony and the government in London prevented a Communist take-over there. Vietnam, Laos, and Cambodia made up the colony of French Indo-China. As the 1950s dawned, the French seemed to be losing their battle to keep Vietnam at once French and non-Communist.

A land of jungles, mountains, and fertile deltas, Vietnam had one of the oldest civilizations in the world. Before they were conquered by the French in the second half of the nineteenth century, the Vietnamese had enjoyed more than nine hundred years of almost uninterrupted independence. Vietnam's civilization had been heavily influenced by the country's giant neighbor to the north, China. The Vietnamese based their laws on Chinese legal codes and used Chinese characters in their written language. Most Vietnamese became disciples of the Buddhist religious faith, which also arrived by way of China. The Vietnamese, however, showed little affection for China. They remembered that their homeland had once been under Chinese domination for almost a thousand years. They always saw China as a threat to Vietnamese independence.

In the second half of the nineteenth century a new danger to Vietnamese independence appeared, the French. In 1861 the French entered the southern tip of the country, Cochin China. The French, who wanted to build a world empire, showed little concern for the rights, traditions, or wishes of the Vietnamese. Gradually they enlarged their control until they had taken over Vietnam and also Laos and Cambodia. The area became known as French Indo-China.

The French undertook ambitious public works programs, encouraged public health and sanitation, and built roads and railways. They introduced new crops and built irrigation systems that brought large tracts of land under cultivation for the first time. They introduced improved techniques of civil administration. They also brought their Roman Catholic religion to Vietnam, and a fair number of Vietnamese became and remained Catholics. Under French control Saigon became known as one of the most beautiful and cosmopolitan cities in East Asia—the "Paris of the Orient." But these programs often seemed designed mainly to advance the interests of French colonists, particularly owners of rubber plantations.

In French Indo-China illiteracy remained high and the schools were conducted in the French language, virtually ignoring Vietnamese history and culture. Taxes were oppressive, medical facilities poor, and death rates high. The result was considerable discontent among the Vietnamese. On a number of occasions they revolted, but the French easily put down insurrections.

Then came 1940-41 and the invasion of Indo-China by Japan during World War II. In the years of the Japanese occupation an intelligent and resourceful Vietnamese patriot, Ho Chi Minh, stepped up his activities.

The son of scholarly parents, Ho was born in 1890. He went to sea as a cabin boy at the age of twenty-one and toured the world. A sensitive young man, he deplored the colonial status of his homeland. After World War I, he urged delegates to the Paris peace conference to take a stand against colonialism and arrange for Vietnam's independence from France. The delegates were not interested.

Ho became absorbed with radical ideas and remained in France. He helped organize the French Communist party (1920), then studied revolutionary theories and techniques in Moscow. In the mid-1920s he went to China as a translator for the government of Chiang Kai-shek. In China he built the foundation for a Communist movement in French Indo-China. He returned to Moscow in 1927, after Chiang expelled Communists from his government. Then, in the early 1930s, he returned to Vietnam, where he had minimal success over the next several years trying to enlist Vietnamese nationalists in his Communist organization.

Then came the Japanese occupation of Vietnam and Ho saw his opportunity. He moved across the border into China, where he organized a band of anti-French Vietnamese patriots, some of whom were Communists, others not. Next he organized the League for the Independence of Vietnam, commonly called the Vietminh.

In March 1945, just five months before the end of World War II, the Japanese granted independence to Vietnam. They made Emperor Bao Dai the head of the new government. The Japanese were trying to rally Vietnamese patriots to their side, but Ho Chi Minh promptly denounced Bao Dai as a Japanese puppet. Ho then moved across the border from China and established his own "liberated area" in the north of Vietnam. At the end of the war in 1945 Bao Dai, who had only been a puppet, abdicated his throne. Ho Chi Minh moved in and set up the Democratic Republic of Vietnam, with its capital at Hanoi. Ho, however, did not have sufficient strength to extend his authority over the southern part of the country.

When World War II was over, there seemed to be some doubt whether the French would return to Indo-China. The Atlantic Charter had pledged support of the idea of self-determination for all people. Here was an eloquent statement of anticolonialism. At the end of the war, however, the United States did not press the issue. Hence, in Southeast Asia the British returned to Malaya and Burma and the Dutch, with British support, to Indonesia. The French, also with the help of the British, returned to Indo-China.

The United States did not make a firm stand in behalf of its anticolonial principles primarily because American leaders felt they would need the continuing goodwill and support of Britain and France. Hence, the United States could not risk alienating those two powers by provoking a quarrel over colonialism.

Civil War in Indo-China

The French had been beaten in World War II, and their nation was still in disarray. They proceeded cautiously upon returning to Indo-China. To stall until they became strong again, they negotiated an agreement with Ho Chi Minh in which they recognized his regime in Northern Vietnam as a free state within the French empire. Ho sensed the true intentions of the French, which led to continuing friction. At last, in December 1946, near Hanoi, hostilities broke out between units of the French army and forces of the Vietminh. Thus began a civil war that continued for eight years, until 1954. It was a brutal war, marked by atrocities on both sides, and claimed the lives of more than seventy thousand soldiers of the French army.

At first the government in Washington maintained a policy of hands off. It saw the war as a local struggle resulting from the legitimate desire of Vietnamese patriots to throw off the shackles of colonialism. Then came the cold war and the Truman Doctrine in 1947, which committed the United States to do battle with communism across the entire world. By the late 1940s it seemed clear to observers in America that Ho Chi Minh was determined to drive the French from his homeland and establish a Communist system. Americans then saw the conflict in Vietnam as a battle between communism and anticommunism, one whose outcome would have great bearing on the cold war.

The triumph of communism in China in 1949 heightened America's interest in the war in Vietnam. When American leaders learned that the new People's Republic of China was providing military assistance to the Vietminh, Secretary of State Acheson announced in May 1950 that the United States would make available economic and military aid to the French and their Indo-Chinese allies.

Seven weeks after Acheson's speech, the Communists of North Korea attacked South Korea. As Americans saw the situation, the wars in Korea and Vietnam were parts of the same Moscow-directed "international Communist conspiracy" which aimed to take over the entire world for communism. Over the next three years, despite the demands of the fighting in Korea, the United States managed to ship bombing planes, guns, and other equipment to Indo-China. By 1953 America was shouldering more than a third of the cost of the war against Ho and his followers.

To attract non-Communist nationalists away from the Vietminh, the French had proclaimed in 1949 that Vietnam, Laos, and Cambodia were "associated states" within the French Union— or empire. Each would be independent in domestic matters, but the French would manage their military and foreign affairs. In Vietnam the former emperor, Bao Dai, became the head of the State of Vietnam. The maneuver had little effect on the attitudes of Vietnam's non-Communists. Most of them had little faith in French pledges and little use for Bao Dai. As for the fighting war, the French concentrated on holding a chain of forts across the country. It was no use. Relying on guerrilla tactics, the Vietminh gained control of the countryside and defeated the French at point after point. By 1952-53, it was clear that the French were losing the war. Still, the government in Paris continued to pour men and equipment into the steaming jungles and swamps of Vietnam.

Fall of Dien Bien Phu

In early 1954 the Vietminh trapped a large French force inside the fortress of Dien Bien Phu. As the battle took shape, it came to have tremendous psychological importance. Within a short time it was evident that if Dien Bien Phu fell, the morale of the French — in France, not in Vietnam — would crack. The government in Paris would then be ready for a settlement on terms favorable to the Vietminh. The siege of Dien Bien Phu continued, week after dreary week.

President Eisenhower in early April 1954 compared the countries in Indo-China and Southeast Asia to a row of dominoes: if the Communists knocked over Vietnam, the other countries — Laos, Cambodia, Thailand, Malaya, Indonesia, the Philippines — would fall, one by one, under Communist domination. If communism gained control of Southeast Asia's great material and human resources, the "international Communist conspiracy" would be strengthened immeasurably. Next came the big question: should the United States, as it had done in Korea, intervene with armed forces to save Vietnam from communism? Despite the unpopularity in America of the war in Korea, Eisenhower gave serious thought to the possibility of a similar intervention in Vietnam. If the British had indicated a willingness to join, he might have issued the necessary orders. But the British would have no part of the war, so he decided to do nothing. Thus, on May 7, 1954, Dien Bien Phu's twelve-thousand-man garrison surrendered to the Vietminh.

Even before the fall of Dien Bien Phu, representatives of several countries, including the United States, the Soviet Union, Great Britain, France, and "Red" China had gathered in Geneva to consider problems left over from the war in Korea and arising from the current situation in Indo-China. The French had no intention of handing Vietnam over to the Communists. They still had a strong army in the field in Vietnam and continued to control large areas of the country. Many Vietnamese, the French knew, feared and despised the Communists. What the French were aiming for, given some support from the West, was a division of the country into two parts, one Communist, the other non-Communist.

The Vietminh, drained by eight years of war, were agreeable to a partitioning agreement, especially with a provision that two years later elections would be held across Vietnam to determine a basis for unification. Because of Ho Chi Minh's stature as a national hero in the country, and also because of their superior organizational abilities, the Communists were confident they would be able to dominate any nationwide elections and take absolute control of the country.

The Geneva Agreement of 1954

The outcome of the conference was the Geneva Agreement of July 1954. Under terms of the agreement the combatants agreed to a cease-fire in Vietnam. Ho Chi Minh and his Communists would withdraw to the north of the seventeenth parallel; the French and their non-Communist Vietnamese allies would withdraw to the south of that line. For a period of three hundred days there would be freedom of movement for all persons wishing to move from one section to the other. (Eighty percent of the subsequent movement was from the Communist north to the south.) Overseeing the movement of people and transfer of military forces, and also supervising the cease-fire, would be an International Control Commission made up of representatives of Canada, India, and Poland. After two years, in July 1956, there would be elections throughout Vietman to determine a basis for the country's reunification. Finally, the Geneva settlement provided for the independence of Laos and Cambodia.

Ho Chi Minh and the Communists looked on the Geneva arrangement as a great victory. All they had to do, they thought, was mark time for two years until the democratic process of elections delivered all of Vietnam to their control. They were unduly optimistic. While the members of the conference were hammering out the Geneva settlement, the French, in June 1954, had granted full independence to Bao Dai's State of Vietnam in the southern half of the country. At the same time an honest and capable Vietnamese patriot, Ngo Dinh Diem, became premier of Bao Dai's government in Saigon.

Diem was determined to do everything within his power to prevent a Communist take-over of the non-Communist part of the country—South Vietnam. The intentions of Diem and the Saigon government were made doubly clear in July 1954 when South Vietnam's representatives refused to put their signatures on the Geneva Agreement. This meant that South Vietnam felt no obligation to honor the settlement, particularly the provision concerning elections in 1956.

The United States continued to believe in Eisenhower's "domino theory" and also continued to view Southeast Asia as an area of immeasurable importance in cold war calculations. The government in Washington set about doing what it could to prevent the remainder of the area, including South Vietnam, from falling to communism. A first step came when the United States, like South Vietnam, refused to sign the Geneva Agreement. Although the American representative pledged that his government would respect the settlement, the United States was not committed to carrying out its terms, thus leaving as much room for maneuver as possible.

Southeast Asia
Treaty Organization

The United States prepared to build a Southeast Asia military alliance. The outcome, in September 1954, was the Manila Pact creating the Southeast Asia Treaty Organization (SEATO). Signers of the pact included the United States, Great Britain, France, Australia, New Zealand, the Philippines, Pakistan, and Thailand. In the event of an attack on any of the members, or an attack on South Vietnam, Laos, or Cambodia, the attack would be considered a threat to the security of all. Each member would then act to meet the common danger in accord with its constitutional processes. In the event of aggression through subversion, the parties agreed to consult one another and agree on common measures to meet the problem.

SEATO had serious shortcomings. It never became the powerful instrument for containing Communist power that NATO had become in Europe. Unlike NATO, it did not have a unified command or joint armed forces. Most of the countries of Southeast Asia and the surrounding area—Burma, Indonesia, India, Ceylon—stayed out of the SEATO alliance in their pursuit of neutrality between East and West. Thailand and the Philippines were the only members of the

alliance located in the vicinity of Southeast Asia. Still, the Manila Pact was a warning to Communists that the United States felt it had a stake in Southeast Asia. And SEATO offered the non-Communist countries of Southeast Asia some assurance of support by the United States.

Diem's Regime

Diem was America's man in Vietnam through the 1950s. He was born in 1901, a member of a family of respected civil servants. Educated mostly in French schools in Vietnam, he was essentially French in outlook and was a Roman Catholic. He entered the French civil service in Vietnam and achieved the highest positions permitted to a Vietnamese. Still, he remained a Vietnamese patriot. In the 1930s, when he concluded that the French would never grant independence to Vietnam, he resigned his position. For the next two decades he worked to free his homeland of colonialism.

Hotly opposed to communism, Diem turned aside offers from Ho Chi Minh and refused to have any connection with Bao Dai's regime, which he considered a French puppet. When Diem became premier of South Vietnam, in 1954, most American observers were pleased. He was a legitimate Vietnamese patriot, was honest, and seemed determined to improve the lot of the ordinary people of his country.

Whatever Diem's qualities, the chances of South Vietnam's survival did not appear bright in 1954. The country's army was weak and the Saigon government did not have strong popular support. Within a year, however, Diem managed to gain effective military and political control over most of South Vietnam. In the autumn of 1955 Diem arranged a national election to decide whether he or Bao Dai would be head of state. Diem won ninety-eight percent of the votes, whereupon he proclaimed South Vietnam a republic with himself as its first president. (Without much supporting evidence, Diem's critics charged that the election had been rigged. They contended that in an honest election Diem could not possibly have won by such an overwhelming majority over Bao Dai.)

The following year, 1956, was scheduled, according to the Geneva settlement of 1954, for the elections to determine the basis for reunification of the country. As 1956 approached, the Communists felt confident of winning the elections and began to demand that they be held. In North Vietnam the Communists had absolute control and could manage a nearly solid vote for their side. In South Vietnam, where many people looked on Ho Chi Minh as a national liberator, they could be sure of a fair percentage of the total vote. The vote of the north plus part of the vote of the south would guarantee a victory. Diem, of course, understood the Vietnam election arithmetic. Urged on by the United States, he refused to consider elections in his part of the country.

Critics of America's policies in Vietnam in subsequent years repeatedly condemned the failure of the United States to insist on elections in Vietnam in 1956. Defenders of the American position argued that the Communists in North Vietnam clearly had no intention of allowing free organization of political parties and free electioneering in their part of the country. Hence, they said, an election would have been a mockery of the democratic process.

Meanwhile Diem, whose regime was neither a democracy nor a tyranny, continued to strengthen his authority and broaden his popular support.

With American assistance, he also reformed and reequipped the South Vietnamese army and made the national police force an effective organization. Economic and technical problems proved more complicated, but with American help Diem was making headway in those areas by the latter 1950s.

North Vietnam felt cheated of the rightful fruits of the victory over the French when the 1956 elections did not take place. The Communists of course had not honored their part of the Geneva settlement. Contrary to their pledge, they had not removed all of their military personnel and equipment from the south of Vietnam. Instead they had left behind as many as fifty thousand military men and political commissars to organize guerrilla activities. They had also hidden quantities of arms and ammunition to be used in the event that the elections of 1956 did not come off or if the elections failed to deliver all of Vietnam to communism. Likewise, the Communists had broken their pledge to grant freedom of movement for three hundred days

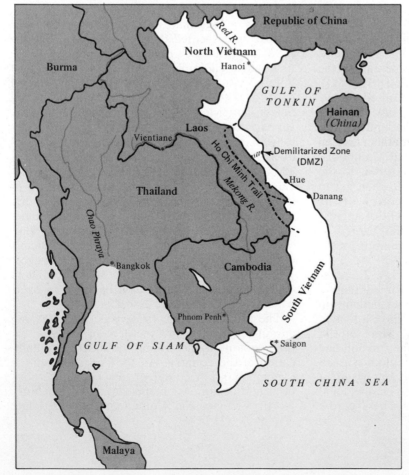

SOUTHEAST ASIA IN THE 1950s

Use this map to locate events which took place in Southeast Asia during the 1940s and 1950s. Note that in 1954 Vietnam was divided into two countries along the Demilitarized Zone, or DMZ, by the terms of the Geneva Agreement. The country remained divided until 1975.

after the cease-fire to anyone in the north of Vietnam who wanted to migrate to the south.

In the years after 1954 the Communists set about consolidating their authority in North Vietnam. To that end they followed conventional Communist tactics of terror, forced confessions, and midnight arrests. Some observers have estimated that during the 1950s Ho Chi Minh's execution squads killed as many as a hundred thousand people. At the same time virtually every citizen above the age of six was compelled to enroll in a Communist cell. These cells conducted indoctrination sessions and urged members to report on individuals, even parents, who were guilty of "reactionary" thought or actions. The press and schools came under rigid government control. "Intellectuals" who criticized the regime were forced to make public apologies or were sent off to forced labor battalions.

When the elections scheduled for 1956 failed to take place, the Communists nonetheless felt confident that Diem's regime in Saigon would fall because of its own lack of competence. By the year 1958, however, it seemed clear that Diem was still gaining popular support across South Vietnam, in part because of some modest attempts at economic and social reform.

Then the Communists switched tactics. Instead of sitting by and waiting for Diem's government to topple, they determined to give it a vigorous shove. So they launched a guerrilla campaign to undermine Diem's authority. The campaign included terrorist attacks against civilians, particularly in the villages. At the same time they set out to wreck Diem's program of land reform. The efforts of the "Viet Cong"—a term of contempt applied to the guerrillas by Diem—were effective. As the decade of the 1950s came to a close, increasing numbers of people in South Vietnam were giving aid and comfort to the Communists. Some of them were moved by promises of a better life under communism. Many more of them were demoralized by failure of the government in Saigon to protect them from Viet Cong attacks.

Diem did not respond by accelerating his program of domestic reform and enlarging the democratic base of his government. On the contrary, he turned to the tactics of repression. Such tactics were an ill omen for South Vietnam.

STUDY GUIDE: In 1949 Chiang Kai-shek and his Nationalist followers fled the China mainland and set up a government on Taiwan (Formosa). During the Korean War, Truman ordered the Seventh Fleet to patrol the Formosa Straits to prevent attack on Taiwan from the Chinese mainland. The fleet was also to prevent Chiang from attacking the mainland.

After his election, Eisenhower told Congress that the Seventh Fleet would no longer restrain Chiang. To guard against a Communist attack on Taiwan, the United States and Chiang signed a mutual defense treaty. Chiang allowed the United States to establish bases in territory under his control.

In 1955 the Communist Chinese began threatening the small Nationalist-held islands of Quemoy and Matsu. Eisenhower asked for the Formosa Resolution. That resolution gave him power to use force to defend Quemoy and Matsu as well as Formosa, the Pescadores, and other islands.

In 1958 the Red Chinese began a continuous shelling of Quemoy and Matsu. Eisenhower sent American ships to the area. He also stepped up the flow of supplies to Chiang. Throughout the 1950s the United States refused to grant diplomatic recognition to the Chinese government in Peking.

France hoped to restore its colonial power in French Indo-China after World War II. But nationalist groups wanted independence. Shortly before the end of the war, Japan had made Emperor Bao Dai head of the Vietnamese government. Ho Chi Minh denounced Bao Dai as a puppet of Japan. When Bao Dai abdicated, Ho set up the Democratic Republic of Vietnam with its capital in Hanoi.

The French recognized Ho's regime in North Vietnam as a free state within the French empire. But in 1946 a civil war broke out. In 1949 France proclaimed Vietnam, Laos, and Cambodia as associated states within the French Union. Bao Dai became head of the State of Vietnam.

By 1952-53 the French were losing their struggle to hold Vietnam. They were opposed by the Vietminh—anti-French Vietnamese patriots, some of whom were Communists. In 1954 the Vietminh trapped a large French force inside the fortress of Dien Bien Phu. After many weeks, the French garrison surrendered.

As a result of the Geneva Agreement of 1954, Vietnam was divided into two parts. Ho Chi Minh and the Communists were to withdraw north of the seventeenth parallel.

The French and non-Communist Vietnamese were to withdraw south of the line. Elections were to be held in 1956 to determine a basis for reunification of the country.

The United States continued to believe in the "domino theory"—that the nations of Indo-China and Southeast Asia would fall like a row of dominoes if the Communists knocked over Vietnam. This was one of the reasons why the United States became involved in Vietnam.

In 1954 the Manila Pact was signed, creating the Southeast Asia Treaty Organization (SEATO). The signers agreed that an attack on any member or on South Vietnam, Laos, or Cambodia would be considered a threat to the security of all. Most of the Southeast Asian nations stayed out of SEATO.

Ngo Dinh Diem became premier of South Vietnam in 1954. Elections were held in 1955. Diem won most of the votes. He then proclaimed South Vietnam a republic with himself as president. Elections were scheduled for 1956 to determine the basis for reunification of the country. Urged on by the United States, Diem refused to consider elections in his part of the country. The North Vietnamese felt cheated when the elections did not take place.

The North Vietnamese had left military personnel and equipment in South Vietnam. They had hidden arms and ammunition to use if the elections failed to deliver Vietnam to the Communists.

By 1958 Diem's regime showed no signs of toppling. The Communists launched a guerrilla campaign to undermine Diem's authority. The guerrillas (called "Viet Cong") were effective. The South Vietnamese became discouraged by failure of the Saigon government to protect them from the Viet Cong. Diem turned to tactics of repression. He did not offer domestic reforms to the people of South Vietnam.

EISENHOWER AND LATIN AMERICA

As in the latter 1940s, the attention of the United States remained riveted on Europe, East Asia, and the Middle East in the early 1950s. Leaders in Washington felt the outcome of the cold war would be determined in these areas. Latin America continued to be an area of secondary impor-

tance in the estimate of the United States. This was apparent in the year 1952 when the government allocated $75 million for foreign aid to Latin America and nearly $6 billion to the rest of the world. Still, American leaders understood that Latin America—a vast area of poverty, illiteracy, and political corruption—provided a classic seedbed for Communist ideas.

When Dwight D. Eisenhower took the presidency in 1953, he decided to take a closer look at the problems of Latin America. In the summer of that year he sent his brother, Milton Eisenhower, a university president, on a "fact-finding" mission to the area.

After visiting ten countries, Milton Eisenhower reported that conditions were worsening in Latin America. What Latin America needed, he thought, was a massive injection of foreign capital. Private investors in North America and Europe were an obvious source of such capital. The president's brother concluded that the governments of Latin America needed to bring an atmosphere of tranquillity and stability to their countries in order to attract outside investors. At the same time, he said, the United States government could stimulate the flow of capital to Latin America by easing tax liabilities of North American companies doing business "south of the border." It could also grant long-term development loans to Latin American governments.

Milton Eisenhower's formula for regenerating Latin America remained more promise than fulfillment. Latin America's governments proved unable to create the kind of business climate that would attract private capital and foreign aid. When measured against Latin America's needs, the increase in business and aid was a mere trickle. And so Latin America continued to languish—and of course remained a fertile ground for communism.

The Threat of Communism

The threat of communism in Latin America became a grim reality in the early 1950s when Communists infiltrated the government of Guatemala. Using tactics of intimidation and even murder, they took over key positions and gained effective control of the government. The Communist-dominated government set in motion a program of social reform. It also took over property of the American-owned United Fruit Company and distributed the company's land to peasants.

To counter the Communist threat in Guatemala, the United States persuaded the Organization of American States (OAS) to approve a resolution condemning the control of any government in the Western Hemisphere "by the International Communist movement." More important, the United States, through its Central Intelligence Agency, encouraged Guatemalan exiles in neighboring Honduras to develop plans to return and take over the government of their homeland. The exiles mounted their "invasion" in mid-June 1954 with three old American-built F-51 Mustang fighter-bombers. The main value of these planes was their psychological effect on the people, but two of them were lost in the first days of the operation. The chief of the CIA told Eisenhower that if the United States did not replace the lost aircraft the chances of the exiles were "about zero." The president ordered immediate delivery of aircraft, and the exile movement continued. At that point the Guatemalan army, which felt no sympathy with communism, would not defend the government. The Communist-oriented government collapsed.

After helping Guatemala get rid of its Communist rulers, the government in Washington continued to be concerned over conditions and events in Latin America. Everywhere in Latin America the population was increasing more rapidly than were agricultural and industrial output. In most countries reactionary military dictatorships were opposed to any meaningful social reform to eliminate poverty and despair. The result was widespread unrest, frequent outbursts of violence, and occasional revolution—as in Argentina in 1955 when rebels ousted the dictator Juan Perón. Frequently attempts at reform met with vigorous repression by authorities. American leaders concluded that it was necessary to break the cycle of poverty–unrest–violence–repression–more poverty–more violence. Otherwise, the Communists would eventually ride Latin America's misery to victory, just as they had done in China.

To meet Latin America's problems the United States might have inaugurated a great program of economic assistance to Latin America—a new "Marshall Plan." It might have denounced the tactics of Latin America's dictators and used its influence to promote democracy. It did neither of those things. By the mid-1950s great numbers of Americans had decided that economic aid to foreign countries was nothing more than a "giveaway." Hence Congress would not approve a program of massive economic assistance to

Compix

On his 1958 goodwill tour of Latin America, Vice President Richard Nixon was met by hostile crowds everywhere. In Lima, Peru, he hurries to his car after being hit by a stone. What U.S. policy toward Latin America caused this reaction to Nixon?

Latin America. As for trying to advance democracy, America's leaders were quite content to tolerate Latin America's dictators so long as they opposed communism.

In the spring of 1958 President Eisenhower sent Vice-President Nixon on a "goodwill tour" of Latin America. The trip turned into a nightmare. In Uruguay, Argentina, Paraguay, Peru, and Venezuela the vice-president was jeered and heckled by leftist students and some working people.

The people of the United States were shocked and outraged. They were also frightened. As a result, in 1959 Congress voted increased funds for economic assistance to Latin America, although not nearly enough to make a significant impact. The Eisenhower administration also took new steps to encourage private investment "south of the border." This renewed interest found a favorable response, as was indicated when President Eisenhower toured the area in early 1960. He was warmly received in virtually every city he visited.

Castro and Cuba

Meanwhile, in January 1959, Fidel Castro took over in Cuba.

As an independent nation after the Spanish-American War in 1898, Cuba had enjoyed a higher level of prosperity than had most countries of Latin America. It was a tourist mecca, and it was able to dispose of much of its sugar

THE
1950s

After World War II the United States quickly adjusted to peacetime conditions. Vast changes in the American way of life took place in the 1950s. Dwight D. Eisenhower was elected president in 1952 and 1956. His administrations dominated the decade. His domestic policy included a program for internal improvements. In foreign affairs he advocated aid to countries threatened by Communist influence.

1

Alaska Pictorial Service

2

1

This portrait of President Eisenhower was painted by Thomas Stephens, an American artist.

2

In 1959, Alaska became the forty-ninth state to be admitted to the Union. It is the largest state, and its industries include fishing, mining, and fur trapping. This is a view of Glacier Bay National Monument in southeastern Alaska.

3

One of the most important events of the 1950s was the successful initiation of the United States space program. The first American earth satellites were launched early in 1958. One of these, *Vanguard 1,* is shown here as it lifted off Cape Canaveral on March 17. Its mission was to make measurements of the earth and its atmosphere.

4

Dr. Martin Luther King, Jr., rose to national prominence in 1955 as leader of a nonviolent bus boycott in Montgomery, Alabama. Two years later, when the Southern Christian Leadership Conference (SCLC) was formed to campaign for civil rights through boycotts and other peaceful means, King was chosen to head it. This photograph was made during a protest which took place several years later in Selma, Alabama.

5

Hawaii was the fiftieth state to join the Union. Its fine climate and scenery make it a favorite vacation spot.

5
Courtesy Hawaii Visitors Bureau

4
Bob Adelman for Magnum

3 NASA

crop and cigar output in the United States. Compared with its rich neighbor to the north, of course, it was a land of poverty and backwardness. Hampering Cuba's economic development were periodic political turmoil, corrupt dictators, and repression of opposing views. In the estimate of Cubans, the island's economic growth also had been retarded by meddling—or the threat of meddling—by the government in Washington. Another obstacle to growth was the fact that much of Cuba's land and industry were owned by North Americans.

Cuba's miseries did not decline in 1952 when Fulgencio Batista seized control of the government. A one-time army sergeant, Batista had dominated Cuba's government off and on since 1933. He did nothing to lighten the burden of the people. He repeatedly put off the elections which he had promised. To keep restlessness from getting out of hand, Batista used the conventional tools of the tyrant: intimidation, torture, and murder. The government in Washington did not approve of Batista's methods. Still, he was keeping order in Cuba and seemed a bulwark against communism in the Caribbean.

Among the Cubans who despised Batista was the son of a wealthy planter and a graduate of the Havana Law School, Fidel Castro. Castro had visions of arranging the downfall of the Batista tyranny and on July 26, 1953, led an attack on army barracks in Santiago in eastern Cuba. The attack failed and its leader landed in jail. Released in 1955, Castro went to Mexico, where he recruited, organized, and trained a small guerrilla force made up mostly of youthful Cubans.

In late 1956 Castro's little band "invaded" Oriente Province in easternmost Cuba. There, operating out of the rugged Sierra Maestra mountains, they mounted guerrilla raids against government installations and organized an anti-Batista "underground" resistance movement in Cuba's cities. This movement employed its own brand of terror tactics against individuals considered to be pro-Batista.

Castro promised sweeping social reforms and democratic government. Such promises won for him the support of most of Cuba's peasants, intellectuals, and students. Batista responded with a campaign of harassment and murder. In addition to failing entirely to eliminate the Castro movement, Batista's terrorism shocked and alienated Cuba's middle class. By mid-1958 he had driven it into the arms of Castro.

The government in Washington, meanwhile, was reassessing its estimate of the Batista regime. This reappraisal stemmed in part from disapproval of Batista's counterrevolutionary tactics. The United States government also suspected that Batista would not be able to resist the revolutionary tide much longer. After an uprising at the Cienfuegos naval base, the Eisenhower administration suspended further arms shipments to the Cuban government in early 1958. At the same time the United States, via the CIA and the FBI, maintained contact with Castro and made little effort to prevent shipment of arms from North America to the Cuban rebel.

Then, rather suddenly, the end came for Batista. By autumn 1958 Castro had won control of the eastern half of Cuba. Batista's army had almost stopped fighting. On January 1, 1959, Batista fled the country. Within a few days Castro, attired in his familiar green fatigue uniform, was parading through the streets of Havana to the cheers of thousands of hysterically happy Cubans.

Most people of the United States were delighted when Batista fell and Castro took power in Havana. Some Batista men were calling Castro a Communist, but North Americans tended to dismiss such charges as the rantings of discredited tyrants. In the view of many Americans Castro in early 1959 was a good-humored patriot who would bring social regeneration and democracy to Cuba.

While not confident of Castro's commitment to democratic principles, leaders of the United States took a hopeful view of the new regime in Havana and tried to establish good relations with it. The government in Washington offered financial assistance to Cuba in early 1959. When Castro visited the American capital in April 1959, Washington leaders showered attention on him.

But then optimism turned to disillusion. First came the "trials" of "criminals" of the Batista era. North Americans were aghast. The accused were hauled into a sports arena in Havana which was packed with cheering Castro partisans. There, in a circus-like atmosphere, "trials" were held. Death before a firing squad was the fate of many. Next Castro set out to nationalize oil refineries, sugar plantations, and other properties owned by foreigners. The government in Washington had no objection to "nationalization," provided the Cubans made "prompt, adequate and effective compensation" to the former owners. The Castro regime soon made it clear that it had no intention of compensating the owners for properties it had seized. At the same time Castro mounted a shrill campaign of anti-Americanism.

By summer 1959 Castro was showing increasing sympathy with Communist ideas. He was purging anti-Communists from his government and enlarging the authority and responsibilities of old-line Cuban Communists. Clearly he had no plans for free elections. He also was becoming increasingly friendly with the Soviet Union. In February 1960 he signed the first of a series of aid and trade agreements with leaders in the Kremlin.

Cuba's drift toward communism seemed especially threatening when Castro announced his determination to export his Communist-style revolution to the other countries of Latin America. In his first six months in power, Castro supported or encouraged revolutionary action against the governments of Panama, Nicaragua, the Dominican Republic, and Haiti. American leaders feared that with support of the Soviet Union he might deliver much of the Western Hemisphere to communism. This would present a threat to the security of the United States.

The United States responded first by cutting back the quota of sugar that Cuba could sell in the United States, then eliminating it altogether. Next, in January 1961, the United States severed diplomatic relations with Castro's government.

The overwhelming view in the United States was that Castro's behavior had forced the United States to sever relations. Many Latin Americans, and also a few critics in the United States, blamed the Eisenhower administration for failing to work out a satisfactory relationship with Castro. There is no reason, however, to believe that the Eisenhower administration at that time hoped for destruction of the new Castro regime. On the contrary, evidence indicates that leaders in Washington viewed the Castro government with a measure of sympathy. Then came Castro's campaign against the United States. Next came the uncompensated nationalization of American-owned properties in Cuba, a step which Castro knew challenged old and strongly held principles in the United States. Then came the drift toward communism and Castro's stated intention to export Communist-style revolution to the rest of Latin America.

In Castro's estimate a drastic revolution was necessary if Cuba was to achieve prosperity and dignity. This revolution would seize foreign property and redistribute the national wealth. It would tolerate no opposition.

Compix

Prime Minister Fidel Castro of Cuba was greeted by Vice President Richard Nixon when he visited Washington, D.C. in 1959.

Castro, then, had little interest in appeasing the United States. Instead he pursued policies which almost seemed calculated to provoke the government in Washington and bring a diplomatic rupture. But what about the North American sugar market? Cuba's economy, after all, rested in large measure on the country's ability to sell much of its sugar crop in the United States. It seems that the Cuban dictator was quite willing to forfeit Cuba's share of the sugar market in the United States. The sugar quota provided an ever-present implement with which the government in Washington could compel Cuba's leaders to behave according to its liking. Loss of the sugar quota would give Castro a new freedom of maneuver. For that reason Cuba's leaders seemed genuinely relieved when the United States first cut back and then eliminated the Cuban quota.

The break with the United States had another attraction for Castro. Open defiance of the "colossus of the north" struck a popular chord in Cuba. It enabled Castro to mobilize behind his regime many patriotic Cubans who on other counts doubted the wisdom of Castroism.

STUDY GUIDE: Eisenhower sent his brother to Latin America in 1953 to examine conditions there. Milton Eisenhower suggested that Latin America needed large amounts of foreign capital. He said the United States government could stimulate the flow of capital there by easing taxes of North American companies doing business in Latin America. But Latin American governments were unable to create the kind of business climate that would attract money from other countries.

In the early 1950s, Communists tried but failed to take over the government of Guatemala.

The United States gave little financial aid to Latin America during the 1950s. In 1958, Vice-President Nixon went on a goodwill tour of Latin America. He was jeered and heckled by leftists in several countries. After the visit, Congress voted increased funds for economic aid to Latin America. In 1960, when Eisenhower toured the area, he was warmly received.

In 1952 Fulgencio Batista seized control of the Cuban government. In 1956, Fidel Castro and some young Cubans began guerrilla raids against installations of the Batista government. In 1958 Eisenhower's administration cut further arms shipments to Cuba. Batista fled from Cuba in 1959. A few days later Castro took power. He soon began showing sympathy with Communist ideas. In 1960 he signed the first of several agreements with Russia.

Castro supported or encouraged revolutionary action in other Latin America nations. Fearing a threat to its security, the United States cut back the amount of sugar that Cuba could sell here. Finally the United States stopped the import of Cuban sugar altogether. In January 1961, the United States broke off diplomatic relations with Castro.

OTHER HIGHLIGHTS

Despite recessions in 1953-54 and 1957-58, the years 1950-59 were a period of prosperity for most Americans. The 1950s were so prosperous that some thoughtful people felt that Americans were too intent upon their private search for wealth. These thoughtful Americans feared that the people of the country were overlooking such serious public problems as urban decay and civil rights. This sentiment received its most eloquent expression in John Kenneth Galbraith's best-selling book, *The Affluent Society,* published in 1958. Other observers of the American scene in the prosperous 1950s included William H.

Whyte, Jr., whose popular book *The Organization Man* appeared in 1956. Whyte believed that Americans were putting aside their faith in individual initiative and instead emphasizing the group or organization as the main source of creativity. The outcome, Whyte and others believed, was the willingness on the part of the individual in America to subordinate himself to the wishes, demands, and ethics of the group.

The years 1950-59 were a period of continuing population growth and business expansion, a time when Americans continued to move from the countryside to the city and from the "inner city" to the suburb. It was a time of increasing mechanization and automation in industry with resultant concern over technological unemployment. There was an ever-increasing array of electronic devices, particularly computers.

The most publicized achievement in the field of medical research came in 1955. In that year Dr. Jonas Salk introduced the vaccine that in a few years would make polio, once a scourge, particularly for children, almost unknown in America.

The people of the United States throughout the 1950s continued their love affair with the automobile. As a result of prosperity the number of families with more than one car increased steadily. The growing congestion of streets and highways and freeways, however, was persuading increasing numbers of Americans to try one of the new "compacts."

Increasing numbers of Americans turned to the airlines. When the Boeing Company introduced its 707 jetliner in 1958, the age of air travel in America and the world had unquestionably arrived. The engines of the 707 could propel the $6 million craft through the sky at a speed in excess of five hundred miles an hour—from New York to Los Angeles in four hours. Meanwhile, many famous passenger trains disappeared from the country's railways, and diesel engines replaced steam locomotives.

Americans in the 1950s consumed increasing quantities of beer, wine, and liquor. They smoked billions of cigarettes each year, although new statistical evidence linked cigarette smoking with lung cancer. The 1950s were the period of "rock and roll" music, the era of Elvis Presley. They were also the decade in which television triumphed over the movie theater as the main source of entertainment for Americans.

In professional sports the 1950s were the era of the New York *Yankees,* Cleveland *Browns,* and Boston *Celtics,* the heyday of Mickey Mantle and Willie Mays in baseball, Otto Graham in football, Bob Cousey in basketball, Rocky Marciano and Floyd Patterson in boxing, Sam Snead and Ben Hogan in golf, Bill Vukovich and Tony Bettenhausen in auto racing. They were the time when the Brooklyn *Dodgers* and New York *Giants* pulled up stakes and moved westward to Los Angeles and San Francisco respectively.

The 1950s saw increasing numbers of young people entering college, thus continuing a trend begun at the end of World War II. A smaller percentage of the youthful population was dropping out of school, although the high school dropout became the subject of growing concern during the decade. The '50s were an era in which Americans exalted the achievements of the scientist and engineer.

The 1950s were the era of Dwight D: Eisenhower and the Democratic party. Eisenhower was the most popular man in American politics in the decade, but he found it impossible to transfer his popularity to the Republican party. As a consequence, the GOP remained a minority party. During the decade the Republicans managed to maintain control of Congress for only two years, 1953-54.

Two political events of the 1950s were particularly important. In September 1955, President Eisenhower suffered a heart attack and was hospitalized for three months. Although he was sixty-five, physicians concluded that he had made a remarkable recovery and would likely be able to meet the demands of the presidency for another four years. He easily defeated his Democratic opponent Adlai E. Stevenson in 1956, but the Democrats managed to keep control of Congress, something they had failed to do back in 1952.

The second important development of the 1950s was the rise to national prominence of a handsome young politician from Massachusetts, John F. Kennedy. Kennedy was an upset winner over Henry Cabot Lodge, Jr., in Massachusett's senatorial election of 1952. He moved to the national spotlight at the Democratic national convention of 1956 in Chicago in a spirited contest against Senator Estes Kefauver of Tennessee for the vice-presidential nomination. Kefauver won, but Kennedy appeared at the speaker's rostrum, smiled, waved, and made a graceful speech in which he congratulated Kefauver and urged Democrats to close ranks behind the ticket. The effect was electric. From that point on, Kennedy seemed a man who was destined for greater things.

The 1950s, at least after the end of the Korean War and the end of Senator Joseph McCarthy, were a relatively calm time for the people of the United States. There were some trouble spots in the world, and it was frustrating when the Soviets put the first earth satellite in orbit. It was also distressing to learn that large numbers of American prisoners-of-war in North Korea had cracked under Communist pressure and collaborated with their captors. But the economy, except for a couple of minor interruptions, hummed along in the 1950s and the cold war went on year after year without breaking into a hot war. Indeed there was increasing confidence among Americans throughout the decade that a nuclear holocaust was unthinkable. The decade of the 1950s was a time when most Americans managed to keep such problems as abuse of racial minorities, urban decay, and poverty in the recesses of their minds. It was a period when there were no serious campus disorders or riots in the cities, a time when most Americans concentrated on making money and living "the good life." Most Americans placed their faith in "Ike" and were inclined to let social problems take care of themselves. However, the 1950s closed on a note of frustration and international tension.

STUDY GUIDE: The 1950s were a time of prosperity for most Americans. There was continuing population growth and business expansion. Americans continued to move to the suburbs. Mechanization and automation continued. There was an increasing use of electronic devices, especially computers. Automobile ownership increased, and highways became more and more crowded.

Rock and roll music was popular in the 1950s. Television became the main source of entertainment. Professional sports gained in popularity. Increasing numbers of young people went to college.

In 1956 Eisenhower again defeated Adlai Stevenson but the Democrats kept control of Congress.

SUMMIT CONFERENCE THAT NEVER WAS

In December 1959 President Eisenhower and the leaders of Great Britain, France, and West

Germany agreed to invite Premier Khrushchev of the Soviet Union to a new summit meeting in Paris the following spring. And while Eisenhower celebrated the arrival of 1960, which would be his last full year in the White House, plans for the meeting were moving forward. At length everything was set, and the president put the final touches on strategy to be employed during his third encounter with the boss of the Soviet empire.

Then it happened. In the first days of May 1960 an American U-2 spy plane, piloted by Francis Gary Powers, was apparently struck by a surface-to-air missile and went down deep inside Soviet territory. Hoping that the pilot had triggered the craft's self-destruction mechanism or that the crash had destroyed evidence of the plane's spy mission, the State Department in Washington issued a "cover story." The story indicated that an American "weather research plane" had strayed over the border perhaps because faulty oxygen equipment had caused the pilot to lose consciousness. Whereupon Khrushchev produced the pilot, who had parachuted to safety, been captured, and confessed the nature of his mission. As further evidence, he produced large chunks of the U-2.

President Eisenhower claimed full responsibility for U-2 flights. He vigorously defended the spy plane program on the ground that "no one wants another Pearl Harbor." A few days later he set out for Paris.

On the morning of May 16 President de Gaulle of France called the opening session of the summit conference to order. Before de Gaulle could finish his introductory remarks, Khrushchev jumped to his feet, demanded the right to speak, and delivered a scalding speech. He demanded that Eisenhower denounce past U-2 flights over Soviet territory, pledge that there would be no flights in the future, and pass "severe judgment" on individuals who had been responsible for violations of Soviet air space. The president promised that there would be no further "overflights" of Soviet territory but refused to apologize for previous flights. At that point Khrushchev stalked from the room. When he failed to show up for the second session of the meeting, the Paris summit conference of 1960 came to an end.

Why did Khrushchev use the U-2 flight as an excuse to break up the summit meeting? After all, he might have refrained from public disclosure of the U-2 incident and quietly warned the Americans that the Soviets had the means

and would shoot down spy planes. Then he could have gone on with the conference as though nothing had happened. Probably the Soviet leader felt that the Paris meeting would not result in any meaningful agreements. Therefore he could not resist using the U-2 incident to humiliate the United States, thus scoring a grand propaganda victory.

Eisenhower returned to a rousing reception in the United States, for most Americans resented the crude treatment which he had endured at the hands of Khrushchev. A few weeks later, the president set out on a goodwill tour of the Western Pacific, only to receive a second humiliation. Japanese leftists, exploiting the U-2 incident, created such disorder that fear was aroused for the safety of the president. Accordingly, Eisenhower's stopover in Japan was canceled.

STUDY GUIDE: In December 1959 Eisenhower and leaders of Britain, France, and West Germany invited Premier Khrushchev to a summit meeting in Paris the following spring. Shortly before the conference, in May 1960, an American U-2 spy plane went down in Soviet territory. At the summit meeting Khrushchev demanded an apology and an end to U-2 flights. When Eisenhower refused the Russians left the meeting room and the summit conference ended.

SUMMING UP THE CHAPTER

Names and Terms to Identify

Syngman Rhee	NASA
Trygve Lie	*Echo I*
Matthew B. Ridgway	Nikita Khrushchev
Panmunjom	Gamal Abdul Nasser
Adlai E. Stevenson	Ho Chi Minh
Atomic Energy Act of 1954	Dien Bien Phu
Sputnik I	Ngo Dinh Diem
Orval Faubus	Viet Cong
Explorer I	Fulgencio Batista

Study Questions and Points to Review

1. What recommendations regarding Korea did the United Nations make in 1947?

2. What action did the UN Security Council take regarding Korea in June 1950? What happened when North Koreans ignored the resolution?

3. Who was the first supreme commander of UN forces for the military operation in Korea?

4. What events in November-December 1950 drastically changed the military situation in Korea?

5. What issue, unresolved by spring 1952, caused the war to drag on for an additional fifteen months?

6. What were two of the major problems confronting President Eisenhower when he took office in 1953?

7. What led to the Army-McCarthy hearings of 1954? What effect did the hearings have on McCarthy?

8. What was the Soil Bank Bill?

9. What position did President Eisenhower take on ownership of offshore lands?

10. Name the legal case in which the Supreme Court made the decision that separate educational facilities are inherently unequal, and that those students in segregated schools were deprived of equal protection of laws guaranteed by the Fourteenth Amendment.

11. What incident caused a crisis in Little Rock, Arkansas in 1957?

12. What organization was created in January 1957 to launch a campaign for Negro rights using methods similar to those used earlier in Montgomery, Alabama?

13. Name the proposal in which major powers would supply each other with complete blueprints of their military establishments and would allow unlimited inspection of their territories by "unarmed peaceful planes." What was Soviet reaction to the proposal?

14. What doctrine was designed to prevent Communists from taking over any governments in the Middle East by providing economic and military aid to those countries?

15. What was the Formosa Resolution?

16. What was Eisenhower's "domino theory"?

17. Name the signers of the SEATO pact.

18. What happened to Vice-President Nixon when he went on a "goodwill tour" of Latin America?

19. When did Fidel Castro take over in Cuba?

20. What incident occurred shortly before the summit meeting in Paris in 1960?

Topics for Discussion

1. Trace the rise and decline of Senator Joseph R. McCarthy. What kind of man was he? What was the nature of the campaign he waged against alleged subversion in America? What was his evidence? Why did many Americans believe in him? What brought his downfall?

2. Why did General Eisenhower choose to seek the presidency in 1952? Why did Adlai E. Stevenson receive the Democratic nomination for president?

What were the main issues of the 1952 campaign? What accounted for Eisenhower's landslide victory?

3. Relying mainly on the cases of *Plessy* v. *Ferguson* and *Brown* v. *Board of Education of Topeka*, describe the main constitutional issues in the controversy over school desegregation. Apart from the constitutional question, why did many white Americans oppose school desegregation and why did black Americans insist on it? What was President Eisenhower's view of the Supreme Court's desegregation decision in 1954? What was the basis for his view?

4. Evaluate Martin Luther King, Jr. What were his origins? What kind of man was he? What accounted for his success as a leader in the civil rights movement in the 1950s?

5. Discuss the policies of the Eisenhower administration toward the Middle East. What were America's principal diplomatic problems in the Middle East in the 1950s?

6. Consider United States relations with China during the 1950s. What were the arguments for and against dealing with Mao Tse-tung's regime in Peking? What were the high points of America's dealings with Chiang Kai-shek during the period?

7. What prompted the creation of the Southeast Asia Treaty Organization. What was the nature of the alliance? How effective was it?

8. What were the major problems which the United States faced in Latin America during the Eisenhower administration? How did Eisenhower meet these problems?

9. Assess the policy of the United States toward Cuba in the years 1953-61. What do you think of United States policy toward the Batista regime? Toward the Castro regime?

Subjects for Reports or Essays

1. Using materials available in your library, write an essay on Senator Joseph McCarthy and "McCarthyism."

2. Investigate the Civil Rights Acts of 1957 and 1960. Compare the two measures and write an evaluation of each.

3. Prepare a report for class presentation on one of the following topics: (a) Eisenhower's "open skies" proposal; (b) Nixon's "Checkers" speech made during the 1952 campaign; (c) Truman's recall of General MacArthur during the Korean War; (d) Eisenhower's handling of the Little Rock crisis of 1957; (e) the U-2 incident of 1960.

4. On the basis of outside reading, write a brief biographical sketch of one of the following: Gamal Abdul Nasser, Mao Tse-tung, Chiang Kai-shek, Ho Chi Minh, Chou En-lai.

5. Write your evaluation of American policy toward French Indo-China during the years 1945-54.

6. Do you agree or disagree with the idea that the United States should have extended diplomatic recognition to the Communist government in China in the 1950s? Write a report setting forth your views.

Projects, Activities, and Skills

1. Conduct a poll among people in your community, including relatives and acquaintances, who were adults during the years 1950-54 when Senator Joseph McCarthy was at the peak of his influence. Ask your interviewees what they can remember about McCarthy and his methods, and what they thought about him and his activities in the early 1950s.

2. Prepare an exhibit on the Korean War. Use maps to show the course of the fighting. Also gather photographs, models, and possibly souvenirs to show the kinds of equipment that were used. Display photographs of some of the major personages, including presidents Truman and Rhee; Kim Il Sung; generals MacArthur, Dean, Walker, Ridgway, Van Fleet, and Clark; and Admiral C. Turner Joy. Write captions briefly describing the part each man played.

3. Prepare a pictorial biography of Dwight D. Eisenhower.

4. Prepare a pictorial biography of Martin Luther King, Jr., from his childhood in Atlanta through his death in 1968.

5. Prepare an exhibit on America's initial leap into outer space. To show the origins of the space program you might include photographs (or models) and specifications of the early German V-1 and V-2 rockets. Also include pictures, models, and data on the Soviet *Sputniks*, as well as similar material on the first rockets and satellites of the United States.

Further Readings

General

Black Bourgeoisie by Franklin E. Frazier. The rise of a new middle class.
The Decline of American Communism by David A. Shannon. The Communist movement in the United States after World War II.
A Generation on Trial: U.S.A. v. Alger Hiss by Alistair Cooke.
Hell in a Very Small Place: The Siege of Dien Bien Phu by Bernard B. Fall.

How Communists Negotiate by C. Turner Joy. A useful study of the Korean truce negotiations.
Korea and the Fall of MacArthur: A Précis in Limited War by Trumball Higgins. A useful study of the Truman-MacArthur controversy.
The Negro Revolt by Louis E. Lomax.
Stride Toward Freedom by Martin Luther King, Jr.
Thud Ridge by Jack Broughton. The Hanoi area in North Vietnam.
Vietnam, a Diplomatic Tragedy: Origins of the United States Involvement by Victor Bator. An early, balanced study of the U.S. commitment to Vietnam.

Biography

In the Court of Public Opinion by Alger Hiss.
John Foster Dulles by John R. Beal.
Manchild in the Promised Land by Claude Brown.
Ordeal by Slander by Owen Lattimore.
Senator Joe McCarthy by Richard H. Rovere.
Soldier by Matthew B. Ridgway. Autobiography.
The White House Years (2 vols.): *Mandate for Change, 1953-1956* and *Waging Peace, 1956-1961* by Dwight D. Eisenhower.
Witness by Whittaker Chambers. An American's account of his years as a Communist, and his side of the Alger Hiss case.

Fiction

Alas, Babylon by Pat Frank. A story about the survivors of a thermonuclear accident that triggered World War III.
The Bridges at Toko-Ri by James Michener. A novel about efforts to destroy Communist supply bridges in Korea.
Fail-Safe by Eugene Burdick and Harvey Wheeler. A modern horror story in which U.S. nuclear bombers threaten to destroy the world.
Ice Palace by Edna Ferber. Epic novel about Alaska.
Invisible Man by Ralph Ellison. The story of a black man seeking his identity.
On the Road by Jack Kerouac. A novel expressing the restless search of the "beat generation" for experience and meaning in the postwar world.
The Spy Who Came in from the Cold by John Le Carré. A realistic novel about cold war espionage.

Pictorial History

This Fabulous Century, 1950-1960, Vol. 6, by the editors of Time-Life Books.

The space program gave Americans a new view of themselves and their planet, but serious problems remained to be solved on earth. This photograph of the earth rising above the horizon of the moon was made during the flight of *Apollo 11* in 1968.

7
THE RECENT PAST

CHAPTER 20

THE KENNEDY-JOHNSON YEARS

IN THE SPRING OF 1960, the people of the United States were keeping watch on a spirited contest for the Democratic party's nomination for president. Eisenhower had easily won election to the two presidential terms allowed him by law, defeating Adlai E. Stevenson in the elections of 1952 and 1956. The election of 1960 seemed to offer the Democrats an excellent chance to win a presidential election. There were several contenders for the Democratic nomination.

THE ELECTION OF 1960

At the beginning of election year 1960 the most talked-about contender for the Democratic party's nomination for president was the wealthy young senator from Massachusetts, John F. Kennedy. Still, Kennedy's nomination seemed far from certain, for the youthful legislator was burdened with several handicaps. Among those handicaps was his age. Many Americans felt that Kennedy, at forty-two, was too young and inexperienced to meet presidential responsibilities. There was also the coolness which a number of "old pros" of the Democratic party felt toward his candidacy. Moreover, he was a Roman Catholic and certain to have the opposition of those Protestants who shuddered at the prospect of a Catholic occupying the White House.

Kennedy entered his name on the ballots of seven states that would hold primary elections to choose convention delegates. His first major primary test came in Wisconsin, where he was opposed by Senator Hubert H. Humphrey of Minnesota. Following a heavily financed campaign, Kennedy won a plurality of votes in the Badger State. Then he turned to West Virginia, a state in which barely two percent of the population was Catholic. Hence it afforded him a chance to prove that he could win in an overwhelmingly Protestant area. Again opposed by Humphrey, Kennedy scored a resounding victory, whereupon the senator from Minnesota withdrew from the contest.

After the balloting in West Virginia, Kennedy was left with one principal opponent, Lyndon B. Johnson of Texas, the dynamic majority leader of the Senate. Johnson had secured pledges of a solid core of convention votes from southern states and was campaigning furiously. But he was able to generate little support outside the South. Kennedy clearly seemed to be the Democrat most apt to defeat the Republican standard-bearer in the election in November. Thus he won the nomination on the first ballot at the national convention in Los Angeles. Then, in a move which stunned people everywhere and angered many of his liberal followers, Kennedy designated Johnson as his vice-presidential running mate.

A short time later, the Republicans assembled in Chicago and nominated Vice-President Nixon for president. Henry Cabot Lodge, Jr., was chosen for his running mate as vice-president.

When the presidential campaign opened, public opinion polls showed that Nixon held a substantial lead. He was able to claim that his eight years in the vice-presidency had given him experience in the executive branch of the government which Kennedy could not match. But Nixon had committed himself to a series of television debates with his rival. During four confrontations Kennedy, in addition to projecting a better image, demonstrated that he was as well informed about affairs of state as Nixon was. He severely weakened the vice-president's arguments regarding his experience.

Meanwhile Lyndon Johnson was moving through the southern states, where Kennedy had generated little enthusiasm. Johnson was persuading great numbers of white southerners that a Kennedy-Johnson victory would be in their interest. The outcome? In popular balloting Kennedy and Johnson edged Nixon and Lodge by barely 100,000 popular votes out of more than 68,000,000. In the electoral college the margin of the Democratic ticket was 303-219.

STUDY GUIDE: John F. Kennedy won the presidential nomination on the first ballot at the Democratic national convention. He requested Lyndon B. Johnson as his vice-presidential

HEADLINE
EVENTS

1960 Twenty-third Amendment ratified
First sit-in demonstrations in the South
Kennedy-Nixon television debates
1961 John F. Kennedy inaugurated president
Kennedy revives Food for Peace program
and organizes the Peace Corps
Kennedy proposes Alliance for Progress
Bay of Pigs invasion
Alan Shepard launched in *Freedom 7*
Kennedy and Khrushchev meet in Vienna
Berlin Wall constructed
Freedom rides in the South
1962 Twenty-fourth Amendment ratified
John Glenn orbits the earth aboard *Friendship 7*
Mariner 2 Venus probe launched
Kennedy federalizes Mississippi national
guard when governor refuses to let James
Meredith enter the state university
Kennedy announces that the Soviets are
placing ballistic missile bases in Cuba;
naval blockade of Cuba begins
Khrushchev offers to remove Soviet weapons from Cuba
Cesar Chavez organizes National Farm
Workers Association (NFW)
Rachel Carson's *Silent Spring* published
1963 Racial trouble in Birmingham; Kennedy
federalizes Alabama national guard
NAACP director Medgar Evers murdered
Kennedy sends new civil rights legislation
to Congress
"Hot line" connects Washington and Moscow
March on Washington
Nuclear test ban treaty signed
Kennedy assassinated; Vice-President Lyndon B. Johnson succeeds to presidency
1964 Johnson signs tax cut bill
Civil Rights Act of 1964
National Defense Education Act extended
Gulf of Tonkin resolution passed
Office of Economic Opportunity created
Johnson wins reelection by a landslide

1965 Johnson inaugurated for a second term
Dr. Martin Luther King, Jr., leads voter registration drive in Selma, Alabama
Voting Rights Act
Antipoverty measures to improve roads and
stimulate industry in Appalachia
Water Quality Act; Federal Water Pollution
Control Administration created (FWPCA)
Elementary and Secondary Education Act
(ESEA)
Department of Housing and Urban Development created; Robert E. Weaver is first
black cabinet member
King-Anderson bill (Medicare) signed
Riots in Watts, California
Johnson sends troops to put down rebellion
in the Dominican Republic
1966 Edward W. Brooke of Massachusetts is
elected first black senator since Reconstruction
Department of Transportation created
Black militancy increases: Stokely Carmichael and Floyd McKissick reject policy
of nonviolence; Huey P. Newton and
Bobby Seale organize the Black Panthers
Betty Friedan founds National Organization
for Women (NOW)
1967 Antiwar sentiment grows
First human heart transplants
Rioting in 75 American cities
Thurgood Marshall becomes first black
Supreme Court justice
Twenty-fifth Amendment ratified
1968 Shirley Chisholm of New York is elected first
black congresswoman
President Johnson's Kerner Commission
Report blames riots on poverty
Poor People's March on Washington
Pueblo incident
Tet offensive
Dr. Martin Luther King, Jr., assassinated
Senator Robert Kennedy assassinated
Richard M. Nixon defeats Vice-President
Hubert Humphrey in presidential election

John F. Kennedy and Richard M.Nixon engaged in four debates during the 1960 presidential campaign. How did these debates disprove Nixon's charges that Kennedy lacked experience?

running mate. During the campaign, Kennedy and Republican candidate Richard M. Nixon met in a series of television debates. Kennedy won the election by a narrow margin of barely 100,000 popular votes. At forty-three, he was the youngest man to be elected to the presidency. He was also the first Roman Catholic to hold the position.

JOHN F. KENNEDY

John Fitzgerald Kennedy was born in Brookline, Massachusetts in May 1917. He grew up as a member of a closely knit and very wealthy family. After graduating from the Choate preparatory school in Connecticut, he entered Harvard University.

During his junior year at Harvard, Kennedy spent a semester traveling in Europe. Because his father, Joseph P. Kennedy, was ambassador to Great Britain, young Kennedy was able to use American embassies as stopping-off places and observation points. Shortly after he returned to America, World War II broke out. Drawing largely on his recent observations, he wrote a senior thesis which analyzed British and French appeasement of Hitler during the Czech crisis of 1938. The thesis received such praise from Harvard faculty members that the twenty-three-year-old Kennedy decided to expand it for publication as a book. The book, entitled *Why England Slept,* won considerable acclaim from critics.

Kennedy graduated from Harvard with honors

in 1940 and enlisted in the navy in 1941. By summer 1943 he was in command of a PT boat operating in waters around the Solomon Islands in the Southwest Pacific. On the night of August 2, 1943, his boat, PT-109, was struck amidships by a Japanese destroyer. Two crewmen were killed immediately. Kennedy swam from island to island until he found friendly natives. They delivered to an American base a coconut on which he had carved a message explaining that he and his men were awaiting rescue. For his heroism Kennedy received the Navy and Marine Corps Medal.

After his service in the navy, in 1945 Kennedy covered the founding of the United Nations at the San Francisco Conference and the British elections as a reporter for the Hearst newspapers. In 1946, he decided to enter politics and won nomination as the Democratic candidate for the House of Representatives from the Eleventh District of Massachusetts. He easily defeated his Republican opponent. Reelected in 1948 and 1950, he decided in 1952 to run for the Senate. In a major upset, he defeated the popular incumbent, Henry Cabot Lodge, Jr.

A short time after entering the Senate Kennedy married Jacqueline Bouvier, an attractive and socially prominent young lady whom he had met two years earlier, while she was a photographer for a Washington newspaper. The following year brought near-tragedy. Suffering severe pain in his back, the result of an old injury, Kennedy submitted to delicate surgery which took him to the edge of death. While recuperating he wrote *Profiles in Courage,* a collection of biographical sketches of United States senators who had displayed unusual courage. The book, a best-seller, won a Pulitzer Prize for biography.

In 1956, Kennedy achieved national prominence when he nearly won the nomination for vice-president at the Democratic national convention. Two years later, in 1958, he won reelection to the Senate by the largest plurality ever given a candidate in Massachusetts. In 1960 came the election to the presidency.

In the weeks after the election Kennedy assembled his new administration. Then came inauguration day, January 20, 1961. After attending Mass and, with Mrs. Kennedy, making a ceremonial call on President and Mrs. Eisenhower at the White House, the president-elect and outgoing president made the traditional drive up Pennsylvania Avenue to the Capitol.

After the swearing-in ceremony Kennedy delivered a stirring inaugural. Declared the new chief executive: "Let the word go forth from this time and place, to friend and foe alike, that the torch has been passed to a new generation of Americans, born in this century, tempered by war, disciplined by a hard and bitter peace, proud of our ancient heritage, and unwilling to witness or permit the slow undoing of those human rights to which this nation has always been committed, and to which we are committed today at home and around the world." He appealed to his fellow Americans: "Ask not what your country can do for you – ask what you can do for your country."

Thus began a presidential administration which would last for 1,036 days.

The New Frontier

When Kennedy entered the White House the country was in the midst of an economic recession. To stimulate economic activity and provide relief for victims of recession distress he took a variety of steps. The most important was a proposal authorizing grants and loans to communities which faced persistent economic difficulty and providing funds for vocational retraining of people who were unemployed. It was approved by Congress in 1961 under the title of the Area Redevelopment Act.

The economy seemed to respond to Kennedy's remedies, but in summer 1962 a new recession threatened. The president again moved to the attack, this time concentrating on assorted benefits; notably in the areas of taxes and credit, which were designed to generate business activity. The latter acts did much to persuade businessmen that Kennedy was not antibusiness. The previous spring he had denounced leaders of the steel industry for raising the price of steel, giving rise to the impression that he was hostile to big business.

Businessmen were encouraged again in 1962 when the president approved the Communications Satellite Act over strong objection by Democratic liberals in Congress. By this legislation the federal government chartered a privately owned corporation to operate the Telstar communications satellite system.

While he was taking action against the economic recession, Kennedy was also working in behalf of trade expansion and trying to deal with America's continuing farm problem.

The trade expansion program grew out of Kennedy's determination to come to grips with the increasing imbalance of America's trade with the countries of the European Common Market.

The imbalance was largely a result of the tariff barriers raised by Common Market countries against countries that were not members of the market. In autumn 1962, Congress approved the Trade Expansion Act which gave the president wide authority to negotiate tariff reductions with other countries, particularly those of Western Europe.

A central problem of agriculture when Kennedy entered the White House was the huge quantity of farm commodities which had passed to ownership of the federal government under the federal subsidy program. These commodities were stored throughout the nation at enormous expense. To deal with the problem of agricultural surpluses, and to counter hunger in underdeveloped countries, the president revived the Food for Peace program which had originated during the Eisenhower presidency. As a result surpluses virtually disappeared and farm prices in America moved upward. Far more important, hunger and malnutrition were relieved in many parts of the world, notably in Africa, Latin America, and Southeast Asia. In India, Egypt, and Algeria shipments under Food for Peace helped prevent massive starvation.

Meanwhile Kennedy's "New Frontier" administration was seeking to win congressional approval of a range of innovations and reforms engineered along the lines of Franklin D. Roosevelt's New Deal in the 1930s. Because the coalition of conservative Democrats from the South and conservative Republicans from the North continued to dominate Capitol Hill, however, the domestic program of the New Frontier made slow headway. It remained more a promise than a reality. Kennedy tried with little success to reform the national tax structure, mainly by closing tax "loopholes." He saw his requests for federal aid to public elementary and secondary schools heavily changed and got nowhere with his proposals for "Medicare" – medical assistance to elderly citizens under the Social Security system.

Still, the record of the New Frontier in the area of domestic innovation and reform was not entirely blank. Kennedy persuaded Congress to approve legislation appropriating $175 million to help medical schools enlarge facilities and another $61 million from which students of medicine, osteopathy, and dentistry could borrow at low interest rates. He also prevailed on Congress to appropriate nearly a half-billion dollars to combat mental illness and retardation. The Drug Industry Act tightening federal control over manufacture and sale of drugs was also passed. Congress also gave its consent to an omnibus housing bill which appropriated $4.9 billion. This money was for construction of middle-income housing; loans to elderly citizens for purchase of houses; urban renewal programs; construction of mass transportation facilities; loans for construction of college dormitories and hospitals; and loans to rural Americans who wanted to purchase or improve houses.

Perhaps the most important reform during Kennedy's administration resulted from the Supreme Court's decision in the case of *Baker* v. *Carr,* brought before the high court by the president's brother, Attorney General Robert F. Kennedy. At issue was the refusal of the lower house of the legislature of Tennessee to reapportion itself in accord with shifting population patterns. Despite much urban growth in Tennessee, legislative districts remained drawn as in the time when the great bulk of the population lived in the countryside. Thus the legislature remained under control of rural politicians.

In *Baker* v. *Carr* the Supreme Court ruled that federal courts had authority to compel state legislatures to apportion themselves in accord with actual distributions of population. As a result, suits demanding reapportionment of legislative districts had been filed within a very short time in more than twenty states. It was clear that the day of rural domination of state governments to the detriment of cities was about to end.

STUDY GUIDE: John F. Kennedy came from a closely knit, wealthy New England family. His father was a former ambassador to Great Britain. Young Kennedy saw combat in the navy during World War II, and was decorated for heroism. In 1946 he entered politics. He won a seat in the House of Representatives and was reelected twice. In 1952 he ran for the Senate and won. As he began his "New Frontier" administration, Kennedy acted first to combat an economic recession with the Area Redevelopment Act. He also worked toward improving America's balance of trade with the Trade Expansion Act. To solve farm surplus problems, he revived the Food for Peace program of the Eisenhower administration. The *Baker* v. *Carr* case dealt with the rules for electing representatives to the state governments. The effect of the Supreme Court's decision was to give more representation to the large cities where many people lived and to take power away from the rural areas where fewer people lived.

EQUAL RIGHTS FOR BLACKS

During his campaign for the presidency in 1960 John F. Kennedy spoke out eloquently in favor of equal rights for black Americans. On election day he received an overwhelming endorsement from Negroes (mainly in the North and West) who were permitted to vote. After taking over the White House he issued an executive order against racial discrimination in federal employment and made a special effort to appoint blacks to high positions in the federal bureaucracy, foreign service, and federal judiciary. He set up the President's Committee on Equal Employment Opportunity, which pressed leaders of business to eliminate discriminatory practices. Kennedy needled whites who urged equal rights but who held membership in social clubs which refused to admit Negroes as members. He gave his brother Robert, the attorney general, a free rein to use the authority of the Justice Department in behalf of equal rights. At the same time, however, the president did not wish to arouse the fury of southern members of Congress who might stop the progress of other parts of the New Frontier program. Therefore—to the disappointment of black leaders—he proposed no new equal rights legislation during his first two years in the White House.

Sit-ins And Freedom Rides

While Kennedy was working for his New Frontier program, increasing numbers of blacks, spurred on by the Reverend Martin Luther King, Jr., were turning to massive nonviolent action. This appeared to be their most effective means of breaking down the walls of segregation and unequal treatment.

In 1960 four black students had been denied service at a segregated lunch counter in Greensboro, North Carolina. They decided to stay seated until the counter closed. Other black Americans began using these tactics. As a result, more than eight hundred "sit-ins" were organized to protest discrimination and segregation. As a result, restaurants in at least eight major cities were desegregated. Moreover, white Americans became increasingly aware of black frustration over racial discrimination.

Then, in spring 1961, came the "freedom rides."

To test discrimination in interstate travel terminals, seven black and six white "freedom riders" boarded a bus in Washington bound for New Orleans. In Virginia, the Carolinas, and Georgia the riders on occasion received full and equal use of facilities. Sometimes, however, they found facilities closed and at times were taunted and harassed by local whites. Then the freedom riders entered Alabama. As they approached the town of Anniston a bus in which part of the group was riding came under attack by a white mob. Tires were slashed, and a fire bomb thrown through a window set the bus on fire. Fortunately all the passengers escaped with only minor injuries. Later, at Birmingham, freedom riders aboard a second bus were attacked as they got off. One of the group sustained injuries which required fifty stitches.

Despite warnings by the Justice Department in Washington, white authorities in Alabama had done nothing to prevent the outrages at Anniston and Birmingham. Nobody was arrested for participation in the attacks. Meanwhile other groups of freedom riders had boarded buses and were heading southward. When it became clear that white officials would not or could not protect them, Attorney General Kennedy sent six hundred federal marshals to Alabama. Despite the efforts of the marshals and, later, the Alabama National Guard, there was violence for another two weeks in Alabama, and in Mississippi, as freedom rides continued. A few months later the Interstate Commerce Commission, prodded by Attorney General Kennedy, issued an order prohibiting discrimination in interstate bus, rail, and air terminals.

James Meredith Enrolls at "Ole Miss"

In September 1962, the nation faced a new outbreak of racial violence. The trouble developed when a black Mississippi air force veteran, James Meredith, supported by a federal court order, tried to enroll at the University of Mississippi. He found his path blocked by Governor Ross Barnett and white students who marched about the campus singing "Glory, Glory Segregation."

Attorney General Kennedy appealed for obedience of the law, and a new federal court order was issued ordering officials in Mississippi

Compix

James Meredith escorted by federal marshals attempted to register at the University of Mississippi on September 20, 1962. Governor Ross Barnett blocked his way. Finally President Kennedy had to call out the Mississippi National Guard to quell riots on the "Ole Miss" campus.

not to interfere with Meredith's registration. Nonetheless, Governor Barnett, aided by a mob of angry whites, prevented a second attempt by Meredith to enroll at the university. At length President Kennedy federalized the Mississippi National Guard to meet wholesale violence if it should erupt on the campus. At this point, Governor Barnett, who also had been charged with civil contempt, agreed that Meredith could register. On the evening of September 30, Meredith, accompanied by federal marshals, made his way to the campus and settled in a dormitory room. He was scheduled to register the next day.

That evening President Kennedy went before television cameras and explained why he had mobilized the power of the federal government to get a black man into a university. He concluded by appealing to students of "Ole Miss" to uphold "the honor of your University." Students at the university jeered and hooted. Whites, some of them armed, shouting and screaming, stepped up an attack on federal marshals which had begun before Kennedy's address. During the rioting, two men were killed and hundreds of people were injured. After troops of the Mississippi National Guard and army paratroops arrived, the battle ended. The next morning Meredith registered. Despite the continuing presence of marshals, the hostility of fellow stu-

A quarter million people came to Washington, D.C., on August 28, 1963, to protest the black man's lack of civil rights. They gathered in front of the Lincoln Memorial and spread around the reflecting pool as far back as the Washington Monument. Did the march accomplish anything in terms of legislation?

dents, and threats against his family, he received his diploma in 1963. Following the Meredith incident, racial barriers soon were falling at hitherto all-white colleges and universities across the entire South.

Trouble at Birmingham and Tuscaloosa

In 1962, President Kennedy signed an order prohibiting discrimination in housing owned or insured by the federal government. In early 1963 he asked Congress to enact legislation strengthening existing voting rights laws and helping schools to desegregate. Then, in April 1963, came a new racial crisis.

The crisis occurred when blacks led by Martin Luther King, Jr., began to march in the streets and stage sit-ins to protest discrimination in shops, restaurants, and employment in Birmingham, Alabama. Predictably, the protesters collided with mobs of militant white citizens who were anti-Negro. In the days and weeks which followed, the blacks and their white allies were taunted with obscenities, assaulted with rocks and bottles, and hauled off to jail by the hundreds. On May 3, authorities turned high-pressure fire hoses on protest marchers and the police commissioner unleashed snarling German shepherd "police" dogs. A photographer snapped a

picture of one of the dogs, its teeth bared, lunging at a black woman. The picture was flashed across the entire world.

Finally authorities in Birmingham and protest leaders agreed to a truce, largely as a result of efforts by the White House. An uneasy calm settled over the Alabama city.

A few weeks later national attention again centered on Alabama when Governor George C. Wallace prevented two black Alabamans from entering the University of Alabama. President Kennedy federalized the Alabama National Guard and made it clear that he would allow no nonsense in Alabama. Wallace stayed away from the campus at Tuscaloosa when the Negroes made their second attempt to register, and the registration proceeded without incident. That same evening President Kennedy, in a television address, related the events at Tuscaloosa and declared that "the rights of every man are diminished when the rights of one man are threatened." He made an eloquent appeal for elimination of second-class citizenship in America. But triumph in the area of equal rights was mixed with tragedy, for later that night Medgar Evers, the highly respected director of the NAACP in Mississippi, was shot to death in front of his house in Jackson, Mississippi.

The March on Washington

In June 1963, President Kennedy sent new equal rights proposals to Capitol Hill. The most notable of these sought to guarantee equal treatment for all citizens in facilities — such as hotels, restaurants, and department stores — soliciting the business of the general public.

To put pressure on Congress to approve Kennedy's proposals, black leaders hit on the idea of a massive "march on Washington." The outcome, on August 28, 1963, was a memorable happening when a quarter-million people gathered in the national capital. The weather was perfect, warm and sunny as the marchers, chanting and singing, wound through the streets of the capital city. Their procession ended at the Lincoln Memorial.

Then Martin Luther King, Jr., made his way to the microphone and delivered the speech that was destined to become his most famous address. Beginning with "I have a dream. . . ," he told of the agony and hope of generations of black Americans. His words have become a classic expression of the goals in the search for justice, equality, and brotherhood.

That evening, as dusk settled over Washington, the marchers departed. Unfortunately they had little effect on Congress. For months the civil rights bill remained bottled up in committee.

STUDY GUIDE: Kennedy set up the President's Committee on Equal Employment Opportunity to help end discrimination in business. In 1960 sit-ins were organized to protest discrimination and segregation. In 1961 freedom riders worked to end discrimination in interstate travel. Their actions secured an Interstate Commerce Commission ruling that prohibited discrimination in interstate bus, rail, and air terminals.

Racial violence broke out in 1962 when Negro air force veteran James Meredith tried to enroll at the all-white University of Mississippi. President Kennedy had to federalize the Mississippi National Guard after attempts were made to block Meredith's registration. More racial unrest broke out in Tuscaloosa and Birmingham, Alabama in 1963. In Jackson, Mississippi, NAACP director Medgar Evers was murdered. That same year, Kennedy asked Congress to make stronger civil rights legislation. A peaceful march on Washington took place during which thousands of people gathered to show support of the civil rights program which Kennedy had sent to Congress.

OUTER SPACE

The triumph of propelling the first man into space went to the Soviet Union when Major Yuri A. Gagarin orbited the earth in a five-ton spacecraft in April 1961. America's first man-in-space venture was to be a suborbital mission, a rather unimposing operation compared to Gagarin's feat.

Less than a month after Gagarin's flight, Lieutenant Commander Alan B. Shepard of the navy, at Cape Canaveral in Florida, sealed himself into a spacecraft called *Freedom 7,* and was launched on a fifteen-minute flight. Shepard traveled up to an altitude of 116.5 miles and across the Atlantic a distance of 302 miles.

Three weeks later, President Kennedy made a dramatic appeal. In a speech to a joint session of Congress, he urged Americans to commit themselves to "achieving the goal before this decade is out of landing a man on the moon and returning him safely to earth."

Meanwhile, scientists and engineers at Cape Canaveral, Florida were preparing a second manned space shot. In July of 1962 Captain Virgil I. ("Gus") Grissom of the air force made a suborbital flight in *Liberty Bell 7* similar to that of Shepard. Then in August 1961 Major Gherman S. Titov of the USSR orbited the earth eighteen times.

Spurred by Soviet accomplishments, officials of the National Aeronautics and Space Administration stepped up plans to put an American in an earth orbit. On the morning of February 20, 1962, Lieutenant Colonel John H. Glenn, Jr., of the marine corps, slipped into *Friendship 7.* While Americans watched nervously via television, the service tower was rolled away, leaving the giant Atlas-Mercury rocket standing alone, gleaming in the sunlight, oxygen vapor spewing from its base. Then, at 9:46, the low, matter-of-fact voice of Lieutenant Colonel John A. ("Shorty") Powers, "the voice of Mercury Control," intoned: "We are at T minus nineteen seconds. T minus ten seconds, eight, seven, six, five, four, three, two, one, zero. Ignition." A great ball of orange flame, a deafening roar, a cloud of white smoke, and four seconds later the Atlas-Mercury gracefully lifted from its pad. Reported Powers: "Pilot John Glenn is reporting that all systems are go." Within a few seconds the streaking Atlas-Mercury and its payload, *Friendship 7,* had vanished. Four hours, fifty-five minutes, and ten seconds after liftoff Glenn's spacecraft, after three orbits of the earth, splashed down in the Atlantic.

Three months later, in May 1962, Lieutenant Commander Malcolm Scott Carpenter of the navy, in *Aurora 7,* duplicated Glenn's three-orbit mission. But in August 1962 the Soviets sent two spacecraft into orbit at the same time, one of which revolved around the earth forty-eight times, the other sixty-four. Americans refused to be discouraged and cheered lustily in October 1962 when Commander Walter M. Schirra, Jr., of the navy, made six revolutions of the earth in *Sigma 7.* Then in May 1963 Leroy Gordon Cooper, Jr., of the air force, in *Faith 7,* made a flight which lasted nearly four hours and took him around the earth twenty-two times.

Although manned space flights received the most attention, an unmanned flight in 1962 seemed at least as important from the standpoint of science. The flight began in late August when an Atlas rocket propelled a 447-pound, instrument-laden spacecraft called *Mariner 2* into orbit. After the spacecraft made one revolution of the earth, controllers at Cape Canaveral pressed buttons which sent *Mariner 2* rocketing in the direction of Venus, a planet about the size of the earth. One hundred and nine days later, in mid-December, the spacecraft, with all systems working, flew past Venus at a distance of 21,598 miles. *Mariner 2*'s sophisticated instruments revealed that Venus was a dry, lifeless ball on which temperatures were 800 degrees Fahrenheit.

STUDY GUIDE: In April 1961, the Soviet Union sent the first man into space. The following month, Lieutenant Commander Alan B. Shepard made a suborbital flight in *Freedom 7*. In February 1962, Lieutenant Colonel John H. Glenn, Jr., became the first American to orbit the earth. Later that year, *Mariner 2*, an unmanned spacecraft, was sent to Venus. The craft passed the planet at a distance of 21,598 miles. Scientific equipment on board gave scientists new information about Venus.

FOREIGN ASSISTANCE

John F. Kennedy felt that his historical reputation as president would rest mainly on the way in which he handled America's foreign relations. He believed that the chief reality in world affairs was the continuing cold war between the Soviet Union and its Communist allies and the so-called free world. He also believed that, to a considerable extent, the battleground of the cold war had shifted from Europe to the underdeveloped countries of Latin America, Africa, and Asia. Many of these countries had only recently secured independence after breaking the chains of colonialism. Nearly all these nations were mired in poverty and seemed receptive to Communist ideas. Declared the youthful president in his inaugural: "To those people in the huts and villages of half the globe struggling to break the bonds of mass misery, we pledge our best efforts to help them help themselves. . . . If a free society cannot help the many who are poor, it cannot save the few who are rich."

Perhaps the most obvious vehicle for assisting underdeveloped nations was the foreign aid program. And it was a vehicle which Kennedy determined to utilize. However, his proposals ran counter to an increasing national sentiment that foreign aid in the form of grants and low-interest loans amounted to a giveaway of the hard-earned money of American taxpayers. Consequently,

Congress appropriated far fewer funds for foreign aid than he requested, although the appropriation did increase each year.

Meanwhile Kennedy was seeking other means of assisting poor countries. He decided that America's stocks of surplus food should be used for foreign aid. To accomplish his purpose he breathed new life into the Food for Peace program. The outcome, although not highly publicized in the United States, was a success. Hunger was relieved in numerous parts of the world; Communist appeals were weakened; and America's standing overseas was strengthened.

The Peace Corps

Kennedy believed that another means of improving the quality of life in the underdeveloped nations was available. For this purpose he directed his attention toward the idealism and spirit of self-sacrifice of bright and energetic Americans. In early 1961, he issued an executive order setting up the Peace Corps. The principal aim of the Peace Corps was to help people help themselves by teaching them basic technical skills. The idea for the Peace Corps had originated several years earlier in the minds of Hubert Humphrey and a few other idealists on Capitol Hill. Later in 1961 Congress, with an obvious lack of enthusiasm, approved a one-year appropriation of $40 million for the Peace Corps.

Directed by the president's brother-in-law Sargent Shriver, the Peace Corps, in spring 1961, selected its first volunteers—twenty-eight surveyors, civil engineers, and geologists to work in Tanganyika. In the months which followed, several hundred more volunteers were chosen and put in training programs. Because of Communist charges that the corps was an arm of the Central Intelligence Agency recruits were told repeatedly that, once overseas, they were not to engage in diplomatic or intelligence activities. Their sole mission was to help people to help themselves. They also were lectured on the importance of conducting themselves with courtesy and dignity and were instructed to lead, by American standards, a Spartan existence while on assignment abroad.

By spring 1963 some five thousand Peace Corps volunteers were working in forty-six countries in Latin America, Africa, the Middle East, Central Asia, Southeast Asia, and the Western Pacific. Critics contended that volunteers were essentially boy and girl scouts who were performing good deeds but that they could not begin to cope with enormous economic and social problems of the underdeveloped nations. Most Americans believed, however, that the corps was worthwhile. Americans grasped the fact that Peace Corps volunteers were lending a hand to people of primitive villages and filth-ridden slums and giving them a fresh image of America. At the same time the volunteers were learning a great deal about the outer world, about other people, and about themselves. By the end of 1963 the corps had won such popular support that Congress dramatically raised the appropriation for the Peace Corps, although at the same time it slashed the president's foreign aid request.

Although President Kennedy felt concern for all the lesser nations, he believed that Latin America was most important to the interests and security of the United States.

The Alliance for Progress

Latin America certainly abounded with problems. A tiny minority—perhaps two per cent—of the population of the area owned more than fifty per cent of the wealth, including most of the land. This minority lived, as it had for generations, in luxury. Families of the wealthy often alternated between luxurious apartments in cities and rural estates with graceful mansions, manicured gardens, and battalions of servants.

Latin America's "masses" presented a startling contrast. Breadwinners of poor families spent their days scrounging about cities in search of odd jobs, laboring in the blistering sun on sugar or coffee plantations for a few pesos, or trying to scratch a living from tiny plots of ground which they owned or rented. The poor found shelter in rat-infested tenements or cardboard and tin shacks in urban slums and in crude huts in squalid villages in the countryside. For most Latin Americans regular medical attention and schooling were only dreams. Reality consisted of pain, hunger, disease, and ignorance.

To help Latin Americans meet their problems —and to weaken the appeal of totalitarian communism, particularly as preached by Fidel Castro —President Kennedy announced the Alliance for Progress in 1961. In this ambitious program, the governments of the Western Hemisphere, working together, would seek to effect a peaceful revolution in the Americas aimed at eliminating poverty.

For a year or so it appeared that the Alliance was making impressive headway, underwritten by generous financial support by the

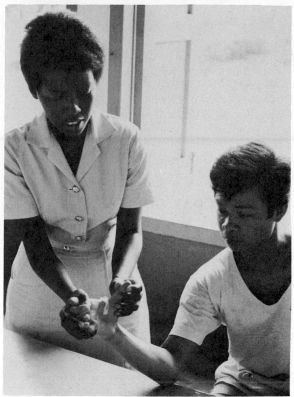
ACTION/Peace Corps

A Peace Corps physical therapist exercises the hand of a leprosy patient in Thailand. Congress was not enthusiastic in voting money for the volunteers. What were some of the arguments for and against the Peace Corps?

United States. But around 1963, optimism began to turn to pessimism. Latin America's wealthy elite was thwarting the reforms designed to redistribute wealth and income. A decline in the world price of sugar and coffee and Latin America's soaring birth rate were also nullifying economic gains. Moreover, North American businessmen were showing scant enthusiasm for the new investments needed to stimulate economic activity south of the border.

Matters worsened after 1965 when the United States escalated its involvement in the war in Vietnam, diverting its attention away from Latin America. By the end of the 1960s the Alliance for Progress was widely viewed as a failure— although some observers felt that it had provided an essential structure in which great advances could be made in years to come.

STUDY GUIDE: Kennedy revived the Food for Peace program to lessen hunger in underdeveloped nations, while using up American food surpluses. To help people of developing nations help themselves by learning technical skills, Kennedy started the Peace Corps in 1961. The Alliance for Progress, also announced in 1961, was a long-range plan to raise living standards in Latin America. The program was not well received among the wealthy people of Latin America, and the program did not work well.

BAY OF PIGS

At the same time that President Kennedy was announcing the Alliance for Progress—which was aimed at stopping the spread of communism in Latin America—his administration was considering a more direct strike against Cuba's bearded revolutionary leader, Fidel Castro.

Many Cubans who had fled Castroism and settled in Florida were eager to return to their homeland and try to overthrow Castro. President Eisenhower, in early 1960, had authorized the Central Intelligence Agency to organize a handful of these exiles into a military force. Recruitment for the exile force got underway at once. By summer 1960 several hundred Cubans had been dispatched to jungle hideaways in Guatemala for military training. While the exile force was taking shape, in autumn 1960, John F. Kennedy won election as president of the United States. By the time he entered the White House, in January 1961, the CIA was working out plans to use the force of fifteen hundred men for an invasion of Castro's island fortress. The CIA hoped an invasion would trigger a rebellion among the Cuban people, who, it was assumed, would jump at the opportunity to topple the Cuban dictator.

When Kennedy learned of the CIA's plans, he was not overly enthusiastic. Still, he was interested. In March 1961, he and members of his administration weighed the merits of an invasion of Cuba by the exile force and found it hard to argue against the CIA's claim that such an operation had an excellent chance of success. After all, the CIA had been dealing with "the Cuban problem" at close range for many months, even years. And the newcomers of the Kennedy administration were hesitant to suggest that men of the CIA were mistaken and that their scheme might lead to disaster. Moreover, the Joint Chiefs of Staff assured the president that, from a military standpoint, the plan seemed sound. Kennedy did not know that the Joint Chiefs had not evaluated the plan carefully. So in early April,

Kennedy gave his consent to the operation. On one point, however, he was absolutely clear: under no circumstances would he commit North American military and naval forces to assure success of the exile invasion. The exiles would be put ashore and after that they would be on their own.

After receiving the "go" signal from Washington, the exile force made final preparations to begin the invasion of Cuba. The first blow against Castro's island came in the early hours of April 15 when two B-26 bombing planes, disguised with the insignia of Castro's air force, swooped down on several airfields in Cuba. After failing to achieve their objective of knocking out Castro's small air force, the bombers roared to Florida and landed. The crewmen claimed that they were Castro's airmen and were defecting to the United States. Meanwhile the exile "army" evacuated camps in Guatemala and boarded cargo ships and landing craft. By the night of April 16, the army of exiles was moving across the Caribbean in a northeasterly direction toward the Bay of Pigs on the lightly defended south coast of Cuba. At one o'clock in the morning of April 17, the exile soldiers landed and moved inland. They met no opposition.

By daybreak, Castro knew of the invasion. With cool efficiency he issued orders which alerted his 250,000-man army and sent advance units racing toward the Bay of Pigs. He directed his secret police to round up and detain individuals suspected of being hostile to the regime who might provide leadership for a civilian uprising. He sent all of his tiny air force toward the Bay of Pigs. At 6:45 A.M., one of the planes dealt a heavy blow to the invaders when it sent rockets crashing into the cargo ship *Houston*. In addition to the usual supplies, the *Houston* carried most of the exile force's communications equipment. The ship ran aground on a sandpit two miles from shore and its cargo of supplies and equipment was lost.

By nightfall of the first day it was clear that the invasion was not going to succeed unless President Kennedy changed his mind and committed United States forces to the combat. The invasion had been based on the assumption that a popular uprising would follow the landing of the invaders. But the action at the Bay of Pigs had failed to touch off any sort of popular action. It was apparent that the fifteen-hundred-man force, standing alone, could not possibly defeat Castro's army of a quarter of a million men. President Kennedy was distressed over the events unfolding in Cuba, but he steadfastly refused to order air and naval forces to go to the aid of the exiles.

The rest was anticlimactic. Effectively supported from the air, Castro's soldiers methodically surrounded the invaders. After four days, the ordeal of the exile force ended. Some three hundred of the invaders had died. Since nobody had thought to work out a plan for evacuating the exiles in the event that the operation turned sour, the remaining twelve hundred men were captured.

In subsequent weeks the United States took an unprecedented barrage of criticism from around the world. Iron Curtain countries called the Bay of Pigs affair a fresh example of capitalist imperialism. Leaders of such neutralist countries as India and Egypt denounced the United States for heavy-handed treatment of a small neighbor. And across Latin America people of all political views protested "Yankee" interference in Latin American affairs. At home President Kennedy came under attack on the one hand for having permitted the United States to get involved in such a dubious operation and on the other for not using United States power to assure success of the invasion.

The Bay of Pigs episode shattered the illusion of New Frontiersmen that somehow any enterprise to which Kennedy gave his attention would turn out all right. And it brought organizational changes in the White House. The president set up procedures for making certain that in future deliberations he and his closest advisers would ask the right questions of intelligence and military people. He also got the White House staff more actively involved in the process of making decisions. The episode sharpened Kennedy's diplomatic skills and thus helped him to respond more successfully to international crises in the months to come.

STUDY GUIDE: When President Kennedy entered the White House, the CIA was working on a plan for an invasion of Cuba by a group of exiled Cubans. The purpose of the invasion was to start a rebellion among the Cuban people against Fidel Castro's revolutionary government. Kennedy approved the plan early in April of 1961. Castro soon learned of the invasion, and when the fifteen-hundred-man force of exiles landed at the Bay of Pigs, Castro's army was waiting. Most of the exiles were captured; the rest died. No escape plan had been worked out. The

U.S. Coast Guard

A sailboat which was found off the coast of Florida carrying Cuban refugees is towed the rest of the way to Miami by a Coast Guard patrol boat. One of the Cubans, who became ill during the voyage, is being airlifted to a hospital. More than 10,000 Cubans have escaped to the United States, many of them in small boats like this one.

This editorial cartoon appeared in newspapers across the U.S. after the unsuccessful Bay of Pigs invasion. As a result of the disaster, what changes in procedure did Kennedy make?

"HELLO, PENTAGON? WHAT THE HELL HAPPENED TO OUR AIR COVER?"

SOUTHEAST ASIA

At the same time that he was weighing the merits of the Cuban invasion, in the early months of his presidency, Kennedy was also concerned with another troubled area—Southeast Asia.

Laos

When Kennedy entered the White House the principal trouble spot in Southeast Asia was Laos. Three factions of the Laotian ruling elite were struggling for control of the country. One faction, supported by an organization called the Pathet Lao, wanted to turn Laos into a Communist state. At the opposite extreme was a conservative faction which wanted to rid Laos of all Communist influence. In the middle was a faction headed by Prince Souvanna Phouma which wanted to make Laos into a neutralist state and bring all political factions of the country, including the Communists, into a coalition government.

Kennedy shared the view of his predecessor, President Eisenhower, that Laos was a "domino." If it fell to the Communists, he felt that South Vietnam, Cambodia, Thailand, Malaya, and Indonesia would fall like dominoes, one by one, under Communist control. Kennedy also shared Eisenhower's belief that it would be a disaster for the non-Communist world if Southeast Asia should become a Communist stronghold.

Kennedy did not share Eisenhower's view, however, that the interests of the non-Communist world required the triumph of the conservative anti-Communists in Laos. On the contrary, he spoke out in favor of a neutralist Laos and threw support to the faction headed by Souvanna Phouma.

Kennedy set about persuading the Pathet Lao, who were the chief stumbling blocks in the way of a neutralist coalition government, that the United States would not stand by and tolerate a Communist takeover of Laos. Hence their only sensible alternative was to fall in behind Souvanna Phouma. At length, in 1962, the Pathet Lao agreed to enter a coalition regime. Delegates from fourteen countries, including the United States, the Soviet Union, and China, met at Geneva and pledged to uphold the independence and neutrality of Laos.

Unfortunately the agony of Laos was not over. The Pathet Lao forces were unwilling to put aside dreams of eventually taking over the country. Bolstered by several thousand North Vietnamese troops who remained in Laos in violation of the Geneva agreement, the members of the Pathet Lao refused to take up positions in the coalition government. They also kept control of territory in northern Laos which was firmly in their grasp. The result, through the remainder of the 1960s, was periodic fighting between troops of Souvanna Phouma and those of the Pathet Lao.

Meanwhile the North Vietnamese, also in violation of the Geneva agreement, stepped up the movement of troops and supplies to South Vietnam via the Ho Chi Minh Trail, which snaked through the jungles of southeastern Laos. Accordingly Laos increasingly became an object of the military calculations of combatants in the conflict in South Vietnam.

South Vietnam

The conflict in South Vietnam of course soon replaced the turmoil in Laos as the central point of President Kennedy's attention in Southeast Asia.

Both Eisenhower and Kennedy viewed South Vietnam as another "domino." And when Kennedy moved into the White House, in early 1961, it was clear that Communist insurgents were enlarging their power in South Vietnam. They were supported by the Communist government of North Vietnam and relied on tactics of terror and strike-and-run. Still, the situation in South Vietnam did not seem as precarious as that in Laos. Then, in September 1961, the insurgents—or Viet Cong—seized a provincial capital and beheaded the governor. At this point the morale of political and military leaders in South Vietnam slipped noticeably.

After analyzing the situation Kennedy concluded that the Communists had not yet won in South Vietnam. He believed that the regime of President Ngo Dinh Diem, if properly guided and supported, stood a good chance of keeping the country out of Communist hands. He decided that the United States would send several thousand additional soldiers to South Vietnam—raising the total number of GIs in the country to perhaps ten thousand—to advise and train South Vietnamese forces. These American troops would also act as an emergency reserve for the South Vietnamese army. At the same time Americans would become more actively involved in the business of counseling political officials in South Vietnam. The result? Through the year 1962 reports from South Vietnam indicated that the new tactics being taught the South Vietnamese army and the program of herding peasants into rural fortresses or "strategic hamlets" were beginning to take the measure of the Viet Cong.

But then, in spring and summer 1963, trouble began. Charging that Diem, a Catholic, was discriminating against them, Buddhists opened a campaign of opposition to the South Vietnamese president. Denied permission by the government to fly Buddhist flags on the 2,587th birthday of Gautama Buddha, Buddhists in the city of Hué staged an unusually hostile demonstration and were fired on by government policemen. When the shooting stopped, twelve demonstrators lay dead in the street. A few weeks later a thousand Buddhist monks and nuns paraded through Saigon, stopped at a main crossroads, and gathered around an elderly monk, Thich Quang Doc. Two monks then stepped forward and doused Quang Doc with gasoline. Whereupon the old man struck a match and touched it to his yellow robe. As the flames roared and black smoke billowed skyward, monks and nuns chanted, and people wept. Ten minutes later the monk's charred body fell back against the pavement.

The self-inflicted martyrdom of Quang Doc sparked new hostility against Diem's regime, which had increasingly resorted to tactics of repression to silence dissent and mobilize the country for the war against the Communists. Diem made concessions. Too late. More street demonstrations. More self-immolations. Then came a hot evening in late August. Without warning Diem's police and elements of the army stormed Buddhist pagodas across South Vietnam. They dragged monks and nuns (whom Diem accused of being Communists in disguise) into the streets and carted them off to jail. People in South Vietnam and around the world were appalled.

Leaders of the United States were becoming increasingly doubtful that Diem ever would lead South Vietnam's non-Communists to victory over the Viet Cong. Still, given their commitment to the "domino theory" and their belief in the importance of a non-Communist Southeast Asia, they were not willing to consider cutting America's losses and abandoning South Vietnam

to its fate. Instead they pressed Diem to reform his government and declare an amnesty for imprisoned Buddhists. Confident that the Americans would not allow his fervently anti-Communist regime to collapse, Diem ignored American appeals.

Meanwhile South Vietnam's military chieftains were stirring. On the afternoon of November 2, 1963, while the citizens of Saigon were enjoying their customary siesta, three battalions of marines overran the police station and naval headquarters. Next, mortar and artillery shells began to crash around Diem's palace and from a captured radio station General Duong Van Minh announced that the armed forces were liberating South Vietnam from "the rotten Diem regime." Delirious with excitement, thousands of residents of Saigon rushed to the streets to celebrate. The battle was not over, however, and through the night guns flashed and shells exploded. Early the following morning, a white flag appeared over the palace. A short time later Diem and his brother, Ngo Dinh Nhu, escaped from the palace, but they were soon captured and shot to death. A new government was formed under the leadership of a civilian, Nguyen Ngoc Tho. Later it was learned that the United States government had helped arrange Diem's overthrow.

STUDY GUIDE: President Kennedy favored a neutral government in Laos. In 1962, the Communist-led Pathet Lao agreed to a coalition government. But the Pathet Lao wanted to take over the country. As a result fighting took place for the rest of the 1960s.

In Vietnam, the Viet Cong seized a provincial capital in 1961. Kennedy sent additional soldiers to Vietnam to act as advisors and train South Vietnamese forces. During 1963 Buddhists demonstrated against President Diem's government. In November Diem was overthrown by a military coup. Both Diem and his brother Ngo Dinh Nhu were killed.

EUROPE

Other nations of the Third World besides those of Southeast Asia and Latin America commanded President Kennedy's attention in 1961–63. Most notable perhaps was the Congo in Central Africa, a newly independent country which threatened to break apart into three warring states, one of them Communist. In part as a result of Kennedy's diplomacy, a measure of peace and unity returned to the Congo and Communist influence was undercut. In terms of America's security and prosperity, however, the most important overseas area was Europe. And when Kennedy moved into the White House he found no absence of European problems with which to wrestle.

The most pressing problem was Berlin, a long-time point of friction between the Communist and non-Communist worlds. In early 1961 the Soviet leader Nikita Khrushchev declared as he had back in 1958, that if a solution to the Berlin question suitable to the Soviet empire was not soon forthcoming, he would sign a separate peace treaty with the satellite government in East Germany and turn over control of access routes to West Berlin to the East Germans. Presumably, as in 1958, he was thinking about turning West Berlin into "an international free city," a step which in the western view merely would be a prelude to a Communist take-over. Only by negotiating with the East German government, which the western powers refused to recognize, could the access routes then be kept open. If the western powers refused to negotiate with the East Germans, they would have to force their way to West Berlin in order to maintain their position in the former German capital. And that would mean war, for, as Khrushchev made clear, the Soviets were determined in such an event to back up the East Germans.

President Kennedy had no intention of surrendering the western position in West Berlin. Largely to impress that fact on Soviet minds he arranged a meeting with Khrushchev in Vienna in June 1961. During the Vienna meeting, Khrushchev refused to give an inch on the Berlin question. Whereupon Kennedy, a short time later, quietly warned the Soviets that it would be a grave mistake for them to underestimate the resolve of the western powers to resist a Soviet power play in West Berlin. He then set about building up America's armed strength—and let the Soviets know what he was doing.

The Soviets made a display of their own determination. A few minutes after midnight on August 13, 1961, East German soldiers and police began closing the crossing points between East and West Berlin by installing road blocks and barbed wire barricades. Four days later the East Germans started construction of the infamous "Berlin wall" along the dividing line between the eastern and western sectors of the city. The purpose of the wall was to stop the westward flow of people, particularly scientists, technicians,

and artisans, whose skills the Communists could ill afford to lose.

The next development in the crisis came at the end of August when the Soviets announced that they were going to end the informal ban on nuclear testing which the superpowers had observed over the past several years. Meanwhile East German police and soldiers contributed to the tension when they gunned down several of their countrymen who tried to escape to the West before completion of the Berlin wall.

But then, in October 1961, only two months before the time in December when Khrushchev had pledged to conclude a treaty with the East Germans, the Soviet leader announced that he would not insist on the treaty at that time. Thus passed the Berlin crisis of 1961.

An uneasy calm enveloped West Berlin through 1962, but the former German capital continued to receive the close attention of American leaders. To demonstrate America's interest in the city, and its determination to keep it out of Communist hands, President Kennedy flew to West Berlin in summer 1963. He visited the wall and told West Berliners that America "will risk its cities to defend yours because we need your freedom to protect ours." Kennedy dramatically announced that he considered himself a Berliner —"Ich bin ein Berliner."

In 1963 relations between the two superpowers, the United States and the Soviet Union, seemed to undergo one of their periodic thaws. Leaders in Washington and Moscow seemed to think less about confrontation and more about peaceful coexistence. When crop failures threatened the Soviet Union with severe food shortages, in autumn 1963, President Kennedy answered an appeal from the Kremlin. Over the objection of some of his countrymen, he approved sale of $250 million of American wheat to the Soviets. Then, to reduce chances of accidental war by making it possible for leaders of the two superpowers to communicate with one another at a moment's notice, the governments in Washington and Moscow agreed, in summer 1963, to set up a direct telephone system—the famous "hot line"—between the two capitals. Finally—in one of the greatest diplomatic achievements of the 1960s—representatives of the two superpowers, in August 1963, signed a test-ban treaty pledging that their governments would not make nuclear tests in the atmosphere, outer space, or under water.

President Kennedy also was much concerned over the state of the North Atlantic alliance.

The alliance had been the cornerstone of the western policy of containing Soviet-Communist power in Europe since 1949, but it was clear in the early 1960s that the alliance had lost a good deal of its former vitality. Americans were convinced that much of the fault for deterioration of the alliance rested with France. The French leader, President Charles de Gaulle, doubted that the Soviets would consider a military strike against the West. He believed that the time had come for Western Europe—led by France of course—to assert its independence from the United States and become a third force between the two superpowers. Kennedy tried to restore the alliance and, more to the point, to bring France back into harness. To no avail. The pace of deterioration continued. In 1966 de Gaulle announced France's withdrawal from NATO's integrated military command and decreed that all NATO and other foreign military headquarters and bases must be removed from French territory by April 1, 1967.

STUDY GUIDE: Early in 1961, Soviet leader Nikita Khrushchev announced that he planned to sign a separate peace treaty with East Germany and give control of routes to Berlin to the East Germans. President Kennedy arranged a meeting with Khrushchev in June 1961 in Vienna. No agreement was reached on Berlin at the meeting. In August, East Germans began constructing the Berlin wall. The Soviets then announced the end of an informal ban on nuclear testing. In late 1961, Khrushchev announced that he would not insist on the treaty with the East Germans. In 1963 relations between the Soviet Union and the United States improved. A direct telephone system—the hot line—was set up between Washington and Moscow. That autumn, Kennedy authorized the sale of wheat to the Soviets. That same year, a test-ban treaty was signed.

Elsewhere in Europe, Kennedy was unsuccessful in his attempts to revitalize NATO. French leader Charles de Gaulle believed the time had come for European nations to assert their independence from the United States.

THE CUBAN MISSILE CRISIS

When pondering the task of managing America's problems in the world President Kennedy at times must have compared himself with a juggler who was trying to keep several fragile plates in the air. Like the juggler, he could not take his eyes off any one of those problems, even momentarily, lest it come crashing down about him. And so it was that while dealing with Laos, Vietnam, the Alliance for Progress, the Congo, West Berlin, and de Gaulle, Kennedy found it necessary to keep a continual watch on Cuba.

A few weeks after his triumph at the Bay of Pigs, in spring 1961, Castro proclaimed officially that Cuba had become a "socialist" country. He set about strengthening Cuba's links with the Soviet Union, and repeated his determination to export his revolution to other parts of the Western Hemisphere. Still, leaders in Washington felt that Castro was beset with endless problems inside Cuba and did not present much of a threat to non-Communist states in the hemisphere. Then, in mid-October 1962, a U-2 spy plane returned from a reconnaissance flight over Cuba. From its cameras came photographs establishing beyond a doubt that launching pads for ballistic missiles were being constructed—obviously by the Soviets—on Castro's island.

Why were the Soviets installing missiles in Cuba? In the estimate of leaders in Washington they had two objectives. First, by putting their medium- and intermediate-range missiles within reach of the United States, they doubled the striking power of missiles targeted on North America. Thus the Soviets hoped to dramatically shift the balance of nuclear power. This would place them in a stronger bargaining position against the Americans on such questions as the future of Berlin. Second, they hoped to weaken the faith of America's allies that the government in Washington, in a showdown, would rally to their defense. For if the United States would tolerate missiles within ninety miles of its own shores, there seemed little reason to believe it would take action when its allies were threatened.

President Kennedy was furious. He recalled Khrushchev's recent assurance that the Soviets would do nothing to stir up trouble in Cuba and, specifically, would not install offensive weapons in the island. The president determined to act. Some of his advisers favored an aerial strike against the missile sites. Such a strike, Kennedy concluded, would be extremely provocative. It likely would result in the death of Soviet technicians and might touch off a nuclear war. Whereupon Kennedy and his advisers began to weigh the possibility of a naval blockade around Cuba which would prevent the Soviets from sending more missiles to the island and might persuade

Two years after the Berlin crisis, the Berlin Wall, or Wall of Shame, was still standing. Here President Kennedy and West Berlin's Mayor Willy Brandt walk around Checkpoint Charlie, the major traffic route between the American protected sector of Berlin and the Russian zone.

them to remove those that already were there.

A blockade—or "quarantine"—could be carried out without shooting and bloodshed. Compared with an air strike on the missile sites, a quarantine would not have the dramatic shock effect which would threaten Soviet prestige and almost certainly invite some sort of immediate retaliation by the Soviets, perhaps a Communist thrust into West Berlin. Finally, if properly managed, a blockade would allow leaders in the Kremlin several days to ponder what was happening in the Western Hemisphere. Unless they wanted a nuclear showdown with the United States, they would have to put aside their project of installing missiles in Cuba. If the Soviets ignored the blockade, tried to send missile-laden ships through the naval barrier, and continued work at the missile sites, the United States of course would be left with no choice. Bombing planes would have to be sent against the sites and an invasion of Cuba might have to be attempted.

From the outset President Kennedy liked the idea of a quarantine—the same sort of measured response to a threat to America's interests and security which had worked so effectively the

This is a U.S. Air Force reconnaissance photograph. It shows the Russian missile site at San Cristobal, Cuba, a scant ninety miles from the U.S. The missiles stored there had a range of a thousand miles. How did Castro try to sabotage the U.S.-Russian agreement to end the missile crisis?

year before during the Berlin crisis. On Monday, October 22, the quarantine went into effect. And in Florida a giant amphibious force began to prepare for a possible invasion of Castro's island. That evening the president, in matter-of-fact tones, explained to his countrymen what was going on in Cuba and what he was doing about it.

Meanwhile work went on at the missile sites. And out in the Atlantic more than twenty Soviet freighters, some of them doubtless carrying missiles, were steaming toward Cuba. It seemed that a great time-bomb — possibly one with a nuclear charge — was ticking away. If the Soviet freighters pressed on toward Cuba and refused to submit to search by America's picket ships, the bomb probably would go off. Or if work at the missile sites continued and the missiles seemed about to become operational, the bomb was certain to explode. In that event President Kennedy doubtless would order air strikes to destroy the missiles before they could be targeted on the United States. Still, the bomb was continuing to tick. And so long as it was ticking there was a chance that Soviet leaders might reassess their Cuban venture and agree to withdraw the missiles.

Then, on Friday, October 26, the Soviets, communicating through John Scali, a diplomatic correspondent of the American Broadcasting Company, hinted that they would remove the missiles from Cuba if the United States would end the blockade and pledge not to invade Cuba. When the State Department, via Scali, indicated that the United States would accept such a deal, Premier Khrushchev made a formal offer in a message to President Kennedy. It seemed that the crisis had passed. But then, the following day, in a new message, Khrushchev demanded that the United States also dismantle its missile bases in Turkey. The bases in Turkey had become obsolete and the government in Washington already had decided to eliminate them. But Kennedy refused to establish a precedent whereby the United States would make concessions in one part of the world whenever the Soviets engineered a crisis in another.

At this point, on the suggestion of his brother Robert, the president made one of the most ingenious moves of the period of the crisis. He ignored Khrushchev's message of Saturday — the one demanding elimination of bases in Turkey — and responded to that of Friday — the one indicating the Soviet Union's willingness to withdraw offensive weapons from Cuba in return for an end to the quarantine and a pledge that the United States would not invade Cuba.

At last, on Sunday, October 28, President Kennedy received a cable from Khrushchev that work on the missile sites would stop and the missiles would be crated up and shipped back to the Soviet Union. The president ordered that there should be no public celebrations and no claims of victory over the Soviets. In a television address he spoke of Khrushchev's statesmanlike decision.

Then, for a brief moment, the settlement seemed in danger. Castro had been the forgotten chief of state during the crisis, and he emerged from the affair looking like a small-time dictator rather than a world leader. He was incensed at the Soviet retreat and announced that he would not allow the inspection of missile sites insisted on by Kennedy. But Kennedy remained calm. Believing that U-2 spy planes and other aircraft could provide adequate surveillance of Cuba, he did not press the point of on-site inspection. In any event, Soviet ships, heading back to their homeland, permitted American aircraft and ships to make "along-side inspection" of missiles lashed to their decks.

Thus passed the most chilling international crisis since World War II.

STUDY GUIDE: A few weeks after the unsuccessful Bay of Pigs invasion, Castro announced that Cuba had become a "socialist" nation. He then set about strengthening ties with the Soviet Union. In October 1962, a U-2 plane brought back photographs showing that launching pads for ballistic missiles were being constructed in Cuba. Then Kennedy ordered a quarantine or blockade of Cuba to prevent the flow of more weapons from the Soviets to the Cubans. On October 22, he told the nation what was happening in Cuba and what action he had taken. On October 26, the Russians hinted that they would remove the missiles if the United States would end the blockade and not invade Cuba. The next day, another message demanded that the United States also dismantle its missile bases in Turkey. Kennedy ignored the second message, and responded to the one of October 26. On October 28, Khrushchev notified Kennedy by cable that the missiles would be removed.

THE DEATH OF A PRESIDENT

In the months after the Cuban missile crisis, President Kennedy increasingly turned his mind to the year 1964 when he expected to seek a second term in the White House. To improve his chances of winning the electoral votes of Texas he decided, in autumn 1963, to fly down to "the Lone Star State" and urge feuding factions of the Democratic party to put aside differences and work together. Thus, on the morning of November 21, the president and Mrs. Kennedy walked out to the White House lawn, climbed aboard a helicopter, and were whisked to Andrews Air Force Base where they boarded Air Force One, the official presidential plane. Soon the glamorous presidential couple was winging through the sky toward San Antonio. After dedicating an aerospace medical center near San Antonio the president flew to Houston, where Kennedy attended a dinner in honor of Representative Albert Thomas. Afterward, the same evening, Kennedy flew on to Fort Worth.

The following morning, November 22, Kennedy emerged from the Hotel Texas and shook hands and exchanged pleasantries with a throng of friendly Texans. Next came a breakfast sponsored by the Fort Worth Chamber of Commerce. The president laughed when presented with a wide-brimmed "cow country" hat and joined the guests in a standing ovation when Mrs. Kennedy made her entrance to the dining room. During an after-breakfast speech he remarked that "we live in a very dangerous and uncertain world." After the speech the president and his group hurried to the airport for the short flight to Dallas, where the president was scheduled to address a luncheon gathering.

At 11:30 A.M. Air Force One touched down at Love Field outside Dallas. After the big plane's jet engines whined to a stop, the cabin door swung open and out stepped Mrs. Kennedy followed by her husband. After the customary round of greetings with local dignitaries there followed several minutes of handshaking and chatting with spectators, who were restrained by a low fence. The presidential couple then joined Governor and Mrs. John B. Connally in the limousine which was to take them through downtown Dallas and on to the Trade Mart where the president was scheduled to give his luncheon speech. Because the day was bright and clear, and also because Kennedy believed that it would obstruct the view of people who wished to see the president, the limousine's bubble top had not been put in place.

Well-wishers waved and cheered as the presidential party moved into Dallas. Then, at 12:20 P.M., the motorcade, like a giant serpent, turned off Main Street and proceeded along Houston Street toward Elm, one block away. People along the curbs and sidewalks continued to wave and clap and cheer. These demonstrations of friendliness prompted Mrs. Connally to turn to Kennedy and say: "No one can say Dallas doesn't love and respect you, Mr. President." Replied Kennedy: "You sure can't." A moment later the motorcade, having slowed to a crawl, was turning left on Elm Street and moving past the Texas School Book Depository. Then several shots rang out. Governor Connally and President Kennedy were hit. Connally was seriously wounded, but Kennedy was not as fortunate. The youthful thirty-fifth president of the United States was pronounced dead an hour later at Parkland Hospital.

On November 22, 1963, the Kennedys rode through Dallas in an open limousine. This photograph was taken seconds before shots were fired. Since then, U.S. presidents have become more protected and less accessible to the people.

Who killed the president? A suspect, Lee Harvey Oswald, was arrested shortly after the assassination but was never brought to trial. He was shot and killed by a small-time club operator, Jack Ruby, while being transferred from a Dallas jail. A commission headed by Chief Justice Earl Warren investigated the assassination and reviewed the evidence, which seemed to point toward Oswald as the killer.

STUDY GUIDE: In November 1963 President Kennedy and his wife went to Texas to improve chances of winning votes there the following year. While traveling in an open car through downtown Dallas, Kennedy was assassinated. Texas Governor Connally who was riding in the car with Kennedy was seriously wounded. Lee Harvey Oswald was arrested as the suspected assassin. Before he could be brought to trial, however, he was killed by Jack Ruby while being transferred from a Dallas jail. The Warren Commission indicated that evidence pointed to Oswald as the president's assassin.

LYNDON B. JOHNSON

The new president, Lyndon Baines Johnson, a descendant of hardy pioneers, was born in Blanco County, Texas in 1908. He grew up in Johnson City, Texas and lived and worked in California for more than a year after graduating from high school. He then returned to Texas and attended Southwest State Teachers College in San Marcos. For a time he taught school, first in a Mexican-American ghetto in Cotulla, Texas, and then in a high school in Houston. But the first love of young Johnson, whose father had served in the Texas legislature, was politics. In 1933 he accepted an invitation to travel to Washington and become secretary to Representative Richard Kleberg of Texas. The following year he married Claudia Alta ("Lady Bird") Taylor.

President Roosevelt recently had established the National Youth Administration and in 1935 he named Johnson to direct the NYA program in Texas. Typically, Johnson threw himself into the new job, drove himself and his subordinates unmercifully, and organized countless projects which gave employment to thousands of young Texans. Then in 1937, death claimed the congressman whose district included Blanco County.

Johnson declared himself a candidate to fill the late representative's unexpired term and won a special election by a wide margin.

Reelected in 1938 and 1940, Johnson in 1941 lost his bid to fill the unexpired term of the late Senator Morris Sheppard. Later that year came the raid at Pearl Harbor. Johnson, a lieutenant commander in the naval reserve, soon was summoned to active duty. By spring 1942 he was in Australia where he inspected military supplies, went on a bombing raid aboard a B-26 bomber which came under attack by Japanese fighter planes, and was awarded the Silver Star Medal. In summer 1942 President Roosevelt ordered all members of Congress who had gone on active duty in the armed forces back to Washington. Johnson spent the balance of the war in the national capital.

Reelected to the House in 1942, 1944, and 1946, Johnson in 1948 again ran for the Senate. After a bruising campaign he won the Democratic primary election by only eighty-seven votes out of 988,000. In the general election the following November he trounced his Republican opponent by a margin of 2-1. During his first term he was elected the Democratic minority leader in the Senate. In 1955, when the Democrats gained control, he became Senate majority leader. In his new role he seemed like a rumbling volcano about to erupt at any moment as he strode the corridors and cloakrooms of the Senate Office Building and Capitol. Chain-smoking cigarettes and barking out orders to aides, he buttonholed fellow senators and persuaded them to accept his point of view. In summer 1955 Johnson suffered a near-fatal heart attack—but after six months of rest he was back in the Senate and operating at the same old pace.

Although he won renown for his talents as a legislative leader, Johnson in the 1950s was not universally liked by his Democratic colleagues in the Senate. Democratic liberals in particular resented his high-pressure tactics of persuasion and his willingness to strike compromises with conservatives. Liberals also believed that Johnson, despite his early support of Franklin Roosevelt's New Deal, was basically conservative. They felt that he would go to any length to protect the interests of the oil and natural gas industries of his home state, never would do any more than give lip-service to the cause of equal rights for Negroes, and would not give much support to liberal programs.

Because he was not trusted by Democratic liberals, Johnson was fighting a lost cause in

Wide World

A little more than an hour after President Kennedy died, Lyndon B. Johnson took the oath of office aboard *Air Force One,* the presidential plane. Kennedy's widow, Jacqueline Kennedy, is on the right. Johnson's wife, who became known as Lady Bird Johnson, is on the left.

1960 when he sought the Democratic nomination for president. The liberal wing of the party, while often overshadowed by conservative Democrats on Capitol Hill, still held the balance of power when delegates gathered at the Democratic national convention in Los Angeles that summer. Liberals were shocked when John F. Kennedy, after winning first place on the Democratic ticket, shrewdly made Johnson his vice-presidential running mate.

Following the narrow electoral victory of the Kennedy-Johnson ticket Johnson took the oath as vice-president in January 1961. President Kennedy, who had great respect for Johnson, set out to make the Texan the most active vice-president in history. Still, Johnson's responsibilities seemed largely ceremonial and unimportant. Moreover, some New Frontiersmen clung to the old liberal stereotype of Johnson, and made little effort to disguise their feelings. And so Johnson, frustrated by his lack of political power and aware that some members of the administration disliked him, was unhappy in the vice-presidency.

Then came the events in Dallas of November 22, 1963 and, suddenly Lyndon B. Johnson was president of the United States.

Johnson Assumes the Presidency

When Lyndon Johnson took over the national leadership, the people of the United States were numbed and grief-stricken. National self-confidence seemed lost but was soon restored as the new chief executive moved calmly and surely. Taking a firm grip on the national helm, Johnson persuaded his countrymen that the nation was not going to founder. On the contrary, it would move forward along the course charted by President Kennedy.

Meanwhile the new president set about picking up the threads of the Kennedy legislative program, most of which had been bogged down for months in Congress. And he decided that his first object would be passage of a bill to heat up the national economy, which had become sluggish in recent months. He proposed to reduce personal and corporate income taxes by more than $11 billion annually. Using his legendary powers of persuasion, recalling past favors, and promising that he would do his best to limit federal spending, he quickly rounded up the necessary votes on Capitol Hill. In late February 1964, only ninety-six days after taking over the White House, Johnson, beaming with satisfaction and exuding warmth and goodwill under the glare of television floodlights, signed the tax cut measure.

The country needed a tax cut to stimulate the economy, but it also desperately needed legislation to remove some of the disabilities and indignities which were part and parcel of the daily lives of black Americans. For it was becoming increasingly clear that the country's Negroes, particularly the young blacks, had grown weary of mild assurances that someday they would achieve civil equality. If they did not soon make more than token strides toward first-class citizenship, they were going to lose what lingering faith they had in "the American dream," recoil against the gentle creed of Martin Luther King, Jr., and turn to violence, either out of anger and frustration or as a calculated means of achieving their ends.

The mood of many black Americans was reflected by increasing interest in a black nationalist cult popularly known as the Black Muslims. The Black Muslims, who observed the rituals of the Muslim faith, were led by a Chicagoan, Elijah Muhammad. Their message was eloquently expressed by an intelligent, sensitive young man known as Malcolm X. They taught that white people were so consumed by evil that they were

Wide World

The Muslim minister Malcolm X called Kennedy's assassination an example of "the chickens coming home to roost"—meaning that because whites had used violence against others, violence would sooner or later be used against them. The next year his views softened and he began to preach brotherhood between blacks and whites, but in 1965 he was assassinated in New York City.

beyond redemption and that blacks should completely separate themselves from white society. They preached that if there was no other way to achieve their goals, blacks should not overlook tactics of violence.

The Civil Rights Act of 1964

And so Johnson set out to persuade Congress to pass the civil rights package put before it many months before by President Kennedy.

Getting the bill through the House of Representatives was no large problem. In February 1964 it won approval of the lower chamber by a vote of 290-130. The Senate was another matter. In the upper chamber of the national legislature eighteen members from states of the old Confederacy determined to do everything in their power to prevent the bill from coming to a vote. For there was no doubt that if given an opportunity to vote a substantial majority of senators would vote "yea."

The beginning of the southern filibuster, which would turn out to be the longest in the history of the Senate, was the signal for the president to bring into play once again his great powers of persuasion. And a central target of those powers was Everett McKinley Dirksen, the Republican minority leader in the Senate. Dirksen, the conservative senator from Illinois, alone could round up the votes needed to invoke cloture—approval of a resolution by three-fourths of the members of the Senate to stop the filibuster and bring the bill to a vote. At length Dirksen—whose smooth tones and flowery phrases had inspired newsmen to refer to him affectionately as "the wizard of ooze"—agreed to support a cloture resolution. The filibuster ended, and the legislation won consent of the Senate by a vote of 73-27.

After the House accepted a few minor amendments by the Senate, President Johnson, on July 2, 1964, signed the Civil Rights Act of 1964. The most sweeping equal rights legislation ever enacted in America, the measure prohibited discrimination on account of race in hotels, restaurants, theaters, and other places of public accommodation. It authorized the attorney general to initiate suits or otherwise intervene in behalf of victims of discrimination. It forbade both employers and labor unions to practice racial discrimination (striking down "white only" charters of numerous labor organizations). It also allowed the withholding of federal funds from projects in which racial discrimination persisted. Finally, it forbade the application of different standards of eligibility to whites and blacks who sought to register and vote.

Economic Opportunity Act

President Johnson believed that much Negro unrest in the country arose from the kinds of indignities and injustices which the Civil Rights Act of 1964 sought to counter. He also felt certain that a central cause of black anger and frustration—which in his first year in the White House produced violent outbursts in New York, Rochester, Jersey City, and Chicago—was the fact that a large percentage of the black population was mired in poverty. To relieve that anger and frustration and bring the poor—both black and white—into the mainstream of American society he believed that Americans must strike hard at the problem of poverty. Hence the president, in early 1964, asked Congress to approve a sweeping antipoverty measure.

Some whites—increasingly taken up in an antiblack "backlash"—opposed new programs designed to benefit Negroes. Prompted by this attitude, conservatives on Capitol Hill reacted

Children in New York's Harlem have nowhere to go but the streets. In 1964, 233,000 people lived in an area of New York 45 blocks long and 11 blocks wide. The Economic Opportunity Act was designed to help to free people from poverty. What were some of the functions of the Office of Economic Opportunity?

negatively to the President's request. Whereupon Johnson swung into action. He coaxed reluctant members of Congress, and, for his part, accepted a few minor amendments to the proposal. As a result the legislation passed. On August 20, 1964, in the Rose Garden of the White House, Johnson put his signature to the Economic Opportunity Act.

Specifically, the measure provided for establishment of rural conservation camps and urban training centers to help forty thousand school dropouts obtain job training, work-training programs to enable two hundred thousand boys and girls to stay in school by providing them with part-time employment, and part-time jobs to help one hundred forty thousand college and university students to remain in school. It provided federal funds to urban and rural communities to help them combat poverty and illiteracy, loans to farmers to help them improve their land, and loans to small businesses to encourage them to hire the chronically unemployed. It provided for job-training programs for heads of families who were on welfare rolls and, finally, established a central agency – the Office of Economic Opportunity – to coordinate the antipoverty program.

While the tax cut, the Civil Rights Act and the Economic Opportunity Act were the major legislative achievements in his first year in the White House, President Johnson also could point to other successes. He persuaded Congress to establish a nine-million-acre wilderness preserve from government-owned lands, enact a housing bill providing for construction of thirty-five thousand low-rent housing units for poor families, and approve a measure whereby the federal government would contribute $375 million over a three-year period to help cities improve and expand public transit facilities. He also prevailed on Congress to appropriate $400 million to continue federal aid to schools in "impacted areas" – schools whose enrollments had been swollen by federal installations or projects. He persuaded Congress to extend the National Defense Education Act until 1968, and amend the measure to provide support for instruction and training in the humanities as well as science.

Johnson also felt the sting of legislative defeat in his first year in the presidency. To counter economic distress and promote economic growth in Appalachia – a poverty-ridden area of eleven states bordering the Appalachian Mountains – he asked for an appropriation of $1 billion. After winning approval of the Senate the measure failed to come up for a vote in the House. Equally disappointing to Johnson was the failure of Medicare – a measure to provide medical assistance to the elderly under the Social Security system – to win consent of Congress.

At the same time that he was laboring to get his legislative proposals through Congress, during his first year in the White House, President Johnson also was dealing with assorted diplomatic problems. The first of these originated in a completely unexpected quarter, Panama. Touching off the difficulty in Panama, in early 1964, was a dispute over the flying of flags in the Canal Zone. But the root of the problem was the conviction of many Panamanians that they were not receiving a fair share of the returns from the Panama Canal. Johnson recognized the validity of some of Panama's complaints. He agreed to negotiations aimed at revising the treaty of 1903 under which the United States owned and operated the Panama Canal. The outcome was a treaty which gave Panama a larger financial return from operation of the canal and an increased role in management of the waterway. The treaty also provided for the gradual integration of North Americans who lived in the Canal Zone into Panamanian life.

The Vietnam Conflict

When Johnson took over the White House, the situation in South Vietnam seemed fluid. Meeting minimal opposition from government troops, the Viet Cong continued to prowl the countryside, extorting taxes from terrified peasants and murdering village chieftains. Meanwhile the new leaders in Saigon – the successors of the late President Diem – struggled to fashion a workable administration. Leaders of the United States continued to believe that America's national interest required a non-Communist South Vietnam. They hoped that somehow, without any substantial increase in America's involvement in the area, the Communists could be thwarted in their ambition to take over the country. But of one thing the Americans were certain: unless the non-Communists of South Vietnam achieved political stability, they stood no chance of overcoming the well-organized and highly disciplined Communists. And political stability continued to elude the country's non-Communists. On the contrary, February 1964 brought another coup in Saigon which propelled a new "strong man," General Nguyen Khanh, to leadership of the government.

Then, on August 2, 1964, the government in Washington announced that North Vietnamese torpedo boats had attacked the American destroyer *Maddox* in international waters in the Gulf of Tonkin off the coast of North Vietnam. Two days later the government announced a second attack in the Gulf of Tonkin, this time on the *Maddox* and the destroyer *C. Turner Joy*. (The "Pentagon Papers" published in 1971 indicate that units under General William C. Westmoreland made an amphibious raid on the North Vietnamese islands of Hon Me and Hon Ngu in the Gulf of Tonkin and that the North Vietnamese boats that attacked the *Maddox* had mistaken the *Maddox* for a South Vietnamese escort vessel.)

Claiming that the Communists had committed aggression against the United States, President Johnson sent American bombing planes on a retaliatory raid against North Vietnamese torpedo boats and their bases. At the same time he asked Congress to approve a resolution expressing approval of the retaliatory raid and authorizing him to do whatever he might consider necessary to counter Communist "aggression" in Southeast Asia. The outcome was the Gulf of Tonkin resolution, voted unanimously in the House and opposed in the Senate by only a handful of members. These senators feared that it might become an instrument for justifying a massive escalation of America's military involvement in Southeast Asia. Still, it did not seem likely that the president would use the resolution for enlarging the war at the time. And in subsequent weeks Johnson on several occasions emphasized that ultimate responsibility for stopping Communist ambitions in Asia rested with Asians.

STUDY GUIDE: After President Kennedy was assassinated, Vice-President Lyndon B. Johnson was sworn in as president. Johnson had been active in politics since the early days of Franklin D. Roosevelt's administration. He served as a congressman from 1937 to 1941. During World War II, he served in the navy. Johnson was reelected to the House in 1942, 1944, and 1946. In 1948 he won a Senate seat. He served as Democratic minority leader during his first term. In 1955, he became Senate majority leader.

Johnson tried to get the Democratic presidential nomination in 1960 but was unsuccessful because of his lack of popularity with liberal Democrats. However, Kennedy named him as his vice-presidential running mate.

As president, Johnson's first target was to improve the nation's lagging economy. He introduced tax-cut measures which were passed by Congress in February 1964. He then set about securing passage of Kennedy's civil rights legislation which had been presented to Congress many months earlier. Then the Senate began the longest filibuster in its history. It ended when Senate minority leader Everett Dirksen agreed to support cloture. The law was passed, and in July the Civil Rights Act of 1964 was signed. It was the most sweeping civil rights law ever enacted in America.

Johnson also supported a broad antipoverty measure. Consequently the Economic Opportunity Act was signed into law in August 1964. It provided for creation of the Office of Economic Opportunity.

Johnson had other legislative achievements and a few defeats during his first year in office. He saw a dispute in Panama result in a treaty which gave Panama more influence in the operation of the Canal.

After an incident in the South China Sea Congress passed the Gulf of Tonkin Resolution. The resolution gave the president power to do whatever he might consider necessary to stop Communist aggression in Southeast Asia.

THE ELECTION OF 1964

At the time Congress was approving the Gulf of Tonkin resolution a national political campaign was gathering momentum, for 1964 was an election year.

By virtue of an active and heavily financed campaign in the months after President Kennedy's assassination, Senator Barry M. Goldwater, a conservative from Arizona, had won the Republican nomination for president at the national convention in San Francisco, despite the obvious fact that a large majority of rank-and-file Republicans across the country opposed his candidacy. Next, at the end of August, the Democrats met at Atlantic City and, in humdrum fashion, nominated Johnson for president and Senator Hubert H. Humphrey of Minnesota for vice-president.

The Goldwater-Johnson contest was dull and uninspiring. Goldwater slashed away at Johnson with the conservative argument that Democrats had shackled the country with "big government" and the charge that Democrats were "soft on communism," a relic of the dark days of Joseph McCarthy. For his part, President Johnson spoke out in generalities for a domestic program to achieve the "Great Society." He suggested that Goldwater was apt to propel the United States into some dangerous confrontation with the Communists, perhaps in Vietnam. Johnson, to be sure, could afford to play it cool. There was little doubt that he was going to win on election day – not because Johnson was particularly popular with voters, but because most Americans shuddered at the prospect that Goldwater, at once extremely conservative in domestic affairs and irrepressibly "hawkish" in foreign affairs, might be installed in the White House.

At length, on November 3, the tedious campaign ended. When ballots were counted Johnson and Humphrey received 43,100,000 votes to 27,100,000 for Goldwater and his running mate William Miller. With sixty-one percent of the popular vote the Democrats achieved what most political observers had considered an impossibility – they ran slightly better than had Franklin D. Roosevelt and John Nance Garner in the Democratic landslide of 1936. In the electoral college the Democratic ticket won by a margin of 486-52.

STUDY GUIDE: President Johnson was the Democratic candidate in the 1964 political campaign. Senator Barry Goldwater of Arizona was the Republican presidential candidate. During a very dull campaign, Johnson spoke out for a "Great Society." Goldwater accused the Democrats of being "soft on communism." In November Johnson won an overwhelming victory. He piled up more popular votes than Franklin Roosevelt had received in the landslide election of 1936.

THE GREAT SOCIETY

Now that he had been elected president in his own right, Lyndon Johnson confidently prepared to get on with the task of building the "Great Society." During 1965 Johnson brilliantly brought into play all his legendary parliamentary skills and immense presidential powers, not to mention the force of his own dynamic personality. He prevailed on Congress to consent to a program of domestic innovation and reform which in its magnitude and impact on American society rivaled the fabled "One Hundred Days" of 1933 when Franklin Roosevelt launched the New Deal.

Medicare

When the new Congress convened in January 1965, Johnson's first legislative proposal urged approval of a measure to provide medical assistance to elderly citizens under the social security program. This was essentially the same proposal that had been rejected the previous year.

For years the American Medical Association had attacked all proposals for medical assistance under social security on the ground that such assistance would be a giant leap toward socialized medicine in America. The AMA quickly organized for its traditional response and opened its treasury to finance a propaganda and lobbying campaign against the King-Anderson Bill, which embodied the president's proposal. To no avail. After several months of debate and legislative maneuvering the bill passed Congress. It provided limited coverage for hospital, posthospital, and nursing home care for most Americans who were sixty-five and older. This coverage would be financed by increases in social security taxes. For elderly citizens who wished to make a three-dollar-a-month supplemental payment, it provided partial coverage for services of physicians and surgeons, home visits by nurses or other health workers, and various additional medical services.

To sign the legislation President Johnson flew to Independence, Missouri, the home of former-President Truman. Back in 1945, Truman had made an impassioned appeal for a national health insurance program. Largely because of the opposition of the AMA, his proposal had gone down to defeat—a defeat which Truman always had considered one of the most disappointing of his years in the White House. Now eighty-one years old, Truman thanked Johnson for the honor of having the King-Anderson Bill signed in the Harry S. Truman Library. He also made a short speech in which he said no elderly citizen should ever be abandoned to the indignity of charity.

Education

While Congress was weighing the question of health care for older citizens, in early 1965, it was also considering a bill—the result of a request by President Johnson—to provide $1.5 billion of federal aid to the country's elementary and secondary schools.

For many years classrooms had been over-crowded, school buildings and equipment often antiquated, and teachers underpaid. Local authorities could not raise the taxes required to meet educational problems. As early as the 1940s, many Americans began to conclude that only the federal government could raise sufficient money to meet the problems of schools. However, every proposal for federal aid to education during the presidencies of Truman, Eisenhower, and Kennedy had come under heavy attack. Political conservatives argued that administration of a federal assistance program would be frightfully expensive and open the way for undesirable federal interference in local school affairs. Segregationists spoke out in fear that federal aid would provide the government in Washington with a powerful instrument for forcing school districts to accept racial integration. Many of the country's Roman Catholics, half of whose children were enrolled in church-operated parochial schools, opposed any proposal for federal aid to education which did not include assistance to parochial schools. But many of the country's Protestants and Jews contended that aid to church-operated schools would violate the provision in the Bill of Rights guaranteeing separation of church and state. Thus, all proposals for federal aid to schools had come to nothing.

Then came the Johnson-Humphrey landslide in the election of 1964. As a result, the old coalition of conservative northern Republicans and segregationist southern Democrats, which had dominated Congress for a quarter-century, went temporarily into eclipse. Hence the arguments of conservatives and segregationists against federal aid to education lost most of their force. Meanwhile a new climate of religious toleration had appeared, in part a result of the ecumenical movement set in motion a few years before by Pope John XXIII. Accordingly Protestants and Jews registered little protest and Catholics expressed delight when President Johnson requested legislation which would allow local school boards to use some of their federal funds to help pupils in parochial and private schools. Such help in part would be in the form of programs in which pupils of public and nonpublic schools would share classrooms for instruction in certain subjects. Funds also would be made available for purchase of certain textbooks and library materials for pupils of parochial and private schools.

At length, in mid-April 1965, Johnson's school aid requests won consent of Congress. A few days later, the president, who as a former school teacher felt a special attachment to the legislation, drove to the tiny one-room building in Blanco County, Texas, where he first had attended school. Sitting on a bench beside seventy-two-year-old Mrs. Kate Deadrich Loney, his first teacher—whom he addressed as "Miss Katie"—he signed the Elementary and Secondary Education Act of 1965.

Voting Rights Act

Of larger importance, or so it seemed in 1965, was the Voting Rights Act.

The main provisions of the Civil Rights Act of 1957 and 1960 concerned Negro voting. The Twenty-fourth Amendment to the Constitution (ratified in 1964) provided that the right of citizens to vote in federal elections should not be denied or abridged because of failure to pay a poll tax or other tax (thus removing a device long used in the South to keep blacks from the voting booth). And Title I of the Civil Rights Act of 1964 prohibited discriminatory standards and procedures and restricted use of literacy tests in determining voting qualifications. Still, only two million of the South's five million black adults were registered voters by the end of 1964. Many blacks were not registered because of ignorance of registration procedures. Some

Representatives of many religious organizations took part in the 1965 voter rights march in Selma, Alabama. Despite southern opposition, Congress passed the Civil Rights Voting Act five months later. Why did Martin Luther King pick Selma as the focal point for his voter registration drive?

others feared loss of employment and even physical harm at the hands of white racists if they tried to register. And others were victims of various devices by which local election officials made Negroes ineligible to vote.

Then, in January 1965, Martin Luther King, Jr. – his prestige at a peak as a result of receiving a Nobel Peace Prize – announced a campaign to get black southerners on voting rolls. To achieve his goal he turned to Selma, Alabama, a city in which racism ran deep and one in which the systematic disfranchisement of Negroes was clearly evident. If white resistance to black voting could be broken in Selma, he calculated, Negroes across the entire South might be encouraged to challenge barriers which were keeping them out of the voting booth. Equally important, his activity was sure to attract reporters, photographers, and television cameramen. It would draw national attention to the fact that Negroes were still being denied the right to vote. King hoped that the outcome would be massive demands by enraged Americans, particularly in the North and West, that obstacles to black voting be smashed.

Events went more or less as King expected. When great numbers of blacks marched to the courthouse in Selma to seek admission to voting rolls they were harassed and hauled off to jail by helmeted sheriff's deputies. To further publicize the voter-registration campaign, five hundred of King's followers set out on a march from Selma to the state capital in Montgomery. They came under brutal attack by deputies and state troopers. While walking along a darkened street in Selma, three white clergymen who had come from the North to support the voter-registration campaign were attacked. Two days later one of the clergymen, the Reverend James J. Reeb, a Unitarian minister, died of multiple skull fractures. Following a court-sanctioned march by voting rights crusaders from Selma to Montgomery, Mrs Viola Gregg Liuzzo, a white mother of five children from Detroit, was shot to death.

Events in Selma produced shock and outrage across the nation. They also persuaded President Johnson to go before a joint session of Congress (and a national television audience) and appeal for new voting rights legislation. He made the speech on March 15, 1965. After declaring that every citizen must have an equal right to vote, the president observed that "it is not just Negroes, but all of us, who must overcome the crippling legacy of bigotry and injustice." Then, slowly, emphatically, dramatically came the next words, taken from the anthem of the black revolution: "And we *shall* overcome." Despite tactics of delay and harassment by southern representatives and senators, the president's proposal moved relentlessly forward. Finally the voting rights legislation was passed by Congress. On August 6, 1965, in the Presidential Room of the Capitol, Johnson put his signature to the Voting Rights Act.

It was generally assumed that the Civil Rights Acts of 1957 and 1960 had failed to open the voting booth to blacks in the South because changes in local voting laws could be triggered only by local action – that is, by suits or complaints by blacks that they had been deprived of their right to vote because of racial discrimination. The 1965 Voting Rights Act set out a formula by which the federal government could go into local areas and register voters. Under this formula, the government would be able to take such action in all counties where, on November 1, 1964, literacy tests or similar restrictions on voting were in effect and where less than half of the voting-age citizens had been registered and actually voted in the presidential election of 1964. All of which meant that the federal government gained authority to register voters in all counties of Alabama, Georgia, Louisiana, Mississippi, South Carolina, and Virginia and thirty-four counties in North Carolina.

Other Reforms

The acts setting up Medicare, providing federal aid to schools, and guaranteeing the right to vote were not the only important achievements of President Johnson and Congress in 1965. There was an antipoverty measure authorizing $1.1 billion mostly to build roads and stimulate industry for Appalachia. Another appropriated $1.8 billion mainly for job retraining and Youth Corps camps. There were acts to combat pollution, including the Water Quality Act, which established a Federal Water Pollution Control Administration. The Water Quality Act increased funds for sewage treatment grants to states and directed states to establish pollution standards for interstate waters. There was legislation authorizing $350 million to aid regional programs for research into treatment of heart disease, cancer, stroke, and related diseases. A law was passed requiring all cigarette packages to carry a warning that smoking is dangerous to health. Other laws provided stronger controls over the distribution of barbiturate and amphetamine drugs. Funds were approved to support mental health centers and to care for retarded children.

To stimulate higher education Congress approved a bill providing $2.3 billion for federal guarantees of loans to college students, federal scholarships for needy college students, and federal grants-in-aid for constructing and equipping college facilities. A new immigration statute abolished the national origins quota system, setting a limit of 170,000 immigrants annually from outside the Western Hemisphere and a limit of 120,000 from within the hemisphere. For would-be immigrants from outside the Western Hemisphere the legislation established priorities for artists, scientists, professional people, skilled or unskilled workers who were needed to meet labor shortages in America, close relatives of American citizens, and refugees from communism or national disaster.

Then Congress created the Department of Housing and Urban Development (HUD). Other legislation included a highway beautification act restricting billboards and requiring screening of junkyards along interstate and primary road systems; passage of the High Speed Ground Transportation Act, which provided for investigation of a national approach to mass-transit problems; and establishment of a National Foundation on the Arts and Humanities. Housing legislation provided rent supple-

ments to low-income families, and the Older Americans Act set up an Administration on Aging. The Public Works and Economic Development Act consolidated and encouraged regional development programs. In addition, Congress approved a measure reducing excise taxes by $4.7 billion.

Despite these legislative triumphs, national attention was dramatically turned away from the accomplishments of the Johnson administration by an eruption of racial violence in Los Angeles. Centered in the Negro ghetto of Watts — an area of substandard housing, broken families, and high unemployment — the rioting came only a week after Johnson signed the Voting Rights Act.

When the rioting ended, great areas of the ghetto were blackened, smoldering ruins. Twenty-five blacks and nine whites had died during the violence.

STUDY GUIDE: Johnson sent legislation through Congress that resulted in better living conditions for the people of America. Included were medical care for the aged under social security, a comprehensive aid-to-education program, and a voting rights act. Other acts included an antipoverty program to stimulate industry in Appalachia, programs for combating water pollution, heart disease and cancer, and a new immigration statute. In 1965 the Department of Housing and Urban Development was created.

FOREIGN AFFAIRS

At the same time that he was engineering his program of domestic innovation and reform of 1965, President Johnson was also making important decisions affecting America's international affairs. Some of those decisions came as a result of an outbreak of civil war in the Dominican Republic.

Dominican Intervention

After gaining independence from Spain early in the 1800s, the Dominican Republic suffered continual turmoil, political instability, and grinding poverty over the next hundred years. Then, in 1930, Rafael Leonidas Trujillo Molina seized power. Over the next three decades he earned a reputation as one of the most corrupt and repressive dictators in history.

On a warm evening in May 1961, while riding in an automobile through the countryside, Trujillo was ambushed and killed by a band of discontented army officers. The following year, 1962, brought the first democratic elections in the Dominican Republic since 1924. When ballots were tabulated, the new president-elect was Dr. Juan Bosch, a white-haired man in his early fifties who had spent the previous twenty-four years in exile. A brilliant scholar, Bosch also was a gifted orator and a fervent idealist. On taking office in early 1963 he set out to establish a program of sweeping social reform. Unfortunately Bosch was a poor administrator, and, more serious, his reformist zeal angered well-to-do businessmen, planters, and military chieftains. The outcome, in September 1963, was a military coup which sent Bosch once more into exile.

Through 1964 and into 1965 the Dominican Republic appeared calm. But then, in April 1965, a band of civilians and young military officers who despised the conservatism, corruption, and heavy-handedness of the ruling military junta, seized a military barracks. From a small radio station the rebels announced that the military regime had been overthrown. Whereupon tens of thousands of Dominicans rushed to the streets to celebrate, waving flags, setting off firecrackers, shouting, singing, and cheering. And in San Juan, Puerto Rico, Juan Bosch prepared for a triumphal return to his homeland. The joy of rebel leaders, local citizens, and Bosch was not shared, however, by officials in the United States embassy in Santo Domingo. On the contrary, men in the embassy felt uneasy about events in the Dominican Republic. They were even more disturbed when the rhetoric beamed forth by rebel-controlled radio and television stations took on tones which sounded vaguely like those of the Castro rebels at the time they took over Cuba in 1958-59. Before long embassy officials decided that the uprising probably was Communist-inspired and Communist-led. Accordingly, Ambassador W. Tapley Bennett, Jr., urged President Johnson to intervene with North American forces to prevent a rebel victory if defeat of the military junta appeared imminent.

Johnson saw no reason to doubt the accuracy of reports coming from the embassy in Santo Domingo. He decided that under no circumstances would the United States stand by and permit a new Castro-style revolution to succeed in the Caribbean. He hoped of course that the junta would be able to take care of the "Communists" without any help from North America. Still, if it appeared that the rebels – who were waging a vigorous fight – were getting the upper hand, he was quite prepared to act. Meanwhile the president faced another problem – the safety of perhaps two thousand North American nationals who had been marooned in the strife-torn Dominican Republic. On the basis of grossly exaggerated reports that the embassy, where many North Americans had found refuge, was under rebel attack, he ordered marines from the helicopter carrier *Boxer* to move into Santo Domingo and offer protection to North Americans and other foreigners.

If the president had used United States forces in the Dominican Republic in April 1965 only to rescue foreign nationals, there would probably have been little criticism of his intervention. But when it became apparent that the rebels were winning the civil struggle, Johnson decided to use the marines, and also army paratroops, for political purposes. His aim was not simply to restore the junta to power but to stop the fighting, arrange for general elections, and return the Dominican Republic to constitutional government. Armed with machine-guns, bazookas, and rifles, the marines and paratroops moved in swiftly and methodically. They occupied strategic points in Santo Domingo and quickly persuaded the rebels and junta to accept a cease-fire.

Next, after several months of delicate negotiations, an agreement emerged. A former member of the Bosch cabinet and one of the most respected men in the Dominican Republic, Héctor García-Godoy, was commissioned to form a provisional government and arrange elections. Quite satisfactory to most rebels, the agreement was accepted by the junta – but only after not-so-gentle arm-twisting by the United States.

President Johnson believed that with little bloodshed he had stopped a civil war, prevented appearance of a new Castro-type regime in the Caribbean, and arranged the return of democratic rule to the Dominican Republic. Most journalists, foreign diplomats, and other observers believed that he had achieved nothing that the rebels could not have achieved for themselves, that is, an end to military rule and a return to democracy. Moreover, they contended that only a handful of the rebels were followers of Castro and that the United States, by its intervention, had resurrected memories of the despised Big Stick policies of a bygone era. Johnson's critics believed his action had offended Latin American sensibilities and weakened North American prestige south of the border — to the advantage of Communists.

Vietnam

While President Johnson was occupied with the intervention in the Dominican Republic, in 1965, the situation in South Vietnam took an abrupt turn for the worse. Inflation in the country was raging out of control, Buddhists again were demonstrating against the government in Saigon, and zealots once more were turning themselves into human torches. In the face of such developments, the government of General Khanh, torn by intrigue and corruption, seemed to be edging toward collapse. Out in the countryside, meanwhile, the South Vietnamese army appeared totally incapable of holding its own against the Communists.

Johnson shared the view of Eisenhower and Kennedy that a Communist take-over of South Vietnam would threaten the security and prosperity of the United States. He concluded that only an escalation of America's military involvement in South Vietnam could save the country from the Communists. Expansion of the air war to include targets in North Vietnam and the arrival of several thousand additional American ground troops in South Vietnam, he thought, would demonstrate America's seriousness of purpose and perhaps persuade the Viet Cong and their North Vietnamese supporters that their goals in South Vietnam were beyond reach. As a consequence, Johnson believed, the Communists, after a year or so, would agree to a negotiated settlement which would recognize South Vietnam's existence as a non-Communist state or, failing that, the war simply would fade away.

And so the president issued orders which increased America's involvement in the war.

How did Johnson's countrymen respond to the escalation? A large majority of them seemed to agree. Most Americans in 1965 accepted the argument that a non-Communist Southeast Asia was important to the interests and security of the United States and that the fall of South Vietnam to communism would open the way for a Communist take-over of Southeastern Asia. Supporters of America's involvement in South Vietnam insisted that the United States must not only prevent the spread of communism in

Southeast Asia but also contain the power of China. Only a few years before, the Chinese had launched a series of attacks on outposts high in the Himalayas on the India-Chinese frontier. The previous autumn they had exploded a nuclear bomb. To Americans, the Chinese seemed increasingly aggressive. They seemed to want to transform all the states on their borders into Communist satellites.

Still, some Americans opposed escalation of the war in Vietnam, including Senators Wayne Morse of Oregon, Mike Mansfield of Montana, and Ernest Gruening of Alaska. According to critics, the idea that the countries of Southeast Asia were like a row of dominoes rested on false logic. These critics argued that Southeast Asia, whatever its human and material resources, had no important bearing on the security and prosperity of the United States. As for China, critics contended that states in Southeast Asia which might become Communist would not necessarily become Chinese satellites. On the other hand, they felt that China, given its size, inevitably would become a dominant factor in the politics of the area.

What was America's interest in staying in Vietnam? In 1964 President Johnson had stated that the goal of the United States was to assure that South Vietnam would remain independent and non-Communist. According to the "Pentagon Papers" made public in 1971, Secretary of Defense Robert S. McNamara indicated in 1964 that the aim of the United States was to test its capacity to help a nation defend itself against a Communist war of liberation. In other words, South Vietnam was only a test case in the worldwide campaign of the United States to contain communism. Later in 1965, McNamara approved a statement by one his assistants that the goal of the United States was "not to help a friend, but to contain China." McNamara's assistant evaluated United States goals differently: 70 percent to avoid the humiliation of defeat, 20 percent to keep South Vietnamese territory from being taken by China, and 10 percent to make it possible for the South Vietnamese to enjoy a better life.

The confusion of American leaders concerning goals of war was shared by most of the population. Supporters of the war, known as "hawks," and opponents of the war, known as "doves," exchanged opinions in bitter words, and emotions ran high.

While Americans were weighing the merits of their country's increasing involvement in the war, in spring 1965, speaking at Johns Hopkins University, President Johnson offered to enter "unconditional" negotiations aimed at bringing peace to Vietnam. He also urged all countries of Southeast Asia, including North Vietnam, to join together with the United States and other industrial nations in a massive program to bring economic and social improvement to the area. Johnson's proposals brought only hoots from Vietnam's Communists. Meanwhile the buildup of American forces in Vietnam continued.

Through 1965 American soldiers and marines stayed close to assorted strong points and had limited contact with the enemy. But pilots of the American air force and navy, zooming off from air strips in South Vietnam and Thailand and carriers in the South China Sea, steered their fighter-bombers on an endless stream of raids. They showered countless targets, claimed to be military, in South and North Vietnam and southeastern Laos with bombs and rockets and napalm.

As 1965 drew to a close, leaders in Washington felt optimistic about prospects in South Vietnam. The arrival of a substantial American force in the country had headed off a military collapse. The political situation apparently had stabilized with the accession to the premiership, in June 1965, of Air Vice-Marshal Nguyen Cao Ky, a swashbuckling "strong man." Thus, American leaders believed, it should be evident to the Communists that a take-over of South Vietnam now was beyond their reach. All they stood to gain from continuing the war was a merciless battering by American air power. If America's ground forces moved out from their strong points (as they doubtless would if the war continued), destruction of Communist regiments seemed inevitable. According to Western logic the conclusion was clear: the Communists ought to be ready to face up to reality and enter serious discussions aimed at achieving a negotiated end of the war. As a result, in late December 1965, President Johnson launched a "peace offensive" which he hoped would bring the war to the conference table. To show his good intentions, he proclaimed a bombing pause over North Vietnam.

The War Drags On

Ho Chi Minh and the Communists of Vietnam, however, did not think along the lines of Western logic. They calculated that if the war in Vietnam became more or less stalemated, American casualty lists became longer, and the expense of carrying on the war began to pinch the national pocket book, the people of the United States would decide that the war was not very important. Americans would then begin to press their leaders to end the war at almost any price. At that point, the Communists thought, the Americans would accept a negotiated settlement which would leave the way open for a Communist take-over. Or they simply would pack up and leave South Vietnam and permit the anti-Communist South Vietnamese to collapse before superior Communist forces.

And so the Ho Chi Minh formula for an eventual Communist victory in South Vietnam was obvious: make no peace settlement, keep up the fight, and wait for the patience of the Americans to become exhausted. Thus, the Communists took advantage of the bombing pause to send men and equipment streaming down the Ho Chi Minh Trail from North Vietnam to reinforce their units in South Vietnam. They responded to Johnson's peace overtures by insisting on conditions which were sure to be rejected. Whereupon, at the end of January 1966, after thirty-seven days, the bombing pause was ended and American fighter-bombers once more began to streak northward over North Vietnam.

B-52 bombers like these extended their raids to North Vietnam on President Johnson's orders. What were some of the arguments for and against escalating the war?

Official U.S. Air Force Photo

Search-and-destroy missions often were carried out in areas like this where dense foliage made it impossible to avoid ambush. By 1966 more than one hundred American soldiers were dying each week in Vietnam. Can their deaths—or the deaths in any war—be justified?

Meanwhile, ground forces began search-and-destroy operations through swamps and jungles. These were massive operations which included GIs backed up by artillery, tanks, and tactical aircraft. But the big American battalions were noisy and unwieldy, and the Communists often were able to ambush them or to slip away into the jungle. As a result, these operations failed, and American casualties mounted. More than one hundred American soldiers were dying in Vietnam every week by the spring of 1966.

Not all of America's combat troops in Vietnam were engaged in search-and-destroy maneuvers. Because the Ho Chi Minh Trail was long and winding, the Communists, in summer 1966, began establishing more direct lines of communication between North and South Vietnam—straight across the demilitarized zone (DMZ) which separated the two sections of the country. The outcome was a series of bloody battles with American marines for the high ground in the vicinity of the DMZ. Notwithstanding high casualties, the marines won and denied the Communists an easier access from North Vietnam to South Vietnam.

Meanwhile there were stirrings far from the main battle areas. Like his predecessors, Premier Ky found himself at odds with the Buddhists. In late summer 1966, following a new wave of antigovernment demonstrations and ceremonial suicides, Ky moved soldiers and police to the Buddhist centers of Hué and Da Nang and effectively crushed the Buddhist revolt. Although they failed to topple Ky's government, the Buddhists nonetheless did succeed in forcing the premier to redeem his pledge to call general elections. Despite a campaign of terror and intimidation by the Communists, more than eighty percent of the citizens who were eligible to vote trooped to polling places in September 1966. Voters elected a 117-member assembly which was commissioned to fashion a new constitution for the country. While the wheels of democracy were beginning to turn in South Vietnam, President Johnson kept up the search for peace via negotiations. To that end, in October 1966, he made a new peace proposal during a seventeen-day trip to the Western Pacific and East Asia. The Communists were not interested.

Through 1967 the war in Vietnam continued to escalate. Despite the loss of many multimillion-dollar aircraft and, more important, their crews—and despite expressions of outrage around the world that strategic bombing was unjustifiable because it sometimes brought death to civilians—the air war was expanded. New targets, particularly bridges and supply dumps and railroads, were brought under attack by American fighter-bombers. In the ground war American soldiers and marines, whose manpower swelled to nearly a half million during the year, continued to resist the Communists along the DMZ and to search and destroy. The Communists continued their terror tactics of strike-and-run against the civil population. During a four-day cease-fire proclaimed in honor of *Tet* — a national holiday period celebrating the lunar New Year in Southeast Asia — the Communists secretly brought long-range rocket launchers and ammunition into South Vietnam. Then they set off a series of surprise attacks against American installations, notably the big base at Da Nang. During 1967, moreover, it became apparent that the Communists, in violation of Cambodian territory, had established base camps and supply stations in Cambodia. The Cambodian bases were being used to reinforce units across the border in South Vietnam.

In 1967 weekly American casualty lists were twice as long as those of 1966 (during which five thousand Americans had died in combat). The Communists were also showing no signs of giving up the fight. Despite such discouraging developments, most American leaders felt optimistic about prospects in South Vietnam as 1967 drew to a close. The rural pacification program in South Vietnam seemed to be gaining momentum. Equally important, the previous September, eighty-three percent of South Vietnam's voters had gone to the polls despite another campaign of terror and harassment by the Communists. In accord with the new constitution drawn up by the assembly chosen the previous year, they elected a president and a national house of representatives. Following the election a constitutional administration headed by General Nguyen Van Thieu had taken the reins of power in Saigon. Thus South Vietnam seemed to be achieving a new measure of political stability. In Washington in November 1967 the American commander in Vietnam, General William C. Westmoreland, expressed the sentiment of most American leaders when he described the situation in Vietnam as "very, very encouraging."

Antiwar Sentiment Grows in America

General Westmoreland's optimism in 1967 made little impression on increasing numbers of Americans. Many of them were coming to believe that America's participation in the war in Vietnam had been a monumental mistake.

War critics were not united in their reasons for challenging America's involvement in the conflict. A great many people were troubled by the grisly pictures of death and destruction which appeared on television newscasts nearly every evening. They saw residential sections of Hanoi hit by stray American bombs and villagers sifting through the rubble of houses shelled by American artillery because of a suspicion that the houses were providing sanctuary for Viet Cong soldiers. They were horrified to see peasants burned by napalm dropped by American airmen in areas where Communist troops were thought to be concentrated. Such people concluded that America's purposes in the war could not possibly justify the cost of the war in terms of the misery and anguish of the Vietnamese people. Other critics emphasized the billions upon billions of dollars which were going to sustain the military effort in Vietnam. They pondered what those billions could do to counter unemployment, slum housing, and inadequate social services in black ghettos of urban America. Then some critics in America were political leftists who wanted to see Ho Chi Minh win.

As antiwar sentiment in America increased, many critics, particularly among the young, expressed their feelings in ways which seemed shocking and even seditious in the view of older generations of Americans. Some young protesters burned American flags, publicly destroyed or burned their draft cards, jeered men in uniform, attacked buildings on college campuses which housed Reserve Officer Training Corps (ROTC) programs, and paraded down main thoroughfares of American cities carrying Viet Cong flags. And in October 1967 some fifty thousand protesters held a rally in front of the Lincoln Memorial in Washington. Afterward, several thousand of them crashed against a line of policemen and paratroops as they sought to storm the Pentagon.

Yet most antiwar protests were peaceful. In every major city, young people demonstrated their opposition to the war in Vietnam by circulating petitions, writing letters, and organizing large marches and rallies.

Criticism of the war also increased on Capitol Hill in 1967. As in previous years, the most outspoken critics were members of President Johnson's own party: Senators J. William Fulbright of Arkansas, George McGovern of South Dakota, Eugene McCarthy of Minnesota, Robert F. Kennedy of New York (who had resigned from Johnson's cabinet and in 1966 won election to the Senate), Frank Church of Idaho, and Vance Hartke of Indiana. Fulbright was particularly prominent among congressional critics.

As chairman of the Senate Foreign Relations Committee, he presided over hearings in which it was charged that the president had exceeded his constitutional authority by committing the United States to a major war in Vietnam. Johnson replied that all of his actions in Vietnam over the past two years had been within limits of authority granted him in the Gulf of Tonkin resolution of 1964. Then, late in 1967, Senator Eugene McCarthy moved into the spotlight by announcing that, because of differences with Johnson over the war, he would run for the Democratic nomination for president in 1968. He at once found that many war critics, notably college and university students and some professors, were rallying to his support.

THE ELECTION OF 1968

At the dawn of 1968, America was in turmoil. The country remained bitterly divided over the war in Vietnam. Legions of young people were in open revolt against the moral values of their elders. Racial unrest was rampant. Still, 1968 was an election year. Perhaps a national referendum on the problems plaguing the country

Becky Young

In the U.S., opposition to the Vietnam war became open and vocal. Many rallies like this one were staged across the country.

would clear the air, generate fresh ideas, and result in the election of imaginative leaders.

President Johnson had begun to feel frustrated by the slow progress of the Vietnam war by the start of 1968. He resented protests by antiwar critics. He worried about the racial violence which had flared in city after city in the past two years. And like most Americans his age, he was puzzled and distressed by the youth rebellion.

Still, Johnson could look back over the past two years with some satisfaction. He had appointed the first black cabinet member, Robert C. Weaver, and the first black justice of the Supreme Court, Thurgood Marshall. He had signed bills to improve public health services, upgrade the national park system, and improve highway safety. He had signed the Truth in Packaging Act, the Model Cities Act, and the Air Quality Act. He had approved a new "GI bill of rights" for veterans, a new minimum wage, a new meat inspection act, a measure to encourage oceanography, and a bill to establish the Department of Transportation. In foreign affairs, Johnson's administration had defused a crisis on Cyprus. Communists had failed in an attempt to take over Indonesia. And America's friend Israel had mauled its Arab enemies in the Six-Day War of 1967.

As a result, Johnson looked forward with cautious optimism to 1968, the last full year of his current term in office. He was confident that he would win reelection. But then came trouble. In late January, North Korean gunboats seized a lightly armed American intelligence vessel, the

U.S.S. Pueblo. Next, a week later, the Communists unleashed a murderous attack on South Vietnam's cities.

The *Tet* Offensive

The North Vietnamese had proposed a week-long cease-fire in January in honor of the lunar New Year, or *Tet.* When United States and South Vietnamese military leaders accepted the proposal, thousands of South Vietnamese soldiers, the main guards of the cities, trooped off to their villages for a few days of companionship and revelry.

Meanwhile, the Communists slipped guerrillas and ammunition into Saigon and twenty-six provincial capitals. Other Communist units advanced to the outskirts of the cities and set up rocket launchers and mortar tubes. Then, on January 30 and 31, the Communists let fly their "*Tet* offensive." While rockets and mortar shells crashed into downtown areas, guerrillas roamed city streets. They killed public officials, blew up utilities, and touched off mass terror. After a week or so, however, American firepower turned the tide of battle in one city after another.

The Communists had failed to achieve their aim of provoking a revolutionary uprising by the people of South Vietnam. They also had lost more than fifty thousand men. But few Americans accepted claims by their military leaders that the *Tet* offensive had been a disaster for the Communists. The fact that the Communists had been able to mount such an offensive indicated that the American military had been too optimistic about the war. Americans also were numbed by television pictures showing the mangled bodies of civilians caught in the inevitable crossfires, American bombers swooping down on houses in which guerrillas were thought to be hidden, and marines blasting their way into ancient temples at Hué.

The *Tet* offensive gave the Communists a magnificent psychological victory—in America. It fired antiwar sentiment in the United States and dramatically reduced the willingness of Americans to continue the war.

President Johnson Withdraws

Then, in March, voters in New Hampshire went to the polls in the first presidential primary election of the year. President Johnson won only 49.4 percent of the Democratic votes. His antiwar challenger, Senator Eugene McCarthy of Minnesota, won a surprising 42.2 percent. Suddenly Johnson's renomination no longer seemed certain. Soon a second challenger, Senator

Robert F. Kennedy of New York, brother of the late President Kennedy, announced that he would compete with Johnson for the Democratic nomination.

Shaken by the *Tet* offensive and the New Hampshire primary, Johnson acted boldly. He denied General William Westmoreland's request that 200,000 more GIs be sent to Vietnam. To encourage the Communists to enter peace talks, he ended bombing raids over most of North Vietnam. Finally, aware that he had become the national symbol of an increasingly unpopular and divisive war, Johnson announced in March that he would not seek reelection.

Dr. King and Senator Kennedy Murdered

Leaders in Hanoi showed a willingness on April 3 to enter peace talks. But the following day brought tragedy in the United States. It happened in Memphis, where Dr. Martin Luther King, Jr., was visiting to support demonstrations by striking sanitation workers. As twilight was settling over the city, King stepped to a balcony outside his room on the second floor of the Lorraine Motel. Suddenly the calm was shattered by the crack of a rifle, fired from a window of a dingy hotel across the street. The champion of nonviolence was killed instantly. James Earl Ray later was convicted of the murder.

Tragedy begot tragedy. Within hours, news of King's murder caused rioting by blacks in the ghettos of America's cities. Violence erupted in 125 cities. In Washington, D.C., residents of a ghetto only a few blocks from the White House vented their anger and frustration in a massive outburst of looting and burning. Millions of Americans were frightened by photographs showing clouds of smoke floating out of the ghetto and over the White House.

As a memorial to King and as a peace gesture to blacks, Congress rammed through the Civil Rights Act of 1968. The law barred discrimination in the sale or rental of eighty percent of the country's housing. But as a tool to pacify black Americans, it failed.

Meanwhile, many citizens were concentrating on the contest to succeed Johnson as president. Former-Vice-President Richard M. Nixon had no serious challenger for the Republican nomination. Thus interest centered on the Democratic competition.

In early June, attention turned to California, where Democratic Senators Kennedy and McCarthy were competing in the last major primary election of the year. When the ballots were counted Kennedy was the winner. But then the

After learning that he had won an important presidential primary election in California, Senator Robert F. Kennedy made a victory speech. Moments after he finished speaking he was fatally shot.

Kennedy campaign ended. After issuing a victory statement at the Ambassador Hotel in Los Angeles, Kennedy was shot by an assassin while walking through a crowded serving pantry. Twenty-four hours later, "Bobby" Kennedy was dead. Sirhan Sirhan later was convicted of his murder.

The Nominating Conventions

As expected, the Republicans nominated Nixon for president at their July convention in Miami. At Nixon's urging they nominated Governor Spiro T. Agnew of Maryland for vice-president. The Democrats met in Chicago three weeks later, and the outcome was a political disaster.

On the eve of the Democratic convention, about 10,000 young people assembled in Chicago. They hoped to persuade delegates to repudiate the war in Vietnam and to nominate McCarthy for president. The upshot was a series of violent clashes between young demonstrators and police outside the convention hall. Millions of Americans watched the drama on television with a mixture of horror and disbelief.

Inside the convention hall, Democrats were holding the most tumultuous political gathering in anyone's memory. Debate raged between supporters of Senator McCarthy and Vice-Presi-

dent Hubert H. Humphrey. The shouting and gavel-pounding reached a peak when antiwar delegates, most of whom supported McCarthy, demanded a platform pledging a dramatic reduction of America's involvement in Vietnam. Other delegates, most of them supporters of Humphrey, wanted to cut back America's involvement only to the extent that the South Vietnamese could take over their own defense.

Over howls of anguish by pro-McCarthy delegates, the Humphrey delegates prevailed. With McCarthy's supporters defeated in the platform struggle, the nomination of Humphrey was assured. Humphrey named Senator Edmund S. Muskie of Maine as his vice-presidential running-mate.

The Voters Choose

It appeared that "the battle of Chicago" had destroyed Democratic unity, and with it any chance of a Democratic presidential victory. But that did not mean that Nixon would win a majority of the electoral votes. For there was another serious candidate for president in 1968, Governor George C. Wallace of Alabama, who had organized his own political party.

A one-time champion of racial segregation and a spokesman for what he called "law and order," Wallace knew he could not win the election. But by carrying most of the South, he hoped to prevent either Nixon or Humphrey from winning a majority of electoral votes. In that event, the election would be resolved by the House of Representatives. Then, in return for his endorsement, Wallace might extract pledges from either Nixon or Humphrey. Wallace hoped that in return for his support either Nixon or Humphrey might agree to end federal programs to secure equal rights for blacks.

Opinion polls showed that Nixon had a commanding lead over Humphrey. Nixon was considered a "hawk"—a supporter of the Vietnam War. To win over antiwar voters—the "doves"—Vice-President Humphrey spoke out in favor of an unconditional end to all bombing of North Vietnam. A short time later the Humphrey campaign began to catch fire. Then, a few days before the election, President Johnson announced a total bombing halt over North Vietnam. In return, the North Vietnamese agreed to begin serious peace talks in Paris. Johnson's announcement added new fuel to Humphrey's campaign.

By election day Nixon and Humphrey were nearly tied. When the votes were counted, Nixon had 31,770,237 to Humphrey's 31,270,533. The Wallace strategy of throwing the election into

Candidates Richard Nixon and Spiro Agnew acknowledge the applause of fellow Republicans at the final session of the 1968 nominating convention. Early in the campaign which followed, Nixon had a substantial lead over Humphrey. What factors helped Humphrey narrow this lead?

Compix

the House of Representatives failed when Nixon won a clear majority of electoral votes: 301 to 191 for Humphrey. Wallace received only 46. Despite Nixon's victory, the Democrats retained control of both houses of Congress.

STUDY GUIDE: At the start of 1968 President Johnson was sure that he could win another term in the White House. But the Communists' impressive *Tet* offensive in South Vietnam produced a new wave of antiwar sentiment in the United States. Then, in early March, Johnson ran poorly in the presidential primary election in New Hampshire. Soon afterward he announced that he would not seek another term.

In April an assassin killed Dr. Martin Luther King, Jr. An outburst of violence in urban ghettos followed. A few weeks after King's murder, Senator Robert Kennedy, a Democratic presidential candidate, also was assassinated.

That summer, the Republicans nominated Richard Nixon for president. The Democrats nominated Vice-President Hubert Humphrey during a convention filled with turmoil over the Vietnam War. George Wallace ran as an independent candidate for president.

Nixon won the 1968 presidential election. However, the Democrats kept control of Congress.

CLOSER TO THE MOON

The moon program which had been launched in 1961 by President Kennedy was continuing under Johnson's administration. Space scientists were designing more and more complex programs, and each success brought them one step closer to their goal of landing a man on the moon.

The Mercury program, the first stage of America's manned space flight program which had begun in 1960, ended in 1963 when Leroy Gordon Cooper splashed down in the Atlantic in the spacecraft *Faith 7*. It was time for the next step: Project Gemini. Its name was taken from the Latin word for twins. Its goal was to put two astronauts in the same spacecraft into orbit around the earth.

By March of 1965 the first two-passenger Gemini spacecraft was ready, and a Titan 2 rocket pushed Virgil I. ("Gus") Grissom and John W. Young into orbit. After three revolutions of the earth they splashed down safely.

In June of 1965, during the fourth Gemini mission, astronaut Edward H. White II became the first American to take a "spacewalk," a feat already performed by the Soviets. After climbing out of the space capsule, White took a twenty-five-minute "walk in space" while dangling at the end of a long, thin, life-support cable.

The Gemini program continued throughout 1965 and 1966. August 1965 brought a trouble-plagued mission which ended safely. In December two spacecraft, launched several days apart, succeeded in coming within 150 feet of one another in space—a "rendezvous," or meeting, which was another essential step in the moon program. A few months later, Neil Armstrong performed a successful docking of two spacecraft in March 1966 when he attached his *Gemini 8* capsule to an unmanned vehicle in space. The next mission failed to achieve a docking, but then came three nearly perfect flights in July, September, and November of 1966. With these three successes, Project Gemini completed its role. Scientists began to prepare for Project Apollo, the program to reach the moon.

Then came tragedy. It happened during a final rehearsal in preparation for the first manned test of the Apollo spacecraft in January 1967. Astronauts "Gus" Grissom, Edward White, and Roger B. Chaffee were sealed in their spacecraft atop a Saturn rocket when fire broke out in the cabin. All three died. Their loss was a severe setback to the Apollo program.

Late in 1967, a giant Saturn 5 rocket—America's largest rocket ever—sent an unmanned Apollo spacecraft into earth orbit on a test flight. The flight proved that the United States had a rocket powerful enough to send a spacecraft to the moon. Its success was followed a few months later, in January 1968, by a successful unmanned flight of a small lunar (moon) module on a flight around the earth. The vehicle would, in a future flight, separate from the command ship as it orbited the moon, carry two astronauts down to the moon's surface, and then return them to the orbiting Apollo craft.

The first manned Apollo flight came in April of 1968. This was a successful test flight in which three astronauts orbited the earth in an Apollo spacecraft and made the first live television broadcasts from outer space.

Next came the most celebrated American space flight since John Glenn orbited the earth in *Friendship 7* back in 1962: the three-man flight of *Apollo 8*. Its mission was to orbit the moon. Its commander, Major Frank Borman of the air force, and two other astronauts, James Lovell and William Anders, lifted off December 21. After two revolutions of the earth, the spacecraft was kicked out of earth orbit and went streaking toward the moon, nearly a quarter of a million miles away.

Three days later, on Christmas Eve, 1968, *Apollo 8* went into orbit around the moon. Near the end of a live telecast, as TV cameras transmitted pictures of the forbidding lunar surface, Borman announced that the crew of *Apollo 8* wished to send a message to the people on earth. Then all three members of the crew took turns reading from *Genesis*, the first book of the *Bible* which tells the story of the Creation.

On Christmas morning, rockets were reignited and *Apollo 8* headed home toward earth and a successful splashdown in the Pacific. The mission had given Americans their closest view yet of the moon.

HEALTH AND COMPUTER SCIENCES

The 1960s were years of impressive scientific and technical accomplishments. The human heart transplant was the most publicized scientific achievement outside the space program. The first heart transplant was performed in 1967 by Dr. Christiaan Barnard of South Africa. The technique captured the world's imagination, and soon other surgeons were performing transplants. In the United States the most active heart transplant surgeon was Dr. Denton Cooley of Houston. Unfortunately, only a fraction of those who received "new" hearts survived for as long as a year. But the limited successes of Barnard and Cooley demonstrated the enormous strides which science was making in the battle against disease.

Meanwhile, other scientists were exploring the depths of the world's oceans, isolating human genes, and developing a vaccine against measles. Some of the most important scientific work of the period was done by teams of agronomists. These agricultural biologists were working to develop hybrid strains of wheat, rice, and other grains which would dramatically increase yield. The outcome was a "green revolution"—a large increase in the output of grains in several areas of the world. Dr. Norman E. Borlaug, an American, won the Nobel Prize for his work. By using his hybrid seeds, India nearly doubled its output of wheat between 1965 and 1970.

The technology of the Kennedy-Johnson era brought development of the Boeing 747 "jumbo jet." But the technical achievement which probably touched Americans most often was the rapid development of the computer. During the 1960s, electronics firms designed increasingly sophisticated computers which revolutionized the operations of corporations and government agencies, hospitals and the armed forces. By the end of the 1960s, engineers and technicians were perfecting computers which could land airplanes and perform medical examinations, teach classes and control urban traffic.

ECONOMIC AND SOCIAL CHANGE IN THE KENNEDY-JOHNSON YEARS

The years of Kennedy and Johnson were a time of unparalleled prosperity in America. Between 1960 and 1967, the annual gross national product, or GNP—the total national output of goods and services—zoomed from $504 billion to $789 billion. The result was a marked improvement in the standard of living of most Americans.

The Kennedy-Johnson era was a time when young people became increasingly active in politics. It was the era of miniskirts, the short skirts that rose several inches above the knee. It was a time when many American males rediscovered the satisfaction of growing long hair, bushy sideburns, and beards. And it was a time when many Americans began to rediscover their own identities.

New Attitudes

The years of Kennedy and Johnson seemed to bring bewildering social change. There was a weakening of old sexual taboos. Part of that weakening resulted from Supreme Court rulings that many laws banning "obscene" books, magazines, movies, and plays were unconstitutional. The court reasoned that such laws violated freedom of expression. In the wake of these rulings, bookstores were flooded with publications which dealt openly with sex, and plays such as *Hair* featured performers in various degrees of nudity.

Other signs of changing attitudes toward sex included an increasing willingness of unmarried couples to live together openly, a new frankness on the subject of homosexuality, and the introduction of sex education courses in high schools.

During the Kennedy-Johnson years, the movement to legalize abortion gathered momentum. Proponents of legal abortion argued that the laws did not prevent abortions, and that women's lives would be saved if they could obtain safe, legal abortions from physicians. They also argued that each woman has a right to decide whether to give birth. Opponents of abortion argued that a human embryo is a person with a right to life, and that

[756]

abortion is an act of murder. (The issue was not resolved until 1973, when the Supreme Court virtually ended the power of the states to limit abortion in the early months of pregnancy.)

Drugs

The Kennedy-Johnson years also were a time when it became fashionable, particularly among younger people, to "turn on" with drugs. It was marijuana—also called "pot," "grass," and a dozen other nicknames—which attracted the most users. Having grown up in the belief that marijuana would destroy the health and spirit of the user, most older Americans were shocked by the sight of young people casually getting "high" on pot. The outcome was a national debate over the effects of smoking marijuana. Unfortunately, the verdict of the scientific community was confused. Some scientists thought that marijuana was harmless. Others suspected that it might hurt both the bodies and the minds of heavy users.

Meanwhile, Americans were learning of a mind-expanding drug called LSD—a chemical compound known as lysergic acid diethylamide, or "acid" to the legions of young people who tried it. LSD caused hallucinations or imaginary "trips." Sometimes these "trips" were sheer ecstasy, but at other times they were so terrifying that they left permanent psychological scars.

More serious was the increase in addiction to the narcotic heroin, or "horse," particularly in cities. Because it was illegal to sell heroin, addicts had to buy shots, or "fixes," from sellers, or "pushers," who were part of a vast underworld network. To finance their habits, addicts often became thieves. In New York City alone, according to some estimates, addicts stole more than a billion dollars a year.

Religion

The religious climate was changing, and organized religion seemed on the defensive during the 1960s. The religious revival which had characterized the decade or so after World War II ran out of steam.

The decline of religious enthusiasm was particularly noticeable among young people. Consumed by visions of improving life in America, many youthful citizens viewed organized religion as an obstacle to social change. Some based their view on the failure of many of the clergy in recent decades to speak out against social evils such as racial discrimination. Other youths rebelled against the rules and restraints imposed by most religious creeds.

THE KENNEDY-JOHNSON YEARS

The period from 1960 to 1968 was a time of sweeping social change in the United States. President Kennedy and President Johnson worked to end discrimination, and women and minority groups began to band together to assert their rights. Each president hoped to prevent South Vietnam from falling under Communist control, but the American people became deeply divided over whether the Vietnam War was right or wrong. It also was a period when the United States lost three leaders through assassination: President Kennedy, Dr. Martin Luther King, Jr., and Senator Robert F. Kennedy.

1

This official portrait of John F. Kennedy by Aaron Shikler hangs in the White House. Kennedy was assassinated just 1,036 days after taking office.

2

Lyndon B. Johnson was sworn in as president a little over an hour after John Kennedy's death. Why were liberals surprised in 1960 when Kennedy chose Johnson as his running mate?

3

Bumper stickers expressed strong feelings about the Vietnam War during the late 1960s. Supporters of the war charged that antiwar critics were unpatriotic Americans who comprised only a vocal minority of the population. Critics questioned the morality of the war and pointed to the devastation which American bombs were causing in a once-beautiful country. Can a democracy exist without differences of opinion?

3

AMERICA
LOVE IT OR LEAVE IT!

★★★ I'M A MEMBER OF THE ★★★
SILENT MAJORITY

VACATION in beautiful VIETNAM

Still, there was new activity within organized religion. Inspired in part by the ecumenical movement — the movement for Christian unity, inspired in part by Pope John XXIII — Protestants and Catholics put aside many old antagonisms. They talked tolerantly and frankly about differences. Both Christians and Jews engaged in cooperative activities, including public worship, which would have been unthinkable a generation before. The clergy increasingly denounced social abuses and took part in the movement for equal rights.

Among Catholics there was pride in the election of the first Catholic president, John F. Kennedy. Later in the 1960s, the ancient Latin liturgy was gradually replaced by English, and the solemn atmosphere of Catholic churches was punctured by the sounds of guitars and folk music.

Jewish Americans took renewed pride and interest in their religion and culture. Jews felt exhilaration over the achievements of the Jewish nation-state, Israel. The continuing Arab threat to Israel's national survival also generated a new sense of Jewish solidarity.

Women and Minorities

During the 1960s, many women began to question their roles in American society. Betty Friedan's *The Feminine Mystique* appeared in 1963, and three years later Friedan founded the National Organization for Women (NOW). NOW's goal was equal rights for women, particularly in employment — "equal pay for equal work." NOW soon became America's largest women's rights group.

But it was black Americans who were most touched by change in the time of Kennedy and Johnson. Blacks took new pride in their African heritage and summed up their feelings in the phrase, "black is beautiful."

At the same time, blacks began to move into the mainstream of American society. New civil rights legislation enabled blacks to use lunchrooms, hotels, and places of amusement which had been closed to them. Blacks moved into previously all-white neighborhoods. They took advantage of new job opportunities. They voted in record numbers, and two black men, Richard Hatcher and Carl B. Stokes, were elected mayors of major cities (Gary, Indiana, and Cleveland). Robert C. Weaver became the first black cabinet member when President Johnson appointed him Secretary of the new Department of Housing and Urban Development, and in 1967 Thurgood Marshall became the first black appointed to the Supreme Court. Edward W. Brooke of Massachusetts was elected the first black senator since Reconstruction in 1966, and Shirley Chisholm of New York, the first black congresswoman, won election in 1968.

For the first time, blacks appeared regularly in television commercials, and Bill Cosby and Diahann Carroll appeared in starring roles on weekly TV shows. On college campuses, "black studies" became a staple of the curriculum.

Still, many black Americans were frustrated by the economic and social inequities of daily life. Militant black leaders began to emerge. One of the earliest was Malcolm X (see pages 738-39). Malcolm renounced violence in 1964. He began to preach brotherhood between blacks and whites, but he was assassinated shortly afterward.

Leaders of two civil rights organizations announced in 1966 that they were abandoning the policy of nonviolence. They were Stokely Carmichael, chairman of the Student Nonviolent Coordinating Committee (SNCC), and Floyd McKissick, head of the Congress on Racial Equality (CORE). Both Carmichael and McKissick said that violence against blacks should be met with violence.

The same year, in 1966, Huey P. Newton and Bobby Seale formed the Black Panthers. The Panthers were organized as a black militant group. Newton and Seale argued that violent revolution was the only way to achieve social and economic equality for blacks.

The oldest and largest civil rights organizations continued to support nonviolence as the only ef-

Secretary of Housing and Urban Development Robert Weaver met in 1967 with the mayors of three major American cities: Carl Stokes of Cleveland, Ohio; Walter Washington of Washington, D.C.; and Richard Hatcher of Gary, Indiana.

Compix

Wide World

Holding a picket sign, Cesar Chavez pauses for a photographer during a protest in Seattle in 1969. Chavez led a nationwide boycott of California grapes to protest low wages paid to grape pickers.

fective means of social and economic change. The National Association for the Advancement of Colored People (NAACP) and the Southern Christian Leadership Conference (SCLC) were active in voter registration drives, peaceful protest marches, and programs aimed at helping blacks own their own businesses.

But other protests erupted spontaneously. During the summer of 1967, riots broke out in the black ghettos of about 75 cities. A five-day riot in Detroit caused 43 deaths and $45 million in property damage. President Johnson appointed a commission—the Kerner Commission—to study the causes of the riots. The report of the Kerner Commission concluded that the riots were largely the result of economic injustice and poverty. For despite the general prosperity of the 1960s, many Americans were poor.

To dramatize the problems of the poor, the Rev. Ralph David Abernathy led a "poor people's march" to Washington, D. C. in 1968. Abernathy had succeeded Dr. Martin Luther King, Jr., as leader of the SCLC. Thousands of poor blacks, Indians, Chicanos, Hispanics, and whites joined the march. For six weeks they camped in tents and huts set up on park land near the Lincoln Memorial.

Black Americans were not the only minority group to become more assertive in the 1960s. Mexican-Americans, or Chicanos, began to express a new pride in their identity and to demand an end to discrimination and social abuses. Most of the country's ten million Mexican-Americans lived in the Southwest, and many were poor. In California, Cesar Chavez organized the National Farm Workers Association (NFW), a new union. Its goal was to gain better wages for poorly-paid grape pickers and other seasonal farm workers, many of whom were Mexican-Americans.

Chavez used nonviolent strikes, boycotts, and picketing to call attention to his cause. The result was much progress toward raising wages and working conditions for seasonal farm workers.

Chicanos also became more influential in government. President Johnson appointed several Americans of Mexican ancestry to high government positions, including Hector P. García, a member of the U. S. delegation to the UN. Joseph Montoya of New Mexico won election to the Senate in 1964.

Protecting the Environment

The idea of protecting the environment—the air, water, land, and all the animals that live there—was not new in the 1960s. National and state parks had been established to preserve segments of the natural environment. Presidents Theodore and Franklin Roosevelt had sponsored measures to protect forests and soil, and Congress had passed some laws to control air and water pollution in the 1950s. But it was not until the years of Kennedy and Johnson that most Americans began to view the environment as a complex whole and to realize that changes made by humans in the balance of nature could cause long-term damage.

Stimulating this new concern was a book called *Silent Spring,* published in 1962. The author was a biologist named Rachel Carson. In simple yet moving prose, she described an imaginary town in the heart of America which always had lived in harmony as it experienced the peaceful turn of seasons. But then a strange blight crept over the area. Spring came and no baby chicks hatched. The fields remained brown. Most frightening of all, no birds sang. What had happened? The people had poisoned everything around them by using DDT, a chemical designed to kill insect pests.

In the years following publication of *Silent Spring,* protection from DDT and other poisonous chemicals and gases, raw sewage, noise, and eyesores became a national concern. By the end of the Kennedy-Johnson years, leaders in Washington had felt that concern. Thus the stage was set for a series of federal measures to protect the environment. Many of these were adopted after Richard Nixon's election to the presidency.

Consumer Protection

Like environmental protection, consumer protection was not new. Its purpose was to protect consumers—people who use, or consume, goods—from products that were unsafe, too expensive, or not what advertisements claimed them to be. Federal laws to guarantee meat inspection and pure food and drugs had existed since 1906 (see pages 413-14). But the idea of consumer protection failed to stir the enthusiasm of large numbers of Americans until the 1960s.

During his presidential campaign in 1960, John F. Kennedy announced: "The consumer is the only man in our economy without a high-powered lobbyist. I intend to be that lobbyist." In 1962 President Kennedy proposed an unprecedented consumer program, a so-called Consumer Bill of Rights. Later that same year, after the discovery that pregnant women who had taken the drug thalidomide had given birth to deformed babies, Congress passed a new drug control bill. Still, the efforts of Kennedy—and also those of his successor, President Johnson—met stiff opposition from the business community. Opponents charged that consumer interests were trying to undermine the system of free enterprise.

But then, in 1965, a lanky young man named Ralph Nader published *Unsafe at Any Speed.* The book charged that the General Motors Corporation had sacrificed safety for profits in producing its Chevrolet *Corvair* automobiles. Almost overnight, consumer protection won the support of millions of Americans—and, inevitably, their representatives in Congress. The outcome was such legislation as the Motor Vehicle Safety Act, the Truth in Lending Act, and the Truth in Packaging Act. The federal government tightened regulations for inspecting meat and poultry. The Federal Trade Commission began to take a strong stand for truth in advertising. State governments reinforced federal consumer programs with countless other measures.

STUDY GUIDE: The Kennedy-Johnson years were prosperous years. They also were a time of social ferment.

Attitudes toward sex changed. A movement to legalize abortion gathered strength. The use of drugs, particularly marijuana, rose dramatically. Support for organized religion declined, but the ecumenical movement brought new harmony among Christians and Jews.

The Kennedy-Johnson era was a time of increasing self-awareness among women and minority groups. The National Organization for Women (NOW) was founded. Blacks saw the weakening of racial discrimination in public places, a new prominence of blacks in politics, and a new interest in "black studies." At the same time, black militants began to emerge. The Black Panthers were formed. However, the country's oldest and largest civil rights groups, such as the NAACP, remained committed to nonviolence.

Mexican-Americans, or Chicanos, also became more assertive. They expressed pride in their identity and called for an end to discrimination. In California, Cesar Chavez organized a new union for poorly-paid farm workers, the National Farm Workers Association (NFW). Chicanos also began to gain a greater voice in government.

Protecting the environment became a national concern. After publication of Rachel Carson's *Silent Spring,* Americans began to demand stronger laws to control pollution. A broad movement to protect consumers also formed after Ralph Nader published *Unsafe at Any Speed.*

ART AND ENTERTAINMENT IN THE 1960S

During the economic boom of the 1960s, most Americans had more money than ever before—and they spent a great deal of it on entertainment.

Music and Literature

The Kennedy-Johnson years were the era of the Beatles, the four mop-haired young men from Liverpool, England who dominated American music until 1970. American performers also captivated vast audiences: Bob Dylan, who composed songs of social protest as well as nostalgia; Joan Baez, the folksinger who sang of love and nonviolence; Aretha Franklin, the "queen of soul"; Jimi Hendrix, the virtuoso rock guitarist; and Johnny Cash, the craggy country balladeer.

Classical music gained new audiences. Leonard Bernstein led the New York Philharmonic Orchestra to a new height of popularity, and the coloratura soprano Beverly Sills emerged as opera's leading prima donna.

During the 1960s, Americans were reading Joseph Heller's *Catch-22*, James Baldwin's *The Fire Next Time* and Truman Capote's *In Cold Blood*. They read poems by Robert Frost. They read novels by Saul Bellow, Katherine Anne Porter, Bernard Malamud, and Mary McCarthy. They read Rachel Carson's *Silent Spring* and Eldridge Cleaver's *Soul on Ice*.

On Broadway, the curtain went up on Edward Albee's *Who's Afraid of Virginia Woolf?*, Robert Bolt's *A Man for All Seasons*, and Howard Sackler's *The Great White Hope*. Musical comedies flourished. Among the most successful were *Hello, Dolly!*, *Fiddler on the Roof*, and *The Man of LaMancha*.

The Visual Arts

The economy of the 1960s produced an "art boom." Galleries prospered, and many regional museums of art were organized. In New York, the king of "pop" art, Andy Warhol, found that his portraits of soup cans had started a trend in paintings of everyday objects. Abstract painting also thrived, and the huge, colorful canvases of Morris Louis, Kenneth Noland, Helen Frankenthaler, and Frank Stella won international acclaim.

Some people thought the American movie industry was dying. Most of the studios were in financial trouble, and the annual output of motion pictures shrank to a fraction of what it had been in the 1930s. Still, the movies continued to attract millions of fans, particularly among young people.

Subject matter varied widely. There were films of social comment such as *Dr. Strangelove*, the caustic antiwar comedy directed by Stanley Kubrick; *The Graduate*, Mike Nichols' portrait of an affluent and thoroughly confused adolescent; and *Guess Who's Coming to Dinner?*, an interracial romantic comedy directed by Stanley Kramer. There were movies about cowboys and movies about bandits, the most popular of which was Arthur Penn's *Bonnie and Clyde*. And there were lavish musical films such as *West Side Story*, *My Fair Lady*, *The Sound of Music*, and *Mary Poppins*.

But the most popular mass medium was television. Among the more popular TV shows in the Kennedy-Johnson years were "The Ed Sullivan Show," "Gunsmoke," and "The Dick Van Dyke Show." Hollywood began to make movies exclusively for TV. The National Geographic Society produced "specials" on nature and geography which won critical acclaim.

TV's coverage of news events became increasingly dramatic, especially as black and white transmission gave way to color. Still, TV came under continual attack. Many people criticized the low artistic and intellectual quality of most TV programs. Others deplored TV's emphasis on violence. And supporters of the war in Vietnam complained that TV's coverage of the military combat was diverting Americans from the political issues of the conflict.

Sports

Spectator sports, particularly professional football, enjoyed a golden era in the time of Kennedy and Johnson. Pro football's unique blend of mayhem and computer-like precision appealed to so many people that a new league was formed in 1960, the American Football League (AFL). The AFL began to compete with the National Football League (NFL) in annual Super Bowl contests. Then, in 1969, the AFL's champion *New York Jets,* led by Joe Namath, defeated the NFL's *Baltimore Colts.* The AFL had proven itself.

Major league baseball, long considered the national pastime, was under criticism for being too slow. Still, it attracted record crowds and expanded into several new cities. In 1961, Roger Maris of the *New York Yankees* hit his sixty-first home run of the season. It was the highest number of homers for a single major league season since Babe Ruth had hit 60 home runs in 1927. Throughout the 1960s, crowds applauded the remarkable batting and throwing abilities of Roberto Clemente of the *Pittsburgh Pirates* and Hank Aaron of the *Braves.*

In boxing, Muhammad Ali emerged as the controversial champion. He had changed his name from Cassius Clay to Muhammad Ali when he became a Black Muslim. He was stripped of the heavyweight title in 1967 after he refused to be drafted into the armed forces because of his religion.

Professional basketball was dominated by such superstars as Bill Russell and Wilt Chamberlain. Professional golf reached new levels of popularity, boosted by Arnold Palmer and Jack Nicklaus. Arthur Ashe became the first black tennis star to win the U. S. Open, and the champion automobile racers A. J. Foyt and Mario Andretti attracted millions of new fans.

Intercollegiate football boasted such superstars as O. J. Simpson. College basketball was dominated by the *UCLA Bruins,* under the direction of Coach John Wooden, and their star center, Lew Alcindor, who later took the Muslim name of Kareem Abdul Jabbar.

STUDY GUIDE: Because people had more money to spend during the Kennedy-Johnson years, all the arts prospered.

The Beatles dominated American music during the 1960s. Some American artists created songs, books, and films of social comment on the war in Vietnam and other issues. At the same time, musical comedies flourished. Art galleries became more popular. The most popular mass medium was television, despite criticism of its quality.

The 1960s were a golden era for spectator sports. The AFL was formed, and collegiate sports also attracted many new fans.

SUMMING UP THE CHAPTER

Names and Terms to Identify

New Frontier	Everett M. Dirksen
Medicare	Appalachia
Baker v. *Carr*	Barry M. Goldwater
freedom rides	Great Society
James Meredith	Robert C. Weaver
Dr. Martin Luther King, Jr.	U.S.S. *Pueblo*
	ecumenical movement
Medgar Evers	Robert F. Kennedy
John H. Glenn, Jr.	Cesar Chavez
Pathet Lao	Shirley Chisholm
Ngo Dinh Diem	Rachel Carson
Lee Harvey Oswald	Ralph Nader

Study Questions and Points to Review

1. Who was John F. Kennedy's Republican opponent in the 1960 presidential race?

2. What program from the Eisenhower administration did Kennedy revive to deal with America's food surpluses and the problem of hunger in underdeveloped nations?

3. What was the purpose of the 1963 March on Washington?

4. Toward which planet was *Mariner 2* directed to gain scientific information?

5. Name the Kennedy-sponsored program that sought to combat poverty in Latin American nations.

6. How many Cuban exiles participated in the Bay of Pigs invasion? Why was the invasion a failure? What had the invaders hoped to accomplish?

7. When and why was the Berlin Wall built?

8. What is the "hot line"? Why was it installed?

9. What two reasons are offered for the installation of missiles in Cuba by the Soviets?

10. Why did President Kennedy choose to ignore Soviet leader Khrushchev's second message during the Cuban missile crisis, and to reply only to the first message?

11. Why did President Kennedy go to Texas in November 1963?

12. Who was seriously injured at the same time that President Kennedy was assassinated?

13. What action did President Johnson take shortly after assuming the presidency to stimulate the nation's lagging economy?

14. What triggered the difficulty between the United States and Panama in 1964? What was the outcome of negotiations?

15. What incident led to passage of the Gulf of Tonkin resolution?

16. Why did the American Medical Association oppose proposals for medical assistance under Social Security?

17. What is the subject of the Twenty-fourth Amendment to the Constitution?

18. What two Cabinet positions were established during the Johnson administration?

19. What events in Vietnam prompted President Johnson to escalate the war in 1965?

20. What made President Johnson decide not to run for reelection in 1968?

21. Why has the Democratic national convention in Chicago in 1968 been called a political disaster?

22. What did Governor George Wallace hope to accomplish in his presidential campaign of 1968?

23. What were some of the social changes which took place during the Kennedy-Johnson years?

Topics for Discussion

1. Trace the life and career of John F. Kennedy down to the time he began to campaign for the presidency. In what ways did Kennedy's experience qualify him—or fail to qualify him—for the presidency?

2. Evaluate the Food for Peace program and the Peace Corps. What in your opinion were the chief merits of these programs? What, if anything, do these

programs reveal to you about the "American character"?

3. Evaluate the Alliance for Progress. What were its origins? What did it hope to achieve? How successful was it in the 1960s?

4. What was the background of the Bay of Pigs operation of 1961? What arguments persuaded President Kennedy to give his consent to the operation? Why did the operation fail? What were the consequences of the failure?

5. Discuss the Berlin crisis of 1961. What were the origins of the crisis? How did President Kennedy respond to the situation? What were the results of the crisis? Assess President Kennedy's leadership during the Berlin crisis.

6. Consider the state of the NATO alliance in the 1960s. What accounted for the apparent weakening of the alliance? Do you agree or disagree that by the 1960s NATO had outlived its usefulness? Explain your answer.

7. What prompted the Cuban missile crisis of 1962? What alternative responses did President Kennedy consider? Why did he choose to respond as he did? What was the outcome of the crisis? What do you think of Kennedy's handling of the crisis?

8. What was the reasoning behind President Johnson's decision to escalate America's involvement in the war in Vietnam? Explain the arguments of those Americans who took a critical view of that escalation. Offer your own evaluation of the reasoning of both the president and his critics.

9. Discuss the antiwar movement in the United States in the latter 1960s. What were the main themes of the movement? What do you think of the arguments of the protesters? Take particular note of the argument that American intervention in the war in Vietnam was immoral.

10. What in your view were some of the principal achievements of Dr. Martin Luther King, Jr.? Do you think the violence in the cities which followed Dr. King's murder was justified? How do you think future generations will assess Dr. King?

11. Evaluate the gains made by black Americans during the Kennedy-Johnson years.

12. What caused the decline in organized religion during the 1960s? What do you think of the criticisms which were being leveled against organized religion during that period?

Subjects for Reports or Essays

1. Write a personal assessment of America's military involvement in Vietnam in the 1960s.

2. Using reference materials in the library — newspapers, magazines, books, or other documents — write your own account and assessment of the events which took place early in 1965 in Selma, Alabama.

3. Read the report of the National Advisory Commission on Civil Disorders (the Kerner Commission Report). On the basis of that report, what were, in your view, the main causes of riots in cities during the 1960s? What do you think should be done to prevent similar disorders? Present your conclusions in an essay.

4. Prepare a report for class presentation on one of the following subjects: (a) the Berlin Wall; (b) the 1963 march on Washington; (c) President Kennedy's assassination; (d) the U.S.S. *Pueblo* incident; (e) the *Tet* offensive; (f) the green revolution.

5. On the basis of outside reading, write a brief biographical sketch of one of the following: Thurgood Marshall, Barry Goldwater, Hubert Humphrey, Dr. Martin Luther King, Rachel Carson, Cesar Chavez.

6. Examine Table 19 in the Appendix, "Employees in Selected Industries: 1950 to 1975." Which industry showed the greatest number of employees in the 1960s? The greatest change? Prepare a brief report giving reasons for these changes.

Projects, Activities, and Skills

1. Prepare a pictorial biography of John F. Kennedy. Collect and display photographs from his childhood through his career as president. You might include a model of the PT-109, a map showing the location of Kennedy's heroics in the waters around the Solomon Islands, and copies of his two books, *Why England Slept* and *Profiles in Courage*.

2. Prepare an exhibit titled "Black Americans in the 1960s." Include pictures of notable black persons of the decade such as Dr. Martin Luther King, Jr., Rev. Ralph David Abernathy, Shirley Chisholm, Malcolm X, Thurgood Marshall, Robert C. Weaver, Edward Brooke, Carl B. Stokes, Medgar Evers, Stokely Carmichael, H. Rap Brown, Eldridge Cleaver, James Baldwin, Muhammad Ali, Willie Mays, Hank Aaron, Arthur Ashe, Bill Russell, O. J. Simpson, Sidney Poitier, James Meredith, Kareem Abdul Jabbar. Include information on the civil rights legislation of 1960, 1964, 1965, and 1968. Add your own short essay on "What the 1960s Meant to Black Americans."

3. Prepare an exhibit on America's space program through Project Gemini. Include models of rockets and space capsules, pictures of astronauts, blast-offs, recoveries, and space walks.

4. Prepare an exhibit on the war in Vietnam. Include a large map of Vietnam and pictures of people

who took a leading part in the war in the 1960s: for example, Ho Chi Minh, Ngo Dinh Diem, Nguyen Van Thieu, Presidents Kennedy and Johnson, and Generals Westmoreland and Abrams. Include pictures and models of weapons and planes. Also include pictures of antiwar demonstrations in the United States. Include a brief essay setting forth arguments for and against American involvement in the war.

5. Make a chart or graph using information available in any of the following Appendix tables: 15, 16, 24, 28, 32, 33, or 34.

6. Prepare an exhibit on "Life in the United States in the 1960s." Include pictures or lists of prominent Americans in government, the military, education, journalism, religion, science, entertainment, and sports. Include pictures of major events, such as presidential inaugurations, assassinations, riots, and space activities. Include a list of the most popular books, movies, plays, and music of the decade. Include information on economic growth and scientific achievements.

7. Prepare an exhibit on the presidential election of 1968. Include pictures of candidates, recordings of speeches, books about the candidates and elections, and maps showing the distribution of votes.

Further Readings

General

America in the Sixties: An Intellectual History by Ronald Berman. A useful collection of source materials on the rights of blacks in America, from Jamestown to the 1960s.
The American Negro Revolution by Benjamin Muse. The evolution of the crusade for equal rights.
Crisis in Black and White by Charles Silberman.
The Death and Life of Great American Cities by Jane Jacobs. A study of urban growth and decay.
The Death of a President by William Manchester. A detailed account of Kennedy's last days.
Enough! The Revolt of the American Consumer by Doris Faber.
The Making of the President, 1960; *The Making of the President, 1964*; and *The Making of the President, 1968* by Theodore H. White. Three detailed, graphic narratives of the presidential sweepstakes.
Nobody Knows My Name by James Baldwin. One person's story of what it was like to be a black American at the turn of the 1960s.
Profiles in Courage by John F. Kennedy.
The Quality of the Environment by James L. McCamy.

Report of the National Advisory Commission on Civil Disorders by the Kerner Commission. The report of the national commission appointed by President Johnson to find the causes of riots in American cities.
Silent Spring by Rachel Carson.
The Struggle for Racial Equality: A Documentary Record ed. by Henry Steele Commager.
Tet! by Don Oberdorfer.
Thirteen Days: A Memoir of the Cuban Missile Crisis by Robert F. Kennedy.
A Thousand Days: John F. Kennedy in the White House by Arthur M. Schlesinger, Jr.
Vantage Point: Perspectives of the Presidency, 1963-1969 by Lyndon B. Johnson.
The Woman in America ed. by Robert J. Lifton. An anthology.

Biography

The Autobiography of Malcolm X by Malcolm X.
John Kennedy: A Political Profile by James M. Burns.
King: A Critical Biography by David Lewis.
Kennedy by Theodore Sorenson.
PT-109: John F. Kennedy in World War II by Robert J. Donovan.
Soul on Ice by Eldridge Cleaver.
Unbought and Unbossed by Shirley Chisholm. Autobiography.
With Kennedy by Pierre Salinger.

Fiction, Drama, Poetry, and Music

Ballads, Blues, and the Big Beat: Highlights of American Folk Singing from Leadbelly to Dylan by Donald Myrus.
Great Songs of the Sixties ed. by Milton Okun. Words and music with social commentary and illustrations.
In White America by Martin B. Duberman. A dramatized review of blacks in America since the 1600s.
Looking for a Place by Richard Margolis. Sensitive poems about life in the ghetto.
The Soul Brothers and Sister Lou by Kristin Hunter. A black girl seeks her identity.
Too Far to Walk by John Hersey. A story about campus unrest.
Tuned Out by Maia Wojciechowska. A teenager discovers that his brother is a drug addict.

Pictorial History

Ebony Pictorial History of Black America, Vol. 3, by the editors of *Ebony*.
This Fabulous Century, 1960-1970, Vol. 7, by the editors of Time-Life Books.

CHAPTER 21

YEARS OF TRIUMPH AND TURMOIL

Thermometers registered near-freezing temperatures in Washington on January 20, 1969. It was Inauguration Day for Richard M. Nixon, the thirty-seventh president. Skies were leaden and the weather seemed to reflect the somber mood of the divided American nation.

In a solemn inaugural address the new president called on Americans to put aside the angry rhetoric of recent years: "We cannot learn from one another until we stop shouting at one another," he said, "until we speak quietly enough so that our words can be heard as well as our voices." Afterward, as Nixon moved back down Pennsylvania Avenue from the Capitol to the White House, militant demonstrators screamed antiwar slogans and threw rocks and beer cans at the presidential limousine.

Still, many Americans hoped that the bitterness and tension of recent years might soon pass.

RICHARD M. NIXON

Born in Yorba Linda, California in 1913, Richard Milhous Nixon was a descendant of Scots-Irish pioneers. During his early years, Nixon and his family lived on the edge of poverty. But after the elder Nixon opened a grocery store in Whittier, California, the family lived in middle-class comfort. Young "Dick" Nixon was an excellent student and a successful debater. He was graduated from high school in 1930 with honors.

At Whittier College Nixon again was an outstanding student and a champion debater. After graduation from Whittier he compiled an excellent academic record at the Duke University law school in North Carolina. He returned to Whittier, joined a law firm, and in 1940 married Thelma ("Pat") Ryan.

In 1942 Nixon took a commission in the navy and helped construct airfields and other facilities on various islands in the South Pacific during World War II. When he returned to California, he decided to run for Congress as a Republican in the election of 1946. Charging that his opponent was a friend of Communists, he won a thumping victory.

On taking his seat in Congress, Nixon was appointed to the House Un-American Activities Committee (HUAC). He gained national prominence through the committee in 1948 when he produced evidence that Alger Hiss, a former official in the State Department, had lied when he testified that he never had known Whittaker Chambers. (Chambers, a former Soviet spy, had accused Hiss of espionage.) In 1950, California Republicans nominated Nixon for the Senate. Again charging that his opponent had been sympathetic with Communist ideas, he won an overwhelming victory.

Then, in 1952, General Dwight D. Eisenhower won the Republican nomination for president. Nixon was chosen as his vice-presidential running-mate. The Eisenhower-Nixon ticket was victorious in 1952 and again in 1956, and Nixon became the most active vice-president to that time. He filled in capably for Eisenhower when the president suffered a heart attack and, later, a stroke. In 1960 Nixon won the Republican nomination for president, only to lose the election by an eyelash to John F. Kennedy.

Nixon returned to California and wrote *Six Crises,* a book about his political career. Then, in 1962, he suffered a stunning defeat when he ran for governor of California. He seemed finished as a politician.

But in 1964 Nixon began a remarkable political comeback. At the Republican national convention he introduced the party's presidential candidate, Senator Barry M. Goldwater of Arizona, to cheering delegates. In the subsequent campaign he traveled across the country in behalf of Goldwater. When Goldwater was defeated, Nixon emerged as the only nationally known Republican who was on good terms with all Republican factions. During the election campaign of 1966 he again traveled about the country in behalf of Republican candidates.

By 1967 Nixon had decided to strike again for the White House. He was not the first choice of most Republicans. But because of his many services to the party, he was the second choice of a large majority. So when other Republican hopefuls such as Governors George Romney and Nelson Rockefeller failed to stir enthusiasm,

HEADLINE
EVENTS

1969 Richard M. Nixon inaugurated president
Neil Armstrong and Edwin Aldrin become the first men to walk on the moon
Peace talks begin in Paris to end the war in Vietnam
Nixon announces troop withdrawals
SALT Talks begin
1970 Environmental Protection Agency (EPA) created
United States troops enter Cambodia; four students killed by national guard troops in an antiwar protest at Kent State University
Radical terrorism erupts repeatedly
Equal Rights Amendment (ERA) approved by Congress
1971 Lieutenant William Calley convicted of murder at My Lai
Daniel Ellsberg leaks the *Pentagon Papers* to the press
Twenty-sixth Amendment ratified
1972 Nixon visits China
Nixon visits the USSR; *détente* becomes a new American foreign policy
Revenue Sharing Act wins approval
Police arrest five men breaking into Democratic national headquarters at the Watergate building in Washington
Nixon defeats Senator George McGovern and is reelected president
Nixon orders bombing of North Vietnam
1973 Cease-fire agreement signed in Paris
Militant members of the American Indian Movement (AIM) occupy Wounded Knee

Cover-up is charged in Watergate case; the Senate's Ervin Committee and a Special Prosecutor begin investigating
Vice-President Spiro Agnew resigns in disgrace; Nixon appoints Gerald Ford to succeed him
Nixon is accused in Watergate hearings; legal battle begins for White House tape recordings of his conversations
Nixon fires the Special Prosecutor; impeachment inquiry begins
1974 Internal Revenue Service asks Nixon to pay more than $400,000 in back taxes
Supreme Court orders Nixon to release tapes of White House conversations
House Judiciary Committee sends three articles of impeachment charging Nixon with crimes to the full House for debate
Nixon admits having known of cover-up and of having tried to stop an FBI inquiry
Nixon resigns
Vice-President Ford becomes president; Nelson Rockefeller becomes vice-president
President Ford pardons Nixon
1975 Worst recession since the Great Depression
Vietnam War ends when Communist troops take Saigon; Communists also capture Cambodia and Laos
Mayaguez incident
1976 Bicentennial year
Jimmy Carter defeats Ford in presidential election
1977 Jimmy Carter inaugurated president

Nixon became the front-runner. At the Republican convention of 1968 he easily won the nomination. The climax of his comeback came in November of 1968, when he edged Hubert Humphrey in the presidential balloting.

STUDY GUIDE: Richard Nixon grew up in Whittier, California. He was an excellent student. He became a lawyer, married Thelma ("Pat") Ryan, and served in the navy in World War II.

Elected to the House of Representatives in 1946, he gained national prominence during the investigation of Alger Hiss. He was elected to the Senate in 1950 and in 1952 won the vice-presidency. He was an active vice-president. He ran for president in 1960, but lost to Kennedy. Two years later he ran for governor of California and lost. It seemed that his political career was over.

In 1964 Nixon began a remarkable political comeback. He campaigned for Republican candidates. When other Republicans faltered, he won the Republican nomination for president in 1968 and defeated Hubert Humphrey.

TO THE MOON

Just weeks before Nixon took the oath of office, *Apollo 8* and its three-man crew had orbited the moon on Christmas Eve. Only a few more tests were needed before the final voyage to land an American on the moon.

Early in 1969 a giant Saturn rocket boosted *Apollo 9* into earth orbit. During the flight the spacecraft's lunar module, which would carry the astronauts from the command ship to the moon's surface, was separated from the command ship and later rejoined to it. Astronaut Russell L. Schweickart took a space walk to test the suit which astronauts would wear while walking on the moon. Next, in May 1969, came the final test of equipment and procedures. After going into orbit around the moon, *Apollo 10*'s lunar module was separated from the command ship, flew within 56,000 feet of the lunar surface, then soared back up to the orbiting spacecraft.

The Voyage of *Apollo 11*

Then came the historic voyage of *Apollo 11*.

The blastoff date was July 16, 1969. On that day perhaps a million people, including President Nixon, Former-President Johnson, and Charles A. Lindbergh, gathered at Cape Canaveral (then called Cape Kennedy). By seven a.m. astronauts Neil A. Armstrong, Edwin E. ("Buzz") Aldrin, Jr., and Michael Collins were strapped into their seats in the command module *Columbia*. Nestled beneath them at the head of a Saturn rocket was the smaller lunar module, *Eagle*. Then, at 9:32 a.m., a brilliant orange flame shot from the base of the rocket, the earth shook, and amid a deafening roar and billowing smoke *Apollo 11* gracefully lifted skyward.

Everything went perfectly. Three days later *Apollo 11* entered moon orbit. On July 20, Armstrong and Aldrin crawled from the *Columbia* into the *Eagle*, and the lunar module was separated from the command ship. The *Eagle* then began its gradual descent to the lunar surface while Collins remained aboard the *Columbia*, orbiting the moon. Less than three hours later the *Eagle* was hovering above the moon's Sea of Tranquility. To avoid craters and to assure an upright landing, Armstrong was manually steering the vehicle. Finally, the *Eagle*'s landing pods settled in the lunar dust. Armstrong shut off the engines and reported, "The *Eagle* has landed."

For several hours Armstrong and Aldrin rested and checked their equipment. Then, as millions of earthlings watched on television, Armstrong stepped out of the *Eagle* and slowly descended a small ladder to the lunar surface. Said the first man to set foot on the moon: "That's one small step for a man, one giant leap for mankind." Twenty minutes later Aldrin joined Armstrong. The two men planted a small American flag in the lunar soil, then began to gather soil and rock samples. They also set up scientific experiments.

After two hours, the astronauts returned to their little spacecraft. Ten hours later Armstrong ignited *Eagle*'s engines, and amid a swirl of dust the craft lifted off. A few hours after that, the *Eagle* docked with the *Columbia* in moon orbit. Armstrong and Aldrin rejoined Collins, and the unmanned *Eagle* was cut loose and cast adrift into space. The astronauts began the long voyage home, and on July 24 splashed down in the Pacific. The goal which President Kennedy had set in 1961 had been achieved.

After *Apollo 11*

After the voyage of *Apollo 11* Americans lost much of their enthusiasm for adventures in outer space. Many complained that the space program was too expensive and should be cut back.

Nevertheless, space exploration continued. Five more manned Apollo flights were made to the moon. Unmanned spacecraft took sophisticated sensing and measuring devices near Mars, Jupiter, Venus, and Mercury. In the winter of 1973-74 three astronauts orbited the earth for eighty-four days in a *Skylab* space station. In 1975, American astronauts and Soviet cosmonauts met in space in a successful joint experiment to dock their vehicles in orbit.

In 1976, two Viking spacecraft completed an eleven-month voyage and landed on Mars. After sending back amazingly clear pictures of the desolate, rock-strewn surface, the sophisticated equipment aboard the Viking landers set about to determine whether life might exist on the fabled "red planet." No life was found, but in other complex experiments the spacecraft confirmed Einstein's general theory of relativity.

STUDY GUIDE: In July 1969 came the historic voyage of *Apollo 11* to the moon. Neil Armstrong and Edwin ("Buzz") Aldrin became the first men to walk on the moon. Although popular enthusiasm for space adventures declined after the success of *Apollo 11*, space exploration continued in the 1970s.

THE VIETNAM WAR

As Nixon's term in the White House unfolded, foreign affairs claimed a large share of attention. The most important of these was the Vietnam War. Nixon hoped to withdraw the United States from the war in Vietnam while preventing the North Vietnamese Communists from gaining control of South Vietnam.

A few days after Nixon entered the White House, peace talks between representatives of North Vietnam, the Viet Cong, South Vietnam, and the United States finally opened in Paris. But it soon became clear that the talks were to be little more than a forum for Communist propaganda.

Still, Nixon believed that the war in Vietnam had become an intolerable burden for the United States. So he set about to prepare for the country's gradual withdrawal from the conflict. Nixon wanted to give South Vietnam's non-Communists the best possible chance of preventing a Communist victory. By removing American troops gradually, he hoped to give the non-Com-

munists time to build up their military forces and strengthen their political institutions.

The Nixon Doctrine

The withdrawal began in the summer of 1969 when Nixon announced that in the next two months 25,000 American troops would leave Vietnam. A short time later, he announced that another 40,500 troops would leave Vietnam by Christmas. Then, in July, he traveled to the Western Pacific and East Asia to explain his policies to America's friends. During a stopover on Guam, he outlined the "Nixon Doctrine." According to this policy, the United States would adopt a "lower profile" in the Far East — a less forceful presence. American troops would not be sent to put down local rebellions. Instead, the United States would encourage Asian countries to defend themselves.

Gradual withdrawal and the Nixon Doctrine did not satisfy antiwar critics in America. Many people continued to demand an immediate and total withdrawal of American forces from Vietnam, even if it resulted in a Communist takeover of the entire country. They argued that no anti-Communist cause could justify the killing and devastation in Vietnam. Others believed the war could never be won.

In September 1969, the leader of Vietnam's Communists, Ho Chi Minh, died. Some Americans hoped that the Communists might compromise. But there was no sign of the slightest change in their goals or strategy.

Antiwar activity continued at a fever pitch through autumn of 1969. The climax came when three hundred thousand persons gathered in Washington for a peaceful demonstration at the Washington Monument. Nixon angrily responded by declaring that national policy would not be made in the streets.

American Troops Enter Cambodia

By spring of 1970, the level of combat in Vietnam had declined substantially. Still, fresh North Vietnamese troops and supplies were streaming down the Ho Chi Minh Trail into South Vietnam. Where did many of these troops and most of these supplies end up? In base camps or "sanctuaries" just inside the border of neutral Cambodia. Arms and supplies also were moving toward the combat area through the Cambodian port of Sihanoukville.

YEARS OF TRIUMPH AND TURMOIL

Some of the proudest and most difficult moments in United States history have occurred during recent years. American astronauts became the first persons to walk on the moon, and the nation celebrated its Bicentennial. During the same period, both President Richard Nixon and Vice-President Spiro Agnew resigned from office in disgrace, and Americans everywhere began to worry about the cost of energy resources.

1

The first persons on the moon, Neil Armstrong and Edwin Aldrin, left behind an American flag and a plaque with the message, "We came in peace for all mankind." They were followed by five more teams of Americans between 1969 and 1972. During the flight of *Apollo 15* in 1971, astronaut James B. Irwin, shown here, posed with a salute to the flag. The lunar module which carried him from the command ship to the moon is at the center of the photograph, and a battery-powered moonmobile, the lunar rover, is on the right.

1 *NASA*

2 *DeSciosi/Photo Researchers*

2

The Ervin Committee, the special Senate committee formed to investigate Watergate, gathered testimony which led to the resignation of President Nixon in 1974. The case was the worst political scandal in the country's history.

3

Although American technology had put men on the moon, it had not solved the problem of how to keep gas tanks filled on earth. Long lines and rationing of gasoline caused widespread frustration among motorists during the summer of 1974.

3 *Mark Godfrey for Magnum*

8-GALLON LIMIT, PLEASE

TO SERVE ALL OUR CUSTOMERS, WE MUST LIMIT INDIVIDUAL GASOLINE PURCHASES. YOUR COOPERATION IS APPRECIATED.

American and South Vietnamese leaders were reluctant to order an all-out attack against the Cambodian sanctuaries. Such action might drive the neutral Cambodian leader, Prince Norodom Sihanouk, to take sides with the Communists.

But then, in early 1970, Prince Sihanouk traveled to France. While he was away he was deposed by a faction led by General Lon Nol. The new regime promptly stopped the flow of Communist supplies through the port of Sihanoukville. It also began to build up Cambodia's ragtag army. As a result, the North Vietnamese began to move out of the sanctuaries and deeper into Cambodia. The outcome was several clashes in which the Vietnamese easily overpowered the Cambodians.

Lon Nol appealed to Nixon for help. It was obvious to Nixon that the Cambodian sanctuaries threatened his goal of keeping South Vietnam out of Communist control after the withdrawal of American troops. Lon Nol's appeal offered Nixon an excuse to clear the Communists from the sanctuaries inside Cambodia.

So in May of 1970 Nixon announced that American and South Vietnamese army units had crossed into Cambodia to drive out the Communists and "clear the sanctuaries." Since the Communists had removed most of their troops to the interior of Cambodia, casualties were light. But American and South Vietnamese soldiers captured large stocks of arms and supplies.

Kent State

Great numbers of Americans were shocked by the news that American troops had entered Cambodia. They viewed the move as a dangerous expansion of the war. Then came tragedy.

Shortly after announcement of the Cambodian operation, antiwar students at Kent State University in Ohio rioted to protest the action. They destroyed property in the city of Kent and burned down the school's ROTC building. Ohio's governor sent national guard troops to the campus. Soon, armed troops faced an angry crowd of students. The troops used tear gas to break up the crowd as the students heckled them. Then it happened: a number of guardsmen raised their rifles and fired into the crowd. When the smoke cleared, four students lay dead, two men and two women. Eleven others were wounded.

Even people who disapproved of the behavior of young demonstrators felt numbed by the deaths at Kent State. The tragedy heightened the rage of critics of the Cambodian operation.

To subdue the wave of protests sweeping the country, President Nixon promised that American troops were under strict orders not to go beyond the sanctuaries to the interior of Cambodia. He also pledged that the GIs would be out of Cambodia in a few weeks.

My Lai

The president kept his pledge. But the antiwar critics would not be silenced. Firing the determination of the critics was news of an alleged massacre at My Lai.

According to the recent news reports, American soldiers had gunned down more than a hundred Vietnamese civilians near the village of My Lai back in 1968. My Lai had been believed to be a hotbed of Viet Cong sympathizers who sheltered Communist soldiers, fired on

When President Nixon sent troops into Cambodia in 1970, a new wave of antiwar demonstrations erupted across the United States. In Ohio, national guardsmen were sent to the Kent State University campus to end a protest there. Here the guardsmen are shown hurling tear gas at a crowd of students and spectators. About twenty minutes later, some of the guardsmen opened fire and killed four students.

Kent State News Service

American troops, and planted booby traps which had maimed or killed several GIs. A platoon of Americans, nervous and angry and tired, had turned its rifles on the unarmed villagers, including women and children.

At length, in 1971, several soldiers who had been charged in the My Lai killings were court-martialed. Lieutenant William L. Calley, Jr., was convicted of murder. The case touched off a new round of verbal fireworks. Antiwar critics charged that Calley had been made a scapegoat for high-ranking officials in the government and the army who, critics insisted, were the real war criminals. Calley's conviction later was overturned by a federal court.

The *Pentagon Papers*

A few months after Calley's conviction in 1971 came publication of the *Pentagon Papers*—documents from a top-secret Pentagon study of United States involvement in Vietnam. One person who had worked on the study, Daniel Ellsberg, gave, or "leaked," the papers to the press. The papers showed that some leaders, including President Johnson, had not told the truth in public statements about what the United States was doing in Vietnam.

Critics charged that Ellsberg had damaged America's foreign relations by revealing national secrets. Ellsberg's defenders praised him as a patriot who had risked a prison term to help Americans learn the truth about their country's involvement in Vietnam.

Searching for Peace

President Nixon continued to search for a negotiated peace in Vietnam. He sent his foreign policy adviser, Henry A. Kissinger, on several secret trips to Paris to meet with Communist delegates to the stalemated peace talks. Kissinger's efforts came to nothing. As a price for peace settlement, the Communists demanded concessions which would assure their control of South Vietnam. Continuing to hope for a non-Communist South Vietnam, Nixon and Kissinger were of no mind to make such concessions.

Then, in January 1972, the president offered an elaborate proposal for a peaceful settlement of the war. The proposal required the Communists to silence their guns. It also required them to accept the will of the voters of South Vietnam regarding the future government of the country. The Communists turned aside the proposal.

STUDY GUIDE: Foreign affairs claimed much of President Nixon's attention at the beginning of his term in 1969. The most important of these was the Vietnam War.

In 1969 peace talks began in Paris. They soon deadlocked. Nonetheless, Nixon set out to remove the United States from the war. His idea was to withdraw troops gradually. He hoped that this would give the South Vietnamese time to build their strength and prevent a Communist take-over.

Threatening Nixon's plan were the "sanctuaries" in neutral Cambodia. These were bases from which the Communists attacked South Vietnam across the border. In the spring of 1970 American and South Vietnamese troops crossed the border into Cambodia and attacked the sanctuaries. In the United States, critics called the action an expansion of the war. During a related protest at Kent State University, national guard troops shot and killed four students. Nixon removed the GIs from Cambodia.

Antiwar criticism mounted with news of an alleged massacre in Vietnam two years earlier at a village called My Lai. One soldier, Lieutenant William Calley, was found guilty by the army of murder. A federal court later overruled the conviction.

Soon afterward came publication of the *Pentagon Papers*. These were top-secret documents from a Pentagon study of the country's involvement in Vietnam. They were given to the press by Daniel Ellsberg, and they showed that President Johnson and other leaders had not told the public the truth.

President Nixon continued to try to negotiate an end to the war. But the peace proposal he offered in 1972 was rejected by the Communists.

NIXON AND CHINA

In his first months as president, Nixon studied dispatches relating a series of bloody clashes between Chinese and Soviet troops along the Sino-Soviet frontier, the border between the People's Republic of China and the USSR. Some observers were predicting all-out war between the two Communist giants. A short time later, Nixon learned that the Chinese had touched off new nuclear explosions.

Unfortunately, the United States had little

influence in China. The governments in Washington and Peking had hardly spoken to one another since the Communists took control of China in 1949. There had been no trade between the two countries. The United States had continued to recognize Chiang Kai-shek's regime on the island of Taiwan as the only legitimate government of China. American and Communist Chinese armies had fought in Korea in 1950-53, and the United States had intervened in Vietnam partly out of a desire to "contain" Chinese Communist influence.

The "Two China" Policy

Then, in spring of 1971, an American table tennis team touring the Far East unexpectedly received an invitation to visit mainland China. Within a few days, astonished people across the world were pondering photographs of Premier Chou En-lai entertaining the American ping-pong players. President Nixon let it be known that he was reevaluating America's policy toward China.

Soon it was clear that Nixon was moving toward a "two China" policy: the United States would maintain ties with Chiang's regime on Taiwan but was prepared to deal with Mao Tse-tung's regime in Peking as the legitimate government of mainland China. Then in July 1971 came a startling announcement: sometime in 1972 President Nixon, formerly a bitter foe of communism everywhere, would travel to the People's Republic of China!

Diplomatic Tremors

Nixon's announcement delighted most Americans. But it sent tremors through the diplomatic community.

Arrangements for the president's invitation to visit China had been made in utmost secrecy. America's allies wondered if this meant the beginning of a new "go-it-alone" style of diplomacy by the United States. The Japanese felt offended that Nixon had acted without consulting them. America's principal adversary, the USSR, also was upset. The Soviets wondered whether Nixon was trying to exploit Soviet-Chinese differences. To ease their fears, Nixon announced that he also would visit Moscow in 1972. Next, he had a series of meetings with leaders of Japan, Canada, France, Britain, and West Germany.

Nixon's plan to visit China had other effects.

The most dramatic occurred at the United Nations.

For two decades a group of American allies had reluctantly supported America's claim that Chiang Kai-shek's government on Taiwan, not that in Peking, should represent China in the UN. But now the United States was making peace gestures to Peking. Therefore, America's allies refused to continue to offend Mao's government by keeping it out of the UN. The United States wanted the UN to admit both Chinese governments. But the UN passed a resolution admitting Mao's representatives and expelling those of Chiang.

Nixon Visits China

The historic presidential visit to China took place in February, 1972. The official greeting of President and Mrs. Nixon in Peking was stiff and formal, and there were no crowds to welcome the presidential motorcade.

Then, suddenly, official restraint gave way to warmth and cordiality. A one-hour discussion between Nixon and the aging Chairman Mao

In 1972 Richard Nixon became the first United States president to visit the People's Republic of China. Below, he and Chinese Premier Chou En-lai (left) inspect a detachment of the People's Liberation Army. The two leaders spent many hours in private talks in Peking and Shanghai, and the result was to soften more than two decades of mutual distrust between the two countries. What events in the United Nations led to the president's trip?

John Dominis, Life Magazine, copyright © 1972 Time Inc.

seemed to break the ice. Banner headlines in newspapers shouted the news to the people. Friendly crowds gathered when the Nixons toured the Ming Tombs, the Forbidden City, and the Great Wall. And a spirit of good fellowship prevailed during a round of dinners and entertainment.

President Nixon and Premier Chou En-lai spent many hours discussing world problems. In Shanghai, at the end of the visit, they issued a joint *communiqué*, or statement. In it they noted differences separating their countries. But they announced that the United States and China accepted the principle of peaceful coexistence, renounced the use of force to settle disputes, and agreed that neither country would try to dominate the Pacific. Nixon acknowledged that Taiwan was a part of China, and indicated that the United States would withdraw its troops from the island. Finally, the two leaders agreed that there should be increased trade and periodic, high-level consultations between their countries.

When he returned home, Nixon spoke of his visit as "the week that changed the world." Many people agreed.

STUDY GUIDE: In 1971 the United States re-evaluated its policy toward Communist China. Nixon accepted an invitation to visit the People's Republic of China. A short time later the United Nations expelled the Nationalist Chinese government of Taiwan headed by Chiang Kai-shek and admitted the Communist government of mainland China headed by Mao Tse-tung. Early in 1972 President Nixon visited Peking.

NIXON AND THE USSR

Like all presidents since 1945, Nixon dreamed of an agreement to end the arms race with the Soviet Union. Nuclear weapons were very expensive, and their capacity for destruction was frightening. To make matters worse, scientists and engineers were perfecting ever-more devastating weapons. Most notable was the Multiple Independently Targeted Re-entry Vehicle (MIRV)—a giant rocket carrying several nuclear warheads designed to strike several targets. An arms agreement seemed more urgent than ever.

SALT Talks Begin

In the past, the Soviets had refused to talk seriously about arms limitation because they were racing to catch up with the United States. But at last the Soviet Union had nearly achieved nuclear equality, or parity, with the United States. So in 1969 the governments in Washington and Moscow sent delegates to Helsinki, Finland for a round of talks on a Strategic Arms Limitation Treaty (SALT).

Because of the complexity of the problem, there was no chance for an early agreement. Still, the talks were cordial, and leaders in Washington and the Kremlin agreed to resume the talks the next year.

In 1969 the United States and the USSR also signed a nonproliferation treaty. The treaty was meant to prevent nuclear weapons from spreading, or proliferating. Both countries promised not to provide nuclear weapons to countries which did not already have them. Nixon also announced that the United States never would engage in biological warfare, and would use chemical weapons only if they were first used against the United States.

Détente

Then, in 1971, the Soviets indicated a desire to further improve relations with the West, particularly the United States. Soviet leaders were worried that the bitter quarrel between the USSR and the People's Republic of China might break into open war. At home, there were economic problems, notably a poor grain harvest. A relaxation of tensions with the West would strengthen the USSR against China. It also might provide Western help in coping with economic problems.

By late 1971 the Soviets were vigorously promoting *détente*, a relaxing of the strained relations between the two nations. Their efforts struck a chord with President Nixon, who embraced *détente* as a new American policy.

The outcome was a visit to the Soviet Union by Nixon in May 1972. During the visit, Nixon and Soviet Chairman Leonid Brezhnev signed a treaty limiting the spread of antiballistic (defensive) missiles. They signed a temporary agreement limiting offensive missiles for five years. During this period, American and Soviet representatives would try to work out a permanent agreement. The two leaders also agreed to cooperate in commerce, science, technology, space, and pollution control.

STUDY GUIDE: Relations between the United States and the Soviet Union improved. The two countries began talking about a Strategic Arms Limitation Treaty (SALT) in 1969. They signed a nonproliferation treaty to stop the spread of nuclear weapons. In 1971 the USSR began promoting *détente*, a relaxing of relations with the United States.

Détente became a new American policy, and in May 1972 Nixon visited the USSR. During his visit he and Soviet Chairman Brezhnev signed a treaty limiting the spread of defensive missiles. They also agreed to cooperate in other areas.

ELSEWHERE IN FOREIGN AFFAIRS

President Nixon found no end to diplomatic matters with which to wrestle. He wanted to improve relations with Japan, which had become the world's third greatest industrial power. To this end, Nixon in 1971 approved a treaty ending American occupation of Okinawa. Through the CIA, he secretly and unsuccessfully tried to prevent a Communist, Salvador Allende, from winning the presidency of Chile.

In the United States he countered attempts in Congress to cut back the American troop commitment to NATO.

The Middle East

The Middle East remained tense. The Israelis continued to occupy land seized from Arab states in the Six-Day War of 1967. Arab leaders refused to meet the Israelis in face-to-face negotiations. The outcome was continuing artillery duels, commando raids, and aerial attacks.

Nixon stood by the policy that any peace settlement in the Middle East must recognize Israel's right to exist. He also believed that the main deterrent to all-out war in the Middle East was Israel's military superiority. So when it appeared that the Arabs, with Soviet support, were approaching military equality with Israel, Nixon approved the sale of fifty Phantom jet fighter-bombers to Israel.

Yet one group of Arabs seemed bent on conflict, whatever the risks: the Palestinians. In 1972 Palestinian guerrillas began a series of terrorist attacks outside the Middle East. Their purpose was to draw attention to their cause of expelling the Israelis from the former Palestinian homeland in Israel. Their campaign of global terrorism climaxed at the 1972 Olympic Games in Munich, when a group of Palestinians murdered two Israeli athletes and kidnapped

An Arab terrorist, masked by a ski cap, peers from the balcony of a building in Munich where Israeli athletes were being held hostage. West German police surrounded the building but were not able to prevent the deaths of nine Israelis.

Wide World

nine other members of the Israeli Olympic team. In a shoot-out between the Palestinians and West German police, all nine Israeli athletes were killed.

STUDY GUIDE: President Nixon was busy with foreign affairs all over the world. While trying to improve relations with Japan, he secretly tried to prevent the Communist candidate, Salvador Allende, from winning the presidential election in Chile.

The Middle East remained tense. Nixon maintained that any settlement there must recognize Israel's right to exist. Meanwhile, Palestinian guerrillas began a campaign of terror against Israel. In 1972 they caused the deaths of nine Israeli athletes at the Olympic Games in Munich.

EVENTS AT HOME

The happenings in Southeast Asia, China, the Middle East, and elsewhere in the world were not the only issues which commanded President Nixon's attention. One of the most serious problems at home was the economy.

The Economy

When Nixon became president in early 1969, Americans were enduring the most serious inflation in years. Attempts to control it were disappointing. In the second half of 1969, industrial production and corporate profits slipped sharply. The stock market suffered its worse decline since the Great Depression. Unemployment increased.

By 1970 the country was in the grip of an economic recession. Unemployment rolls lengthened. The stock market slide continued. Sales of new cars slumped. The giant Penn Central Railroad went bankrupt. Even worse, prices did not drop. Instead, they continued to inch upward.

In August 1971, Nixon announced a far-reaching economic program. To encourage foreigners to make purchases in the United States, he brought about a devaluation of the dollar. To discourage the sale of foreign goods in the country, he raised tariff barriers. He granted tax credits to businesses which invested in new machinery. And he proclaimed a ninety-day freeze on wages and prices.

It seemed in 1972 that Nixon's economic plan had succeeded. The gross national product rose. Personal income and corporate profits soared. Automobile sales climbed sharply. Stock prices zoomed to their highest level ever. Equally encouraging, the rate of inflation fell, and unemployment declined slightly.

Supreme Court Appointments

Four vacancies appeared on the Supreme Court during Nixon's term. The Senate readily confirmed Warren E. Burger, a strict constructionist of the Constitution, to succeed the liberal Earl Warren as chief justice. But the Senate humiliated the president by rejecting his next two nominees, Clement Haynsworth and G. Harrold Carswell, as unfit. After that came confirmation of the conservatives Harry A. Blackmun, Lewis F. Powell, Jr., and William H. Rehnquist. Liberals were unhappy because these appointments gave the court a conservative majority which was expected to continue for many years.

Successes and Setbacks in Congress

Successes alternating with setbacks became the pattern of Nixon's dealings with Congress. Although Nixon was a Republican president, the Democrats controlled Congress.

At the president's request, Congress approved a bill to convert the Post Office Department into a government-owned corporation. Congress also passed several laws to prevent drug abuse and fight crime. It approved a range of environmental protection measures, set up the Consumer Protection Agency, and passed a military draft lottery bill. After a long debate, it narrowly approved funds for the *Safeguard* antiballistic missile (ABM) system.

Nixon and Congress managed to agree on other important measures. The Twenty-sixth Amendment to the Constitution lowered the voting age from twenty-one to eighteen. New legislation banned cigarette advertising on radio and television, supported research on cancer and sickle cell anemia, and expanded the federal birth control program. The president and Congress agreed to create a government corporation (AMTRAK) to operate the country's passenger trains. They compromised on legislation enlarging social security benefits.

Nixon's most satisfying legislative triumph came in 1972 when Congress passed the Revenue Sharing Act. Through this act, state and city governments, nearly all of them strapped for funds, were to receive more than $30 billion in federal tax money over a five-year period. Fearing that state and city officials might misuse the money, liberals were suspicious of revenue sharing. But conservatives, including the president, viewed it as a successful reversal of the forty-year trend toward concentration of authority in Washington.

Nixon also suffered legislative setbacks. The most disappointing came when Congress rejected his welfare and family assistance program. By 1970 nearly everyone agreed that America's welfare system was a mess. To reform the system Nixon wanted to guarantee individuals and families a minimum annual income. He wanted to allow poor people to hold low-paying jobs and still receive part of their guaranteed incomes. He also wanted to require the poor to accept jobs whenever jobs were available or to undergo job training. Critics of the plan pointed out that many people on welfare were old persons, disabled persons, or children. Nixon could not win the necessary support from Congress, so legislation embodying his ideas failed.

Radical Terrorism Erupts

The spirit of radicalism and rebellion which had begun in the 1960s reached a peak in 1970.

Early in 1970 the trial of the "Chicago 7" was concluding in Chicago. The seven (originally called the "Chicago 8" before Bobby Seale was ejected from the trial) were political radicals charged with conspiring to cause a riot at the 1968 Democratic convention. When they were found guilty of crossing state lines to incite violence, more violence erupted in several cities.

During the next few months, hardly a week passed without new violence. In San Francisco a bomb exploded in a police station, killing one person and injuring nine others. Students from the Santa Barbara campus of the University of California burned a bank, pelted police with rocks, and destroyed a patrol car. In New York a group known as "Revolutionary Force 9" set off explosions in the offices of three large corporations. In Cambridge, Maryland another bomb ripped off the corner of the courthouse where black militant H. Rap Brown was to stand trial.

The next month, radicals rioted in Harvard Square in Cambridge, Massachusetts and caused $100,000 in property damage. At the University

of Wisconsin a bomb gutted the building which housed the army's mathematics research center. One man died and three persons were injured. Other riots and explosions occurred elsewhere around the country.

Environmentalists and Feminists

Other Americans sought change in peaceful ways, particularly environmentalists and feminists.

Americans recently had become increasingly conscious of the fragile nature of the environment, as mentioned in Chapter 20. They were appalled to learn the extent of the pollution of lakes and rivers. They were shocked to learn that pollution of the atmosphere might one day threaten human survival. The outcome was a

After Congress passed the Equal Rights Amendment (ERA) in 1970, women's groups began to campaign in marches like this one for its approval by the states. Other groups of women spoke out against it.

Wide World

Some scientists are worried that mankind may pollute the environment so badly that the earth will become unfit for humans. Even cities which have little industry, such as Washington, D.C., suffer from pollution. Which environmental problems affect your own community most? What is being done to solve them?

loosely organized movement to clean up the environment and preserve the balance of nature.

The environmentalists found a friend in the White House. In 1969 President Nixon established the Environmental Protection Agency (EPA). That same year he persuaded Congress to pass the National Environmental Quality Act committing the federal government to preserve the natural environment. Then, in 1970, he sent to Congress the most comprehensive environmental message ever prepared by a president. The result was several more laws to protect the environment.

Then there was the women's liberation movement. The feminists' movement to liberate women from social and economic injustice gath-

ered momentum in the United States while Nixon was president. Feminist leaders increasingly concentrated on discrimination against women in employment and wages and on divorce and abortion laws. Accordingly, millions of women began to close ranks with the movement. National magazines featured articles by leading feminists such as Betty Friedan and Gloria Steinem. Two feminist magazines, *Ms.* and *New Women,* began publication. Kate Millet's *Sexual Politics* and Germaine Greer's *The Female Eunuch* became best-sellers.

Leaders of the women's movement pressed their objectives in the political arena. As a result, in 1970 the House of Representatives overwhelmingly approved the Equal Rights Amendment (ERA) to the Constitution. Bottled up in the House since 1923, the amendment stated: "Equality of rights under the law shall not be abridged by the United States or by any State on account of sex." The Senate also approved ERA, and women's groups began working to obtain approval by the thirty-eight state legislatures required to make it law.

The American Indian Movement

Other Americans who were pressing for social change in the early 1970s included members of the American Indian Movement (AIM).

Militant supporters of AIM occupied the national offices of the Bureau of Indian Affairs (BIA) in Washington for a week during November 1972. They demanded renegotiation of a number of treaties which had been made between Indian peoples and the United States, and they called for an end to BIA's practice of appointing officials to their tribal councils.

The following winter, in February, about 200 members of AIM occupied Wounded Knee, a village within the Ogala Sioux reservation in South Dakota. Wounded Knee had been the site of the last major battle between an Indian people and the United States, a battle which had resulted in a massacre of hundreds of Sioux by United States cavalry in 1890. (See Chapter 10.)

The 1973 occupation of Wounded Knee lasted 70 days. Armed protesters demanded a review of more than 300 treaties, an investigation of the BIA, and administrative changes which would provide for election rather than appointment of tribal council officials.

Shooting broke out between protesters and federal marshals several times. In all, two In-

During the occupation of Wounded Knee in 1973, members of the militant American Indian Movement acted as lookouts to keep track of movements by government officials. What were the demands made by the militants? Do you think their demands were justified? What do you think of the methods they used?

dians died during the protest, and ten Indians and two marshals were wounded.

The occupation ended with a cease-fire in May. The government promised to send representatives of the White House to the reservation to discuss charges of broken treaties, and to investigate operations of the tribal government.

STUDY GUIDE: At home, economic problems commanded President Nixon's attention. By 1970 the United States was in the grip of a recession, but in 1972 it passed and the economy boomed.

Nixon was a Republican president, but the Democrats controlled Congress. The Senate rejected two of his nominees as unfit for the Supreme Court but confirmed four others. These appointments gave the court a conservative majority. Nixon's greatest success in his dealings with Congress was the Revenue Sharing Act. His most disappointing setback was his failure to win passage of a welfare program.

Radical terrorism reached a high point during the Nixon presidency. By contrast, environmentalists and feminists sought change through new laws. As a result, the Environmental Protection Agency (EPA) was formed, and the Equal Rights Amendment (ERA) was approved by Congress. Other Americans who pressed for change in the early 1970s included members of the American Indian Movement

(AIM), who in 1973 occupied Wounded Knee, an Ogala Sioux village in South Dakota, to demand reforms in Indian affairs.

NIXON: A YEAR OF TRIUMPH

President Nixon began the final year of his first term in January 1972. In the months which followed it seemed that his career had reached high tide. Nixon visited China and the Soviet Union. In both Peking and Moscow he signed documents which seemed to signal a new era of harmony. Congress approved his revenue-sharing proposal. The economy was booming.

Although peace talks in Paris had broken down, the withdrawal of United States troops from Vietnam was continuing. By spring of 1972, only 70,000 American fighting men remained in Vietnam, compared with 550,000 when Nixon entered the White House in 1969.

Even a new display of toughness by North Vietnam proved no setback for Nixon. When the Communists launched a new offensive in spring of 1972, Nixon ordered the resumption of full-scale bombing of North Vietnam. He also announced that mines would be planted in North Vietnam's main harbor, Haiphong. Mining Haiphong was risky because a mine might sink a Soviet ship. Still, most Americans accepted

Nixon's firmness, especially since he showed no inclination to end troop withdrawals.

Not even hints of misdeeds touching Nixon's administration seemed to weaken his popular standing. First came charges that his administration had agreed to settle an antitrust suit against the International Telephone and Telegraph Company (ITT) in return for a large contribution to the Republican party.

Then, in June 1972, police arrested five men during a break-in at Democratic national headquarters in the Watergate apartments in Washington. What were the five intruders up to? Apparently they were trying to hide listening devices, or "bugs," in the offices of Democratic leaders. One of the five was a security coordinator for a rival organization, the Republican committee to reelect Nixon. In addition, two White House aides were accused of helping to plan the break-in. Nixon denied that any of his staff had broken the law. Most Americans believed him.

The Election of 1972

Nixon's renomination for a second term was a foregone conclusion when in August 1972 the Republicans met in Miami Beach. Delegates also renominated Vice-President Spiro T. Agnew.

Events did not proceed so smoothly for the Democrats. At the start of the election year Senator Edmund S. Muskie of Maine seemed the most likely candidate for the Democratic presidential nomination. But Muskie's campaign faltered, and he withdrew. His withdrawal left the field largely to Governor George C. Wallace of Alabama, Senator George S. McGovern of South Dakota, and the Democratic candidate of 1968, former Vice-President Hubert H. Humphrey. But then a would-be assassin reduced the field to two when he shot and seriously wounded Wallace at a political rally in Maryland, leaving the governor paralyzed below the waist.

McGovern emerged as the front-runner. He demanded America's immediate and total withdrawal from the war in Vietnam and urged a cutback in America's commitments around the world. His solutions to domestic problems struck millions of Americans as radical. In fact, his positions appealed to only a minority of Democrats. But McGovern had an efficient organization. When the Democrats convened at Miami Beach in July 1972 he won the nomination on the first ballot. For his vice-presidential runningmate he turned to Senator Thomas F. Eagleton of Missouri.

From the start everything seemed to go wrong for the McGovern campaign. Most serious was the news that Eagleton had undergone shock treatments for mental depression. Millions of

A saddened Senator Thomas Eagleton listens with bowed head as Senator George McGovern announces that Eagleton is withdrawing as the Democratic candidate for vice-president. The announcement followed news that Eagleton had had shock treatments for mental depression.

Americans felt worried that a man with a history of depression might one day become president. McGovern forced Eagleton to withdraw and chose R. Sargent Shriver, brother-in-law of the late President Kennedy, as his running-mate. The episode was a severe embarrassment for McGovern and the Democrats.

During the next three months the McGovern campaign continued to sputter. Efforts to exploit the Watergate break-in had little effect. Most Americans seemed satisfied with Nixon's claims of innocence in the bizarre episode. Then, two weeks before the election, Henry Kissinger dramatically predicted that "peace is at hand" in Vietnam.

It was clear by election day that the McGovern-Shriver ticket, abandoned in droves by middle-of-the-road Democrats, was headed for overwhelming defeat. When votes were tallied, Nixon and Agnew had won a staggering sixty-one percent of the popular vote. They had carried forty-nine states and won the electoral vote 520-17. Still, the Democrats retained control of the House of Representatives by a large margin and strengthened their majority in the Senate by capturing two seats from the Republicans.

"Peace with Honor"

Despite his victory, Nixon felt frustrated in the weeks following the election. Contrary to Kissinger's claim, peace did not seem to be at hand.

The president decided to put new pressure on the North Vietnamese by ordering a steep escalation of the bombing. In what came to be called the "Christmas bombing," B-52s ravaged North Vietnam's cities, particularly Hanoi. Pictures of the devastation were shocking. The bombing achieved Nixon's purpose, and in January 1973 Nixon declared that he had attained his goal of "peace with honor"—a peace that would not humiliate the United States. Nixon announced that a cease-fire agreement would be signed in Paris ending the war.

Nixon knew that the war was far from over. But the cease-fire would give a temporary appearance of peace. It thus would provide a cover for the withdrawal of all remaining Americans. It also brought the release of 587 American prisoners of war. In late January 1973 Nixon's popular-approval rating soared to sixty-eight percent.

STUDY GUIDE: Nixon's career reached high tide in January 1972-January 1973. The president visited China and the Soviet Union. The economy recovered from the recession of 1970-71. The news that a man connected with Nixon's Republican campaign committee had been arrested while trying to "bug" Democratic headquarters in the Watergate building did little to damage the president's popularity.

Nixon and Vice-President Agnew won renomination at the Republican convention in 1972. Senator George McGovern won the Democratic nomination for president, but many Democrats viewed him as a radical. Nixon and Agnew were overwhelmingly re-elected.

To persuade the North Vietnamese Communists to sign a cease-fire, Nixon ordered new bombing raids over North Vietnam in December 1972. The plan worked, and Nixon's popularity soared as troop withdrawals continued.

WATERGATE

Even as President Nixon's approval rating rose, trouble was brewing. The biggest problem was the continuing controversy over the break-in at Democratic headquarters in the Watergate back in June of 1972. Eventually the Watergate case would become the worst political scandal in United States history.

While Americans were celebrating the "cease-fire" in Vietnam, the seven charged in the Watergate burglary were undergoing trial in a federal district court in Washington. Five of them pleaded guilty, and the other two were convicted. It was learned that each had been employed either directly or indirectly by the Republican campaign committee to reelect Nixon.

The Investigation Begins

The trial judge, John J. Sirica, announced that he was not satisfied that all the facts about Watergate had come out. He urged a congressional inquiry. The Senate responded by creating a special seven-member committee to investigate political spying during the 1972 presidential campaign. The committee soon was nicknamed the Ervin Committee after its colorful and outspoken chairman, Sam J. Ervin, Jr., a Democratic senator from North Carolina.

Because he suspected something, John J. Sirica, a federal district judge in Washington, called on Congress to investigate Watergate.

It was Judge Sirica, however, who produced the first major break in the case. By threatening a heavy sentence, he prompted a letter in March 1973 from James W. McCord, Jr., one of those convicted in the Watergate break-in. McCord wrote that the Watergate defendants had been under political pressure to plead guilty and keep silent. He also claimed that perjury had been committed and that the facts of the case had been covered up.

McCord's letter increased suspicions that the White House had been involved. Nixon on April 17 announced that he had begun his own investigation of Watergate. He declared that not even important members of his administration should be free from prosecution. Two days later the president's counsel, John W. Dean III, announced that he would not "become a scapegoat."

By the end of April, Dean and three other important officials had resigned, including Nixon's two closest advisers: H. R. Haldeman, the president's chief of staff, and John D. Ehrlichman, the president's chief adviser for domestic affairs.

New bombshells rocked the Nixon presidency in May. It was learned that in 1971 two of the men convicted in the Watergate break-in had burglarized the files of Daniel Ellsberg's former psychiatrist. (Ellsberg was the man who had outraged the White House by leaking the *Pentagon Papers*.) In response, Nixon emphasized his innocence in the Watergate affair. But he conceded that members of his administration had tried to conceal some aspects of the case. Three days later, Archibald Cox, a Harvard law professor, took the oath as special prosecutor with a broad mandate to investigate Watergate.

Nixon is Accused in Hearings

Meanwhile, the Ervin Committee had begun televised hearings on May 17. For Nixon the hearings proved disastrous.

Witnesses explained how $400,000 in Nixon campaign funds had been channeled to the Watergate defendants to buy their silence. The deputy director of the Nixon reelection committee, Jeb Stuart Magruder, testified that

As millions watched on television, Senator Sam Ervin of North Carolina and other members of a special Senate committee tried to find out the truth about what had happened in 1972.

John Dean, who had been President Nixon's lawyer, told the Ervin Committee that Nixon was lying about his role in the cover-up. But he had no proof.

Nixon's friend, former Attorney General John N. Mitchell, had approved the bugging of Democratic headquarters. But the most explosive testimony came from the president's former counsel, John Dean.

In matter-of-fact tones, Dean charged that Nixon himself had tried to cover up the fact that Haldeman, Ehrlichman, and other White House aides were involved. If what Dean said was true, the president had taken part in an illegal conspiracy and then lied about it.

Many Americans believed Dean. But without evidence, it was Dean's word against Nixon's. Who was telling the truth? Then, on July 16, came another bombshell.

It was learned that "for historical purposes" Nixon had installed a tape recording system which automatically recorded conversations in his offices at the White House and the Executive Office Building. Thus there must be tape recordings of talks recalled by Dean which would prove Nixon's involvement in the Watergate cover-up. Two days later Special Prosecutor Cox requested eight of the tapes. But Nixon re-fused to provide them on the grounds that a president's private conversations are beyond the reach of the law—the principle of executive privilege.

The Battle for the Tapes

A legal battle then began between Cox and Nixon which continued for the rest of the summer and into the fall. For more than three months the special prosecutor tried to obtain the tapes from the president. In late October, after Cox refused to stop trying to obtain the tapes, Nixon had him fired and announced that he had abolished his job. The action caused a public outcry that it was Nixon, not Cox, who should be removed from office. The public was so outraged that Nixon felt compelled to appoint a new special prosecutor, Leon Jaworski, a highly respected Texas attorney.

Then came a new shock. The White House announced that tapes of several critical conversations pertaining to Watergate were missing. Moreover, an eighteen-minute segment of another critical tape had been mysteriously erased.

The Fall of Agnew

Another bombshell rocked the Nixon administration in October of 1973—one totally unrelated to Watergate. Federal investigators had found evidence that Vice-President Agnew had accepted bribes from contractors while he was governor of Maryland and also after becoming vice-president. Other materials indicated that Agnew had evaded income taxes while he was vice-president.

Agnew struck a bargain with federal prosecutors. He would not contest the charge of income tax evasion and he would resign. In return he would not be sent to jail. On October 10 Agnew became the second vice-president in United States history to resign. (John C. Calhoun was the first, in 1832.)

Acting under the Twenty-fifth Amendment, President Nixon nominated Representative Gerald R. Ford, Jr., a Republican from Michigan, to succeed Agnew. Confirmed by Congress, Ford took the vice-presidential oath on December 6, 1973. He was the first vice-president to be appointed under the Twenty-fifth Amendment.

Impeachment Proceedings Begin

In his State of the Union address in January 1974, President Nixon announced that "one year of Watergate is enough." But Special

H. R. Haldeman, Nixon's chief of staff and one of his two top aides, resigned as the Watergate hearings continued. He later was convicted of taking part in a conspiracy to cover up the case, along with former Attorney General John Mitchell and others.

Like Haldeman, John Ehrlichman, who was Nixon's adviser for domestic affairs, resigned. He later went to prison for his role in the Watergate cover-up and for helping to plan a burglary of an office containing the psychiatric files of Daniel Ellsberg.

Prosecutor Jaworski was pressing the case as vigorously as had his predecessor. The outcome, in March 1974, was a series of grand jury indictments charging that important officials of the Nixon administration, including Haldeman and Ehrlichman, had conspired to block the Watergate investigation. If the charge was true, Nixon's two top aides had been guilty of the crime of obstructing, or blocking, justice. (Both Haldeman and Ehrlichman later were convicted, as was former Attorney General Mitchell. Among others convicted of Watergate crimes were Dean, Nixon's former counsel, and Magruder, Nixon's deputy campaign director.)

A short time after the grand jury indictments came news that the jury had not indicted Nixon only because of the constitutional provision that a president may not be prosecuted while in office. Instead, the jury named Nixon an "unindicted co-conspirator." This meant that the jury was accusing Nixon of taking part in the cover-up, even though he could not be indicted.

The only legal action that may be taken against a president is impeachment. Impeachment is a legal process in which the House of Representatives weighs evidence to determine whether the president or any other federal official suspected of "high crimes and misdemeanors" should be impeached—that is, charged with a crime. If a majority of the representatives present and voting decides that the evidence against the accused is persuasive, the official is thereby impeached, or charged. Next comes a trial in which the Senate acts as a jury. If two-thirds of the senators vote for conviction, the accused is removed from office.

When the grand jury's findings became public in the spring of 1974, an impeachment inquiry by the House Judiciary Committee was already underway. It had begun the previous autumn in the aftermath of the firing of Special Prosecutor Archibald Cox. Led by Chairman Peter W. Rodino, Jr., Democrat of New Jersey, the committee had moved cautiously at first. But by March of 1974 the inquiry was picking up steam. When Nixon again refused to hand over taped conversations relating to Watergate, the committee voted to subpoena them.

Fearing that defiance might hasten his impeachment, Nixon acted dramatically. In a televised address on April 29 he announced that he would provide the committee with edited, printed transcripts of the tapes (but not the tapes themselves). He also promised to release to the public more than twelve hundred pages of transcripts. Although these papers would embarrass him, Nixon said, the transcripts would prove his innocence.

Nixon had miscalculated. The transcripts of his conversations actually heightened the suspicions of millions of Americans that he had indeed been involved in the Watergate cover-up. The transcripts were filled with gaps and profanity. Even prominent Republicans joined the swelling national chorus demanding Nixon's resignation. The president responded by declaring that he never would resign.

Nixon Asked to Pay Back Taxes

A controversy over Nixon's personal finances climaxed earlier in April when a congressional committee announced that the president owed more than $400,000 in back taxes.

After several months of study, the committee had decided—and the Internal Revenue Service agreed—that Nixon should have reported a profit on the sale of some property in California. Nixon also had claimed a large tax deduction for donating his vice-presidential papers to the country, but he had made the donation nearly a year after such deductions had become illegal. Nixon announced that he would pay the tax.

Nixon Resigns

The final act of the Watergate tragedy began to unfold within weeks. On May 22 Nixon told Chairman Rodino that he would honor no further subpoenas for materials. The House Judiciary Committee warned that this "might constitute a ground for impeachment." When Nixon still would not yield, Special Prosecutor Jaworski asked the Supreme Court to decide the matter. If the court decided in favor of Jaworski, it was certain that Rodino's committee—and the public —would gain access to the same materials.

By July the end was near. The committee released evidence that the White House had used confidential tax information to hurt its political enemies and had placed secret wiretaps on the telephones of some members of government and the press. On July 24 the Supreme Court ruled

When it became clear that he would be forced out of office, President Nixon went on television to announce his resignation to the American people.

unanimously that Nixon must hand over the tapes. That same day, before a national TV audience, the Judiciary Committee began formal debate on the question of impeachment.

Within a week the Judiciary Committee voted to send three articles of impeachment to the floor of the House for consideration. These articles charged Nixon with obstructing justice in the Watergate cover-up, abusing presidential powers, and attempting to block the impeachment process by denying requests for evidence. It seemed certain that the House would vote to impeach the president and order a trial by the Senate. Still, Nixon clung to the hope that two-thirds of the senators would not vote to remove him from office.

That hope soon faded. Transcripts of one of the tapes released under the Supreme Court order disclosed that six days after the Watergate break-in the president had approved a cover-up for political reasons. It was clear that Nixon had been lying about his role in the cover-up for more than a year. Nixon then made a statement admitting that he had known about the cover-up, but he concluded by saying that this action did not justify impeachment.

However, with that statement, Nixon's support in Congress disappeared. Republican leaders in the Senate urged Nixon to resign before he was forced out of office.

So on August 8 the president went before TV cameras to announce his resignation, effective at noon the following day. It was the first time in United States history that a president had resigned.

The next morning, August 9, 1974, Nixon made an emotional farewell speech to his staff in the East Room of the White House. A short time later in that same room—while Nixon was flying home to California—Vice-President Gerald Ford repeated the presidential oath.

STUDY GUIDE: As controversy over Watergate continued, the Senate established a special committee to investigate political spying in the 1972 presidential campaign. One of the Watergate burglars claimed that he and other defendants had been under political pressure to keep silent. In May 1973 Nixon emphasized that he was innocent in the Watergate case. But he admitted that members of his administration had tried to cover it up. Archibald Cox was appointed special prosecutor to investigate.

Meanwhile, televised hearings of the Senate's investigating committee (the Ervin Committee) opened. Nixon's former counsel, John Dean, charged that Nixon himself had taken part in the Watergate cover-up. Then came the news that a recording system had taped White House conversations. When Special Prosecutor Cox demanded the tapes, Nixon had him fired. But Cox's successor, Leon Jaworski, pressed the investigation as vigorously as had Cox.

Adding to Nixon's embarrassment was evidence that Vice-President Agnew had taken bribes and evaded income taxes. To avoid a possible jail sentence, Agnew resigned. His successor was Gerald Ford.

In March 1974 a grand jury charged several former Nixon aides with obstructing justice in the Watergate cover-up. It also expressed the view that Nixon had been involved. The House Judiciary Committee already had begun an impeachment inquiry, and in April 1974 it demanded tapes of White House conversations about Watergate.

Nixon refused to hand over the tapes, but the Supreme Court ordered him to do so. That same day the House Judiciary Committee began impeachment hearings. The committee voted to charge Nixon with obstructing justice, abusing his power, and blocking the im-

peachment process. It seemed certain that Nixon would be impeached and tried by the Senate.

Nixon became convinced that two-thirds of the Senators would vote to remove him from office. On August 9, 1974, he resigned. The same day, Gerald Ford became the thirty-eighth president.

GERALD FORD

Leslie King, Jr., was born in Omaha, Nebraska in 1913. A short time later his mother divorced Leslie King, Sr., and with her infant son moved to Grand Rapids, Michigan. There she married Gerald Rudolph Ford, a paint manufacturer. Ford adopted his new wife's young son, and Leslie King, Jr., became Gerald R. Ford, Jr.

Ford's main interest in his youth was athletics. In high school he was an all-state center in foot-

Leadership of the country fell to Gerald Ford after first the vice-president and then the president resigned in disgrace. The peaceful, orderly way in which power changed hands reminded the American people that the office of president is more important than any single person who holds it.

ball. In 1931 he entered the University of Michigan, and played center on Michigan's undefeated national championship football teams of 1932 and 1933. In 1935 he was a member of the college all-star football team. After graduation from Michigan he entered the Yale Law School, and was an assistant football coach and freshman boxing coach. In 1941 he received his law degree.

Ford then joined a law firm in Grand Rapids. After Japan's raid on Pearl Harbor he joined the navy and took part in carrier operations in the Pacific. When he was discharged in 1946 with the rank of lieutenant commander, Ford returned to the practice of law in Grand Rapids.

The law did not remain his principal interest. Ford became active in the Republican Party, and in 1948 won election to Congress. Less than a month before the election he married Elizabeth Bloomer, a former dancer who was then a fashion coordinator in Grand Rapids. The Fords later became the parents of three sons and a daughter.

Ford held his seat in the House of Representatives from 1949 to 1973, when he gave it up to become vice-president. During his years as a congressman, Ford proved hard-working and conscientious. On most domestic issues he voted with the conservative wing of the Republican Party. In foreign affairs he advocated toughness in dealing with the Soviet Union.

By 1960 Ford was extremely well known on Capitol Hill. No one viewed him as an imaginative legislator. But Republicans admired his loyalty to the party, and both Democrats and Republicans found him likable. Ford also had won a reputation for honesty. In part because of that reputation, President Johnson appointed him to the Warren Commission to investigate the assassination of President Kennedy. In 1965 the Republicans of the House elected Ford their leader.

Then came the resignation of Vice-President Agnew in 1973. To fill the vacancy President Nixon wanted a loyal Republican who shared his political views. He wanted a person of spotless personal reputation. And he wanted someone who enjoyed good relations with both Republicans and Democrats in Congress. The one who best met those qualifications, he decided, was Gerald Ford.

As the Watergate scandal closed in on Nixon in 1974, Vice-President Ford found his position delicate. On one hand, he felt compelled to express loyalty to the president. On the other hand, it seemed necessary to keep a discreet distance from Nixon. Ford handled the situation with skill. When Nixon resigned and Ford took the presidential oath in August 1974, there were no complaints that Ford had contributed to the collapse of the Nixon presidency or allowed himself to be discredited by Watergate.

STUDY GUIDE: Gerald R. Ford, Jr., was born in Nebraska and grew up in Grand Rapids, Michigan. He was a star football player at the University of Michigan and earned a law degree at Yale. He served in the navy in World War II, practiced law after the war, and in 1948 was elected to Congress. As a congressman, Ford was a conservative who worked hard. He served on the Warren Commission which investigated the assassination of President Kennedy, and in 1965 he became the Republican leader of the House of Representatives. After the resignation of Vice-President Agnew in 1973, he was appointed vice-president by Nixon. In 1974, when President Nixon resigned, Ford became president.

THE FORD PRESIDENCY

Most Americans felt a sense of relief when Ford became president. For many, it seemed that the Watergate scandal—which Ford called "our long national nightmare"—was over. The new president seemed modest, open, and honest. It was an image which many Americans thought contrasted sharply with that of Nixon.

Ford Pardons Nixon

But then came a new thunderclap. A month after taking the presidential oath, Ford issued a "full, complete, and absolute" pardon to Nixon for any illegal acts committed as president. This meant that Nixon could not be prosecuted as a private citizen for his part in Watergate. As a result, the issue of his innocence or guilt never could be fully resolved. Great numbers of Americans were furious that the new chief executive had put Nixon beyond the reach of the law.

Meanwhile, Ford set about to act under the Twenty-fifth Amendment to nominate a new vice-president. He turned to Nelson A. Rockefeller, a Republican who had been governor of New York. Rockefeller won confirmation by Congress, but the more liberal "Rocky" never seemed to fit in with the Ford administration. Relations between the president and vice-president cooled. In late 1975 Rockefeller announced that

AMERICAN BUSINESS ACTIVITY: 1960-1975

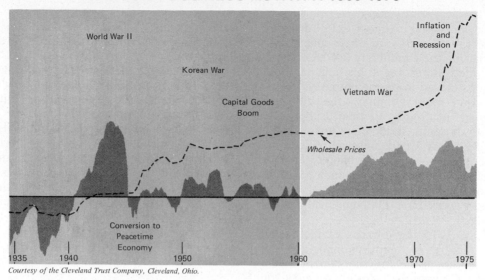

World War II

Korean War

Capital Goods
Boom

Vietnam War

Inflation
and
Recession

Wholesale Prices

Conversion to
Peacetime
Economy

1935   1940   1950   1960   1970   1975

Courtesy of the Cleveland Trust Company, Cleveland, Ohio.

he would not be Ford's running-mate if Ford won the Republican nomination for president in 1976.

Other Domestic Issues

A series of problems crowded in about Ford. There were disclosures that the Federal Bureau of Investigation (FBI) and the Central Intelligence Agency (CIA) had been spying on citizens of their own country through illegal "snooping" activities within the United States. It also was learned that the CIA had tried to arrange the assassination of certain foreign leaders, including Premier Fidel Castro of Cuba.

The government of the largest city in the country, New York, was edging toward bankruptcy. In Boston and Louisville, white parents reacted angrily when federal judges ordered the busing of children far from their own neighborhoods to achieve racial balance in schools.

Of larger concern were economic problems. When Ford took office, the rate of inflation was the highest in decades. Production of automobiles sagged and the building industry was depressed. Prices of common stocks had plunged. By the end of 1974, unemployment had passed seven percent, the highest level in years.

Contributing to the economic disarray, around the world as well as in the United States, was the "energy crisis." The crisis actually was an energy squeeze—a drastic increase in oil prices imposed by a small group of countries, mainly in the Middle East, which produced much of the world's petroleum. The increase in oil prices led to sharp increases in the cost of a wide variety

of goods, from gasoline to agricultural produce. Efforts by the president and Congress to plan a national energy policy to make the United States less dependent on foreign oil made little headway.

By 1975 there was no denying that the United States was in the grip of a major economic recession. Statistics later showed that the recession was the worst economic crisis since the Great Depression.

Foreign Affairs: The End of the War

On taking the presidency, Ford made it clear that he would encourage anti-Communists in their continuing struggle in Vietnam, support NATO, and continue the pursuit of *détente* with the Soviet Union.

In foreign affairs Ford relied heavily on Henry Kissinger, Nixon's former foreign policy adviser who had become secretary of state in 1973. A war between Arabs and the Israelis had ended in a standoff in 1973, and in 1974 Kissinger began a round of diplomatic talks in the Middle East. The outcome was several agreements designed to reduce tensions and prevent a new Middle Eastern war.

But from Southeast Asia came news of defeat. By the spring of 1975, Americans were forced to admit that the enormous investment which the United States had made in Southeast Asia over the past two decades—an investment of more than fifty thousand American lives and scores of billions of dollars—had failed.

First, the anti-Communists of Cambodia, despite continuing American support, gave in to

Communist pressure. Almost with disbelief, Americans saw pictures of their ambassador glumly departing the capital city of Phnom Penh, a folded United States flag in his hand, as Communist troops closed in on the embassy.

Second—and more stunning—the anti-Communist forces of South Vietnam simply collapsed. With dramatic suddenness and astonishing ease the North Vietnamese and Viet Cong swept through the country, jubilantly entering South Vietnamese cities whose names had become almost as familiar to Americans as Des Moines and Peoria: Hué, Da Nang, and then the capital, Saigon.

In April of 1975 the citizens of the United States saw pictures of their diplomatic and military representatives fleeing the American embassy as the Communists closed in on Saigon. Soon the president of South Vietnam formally surrendered the country to the Communists. The war was over. Finally, in a series of political and military maneuvers, the Communists also took control of Laos.

Relations with Cambodia and the USSR

Two weeks after the fall of Saigon, in May 1975, Cambodian naval patrol boats seized the American cargo ship *Mayaguez* and its forty-man crew sixty miles off the coast of Cambodia. Instead of using diplomacy, President Ford responded with force. American planes bombed three Cambodian gunboats and a Cambodian air base while two hundred marines landed on a Cambodian island. The Cambodians released the *Mayaguez* and its crew. But the president's show of force cost the lives of forty-one marines, all of whom died in the attack on Cambodia. When the public learned of the deaths, Ford was widely criticized.

In his relations with the Soviet Union, Ford gave full support to the SALT talks. He had a dramatic summit meeting with Chairman Leonid Brezhnev at Vladivostok. There the two men signed an agreement to hasten strategic arms limitation.

Unfortunately, the Soviets could not resist the temptation to take advantage of a new isolationist spirit which had settled over the United States following the Communist victory in Vietnam. Thus they encouraged the Communist faction which was struggling for power in Portugal.

When civil war broke out in the former Portuguese colony of Angola, the Soviets sent tanks and guns to assist the Communist faction. There also were signs that the Soviets had cheated on the arms limitation agreements they had made with Presidents Nixon and Ford. By 1976 *détente* was under considerable strain.

STUDY GUIDE: Most Americans were relieved when Ford entered the White House. But Ford provoked widespread criticism when he pardoned Nixon for any wrongs committed while president. Nelson Rockefeller became the new vice-president.

A series of problems confronted Ford. There were disclosures of illegal activities by the FBI and CIA. Economic problems, caused in part by an energy squeeze, developed into the worst recession in forty years.

Secretary of State Henry Kissinger worked out an agreement to keep the peace in the Middle East. But in the spring of 1975 it was clear that America's enormous investment in Southeast Asia had failed when Communists completed the conquest of Cambodia, South Vietnam, and Laos. Soon afterward, when the Cambodian navy seized the United States cargo ship *Mayaguez*, Ford's show of force resulted in the deaths of forty-one marines. Ford supported *détente*, but by 1976 relations with the Soviet Union were strained.

A scramble to leave South Vietnam took place when Communists won control of the capital city of Saigon. As the United States began evacuating the staff of its embassy there by helicopter, hundreds of Vietnamese civilians climbed over walls and barbed wire onto the grounds of the embassy, hoping to be taken to the United States.

Wide World

THE BICENTENNIAL YEAR

At the start of 1976 Americans seemed troubled and uncertain. The national economy remained weak. Several million people were out of work. The energy squeeze continued. Then there were the memories of Vietnam and Watergate. Americans wondered if their country had lost its sense of direction.

Still, Gerald Ford, a president who appeared steady and forthright, was presiding over the national destiny. No Americans were facing the shot and shell of an enemy. The urban ghettos were quiet. Radical terrorism had nearly ended. In 1976, moreover, Americans would celebrate their national bicentennial—the two-hundredth anniversary of the signing of the *Declaration of Independence*. And they would participate in that wonderful madness which happens every four years in America, the election of a president.

An Uncertain Beginning

Good news and bad confronted Americans as 1976 unfolded. The economy showed signs of rebounding from the recession. Automobile production took an upward turn. The rate of inflation slowed. But unemployment remained high—more than seven percent. This meant that as many as twenty million Americans (the unemployed and their families) faced severe hardship.

Abroad, the Middle East remained tense, but the truce between the Israelis and Arabs was holding. The Soviets ignored American warnings that their actions in Angola were jeopardizing *détente*, the policy of relaxing tensions between the United States and the Soviet Union. The Soviets continued to support Communist-led guerrillas in Angola, and by mid-1976 the guerrillas had won control. From another part of Africa the news was slightly better. In the autumn, Secretary of State Henry Kissinger worked out a tentative agreement by which the black majority would eventually gain control of strife-torn Rhodesia.

In China, meanwhile, the death of Mao Tse-tung in September 1976 led to a power struggle among factions of the ruling Communist party. By the end of the year the less radical faction led by Hua Kuo-feng had gained the upper hand. In the United States there was hope that improved relations with China would continue.

Americans Celebrate the Bicentennial

Whatever their concerns, millions of Americans determined to celebrate the bicentennial of their

George Holton/Photo Researchers

Birthday fireworks exploded across the country on July 4, 1976. This display took place in New York City around the Statue of Liberty.

national independence. Their imaginations ran rampant. They paraded in "Uncle Sam" suits, flew flags of 1776 vintage and staged mock battles in Revolutionary War uniforms. They decorated fireplugs and basketball goals in patriotic red, white, and blue. *The American Freedom Train,* powered by steam locomotives, moved across the landscape, pausing intermittently to allow citizens to tour its cars filled with symbols of the national past.

The grand climax came on July 4. Nearly every city and town was the scene of parades, rousing music, and fireworks. A great fleet of tall-masted sailing ships majestically entered New York harbor. But what was most notable was the spirit which settled over the republic in those few hours. People of all ages and creeds and colors let themselves go in a frenzy of celebration. Millions of Americans were momen-

During its Bicentennial year the United States took special pride in seven of its citizens who won all the Nobel Prizes awarded in 1976. It was the first year a single country had won every Nobel, the world's most prestigious prize. At left, being congratulated by Sweden's King Carl Gustav, is Dr. Baruch Blumberg, who with Dr. Carleton Gajdusek won the Nobel Prize for medicine. Other winners were Saul Bellow for literature; Milton Friedman for economics; Dr. William Lipscomb for chemistry; and Dr. Burton Richter and Dr. Samuel Ting for physics.

Wide World

tarily consumed by a sense of national pride and unity which the world's longest-surviving democratic republic had not experienced since World War II.

Carter Wins Democratic Nomination

Of larger importance to many Americans was another event which was taking place: the election of a president.

At the start of 1976 Democrats were optimistic. President Ford, a Republican, had not won high marks as a dynamic national leader. His relations with Congress were poor. Many Americans remained angry over Ford's pardon of former-President Nixon. Then there was the economic recession. Economic troubles always rebounded against the party controlling the White House. And, of course, there was Watergate. How could voters possibly give the Republican party another four years in the White House in view of the fact that in 1972 the Republicans had given the country Nixon and Agnew?

Another reason for Democratic optimism was the fact that the divisions which had torn the party in 1968 and 1972 were largely healed. And since theirs was clearly the majority party, claiming twice as many followers as the Republican party, Democrats believed that simple arithmetic assured them victory if they remained united.

Such optimism encouraged a dozen persons to seek the Democratic presidential nomination. One of these was an obscure former governor of Georgia named Jimmy Carter. His easy smile,

southern accent, and Baptist religious faith appealed to some people and annoyed others. Few observers thought he had a chance. After all, only one presidential candidate from the Deep South, Zachary Taylor, had been elected in the last hundred years.

But then millions of voters registered preferences in a series of primary elections. Many voters viewed Carter as a person who had not been tarnished by Vietnam and Watergate, and Carter amazed the experts by winning most of the Democratic primaries.

When the Democratic national convention was called to order in New York City in July 1976, delegates carefully avoided the battles which had divided their party in 1968 and 1972. They adopted a platform reflecting Jimmy Carter's views. They nominated Carter for president. At Carter's request they nominated Walter F. Mondale, a liberal senator from Minnesota, for vice-president.

In the aftermath of the convention, opinion polls indicated that more than sixty percent of the electorate favored Carter and Mondale over whomever the Republicans might nominate.

Ford Wins Republican Nomination

Who would the Republican nominee be? Until the Republicans convened in Kansas City in August, no one could be certain.

Traditionally any president, even an unpopular one, easily wins his party's nomination. But Gerald Ford was unique. Unlike every other president, he had never been elected either president or vice-president. He had become president not by election, but as a result of two resignations: first Spiro Agnew's, and later Richard Nixon's. Thus Ford's claim to the White House seemed flawed.

Although Ford was a conservative, he had made Republican conservatives unhappy by violating a basic rule of conservatism. That rule was that a president must bend heaven and earth to balance the federal budget. Ford had broken that rule by supporting massive deficit financing to stimulate the economy. For the fiscal year 1975-76 it was estimated that the deficit would be an incredible $60 billion. Republican conservatives also were suspicious of the Nixon-Kissinger-Ford policy of *détente* with the Soviet Union.

The result was a determined bid for the Republican nomination by the conservative Ronald Reagan, a former film actor and more recently the governor of California. An effective campaigner, Reagan defeated Ford in several primary elections. But shortly before the Republican convention the president was able to win over a number of wavering delegates. At the convention, the most boisterous Republican gathering since 1952, Ford won a narrow victory over Reagan. For his vice-presidential running-mate he turned to Senator Robert Dole, a conservative from Kansas.

The Election of 1976

In a stirring acceptance speech at the Republican convention, Ford challenged Carter to a series of televised debates. Carter accepted. In view of Ford's many years of experience in legislative debate in Congress and his first-hand knowledge of the presidency, it was widely thought that the debates would help him. Still, the opinion polls showed a large lead for Carter. Few thought the president could catch up.

Such an estimate turned out to be wrong. Although he made a serious slip of the tongue by saying that the Soviet Union did not dominate Eastern Europe, Ford did well in the TV debates. He struck a popular chord by pointing out that the economy had improved, the country was not at war, and that he had restored integrity to the White House. He charged that Carter lacked experience in national affairs and warned that Carter's programs would result in sharp tax increases.

For his part, Carter hurt his own campaign in several ways. He granted an interview to *Playboy* magazine which millions of Americans found in poor taste. He seemed vague in spelling out details of his proposals. And he made several statements which he was forced to retract or revise. By election day, Ford had overcome Carter's lead in the opinion polls, and experts described the contest as "too close to call." Many observers believed that the election might turn on the votes won by an independent candidate, Eugene McCarthy. McCarthy, a former senator from Minnesota, appealed to Democratic liberals. If forced to choose between Ford and Carter, these liberals would vote for Carter. But if they voted for McCarthy instead of Carter, they might cost Carter enough votes to tip the election to Ford.

As it turned out, most Democratic liberals voted for Carter. Thanks to Carter's southern origins—and the overwhelming support of blacks

Jimmy Carter (left) and Gerald Ford competed for votes in a series of televised debates during the 1976 campaign. It was the second series of TV debates by presidential candidates (see Chapter 20), and a debate also was held between the vice-presidential candidates. In 1976, as in 1960, the Democrats won the election.

Wide World

—he carried every southern state except Virginia. The vigorous support of northern blacks and of organized labor, which blamed the Republicans for the recession and high unemployment, also helped Carter in the heavily populated northeastern states. Carter won fifty-one percent of the popular vote to Ford's forty-eight percent. In the electoral college, the final vote was 297 for Carter and 240 for Ford. Reagan received one vote. The Republicans made no gains in Congress: both the House and Senate remained under Democratic control.

STUDY GUIDE: Americans were troubled at the start of 1976. But they looked forward to their nation's bicentennial celebration and a presidential election. As 1976 unfolded, the best news was that the country seemed to be recovering from its economic recession. Americans celebrated the bicentennial in grand style.

Democrats were optimistic at the start of the 1976 presidential campaign. The result was a scramble for the Democratic nomination. The surprise winner of the contest was a southerner, Jimmy Carter. President Ford won the Republican nomination after a hard-fought battle with Ronald Reagan. As the Carter-Ford contest began it seemed that Ford had little chance. But the president waged an effective campaign. By election day the contest was "too close to call." When the votes were counted, Carter had scored a narrow victory.

JIMMY CARTER

Born in 1924 in the little town of Plains in southwestern Georgia, James Earl Carter, Jr., grew up in the nearby community of Archery. His father was hard-working, thrifty, and shrewd; he owned four thousand acres of farmland and timberland, and operated a number of business enterprises. The elder Carter took his children to the Baptist church on Sundays, and never questioned racial segregation. The mother of the future president, Lillian Carter, valued books. She also was sensitive to the feelings of blacks. Both Carters influenced their eldest son, who even as an adult preferred to be called Jimmy. From his father he learned discipline and thrift, and from his mother tolerance and respect for learning.

Slightly built and rusty-haired, Jimmy Carter enjoyed a secure childhood. At his father's insistence he worked in the cotton and peanut fields. But he also had time for outdoor pursuits, often with black companions. He was mischievous, good-humored, and highly competitive. Only because he played hooky to see a movie was he ranked second in his high school graduating class.

After graduation from high school in 1941, Carter entered the U.S. Naval Academy at Annapolis. Only moderately studious, he was graduated fifty-ninth in a class of 820. While still a midshipman he married his hometown sweetheart, Rosalynn Smith, and later they had three sons and a daughter. From the naval academy Carter went to sea and quickly proved himself a forceful and competent leader. He was particularly interested in submarines and became a member of a select group of officers working with Admiral Hyman Rickover to develop nuclear submarines.

But then, in the late 1950s, his father died. Jimmy, the eldest son, resigned from the navy and returned to Plains to take over the family's business enterprises, which had become troubled. Within a few years business was thriving, particularly the family's peanut farm, and Carter had become a man of considerable wealth. However, he was restless. He entered politics and won election to the Georgia Senate. Next, in 1966, he ran for governor—and lost.

The defeat depressed Carter. During his depression he found a fresh source of strength. He experienced a spiritual rebirth—he was "born again." After that, prayer, religious meditation, and church activities were central parts of his life.

Still, he had not abandoned politics, and in 1970 he ran again for governor. Openly courting Georgia's segregationists, he won. Then, at his inauguration in January 1971, he dramatically announced that "the time for racial discrimination is over." The outcome was an administration which showed more interest in equal rights for blacks than any in Georgia's history. Carter also reorganized the state government, made appointments on the basis of merit, and quarreled continually with the state legislature.

In late 1972 Carter decided to seek the presidency in 1976. The result was a long, careful, and tireless campaign to make himself known throughout the country. He tried to impress upon people that he was a man of intellect and high moral standards. In December 1974 he formally announced his candidacy, a year and a half before the nominating convention. Few people thought he could win. But at a time when Americans were still smarting over the deceptions of Vietnam and the corruption of Watergate—deceptions and corruption produced by politicians in Washington—the appeal to morality by a Washington outsider was attractive. The result was victory for Carter.

On January 20, 1977, on the front steps of the Capitol, Jimmy Carter repeated the oath of office to become the thirty-ninth president of the United States. In a restrained statement Carter said, "Let us learn together and laugh together and work together and pray together—confident that in the end we will triumph together."

Shortly afterward, to the delight of people all over the country, the new president walked down Pennsylvania Avenue, hand in hand with his wife Rosalynn, to begin his term in the White House.

Jimmy Carter won over many voters by promising to tell the truth. Is it ever necessary for a president to mislead the American people?

© Wally McNamee/Woodfin Camp & Associates

SUMMING UP THE CHAPTER

Names and Terms to Identify

Apollo 11	Twenty-sixth Amendment
Sihanoukville	Revenue Sharing Act
My Lai	Thomas Eagleton
Pentagon Papers	John Sirica
Chou En-lai	Ervin Committee
SALT	John Dean
détente	impeachment
G. Harrold Carswell	"energy crisis"

Study Questions and Points to Review

1. What were the high points in the life and career of Richard Nixon before he became president?

2. Why was Nixon able to make a political comeback in the years after his defeat in the California gubernatorial campaign in 1962?

3. When did the first persons walk on the moon? Who were they?

4. Why and how did Nixon propose to bring about America's withdrawal from the war in Vietnam?

5. Why did Nixon send United States troops into Cambodia in 1970? What was the reaction at home?

6. Why did President Nixon decide to revise Amer-

ica's policy toward China? What were the results of the revision?

7. Why were the Soviets willing to consider a limitation in strategic arms by 1969?

8. What is the meaning of the word *détente*? Why did the United States and the Soviet Union choose to pursue *détente* in the years Nixon was president?

9. What did Nixon do in the summer of 1971 to counter the economic recession? What was the result?

10. How did Nixon's Supreme Court nominees fare in the Senate? How did the court change as a result of Nixon's appointments?

11. What were some of Nixon's successes and setbacks in his dealings with Congress?

12. What were the goals of the environmentalists, the feminists, and members of the American Indian Movement?

13. Why did it seem that Nixon's career had peaked in the period between January 1972 and January 1973?

14. What were the major events which led to Nixon's resignation?

15. What issues and problems troubled President Ford during his term in the White House?

16. Who were the candidates, what were the issues, and what was the outcome of the presidential election of 1976?

Topics for Discussion

1. Consider the life and career of Richard Nixon, Gerald Ford, or Jimmy Carter up to the time he became president. In what way did his experience qualify him — or fail to qualify him — for the presidency?

2. Explain the Nixon Doctrine. What do you think of this policy?

3. Describe President Nixon's approach to the problem of withdrawing the United States from the Vietnam War. How did he respond to antiwar protesters in the United States?

4. What was America's policy toward China between 1949 and 1971? What prompted Nixon to change this policy? What were the results? Do you think America's policy toward China between 1949 and 1971 made sense? Do you think it was a good idea to make a change in the policy in 1971?

5. Evaluate the policy of *détente* with the Soviet Union. What were the origins of *détente*? What, in your judgment, were the best arguments for and against *détente*?

6. Consider Nixon's policy toward Vietnam and other Asian countries from 1969 to 1973, from his inauguration to the "cease-fire." What were the main points of the policy? Do you think Nixon followed a

wise course in dealing with Vietnam? What, if anything, should he have done differently?

7. What is revenue sharing? Do you think it is a good idea?

8. What were the goals of the environmentalists, the feminists, and members of the American Indian Movement in the early 1970s? Do you think their grievances were legitimate?

9. What were the high points in the Watergate drama? Do you think that Nixon's involvement in the Watergate cover-up was reason enough to remove him from office? Why or why not? Do you think President Ford should have pardoned him? What would you have done?

10. What were the most important successes and failures of the Nixon presidency? How do you think future generations will judge Nixon as a president?

11. Consider the presidency of Gerald Ford. What in your judgment were Ford's strengths and what were his shortcomings as president? On the whole, do you think he did a good job?

Subjects for Reports or Essays

1. Do you agree or disagree with the critics who felt that the American space program was a misuse of billions of dollars? Write a report setting forth your view.

2. On the basis of outside reading, write a biographical sketch of one of the following: Neil Armstrong, Spiro Agnew, Henry Kissinger, Peter Rodino, Leon Jaworski, John Sirica, or Sam Ervin.

3. Prepare a report for class presentation on one of the following: (a) the voyage of *Apollo 11*; (b) the My Lai controversy; (c) the Watergate break-in; (d) the Watergate hearings; (e) the "energy crisis"; (f) the main issues in the presidential election of 1976.

4. Do you agree or disagree that previous treatment for mental depression should have disqualified Senator Thomas Eagleton for the vice-presidency? Set out your views in a classroom report.

5. Write an essay on the American investment in Vietnam. Speculate on how the history of this country might have been different had the United States not entered the war.

6. Do you think Daniel Ellsberg did the right thing in giving the *Pentagon Papers* to the press? Explain your viewpoint in a classroom report.

7. Read part of the edited transcripts of White House conversations relating to Watergate which Nixon released to the public in the spring of 1974. What do the conversations tell you? What do they indicate concerning Nixon's involvement in the Watergate cover-up? Present your conclusions in an essay.

8. Prepare a report on the testimony of John Dean during the Senate Watergate hearings in 1973. Or prepare a report on the articles of impeachment prepared by the House Judiciary Committee in July 1974.

9. Do you think President Ford was right to pardon Nixon? Set out your conclusions in a classroom report.

Projects, Activities, and Skills

1. Create a pictorial biography of Richard Nixon, Gerald Ford, or Jimmy Carter. Collect and display photographs and printed materials describing him and his career.

2. Prepare a group of charts and graphs showing the ups and downs of the economy since 1969. Take note of the gross national product, unemployment, personal income, corporate profits, the stock market, automobile production, and the consumer price index.

3. Organize an exhibit about President Nixon's trip to China in 1972 or his trip to the Soviet Union the same year.

4. Make a display relating to the Watergate case. Include pictures of the Watergate building, a map of Washington showing the location of the building, pictures of the central figures in the case, pictures of the Senate hearings, and copies of documents, speeches, or testimony given during the investigation of the case.

5. Poll a cross-section of persons in your classroom or your community and ask them whether they agree or disagree with the statement, "Richard Nixon was an outstanding president." Make notes on comments about Nixon made by those you interview and tabulate your findings in a classroom report.

6. Prepare an exhibit on the presidential election of 1976. Include photographs of the candidates, recordings or quotations from speeches, books about the candidates and the election, and maps showing the distribution of popular votes.

Further Readings

General

The American Woman: Her Changing Social, Economic, and Political Roles, 1920-1970 by William H. Chafe.
A Heartbeat Away: The Investigation and Resignation of Vice-President Spiro T. Agnew by Richard Cohen and Jules Witcover.
Kent State by James A. Michener.
The Making of the President, 1972 by Theodore H. White.

Mission to the Moon: A Critical Examination of NASA and the Space Program by Erlend A. Kennan and Edmund H. Harvey, Jr.
My Lai Four: A Report on the Massacre and Its Aftermath by Seymour M. Hersh.
Nixon's Good Deed: Welfare Reform by Vincent J. Burke and Vee Burke.
Nixon's Quest for Peace by Frank Van der Linden.
The Papers and the Papers: An Account of the Legal and Political Battle over the Pentagon Papers by Sanford J. Ungar.
A Peace Denied: The United States, Vietnam, and the Paris Agreement by Gareth Porter.
Test of Loyalty: Daniel Ellsberg and the Rituals of Secret Government by Peter Schrag.
Thirteen Seconds: Confrontation at Kent State by Joe Eszterhas and Michael D. Roberts.

Watergate

All the President's Men by Carl Bernstein and Bob Woodward.
An American Life by Jeb Stuart Magruder.
Before the Fall: An Inside View of the Pre-Watergate White House by William Safire.
Breach of Faith: The Fall of Richard Nixon by Theodore H. White.
The Fall of the President by the staff of the *Washington Post.*
The Pentagon Papers with commentary by Neil Sheehan and others.
Perfectly Clear: Nixon from Whittier to Watergate by Frank Mankiewicz.
A Piece of Tape; The Watergate Story, Fact and Fiction: Reference Handbook to the Watergate Cases by James W. McCord, Jr.
They Could Not Trust the King by Stanley Tretick and William V. Shannon.

Biography

A Ford, Not a Lincoln by Richard Reeves.
Just a Country Lawyer: A Biography of Senator Sam Ervin by Paul R. Clancy.
Kissinger by Marvin Kalb and Bernard Kalb.
Kissinger: The Uses of Power by David Landau.
One Man Alone: Richard Nixon by Ralph De Tolano.
The Resurrection of Richard Nixon by Jules Witcover.
Roots by Alex Haley. Autobiography. The story of an American's African ancestry.
Six Crises by Richard M. Nixon. Autobiography.
Why Not the Best? by Jimmy Carter. Autobiography.

STATISTICAL APPENDIX

For Serious Searchers

The map, tables, and graphs of this appendix are for the student's use in verifying and evaluating concepts and statements in the text. They are also designed as a basis for making further investigations and inquiries. Suggested inquiries and problems, called "Figure It Out," are given with each item of the appendix. Groups or individuals may wish to devise other investigations using graphs and tables of the appendix.

Information in the Statistical Appendix has been compiled from the Bureau of the Census publications *Historical Statistics of the United States, 1789–1945, Historical Statistics to 1957,* and the most recent editions of the annual *Statistical Abstract.*

1. Territorial Expansion of the United States

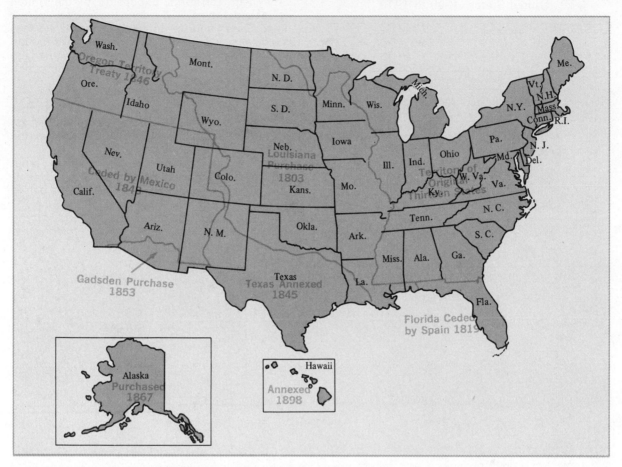

2. States: Date of Entry, Population, and Capital

State	Date of Entry	Population	Capital	State	Date of Entry	Population	Capital
Delaware	1787	548,000	Dover	Michigan	1837	8,875,000	Lansing
Pennsylvania	1787	11,794,000	Harrisburg	Florida	1845	6,789,000	Tallahassee
New Jersey	1787	7,168,000	Trenton	Texas	1845	11,197,000	Austin
Georgia	1788	4,590,000	Atlanta	Iowa	1846	2,825,000	Des Moines
Connecticut	1788	3,032,000	Hartford	Wisconsin	1848	4,418,000	Madison
Massachusetts	1788	5,689,000	Boston	California	1850	19,953,000	Sacramento
Maryland	1788	3,922,000	Annapolis	Minnesota	1858	3,805,000	St. Paul
South Carolina	1788	2,591,000	Columbia	Oregon	1859	2,091,000	Salem
New Hampshire	1788	738,000	Concord	Kansas	1861	2,247,000	Topeka
Virginia	1788	4,648,000	Richmond	West Virginia	1863	1,744,000	Charleston
New York	1788	18,237,000	Albany	Nevada	1864	489,000	Carson City
North Carolina	1789	5,082,000	Raleigh	Nebraska	1867	1,483,000	Lincoln
Rhode Island	1790	947,000	Providence	Colorado	1876	2,207,000	Denver
Vermont	1791	444,000	Montpelier	North Dakota	1889	618,000	Bismarck
Kentucky	1792	3,219,000	Frankfort	South Dakota	1889	666,000	Pierre
Tennessee	1796	3,924,000	Nashville	Montana	1889	694,000	Helena
Ohio	1803	10,652,000	Columbus	Washington	1889	3,409,000	Olympia
Louisiana	1812	3,641,000	Baton Rouge	Idaho	1890	713,000	Boise
Indiana	1816	5,194,000	Indianapolis	Wyoming	1890	332,000	Cheyenne
Mississippi	1817	2,217,000	Jackson	Utah	1896	1,059,000	Salt Lake City
Illinois	1818	11,114,000	Springfield	Oklahoma	1907	2,559,000	Oklahoma City
Alabama	1819	3,444,000	Montgomery	New Mexico	1912	1,016,000	Santa Fe
Maine	1820	992,000	Augusta	Arizona	1912	1,771,000	Phoenix
Missouri	1821	4,677,000	Jefferson City	Alaska	1959	300,000	Juneau
Arkansas	1836	1,923,000	Little Rock	Hawaii	1959	769,000	Honolulu
				District of Columbia	(1791)	757,000	

3. Area and Population of the United States: 1790 to 1970

Year	Area (square miles)			Population	
	Gross area	Land	Water	Number	Per square mile of land area
1790	888,811	864,746	24,065	3,929,214	4.5
1800	888,811	864,746	24,065	5,308,483	6.1
1810	1,716,003	1,681,828	34,175	7,239,881	4.3
1820	1,788,006	1,749,462	38,544	9,638,453	5.6
1830	1,788,006	1,749,462	38,544	12,866,020	7.4
1840	1,788,006	1,749,462	38,544	17,069,453	9.8
1850	2,992,747	2,940,042	52,705	23,191,876	7.9
1860	3,022,387	2,969,640	52,747	31,443,321	10.6
1870	3,022,387	2,969,640	52,747	39,818,449	13.4
1880	3,022,387	2,969,640	52,747	50,155,783	16.9
1890	3,022,387	2,969,640	52,747	62,947,714	21.2
1900	3,022,387	2,969,834	52,553	75,994,575	25.6
1910	3,022,387	2,969,565	52,822	91,972,266	31.0
1920	3,022,387	2,969,451	52,936	105,710,620	35.6
1930	3,022,387	2,977,128	45,259	122,775,046	41.2
1940	3,022,387	2,977,128	45,259	131,669,275	44.2
1950	3,615,211	3,552,206	63,005	151,325,798	42.6
1960	3,615,123	3,540,911	74,212	179,323,175	50.5
1970	3,615,122	3,536,855	78,267	203,184,772	57.4

FIGURE IT OUT

The map Territorial Expansion of the United States and tables 2–5 show the growth of the United States and its population. Tables 4 and 5 provide a basis for study of origins and distribution of population in the colonial period. Comparison with Table 8 is useful in studying later immigration to the United States.

Find your own state in Table 2 and on Map 1. Using the index and table of contents, find other maps and passages in the book describing domestic and foreign affairs when your state entered the Union.

According to Table 4, which countries, other than England, contributed the greatest percentages of immigrants to the United States before 1790?

Refer to Table 5 and determine the period during which the Negro population of the colonies increased at the greatest rate.

4. Percent Distribution of the White Population, by National Origin: 1790

	Total	English	Scotch	Irish		German	Dutch	French	Swedish	Unassigned
				Ulster	Free State					
Total	**100.0**	**60.9**	**8.3**	**6.0**	**3.7**	**8.7**	**3.4**	**1.7**	**0.7**	**6.6**
Maine	100.0	60.0	4.5	8.0	3.7	1.3	0.1	1.3	....	21.1
New Hampshire	100.0	61.0	6.2	4.6	2.9	0.4	0.1	0.7	....	24.1
Vermont	100.0	76.0	5.1	3.2	1.9	0.2	0.6	0.4	....	12.6
Massachusetts	100.0	82.0	4.4	2.6	1.3	0.3	0.2	0.8	....	8.4
Rhode Island	100.0	71.0	5.8	2.0	0.8	0.5	0.4	0.8	0.1	18.6
Connecticut	100.0	67.0	2.2	1.8	1.1	0.3	0.3	0.9	....	26.4
New York	100.0	52.0	7.0	5.1	3.0	8.2	17.5	3.8	0.5	2.9
New Jersey	100.0	47.0	7.7	6.3	3.2	9.2	16.6	2.4	3.9	3.7
Pennsylvania	100.0	35.3	8.6	11.0	3.5	33.3	1.8	1.8	0.8	3.9
Delaware	100.0	60.0	8.0	6.3	5.4	1.1	4.3	1.6	8.9	4.4
Maryland and District of Columbia	100.0	64.5	7.6	5.8	6.5	11.7	0.5	1.2	0.5	1.7
Virginia and West Virginia	100.0	68.5	10.2	6.2	5.5	6.3	0.3	1.5	0.6	.9
North Carolina	100.0	66.0	14.8	5.7	5.4	4.7	0.3	1.7	0.2	1.2
South Carolina	100.0	60.2	15.1	9.4	4.4	5.0	0.4	3.9	0.2	1.4
Georgia	100.0	57.4	15.5	11.5	3.8	7.6	0.2	2.3	0.6	1.1
Kentucky and Tennessee	100.0	57.9	10.0	7.0	5.2	14.0	1.3	2.2	0.5	1.9
Northwest Territory	100.0	29.8	4.1	2.9	1.8	4.3	.....	57.1	....	......

5. Estimated Population of American Colonies: 1610 to 1780

Colony	1610	1620	1630	1640	1660	1680	1700	1720	1740	1760	1770	1780
WHITE AND NEGRO												
Total	**350**	**2,302**	**4,646**	**26,634**	**75,058**	**151,507**	**250,888**	**466,185**	**905,563**	**1,593,625**	**2,148,076**	**2,780,369**
Maine (counties)[1]	....	....	400	900	....	....	....	....	....	....	31,257	49,133
New Hampshire	....	....	500	1,055	1,555	2,047	4,958	9,375	23,256	39,093	62,396	87,802
Vermont	....	....	....	....	....	....	....	....	....	....	10,000	47,620
Plymouth[2]	....	102	390	1,020	1,980	6,400	....	....	....	....	....	....
Massachusetts[1][2]	....	....	506	8,932	20,082	39,752	55,941	91,008	151,613	222,600	235,308	268,627
Rhode Island	....	....	....	300	1,539	3,017	5,894	11,680	25,255	45,471	58,196	52,946
Connecticut	....	....	....	1,472	7,980	17,246	25,970	58,830	89,580	142,470	183,881	206,701
New York	....	....	350	1,930	4,936	9,830	19,107	36,919	63,665	117,138	162,920	210,541
New Jersey	....	....	....	....	....	3,400	14,010	29,818	51,373	93,813	117,431	139,627
Pennsylvania	....	....	....	....	....	680	17,950	30,962	85,637	183,703	240,057	327,305
Delaware	....	....	....	....	540	1,005	2,470	5,385	19,870	33,250	35,496	45,385
Maryland	....	....	....	583	8,426	17,904	29,604	66,133	116,093	162,267	202,599	245,474
Virginia	350	2,200	2,500	10,442	27,020	43,596	58,560	87,757	180,440	339,726	447,016	538,004
North Carolina	....	....	....	....	1,000	5,430	10,720	21,270	51,760	110,442	197,200	270,133
South Carolina	....	....	....	....	....	1,200	5,704	17,048	45,000	94,074	124,244	180,000
Georgia	....	....	....	....	....	....	....	....	2,021	9,578	23,375	56,071
Kentucky	....	....	....	....	....	....	....	....	....	....	15,700	45,000
Tennessee	....	....	....	....	....	....	....	....	....	....	1,000	10,000
NEGRO												
Total	....	**20**	**60**	**597**	**2,920**	**6,971**	**27,817**	**68,839**	**150,024**	**325,806**	**459,822**	**575,420**
Maine (counties)[1]	....	....	....	....	....	....	....	....	....	....	475	458
New Hampshire	....	....	....	30	50	75	130	170	500	600	654	541
Vermont	....	....	....	....	....	....	....	....	....	....	25	50
Massachusetts[1]	....	....	....	150	422	170	800	2,150	3,035	4,866	4,754	4,822
Rhode Island	....	.	....	....	65	175	300	543	2,408	3,468	3,761	2,671[3]
Connecticut	....	....	....	15	25	50	450	1,093	2,598	3,783	5,698	5,885[3]
New York	....	....	10	232	600	1,200	2,256	5,740	8,996	16,340	19,112	21,054
New Jersey	....	....	....	....	....	200	840	2,385	4,366	6,567	8,220	10,460
Pennsylvania	....	....	....	....	....	25	430	2,000	2,055	4,409	5,761	7,855
Delaware	....	....	....	....	30	55	135	700	1,035	1,733	1,836	2,996
Maryland	....	....	....	20	758	1,611	3,227	12,499	24,031	49,004	63,818	80,515
Virginia	....	20	50	150	950	3,000	16,390	26,559	60,000	140,570	187,605	220,582
North Carolina	....	....	....	....	20	210	415	3,000	11,000	33,554	69,600	91,000
South Carolina	....	....	....	....	....	200	2,444	12,000	30,000	57,334	75,178	97,000
Georgia	....	....	....	....	....	....	....	....	....	3,578	10,625	20,831
Kentucky	....	....	....	....	....	....	....	....	....	....	2,500	7,200
Tennessee	....	....	....	....	....	....	....	....	....	....	200	1,500

[1] For 1660–1760, Maine Counties included with Massachusetts.
[2] Plymouth became part of the Province of Massachusetts in 1691.
[3] Includes some Indians.

6. Values of Exports to and Imports from England, by American Colonies: 1697 to 1776

[In pounds sterling]

Year	Exports	Imports	Year	Exports	Imports
1697	279,852	140,129	1740	718,416	813,382
1700	395,021	344,341	1745	554,431	535,253
1705	150,961	291,722	1750	814,768	1,313,083
1710	249,814	293,659	1755	939,553	1,112,997
1715	297,246	452,366	1760	761,099	2,611,764
1720	468,188	319,702	1765	1,151,698	1,944,114
1725	415,650	549,693	1770	1,015,535	1,925,571
1730	572,585	536,860	1775	1,920,950	196,162
1735	652,326	668,664	1776	103,964	55,415

FIGURE IT OUT

Exports to and imports from England by the American colonies are illustrated in Table 6. Does this table demonstrate the principles of mercantilism described in the text? In which years did exports exceed imports?

7. Value of Exports and Imports: 1790 to 1970

[In millions of dollars]

Year	Exports	Imports	Excess of exports (+) or imports (−)
1790	20	23	− 3
1795	48	70	− 22
1800	71	91	− 20
1805	96	121	− 25
1810	67	85	− 19
1815	53	113	− 60
1820	70	74	− 5
1825	100	96	+ 3
1830	74	71	+ 3
1835	122	150	− 28
1840	132	107	+ 25
1845	115	117	− 3
1850	152	178	− 26
1855	275	261	+ 14
1860	400	362	+ 38
1865	234	249	− 15
1870	451	462	− 11
1875	606	554	+ 52
1880	853	761	+ 92
1885	784	621	+ 164
1890	910	823	+ 87
1895	921	789	+133
1900	1,499	930	+ 570
1905	1,660	1,199	+ 461
1910	1,919	1,646	+ 273
1915	2,966	1,875	+ 1,091
1920	8,664	5,784	+ 2,880
1925	5,272	4,419	+ 852
1930	4,013	3,500	+ 514
1935	2,304	4,143	− 1,839
1940	4,030	7,433	− 3,403
1945	10,097	4,280	+ 5,816
1950	10,816	9,125	+ 1,691
1955	15,563	11,562	+ 4,001
1960	20,577	15,406	+ 5,531
1965	28,661	21,377	+ 7,294
1970	43,226	39,963	+3,263

8. Immigrants: 1820 to 1970

Year	Africa	America	Asia	Europe	All other
1820	1	387	5	7,691	301
1825	1	846	1	8,543	808
1830	2	2,296	−	7,217	13,807
1835	14	3,312	17	41,987	44
1840	6	3,815	1	80,126	118
1845	4	5,035	6	109,301	25
1850	−	15,768	7	308,323	45,882
1855	14	9,260	3,540	187,729	334
1860	126	6,343	5,476	141,209	486
1865	49	22,778	2,947	214,048	8,298
1870	31	42,658	15,825	328,626	63
1875	54	26,640	16,499	182,961	1,344
1880	18	101,692	5,839	348,691	1,017
1882	60	100,129	39,629	648,146	988
1885	112	41,203	198	353,083	750
1890	112	3,833	4,448	445,680	1,229
1895	36	3,508	4,495	250,342	155
1900	30	5,455	17,946	424,700	441
1905	757	25,217	23,925	974,273	2,327
1910	1,072	89,534	23,533	926,291	1,140
1915	934	111,206	15,211	197,919	1,430
1920	648	162,666	17,505	246,295	2,887
1921	1,301	124,118	25,034	652,364	2,411
1924	900	318,855	22,065	364,339	737
1925	412	141,496	3,578	148,366	462
1929	509	116,177	3,758	158,598	636
1930	572	88,104	4,535	147,438	1,051
1935	118	11,174	682	22,778	204
1940	202	17,822	1,913	50,454	365
1943	141	18,162	334	4,920	168
1945	406	29,646	442	5,943	1,682
1946	1,516	46,066	1,633	52,852	6,654
1950	849	44,191	3,779	199,115	1,253
1955	1,203	110,436	10,935	110,591	4,625
1960	1,925	119,525	21,604	120,178	1,166
1965	1,949	171,019	19,675	101,833	2,221
1968	3,220	262,736	55,973	129,347	3,172
1970	7,099	161,727	89,720	111,148	3,632

FIGURE IT OUT

Some of the ups and downs of the national economy can be traced in Table 7. Compare this table with economic graphs in the text and find explanations for an excess of imports over exports in the years when this occurred.

FIGURE IT OUT

Immigration from major areas of the world is shown in the table above. In which periods did immigration decline? How can you account for this? Find passages in the text to explain your findings. Note the periods in which immigration was greatest and find explanations in the text.

9. Expenditures of the Federal Government: 1789 to 1899

[In thousands of dollars]

Year	Total	Department of the Army (formerly War Department)	Department of the Navy	Interest on the public debt	Other
1789–1791	4,269	633	1	2,349	1,286
1795	7,540	2,481	411	3,189	1,459
1800	10,786	2,561	3,449	3,375	1,402
1805	10,506	713	1,598	4,149	4,047
1810	8,157	2,294	1,654	2,845	1,363
1815	32,708	14,794	8,660	5,755	3,499
1820	18,261	2,630	4,388	5,126	6,116
1825	15,857	3,660	3,049	4,367	4,781
1830	15,143	4,767	3,239	1,914	5,223
1835	17,573	5,759	3,865	58	7,891
1840	24,318	7,097	6,114	175	10,932
1845	22,937	5,753	6,297	1,040	9,847
1850	39,543	9,400	7,905	3,782	18,456
1855	59,743	14,774	13,312	2,314	29,342
1860	63,131	16,410	11,515	3,177	32,029
1865	1,297,555	1,031,323	122,613	77,398	66,221
1870	309,654	57,656	21,780	129,235	100,982
1875	274,623	41,121	21,498	103,094	108,912
1880	267,643	38,117	13,537	95,758	120,231
1885	260,227	42,671	16,021	51,386	150,149
1890	318,041	44,583	22,006	36,099	215,352
1895	356,195	51,805	28,798	30,978	244,615
1899	605,072	229,841	63,942	39,897	271,392

FIGURE IT OUT

Compare expenses for each major function of the federal government in the recent period and in an earlier period. What trends can you establish? What new functions has the federal government undertaken in the modern period? Which function shown for the most recent year makes up the greatest percentage of total expenditures? Compare expenditures for other functions as percentages of the total.

10. Expenditures of the Federal Government, by Major Function: 1900 to 1945

[In millions of dollars]

Year	Total	Major national security	International affairs and finance	Veterans services and benefits	Interest	All other
1900	521	191	(1)	141	40	149[1]
1905	567	244	(1)	142	25	156[1]
1910	694	284	(1)	161	21	228[1]
1915	746	297	5	176	23	245
1919	18,448	13,548	3,500	324	616	460
1920	6,357	3,997	435	332	1,024	569
1925	2,881	591	15	741	882	652
1930	3,320	734	14	821	697	1,054
1935	6,521	711	19	607	826	4,358
1940	9,062	1,498	51	552	1,056	5,914
1945	98,416	81,216	3,312	2,095	3,662	7,881

[1] Prior to 1912, figures for "International affairs and finance" included with "All other."

11. Governmental Expenditure, by Function: 1950 to 1973

[In millions of dollars]

Year	Total	National defense and international relations	Veterans services	Interest on general debt	Housing and urban renewal	Highways	Natural resources	Social insurance	Health education and welfare	Space research and technology	All other[1]
1950	70,300	18,400	3,300	4,900	600	3,900	5,000	6,900	15,300	(2)	12,200
1955	110,700	43,500	3,100	5,700	600	6,500	6,300	9,000	19,300	(2)	16,700
1960	151,300	47,500	3,800	9,300	1,100	9,600	8,400	17,600	29,100	400	24,500
1965	205,600	55,800	4,200	11,400	2,200	12,300	11,000	24,900	43,700	5,100	35,100
1970	333,000	84,300	5,400	18,400	3,200	16,700	11,500	48,500	86,900	3,700	54,400
1973	432,600	79,600	7,400	25,100	7,300	19,200	16,400	75,300	121,400	3,300	75,500

[1] Includes postal services, police protection, local fire protection, sanitation, local parks and recreation, financial administration, general control, utility and liquor stores expenditure, and other.
[2] Not applicable.

12. Public Debt of the Federal Government: 1791 to 1974

[Selected years]

Year	Total gross debt	
	Amount	Per capita[1]
	1,000 dollars	*Dollars*
1791	75,463	
1796	83,762	
1803	77,055	
1804	86,427	
1809	57,023	
1812	45,210	
1814	81,488	
1816	127,335	
1821	89,987	
1826	81,054	
1830	48,565	
1832	24,322	
1833	7,012	
1834	4,760	
1835	38	
1836	38	
1837	337	
1838	3,308	
1839	10,434	
1840	3,573	
1841	5,251	
1842	13,594	
1843	32,743	
1844	23,462	
1845	15,925	
1846	15,550	
1847	38,827	
1851	68,305	2.85
1857	28,701	.99
1861	90,582	2.80
1862	524,178	15.79
1863	1,119,774	32.91
1864	1,815,831	52.08
1865	2,677,929	75.01
1866	2,755,764	75.42
1871	2,322,052	56.72
1877	2,107,760	44.71
1881	2,019,286	39.18
1882	1,856,916	35.16
1889	1,249,471	20.23
1891	1,005,807	15.63
1892	968,219	14.74
1893	961,432	14.36
1899	1,436,701	19.21
1905	1,132,357	13.51
1910	1,146,940	12.41
1915	1,191,264	11.85
1916	1,225,146	12.02
1917	2,975,619	28.77
1918	12,455,225	119.13
1919	25,484,506	242.56
	1,000,000 dollars	
1925	20,516	177
1930	16,185	132
1935	28,701	226
1941	48,961	367
1942	72,422	537
1943	136,696	1,000
1944	201,003	1,452
1945	258,682	1,849
1946	269,422	1,905
1951	255,222	1,654
1957	270,527	1,580
1961	288,971	1,573
1967	326,221	1,637
1970	370,900	1,811
1971	398,100	1,923
1972	427,200	2,046
1973	458,100	2,177
1974	475,100[2]	2,242[2]

[1] Not available prior to 1850.
[2] Preliminary.

13. Tax Revenue, by Level of Government: 1942 to 1973

Year	[In millions of dollars]			Per capita [dollars]	
	Federal	State	Local	Federal	State and local
1942	12,265	3,903	4,625	91	63
1950	35,186	7,930	7,984	232	105
1955	57,589	11,597	11,886	348	142
1960	77,003	18,036	18,081	428	201
1965	93,710	26,126	25,116	483	264
1970	146,082	47,962	38,833	719	427
1973	165,493	68,069	53,032	789	577

FIGURE IT OUT

Find newspaper and magazine articles describing some recent proposals for tax reforms. Take a poll in your community of attitudes toward state and local taxes. In a dictionary and textbooks on economics and government look up the definition of "regressive" taxes. Can you find examples of regressive taxes in your own community?

FIGURE IT OUT

In which years was the public debt of the federal government highest? What factors do you believe have contributed most to increase in the public debt? See economic graphs in the text and determine whether the public debt rose or declined in periods of prosperity. Find articles by economists explaining their theories concerning the public debt.

14. Social Welfare Expenditures Under Public Programs: 1929 to 1974

Year	Total (millions)	Per capita						
		Total	Social insurance	Public aid	Health and medical programs	Veterans programs	Education	Other social welfare
1929	$3,900	$32	$3	(1)	$3	$5	$20	$1
1935	6,500	51	3	$23	3	5	16	1
1940	8,800	66	9	27	5	5	19	1
1945	9,200	65	10	7	17	8	22	1
1950	23,400	153	32	16	13	44	43	3
1955	32,500	195	59	18	19	28	67	4
1960	52,100	285	106	23	25	30	97	6
1965	76,900	391	142	32	32	30	143	11
1970	145,500	701	262	79	47	43	245	(3)
1974	241,700[2]	1,126[2]	456[2]	157[2]	65[2]	64[2]	339[2]	(3)

[1] Less than $0.50.
[2] Preliminary.
[3] Not available.

14-A. Federally Assisted Welfare Population—1971

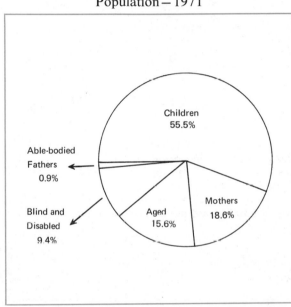

FIGURE IT OUT

The amount of money which is spent for social welfare changes regularly, just as Congress and federal policies change. Use the tables and the graph on this page to learn how much money was spent for social welfare in the United States during certain years. Then use Table 11 to find out what percentage of the total federal expenditure was used for social welfare. Compare this figure with the portion being spent under the current administration. Or, poll your classmates for their opinions about spending money for social welfare and make a summary of your findings.

15. Old-Age, Survivors, Disability, and Health Insurance — Number and Age of Persons Receiving Retirement Benefits: 1940 to 1974

Year	Male						Female					
	Number (1,000)	Average age	Percent of retired workers aged[1]				Number (1,000)	Average age	Percent of retired workers aged[1]			
			62–64	65–69	70–74	75 and over			62–64	65–69	70–74	75 and over
1940	99	68.8	(2)	74.4	17.4	8.2	13	68.1	(2)	82.6	12.8	4.5
1945	447	71.7	(2)	39.9	40.2	19.8	71	70.8	(2)	47.1	40.0	12.8
1950	1,469	72.2	(2)	39.1	33.7	27.3	302	71.1	(2)	48.4	32.9	18.7
1955	3,252	72.7	(2)	35.7	34.8	29.5	1,222	71.3	(2)	47.8	32.3	19.8
1960	5,217	73.2	(2)	33.8	33.1	33.2	2,845	71.0	12.6	36.3	29.0	22.2
1965	6,825	72.9	6.9	29.7	29.5	33.9	4,276	71.8	12.2	31.6	28.1	28.1
1970	7,688	72.6	7.5	30.1	26.9	35.5	5,661	72.0	11.5	30.1	25.4	33.1
1974	8,832	(3)	(3)	(3)	(3)	(3)	7,126	(3)	(3)	(3)	(3)	(3)

[1] Age at birthday in stated year.
[2] Not applicable.
[3] Not available.

16. Median Money Income, by Sex and Occupation: 1947 to 1969

Sex and Occupation	1947	1950	1955	1960	1965	1969
Male employed civilians	**$2,406**	**$2,831**	**$3,797**	**$4,822**	**$5,907**	**$7,659**
Professional, technical, and kindred workers	3,972	4,073	5,429	6,692	8,313	11,062
Farmers and farm managers	1,456	1,496	1,283	1,941	2,985	3,887
Managers, officials, proprietors, except farm	3,354	3,814	5,228	6,519	8,143	10,822
Clerical and kindred workers	2,654	3,103	3,950	5,011	5,772	7,458
Salesworkers	2,687	3,137	4,472	4,990	6,033	7,876
Craftsmen, foremen, and kindred workers	2,746	3,293	4,423	5,582	6,592	8,344
Operatives and kindred workers	2,373	2,790	3,695	4,477	5,395	6,741
Service workers, except private household	2,096	2,303	3,036	3,412	4,161	5,041
Farm laborers and foremen	846	854	1,039	1,103	1,411	2,124
Laborers, except farm and mine	1,707	1,909	2,599	2,868	3,405	4,464
Female employed civilians	**$1,372**	**$1,559**	**$1,926**	**$2,348**	**$2,771**	**$3,598**
Professional, technical, and kindred workers	1,889	2,175	2,994	3,870	4,732	6,054
Managers, officials, proprietors, except farm	1,858	1,674	2,375	2,948	3,495	5,346
Clerical and kindred workers	1,728	2,074	2,667	3,122	3,525	4,271
Salesworkers	1,118	1,109	1,300	1,505	2,063	2,222
Craftsmen, foremen, and kindred workers	(1)	(1)	(1)	3,125	3,529	4,457
Operatives and kindred workers	1,406	1,661	2,110	2,489	2,832	3,700
Private household workers	428	427	610	614	728	800
Service workers, except private household	913	913	1,246	1,636	1,764	2,321
Farm laborers and foremen	(1)	(1)	(1)	412	713	839
Laborers, except farm and mine	(1)	(1)	(1)	(1)	(1)	2,957

[1] Not shown; base too small.

FIGURE IT OUT

Which occupations shown in Table 16 had the greatest increase in earnings over the period shown? Which groups had the smallest increase? Compare the earnings for women with those of men in the same occupation for the years shown. Using the graph Decline in the Value of the Dollar (number 34 in the Appendix), compare actual dollar value of 1950 with that of 1965. How does this affect your interpretation of the table above?

FIGURE IT OUT

Use tables 17–19 to make graphs or charts showing industries that grew or declined in the period illustrated. Make a list of occupations existing today that did not exist fifty years ago. Make a list of occupations that were important one hundred years ago but are no longer important.

17. Average Annual Earnings in Selected Industries and Occupations: 1890 to 1926

Year	Wage earners, manufacturing	Wage earners, steam railroads	Street railways	Telephones	Telegraphs	Gas and electricity	Clerical workers, mfg. and steam railroads	Bituminous coal mining	Farm labor	Federal employees	Postal employees	Public school teachers
1890	$439	$560	$557	....	....	$687	$848	$406	$233	....	$878	$256
1892	446	563	535	....	....	625	885	393	238	$1,096	899	270
1894	386	546	508	....	....	670	928	292	214	1,110	919	283
1896	406	544	531	....	....	665	954	282	220	1,084	944	294
1898	412	542	558	....	....	698	1,010	316	228	1,025	939	306
1900	435	548	604	....	....	620	1,011	438	247	1,033	925	328
1902	473	562	576	$408	$544	.....	1,025	490	264	1,061	934	346
1904	477	600	610	392	601	556	1,056	470	290	1,066	931	377
1906	506	607	662	412	592	581	1,074	537	315	1,084	921	409
1908	475	667	650	420	639	595	1,111	487	324	1,102	987	455
1910	558	677	681	417	649	622	1,156	558	336	1,108	1,049	492
1912	550	721	674	438	669	641	1,209	614	348	1,128	1,091	529
1914	580	795	737	476	742	651	1,257	543	351	1,140	1,157	564
1916	651	867	798	567	806	679	1,359	750	388	1,211	1,175	605
1918	980	1,424	1,111	690	831	1,092	1,697	1,211	604	1,380	1,339	689
1920	1,358	1,817	1,608	980	1,145	1,432	2,160	1,386	810	1,648	1,844	936
1922	1,149	1,591	1,436	1,064	1,110	1,343	2,067	954	508	1,625	1,844	1,188
1924	1,240	1,570	1,544	1,104	1,150	1,436	2,196	1,120	574	1,708	1,934	1,247
1926	1,309	1,613	1,566	1,117	1,215	1,477	2,310	1,247	593	1,809	2,128	1,277

18. Industrial Distribution of Gainful Workers: 1820 to 1940

[In thousands]

Year	Agriculture, forestry and fisheries	Mining	Manufacturing and hand trades	Construction	Transportation and other public utilities	Trade	Finance and real estate	Educational service	Other professional service	Domestic service	Personal service	Government not elsewhere classified
1820	2,070²	(1)	350			(1)				(1)		
1860	6,260	170	1,930			780				1,310		
1900	10,920	760	6,340	1,660	2,100	2,760		650	500	1,740	970	300
1940	9,140	1,110	11,940	3,510	4,150	7,180	1,550	1,680	2,320	2,610	3,100	1,690

¹ Not available.
² Agriculture only (forestry and fisheries not available).

19. Employees in Selected Industries: 1950 to 1975

[Number in thousands]

Year	Manufacturing	Wholesale and retail trade	Government	Services	Transportation and public utilities	Finance, insurance, and real estate	Contract construction	Mining	Goods related¹	Service related and all other	Agriculture
1950	15,241	9,386	6,026	5,382	4,034	1,919	2,333	901	22,509	22,713	7,408
1960	16,796	11,391	8,353	7,423	4,004	2,669	2,885	712	24,397	29,836	5,176
1970	19,349	15,040	12,561	11,621	4,504	3,687	3,536	623	28,011	47,412	3,126
1975	17,936²	16,664²	15,064²	13,787²	4,468²	4,147²	3,320²	694²	26,418²	54,130²	2,747²

¹ Includes mining, construction, manufacturing, transportation, and public utilities.
² Preliminary.

20. Labor Union Membership, Selected Industries: 1897 to 1934

[In thousands]

Year	Total union membership	Mining, quarrying, and oil	Building, construction	Metals, machinery, shipbuilding	Textiles	Leather and shoes	Clothing	Lumber and woodworking	Paper printing, and bookbinding	Chemicals, clay, glass, stone	Food, liquor, tobacco	Transportation and communication	Public service	Theaters and music	Other
1897	447	21	67	50	8	15	15	6	38	23	46	116	11	7	24
1900	868	131	153	81	8	10	25	26	48	30	69	189	15	9	74
1905	2,022	297	373	166	14	41	63	42	91	51	104	446	24	38	272
1910	2,140	275	459	196	21	47	98	28	90	60	123	480	58	60	145
1915	2,583	332	533	224	22	53	174	21	116	53	119	576	90	87	183
1920	5,048	439	888	859	149	113	374	24	164	52	181	1,256	161	99	289
1925	3,519	439	837	205	36	54	292	10	156	42	75	893	193	110	177
1930	3,393	230	904	203	35	44	230	13	165	35	62	882	264	134	192
1933	2,973	355	583	180	16	76	336	8	153	27	58	609	296	127	149
1934	3,609	579	605	222	40	117	405	10	162	47	82	645	299	127	269

21. Labor Union Membership: 1935 to 1972

[In thousands]

Year	Total union membership
1935	3,728
1940	8,944
1945	14,796
1950	15,000
1955	17,749
1960	18,117
1965	18,519
1970	20,752
1972	20,894

FIGURE IT OUT

Using tables 20 and 21 find total union membership as a percentage of the total population (Table 3) for selected years. In which years shown was labor union membership lowest? In which years was it highest? Find passages in the text to explain increase or decrease in union membership. Using economic graphs in the text, draw your own conclusions as to whether union membership increased during times of prosperity.

22. Farms, Land in Farms: 1850 to 1975

Year	Number of farms	Land in farms
	1,000 farms	*1,000,000 acres*
1850	1,449	294
1860	2,044	407
1870	2,660	408
1880	4,009	536
1890	4,565	623
1900	5,737	839
1910	6,406	879
1915	6,458	917
1920	6,518	956
1925	6,471	924
1930	6,546	987
1935	6,814	1,055
1940	6,350	1,061
1945	5,967	1,142
1950	5,648	1,202
1955	4,654	1,202
1960	3,963	1,176
1965	3,356	1,140
1970	2,954	1,103
1975	2,819[1]	1,086[1]

[1] Preliminary.

FIGURE IT OUT

In which year of those shown were there the most farms? What was the average size of a farm in that year? (Divide the amount of land in farms by the number of farms.) Look up explanations in the text concerning the condition of farmers about 1890 and about 1960. How do the graphs and table on this page illustrate the trends described in the text?

23. Farm Population: 1920 to 1973

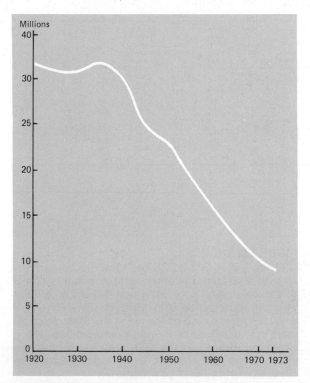

24. Farm Production Index: 1930 to 1976

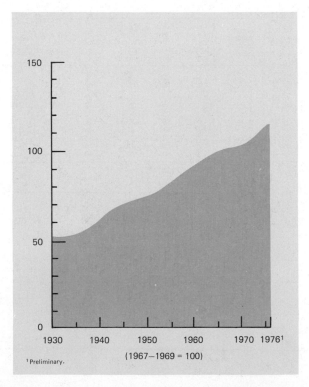

[1] Preliminary.

(1967–1969 = 100)

25. Retail Prices of Selected Foods in U.S. Cities: 1890 to 1975

[In cents per unit indicated]

Year	Bread	Round steak	Eggs	Milk, delivered	Oranges	Potatoes
	Lb.	*Lb.*	*Doz.*	*Qt.*	*Doz.*	*10 lb.*
1890	......	12.3	20.8	6.8	......	16.0
1892	......	12.4	22.1	6.8	......	14.0
1893	......	12.4	22.4	6.8	......	17.0
1895	......	12.3	20.6	6.8	......	14.0
1896	......	12.4	19.2	6.8	......	12.0
1898	......	12.7	19.9	6.7	......	16.0
1899	......	12.9	20.9	6.7	......	15.0
1901	......	13.8	21.9	6.8	......	18.0
1902	......	14.7	24.7	7.0	......	18.0
1904	......	14.1	27.1	7.2	......	18.0
1905	......	14.0	27.2	7.2	......	17.0
1907	......	15.2	29.0	7.8	......	18.0
1908	......	15.9	29.7	8.0	......	19.0
1910	......	17.4	33.7	8.4	......	17.0
1911	......	17.5	32.3	8.5	......	22.0
1913	5.6	22.3	34.5	8.9	......	17.0
1914	6.3	23.6	35.3	8.9	......	18.0
1916	7.3	24.5	37.5	9.1	......	27.0
1917	9.2	29.0	48.1	11.2	......	43.0
1919	10.0	38.9	62.8	15.5	53.2	38.0
1920	11.5	39.5	68.1	16.7	63.2	63.0
1922	8.7	32.3	44.4	13.1	57.4	28.0
1923	8.8	34.3	49.9	13.9	49.7	30.0
1925	9.3	36.2	55.4	13.9	57.1	36.0
1926	9.3	37.1	51.9	14.0	51.6	49.0
1928	8.9	43.7	50.3	14.2	58.6	27.0
1929	8.8	46.0	52.7	14.4	44.7	32.0
1931	7.7	35.4	35.0	12.6	35.0	24.0
1932	7.0	29.7	30.2	10.7	30.2	17.0
1934	8.3	28.1	32.5	11.2	34.1	23.0
1935	8.3	36.0	37.6	11.7	32.0	19.1
1937	8.6	39.1	36.2	12.5	38.9	27.9
1938	8.6	34.9	35.5	12.5	26.7	21.3
1940	8.0	36.4	33.1	12.8	29.1	23.9
1941	8.1	39.1	39.7	13.6	31.0	23.5
1943	8.9	43.9	57.2	15.5	44.3	45.6
1944	8.8	41.4	54.5	15.6	46.0	46.5
1946	10.4	52.1	58.6	17.6	49.9	46.8
1947	12.5	75.6	69.6	19.6	43.4	50.3
1949	14.0	85.3	69.6	21.1	51.8	54.6
1950	14.3	93.6	60.4	20.6	49.3	46.1
1952	16.0	111.2	67.3	24.2	50.6	76.0
1953	16.4	91.5	69.8	23.4	49.0	53.8
1955	17.7	90.3	60.6	23.1	52.8	56.4
1956	17.9	88.2	60.2	24.2	58.3	67.7
1958	19.3	104.2	60.4	25.3	76.0	63.0
1959	19.7	107.3	53.0	25.3	66.4	63.0
1961	20.9	103.6	57.3	26.2	77.7	63.0
1962	21.2	107.8	54.0	26.1	79.3	63.0
1964	20.7	103.9	53.9	26.4	88.1	76.0
1965	20.9	108.4	52.7	26.3	77.8	94.0
1967	22.2	110.3	49.1	28.7	76.6	75.0
1968	22.4	114.3	52.9	30.2	96.6	76.0
1970	24.3	130.2	61.4	32.9	86.4	90.0
1971	25.0	136.1	52.9	33.8	94.3	86.0
1972	24.7	147.7	52.4	34.5	94.2	93.0
1973	27.6	174.6	78.1	37.6	105.3	137.0
1974	34.5	179.8	78.3	(2)	111.4	166.0
1975	36.8[1]	171.0[1]	77.2[1]	(2)	108.3[1]	100.0[1]

[1] Preliminary.
[2] Not available.

FIGURE IT OUT
Use Graph number 34 (Decline in the Value of the Dollar) to compare actual costs of items shown in the table of retail prices shown in Table 25 above. After accounting for the decline in value of the dollar, does the table reflect a rise in cost between 1940 and 1970? Why is it important in using statistical information to account for differences in the value of money over a period of time?

26. Institutions of Higher Education — Degrees Conferred, by Sex: 1870 to 1970

School year ending —	All degrees		
	Total	Male	Female
1870	9,372	....	....
1880	13,829	....	....
1890	16,703	....	....
1900	29,375	23,812	5,563
1910	39,755	30,716	9,039
1920	53,516	35,487	18,029
1930	139,752	84,486	55,266
1940	216,521	128,915	87,606
1950	496,874	376,051	120,823
1960	479,215	315,242	163,973
1970	1,073,000	638,900	433,000

FIGURE IT OUT
Compare the number of persons receiving degrees (Table 26) in 1870, 1900, and 1970 as percentages of the total population. Use Table 14 to find the amounts of federal expenditures for education in years between 1929 and 1970. As a percentage of the total federal budget (see tables 10 and 11) how much did federal expenditure for education increase between 1929 and 1970?

27. Illiteracy in the United States, by Percentage of the Population: 1870 to 1970

[Data for 1870 to 1940 are for population 10 years old and over; data for 1950 to 1970 are for population 14 years old and over]

Year	Percentage	Year	Percentage
1870	20.0	1930	4.3
1880	17.0	1940	2.9
1890	13.3	1950	3.2
1900	10.7	1960	2.4
1910	7.7	1970	1.2
1920	6.0		

FIGURE IT OUT
Among what groups of people would you expect to find the greatest percentage of illiteracy? Give the reasons for your answer.

FIGURE IT OUT

Which of the three kinds of transportation described in the tables on this page had the most rapid development in the 1830s? The 1940s? What do you consider to be the most urgent problems of transportation in your own community?

30. Miles of Railroad Built: 1830 to 1925

Year	Miles	Year	Miles
1830	40		
1831	99	1876	2,575
1832	191	1877	2,280
1833	116	1878	2,428
1834	214	1879	5,006
1835	138		
1836	280		
1837	348		
1838	453		
1839	386		
1840	491		
1841	606		
1842	505		
1843	288	1893	3,024
1844	180	1894	1,760
1845	277	1895	1,420
1846	333	1896	1,692
1847	263	1897	2,109
1848	1,056	1898	3,265
1849	1,048	1899	4,569
1850	1,261	1900	4,894
1851	1,274	1901	5,368
1852	2,288	1902	6,026
1853	2,170	1903	5,652
1854	3,442	1904	3,832
1855	2,453	1905	4,388
1856	1,471	1906	5,623
1857	2,077	1907	5,212
1858	1,966	1908	3,214
1859	1,707	1909	3,748
1860	1,500	1910	4,122
1861	1,016	1911	3,066
1862	720	1912	2,997
1863	574	1913	3,071
1864	947	1914	1,532
1865	819	1915	933
1866	1,404	1916	1,098
1867	2,541	1917	979
1868	2,468	1918	721
1869	4,103	1919	686
1870	5,658	1920	314
1871	6,660	1921	475
1872	7,439	1922	324
1873	5,217	1923	427
1874	2,584	1924	579
1875	1,606	1925	644

28. Scheduled Air Transportation: 1926 to 1974

[All data reflect scheduled operations exclusively]

Year	Aircraft in service	Persons employed	1000 passengers carried
1926	[1]	[1]	6
1930	600	3,475	418
1935	464	8,352	790
1940	437	22,051	2,686
1945	518	68,281	7,052
1950	1,200	82,800	19,000
1955	1,400	122,200	41,400
1960	1,900	162,800	62,300
1965	1,900	206,800	103,000
1970	2,400	391,000	169,000
1974	2,200	305,000	207,000

29. Mileage and Cost of Federal-Aid Highway Improvements: 1917 to 1974

Year or period	Miles of highway (1,000)		Cost ($1,000,000)
	Total designated as part of federal systems	Completed during year	Total federal funds and state funds
1917–1921	[1]	13	222
1925	179	11	221
1930	193	10	237
1935	214	13	242
1940	234	12	269
1945	233	3	101
1950	641	20	753
1955	742	23	1,287
1960	867	21	3,264
1965	909	17	4,569
1970	919	11	4,625
1974	[1]	7	4,118

[1] Not available.

31. Motor Vehicles — Factory Sales and Registrations: 1900 to 1974

Year	Factory Sales Number (1,000)			Registrations (1,000)		
	Total cars, trucks, buses	Passenger cars	Trucks and buses	Total cars, trucks, buses	Passenger cars and taxis	Trucks and buses
1900	4	4	....	8	8	....
1910	187	181	6	470	458	10
1920	2,227	1,906	322	9,251	8,131	1,108
1930	3,363	2,787	575	26,794	23,035	3,715
1940	4,472	3,717	755	32,525	27,466	4,987
1945	725	70	656	31,106	25,797	5,238
1950	8,003	6,666	1,337	49,300	40,339	8,823
1955	9,169	7,920	1,249	62,870	52,145	10,544
1960	7,869	6,675	1,194	73,869	61,682	12,187
1965	11,057	9,306	1,752	90,341	75,241	15,100
1970	8,239	6,547	1,692	108,375	89,230	19,145
1974	10,059	7,331	2,727	130,751[1]	105,287[1]	25,464[1]

[1] Estimated.

32. Electric Energy Production: 1940 to 1970

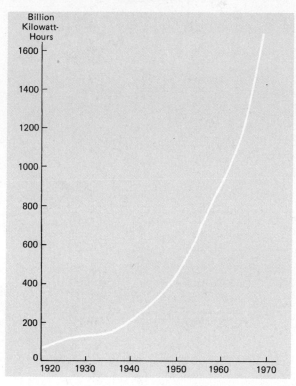

FIGURE IT OUT
In which ten-year period did production of electric energy increase most rapidly?

33. Crime Rates for Selected Crimes: 1960 to 1974

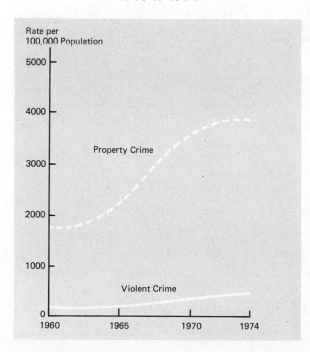

34. Decline in the Value of the Dollar: Purchasing Power, 1940 to 1975

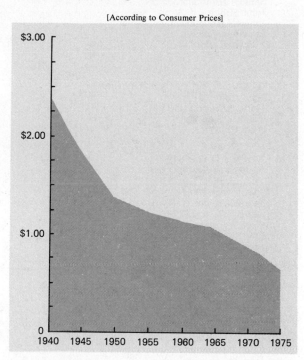

[According to Consumer Prices]

FIGURE IT OUT
How does a decline in the value of the dollar reflect inflation? Can you find passages in the text that offer explanations of inflationary trends in the economy? Do you agree with the explanations given? How much more was a dollar worth in 1940 than in 1967? Compare the value of the dollar in 1967 with its value in 1975.

FIGURE IT OUT
What do you consider to be the major causes of crime? What do you believe might be the best means of decreasing the crime rate? How is your life affected by a growing crime rate? How is your community affected by crime?

35. Presidential Elections, 1789 to 1976, and Political Parties Represented in Opening Sessions of Congress

CANDIDATES	POPULAR VOTE	ELECTORAL VOTE	CONGRESS	MAJORITY PARTY	MINORITY PARTIES
1789 GEORGE WASHINGTON	—[1]	69	1st Senate	AD–17	OP–9
John Adams	—	34	House	AD–38	OP–26
John Jay	—	9	2nd Senate	F–16	DR–13
R. H. Harrison	—	6	House	F–37	DR–33
John Rutledge	—	6			
John Hancock	—	4			
George Clinton	—	3			
Samuel Huntington	—	2			
John Milton	—	2			
James Armstrong	—	1			
Benjamin Lincoln	—	1			
Edward Telfair	—	1			
(Not voted)	—	12			
1792 GEORGE WASHINGTON (F)	—	132	3rd Senate	F–17	DR–13
John Adams (F)	—	77	House	DR–57	F–48
George Clinton (DR)	—	50	4th Senate	F–19	DR–13
Thomas Jefferson	—	4	House	F–54	DR–52
Aaron Burr	—	1			
1796 JOHN ADAMS (F)	—	71	5th Sentate	F–20	DR–12
Thomas Jefferson (DR)	—	68	House	F–58	DR–48
Thomas Pinckney (F)	—	59	6th Senate	F–19	DR–13
Aaron Burr (AF)	—	30	House	F–64	DR–42
Samuel Adams (DR)	—	15			
Oliver Ellsworth (F)	—	11			
George Clinton (DR)	—	7			
John Jay (IF)	—	5			
James Iredell (F)	—	3			
George Washington (F)	—	2			
John Henry (I)	—	2			
S. Johnston (IF)	—	2			
C. C. Pinckney (IF)	—	1			
1800 THOMAS JEFFERSON (DR)	—	73[2]	7th Senate	DR–18	F–13
Aaron Burr (DR)	—	73	House	DR–69	F–36
John Adams (F)	—	65	8th Senate	DR–25	F–9
C. C. Pinckney (F)	—	64	House	DR–102	F–39
John Jay (F)	—	1			
1804 THOMAS JEFFERSON (DR)	—	162	9th Senate	DR–27	F–7
George Clinton[3]			House	DR–116	F–25
C. C. Pinckney (F)		14	10th Senate	DR–28	F–6
			House	DR–118	F–24
1808 JAMES MADISON (DR)	—	122	11th Senate	DR–28	F–6
George Clinton	—	6*	House	DR–94	F–48
C. C. Pinckney (F)	—	47	12th Senate	DR–30	F–6
(Not voted)	—	1	House	DR–108	F–36
1812 JAMES MADISON (DR)	—	128	13th Senate	DR–27	F–9
Elbridge Gerry			House	DR–112	F–68
DeWitt Clinton (Fusion)	—	89	14th Senate	DR–25	F–11
(Not voted)	—	1	House	DR–117	F–65

AD–Administration   AF–Anti-Federalist   DR–Democratic Republican   F–Federalist   I–Independent
IF–Independent Federalist   OP–Opposition   President–capital letters   Vice-President—*italics*

[1] In our earliest elections, the electors were chosen by the state legislatures.
[2] Election was decided in the House of Representatives.
[3] Because of the 12th Amendment, the vice president was the president's running mate from here on.
* Clinton received 6 electoral votes for president while a vice-presidential candidate on the Democratic-Republican ticket.

CANDIDATES	POPULAR VOTE	ELECTORAL VOTE	CONGRESS	MAJORITY PARTY	MINORITY PARTIES
1816 JAMES MONROE (DR)	–	183	15th Senate	DR–34	F–10
Daniel D. Tompkins			House	DR–141	F–42
Rufus King (F)	–	34	16th Senate	DR–35	F–7
(Not voted)	–	4	House	DR–156	F–27
1820 JAMES MONROE (DR)	–	231	17th Senate	DR–44	F–4
Daniel D. Tompkins			House	DR–158	F–25
John Q. Adams (IR)	–	1	18th Senate	DR–44	F–4
(Not voted)	–	3	House	DR–187	F–26
1824 JOHN Q. ADAMS[4]	108,740	84[5]	19th Senate	AD–26	J–20
John C. Calhoun			House	AD–105	J–97
Andrew Jackson	153,544	99	20th Senate	J–28	AD–20
Henry Clay	47,136	37	House	J–119	AD–94
W. H. Crawford	46,618	41			
1828 ANDREW JACKSON (D)	647,286	178	21st Senate	D–26	NR–22
John C. Calhoun			House	D–139	NR–74
John Q. Adams (NR)	508,064	83	22nd Senate	D–25	NR–21; Other –2
			House	D–141	NR–58; Other–14
1832 ANDREW JACKSON (D)	687,502	219	23rd Senate	D–20	NR–20; Other–8
Martin Van Buren			House	D–147	AM–53; Other–60
Henry Clay (NR)	530,189	49	24th Senate	D–27	W–25
William Wirt (AM)	–	7	House	D–145	W–98
John Floyd (NUL)	–	11			
(Not voted)	–	2			
1836 MARTIN VAN BUREN (D)	765,483	170	25th Senate	D–30	W–18; Other–4
Richard M. Johnson			House	D–108	W–107; Other–24
William H. Harrison (W)		73	26th Senate	D–28	W–22
Hugh L. White (W)	739,795[6]	26	House	D–124	W–118
Daniel Webster (W)		14			
W. P. Mangum (AJ)	–	11			
1840 WILLIAM H. HARRISON (W)	1,274,624	234	27th Senate	W–28	D–24; Other–2
John Tyler			House	W–133	D–102; Other–6
Martin Van Buren (D)	1,127,781	60	28th Senate	W–28	D–25; Other–1
			House	D–142	W–79; Other–1
1844 JAMES K. POLK (D)	1,338,464	170	29th Senate	D–31	W–25
George M. Dallas			House	D–143	W–77; Other–6
Henry Clay (W)	1,300,097	105	30th Senate	D–36	W–21; Other–1
James G. Birney (L)	62,300	–	House	W–115	D–108; Other–4
1848 ZACHARY TAYLOR[8] (W)	1,360,967	163	31st Senate	D–35	W–25; Other–2
Millard Fillmore			House	D–112	W–109; Other–9
Lewis Cass (D)	1,222,342	127	32nd Senate	D–35	W–24; Other–3
Martin Van Buren (FS)	291,263	–	House	D–140	W–88; Other–5
1852 FRANKLIN PIERCE (D)	1,601,117	254	33rd Senate	D–38	W–22; Other–2
William R. King			House	D–159	W–71; Other–4
Winfield Scott (W)	1,385,453	42	34th Senate	D–40	R–15; Other–5
John P. Hale (FS)	155,825	–	House	R–108	D–83; Other–43

AD–Administration   AJ–Anti-Jackson   AM–Anti-Masonic   D–Democratic   DR–Democratic Republican
F–Federalist   FS–Free Soil   IR–Independent-Republican   J–Jackson   L–Liberty   NR–National Republican
NUL–Nullifiers   W–Whig   R–Republican

[4] No distinct party designations.   [5] No electoral majority; election decided in House of Representatives.
[6] Whig tickets were pledged to various candidates in various states.
[7] W. H. Harrison died in office and John Tyler became president 1840–1844.
[8] Taylor died in office and Millard Fillmore became president 1850–1852.

	CANDIDATES	POPULAR VOTE	ELECTORAL VOTE	CONGRESS		MAJORITY PARTY	MINORITY PARTIES
1856	JAMES BUCHANAN (D)	1,832,955	174	35th	Senate	D–36	R–20; Other–8
	John C. Breckinridge				House	D–118	R–92; Other–26
	John C. Frémont (R)	1,339,932	114	36th	Senate	D–36	R–26; Other–4
	Millard Fillmore (A)	871,731	8		House	R–114	D–92; Other–31
1860	ABRAHAM LINCOLN (R)	1,865,593	180	37th	Senate	R–31	D–10; Other–8
	Hannibal Hamlin				House	R–105	D–43; Other–30
	J. C. Breckinridge (D-S)	848,356	72	38th	Senate	R–36	D–9; Other–5
	Stephen A. Douglas (D)	1,382,713	12		House	R–102	D–75; Other–9
	John Bell (CU)	592,906	39				
1864	ABRAHAM LINCOLN[9] (R)	2,206,938	212	39th	Senate	U–42	D–10
	Andrew Johnson				House	U–149	D–42
	George B. McClellan (D)	1,803,787	21	40th	Senate	R–42	D–11
	(Not voted)	–	81		House	R–143	D–49
1868	ULYSSES S. GRANT (R)	3,013,421	214	41st	Senate	R–56	D–11
	Schuyler Colfax				House	R–149	D–63
	Horatio Seymour (D)	2,706,829	80	42nd	Senate	R–52	D–17; Other–5
	(Not voted)	–	23		House	R–134	D–104; Other–5
1872	ULYSSES S. GRANT (R)	3,596,745	286	43rd	Senate	R–49	D–19; Other–5
	Henry Wilson				House	R–194	D–92; Other–14
	Horace Greeley (D)	2,843,446	–[10]	44th	Senate	R–45	D–29; Other–2
	Charles O'Connor (SD)	29,489	–		House	D–169	R–109; Other–14
	Thomas A. Hendricks (ID)	–	42				
	B. Gratz Brown (D)	–	18				
	Charles J. Jenkins (D)	–	2				
	David Davis (D)	–	1				
	(Not voted)	–	17				
1876	RUTHERFORD B. HAYES (R)	4,036,572	185	45th	Senate	R–39	D–36; Other–1
	William A. Wheeler				House	D–153	R–140
	Samuel J. Tilden (D)	4,284,020	184	46th	Senate	D–42	R–33; Other–1
	Peter Cooper (G)	81,737	–		House	D–149	R–130; Other–14
1880	JAMES A. GARFIELD[11] (R)	4,453,295	214	47th	Senate	R–37	D–37; Other–1
	Chester A. Arthur				House	R–147	D–135; Other–11
	Winfield S. Hancock (D)	4,414,082	155	48th	Senate	R–38	D–36; Other–2
	James B. Weaver (GL)	308,578	–		House	D–197	R–118; Other–10
	Neal Dow (Proh.)	10,305	–				
1884	GROVER CLEVELAND (D)	4,879,507	219	49th	Senate	R–43	D–34
	Thomas A. Hendricks				House	D–183	R–140; Other–2
	James G. Blaine (R)	4,850,293	182	50th	Senate	R–39	D–37
	Benjamin F. Butler (GL)	175,370	–		House	D–169	R–152; Other–4
	John P. St. John (Proh.)	150,369	–				
1888	BENJAMIN HARRISON (R)	5,447,129	233	51st	Senate	R–39	D–37
	Levi P. Morton				House	R–166	D–159
	Grover Cleveland (D)	5,537,857	168	52nd	Senate	R–47	D–39; Other–2
	Clinton B. Fisk (Proh.)	249,506	–		House	D–235	R–88; Other–9
	Anson J. Streeter (UL)	146,935	–				
1892	GROVER CLEVELAND (D)	5,555,426	277	53rd	Senate	D–44	R–38; Other–3
	Adlai E. Stevenson				House	D–218	R–127; Other–11
	Benjamin Harrison (R)	5,182,690	145	54th	Senate	R–43	D–39; Other–6
	James B. Weaver (P)	1,029,846	22		House	R–244	D–105; Other–7
	John Bidwell (Proh.)	264,133	–				
	Simon Wing (SL)	21,164	–				

A–American   CU–Constitutional Union   D–Democratic   D-S–Democratic-Southern   G–Greenback   GL–Greenback Labor   ID–Independent Democratic   P–People's   Proh.–Prohibition   R–Republican   SD–Straight Democratic SL–Socialist Labor   U–Unionist   UL–Union Labor

[9] Lincoln was assassinated and Andrew Johnson became president 1865–1868.
[10] Greeley died shortly after the election and the electors supporting him cast their votes as shown.
[11] Garfield was assassinated in office and Chester Arthur became president 1881–1884.

CANDIDATES	POPULAR VOTE	ELECTORAL VOTE	CONGRESS		MAJORITY PARTY	MINORITY PARTIES
1896 WILLIAM McKINLEY (R)	7,102,246	271	55th Senate		R–47	D–34; Other–7
Garret A. Hobart				House	R–204	D–113; Other–40
William J. Bryan (D)	6,492,559	176				
John M. Palmer (ND)	133,148	—	56th Senate		R–53	D–26; Other–8
Joshua Levering (Proh.)	132,007	—		House	R–185	D–163; Other–9
Charles H. Matchett (SL)	36,274	—				
Charles E. Bentley (N)	13,969	—				
1900 WILLIAM McKINLEY[12] (R)	7,218,491	292	57th Senate		R–55	D–31; Other–4
Theodore Roosevelt				House	R–197	D–151; Other–9
William J. Bryan (D)	6,356,734	155				
John C. Wooley (Proh.)	208,914	—	58th Senate		R–57	D–33
Eugene V. Debs (S)	87,814	—		House	R–208	D–178
Wharton Barker (P)	50,373	—				
Jos. F. Malloney (SL)	39,739	—				
1904 THEODORE ROOSEVELT (R)	7,628,461	336	59th Senate		R–57	D–33
Charles W. Fairbanks				House	R–250	D–136
Alton B. Parker (D)	5,084,223	140				
Eugene V. Debs (S)	402,283	—	60th Senate		R–61	D–31
Silas C. Swallow (Proh.)	258,536	—		House	R–222	D–164
Thomas E. Watson (P)	117,183	—				
Charles H. Corregan (SL)	31,249	—				
1908 WILLIAM H. TAFT (R)	7,675,320	321	61st Senate		R–61	D–32
James S. Sherman				House	R–219	D–172
William J. Bryan (D)	6,412,294	162				
Eugene V. Debs (S)	420,793	—	62nd Senate		R–51	D–41
Eugene W. Chafin (Proh.)	253,840	—		House	D–228	R–161; Other–1
Thomas L. Hisgen (I)	82,872	—				
Thomas E. Watson (P)	29,100	—				
August Gillhaus (SL)	14,021	—				
1912 WOODROW WILSON (D)	6,296,547	435	63rd Senate		D–51	R–44; Other–1
Thomas R. Marshall				House	D–291	R–127; Other–17
Theodore Roosevelt (Prog.)	4,118,571	88				
William H. Taft (R)	3,486,720	8	64th Senate		D–56	R–40
Eugene V. Debs (S)	900,672	—		House	D–230	R–196; Other–9
Eugene W. Chafin (Proh.)	206,275	—				
Arthur E. Reimer (SL)	28,750	—				
1916 WOODROW WILSON (D)	9,127,695	277	65th Senate		D–53	R–42
Thomas R. Marshall				House	D–216	R–210; Other–6
Charles E. Hughes (R)	8,533,507	254				
A. L. Benson (S)	585,113	—	66th Senate		R–49	D–47
J. Frank Hanly (Proh.)	220,506	—		House	R–240	D–190; Other–3
Arthur E. Reimer (SL)	13,403	—				
1920 WARREN G. HARDING[13] (R)	16,143,407	404	67th Senate		R–59	D–37
Calvin Coolidge				House	R–301	D–131; Other–1
James M. Cox (D)	9,130,328	127				
Eugene V. Debs (S)	919,799	—	68th Senate		R–51	D–43; Other–2
P. P. Christensen (FL)	265,411	—		House	R–225	D–205; Other–5
Aaron S. Watkins (Proh.)	189,408	—				
James E. Ferguson (A)	48,000	—				
W. W. Cox (SL)	31,715	—				

A–American   D–Democratic   FL–Farmer-Labor   I–Independence   N–Nationalist   ND–National Democratic
P–People's   Prog.–Progressive   Proh.–Prohibition   R–Republican   S–Socialist   SL–Socialist Labor

[12] McKinley was assassinated and Theodore Roosevelt became president 1901–1904.
[13] Harding died in office and Calvin Coolidge became president 1923–1924.

CANDIDATES	POPULAR VOTE	ELECTORAL VOTE	CONGRESS	MAJORITY PARTY	MINORITY PARTIES
1924 CALVIN COOLIDGE (R)	15,718,211	382	69th Senate	R–56	D–39; Other–1
Charles G. Dawes			House	R–247	D–183; Other–4
John W. Davis (D)	8,385,283	136	70th Senate	R–49	D–46; Other–1
Robert M. LaFollette (Prog.)	4,831,289	13	House	R–237	D–195: Other–3
Herman P. Faris (Proh.)	57,520	—			
Frank T. Johns (SL)	36,428	—			
William Z. Foster (W)	36,386	—			
Gilbert O. Nations (A)	23,967	—			
1928 HERBERT C. HOOVER (R)	21,391,993	444	71st Senate	R–56	D–39; Other–1
Charles Curtis			House	R–267	D–167; Other–1
Alfred E. Smith (D)	15,016,169	87	72nd Senate	R–48	D–47; Other–1
Norman Thomas (S)	267,835	—	House	D–220	R–214; Other–1
Verne L. Reynolds (SL)	21,603	—			
William Z. Foster (W)	21,181	—			
William F. Varney (Proh.)	20,106	—			
1932 FRANKLIN D. ROOSEVELT (D)	22,809,638	472	73rd Senate	D–60	R–35; Other–1
			House	D–310	R–117; Other–5
John N. Garner			74th Senate	D–69	R–25; Other–2
Herbert C. Hoover (R)	15,758,901	59	House	D–319	R–103; Other–10
Norman Thomas (S)	881,951	—			
William Z. Foster (Comm.)	102,785	—			
William D. Upshaw (Proh.)	81,869	—			
William H. Harvey (L)	53,425	—			
Verne L. Reynolds (SL)	33,276	—			
1936 FRANKLIN D. ROOSEVELT (D)	27,752,869	523	75th Senate	D–76	R–16; Other–4
			House	D–331	R–89; Other–13
John N. Garner			76th Senate	D–69	R–23; Other–4
Alfred M. Landon (R)	16,674,665	8	House	D–261	R–164; Other–4
William Lemke (U)	882,479	—			
Norman Thomas (S)	187,720	—			
Earl Browder (Comm.)	80,159	—			
D. Leigh Colvin (Proh.)	37,847	—			
John W. Aiken (SL)	12,777	—			
1940 FRANKLIN D. ROOSEVELT (D)	27,307,819	449	77th Senate	D–66	R–28; Other–2
			House	D–268	R–162; Other–5
Henry A. Wallace			78th Senate	D–58	R–37; Other–1
Wendell L. Willkie (R)	22,321,018	82	House	D–218	R–208; Other–4
Norman Thomas (S)	99,557	—			
Roger Q. Babson (Proh.)	57,812	—			
Earl Browder (Comm.)	46,251	—			
John W. Aiken (SL)	14,892	—			
1944 FRANKLIN D. ROOSEVELT[14] (D)	25,606,585	432	79th Senate	D–56	R–38; Other–1
			House	D–242	R–190; Other–2
Harry S. Truman			80th Senate	R–51	D–45
Thomas E. Dewey (R)	22,014,745	99	House	R–245	D–188; Other–1
Norman Thomas (S)	80,518	—			
Claude A. Watson (Proh.)	74,758	—			
Edward A. Teichert (SL)	45,336	—			
1948 HARRY S. TRUMAN (D)	24,105,812	303	81st Senate	D–54	R–42
Alben W. Barkley			House	D–263	R–171; Other–1
Thomas E. Dewey (R)	21,970,065	189	82nd Senate	D–49	R–47
J. Strom Thurmond (SR)	1,169,063	39	House	D–234	R–199; Other–1
Henry Wallace (Prog.)	1,157,172	—			
Norman Thomas (S)	139,414	—			
Claude A. Watson (Proh.)	103,224	—			
Edward A. Teichert (SL)	29,244	—			
Farrell Dobbs (SW)	13,613	—			

A–American   Comm.–Communist   D–Democratic   L–Liberty   Prog.–Progressive   Proh.–Prohibition
R–Republican   S–Socialist   SL–Socialist Labor   SR–States' Rights   SW–Socialist Workers   U–Union   W–Workers

[14] Franklin D. Roosevelt died in office and Harry S. Truman became president 1945–1948.

CANDIDATES	POPULAR VOTE	ELECTORAL VOTE	CONGRESS	MAJORITY PARTY	MINORITY PARTIES
1952 DWIGHT D. EISENHOWER (R)	33,936,234	442	83rd Senate	R–48	D–47; Other–1
Richard M. Nixon			House	R–221	D–211; Other–1
Adlai E. Stevenson (D)	27,314,992	89	84th Senate	D–48	R–47; Other–1
Vincent Hallinan (Prog.)	140,023	–	House	D–232	R–203
Stuart Hamblen (Proh.)	72,949	–			
Eric Hass (SL)	30,267	–			
Darlington Hoopes (S)	20,203	–			
Douglas A. MacArthur (Const.)	17,205	–			
Farrell Dobbs (SW)	10,312	–			
1956 DWIGHT D. EISENHOWER (R)	35,590,472	457	85th Senate	D–49	R–47
Richard M. Nixon			House	D–233	R–200
Adlai E. Stevenson (D)	26,022,752	73	86th Senate	D–64	R–34
T. Coleman Andrews (SR)	107,929	–	House	D–283	R–153
Eric Hass (SL)	44,300	–			
Enoch A. Holtwick (Proh.)	41,937	–			
Walter Jones[15]	–	1			
1960 JOHN F. KENNEDY[16] (D)	34,227,000	303	87th Senate	D–65	R–35
Lyndon B. Johnson			House	D–263	R–174
Richard M. Nixon (R)	34,108,000	219	88th Senate	D–67	R–33
Eric Hass (SL)	46,560	–	House	D–258	R–177
Rutherford Decker (Proh.)	46,203	–			
Orville Faubus (SR)	44,977	–			
Farrell Dobbs (SW)	39,541	–			
Senator Harry F. Byrd[15]	–	15			
1964 LYNDON B. JOHNSON (D)	43,129,000	486	89th Senate	D–68	R–32
Hubert H. Humphrey			House	D–295	R–140
Barry Goldwater (R)	27,178,000	52	90th Senate	D–64	R–36
Eric Hass (SL)	45,186	–	House	D–246	R–187
Clifton DeBerry (SW)	32,705	–			
E. Harold Munn (Proh.)	23,267				
1968 RICHARD M. NIXON (R)	31,770,237	301	91st Senate	D–57	R–43
Spiro T. Agnew			House	D–243	R–192
Hubert H. Humphrey (D)	31,270,533	191	92nd Senate	D–54	R–44; Other–2
George C. Wallace (AI)	9,906,141	46	House	D–254	R–180
Henning A. Blomen (SL)	52,588	–			
Dick Gregory (PAF)	47,097				
Fred Halstead (SW)	41,300	–			
Eldridge Cleaver (NPol)	36,385	–			
Eugene McCarthy (NP)	25,858	–			
E. Harold Munn (Proh.)	14,519	–			
1972 RICHARD M. NIXON[17] (R)	47,169,911	520	93rd Senate	D–56	R–42; Other–2
Spiro T. Agnew[18]			House	D–239	R–192; Other–1; Vacant–3
George S. McGovern (D)	29,170,383	17			
John Schmitz (A)	1,099,482	–	94th Senate	D–60	R–37; Other–3
Benjamin Spock (P)	78,756	–	House	D–291	R–144
Linda Jenness (SW)	66,677	–			
Louis Fisher (SL)	53,814	–			
Gus Hall (C)	25,595	–			
Earl Munn, Jr. (Proh.)	13,505	–			
John Hospers (L)	3,673*	1			
John Mahalchik (AF)	1,743*	–			
Gabriel Green (U)	220*	–			

A–American   AF–America First   AI–American Independent   C–Communist   Const.–Constitution
D–Democratic   L–Libertarian   NP–New Party   NPol–New Politics   P–Peoples'   PAF–Peace and Freedom
Prog.–Progressive   Proh.–Prohibition   R–Republican   S–Socialist   SL–Socialist Labor   SR–States' Rights
SW–Socialist Workers   U–Universal

[15] Was not a candidate.
[16] John F. Kennedy was assassinated and Lyndon B. Johnson became president, 1963–1964.
[17] Richard M. Nixon resigned in 1974 and Gerald Ford became president, 1974–1976.
[18] Spiro T. Agnew resigned in 1973 and Gerald Ford was appointed vice-president, 1973–1974. When President Nixon resigned in 1974 and Ford became president, Nelson A. Rockefeller became vice-president, 1974–1976.
* Unofficial estimate.

	CANDIDATES	POPULAR VOTE	ELECTORAL VOTE	CONGRESS	MAJORITY PARTY	MINORITY PARTIES
1976	JIMMY CARTER (D)	40,127,169*	297	95th Senate	D–61	R–38; Other–1
	Walter F. Mondale			House	D–292	R–143
	Gerald R. Ford (R)	39,118,228*	240			
	Eugene McCarthy (I)	749,296*	–			
	Roger L. MacBride (L)	172,191*	–			
	Lester G. Maddox (AI)	168,457*	–			
	Thomas Jefferson Anderson (A)	157,223*	–			
	Peter Camejo (SW)	90,381*	–			
	Gus Hall (C)	58,945*	–			
	Margaret Wright (I)	49,022*	–			
	Lyndon H. Larouche, Jr. (USL)	40,035*	–			
	Benjamin Bubar (Proh.)	15,854*	–			
	Julius Levin (SL)	9,569*	–			
	Frank P. Zeidler (S)	6,010*	–			
	Ronald W. Reagan (R)	**	1			

A–American   AI–American Independent   C–Communist   D–Democratic   I–Independent   L–Libertarian
Proh.–Prohibition   R–Republican   S–Socialist   SL–Socialist Labor   SW–Socialist Workers
USL–United States Labor

* Unofficial estimate.
** Not available.

DECLARATION OF INDEPENDENCE

In Congress, July 4, 1776

The Unanimous Declaration of the Thirteen United States of America

When, in the course of human events, it becomes necessary for one people to dissolve the political bands which have connected them with another, and to assume, among the powers of the earth, the separate and equal station to which the laws of nature and of nature's God entitle them, a decent respect to the opinions of mankind requires that they should declare the causes which impel them to the separation.

We hold these truths to be self-evident: That all men are created equal; that they are endowed by their Creator with certain unalienable rights; that among these are life, liberty, and the pursuit of happiness. That, to secure these rights, governments are instituted among men, deriving their just powers from the consent of the governed; that, whenever any form of government becomes destructive of these ends, it is the right of the people to alter or to abolish it, and to institute new government, laying its foundation on such principles, and organizing its powers in such form, as to them shall seem most likely to effect their safety and happiness. Prudence, indeed, will dictate that governments long established should not be changed for light and transient causes; and accordingly all experience hath shown that mankind are more disposed to suffer while evils are sufferable, than to right themselves by abolishing the forms to which they are accustomed. But when a long train of abuses and usurpations, pursuing invariably the same object, evinces a design to reduce them under absolute despotism, it is their right, it is their duty, to throw off such government, and to provide new guards for their future security. Such has been the patient sufferance of these colonies; and such is now the necessity which constrains them to alter their former systems of government. The history of the present King of Great Britain is a history of repeated injuries and usurpations, all having in direct object the establishment of an absolute tyranny over these states. To prove this, let facts be submitted to a candid world.

He has refused his assent to laws the most wholesome and necessary for the public good.

He has forbidden his governors to pass laws of immediate and pressing importance, unless suspended in their operation till his assent should be obtained; and, when so suspended, he has utterly neglected to attend to them.

He has refused to pass other laws for the accommodation of large districts of people, unless those people would relinquish the right of representation in the legislature, — a right inestimable to them, and formidable to tyrants only.

He has called together legislative bodies at places unusual, uncomfortable, and distant from the depository of their public records, for the sole purpose of fatiguing them into compliance with his measures.

He has dissolved representative houses repeatedly, for opposing with, manly firmness, his invasions on the rights of the people.

He has refused, for a long time after such dissolutions, to cause others to be elected, whereby the legislative powers, incapable of annihilation, have returned to the people at large for their exercise; the state remaining, in the mean time, exposed to all the dangers of invasions from without and convulsions within.

He has endeavored to prevent the population of these states; for that purpose obstructing the laws for the naturalization of foreigners, refusing to pass others to encourage their migration hither, and raising the conditions of new appropriations of lands.

He has obstructed the administration of justice, by refusing his assent to laws for establishing judiciary powers.

He has made judges dependent on his will alone or the tenure of their offices, and the amount and payment of their salaries.

He has erected a multitude of new offices, and sent hither swarms of officers to harass our people and eat out their substance.

He has kept among us, in times of peace, standing armies without the consent of our legislatures.

He has affected to render the military independent of, and superior to, the civil power.

He has combined with others to subject us to a jurisdiction foreign to our constitutions, and unacknowledged by our laws; giving his assent to their acts of pretended legislation:

For quartering large bodies of armed troops among us;

For protecting them, by a mock trial, from punishment for any murders which they should commit on the inhabitants of these states;

For cutting off our trade with all parts of the world;

For imposing taxes on us without our consent;

For depriving us, in many cases, of the benefits of trial by jury;

For transporting us beyond seas to be tried for pretended offenses;

For abolishing the free system of English laws in a neighboring province, establishing therein an arbitrary government, and enlarging its boundaries, so as to render it at once an example and fit instrument for introducing the same absolute rule into these colonies;

For taking away our charters, abolishing our most valuable laws, and altering fundamentally, the forms of our governments;

For suspending our own legislatures, and declaring themselves invested with power to legislate for us in all cases whatsoever.

He has abdicated government here, by declaring us out of his protection and waging war against us.

He has plundered our seas, ravaged our coasts, burned our towns, and destroyed the lives of our people.

He is at this time transporting large armies of foreign mercenaries to complete the works of death, desolation, and tyranny already begun with circumstances of cruelty and perfidy scarcely paralleled in the most barbarous ages, and totally unworthy the head of a civilized nation.

He has constrained our fellow-citizens, taken captive on the high seas, to bear arms against their country, to become the executioners of their friends and brethren, or to fall themselves by their hands.

He has excited domestic insurrection among us, and has endeavored to bring on the inhabitants of our frontiers the merciless Indian savages, whose known rule of warfare is an undistinguished destruction of all ages, sexes, and conditions.

In every stage of these oppressions we have petitioned for redress in the most humble terms; our repeated petitions have been answered only by repeated injury.

A prince whose character is thus marked by every act which may define a tyrant is unfit to be the ruler of a free people.

Nor have we been wanting in our attentions to our British brethren. We have warned them, from time to time, of attempts by their legislature to extend an unwarrantable jurisdiction over us. We have reminded them of the circumstances of our emigration and settlement here. We have appealed to their native justice and magnanimity; and we have conjured them by the ties of our common kindred to disavow these usurpations, which would inevitably interrupt our connections and correspondence. They, too, have been deaf to the voice of justice and consanguinity. We must, therefore, acquiesce in the necessity which denounces our separation, and hold them, as we hold the rest of mankind, enemies in war, in peace friends.

We, therefore, the representatives of the United States of America, in General Congress assembled, appealing to the Supreme Judge of the world for the rectitude of our intentions, do, in the name and by the authority of the good people of these colonies, solemnly publish and declare, That these united colonies are, and of right ought to be, free and independent states; that they are absolved from all allegiance to the British crown, and that all political connection between them and the state of Great Britain is, and ought to be, totally dissolved; and that, as free and independent states, they have full power to levy war, conclude peace, contract alliances, establish commerce, and do all other acts and things which independent states may of right do. And, for the support of this declaration, with a firm reliance on the protection of Divine Providence, we mutually pledge to each other our lives, our fortunes, and our sacred honor.

Constitution of the United States

PREAMBLE

We the people of the United States, in order to form a more perfect union, establish justice, insure domestic tranquility, provide for the common defense, promote the general welfare, and secure the blessings of liberty to ourselves and our posterity, do ordain and establish this Constitution for the United States of America.

Article I

LEGISLATIVE DEPARTMENT

Section 1

CONGRESS

Legislative powers vested. All legislative powers herein granted shall be vested in a Congress of the United States, which shall consist of a Senate and House of Representatives.

Section 2

HOUSE OF REPRESENTATIVES

1. *Election.* The House of Representatives shall be composed of members chosen every second year by the people of the several States, and the electors in each State shall have the qualifications requisite for electors of the most numerous branch of the State legislature.

2. *Qualifications.* No person shall be a representative who shall not have attained to the age of twenty-five years, and been seven years a citizen of the United States, and who shall not, when elected, be an inhabitant of that State in which he shall be chosen.

3. *Apportionment.* Representatives and direct taxes shall be apportioned among the several States which may be included within this Union, according to their respective numbers, which shall be determined by adding to the whole number of free persons, including those bound to service for a term of years, and excluding Indians not taxed, three fifths of all other persons. The actual enumeration shall be made within three years after the first meeting of the Congress of the United States, and within every subsequent term of ten years, in such manner as they shall by law direct. The number of representatives shall not exceed one for every thirty thousand, but each State shall have at least one representative; and until such enumeration shall be made, the State of New Hampshire shall be entitled to choose three, Massachusetts eight, Rhode Island and Providence Plantations one, Connecticut five, New York six, New Jersey four, Pennsylvania eight, Delaware one, Maryland six, Virginia ten, North Carolina five, South Carolina five, and Georgia three.

4. *Vacancies.* When vacancies happen in the representation from any State, the executive authority thereof shall issue writs of election to fill such vacancies.

5. *Officers; impeachment.* The House of Representatives shall choose their speaker and other officers, and shall have the sole power of impeachment.

Section 3

SENATE

1. *Election.* The Senate of the United States shall be composed of two senators from each State, chosen [by the legislature thereof] for six years; and each senator shall have one vote.

2. *Classification.* Immediately after they shall be assembled in consequence of the first election, they shall be divided as equally as may be into three classes. The seats of the senators of the first class shall be vacated at the expiration of the second year, of the second class at the expiration of the fourth year, and of the third class at the expiration of the sixth year, so that one third may be chosen every second year; [and if vacancies happen by resignation, or otherwise during the recess of the legislature of any State, the executive thereof may make temporary appointments until the next meeting of the legislature, which shall then fill such vacancies.]

3. *Qualifications.* No person shall be a senator who shall not have attained to the age of thirty years, and been nine years a citizen of the United States, and who shall not, when elected, be an inhabitant of that State for which he shall be chosen.

4. *President of Senate.* The Vice-President of the United States shall be President of the Senate, but shall have no vote, unless they be equally divided.

5. *Other officers.* The Senate shall choose their other officers, and also a president *pro tempore,* in the absence of the Vice-President, or when he shall exercise the office of President of the United States.

6. *Trial of impeachments.* The Senate shall have the sole power to try all impeachments. When sitting for that purpose, they shall be on oath or affirmation. When the President of the United States is tried, the chief justice shall preside: and no person shall be convicted without the concurrence of two thirds of the members present.

7. *Judgment in case of conviction.* Judgment in cases of impeachment shall not extend further than to removal from office, and disqualification to hold and enjoy any office of honor, trust, or profit under the United States: but the party convicted shall nevertheless be liable and subject to indictment, trial, judgment, and punishment, according to law.

Section 4

ELECTION AND MEETINGS

1. *Election.* The times, places, and manner of holding elections for senators and representatives, shall be prescribed in each State by the legislature thereof; but the Congress may at any time by law make or alter such regulations, except as to the places of choosing senators.

2. *Meetings.* The Congress shall assemble at least once in every year, [and such meeting shall be on the first Monday in December, unless they shall by law appoint a different day.]

Section 5

ORGANIZATION OF CONGRESS

1. *Organization.* Each House shall be the judge of the elections, returns, and qualifications of its own members, and a majority of each shall constitute a quorum to do business; but a smaller number may adjourn from day to day, and may be authorized to compel the attendance to absent members, in such manner, and under such penalties as each House may provide.

2. *Rules.* Each House may determine the rules of its proceedings, punish its members for disorderly behavior, and, with the concurrence of two thirds, expel a member.

3. *Journal.* Each House shall keep a journal of its proceedings, and from time to time publish the same, excepting such parts as may in their judgment require secrecy; and the yeas and nays of the members of either House on any question shall, at the desire of one fifth of those present, be entered on the journal.

4. *Adjournment.* Neither House, during the session of Congress, shall, without the consent of the other, adjourn for more than three days, nor to any other place than that in which the two Houses shall be sitting.

Section 6

PRIVILEGES AND RESTRICTIONS

1. *Pay and privileges.* The senators and representatives shall receive a compensation for their services, to be ascertained by law, and paid out of the Treasury of the United States. They shall in all cases, except treason, felony, and breach of the peace, be privileged from arrest during their attendance at the session of their respective Houses, and in going to and returning from the same; and for any speech or debate in either House, they shall not be questioned in any other place.

2. *Prohibitions on members.* No senator or representative shall, during the time for which he was elected, be appointed to any civil office under the authority of the United States, which shall have been created, or the emoluments thereof shall have been increased during such time; and no person holding any office under the United States shall be a member of either House during his continuance in office.

Section 7

METHOD OF PASSING LAWS

1. *Revenue bills.* All bills for raising revenue shall originate in the House of Representatives; but the Senate may propose or concur with amendments as on other bills.

2. *How bills become laws.* Every bill which shall have passed the House of Representatives and the Senate, shall, before it become a law, be presented to the President of the United States; if he approve he shall sign it, but if not he shall return it, with his objections to that House in which it shall have originated, who shall enter the objections at large on their journal, and proceed to reconsider it. If after such reconsideration two thirds of that House shall agree to pass the bill, it shall be sent, together with the objections, to the other House, by which it shall likewise be reconsidered, and if approved by two thirds of that House, it shall become a law. But in all such cases the votes of both Houses shall be determined by yeas and nays, and the names of the persons voting for and against the bill shall be entered on the journal of each House respectively. If any bill shall not be returned by the President within ten days

(Sundays excepted) after it shall have been presented to him, the same shall be a law, in like manner as if he had signed it, unless the Congress by their adjournment prevent its return, in which case it shall not be a law.

3. *The President's veto power.* Every order, resolution, or vote to which the concurrence of the Senate and House of Representatives may be necessary (except on a question of adjournment) shall be presented to the President of the United States; and before the same shall take effect, shall be approved by him, or being disapproved by him, shall be repassed by two thirds of the Senate and House of Representatives, according to the rules and limitations prescribed in the case of a bill.

Section 8

POWERS GRANTED TO CONGRESS

1–17. *Enumerated powers.* 1. The Congress shall have power to lay and collect taxes, duties, imposts, and excises, to pay the debts and provide for the common defense and general welfare of the United States; but all duties, imposts, and excises shall be uniform throughout the United States;

2. To borrow money on the credit of the United States;

3. To regulate commerce with foreign nations, and among the several States, and with the Indian tribes;

4. To establish an uniform rule of naturalization, and uniform laws on the subject of bankruptcies through the United States;

5. To coin money, regulate the value thereof, and of foreign coin, and fix the standard of weights and measures;

6. To provide for the punishment of counterfeiting the securities and current coin of the United States;

7. To establish post offices and post roads;

8. To promote the progress of science and useful arts by securing for limited times to authors and inventors the exclusive right to their respective writings and discoveries;

9. To constitute tribunals inferior to the Supreme Court;

10. To define and punish piracies and felonies committed on the high seas, and offenses against the law of nations;

11. To declare war, grant letters of marque and reprisal, and make rules concerning captures on land and water;

12. To raise and support armies, but no appropriation of money to that use shall be for a longer term than two years;

13. To provide and maintain a navy;

14. To make rules for the government and regulation of the land and naval forces;

15. To provide for calling forth the militia to execute the laws of the Union, suppress insurrections, and repel invasions;

16. To provide for organizing, arming, and disciplining the militia, and for governing such part of them as may be employed in the service of the United States, reserving to the States respectively the appointment of the officers, and the authority of training the militia according to the discipline prescribed by Congress;

17. To exercise exclusive legislation in all cases whatsoever, over such district (not exceeding ten miles square) as may, by cession of particular States and the acceptance of Congress, become the seat of the government of the United States, and to exercise like authority over all places purchased by the consent of the legislature of the State in which the same shall be, for the erection of forts, magazines, arsenals, dockyards, and other needful buildings; and

18. *Implied powers.* To make all laws which shall be necessary and proper for carrying into execution the foregoing powers, and all other powers vested by this Constitution in the government of the United States, or in any department or officer thereof.

Section 9

POWERS FORBIDDEN TO CONGRESS

1. The migration or importation of such persons as any of the States now existing shall think proper to admit, shall not be prohibited by the Congress prior to the year one thousand eight hundred and

eight, but a tax or duty may be imposed on such importation, not exceeding ten dollars for each person.

2. The privilege of the writ of *habeas corpus* shall not be suspended, unless when in cases of rebellion or invasion the public safety may require it.

3. No bill of attainder or *ex post facto* law shall be passed.

4. No capitation, or other direct, tax shall be laid, unless in proportion to the census or enumeration herein before directed to be taken.

5. No tax or duty shall be laid on articles exported from any State.

6. No preference shall be given by any regulation of commerce or revenue to the ports of one State over those of another: nor shall vessels bound to, or from, one State be obliged to enter, clear, or pay duties in another.

7. No money shall be drawn from the treasury, but in consequence of appropriations made by law; and a regular statement and account of the receipts and expenditures of all public money shall be published from time to time.

8. No title of nobility shall be granted by the United States: and no person holding any office of profit or trust under them, shall, without the consent of the Congress, accept of any present, emolument, office, or title of any kind whatever, from any king, prince, or foreign State.

Section 10

POWERS FORBIDDEN TO STATES

1. No State shall enter into any treaty, alliance, or confederation; grant letters of marque and reprisal; coin money; emit bills of credit; make anything but gold and silver coin a tender in payment of debts; pass any bill of attainder, *ex post facto* law, or law impairing the obligation of contracts, or grant any title of nobility.

2. No State shall, without the consent of the Congress, lay any imposts or duties on imports or exports, except what may be absolutely necessary for executing its inspection laws: and the net produce of all duties and imposts laid by any State on imports or exports, shall be for the use of the treasury of the

United States; and all such laws shall be subject to the revision and control of the Congress.

3. No State shall, without the consent of Congress, lay any duty of tonnage, keep troops, or ships of war in time of peace, enter into any agreement or compact with another State, or with a foreign power, or engage in war, unless actually invaded, or in such imminent danger as will not admit of delay.

Article II
EXECUTIVE DEPARTMENT
Section 1
PRESIDENT AND VICE-PRESIDENT

1. *Term.* The executive power shall be vested in a President of the United States of America. He shall hold his office during the term of four years, and, together with the Vice-President, chosen for the same term, be elected as follows:

2. *Electors.* Each State shall appoint, in such manner as the legislature thereof may direct, a number of electors, equal to the whole number of senators and representatives to which the State may be entitled in the Congress: but no senator or representative, or person holding an office of trust or profit under the United States, shall be appointed an elector.

Former method of election. [The electors shall meet in their respective States, and vote by ballot for two persons, of whom one at least shall not be an inhabitant of the same State with themselves. And they shall make a list of all the persons voted for, and of the number of votes for each; which list they shall sign and certify, and transmit sealed to the seat of the government of the United States, directed to the president of the Senate. The president of the Senate shall, in the presence of the Senate and House of Representatives, open all the certificates, and the votes shall then be counted. The person having the greatest number of votes shall be the President, if such number be a majority of the whole number of electors appointed; and if there be more than one who have such majority, and have an equal number of votes, then the House of Representatives shall immediately choose by ballot one of them for President; and if no person have a majority, then from the five highest on the list the said house shall in like manner choose the President. But in choosing the President, the votes shall be taken by States, the representation from each State having one vote; a quorum for this purpose shall consist of a member or members from two thirds of the States, and a majority of all the States shall be necessary to a choice. In every case, after the choice of the President, the person having the greatest number of votes of the electors shall be the Vice-President. But if there should remain two or more who have equal votes, the Senate shall choose from them by ballot the Vice-President.]

3. *Time of choosing electors*. The Congress may determine the time of choosing the electors, and the day on which they shall give their votes; which day shall be the same throughout the United States.

4. *Qualifications of the President.* No person except a natural born citizen, or a citizen of the United States, at the time of the adoption of this Constitution, shall be eligible to the office of President; neither shall any person be eligible to that office who shall not have attained to the age of thirty-five years, and been fourteen years a resident within the United States.

5. *Vacancy*. In case of the removal of the President from office, or of his death, resignation, or inability to discharge the powers and duties of the said office, the same shall devolve on the Vice-President, and the Congress may by law provide for the case of removal, death, resignation, or inability, both of the President and Vice-President, declaring what officer shall then act as President, and such officer shall act accordingly, until the disability be removed, or a President shall be elected.

6. *Salary*. The President shall, at stated times, receive for his services a compensation, which shall neither be increased nor diminished during the period for which he shall have been elected, and he shall not receive within that period any other emolument from the United States, or any of them.

7. *Oath*. Before he enter on the execution of his office, he shall take the following oath or affirmation:—"I do solemnly swear (or affirm) that I will faithfully execute the office of President of the United States, and will to the best of my ability, preserve, protect, and defend the Constitution of the United States."

Section 2

POWERS OF THE PRESIDENT
1. *Military powers; reprieves and pardons.* The President shall be commander in chief of the army and navy of the United States, and of the militia of the several States, when called into the actual service of the United States; he may require the opinion, in writing, of the principal officer in each of the executive departments, upon any subject relating to the duties of their respective offices, and he shall have power to grant reprieves and pardons for offenses against the United States, except in cases of impeachment.

2. *Treaties; appointments*. He shall have power, by and with the advice and consent of the Senate, to make treaties, provided two thirds of the senators present concur; and he shall nominate, and by and with the advice and consent of the Senate, shall appoint ambassadors, other public ministers and consuls, judges of the Supreme Court, and all other officers of the United States, whose appointments are not herein otherwise provided for, and which shall be established by law: but the Congress may by law vest the appointment of such inferior officers, as they think proper, in the President alone, in the courts of law, or in the heads of departments.

3. *Filling of vacancies*. The President shall have power to fill up all vacancies that may happen during the recess of the Senate, by granting commissions which shall expire at the end of their next session.

Section 3

DUTIES OF THE PRESIDENT
He shall from time to time give to the Congress information of the state of the Union, and recommend to their consideration such measures as he shall judge necessary and expedient; he may, on extraordinary occasions, convene both Houses, or either of them, and in case of disagreement between them with respect to the time of adjournment, he may adjourn them to such time as he shall think proper; he shall receive ambassadors and other public ministers; he shall take care that the laws be faithfully executed, and shall commission all the officers of the United States.

Section 4

IMPEACHMENT
The President, Vice-President, and all civil officers of the United States, shall be removed from office on impeachment for, and conviction of, treason, bribery, or other high crimes and misdemeanors.

Article III

JUDICIAL DEPARTMENT

Section 1

FEDERAL COURTS

The judicial power of the United States shall be vested in one Supreme Court, and in such inferior courts as the Congress may from time to time ordain and establish. The judges, both of the Supreme and inferior courts, shall hold their offices during good behavior, and shall, at stated times, receive for their services, a compensation which shall not be diminished during their continuance in office.

Section 2

JURISDICTION OF FEDERAL COURTS

1. *Federal courts in general.* The judicial power shall extend to all cases, in law and equity, arising under this Constitution, the laws of the United States, and treaties made, or which shall be made, under their authority;—to all cases affecting ambassadors, other public ministers and consuls;—to all cases of admiralty and maritime jurisdiction;—to controversies to which the United States shall be a party;—to controversies between two or more States;—between a State and citizens of another State;—between citizens of different States,—between citizens of the same State claiming lands under grants of different States, and between a State, or the citizens thereof, and foreign States, citizens or subjects.

2. *Supreme Court.* In all cases affecting ambassadors, other public ministers and consuls, and those in which a State shall be party, the Supreme Court shall have original jurisdiction. In all the other cases before mentioned, the Supreme Court shall have appellate jurisdiction, both as to law and fact, with such exceptions, and under such regulations, as the Congress shall make.

3. *Trials.* The trial of all crimes, except in cases of impeachment, shall be by jury; and such trial shall be held in the State where the said crimes shall have been committed; but when not committed within any State, the trial shall be at such place or places as the Congress may by law have directed.

Section 3

TREASON

1. *Definition.* Treason against the United States, shall consist only in levying war against them, or in adhering to their enemies, giving them aid and comfort. No person shall be convicted of treason unless on the testimony of two witnesses to the same overt act, or on confession in open court.

2. *Punishment.* The Congress shall have power to declare the punishment of treason, but no attainder of treason shall work corruption of blood, or forfeiture except during the life of the person attainted.

Article IV

RELATIONS OF THE STATES

Section 1

PUBLIC RECORDS

Full faith and credit shall be given in each State to the public acts, records, and judicial proceedings of every other State. And the Congress may by general laws prescribe the manner in which such acts, records, and proceedings shall be proved, and the effect thereof.

Section 2

PRIVILEGES OF CITIZENS

1. *Privileges of citizens.* The citizens of each State shall be entitled to all privileges and immunities of citizens in the several States.

2. *Fugitives from justice.* A person charged in any State with treason, felony, or other crime, who shall flee from justice, and be found in another State, shall on demand of the executive authority of the State from which he fled, be delivered up to be removed to the State having jurisdiction of the crime.

3. *Fugitive slaves.* No person held to service or labor in one State, under the laws thereof, escaping into another, shall, in consequence of any law or regulation therein, be discharged from such service or labor, but shall be delivered up on claim of the party to whom such service or labor may be due.

Section 3

NEW STATES AND TERRITORIES

1. *New states.* New States may be admitted by the Congress into this Union; but no new State shall be formed or erected within the jurisdiction of any other State; nor any State be formed by the junction of two or more States, or parts of States, without the consent of the legislatures of the States concerned as well as of the Congress.

2. *Territory and property.* The Congress shall have power to dispose of and make all needful rules and regulations respecting the territory or other property belonging to the United States; and nothing in this

Constitution shall be so construed as to prejudice any claims of the United States, or of any particular State.

Section 4

PROTECTION OF THE STATES

The United States shall guarantee to every State in this Union a republican form of government, and shall protect each of them against invasion; and on application of the legislature, or of the executive (when the legislature cannot be convened), against domestic violence.

Article V

AMENDMENTS

The Congress, whenever two thirds of both Houses shall deem it necessary, shall propose amendments to this Constitution, or, on the application of the legislatures of two thirds of the several States, shall call a convention for proposing amendments, which, in either case, shall be valid to all intents and purposes, as part of this Constitution, when ratified by the legislatures of three fourths of the several States, or by conventions in three fourths thereof, as the one or the other mode of ratification may be proposed by the Congress; Provided that no amendment which may be made prior to the year one thousand eight hundred and eight shall in any manner affect the first and fourth clauses in the ninth section of the first article; and that no State, without its consent, shall be deprived of its equal suffrage in the Senate.

Article VI

THE SUPREME LAW OF THE LAND

1. *Public debt.* All debts contracted and engagements entered into, before the adoption of this Constitution, shall be as valid against the United States under this Constitution, as under the Confederation.

2. *Supreme law of the land.* This Constitution, and the laws of the United States which shall be made in pursuance thereof; and all treaties made, or which shall be made, under the authority of the United States, shall be the supreme law of the land; and the judges in every State shall be bound thereby, anything in the Constitution or laws of any State to the contrary notwithstanding.

3. *Oath.* The senators and representatives before mentioned, and the members of the several State legislatures, and all executive and judicial officers, both of the United States, and of the several States, shall be bound by oath or affirmation to support this Constitution; but no religious test shall ever be re-

quired as a qualification to any office or public trust under the United States.

Article VII

RATIFICATION

OF THE CONSTITUTION

The ratification of the conventions of nine States shall be sufficient for the establishment of this Constitution between the States so ratifying the same.

Done in Convention by the unanimous consent of the States present the seventeenth day of September in the year of our Lord one thousand seven hundred and eighty-seven, and of the independence of the United States of America the twelfth. In witness whereof we have hereunto subscribed our names,

G°: Washington—
Presd.^t and Deputy from Virginia.

(Signed also by thirty-eight other delegates, from twelve states.)

Amendments to the Constitution

Article I

FREEDOM OF RELIGION, SPEECH, AND PRESS

Congress shall make no law respecting an establishment of religion, or prohibiting the free exercise thereof; or abridging the freedom of speech, or of the press; or the right of the people peaceably to assemble, and to petition the government for a redress of grievances.

Article II

RIGHT TO BEAR ARMS

A well regulated militia, being necessary to the security of a free State, the right of the people to keep and bear arms, shall not be infringed.

Article III

QUARTERING OF SOLDIERS

No soldier shall, in time of peace, be quartered in any house, without the consent of the owner, nor in time of war, but in a manner to be prescribed by law.

Article IV

SEARCH WARRANTS

The right of the people to be secure in their persons, houses, papers, and effects, against unreasonable searches and seizures, shall not be violated, and no warrants shall issue, but upon probable cause, supported by oath or affirmation, and particularly describing the place to be searched, and the persons or things to be seized.

Article V
RIGHTS IN CRIMINAL CASES

No person shall be held to answer for a capital, or otherwise infamous, crime, unless on a presentment or indictment of a grand jury, except in cases arising in the land or naval forces, or in the militia, when in actual service in time of war or public danger; nor shall any person be subject for the same offense to be twice put in jeopardy of life or limb; nor shall be compelled in any criminal case to be a witness against himself, nor be deprived of life, liberty, or property, without due process of law; nor shall private property be taken for public use without just compensation.

Article VI
RIGHTS IN CRIMINAL CASES

In all criminal prosecutions, the accused shall enjoy the right to a speedy and public trial, by an impartial jury of the State and district wherein the crime shall have been committed, which district shall have been previously ascertained by law, and to be informed of the nature and cause of the accusation; to be confronted with the witnesses against him; to have compulsory process for obtaining witnesses in his favor, and to have the assistance of counsel for his defense.

Article VII
RIGHT OF TRIAL BY JURY

In suits at common law, where the value in controversy shall exceed twenty dollars, the right of trial by jury shall be preserved, and no fact tried by a jury shall be otherwise reexamined in any court of the United States, than according to the rules of the common law.

Article VIII
BAIL, FINES, PUNISHMENT

Excessive bail shall not be required, nor excessive fines imposed, nor cruel and unusual punishments inflicted.

Article IX
RIGHTS RESERVED BY THE PEOPLE

The enumeration in the Constitution of certain rights shall not be construed to deny or disparage others retained by the people.

Article X
POWERS RESERVED TO THE STATES

The powers not delegated to the United States by the Constitution, nor prohibited by it to the States, are reserved to the States respectively, or to the people.

Article XI
SUITS AGAINST STATES
(Amendment to Article III, Section 2, Clause 1)

The judicial power of the United States shall not be construed to extend to any suit in law or equity, commenced or prosecuted against one of the United States, by citizens of another State, or by citizens or subjects of any foreign State.

Article XII
ELECTION OF PRESIDENT
AND VICE-PRESIDENT
(Amendment to Article II, Section I, Clause 2)

The electors shall meet in their respective States, and vote by ballot for President and Vice-President, one of whom, at least, shall not be an inhabitant of the same State with themselves; they shall name in their ballots the person voted for as President, and in distinct ballots the person voted for as Vice-President, and they shall make distinct lists of all persons voted for as President and of all persons voted for as Vice-President, and of the number of votes for each, which lists they shall sign and certify, and transmit sealed to the seat of government of the United States, directed to the president of the Senate;—The president of the Senate shall, in the presence of the Senate and House of Representatives, open all the certificates and the votes shall then be counted;—The person having the greatest number of votes for President shall be the President, if such number be a majority of the whole number of electors appointed; and if no person have such majority, then from the persons having the highest numbers not exceeding three on the list of those voted for as President, the House of Representatives shall choose immediately, by ballot, the President. But in choosing the President, the votes shall be taken by States, the representation from each State having one vote; a quorum for this purpose shall consist of a member or members from two thirds of the States, and a majority of all the States shall be necessary to a choice. And if the House of Representatives shall not choose a President whenever the right of choice shall devolve upon them, [before the fourth day of March next following,] then the Vice-President shall act as President, as in the case of the death or other constitutional disability of the President. The person having the greatest number of votes as Vice-President shall be the Vice-President, if such number be a majority of the whole number of electors appointed, and if no person have a majority, then from the two highest numbers on the list, the Senate shall choose the Vice-President; a quorum for the purpose shall consist of two thirds of the whole number of senators, and a majority of the whole number shall be necessary to a choice. But no person constitutionally ineligible to the office of President shall be eligible to that of Vice-President of the United States.

Article XIII
ABOLITION OF SLAVERY
Section 1
Neither slavery nor involuntary servitude, except as a punishment for crime whereof the party shall have been duly convicted, shall exist within the United States, or any place subject to their jurisdiction.

Section 2
Congress shall have power to enforce this article by appropriate legislation.

Article XIV
CIVIL RIGHTS
Section 1
Protection of political privileges. All persons born or naturalized in the United States, and subject to the jurisdiction thereof, are citizens of the United States and of the State wherein they reside. No State shall make or enforce any law which shall abridge the privileges or immunities of citizens of the United States; nor shall any State deprive any person of life, liberty, or property, without due process of law; nor deny to any person within its jurisdiction the equal protection of the laws.

Section 2
Apportionment of representatives. Representatives shall be apportioned among the several States according to their respective numbers, counting the whole number of persons in each State, excluding Indians not taxed. But when the right to vote at any election for the choice of electors for President and Vice-President of the United States, representatives in Congress, the executive and judicial officers of a State, or the members of the legislature thereof, is denied to any of the male inhabitants of such State, being twenty-one years of age, and citizens of the United States, or in any way abridged, except for participation in rebellion, or other crime, the basis of representation therein shall be reduced in the proportion which the number of such male citizens shall bear to the whole number of male citizens twenty-one years of age in such State.

Section 3
Loss of political privileges. No person shall be a senator or representative in Congress, or elector of President and Vice-President, or hold any office, civil or military, under the United States, or under any State, who, having previously taken an oath, as a member of Congress, or as an officer of the United States, or as a member of any State legislature, or as an executive or judicial officer of any State, to support the Constitution of the United States, shall have engaged in insurrection or rebellion against the same, or given aid or comfort to the enemies thereof. But Congress may by a vote of two thirds of each House, remove such disability.

Section 4
Public debt. The validity of the public debt of the United States, authorized by law, including debts incurred for payment of pensions and bounties for services in suppressing insurrection or rebellion, shall not be questioned. But neither the United States nor any State shall assume or pay any debt or obligation incurred in aid of insurrection or rebellion against the United States, or any claim for the loss or emancipation of any slave; but all such debts, obligations, and claims shall be held illegal and void.

Section 5
Enforcement. The Congress shall have power to enforce, by appropriate legislation, the provisions of this article.

Article XV
NEGRO SUFFRAGE
Section 1
Right to vote. The right of citizens of the United States to vote shall not be denied or abridged by the United States or by any State on account of race, color, or previous condition of servitude.

Section 2
Enforcement. The Congress shall have power to enforce this article by appropriate legislation.

Article XVI

INCOME TAXES

The Congress shall have power to lay and collect taxes on incomes, from whatever source derived, without apportionment among the several States, and without regard to any census or enumeration.

Article XVII

DIRECT ELECTION OF SENATORS

(Amendment to Article I, Section 3, Clauses 1 and 2)

The Senate of the United States shall be composed of two senators from each State, elected by the people thereof, for six years; and each senator shall have one vote. The electors in each State shall have the qualifications requisite for electors of the most numerous branch of the State legislatures.

When vacancies happen in the representation of any State in the Senate, the executive authority of such State shall issue writs of election to fill such vacancies: *Provided,* That the legislature of any State may empower the executive thereof to make temporary appointments until the people fill the vacancies by election as the legislature may direct.

Article XVIII

PROHIBITION OF LIQUOR

Section 1

After one year from the ratification of this article the manufacture, sale, or transportation of intoxicating liquors within, the importation thereof into, or the exportation thereof from the United States and all territory subject to the jurisdiction thereof for beverage purposes is hereby prohibited.

Section 2

The Congress and the several States shall have concurrent power to enforce this article by appropriate legislation.

Section 3

This article shall be inoperative unless it shall have been ratified as an amendment to the Constitution by the legislatures of the several States, as provided in the Constitution, within seven years from the date of the submission hereof to the States by the Congress.

Article XIX

WOMAN SUFFRAGE

Section 1

The right of citizens of the United States to vote shall not be denied or abridged by the United States or by any State on account of sex.

Section 2

Congress shall have power, by appropriate legislation, to enforce the provisions of this article.

Article XX

TERMS OF PRESIDENT AND CONGRESS

Section 1

The terms of the President and Vice-President shall end at noon on the 20th day of January, and the terms of senators and representatives at noon on the 3d day of January, of the years in which such terms would have ended if this article had not been ratified; and the terms of their successors shall then begin.

Section 2

The Congress shall assemble at least once in every year, and such meeting shall begin at noon on the 3d day of January, unless they shall by law appoint a different day.

Section 3

If, at the time fixed for the beginning of the term of the President, the President-elect shall have died, the Vice-President-elect shall become President. If a President shall not have been chosen before the time fixed for the beginning of his term, or if the President-elect shall have failed to qualify, then the Vice-President-elect shall act as President until a President shall have qualified; and the Congress may by law provide for the case wherein neither a President-elect nor a Vice-President-elect shall have qualified, declaring who shall then act as President, or the manner in which one who is to act shall be selected, and such persons shall act accordingly until a President or Vice-President shall have qualified.

Section 4

The Congress may by law provide for the case of the death of any of the persons from whom the House of Representatives may choose a President whenever the right of choice shall have devolved upon them, and for the case of the death of any of the persons from whom the Senate may choose a Vice-President whenever the right of choice shall have devolved upon them.

Section 5

Sections 1 and 2 shall take effect on the 15th day of October following the ratification of this article.

Section 6

This article shall be inoperative unless it shall have been ratified as an amendment to the Constitution by the legislatures of three fourths of the several States within seven years from the date of its submission.

Article XXI
REPEAL OF PROHIBITION OF LIQUOR

Section 1

The eighteenth article of amendment to the Constitution of the United States is hereby repealed.

Section 2

The transportation or importation into any State, Territory, or possession of the United States for delivery or use therein of intoxicating liquors, in violation of the laws thereof, is hereby prohibited.

Section 3

This article shall be inoperative unless it shall have been ratified as an amendment to the Constitution by conventions in the several States, as provided in the Constitution, within seven years from the date of submission hereof to the States by the Congress.

Article XXII
PRESIDENT LIMITED TO
TWO TERMS OF OFFICE
(Amendment to Article II, Section 1, Clause 1)

Section 1

No person shall be elected to the office of the President more than twice, and no person who has held the office of President, or acted as President, for more than two years of a term to which some other person was elected President shall be elected to the office of the President more than once. But this article shall not apply to any person holding the office of President when this article was proposed by the Congress, and shall not prevent any person who may be holding the office of President, or acting as President, during the term within which this article becomes operative from holding the office of President or acting as President during the remainder of such term.

Section 2

This article shall be inoperative unless it shall have been ratified as an amendment to the Constitution by the legislatures of three fourths of the several States within seven years from the date of its submission to the States by the Congress.

Article XXIII
SUFFRAGE FOR DISTRICT OF COLUMBIA
IN ELECTION OF PRESIDENT
AND VICE-PRESIDENT
(Amendment to Article II, Section 1)

Section 1

The District constituting the seat of Government of the United States shall appoint in such manner as the Congress may direct:

A number of electors of President and Vice-President equal to the whole number of senators and representatives in Congress to which the District would be entitled if it were a State, but in no event more than the least populous State; they shall be in addition to those appointed by the States, but they shall be considered, for the purposes of the election of President and Vice-President, to be electors appointed by a State; and they shall meet in the District and perform such duties as provided by the twelfth article of amendment.

Section 2

The Congress shall have power to enforce this article by appropriate legislation.

Article XXIV
POLL TAX

Section 1

The right of citizens of the United States to vote in any primary or other election for President or Vice-President, for electors for President or Vice-President, or for senator or representative in Congress, shall not be denied or abridged by the United States or any state by reason of failure to pay any poll tax or other tax.

Section 2

The Congress shall have the power to enforce this article by appropriate legislation.

Article XXV
PRESIDENTIAL DISABILITY
AND SUCCESSION
(Amendment to Article II, Section 1, Clause 5)

Section 1

In case of the removal of the President from office or his death or resignation, the Vice-President shall become President.

Section 2

Whenever there is a vacancy in the office of the Vice-President, the President shall nominate a Vice-President who shall take the office upon confirmation by a majority vote of both houses of Congress.

Section 3

Whenever the President transmits to the President pro tempore of the Senate and the Speaker of the House of Representatives his written declaration that he is unable to discharge the powers and duties of his office, and until he transmits to them a written declaration to the contrary, such powers and duties shall be discharged by the Vice-President as Acting President.

Section 4

Whenever the Vice-President and a majority of either the principal officers of the executive departments or of such other body as Congress may by law provide, transmit to the President pro tempore of the Senate and the Speaker of the House of Representatives their written declaration that the President is unable to discharge the powers and duties of his office, the Vice-President shall immediately assume the powers and duties of the office as Acting President.

Thereafter, when the President transmits to the President pro tempore of the Senate and the Speaker of the House of Representatives his written declaration that no inability exists, he shall resume the powers and duties of his office unless the Vice-President and a majority of either the principal officers of the executive department or of such other body as Congress may by law provide, transmit within four days to the President pro tempore of the Senate and the Speaker of the House of Representatives their written declaration that the President is unable to discharge the powers and duties of his office. Thereupon Congress shall decide the issue, assembling within 48 hours for that purpose if not in session. If the Congress, within 21 days after receipt of the latter written declaration, or, if Congress is not in session, within 21 days after Congress is required to assemble, determines by two-thirds vote of both houses that the President is unable to discharge the powers and duties of his office, the Vice-President shall continue to discharge the same as Acting President; otherwise, the President shall resume the powers and duties of his office.

Article XXVI

VOTING AGE LOWERED TO EIGHTEEN

Section 1

The right of citizens of the United States, who are eighteen years of age or older, to vote shall not be denied or abridged by the United States or any state on account of age.

Section 2

The Congress shall have the power to enforce this article by appropriate legislation.

Index

Page numbers which refer to illustrations are in *italic* type.

Carlyle, Thomas, 3
Carmichael, Stokely, 758
Carnegie, Andrew, 240–42
Carnegie Institute of Technology, 242
Carnegie Steel Co., 241–42, 243, 253, 260
Carolinas, 19, 31–32, 333. *See also* North Carolina; South Carolina.
Caroline Islands, 587, 588
Carousel, 629
Carpenter, Malcolm Scott, 687, 725
Carpenter's Hall, Phila., 50
carpetbaggers, 194, 228
carpetbag governments, 195–97, 285, 289, 297, 301
Carranza, Venustiano, 385
Carroll, Diahann, 758
Carson, Kit, 336
Carson, Rachel, 759, 761
Carson City, Nev., 331
Carswell, G. Harrold, 775
Carter, Jimmy, 790; early career, 792; election of 1976, *791–93*
Cartier, Jacques, 19
cartographers, *13*, 14, 15, 16
Carver, George Washington, 273
Casablanca Conference, 587, 604
Casa Grandes, Mexico, *12*
Cascina, Italy, *599*
Case, Francis P., 675
Cash, Johnny, 760
Cashtown, Pa., 165
Cass, Lewis, 126, 131
Cassatt, Mary, 283
caste system, Indian, 10
Castile, Spain, 8
Castro, Fidel, 707, *710–11*, 787; Bay of Pigs, 727–29; missile crisis, 733–35
Catch-22 (Heller), 761
Cather, Willa, 400
Catholic-baiting, 479
Catholic church, *see* Roman Catholic church.
Catholic Sovereigns, 17–18
cattle industry, 342–43
caucus, congressional, 97
CCC, *see* Civilian Conservation Corps.
Cedar Creek, Va., 169
Celebrated Jumping Frog of Calaveras County, The (Twain), 282
Cemetery Ridge, 165
censorship, wartime, 446–47
census: (1850), 136; (1860), 136; (1890), 324; (1910), 396; (1940), 626; (1950), 626
Census, Bureau of, 428
CENTO, *see* Central Treaty Organization.
Central America, 10, 18, 41, 44

Central City, Colo., 327
Central Intelligence Agency (CIA), 622, 662, 707, 710, 726, 728, 774, 787
Central Pacific Rrd., 218–21
Central Treaty Organization (CENTO), 696
Century of Dishonor, A (Jackson), 339–40
certificates of indebtedness, 67
Cervera y Topete, Pascual, 376–78
Ceylon, 44, 703
Chaffee, Roger B., 755
Chamberlain, Wilt, 761
Chambers, Whittaker, 652, 765
Chamoun, Camille, 696
Champs-Elysées, 450
Chancellorsville, Battle of, 164, 167
Charles I, King of England, 25, 26, 31
Charles II, King of England, 28, 30, 31
Charleston, S.C., 69, 100, 141, 143, 414; in American Revolution, 57, 62; in Civil War, 146, 171; colonial, 37, 39; founding of, 31
Charleston, W. Va., 206, 207
Charlestown, Mass., 26
Charles Town, Va., 141
Charlotte, Queen of England, 58
Charlotte, N.C., 420
Charlottesville, Va., 62
Charter of Privileges, 31
charters, colonial, 22, 59
Chase, Salmon P., 190, 291
Château-Thierry, 453, 455
Chattahoochee River, 167
Chattanooga, 201; Battle of, 166–67
Chautauqua, 349
Chavez, Cesar, 759
check-off (union), 622
checks and balances, 190
Chemin des Dames, 449, 450, 452
chemistry, 14, 107
Chengte, Jehol Province, Manchuria, 547
Cherokee Indians, *12*, 94, 99, 100, 334, 336
Chesapeake (frigate), 82
Chesapeake and Ohio Canal, 218
Chesapeake and Ohio Rrd., 224, 243
Chesapeake Bay, 22, 58, 62, 86, 155, 224
Chesnutt, Charles Waddell, 283
Chevrolet, 485, 504, 760
Cheyenne Indians, 336
Chiang Kai-shek, 546, 561, 588, 604–06, 635, 643–46, 652, 698–99, 772
Chicago, Ill., 170, 186, 260, 266, 355, 422, 487, 509; Democratic convention of 1968, 753,

776; politics, 313; population, 271–72; railroads, 220–21, 224, 220, sanitation, 277; South Side, 625; transportation, 274
Chicago and North Western Rrd., 220
Chicago, Burlington and Quincy Rrd., 220, 413
Chicago, Burlington & Quincy R.R. v. Iowa, 231
Chicago 8, 776
Chicago, Rock Island, and Pacific R.R., 220
Chicago 7, 776
Chicago *Tribune*, 183, 520
Chicanos, 759
Chickamauga, Battle of, 166, 306
Chickasaw Indians, 334, 336
Chief Joseph, *339*
child labor, 257, 261, 279, 396, *407*, 424, 500, 515
Child Labor Act, 491
Children's Bureau, 419
Chile, 372, 385, 642, 774
Chilkat Tlingit Indians, 20
China, 235, 486, 772; Boxer Rebellion, 387; Chiang *v.* Mao, 644–45; communism in, 643–46, 652, 697; dollar diplomacy, 389; immigrants from, 219, 267, 269, 308; and Japan, 370, 388–89, 541, 545–48, *551–52*, 563; long march, 644; medieval trade with, 15–16; Nationalist, *see* Nationalist China; Open Door policy, 386–87, 541–42; post-World War II, 645–46; trade treaty, 114; in World War II, 587, 588, 592, 606, 645. *See also* People's Republic of China.
Chinese Exclusion Act, 269
Chisholm, Shirley, 758
Chisholm Trail, 342
Choctaw Indians, 334, 336
Chou En-lai, 699, 773
Christianity: and ecumenism, 758; in Middle Ages, 14–15; and slavery, 39–40
"Christmas bombing," 780
Christy, Howard Chandler, *435*
Chrysler Corp., 525
Church, Frank, 750
church and state, separation of, 28, 59, 743
Churches of God, 628
Churchill, Winston, 582; Atlantic Conference, *559–60*, 570; destroyer deal, 557–58; Iron Curtain speech, 634; Potsdam Conference, 592,

605, 607–08; wartime conferences, 604–05; Yalta Conference, 603, 605–06
CIA, *see* Central Intelligence Agency.
Cibola, 18
Cicero, 2
Cicero, Ill., 625
Cienfuegos Naval Base, Cuba, 710
cigarette: industry, 233; smoking, 712, 745, 775
Cigarmakers' Union, 259
Cincinnati, Ohio, 105, 134, 159, 224, 264, 272, 300, 319, 352, 415, 416–17, 447
Cincinnati Law School, 353, 416
CIO, *see* Congress of Industrial Organizations.
cities: advantages of, 281–82; colonial, 37–38; communication in, 275; decay, 627; growth of, 271–72, 405–06; housing, 278–79; immigration and, 272; and industry, 249, 271; lighting in, 276–77; migrations to, 234, 253, 272–73, 597; nineteenth-century, 106; pollution, 277–78; population, 271–72, 398; post-World War II, 627; rioting in, 752, 759; and suburban growth, 627, 712; traffic and transportation, 273–75; water and waste, 277–78; women in, 281
citizenship: black Americans, 139; Fourteenth Amendment, 185–86; Indians and, 185; Puerto Ricans, 392; territories and, 380, 390
civil disobedience, 52, 683
Civilian Conservation Corps (CCC), 521–22, 523, 530
civilization: Eastern, 14; European, 15; and pragmatism, 405
civil liberties, 67, 183, 198, 483
civil rights, 185, 187, *189*, 196, 623–24, 679–82, 723–25, 738, 739, 743, 752, 758–59
Civil Rights acts: (1866), 185, 187, *189*; (1957), 682, 743; (1960), 682, 743; (1964), 196, 739; (1968), 624, 752, 753
Civil Rights Commission, 624, 682
Civil service, 319–20; list, 309, 315; reform, 308–09; and spoils system, 290, 301, 308
Civil Service Commission, 309, 315, 320, 411, 417
Civil War, *113*, *148*, 306, 319, 364; beginning of,

143; behind the lines, 160–64; black Americans, 158, 160–61, *205*, 206; blockade, 146, 156, 162, 163; campaigns, 149–50, 153–59, 164–72; comparison of North and South, 146, 148; conscription, 160, 242, 314; consequences of, 146; Copperheads, 159, 161, 170; cost of, 146; demobilization, 181, 183; diplomacy, 150–51, 158, 162; disloyalty, 161; in East, 154–58; and election of 1864, 169–70; Emancipation Proclamation, 158–59; end of, 172–73; equipment, 163, 214; financing, 149, 161, 220, 286; foreign aid, 146, 150–51; Indians in, 336; industry during, 146, 163, 214, 238; internal politics, 151; Lincoln's contribution, 148–49; morale, 150, 156; naval war, 148, 151, 154, 155, 162, 168; objective of, 143; prisons and prisoners, 161, *163–64*; purpose of, 146, 148; secession, 142–43; strategy, 149–50; subversion, 161–62; transportation, 240; turning point, 164–65; veterans of, 315–16, 320; in West, 153–54, 159, 171; wounded, 157, 164. *See also* Confederate Army; Confederate States of America; North (Union side in Civil War); reconstruction, names of armies and battles.
Civil Works Administration (CWA), 519
Clark, Beauchamp ("Champ"), 421
Clark, George Rogers, 62, 69, 80
Clark, J. Reuben, 554
Clark, Mark, 575
Clark, William, 80
Clark & Rockefeller, 238
Clark Field, Philippines, 583
Clark memorandum, 554
Clay, Cassius M., *see* Ali.
Clay, Henry: American System, 87, 114; Bank of the U.S., 101; Compromise of 1850, 128–29; election of 1824, 93; and slavery, 118, 128; and tariffs, 100; and J. Tyler, 114; and warhawks, 85; Whig party, 114, 122, 138
Clearwater River, 80
Cleaver, Eldridge, 761
Clemenceau, Georges, 464, 466

Clemens, Samuel L. (Mark Twain), 282–83
Clemente, Roberto, 761
Clermont (steamboat), 106
Cleveland, Grover, 245, 311, 411; campaign of 1884, 313; defeated for presidency, 317–18; early career, 314; election of 1892, 352–53; first administration, 314–17; gold crisis, 354–55; and Hawaii, 370; and immigration, 270; second administration, 320, 353–55; and tariff, 354
Cleveland, Ohio, 186, 238–39, 266, 272, 406, 493, 531, 758
Cleveland *Browns*, 712
Clinton, George, 69
Clinton, Henry, 61–62
Clinton, N.Y., 314
closed shop, 254, 255, 622
coal, 228, 232; industry, 224, 232, 476, 500; "roads," 224; strikes, 414
Cobb, Frank I., 428
Cobb, Ty, 400
Coburg, Nebr., *345*
Cochin China, 700
Cody, William ("Buffalo Bill"), 338
Coercive laws, 50
Cohens v. *Virginia*, 88
Cohn, Roy, 670
coins: gold, 513; silver, 303. *See also* currency; money.
Cold Harbor, Battle of, 168
cold war, 633–34, 639, 726
Colfax, Schuyler, 292
collective bargaining, 261, 473, 514, 515
College of William and Mary, 76, 88, 89, 114
colleges: black, 204, 207–08, *626*; land-grant, 161; segregation in, 626, 680, 723–24. *See also* education; schools.
Collier, John, 528
Collier's, 419, 629
Collins, Michael, 767
Cologne, Germany, 581
Colombia, 105–06, 380–93
colonies, black, 118
colonies, Dutch, 28–30, 39
colonies, English: agriculture, 23–25, 31, 34; cities, 37–38; early, 19, 21–22; economy of, 23, 32, 44; education in, 27; government, 30, 44, 46, 48–49; industry, 34–36; labor in, 36–37; religion, 24–28, 30, 39–40; slavery, 24–25, 27, 36–37; trade in, 27, 29, 31–32; transportation, 34; wars, 46–48. *See also* names of colonies.
colonies, French, 19, 41,

46, 47–48
colonies, Spanish, 18–19, 32, *41*, 63, 64, 70, 92, 96
Colorado, 18, 123, 128, 336, 341; agriculture, 342; mining, 327–28; statehood, 320, 345
Colorado River, *121*, 507
Colorado Springs, Colo., 678, *693*
Colored American Magazine, 414
Colt, Samuel, 107
Columbia (command module), 767
Columbia, S.C., 420
Columbia River, 80, 524
Columbia University, 508, 668
Columbus, Christopher, 8, 16–18
Columbus, N.M., 385
Columbus, Ohio, 272
Comanche Indians, 336
commerce, *see* trade.
Commerce, Department of, 491, 497, 500
Commerce and Labor, Department of, 413
Committee for Industrial Organizations, 525
Committee of Correspondence, 50
Committee on Public Information, 446
Commodity Credit Corporation, 512
commodity price index, 513
common law, 23
Common Market, 721
Common Sense (Paine), 52
communication: cities, 275–76; in Civil War, 151; in colonies, 55; satellites, 721; telegraph, 122, *160*, 168, 220, 231, 236, 276, 331; telephone, 236, 275–76. *See also* mail.
Communications Satellite Act, 721
Communists and communism, 3, 279; Bolshevik revolution, 439, 458, 476; in China, 643–46, 652, 697, 772, 789; cold war, 633–34, 639, 726; in Cuba, 707, 710–11; in Europe, 633–34, 637–41; in Latin America, 641–42, 706–07, 710–11, 727, 774; McCarthyism, 656, 658–59; "red scare," 476–78; in Vietnam, 700–01, 750, 752, 768, 779, 788; in Yugoslavia, 633, 642–43
comparative advantage, 231, 252
compass, 15
competition (business), 214, 229, 231, 244, 246, 249; and NRA, 514; and tariffs, 309, 316
Compiègne Forest, 455, 460

Compromise of 1820, *see* Missouri Compromise.
Compromise of 1850, 128, 129, 130–31, 134, 327
Compton, Arthur and Karl, 594
computers, 712, 755
Comstock, Henry T. P., 327
Comstock Lode, 233, 303, 327
Conant, James B., 594
concentration camps, 581–82
"Concerto in F" (Gershwin), 488
Concord, Mass., 51
Confederate army, *113*, 149; black troops in, 161; morale, 156; prison camps, 163–64. *See also* Civil War; Confederate States of America; North (Union side in Civil War); Union Army; names of specific armies and battles.
"Confederate" reconstruction, 181–87, 194, 196, 197, 203
Confederate States of America, *113*; advantages, 149; and blockade, 146, 156, 163; constitution of, 142; creation of, 116, 142; diplomacy, 150–51; finances, 146; industry, 146; last days of, 171–73; navy, 148; population of, 146; post-war, 181–82; transportation, 146–48. *See also* Civil War; Confederate army; North (Union side in Civil War); reconstruction; Union Army.
Confederation Congress, 63–64, 66, 76, 83, 89, 117
Confederation Period, 63
Confiscation Act, 158
Congo, 731–32
Congregational church, 39, 40
Congress, Continental, *see* First Continental Congress; Second Continental Congress.
Congress, Stamp Act, 49
Congress, U.S., 4; black Americans in, *193*, 758; and immigration, 271; and Indians, 335, 340; interstate commerce, 231; and labor, 261; Missouri Compromise, 91–92; and Nixon, 775–76; and railroads, 219; during Reconstruction, 181, 191, 196; salary grab, 292; and slavery, 128, 136. *See also* House of Representatives; Senate.
Congressional Globe, 4
Congressional Record, 4

Congress of Industrial Organizations (CIO), 259; AFL merger, 623, 674; creation of, 525

Congress on Racial Equality (CORE), 758

Conjure Woman, The (Chesnutt), 283

Conkling, Roscoe, 301, 303, 308, 320

Connecticut, 189; colonial, 39, *41;* settlement of, 28

Connecticut Compromise, 65

Connecticut River and Valley, 28, 29, 30, 332

Connelly, Marc, 488

conscription: Civil War, 160, 161, 242; peacetime, 570; World War I, 443–44

conservation: Ballinger-Pinchot controversy, 418–19; New Deal and, 521–22; T. Roosevelt and, 414; soil banks, 673; TVA, 522–24, 530, 675

Constantinople, 16

Constitution (frigate), 85

Constitution, U.S.: amendments to, 66, 67, 83; and Articles of Confederation, 63; Bill of Rights, 66, 67, 83; and citizenship, 185–86, 380; 389–90; and Congress, 184; *Federalist* and, 66; framing of, 65; and impeachment, 190; and internal improvements, 87; and post offices, 65; and president, 65–66, 162, 621; and property, 230; ratification of, 66, 88, 89; and Reconstruction, 179; rigid interpretation of, 114; signers, 53; slavery and, 65, 159, 183; suffrage and, 186, 188, 196, 198; and taxation, 65; and trade, 65; and treaties, 65; and vice-president, 70, 621

Constitutional Amendments, *see* amendments, by number.

Constitutional Convention, 65–66, 83

Constitution Hall, Wash., D.C., 529, 530

constitutions, state, 59, 96, *133,* 178, 180, 184, 188, 195, 358

consumer protection, 760

Consumer Protection Agency, 775

Continental Army, 54, 61, 67; black soldiers in, 56–57; G. Washington and, 51, *56,* 71. *See also* American Revolution.

Continental Congress, *see* First Continental Congress; *see also* Second

Continental Congress.

Continental system, 82

conventions, political, 97. *See also* elections.

convicts: in colonies, 36; labor, 256, 257, 258

convoy system, 448, 560

Cook, James, 369

Cooke, Jay, 220, 243

Cooley, Denton, 755

Coolidge, Calvin, *493;* and election of 1920, 472, 473; election of 1924, 493; president, 492–94, 542

Coolidge, William D., 400

cooling-off period, 622

Cooper, Gary, 629

Cooper, James Fenimore, 108

Cooper, Leroy Gordon, Jr., 687, 725, 754

Cooper, Peter, 350

cooperatives, farm, 502

Copperheads, 159, 161, 170, 285, 288

Coral Sea, Battle of, 585

CORE, *see* Congress on Racial Equality.

Corinth, Miss., 154

Cornell University, 513

Cornstalk, 333

Cornwallis, Lord, 57, 62, 76

Coronado, Francisco Vásquez de, 18

corporate colony, 25

corporate state, 505

corporations, 239–46, 755; control of, 357, 426; and labor, 252, 408; profits, 485, 500; and strikes, 253; T. Roosevelt and, 412. *See also* business.

Corporations, Bureau of, 413

Corregidor, 376, 584, 590

"corrupt bargain," 93

corruption: national government, 286, 290–93, 406, 491; railroads, 219, 228–30; state government, 310–11

Cosby, Bill, 758

Cosmopolitan, 408

Costa Rica, 18

cotton: and Civil War, 146, 150–51; and slavery, 117

cotton gin, 117

cotton picker, 487

cotton plowup (1933), 516

cotton states, 141, 155

Cotton States and International Exposition, 208

Cotulla, Tex., 737

Coughlin, Charles E., 505, 531

Coughlin, John J. ("Bathhouse John"), 313

Council of Foreign Ministers, 607

Council of National Defense, 445

Cousey, Bob, 713

cowboy diplomacy, 383

cowboys, 342, 345, 378

Cowpens, Battle of, 62

Cox, Archibald, 781–83

Cox, James M., 472–73, 490

Coxey, Jacob S., 353, 356

Coxey's Army, 353–54

craftsmen: colonial, 34, 35, 255; and mechanization, 251

craft unions, 255, 259, 260, 525, 530

Crane, Stephen, 283

Crawford, William H., 93

Crazy Horse, 337

credit, 98, 102, 510–12

Crédit Mobilier, 219, 228, 292, 305

creditors, 64, 68

Creek Indians, 94, 96, 334, 336, 348

Creek War, 334

Creel, George, 446

Creoles, 86

"Crime Against Kansas," 134, 184

crime, 775

Crimea, 573, 576, 601

Crimean War, 150, 237, 631

"Crime of '73," 303

Cripple Creek, Colo., 327

Crisis, 401, 456

Cristóbal Colón (ship), 377

Crittenden, John J., 142

Crittenden Compromise, 142

Crocker, Charles, 219

crop lien system, 201

crops, 352; colonial, 34; failures and climate, 516–17; and rainfall, 343, 349; and pesticides, 759; and prices, 349; rotation of, 34; sharing, 200–01; soil conserving, 517–18; soil-depleting, 517; staple, 23, 120, 201; surpluses, 349, 352, 516–17. *See also* Agriculture; names of crops.

Crosby, Bing, 629

"cross of gold," 347, 355

Crozer Theological Seminary, 683

Crum, William D., 414

Crusade in Europe (Eisenhower), 668

Crusades, 14

C. Turner Joy (destroyer), 741

Cuba, 125, 642; Bay of Pigs, 728–29; communism in, .707, 710–11; discovery of, 18; missile crisis, 733–35; Ostend Manifesto, 134; Platt Amendment, 383, 554; refugees, 729; revolt, 296; in Spanish-American War, 373–79; yellow fever, 402–03

Cullen, Countee, 488

Culpeper Minutemen, 87

Culp's Hill, 165

cultures: immigrants, 268–69; Indians, 10, *12, 332;* medieval Europe, 14

Cumberland River, 62, 96, 153–54, 159

cummings, e. e., 488

currency, 59, 97–98, 424; expansion of, 256, 320, 357; Specie Circular, 104; uniform, 308. *See also* coins; money; paper money.

Currency Acts: (1764), 49; (1900), 366, 409

Curtis, Charles, 494, 500, 510

Curzon Line, 605

Custer, George A., 337

Custer's Last Stand, 337–38

Cuyahoga County, Ohio, 306

CWA, *see* Civil Works Administration.

Cyprus, 751

Czechoslovakia: immigrants from, 254, 266; post-World War II, 614, 633, 637, 640, 643; World War I, 458; World War II, 553, 555

Czolgosz, Leon, 270, 410

Dachau, 581

Daimler, Gottlieb, 398

Daiquiri, Cuba, 378

Dairen, Manchuria, 606

Daisy Miller (James), 283

Dakota Territory, 345, 411

Dallas, Tex., 736

Da Nang, Viet., 749, 750, 788

Danbury Hatters' case, 246

Dandelion (gunboat), 171

Danish West Indies, 295, 393

Danzig, 581

"dark horse," 122, 558

Darlan, Jean, 574

Darrow, Clarence, 483–84

Dartmouth College, 184

Darwin, Charles, 214, 216, 404, 483

Darwin, Australia, 584

Darwinian theory: and Scopes trial, 483–84; and Social Darwinism, 214, 216

Daugherty, Harry M., 472, 490, 491

Daughters of Revolution (Wood), *499*

Daughters of the American Revolution, 281, 529

Davidson College, 420

Davis, Jefferson, *113, 132,* 141, 142; and Confederacy, 146, 148, 162, 165, 167, 171, 172, *182*

Davis, John W., 492

Dawes, Charles Gates, 492, 544

Dawes, Will, 51

Dawes Act, 317, 340–41
Dawes Plan, 544
Dawson, Yukon, 328, 329, 392
Day, Benjamin H., 108
Day, William R., *371*
Dayton, Ohio, 401
Dayton, Tenn., 483–84
DDT, 759
Dean, "Dizzy," 506
Dean, John W., III, 781–83
Dearborn *Independent*, 479
Debs, Eugene V., 354, 409, 412, 425, 447
debtors, 32, 36; and deflation, 64; and Great Depression, 504; and greenbacks, 287, 302–03; imprisoning, 97, 108, 195; money question, 302
debts, foreign, 384, 544–45
Decatur, Stephen, 79
Declaration of Independence, 6–7, 52, 54, 65; bicentennial of, 789; drafting of, 61, 76; signers, 105, 319; and slavery, 118
Declaration of Rights and Grievances, 51
Declaratory Act, 49
Deere, John, 107
de facto segregation, 680
Defense, Department of, 621–22
Defense Transportation, Office of, 596
deflation, 64, 512
De Gaulle, Charles, 580, 714, 733
de jure segregation, 680
Delaware, 141, 159, 245, 680; and Civil War, 143; colonial, *41;* settlement of, 28–31
Delaware, Ohio, 300
Delaware Bay, 29
Delaware Indians, 335
Delaware River, 30, 31, 57, 61
demilitarized zone (DMZ), 749–50
democracy: in colonies, 31; Jacksonian, 97; political, 509
Democratic party, 95, 114, 122, 126, 131, 134, 135, 161, 464, 466; in Civil War, 169–70, 178, 285; "free silver," 335; "gold-bug," 353, 356; and immigrants, 264; and Philippines, 394; Reconstruction, 187, 195; split in, 141; and tariff, 310. *See also* elections, presidential.
Democratic - Republican party, 95, 103
Dempsey, Jack, 486
Denmark: and Virgin Islands, 295; in World War II, 556, 559
Denver and Rio Grande

Railroad, 220
Dependent Pension Bill, 316
deportation, 477
depressions, 82, 234, 237, 239, 241, 369; (1819), 90; (1837), 104; (1873), 202; (1893), 221; and immigration, 265; and labor, 256–57; (1920s), 485. *See also* Great Depression; business activity.
Descent of Man (Darwin), 214
Des Moines, Iowa, 751
De Soto, Hernando, 18
destroyer deal, 557–58
détente, 773, 787, 788, 791
Detroit, Mich., 85, 86, 186, 266, 272, 599, 759
Devil's Dictionary, 1
Dewey, George, 376, 396
Dewey, Thomas E., 600, 618, 625, 650
Dias, Bartholomew, 16
Diaz, Porfirio, 384
Dickinson, Emily, 283
Dickinson, John, 59
Dickinson College, 135
"Dick Van Dyke Show," 761
Diem, Ngo Dinh, 702–05, 730–31, 741
Dien Bien Phu, 702
diesel engine, 235
Di Maggio, Joe, 629
diplomacy: in American Revolution, 59; with Asia, 386–89; in Civil War, 150–51, 158, 162; "cowboy," 383; "dollar," 389; Monroe, 92–93; pre-World War II, 561, 563
diplomatic service, 366–67
Dingley Tariff Act, 366
Directory, The, 71, 72
Dirksen, Everett McK., 739
disadvantaged, aid for, 195
disarmament: post-World War I, 541–45, 548; post-World War II, 689–90
Disciples of Christ, 306
discrimination: against Asians, 269; against blacks, 186, 479, 623–25, 722–23, 744, 752; in housing, 724, 752; immigrants, 269–70; in public facilities, 723–24; and religion, 756; against women, 777
disease, 22, 37, 277, 755
disfranchisement, 179, 187, 188, 194, 202–03, 358
Disney, Walt, 486
Displaced Persons Bill, 677–78
District of Columbia, 205, 301; slavery in, 128, 130, 158. *See also* Washington, D.C.
divorce, 195, 777

Dix, Dorothea, *108,* 109
"Dixie," 175
Dixiecrat party, 650
Dixon, Edgar H., 675
Dixon-Yates contract, 675
DMZ, *see* demilitarized zone.
Dnieper River, 576
Dr. Strangelove (Kubrick), 761
Dodge, Grenville, 219
Dodge City, Kans., 347
Doenitz, Karl, 582
Doheny, E. L., 491
Dole, Robert, 791
Dole, Sanford B., *369*
dollar: devaluation of, 513, 775; value of, 302
"dollar diplomacy," 389
Domestic Allotment Act, 517
Dominican Republic, 18, 383–84, 711; U.S. intervention, 745–46
domino theory, 702, 703, 730, 731
Dooley, Mr., 418
Doolittle, James H., 584
Dorchester, Mass., 26, 269
Dos Passos, John, 488, 506
doughboys, 450
"doughface," 134
Douglas, Stephen A., 132–33, 137, 186; election of 1860, 141; Kansas-Nebraska Bill, 132–33, 141; Lincoln debates, 139–40; popular sovereignty, 130, 133, 136, 139
Douglas Aircraft, 506
Douglass, Frederick, 204–05, 206, 208, 301
Dove (ship), 25
Dover, Strait of, 21, 448
"doves," 747, 753
draft, *see* conscription.
Drake, Edwin L., 233, 239
Drake, Francis, 19, 21, 369
drama: Civil War, 160; twentieth-century, 629. *See also* theater.
Dred Scott decision, 136, 139, 140, 141, 185
Dreiser, Theodore, 216, 400, 488
Drew, Daniel, 228–29
Drug Industry Act, 721–22
drugs: abuse, 756, 775; antibiotic, 506, 628; control of, 413–14; 721–22, 756, 760
dry farming, 344
Dubinsky, David, 525
Du Bois, W.E.B., 283, 400, *401,* 428, 456, 488
Duesenberg, 485
Duke University, 765
Dulles, John Foster, 688, 692, 699
Dumbarton Oaks Plan, 601, 605
Dunbar, Paul Laurence, 283
Dunkirk, 566; Treaty of, 640
Dunne, Finley Peter, 418

Du Pont Co., 506
Durant, Thomas C., 219
Durkin, Martin, 673–74
Duryea, Charles E., 236, 398
Duryea, J. Frank, 398
dust bowl, *517*
Dutch East India Company, 28
Dutch East Indies, 28, 561
Dutch Reformed church, 39
Dutch West India Company, 29
Dylan, Bob, 760
dynamo, 235, 274, 276, 277

Eads Bridge, 275
Eagle (lunar module), 767
Eagleton, Thomas F., 779
Eakins, Thomas, 362
Early, Jubal, 168
Eastern Europe, 646; post-World War II, 638; World War I, 459; World War II, 605
Eastern front: World War I, 450, 458–59; World War II, 574–76, 581
East Germany, 638, 688, 690–91, 732
East Jersey, 30
Eastland, James O., 682
Eastman, George B., 236
East Saint Louis, Ill., 275, 456
Eaton, John H., 99
Eaton, Peggy O'Neale, 98–99
Eberton, N.J., 307
ECA, *see* Economic Cooperation Administration.
Eccles, Marriner, 526
Echo I, 686
Economic Cooperation Administration (ECA), 637
Economic Opportunity, Office of, 740
Economic Opportunity Act, 739–40
economics, 3; and foreign policy, 368
economy: and American System, 87, 114; and Civil War, 146, 148; of colonies, 23, 32, 39; and competition, 243–46; and credit, 511; Eisenhower era, 672–73; in Ford era, 787, 789, 791; in "good years," 396, 398; and Great Depression, 503, 507–14, 519; and immigration, 264–65, 266, 269, 271; and industry, 237–38, 249; in Jacksonian era, 101–02; New Deal, 510–14; and Nixon, 775; North/South differences, 146; post-Civil War, 194, 197, 214; post-reconstruction, 200–03; post-

Forrest, Nathan Bedford, 156, 197
Forrestal, James V., 621
Fort Bridger, 331
Fort Detroit, 47
Fort Donelson, 153
Fort Duquesne, 46, 47, 55
Fort Edward, 58
Fort Frontenac, 47
Fort Harrod, 49
Fort Henry, 153
Fort Kearny, 331
Fort Laramie, 331
Fort Leavenworth, 124
Fort Lyon, 336
Fort McHenry, *85*, 86
Fort Morgan, 168, 170
Fort Necessity, 46, *47*
Fort Niagara, 47
Fort Peck Dam, 524
Fort Pickens, 143
Fort Pitt, 62
Fort Ross, 92
Fort Saint Pierre, *41*
Fort Sill, 337
Fort Smith, 330
Fort Stanwix, 58
Fort Sumter, 143, 148, 156
Fort Ticonderoga, 47, 51, 58, 61
Fort Worth, Tex., 736
Fort Yuma, 330
forty-eighters, 264
forty-niners, 326, 327
forty-ninth parallel, 92
Forty-second ("Rainbow") Division, 454, 456
Forty-second Ohio Volunteer Infantry, 306
Foster, William Z., 476
Four Freedoms (Rockwell), 602
Fourteen Points, 459–60, 464, 466, 468
Fourteenth Amendment, 185–86, 187, 188, 196, 230
Fox, George, 30
Fox Indians, 127, 334
Foxx, Jimmy, 506
Foyt, A. J., 761
France, *391*, 772; and American Revolution, 60–61; and Civil War, 162; European Defense Community, 688; Five-Power Treaty, 541–42; Four-Power Treaty, 541–42; B. Franklin and, 60–61; French and Indian War, 46–48; and Great Britain, 46–48, 82; immigrants from, 30; in Indo-China, 583, 587, 697, 700–02; industry, 232; Kellogg-Briand Pact, 543–44; League of Nations, 467; Louisiana Purchase, 89; Macon's Bill No. 2, 84; and Middle East, 694–95; Napoleon I, 80, 84–85, 263–64; Napoleon III, 162, 192; NATO, 640–41, 733; post-World War II, 637; revolution in, 69, 72, 78;

Santo Domingo, 80; SEATO, 703; trade with, 78, 237; Treaty of Alliance (1778), 61, 69; Treaty of Paris (1763), 48; Treaty of Paris (1783), 62–63; Vichy government, 561, 574; World War I, 431, 433–34, 449–59, 464; World War II, 556, 561, 574, 579–80; XYZ affair, 71–72
Francis I, King of France, 19
Francis Ferdinand, Archduke, 431
Franck, James, 594
Franco, Francisco, 551, 574, 688
Franco-Prussian War, 243, 294, 431
Frankenthaler, Helen, 761
Frankfort, Ky., 143, 159
Franklin, Aretha, 760
Franklin, Benjamin, *38*, 216; Albany Plan, 60; Constitutional Convention, 65; Declaration of Independence, 61; in France, 60–61; quoted, 36; scientist, 60; Treaty of Paris, 62–63
Franklin, John Hope, 193
Franklin County, Va., 206
Franklin stove, 60
Fredericksburg, Battle of, 159, *160*
"free breakfast table," 321
Freedmen's Bureau, 181–82, 185, 196–97, 200
Freedom 7, 725
freedom rides, 723
free-enterprise system, 254, 412, 423, 509, 515, 760
Freeport Doctrine, 139–40, 141
free silver, 303, *347*, 353, 355, 357, 409
Free-Soil party, 126, 184
Frémont, John C., 124, 134, 135, 308
French, Daniel Chester, 282
French and Indian War, 44, 55, 60, 333; campaigns, 46–47; causes, 46; results of, 48, 49
French Indo-China, 583, 587, 697, 700–02
French Revolution, 69, 72, 78, 89, 263, 264
Freud, Sigmund, 487
Friedan, Betty, 758, 777
Friendship 7, 755
Frisco, Utah, *346*
frontier: closing of, 324, 346; housing, 345; mining, 324, 326–29; politics on, 327; transportation, 329, 343–44; Washington and, 68. *See also* pioneers; West.
Frost, Robert, 761
Fuchs, Klaus, 652
Fuel Administration, 446

Fugitive Slave Law, 130, 133, 140, 184
Fulbright, J. William, 750
Full Employment Act, 616
Fulton, Robert, 106
Fulton, Mo., 634
fundamentalists, 482–83
fur trade, 28–29, 41, 221

Gable, Clark, 506, 629
Gadsby's Hotel, 98
Gadsden, James, 132
Gadsden Purchase, 132, 221
Gagarin, Yuri, 725
Galbraith, John Kenneth, 712
Galena, Ill., 153
Gall, 337
Gama, da, Vasco, 16
Gandhi, Mohandas K., 683
GAR, *see* Grand Army of the Republic.
Garbo, Greta, 486
García, Hector P., 759
García-Godoy, Héctor, 746
Gardner, Erle Stanley, 506
Garfield, James A., 304–05, 620; administration, 306; assassination, 307, 309
Garfield, James R., 418
Garland, Hamlin, 216, 272
Garner, John Nance, 509–10, 553
Garrison, William Lloyd, 118–19, 120, 206
Garvey, Marcus, 683
Gary, Ind., 758
gasoline engine, 235
Gastineau Channel, 328
Gates, Horatio, 58
Gautama Buddha, 731
Gaza Strip, 695
Gehrig, Lou, 506
Gemini program, 754
General Electric, 419
General Motors, 399, 525, 616, 760
Genêt, Edmond, 69
Geneva, Switzerland, 295
Geneva Agreement (1954), 702–04
Geneva Conference (1955), 689–90
Geneva Conference (1962), 730
Genoa, Italy, 16
gentleman's agreement, 229; with Japan, 270, 388
geographers and geography, 15, 16
George II, King of England, 32
George III, King of England, 49, 52, 58
George, Walter, 533
Georgetown, Ohio, 152
Georgia, 681, 744, 790; agriculture, 201; in American Revolution, 57, 62; in Civil War, 166–67, 170–71; colonial, *41*; founding of, 32–33; Indians in, 94, 99, 334; re-

construction, 180, *188*, 195, 198; secession, 142; slavery in, 33, 57
German-Americans, 30, 106, 108, 134, 254, 263–65, 269, 272, 447, 598
German Reformed church, 39
Germantown, Battle of, 58, 87
Germany, 546; civil wars in, 264; Czechoslovakia and, 553, 555; Franco-Prussian war, 294; Hitler, 548, 552–53, 556–57; immigration from, 30, 106, 108, 134, 254, 263–64, 265, 269, 272; League of Nations, 466; Munich Agreement, 553; Naziism, 548; and Poland, 555; post-World War II, 637–40; reparations, 544, 608, 638; and Samoa, 368–69; Soviet pact, 555; trade, 237; Versailles treaty, 459, 460, 541, 544, 548; World War I, 431, 433–60, 464; World War II, 570–82, 608; Zimmermann telegram, 440–41. *See also* East Germany; West Germany.
germ theory, 278
Geronimo, 337
Gershwin, George, 488
Gettysburg, Battle of, *113*, 164–65, 305
Gettysburg Address, 148
Ghana, 40, 44, 400
Ghent, Treaty of, 86, 94
ghettos, 750, 752, 759
ghost dances, 341
Gibbons, James, 280
GI Bill of Rights, 615, 628, 751
Gibraltar, 40, 488
"Gibraltar of the Mississippi," 154
gift tax, 526
Gilbert, Humphrey, 21
Gilbert Islands, 583, 587, 588
Glacier Bay National Monument, *708*
glass, *35*, 506
Glass-Steagall Act, 525
Glazer, Nathan, 281
Glenn, John H., Jr., 687, 725
Glidden, Joseph F., 344
GNP, *see* gross national product.
Goddard, Robert H., 400, 572
Goethals, George W., 404
"Goin' Down the Road," *499*
gold, 233, 337; in Alaska, 328–29; California, 128, 324; Colorado, 327; and greenbackism, 286, 290, 302
Gold Beach, 578
"goldbug" Democrats, 353, 356

nam peace talks, 753, 768, 771; World War I, 434, 453, 454; World War II, 557, 579–80
Paris, Pact of, *see* Kellogg-Briand Pact.
Paris Peace Conference (1919), 466–68, 544, 646
Paris treaties: (1763), 48; (1783), 62–63, 71; (1898), 371, 379–80
Parker, Alton B., 412
Parker, Dorothy, 488
Parks, Rosa, 684
Parliament, 26, 36, 49–50
Pasteur, Louis, 164
patent (grant), 24, 29
Pathet Lao, 730
Patterson, Floyd, 713
Patterson, Robert, 149
Patton, George S., Jr.: World War I, 457; World War II, 574, 575, 581
Patton tank, 570, 661
Pawnee Indians, 335
Payne-Aldrich Bill, 418
Peabody, George, 204
Peace Corps, 726–27
peaceful coexistence, 732, 773
peace groups, 538, 540, 551, 750-51, 752, 768, 770
"peace with honor," 780
Peary, Robert, 402
Pecora, Ferdinand, 525–26
"peculiar institution," 91
Peik v. Chicago & North Western R.R., 231
Peiping, 551
Peking, 387, 772, 778
Pendergast, Thomas J. ("Boss"), 612, 614
Pendleton Civil Service Reform Act, 309, 315
peninsular campaign, 155–56
Penn, Arthur, 761
Penn, William, 30, 41, 333
Penn Central Rrd., 221, 224, 775
Pennsylvania, 68, 69, 135, 184, 189; American Revolution in, 57–58; Civil War in, 164–65, 168, 170; Indians of, 333; industry in, 232–33, 239; religion, 30, 39; settlement of, 28, 30–31
Pennsylvania Avenue, Wash., D.C., 176, 191, 505, 793
Pennsylvania Gazette, 60
Pennsylvania Hospital, *38*
Pennsylvania Rrd., 224, 225, 240
penny press, 108
Pensacola, Fla., 92, 143
pensions, 527, 617
Pentagon Papers, 741, 747, 771, 781
Pentecostal Assemblies, 628
People's party, 352, *353*
People's Republic of

China, 661–63, 698–701, 789; Chiang *v.* Mao, 644–45; Nixon and, 771–72, 778; nuclear bomb, 747, 771. *See also* China.
Pequot Indians, 332
Perkins, Frances, 527
Permanent Court of International Justice, *540,* 543
Permanent Investigation Committee (Senate), 670
Perón, Juan, 707
Personal Memoirs (Grant), 297
Perry, Matthew C., 131, *132*
Perry, Oliver Hazard, 86
Perryville, 159, 166
Pershing, John J., 385, 449–50, 451, 452, 455
Persian Gulf, 634, 647
Peru, 19, 707
Pescadores, 699
pesticides, 759
Pétain, Henry Philippe, 449
pet banks, 102, 104
Petersburg, Battle of, 168, 172
petroleum, 233, 239, 787
Phantom jet fighters, 774
Phelan, James D., 406
Philadelphia, Pa., 105, 193, 531; in American Revolution, 59, 61; colonial, 34, 37–38, 39, 47, 49, 255; Constitutional Convention, 65; Continental Congress, 50–52; founding of, 31, 333; immigrants in, 272; as national capital, 67, 78, 79; nineteenth-century, 146, 264; transportation, 224–25, 274, 275
Philadelphia and Reading Rrd., 243
Philadelphia Centennial Exposition, 236, *299*
Philadelphia Free Library, 60
Philadelphia Negro, The (Dubois), 283
Philadelphia Public *Ledger,* 4
philanthropists, 204, 207, 239–40, 241–42
Philip II, King of Spain, 21
Philippine Insurrection, 380, 393
Philippine Islands, 541, 564, 702; fall of, 584; independence, 394, 697; Japan attacks, 565; SEATO, 703; Spanish-American War, 376–80; W. H. Taft and, 417; Treaty of Paris, 379–80; as unorganized territory, 394; World War II, 394, 587, 589–90
Philippine Sea, Battle of, 589
Philippoteaux, Paul, *113*

philosophy: ancient, 14, 15, 20; pragmatism, 404–05; transcendentalism, 108, 414. *See also* Social Darwinism.
Phnom Penh, Cambodia, 788, 704
phonograph, 236, 237, 276
Phony War, 556
photography, *236*
picketing, 674
Pickett, George, 165
Pierce, Franklin: early career, 131; presidency, 133, 134, 335
Pierce Arrow, *426, 485*
Pike, Zebulon M., 80
Pike's Peak, 80, 327
Pilgrims, 25–26, 332
Pilgrim's Progress, 408
Pinchot, Gifford, *410,* 418–19
Pinckney, Charles C., 72, 82
Pinckney, Thomas, 70
Pinckney's Treaty, 70, 92
Pine Ridge, S.D., *339*
Pinkerton Detective Agency, 190, 260
Pinta, 8, 17–18
pioneers, 254; Great Plains, 400; and Proclamation Line of 1763, 49. *See also* frontier; West.
pirates: Barbary states, 79–80; English, 18; industrial, 242, 243
Pistoia, Italy, *549*
Pitt, William, 47, 49
Pittsburg Landing, Tenn., 154
Pittsburgh, Pa., 47, 55, 62, 187, 224, 242, 259, 266, 275
Pittsburgh *Pirates,* 761
Plains, Ga., 792
Plains of Abraham, 48
plantations, 23, 24, 32, 200, 202
plastics, 400
Platt, Thomas C. ("Boss"), 409
Platt Amendment, 383, 554
Platte River, 331
Plattsburg, N.Y., 86
Playboy, 791
Plessy v. *Ferguson,* 358, 680
Ploesti, Rumania, 581
plows, 34, 107, 236
Plunkitt, George Washington, 312–13
Plymouth (automobile), 504
Plymouth colony, 26, 39
Plymouth Company, 22
Plymouth Notch, Vt., 492
pneumatic tire, 236
Pocahontas, 23, 332
pocket veto, 179
poetry: Civil War, 160; nineteenth-century, 283; twentieth-century, 488
Point Four Program, 642
Point Pleasant, Ohio, 152

Poland: and American Revolution, 58; immigrants from, 234, 254, 266–67; post-World War II, 633; World War I, 459; World War II, 555, 581, 601, 605–06
Poland, Ohio, 364
Polaris program, 686
polaroid glass, 506
polio, 629, 712
Polish National Alliance, 269
political parties, 93; differences in, 310; formation of, 68, 95; fourth party, 141; and labor unions, 257, 260; machines, 97; and spoils system, 97, 104; third party, 134, 141. *See also* names of parties.
politicians: local, 312–13; state, 310–11
Polk, James K., 135, 148; and California, 123; early career, 122; Mexican War, 124–26, 138; Slidell Mission, 123–24
poll tax, 358, 530, 743
pollution, 277–78, 759, 776–77
Polo, Marco, 15
polygamy, 308
Ponce de León, Juan, 18
Pontiac, 47, 333
Pontiac's Uprising, 333
pony express, 330–31
pools, 229, 244–45, 525
"poor people's march," 759
Poor Richard's Almanac, 60
poor whites, 182–83, 194, 200–01, 203–04
"pop" art, 761
Pope, Alexander, 87
Pope, John S., 156–57
popery, 479
Pope's Day, 38
"Popish peril," 134
popular sovereignty, 130, 133, 136, 139; def., 130
population: city, 271–72; and labor, 234; in North, 149; and politics, 107; post-World War II, 626–27; and reapportionment, 722; shifts, 597; and South, 149; statistics, 263, 398; in West, 136. *See also* census.
populism, 352, *353*
Populist party, 352–58, 406
Populist revolt, 324, 406
pork-barrel legislation, 308, 317
pornography, 756
Port Arthur, 387, 606, 659
Port Conway, Va., 82
Porter, Katherine Anne, 488, 761
Port Gibson, 166
Port Hudson, 154, 166
Port Moresby, New Guinea, 585

Portrait of a Lady (James), 283

Portrait of the Artist's Mother (Tanner), 363

Port Royal, 46, 47

Portsmouth, N.H., 387

Portsmouth Treaty, 387–88

Portugal, 16, 39, 267, 641, 788

postal savings system, 357, 419

postal services, 59

Post Office Department, 308, 428, 775

potash industry, 34–35

potato famine, 263

Potomac (yacht), 559

Potomac River, 23, 24, 25, 55, 150, 155, 165, 168, 218

Potsdam Conference, 592, 593, 605, 607–08, 659–60

Pottawatomie Massacre, 140

poverty, 214, 740, 759, 776

Powderly, Terence V., 257–58

Powell, Lewis F., Jr., 775

power: electric, 235; gasoline, 235; nuclear, 619; private companies, 619, 675; public v. private, 675–76; steam, 235; water, 234, 235. See also Tennessee Valley Authority.

Powers, Abigail, 129

Powers, Francis Gary, 714

Powers, John A. ("Shorty"), 725

Powhatan, 22, 23, 332

Poznan, Poland, 581

pragmatism, 404–05

Pratt, Julius W., 551

Presbyterians, 39

Prescott, Samuel, 51

predestination, 27

president(s): and Constitution, 65–66, 162; and corruption, 285, 290–92; disability, 308, 620–21; election of, 65; impeachment of, 65, 783; resignation of, 785; salary, 292; succession, 620–21; terms, 621

Presidential Succession Act, 620

President's Committee on Equal Employment Opportunity, 722

President's Reemployment Act, 515

Presley, Elvis, 712

Price Administration, Office of, 596, 617

prices: controls, 617; and depression, 504–05, 512, 515–18; and economy, 355; freeze on, 775; and inflation, 512. See also business activity.

"priming the pump," 519–21, 523

Prince of Wales (Br. ship), 559, 583

Princeton, N.J., 57

Princeton University, 82, 420, 421

printing, 27, 60

prisoners of war, 780

prison lessee system, 203, 258

prisons, 182, 405; Civil War, 163–64; reform, 108

privateering, 69, 151

Proclamation Line of 1763, 49, 333

Proclamation of Amnesty and Reconstruction, 178–79

Profiles in Courage (Kennedy), 720

profit: corporate, 485, 500; excess, 309; sharing, 241

progressive era, 396–419

progressive movement, 404–08; aims of, 405–06; and black Americans, 414–15; literature, 408; national politics, 412–13; New Nationalism and, 423–24; and Populist revolt, 406; state politics, 406–08; W. H. Taft and, 418

Progressive party (1912), 406; (1924), 493; (1948), 650

Prohibition, 474, 492, 494; amendments, 481–82; repealed, 507; and states, 481; and temperance movements, 480–81

Prohibition party, 481

Promontory Point, Utah, 220, 226, 331

propaganda, 446

property, 230; as voter qualification, 97, 195

Prophet's Town, 105

proprietary colony, 25, 30, 32, 61

prospectors, 324, 325–29

protective tariffs, 97, 241, 316, 320, 356, 366, 409, 424, 425, 544. See also tariffs.

Protestants and Protestantism, 25, 27, 28, 29, 39, 108, 263; and ecumenism, 758; and Prohibition, 481–82; and urbanization, 279–80. See also religion; names of denominations.

protectorates, U.S., 368, 370, 384

Providence, R.I., 28

Prussia, 69, 92, 434

Ptolemy, Claudius, 14

PT-109, 720

public accommodations, 196, 722–23

public health services, 751

public utilities, 526; Federal Power Commission, 675; public v. private,

230–31, 523–24; TVA, 522–24

public works, 507, 512, 519

Public Works Administration (PWA), 519

Public Works and Economic Development Act, 745

Puck, 246, 305

Pueblo, Colo., 471

Pueblo Incident, 752

Pueblo Indians, 10, 528

Puerto Rico, 18; administration of, 392–93; as federal territory, 392; independence movement, 393; Spanish-American War, 379; U.S. citizenship, 392

Pujo, Arsène, 243

Pujo Committee, 243

Pulaski, Count Casimir, 58

Pulaski, Tenn., 197

Pulitzer, Joseph, 2

Pulitzer Prize, 488

Pullman sleeping car, 227

Pullman strike, 246, 253, 354, 409

Pure Food and Drug Act, 413–14

Puritans and Puritanism, 25–28, 29, 35, 39, 214, 254, 263, 332–33

Pusan, S. Korea, 661, 662

PWA, see Public Works Administration.

Pyong Yang, N. Korea, 660–62

Quadrant Conference, 604

Quakers, see Society of Friends.

Quang Doc, Thich, 731

quarantine, Cuban, 733–35

"quarantine" speech, 552

Quartering Act, 49

Quay, Matthew S., 318

Quebec, 41, 46–48, 51, 604–05

Queen, Ellery, 506

Queen Anne's War, 46

Quemoy, 699

Quezon, Manuel L., 394

Quick, Herbert, 272

Quincy, Mass., 70, 72

quota system, 742

Rabaul, 588

Rabbit Creek, Yukon, 328

Rabi, Isidore, 594

racketeers, 482–83

radar, 570

Radical Republicans, 151–52, 170, 175, 179–81, 188–91, 194–96, 198, 203–04, 285, 289

radicals and radicalism, 776, 789; "red scare," 473, 476

radio, 400, 484, 486, 487, 506, 598, 630; FM, 506

ragtime, 487

Railroad Retirement Bill, 527

railroads, 199, 214, 243, 500, 506, 712, 775; abuses, 405, 408; competition, 229, 231, 412–13; contributions of, 231–32; decline of, 218; development of, 106–07, 218; and farmers, 230, 350; land, 219, 317; mileage, 220; pools, 229; post-World War II, 628–29; rate controls, 219, 229–31, 413; rebates, 230, 239, 245, 413; safety, 226–27, 261, 419; scandals, 219, 228; schedules, 225; standardizing of, 225, 252; strikes, 246, 253, 257, 258, 293, 617; time, 225; transcontinental, 132, 161, 218–21, 226, 228, 330, 331, 335. See also names of railroads.

Railroad Safety Appliance Act, 227

Raleigh, Walter, 13, 21, 23, 31

Raleigh, N.C., 177

Raleigh Tavern (Va.), 50

Randolph, A. Philip, 599

Randolph, Edmund, 65

Randolph, John, 117

Rankin, Jeanette, 565

Rapidan River, 165

Rappahannock River, 23, 158, 159

rationing, wartime, 597, 598

Ray, James Earl, 752

Rayburn, Sam, 693

Raymond, Miss., 166

rayon, 400

REA, see Rural Electrification Administration.

Reagan, Ronald, 791

reaper, 107

reapportionment, 722

rebates, 230, 239, 245, 413

recessions, 672, 721, 787, 789, 790

reciprocal trade agreements, 514, 554

reconstruction: amnesty, 181–82; and black Americans, 179–86; "Confederate," 181–87, 194, 196, 197, 203; and Congress, 181–85; corruption, 181, 196–97; election of 1868, 285–86, 288; end of, 200, 301; Freedmen's Bureau, 181–82, 184; Grant administration, 289; Johnson's plan, 180–81, 184, 193; Lincoln's plan, 175, 178–80, 181, 193; military districts, 188, 193, 195; secret societies, 197–98; and state governments, 178–80, 184, 188, 193, 200; violence, 182–83;

lied intervention in, 458–59, 541; Bolshevik revolution, 439–40, 458, 476; immigrants from, 254, 266–68; and Korea, 659; in Northwest, 92; trade with, 237; World War I, 431, 451, 458–59; World War II, 573–76. *See also* Soviet Union.

Russo-Japanese War, 387, 545, 606, 631

Russo-Turkish War, 266

Rust, John Daniel, 487

Rust, Mack Donald, 487

Ruth, Babe, 486, 761

Ryukyu Islands, 591

Sabin, Albert, *629*

sabotage (union), 261

Sacco, Nicola, 477–78

Sachs, Alexander, 593

Sac Indians, 359

Sackler, Howard, 761

Sacramento, Calif., 128, 219, 324, 331

Sacramento River, 324, 331, 335

Safeguard (ABM), 775

safety: factory, 254; railroad, 230–31

Sagamore Hill, 411

Saigon, Viet., 583, 700, 731, 752, *788*

Saint Antoine, *41*

Saint Christopher, 41

Saint Helena, 40, 263

Saint John's River, Fla., 18

Saint Joseph, Mo., 331

Saint Lawrence River, 19, 46, 47–48, 58, 62, 295

Saint Lawrence Seaway, 678, *679*, 709

Saint Leger, Barry, 58

Saint Louis, Mo., 47, 80, 136, 153, 154, 187, 275, 317, 330, 352, 356, 400, 482, 492, 497; desegregation in, 625; and immigration, 264, 265, 272; and railroads, 224, 227, 229

Saint Mary's, Md., 25

Saint-Mihiel, France, 449, 455

Saint Paul, Minn., 221, 229, 265, 272

Saint Paul & Pacific Co., 221

Saint Petersburg, Russia, 94

Saipan, Mariana Is., 588–89, 590, 591

Sakhalin Island, 606

Salamaua, New Guinea, 588

salary grab, 292

Salem, Peter, 56

Salem, Mass., 27, 37

Sale of Securities Bill, 525

Salerno, Italy, 575

Salisbury, N.C., 96

Salk, Jonas, *629*, 712

SALT, *see* Strategic Arms Limitation Talks.

Salt Lake City, 331

Sampson, William T., 377–78

San Antonio, Tex., *41, 81*, 121, 736

San Cristobal, Cuba, 734

San Diego, Calif., 124

Sandys, Edwin, 26

San Francisco, Calif., 221, 270, 274, 324, 330, 331, 388, 406, 472, 487; earthquake, 396; terrorist bombings, 776; UN Conference, 605, 720

Sangamon County, Ill., 4

sanitation, 38, 277

San Jacinto, Tex., 121

San Jacinto, U.S.S., 151

San Joaquin Valley, 221

San Juan, P.R., 392

San Juan Hill, Battle of, 378, 412

San Juan Islands, 295

San Salvador, 8, 17

Sansapor, 589

Santa Anna, Antonio López de, 121, 125

Santa Barbara, Calif., 776

Santa Fe, N.M., *41, 80*, 124, 221

Santa Fe Rrd., *220*, 348

Santa Fe Trail, 220, 331

Santa Maria, 8, 17–18

Santayana, George, 2

Santee Sioux, 336

Santiago, Cuba, 377–79

Santo Domingo, 80, 295–96, 746

Sarajevo, Bosnia, 431

Saratoga, Battle of, 58, 61

Saratoga (carrier), 585

satellites, space, 679, 686, *709*, 721. *See also* names of satellites.

Sato, Eisaku, 758

Saturday Evening Post, 629

Saturn rocket, 755

Sauk Indians, 127, 334

Sault Sainte Marie Canal, 404

Savage Station, Battle of, *156*

Savannah, Ga., 32, 37, 39, 170–71

Savannah River, 32

Savo Island, 586

scalawags, 194–95, 196

Scali, John, 735

Scandinavia, 10, 254, 265, 272

Schechter Poultry Corporation v. *U.S.*, 515

Schenectady, N.Y., 307

Schine, G. David, 670

Schirra, Walter M., 687, 725

schism, 14

Schley, Winfield S., 377

Schmelling, Max, 530

schools: and biological evolution, 483–84; black Americans, 181, *182*, 195, 204, 207, 626; busing, 787; city, 281–82; colonial, 31; dropouts,

713; integration of, 680–81; medical, 619, 721; parochial, 479, 628, 743; private, 680, 743; public, 76, 182, 195, 196; segregated, 195, 204, 270, 358, 388, 414, 677, 679, 682. *See also* colleges; education.

Schuylkill River, 31, 275

Schweickart, Russell L., 767

science: and history, 4–5; and industry, 235; in Middle Ages, 15; nineteenth-century, 107–08; twentieth-century, 400, 487, 628, 755; World War II, 570, 594–95

SCLC, *see* Southern Christian Leadership Conference.

Scopes, John Thomas, 483–84

Scotland, 21; immigrants from, 262, 263, 265

Scott, Dred, 136

Scott, Thomas A., 240

Scott, Winfield, 125, 130, 131, 149, 150, 153, 155

Scottsboro affair, 529

sculpture, 15, 282

Seaboard Air Line, 224

Seaboard Coast Line, 224

Seale, Bobby, 758, 776

Sea of Darkness, 17, 18

SEATO, *see* Southeast Asia Treaty Organization.

Seattle, Wash., 221, 491

Sebastopol, 573

SEC, *see* Securities and Exchange Commission.

secession, 99, 116, 128, 142, 177, 178, 180, 194

Second Continental Congress, 56, 61, 71, 83; and Articles of Confederation, 59; creates Continental Army, 51; and Declaration of Independence, 52, 76; and navy, 59

Second Infantry Division, 453–55

Second Treatise on Government (Locke), 52

secret ballot, 203, 350, 352, 357

secret societies, 134, 197–98

sectionalism, 94, 107

Section 7 (NRA), 514–15

Securities and Exchange Act, 525

Securities and Exchange Commission (SEC), 525, 526

Security Council (UN), 661

Sedalia, Mo., 342

Sedan-Mézieres Rrd., 452

Sedition Act (1798), 72

Sedition Act (1918), 447

segregation, 358, 428–29, 624; *de facto*, 680; *de jure*, 680; of public fa-

cilities, 722–23; in schools, 195, 204, 270, 358, 388, 414, 625, 679–82, 771

Selden, George B., 235, 236

Selective Service Acts: (1917), 443–44; (1948), 614

self-determination, 464, 467

selling short (stock market), 228–29

Selma, Ala., 744

Seminary Ridge, 165

Seminole Indians, 96, 100, 127, 334, 336, 348

Senate: election of, 350, 352, 357, 419; and impeachment, 190–91; president pro tempore, 620; and Watergate, 780–81. *See also* Congress, U.S.

Senate Committee on Banking and Currency, 525

Seneca Falls, N.Y., *401*

Senegal, 40

Senegambia, 40

senior citizens, *see* aged.

Seoul, S. Korea, 660–61, 662

separate-but-equal decision, 358, 680

Separatists, 25–26

Sequoya, *100*

Serbia, 266

Service, Robert W., 329

Servicemen's Readjustment Act, 615

Seven Days' Battle, 156

Seven Pines, Battle of, 156

Seventeenth Amendment, 357, 419

Seventh Cavalry, 337

Seventh Fleet, 698

Seventieth Regiment, Indiana Volunteer Inf., 319

Seven Years' War, 46, 63

Seville, Spain, 17

Sewall, Arthur, 356

Seward, William H., 148, 151, 158, 162, *192*, 366

"Seward's folly," 192

sewing machine, 236, *407*

sex, changing attitudes toward, 770

Sexual Politics (Millet), 777

Seymour, Horatio, 192, 288, 314

Shafter, William R., 377–78

Shame of the Cities, The (Steffens), 408

Shanghai, China, 552, 773

Shantung, China, 541

sharecroppers, 200–01, 518

"Share Our Wealth" clubs, 506

Sharpsburg, Battle of, 157

Shawnee Indians, 105, 333

Shays's Rebellion, 64, 65

Sheen, Fulton J., 628

sheep raising, 343
Sheik, The, 475
Shenandoah Valley, 55, 149, 155, 165, 168, 170, 172, 364
Shepard, Alan B., Jr., 687, 725
Sheppard, Morris, 737
Sheridan, Philip, 166, 168, 172, 336
Sherman, John, 304
Sherman, William Tecumseh, 165, 167, 170–71, 319, 337
Sherman Antitrust Act, 231, 245–46, 321, 357, 413–14, 424
Sherman Silver Purchase Act, 320–21, 353
Sherwood, Robert E., 488
Shikler, Aaron, 757
Shiloh, Battle of, 154, 167
ships and shipping: Civil War and, 151, 162; of Columbus, 8, 17–18; destroyer deal, 557–58; foreign interference, 82; medieval, 15; and neutrality, 550–51; slave, 23, 37; steam-powered, 106, 107, 227; Viking, 11; Washington Conference, 541–42; World War I, 437–38, 448–49; World War II, 570, 575
Sholes, Christopher, 236
Showboat, 488
Shriver, Sargent, 726, 780
Siberia, 8, 10, 458–59, 595
Sicily, 575
sickle cell anemia, 775
Sierra Nevadas, 331
Sihanouk, Norodom, 770
Sihanoukville, Cambodia, 768, 770
"silent majority," 757
Silent Spring (Carson), 759, 761
Silliman, Benjamin, Jr., 107, 233
Sills, Beverly, 761
silver, 233; coinage of, 303, 351, 352, 353, 355; demonetization of, 303; free, 303, 353, 355, 357, 409; mines, 233, 303, 320, 327, *328, 346;* money issue, 320–21; Sherman Silver Purchase Act, 320–21, 353. *See also* money.
Simmons, William Joseph, 479–80
Simpson, O. J., 762
Sims, William S., 448
Sinai peninsula, 695
Sinclair, Harry, 491
Sinclair, Upton, 400, 413
Singapore, 563, 583–84, 587
Singer, Isaac, 236
Sioux Indians, 219, 335, 337–41, 777–78
Sioux Wars, 337–38
Sirhan, Sirhan, 753
Sirica, John J., 780–*81*
Sissle, Noble, 487

Sister Carrie (Dreiser), 400
sit-down strikes, 525, 533
sit-in demonstrations, 722, 723
Sitting Bull, 337, 341
Six Crises (Nixon), 765
Six-Day War, 751, 774
Sixteenth Amendment, 419
Sixth Circuit Court of Appeals, 417
Sixth Corps, U.S., 576
Sixth Massachusetts Regiment, 143
Skagway, Alas., 329
Skylab, 768
slackers, 447
Slater, John, 204
slaves and slavery: abolition of, 118, 146, 151 (*see also* abolition movement); in American Revolution, 56–57, 59; Bible and, 120; colonization attempts, 118; Compromise of 1850, 128–29, 130; and Congress, 128; and Constitution, 65, 159; and cotton industry, 117; in District of Columbia, 128, 138, 158; Dred Scott decision, 136, 139; early criticism of, 117; early use of, 24, 25, 117; and economy, 37, 41, 117; and education, 181, 182; Emancipation Proclamation, 158–59; free, 180; fugitive, 130, 133, 158; Great Britain and, 41; importation of, 23, 59, 117, 140; and Indians, 36, 336; Kansas-Nebraska Bill, 132, 133; life of, 117; Lincoln-Douglas debates, 139–40; Louisiana Territory, 91, 92; Missouri Compromise, 90–92, 126, 133, 136; morality of, 139, 141; in New England, 57; Northwest Ordinance, 78, 117; and plantation, 32; as political issue, 126, 131; popular sovereignty, 130, 133; proslavery arguments, 120; and reconstruction, 181, 182; religion and, 39–40; revolts, 80, 118, 120; and state representation, 65; and suffrage, 178; in territories, 91, 126, 127, 136, 138, 139–42, 158; in Texas, 120–21; treatment of, 117. *See also* black Americans; slave trade.
slave trade, 262–63; in District of Columbia, 117, 128, 130; early, 23, 37; ended in U.S., 59, 117, 140; triangular, 37
Slayton, Donald K., 687

Slidell, John, 123, 151
Slidell Mission, 123–24
Sloat, John, 124
smallpox, 55, 335
Smith, Alfred E., 492, 494
Smith, Bessie, 487
Smith, Donald, 221
Smith, E.D. ("Cotton Ed"), 533
Smith, Edmund Kirby, 159
Smith, Gerald L.K., 531
Smith, James ("Sugar Jim"), 421
Smith, John, 22
Smith, Joseph, 108
Smith, Margaret Chase, 658
Smith, Milton H., 224
Smith-Hughes Act, 428
Smith-Lever Act, 426
smoking, 23, 712, 745, 756
Smolensk, USSR, 573, 576
Smoot-Hawley Tariff Bill, 502
Snake River, 80, 338, 675
SNCC, *see* Student Nonviolent Coordinating Committee
Snead, Sam, 713
social compact, 52
Social Darwinism, 214, 216–18, 228, 232, 246, 254, 262, 285, 312, 367, 368
Social Darwinism in American Thought (Hofstadter), 216
social gospel movement, 279–80
socialism, 257, 260, 551
Socialist-Labor party, 257
social reform, 108–09, 407
social security, 527, 617, 676, 721, 740
Social Security Act, 527, 531, 532
Society of Friends, 30, 39, 333
sod houses, 345
Soil Bank Bill, 673
Soil Conservation and Domestic Allotment Act, 517
Soil Conservation Service, 522
Soil Erosion Service, 522
Soissons, France, 455
Solingen, Germany, 578
Solomon Islands, 583, 586–88, 720
Somme River, 439, 451
songs: colonial, 38; depression era, *499;* of 1960s, 760; post-World War I, 487–88; progressive era, *407;* World War I, 435. *See also* music.
Sons of Liberty, 49
Soul on Ice (Cleaver), 761
Sound of Music, The, 761
sourdoughs, 328
South: in Civil War, *see* Confederate States of America; economy of, 182; education in, 181, 182; industry, 149, 199,

201; post-World War I, 478; and reconstruction, 178, 185–86, 288, 289; transportation, 224. *See also* names of states.
South Africa, 44, 233, 265, 373, 381
South America, 44, 128, 149; discovery of, 18; early man in, 10; Pan-Americanism, 321–22, 370. *See also* Latin America; names of countries.
Southampton County, Va., 120
South Braintree, Mass., 477
South Carolina, 95, 177, 625, 681; in American Revolution, 57, 62; in Civil War, 143, 171; colonial, *41;* constitution, 195; nullification crisis, 100; reconstruction, 180, 188, 193, 195, 196, 197, 198, 199, 200, 297, 301; religion, 39; secession, 142; settlement, 31–32; slavery, 57
South China Sea, 748
South Dakota, 327, 351; agriculture, 342; Indians, 335, 337, *339, 341, 346;* statehood, 320, 345
Southeast Asia, 28, 561, 697, 787; Eisenhower and, 700–05; Kennedy and, 730–31; in 1950s, 705; Nixon Doctrine, 768
Southeast Asia Treaty Organization (SEATO), 703
Southern Alliance, 350–52
Southern Christian Leadership Conference (SCLC), 684–85, 759
Southern Pacific Rrd., 221, *671*
Southern Railway system, 243, 601
Southern Regional Council, 600
South Korea, 659–64, 699, 701
South Manchuria Railway, 546–47, 606
South Pacific, 629
South Sea Islands, 44
South Vietnam, 700–05, 730–31, 740–41, 747–50, 768, 788. *See also* Vietnam; Vietnam War.
Southwest: exploration of, 18; Indians of, 10, 336
Southwest State Teachers' College, 737
Souvanna Phouma, Prince of Laos, 730
Soviet Union (USSR), 477, 545, 631, 714, 732; and Angola, 788, 789; and China, 772; and Cuba, 711; and Middle East, 692–96; and Nixon,

773, 778; nuclear arms, 688, 773; SALT, 773, 788; space programs, 677, 686, 725, 768; World War II, 555, 559, 562, 573, 574–76, 592, 601, 604–06. *See also* *détente*; Russia.

Spaatz, Carl A. ("Tooey"), 577

space programs, 677, 686–87, 709, 725, 754–55, 767–68, *769. See also* names of programs.

Spain: and American Revolution, 60, 61; Armada defeated, 21; civil war in, 550, 551; colonies of, 18–19; and Cuba, 296, 374–79; explorations by, 17–19; and Florida, 32, *41,* 63, 64, 70, 92, 96; and France, 80; and Great Britain, 32, 63; and Mexico, 162; Pinckney's Treaty, 92; U.S. bases in, 688

Spanish-American War: background to, 373–76; campaigns, *371,* 376–79; declared, 376; effect on America, 379–80; peace treaty, *371,* 379–80; and Philippines, 380–81; and yellow fever, 402

Spanish Armada, 21

Spanish Civil War, 550, 551

Spanish Florida, 32, *41,* 63, 64, 70, 80, 92, 96

Spanish Main, 21

Sparkman, John J., 666, 682

speakeasy, 474, 482, 507

Specie Circular, 102, 104

Specie Redemption Act, 290, 302

speculation, 90, 229; gold, 291–92; stock market, 502–03

Spencer, Herbert, 216–17

Spencer City, Ill., 137

Sperry, Elmer A., 400

"spheres of interest," 386

Spindletop, 233

spinning wheels, 34

Spirit of St. Louis, 488–89

spoils system, 97, 104, 290, 319

Spokane, Wash., 419

sports: nineteenth-century, 160; twentieth-century, 400, 486, 506, 598, 625–26, 629, 712–13, 761–62

"spot resolutions," 138

Spotsylvania, Battle of, 168

Springfield, Ill., 137

Springfield, Mass., 64, 65, 398

Spruance, Raymond A., 589, 591

Sputnik: (I), 677; (II), 686

Squanto, 26, 332

Stafford, Jo, 629

stagecoaches, 308, 330

Stagg Field, Chicago, 594

Stalin, Josef, 592, *603,* 604–*08,* 643, 669

Stalingrad, 573; Battle of, 574–75

Stalwarts, 303–04, 307, 310

Stamp Act, 49, 70

Stamp Act Congress, 49

standard of living, 217–18, 251, 252, 515, 756

Standard Oil Co., 230, 238–39, 245, 408, 419

standard time, 225, 308

Standish, Miles, 26

Stanford, Leland, 220, 221

Stanton, E. Cady, *401*

Stanton, Edwin M., 152, 154, 155, 175, 189–91

staple crops, 23, 120, 201

Stark, John, 58

"star-route" frauds, 308

"Star-Spangled Banner," 86

state banks, 90, 97–98, 102, 104, 161

State Department, 83, 294, 622, 635, 645; McCarthyism, 656, 658; U-2 spy plane, 713

state government: and business, 245; corruption in, 310–11; and progressive movement, 405–07; and railroads, 230; and reconstruction, 178–89, 193, 195–96, 286; reforms, 310–11. *See also* government.

Staten Island, 57

state rights, 94, 99, 100, 114, 116, 128, 142

states: border, 142, 143, 158; and Constitution, 65; cotton, 141, 155; free, 41, 141, 143; slave, 41, 143, 158; and statehood, 63; trade between, 65, 231, 246, 261, 413

States' Rights party, 650

"state suicide," 178, 184

Statue of Liberty, 269, *791*

Staunton, Va., 419, 427

steam: boats, 106, *107,* 227–28; engines, 235; locomotives, 107, 274; power, 235; railroads, 218

steel: industry, 194, 201, 223, 232–33, 236–37, 241, 254, 396–97, 491; 721; strikes, 476

Steffens, Lincoln, 408

Stegomyia mosquito, 403

Stein, Gertrude, 488

Steinbeck, John, 506, 518

Steinem, Gloria, 777

Stella, Frank, 761

Stephens, Thomas, *708*

Stephens, Uriah, 257–58

Steuben, Baron von, 62, 447

Stevens, John L., 370

Stevens, Thaddeus, 184–

86, 187, *189,* 190, 199, 300

Stevens Trade Commission Bill, 425

Stevenson, Adlai E., 352, 409; (grandson), 659, 666–67, 713

Stilwell, Joseph W. "Vinegar Joe"), 588, 645

Stimson, Henry L., 543, 547–48, 551, 592, 594, 599

Stimson Doctrine, 547–48

stock, 228–29

stockholders, 262

stock market, 775; collapse, 503; and New Deal, 525–26; speculation, 502–03

Stock ticker, 276

Stockton, Robert F., 124

Stokes, Carl B., *758*

Stone River, 116

Stony Point, Battle of, 87

Story, Joseph, 98

Stowe, Harriet Beecher, 132

Strange Career of Jim Crow, The (Woodward), 202

Strasbourg, 580

Strasburg, Va., 168–69

Strategic Arms Limitation Talks (SALT), 773, 788

Stratford, Va., 154

streets, 37, 273

Stride Toward Freedom (King), 684

strikes, 252–55, 258–60, 293; government intervention, 257, 414; post-World War I, 473, 476; post-World War II, 616–17, 622; sit-down, 525, 533; wildcat, 258. *See also* labor unions.

Strong, Josiah, 367

Stuart, Gilbert, 84

Student Nonviolent Coordinating Committee (SNCC), 758

Studs Lonigan (Farrell), 506

Stuka (plane), 570

Stutz (automobile), 485

Stuyvesant, Peter, 29–30

submarines: nuclear, 686, 792; World War I, 436–38, 440–41, 448, 460; World War II, 559–60, 570, 575, 589

Submerged Lands Act, 674

subsidies, 650, 673

Subsistence Housing Division, 526

subtreasury, 352, 357

suburbs, 627, 712

subversives, 678

subways, 275

Sudetenland, 553

Suez Canal, 380, 388, 404, 559, 692–94

suffrage: black Americans, 180, 185–86, 188, 189, 195–96, 198, 623, 682, 758; and Constitution, 198; literacy tests,

358, 743; slaves, 178; universal, 195; women, *199, 401,* 427, 428, 487. *See also* voting.

sugar: Cuba, 373, 707, 710, 711; "free," 321; Hawaii, 267, 369; industry, 245–46, 321; Philippines, 394; triangular trade, 35

Sugar Act, 49

Sullivan, Louis, 282

Sully, Thomas, 81

Sumner, Charles, 134, 184–86, *189,* 192, 199, 296

Sumner, William Graham, 217

Sunday, Billy, 400, 477

Sun Yat-sen, 644

Super Chief (train), 628

Super Bowl, 761

Supreme Court, 523; and abortion, 756; *Baker* v. *Carr,* 722; and black Americans, 185, 358, 529, 530, 679–81, 751, 758; and business, 246, 413; and citizenship, 389–90; Dred Scott decision, 136, 139; *ex parte Milligan,* 162; income tax, 354; Indians and, 99, 100; interstate commerce, 231, 261; and labor, 491; *Marbury* v. *Madison,* 79; and J. Marshall, 79, 88–89; *McCulloch* v. *Maryland,* 88; Nixon appointments, 775; Nixon tapes, 784; and NRA, 515, 524; packing episode, 531–33; *Plessy* v. *Ferguson,* 358, 680; and obscenity, 756; prayers in school, 770; and public utilities, 230–31; and segregation, 679, 684

survival of fittest, 216–17

Sussex (steamer), 438

Sutter, John A., 324

Sutter's Sawmill, 128, 324

"sweatshops," 278

Sweden: colony in America, 29; immigrants from, 263, 265; World War II, 595

Switzerland: immigrants from, 263; World War II, 595

Sword Beach, 578

Sylvis, William, 256

synthetics, 400, 628

Syria, 267, 696

Taft, Robert A., 417, 558, 623, 641, 650, 658, 665–67

Taft, William Howard, 270, 357, 417, 466; administration, 418–19; Ballinger-Pinchot controversy, 418; chief justice, 418; "dollar diplo-

770–71; Paris peace talks, 753, 768, 771; *Tet* offensive, 752
vigilantes, 209
Viking spacecraft, 768
Villa, Francisco ("Pancho"), 385
Vincennes, Ind., 62, 105
Vinland, 11
Virginia (ironclad), 155
Virginia, 21, 59, 66, 68, 76, 83, 88, 89, 114, 126, 141, 142, 224, 744; agriculture, 23–24, 201; in American Revolution, 62; in Civil War, 143, 149–50, 155–56, 163, 167–68, 172–73; colonial, 22–25, *41*, 50; Indians of, 22–24, 332, 333; and Reconstruction, 180, 188, 195, 198; religion in, 39; secession, 143; segregation in, 358, 680–81; slavery in, 23–24
Virginia City, Nev., 327
"Virginia dynasty," 90
Virginia Plan, 65
Virgin Islands, 295, 393, 554, 625
Virginius (ship), 296
Visscher, Nicholas, *13*
Vladivostok, USSR, 458–59, 788
Voice of America, 669
Volga River, 573
Volturno River, 575
Von Braun, Wernher, 685
V-1 (buzz bomb), 570, 579, 685
vote recorder, 276
voters: lowered age, 775; qualifications of, 97; in reconstruction South, 193–95; and secret ballot, 203, 350, 352, 357. *See also* suffrage.
voting machines, *318*
voting reforms, 682
Voting Rights Act (1965), 743–44
V-2 (rocket), 570, 579, 685
Vukovich, Bill, 713

Wabash Rrd., 258
Wabash rate case, 231
Wade-Davis Bill, 170, 175, 178–79
Wade-Davis manifesto, 179
Wadke, 589
wages: in colonies, 36; freeze on, 763–64; in Great Depression, 504–05, 515, 525; minimum, 424, 515, 617, 751; and women, 777
Wages and Hours Act, 525
Wagner, Honus, 400
Wagner, Robert F., 524
Wagner Labor Relations Act, 524, 531, 532, 622
Wagner-Steagall Act, 526
Wainwright, Jonathan M., 584

Wake Is., 583, 662
Wales, immigration from, 30, 262, 263, 265
Walker, Thomas ("Fats"), 487
Wallace, George C., 724, 753, 754, 779
Wallace, Henry A., 516, 600, 614, 636–37, 650
Wall Street, 228–29, 243, 292, 355, 477
war: "brush-fire," 687; global, 631; outlawing, 540, 545. *See also* names of wars.
War, Department of, 89, 152, 175, 176, 190, 598, 621
War Between the States, *see* Civil War.
war crimes, 632–33
Ward, Lester, 404–05
war debts: American Revolution, 63, 67; Civil War, 180, 186; World War, I, 544–45
"war Democrats," 169–70, 178
Warehouse Act, 357, 427
warhawks, *84*, 85
Warhol, Andy, 761
War Industries Board, 444
War Labor Board, 446
War Loan Act, 444
War Manpower Commission, 596
Warm Springs, Ga., 601
War of 1812, *81*, 89, 127, 334; campaigns of, 85–86; causes of, 84, 85; declared, 85; Treaty of Ghent, 86; in West, 85
War Production Board, 596
Warren, Earl, 650, 680, 737, 764
Warren, George F., 513
Warren Commission, 737, 786
Warsaw, Poland, *556*, 581, 757
Washington, Booker T., 206–07, 208, 400, 414
Washington, George, *56*, 106; in American Revolution, 51, 54, 55–57, 61–62, 71; Constitutional Convention, 65; Farewell Address, 70, 469, 538; foreign policy, 69, 89; French and Indian War, 46, 55; inauguration, 67; and Indians, 333; and neutrality, 69; and slavery, 56; and West, 68–69
Washington, Laurence, 55
Washington, Martha Dandridge Custis, 55, 155
Washington, Walter, 758
Washington (state), 320, 342; statehood, 345
Washington, D.C., 78, 79, 224, 236, 751; Bonus March on, 505; British invasion of, *84*, 86; and Civil War, 155, 168,

240; march on, 724–25; "poor people's march," 759; racial violence in, 752; telegraph in, 122
Washington, Treaty of, 295
Washington Bridge, N.Y.C., 275
Washington Conference (World War II), 604
Washington Conference for the Limitation of Armaments, 490, 540–42
Washington Monument, 768
Washita Valley, 337
Wasp (ship), 585, 586
Watauga, Tenn., 49
watered stock, 228
Watergate case, 769, 779, 780–85
Waterloo, Belgium, 263
water pollution, 745
water power, 234, 235
Water Quality Act, 745
water supply, 282, 344
Watertown, Mass., 26
water transportation, 218, 227–28
Watkins, Arthur V., 670
Watson, Thomas E., 356, 412
Watts, Calif., 745
"waving the bloody shirt," 187, 199, 288, 291, 305
Waxhaw, S.C., 95
Wayne, Anthony, 62, 69, 105, 333
Ways and Means Committee (House), 122, 665
WCTU, *see* Woman's Christian Temperance Union.
weapons, 107, 236; conventional, 687; Middle Ages, 15; nuclear, *603*, 686–87, 747, 773; World War II, 570. *See also* names of bombs and missiles.
Weaver, James B., 352–53, 356
Weaver, Robert C., 529–30, 751, *758*
Webb Kenyon Bill, 481
Webster, Daniel, 99, 102, 114, 129
Webster-Ashburton Treaty, 114
Webster-Hayne debate, 99
Wehrmacht, 570
welfare reform, 196, 776
Wells Fargo Co., 330, *331*
Wesleyan Female College, 300
Wesleyan University, 421
West: and American Revolution, 62; exploration of, 80; expansion to, 136, 232; Indians and, 333–41; and politics, 107; post-Civil War, 199; and Proclamation of 1763, 49; sale of public lands, 99. *See also* frontier; pioneers.

West Branch, Iowa, 497
Western European Union (WEU), 688–89
Western Front, 438–39, 449–56, 460
Western Union Co., 236, 276
West Germany, 608, 772; Marshall Plan, 637, 639; NATO, 688–89
West Indies, 21, 22, 23, 37, 44, 49, 63, 67, 69
Westinghouse, George, 226
Westinghouse Electric Co., 227
West Jersey, 30
Westminster College, 634
Westmoreland, William C., 741, 750, 752
Westmoreland County, Va., 55, 89
West Point, 150, 152, 155, 667–68
West Side Story, 761
West Virginia, 150, 159, 224, 232–33, 245, 680, 718; statehood, 143, 161
WEU, *see* Western European Union.
Weyler, Valeriano, 373
WGN (radio station), 484
whaling industry, 35, 369
wheat, 151, 236, 516–17, 755
Wheeler, Burton K., 558, 561
Wheeler, Schuyler Skaats, 236
Wheeler-Howard Indian Reorganization Act, 528
Wheeler-Rayburn Holding Company Act, 526
Wheeling, W. Va., 143, 656
Whig party, 102, 104, 114, 122, 125, 126, 130, 131, 195, 305; decline of, 133, 134
whiskey: and Indians, 335; tax on, 68, 69, 78
Whiskey Rebellion, 69
Whiskey Ring, 293
Whistler, James McNeill, 282, *362*
White, Edward II., 754, 755
White, George, 488
White, Henry, 466
White, Hugh Lawson, 102
White, John, *13*, *20*, *21*
White, Walter, 529
White Brotherhood, 197
Whitefield, George, 40
White Girl, The (Whistler), *362*
White House, 78, 175, *302*, *316*, 354, 414, 752, 782; burning of, 84, 86; electricity in, 319; naming of, *415*
White League, 197
White Line, 197
Whiteman, Paul, 487, 506
White Plains, N.Y., 62
Whitney, Eli, 117
Whittier, Calif., 765

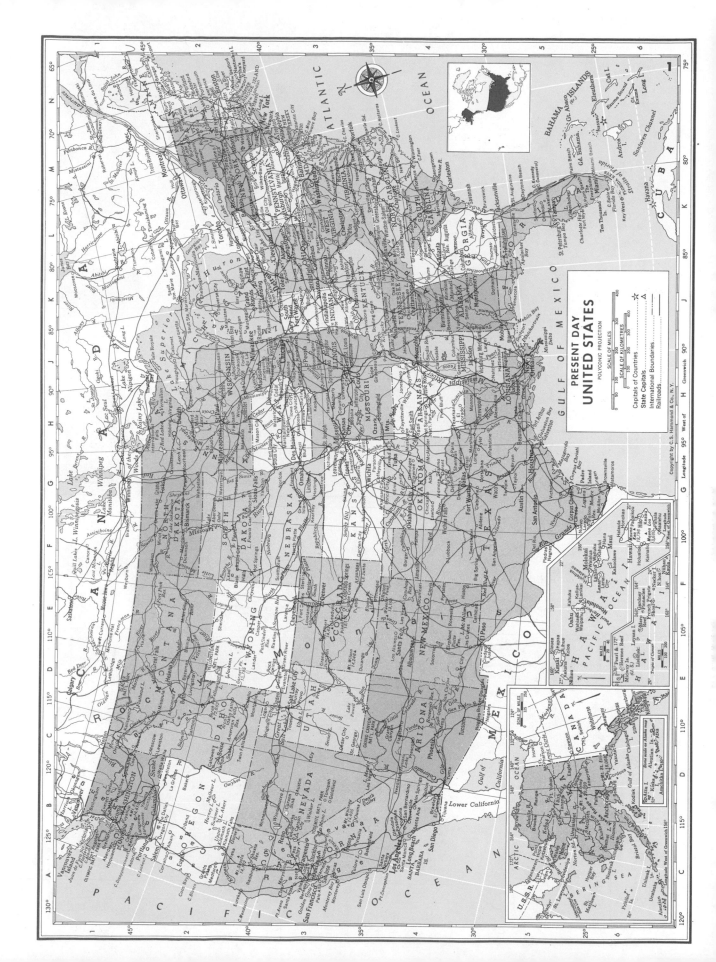

PRESENT DAY
UNITED STATES
POLYCONIC PROJECTION

SCALE OF MILES

SCALE OF KILOMETRES

Capitals of Countries . . . . ★
State Capitals . . . . ▲
International Boundaries . . . .
Railroads . . . .

Copyright by C.S. Hammond & Co., N.Y.

1

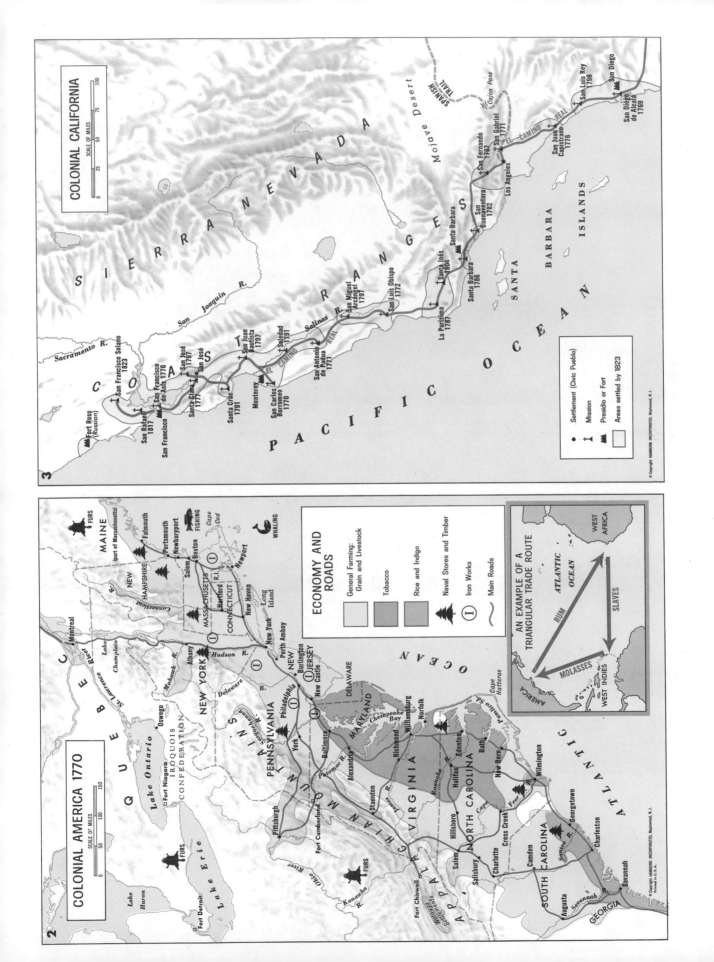

COLONIAL CALIFORNIA

SCALE OF MILES

0 25 50 75 100

3

SIERRA NEVADA

Mojave Desert

SPANISH TRAIL

Cajon Pass

San Luis Rey 1798

San Diego

San Gabriel 1771

EL — CAMINO — REAL

San Juan Capistrano 1776

San Diego de Alcalá 1769

San Fernando 1797

Los Angeles

San Buenaventura 1782

SANTA BARBARA ISLANDS

Santa Barbara

Santa Inés 1804

Santa Barbara 1786

La Purísima 1787

San Luis Obispo 1772

San Miguel Arcángel 1797

COAST

RANGES

San Joaquin R.

San Juan Bautista 1797

Salinas R.

Soledad 1791

San Antonio de Padua 1771

EL CAMINO REAL

Sacramento R.

San Francisco Solano 1823

San José 1797

San José

San Juan Bautista 1797

San Carlos Borromeo 1770

Monterey

Santa Cruz 1791

San Rafael 1817

San Francisco de Asís 1776

Santa Clara 1777

San Francisco

Fort Ross (Russian) 1812

PACIFIC OCEAN

• Settlement (Civic Pueblo)
† Mission
▲ Presidio or Fort
☐ Areas settled by 1823

© Copyright HAMMOND INCORPORATED, Maplewood, N.J.

COLONIAL AMERICA 1770

SCALE OF MILES

0 50 100 150

2

FURS

MAINE (part of Massachusetts)

Falmouth

NEW HAMPSHIRE

Portsmouth

Newburyport

Salem

Boston

FISHING

Cape Cod

WHALING

Connecticut R.

Hartford

New Haven

R.I.

Newport

Long Island

MASSACHUSETTS

CONNECTICUT

New York

Perth Amboy

Albany

Hudson R.

Mohawk R.

NEW YORK

Oswego

Fort Niagara

IROQUOIS CONFEDERATION

Lake Ontario

Lake Erie

FURS

Fort Detroit

Lake Huron

Q U E B E C

St. Lawrence River

Lake Champlain

Montreal

NEW JERSEY

Burlington

New Castle

PENNSYLVANIA

Philadelphia

York

DELAWARE

Baltimore

MARYLAND

Chesapeake Bay

Susquehanna R.

Delaware R.

Pittsburgh

Fort Cumberland

A P P A L A C H I A N   M O U N T A I N S

Staunton

Alexandria

Richmond

Williamsburg

Norfolk

VIRGINIA

James R.

Potomac R.

Roanoke R.

Halifax

Edenton

New Bern

Bath

NORTH CAROLINA

Pamlico Sd.

Cape Hatteras

Hillsboro

Salem

Salisbury

Charlotte

Cross Creek

Wilmington

Cape Fear R.

Camden

SOUTH CAROLINA

Georgetown

Charleston

Santee R.

Augusta

Savannah R.

GEORGIA

Savannah

Kanawha R.

Wataga Settlements

Fort Chiswell

Ohio River

FURS

ATLANTIC OCEAN

ECONOMY AND ROADS

General Farming: Grain and Livestock

☐ Tobacco

☐ Rice and Indigo

🌲 Naval Stores and Timber

Ⓘ Iron Works

〜 Main Roads

AN EXAMPLE OF A TRIANGULAR TRADE ROUTE

ATLANTIC OCEAN

WEST AFRICA

RUM

SLAVES

MOLASSES

AMERICA

WEST INDIES

© Copyright HAMMOND INCORPORATED, Maplewood, N.J.
Printed in U.S.A.

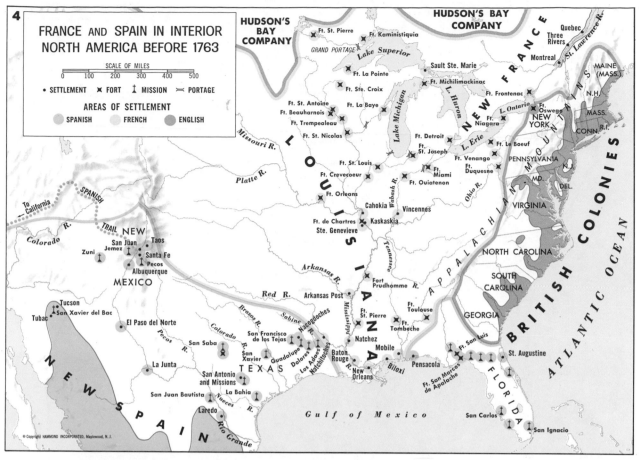

4

FRANCE AND SPAIN IN INTERIOR NORTH AMERICA BEFORE 1763

SCALE OF MILES

0 100 200 300 400 500

• SETTLEMENT ✗ FORT ⚐ MISSION ⚔ PORTAGE

AREAS OF SETTLEMENT

SPANISH   FRENCH   ENGLISH

HUDSON'S BAY COMPANY

HUDSON'S BAY COMPANY

Ft. St. Pierre   Ft. Kaministiquia   Quebec   Three Rivers
GRAND PORTAGE   Lake Superior   Montreal   St. Lawrence R.
Ft. La Pointe   Sault Ste. Marie   MAINE (MASS.)
Ft. Ste. Croix   Ft. Michilimackinac
Ft. St. Antoine   Ft. La Baye   Ft. Frontenac   N.H.
Ft. Beauharnois   L. Huron   Ft. Oswego   MASS.
Ft. Trempealeau   Lake Michigan   L. Ontario   CONN.   R.I.
Ft. St. Nicolas   Ft. Detroit   Ft. Niagara   NEW YORK
Ft. St. Louis   L. Erie   Ft. Le Boeuf   PENNSYLVANIA
Ft. Crevecoeur   Ft. St. Joseph   Ft. Venango   N.J.
Ft. Miami   Ft. Duquesne   MD.   DEL.
Ft. Orleans   Ft. Ouiatenon   Ohio R.   VIRGINIA
Cahokia   Vincennes   Wabash R.
Ft. de Chartres   Kaskaskia   NORTH CAROLINA
Ste. Genevieve

Missouri R.

Platte R.

LOUISIANA

SPANISH
To California
TRAIL   NEW
Colorado R.   San Juan   Taos
Zuni   Jemez   Santa Fe
Pecos   Albuquerque
MEXICO

Arkansas R.
Fort Prudhomme
Tennessee R.
Red R.   Arkansas Post
Brazos R.   Ft. St. Pierre   Ft. Toulouse
Colorado R.   Sabine R.   Nacogdoches   Natchez   Ft. Tombeche
San Francisco de los Tejas   Mobile
Tucson   San Saba   Guadalupe   Dolores   Baton Rouge   Biloxi   Pensacola
San Xavier del Bac   San Xavier   Los Adaes   Natchitoches
Tubac   El Paso del Norte   La Junta   New Orleans
Pecos R.   TEXAS   Ft. San Marcos de Apalache
San Antonio and Missions   La Bahia
San Juan Bautista   Nueces R.
Laredo   Rio Grande

NEW SPAIN

SOUTH CAROLINA
GEORGIA
BRITISH COLONIES
Ft. San Luis   St. Augustine
FLORIDA
ATLANTIC OCEAN
APPALACHIAN MOUNTAINS
NEW FRANCE

Gulf of Mexico   San Carlos
San Ignacio

© Copyright HAMMOND INCORPORATED, Maplewood, N.J.

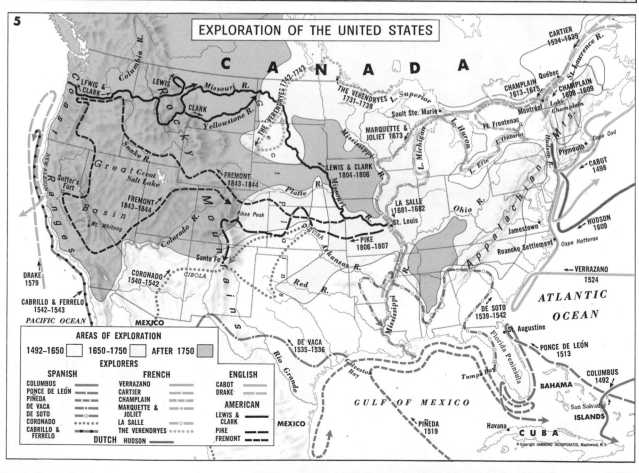

5

EXPLORATION OF THE UNITED STATES

C A N A D A

Columbia R.   LEWIS & CLARK   LEWIS   Missouri R.   THE VERENDRYES 1742-1743   CARTIER 1534-1535
CLARK   Yellowstone R.   THE VERENDRYES 1731-1738   Québec   St. Lawrence R.
LEWIS   ROCKY   Sault Ste. Marie   L. Superior   CHAMPLAIN 1613-1615   CHAMPLAIN 1608-1609
Snake R.   MARQUETTE & JOLIET 1673   Montréal   Lake Champlain
Great Salt Lake   Great   L. Michigan   L. Huron   Ft. Frontenac   Hudson R.
FREMONT 1843-1844   Basin   LEWIS & CLARK 1804-1806   L. Ontario   L. Erie   Plymouth   Cape Cod
Sutter's Fort   MOUNTAINS   Platte   CABOT 1498
FREMONT 1843-1844   Colorado R.   LA SALLE 1681-1682   Ohio R.   HUDSON 1609
NEW ALBION   Mt. Whitney   Pikes Peak   Platte R.   St. Louis   Jamestown
Santa Fe   QUIVIRA   PIKE 1806-1807   Mississippi R.   Roanoke Settlement   Cape Hatteras
DRAKE 1579   Arkansas R.   VERRAZANO 1524
CABRILLO & FERRELO 1542-1543   CORONADO 1540-1542   CIBOLA   Red R.   DE SOTO 1539-1542   ATLANTIC OCEAN
PACIFIC OCEAN   MEXICO   St. Augustine
DE VACA 1535-1536   PONCE DE LEÓN 1513
Rio Grande   Florida Peninsula
Galveston Bay   COLUMBUS 1492
DE VACA   Tampa Bay   BAHAMA
GULF OF MEXICO   ISLANDS
MEXICO   PIÑEDA 1519   San Salvador
Havana   CUBA

AREAS OF EXPLORATION

1492–1650   1650–1750   AFTER 1750

EXPLORERS

SPANISH	FRENCH	ENGLISH
COLUMBUS	VERRAZANO	CABOT
PONCE DE LEÓN	CARTIER	DRAKE
PIÑEDA	CHAMPLAIN	**AMERICAN**
DE VACA	MARQUETTE & JOLIET	LEWIS & CLARK
DE SOTO	LA SALLE	PIKE
CORONADO	THE VERENDRYES	FREMONT
CABRILLO & FERRELO		

DUTCH   HUDSON

© Copyright HAMMOND INCORPORATED, Maplewood, N.J.

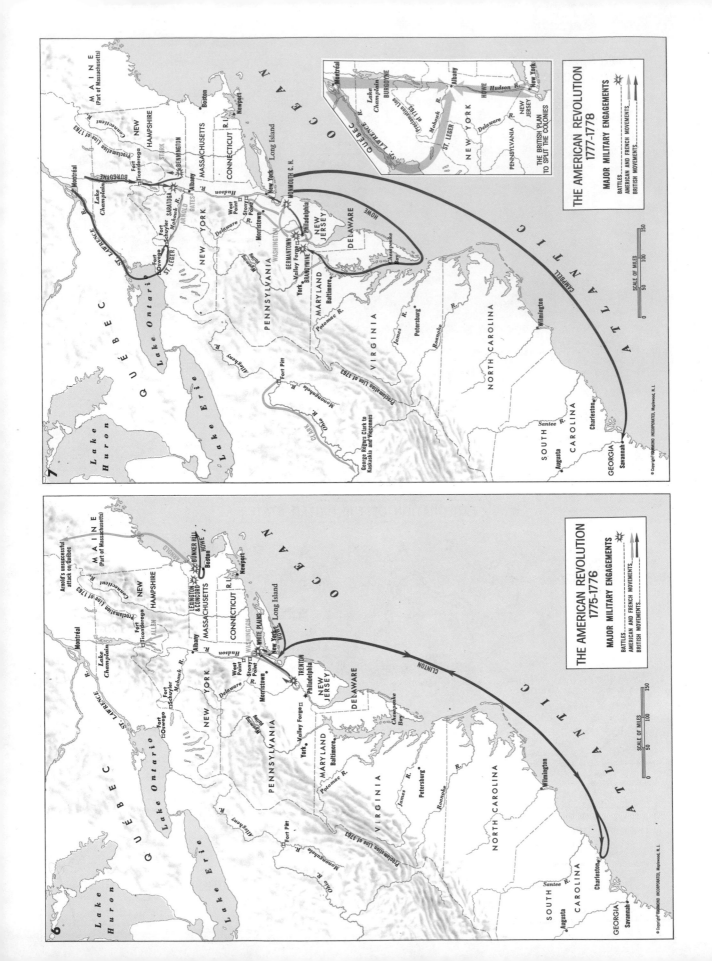

**THE AMERICAN REVOLUTION
1777-1778**

MAJOR MILITARY ENGAGEMENTS

BATTLES
AMERICAN AND FRENCH MOVEMENTS
BRITISH MOVEMENTS

THE BRITISH PLAN
TO SPLIT THE COLONIES

SCALE OF MILES
0   50   100   150

George Rogers Clark to
Kaskaskia and Vincennes

© Copyright HAMMOND INCORPORATED, Maplewood, N.J.

**THE AMERICAN REVOLUTION
1775-1776**

MAJOR MILITARY ENGAGEMENTS

BATTLES
AMERICAN AND FRENCH MOVEMENTS
BRITISH MOVEMENTS

SCALE OF MILES
0   50   100   150

Arnold's unsuccessful
attack on Québec

© Copyright HAMMOND INCORPORATED, Maplewood, R.I.

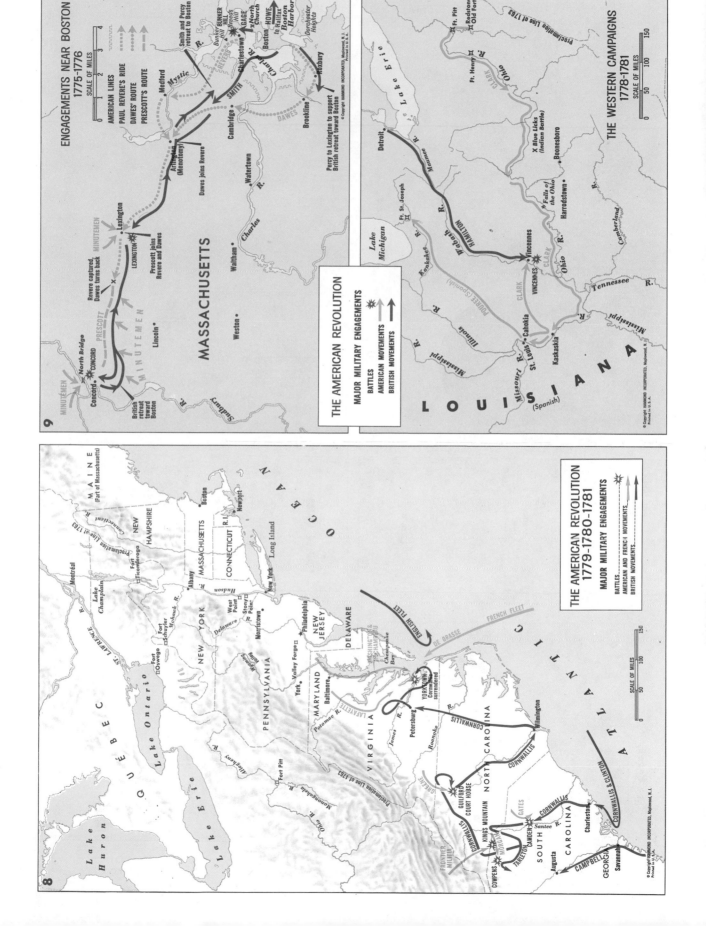

ENGAGEMENTS NEAR BOSTON
1775-1776

SCALE OF MILES
0   1   2   3   4

AMERICAN LINES
PAUL REVERE'S RIDE
DAWES' ROUTE
PRESCOTT'S ROUTE

© Copyright HAMMOND INCORPORATED, Maplewood, N.J.
Printed in U.S.A.

Smith and Percy
retreat to Boston

BUNKER
HILL
Breed's
Hill
North
Church
GAGE
Boston
Charlestown
HOWE,
to Halifax

Dorchester
Heights

Boston
Harbor

Roxbury

Brookline

Medford

Mystic

Cambridge

Watertown

Charles R.

Arlington
(Menotomy)

Dawes joins Revere

Waltham

Weston

Lincoln

Lexington

Revere captured,
Dawes turns back

Prescott joins
Revere and Dawes

MINUTEMEN

North Bridge

Concord

CONCORD

MINUTEMEN

British retreat
toward Boston

Sudbury R.

MASSACHUSETTS

Percy to Lexington to support
British retreat toward Boston

PRESCOTT

SMITH

REVERE

DAWES

LEXINGTON

MINUTEMEN

9

THE WESTERN CAMPAIGNS
1778-1781

SCALE OF MILES
0   50   100   150

Ft. Pitt
Radstone
Old Fort

Proclamation Line of 1763

Lake Erie

Detroit

Ft. Henry

Maumee R.

HAMILTON

Ohio R.

X Blue Licks
(Indian Battle)

Boonesboro

Falls of
the Ohio

Harrodstown

Lake
Michigan

Ft. St. Joseph

St. Joseph R.

Kankakee R.

Wabash R.

Vincennes

VINCENNES

CLARK

HAMILTON

CLARK

Cumberland R.

Tennessee R.

Illinois R.

POUGE (Spanish)

Missouri R.

St. Louis

Cahokia

Kaskaskia

Mississippi R.

Ohio R.

Mississippi R.

L O U I S I A N A
(Spanish)

© Copyright HAMMOND INCORPORATED, Maplewood, N.J.
Printed in U.S.A.

THE AMERICAN REVOLUTION

MAJOR MILITARY ENGAGEMENTS

BATTLES
AMERICAN MOVEMENTS
BRITISH MOVEMENTS

THE AMERICAN REVOLUTION
1779-1780-1781

MAJOR MILITARY ENGAGEMENTS

BATTLES
AMERICAN AND FRENCH MOVEMENTS
BRITISH MOVEMENTS

SCALE OF MILES
0   50   100   150

© Copyright HAMMOND INCORPORATED, Maplewood, N.J.
Printed in U.S.A.

MAINE
(Part of Massachusetts)

ST. LAWRENCE R.

Montréal

Lake Champlain

Fort Ticonderoga

NEW HAMPSHIRE

Connecticut R.

Boston

MASSACHUSETTS

Newport

CONNECTICUT

Long Island

Albany

Hudson R.

West
Point

Stony
Point

New York

NEW
YORK

Fort
Schuyler

Mohawk R.

Fort
Oswego

Lake Ontario

Lake Erie

Lake Huron

Q U É B E C

Proclamation Line of 1763

Allegheny R.

Fort Pitt

Monongahela R.

Ohio R.

PENNSYLVANIA

Morristown

Valley Forge

York

Reading

Philadelphia

NEW
JERSEY

DELAWARE

MARYLAND

Baltimore

Potomac R.

WASHINGTON &
ROCHAMBEAU

Chesapeake
Bay

VIRGINIA

James R.

Petersburg

LAFAYETTE

YORKTOWN
Cornwallis
surrendered

DE GRASSE

ENGLISH FLEET

FRENCH FLEET

Roanoke R.

CORNWALLIS

Wilmington

NORTH
CAROLINA

GREENE

GUILFORD
COURT HOUSE

CORNWALLIS

KINGS MOUNTAIN

GATES

Santee R.

Camden

MORGAN

COWPENS

TARLETON

FRONTIER
MILITIA

SOUTH
CAROLINA

Charleston

Augusta

CAMPBELL

Savannah

GEORGIA

CORNWALLIS & CLINTON

ATLANTIC OCEAN

8

SETTLEMENT OF THE UNITED STATES 1770–1890

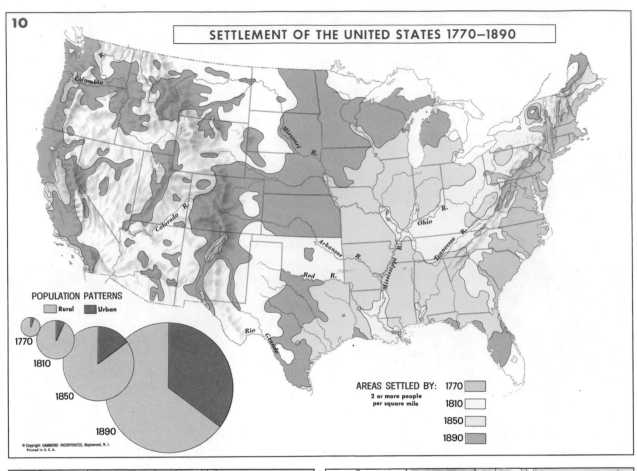

POPULATION PATTERNS

Rural   Urban

1770
1810
1850
1890

© Copyright HAMMOND INCORPORATED, Maplewood, N. J.
Printed in U.S.A.

AREAS SETTLED BY: 1770
2 or more people
per square mile
1810
1850
1890

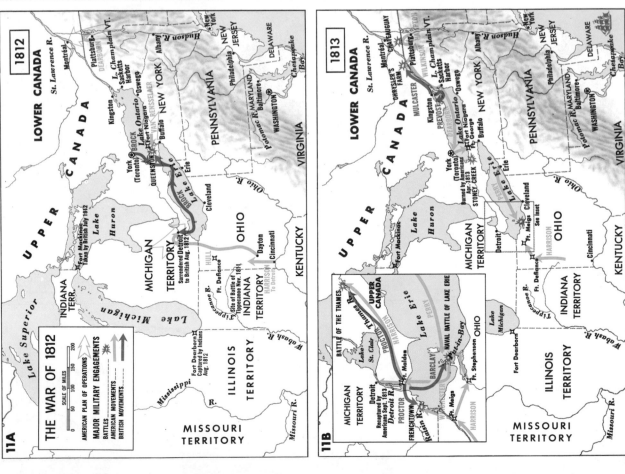

1812

THE WAR OF 1812

SCALE OF MILES
0   50   100   150   200

AMERICAN PLAN OF OPERATIONS
MAJOR MILITARY ENGAGEMENTS
BATTLES
AMERICAN MOVEMENTS
BRITISH MOVEMENTS

11A

1813

11B

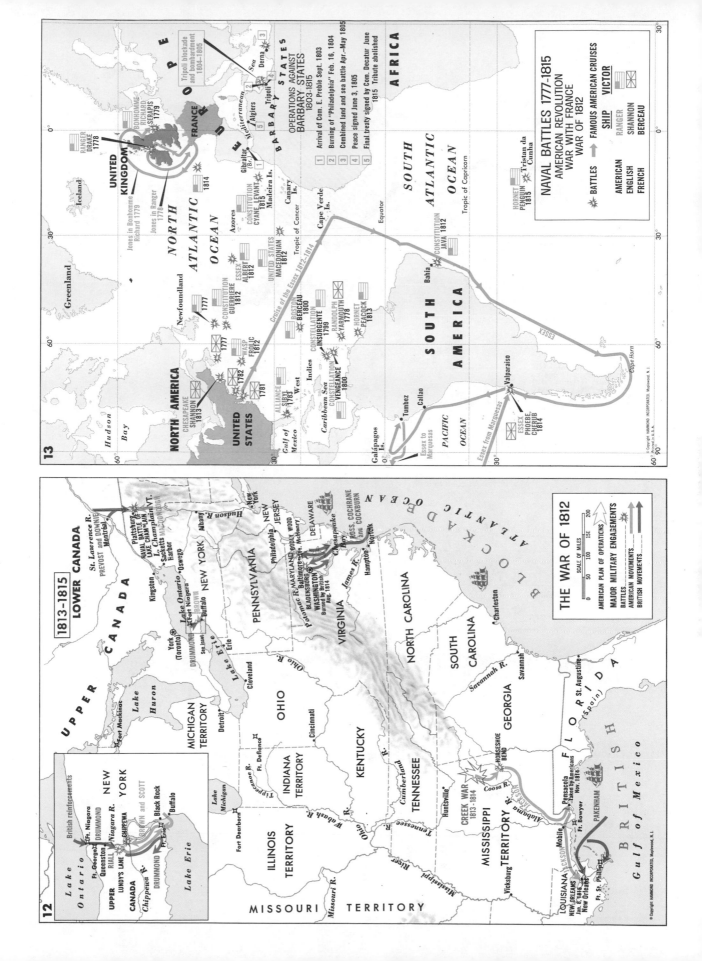

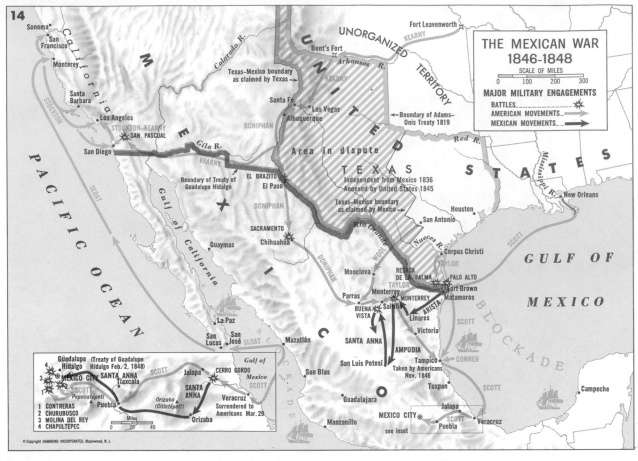

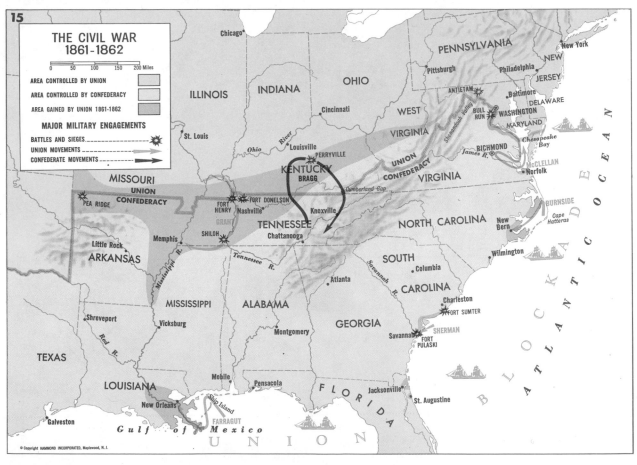

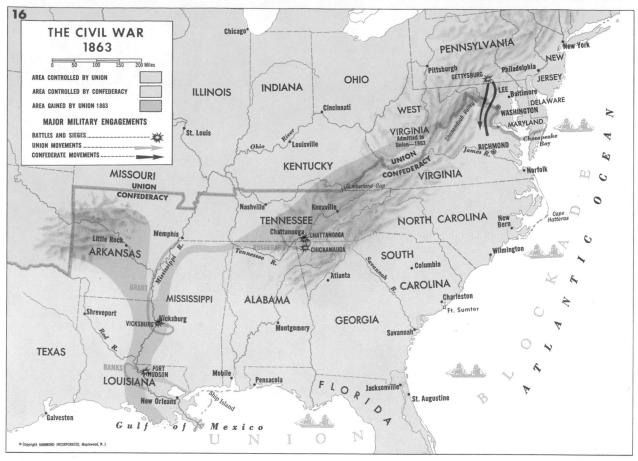

16

THE CIVIL WAR 1863

0 50 100 150 200 Miles

AREA CONTROLLED BY UNION
AREA CONTROLLED BY CONFEDERACY
AREA GAINED BY UNION 1863

MAJOR MILITARY ENGAGEMENTS

BATTLES AND SIEGES
UNION MOVEMENTS
CONFEDERATE MOVEMENTS

© Copyright HAMMOND INCORPORATED, Maplewood, N.J.

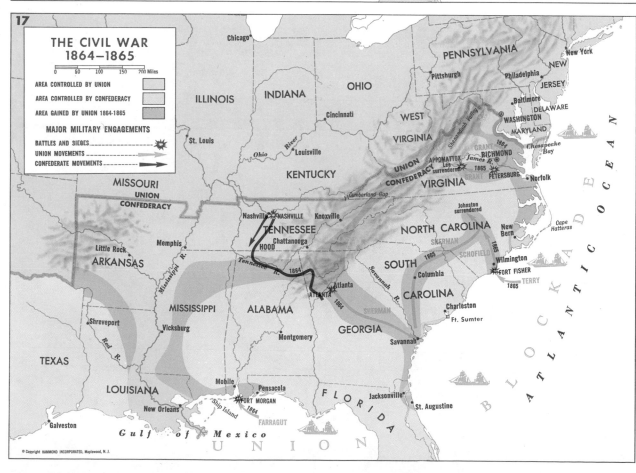

17

THE CIVIL WAR 1864–1865

0 50 100 150 200 Miles

AREA CONTROLLED BY UNION
AREA CONTROLLED BY CONFEDERACY
AREA GAINED BY UNION 1864-1865

MAJOR MILITARY ENGAGEMENTS

BATTLES AND SIEGES
UNION MOVEMENTS
CONFEDERATE MOVEMENTS

© Copyright HAMMOND INCORPORATED, Maplewood, N.J.

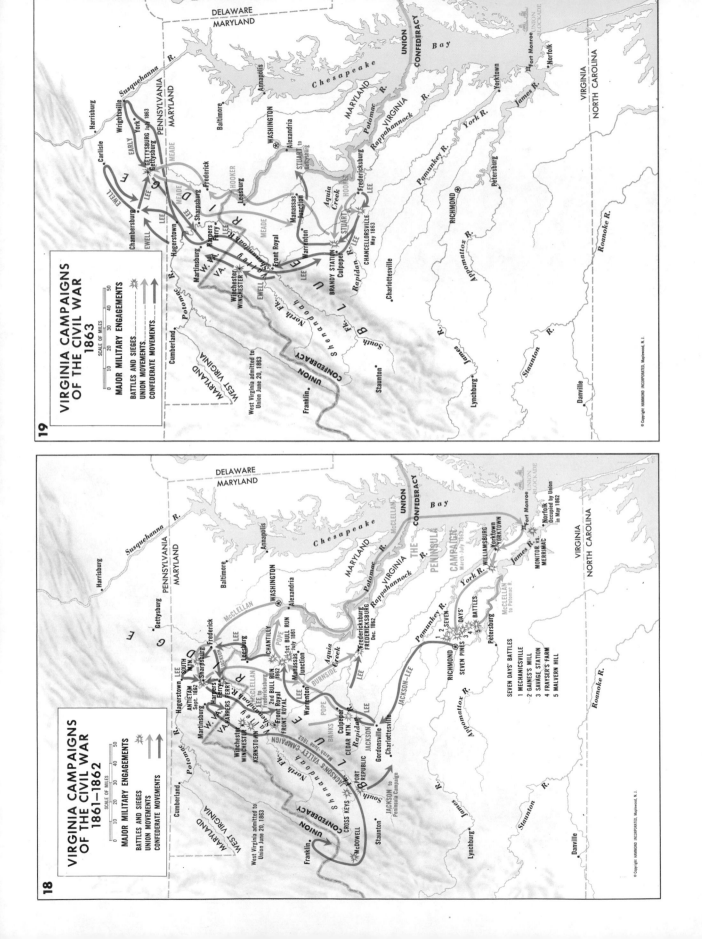

VIRGINIA CAMPAIGNS OF THE CIVIL WAR 1863

SCALE OF MILES
0 10 20 30 40 50

MAJOR MILITARY ENGAGEMENTS

BATTLES AND SIEGES
UNION MOVEMENTS
CONFEDERATE MOVEMENTS

West Virginia admitted to
Union June 20, 1863

© Copyright HAMMOND INCORPORATED, Maplewood, N.J.

VIRGINIA CAMPAIGNS OF THE CIVIL WAR 1861-1862

SCALE OF MILES
0 10 20 30 40 50

MAJOR MILITARY ENGAGEMENTS

BATTLES AND SIEGES
UNION MOVEMENTS
CONFEDERATE MOVEMENTS

West Virginia admitted to
Union June 20, 1863

SEVEN DAYS' BATTLES
1 MECHANICSVILLE
2 GAINES'S MILL
3 SAVAGE STATION
4 FRAYSER'S FARM
5 MALVERN HILL

© Copyright HAMMOND INCORPORATED, Maplewood, N.J.

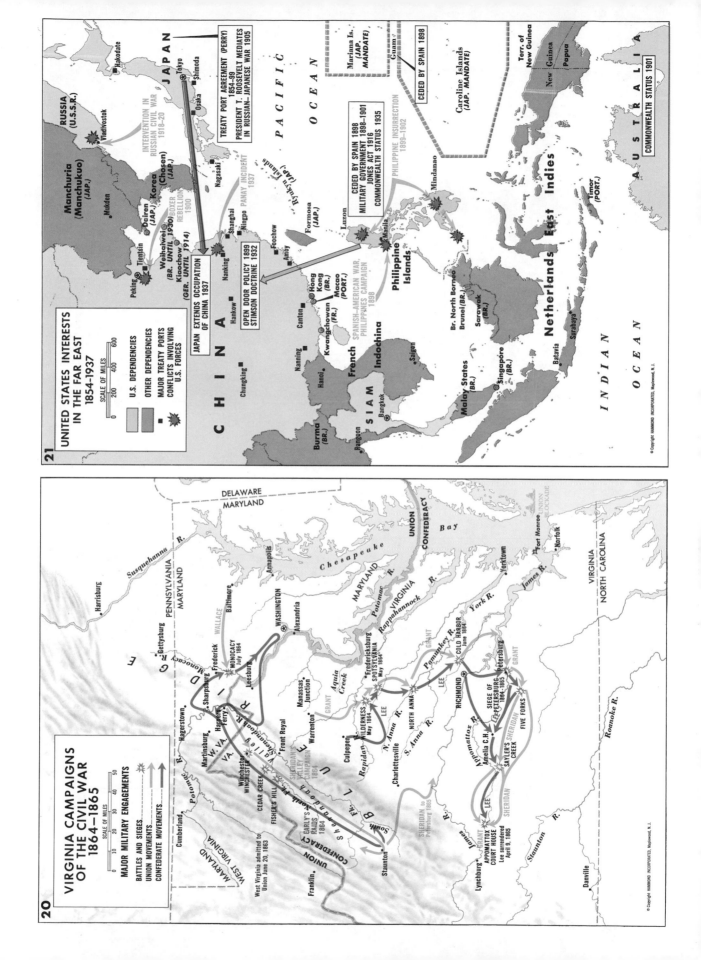

21 UNITED STATES INTERESTS IN THE FAR EAST 1854-1937

20 VIRGINIA CAMPAIGNS OF THE CIVIL WAR 1864-1865

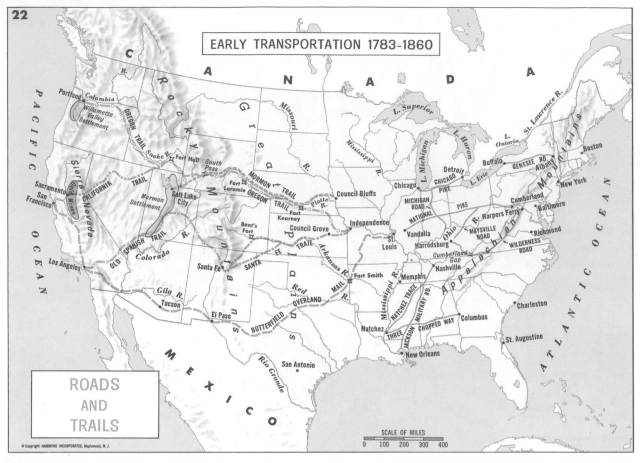

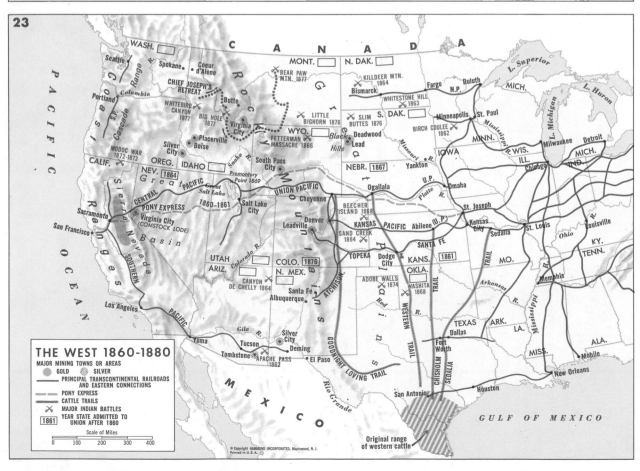

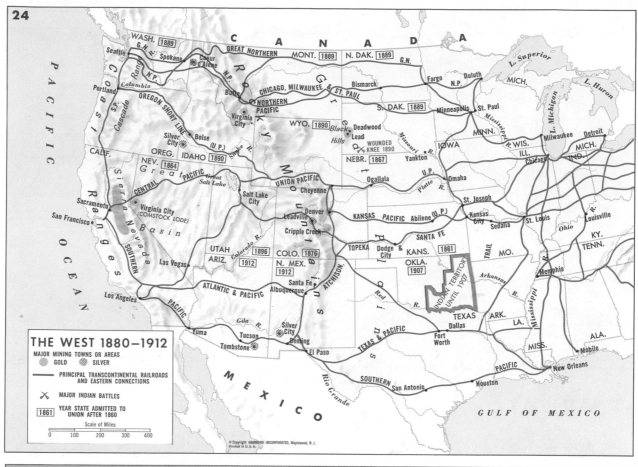

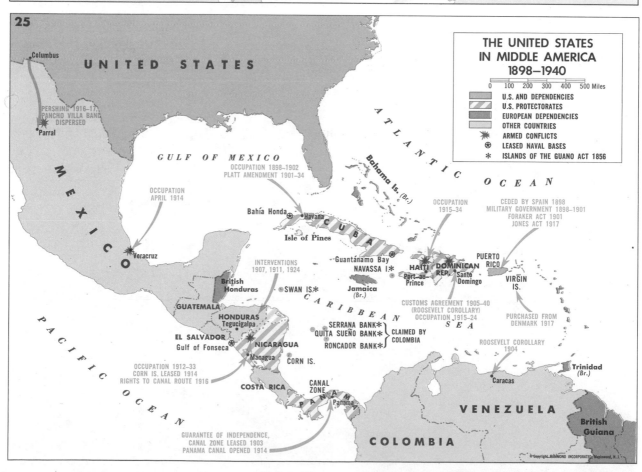

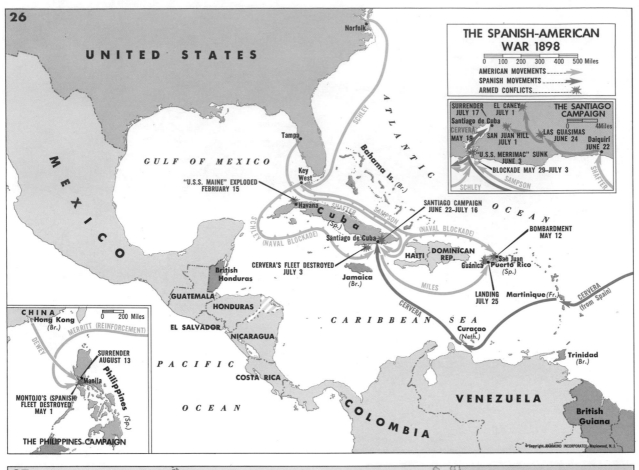

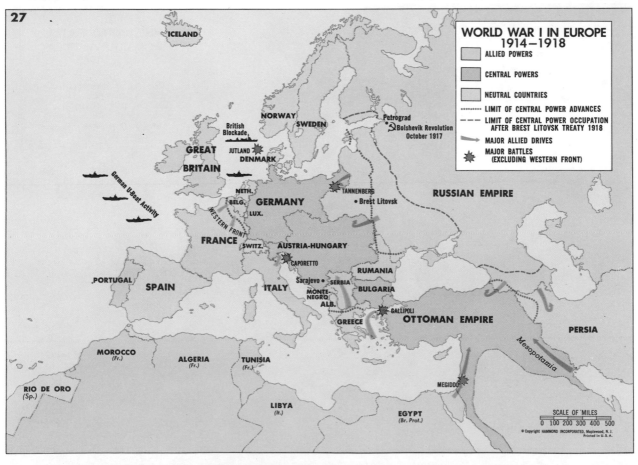

28

WORLD WAR II
EUROPEAN THEATER
1940-1942

Allied Nations and Allied
controlled Nations

Axis Powers and Axis
controlled Nations

Neutral Nations

Vichy France; Vichy controlled
Areas (later to Allies)

Areas occupied by Axis

German Air Strikes

Famous Battles or Sieges

German Advances

Allied Advances

Western Front

Eastern Front

British occupation 1940
U.S. occupation 1941
Independent 1944

ICELAND

SUPPLY ROUTE FROM U.S. & BRITISH COMMONWEALTH

NORWEGIAN
SEA

NORTH
SEA

Murmansk

SWEDEN

NORWAY

FINLAND

1941

Leningrad

EST.

LATVIA
LITH.

1941

Moscow

UNITED
KINGDOM

IRELAND

DENMARK

NETH.

Berlin

BELG.
Lux.

GERMANY

POLAND

1941

1941

UNION OF SOVIET
SOCIALIST REPUBLICS

SUPPLY ROUTE FROM U.S.

London

Paris

Ukraine

1941

1942

Stalingrad

German U-boat
Blockade

VICHY
FRANCE

SWITZ.

Austria

HUNGARY

SLOVAKIA

1941

RUMANIA

1942

CASPIAN
SEA

ATLANTIC

OCEAN

SPAIN

PORTUGAL

ITALY

Corsica

Rome

Sardinia

YUGOSLAVIA

BULGARIA

ALB.
(It.)

GREECE

1941

BLACK SEA

TURKEY
Neutral until Feb. 1945

Axis influence removed
after British and Russian
invasion 1941

ALLIED SUPPLY ROUTE TO U.S.S.R.

IRAN

IRAN

Gibraltar
(Br.)

MEDITERRANEAN

Sicily

Malta
(Br.)

Crete

Cyprus
(Br.)

SYRIA
(Fr.)

IRAQ

SP. MOR.

Casablanca

Oran

Algiers

Tunis

SEA

PALESTINE
(Br. Mandate)

TRANS-
JORDAN
(Br. Mandate)

Persian
Gulf

Canary Is.
(Sp.)

MOROCCO
(Fr.)

ALGERIA
(Fr.)

TUNISIA
(Fr.)

Tripoli

El Alamein

1940

1942

1941

1942

Cairo

Pro-Axis government
removed by British 1941

SAUDI ARABIA
Neutral until Mar. 1945

RIO DE ORO
(Sp.)

LIBYA
(It.)

EGYPT

SCALE OF MILES
0 100 200 300 400 500

© Copyright HAMMOND INCORPORATED, Maplewood, N.J.

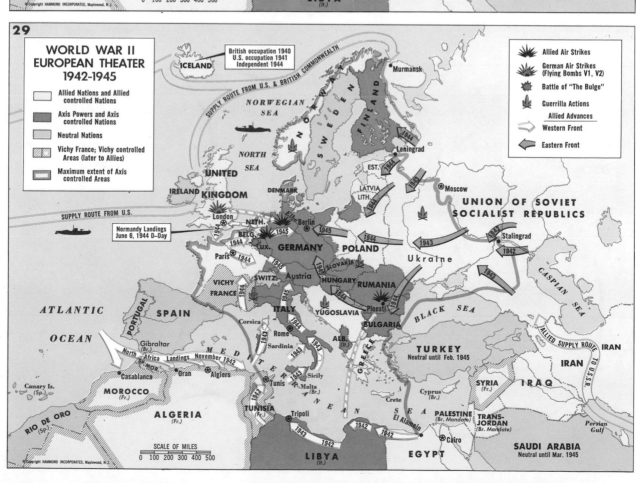

29

WORLD WAR II
EUROPEAN THEATER
1942-1945

Allied Nations and Allied
controlled Nations

Axis Powers and Axis
controlled Nations

Neutral Nations

Vichy France; Vichy controlled
Areas (later to Allies)

Maximum extent of Axis
controlled Areas

Allied Air Strikes

German Air Strikes
(Flying Bombs V1, V2)

Battle of "The Bulge"

Guerrilla Actions

Allied Advances

Western Front

Eastern Front

British occupation 1940
U.S. occupation 1941
Independent 1944

ICELAND

SUPPLY ROUTE FROM U.S. & BRITISH COMMONWEALTH

NORWEGIAN
SEA

NORTH
SEA

Murmansk

SWEDEN

NORWAY

FINLAND

1944

Leningrad

EST.

1944

LATVIA
LITH.

1943

Moscow

UNITED
KINGDOM

IRELAND

DENMARK

SUPPLY ROUTE FROM U.S.

London

NETH.

Elbe

Berlin

1945

BELG.

1944

Lux.

GERMANY

1944

POLAND

1944

1943

Stalingrad

1942

Normandy Landings
June 6, 1944 D-Day

Paris

1944

1945

SWITZ.

Austria

1945

SLOVAKIA

HUNGARY

RUMANIA

1944

Ploesti

1944

1943

UNION OF SOVIET
SOCIALIST REPUBLICS

Ukraine

1942

CASPIAN
SEA

VICHY
FRANCE

1944

ATLANTIC

OCEAN

SPAIN

PORTUGAL

ITALY

1944

Corsica

Rome

Sardinia

1943

YUGOSLAVIA

1944

BULGARIA

ALB.
(It.)

GREECE

BLACK SEA

TURKEY
Neutral until Feb. 1945

ALLIED SUPPLY ROUTE TO U.S.S.R.

IRAN

IRAN

Gibraltar
(Br.)

North Africa
Landings November 1942

SP. MOR.

Casablanca

Oran

Algiers

MEDITERRANEAN

1943

Tunis

Sicily

1943

Malta
(Br.)

Crete

Cyprus
(Br.)

SYRIA
(Fr.)

IRAQ

SEA

PALESTINE
(Br. Mandate)

TRANS-
JORDAN
(Br. Mandate)

Persian
Gulf

Canary Is.
(Sp.)

MOROCCO
(Fr.)

ALGERIA
(Fr.)

TUNISIA
(Fr.)

Tripoli

1943

1942

El Alamein

1942

1942

Cairo

SAUDI ARABIA
Neutral until Mar. 1945

RIO DE ORO
(Sp.)

LIBYA
(It.)

EGYPT

SCALE OF MILES
0 100 200 300 400 500

© Copyright HAMMOND INCORPORATED, Maplewood, N.J.

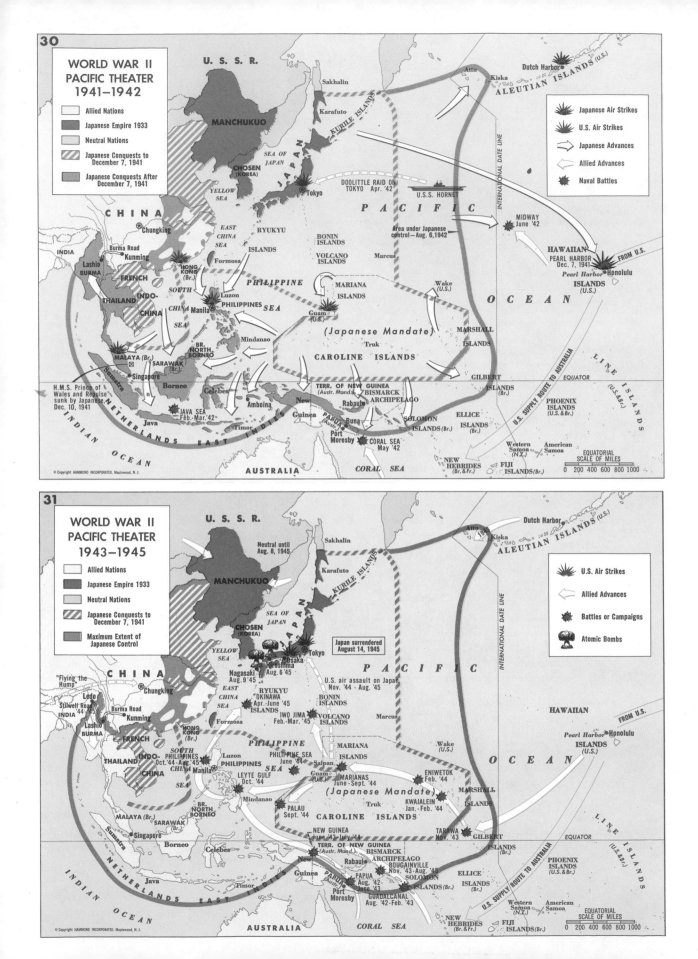

30

WORLD WAR II
PACIFIC THEATER
1941–1942

	Allied Nations
	Japanese Empire 1933
	Neutral Nations
	Japanese Conquests to December 7, 1941
	Japanese Conquests After December 7, 1941

Japanese Air Strikes
U.S. Air Strikes
Japanese Advances
Allied Advances
Naval Battles

U.S.S.R.

Sakhalin

Karafuto

KURILE ISLANDS

ALEUTIAN ISLANDS (U.S.)
Attu
Kiska
Dutch Harbor

MANCHUKUO

CHOSEN (KOREA)

SEA OF JAPAN

JAPAN

Tokyo

DOOLITTLE RAID ON TOKYO Apr. '42

U.S.S. HORNET

P A C I F I C

INTERNATIONAL DATE LINE

CHINA

Chungking

YELLOW SEA

EAST CHINA SEA

RYUKYU ISLANDS

BONIN ISLANDS

VOLCANO ISLANDS

Marcus

Area under Japanese control—Aug. 6, 1942

MIDWAY June '42

O C E A N

INDIA

Burma Road
Kunming

Lashio
BURMA

FRENCH

Formosa

HONG KONG (Br.)

PHILIPPINE

PHILIPPINE SEA

MARIANA ISLANDS

Wake (U.S.)

HAWAIIAN PEARL HARBOR Dec. 7, 1941

Honolulu

FROM U.S.

THAILAND
INDO-CHINA

SOUTH CHINA SEA

Luzon
Manila
PHILIPPINES

Guam (U.S.)

(Japanese Mandate)

Truk

MARSHALL ISLANDS

Pearl Harbor
ISLANDS (U.S.)

Mindanao

CAROLINE ISLANDS

MALAYA (Br.)

SARAWAK (Br.)

BR. NORTH BORNEO

GILBERT ISLANDS (Br.)

LINE ISLANDS (U.S. & Br.)

EQUATOR

U.S. SUPPLY ROUTE TO AUSTRALIA

Sumatra

Singapore

Borneo

Celebes

Amboina

New Guinea

TERR. OF NEW GUINEA (Austr. Mand.)

BISMARCK ARCHIPELAGO

Rabaul

PHOENIX ISLANDS (U.S. & Br.)

H.M.S. Prince of Wales and Repulse sunk by Japanese Dec. 10, 1941

JAVA SEA Feb.-Mar. '42

Java

Timor

PAPUA (Austr.)

Buna

Port Moresby

SOLOMON ISLANDS (Br.)

ELLICE ISLANDS (Br.)

INDIAN OCEAN

NETHERLANDS EAST INDIES

CORAL SEA May '42

NEW HEBRIDES (Br. & Fr.)

Western Samoa (N.Z.)

American Samoa

FIJI ISLANDS (Br.)

EQUATORIAL SCALE OF MILES
0 200 400 600 800 1000

AUSTRALIA

CORAL SEA

© Copyright HAMMOND INCORPORATED, Maplewood, N.J.

31

WORLD WAR II
PACIFIC THEATER
1943–1945

	Allied Nations
	Japanese Empire 1933
	Neutral Nations
	Japanese Conquests to December 7, 1941
	Maximum Extent of Japanese Control

U.S. Air Strikes
Allied Advances
Battles or Campaigns
Atomic Bombs

U.S.S.R.

Sakhalin

Neutral until Aug. 8, 1945

Karafuto

KURILE ISLANDS

ALEUTIAN ISLANDS (U.S.)
Attu
Kiska
Dutch Harbor

MANCHUKUO

CHOSEN (KOREA)

SEA OF JAPAN

JAPAN

Tokyo
Osaka
Hiroshima Aug. 6 '45

Japan surrendered August 14, 1945

P A C I F I C

INTERNATIONAL DATE LINE

"Flying the Hump"

Ledo

Stilwell Road '44-'45

CHINA

Chungking

YELLOW SEA

Nagasaki Aug. 9 '45

EAST CHINA SEA

RYUKYU OKINAWA ISLANDS Apr.-June '45

U.S. air assault on Japan Nov. '44 - Aug. '45

BONIN ISLANDS

VOLCANO ISLANDS

Marcus

HAWAIIAN

INDIA

Burma Road
Kunming

Lashio
BURMA

FRENCH

Formosa

HONG KONG (Br.)

IWO JIMA Feb.-Mar. '45

Wake (U.S.)

Pearl Harbor

Honolulu

FROM U.S.

THAILAND
INDO-CHINA

SOUTH CHINA SEA

PHILIPPINE

Luzon
Manila

PHILIPPINES
Oct.'44-Aug.'45

PHILIPPINE SEA June '44

Saipan

MARIANA ISLANDS

ISLANDS (U.S.)

O C E A N

LEYTE GULF Oct. '44

Guam (U.S.)

MARIANAS June-Sept. '44

ENIWETOK Feb. '44

Mindanao

(Japanese Mandate)

Truk

KWAJALEIN Jan.-Feb. '44

MARSHALL ISLANDS

BR. NORTH BORNEO

MALAYA (Br.)

SARAWAK (Br.)

PALAU Sept. '44

CAROLINE ISLANDS

TARAWA Nov. '43

GILBERT ISLANDS (Br.)

LINE ISLANDS (U.S. & Br.)

EQUATOR

Singapore

Borneo

Celebes

NEW GUINEA June '43-July '44

TERR. OF NEW GUINEA (Austr. Mand.)

BISMARCK ARCHIPELAGO

Rabaul

BOUGAINVILLE Nov. '43-Aug. '45

PHOENIX ISLANDS (U.S. & Br.)

U.S. SUPPLY ROUTE TO AUSTRALIA

Sumatra

Java

Timor

New Guinea

PAPUA (Austr.)

PAPUA Aug. '42-Jan. '43

Port Moresby

SOLOMON ISLANDS (Br.)

GUADALCANAL Aug. '42-Feb. '43

ELLICE ISLANDS (Br.)

INDIAN OCEAN

NETHERLANDS EAST INDIES

CORAL SEA

NEW HEBRIDES (Br. & Fr.)

Western Samoa (N.Z.)

American Samoa

FIJI ISLANDS (Br.)

EQUATORIAL SCALE OF MILES
0 200 400 600 800 1000

AUSTRALIA

© Copyright HAMMOND INCORPORATED, Maplewood, N.J.